Black Women in America

BLACKS IN THE DIASPORA

Darlene Clark Hine, John McCluskey, Jr., and David Barry Gaspar
General Editors

Black Women in America
An Historical Encyclopedia

Editors

DARLENE CLARK HINE

ELSA BARKLEY BROWN

ROSALYN TERBORG-PENN

VOLUME I

A–L

INDIANA UNIVERSITY PRESS
BLOOMINGTON & INDIANAPOLIS

First published in 1993 by Carlson Publishing, Inc.
First Indiana University Press Edition 1994

The paper used in this publication meets the minimum requirements of American
National Standard for Information Sciences–Permanence of Paper for Printed
Library Materials, ANSI Z39.48-1984.

Manufactured in the United States of America

Library of Congress Cataloging-in-Publication Data

Black women in America : an historical encyclopedia / edited by Darlene
Clark Hine, Elsa Barkley Brown, and Rosalyn Terborg-Penn.
    p. cm. – (Blacks in the diaspora)
    Originally published: Brooklyn, N.Y. : Carlson Pub., 1993.
    Includes bibliographical references and indexes.
    ISBN 0-253-32774-1 (set, pbk.)
    1. Afro-American women–Encyclopedias. I. Hine, Darlene Clark.
II. Brown, Elsa Barkley. III. Terborg-Penn, Rosalyn.
E185.86.B542   1994
920.72'089'96073–dc20
[B]   93-14369
    ISBN 0-253-32775-X (v. 1, pbk.)
    ISBN 0-253-32776-8 (v. 2, pbk.)

1 2 3 4 5 99 98 97 96 95 94

Cover photo: Anna Julia Cooper (1858-1964), scholar and educator;
principal of M Street High School in Washington, D.C.; president of
Frelinghuysen University; author of *A Voice from the South by a
Black Woman of the South* (1892). (Scurlock Studio, Washington, D.C.)

Cover design: Harakawa Sisco Inc.

Contents

043379

Volume I

Volume II

Contents Listed by Topic

The following list includes all entries not devoted to individual Black women.
For a classified list of biographical entries, see pages 1,345-1,352 in Volume II.

Editorial Advisory Board

(For biographies of the Board, please see the section at the end of Volume II.)

Sponsors

The following individuals provided essential financial support for this project. We gratefully acknowledge their assistance.

Delores P. Aldridge

Randall K. Burkett

Carolyn A. Dorsey

David J. Garrow

Betty K. Gubert

Darlene Clark Hine

Wilma King

Richard Newman

Nell Irvin Painter

Arvarh Strickland

Acknowledgments

This project required an extraordinary amount of energy, enthusiasm, and hard work from literally hundreds of friends, colleagues, scholars, writers, students, librarians, and archivists. I thank each and every one. In particular, I owe an enormous debt of gratitude to my special assistant, Linda Werbish, who not only typed my entries but also secured photographs and attended to a thousand details. My sisters, Barbara Ann Clark and Alma Jean Mitchell, gave abundant moral and spiritual support and encouragement throughout the duration of this project. My associate editors, Elsa Barkley Brown and Rosalyn Terborg-Penn, provided wise counsel and invaluable intellectual assistance. The members of the advisory board gave generously of time and advice and labor. But it was Ralph Carlson who made all of this happen. Without him and without the sponsors, editors, and the work of an earlier generation of Black women archivists, compilers, and historians, this historical encyclopedia of Black women would not exist.

D.C.H.

My primary debts are to the archivists and early historians who preserved the record and to the many scholars who took time from their already full schedules to contribute to this volume. Additionally, I thank Tracy Boisseau and Lisa Hill, who helped develop the initial list of entries; the Center for Afro-american and African Studies, University of Michigan, and Jamie Hart for the research on which the chronology is based; Christine Lunardini, who got us organized and persistently cajoled and nudged us forward; Mary Wyer, whose sharp editorial eye is always a blessing; and Nataki H Goodall, whose assistance during the final stages of editing was invaluable.

E.B.B.

Many thanks go to my colleagues and graduate students who responded to my call and wrote the many fine essays and biographical sketches that helped to make this work possible. I owe special thanks to Vivian Fisher, Special Collections Librarian, Soper Library at Morgan State University, for identifying a significant number of individuals and organizations for the initial list of entries. I am particularly indebted to my officemate, Professor Jo Ann O. Robinson; my daughter, Jeanna C. Terborg Penn, a student at Morgan State University; and my mother, Jeanne Terborg, for critiquing the essays and sketches I wrote. Finally, I thank our editorial team for making this project work so well.

R.T.-P

Editor's Preface

Darlene Clark Hine

This historic encyclopedia project was initiated to reclaim and to create heightened awareness about individuals, contributions, and struggles that have made African-American survival and progress possible. We cannot accurately comprehend either our hidden potential or the full range of problems that besiege us until we know about the successful struggles that generations of foremothers waged against virtually insurmountable obstacles. We can, and will, chart a coherent future and win essential opportunities with a clear understanding of the past in all its pain and glory.

History has its own power and Black women more than ever before need its truths to challenge hateful assumptions, negative stereotypes, myths, lies, and distortions about our own role in the progress of time. Black women need to know the contradictions and ironies that our unique status presents to a country founded on the proposition that all men are created equal and endowed with the inalienable rights of life, liberty, and opportunity to pursue happiness. Yet it is not enough only to know about the injustices and exploitation Black women endured. We also owe it to ourselves to experience the thrill of knowing about the heroism of Harriet Tubman, share in the pride of Madam C. J. Walker's business acumen, and delight in the tremendous creative artistry of a pantheon of Black women writers, performers, and thinkers. As we garner the inspiration contained in past and present

Black women's lives, we acquire the power to take history further and the will to use the power of history to construct a better future. The realities of history as unearthed and presented in the essays, photography, and biographies in these volumes promise to liberate us all from ignorance, intolerance, and apathy, our most formidable enemies in this postmodern world.

My personal odyssey toward editing this historic encyclopedia of Black women in America represents over a decade of reflection, research, and writing. When I first became a historian, few of my colleagues considered Black women as worthy of separate and distinct study. The generic Black was male and the generic woman was white. Black women found no space in the history books and in 1975 few questioned their absence. My transformation into a historian of Black women began rather inauspiciously in 1980 with a telephone call from Shirley Herd, an Indianapolis primary school teacher. Inasmuch as this call shook the foundations of my career as a scholar, it is only fitting that I now recapture that conversation.

I was sitting in my home in West Lafayette, Indiana, where I was an associate professor of American history at Purdue University. I was, as my mother would say, minding my own business. The telephone rang. The voice on the other end identified herself as Shirley Herd, president of the Indianapolis section of the National Council of Negro Women. In response to her query, I indicated that, yes, I am Darlene Clark

Hine, the historian. Herd then informed me that she was calling to ask me to write a history of Black women in Indiana. Though this was without question the strangest request I had ever heard, I remember thinking that her call presented me with an excellent opportunity to explain to a lay person how we scholars work. In a patronizing manner, I proceeded to explain to her that she could not call up a historian and order a book the way you drive up to Wendy's and order a hamburger. Herd remained silent as I launched into a long description of how historians select a topic, undertake years of research in libraries and archives, prepare a draft manuscript, submit it to a publisher, and with luck have it accepted, pending revisions. If it is rejected, then you send it to another press until you hit pay dirt. I added that the entire process takes several years, often as many as ten, and in some cases even longer.

To her credit, Herd was patient (even tolerant) of my thinly veiled arrogance. She stubbornly insisted, however, that she wanted me to write a book on the history of Black women in Indiana. At her insistence, I thought it best to take a different tack. It was clear that I was not getting through to her, so I elaborated that I could not write such a book because I did not know anything about the history of Black women. I had never studied about them in all the history courses that I had taken as an undergraduate student at Roosevelt University in Chicago where I had earned my B.A. in 1968, nor had I thought about Black women during my entire graduate study at Kent State University in Kent, Ohio, where I earned my Ph.D. in 1975. I tried to impress upon Herd that the only Black women whose names and exploits I had ever heard of throughout my formal education were Phillis Wheatley, Harriet Tubman, and Sojourner Truth. I then declared that it was impossible to write any history of Black women because to my knowledge there were no manuscript collections or other primary documents and sources in the libraries and archives. I added that no one could write a history of Black women without records. That Herd's response floored me is an understatement. She spoke, and I pictured her in my mind's eye with her hand on her hip, "Now, let me get this straight. You are a Black woman?"

I said, "Yes."

And she continued, "You are a historian?"

"Yes."

Then she exploded, "You mean to tell me that you can't put those two things together and write a history of Black women in Indiana?" Before I could reply, she let loose. "About the sources, the members of the Indianapolis section of the National Council of Negro Women just spent the last two years collecting the papers and records of Black women from across the state. We have all the sources you need. We could write our own history book, but this will not change things because we don't know what their lives mean in relation to everybody else in this society. I do know that I am sick and tired of teaching social studies and telling my students all that white men, Black men, and white women have done and never having anything to say or teach about Black women. So you are going to write us something so that we can change the history books."

I knew then that I had no recourse other than to invite Herd to bring me the records that she and her club members had collected. The following Saturday Herd and her best friend, Virtea Downey, another primary school teacher, arrived at my house in a white station wagon loaded with dozens of boxes filled with every conceivable type of record. They put the boxes on my living room floor, we talked, and as they went out the door, Herd paused and said, "We'll be back in six months for our book."

It took me six months to go through and to arrange the material. They had collected diaries, obituaries, club minutes, church programs, newspaper clippings, rent receipts, photographs, family bibles, brochures, posters, typescript histories, marriage licenses, ledgers, and letters. As I sifted through the mountain of paper, I felt as if I had discovered another universe. The records revealed a history of Black women's activism and agency. These community builders and religious workers had created and helped to sustain the entire institutional infrastructure of Black life and culture in disparate communities across the state. Black women in Indiana had founded schools and settlement houses, provided welfare for orphaned children, homes for the aged, clinics for the sick, and money for scholarships. They were tireless political workers, as well as nurses, teachers, social workers, and librarians on the one hand and domestic servants, laundresses, and beauticians on the other. Black churches were utterly dependent on their fundraising labors. They organized celebrations, festivals, balls, symposia, lectures, and recitals. How could I have been so blind and ignorant of the contributions and significance of Black women to the survival of Black America?

Though I learned much from the documents and did write the book, *When the Truth Is Told: Black Women's Community and Culture in Indiana, 1875-1950* (1981), questions about the nature and politics of history hounded me. For the first time I thought seriously about how historians determine what is relevant and important, who merits inclusion and discussion, and what constitutes legitimate evidence in the construction of historical narrative. The women were pleased with *When the Truth Is Told* and Herd thought the subject closed, but my relief soon gave way to guilt. I knew that I had not addressed the fundamental problem that had provoked the call from Herd.

As a historian, I knew that the surest way to change the writing of history was to make accessible abundant archival sources. A few months after the publication of *When the Truth Is Told*, Herd, Downey, and the other council members returned to the original donors every document so painstakingly collected. Thus the records that are so essential to historians were again to be stashed away in basements, attics, closets, drawers, and shoe boxes.

Finally, in 1982, I called Herd. I described my feelings of guilt and pain and asked her to help me start over again, but this time the objective would be to create a permanent Black women's history archive. Herd, Downey, and a young white male historian at Purdue University, Patrick Biddleman, and I initiated the Black Women in the Middle West project. We secured a $150,000 grant from the National Endowment for the Humanities (NEH) which, among other things, facilitated the development of a network of over 1,500 midwestern women and men, Black and white, academics and community-based individuals who actually identified and amassed substantial paper and photographic records pertaining to the lives of Black women. Initially the project aimed to collect records from and about Black women in Illinois, Indiana, Michigan, Ohio, and Wisconsin. The NEH grant stipulated, however, that we concentrate only on two states. We selected Illinois and Indiana and worked closely with archivists at the Chicago Historical Society, the Illinois State Library, and the Indiana Historical Society. These and other agencies received the approximately 300 different record collections gathered during the eighteen months of this historic reclamation project.

As the Black Women in the Middle West project evolved, so did my commitment to writing Black women's history. In 1983, I coordinated a major conference sponsored by the American Historical Association and edited the papers presented, *The State of Afro-American History, Past, Present, and Future* (1986). The only essay included in the volume that was not delivered at the conference was the one I wrote, "Lifting the Veil, Shattering the Silence: Black Women's History in Slavery and Freedom." The

members of the planning committee agreed that the volume would benefit from having an essay devoted exclusively to Black women's history and that it should stress the need for more work in this area. At that time, at least six Black women scholars were already at work on what would become significant groundbreaking studies in Black women's history. Many of these scholars belonged to the newly formed Association of Black Women Historians, and they joined me on the advisory board of this historical encyclopedia project.

When Shirley Herd called in 1980, I was involved in researching the history of Black Americans in the medical profession. I had collected scattered references on Black women nurses, but the primary focus of my study was Black male physicians. My first book, *Black Victory: The Rise and Fall of the White Primary in Texas* (1979), had contained scant mention of any Black women. In the aftermath of the Black Women in the Middle West project everything changed. Within a couple of years my research and writing switched from medicine to nursing. In 1989, I published *Black Women in White: Racial Conflict and Cooperation in the Nursing Profession, 1890-1950*. My scholarship had been transformed.

The transformation and culmination of my work on Black women is witnessed in my two collaborative projects with Ralph Carlson, president of Carlson Publishing. By the time Carlson contacted me in 1987, I had left Purdue University to become John A. Hannah Professor of History at Michigan State University. Carlson invited me to be the editor of a series of essay collections in Black women's history. Again, my first response was ambivalence. I knew a series of such books would greatly facilitate future research on Black women's history. I doubted, however, that more than fifty first-rate articles existed. To my surprise and delight we located close to 250 articles—an impressive testament to the volume and quality of work completed in the past decade. The sixteen volumes of *Black Women in United States History* (1990) benefitted from the advice and assistance of associate editors Elsa Barkley Brown, Tiffany Patterson, and Lillian Williams, and the research assistance of Earnestine Jenkins.

At this juncture it would be easy to conclude that Black women's history is alive and flourishing and that our goals have been achieved. While much has been accomplished in a remarkably short period, troubling and tiresome problems remain. It is especially irritating these days to read any scholarly rationalization as to why Black women's history is not addressed in women's history or in African-American history books and courses. Some white women historians insist that they do not know how to deal with questions of race. Likewise, some African-American male historians persist in avoiding gender issues and the intersections of gender constructions with those of race and class. In most general U.S. history survey texts, Black women are never mentioned or at best are relegated to marginal roles in history. In popular culture, negative and demeaning stereotypes of Black women abound. In political discourse, Black women are all too often villainized as the ubiquitous welfare queens or mothers of illegitimate, impoverished, and delinquent children. Daily bombardment of negative images, too little hope combined with too many barriers to enumerate, adversely affects the self-esteem of young Black girls. Too often, their caretakers are equally vulnerable to relentless assaults on their dignity as human beings, leaving few internal and external resources to do battle with multidimensional oppression.

Before sharing my final thoughts about the objectives of this encyclopedia, I would like to thank my family. I am the sum of what I believe and do. Several significant individuals, however, played pivotal roles in providing the essential lessons and ideas that I needed to become the Black woman, scholar, mother, aunt, sister, daughter, companion, and friend that I imagine myself now to be. I am grateful to them all.

I was born on February 7, 1947, in Morley, Missouri, but spent my formative years on my maternal grandparents' farm in Villa Ridge, Illinois. My grandmother, Fannie Venerable Thompson, was the most influential person in my early childhood. She taught me my manners, the Lord's Prayer, and the Twenty-third Psalm. My grandfather, Robert Lee Thompson, taught me the virtue of listening and how to be silent. When I joined my nuclear family in Chicago, I learned additional lessons. My mother, Lottie Mae Thompson Clark, taught me that "God don't like ugly and he ain't crazy about pretty either." I always took that saying to mean I should be bal-anced, avoid extremes, and look beyond the surface to understand substance. She instilled in me a sense of responsibility and self-respect, and nourished a take-charge attitude. From my mother's example, I learned that laziness and ignorance were sins, but the highest immorality was to be unkind to children. It is because of the exquisite simplicity and profound impact of her teachings on my development that I dedicate to her memory this historical encyclopedia.

From my father, Levester Clark, I inherited the gift of humor, an aesthetic appreciation, and an ability to love unconditionally. I had one very special brother, Orlando Stanley Clark, now deceased, and I have two supportive and loyal sisters, Barbara Ann Clark and Alma Jean Mitchell, who remind me that it is okay to have fun. My daughter, Robbie Davine, born on August 10, 1965, is without question the dearest part of my life. My brother-in-law Sylvester Clark and my sister-in-law Dorothy Clark have offered unfailing encouragement of all my efforts. Among those for whom I feel considerable responsibility for their education and well-being are my nine nieces and nephews: Joyce, Barbie Darlene, Tina, Jimmy, Steven, Jammie, Orlando, Jr., Charles, and Derrick. From the very beginning of my work on the history of Black women, Johnny E. Brown was there for me. Finally, I would like to thank my friend James D. Anderson.

What Black women really need today is power. Although there are many kinds of power, I have learned in the past decade of working with and listening to thousands of Black women from all walks of life that special kinds of power exist in our history. I hope that this encyclopedia will bring others to the self-education and empowerment I experienced. I trust that it will encourage the keepers of our people's histories to continue their struggles to be heard.

EAST LANSING, MICHIGAN
OCTOBER 1992

Reader's Guide

This encyclopedia consists of 804 entries, 641 of which are biographies of individual Black women and 163 of which deal with general topics and organizations.

The task of deciding which individuals and topics to include was not an easy one. We wanted to provide as much information as possible, while at the same time keeping the publication to a manageable length. A number of editorial decisions have defined the publication. First, the biographies included are only those of Black women. This might seem obvious, but some of the most active champions of Black women have been white and/or male. We did include entries on the involvement with and ideas about Black women of four Black men—W.E.B. Du Bois, Frederick Douglass, Booker T. Washington, and Marcus Garvey. The encyclopedia would have been incomplete without the presentation of their ideas (note that the information on Garvey is presented under his organization—the Universal Negro Improvement Association).

Biographies were included of individuals who played a role on the national stage or who made national news. We have also included some people who were prominent only in their local communities, but who were typical of women throughout the country. Using these parameters, we tried to include as many people as possible, with a special emphasis on women about whom information could not easily be found in other reference books. Conversely, we have slighted contemporary women who are in mid-career and are in virtually every reference book. Their entries are shorter than their accomplishments deserve.

The entries on organizations include only those of Black women. Again, we could have included many white organizations, but we chose not to. And, of course, there are exceptions to every rule. There are entries here on national Black organizations such as the National Association for the Advancement of Colored People, the National Urban League, the Baptist Church, and other organizations in which Black women played a central part—organizations which also played a central part in Black women's history.

HOW TO USE THE ENCYCLOPEDIA

Many of the alphabetically arranged entries in the *Encyclopedia* deal with general topics. For the reader's convenience, we have included a list of all such entries, which appears on pages xi-xii. You can scan this list to find the entries that contain the information you need.

If you are interested in knowing about women in specific fields of endeavor, you should consult the Classified List of Biographical Entries at the end of Volume II. There you can find listings of all the lawyers, educators, politicians, etc., whose biographies appear in the publication.

We are especially proud of the detail presented in the general index to these volumes and urge you to become familiar with it. It presents tens of thousands of access points to the encyclopedia.

FACT-CHECKING

Fact-checking for *Black Women in America* was undertaken as part of the editorial process managed by the Durham, North Carolina, editorial office. The Durham Public Library, North Carolina Central University Library, North Carolina State Library, and Duke University Libraries all proved to be valuable sources of information. We also consulted the Schomburg Center for Research in Black Culture of The New York Public Library, and the Alumnae Affairs Office at Tuskegee University.

The research staff provided fact-checking whenever information provided seemed implausible, when sources gave conflicting information, spellings differed, or basic facts were accessible only in rare or distant sources. Whenever possible, we located at least two published sources to confirm background information. However, one great strength of this encyclopedia is that an unusually high percentage of entries are based on new sources. Many of the people and topics here have not previously appeared in standard sources. These contributions are based on archival or other unpublished sources of information (including in some cases family Bibles, personal collections of papers, and interviews). In a few cases, we were able to confirm biographical information with the subject of the entry herself. This was an especially important task, we felt, for those whose achievements may have been overlooked in the available historical accounts. Though we spent hundreds of hours in this fact-checking, in a publication of this magnitude we

have, of necessity, relied heavily on the expertise of the contributors.

CHRONOLOGY

We are very pleased to include with the *Encyclopedia* "Black Women in the United States: A Chronology." It appears on pages 1,309-1,332. It contains elements of Black women's history which we have not been able to include in more detail in the individual entries as well as provides a broad historical context for those individuals, organizations, and activities that are detailed within these two volumes.

BIBLIOGRAPHICAL CITATIONS

The bibliographical citations at the end of the entries contain the sources that the author used to write the entry and/or provide additional information. They do not necessarily include all the standard sources. Nonetheless, many standard sources have been consulted routinely. These are cited using abbreviations; a complete list of these abbreviations follows.

FUTURE EDITIONS

This *Encyclopedia* includes an unprecedented amount of information on Black women in the United States, yet it is far from comprehensive. Many important topics (and individuals) are still to be researched.

Research on Black women over the last several decades has grown exponentially, and we hope and expect that it will continue to grow at this rate. We plan to keep up with the latest research by publishing supplemental editions of *Black Women in America* on a regular basis.

Abbreviations

The following abbreviations are used for reference works
frequently cited in the bibliographies to the entries.

AAW1   Trudier Harris and Thadious Davis, eds., *Afro-American Writers before the Harlem Renaissance*. Vol. 50 in *Dictionary of Literary Biography* (Detroit: Gale Research Company, 1986).

AAW2   Trudier Harris and Thadious Davis, eds., *Afro-American Writers from the Harlem Renaissance to 1940*. Vol. 51 in *Dictionary of Literary Biography* (Detroit: Gale Research Company, 1987).

AAWW   Ann Allen Shockley, *Afro-American Women Writers, 1746-1933: An Anthology and Critical Guide* (Boston: G. K. Hall, 1988).

AWW   Narda L. Schwartz, ed., *Articles on Women Writers* (Santa Barbara, Calif.: ABC-Clio, 1977, 1986).

BABB   *Selected Black American, African, and Caribbean Authors: A Bio-Bibliography*, compiled by James A. Page and Jae Min Roh (Littleton, Colo.: Libraries Unlimited, 1985).

BAFT   Donald Bogle, *Blacks in American Films and Television* (New York: Garland Publishing, 1988).

BAR   Mabel M. Smythe, *The Black American Reference Book* (Englewood Cliffs, N.J.: Prentice-Hall, 1976).

BAW   Theressa Gunnels Rush, Carol Fairbanks Myers, and Esther Spring Arata, *Black American Writers Past and Present: A Biographical and Bibliographical Dictionary* (Metuchen, N.J.: Scarecrow Press, 1975).

BDAAM   Eileen Southern, *Biographical Dictionary of Afro-American and African Musicians* (Westport, Conn.: Greenwood Press, 1982).

BI   *Biography Index* (New York: H. H. Wilson, 1984).

BW   Linda Metzger, ed., *Black Writers: A Selection of Sketches from Contemporary Authors* (Detroit: Gale Research, 1989).

BWW   Sheldon Harris, *Blues Who's Who: A Biographical Dictionary of Blues Singers* (New Rochelle, N.Y.: Arlington House, 1979).

CA   *Contemporary Authors* (Detroit: Gale Research, 1986).

CBWA   Marianna W. Davis, *Contributions of Black Women to America* (Columbia, S.C.: Kenday Press, 1982).

DANB   Rayford W. Logan and Michael R. Winston, eds., *Dictionary of American Negro Biography* (New York: Norton, 1982).

DBT   Allan Woll, *Dictionary of the Black Theatre: Broadway, Off-Broadway, and Selected Harlem Theatre* (Westport, Conn.: Greenwood Press, 1983).

DLB   *Dictionary of Literary Biography* (Detroit: Gale Research, 1986).

EAL   Mari Jo Buhle, Paul Buhle, and Dan Georgakas, eds., *Encyclopedia of the American Left* (New York: Garland Publishing, 1990).

EBA   W. Augustus Low and Virgil A. Clift, eds., *Encyclopedia of Black America* (New York: McGraw-Hill, 1981).

IWW   *International Who's Who* (London: Europa Publications, 1983).

LBAA   Ann Allen Shockley and Sue P. Chandler, *Living Black American Authors: Biographical Directory* (New York: R. R. Bowker, 1973).

NA   Harry A. Ploski and James Williams, eds., *The Negro Almanac: A Reference Work on the African American* (Detroit: Gale Research, 1989).

NAW   Edward James, Janet Wilson James, and Paul S. Boyer, eds., *Notable American Women, 1607-1950: A Biographical Dictionary* (Cambridge, Mass.: Harvard University Press, 1971); Barbara Sicherman and Carol Hurd Green, eds., *Notable American Women: The Modern Period* (Cambridge, Mass.: Harvard University Press, 1980).

NBAW   Jessie Carney Smith, ed., *Notable Black American Women* (Detroit: Gale Research, 1992).

NWAT   Alice M. Robinson, Vera Mowry Roberts, and Milly S. Barranger, eds., *Notable Women in the American Theatre: Biographical Dictionary* (Westport, Conn.: Greenwood Press, 1989).

NYTBS   *New York Times Biographical Service* (Ann Arbor, Mich.: University Micro International, 1986).

RLBA   Harry A. Ploski and James Williams, eds., *Reference Library of Black America* (Detroit: Gale Research, 1990).

SBAA   James A. Page, *Selected Black American Authors: An Illustrated Bio-Bibliography* (Boston: G. K. Hall, 1977).

WA   Ute Gacs, Aisha Khan, Jerrie McIntyre, and Ruth Weinberg, eds., *Women Anthropologists: A Biographical Dictionary* (Westport, Conn.: Greenwood Press, 1988).

WWBA   *Who's Who among Black Americans* (Detroit: Gale Research, 1975-92).

WWCA   Thomas Yenser, ed., *Who's Who in Colored America* (New York: Who's Who in Colored America Corp., 1927-50).

Black Women in America

THE ENTRIES

A-L

A

ABOLITION MOVEMENT

O, ye daughters of Africa, awake! awake! arise!
No longer sleep nor slumber, but distinguish
yourselves. Show forth to the world that ye are
endowed with noble and exalted faculties.
(Maria Stewart 1831)

Maria Stewart was exceptional. Born in 1803 in
Hartford, Connecticut, Stewart was orphaned at the
age of five and bound out to a clergyman's family as a
domestic apprentice. She spent years in this family
home, cleaning, cooking, serving, and hoping for an
opportunity to better her "condition." She was especially interested in gaining a formal education but
instead received an introduction to religious rhetoric
and deep philosophical convictions of self-help and
service to one's community. These attributes profoundly colored her life and her work as an advocate
of abolition and free African-American equality. In
1831, fired by her belief that God had ordained her
with a "holy zeal" to these causes, she began to write
and lecture. Remarkably, this poor, informally educated domestic servant became the first American-
born woman of any color to hold a series of public
lectures before racially mixed audiences of men and
women.

During her brief stint on the Boston lecture circuit, Stewart spoke about every major issue of concern
to African-Americans of her generation—abolition,
colonization, the expansion of rights for free people of
color, the necessity of educational and occupational
opportunities for African-Americans, racial unity, racial pride, and self-determination. During her later
life, she became a teacher in New York and eventually
established two schools for free African-American children in Washington, D.C.

Maria Stewart was an exceptional woman, but she
was not alone. Many other women took similar paths,
dedicating their lives to abolition and Black rights.
Accordingly, her 1832 call to the "daughters of Africa" for activism and self-improvement was
provocatively timed. In 1829, just two years before
Stewart began her public reform efforts, a friend and
mentor, David Walker, published what his critics
called his "incendiary" *Appeal to the Coloured Citizens of
the World.* The following year, forty Black delegates
(all men) from eight states met in a convention to
consider the problems of African-Americans. Then,
in 1831, William Lloyd Garrison initiated his *Liberator* magazine, and activists soon formed the American
Anti-Slavery Society and numerous other regional
and local organizations. These activities were centered in the Northeast, but in August 1831 another
abolitionist effort was initiated in the rural Virginia
county of Southampton, where Nat Turner riveted
the nation as the leader of a slave rebellion that left
sixty Anglo-Americans dead, sparked the murder of

countless African-Americans, and influenced the on-slaught of new, discriminatory legislation aimed at free people of color.

Thus, Stewart's challenge to her community of women occurred at a time when abolition and other reform efforts were becoming more organized and gaining a national audience. The slave population was growing rapidly, increasing from approximately 1.5 million persons in 1820 to more than 2 million in 1830. A "cotton kingdom" dependent on slave labor was being established in the South and Southwest, which meant widespread territorial expansion of the institution of slavery. Clearly slavery was not dying out, as optimists had hoped at the end of the eighteenth century.

The movement to end slavery not only grew during the second half of the antebellum era, it also changed substantially. Although some ideological and methodological splintering did occur over the years, most abolitionists of the post-1830 era could not support efforts of gradual emancipation as their predecessors had. Immediate abolition became the call of most, and among African-Americans it held virtually universal appeal. Therefore, the issue of slavery, its fate and its impact on the socioeconomic and political character of the country, summoned a growing corps of abolitionists into conflict with proslavery advocates, a clash that would propel a second generation into national division and warfare.

Slavery was not the only issue at hand, however. Intimately related to this cause was the position—social, economic, and political—of free people of color who were victims of increasing legal and customary discrimination. Most southern states, for example, required free people of color to carry evidence of their status, or "certificates of freedom," wherever they went. Those who could not immediately produce this kind of documentation were held in jail until they could; some eventually were sold back into slavery. Many southern jurisdictions also demanded that free people of color register with the local police or court authorities—Florida, Georgia, and Alabama even required them to have a white guardian. Most antebellum southern states also forced those who were recently emancipated to leave within twelve months of their manumission or risk reenslavement. These laws and hostile customs forced many free people of color to leave the South. Those who remained faced mounting restrictions, including mandatory curfews, an end to free assembly, and exclusion from schools as well as many trades and occupations. Southern political and judicial systems were just as discriminatory. Black southerners gener-

ally could not vote, serve on juries, or testify against white defendants in a court of law, and they usually received stiffer criminal penalties than did white convicts for the same offenses.

The Northwest and West provided few additional expressions of freedom for the Black minority. Many of the so-called Black laws enacted in these regions were drawn directly from southern legislation and tradition. Free people of color fared better in the Northeast than other parts of the nation, but it was far from welcoming. Where discrimination was not founded in law, custom was often the basis. None of the northern states, for example, legislatively ousted Black persons from the courtroom, but social convention often prevented free people of color from sitting on juries everywhere except Massachusetts. Likewise, northern free people of color generally were not segregated in places of public accommodation or in publicly owned institutions, except schools, but they routinely were denied admission to hotels, restaurants, theaters, public lyceums, hospitals, and even cemeteries patronized by white residents.

It was not just that free African-Americans faced growing opposition, which limited their opportunities, resources, and fundamental rights; there also was an attempt mounting to force Black people out of the country permanently. The American Colonization Society was formed in 1816 for that express purpose. The Black community widely opposed colonization, and their campaign against this effort, coupled with the inability of the society to fund removal, kept the organization from being successful. In the end, only about 1,400 persons moved to the West African colony of Liberia, despite the support of leading U.S. statesmen and the federal government. Instead of the number of free Black people in the population diminishing, there actually was a steady increase from 108,435 persons in 1800 to 233,634 in 1820, to 386,293 in 1840, and to almost one-half million, 488,070, in 1860. The majority were located in the Northeast, although Maryland and Virginia contained the largest population within state boundaries. Baltimore, with a population in excess of 25,000 in 1860, contained the largest number of free African-Americans residing in a city. While most free people of color south of Maryland lived in rural locales, north of Maryland they tended to congregate in urban centers, cities, and towns, and it was in such places that their abolitionist activities were centered.

Women constituted a major part of the free Black community, about 52 percent of the nineteenth-century Black population. Their numerical superiority was not reflected in their social or economic status, however. Because of extremely limited educational resources and exclusion from lucrative employment due to racial and gender bias, few free women of color were able to acquire a comfortable lifestyle independently of men. Only a small number found work in the expanding industrial sector of the northern urban economy or were able to invest in their own businesses in any section of the country. Likewise, the number of free women of color who owned farmland and who had access to labor resources in the overwhelming agrarian South was minuscule. The free Black woman, therefore, most readily found employment as a washerwoman, maid, cook, day laborer, or seamstress. Most women worked all of their lives, beginning as older children and continuing through old age, yet rarely achieved financial security. In Philadelphia in 1849, for example, 46 percent of free Black women were washerwomen. They fared similarly in the Midwest and South. Sixty percent of free women of color in Cincinnati, Ohio, in 1835, for example, were described as laundresses, as were 36 percent of those in Richmond County, Georgia, in 1819. Their

poverty had an incredible social impact on the free African-American community because these women headed a significant minority of households. Given the tragic effect of racial oppression on their daily lives, it is no small wonder that many free women of color became involved in efforts to expand the rights of Black Americans.

In the most fundamental sense, African-American women's participation in abolitionist efforts began with African girls and women who resisted their enslavement at every juncture. Their desire to be free fueled their participation in innumerable individual and group acts of resistance and rebellion throughout the colonial and antebellum eras. This tradition is perhaps most readily symbolized in the courageous work of Harriet Tubman, a slave woman from Maryland who was not content to acquire her own freedom but risked her life at least nineteen times in order to help approximately 300 other slaves find their way to safety and freedom. Tubman's determination to end slavery did not end with these brilliantly planned and executed escapes funded principally by her own spo-

Harriet Tubman, a slave woman from Maryland, was not content to secure her own freedom; she risked her life at least nineteen times in order to help some 300 other slaves reach freedom. Here she stands (far left) with some of the passengers on the Underground Railroad. [Schomburg Center]

radic work as a domestic. She also served as nurse, scout, and spy for the Union Army during the Civil War. Like her, some of the most important female participants in organized abolition during the antebellum era were fugitive slave women.

African-American women involved in abolition derived much of their inspiration and legitimacy from the self-help and self-improvement traditions of the Black community. Many of the earliest female societies first formed as auxiliaries to male groups. Women who belonged to gender-integrated societies sometimes faced male opposition to their membership or, once admitted, were not allowed to fill leadership positions. Some women believed that their gender distinguished both their agenda and their strategies for service and reform, and they resented having to seek the approval of men when trying to express these differences. In the early nineteenth century, free women of color began to create many of their own literary, debating, insurance, and abolitionist societies. In so doing, they helped create a community of women who shared a common sense of sociopolitical and cultural identity and who had a moral, civic, and intellectual agenda that embraced, among other causes, abolition.

Their organizations generally had three important priorities: service and charity to members and the adjoining Black community; individual and group intellectual development; and moral instruction appropriate for Christian women. The preamble to the constitution of the Afric-American Female Intelligence Society of Boston is exemplary:

Whereas the subscribers, women of color of the Commonwealth of Massachusetts, actuated by a natural feeling for the welfare of knowledge, the suppression of vice and immorality, and for cherishing such virtues as will render us happy and useful to society, sensible of the gross ignorance under which we have too long labored, but trusting, by the blessing of God, we shall be able to accomplish the object of our union—we have therefore associated ourselves under the name of the Afric-American Female Intelligence Society.

Many such organizations formed throughout the Northeast as well as in southern cities such as Baltimore, Alexandria, Richmond, Charleston, and New Orleans. Most, however, were centered in northeastern urban centers, for example, the African Female Benevolent Society of Newport, Rhode Island, formed in 1809; the Colored Female Religious and Moral Society of Salem, Massachusetts, in 1818; the Coloured Female Roman Catholic Beneficial Society of Washington, D.C., in 1828; the Colored Female Charitable Society of Boston in 1832; the Minerva Literary Association of Philadelphia in 1834; the Ladies Literary Society and the Female Literary Society, both of New York City, in 1834 and 1836; the Ladies Literary and Dorcas Society of Rochester in 1836; and the Young Ladies Literary Society of Buffalo in 1837.

The majority of African-American women reformers were middle-class or relatively well-to-do women who had received some formal education and were involved in numerous self-help and community-improvement ventures. Many represented second- and third-generation activists who had the benefit of growing up in homes and among friends who, as influential reformers and revolutionaries in their own right, set rigid standards for their younger kin to emulate. The number of elite Black people in many communities was so small that some of their self-help and reform organizations resembled extended families. Therefore, race, class, gender, and sometimes even family lines influenced the development of the work they performed. Of course, there were many exceptions to this middle-class standard. The Daughters of Africa in Philadelphia, for example, consisted of working women who pooled small amounts of their income in order to provide a collective fund to serve their members in times of emergency. Yet it was difficult for individuals, particularly pioneers such as Maria Stewart, to have a significant impact on the African-American community or the abolitionist movement without the benefit and support of a network of sponsoring Black reformers.

Literary societies were popular among free women of color throughout the antebellum years. Given the lack of educational opportunities or intellectual and artistic outlets for Black women, it is not difficult to imagine why many joined these organizations. Yet the African-American women who supported these literary and debating societies had a political agenda as well. Many were as equally invested in abolition and issues of equality as in literary development and intellectual exercise. As the decades passed and abolition became the dominant reform issue, however, some organizations shifted their emphasis to address this priority. Therefore, although the title of a group might suggest only a literary society, often the favored interests of its members were abolition and the expansion of Black rights. Many raised money to support these movements by selling some of their original texts, writing letters for persons who were illiterate, hosting bake sales, and holding fairs. The

Ladies Literary Society of New York, for example, held numerous fund-raising activities in September 1837 in order to assist the *Colored American*, an African-American antislavery journal. They also donated funds to the New York Vigilance Committee.

Even at the most fundamental level, African-American women who were active in literary groups believed that their goals supported abolition and Black rights activism, maintaining that the intellectual acuity and high moral standards demonstrated by their work undermined racist notions of innate Black inferiority and debasement. "As daughters of a despised race," the Female Literary Association of Philadelphia asserted in 1831, "it becomes a duty . . . to cultivate the talents entrusted to our keeping that by so doing, we may break down the strong barrier of prejudice" (Porter 1936).

Their intellectual endeavors also helped inspire a core of dedicated teachers who worked among free Black people and, later, southern freedmen. Many abolitionist women, including Maria Stewart, Mary Ann Shadd Cary, Margaretta and Charlotte Forten, Frances Ellen Watkins Harper, and Sarah Douglass, believed that their teaching careers were laudable expressions of their abolitionist sentiment. As Frances Harper declared in 1852:

> There are no people that need all the benefits resulting from a well-directed education more than we do. The condition of our people, the wants of our children, and the welfare of our race demand the aid of every helping hand. It is a work of time, a labor of patience, to become an effective school teacher; and it should be a work of love in which they who engage should not abate heart or hope until it is done (Still 1968).

Free women of color used their talents and accomplishments, honed in their literary societies, to protest slavery and racial discrimination on several fronts. Indeed, many of the literary texts written by African-American women promoted their sociopolitical assertions. Harriet Wilson, Charlotte and Sarah Forten, Harriet Jacobs, Maria Stewart, Ann Plato, and Frances E. W. Harper were foremost among the early Black female realists and protest writers. Their literature not only carried powerful statements affirming the African-American cause; it also credited some of them with tremendous firsts. Mary Prince's *The History of Mary Prince, A West Indian Slave* (1831), a horrifying document of Caribbean slavery, was the first slave narrative written by a

Black woman in the Americas. The following year, Maria Stewart became the first free African-American woman to publish a book of hymns and meditations. In 1835, Stewart also published a collection of her works, including political speeches, essays, and religious meditations. Ten years later, Ann Plato became the first African-American to publish a book of essays, and Harriet Wilson was the first Black person in the United States to publish a novel. Her 1859 text, *Our Nig: or, Sketches from the Life of a Free Black*, details some of the excruciating problems of free families of color, and the abuse of African-American servant children and female domestics, whose only chance of financial survival was to work under conditions similar to those of chattel slavery. Two years later, Harriet Jacobs's *Incidents in the Life of a Slave Girl* personalized the plight of the southern female slave by detailing episodes of psychological torture, sexual abuse, physical intimidation, and loss of family in her own life. Jacobs's testimony, which expresses her determination to resist abuse and claim her humanity and femininity as much as it describes her life as a slave, was an invaluable defense of abolition and the Black female character.

Some women also published in various antislavery journals and literary magazines. The writings of Charlotte Forten, for example, appeared in the *Liberator*, the *Christian Recorder*, the *Anglo-African Magazine*, the *National Anti-Slavery Standard*, the *Atlantic Monthly*, and the *New England Magazine*. An avid scholar and educator, Forten also impressed her "society" of friends with her linguistic abilities, translating for publication the French novel *Madame Thérèse: or, The Volunteers of '92* by Emile Erckmann and Alexandre Chatrian.

One of the most prolific writers of her generation was Frances E. W. Harper, a free woman of color from Baltimore who had worked as a domestic, seamstress, and teacher before turning to writing and lecturing for the Maine Anti-Slavery Society on a full-time basis. Harper's poems were published in three volumes: *Poems on Miscellaneous Subjects* (1854), *Poems* (1871), and *Sketches of Southern Life* (1872). Eager to provide financial support as well as inspiration and information to the abolitionist movement, Harper used much of the income derived from her first book of poems to support William Still and his efforts on behalf of the Underground Railroad.

Mary Ann Shadd [Cary] not only was an influential abolitionist writer and activist but also was the first African-American female editor. Determined not to have her political views or social critiques censored, Shadd Cary created her own newspaper, the

Provincial Freeman, in 1853. For six years Shadd Cary juggled key positions on the fledgling antislavery and emigrationist journal, serving as its editor, writer, promoter, and fund-raiser. She was a pioneer in an all-male profession, however, and few were willing to provide her with long-term support. Shadd Cary herself once described the situation she faced as an editor:

> To colored women, we have a word. We have "broken the editorial ice" for your class in America; so go to editing, as many of you as are willing, and able; and to those who will not, we say help us when we visit you, by subscribing to the paper, paying for it, and getting your neighbors to do the same (*Provincial Freeman*, August 22, 1855).

Shadd Cary's personal cause was not helped by her conflict with Henry Bibb, a fugitive slave of considerable power in abolitionist circles whom she accused of illegal and unethical activities. Exposing Bibb's activities resulted in the loss of funding from the American Missionary Association for a school she had founded in Windsor. Shadd Cary continued to agitate, however, and part of her rhetoric included a scorching criticism of Black male sexism. "Better far to have a class of sensible, industrious wood-sawyers, than of conceited poverty-starved lawyers, superficial professors, or conceited quacks," she asserted regarding the African-American male leadership in the United States and Canada (*Provincial Freeman*, May 5, 1855).

Shadd Cary was born in Wilmington, Delaware, but grew up in Pennsylvania. Like many of her female peers, she was reared in an African-American abolitionist household and as a child came to understand the kinds of sacrifices that one had to make in order to promote Black freedom and equality. Yet her solutions differed substantially from those of many others. For one thing, Mary Ann Shadd Cary supported immigration to Canada, and she spent much of her time and energy during the 1850s promoting the exodus that eventually included approximately 15,000 people. In 1852, she wrote a lengthy pamphlet entitled, *A Plea for Emigration or, Notes of Canada West, in its Moral, Social and Political Aspect.* Like other emigrationists, she believed that free Black people would live better outside the United States; she also knew that Canada was one of the few places on the continent where fugitive slaves could live without constant fear of being captured.

During the 1830s, 1840s, and 1850s, free women of color were at the forefront of establishing and maintaining female antislavery societies. For example, they are credited with founding the first women's abolitionist society, the Salem (Massachusetts) Female Antislavery Society, in 1832. Although many of these organizations did not include white members, some were racially integrated. The Philadelphia Female Anti-Slavery Society, for example, was founded in 1833 by both white and at least seven women of color, including four from the prominent Forten family. Other integrated organizations were established in Rochester, New York, and Lynn and Boston, Massachusetts. Members sponsored numerous revenue-producing projects, public lyceums, exhibitions, and lectures, and they circulated abolitionist literature and various petitions directed at local, state, and national government agencies. Gaining a sense of their unique contributions to, and their general self-assurance within, these politically charged reformist circles, Black women acted as representatives to regional and national antislavery conventions as well as helped initiate the earliest organized strivings for women's rights.

Integrated abolitionist societies, however, did not eliminate demonstrations of racial bias. Many Euro-American abolitionists did not believe in racial equality or social integration. Often they refused to socially embrace Black antislavery advocates, allow them to take leadership positions in various organizations, or support African-American journalists and lecturers. Many spoke to or about Black abolitionists in a condescending or patronizing manner, willing to tolerate some African-American participation in the movement but demanding that Euro-American activists retain ultimate control. Black women abolitionists did not ignore these conflicts when they arose in their integrated meetings. "Our skins may differ, but from thee we claim / A sister's privilege and a sister's name," Sarah Forten wrote in a poem commissioned for the 1837 Convention of American Women. That same year she noted bitterly in a letter to Angelina Grimké, regarding the "effect of Prejudice," that:

> No doubt but there has always existed the same amount of prejudice in the minds of Americans towards the descendants of Africa. Even our professed friends have not yet rid themselves of it. To some of them it clings like a dark mantle obscuring their many virtues and choking up the avenues of higher and nobler sentiments. I recollect the words of one of the best and least prejudiced men in the Abolition ranks. "Ah," said he, "I can recall the time when in walking with a colored brother, the darker the night, the

better Abolitionist was I." . . . how much of this leaven still lingers in the hearts of our white brethren and sisters is oftentimes made manifest to us (Sterling 1984).

A few people were able to move beyond the bounds of racism and sexism not only to participate in local abolitionist organizations, but also to lecture as representatives of some of the largest and most powerful national antislavery societies. Younger generations of African-American women were able to take advantage of the opportunities painfully created by their predecessors. Sarah Parker Remond, for example, born in Salem, Massachusetts, to a family of activists and a member of several antislavery groups, became lecturer for the American Anti-Slavery Society in 1856. She lectured throughout the Northeast, England, Scotland, and Ireland from 1859 through the Civil War era, at first supporting the cause of abolition and then hoping to influence the British not to support the Confederacy.

Sarah Remond's stint on the lecture circuit followed in the tradition established by Maria Stewart in 1832. Branded as "promiscuous," however, Stewart eventually was subdued by criticism that her behavior was not befitting a woman; after giving only four public speeches in Boston, she was forced to retire. Yet Stewart did not retire or leave the lecture circuit before she chastised men for trying to limit her contributions as an abolitionist because of her sex:

> Be no longer astonished . . . my brethren and friends that God at this eventful period should raise up your own females to strive by their example . . . to assist those who are endeavoring to stop the strong current of prejudice that flows so profusely against us at present. No longer ridicule their efforts. It will be counted for sin. For God makes use of feeble means sometimes to bring about his most exalted efforts ("Farewell Address to Her Friends in the City of Boston," September 21, 1833).

Feeble was the word to use to describe a convention of nineteenth-century feminine identity that many Black female abolitionists seemed to defy. Consider, for example, the life and work of Sojourner Truth. Born a slave in New York State at the end of the eighteenth century, Truth (named Isabella Bomefree while a slave) was the victim of a series of cruel masters and devastating personal experiences, including separation from her parents as a child and having her own children sold away from her. Taking her

freedom in 1826, Sojourner Truth embraced Christianity and later came to believe that it was her religious duty to further the cause of Black men and women, slave and free. She was a tireless lecturer, often appearing unexpectedly but fascinating a charged crowd whenever she spoke. Refusing to be turned away by antagonists, Truth helped redefine womanhood in order to embrace the African-American woman's experience. "Nobody ever helps me into carriages, or over mud puddles, or gives me any best place!" she declared at a woman's rights convention in Akron, Ohio, in 1851. "And ain't I a woman?" She proved that she was indeed a woman in 1858 when she stood up to a heckler who had challenged her to prove that she was a woman. Truth bared her breasts and, referring to her work as a slave wet nurse, asked if there was anyone in her audience who wanted to suck. Clearly few could argue with the effectiveness of her lecturing style in support of abolition and the recognition of Black womanhood.

Free women of color continued their various activities in support of abolition and Black rights through the antebellum era and beyond. Not content to end their efforts with the initiation of the Civil War, they continued their agitation, hoping to convince the U.S. government and the American people to mandate general emancipation as a condition for peace. Others joined forces to collect food, clothing, school books, and medical supplies for the thousands of slaves who escaped to Union lines during the war. Their efforts inspired younger activists, many just finishing their formal education, to travel to the South during and after the Civil War to educate Black southerners. Teachers such as Charlotte Forten, Sara Stanley, Lucie Stanton Day, and Blanche Harris helped create the first generation of literate ex-slaves. As always, their work, pursued under trying social and economic conditions, was part of their determination to fulfill their twofold duty as women and African-Americans.

> In the earnest path of duty
> With the high hopes and hearts sincere,
> We, to useful lives aspiring,
> Daily meet to labor here.
> Not the great and gifted only
> He appoints to do his will,
> But each one, however lowly,
> Has a mission to fulfill.
> Knowing this, toil we unwearied,
> With true hearts and purpose high;
> We would win a wreath immortal
> Whose bright flowers ne'er fade and die.
> (Charlotte Forten, 1856)

BIBLIOGRAPHY

Bell, Howard. "National Negro Conventions of the Middle 1840's: Moral Suasion vs. Political Action," *Journal of Negro History* (October 1957); Brown, Jean Collier. "The Economic Status of Negro Women," *Southern Workman* (October 1931); Craft, William. *Running a Thousand Miles for Freedom: or the Escape of William and Ellen Craft from Slavery* (1860); Curry, Leonard P. *The Free Black in Urban America, 1800-1850: The Shadow of the Dream* (1981); Foner, Philip and Ronald Lewis, eds. *The Black Worker to 1869* (1978); Greene, Lorenzo and Carter Woodson. *The Negro Wage Earner* (1930); Hughes, Langston and Arna Bontemps, eds. *The Poetry of the Negro, 1746-1970* (1949); Jacobs, Harriet. *Incidents in the Life of a Slave Girl* ([1861] 1988); Litwack, Leon. *North of Slavery: The Negro in the Free States, 1790-1860* (1961); Loewenberg, Bert and Ruth Bogin, eds. *Black Women in Nineteenth-Century American Life: Their Words, Their Thoughts, Their Feelings* (1978); Pennsylvania Society for Promoting the Abolition of Slavery. *Register of the Trades of the Colored People in the City of Philadelphia* (1849), and *Statistical Inquiry into the Condition of the People of Color of the City and Districts of Philadelphia* (1849); Plato, Ann. *Essays, Including Biographies and Miscellaneous Pieces in Prose and Poetry* (1841); Porter, Dorothy. "The Original Educational Activities of Negro Literary Societies," *Journal of Negro Education* (October 1936); Prince, Mary. "The History of Mary Prince, A West Indian Slave." In *Six Women's Slave Narratives* ([1831] 1988); Richardson, Marilyn, ed. *Maria W. Stewart, America's First Black Woman Political Writer* (1987); Smith, Amanda Berry. *An Autobiography of Mrs. Amanda Smith, the Colored Evangelist* (1893); Sterling, Dorothy, ed. *We Are Your Sisters: Black Women in the Nineteenth Century* (1984); Stevenson, Brenda E., ed. *The Journals of Charlotte Forten Grimké* (1988); Still, William, ed. *The Underground Railroad, A Record of Facts, Authentic Narratives, Letters, Etc.* ([1872] 1968); Sumler-Lewis, Janice. "The Fortens of Philadelphia: An Afro-American Family and Nineteenth-Century Reform," Ph.D. diss. (1978); U.S. Bureau of the Census. *Historical Statistics of the United States: Colonial Times to 1957* (1960), and *The Social and Economic Status of the Black Population in the United States: An Historical View, 1790-1978* (1979); Wesley, Charles. *Negro Labor in the United States, 1850-1925: A Study in American Economic History* (1927); Wilson, Harriet E. *Our Nig: or, Sketches from the Life of a Free Black*, ed. Henry Louis Gates (1983).

BRENDA E. STEVENSON

ADAMS, OSCEOLA *see* ARCHER, OSCEOLA MACARTHY

ADAMS-ENDER, CLARA LEACH (1939-)

Her 1987 appointment as chief of the Army Nurse Corps and director of personnel clearly indicated that Brigadier General Clara Adams-Ender, a sharecropper's daughter, had gone from "rags to respect." While not the first Black woman to hold the highest position in the more than 40,000-member nurse corps (Hazel Johnson was first), Adams-Ender was a pacesetter in her own right.

In 1967, she became the first female in the army to qualify for and be awarded the Expert Field Medical Badge. Less than ten years later she became the first woman to be awarded the Master of Military Art and Science degree from the Command and General Staff College at Ft. Leavenworth, Kansas, in 1976. Four years later, she was selected as the first female to serve as senior marcher for 700 soldiers in the four-day, 100-mile Nijmegan March in Nijmegan, Holland. In 1982, she became the first Black Army Nurse Corps officer to graduate from the U.S. Army War College. In 1984, she was named chief of the Department of Nursing at Walter Reed Army Medical Center, making her the first Black nurse to hold that position.

Clara Adams was born July 11, 1939, and grew up in Wake County, North Carolina, with her five sisters and four brothers. She entered the Army Student Nurse Program during her third year of studies at North Carolina A & T State University in 1959. She married her husband, German-born Heinz Ender, in 1981.

In addition to her many firsts, Adams-Ender has served the military in the United States, Europe, and Korea and has held academic appointments in the nursing schools at the University of Maryland, Georgetown University, and Oakland University. She has also served as a member of the Defense Advisory Committee on Women in the Services and as a consultant for a children's television workshop in New York City.

An avid reader and physical fitness enthusiast, Adams-Ender is also an accomplished writer. Articles she has authored or coauthored have appeared in *Perspectives on Nursing, Today's O.R. Nurse, Medical Bulletin,* and *Nursing Management.* She is a contributor to *Ethical Decision-Making in Nursing Administration,* ed. Mary Cipriano Silva (1990).

Fluent in German, Adams-Ender is one of the most sought-after military speakers in the country. Her resume indicates that she gave fifty-four professional presentations in 1990 alone. Yet she also found time for the community, her personal interests, her stepson, and her husband, who is a retired orthodontist and oral surgeon. She has a life membership in the National Association for the Advancement of Colored People, is a Red Cross nurse, and has served on the board of the Northeast Illinois Council of the Boy Scouts of America. She was recently inducted into Delta Sigma Theta Sorority as an honorary member and is also a member of the National Council of Negro Women and the National Association for Female Executives.

Adams-Ender is a tireless worker whose many awards and honors include the military's Distinguished Service Award and Meritorious Service Medal with three oak leaf clusters; Roy Wilkins Meritorious Service Award of the NAACP; Female Athlete of the Year; Regents' Distinguished Graduate Award of the University of Minnesota; Outstanding Young Woman of America; and a place on *Washingtonian* magazine's 1989 list of the 100 most powerful women in Washington, D.C.

BIBLIOGRAPHY

Army records. General Officer Management Office, Headquarters, Department of the Army, Washington, D.C.; Cheers, Michael. "Brig. Gen. Clara Adams-Ender: Army Nurse Corps Chief," *Ebony* (June 1989); *Essence*, "Women in the Military" (April 1990); *NA*.

LINDA ROCHELLE LANE

ADDISON, ADELE (1925-)

Adele Addison, soprano, is best known as a recitalist but has made distinguished appearances and recordings in oratorio and opera; she is also recognized as a teacher and scholar with special interests in German lieder. She was born July 24, 1925, in New York City. Her early education took place in Springfield, Massachusetts, where her family moved during her childhood. She received the B.Mus. from Westminster Choir College in 1946 and then studied with Boris Goldovsky at the Berkshire Music Center and Povla Frijsh in New York City.

Addison made her recital debut in Jordan Hall, Boston, Massachusetts, in April 1948, and four years later gave a recital in Town Hall, New York City. Her career continued with tours of the United States and Canada interspersed with teaching. In 1962, she was soloist in the opening concert at Philharmonic Hall at Lincoln Center, and in 1963, she made an acclaimed tour of the Soviet Union under a cultural exchange program. She has taught at the Eastman

School, Philadelphia College of the Performing Arts, Aspen Music School, and the State University of New York, Stony Brook.

Indicative of Adele Addison's standing among American singers and her intelligent musicianship is the fact that she has participated in several significant world premieres of contemporary music, such as John La Montaigne's *Fragments from Song of Songs* with the New Haven Symphony (1950); Poulenc's *Gloria* with the Boston Symphony Orchestra (1961); and Lukas Foss's *Time Cycle* with the New York Philharmonic Orchestra. In addition, she has appeared with most of the other major American symphony orchestras. She was awarded an honorary doctorate by the University of Massachusetts in 1963.

BIBLIOGRAPHY

BDAAM; Hitchcock, Wiley and Stanley Sadie, eds. *The New Grove Dictionary of American Music* (1986); Story, Rosalyn M. *And So I Sing* (1990); *WWBA* (1981).

DORIS EVANS McGINTY

Acclaimed soprano Adele Addison was soloist at the opening concert of Philharmonic Hall at Lincoln Center in 1962. [Library of Congress]

AFRICAN METHODIST EPISCOPAL PREACHING WOMEN OF THE NINETEENTH CENTURY

Throughout the nineteenth century, hundreds of African-American women traveled the country preaching the gospel of Christianity. Fewer than three were ever officially ordained into the ministry though most were successful in the type of ministry they practiced. Within the African Methodist Episcopal (AME) church, the collective efforts of preaching women served as a cutting edge that pierced the fabric of the all-male church hierarchy. When the denomination was organized in 1816, there was no organizational position for women. By 1900, however, church structure had been expanded to include three positions for women's service. In addition, the radical question of ordaining women to the ministry had been considered by church officials on eight occasions. The existence and success of preaching women were major reasons for church actions to officially include women and their service.

Nineteenth-century AME preaching women would never have considered themselves a radical element in their church, but they were extremely committed to their supreme call to preach the gospel and were devoutly religious in their Christian faith. To surrender a call from their God because a worldly organization did not approve would have meant a serious breach of their religious beliefs. However, throughout the century, preaching women carrying out their call consistently caused church officials to reconsider women's absence in denominational structure.

Jarena Lee was the earliest woman preacher of the AME church, and she began her gospel work before African Methodism was organized; in fact, no one has been found who precedes her in preaching activities.

Between 1816 and 1849, the year Lee published her autobiographical *Journal*, a number of women were active as preachers within the AME church network. Sophie Murray, for example, was an early member of the Philadelphia Bethel African Methodist Church, as was Elizabeth Cole. Each woman was referred to as an evangelist of the congregation and was reported to have "held many glorious prayer meetings [where] many souls were brought to the saving knowledge." In New Jersey, Rachel Evans distinguished herself as a better preacher than her acclaimed husband and was referred to as "a preacheress of no ordinary ability. She could rouse a congregation at any time." In Washington, D.C.,

Harriet Felson Taylor also earned a reputation for her preaching abilities. As one of the first members of that city's 1840 Union Bethel congregation, Taylor was identified as "first female exhorter and local preacher." Similarly, Zilpha Elaw was a preaching woman within African Methodism from 1816 to 1849. Not only did she visit the annual conference of the Bethel AME Church of Baltimore in 1828, but, like Lee, she published an autobiography.

None of these women, or the many others not named, was ordained. In the context of Christianity of the time, there was no authority that sanctioned women as preachers. Independent denominations like the AME church had separated themselves from white bodies over issues of a racially inclusive worship, but no group had ever questioned the church's patriarchy or the authority of an exclusively male clergy. The preaching women themselves were not as interested in altering the organizational arrangements of their church as they were in garnering recognition for their right to preach. However, their activities and their reputations as successful preachers threatened the exclusive authority of men to the ministry.

Although the AME church had not formally responded to women preachers, by the 1844 meeting of the General Conference the issue had gained so much public attention that it required official consideration. Rev. Nathan Ward and others, as authorized members of the decision-making body, presented a petition requesting that the church "make provisions for females to preach and exhort." This petition was defeated, but at the next meeting of the conference, in 1848, another request was made that women be licensed to preach in connection with "ministerial privileges, akin to those of men."

The significance of the challenge posed by these petitions is reflected in the fact that the reigning church thinker of 1848, Rev. Daniel Payne, soon to be bishop, "filed a protest against the licensing of females to travel in the connection." In writing an official history of the church in 1891, after serving thirty-nine years as bishop, Payne trivialized women's preaching activities and the petitions for their licensing:

> The origin of the question is found in the fact that certain women members of the AME Church, who believed themselves divinely commissioned to preach by formal licenses, subsequently organized themselves into an association with avowed intention of laying out a field of usefulness for themselves, and making out appointments for such a field after the

manner of our Annual Conferences. They held together for a brief period, and then fell to pieces like a rope of sand. (*The Budget*, c. 1888; cited in Tanner 1884 and Payne 1891)

None of this stopped women from preaching, and at the next meeting of the General Conference a distinct action, as called for in the episcopal address of Bishop William Paul Quinn, was secured. By a large majority vote, the all-male body defeated the bishop's 1852 request that the church consider licensing women to preach. The question of authorizing women preachers quieted for a while, but the women's activities did not. More significantly, the issue reflected the larger problem of a lack of positions for women within the denominational structure.

Between 1816 and 1852, the AME church expanded its membership tremendously, and women were the majority participants in that expansion. Individually and collectively, women were the essence of African Methodism: they helped construct church buildings; they supported denominational programs; they converted and socialized new members; they led worship; they sustained fledgling congregations; they fed and clothed ministers; they visited the sick in the name of the church; they buried the dead; and they financed church work. However, every officially designated position of denominational structure was reserved for men.

In 1868, male leadership could no longer avoid taking some type of action to correct this serious omission. They had dismissed the question of women's ordination at the 1864 General Conference by not discussing it. However, they could no longer justify women's absence from church positions, given their overwhelming majority in the growth and development of African Methodism. At the 1868 conference, delegates created the position of stewardess and allowed pastors to nominate a board of stewardesses. As conditional and male-dependent as this was, it was still the first and only official position for women in the denomination.

Preaching women were not seeking just any service, however; they had been called to proclaim the Christian gospel. Stewardess might suffice for the services of many AME women, but there remained a group who would continue to preach. Between 1868 and 1900, the number of women functioning as preachers increased tremendously, and their work did not go unnoticed. Amanda Berry Smith was among the more internationally known preaching women of the period, and Margaret Wilson of the New Jersey Annual Conference was known for her work at the Haleyville

Mission in 1883. Emily Calkins Stevens as well as Harriet A. Baker had support from bishops of the church, including Bishop John Mifflin Brown. Lena Doolin Mason was exceptionally active in her preaching.

By the 1884 meeting of the General Conference, the preponderance of women preachers, and their renowned successes, were once again challenging the male-dominated church hierarchy. Part of the problem was the increasing number of pastors willing to give license to female evangelists in order that their congregations be the beneficiaries of the women's successful proselytizing work. These local licenses were not under control of the denominational church, and the 1884 conference was urged to take action.

To concede the reality of preaching women and their success, the conference gave denominational approval to licensing women, but with severe restrictions. The concession of the female evangelist position was the second organizational change made by the church to accommodate its women members. However, the change did not sanction women's call to the gospel ministry, and it did not authorize them to ordination. Preaching women refused to be satisfied and continued their activities. The issue was brought to a head again with the 1885 ordination of Sarah A. H. of North Carolina. The 1888 meeting of the General Conference once again had to consider the topic of ordaining women.

The all-male leadership of the conference began making a definitive decision by first reprimanding Bishop Henry McNeal Turner for ordaining a woman. They then proceeded to issue a strongly worded resolution absolutely prohibiting women's ordination. The resolution passed, and bishops were officially "forbidden to ordain a woman to the order of a deacon or an elder" (James n.d.).

In spite of limitations from the denomination, women persevered with their work. Mary C. Palmer, Melinda M. Cotton, Emma V. Johnson, and Mary L. Harris made extensive reports of their 1896-98 preaching activities to the Philadelphia Annual Conference, for example. Margaret Wilson also continued and reported on preaching success to the 1897 New Jersey Annual Conference meeting. African Methodist women labored to preach despite church restrictions.

As the nineteenth century came to a close, the male hierarchy of the church made another attempt to channel women's activities from those that challenged men's exclusive authority to ministry. At the 1900 meeting of the General Conference, delegates agreed to create another position for women. This final organizational, gender-specific change of the century was the position of deaconess. There were formal rituals for becoming a deaconess, but the position was never part of the ordained ministry like that of the deacon position for men.

It would be another forty-eight years before the African Methodist Episcopal church would authorize women into the ordained ministry, but without the persistence of preaching women, the inclusion of women's activities by way of other structural positions might have been delayed.

BIBLIOGRAPHY

Christian Recorder (July 1, 1851); Cook, John Francis. "Outstanding Members of the First Church—September 1, 1840" (c. 1841); Elaw, Zilpha. *Memoirs of the Life, Religious Experience, Ministerial Travels and Labours of Mrs. Zilpha Elaw: An American Female of Colour* (1846); Handy, James A. *Scraps of African Methodist Episcopal History* (n.d.); Payne, Daniel Alexander. *History of the African Methodist Episcopal Church* (1891); Smith, Charles Spencer. *A History of the African Methodist Episcopal Church* (1922); Tanner, Benjamin Tucker. *An Outline of Our History and Government for African Methodist Churchmen* (1884); Thompson, Joseph. *Bethel Gleanings* (1881); Wayman, Alexander. *Cyclopaedia of African Methodism* (1882).

JUALYNNE E. DODSON

AFRICAN MISSIONARY MOVEMENT

American Protestant missionary societies began to focus on the continent of Africa at the beginning of the nineteenth century. By 1840, Congregationalist, Baptist, Methodist, Episcopalian, and Presbyterian denominations had organized foreign mission societies. Although American Protestant missionary activity among Native Americans began in the mid-seventeenth century, the first foreign missionary society in the country was the interdenominational American Board of Commissioners for Foreign Missions (ABCFM), formed in 1810. However, with the rise of denominationalism, all the non-Congregationalists withdrew from the ABCFM and founded separate societies.

The Baptists established a separate missionary society in 1814. In May 1845, southern Baptists seceded over the questions of slavery and denominational organization, and formed their own convention. The Foreign Mission Board of the Methodist Episcopal Church was created in 1819. After the Methodist Episcopal Church split in 1844, the Southern Meth-odist Episcopal Church initiated foreign missionary activity in 1848. The Domestic and Foreign Missionary Society of the Protestant Episcopal Church in the United States began operation in 1820 and the Foreign Mission Board of the Presbyterian Church was organized in 1837.

The African Methodist Episcopal (AME) Church began mission activity in 1822 with the appointment of its first official foreign missionary, Charles Butler. However, Butler never left the United States for his assignment and John Boggs became the earliest commissioned AME Church missionary to reach Africa, arriving in Liberia in 1824. In 1876, the AME Zion Church began its foreign missionary activities in Liberia. The Baptist Foreign Mission Convention of the United States was established in 1880 and sent six missionaries to Liberia in 1883.

By the mid-nineteenth century, women, who were denied ordination, voting privileges, and authority in the church, began to channel their energies and abilities into other areas of religious leadership. The expanded status and role of women in the church came with the formation of church groups for women only, especially home and foreign mission societies and deaconesses' orders. Church women collected thousands of dollars from the "mite boxes" to support mission programs, which included sending single female workers into home and foreign fields. Between 1861 and 1894 home missionary societies were organized by and for women in seventeen denominations and foreign missionary societies were formed in thirty-three. Thus, through their own self-created separatist groups, women were able to broaden their church involvement.

After 1900, women's societies were pressured to merge with the denominational boards with the argument that women's societies drained off funds. By 1950, not only had most women's societies merged, but few women held leadership positions in these reconstituted boards.

Black Americans assumed a role in the evangelization of Africa because of a belief in their duty and moral obligation to their ancestral homeland. Yet African-Americans had an ambiguous alliance with the continent because of the Western image of Africa as the "Dark Continent." Nevertheless, Black missionaries had a genuine sense of obligation for Africa and their attitudes toward Africa and Africans were far less patronizing than those of white Americans. At the schools and colleges that they attended, Black students were indoctrinated with a strong dose of propaganda about their special mission in Africa.

Married male missionaries assigned to mission work often were accompanied by wives who shared in missionary duties. American church officials eventually came to the conclusion that wives were indispensable to the success of mission work. However, missionary wives, designated assistant missionaries, received little recognition for their efforts and no financial compensation because the church maintained that married women missionaries were primarily wives, mothers, and homemakers and only secondarily missionaries.

As a result of this view of the role of married women, religious leaders decided that single women could play a role in mission work. Single women also were designated "assistant missionaries." Their work was devalued, they were paid less than single or married male missionaries, and they seldom were asked to write mission reports or carry mission work into the interior, as did men. Missionary men often objected to the full participation of women in mission work. Full missionary status belonged only to ordained ministers and women were excluded from the ordained ministry.

Women who went to Africa, either as missionary wives or as single commissioned missionaries, generally aided in efforts to transform the lives of African women and children, since the social transformation philosophy of the late nineteenth and early twentieth centuries emphasized that women missionaries be engaged in "women's work for women, wife to wife, sister to sister" (White 1988). Women missionaries, Black and white, taught in or were principals in day, industrial, and Sunday schools; supervised or worked in nurseries, orphanages, or boarding schools; made house-to-house visitations; did evangelistic work; conducted Bible classes; prepared vernacular literature; and dispensed medical care to women and children as nurses or physicians.

As early as 1830, women constituted 49 percent of the American Protestant missionary force overseas. The number increased to 57 percent by 1880 and 60 percent by the late nineteenth century. Today women make up about 60 percent of North American overseas missionaries.

The American Protestant mission movement has relied heavily on the contribution of women, both Black and white. Almost half of the Black American missionaries sent to Africa from 1820 to 1980 were women. Women were and are today the most numerous and consistent supporters of missions, both in financial support and volunteerism. American women rallied to the cause of overseas missions. As leaders in

missionary societies and as married and single missionaries, women found a status and role that had been denied them in other areas of the church.

BIBLIOGRAPHY

Beaver, R. Pierce. *American Protestant Women in World Mission: History of the First Feminist Movement in North America* (1980); Beck, James P. "Women in Missions: A Pilot Study," *Journal of Psychology and Theology* (Fall 1986); Brooks, Evelyn. "Religion, Politics and Gender: The Leadership of Nannie Helen Burroughs," *Journal of Religious Thought* (Winter-Spring 1988); Burrow, Rufus, Jr. "Sexism in the Black Community and the Black Church," *Journal of the Interdenominational Theological Center* (Spring 1986); Carpenter, Delores C. "Black Women in Religious Institutions: A Historical Summary from Slavery to the 1960s," *Journal of Religious Thought* (Winter-Spring 1989-90); DeVries, Susan B. "Wives: Homemakers or Mission Employees," *Evangelical Mission Quarterly* (October 1986); Edwards, Lillie Johnson. "Mothers, Wives, and Missionaries: Afro-American Women in Africa, 1885-1940," Southeastern Regional Seminar in African Studies, Charlottesville, Virginia (1983); Heuser, Frederick J., Jr. "Women's Work for Women: Belle Sherwood Hawkes and the East Persia Presbyterian Mission," *American Presbyterians, Journal of Presbyterian History* (Spring 1987); Jacobs, Sylvia M. "African-American Women Missionaries and European Imperialism in Southern Africa, 1880-1920," *Women's Studies International Forum* (1990), and "Afro-American Women Missionaries Confront the African Way of Life." In *Black Women in United States History: The Twentieth Century*, ed. Darlene Clark Hine (1990), and *Black Americans and the Missionary Movement in Africa* (1982), and "Give a Thought to Africa: Black Women Missionaries in Southern Africa." In *Complicity and Resistance: Western Women and Imperialism*, ed. Nupur Chaudhuri and Margaret Strobel (1992), and " 'Say Africa When You Pray': The Activities of Early Baptist Women Missionaries among Liberian Women and Children," *Sage: A Scholarly Journal on Black Women* (Fall 1986), and "Three Afro-American Women: Missionaries in Africa, 1882-1904." In *Women in New Worlds*, ed. Rosemary Skinner Keller, Louise L. Queen, and Hilah F. Thomas (1982); Keller, Rosemary Skinner. "Lay Women in the Protestant Tradition" and "Patterns of Laywomen's Leadership in Twentieth-Century Protestantism." Both in *Women and Religion in America*, ed. Rosemary Radford Ruether and Rosemary Skinner Keller (1981); Martin, Sandy D. *Black Baptists and African Missions: The Origins of a Movement, 1880-1915* (1989), and "Spelman's Emma B. DeLaney and the African Mission," *Journal of Religious Thought* (Spring-Summer 1984); Patterson, Virginia. "Women in Missions: Facing the Twenty-First Century," *Evangelical Mission Quarterly* (January 1989); Tucker, Ruth. "Female Mission Strategists: A Historical and Contemporary Perspective," *Missiology* (January 1987); Welter, Barbara. "She Hath Done What She Could: Protestant Women's Missionary Careers in

Nineteenth-Century America," *American Quarterly* (Winter 1978); White, Ann. "Counting the Cost of Faith: America's Early Female Missionaries," *Church History* (March 1988); Williams, Walter L. *Black Americans and the Evangelization of Africa, 1877-1900* (1982).

SYLVIA M. JACOBS

AKERS, DORIS (1923-)

At a very young age, Doris Akers (gospel composer, choir director, singer, and publisher) listened to sermons to get ideas for songs. She became one of the most prolific, influential composers in the history of gospel music. She was born May 21, 1923, in Brookfield, Missouri. Her family moved to Kirksville, Missouri, when she was five. By the time she was six years old, she was playing the piano "by ear." Her first song, "Keep the Fire Burning in Me," was written when she was ten. As a young person, not only did she play at church and school activities, she also organized a five-piece band called "Dot Akers and Her Swingsters" that featured swing jazz and other styles of popular music in vogue during the 1930s and 1940s.

After her arrival in Los Angeles in 1945, Akers performed with the Sallie Martin Singers for a year and later organized her own gospel group, the Doris Akers Singers. In 1948, she joined Dorothy Simmons to form the Simmons-Akers Singers. During the ten years that the group was together, the Simmons-Akers Singers became nationally known through concert tours, recordings, and the establishment of a publishing company, the Simmons and Akers Music House. The company published and distributed songs written by Akers. Akers came into greater prominence in the late 1950s and the 1960s when she became a solo artist and director of the Sky Pilot Choir, one of the first racially mixed choirs in Los Angeles that featured the singing of Black gospel music. In the late 1950s she also became affiliated with the white-owned publishing company Manna Music, giving her music even wider distribution. Thus, she is noted as one of the first musicians to bridge the gap between Black and white gospel music.

In 1970, Akers moved to Ohio. Before leaving, she made several recordings with RCA, Capitol, and Christian Faith; appeared on nationwide television on many occasions; and received numerous awards for her contributions to gospel music. For example, in 1961 Akers was acknowledged as "Gospel Composer of the Year." During the 1970s and 1980s she continued to be active in the field of gospel music, particularly within the white Christian community.

She became known as an established gospel composer in 1947 with the publication of "A Double Portion of God's Love" by Martin and Morris Music; such standards as "Grow Closer" (1952), "Lead Me, Guide Me" (1953), "God Is So Good" (1957), "You Can't Beat God Giving" (1957), and "Sweet, Sweet Spirit" (1962) are just a few of the hundreds of songs that she has composed. Not only are her songs found in various hymn and religious song books of all denominations, but some have been used as themes for musicals (e.g., *Praise House* and *Me and Bessie*) as well as the titles of hymn books (*Lead Me, Guide Me*).

BIBLIOGRAPHY

Akers, Doris. Interviews (February 8, 1988, and September 4, 1989); Boyer, Horace. "Akers, Doris." In *The New Grove Dictionary of American Music*, ed. H. Wiley Hitchcock and Stanley Sadre (1986); DjeDje, Jacqueline Cogdell. "A Historical Overview of Black Gospel Music in Los Angeles," *Black Music Research Bulletin* (Spring 1988), and "Gospel Music in the Los Angeles Black Community: A Historical Overview," *Black Music Research Journal* (Spring 1989); Heilbut, Tony. *The Gospel Sound: Good News and Bad Times* (1975); *Lead Me, Guide Me: The African American Catholic Hymnal* (1987).

JACQUELINE COGDELL DJEDJE

ALBERT, OCTAVIA VICTORIA ROGERS (1853-c. 1890)

Octavia Victoria Rogers Albert was a teacher and author, known for her religious commitment and for writing a collection of slave narratives. She was born a slave on December 24, 1853, in Oglethorpe, Georgia. After Emancipation, she attended Atlanta University, where she trained to become a teacher. Her first teaching position was at a school in Montezuma, Georgia, where she met A.E.P. Albert in 1873. On October 21, 1874, they married and moved to Houma, Louisiana. They had one child.

In 1875, she joined the African Methodist Episcopal (AME) Church in Oglethorpe, under the leadership of Bishop Henry McNeal Turner. When her husband was ordained a minister in the Methodist Episcopal Church in 1877, she converted to Methodism and was baptized in 1878.

Albert's home in Houma became a gathering place for former slaves. She taught them to read and write, read them the Scriptures, and encouraged them

One of the most prolific and influential composers in the history of gospel music, Doris Akers was one of the first musicians to bridge the gap between the Black and white gospel traditions. [J. C. DjeDje]

to discuss their lives during slavery. A skilled interviewer and writer, Albert recorded their experiences. Having been freed from slavery before she was old enough to understand the institution, Albert felt compelled to create an accurate record of slavery in the United States. The resulting book, *The House of Bondage*, was published posthumously in 1890 by her husband and daughter. It consists of seven slave narratives, recorded fifteen years after the end of slavery. The narratives are vivid accounts of the inhumane treatment of slaves. She also records the progress of some freedmen during the Reconstruction period.

Albert wrote to correct and re-create history, not just to satisfy her artistic talent. Her evangelism was evident in her writings. She believed that God would make the entire nation accountable for the sins of slavery and charged that slavery under Catholic slaveholders was more oppressive than under Protestants.

She compared slavery in the United States to the Egyptian bondage of the people of Israel. Noting the differences between Black and white racial attitudes, she preached a gospel of spiritual development. Albert shows that Christianity survived in the Black community despite slaveowners' refusal to allow slaves to practice religion.

BIBLIOGRAPHY

DANB; Majors, Monroe A. *Noted Negro Women: Their Triumphs and Activities* ([1893] 1986).

VIVIAN NJERI FISHER

ALDRIDGE, AMANDA IRA CHRISTINA ELIZABETH *see* COMPOSERS

ALEXANDER, SADIE TANNER MOSSELL (1898-1989)

In an interview in 1981, Sadie Tanner Mossell Alexander provided this advice for young Black men and women: "Don't let anything stop you. There will be times when you'll be disappointed, but you can't stop. Make yourself the best that you can make out of what you are. The very best" (Polak 1981). Alexander, the first Black woman to earn a Ph.D. in economics, a lawyer, and a civil rights activist, could truthfully say that she had always been the best that she could be, and this was usually more than the U.S. society wanted her and other Black women to be.

Sadie Tanner Mossell was born into a prominent Philadelphia family on January 2, 1898. Her father, Aaron Mossell, was the first African-American to receive a law degree from the University of Pennsylvania. Her grandfather, Benjamin Tucker Tanner, was a well-known author, a bishop in the African Methodist Episcopal Church, and editor of the country's first African-American scholarly journal, the *African Methodist Episcopal Review*. The famous painter Henry Ossawa Tanner was her uncle. At the turn of the century, the Tanner home was a gathering place and intellectual center for the Black community.

Mossell was educated in the public schools of Philadelphia and Washington, D.C. In 1915, she graduated from M Street High School and was awarded a scholarship to Howard University. Her mother, however, was convinced that opportunities

for graduate training would be better if her daughter received a Bachelor's degree from the University of Pennsylvania. Mossell went along with her mother's wishes.

Sadie Mossell found her college course work to be extremely difficult, but she graduated with a B.A. with honors in education in 1918, completing a four-year program in three years. Continuing her studies in economics, she obtained an M.A. in 1919, became a Frances Sergeant Pepper Fellow, and earned a Ph.D. on June 6, 1921. Only one day later than Georgiana Simpson, she became the second African-American woman in the United States to receive a doctoral degree and the first to receive a Ph.D. in economics.

The first Black woman to receive a doctorate in economics in the United States, Sadie Tanner Mossell Alexander was also the first to be admitted to the bar and practice law in the state of Pennsylvania. She was a founder of the National Bar Association and helped to draft the 1935 Pennsylvania public accommodations law. [Schomburg Center]

Finding employment that measured up to her abilities and qualifications was her next challenge. Mossell found that her Ph.D. was useless in the job market and did not enable her to secure a job at any of the large white insurance companies. Despite excellent recommendations from her professors, no one would hire an African-American woman, even in positions for which she was clearly overqualified. Her professors threatened, to no avail, not to refer any other students to the insurance companies unless she was hired. Then Mossell decided to utilize her minor in insurance and actuarial science to take a position as assistant actuary for the North Carolina Mutual Life Insurance Company, an African-American firm in Durham. She remained there for two years, until she returned to Philadelphia in 1923 to marry her college sweetheart, Raymond Pace Alexander, who had just finished Harvard University Law School.

Sadie Alexander abhorred domestic life, and after twelve months of running the house she expressed her discontent to her husband. When asked what she would rather do, she replied that she wanted to go to law school.

In September 1924, she entered the University of Pennsylvania Law School and quickly earned honors and became a member of the Law Review Board. Upon graduation in June 1927, she became the first African-American woman to enter the bar and practice law in the State of Pennsylvania. She and her husband entered into private practice as one of the earliest husband-wife legal teams in the United States. The partnership lasted until her husband became a judge in the Philadelphia Court of Common Pleas in 1959. Alexander was appointed assistant city solicitor for Philadelphia, serving from 1928 to 1930 and from 1934 to 1938. Returning to private practice, she specialized in probate law, divorce, and domestic relations matters. In 1925, she and her husband were among the founders of the National Bar Association, the professional organization for African-American lawyers.

During the 1920s and 1930s, the Alexanders were personally responsible for ending overt discrimination against Black Americans in Philadelphia hotels, restaurants, and theaters. Tired of sitting in the "Coloreds Only" sections of movie houses and theaters, they helped to draft the 1935 Pennsylvania state public accommodations law, which prohibited discrimination in public places. Following its passage, the Alexanders tested the law at a Philadelphia theater that refused to admit African-Americans. They made several attempts to gain admittance but were turned away each time by the manager; they had him arrested. After several nights in jail, the manager relented. The Alexanders used the same technique to end discrimination in several of the city's hotels and restaurants.

During the 1940s, the Alexanders pressed for the hiring of African-Americans on the faculty of the University of Pennsylvania and for the integration of the U.S. Armed Forces. In 1946, President Harry S. Truman appointed Alexander to the Commission to Study the Civil Rights of All Races and Faiths, on which she served until 1948. The commission's report, *To Secure These Rights* (1948), recommended the desegregation of the armed services, and this occurred in 1949. Alexander also served on President John F. Kennedy's Lawyers' Committee for Civil Rights under Law in 1963 and was chair of President Jimmy Carter's White House Conference on Aging in 1979 and 1980.

Alexander also held a number of other important professional positions throughout her distinguished career. Between 1919 and 1923, she served as the first national president of Delta Sigma Theta Sorority. She maintained a long association with the American Civil Liberties Union and for twenty-five years served as a national secretary for the National Urban League. Between 1950 and 1967, she was a member of the Philadelphia Commission on Human Relations and for a time she served as the chair. For several years she served as chair of, and the only female on, the Philadelphia Bar Association's subcommittee on human rights.

Alexander received many awards and honors. She was elected to Phi Beta Kappa at the University of Pennsylvania in 1970. She received honorary degrees from the University of Pennsylvania, Swarthmore College, Drexel University, Lincoln University, and the Medical College of Pennsylvania. On April 15, 1980, she received the Distinguished Service Award from the University of Pennsylvania. In 1987, the Philadelphia Bar Association named its public service center in her honor.

Alexander practiced law in Philadelphia until she was eighty-five years old. She died on November 6, 1989, of complications from Alzheimer's disease, Parkinson's disease, and pneumonia. She died in her home in the Roxborough section of Philadelphia, where she had lived since 1983.

In her 1981 interview, Alexander summarized her career and approach to life by declaring, "I haven't worked for the money. There's only so much you can eat, and you can only sleep in one bed—but I always wanted to do something where you can contribute something" (Polak 1981).

BIBLIOGRAPHY

CBWA; Dannett, Sylvia. *Profiles of Negro Womanhood* (1964-66); Franklin, V. P. *The Education of Black Philadelphia: The Societal and Educational History of a Minority Community, 1900-1950* (1979); Greenlee, Marcia McAdoo. Interview with Sadie Tanner Mossell Alexander, Transcript, Schlesinger Library, Radcliffe College, Cambridge, Massachusetts, January 26, 1977; *NA*; Polak, Maralyn Lois. "Sadie Alexander: At 83, a Woman for Any Age," *Philadelphia Inquirer Magazine* (March 29, 1981).

V. P. FRANKLIN

ALEXANDER, VIRGINIA M. (1900-1949)

Virginia M. Alexander, physician, was born in Philadelphia in 1900. She was one of four children. Her mother died when Alexander was four years old, and her father lost his once-successful livery stable when she was thirteen.

Despite financial burdens, Alexander and her siblings managed to continue their educations. Both she and her oldest brother, Raymond, received scholarships to the University of Pennsylvania. Raymond completed his studies at Harvard Law School and went on to become one of the most influential Black lawyers in Philadelphia. To support herself in college, Virginia worked as a waitress, maid, and clerk. A philanthropic friend of the family provided financial assistance so that she could attend the Woman's Medical College of Pennsylvania.

At Woman's Medical College, Alexander had to endure attempts by teaching staff to discourage Black medical students. She persevered, however, and during her first year ranked second highest among medical aptitude test examinees. For a time following her graduation from medical school in 1925, she had trouble obtaining an internship because of her race and gender. After many refusals she was reluctantly accepted at Kansas City (Missouri) General Hospital, becoming the first female member of the hospital staff.

In 1928, Alexander returned to North Philadelphia to set up a general practice. She became increasingly concerned with the poor health care provided to women and children in Black neighborhoods. In 1931, she established the Aspiranto Health Home in her own three-story dwelling to provide health care facilities and instruction to pregnant women and their children.

Following a severe illness that temporarily forced her to discontinue her practice, Alexander renewed her interest in public health matters. During the summer of 1936, she toured several European countries to observe health care techniques and practices. With this new knowledge, she felt she needed additional education to carry out her goal in the United States. In 1937, she received a Master's degree in public health from Yale University.

Alexander worked in the public health field for nearly nine years, first in Washington, D.C., as a member of the U.S. Department of Health and as a staff physician at Howard University Medical School, and later at Schlossfield Hospital in Birmingham, Alabama. In 1941, she returned to private practice in Philadelphia. She was also on the courtesy staff of the Woman's Medical College of Pennsylvania. She continued practicing medicine until her death from lupus in 1949 at the age of forty-nine.

BIBLIOGRAPHY

Alexander, Virginia M. file. Archives and Special Collections on Women in Medicine. Medical College of Pennsylvania, Philadelphia, Pennsylvania.

BRENDA GALLOWAY-WRIGHT

ALLEN, DEBBIE (1950-)

She is the director of a successful, long-running television series, and that achievement, which would mark a career high for almost any Black woman in show business today, is just something she has done by the way.

Debbie Allen was born into a remarkable family on January 16, 1950, in Houston, Texas. Her father, Andrew Allen, was a dentist, and her mother, Vivian Ayers Allen, a poet who has been nominated for the Pulitzer Prize. Her sister, Phylicia Rashad, has become a well-known actress, and one of her brothers is Andrew "Tex" Allen, a jazz musician.

Allen decided early that she wanted to be a dancer. She began her training when she was three, and by the time she was eight, she had decided to go into musical theater. When she tried to enroll in the school of the Houston Foundation for Ballet, she was rejected for reasons her mother considered discriminatory. As a result, her family first hired a former dancer in the Ballets Russes to give Allen private lessons, and then her mother took the three oldest children to Mexico City so that Allen could train with the Ballet Nacional de Mexico. At fourteen, she went back to the Houston Foundation for Ballet and was admitted on a full scholarship.

Allen hoped, after graduation from high school, to attend the North Carolina School of the Arts, but again she was rejected. This time, discouraged, she abandoned her dance training and went to Howard University to study speech and theater. She was not there long, however, before choreographer Mike Malone drew her back into the dance world. She joined his dance troupe, began to perform with other students at the university, and studied at the National Ballet School. She also became head of the dance department of the Duke Ellington School of the Performing Arts and graduated cum laude from Howard in 1971. She left immediately for New York City.

Allen was soon hired to appear in the chorus of *Purlie*, a musical version of Ossie Davis's *Purlie Victorious*. In 1973, after a stint as a principal dancer in the Universal Dance Experience with George Faison, she went back to Broadway for *Raisin*, a musical adaptation of Lorraine Hansberry's *A Raisin in the Sun*, in which she played Beneatha and received excellent reviews. She remained with the show for almost two years. When it closed in 1975, she began working in television.

Allen made individual appearances on a variety of shows, such as *The Love Boat* and *Good Times*, and worked as choreographer on others. She also made a pilot for NBC called *3 Girls 3*, but it was not successful. She worked on a Ben Vereen special and appeared with Jimmy Walker in a made-for-television movie called *The Greatest Thing That Almost Happened*. Three more Broadway appearances, in *Guys and Dolls*, a disco version of *Alice in Wonderland*, and *Ain't Misbehavin'*, failed to put Allen on top, as did her role as Alex Haley's wife in *Roots: The Next Generation*.

Then, in 1980, Allen went back to Broadway for a revival of *West Side Story*. This time she received critical and popular acclaim. In that same year, she appeared in the tiny role in the movie *Fame* that would change her life. The tough dance teacher Lydia spoke only two lines, but she made an impact. When the movie became a television series, Allen was there, as actress and eventually as choreographer, director, and producer.

In 1981, Allen appeared in the film *Ragtime*, and in 1986 she was Richard Pryor's bitter, disappointed wife in *Jo Jo Dancer, Your Life Is Calling*. Also in 1986, she appeared on Broadway in Bob Fosse's revival of *Sweet Charity*. In the meantime, she continued to work on *Fame* and direct episodes of other television series, including *Family Ties* and *Bronx Zoo*. In 1988, she took over as director of the flagging series *A Different World* and turned it around. In the 1988-89 season, Allen appeared in her first television special

In show business, Debbie Allen is the contemporary equivalent of a Renaissance woman. A singer, dancer, actor, and choreographer, Allen is also director of the successful television series A Different World. *[Donald Bogle]*

and choreographed a Black adaptation of the Pollyanna stories, in which she worked with her sister, Phylicia Rashad. In 1992 she directed the made-for-television movie *Stompin' at the Savoy.*

Debbie Allen married Winfred Wilford in 1975, and the couple were divorced in 1983. In 1984, she married Norman Nixon. They have two children, Vivian Nichole and Norman Nixon, Jr.

[*See also* TELEVISION.]

BIBLIOGRAPHY

BAFT; CBWA; NA; NBAW; WWBA (1992).

KATHLEEN THOMPSON

ALLEN, GERI (1959-)

Detroit-born pianist-composer Geri Allen sets modern standards that stem from patterns laid out by jazz greats, from various continental styles, and from a personal sensibility that honors and preserves past traditions. Allen is respected as an intelligent and gifted musician, with connections to the pulse of modern music, and a creative mediator of fused sounds.

Geri Allen's encyclopedic use of sounds grows out of the vocabulary built by the grammarians of keyboard jazz composition—Mary Lou Williams, Thelonious Monk, and Duke Ellington—but her expansions fuse the funk, hip-hop, and soul styles that are closer to the taste of her generation with the ancestral musical sounds of Africa, the Caribbean, and South America. Her concept of musical inclusiveness may be called postmodernism in music.

Allen was graduated with a Bachelor's degree in jazz studies from Howard University in Washington, D.C., and, after several years as a touring performer, earned a Master's degree in ethnomusicology at the University of Pittsburgh. Her musical colleagues include avant-garde saxophonist Oliver Lake, flutist James Newton, and Motown's Mary Wilson. She also has been active with the radical groups M-Base and Black Rock Coalition.

Her 1991 recording, *The Nurturer,* features and honors her mentor, trumpeter Marcus Belgrave. Three of the nine tunes on the album were composed by Allen, and the others (except one by Lawrence Williams) were composed by members of the sextet. This democratic assignment of talent, as well as the musical qualities of the album, suggest a dedication to experimentation and newness. The album's title piece, Allen's "Silence and Song/The Nurturer," comprises piano statements that range from clean lyricism to mystical harmonic coloring to aggressive and complex rhythmic statements that delicately balance the horn and percussion lines.

Other projects include the recording of Jimi Hendrix's compositions (scored for three pianos, not yet released) and the composition of a large experimental work commissioned by the avant-garde American Music Theater Festival in Philadelphia. Her album *Maroons* (1992) is an "improvisation-happening" that recognizes ex-slaves as warriors who freed themselves and who created their own cultures in the Americas. Allen leads her own trio, the Geri Allen Trio, that tours Europe, Japan, and the U.S.

BIBLIOGRAPHY

Futterman, Steve. "A Jazz Pianist Who Dares to Follow an Unmarked Road," *New York Times* (July 21, 1991); Palmer, Don. "Geri Allen: Real-life Music Comes to Town," *Downbeat* (July 1988).

SELECTED DISCOGRAPHY

In the Middle/Open on All Sides, Polygram (1987); *In the Year of the Dragon*, Polygram (1989); *Twylight*, Polygram (1989); *The Nurturer*, Blue Note (1991); *Segments*, DIW Records (n.d.).

LORNA McDANIEL

ALLEN, SARAH (1764-1849)

Although she is usually ignored, or thought of only as the wife of Richard Allen, first bishop of the African Methodist Episcopal (AME) Church, Sarah

When she saw the bedraggled state of her husband and his colleagues at the African Methodist Episcopal Church's first annual conference, Sarah Allen formed a group of women to clothe and feed the dedicated Black ministers. Daughters of Conference, Allen's group, became a crucial part of the support system for impoverished Black churches and their clergy.
[Schomburg Center]

Allen was also instrumental in establishing the first official role of women within the church and providing the assistance necessary for AME ministers to carry out their mission. Most biographers accept that Sarah Allen was born in 1764 on the Isle of Wight, but no verification has been found. At the age of eight, she was brought as a slave to Philadelphia, and though we have yet to discern how she acquired freedom, she married Richard Allen in 1800. She died July 16, 1849, in Philadelphia at the home of her daughter Ann.

Most of Allen's life was devoted to raising her four sons and two daughters while securing the household resources and home atmosphere that fostered the ministry of her husband. She was undoubtedly, however, the guiding force behind the formation of Daughters of Conference organizations of the predominantly African-American AME Church.

As the small group of itinerant ministers of African Methodism returned to Philadelphia for the young church's first annual conference, their appearance and clothing were at best bedraggled. Allen organized women of the church to remedy the condition of the men's attire.

Allen continued to lead conference women in feeding, repairing garments for, and improving the appearance of AME pastors. These activities spread beyond Philadelphia as a tradition was formed. In 1827, the organizations were officially designated Daughters of Conference, wherein AME women assumed responsibility to provide material improvements for ministers assigned to their annual conferences.

Long after Allen's death, the Daughters of Conference organizations provided an essential supplement to AME ministers' meager salaries and insured the survival of church clergy.

BIBLIOGRAPHY

Berry, Llewylen L. *A Century of Missions of the African Methodist Episcopal Church, 1840-1940* (1942); Wright, Richard R. *The Encyclopedia of the African Methodist Episcopal Church* (1947).

JUALYNNE E. DODSON

ALLENSWORTH, JOSEPHINE LEAVELL (1855-1939)

Josephine Leavell Allensworth was one of the guiding forces in the creation of the all-Black "race colony" of Allensworth, California, in 1908. Due, in part, to her efforts, the community of Allensworth became a beacon of social change and a symbol of racial advancement.

Born in Bowling Green, Kentucky, on May 3, 1855, Josephine Leavell married Allen Allensworth, a Civil War veteran and local Baptist minister on September 20, 1877. During the next decade, Allensworth supported her husband's religious efforts as they ministered to congregations in Kentucky and Ohio. They had two daughters, Eva and Nella. In 1886, Allen Allensworth became the chaplain for the United States Army Twenty-Fourth Infantry (Colored). For twenty years, Josephine worked with her husband addressing the spiritual and educational needs of soldiers in forts throughout the American West.

After retiring from the army in 1906, the Allensworths settled in Los Angeles. Disappointed in the racial climate of the city, Josephine and Allen decided to create a "race colony" so that Black people could live "free from the restrictions of race." To Josephine Allensworth, a successful colony would prove that African-Americans were worthy of fair and equitable treatment, and it could provide a home for Black soldiers, a reward for their years of service. In 1908, the community of Allensworth was established in rural Tulare county, thirty miles north of Bakersfield, California. By 1912, Allensworth had a population of 100, two general stores, several large farms, and a number of modest businesses.

While much of the credit for the colony must go to the chaplain, Josephine Allensworth exerted great influence over the operation and direction of the enterprise. She served as the president of the school board, created a library system for the colony, and sponsored educational and social organizations like the Women's Improvement Association.

The colony's success was shortlived, due to declining water resources and the death of Allen Allensworth in 1914. While the town continued into the 1950s, the colony's expansion ended by 1925. Josephine Allensworth left the community in 1920 and spent the rest of her life with her daughter Nella in Los Angeles. She died on March 27, 1939, in Los Angeles.

BIBLIOGRAPHY

Archives. Allensworth State Historical Park, Allensworth, California; Beasley, Delilah. *The Negro Trail Blazers of California* (1969); Bunch, Lonnie. "Allensworth: The Life, Death, and Rebirth of an All-Black Community," *Californians* (November 1987); Ramsey, Eleanor. "Allensworth, A Study in Social Change," Ph.D diss. (1972); Oral histories are also available at the California Afro- American Museum in Los Angeles and the California Department of Parks and Recreation in Sacramento.

LONNIE BUNCH

ALPHA KAPPA ALPHA SORORITY

Summer 1935 in the heart of the Mississippi Delta was typical—full of famine and disease. Malnutrition and no medical attention continued to lead to a rampant growth of diphtheria, smallpox, and syphilis, and other venereal diseases went unchecked. Child mortality increased. After years of being held hostage, people in the mud-sogged, fever-infested region accepted their plight and learned to subsist in spite of the conditions. They were hostages who did not expect to be released.

Still, by summer's end, the people in Holmes County had been given a reason to hope. Mobile health units staffed by twelve visiting doctors, nurses, and health care providers—unheard of in Mississippi or elsewhere—had traveled 5,324 miles to even the most remote areas to administer more than 2,000 immunizations to the children, give medical attention to 2,267, and distribute 6,800 health pamphlets. The mobile health clinics would continue to bring hope for eight years, expanding both the territory covered and the services rendered, and assisting more than 15,000.

Called the Mississippi Health Project (MHP), the clinics were the first national show of strength for twenty-seven-year-old Alpha Kappa Alpha (AKA) sorority. The impact was noted far and wide—from articles in periodicals such as the *Journal of Public Health* to magazines such as *Reader's Digest* to commendations by the surgeon-general of the U.S. Public Health Service, Thomas Parren, who called MHP one of the finest jobs of volunteer public health work he had ever seen.

With the clinic, AKA—founded January 15, 1908, at Howard University as the first Black Greek-letter organization for Black women—was at the vanguard of a movement, and the exigencies of the times determined the response. The same was true in 1908. Then, there were a small number of women enrolled at Howard, limited opportunities for cultural enrichment, and the awareness that membership in this privileged class obligated Black women to develop their potential to its fullest. The combination of circumstances led undergraduate Ethel Hedgeman Lyle and her eight associates to draft a blueprint that incorporated self-pride, social interaction, ethical standards, cultural stimulation, and scholarly pursuits: issues that had to be addressed to improve the quality of life for themselves and their people.

One of the earliest projects was the presentation of a concert in Rankin Chapel by AKA members during spring 1908. By 1913, the cultural program included national figures such as Nathaniel Guy, an elocutionist in classical repertoire, and Jane Addams of Hull House. AKA women also worked cooperatively with groups that fostered social action, marching for women's rights in suffragette parades, giving countless hours of service to aid Black Americans migrating from the Deep South in 1917 and 1918, and taking leadership roles in the National Association for the Advancement of Colored People (NAACP), the Young Women's Christian Association, and other organizations that worked for the betterment of humankind.

In the 1920s, as AKA, having been incorporated in 1913, grew into a national organization, a national agenda began to take shape. Beginning in 1921, AKA chapters used their January founders' day celebrations to feature programs that increased race consciousness. By 1922, national programs to foster "aesthetic development of the public" and increased community involvement had been added (Parker 1990).

The 1930s, reeking with the Great Depression and intense anti-Black feelings, signaled the need for social action programs. At its 1934 national meeting, AKA developed plans for a summer school for rural teachers, the precursor to the Mississippi Health Project; laid the groundwork to pressure Congress to pass the Costigan-Wagner Anti-Lynching Bill; and joined forces with other fraternal groups and the NAACP in monitoring fair employment and lynching legislation. In 1938, feeling the need to do even more to promote and safeguard the interests of Black Americans, AKA established a full-time lobby to secure decent living conditions, permanent jobs, and a voice for determining working conditions.

The lobby continued to be a focal point during the 1940s, adding as targets the elimination of discrimination, disfranchisement, lynching, and inequities in federal housing and hospitalization programs. In 1946, buoyed by the lobby's success and excited about its potential, AKA invited the seven other Greek-letter organizations (sororities Delta Sigma Theta, Zeta Phi Beta, and Sigma Gamma Rho and fraternities Alpha Phi Alpha, Kappa Alpha Psi, Omega Psi Phi, and Phi Beta Sigma) to become partners, and the American Council of Human Rights (ACHR) was created, with the elimination of racial discrimination and inequality as its primary goals.

The awarding of grants during the 1950s brought another dimension to the program. In 1952, AKA gave its first grant-in-aid—$6,000 over a three-year period—to the Howard University College of Medicine for research in child development. Sickle cell anemia was the focus for additional grants, with $15,000 contributed between 1958 and 1961.

The 1960s dictated further program expansion. As a response to the increase in Black poverty, AKA developed a partnership with the federal government to prepare young women for economic independence under the aegis of the Anti-poverty Program. A $4 million grant resulted, and in 1965 AKA began its operation of the Cleveland Job Corps Center, thereby becoming the federal government's first women's Job Corps contractor. Subsequent awards of more than $40 million over a twenty-five-year period and a 1991 award of $15 million attested to the center's effectiveness, providing a second chance for more than 20,000 youths. AKA also developed its interest in the preservation of Black culture, instituting a domestic travel tour on historical Black figures, events, and places and a heritage publication series on Black women in the judiciary, politics, business, medicine, and dentistry.

The 1970s ushered in an era when AKA could give large awards to others. A $20,000 award was given to underwrite the purchase of Dr. Martin Luther King's birthplace; Central State University received $25,000 to restore a rare book collection destroyed by a tornado in 1974; the NAACP was given $50,000; and AKA presented the final installment on its pledge of $500,000 to the United Negro College Fund. AKA also launched its Educational Advancement Foundation, which by 1991 was making annual awards of $300,000 for scholarly pursuits.

With the realization that the world was becoming smaller, global initiatives became program targets in the 1980s. More than 300 African villages were adopted by AKA chapters in partnership with AfriCare. Additional support also was given to education through the award of $200,000 to historically Black colleges.

In the 1990s, education, heritage, Black economic development, and benevolent support continued. The Ivy AKAdemy, a community-based comprehensive learning center, opened in January 1991 in communities across the nation. The donation in October of a memorial honoring World War II hero Dorie Miller marked the inauguration of Black Faces in Public Places, a campaign by AKA to increase the number of Black images on government property and in public parks. The inauguration of Black Family Month re-emphasized the strength of the Black family. A Black Dollar Day campaign called attention to the plight of Black businesses and promoted a "buy Black philosophy." Other special programs raised thousands of dollars for victims of an economy in distress.

When the leadership changed in 1990, AKA's president outlined the critical issues that require responses if AKA is to move itself and Black people into the next century. Although she found herself addressing a membership that had grown from the original nine in a single chapter to more than 120,000 in more than 800 chapters in the United States, West Africa, Germany, the Virgin Islands, and the Bahamas, the approach used by Mary Shy Scott paralleled the one used by Ethel Hedgeman Lyle when she established AKA in 1908: developing a program that would improve the quality of life for AKA and its people was still the order of the day.

BIBLIOGRAPHY

Boyer, Sallie C. Personal interview with Ethel Hedgeman Lyle (Spring 1941); *Ivy Leaf.* "Life of Alpha Kappa Alpha's Founder Given against Colorful, Historical Background" (December 1948); Parker, Marjorie. *Alpha Kappa Alpha in the Eye of the Beholder* (1978), and *Alpha Kappa Alpha 1908-1958* (1958), and *Alpha Kappa Alpha Sorority: Sixty Years of Service* (1966), and *Alpha Kappa Alpha through the Years 1908-1988* (1990).

EARNESTINE GREEN McNEALEY

ALPHA SUFFRAGE CLUB

The Alpha Suffrage Club, organized in 1913, was a counterforce to the racist activities of the National American Woman Suffrage Association (NAWSA) and state suffrage clubs. Ida B. Wells-Barnett and a white colleague, Belle Squire, established the club to place Black women in the state and national suffrage arena, to increase political awareness and knowledge among female constituents, and to politicize Black women in Chicago, who had gained the vote on June 26, 1913, when Illinois became the first state east of the Mississippi River to enfranchise women. This partial suffrage bill enabled women to vote for all offices not mentioned in the state constitution including presidential electors, mayors, aldermen, municipal court judges, sanitary trustees, and most local officers. Passage of the bill sent women throughout the state on quests to organize and educate female constituents. Most of these efforts were among white women.

In addition, the strategy of national white women's suffrage groups was to implement a restricted suffrage, one that would not enfranchise Black women. Throughout the 1890s until the passage of the Nineteenth Amendment in 1920, NAWSA embraced the state's rights stance, supported restricted female suffrage, and courted white southern women.

Two hundred Black female members joined with officers Ida B. Wells-Barnett (president), Mary Jackson (vice president), Viola Hill (second vice president), Vera Wesley Green (recording secretary), Sadie L. Adams (corresponding secretary), Laura Beasley (treasurer), and K. J. Bills (editor) in building a power base among Black women. They implemented a block system to canvass neighborhoods and they organized once-a-week meeting sessions as learning centers on the rights and duties of citizens. Several women worked as clerks in the registration process and provided the necessary civic education.

The club integrated gender obligations with race obligations by holding membership in national, state, and local female and Black organizations. Members sent their president, Ida B. Wells-Barnett, to the National American Woman Suffrage Association's suffrage parade on March 3, 1913, in Washington, D.C. Although snubbed by white delegates, Wells-Barnett successfully completed the march. Moreover, she integrated the suffrage movement, both nationally and in Illinois, by joining the Illinois contingent rather than the all-Black delegates section that was relegated to the back of the line.

Early political efforts of the Alpha Suffrage Club disturbed some men. In the February 1914 primary election in the predominantly Black Second Ward in Chicago, some Black men unaccustomed to female political activity dismissed their efforts by heckling and suggesting that the women should be at home caring for their children. Despite male skepticism, the club canvassers played a significant role in garnering the sixth highest registration numbers of the thirty-five wards in the city. Encouraged by this showing, Black male politicians began to utilize the techniques and voting power of the club by developing a political partnership.

In the February 1915 Republican party primary, the Suffrage Club headquarters served as a forum for the three Black alderman candidates. Oscar DePriest, Louis Anderson, and Charles Griffin presented their political platforms and entertained questions. The club eventually endorsed Oscar DePriest through its newsletter, the *Alpha Suffrage Record,* and pressed each club in the Second Ward to support DePriest. On February 27, 1915, Oscar DePriest won the primary and in April he became the first Black alderman of Chicago.

The organization of the club, the politicization of Black women in Chicago, and the acceptance by political leaders that followed the success of DePriest's election strengthened the role of Black women in the political arena. Black and white Republican politicians actively sought the support of these women. In return, Black women expected them to commit to encouraging Black community political involvement, reform efforts, and economic parity.

BIBLIOGRAPHY

Alpha Suffrage Record (March 18, 1914); *Chicago Daily Tribune* (March 4, 1913); Duster, Alfreda, ed. *Crusade for Justice: The Autobiography of Ida B. Wells* (1970); Williams, Katherine E. "The Alpha Suffrage Club," *The Half Century Magazine* (September 1916).

WANDA HENDRICKS

AMERICAN TEACHERS ASSOCIATION

"We Win Battles by Social Action, Education Will Win Social War: The American Teachers Association and Black Women Educators . . . Support Freedom through Education."

These statements headed an advertisement in the *Negro History Bulletin* for a joint membership in the American Teachers Association (ATA) and the Association for the Study of Negro Life and History (ASNLH) in 1965, one year before the ATA merged with the National Education Association (NEA). For the twenty-six years of its existence, the ATA represented Black schoolteachers struggling to achieve parity with their white counterparts while simultaneously educating young Black men and women to have pride in their race and its achievements. This dual struggle, for equity and autonomy, marked the transition from the separate institutions of the segregated South to integrated institutions.

Although Black women have been in the forefront of the struggle for education, their role in that history has been relegated to biographical sketches of prominent educators and school founders such as Mary McLeod Bethune, Charlotte Hawkins Brown, Fanny Jackson Coppin, and Nannie Helen Burroughs. However, by the last decade of the nineteenth century, their numbers began to exceed those of Black male teachers. By 1900, Black women teachers outnumbered Black men two to one and represented a major force in the teaching profession. In many school districts married women were barred from teaching until the 1920s, and those women who did find jobs tended to work in rural schools for wages that fell below those of white male and female teachers and Black male teachers. Despite these barriers, Black women increasingly moved into teaching because it offered status and autonomy for educated women within the bounds of the community's accepted norms of women's roles. The history of these Black women schoolteachers and their struggle for autonomy is reflected in the institutional history of the organizations in which they were active, as well as their individual biographies.

The ATA represents one such organization. In 1939, the National Association of Teachers in Colored Schools (NATCS), an organization of Black schoolteachers founded in 1904, became the ATA. Carter G. Woodson's ASNLH worked closely with the NATCS and later the ATA to promote the teaching of Black history in America's schools. In addition to publishing the *Journal of Negro History*, Woodson began in 1937 to publish the *Negro History Bulletin* specifically for the many public school teachers and administrators who were establishing local branches of ASNLH. This latter publication publicized the activities of NATCS members as well as ATA plans and programs. Mary McLeod Bethune wrote in 1938 on the importance of teaching Black history, "Through accurate research and investigation, we serve so to supplement, correct, re-orient, and annotate the story of world progress as to enhance the standing of our group in the eyes of all men. In the one hand, we bring pride to our own; in the other, we bear respect from the others." This statement, and the work of ATA (and NATCS) in conjunction with ASNLH to promote "Negro history," reflects the dual goals of empowering Black students and educating the white community about the accomplishments and needs of Black people.

In July 1926, an interracial committee of the NEA and the NATCS was formed to investigate issues surrounding Black education. Originally titled "A Committee on Problems in Colored Schools," in 1928 it was reorganized and became the "Committee to Cooperate with the National Association of Teachers in Colored Schools." The committee's three major areas of study were the portrayal of Black people in textbooks, the unequal distribution of federal funds for education along racial lines, and the development of materials on race relations for teacher training and classroom usage. Several of the NATCS members on the committee also served on the White House Conference on Child Health and Protection during the early 1930s and brought issues of Black child health to the attention of the NEA. In addition the committee put together plans for a film that would portray Black history in America, focusing on Black people's successes in literature, art, business, education, and music.

The joint committee of the NATCS and NEA, by working together, forged a relationship that initiated the overall process of integration. For example, after World War II two publications designed by Ambrose Caliver, a member of the joint committee and a prominent Black educator from Washington, D.C., were circulated in cooperation with the Commission on the Defense of Democracy through Education—"Education of Teachers for Improving Majority-Minority Relationships," and "Sources of Instructional Materials on Negroes." These publications were typical of the joint committee's materials designed to broaden educators' knowledge of race relations and Black history.

A five-year program that expanded and consolidated the NEA after World War II accelerated the organization's efforts to enlist Black teachers among its ranks. Mildred Fenner, in her 1945 history of the NEA, recalled a founding principle of the organization when writing of this program—"What we want is an Association which embraces all the teachers of our whole country." In 1947, the joint committee officially called for the integration of Black teachers into the NEA. In the past, individual Black teachers, as well as delegates from local associations, had participated in annual conventions; however, it was not until 1947 that state associations permitted direct affiliation with the NEA, following rules changes. Thus Black teachers were able to participate in the NEA before southern schools were desegregated, marking a transition from separate professional associations to a more integrated national system. The ATA's work in bringing racial issues to the forefront of the NEA agenda was central to this transformation.

In 1955, the NEA agreed to work for school desegregation in accordance with the *Brown* v. *Board of Education* decision a year before. Reporting to the annual NEA convention, the joint committee stated in 1955, "All efforts toward cooperative work were encouraged among teachers on common professional problems in those states where segregated teachers associations exist." However, it was not until after the Civil Rights Act of 1964 was passed that the merging of the ATA and NEA was accomplished, on June 28, 1966. Although ATA was wooed initially by the American Federation of Teachers (AFT) for a possible

merger after the passage of the Civil Rights Act, its long-term relationship with the NEA made a better match. Because the joint committee had developed a plan for such a merger years before, the transition itself was relatively smooth. The NEA accepted all ATA life members as life members of the NEA, transferred the assets of the ATA into a fund to promote the civil rights of Black teachers, and accepted two of the ATA staff as employees of the NEA. At the time of the merger the ATA had a membership of 41,000; however, over 90 percent of these ATA members also held NEA membership in the dual affiliates of previously segregated southern states.

Two years after the merger, a Black educator from North Carolina, Elizabeth D. Koontz, was elected president of the NEA. Mary L. Williams, a Black woman from West Virginia, had acted as president of the ATA from 1941-44, as had Lillian Rogers Johnson from Mississippi in 1955, and Leila A. Bradby from South Carolina in 1961. These women, who rose to positions of relative power within the ATA, symbolized the thousands of female rank-and-file members who worked among the segregated classrooms of the North and South.

The first one hundred years of post-emancipation education focused on the empowerment and uplifting of the race within a segregated system. Separation gave Black educators the room to explore cultural differences, through organizations such as the ASNLH, that in an integrated atmosphere became threatening to the status quo. Thus desegregation represented an answer to the call for equity but also marked the end of an era. In 1958, when prominent educator Anna Julia Cooper, at the age of one hundred, was asked about her reaction to the *Brown* v. *Board of Education* decision, she said she opposed it because during segregation Black children were taught race pride and Black history. Cooper's remark places her within a lifetime of struggle that focused on empowerment within the Black community. The nature of this search for empowerment was at times contradictory. Hence, the ATA brought the inequities of segregation to the attention of powerful organizations such as the NEA. Ironically, however, the move toward group empowerment and social integration did not eliminate all contradictions because the NEA both assisted in the education of Black Americans and yet often proved institutionally removed from the Black community. The ATA brought the inequities of segregation to the attention of powerful organizations such as the NEA, and so empowered the Black community to make the demands that brought about integration.

BIBLIOGRAPHY

American Teachers Association Bulletin. Tuskegee Institute, Alabama (October 1922-February 1938); Bethune, Mary McLeod. "Clarifying Our Vision with the Facts," *Journal of Negro History* (January 1938); Berry, Mary Frances. "Twentieth-century Black Women in Education," *Journal of Negro Education* (1982); Chateauvert, Melinda. "The Third Step: Anna Julia Cooper and Black Education in the District of Columbia, 1910-1960," *Sage* (1988); Collier-Thomas, Bettye. "The Impact of Black Women in Education," *Journal of Negro History* (1982); Dewing, Rolland. "Desegregation of State NEA Affiliates in the South," *Journal of Negro Education* (1969); "Elizabeth Duncan Koontz: President of the NEA's Department of Classroom Teachers," *Negro History Bulletin* (1964); Fenner, Mildred Sandison. *NEA History* (1945); Hoffman, Nancy. *Woman's True Profession: Voices from the History of Teaching* (1981); Meier, August and Elliott Rudwick. *Black History and the Historical Profession, 1915-1980* (1986); National Education Association. *The National Education Association of the United States Addresses and Proceedings* (1928, 1930, 1947, 1955); National Education Association. *Equal Opportunity for All* (1967); *Negro History Bulletin*, Advertisement (April 1965); Schultz, Michael John, Jr. *The National Education Association and the Black Teacher* (1970); Tyack, David and Elizabeth Hansot. *Managers of Virtue—Public School Leadership in America, 1820-1980* (1982).

EARL LEWIS
VICTORIA WOLCOTT

A graduate of the Women's Medical College, Caroline V. Still Anderson was one of Philadelphia's celebrated nineteenth-century Black women physicians. [Schomburg Center]

ANDERSON, CAROLINE VIRGINIA STILL WILEY (1848-1919)

One of Philadelphia's celebrated nineteenth-century Black women physicians, Caroline Virginia Anderson was born in that city on November 1, 1848. Her parents, Letitia and William Still, were founders of the Underground Railroad in antebellum Philadelphia.

Anderson completed her primary and secondary education at Mrs. Henry Gordon's Private School, the Friends Raspberry Allen School, and the Institute for Colored Youth (now Cheyney University). In 1865, she entered Oberlin College. She graduated from the literary course in 1868, the youngest graduate and only Black woman in a class of forty-five. During commencement ceremonies she was asked to preside over the college's Ladies Literary Society, an honor never before presented to one of her race.

After graduation Anderson returned to Philadelphia to teach school. On December 28, 1869, at her parents' home, Anderson married former slave Edward A. Wiley, whom she had met at Oberlin. The wedding made news headlines and was attended by Lucretia Mott, Dilwyn Parrish, Robert Purvis, and many other prominent figures of the abolitionist movement.

Following the untimely death of her husband in 1873, Anderson accepted a post at Howard University in Washington, D.C., where she taught elocution and drawing classes. While still teaching, she matriculated at Howard Medical School in 1875. The next year she transferred to the Woman's Medical College in Philadelphia, from which she graduated in March 1878. The other Black woman in her class was Georgiana E. Patterson Young from New York.

On August 17, 1880, she married Matthew Anderson of Green Castle, Pennsylvania. A prominent minister and educator, he received a B.A. from Oberlin in 1874 and a doctor of divinity from Lincoln University in Philadelphia. Together, the Andersons helped to found the Berean Manual Training and Industrial School in 1889. The school provided training in many industrial fields as well as instruction in the liberal arts. Anderson was assistant principal of the school for thirty-two years.

Anderson also took an active interest in the concerns of the Philadelphia community. She was appointed treasurer of the Woman's Medical College Alumnae Association in 1888; was a board member of the Home for the Aged and Infirmed Colored People of Philadelphia; was president of the Berean Women's Christian Temperance Union; and helped to organize Black Young Men's Christian Associations (YMCAs) in Philadelphia.

Anderson died in her Philadelphia home on June 1, 1919.

BIBLIOGRAPHY

Anderson, Caroline Virginia Still Wiley. File in Black Women Physicians Collection, Archives and Special Collections, Women in Medicine, Medical College of Pennsylvania, Philadelphia, Pennsylvania; Blockson, Charles L. *Pennsylvania's Black History* (1975); *Loraine County News* (January 20, 1870). Oberlin College Archives, Oberlin, Ohio; Still, Caroline. Papers and Personal Letters, Charles Blockson Afro-American Collection, Temple University, Philadelphia, Pennsylvania.

BRENDA GALLOWAY-WRIGHT

ANDERSON, ERNESTINE (1928-)

Ernestine Anderson was described by *Time* magazine in 1958 as "the best new voice in the business." That voice has gotten even better over the years, and Anderson should easily make anyone's list of the top ten jazz vocalists active in the 1990s.

Born in Houston, Texas, on November 11, 1928, Anderson was exposed very early to the blues. Her parents played blues records constantly, giving their daughter an early taste of bluesmen such as John Lee Hooker and Muddy Waters. This may account for Anderson's strong blues-based style. The church also was a big influence; young Ernestine sang hymns in her neighborhood Baptist church. She also heard jazz whenever the bands of Jimmie Lunceford, Billy Eckstine, Erskine Hawkins, and Count Basie came through Houston.

As a teenager Anderson began singing at Houston's El Dorado Ballroom and at other venues outside the church. When the family moved to Seattle, Washington, she continued to sing with local bands. She toured with several groups led by Russell Jacquet, Johnny Otis, Eddie Heywood, and, finally, in 1952 and 1953, Lionel Hampton.

In 1956, Anderson found herself in Sweden with an all-star jazz group led by trumpeter Rolf Ericson. Although she had made her first recording the previous year with Gigi Gryce, it was the album *Hot Cargo*, recorded in Sweden, that made U.S. critics and audiences take note of her.

Critical acclaim notwithstanding, Anderson's popularity waned in the early 1960s, and in 1965 she moved to England. When she returned to Los Angeles a few years later, she decided to retire from singing and took a succession of nonmusical day jobs. She also took up Nichiren Shosha Buddhism.

In the 1970s, several musicians, including Ray Brown and Benny Carter, urged Anderson to resume her professional career. She signed a recording contract with Concord Jazz and has made a number of excellent albums for the label and garnered several Grammy nominations. Her concert and club appearances have further enhanced her reputation as one of the best song stylists on the scene today.

BIBLIOGRAPHY

Ahlgren, Calvin. "Sunny Side of the Street Now for Ernestine Anderson," *San Francisco Chronicle* (May 30, 1982); Stokes, W. Royal. "Ernestine Anderson: Feeling Good," *Jazz Times* (September 1987).

SELECTED DISCOGRAPHY

As leader: *Hello Like Before*, Concord Jazz CCD-4031 (1976); *Never Make Your Move Too Soon*, Concord Jazz CCD-4147 (1982); *Big City*, Concord Jazz CCD-4214 (1983); *When the Sun Goes Down*, Concord Jazz CCD-4263 (1984); *Be Mine Tonight*, Concord Jazz CCD-4407 (1986). As sideman: *Capp/Pierce Juggernaut: Live at the Alley Cat*, Concord Jazz CCD-4336 (1987); *Clayton-Hamilton Jazz Orch.: Boogie Down*, Concord Jazz CCD-4407 (1989).

VINCENT PELOTE

ANDERSON, MARIAN (1902-)

In 1910, when she was eight years old, Marian Anderson sang on a church program in which she was presented as the "Baby Contralto." Her aunt, who had arranged the program to help raise funds for the church, asked her to sing. Two years earlier, Anderson had joined the junior choir at her church, Union Baptist Church in Philadelphia. She loved to sing more than anything. Music and musical instruments always caught her attention at home and in school.

Anderson was born on February 17, 1902. Her parents, John and Annie, were hard-working but not well off financially. In her autobiography, *My Lord, What a Morning,* Anderson recalled her father's devotion to his family and the warmth and joy they all felt when they were together. For a time before she was two years old, the Andersons lived with John's parents. After her sister Alyce was born, the family rented a small house near the grandparents. Another sister, Ethel, was born while they lived there.

Anderson recalled playing "music" on a table while her mother worked. She pretended the table was a piano and kept rhythm with her feet and hands as she sang a melody with nonsense syllables. She always enjoyed singing with her family at home. Neither of her parents had been particularly talented singers, but Annie Anderson had sung in church choirs.

John Anderson was very active in his church. He served as an usher and took his daughter with him every Sunday to attend Sunday school and morning worship services. She loved hearing the choirs and singing in the congregation. When she was six, she joined the church's children's choir. The choir responded well to volunteer director Alexander Robinson, singing with great spirit and enthusiasm. In a short time Robinson noticed her beautiful voice

and vitality and selected her to sing a duet with her friend, a soprano, in both Sunday school and the worship service. It was Marian's first public appearance.

Anderson was about eight years old when her father bought a piano from his brother. She tried to play immediately, even attempting a major scale by placing her thumb under her fingers as she had seen others play. With no money for music lessons, she taught herself by means of a card with the names of the keys and notes that could be slipped directly behind the keys. Later she saw a Black woman playing the piano and decided that she too could develop her skill.

She also made an attempt at being a violinist. She had seen a violin in a pawn shop and, to earn money to buy it, worked at scrubbing her neighbors' steps. She saved $4 and bought the violin for $3.98. Again she tried to teach herself, but it was not long before she decided the violin was not her instrument.

When she was ten, her father received an accidental blow to his head at work and never recovered.

Marian Anderson traveled throughout the world to perform. She is shown here in 1943 receiving the Liberian Redemption Award from Walter Walker, Liberian Consul General. Eleanor Roosevelt looks on. [National Archives]

Following his death, the family returned to his parents' home.

After grammar school, Anderson went to William Penn High School with the idea of following a commercial education course to prepare her for a job so that she could earn money to help care for her mother and sisters. These studies did not interest her, but she did enjoy her once-a-week music class. The music teacher noticed her talent and invited her to sing with the school chorus, and she was occasionally given solos. After singing solo in a school assembly, she was called to the principal's office and encouraged to change to a college preparatory course, which would permit her to pursue more music studies. She transferred to South Philadelphia High School and continued to perform in assemblies with the support of her new principal, Dr. Lucy Wilson.

In the meantime, her singing began to attract attention at church, where she had joined the senior choir and visited other churches with the choir. As she became increasingly well known, she learned to play the piano well enough to accompany herself. She accepted invitations to sing at other churches and at larger church-related events. In 1919, she sang at the national meeting of the National Baptist Convention, U.S.A., Inc., in Atlantic City. Gospel composer Lucie Campbell, the convention's music director, introduced Anderson to the thousands attending the meeting and accompanied her.

Along with the many opportunities to perform and her growing success, Anderson felt the need for formal training. While still in high school she began vocal studies with Black music teacher Mary Saunders Patterson. Teaching without charge, although a family friend agreed to pay for the lessons, Patterson made Anderson aware of vocal technique and inspired her to find an accompanist to work with her on a permanent basis. She also studied with Agnes Reifsnyder for a short time.

At this point she was encouraged by her mother and others to consider attending a music school, and she decided to get information about enrolling in a school in downtown Philadelphia. She was abruptly turned down because of her race. When she described the humiliating rebuff, her mother encouraged her to keep her faith and never give up the pursuit of her dreams.

During her senior year in high school, her principal introduced Anderson to Giuseppe Boghetti, a teacher of great reputation, but she could not afford his expensive fees. When it appeared that she would have to wait until she could save enough for lessons, church members and friends came to her rescue. A

It was Harold Ickes who, as Secretary of the Interior, paved the way for Marian Anderson's 1939 concert in front of the Lincoln Memorial. She is shown here singing in the same location at the 1952 memorial service for Ickes. [Library of Congress]

special concert at the church was arranged, with Roland Hayes, whom she admired and respected, as one of the soloists. She was greatly moved by this gesture, and considered singing on the same program

Marian Anderson as Ulrica in Verdi's Un Ballo in Maschera *at the Metropolitan Opera in 1955. [Schomburg Center]*

with Hayes to be one of the highlights of her life. The concert raised $600 for her singing lessons.

Boghetti further developed her technique—especially her breathing—and taught her songs by Schubert, Brahms, and other classical composers. She learned songs in German, Italian, and French.

Her accompanist, Billy King, was a talented musician who served as organist at an Episcopal church and had accompanied artists such as Roland Hayes. Eventually King took over the duties of managing her concerts and publicity. Sponsored by a variety of Black organizations, Anderson toured and gave concerts at colleges and churches and other venues with Black audiences. As her earnings increased, she was able to help her mother purchase a home, in which she set up a studio for her music practice.

Her growing audiences and larger fees also gave her assurance that she was ready to advance in her career. At twenty-one, she felt she could gain national recognition by performing at Town Hall in New York City. On the night of the concert, she was shattered by the poor attendance, and her confidence was shaken by a performance she felt was not especially good. The few reviews verified that her New York debut was premature. The incident threatened to end her career, and she retreated for some time.

However, with the comfort and encouragement of her mother, she recovered and continued singing.

Entering a contest sponsored by Philadelphia's Philharmonic Society, Anderson won, marking the first time a Black American had won first prize. In 1925, she won a competition held in New York City under the sponsorship of Lewisohn Stadium Concerts. The prize was an appearance with the New York Philharmonic at Lewisohn Stadium, and many of her friends and family members were able to hear her perform. This tremendous career boost enabled her to change to professional management, and she signed with the organization of Arthur Judson, a top concert manager. Her career advanced for a while, but eventually she felt the need for further study and considered going abroad to try to gain a reputation in Europe, as Roland Hayes and others had done. In New York she studied briefly, on a scholarship, with Frank La Forge, vocal teacher to several famous singers. La Forge felt she did not need to go abroad and he was not particularly encouraging when she decided to do so.

In the summer of 1929, armed with names of people she could contact for assistance, Anderson sailed to England on a second-class ticket. Billy King had given her a letter of introduction to Roger Quilter, who had assisted and encouraged Roland Hayes. Lawrence Brown, Hayes's accompanist, had written to Raimund von zur Muhlen, a famous teacher of German lieder.

Upon arrival in England, she called Quilter, only to discover that he was in a nursing home. Remembering Black actor John Payne, who had visited her home in Philadelphia, she reached him and was invited to stay in his home. Later she telephoned Muhlen and made an appointment to sing for him at his house. When he accepted her as a student, she moved closer to his home, but unfortunately, after only two lessons, he became ill and discontinued all teaching. Quilter, somewhat recovered, recommended Mark Raphael, a student of Muhlen and a specialist in lieder. Although Raphael was a good teacher, Anderson was quite disappointed about not being able to continue with Muhlen.

After a concert in 1931 for the Alpha Kappa Alpha Sorority (she was an honorary member), Anderson was greeted backstage by a representative of the Rosenwald Fund. Upon learning of her desire to study in Germany, he encouraged her to apply for a fellowship, which she received. During her studies in Berlin she gave concerts throughout Europe for the next several years. When she sang in Finland at the home of composer Jean Sibelius, he remarked, "My roof is too low for you" (Anderson 1956). Her popularity, after two successful Scandinavian tours, was noted in Nazi Germany, and she was invited to sing there until it was discovered she was not 100 percent Aryan.

In June 1934, at her third Paris recital, she met and signed with the internationally known American concert manager Sol Hurok, beginning a long professional relationship. In spring 1935, she sang two concerts at Vienna's Wiener Konzerthaus and one at Salzburg's Mozarteum. A second Salzburg recital, held in a hotel ballroom, was arranged by American Gertrude Moulton. Following this concert the great conductor Arturo Toscanini uttered his famous statement, "Yours is a voice such as one hears once in a hundred years" (Anderson 1956). Her first trip to the Soviet Union came in 1935. Returning briefly to the United States, she performed at Town Hall again on December 30, 1935. This time the outcome was much more successful. In 1936 she made a second, more extensive trip to the Soviet Union.

Although her fame throughout the world had helped break some racial barriers, Anderson was still denied many opportunities. Hurok's organization attempted to protect her from the prejudice they met when they tried to book her in certain areas. However, the most infamous incident associated with her career was the refusal in 1939 of the Daughters of the American Revolution (DAR) to allow her to perform in Constitution Hall in Washington, D.C. During a great surge of public protest, Eleanor Roosevelt resigned from the DAR and was instrumental in getting Secretary of the Interior Harold L. Ickes to issue Anderson an invitation to sing at the Lincoln Memorial. On Easter Sunday, April 9, 1939, she sang before a crowd of 75,000 in one of the most significant concerts in American music history. Eventually the policy of prohibiting Black performers in Constitution Hall was changed.

In 1943, Anderson married architect Orpheus H. Fisher. They had met years before, become friends, and remained in touch through the years. They made their home on a farm in Connecticut.

After World War II, Anderson resumed her travels abroad. She made her television debut on *The Ed Sullivan Show* in 1952, and toured South America, Korea, and Japan in 1953. Her historic debut with the Metropolitan Opera Company in January 1955 marked the first time a Black singer had ever sung at the Met. She sang the role of Ulrica in Verdi's *Un Ballo in Maschera*. In 1957, she traveled 40,000 miles throughout Asia as a goodwill ambassador sponsored by the U.S. State Department. The tour, recorded by

CBS television, included Thailand, Korea, Vietnam, Singapore, Taiwan, Burma, Malaysia, and India. Both Anderson and her program, *The Lady from Philadelphia*, won praise.

During her career Anderson received numerous awards and honors, including the Spingarn Medal, Bok Award, and Page One Award. President Eisenhower asked her to sing the national anthem at his inauguration and in June 1958 appointed her to the American delegation to the United Nations. In 1964 and 1965, she gave more than fifty farewell concerts before retiring from a rich career that lasted more than thirty years.

[*See also* AUTOBIOGRAPHY.]

BIBLIOGRAPHY

Anderson, Marian. *My Lord, What a Morning* (1956); *BDAAM*; Cuney-Hare, Maude. *Negro Musicians and Their Music* ([1936] 1974); *Ebony*, "The Survivors" (November 1990); Hughes, Langston. *Famous Negro Music Makers* (1955); Locke, Alain. *The Negro and His Music* ([1936] 1968); Patterson, Charles. *Marian Anderson* (1988); Roach, Hildred. *Black American Music: Past and Present* (1985); Southern, Eileen. *The Music of Black Americans: A History* (1983); Tobias, Tobi. *Marian Anderson* (1972).

MILDRED DENBY GREEN

ANDERSON, NAOMI BOWMAN TALBERT (b. 1843)

Developing survival strategies for herself and the people of her race characterized Naomi Anderson's adult life. Born free in Indiana during the antebellum period, Anderson exemplified nineteenth-century feminism, self-help, and westward migration, and she was a pioneer in the Black woman's club movement.

Naomi Bowman was born March 1, 1843, in Michigan City, Indiana. Her parents, Elijah and Guilly Ann Bowman, were free Black Americans, natives of Ohio. Her mother's goal was to educate Naomi so that she could graduate from Oberlin College, but Guilly Ann's death in 1860 prevented Naomi from going to college.

From that time on, Naomi Bowman shared the plight of African-American women during the Civil War and postwar period. Her marriage to William Talbert in 1863 marked a hopeful time, but the events that followed—the deaths of Naomi's brother, sister, and her first born of four children, plus her husband's failing health—brought hardships. Throughout this period, Naomi Talbert struggled to keep the family together. Her husband died in 1877, after the family had moved three times, settling in Chicago.

Despite the tragedy, Talbert began a career of feminism and public service, including temperance and suffrage work. She delivered a controversial pro-woman suffrage speech at the woman's rights convention held at Chicago in 1869 and engaged in the temperance work of the International Organization of Grand Templars (IOGT). Throughout the late 1870s, Naomi Talbert made several lecture tours in Illinois, Indiana, and Ohio, promoting women's rights issues and, while living in Portsmouth, Ohio, she helped to organize a home for orphaned African-American children.

After William Talbert's death, Naomi became the main provider for her three surviving children and her aging father. She learned the hairdressing trade and later passed the Ohio Board of Examiners examination for public school teachers. By 1879, she and her family had moved to Columbus, Ohio, where she practiced cosmetology and wrote articles on temperance and woman's rights. Talbert was part of a growing

As one of the strongest Black voices in the woman's suffrage movement, Naomi Anderson gained the respect and affection of Susan B. Anthony and Elizabeth Cady Stanton for her fight against racism. [Schomburg Center]

number of African-American women who felt the sting of both racism and sexism and decided to speak against them.

Talbert met Lewis Anderson in Columbus. They married in 1881 and moved to a farm outside of the city. "Kansas fever" attracted them, however, and like many African-Americans, they headed west, settling in Wichita, Kansas, in 1884. Anderson became a successful financier, freeing Naomi to campaign for woman's rights.

In Kansas, Naomi Anderson promoted the efforts of the woman suffrage movement and the Women's Christian Temperance Union (WCTU). In 1892, she campaigned with white suffragists for the state woman suffrage referendum, only the second in the nation. Nonetheless, she realized the prejudices of white women in both the suffrage and the temperance movements. As a result, she sought to convince her white neighbors that African-Americans were not foreigners, but Americans entitled to full rights of citizenship. An example of the prejudice she fought occurred when the white clubwomen of Wichita organized a children's home that barred Black children. In response, Anderson organized the women of her race to raise funds for a children's home for African-Americans. By 1890, the women had rented a small facility and obtained a monthly stipend from the county to help support it.

By 1895, Naomi Anderson had left Kansas for California. Whether she was joined by her husband and her adult children is not known. However, in San Francisco, Anderson, then in her fifties, became active in the woman suffrage movement, representing the African-American women at the state level in their efforts to lobby the legislature for woman suffrage. In so doing, she earned praise for her work from noted woman suffragists Susan B. Anthony and Elizabeth Cady Stanton.

Apparently Anderson continued a life of service to women and to Black people, leaving legacies throughout her westward trek from Ohio, to Kansas, to California. After 1895, her name did not appear again in the proceedings of the National American Woman Suffrage Association. Presumably she remained in California until her death, the date of which has yet to be established.

BIBLIOGRAPHY

Anthony, Susan B. and Ida Husted Harper. *The History of Woman Suffrage* (1902); Majors, M. A., ed. *Noted Negro Women* (1893).

ROSALYN TERBORG-PENN

In the 1920s, Violette Anderson made legal history when she became the first Black woman to practice law in Illinois and then the first to argue a case before the U.S. Supreme Court. [Schomburg Center]

ANDERSON, VIOLETTE N.
(1882-1937)

Born in 1882 in London, England, Violette Anderson was the first Black woman to practice law in the state of Illinois. Anderson was a graduate of the University of Chicago Law School in 1920. She attended the Chicago Athenaeum and the Chicago Seminar of Sciences. Anderson further distinguished herself by becoming, in 1926, the first Black woman to practice law in the U.S. Supreme Court, in the U.S. District Court in the Eastern District of Illinois, and in Chicago as the Assistant City Prosecutor.

Anderson was a member of the Federation of Colored Women's Clubs, president of the Friendly Big Sisters' League of Chicago, first vice president of the Cook County Bar Association, an executive board member of the Chicago Council of Social Agencies, and a member of the Zeta Zeta Chapter of the Zeta Phi Beta Sorority. Anderson died in 1937.

BIBLIOGRAPHY

EBA; Gerrett, Romeo E. *Famous First Facts about Negroes* (1972); *NA*; *RLBA*; *WWCA*.

WENDY BROWN

ANDREWS, REGINA M. ANDERSON
(c. 1900-)

"All ethnic groups and peoples need the dramatic forms of cultural expression." In the 1920s, this was how Regina Andrews answered the question, "Does Harlem need its own theater?" She has lived her answer as a founder and promoter of, and playwright for, the Harlem little theater movement.

Although she was born in Chicago around the turn of the century, Andrews has spent most of her adult life in New York City. Before she married New York Assemblyman William T. Andrews, the apartment she shared with Ethel Ray Nance was always filled with aspiring artists who came to discuss their creations and receive the encouragement they needed. Later, Andrews and her husband were very much involved in the social, political, and cultural affairs of the city.

As assistant to Ernestine Rose at the 135th Street Branch of the New York Public Library, and later as head librarian, Andrews helped set up a theater in the basement where various drama groups and street corner orators could perform. One of the drama groups with which she was actively associated was W.E.B. Du Bois's Krigwa Players, which emphasized Black theater about, by, for, and *near* Black people. In February 1929, after the Krigwa Players had disbanded, Andrews and Dorothy Peterson, aided by such community leaders as Theophilus Lewis, Ira De Augustine Reid, Jessie Fauset, and Harold Jackman, established the Negro (Harlem) Experimental Theatre in the basement of the library. Because of her professional association with the library, Andrews wrote numerous dramas for the group under the pseudonym Ursala Trelling. Her most popular play was *Climbing Jacob's Ladder*, which was performed in 1931 after the group had moved to the Saint Philips Protestant Episcopal Church parish house on 133rd Street. Andrews had been inspired to write this drama about a late-nineteenth-century lynching in the United States by the great journalist and humanitarian, Ida B. Wells-Barnett. Other plays by Andrews include *The Man Who Passed*, *Matilda*, and *Underground*.

Regina Andrews was to have written a chronology for the *Harlem on My Mind* exhibition at the Metropolitan Museum in August 1968, but it was not finished in time. She has since expanded the chronology into a two-volume manuscript about Black New Yorkers, which has yet to be published.

BIBLIOGRAPHY

Anderson, Jervis. *This Was Harlem: A Cultural Portrait, 1900-1950* (1981); Jefferson, Annetta. Personal interviews with Jean Hutson (April 15 and September 29, 1991); Kellner, Bruce. *The Harlem Renaissance: A Historical Dictionary for the Era* (1987); Mitchell, Loften. *Black Drama* (1967), and *Voices of the Black Theatre* (1975); Perkins, Kathy A. *Black Female Playwrights: An Anthology of Plays Before 1950* (1990).

ANNETTA JEFFERSON

ANGELOU, MAYA (1928-)

"You're going to be famous," Billie Holiday told Maya Angelou in 1958, "but it won't be for singing." The first part of the prophecy, of course, was fulfilled. The second part, in the most superficial sense, was true as well. Angelou's fame did not grow from the nightclub singing she was then doing to support herself and her son. Yet in another sense, Holiday was wrong. Since she first put pen to paper, Maya Angelou has been singing.

Angelou's early life is familiar to anyone who has read the several volumes of her highly acclaimed autobiography. She was born Marguerite Johnson on April 4, 1928, in St. Louis, Missouri. Her father, Bailey Johnson, was a doorman and, later, a dictician for the navy. Her mother, Vivian Johnson, was a registered nurse. When Angelou was three years old, her parents were divorced. They sent her and her four-year-old brother, Bailey, Jr., to live with their paternal grandmother, Annie Henderson, in Stamps, Arkansas. Henderson ran a small general store and managed to scrape by. She continued to do so after her grandchildren joined her.

Angelou's grandmother was one of many strong women who trained her, helped her, and provided her with role models. The people of her church also nurtured her and gave her a sense of belonging to a community. For the rest, childhood in the South was a nightmare. Speaking of Stamps to *Ebony* in 1982, Angelou said:

My town was mean. Mean and poor. All its inhabitants, save for a few whites who owned the dying cotton gin and the faded stores along the one-block downtown area, were farmers. On our side of town, called quarters (a lingering term used wistfully by whites), all the men were dirt farmers, and those women who did not work with their husbands in the bottom land, and many who did, took in washing, ironing, or actually left their homes to go to care for the houses of women only a little better off than they, economically, but who believed that their white skin gave them the right to have Negro servants. When I was taken to California by my grandmother, who had raised me, I vowed never to return to the grim, humiliating South. Except for a tentative trip to visit when I was eighteen, I didn't break my promise until I was forty years old.

When she was seven and a half, Angelou left Stamps for a visit with her mother. While there, she was raped by her mother's boyfriend. He was tried, found guilty, and kicked to death in prison. The confused little girl felt responsible for his death and withdrew into herself. "I was mute for five years," she said in an interview for *I Dream a World* (Lanker 1989). "I wasn't cute and I didn't speak." In frustration, her mother sent her back to Stamps. Her emotional withdrawal caused many to dismiss Angelou as backward, but her grandmother did not give up on her. "I don't know what would have happened to me had I been in an integrated school. In another society, I'm sure I would have been ruled out. But my grandma told me all the time, 'Sister, Mama don't care what these people say about you being a moron, being a idiot. Mama don't care. Mama know, Sister, when you and the good Lord get ready, you're gonna be a preacher.'" Angelou was also helped by a woman named Bertha Flowers, who introduced her to literature. By the time of her graduation from eighth grade, she was at the head of her class.

At this point, Angelou and her brother went to live with their mother in San Francisco. Vivian Baxter Johnson was by then a professional gambler. Her milieu was infinitely more sophisticated and somewhat more dangerous than the world Angelou had left behind in Stamps. She began to pick up some of that sophistication, while at the same time attending George Washington High School and taking drama and dance lessons at the California Labor School. One summer, she went to stay with her father, quarreled with his girlfriend, and ran away. For a month she lived with other runaway or homeless children in an abandoned van. Back at home in San Francisco, the teenager decided she wanted to be a streetcar conductor; she was attracted to the uniform. Although San Francisco had never had a Black conductor and was not eager to hire one, she persisted and, with her mother's support, managed to attain her goal.

At sixteen, Angelou gave birth to her son, Guy. She had not planned her pregnancy but has always been deeply grateful that it happened. "The greatest gift I've ever had was the birth of my son," she said in an interview for *Essence* in 1985, and then went on to tell of the ways he changed her life. "Because, when he was small, I knew more than he did, I expected to be his teacher. So because of him I educated myself. When he was four . . . I taught him to read. But then he'd ask questions and I didn't have the answers, so I started my lifelong love affair with libraries. . . . I've learned an awful lot because of him."

Still, Angelou's life at this time was not easy. In addition to teaching her son, she also had to support him. She could not get a job as a telephone operator. The Women's Army Corps Service (WACS) turned her down because the California Labor School where she had taken dance classes was tainted with the rumor of communism. She was a cook and a night-club waitress and, for a short time, "madam" for two lesbian prostitutes. She began doing drugs but then quit after seeing what drugs had done to her brother.

When she was twenty-two, Angelou married Tosh Angelos, a white former sailor. Two and a half years later, she left him and became a professional dancer. Eventually, she moved to New York to pursue that career and study with Pearl Primus. In 1954, she was cast in a production of *Porgy and Bess* that toured Europe and Africa. When she came back to the United States, she wrote, with Godfrey Cambridge, a revue called *Cabaret for Freedom* to raise funds for the Southern Christian Leadership Conference (SCLC). In 1960-61, she was northern coordinator of SCLC. Of that time, she later told *Ebony*, "I met the heroic men who came North. Martin Luther King, Ralph Abernathy, Wyatt Tee Walker, and Andrew Young. The matter they brought to New York was decidedly national and even international in its concern, but it was particularly southern. That region had formed their speech; they spoke in sugary slow accents and talked of southern atrocities and southern protest to those same atrocities." In spite of her affinity with these Black southerners, however, Angelou stayed resolutely away from the scenes of her childhood.

Also in 1961, she appeared in an acclaimed off-Broadway production of *The Blacks*, by Jean Genet. The cast was a remarkable array of talent, including Louis Gossett, Jr., James Earl Jones, and Cicely Tyson.

The show was highly successful and ran until 1964, but Angelou stayed with it only a short time because the director-producer refused to pay for music she had written for the show with Ethel Ayer.

By this time, Angelou was writing poetry, short stories, and songs. Her reputation was growing. Then, in 1961, she and her son went to Africa with South African freedom fighter Vusumzi Make. They lived for a time in Cairo. However, Make became angry when Angelou applied for a job as editor of the *Arab Observer* and, combined with other problems, the quarrel led to a break-up. Angelou and her son moved to Ghana, where they remained for several years. She worked as a journalist and taught at the University of Ghana, returning to the United States in 1966. Shortly after her return, as she retells it in a 1975 *Writer's Digest* interview:

> My friend and brother, James Baldwin, took me to Jules and Judy Feiffer's home one evening, and the four of us sat up and drank and laughed

Few books have so powerfully communicated the pain and joy of the Black experience as has Maya Angelou's classic I Know Why the Caged Bird Sings. *[Moorland-Spingarn]*

and told stories until about 3:30 or 4:00 in the morning. And the next morning, Judy Feiffer called the man who later became my editor and said "Do you know the poet Maya Angelou? If you can get her to write a book, you might have something." So he asked me, and I said, "No." I came out to California, and he phoned, and about the third phone call he said, "Well, I guess you're very wise not to do it, because autobiography is the most difficult art form." So I said I would do it, and I did. It was like that. He should have told me that first.

In 1970, *I Know Why the Caged Bird Sings* was published. It became a best-seller and an almost instant classic. It was nominated for a National Book Award. In 1971, Angelou's screenplay *Georgia, Georgia* was made into a film, making her the first Black woman to have an original screenplay produced. The four other volumes of her autobiography are, to date, *Gather Together in My Name* (1974), *Singin' and Swingin' and Gettin' Merry Like Christmas* (1976), *The Heart of a Woman* (1981), and *All God's Children Need Traveling Shoes* (1986). She has also published several volumes of poetry and has been nominated for the Pulitzer Prize in poetry for one of them, *Just Give Me a Cool Drink of Water 'fore I Diiie* (1971).

Maya Angelou has continued to live the varied life that makes her autobiographical books so fascinating. She appeared on Broadway in 1973 in *Look Away* and was nominated for a Tony Award. That same year, she married writer/cartoonist Paul de Feu. She adapted Sophocles' *Ajax* for the Mark Taper Forum in 1974. In 1977, she received an Emmy nomination for her performance in the miniseries *Roots*. She was appointed to the Bicentennial Commission by President Gerald Ford and to the Commission of International Woman's Year by President Jimmy Carter. In 1979, *I Know Why the Caged Bird Sings* became a made-for-television movie.

In 1981, Angelou and de Feu were divorced, and Angelou moved back to the South. She accepted a lifetime appointment as Reynolds Professor of American Studies at Wake Forest University in Winston-Salem, North Carolina, joined a local church, and began to grow back into a southern community. The community and her place in it are very different, making her return possible, but she seems also to have found something she left behind a long time ago. Perhaps that something is the spirit that once helped a small girl speak again so that the world might someday hear her truly magnificent voice.

BIBLIOGRAPHY
Benson, Carol. "Out of the Cage and Still Singing," *Writer's Digest* (January 1975); *EBA*; *Ebony*, "Prominent, Southern-born Author Talks about the South, Southerners, and the Long Road Home" (February 1982); Julianelli, Jane. "Maya Angelou," *Harper's Bazaar* (November 1972); Lanker, Brian. *I Dream a World: Portraits of Black Women Who Changed America* (1989); *NA*; *NBAW*; Oliver, Stephanie Stokes. "Maya Angelou: The Heart of the Woman," *Essence* (May 1985); Sorel, Nancy Caldwell. "Maya Angelou and Billie Holiday," *Atlantic Monthly* (September 1990); *WWBA* (1992).

KATHLEEN THOMPSON

ANTILYNCHING MOVEMENT

Black women played a pivotal role in the struggle against racial violence. That battle, in turn, served as the catalyst for a Black women's movement dedicated to the eradication of racism and sexism alike.

Ida B. Wells-Barnett (1862-1931), a teacher-turned-journalist who was the co-owner of the Memphis *Free Speech*, launched the first phase of the antilynching movement in 1892, after a mob murdered three Memphis storeowners, one of whom was a close friend. She urged African-Americans to fight back, with guns if necessary but mainly through economic pressure. Spurred by her scathing editorials, thousands migrated to Oklahoma while those who stayed boycotted the newly opened streetcar line. Wells-Barnett began investigating other lynchings, and she soon discovered that few lynch victims were even accused of rape and that behind many rape charges lay interracial affairs. When she published an editorial arguing that "nobody in this section of the country believes the old threadbare lie that Negro men rape white women," a white mob destroyed her press and warned Wells-Barnett, who was in New York at the time, not to return to Memphis at the cost of her life.

Far from being silenced by this attack, Wells-Barnett transformed herself from a local leader into the architect of an international crusade. She wrote for the *New York Age* and published two pamphlets, *Southern Horrors* (1892) and *A Red Record* (1895), which offered an incisive analysis of the economic roots of lynching and linked violence against Black men with the sexual exploitation of Black women. She lectured throughout the North and West. In 1893 and 1894, she traveled to England, where she inspired the formation of the British Anti-Lynching Society.

Ida B. Wells-Barnett became a leader in the antilynching movement when her close friend Tom Moss was murdered by a mob. She is pictured here (left) with his wife, Betty, and his children, Maureen and Tom, Jr. (c. 1893). [The Joseph Regenstein Library, The University of Chicago]

Although Wells-Barnett continued to advocate Black militancy and self-help, she also hoped to turn white public opinion against the South. The lynching-for-rape myth, accepted by white people, North and South, depicted white men as the manly protectors of virtuous white women against uncivilized Black men. Wells-Barnett's genius lay in her ability to reverse this trope, casting white southern men as the lustful rapists of Black women and the hypocritical murderers of innocent Black men. In short, she subverted the equation between whiteness, manliness, and civilization, an equation that lay at the heart of Victorian notions of manhood and that helped to justify imperialism throughout the world. By the end of her second British tour, Wells-Barnett had made lynching a cause célèbre among British reformers, and white American men found that their tolerance of racial violence had placed them in the uncomfortable position of unmanly savages in the eyes of the "civilized" world. Her skillful manipulation of dominant cultural themes did not stop lynching, but it did put mob violence on the American reform agenda.

Wells-Barnett relied from the outset on the support of a network of Black women. A fund-raising event held in New York's Lyric Hall—Wells-Barnett described it as "the greatest demonstration ever attempted by race women for one of their own number"—made possible the publication of *Southern Horrors*. When the president of the Missouri Press Association reacted to Wells-Barnett's British tour by maligning the morality of Black women, Josephine St. Pierre Ruffin (1842-1924), head of Boston's New Era Club, used the incident as the occasion for founding the National Federation of Afro-American Women, which merged in 1896 with two other groups to form the National Association of Colored Women (NACW). NACW antilynching committees at the local and national levels made a special point of publicizing the lynching of Black women. Relief work during World War I spurred organizational growth, and after the armistice the NACW drew on the skills and interorganizational contacts acquired during the war to inaugurate a new phase of the antilynching drive.

President of the NACW and Spingarn Medal winner Mary B. Talbert (1866-1923) guided this effort. Both Talbert and Wells-Barnett had long advocated federal antilynching legislation. Wells-Barnett had urged the National Association for the Advancement of Colored People (NAACP) to lobby for federal action at its founding meeting in 1909, and Talbert had worked with Congressman L. D. Dyer, sponsor of the Dyer Antilynching Bill, when the NAACP was still reluctant to commit itself to a legislative strategy. When the NAACP resolved to channel its resources into a lobbying campaign in 1919, Talbert mobilized women's networks behind the endeavor. In July 1922, she formalized these efforts in a group called the Anti-Lynching Crusaders. Within three months after its founding, the group's sixteen original members had expanded to 900. Broader based than the NAACP, the Crusaders pledged to "unite one million women to suppress lynching."

The Anti-Lynching Crusaders had an unpaid staff and a leadership made up of veterans of settlement houses, state federations of Black women's clubs, the Young Women's Christian Association (YWCA), the Woman's Committee on the Council of National Defense, and the NAACP. Based mainly in the Northeast, these women asked Black state and local women's groups to petition public officials, persuade ministers to deliver antilynching sermons, and hold "sacrifice weeks" in which women were urged to contribute a dollar apiece to the campaign. The Crusaders were also determined to win white women to the cause and to take their campaign into the South, a strategy that would have been unthinkable when Ida B. Wells-Barnett first embarked on her antilynching campaign.

The groundwork for this effort was laid by a network of southern Black women educators and church leaders, who had begun building tenuous alliances with white women through the YWCA and the church more than a decade before. In 1919, Charlotte Hawkins Brown, president of Palmer Memorial Institute in Sedalia, North Carolina, persuaded the white North Carolina Federation of Women's Clubs to pass an antilynching resolution. A year later, her stirring address to the founding meeting of the Woman's Committee of the Commission on Interracial Cooperation (CIC) encouraged the group to attack the double standard that excused white sexual exploitation of Black women while condemning to death Black men accused of crossing the color line.

The Crusaders enjoyed some success in this attempt to secure white women's moral and financial support. The National Council of Women, representing some 30 million women nationwide, endorsed the campaign, and some leaders of the CIC Woman's Committee indicated their support, but the hoped-for outpouring of response from southern white women did not materialize until 1930, with the formation of the Association of Southern Women for the Prevention of Lynching (ASWPL).

It is a testament to the power of segregation that Jessie Daniel Ames, founder of the ASWPL, seems not to have known about or read the trenchant writings of Ida B. Wells-Barnett. She may nevertheless have been influenced by Wells-Barnett's ideas as they had filtered into reform discourse or were conveyed to her by the Black women with whom she worked in the CIC. In any case, it was Wells-Barnett who first exposed white women's complicity in the violence perpetuated in their name, and the repudiation of that role served as the chief rhetorical strategy of the ASWPL. Wells-Barnett attacked the assumptions that equated white men with civilization; the ASWPL, in turn, rejected the white woman's role as the object of the Black man's desire and the excuse for the white man's violence. Throughout the 1930s, Black CIC women prodded the ASWPL to endorse federal antilynching legislation. Ames refused to do so, but state branches of the ASWPL, as well as its major constituent organization, the Woman's Missionary

Council of the Methodist Church, South, lined up behind the Anti-Lynching Crusaders' legislative drive.

The Black women's antilynching campaign did not succeed in pushing an antilynching bill through the U.S. Congress, but it did help to bring about a change in public opinion: by 1942 a Gallup poll indicated that an overwhelming majority of whites, North and South, favored making lynching a federal crime. The campaign also served as a rallying point for a larger Black women's movement, whose initiative in building welfare institutions and defending Black rights during the era of segregation historians have only now begun fully to appreciate and explore.

BIBLIOGRAPHY

Aptheker, Bettina. "Woman Suffrage and the Crusade against Lynching, 1890-1920." In *Woman's Legacy: Essays on Race, Sex, and Class in American History* (1982); Bederman, Gail. "Civilization, the Decline of Middle-Class Manliness, and Ida B. Wells's Anti-Lynching Campaign, 1892-1894," *Radical History Review* (Winter 1992); Carby, Hazel V. " 'On the Threshold of Woman's Era': Lynching, Empire, and Sexuality in Black Feminist Theory." In *"Race," Writing, and Difference*, ed. Henry Louis Gates, Jr. (1985); Duster, Alfreda M., ed. *Crusade for Justice: The Autobiography of Ida B. Wells* (1970); Giddings, Paula. "Ida Wells-Barnett, 1862-1931." In *Portraits of American Women from Settlement to the Present*, ed. G. J. Barker-Benfield and Catherine Clinton (1991); Grant, Donald Lee. "The Development of the Anti-Lynching Reform Movement in the United States, 1883-1932," Ph.D. diss. (1972); Hall, Jacquelyn Dowd. " 'The Mind That Burns in Each Body': Women, Rape, and Racial Violence." In *Powers of Desire: The Politics of Sexuality*, ed. Ann Snitow, Christine Stansell, and Sharon Thompson (1983), and *Revolt against Chivalry: Jessie Daniel Ames and the Women's Campaign against Lynching* (1979); Holt, Thomas C. "The Lonely Warrior: Ida B. Wells-Barnett and the Struggle for Black Leadership." In *Black Leaders of the Twentieth Century*, ed. John Hope Franklin and August Meier (1982); Hutton, Mary Magdelene Boone. "The Rhetoric of Ida B. Wells: The Genesis of the Anti-Lynch Movement," Ph.D. diss. (1975); Salem, Dorothy. *To Better Our World: Black Women in Organized Reform, 1890-1920* (1990); Sterling, Dorothy. *Black Foremothers: Three Lives* (1988); Terborg-Penn, Rosalyn. "African-American Women's Networks in the Anti-Lynching Crusade." In *Gender, Race, and Reform in the Progressive Era*, ed. Noralee Frankel and Nancy S. Dye (1991); Thompson, Mildred. "Ida B. Wells-Barnett: An Exploratory Study of an American Black Woman, 1893-1930," Ph.D. diss. (1979); Tucker, David M. "Miss Ida B. Wells and Memphis Lynching," *Phylon* (Summer 1971).

JACQUELYN DOWD HALL

ARCHER, OSCEOLA MACARTHY (ADAMS) (1890-1983)

"I know one race—the human race," Osceola Archer said once. "We are becoming more and more fragmented . . . in every direction. We are creating our own destruction." She was comparing the Negro Ensemble Company, a product of the 1960s, with the American Negro Theatre where, during the 1940s, she had directed plays and taught Sidney Poitier, Harry Belafonte, and Ossie Davis, among others.

Osceola Macarthy was born in Georgia in 1890. Of Black, white, and Indian ancestry, she fit into an elusive racial category. She told a *New York Times* reporter in 1968 that she was often turned down for jobs with the comment, "You're not Negroid enough, you're too light, you will photograph too white, your speech is too perfect."

Macarthy graduated from Howard University in Washington, D.C., in 1913. At Howard she studied with renowned Rhodes scholar Alain Locke and sociologist Kelly Miller. She also studied classical Greek and was a member of the Howard Players. Delta Sigma Theta, the sorority she cofounded with twenty-one other women, was at the time of her death on November 20, 1983, the largest sorority in the country, with over 713 chapters.

Osceola Macarthy became Osceola Adams in 1915 when she married Numa P. G. Adams, first dean of Howard University's medical school. The family lived in Chicago for ten years, from 1919 to 1929, where Numa Adams attended medical school. While there, Osceola Adams worked as a dress designer under the name of Mrs. Adams and attended the University of Chicago. Her artistic bent also expressed itself in painting, which she did on Sundays. Once their only son finished high school, Dr. Adams encouraged his wife to return to school for her Master's degree so that she could ensure her own future. She earned a graduate degree in drama from New York University in 1936, by then adopting the stage name of Osceola Archer.

Osceola Archer debuted on Broadway in *Between Two Worlds*, the Elmer Rice play that opened at the Belasco Theatre in October 1934. She played Rose Henneford, a maid with exquisite taste and manners, more refined in fact than the woman for whom she worked. Henneford, trained as a librarian, was married to a doctor whose career was hurt by discrimination. The role was not terribly far from Archer's own life.

Osceola Archer then appeared in 1935 in Archibald MacLeish's short-lived *Panic*, along with

Rose McClendon and Orson Welles. Martha Graham choreographed and Virgil Thomson supplied the music. Her husband advised her that she had entered a precarious profession and should consider teaching for a while. She taught at Bennett College in North Carolina, but the professional stage was a much stronger magnet than academia. Her husband died in 1940 while she was on tour with *The Emperor Jones*. At that point, she moved to New York permanently. In 1946, she became resident director at Putnam County Playhouse in Mahopac where she stayed for ten happy years.

Osceola Archer performed almost exclusively in classics of the modern stage, among them *Riders to the Sea, The Skin of Our Teeth, The Crucible, The Sea Gull, Ring around the Moon,* and *Blood Wedding*. She performed with the New York Shakespearean Festival in 1960. She also appeared on television in the 1950s and 1960s in productions such as *Teahouse of the August Moon, Rashomon, The Power and the Glory,* and *Pygmalion*. She filmed *An Affair of the Skin* in 1963, appearing with Diana Sands, Viveca Lindfors, and Herbert Berghof.

Osceola Archer was a pioneering Black director and an actress who fought relentlessly against racial barriers. She participated on a panel against bias in the entertainment industry when she was nearing eighty. She belonged to the Actors' Equity Committee for Minority Affairs and was also a member of the executive committee of the Stage Door Canteen. Playwright Philip Hayes Dean remembers her as an elegant and eloquent woman. Paul Robeson always greeted Osceola Archer with "Hello, Lady." Archer and Robeson toured together in *The Emperor Jones* during the summer of 1935. Osceola Archer died in New York at the age of ninety-three.

BIBLIOGRAPHY

Adams, Charles Macarthy. Personal interview (December 6, 1991); Clipping file, Osceola Archer, Billy Rose Theatre Collection, New York Public Library for the Performing Arts, New York City; Dean, Philip Hayes. Personal interview (December 1, 1991); Jones, Robert Earl. Personal interview (December 11, 1991); Tanner, Jo. "The Emergence and Development of the Black Dramatic Actress," Ph.D. diss. (1989).

BARBARA LEWIS

ARMSTRONG, LILLIAN ("LIL") HARDIN (1898-1971)

Singer, pianist, and composer Lillian Hardin Armstrong was an internationally celebrated musician and one of the first women to become a giant in the jazz world and then successfully maintain an elevated position for the duration of her long—and "hot"—career.

Lillian Hardin was born on February 3, 1898, in Memphis, Tennessee. Classically trained in a childhood environment where popular music was considered vulgar, Armstrong received piano and organ lessons as a child and went on to play for both her church and school. Her family moved to Chicago in 1914 or 1915, whereupon Armstrong's formal music education moved from Fisk University to the Chicago College of Music, where she earned her teacher's certificate in 1924. In 1929, she graduated from the New York College of Music.

One of her first jobs was selling sheet music as a song-plugger at Jones's Music Store in Chicago. Learning and demonstrating the store's music, "the jazz wonder child," as Hardin was billed, developed her abilities as a player of popular music and made many contacts with musicians who later would become useful to her in her career as a jazz pianist; among these is said to have been Jelly Roll Morton, one of the greatest jazz pianists of the era, who swayed her toward the musical style for which she became famous, a hard-note hitting, powerful rhythmic style.

Her early jobs involved accompanying singers, among them Alberta Hunter. Her first major break came with the Original New Orleans Creole Jazz Band, playing the swinging New Orleans style to audiences full of such prominent artists as Bill ("Bojangles") Robinson and Sophie Tucker. One night Hardin was heard by King Oliver and Johnny Dodds, who were so impressed with what they heard that they invited her to join their band, King Oliver's Creole Jazz Band, one of the great jazz bands of the era, bringing the New Orleans style north to Chicago's Lincoln Gardens. A short time later, Louis Armstrong joined the band. The two musicians hit it off from the start and were married in 1924. During this period, Armstrong is credited with aiding and encouraging Louis Armstrong in his career, teaching him how to read music more proficiently and urging him to form his own band. Thus, between 1925 and 1928, the Hot Five and the Hot Seven were formed, bands that Lillian Armstrong played with during many of their concerts and recordings and for whom she composed such hits as "Lonesome Blues" and "Jazz Lips." During these busy years she also appeared in the Broadway shows *Hot Chocolates* (1929) and *Shuffle Along* (1933).

Armstrong's talent and determination enabled her to ride out the difficult years of the Great Depression as a musician, playing in several bands, such as those of Oliver, Freddie Keppard, and Elliot Washington. A combo of her own making was the all-women swing band the Harlem Harlicans, which played between 1932 and 1936, as well as another group out of Buffalo that comprised former members of Stuff Smith's band.

Although the couple were divorced in 1938, Lillian Armstrong's career suffered no setback. During the late 1930s, she recorded under the name Lil Hardin and worked as a session pianist for Decca Records. Armstrong returned to Chicago in the 1940s, playing local venues such as the Three Deuces. She toured several times, including one tour of Europe in 1952. Two of her songs, "Bad Boy" and "Just for a Thrill," became huge hits in the 1960s. In 1971, Armstrong collapsed and died of a heart attack on stage at Chicago's Civic Center Plaza during a memorial concert in honor of her former husband.

Composing and playing some of the greatest music in jazz history, Lillian Hardin Armstrong was a key player in an era that set the tone in the development of jazz. Her style of "hot" jazz succeeded in setting new standards within the industry. Many of Armstrong's superb compositions remain popular today, with fans both old and young.

BIBLIOGRAPHY

Berendt, Joachim E. *The Jazz Book* (1981); Cerulli, Dom, Burt Korall, and Mort L. Nasatir. *The Jazz World* (1987); Chilton, John. *Who's Who of Jazz: Storyville to Swing Street* (1972); Collier, James L. *Louis Armstrong: An American Genius* (1983); Dahl, Linda. *Stormy Weather: The Music and Lives of a Century of Jazzmen* (1984); *EBA*; Foster, George M. *Pops Foster* (1971); Harrison, Max, Charles Fox, and Eric Thacker. *The Essential Jazz Records, Vol. 1: Ragtime to Swing* (1984); Hazeldine, Mike. "Lill(ian) Armstrong." In *New Grove's Dictionary of Jazz*, ed. Barry Kernfeld (1988); Hodeir, André. *Jazz: Its Evolution and Essence* (1956); Jones, Max and John Chilton. *Louis: The Louis Armstrong Story* (1988); Mezzrow, Milton. *Really the Blues* (1946); *NA*; Nanry, Charles. *The Jazz Text* (1979); *NBAW*; Placksin, Sally. *American Women in Jazz: 1900 to the Present* (1982).

FENELLA MACFARLANE

ARROYO, MARTINA (1937–)

" 'The keeper of the seal of Italian melody' was the title Verdi is said to have conferred on Puccini, as his successor; but singers as well as composers are needful guardians of that historic possession. In the nineteen-twenties it left its native land for a time, won by the more fluent and lyrical Germans and Austrians. In the sixties, like a good many European treasures, it appears to have crossed the Atlantic. . . . It is hardly Anglo-Saxon, however, when one reflects that a very considerable part of the American achievement has been played by . . . Price, Arroyo, Bumbry, and Verrett." Thus wrote J. B. Steane in his 1974 book, *The Grand Tradition*.

Born in February 1937 of African-American, Native American, and Spanish descent, Martina Arroyo was encouraged by her parents to follow her dreams, but to always have something to fall back on. Thus, her work as a schoolteacher and as a case worker for the New York Welfare Department might appear simply to have been vocational insurance. However, although singing lessons, opera workshops, and the selected movies her parents took the family to all stimulated her interest in opera, Arroyo thought of teaching as equally glamorous, and her career offers ample evidence that she sees service to humanity as much more important than mere personal glory or attainment.

Arroyo studied music and ballet as a child and in high school began voice lessons with Marinka Gurewich, who remained her principal teacher and mentor until Gurewich's death in December 1990. Even as a teenager Arroyo was described as self-directed, able to stand up to bullies, and not put off by the jealousy of peers who could not understand why she aspired to more than the usual. As her teacher later recounted, "How far a voice will go you can only guess. To be a great singer means more. . . . What struck me was this personality of straightforward determination without any of the unkindness that is so often included" (Levy 1972). Arroyo took the initiative in figuring out what she needed to study. "[She] had her own program for herself, which is rare in a teenager. . . . [She had] intelligence and talent centered in just the right way, plus the awareness that being a human being is still the main thing in life" (Levy 1972).

Arroyo raced through Hunter College in only three years, graduating in 1956, all the while keeping up with her academic studies, her deep involvement in music, and taking part in all the usual college activities. Within two years of graduation she had made her New York debut in the American premiere of Pizzetti's *L'assassinio nella Cattedrale* at Carnegie Hall on September 17, 1958. Her debut at the Metropolitan Opera on March 14, 1959, was as the offstage celestial voice in *Don Carlos*. Onstage stardom at the Met came as the result of her last-minute substitution for Birgit Nilsson as Aida on February 6, 1965. As the performance progressed, the originally disappointed audience was transformed into a wildly enthusiastic fan club. For more than a decade after that, Arroyo was a mainstay of Met casting, known particularly as a superb interpreter of Verdi. She starred in numerous major roles, especially in *Ernani, Il Trovatore, Lohengrin, Don Giovanni, Aida, Un ballo in maschera, La forza del destino, Andrea Chenier, Madama Butterfly,* and, more recently, *The Flying Dutchman* and *Turandot*. She was the first soprano in twenty years to sing two consecutive opening nights at the Met—as Elvira in *Ernani* in 1970-71 and as Elizabeth in *Don Carlos* in 1971-72—followed by a third opening night as Leonora in *Il Trovatore* in 1972-73.

Beginning in 1958, Arroyo began to expand her activity beyond the Met, touring in Europe, South America, and South Africa, as well as middle America. During this time she built an impressive international reputation for her singing, not only of opera but also of oratorio and other large works for voice and orchestra. Unlike most dramatic opera singers, she also is known for her technical mastery of works by contemporary composers such as Varèse, Dallapiccola, and Stockhausen. "It is not every dramatic soprano who knows how to hum one note while whistling another one a third higher" (Movshon 1968).

In 1959, Arroyo embarked on her first of many major tours of Europe, appearing at the Vienna and Berlin state operas and in the opera houses of Frankfurt, Dusseldorf, and Zurich. Her initial engagements in Britain in 1968 were a London concert performance of *Les Huguenots* and a Covent Garden appearance as Aida. In 1973, she made her Paris Opera debut. At home, in addition to her performances at the Met, she was a frequent soloist with the New York Philharmonic and other top orchestras, and a favorite soloist of conductors such as Bernstein, Giulini, Bohm, Schippers, Hindemith, and Mehta.

Throughout her career Arroyo has garnered consistent praise for her vocal opulence and technical control in the classics as well as in the contemporary repertoire. Her vocal presentation has been described as "rich, powerfully projected, staggering in size and beauty . . . heard to greatest advantage in the Verdi spinto roles . . . yet flexible enough for Mozart" (Blyth 1980); as "flooding the vast auditorium with wave after wave of golden sound" (Barber 1968); and as "tenderly sung, excels in the clarity of its triplets and the florid whorl of the second part" (Steane 1974).

Of a 1965 performance with the Cleveland Orchestra, R. Widder wrote that Arroyo "contributed her formidable vocal talents to two widely diversified numbers and . . . scaled the heights of expressive vocalism in both. Her classic style (in Scarlatti) left nothing to be desired, but in [Barber's concert scene, 'Andromache's Farewell'] Arroyo realized a stunning performance of a magnificent composition. Her success and the acclaim of this tremendous work by an enthusiastic audience was overwhelming" (Widder 1965).

Referring to 1968 as "the winter of her content," J. Frymire wrote of Arroyo's January 29, 1968, debut as Elsa in *Lohengrin* as "a performance which should establish her in the front rank of contemporary sopranos . . . a diversified exhibition of the lyric art . . . not seen since Rethberg was in her prime. A full-throated voice of great beauty is given free rein but never pushed; and it is backed by first-rate musical taste, vocal technique, and dramatic credibility."

Of her performance of Leonora's aria "Pace, pace, mio dio" from Act IV of *La forza del destino*, J. B. Steane wrote that probably no performance stays more "in the memory . . . than Arroyo's saddened tone at 'profondo il mio sospir' and her vividly acted change of mood at the start of the final section. In all respects—beauty of voice, technical control, musical and dramatic feeling—she belong[s] to the tradition" (Steane 1974).

In his review of the recording "There's a Meeting Here Tonight," Irving Kolodin described the fully versatile Arroyo performing with Dorothy Maynor as "a meeting in *time* of two particular people whose voices together symbolize what has happened in civil rights to correct uncivil wrongs over the last few decades." Referring to the emotional force of Arroyo, who by that time was an established personality on television as well as in concert halls, he added that "success has not deflected her from fidelity to the objectives to which she originally addressed herself nor . . . has it imparted the least bit of pretension to her as a performer" (Kolodin 1974).

The list of her recordings is astonishing. In 1974, Steane observed, "If she were to record nothing more than she has done up to the present, she would still have earned an honourable place among her contemporaries . . . or indeed, among the century's singers."

Aspiring young artists can benefit from Arroyo's clear-eyed perspective expressed in her comments: "While it's great to be Black and beautiful ... it's even better to be Black and beautiful and prepared" and "work is the key ... to me, charisma is just a fancy word for rehearsals" (Levy 1972).

Martina Arroyo continues to embrace the multiple loves of her life as they appeared to her when she was a teenager. In addition to performing all over the world, she has followed up her first Master's class at the Mozarteum in Salzburg (1983) with classes at other locales around the globe and serves on the music faculty at Louisiana State University.

BIBLIOGRAPHY

Abdul, Raoul. "Martina Arroyo." In *Famous Black Entertainers of Today* (1974), and "Martina Arroyo: A Conversation." In *Blacks in Classical Music* (1977); Barker, F. G. "Albert Hall: Opera for Seven Stars," *Music and Musicians* (March 1968); Blythe, Alan. "Arroyo, Martina," *The New Grove Dictionary of Music and Musicians* (1980); Chism, Olin. "Dallas: A Star-Crossed Opera Season," *Ovation* (April 1984); Chiusana, M. and Donal Henahan. "Metropolitan Opera," *Music and Artists* (February/March 1968); Ewen, David. "Arroyo, Martina, 1940- ." In *Musicians Since 1900: Performers in Concert and Opera*, ed. David Ewen (1978); Frymire, J. "Metropolitan Opera," *Music and Artists* (February/March 1968); Gruen, John. "Martina Arroyo Is Back after a Five-Year Absence," *New York Times* (April 17, 1983); Housewright, W. "Dubrovnik," *Musical Courier* (August 1961); Jacobson, Robert. "If You're Really Famous, Why Aren't You on Ed Sullivan?" *After Dark* (September 1970); Kolodin, Irving. "Music to My Ears," *Saturday Review* (February 20, 1965), and "Music to My Ears," *Saturday Review* (February 10, 1968), and "Music to My Ears," *Stereo Review* (July 1974); Lang, Nancy. "Recital, New York," *Musical Courier* (April 1961); Levy, Alan. "Life at the Opera with Madame Butterball," *New York Times* (May 14, 1972), and "A Look at the Future: Nine Young Artists," *Musical America* (July 1963); Movshon, George. "Musician of the Month: Martina Arroyo," *High Fidelity/Musical America* (June 1968), and Operascope: "Martina Arroyo," *Opera News* (September 1986), and Operascope: "Martina Arroyo," *Opera News* (February 13, 1988), and "Recital, New York," *Musical America* (April 1961); Rich, Maria. "Martina Arroyo." In *Who's Who in Opera* (1976); Rogers, E. B. "High Honors," *Musical America* (January 1961); Rothe, Anna, ed. *Current Biography* (1963); Slonimsky, Nicolas. "Arroyo, Martina." In *Baker's Biographical Dictionary of Musicians* (1978); Steane, J. B. *The Grand Tradition* (1974); Widder, R. "Cleveland," *Musical Leader* (January 1965).

EILEEN T. CLINE

ASHBY, DOROTHY JEANNE THOMPSON (1932-1986)

Jazz harpist and bandleader Dorothy Jeanne Ashby was born August 6, 1932, in Detroit, Michigan, and died April 13, 1986, in Santa Monica, California. Ashby began as a pianist and switched to harp in 1952. Her father, Wiley Thompson, a jazz guitarist, taught her harmony. She continued her musical education at Bass Technical High School and Wayne State University, where she pursued advanced studies in harp, piano, and vocal technique; she also played harp in the university orchestra.

In 1953, she began her professional career as a harpist, performing in Detroit and throughout the Midwest and Northeast. From 1960 to 1966, she was both a staff harpist and show hostess for radio music programs and a harpist in pit orchestras for musicals produced by her husband, John Ashby, and her father. During her career, Ashby performed or recorded with a diverse group of jazz musicians, including Louis Armstrong, Duke Ellington, and Woody Herman, and she made recordings with Jimmy Cobb, Miles Davis, Richard Davis, Roy Haynes, Terry Pollard, Art Taylor, Gene Wright, and Frank Wess. Ashby also toured regularly with her own trio, appearing in concert halls, nightclubs, and on television shows. In addition to her performance credits, Ashby also was active in other areas; she participated in the Detroit public schools harp programs, hosted a Detroit jazz radio show, composed several jazz tunes, and wrote a book about modern harmony for harp and piano.

After moving to California in the early 1970s, Ashby became a much-sought-after studio musician. Ashby's harp style combined traditional harp and jazz performing techniques. Known for her unique choral voicings and impeccable technique, which led scholars such as Linda Dahl to compare her with Wes Montgomery, Dorothy Jeanne Ashby was one of the best jazz harpists of her time.

BIBLIOGRAPHY

BDAAM; Dahl, Linda. *Stormy Weather: The Music and Lives of a Century of Jazz Women* (1984); Kernfield, Barry, ed., *The New Grove Dictionary of Jazz* (1988); Placksin, Sally. *American Women in Jazz, 1900 to the Present: Their Words, Lives, and Music* (1982).

SELECTED DISCOGRAPHY

Soft Winds, Jazz Land LP-61 (1961); *Jazz Harpist*, Regent M6-6039 (1962); *The Fantastic Harp of Dorothy Ashby*, Atlantic 1447 (1965); *Afro-Harping*, Cadet 690 (1968);

Best of Dorothy Ashby, Prestige 7638 (1969); *Dorothy Ashby Plays for the Beautiful People*, Prestige 7639 (1969).

EDDIE S. MEADOWS

ASSOCIATION FOR THE STUDY OF AFRO-AMERICAN LIFE AND HISTORY

The Association for the Study of Negro Life and History (ASNLH), now the Association for the Study of Afro-American Life and History, was organized in Chicago by Dr. Carter G. Woodson on September 9, 1915. In attendance at the meeting were George Cleveland Hall, W. B. Hartgrove, and J. E. Stamps. The purpose of the organization, according to Dr. Woodson, was to collect sociological and historical data on the Negro, to study the peoples of African blood, to publish books in the field, and to promote harmony between the races by acquainting one with the achievements of the other.

In January 1916, four months after the founding of the association, Dr. Woodson began publishing the *Journal of Negro History*, and in 1937 he inaugurated the popular magazine the *Negro History Bulletin*. For a number of years, Mary McLeod Bethune (both as a member of ASNLH and as president) had encouraged Woodson to devise new ways to reach primary and secondary school teachers, children, and the masses of African-Americans; the *Negro History Bulletin* was designed to accomplish this end. Following the publication of the first edition of the *Journal of Negro History*, scholars such as W.E.B. Du Bois, Frederick Jackson Turner, F. W. Shepardson, Oswald Garrison Villard, and major newspapers such as the *New York Evening Post*, the *Boston Herald*, and the *Southern Workman*, were enthusiastic in their praise of the *Journal*. The *Boston Herald* concluded in its comments: "Hitherto, the history of the Negro race has been written chiefly by white men; now the educated Negroes of this country have decided to search and tell the historic achievements of their race in their own way and from their own point of view. Judging from the first issue of their publication, they are going to do it in a way that will measure up to the standards set by the best historical publications of the day" (*Journal of Negro History* 1916).

In 1940, on the occasion of the twenty-fifth anniversary of the association, Professor W. B. Hesseltine of the University of Wisconsin concluded that the association had made a major contribution to scientific history in two respects. By doing scholarly research on the Negro, the association had prompted a reconsideration and a consequent revision of the older concepts of the Negro's role in American history and furnished an example of the interrelationship between history and sociology. The first enriched the content of American history and the second improved the methods of scientific research.

Recognizing the difficulties faced by Black scholars in getting their work published, Carter Woodson organized Associated Publishers in 1920 as the publishing arm of the association. Dr. Charles Wesley, coauthor with Dr. Woodson of *The Negro in Our History* (1992), quotes Woodson as saying that "The Negro faces . . . a stone wall when he presents scientific productions to the publishing houses. If the Negro is to settle down to publishing merely what others permit him to bring out, the world will never know what the race has thought and felt and attempted and accomplished and the story of the Negro will perish with him."

In February 1926, Dr. Woodson inaugurated Negro History Week to coincide with the birthdays of Abraham Lincoln and Frederick Douglass. This celebration enlarged the scope of Woodson's work beyond the circle of scholars to school systems and school curricula. The observance of Negro History Week led to the demand for books, literature, and pictures on the Negro. In 1976, in honor of the nation's bicentennial observance, the week was expanded to National Black History Month. The association, through Associated Publishers, continues to establish the theme for each year's celebration.

Since the association's founding, women have played a significant role in virtually every aspect of the organization. Two women, Mary McLeod Bethune (1936-51) as president and Lorraine Williams (1974-76) as editor, worked at the *Journal of Negro History*—the only women who have served in these positions. During Lorraine Williams's years as editor, the editorial board became more reflective of women and younger scholars. Women have served as vice president (Jeannette Cascone and Darlene Clark Hine), secretary (Janet Sims-Wood), and treasurer (Janette Hoston Harris and Mauree Ayton) of the organization, on its executive council, and on the editorial boards of the *Journal of Negro History* and the *Negro History Bulletin*.

Lucy Harth-Smith, a school principal from Lexington, Kentucky, was the first woman named to the executive council, in 1935. Later, Wilhelmina Crosson, Vivian Cook, and Edith Ingraham served on the council.

For a number of years, Lois Mailou Jones, the well-known artist, illustrated books for Associated Publishers, and Dorothy Porter Wesley lent her considerable skills as an author and archivist to numerous activities of the association, including working with the Committee for the *Encyclopedia Africana*. W. Leona Miles, after more than forty-five years at the association in a variety of positions, oversees the affairs of Associated Publishers as managing director.

Women have also been represented as authors and as subjects in the *Journal of Negro History*. As of 1950, more articles by women authors had appeared in the *Journal of Negro History* than in any other historical journal. During the twenty years from 1958 to 1978, 12 percent of the articles in the *Journal of Negro History* were contributed by women. Among the Black women represented were Merze Tate, Bettye Gardner, Bettye Collier-Thomas, and Martha Cobb.

The Association for the Study of Afro-American Life and History continues the work begun by Carter G. Woodson, with Black History Month, an annual convention, and two Ford Foundation-funded projects.

BIBLIOGRAPHY

Bethune, Mary McLeod. "The Association for the Study of Negro Life and History: Its Contribution," *Journal of Negro History* (October 1935); Collier-Thomas, Bettye. "Mary McLeod Bethune and the Black History Movement, 1920-55," Unpublished manuscript (1990); Goggin, Jacqueline. "Countering White Racist Scholarship: Carter G. Woodson and the *Journal of Negro History*," *Journal of Negro History* (Fall 1983); Hesseltine, W. B. "A Quarter

The prominent Black leader Mary McLeod Bethune served as president of the Association for the Study of Negro Life and History from 1936 to 1951. She is seen here at a WAC center luncheon during a National Civilian Advisory Committee inspection tour in 1945. [National Archives]

Century of the Study of Negro Life and History," *Journal of Negro History* (October 1940); "How the Public Received the *Journal of Negro History*," *Journal of Negro History* (April 1916); Jackson, Luther P. "The Work of the Association and the People," *Journal of Negro History* (October 1935); Logan, Rayford W. "An Evaluation of the First Twenty Volumes of the *Journal of Negro History*," *Journal of Negro History* (October 1935); Miles, W. Leanna. Interview (November 26, 1991); "Proceedings of the Biennial Meeting of the Association for the Study of Negro Life and History," *Journal of Negro History* (October 1917); Woodson, Carter G. and Charles H. Wesley. *The Negro in Our History* (1922).

BETTYE J. GARDNER

ASSOCIATION OF BLACK WOMEN HISTORIANS, INC.

In 1977, recognizing the need for a uniquely focused organizational structure within their profession, three Black women historians spearheaded the move to recruit other Black women nationwide. Rosalyn Terborg-Penn, Eleanor Smith, and Elizabeth Parker initiated a series of meetings held in South Hadley, Massachusetts, and in two California cities, Los Angeles and San Francisco.

After Parker's death, Terborg-Penn and Smith sustained the first organizational efforts by convening a steering committee in Cincinnati, Ohio. Gloria Dickerson, Juanita Moore, Darlene Clark Hine, and Janice Sumler-Lewis (later Sumler-Edmond) met with Terborg-Penn and Smith in February 1979 to create a governance and structural framework for the new organization. The committee selected the name Association of Black Women Historians (ABWH) and unanimously endorsed Dickerson's suggestion to call their newsletter *Truth*. It was decided that membership should be reserved for trained Black women historians and other persons interested in Black women's history and in the professional development of Black women historians. Smith agreed to ask noted artist Gilbert Young to create a logo for the new organization.

In October 1979, approximately fifty Black women attended ABWH's first annual gathering in New York City. A business meeting and an address by Gwendolyn Baker of the U.S. Department of Education marked the official beginning of the ABWH organization. While still in New York, the membership asked Marquita James to draft the ABWH constitution, which was later approved by the group's executive council when it met in Chicago in spring 1980.

The ABWH constitution outlines four organizational goals: to establish a network among the membership; to promote Black women in the profession; to disseminate information about opportunities in the field; and to make suggestions concerning research topics and repositories. Apart from amendments concerning dues, the constitution has undergone few revisions since its adoption.

Starting with the 1979 gathering in New York, ABWH annual meetings have been held every fall in conjunction with the convention of the Association for the Study of Afro-American Life and History (ASALH). This consolidation of meetings saves ABWH members additional travel expense. Over the years ABWH-sponsored sessions have become an integral part of the ASALH convention. At the second ABWH annual meeting in New Orleans, the membership elected Terborg-Penn as the group's first national director, a position she held for two consecutive terms. In 1980, with a view toward the organization's continued stability and growth, Terborg-Penn and other members of the executive council instructed National Treasurer Bettye J. Gardner to incorporate ABWH under the laws of the District of Columbia.

In 1980, ABWH collaborated with the Organization of American Historians and the Fund to Improve Post-Secondary Education to complete a Black History Project. The following year, ABWH members coordinated their efforts with the American Historical Association to develop a *Directory of Women Historians* (1981). During the summer of 1983, ABWH members organized a conference on women in the African diaspora held at Howard University. Other ABWH projects and activities are local in character and focus. The four regional areas, consisting of a far west region, a midwest region, a southern region, and an eastern region, comprise the ABWH organizational framework. The four regional directors plan miniconferences, luncheons, and seminars for the members in their regions.

First initiated in 1981, the ABWH annual luncheon, featuring a keynote address, takes place on the afternoon of the general membership meeting and serves as an organizational fund-raiser and opportunity for networking. Publication prize awards, created in 1983 to honor the now deceased Black historian Letitia Woods Brown, recognize excellence in scholarship. The Brown Prize recipients receive their awards during the luncheon.

In 1987, the ABWH Executive Council announced the Lorraine Anderson Williams Leadership

Award, to be given to distinguished Black women leaders. This award honors Williams, professor emeritus of Howard University and mentor to many Black women historians. The Drusilla Dunjee Houston Scholarship is reserved for outstanding Black women graduate students. The Houston award, created in 1989 as a collaborative effort between ABWH and the Black Classic Press of Baltimore, Maryland, celebrates the life and work of Drusilla Dunjee Houston (1876-1941), a teacher, journalist, and self-taught historian.

Through the various awards and activities, emphasizing excellence in scholarship and leadership, the ABWH remains committed to strengthening networks among historians and to its founders' goals as set forth in its constitution.

BIBLIOGRAPHY

Sumler-Lewis, Janice. "The Association of Black Women Historians' First Decade." *NWSAction* (Summer 1989), and "The History of the Association of Black Women Historians' First Decade," with an introduction by Nancy Hewitt. *Newsletter of the Coordinating Committee on Women in the Historical Profession* (March 1991); Terborg-Penn, Rosalyn. "A History of the Association of Black Women Historians, 1977-1981." *Truth: Special Issue* (1981).

JANICE SUMLER-EDMOND

ASSOCIATION OF DEANS OF WOMEN AND ADVISERS TO GIRLS IN NEGRO SCHOOLS

On Black college campuses in the early twentieth century, Black women were virtually absent from boards of trustees, administrations, and faculties; they were paid less than their male counterparts for comparable work; and they were subjected to deplorable living conditions as students. Determined to confront this situation, Lucy Diggs Slowe, the first permanent dean of women at Howard University in Washington, D.C., and founder of the National Association of College Women (NACW), convened a conference of deans and advisers to girls in Negro schools on March 1-2, 1929. This conference, initiated by the NACW committee on standards, gave birth to the Association of Deans of Women and Advisers to Girls in Negro Schools and to twenty-five years of advocacy for Black women in the academy.

Attending the meeting at Howard were women representing ten Black colleges and public schools. Among the participants were Helen Brown, Carol Cotton, Otelia Cromwell, Marian Cuthbert, Sadie Daniels, Hilda A. Davis, Johanna Houston (Ransom), Juanita Howard (Thomas), Ruth Howard (Beckham), Bertha McNeil, Anna Payne, Ruth Rush, Lucy Diggs

This photograph is identified in the Moorland-Spingarn photo collection as a "meeting with colored deans." Lucy Diggs Slowe is the sixth from the left. [Moorland-Spingarn]

Slowe, Georgiana Simpson, Aletha Washington, Tossie Whiting, and Gertrude Woodard. By the close of the conference, five problems had been identified in Black institutions: the underrepresentation of Black women on boards of trustees and college administrations; the need for academically qualified and equitably salaried deans of women and advisers to girls; the lack of adequate and properly equipped housing for female college students; the absence of wholesome extracurricular and well-planned recreational activities for female college students; and the need for separate housing as well as developmentally appropriate regulations and activities for girls attending high school on college campuses.

Having outlined the poor circumstances of women on Black campuses, the conferees decided to meet annually under the sponsorship of the NACW, and for the next five years they assembled to discuss and examine mutual problems and concerns. These meetings were held at Fisk University, Nashville, Tennessee, 1930; Talladega College, Talladega, Alabama, 1931; Tuskegee Institute, Tuskegee, Alabama, and Virginia State College, Petersburg, Virginia, 1932; and Hampton Institute, Hampton, Virginia, 1934. No meeting was held in 1933.

A sixth conference was held at Howard University in March 1935; attending were twenty-eight women from eleven states and the District of Columbia. As with previous gatherings, this one was chaired by Slowe, but the conferees set an important new course by voting to establish an independent organization. Elected to office were Lucy Diggs Slowe of Howard University, president; Dorothy Hopson of Hampton Institute, first vice president; Georgia Myrtle Teale of Wilberforce University, Wilberforce, Ohio, second vice president; Eva Burrell Holmes of Howard University, secretary; and Tossie P. Whiting of Virginia State College, treasurer. A year later the seventh conference—the organization's first as an autonomous body—was held at Wilberforce University.

No meeting was held in 1937 because of the death of Slowe, and without her leadership the group nearly disintegrated. Fortunately, several members who had attended the 1929 conference urged a reconvening, and Georgia Myrtle Teale assumed the presidency. The dean of women at Tuskegee Institute hosted a conference in 1938, and at this, the ninth annual meeting, the first constitution was presented and adopted. The organization took as its name the Association of Deans of Women and Advisers to Girls in Negro Schools. Its threefold purpose was: to bolster a spirit of unity and cooperation among deans and advisers of Negro women and girls; to

create a recognized professional status for deans, advisers, counselors, and others engaged in the building up of girls and young women physically, mentally, socially, and morally, both in the field of education and in civic and economic life; and to study the best methods of counseling girls and young women.

Also established were membership criteria as well as a dues and leadership structure. Elected as officers of this reconstituted organization were Hilda A. Davis of Talladega College, president; Mamie Mason Higgins of Bethune-Cookman College, Daytona Beach, Florida, vice president; Emma C. W. Gray of Paine College, Augusta, Georgia, secretary; Mary Turner of Shaw University, Raleigh, North Carolina, treasurer; and Hazel B. Williams, Louisville Municipal College, Louisville, Kentucky, membership committee chair.

For the next sixteen years, the association met annually on Black college campuses: Louisville Municipal College, 1939; South Carolina State College, Orangeburg, South Carolina, 1940; Fisk University, 1941; Howard University, 1942; Florida Agricultural and Mechanical College, Tallahassee, Florida, 1943; North Carolina State College, Durham, North Carolina, 1944; Lincoln University, Jefferson City, Missouri, 1945; Dillard University, New Orleans, Louisiana, 1946; Tuskegee Institute, 1947; Howard University, 1948; Florida Agricultural and Mechanical College, 1949; Southern University, Baton Rouge, Louisiana, 1950; North Carolina Agricultural and Technical College, Greensboro, North Carolina, 1951; Morgan State University, Baltimore, Maryland, 1952; Virginia State College, 1953; and Howard University, 1954.

Succeeding Slowe (1929-37), Teale (1937-38), and Davis (1938-40) in the presidency were Ina A. Bolton, 1940-42; Flemmie P. Kittrell, 1942-44; Mayme U. Foster, 1944-46; T. Ruth Brett, 1946-48; Emma C. W. Gray, 1948-50; Virginia S. Nyabongo, 1950-52; and Louise Latham, 1952-54.

In 1946, the association held its first joint conference with the National Association of Personnel Deans and Advisers of Men in Negro Institutions. Seven years earlier the female deans had passed a recommendation that the deans of men be contacted "for the purpose of having joint annual meetings, since their problems are so closely woven." As these combined meetings became a tradition, which was especially beneficial to the male deans because their association was not as organized as the women's, many questioned the need for two independent associations. Eight years later, at a joint meeting hosted by Howard University in 1954, both groups voted to merge. Some women were unhappy about merging their vibrant and growing association with the men's group, which was seen as moribund. The prevailing sentiment was for unification, however, and the two groups dissolved, later forming a new body known as the National Association of Personnel Workers (NAPW). The female deans contributed substantially to the NAPW's leadership. Among the founding officers were Sadie M. Yancey of Howard University, president; Arlynne Jones of Grambling State University, Grambling, Louisiana, recording secretary; Jean Spinner of North Carolina Agricultural and Technical College, assistant recording secretary; and Valleta H. Bell Linnette of Virginia State College, first regional vice president.

In its twenty-five-year history, the Association of Deans of Women and Advisers to Girls in Negro Schools played a critical role in the academy. First, it was a professional and social support network for female deans and related educators, many of whom felt discouraged and embattled. Second, it provided a comfortable setting where women could observe role models and discuss institutional politics. Third, its conferences represented one of the few training opportunities for Black women, who were routinely denied full participation at meetings of white associations where similar activities took place. Fourth, it became a national voice for Black women's educational concerns, as its members were typically the highest placed and most articulate women on the campus and in the nation.

In sum, the Association of Deans of Women and Advisers to Girls in Negro Schools laid the framework for a philosophy of higher education that was sensitive to the unique circumstance of Black women and girls. This framework, and the issues articulated by the association, have influenced educational debate and practice throughout the twentieth century.

BIBLIOGRAPHY

Bell-Scott, Patricia. "The Business of Being Dean of Women: A Letter from Lucy Diggs Slowe to Howard University Board of Trustees," *Initiatives* (1991); Carter, Mary M. "The Educational Activities of the National Association of College Women, 1923-1960," Master's thesis (1962); Cuthbert, Marion. "The Dean of Women at Work," *Journal of the National Association of College Women* (April 1928); Davis, Hilda A. "The Fifth Deans' Conference Meets," *Journal of the National Association of College Women* (1933-34); Davis, Hilda A. and Patricia Bell-Scott. "The Association of Deans of Women and Advisers to Girls in Negro Schools, 1929-1954: A Brief Oral History," *Sage* (Summer 1989); *NBAW*; "Proceedings of the Eleventh Annual Meeting of the Association of Deans of Women and Advisers to Girls in Negro Schools," *Quarterly Review of Higher Education among Negroes* (October 1940); "Proceedings of the Twelfth Annual Meeting of the Association of Deans of Women and Advisers to Girls in Negro Schools," *Quarterly Review of Higher Education among Negroes* (October 1941); "Remarks of the President at the Public Session, Eleventh Annual Conference, Association of Deans of Women and Advisers to Girls in Negro Schools," *Quarterly Review of Higher Education among Negroes* (October 1940); Slowe, Lucy. "A Colored Girl Enters College: What Shall She Expect?" *Opportunity* (September 1937), and "The Dean of Women in a Modern University," *The Howard University Alumni Journal* (December 1933); and "The Deans' Conference at Fisk," *National Association of College Women Journal* (April 1929), and "Higher Education for Negro Women," *Journal of Negro Education* (July 1933), and "Some Impressions from Two Conferences of Deans of Women," *Journal of the National Association of College Women* (1935), and "Summary of the Conference of Deans and Advisers to Women in Colored Schools," *National Association of College Women Journal* (April 1928), and "What Is a Dean of Women?" *Journal of the National Association of College Women* (April 1926); "Summary of Seventh Deans' Conference," *Journal of the National Association of College Women* (1936); "Summary of the Conference of Deans and Advisors to Women in Colored Schools," *Journal of the National Association of College Women* (April 1928); Tancil, Elaine. "The Deans of Women Hold Their Second Conference," *National Association of College Women Journal* (1930-31).

HILDA A. DAVIS
PATRICIA BELL-SCOTT

ASSOCIATIONS FOR THE PROTECTION OF NEGRO WOMEN

At the beginning of the twentieth century, urban reformers were concerned about the poor and less fortunate in American society. In particular, New York reformers attempted to uplift the masses by establishing settlement houses, conducting social work among the poor, and writing about the social and economic conditions of Black Americans in the North. The Associations for the Protection of Negro Women were among several social welfare organizations established by prominent Black and white reformers during the Progressive era.

Frances A. Kellor was the leading organizer of the associations. A social worker, she received a fellowship from the College Settlements Association in 1902 that enabled her to study New York City's employment agencies. Kellor and eight assistants spent two years investigating employment agencies in New

York, Chicago, Philadelphia, and Boston. She published the results of the study in her book, *Out of Work* (1904).

Kellor's book exposed the vicious exploitation of Black migrant women from the South. There was no protection for Black women at the docks or at the train stations. Agents in large southern cities persuaded women from the rural districts to move to the North. If the young woman or her relatives could not pay her transportation fee, the employment office loaned it to her, and the woman paid it back at high interest rates.

In April 1905, the Inter-Municipal Committee on Household Research began organizing associations for the protection of Black women in New York City and Philadelphia. Kellor was secretary and later director of the committee, which was composed of representatives from several New York City organizations concerned with the problems of domestic employment. Officers in the New York City association in 1905 were Frances A. Kellor, Dr. William L. Buckley, Mary E. Dreier, Dr. Verina Morton Jones, and Mary White Ovington. Fred Moore, editor of the *Colored American Magazine* and the *New York Age*, was then president of the state association.

The activities of the Associations for the Protection of Negro Women were divided into travelers' aid, lodging houses, education, employment agencies, finances, and membership. The association placed an agent at the docks and stations to meet the migrant women and take them to lodging houses established to help them until they could find work. Employment agencies also were established in Black neighborhoods and a travelers' aid network was established in Baltimore, Washington, Richmond, and Savannah. Sometimes the association paid the fare so that women who could not compete in the industrialized North could return home. Mrs. S. Layten, the Philadelphia agent, asserted that the associations reached only about a third of the women who needed help.

The Associations for the Protection of Negro Women made considerable advances in providing lodging, employment, and other social services for Black women living in cities. One, for instance, opened an attractive home for forty women in Philadelphia in the fall of 1905 at 714 South Seventeenth Street. The New York association did not set up a home and, instead, cooperated with the Colored Mission, the Young Women's Christian Association in Brooklyn, and the White Rose Mission.

In 1906, the associations united to become the National League for the Protection of Colored Women. Kellor was secretary of both the New York association and the National League for the Protection of Colored Women. The National League, like the White Rose Mission, placed travelers' aid agents at all of the major terminals in New York City. Through its local associations, the National League extended its travelers' aid service to Philadelphia, Baltimore, Memphis, and Norfolk.

The National League for the Protection of Colored Women was one of several organizations established to offer services to disadvantaged groups in New York City. The Committee for Improving the Industrial Conditions of Negroes (CIICN) in New York City, also organized in 1906, was dedicated to increasing employment opportunities for Black workers and providing vocational training. The motivator of the group was William Lewis Buckley, a former public school principal in New York City. The CIICN joined the National League and other reform agencies in sending workers to the docks to assist migrant Black women.

On October 16, 1911, the National League, the CIICN, and the Committee on Urban Conditions among Negroes (which was organized on September 29, 1910, by George E. Haynes) merged to form the National League on Urban Conditions among Negroes (NLUCAN).

BIBLIOGRAPHY

Kellor, Frances A. "Assisted Emigration from the South: The Women," *Charities* (October 7, 1905), and "Associations for Protection of Colored Women," *Colored American Magazine* (December 1905), and "Opportunities for Southern Negro Women in Northern Cities," *Voice of the Negro* (July 1905), and *Out of Work: A Study of Employment Agencies, Their Treatment of the Unemployed, and Their Influence upon Homes and Businesses* (1904), and "Southern Colored Girls in the North: The Problem of Their Protection," *Charities* (March 18, 1905); Wood, L. Hollingsworth. "The Urban League Movement," *Journal of Negro History* (April 1924).

FLORIS BARNETT CASH

ATKINS, HANNAH DIGGS (1923-)

Hannah Diggs Atkins, Oklahoma state legislator, 1969-80, traces her interest in political involvement to watching her father coming home late at night bloody and beaten for trying to vote during her childhood in North Carolina. She has had a long, distinguished career in politics and government, ranging from work in voter registration drives to membership on the Democratic National Committee. Describing herself as a "gadfly to prick the moral conscience of legislators," she worked for reform legislation in education, civil rights, mental health, employment, criminal justice, housing, women's rights and child care as an Oklahoma lawmaker (Atkins 1992).

Born in Winston-Salem, North Carolina, November 1, 1923, to James Thackeray Diggs and Mabel Kennedy Diggs, Hannah Diggs received her B.A. from Saint Augustine's College (1943), her B.L.S. from the University of Chicago (1949), and later studied at Oklahoma City University Law School and the University of Oklahoma (where she received an M.P.A. in 1989). Professionally she worked as a news reporter, teacher, biochemical researcher, school librarian, law librarian, and chief of the general reference division, Oklahoma state legislature. After leaving the legislature she served as the assistant director of human services for Oklahoma, 1983-87. From 1987 to 1991, as both secretary of human resources and secretary of state, she was the highest-ranking woman in Oklahoma state government. In 1980, President Jimmy Carter named her delegate to the United Nations, Thirty-fifth Assembly.

She married Charles N. Atkins, and they have three children: Edmund Earl, Charles N., and Valerie Ann.

BIBLIOGRAPHY

Atkins, Hannah Diggs. Personal interview (February 3, 1992); *Daily Oklahoman,* "State Legislator to Be Y Speaker" (January 29, 1973); Oklahoma Department of Libraries. "Who Is Who in the Thirty-fourth Oklahoma Legislature" (1973); Press, Jacques Cattell, ed. *Who's Who in American Politics 1983-84* (1983).

JEWEL LIMAR PRESTAGE

AUNT JEMIMA

Aunt Jemima™ is one of the most enduring advertising trademarks and thus one of the most subversive racial stereotypes. As depicted on Aunt Jemima pancake mix boxes for most of the twentieth century, she is a plump Black woman with exaggerated features. Her eyes are opened wide; her skin is dark and shiny. Her generous grin reveals prominent, startlingly white teeth. Her dress is simple, and her head is covered by a handkerchief, knotted over her broad forehead. She radiates satisfaction and pride—as if someone had just complimented her pancakes.

Aunt Jemima is perhaps one of the most enduring of advertising trademarks and thus one of the most subversive of racial stereotypes, utilized in a range of memorabilia, such as the button illustrated here. [Kenneth Goings]

In her physical appearance, Aunt Jemima closely resembles the Mammy stereotype, and the two share other characteristics as well. Indeed, for many, the two are interchangeable. Both Mammy and Aunt Jemima evoke a mythic antebellum southern past. Their invariably good-natured smiles demonstrate their willingness to serve their white masters and mistresses, usually at the expense of their own families. They both possess a sassy sense of humor, although some critics define Aunt Jemima as more polite and less headstrong than Mammy. Finally, both serve as nurturers for white children: Mammy as the children's caretaker and Aunt Jemima as an indulgent cook who specializes in pancakes.

The company that made the name Aunt Jemima famous was founded in the early 1890s by a white man named Chris L. Rutt. His revolutionary product, a premade pancake mix, proved successful, and Rutt decided that he needed a spokesperson. He hired Nancy Green, a Black woman, to dress in costume and flip pancakes at the 1893 World's Fair. Green gave the mix visual impact, and in 1898 her character was christened as Aunt Jemima.

Although it was common for white southerners in the nineteenth and early twentieth centuries to term older Black women and men "aunt" and "uncle," the exact origin of the name "Jemima" is uncertain. Quaker Oats, which now owns Aunt Jemima Breakfast Products, can only say that Rutt got the name from an unidentified popular song of the time. Yet the historical precedent for an Aunt Jemima stereotype extends back to the mid-1800s, when the image of a lovable, happy slave was a useful weapon by which to claim that Black slaves were content with their enslavement. Yet abolitionists also used the image to generate sympathy for their cause. Helping people who were as helpless and charming as children was an appealing, unintimidating concept. The most celebrated example of the latter is in Harriet Beecher Stowe's *Uncle Tom's Cabin*. The 1851 novel's endearing slave characters, including an Aunt Jemima-like Aunt Chloe, won many white supporters to the abolitionist cause.

After the Civil War ended in 1865 and well into the twentieth century, nostalgic portraits of antebellum southern life proliferated in novels, films, plays, cartoons, and on radio and television shows. Without fail, an Aunt Jemima would be bent over the grill, concocting griddle cake for the children of the white household. The most famous of these wistful historical tableaux was 1939's film *Gone with the Wind*.

Over the years Aunt Jemima characters also appeared in modern dress as dedicated servants to both northern and southern white families. Fannie Hurst's popular 1932 novel, *Imitation of Life*, detailed the life and times of Bea, a northern white woman who becomes rich by marketing her roly-poly Black maid's pancake mix. The book's success led to the 1934 Hollywood version with Louise Beavers as Delilah, the maid. In the 1959 version of the story, Delilah became Annie Johnson and was played by the slender Juanita Moore. Even in many recent Hollywood movies, such as 1990's *Ghost*, Black women have played sassy characters who cater to the needs of white people at the expense of their own.

The "real" Aunt Jemima also metamorphosed. In the 1960s, in response to the civil rights movement, the figure on pancake boxes acquired earrings and wore a headband instead of a turban. Then, in 1990, Aunt Jemima changed into her current incarnation. She has nothing on her head except a stylish hairdo, and she wears businesslike clothing and modest pearl earrings. Yet she is still called Aunt Jemima, and she still smiles hard enough to show all of her teeth. Her overwhelming desire to feed people pancakes, to serve, still wields enormous appeal to white America.

[*See also* MEMORABILIA.]

BIBLIOGRAPHY

Bogle, Donald. *Toms, Coons, Mulattoes, Mammies, and Bucks* (1989); Seidel, Kathryn Lee. *The Southern Belle in the American Novel* (1985).

SARAH P. MORRIS

AUSTIN, LOVIE (1887-1972)

One of the outstanding blues pianists on the Chicago jazz scene from the 1920s through the 1940s was Lovie Austin. Born Cora Calhoun in Chattanooga, Tennessee, in 1887, Austin was formally trained in music theory and piano at Roger Williams University in Nashville, Tennessee, and later at Knoxville College. Her musical talents and training enabled her to play, record, and arrange for some of the great early blues singers.

In the early 1900s, after a brief first marriage to a movie house operator in Detroit, Michigan, Austin worked the vaudeville circuit as piano accompanist to her second husband, Tommy Ladnier. However, she continued to use her first husband's last name, Austin. She had a great predilection for musicals and revues and formed her own band, the Blues Serenaders, a trio featuring Tommy Ladnier on trumpet and Jimmy O'Bryant on clarinet, with whom she toured the Midwest and the South. Austin also managed, composed, arranged, and directed her own musical shows, including *Sunflower Girls* and *Lovie Austin's Revue*, which played Club Alabam, a Black nightspot in New York.

Austin was one of the first female pianists to accompany early blues singers such as Ida Cox, Ma Rainey, Chippie Hill, Edmonia Henderson, and Ethel Waters. After recording companies started using Black artists, Austin made her first recording for Paramount Records in 1923 with Ida Cox, with whom she worked for many years. She played with jazz musicians Buster Bailey, Louis Armstrong, Kid Ory, Johnny Dodds, and Alberta Hunter. Austin and Hunter shared composer credits on two hit records, "Nobody Knows You When You're Down and Out" and "Down Hearted Blues." The latter became a huge success when Bessie Smith sang it in 1923, and Austin later wrote "Graveyard Blues" for Smith. Among her hundreds of early records, Austin's other hits included "Steppin on the Blues" and "Travelin Blues" in 1924 and "Heebie Jeebie" and "Peepin Blues" in 1925.

In the mid- and late 1920s, Austin composed and arranged music for many so-called race records. She arranged vaudeville-improvised tunes for the orchestra at Chicago's Old Monogram Theater, where she remained as musical director for twenty years. During the Great Depression, which put most Black women artists out of work, Austin became well known as director of theater pit bands at the Monogram, and she played with many of the great performers of the period. After leaving the Monogram, she worked for nine years at Joyland Theater.

During World War II and in the late 1940s, Austin toured her own shows for a time and then became pianist at Jimmy Payne's Dancing School in Chicago. In 1946, when Chippie Hill recorded on the Circle label, she was backed by Austin on piano, Lee Collins on trumpet, John Lindsay on bass, and Baby Dodds on drums.

Austin was a well-respected musician with a powerful, rhythmic style of piano playing. In 1926, a writer for the *Chicago Defender* newspaper described her approach as "percussive, pushing the beat along, filling in the bass parts with her right hand maintaining a steady flow of countermelody." She was a pioneer at the piano and had a consistent and dependable musicianship that supported the performances of other singers and performers. She kept a balance and completeness of sound while making use of stop-time, arranging the chords and harmonies in such a way as to occasionally require the musicians to play in double-time.

Austin's well-rounded musicianship and musicality made her a role model for women pursuing a career in music. Famous jazz pianist, composer, and arranger Mary Lou Williams described how she, as a young performer, felt after seeing Austin perform at a Pittsburgh theater:

> On seeing this great woman sitting in the pit and conducting a group of five or six men, her legs crossed, a cigarette in her mouth, playing the show with her left hand and writing music for the next act with her right. WOW! . . . My entire concept was based on the few times I was around Lovie Austin. She was a fabulous woman and a fabulous musician, too. I don't believe there's any woman around now who could compete with her. (Driggs 1977)

Williams was so fascinated by Austin, finding her superior to many men of the period, that she later incorporated some of Austin's playing style into her own.

With new jazz styles coming onto the national scene and the number of positions for Black women artists waning, Austin's career took a drop in the 1950s. Complicated legal problems kept her from enjoying any financial benefit from most of her reissued recordings and compositions. She made her last recording with Alberta Hunter in Chicago in 1961. She died in Chicago in 1972.

[*See also* BLUES AND JAZZ.]

BIBLIOGRAPHY

Block, Adrienne Fried, and Carol Neuls-Bates, eds. *Women in American Music: A Bibliography in Music and Literature* (1979); Dahl, Linda. *Stormy Weather: The Music and Lives of a Century of Jazzwomen* (1984); Driggs, Frank. "Women in Jazz: A Survey." Pamphlet in *Jazzwomen: A Feminist Retrospective*, Stash Records ST-109 (1977); Handy, Antoinette D. *Black Women in American Bands and Orchestras* (1981); Kernfield, Berry, ed. *The New Grove Dictionary of Jazz* (1988); Placksin, Sally. *American Women in Jazz: 1900 to the Present* (1982); Pool, Jeannie G. *Women in Music History: A Research Guide* (1977); Skowronski, Joann. *Women in American Music: A Bibliography* (1978).

DELORES WHITE

AUTOBIOGRAPHY

In the early part of the twentieth century, William Dean Howells, one of the nation's most eminent men of letters at the time, declared that, for Americans, autobiography had proved to be the most "democratic province in the republic of letters" (*Harper's Monthly Magazine*, October 1909). As the century advanced, contemporary scholars continued to validate his statement, and the study of autobiography, although slow in its beginnings, now equals that of other genres. It is interesting to note that the first book to appear in the critical tradition, one that went almost unnoticed by the literary establishment, was *Witnesses for Freedom: Negro Americans in Autobiography* (1948) by Rebecca Chalmers Barton. *Witnesses* contained twenty-three textual portraits of prominent black Americans, many of them women. Although the form is not unique to this country—in Western culture its origins date back to the early fifth century and the *Confessions* of St. Augustine—its peculiar characteristics have been particularly compatible with the American temperament and its inclination to support the principles of individual rights. In this respect, even marginal voices, including those of Native Americans, African-Americans, and women from diverse groups, have, over time, broken through the boundaries of race, gender, class, and sexual identity to join in making this new form of literature the country's preeminent literary genre.

The writing of American autobiography began in the seventeenth century with the narratives of early European settlers by way of the explorer, travel, spiritual, and Indian captivity narratives (the first form of self-writing unique to this country). Toward the end of the eighteenth century, written between 1771 and 1789, the life story of Benjamin Franklin launched what has become the prototype of the secular model of the American self-in-writing. However, although African slavery became an American institution in the 1700s (slavery existed in some parts of the country from the mid-1600s, but the first slave codes did not appear until early in the seventeenth century), little was made of the presence of members of this group in the development of the early literature of this country because slaves were considered to be nonpersons.

In spite of the denial of their humanity by those who enslaved them, Africans in America did not believe themselves to be inferior to whites, and black autobiography, the earliest prose writings to come from this community, emerged in the eighteenth century. Between 1760 and 1798, five stories, four of them self-written, appeared about African men who had been forcibly taken from their homeland and made to endure various cruelties at the hands of their white captors. By offering partial revelations of their lives, the men sought to establish identities other than those that branded them as slaves. By the early nineteenth century, as more such writings were published, the prominent patterns established in black autobiography were the slave (the second uniquely American autobiographical form) and the spiritual or conversion narratives.

Black women entered the autobiographical tradition with Jarena Lee's 1836 text, *The Life and Religious Experiences of Jarena Lee, a Coloured Lady, Giving an Account of Her Call to Preach the Gospel. Revised and Corrected from the Original Manuscript, Written by Herself.* The first female slave narratives did not emerge until the 1860s. In their search for self through writing, black women who wrote about their lives in the nineteenth century, like their male counterparts, were seeking autonomy in a world dominated by white male racist views; in addition to the motivations of black men, however, they also were concerned with issues of gender inside and outside of their home community. In the spiritual narratives, black women challenged, defied, and defeated the male hierarchy of the black church that had prohibited women from becoming ministers of the gospel. In the slave narratives, they revised the one-dimensional perceptions that black men held of them, and their stories embody a distinct ethos based on their position in the community as black women.

Although generally less political than the slave narratives, spiritual narratives of the nineteenth century served an essential function in the black struggle for freedom. These stories about black women and men who had experienced religious conversion denied the superiority of the white dominant society by claiming equal access to the love and forgiveness of the Christian God. In establishing their full humanity in this manner, the writers of these narratives offered their readers a radical revision of prevailing white myths and ideals of black life in America. Also, as charismatic evangelical ministers and missionaries who traveled extensively, preaching the gospel and saving souls, Jarena Lee and other black women spiritual autobiographers of this period disseminated their messages to large audiences of black and white people in many parts of the country and abroad. In these writings they participated in the black quest for freedom through literacy by claiming their right to read and expound on the Bible through their own powers of understanding.

Black women who wrote spiritual autobiographies in the nineteenth century made use of their religious faith to gain autonomy in a society that deprived them of selfhood. As itinerant preachers and missionaries to other countries, they both refuted the idea of women's sphere and escaped the backbreaking physical labor that otherwise was their lot. Denied education, other opportunities for self-improvement, or less dehumanizing means of making their livelihoods, they found work with dignity on the religious frontier. At the same time, their narratives expanded the boundaries of the black male autobiography through the expression of a black female identity that gave them pride in themselves and control over their lives. These works record an important chapter in black women's history.

Female slave narratives were addressed largely but not exclusively to a sympathetic white female audience. Like male slave narratives, they too were accounts by escaped slaves in search of psychological freedom, serving as propaganda weapons in the struggle for the abolition of slavery. The belief that inspired the slave narrative was that, if given accurate information on the conditions under which slaves existed, moral and just white people, especially northerners, would be convinced of the evil of what British abolitionists called a "peculiar" institution and, therefore, would be moved to call for its eradication. Toward this end, narrators described the

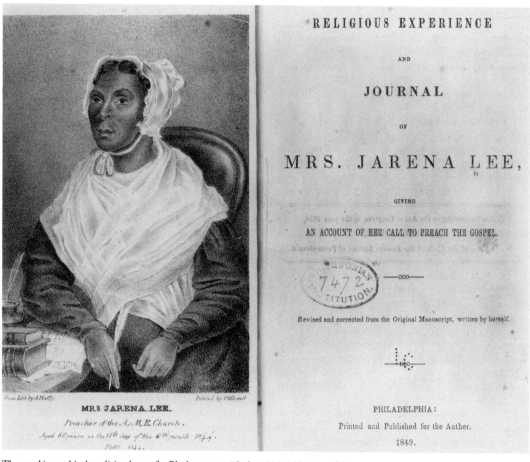

The autobiographical tradition began for Black women with the 1836 publication of Jarena Lee's Life and Religious Experience of Jarena Lee. She was the first woman known to petition the African Methodist Episcopal Church for permission to preach. Reproduced here are the title page and frontispiece of her 1849 autobiography. [Library of Congress]

atrocities of slavery and championed the cause of freedom for all who were suffering under its dehumanizing effects.

The most well-known female slave narrative is Harriet Jacobs's *Incidents in the Life of a Slave Girl* (1861). Unlike many slaves, Jacobs, who lived in Edenton, North Carolina, spent her early childhood with her parents, brother, and grandmother in an environment that did not impress the condition of servitude on her. However, by the time she was twelve years old, in the wake of the death of her parents and a kind mistress, she became the property of a man who was determined to have her submit to him sexually. However, she vowed never to become his victim, and in 1842, after years of struggling against him, she escaped from the South. Jacobs's narrative was the first by a black woman to make her own plea against the sexual tyranny of the slave master.

While male slave narratives portray the experiences of slave women through conventional nineteenth-century male notions of a woman's place, often stereotyping women as sexual victims, female slave narrators present complex images of their lives and experiences. Jacobs, for instance, details the extraordinary events of slave life in Edenton and surrounding communities; the strategies she adopted to confound her master, including deliberately becoming the mother of two children by another white man and hiding in a crawl space of her grandmother's house for seven years; her struggle to free her children; and the existence in Edenton of an antipatriarchal interracial community of women who aided her and made possible her long seclusion. This narrative was very successful in its handling of the sexual exploitation of slave women, in the way that Jacobs appeals to a northern, white, middle-class audience through the conventions of sentimental fiction, and in this slave woman's perceptive analysis of the meaning of freedom.

Although autobiography was the preeminent literary form in nineteenth-century black letters, in the twentieth century emphasis has been placed on writing fiction and poetry. Nevertheless, many women and men also have written personal narratives in this century. The stories by women, no longer constrained by the pressing needs of the slave or spiritual narratives, expand the genre in several directions. Nonetheless, like women slave narrators, many twentieth-century female autobiographers look closely at their lives in relationship to family, community, and the struggles that women face in a world in which they must function as best they can in the face of race and gender oppression.

Many black women's autobiographies focus on the problems of young girls through growing-up stories as well as on work within the community. One of the best known of the growing-up stories is Maya Angelou's *I Know Why the Caged Bird Sings* (1970), the first of her five autobiographical volumes. In this work, Angelou traces her life from the time when, as a child of three, she and her four-year-old brother traveled alone by train across country from their newly divorced parents' home in California to Stamps, Arkansas, the home of their paternal grandmother. Angelou skillfully unfolds the development from her self-conscious, insecure childhood to early maturation, beginning in the small southern town against its background of desperate black poverty and white racism. She pays special tribute to the strength of her religious and independent grandmother and her proud, but physically handicapped, uncle; she looks critically at visits and brief periods with her parents; she relives the pain of her rape by her mother's boyfriend when she was eight years old; and she shows readers how she finally is able to take responsibility for her own life. Psychological details of this development, to an

end that critics characterize as transcendent, dominate Angelou's story.

Other black female autobiographers who have focused at least partially on childhood include activists Mary Church Terrell, Pauli Murray, and Anne Moody. Terrell was born to middle-class parents in the South shortly after the Emancipation Proclamation of 1862. However, in an effort to give her an education better than the one she would receive in the South, her parents sent her, at age six, to live with friends in Ohio. Terrell did well and became one of the first black women to attend Oberlin College. She later worked as a teacher and social activist and was a prime leader in the black women's club movement. Murray, whose narrative also covers much of her life, begins with her growing up with proud grandparents in North Carolina; then it meanders through a series of career choices, revealing her successes as a writer, lawyer, and civil rights activist, roads that eventually led this profoundly religious woman to the Episcopalian priesthood. Moody delineates the life of the daughter of sharecropper parents who, critically assessing the difficult life of her mother, breaks out of the cycle of poverty and ignorance to obtain a college degree while, in spite of racial threats to her life, working as a leader in the civil rights movement in Mississippi.

Autobiographies that focus largely on political action by their protagonists are common among Black women in this century. The antilynching campaign of Ida B. Wells-Barnett in the late nineteenth century when this atrocity was rampant; Shirley Chisholm's campaign for president; and Septima Clark's struggle for better schools for black children are among this group. Stories of service to the black community are sometimes more modest than those that end up in overt political arenas, however. Narratives by schoolteachers, social workers, and nurses, for instance, speak to a commitment to the welfare of black people in general, especially to children, but do not always see the public spotlight.

One group of black women's autobiographies includes those of entertainers and sports figures, such as singers Pearl Bailey and Lena Horne and tennis star Althea Gibson. One of the most moving narratives is Marian Anderson's *My Lord, What a Morning* (1956). Anderson rose from a humble but close-knit Philadelphia background to become the world's leading contralto of her time and perhaps the world's best-known black singer. Her narrative describes the family and community values that shaped this extraordinary woman, and it gives an account of how she carefully navigated the dangerous roadblocks that threatened to turn her away from her course. Her courage and strength in the face of major difficulties are impressive, as is the quiet dignity that enabled her to live above the debilitating racism and sexism that met her at every turn.

Few black women among twentieth-century creative writers have written autobiographies; Maya Angelou is the exception by having chosen this genre over fiction. Writing in kind, however, have been Zora Neale Hurston, who also wrote celebrated fiction; Pauli Murray, who wrote poetry as well; Gwendolyn Brooks, who received a Pulitzer Prize for her poetry and also wrote a novel; Nikki Giovanni, a poet; and Ellen Tarry, an author of stories for children and adolescents.

Although widely diverse in their personalities, ambitions, and goals, and coming from backgrounds widely divided by class, political ideology, and personal differences, black women who write autobiography are joined together by their awareness of the impact that race and gender have had on their lives. This common ground accounts for a strain of radical resistance that runs through even the least overtly political among the group. Black women who write autobiography show their determination to take control of their lives, refusing to yield their autonomy to either the racism of white people or the sexism of black or white men. Instead, they choose identities and actions that defy society's expectations of them and in so doing add a unique voice to the most democratic form of American letters.

BIBLIOGRAPHY

Braxton, Joanne. *Black Women Writing Autobiography* (1989); Foster, Frances Smith. " 'In Respect to Females . . .': Differences in the Portrayals of Women by Male and Female Narrators," *Black American Literature Forum* (1981); McKay, Nellie. "From the Far Corners of the Horizon: Race, Gender, and Cultural Context in Hurston's *Dust Tracks on a Road*." In *Lifelines: Theoretical Essays on Women's Autobiographies*, ed. Bella Brodzki and Celeste Schenck (1988), and "Nineteenth-Century Black Women's Spiritual Autobiographies: Religious Faith and Self-Empowerment." In *Interpreting Women's Lives*, ed. Personal Narratives Group (1989); Smith, Sidonie Ann. "The Song of a Caged Bird: Maya Angelou's Quest after Self-Acceptance," *Southern Humanities Review* (1973).

SELECTED AUTOBIOGRAPHIES

Adams, Effie Kay. *Experiences of a Fulbright Teacher* (1956); Adams, Elizabeth Laura. *Dark Symphony* (1942); Anderson, Marion. *My Lord, What a Morning* (1956); Anderson, Rosa Claudette. *River, Face Homeward* (1956); Angelou, Maya. *All God's Children Need Travelling Shoes* (1986), and *The Heart of a Woman* (1981), and *Gather Together in My Name* (1974), and *I Know Why the Caged Bird Sings* (1969); Bailey, Pearl. *Between You and Me* (1989), and *Talking to Myself* (1971), and *The Raw Pearl* ([1968] 1969); Barlow, Leila Mae. *Across the Years: Memoirs* (1959); Barnett, Ida B. Wells. *Crusade for Justice*, ed. Alfreda Duster (1970); Bass, Charlotte A. *Forty Years: Memoirs from the Pages of a Newspaper* (1969); Bates, Daisy. *The Long Shadow of Little Rock* (1970); Brehan, Delle. *Kicks Is Kicks* (1970); Brent, Linda. *Incidents in the Life of a Slave Girl* (1861); Brooks, Gwendolyn. *Report from Part One* (1972); Broughton, Virginia. *Twenty Years Experience of a Missionary* (1907); Brown, Julia Clarice. *I Testify: My Years as an Undercover Agent for the F.B.I.* (1966); Browne, Rose Butler. *Love My Children: An Autobiography* (1969); Burton, Annie L. *Memoirs of Childhood's Slavery Days* (1909); Campbell, Bebe Moore. *Sweet Summer: Growing Up with and without My Dad* (1989); Chisholm, Shirley. *The Good Fight* (1973), and *Unbought and Unbossed* (1970); Clark, Septima Poinsette. *Ready from Within*, ed. Cynthia S. Brown (1986), and *Echo in My Soul* (1962); Cliff, Michelle. *Claiming an Identity They Taught Me to Despise* (1980); Cooper, Anna Julia. *A Voice from the South by a Black Woman of the South* (1892); Coppin, Fannie Jackson. *Reminiscences of School Life and Hints on Teaching* (1913); Cotton, Ella Earls. *A Spark for My People: A Sociological Autobiography of a Negro Teacher* (1954); Cornwell, Anita. *Black Lesbian in White America* (1983); Craft, William and Ellen Craft. *Running a Thousand Miles for Freedom* (1860); Dandridge, Dorothy and Earl Conrad. *Everything and Nothing: The Dorothy Dandridge Tragedy* (1970); Davis, Angela. *An Autobiography* (1974); Day, Helen Caldwell. *Color Ebony* (1951), and *Not Without Tears* (1951); DeLaney, Lucy A. Berry. *From Darkness Cometh the Light or Struggles for Freedom* (1891); Dunbar-Nelson, Alice. *The Diary of Alice Dunbar-Nelson*, ed. Gloria T. Hall (1984); Dunham, Katherine. *A Touch of Innocence* (1959); Everett, Syble Ethel Byrd. *Adventures with Life* (1945); Ferris, Louanne [pseud.]. *I'm Done Crying* (1969); Fields, Mamie Gavin with Karen Fields. *Lemon Swamp and Other Places* (1983); Foote, Julia A. J. *A Brand Plucked from the Fire* (1913); Forten, Charlotte. *The Journals of Charlotte Forten-Grimké*, ed. Brenda Stevenson (1988); Gaudet, Francis Joseph. *He Leadeth Me* (1913); Gibson, Althea. *I Always Wanted to Be Somebody* (1958); Gibson, Althea with Richard Curtis. *So Much to Live For* (1968); Giovanni, Nikki. *Gemini: An Extended Autobiographical Statement* (1971); Golden, Marita. *Migrations of the Heart: An Autobiography* (1983); Goodwin, Ruby Berkley. *It's Good to Be Black* (1969); Hansberry, Lorraine. *To Be Young, Gifted and Black* (1969); Harrison, Junita. *My Great, Wild, Beautiful World* (1936); Hedgeman, Anna Arnold. *The Trumpet Sounds: A Memoir of Negro Leadership* (1964); Hicks, Estelle Bell. *The Golden Apples: Memoir of a Retired Teacher* (1959); Holiday, Billie with William Duffy. *Lady Sings the Blues* (1956); Horne, Lena with Helen Arnstein and C. Moss. *In Person: Lena Horne* (1950); Horne, Lena with Richard Schickel. *Lena* (1966); Houston, Ruby R. *I Was Afraid to Be Happy* (1967); Hunter, Jane Edna Harris. *A Nickel and a Prayer* (1940); Hunton,

Addie W. and Kathryn M. Johnson. *Two Colored Women in the American Expeditionary Forces* (1920); Hurston, Zora Neale. *Dust Tracks on a Road* (1942); Jackson, Mahalia with Evan McLeod Wylie. *Moving On Up* (1966); Keckley, Elizabeth. *Behind the Scenes: or Thirty Years a Slave and Four Years in the White House* (1868); King, Coretta. *My Life with Martin Luther King, Jr.* (1969); Kitt, Eartha. *Tuesday's Child* (1956); Lee, Jarena. *The Life and Religious Experiences of Jarena Lee* (1836); Lee, Reba [pseud.]. *I Passed for White* (1955); Mix, Sarah (Mrs. Edward). *In Memory of Departed Worth* (1884); Moody, Anne. *Coming of Age in Mississippi* (1970); Moore, Martha Edith. *Unmasked: The Story of My Life* (1964); Morton, Lena Beatrice. *My First Sixty Years: Passion for Wisdom* (1965); Murray, Pauli. *Song in a Weary Throat* (1987); Parks, Lillian Rogers with Frances Spatz Leighton. *My Thirty Years at the White House* (1961); Patterson, Kathryn. *No Time for Tears* (1965); Prince, Nancy. *Narrative of the Life and Travels of Mrs. Nancy Prince* (1850); Ray, Emma J. Smith. *Twice Sold, Twice Ransomed: Autobiography of Mr. and Mrs. L. P. Ray* (1926); Rutland, Eva. *The Trouble with Being a Mama* (1964); Schuyler, Philippa Duke. *Adventures in Black and White* (1960); Smith, Amanda. *An Autobiography of Mrs. Amanda Smith, the Colored Evangelist* (1893); Tarry, Ellen. *The Third Door: The Autobiography of an American Negro Woman* (1955); Taylor, Susie King. *Reminiscences of My Life in Camp with the Thirty-third U.S. Colored Troops* (1902); Terrell, Mary Eliza Church. *A Colored Woman in a White World* (1940); Thompson, Era Bell. *American Daughter* (1946); Truth, Sojourner. *Narrative of Sojourner Truth, Northern Slave* (1850); Turner, Mae Caesar. *Memory Lane in My Southern Home* (1968); Turner, Zatella Rowena. *My Wonderful Year* (1939); Veney, Bethany. *The Narrative of Bethany Veney, A Slave Woman* (1889); Waters, Ethel with Charles Samuels. *His Eye Is on the Sparrow: An Autobiography* (1951); Ethel Waters. *To Me It's Wonderful* (1972); Williams, Rose Berthena Clay. *Black and White Orange: An Autobiography* (1961); Wright, Charlotte. *Beneath the Southern Cross* (1955); Young, Rosa. *Light in the Dark Belt: The Story of Rosa Young as Told by Herself* (1929).

NELLIE Y. McKAY

AVERY, BYLLYE Y. (1937-)

Byllye Y. Avery, the founding president of the National Black Women's Health Project (NBWHP), has been a women's health activist since the early 1970s. As a dreamer and visionary, Avery has combined activism and social responsibility in developing a national forum for the exploration of health issues affecting African-American women. In 1981, as a board member of the National Women's Health Network, Avery moved to Atlanta, Georgia, to pilot a health program that focused on Black women. Under Avery's tireless leadership, the NBWHP grew from an "idea

whose time had come" to the sponsorship in 1982 of the First National Conference at Spelman College in Atlanta, the catalyst to the incorporation of the NBWHP in 1984 as a national organization for and of Black women.

Before moving to Atlanta, Avery was involved in providing direct health service as cofounder of the Gainesville Women's Health Center and cofounder of Birthplace, an alternative birthing center in Gainesville, Florida. Prior to her involvement in health care, Avery taught special education to emotionally disturbed students and served as a consultant to the public schools throughout the state of Florida. Avery, a graduate of Talladega College, Talladega, Alabama, received a Master of Education degree in special education in 1969 from the University of Florida. Since that time, she has received honorary doctorates of Humane Letters from the State University of New York in Binghamton and the Thomas Jefferson University in Philadelphia.

As a proponent of self-help and as executive director of the NBWHP, Avery transformed the women's health movement by mobilizing thousands of Black women to take charge of their life and join the campaign to improve their health status. In recognition of her commitment to promoting self-help as the key to empowerment of African-American women and her commitment to building an organization devoted to identifying and defining health issues for Black women, Avery was awarded a MacArthur Foundation Fellowship for social contributions in 1989.

Since 1990, Byllye Avery, as the founding president of the NBWHP and national messenger of wellness for Black women's health, has written and lectured on how the intersection of race, sex, and class affects empowerment and self-help in the women's health movement. As an international consultant, she has assisted in establishing a health agenda for the Geledes Black Women's Institute in São Paulo, Brazil; the Belize Rural Women's Association, Belize; and Caribbean women at the University of the West Indies, St. Michael, Barbados. She has organized "self-health" groups for the World Council of Churches in Kisumu, Kenya, and in other African countries. In addition, Avery consults on health issues in Southern Africa, Latin America, and the United States as an adviser to the Kellogg Foundation International Leadership Program.

She is the recipient of numerous awards and citations for her selfless labor and outstanding service to women. Her more recent awards are: Community Service Award, Spelman College, 1991; the Ortho Woman of the Twenty-first Century Award, 1991;

the Essence Award for Community Service in Science, Health, and Technology, 1989; and the Outstanding Service to Women and Children, Children's Defense Fund, 1988. She has served on the board of the Global Fund for Women, the International Women's Health Coalition, and the Boston Women's Health Book Collective. Her previous board memberships include the New World Foundation (1986-91), Committee for Responsive Philanthropy (1988-89), and the National Women's Health Network (1976-81).

Byllye Avery is a visiting fellow at the Harvard School of Public Health, where she is developing a Walking for Wellness Program for the National Black Women's Health Project.

BIBLIOGRAPHY

Avery, Byllye. "Breathing Life into Ourselves: The Evolution of the National Black Women's Health Project." In *The Black Women's Health Book*, ed. Evelyn C. White (1990).

ELEANOR HINTON HOYTT

B

BAHA'I FAITH

> Weary and heart sore, discouraged with the Churches that close their doors to them, the silent pulpits that should thunder forth in trumpet tones against the iniquities in the pews, it were strange indeed if the Baha'i teachings wakened no response of great hope in the hearts of colored people. (Coralie Franklin Cook, March 2, 1914)

With these words Coralie Cook declared her commitment to the Baha'i Faith and her expectation that this new religion would unite Black and white believers as was promised in its holy scriptures. Coralie and her husband, George William, became Baha'is around 1913, but had learned about the religion as early as 1910. Coralie Cook was educated at Storer College, Emerson College, and Shoemaker School of Oratory. She served as superintendent of the Washington Home for Destitute Colored Women and Children, and was chair of oratory at Howard University. An outstanding speaker and educator, Cook was appointed to the District of Columbia Board of Education in 1914 and served until 1926, the longest term of any board member at that time.

Cook and her husband were married in 1898 and had one son, George Will, Jr. George Cook was born into slavery in 1855, but escaped and later earned degrees from Howard University. He taught at Howard and became dean of the university's School of Commerce and Finance. The couple devoted their energy to making Howard University a first-rate institution of higher learning. In addition, Coralie was deeply involved in community affairs and was a veteran of the Colored Women's League founded in 1892. She maintained a close friendship with Susan B. Anthony and represented the "women of the Race" at the Susan B. Anthony eightieth anniversary mass meeting in Washington, D.C. Coralie Cook was an ardent civil rights and women's rights activist who brought the same zeal for these issues to the Baha'i Faith, a religion based on the principle of the oneness of mankind and the equality of women and men. She was a masterful rhetorician who published several essays in the National Association for the Advancement of Colored People journal, the *Crisis*.

Coralie and George Cook are just two examples of African-Americans who were attracted to the Baha'i Faith in its early days in the United States. An independent world religion, the Baha'i Faith was founded in Iran in 1844 and spread to the United States in the early 1890s. Baha'u'llah, the Prophet-Founder of the Faith, focused his teachings on a fundamental principle of unity: unity or oneness of God, religion, and mankind. Baha'i tenets revolve around the principle that mankind must unite in a spirit of peace and harmony. Animosity and strife between the races must be eliminated just as all other prejudices must be condemned and abolished. Other principles include the equality of women and men, compulsory education for all children, eradication of extremes of wealth and poverty, and the belief that the primary purpose of religion is the promotion of concord among the peoples of the world.

There are more than five million Baha'is worldwide, and over 100,000 in the United States. Among the followers of the Baha'i Faith are people from all religious backgrounds, nationalities, racial groups, and social classes. More than 2,100 ethnic groups and tribes are represented. Baha'i literature has been translated into more than 700 languages and dialects. The Baha'i Faith has no clergy. Its affairs are administered by democratically elected spiritual assemblies on both local and national levels.

Approximately seventy-five years before the Cooks became Baha'is, Robert Turner was the first Black American to embrace the religion in 1898. He was the butler of Phoebe Apperson Hearst, a philanthropist and mother of William Randolph Hearst, the publishing magnate. Turner lived with his wife and mother-in-law in San Francisco. Nearly one year later, Olive Jackson was the first Black American woman to become a Baha'i. She was a dressmaker who lived in New York City. Information about these first Black American Baha'is is sketchy, but suggests that the Black community was aware of this new religion from its infancy in the United States.

Some of the earliest Black American believers include several Black citizens who enrolled in the Faith when Abdu'l-Baha', son of Baha'u'llah, visited the United States in 1912. Harriet Gibbs Marshall was one of them. She was born in Victoria, on Vancouver Island, in British Columbia in 1870 and grew up in Oberlin, Ohio. She died February 25, 1941. Harriet was the daughter of Judge M. W. Gibbs and Marie Alexander. She married Army Captain Napoleon B. Marshall, a Harvard graduate in the class of 1897.

Talented and well-educated, Harriet Gibbs Marshall was the first Black American woman to graduate from the Oberlin College Conservatory of Music, in 1889. She studied piano in Paris, France, with Moskowski and in 1900 was appointed director of music for the public schools of Washington, D.C. In 1903, she founded the Washington Conservatory of Music and School of Expression for the purpose of providing Black students with the opportunity to study music through a conservatory approach. In 1937, she established the National Negro Music Center as part of the conservatory. The center was designed to be a resource in the research and preservation of Black American music. The conservatory was closed in 1960. Harriet Gibbs Marshall was an active Baha'i and offered the conservatory for Baha'i meetings at a time when few other public facilities would allow integrated gatherings.

A prominent Cleveland couple, Mary B. Martin, a school teacher, and her husband Alexander, an attorney, became Baha'is in 1913. They were initially invited to Baha'i meetings by Louis Gregory, an outstanding, high ranking Black Baha'i who also was an attorney. Mary was born in North Carolina on May 31, 1877, and she died in 1939. She was active in the suffragists' movement and in 1929 was elected to the Cleveland Board of Education. She was the first Black American and the second woman to serve on the board. Mary again was elected to the board in 1933 and in 1939 by nonpartisan ballot. She passed away only two weeks after the 1939 election. Hundreds of people attended her funeral and in 1965 the Cleveland Board of Education named a new elementary school after her, the Mary B. Martin Elementary School. Of her four children, two boys and two girls, Lydia Martin and Sarah Martin Pereira became well-known Baha'is who introduced the religion to people around the world.

Sadie and Mabry Oglesby enrolled as Baha'is in 1914. Sadie Oglesby and her daughter, Bertha Parvine, became the first Black American women to make a pilgrimage to the Baha'i holy places in Haifa, Israel, in 1927. This trip created a dramatic change in Oglesby's life. While on pilgrimage, Shoghi Effendi, grandson of Abdu'l-Baha', urged her to actively help Baha'is understand and bring about racial unity among themselves and the world at large. Sadie Oglesby reported that during most of the pilgrimage Shoghi Effendi focused on issues of racial harmony and constantly encouraged her to play a key role in this "most challenging issue" (Effendi 1971). She agreed to take up this task and immediately upon her return to the United States began giving public speeches on the need for unity among the races. She constantly brought the issue to the floor of Baha'i conventions and exchanged several letters with Shoghi Effendi regarding her plans and progress. Subsequent reports of Baha'i activities indicate that Sadie was indeed successful in generating unity among the races.

Zylpha O. Johnson was born on October 7, 1890, in Boston, Massachusetts, and became a Baha'i in September 1916. She raised her five children as Baha'is. Her husband, Alexander Mapp, was an architect from Barbados, West Indies.

In 1908, Zylpha Mapp became the first Black American woman to graduate from Plymouth High School. Her father, William Johnson, had been the first Black American to graduate from that same high school in the mid-1880s.

On her own property Zylpha Mapp established a camp for underprivileged children from the Boston area. The project was cosponsored ·by the Boston Urban League. While her children were still in school Zylpha Mapp enrolled in law school, but after two and one-half years she had to quit due to the illness and death of her father, and the Great Depression. In 1960, she became active in the Springfield Federation of Women's Clubs. She became its first Black president and served for four consecutive years. During that time she made fifty to sixty dresses a year as a service for the Indian children that the club supported. In her spare time Zylpha wrote eloquent poetry about various subjects, including her acquaintance with Eleanor Roosevelt.

Elected to the Boston Spiritual Assembly in 1929, Zylpha Mapp served until 1934. She corresponded regularly with Shoghi Effendi and Louis Gregory, with whom she later worked in leading discussion groups at the Green Acre Baha'i summer school. Zylpha Mapp Robinson, her daughter, continued in the tradition of her mother and became an extraordinary Baha'i in her own right.

The end of the decade of this first generation of Black Baha'is was highlighted by the enrollment of Dorothy Champ in 1919. That same year Champ became the first Black American to be elected to the New York City Spiritual Assembly. She was a Broadway dancer and actress who gave up her career in order to promote the Baha'i Faith in New England. Born in Virginia on February 23, 1893, Champ passed away in Rhode Island on November 28, 1979. She was remembered as a dedicated, steadfast, and unifying force within the Baha'i community: "Her love for God and His Cause was so strong that the fire would flash from her blazing eyes, galvanizing those who heard her speak" (*Eulogy*, Champ papers).

The Baha'i Faith continues to be enriched by the contributions of Black American women who carry on the legacy of the early believers. Such women include Dr. Wilma Ellis, Administrator-General for the Baha'i International Community and member of the Baha'i Continental Board of Counselors for the Americas; the late Dr. Magdalene Carney, member of the Baha'i International Teaching Center; Attorney H. Elsie Austin, Baha'i trustee; Dr. Alberta Deas, member of the United States Baha'i National Spiritual Assembly; Dr. Sarah Pereira, member of the Baha'i Continental Board of Counselors; Dr. June Thomas, Michigan State University professor and member of the Baha'i Auxiliary Board; Zylpha Mapp Robinson, international educator and Baha'i pioneer; and Ethel Crawford, staff member at the Baha'i International Center. Black women are represented at various levels within the Baha'i Faith. Not all are professional women; they come from a wide range of backgrounds and experiences. They have devoted themselves to active roles in a new religion as exemplified by the words of Annie K. Lewis, who became a Baha'i in 1917: "My only desire is . . . to work interracial till all mankind can live in peace, love, and harmony and go forward with courage in the Cause of God" (Baha'i Historical Record Cards).

BIBLIOGRAPHY

Cook, Coralie Franklin. "A Slave for Life," *Opportunity* (June 1929); Danish, Hossain. "The Baha'i Peace Program,"

Dorothy Champ, who gave up her Broadway acting career to promote the Baha'i faith, was one of many Black people who believed that this multicultural religion could unite the races. [National Baha'i Archives]

In reviewing the 1960 film All the Fine Young Cannibals, *the critic for* Variety *noted that Pearl Bailey gave the best performance, but that "even she can barely cope with a preposterous role of a celebrated blues singer who dies of a broken heart when jilted by 'that man who played blues for her' [Robert Wagner]. Fortunately, the plot takes a brief break to enable Miss Bailey to render one or two numbers in her inimitably casual, well-timed and phrased style."*
[Donald Bogle]

World Encyclopedia of Peace (1986); Effendi, Shoghi. *The Advent of Divine Justice* (1971); Giddings, Paula. *When and Where I Enter: The Impact of Black Women on Race and Sex in America* (1984); Grahame, Roberta and Catherine Blakeslee. *Women of Springfield's Past* (1976); Phoebe Apperson Hearst Collection. Bancroft Library, University of California, Berkeley; Moorland-Spingarn Research Center. Howard University, George William Cook Papers, Washington, D.C.; Morrison, Gayle. *To Move the World: Louis Gregory and the Advancement of Racial Unity in America* (1982); National Baha'i Archive, Wilmette, Illinois: Baha'i Historical Record Cards, Hannen-Knobloch Papers, Lydia Martin Papers, Ober Papers, Robarts Papers, Lunt Papers, Hilda Strauss Papers, Bedikian Papers, Dorothy Champ Papers; National Spiritual Assembly of the Baha'is of the United States. *The Vision of Race Unity: America's Most Challenging Issue* (1991); Robinson, Zylpha Mapp. Interview (June 6, 1988); Stockman, Robert. *The Baha'i Faith in America: Origins 1892-1900* (1985); Universal House of Justice. *The Promise of World Peace: To the Peoples of the World* (1985); WWCA.

GWENDOLYN ETTER-LEWIS

BAILEY, PEARL (1918-1990)

Born Pearlie Mae Bailey on March 29, 1918, to Joseph James Bailey and Pearl Bailey, this versatile entertainer spent her earliest years in Newport News, Virginia. When she was four, her family moved to Washington, D.C., but her mother and father, who was a preacher, soon separated. Although Bailey initially remained with her father, she eventually joined her three older siblings—Virgie, Willie, and Eura—in Philadelphia, where their mother had remarried.

By the time Bailey reached her early teens, her brother Willie (now calling himself "Bill") had established himself as a successful tap dancer. Through his encouragement she entered and won first prize as a singer in an amateur contest at the Pearl Theater in Philadelphia. She was fifteen. Although she originally wanted to become a teacher, her attendance at William Penn High School became sporadic after the Pearl Theater performance. When she won another amateur night a few months later at the prestigious Apollo Theatre in New York City, any residual teacherly ambitions vanished. From then on she devoted herself to show business full-time.

Throughout the rest of the 1930s Bailey performed extensively as a singer and dancer on the Philadelphia-area entertainment circuit. One summer she toured with singer Noble Sissle's band as a specialty dancer. Another summer during her late teens she performed in the red-light districts of tough Pennsylvania mining towns like Pottsville, Wilkes-Barre, and Scranton. It was during this wild time that she married for the first time; the marriage—to a drummer—lasted only eighteen months.

In 1940, after her mining-town stint, Bailey moved to Washington, D.C. Soon after her arrival she landed a job as a vocalist with pianist-composer Edgar Hayes's band. For the next few years she found herself on the move. With the Hayes band and later with the Sunset Royal Band, she performed in high-caliber New York City nightspots such as the Savoy Ballroom and Apollo Theatre, as well as in Washington, D.C., and Baltimore clubs. When the United States went to war in December 1941, Bailey did her part by singing for the troops in a cross-country tour with the USO—the first of many USO tours she made during her long career. The tour ended in Los Angeles, where Bailey lingered long enough to perform at the Flamingo Club.

When Bailey headed back to New York to sing in jazz trumpeter Cootie Williams's band, she stayed put. In 1944, she began performing solo at the Village Vanguard, a popular nightspot. Her manager, Chauncey Oldman, lined up an eight-month stint at the Blue Angel, another famous New York club. Her successes at these two clubs led to a run at the Strand Theater with Cab Calloway in 1945. Although she was to have been only a temporary fill-in for ailing diva Sister Rosetta Tharpe, Bailey found herself booked permanently. She was soon performing regularly with Calloway at the Zanzibar nightclub on Broadway.

In 1946, Bailey made her Broadway theater debut as Butterfly in *St. Louis Woman*, a musical extravaganza. Even though she appeared in only two numbers ("Legalize My Name" and "A Woman's Prerogative"), Bailey upstaged the rest of the cast, including the celebrated tap-dancing Nicholas Brothers. With her appealing mix of comedy and sensuality, she won the 1946 Donaldson Award for most promising newcomer of the year.

Following the success of *St. Louis Woman*, Bailey kept busy both on Broadway and in Hollywood. She appeared onstage as Connecticut in *Arms and the Girl* (1950) and as Madame Fleur in *House of Flowers* (1954)

and performed in the revue *Bless You All* (1954). After making her film debut in *The Variety Girl* (1947), she acted in numerous other films, including *Isn't It Romantic?* (1948), *Carmen Jones* (1955), *That Certain Feeling* (1956), *St. Louis Blues* (1958), *Porgy and Bess* (1959), and *All the Fine Young Cannibals* (1960).

Between these movie and stage jobs, Bailey was constantly in motion, performing in nightclubs across America and sometimes appearing with Count Basie's band throughout the 1950s and 1960s. She was often booked in glitter meccas such as Las Vegas and Atlantic City. Her albums did brisk business: *The Bad Old Days*, *The Cole Porter Song Book*, *For Adult Listen-*

From the red-light districts of tough Pennsylvania mining towns to the glories of Broadway, Hollywood, and television, Pearl Bailey supercharged her performances and her audiences. [Schomburg Center]

ing, *Tired, It Takes Two to Tango, Legalize My Name,* and *Echoes of an Era.* Some of Bailey's own compositions were included on these albums: "A Five Pound Bag of Money," "I'm Gonna Keep on Doin'," "Don't Be Afraid to Love," and "Jingle Bells Cha Cha Cha." During this period she also became a television variety show fixture, appearing primarily on the Ed Sullivan and Perry Como shows.

In 1952, Bailey married Louis Bellson, another drummer. Although controversial because Bellson was white, their union was by far Bailey's happiest. In addition to her brief early marriage, she endured a turbulent 1948-52 marriage to John Randolph Pinkett, Jr., with whom she had a son, Tony, and daughter, DeeDee.

The late 1960s to mid-1970s saw a continued flowering and diversification of Bailey's career. In 1967, she was named entertainer of the year by *Cue Magazine.* In 1968, she won a special Tony Award for her performance as the title character in an all-Black production of *Hello, Dolly!* on Broadway (1967-69); in the same year she won the March of Dimes Award. In 1969, she was named the United Service Organization Woman of the Year. She penned several books, ranging from her 1968 autobiography, *The Raw Pearl,* to a 1976 collection of poetry and personal observations, *Hurry Up America and Spit.* Her other books were *Talking to Myself* (1971), *Pearl's Kitchen* (1973), and *Duey's Tale* (1975). She appeared in a film drama, *The Landlord* (1970), and starred in her own ABC-TV series, *The Pearl Bailey Show* (1971).

Even after announcing in 1975, at the age of fifty-seven, that she was retiring from show business, Bailey remained in the public eye. She made numerous TV appearances on commercials, game shows, sitcoms, dramas, and specials. In 1975, she was named a special advisor to the U.S. mission of the United Nations General Assembly. She costarred with comedian Redd Foxx in the 1976 film comedy *Norman . . . Is That You?* She received a Britannica Life Achievement Award in 1978 and was feted with an "all-star" TV tribute in 1979. In 1981, she provided the voice for Big Mama, the owl in *The Fox and the Hound,* an animated film.

In the early 1980s, Bailey went back to school to complete the education she had abandoned in the 1930s, and in 1985 she received a B.A. in Theology from Georgetown University in Washington, D.C. Her last book, *Between You and Me* (1989), detailed Bailey's experiences with higher education. She was awarded the Presidential Medal of Freedom by Ronald Reagan in October 1988.

She died on August 17, 1990, in Philadelphia.

BIBLIOGRAPHY

Bailey, Pearl. *The Raw Pearl* (1968); Bogle, Donald. *Toms, Coons, Mulattoes, Mammies and Bucks* (1989); Rigdon, W., ed. *Notable Names in the American Theater* (1976).

SARAH P. MORRIS

BAKER, AUGUSTA BRAXSTON (1911-)

Augusta Baker, distinguished children's librarian, storyteller, teacher, administrator, and anthologist, spent her thirty-seven-year career at the New York Public Library. She began as a children's librarian in 1937 at the 135th Street Branch (now the Countee Cullen Regional Branch) and retired as coordinator of children's services in 1974.

Augusta Baker was born on April 1, 1911, in Baltimore, Maryland, the daughter of teachers Winfort J. and Mabel Gough Braxston. She was educated in the public schools of Baltimore and graduated with honors from high school. Her father encouraged her to attend an integrated college where, he thought, contact with people from other cultures would broaden her outlook. She studied for two years at the University of Pittsburgh and then transferred to New York State Teachers College in Albany, where she received a Bachelor of Arts in 1933 and a Bachelor of Science degree in library science the following year. Having grown up in a family that valued scholarship, good books, and a career in teaching, Baker taught school briefly before finding her true calling in public library work. When she became an assistant children's librarian at the 135th Street Branch of the New York Public Library in 1937, the Harlem facility already housed a sizable collection of books on Black history and culture. Under the leadership of Ernestine Rose, branch librarian, and Arthur Schomburg, curator of the Negro Collection, the library had established programs on popular culture and education and had developed services directed especially at the Black community.

Baker plunged into children's work, telling stories and organizing clubs, trips, and concerts. As part of a dedicated staff, she worked with parents, teachers, and community groups to enrich the cultural lives of children, noting that the children who used the library did not know very much about their heritage. Moreover, she found few books that would instill pride in, or encourage children to read about, Black culture. With the assistance of a group of women from the community, Baker tried to correct this problem by collecting worthwhile books that were available. This landmark collection of children's literature, called the James Weldon Johnson Memorial Collection, was selected according to language, theme, and illustration. A bibliography of this pioneering collection was published in 1957 as *Books about Negro Life for Children*; the list has gone through successively larger revisions and eventually was retitled *The Black Experience in Children's Books*.

In 1953, Baker became the first Black librarian to be appointed to an administrative position in the New York Public Library, one of the largest public library systems in the world. As assistant coordinator of children's services for the New York Public Library, she was well regarded for her hard work and effectiveness as a children's librarian at the now renamed Countee Cullen Branch. In her new position, she used her skills as a creative manager and experienced storyteller to bring children and books together and to help parents understand the importance of reading. She was a persistent and convincing spokesperson for the improvement of children's literature about Black people by promoting sensitivity to pictorial, cultural, and intellectual standards. She talked to editors, authors, and publishers about the need for better books about Black life, enlisting the help of interracial organizations in the cause. In so doing, Baker helped to advance the idea that books can help children of different cultures and traditions understand and respect one another while instilling pride in their own cultural traditions. Her commitment to locating materials that would meet this end led Baker to study African folklore and to publish folk tales in anthologies for children. She believed that "folklore makes one aware of the brotherhood of man" (*Negroes of Achievement in Modern America* 1970).

During the 1950s, Baker received nationwide recognition for her efforts. She was the recipient of the first E. P. Dutton-John Macrae Award of the American Library Association (ALA). Her project was to assess the role of books in intercultural education and survey libraries around the country. As a consultant, she organized children's services of the Trinidad Public Library in Port-of-Spain, Trinidad. She taught children's literature, storytelling, and library work with children at Columbia University and the New

When Augusta Baker was appointed assistant coordinator of children's services in 1953, she became the first Black woman to hold an administrative position with the New York Public Library, one of the world's largest public library systems. Later promoted to coordinator of children's services, she used her experience as a storyteller to bring children and books together. [Schomburg Center]

School for Social Research and was invited by other universities here and abroad to lecture and conduct workshops.

In 1961, Baker was appointed to the highest position in the New York Public Library's Office of Work with Children. As coordinator of children's services, she was responsible for the development and coordination of policies and programs for children throughout the system's eighty-two branches and six bookmobiles. She expanded the children's collections by adding audio-visual and other special materials.

Following in the tradition of her predecessors and mentors, Frances Lander Spain, Frances Clarke Sayers, and Anne Carroll Moore, Baker encouraged flexibility, relating library services to the various needs of children from the culturally and economically diverse communities of New York City. Working with a varied staff of more than one hundred, Baker forged relationships and maintained dialogue with schools and community groups, including those involved in the war on poverty. As an adviser to publishers and authors of children's books, a consultant for the television program *Sesame Street*, and a moderator of TV and radio programs, Baker was a visible and vocal advocate for children's services. Following her retirement from the New York Public Library in 1974, she was appointed storyteller-in-residence at the University of South Carolina in Columbia.

Throughout her career Baker was an active participant in professional, literary, and civil rights organizations. She held important offices at the ALA, including chair, Newbery-Caldecott Awards Committee, 1966-67; president, Children's Services Division, 1967-68; and member, executive board, 1968-73. Among her many awards for lifelong contributions to library work with children, children's literature, and to books and American culture are the Parents Magazine Medal Award (1966), the ALA Grolier Award (1968), the Women's National Book Association, Constance Lindsay Skinner Award (1971), the Distinguished Alumni Award from the State University of New York at Albany (1975), honorary membership, American Library Association (1976), an honorary doctorate from St. John's University (1980), and the Catholic Library Association's Regina Medal (1981).

Baker is the widow of James Baker and has a son, James. She is now married to Gordon Alexander.

BIBLIOGRAPHY

ALA World Encyclopedia of Library and Information Services (1986); Baker, Augusta. "My Years as a Children's Librarian." In *The Black Librarian in America*, ed. E. J. Josey (1970); Chepesiuk, R. "Special Report: A Master Storyteller," *Wilson Library Bulletin* (May 1986); Commire, Anne. *Something about the Author* (1972); Flynn, James J., ed. *Negroes of Achievement in Modern America* (1970).

SELECTED WORKS BY AUGUSTA BAKER
Books about Negro Life for Children (1957); *The Golden Lynx and Other Tales* (1960); "Pioneer in the War on Poverty: NYPL," *Library Journal* (September 15, 1965); "Reading for Democracy," *Wilson Library Bulletin* (October 1943); "Readings for Children," New York Library Association (1964); *Storytelling: Art and Technique*, with Ellin Greene (1977); *The Talking Tree* (1960); *The Young Years: Best Loved Stories and Poems for Little Children* (1960).

BETTY L. JENKINS

BAKER, ELLA JOSEPHINE (1903-1986)

Ella Josephine Baker was a pivotal behind-the-scenes figure in progressive African-American political movements from the 1930s until her death in 1986. She helped to organize Black cooperative campaigns in Harlem during the Great Depression; worked as a grass-roots organizer and national leader of the National Association for the Advancement of Colored People (NAACP) in the 1940s; and served as the first interim director of the Southern Christian Leadership Conference (SCLC) in the 1950s. She was a colleague and critic of Martin Luther King, Jr., and was one of the founders and chief sources of inspiration for the Student Nonviolent Coordinating Committee (SNCC), which was founded in 1960. Ella Baker's life, which spanned more than eighty years, was literally immersed in political activity. She was affiliated with nearly fifty organizations and coalitions over the course of her life and thus left an indelible mark on twentieth-century African-American political history. Her life was first documented in an award-winning film, *Fundi: The Ella Baker Story* (1983), by producer Joanne Grant, and more recently in a children's book by Shyrlee Dallard, as well as in several articles and essays.

Although Ella Baker is best known for her activities in the civil rights organizations of the 1950s and 1960s, that involvement did not mark the beginning of her long political career. In many ways her childhood experiences in the South formed the basis of her early political awakening. Born in Norfolk, Virginia, in 1903, Ella Baker grew up in the small town of Littleton, North Carolina. Her parents, Blake Baker and Georgianna Ross Baker, were both educated children of former slaves. For most of Ella Baker's childhood, her father worked as a waiter on a steamship that traveled between Norfolk and Washington, D.C. Her mother had worked as a schoolteacher before her marriage, after which she engaged in volunteer work for the Baptist Missionary Society, raised three children, and earned extra money by taking in an occasional boarder. Ella had two siblings—a younger sister, Margaret, affectionately known as Maggie, and an older brother, Curtis.

Ella Baker's early life was steeped in southern Black culture. Her most vivid childhood memories were of the strong traditions of self-help, mutual cooperation, and sharing of economic resources that encompassed her entire community. In a similar vein, the concept of extended family and fictive kinships further bonded the small, close-knit community into a network of mutual obligations.

Mitchell Ross, Ella's maternal grandfather, was a very important figure in her early development. An independent and hard-working farmer, Ross was proud of the fact that he had purchased a portion of the North Carolina land he had once lived on as a slave. A minister and recognized community leader, Ross was an ardent proponent of equal rights and Black suffrage. He was proud and defiant, and young Ella admired him greatly. Similarly, Baker's maternal grandmother, Josephine Elizabeth, after whom Ella was named, was also a fighter. As a slave she had stubbornly refused to marry a man selected for her by her white mistress, choosing Mitchell Ross instead. Ella Baker also recalled her grandmother as an avid storyteller who passed on the tales of oppression and struggle she had witnessed in the antebellum South. This upbringing, rooted in a tradition of racial pride, resistance to oppression, and a deep sense of community cooperation, formed the core of her strong social conscience.

Because there was no local secondary school, in 1918, when Ella was fifteen years old, her parents sent her to Shaw boarding school in Raleigh, the high school academy of Shaw University. Founded in the mid-nineteenth century by the American Baptist Home Mission Society, Shaw, like most Black colleges at that time, was a conservative institution, run by paternalistic northern white benefactors. The curriculum was "classical," in contrast to the basic vocational training offered at many other Black schools of that era. Shaw students studied literature, philosophy, foreign languages, and mathematics. Ella excelled academically at Shaw, graduating as valedictorian of her college class in 1927. However, she never fully accepted the school's conservative philosophy on many

issues. She joined with classmates on several occasions to protest the rigid regulations imposed on students and refused to comply with practices she deemed degrading. On one occasion she acted as the spokesperson for a group of female students who petitioned the dean to allow them to wear silk stockings on campus. On another occasion she refused a request by the college president to join other students in singing spirituals for a group of northern white guests visiting the campus.

After her graduation from Shaw University, Baker migrated to New York City on the eve of the Great Depression, determined to find an outlet for her intellectual curiosity and growing compassion for social justice. She was deeply moved by the abysmal conditions she witnessed on the streets of Harlem during the 1930s; scenes of poverty, hunger, and desperation were ubiquitous. These scenes of suffering, and the growing radical political culture in New York City in the 1930s, had a tremendous impact on Baker's evolving political consciousness. She traveled throughout the city, attending political meetings, rallies, forums, and discussions. This period proved to be a turning point in her life. It was during her first few years in Harlem that Baker began to define the radical perspective that would inform her political activity for the rest of her life.

The first political organization she joined after moving to Harlem was the Young Negroes Cooperative League (YNCL), founded by the iconoclastic writer George Schuyler in December 1930. The expressed purpose of the group was to gain economic power through consumer cooperation. The YNCL was headquartered in New York City and was made up of nearly two dozen affiliate councils scattered throughout the Northeast and Midwest. Affiliates were organized into buying clubs, cooperative grocery stores, and cooperative distribution networks. In 1931 Baker was elected to serve as the group's first national director.

Baker and many of her idealistic young comrades felt the cooperative movement was much more than a survival strategy to ameliorate the suffering of a handful of Black participants; it was also a proving ground for the principles of communalism and cooperation and an alternative to the cutthroat mode of competition that many felt had led to the 1929 stock market crash and the ensuing social disaster. Cooperative ventures would, they hoped, demonstrate, on a small scale, the efficiency of collective economic planning and simultaneously promote the values of interdependency, group decision making, and the sharing of economic resources. The league was also an organization structured around democratic principles, emphasizing nonhierarchical leadership, the full inclusion of women, and the importance of grass-roots involvement and empowerment. As sociologist Charles Payne points out, this egalitarian vision echoed the treasured memories Baker had of her childhood in the South. In many respects the YNCL experiment foreshadowed a very similar youth organization with which Baker would be closely affiliated some thirty years later—the Student Nonviolent Coordinating Committee.

Another important experience that helped to shape Baker's evolving political consciousness during the Depression was her employment with the Workers Education Project (WEP) of the Works Progress Administration (WPA), a program designed to equip workers with basic literacy skills and to educate them about topics of concern to members of the work force. Classes ranged from instruction in basic arithmetic for sharecroppers to English courses for foreign-born workers. The WEP, like many WPA projects, became a gathering place for a variety of left-wing activists living in New York during the 1930s. The staff engaged in constant debates about political theory, world affairs, and revolution. The WEP also had very close ties to the Congress of Industrial Organizations and the growing trade union movement, and Baker worked closely with a number of militant trade unionists. Given their radical political orientation, Baker and her coworkers were not satisfied to limit curriculum to labor and consumer issues alone. Rather, they sought to link these topics to broader world issues, ranging from the rise of fascism in Europe to colonialism in Africa. While the YNCL was Baker's formal introduction to progressive politics, the WEP was where many of her ideas were forged and molded into a more concrete, radical political analysis.

During the 1930s, Baker also began to grapple with the issue of women's equality and her own identity as an African-American woman. She supported and worked with various women's groups, such as the Women's Day Workers and Industrial League, a union for domestic workers; the Harlem Housewives Cooperative; and the Harlem YWCA. Baker refused to be relegated to a separate "woman's sphere," either personally or politically. She often participated, without reservation, in meetings where she was the only woman present, and many of her closest political allies over the years were men. Similarly, in her personal life Baker refused to comply with prevailing social norms about women's place or women's behavior. When she married her longtime friend, T. J.

Roberts, in the late 1930s, the marriage was anything but conventional, which typified her rebellious spirit. Baker never assumed her husband's name, an unusual act of independence in those days. Also, even though she was married for over a decade, she never framed her identity as a woman around that of her husband and apparently never allowed domestic obligations to interfere with her principal passion, which was politics.

While in Harlem in the 1930s Baker also worked as a reporter and editor for a variety of publications, including the *West Indian News* and the *National News*, a short-lived publication run by her close friend George Schuyler. In 1935 she coauthored an investigative article that exposed the plight of African-American domestic workers in New York during the Depression, which was published in the *Crisis*, the magazine of the NAACP. Among her political friends and associates in Harlem during this period were labor leader A. Philip Randolph, Lester Granger of the National Urban League, Communist party lawyer Conrad Lynn, and George Schuyler.

The next important phase of Baker's political career, which further solidified her evolving views of political struggle and social change, was the beginning of her involvement in the NAACP in 1940. Throughout her relationship with the NAACP, first as a field secretary and later as director of branches (1943-46), Baker fought to democratize the organization and to move it away from legalism as a primary strategy for combating discrimination. She was a staunch advocate of campaigns and strategies that she felt could involve and engage the masses of the NAACP's membership and of linking strategies for racial equality.

Through her fieldwork for the NAACP, Baker established a vast network of contacts in grass-roots African-American communities throughout the South. It was this network of relationships and contacts that formed the foundation for much of the civil rights activity of the 1950s and 1960s. For example, when Baker conducted outreach for the SCLC's Crusade for Citizenship in 1957 and when SNCC volunteers engaged in voter registration and desegregation campaigns in the early 1960s, Baker's web of contacts in the South proved to be an indispensable resource.

Baker remained on the staff of the NAACP until 1946, when, fed up with the top-down bureaucratic structure of the organization and its legalistic strategy for social change, she resigned as director of branches. Another factor that influenced her resignation was the added responsibilities she assumed when she took custody of her nine-year-old niece, Jackie. Baker continued to work with the NAACP in a volunteer capacity as the president of the New York branch, the first woman to hold that post. In that role Baker was a leader of school reform campaigns that sought the desegregation of New York City schools and greater parent involvement in school decision making. She headed a coalition called Parents against Discrimination in Education, which held numerous forums and rallies throughout the city and eventually met with the mayor of the city in 1957 to express its concerns. It was also during the 1950s that Baker became associated with the Liberal party and ran unsuccessfully as its candidate for the New York City Council in 1951. During the late 1950s, she spoke out against McCarthyism and the growing anti-Communist sentiments in the nation.

In January 1956, Baker and two of her closest political allies in New York, Stanley Levison and Bayard Rustin, founded the northern-based organization In Friendship, to help raise funds for the growing southern civil rights struggle. Baker served as executive secretary of the group, staffing its office, handling correspondence, and doing outreach to other organizations and individuals. A. Philip Randolph served briefly as nominal head of the coalition, and the noted Socialist party leader Norman Thomas was a prominent member of the group. In Friendship sponsored several major fund-raisers to aid the Montgomery Improvement Association, which had coordinated the historic Montgomery bus boycott of 1955-56, as well as a number of Black sharecroppers who had been evicted from their farms as retribution for their civil rights activities. In Friendship eventually faded out of existence with the founding in 1957 of the Southern Christian Leadership Conference, formed as a regional coalition in order to sustain and build upon the momentum of the successful Montgomery boycott.

Upon the urging of her friends Rustin and Levison, both of them advisers to Martin Luther King, Jr., in January 1958 Baker agreed to move to Atlanta to coordinate the Crusade for Citizenship, a voter rights campaign launched by the fledgling SCLC. In this new organizational context, Baker took up the fight she had waged within the NAACP some ten years earlier to decentralize decision making and to create accessible channels through which local grassroots people could participate more fully. Although she respected King, SCLC's president, she also felt that the increasing reliance on his public persona and charisma to mobilize people was dangerously channeling the movement's energies in the wrong direction. Baker's message was simply that "strong people don't

One of the founders and chief source of inspiration for the Student Nonviolent Coordinating Committee, Ella Baker believed firmly in participatory democracy at all levels in organizations. "Strong people don't need strong leaders." [Schomburg Center]

need strong leaders." Baker eventually felt that as a woman, a noncleric, and a staunch egalitarian, she never received the respect and recognition she deserved from the male ministers who ran the organization from the top down.

Consequently, when the student-led desegregation sit-in campaign erupted in Greensboro, North Carolina, on February 1, 1960, Baker, already dissatisfied with the leadership of the SCLC, immediately shifted her attention to what would prove to be the cutting edge of the growing Black freedom movement. Just as she had sought to extend the gains of the Montgomery boycott through her work with the SCLC, Baker once again strove to maximize the momentum of this new upsurge in mass direct action among African-American youth. After leaving the SCLC, Baker took a paid position in the regional student office of the YWCA in order to remain close to and assist with the growth of the embryonic student civil rights movement and to use the YWCA as a base of operation to generate resources and recruit student members for a new organization.

Anticipating that the activity would either fizzle out or be co-opted by more moderate African-American leaders, Baker moved quickly to help create a launching pad for a new independent youth organization that would be militant in its tactics and egalitarian in its structure. She called a conference of sit-in leaders in April 1960 at her alma mater, Shaw University. This gathering led to the formation of the Student Nonviolent Coordinating Committee in October of that year. The founding of SNCC as an independent organization represented an alternative to the more politically moderate and hierarchical civil rights organizations that predated it. From its inception SNCC was based upon the principles of grass-roots democracy and decentralized, group-centered leadership. SNCC's fluid, localized structure offered women, poor people, and youth—three forces Ella Baker saw as the backbone of the movement—an important entry point into leadership circles and the ability to contribute to the organization, initiate projects, and influence strategy. SNCC distinguished itself from other civil rights organizations by its aggressive use of mass direct-action tactics and the willingness of its organizers to go into rural regions of the Deep South, where racism and vigilante violence were most intense. Perhaps more than any other organization with which she was affiliated, SNCC embodied the principles and politics Baker had fought for most of her adult life. She served as an adult adviser, role model, and intellectual mentor to many of the young SNCC leaders throughout the existence of the organization.

In 1964, SNCC leaders, including Baker, helped to launch the Mississippi Freedom Democratic Party (MFDP), a grass-roots political party to challenge the hegemony of the segregated, all-white, Mississippi Democratic party. Baker went to Washington, D.C., to manage the national office of the MFDP. In the summer of 1964, at the Democratic party convention in Atlantic City, New Jersey, MFDP delegates confronted Democratic party leaders, urging them to refuse to seat the all-white Mississippi delegation on the grounds that the state Democratic party had discriminated against Mississippi's Black electorate, and to seat the openly elected MFDP delegates instead. The MFDP was ultimately not seated, but its actions were the impetus for subsequent reforms in the Democratic party structure that prohibited discriminatory practices in local primaries.

During the early 1960s, Baker also worked briefly for white antiracist activists Carl and Anne Braden as a staff consultant to the Southern Conference Education Fund (SCEF), an interracial group that worked for racial and social justice in the South. While working for SCEF, she traveled around the country speaking on the importance of linking the fight for civil liberties with the fight for civil rights and thereby helping to forge coalition efforts between white liberals and Black civil rights organizers.

Baker's influence on political movements of the 1960s extended beyond the bounds of the organizations with which she was directly affiliated. Former SNCC members and others who were inspired by her teachings went on to work in organizations ranging from the antiwar group Students for a Democratic Society (SDS), to the Black Panther party, to mainstream electoral politics, and to the women's liberation movement of the 1970s. Throughout the 1970s and 1980s, despite failing health, Baker continued to serve as an adviser to dozens of organizations, activists, and politicians throughout the country. Although Baker's specific ideological imprint upon the civil rights organizations of the 1950s and 1960s is, no doubt, her most significant contribution to the African-American liberation struggle of the twentieth century, one overriding theme stands out in bold relief as we survey the long and rich history that characterizes her political life. Ella Baker was, above all, a bridge connecting young people to their elders, northerners to southerners, Black people to white people, and intellectuals to common folk in a web of organizational and personal relationships. Moreover, she was a historical bridge connecting the social movements of the 1950s and 1960s to the legacy of Black resistance and social protest in the decades that followed.

[See also CIVIL RIGHTS MOVEMENT; FEMINISM IN THE TWENTIETH CENTURY; STUDENT NONVIOLENT COORDINATING COMMITTEE.]

BIBLIOGRAPHY

Baker, Ella Jo. "Bigger than a Hamburger," *Southern Patriot* (June 1960), and "Developing Community Leadership." In *Black Women in White America*, ed. Gerda Lerner (1972); Cantarow, Ellen and Susan Gushee O'Malley. "Ella Baker: Organizing for Civil Rights." In *Moving the Mountain: Women Working for Social Change*, ed. Ellen Cantarow et al. (1980); Dallard, Shyrlee. *Ella Baker: A Leader behind the Scenes* (1990); Forman, James. *The Making of Black Revolutionaries* (1972); Grant, Joanne. *Fundi: The Story of Ella Baker*. New Day Films (1981), and "Mississippi Politics—A Day in the Life of Ella Baker." In *The Black Woman*, ed. Toni Cade (1970); Morris, Aldon D. *Origins of the Civil Rights Movement* (1984); Payne, Charles. "Ella Baker and Models of Social Change," *Signs* (Summer 1989).

BARBARA RANSBY

BAKER, JOSEPHINE (1906-1975)

Josephine Baker was the first and greatest Black dancer to emerge in the genre now called performance art. She epitomized through dance what freedom of expression and artistic expression really meant for generations of artists worldwide. Baker was one of the few artists in the world who were acclaimed and awarded for being themselves. Her genius resided in her conception of music, dance, and comedy. She had a musician's sense of timing, a dancer's instinct for cutting a phrase, and a comedian's ability to deliver the punchline even when it was in the song or gesture. Not merely an entertainer, Baker was in every sense of the word an artist, and it was as an artist that she made her mark on the world.

Baker was also a humanitarian who, in her own unique and eccentric way, tried to live by example. She symbolized beauty, elegance, grace, and, most important, intelligence. Baker helped usher in a new era for Black and white Americans that furthered and fostered mutual understanding between the races. Dance was not only the vehicle for her own transformation into racial awareness, it was also the connector for thousands of her admirers.

Josephine Freda MacDonald was born on June 3, 1906, in St. Louis, Missouri, to Eddie Carson and Carrie MacDonald. She made a name for herself as a singer and dancer in Noble Sissle and Eubie Blake's all-Black musical *Shuffle Along* in 1921. This revue was seen as the Black musical theatrical event of its day and helped to usher in the Harlem Renaissance. It was also a major attraction for white Americans seeking the exotic, which they found in Baker, a fifteen-year-old chorus girl who became the surprise hit of the show.

Baker also toured with Bessie Smith, the "Empress of the Blues," and in 1924 she was featured dancing the Charleston and the Black Bottom at the Old Plantation Club in New York. Baker continued to work with composers Sissle and Blake and returned to Broadway in 1924 in their new revue, *Chocolate Dandies*.

In 1925, she went to Paris and became a sensation in the American production *La Revue Nègre*, symbolizing the quintessential exotic Black woman. She usually performed as an exotic dancer at the Folies-Bergère and the Casino de Paris. She appeared in two films, *La Revue des Revues* and *La Sirène des Tropiques*, in 1927. In the film *ZouZou* (1934), her first talkie, she sang and danced; one song from *ZouZou*, "C'est lui," stayed in her repertoire for years. In 1934, Baker starred in a remake of Offenbach's 1875 comic opera *The Créole*, in which she had one of her greatest artistic successes. *Princesse Tam Tam*, her second talkie, made in 1935, was shot on location in North Africa and told the story of an African beauty

A legend to several generations who found her performances irresistible, Josephine Baker is shown here in one of the spectacular gowns created for her 1951 American tour. She made headlines during this trip to the United States when she protested discrimination against her at the Stork Club. [AP/Wide World Photos]

who is presented to Parisian society as a princess. Baker appeared in New York in the Ziegfeld Follies in 1936 and 1938.

Baker introduced the Charleston and Black Bottom dances to Europe. The influx of Black talent in the chorus line, including Baker and Florence Mills, helped to change dance and fashion in America and Europe. The chorus line was now a precision vehicle performed by women dancing closely together to a swinging rhythm. Langston Hughes said of Baker, "There was something about her rhythm, her warmth, her smile, and her impudent grace that made her stand out" from others in the chorus line.

"La Baker," as she was called in France and abroad, came from a poor community in St. Louis, Missouri, to be feted and toasted in her adult life by European royalty, including Princess Grace of Monaco and Queen Elizabeth of England. Baker also became a friend to many other contemporaries who went on to make national and international contributions. Alexander Calder, an American sculptor and mobile artist, sketched Baker. Novelist Ernest Hemingway proclaimed her the most beautiful woman he had ever seen. She became friends with anthropologist and choreographer Katherine Dunham after seeing her company perform at the Théâtre des Champs-Elysées. Baker said that Dunham should be called "Katherine the Great," evidence of her admiration for a fellow artist and Black American. George Balanchine, the great choreographer, created a dance for Baker in a Ziegfeld revue. Legendary boxer Joe Louis was another admirer and friend and often called on Baker when he was in Paris. Poet e.e. cummings wrote of Baker's performances: "She resembled some tall, vital, incomparably fluid nightmare which crossed its eyes and warped its limbs in a purely unearthly manner—some vision which opened new avenues of fear, which suggested nothing but itself and which consequently was strictly aesthetic."

It was an irony of the times that Baker's performances were considered aesthetic and artistic. Black dance forms lagged behind the other art disciplines in gaining acceptance from the white artistic community, but Baker was instrumental in helping to make that transition. Although she was initially regarded as primitive and exotic, she quickly and skillfully redefined those terms as much as she redefined dance.

In Paris, clothing, perfumes, and hairstyles were all promoted under her name. Baker was known for her spectacular costumes and elaborate headdresses. Dior, Lanvin, Poiret, and Balenciaga, the great European designers, designed clothes especially for her. She was known to make as many as seven costume changes in one performance. Baker wore a shorter dress to accommodate the high kicks and freewheeling movements of the Charleston and the Black Bottom. The shorter fashions which she helped make popular freed women from a Victorian and puritanical look. Baker's influence also contributed to the elimination of the corset. Inspired by Baker, designer Paul Poiret revolutionized the fashion world by discarding the corset in order to permit women to dance more freely. Baker's costumes, especially the fan and banana costumes, became part of French iconography. A banana flan was named after her in honor of the banana outfit.

Baker's ability to sing in six languages (Hebrew, Spanish, German, Portuguese, French, and English) combined with her influence in dance and fashion to remove her from the realm of the savage, in the minds of Europeans, and into the realm of the citizen extraordinaire. She fulfilled the role that had become embedded in the European psyche: the super-sexy Black woman who had a completely free spirit and danced with wild exuberance.

André Levinson, the Russian who became France's first modern dance critic, described Baker and her dancing as "a sinuous idol that enslaves and incites mankind." He also said, "Thanks to her carnal magnificence, her exhibition comes close to pathos. It was she who led the spellbound drummer and the fascinated saxophonist in the harsh rhythm of the blues. It was as though the jazz, catching on the wing the vibrations of this mad body, were interpreting, word by word, its fantastic monologue. The music is born from the dance, and what a dance!"

The long-legged, cocoa-colored beauty was known for her comedic abilities as well as for her sensuous dancing, which often involved dancing topless. This image of "Le Savage" dancing with a string of bananas around her hips tantalized wartorn Europe and fulfilled fantasies and philosophies alike for the masses, the literati, and the intelligentsia. Baker was able to appeal to them all. Sadly, despite all her fame abroad, she was unable to capture the same sort of critical adoration and adulation in America.

Although she made repeated trips to America in the early part of her stay in France, she chose to become a French citizen in 1937 because there she did not face the same level of racial discrimination and prejudice. The indignity of performing before segregated or abusive audiences prevented her from ever seriously considering a return to the United States. Unlike her contemporaries, singers Bessie Smith and Billie Holiday, Baker refused to suffer the habitual and pervasive abuse meted out to Black female entertainers in America. In addition, she resisted what she considered to be the stereotyped image of the Black female performer. When asked about returning to America she said, "They would make me sing mammy songs and I cannot feel mammy songs, so I cannot sing them." On a tour of southern states with musician Artie Shaw, she had a confrontation with a racist who appreciated her music but referred to her as a "nigger wench." Baker insisted on retaliation, and her speaking out often got her in trouble with a nation of audiences accustomed to Black entertainers who smiled and stayed silent, regardless of the verbal and physical abuse heaped upon them.

The "Black Venus" of France, as she was also known, entertained Allied soldiers in North Africa during World War II. As a Red Cross volunteer, she worked as an ambulance driver on the Belgian front. After the German invasion in 1940, she became involved in underground intelligence and made numerous trips throughout Europe and North Africa for the Free French Resistance; for her efforts, Charles De Gaulle later awarded her the Legion of Honor and Rosette of Resistance decorations. After the liberation of Paris in 1944, Baker resumed her performing career at the Théâtre aux Armées, and after the war, she performed at the Folies-Bergère.

Baker's life was not without political controversy. While on tour in Italy, she heard Mussolini advocating the takeover of Ethiopia. She was misquoted or misinterpreted as supporting Mussolini and was roundly condemned by the Black press in the United States. In Argentina, she made anti-American statements that were denounced by Congressman Adam Clayton Powell, Jr., who accused her of letting herself be manipulated by foreign interests. Her tendency to disparage American audiences further distanced her from Americans, including Black Americans; this distance was bridged only when she began to support civil rights issues in subsequent visits to the United States.

Baker was married four times and divorced three times. About her first husband, Willie Wells, little is known, and Baker rarely spoke of him. The greatest contribution of her second marriage, to Will Baker, was his surname. Her third husband, Count Pepito Abatino, orchestrated a disastrous Ziegfeld Follies tour. After Baker got out of her contract with the Follies, the marriage broke up, even though Abatino was then dying of cancer. Later, she married musician and bandleader Jo Bouillon, but they were separated at the time of her death and had been so for some time.

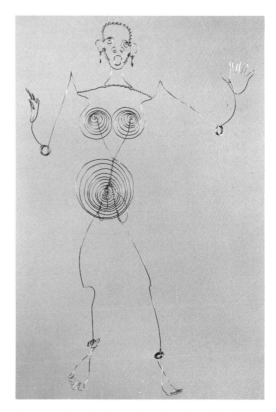

As an expatriate American performing in Paris, Josephine Baker imprinted herself on the consciousness of Parisians. Alexander Calder, who was living in Paris when she took the city by storm in the 1920s (but who probably never saw her perform), did a number of sculptures of her. [Iron wire construction, 39 × 22⅜ × 9¾". Collection, The Museum of Modern Art, New York City]

Although Baker was well known as an animal lover—and owner of a menagerie that included snakes, cheetahs, monkeys, and a pig named Albert—she also loved children. In the 1950s, she embarked on what she called her "experiment in humanity"; she began to adopt orphaned children of different races and nationalities to make a point about humanity and racism. With husband Jo Bouillon, she adopted twelve children and settled into a fifteenth-century chateau, Les Milandes, in France's Dordogne Valley. In 1956, she retired from show business to take care of the children full time. It was a noble experiment, but it was ill-fated; with no income from performing, the expense of keeping such a large, unique family in the extravagant style to which she was accustomed grew prohibitive and strained her marriage.

Forced to return to show business, Baker made her second Paris debut in 1959, at the Olympia de Paris in *Paris, Mes Amours*, a revue based loosely on her own life. Baker and her "Rainbow Tribe," as she called her children, moved into a house in Roguebrune, France, provided by Princess Grace as a testament to Baker's belief in racial harmony and equality.

On a visit to the United States in 1951, Baker said, "My greatest desire will always be to see my people happier in this country." In 1963, she demonstrated her activism and her faith in the civil rights movement by flying in for the march on Washington, D.C., and a Carnegie Hall civil rights benefit at which she performed. In 1964, her appearances at the Brooks Atkinson and Henry Miller theaters in New York were favorably received by both critics and audiences, who marveled at the preservation of her voice and body.

Trying to support her children, the sixty-seven-year-old Baker returned to the United States again in 1974 and 1975 on a tour of major cities that ended in a sold-out performance at Carnegie Hall. The response was the unadulterated appreciation of a living legend. Many Americans had only heard of her and found it a special treat to see and hear the real star. There was ambivalence, however, from the Black community. Although Baker was appreciated for her legacy and stature in the world community, her expressed intolerance of the Black Power movement—a movement based solely on race—made many feel that she was of little help to the cause of Black Americans.

Baker died on April 12, 1975, in Paris after a performance and a dinner party in her honor. She was still adored by millions of fans throughout the world, and she was given a twenty-one-gun salute, the only such honor to be given by France to an American-born woman citizen. At a memorial service in New York, Rosetta LeNoire, the African-American stage and television actress, eulogized Baker this way: "She died in triumph, a woman nearing seventy seemingly transformed to her youth in voice, figure, and vitality, joining her damaged heart with the hearts of cheering audiences which welcomed her back to her beloved Paris."

Baker herself may have said it best in 1927. When a reporter asked about her future, she answered, "I shall dance all my life, I was born to dance, just for that. To live is to dance, I would like to die, breathless, spent, at the end of a dance."

BIBLIOGRAPHY

EBA; Emory, Lynne Fauley. *Black Dance in the United States from 1619 to Today* (1988); Long, Richard. *The Black Tradition in American Concert Dance* (1990); *NA*; *NWAT*; Patterson, Lindsay, ed. *Anthology of the Afro-American in the Theater: A Critical Approach* (1978); Rollins, Charlemae. *Negro Entertainers of Stage, Screen, and TV* (1967); Toppin, Edgar A. *A Biographical History of Blacks in America since 1528* (1971); *WWBA* (1990).

KARIAMU WELSH ASANTE

BAKER, LaVERN (1929-)

Influenced by her aunt, blues great Memphis Minnie, LaVern Baker began her illustrious singing career in 1947. Credited with many popular rhythm-and-blues anthems, including "Tweedle Dee," "Jim Dandy," "Tra La La," and "I Cried a Tear," Baker is known as one of the pioneer rhythm-and-blues artists of the century, with a style *Billboard* magazine once described as "full-throated, vibrant belting with a sexy tease."

Born Delores Williams in Chicago, Illinois, on November 11, 1929, Baker made her singing debut in the Baptist church at the age of twelve. She was dubbed "little Miss Sharecropper," perhaps to compete with the popularity of a singer known as "little Miss Cornshucks" (Shaw 1978). Her astounding vocal abilities led her to make her professional debut while still a teenager. With a powerful, commanding vibrato and a mastery of melodic explorations, she began performing at Chicago's famed Club DeLisa in 1946, receiving an almost unprecedented six-month booking. She moved on to appear at the Flame, a show bar in Detroit, Michigan, where she cut a test record for Columbia Records under the direction of legendary manager Al Green. In 1949, she made her recording debut on RCA-Victor with the Eddie Penigar band. In 1952, she joined the Todd Rhodes Orchestra and toured internationally, both with the orchestra and as a solo artist.

Baker's repertoire, aptly described as raucous, consisted of jazz and urban blues. Her short-lived contracts with Columbia and, later, King Records generally were unrewarding, and in 1953 she signed with Atlantic Records, which was then developing a historic roster of rhythm-and-blues artists. From 1955 to 1960, Baker topped the pop and rhythm-and-blues charts with a stream of hits for Atlantic Records, becoming one of the first rhythm-and-blues artists to cross over to white audiences. In 1958, she recorded a compilation of songs made famous by the great Bessie Smith, with a command of both the blues and the lyrical content that landed her rave reviews.

Although Baker had hits with white audiences, racism kept her from being successful on the pop chart. An unabashedly imitative cover, or remake, of "Tweedle Dee" by white artist Georgia Gibbs went gold, effectively derailing Baker's chances of a pop hit. Not one to sit idly by, she lobbied her congressman to introduce a bill that would make it illegal to copy an arrangement, but to no avail. Several years and thirty-three singles later, Baker left Atlantic in 1965 for Brunswick Records. The following year, "Think Twice," a duet with Jackie Wilson, rose only to number thirty-seven after three weeks on the charts.

In 1965, Baker began working with the United Service Organizations (USO), entertaining American troops with her rich, soulful stylings. Her USO tours crossed Europe and the Far East, including Japan, Taiwan, Vietnam, Guam, and the Philippines. In the Philippines, Baker served as show director, mistress of ceremonies, and vocalist for the U.S. Marine Corps at Subic Bay.

In 1988, Baker made a triumphant return to the States for Atlantic Records's Fortieth Anniversary Celebration at Madison Square Garden. It was an honor to be included as part of the pioneer artists for Atlantic Records. In November 1989, she was honored by the Rhythm and Blues Foundation during its first annual Career Achievement Awards Celebration, receiving an award of $15,000 in recognition of her contributions to rhythm-and-blues music. Later that year two of her songs were featured on the soundtrack of the movie *Shag*, and Baker was signed to perform a new song written by legendary songwriter Doc Pomus for the 1990 film *Dick Tracy*. In February 1990, performing on the U.S. mainland for the first time since 1969, Baker appeared at the John F. Kennedy Center for the Performing Arts in Washington, D.C.

LaVern Baker lives in New York City, where she continues to perform with gusto.

BIBLIOGRAPHY

Clarke, Donald. *Penguin Encyclopedia of Popular Music* (1989); George, Nelson. *The Death of Rhythm and Blues* (1989); Harrington, Richard. "LaVern Baker, Singing Stateside—The R & B Expatriate Redefines Her Base," *Washington Post* (February 23, 1990); Hirshey, Gerri. *Nowhere to Run* (1984); Shaw, Arnold. *Honkers and Shouters* (1978); Whitburn, Joel. *Top R & B Singles, 1942-1988* (1988).

SUZAN E. JENKINS

BALDWIN, MARIA LOUISE (1856-1922)

"I dare not fail," said the distinguished educator Maria Louise Baldwin. She did not fail. For four decades she dedicated her mind and her voice to education.

Maria Louise Baldwin was born on September 13, 1856, in Cambridge, Massachusetts, to Mary E. and Peter L. Baldwin one year after the Massachusetts legislature passed the 1855 act desegregating all public schools in the state. Maria attended the Sargent Primary School, the Allston Grammar School, and the Cambridge High School, from which she graduated in June 1874. In June 1881, she graduated from the Cambridge Training School for Teachers. Almost immediately she taught for one or two terms in Chestertown, Maryland.

Several Black citizens of Cambridge who knew of Baldwin's excellent scholastic record and her futile attempts to secure a teaching position in Cambridge formed a committee to urge the school board to appoint her to a teaching position. As a result, Baldwin was appointed in 1887 as an elementary school teacher of all seven grades in the interracial Agassiz Grammar School. A competent scholar and excellent disciplinarian, Baldwin was selected in 1889 as principal of the school, a position she held for over thirty years.

The deteriorating Agassiz school building was demolished in 1915, and a new $60,000 structure was built in its place. When the school reopened in the fall of 1916, the position of principal was elevated to master. Baldwin became one of only two female masters in Cambridge and the only Black master in New England. In this capacity she directed the work of a dozen white teachers who taught more than 500 students, most of whom were white and many of whose parents were on the faculty of Harvard University. Baldwin held this position with great distinction and efficiency for the remainder of her life.

Maria Louise Baldwin continued her education by enrolling in courses at Boston University and Harvard University. She also collected a large number of books. Her library was used by many friends and literary associates who were frequent visitors to her home on Prospect Street in Cambridge. Among her many friends were Thomas Wentworth Higginson, a Harvard-trained Unitarian minister, and Edward Everett Hale, a writer of New England history and a chaplain of the U.S. Senate. Baldwin enjoyed the friendship and wise counsel of numerous Black persons whose views she shared, such as William H.

On the evening of January 9, 1922, while Baldwin was addressing members of the Council of the Robert Gould Shaw House Association at the Copley-Plaza in Boston, she collapsed and died of a heart attack.

Many tributes were expressed for the life of this unique woman. Memorials were named for her—scholarships, libraries, halls—and in 1952 a new women's dormitory at Howard University in Washington, D.C., was named Maria Baldwin Hall.

Perhaps no teacher has inspired so many or been loved more. Funeral services were held on January 12, 1922, at the Arlington Street Church in Boston. Her ashes were buried in Forest Hill Cemetery. Baldwin was survived by a sister and a brother.

BIBLIOGRAPHY

A.M.E. Church Review (April 1922); *DANB*; Daniel, Sadie Iola. *Women Builders* (1969); Du Bois, W.E.B. "Maria Baldwin," *Crisis* (April 1922); "Funeral Services for Miss Maria L. Baldwin," *Boston Globe* (January 13, 1922); *NAW*; Porter, Dorothy B. "Maria Baldwin, 1856-1922," *Journal of Negro Education* (Winter 1952); Solomons, Olivia S. "Maria Louise Baldwin," *Negro History Bulletin* (October 1941).

DOROTHY PORTER WESLEY

Little more than two decades after Black Americans emerged from slavery, Maria Louise Baldwin was serving as principal of an interracial grammar school in Cambridge, Massachusetts, supervising the education of children of Harvard faculty members. [Moorland-Spingarn]

Lewis, once assistant attorney general of the United States; William Monroe Trotter, publisher and editor of the *Boston Guardian*; and the Honorable Archibald Grimké, a Harvard Law School graduate and editor of the *Hub* newspaper in Boston.

Baldwin frequently lectured, particularly to her own people. She opposed all forms of racial discrimination and praised the achievements of Black Americans. One of her important addresses was delivered at the annual George Washington Birthday Memorial before the Brooklyn Institute in 1897. This was the first time in the fifty-year history of the New York Institute that a woman had given this address. Her speech was entitled "The Life and Services of the Late Harriet Beecher Stowe." The applause was so great she had to stand repeatedly to acknowledge it. As a result of this historic speech, Baldwin was offered another teaching position at twice her salary at Agassiz, and she was sought often for speaking engagements.

BAMBARA, TONI CADE (1939-)

"It's a tremendous responsibility—responsibility and honor—to be a writer, an artist, a cultural worker . . . whatever you call this vocation. One's got to see what the factory worker sees, what the prisoner sees, what the welfare children see, what the scholar sees, got to see what the ruling-class mythmakers see as well, in order to tell the truth and not get trapped." To tell the truth and not get trapped in the maze of prevailing stereotypes of the Black community: this is the writer/cultural nationalist Toni Cade Bambara's self-proclaimed mission as she explained it in a 1983 interview with the critic/scholar Claudia Tate.

The statement reflects the political and social commitment to improving the welfare of the African-American community (especially the urban community) that Bambara first exhibited in the 1950s and 1960s. Moreover, the statement explains Bambara's focus on social messages in all of her short stories and in the two anthologies she edited during the 1970s. Her two short-story collections, *Gorilla, My Love* (1972) and *The Sea Birds Are Still Alive* (1977), cover a wide range of African-American experiences and personalities—those of children and young adults, men and women, the elderly, the political activist, and the blues singer. One anthology of essays, poetry, and prose, entitled *The Black Woman* (1970), was unprecedented in American letters. It was designed to allow Black women from a variety of ages, classes, and occupations to speak their minds on issues relevant to their lives that the civil rights and women's liberation movements at the time did not address. *The Salt Eaters* (1980), Bambara's first and only novel, grew out of a short story intended to expose the division within the African-American community among the political, psychic, and spiritual forces that had sustained it in its earlier history. The novel proposes a fusion among these internal factions and a linking between the African-American community and other ethnic communities in the United States, namely Asian-Americans, Hispanic-Americans, Native Americans, and Americans of Caribbean descent. Hence, Bambara's understanding of the complexities of African-American life informs all of her work.

Named Toni Cade at her birth in 1939 in New York City to Helen Brent Henderson Cade, she adopted the name Bambara in 1970 when she discovered it as part of a signature on a sketchbook she found in her great-grandmother's trunk. Toni and her brother grew up with their mother in New York City (Harlem, Bedford-Stuyvesant, and Queens) and in Jersey City, New Jersey. She attended various public and private schools in New York, New Jersey, and the southeastern United States. When asked in interviews who encouraged and influenced her writing, Bambara always names her mother. Helen Cade had lived in Harlem during the 1920s, when Black writers like Countee Cullen, Langston Hughes, Claude McKay, and Wallace Thurman were publishing poetry, fiction, and drama. She developed a respect not only for their literature but for all types of reading materials. When her children were young, Helen Cade, according to Bambara, encouraged them to daydream, to get in touch with their imaginations, and to follow their inner motives. She encouraged Toni Cade's early efforts to write fiction.

Cade published her first short story, "Sweet Town," in *Vendome* magazine in January 1959. That same year she received her B.A. in theater arts/English and the John Golden Award for Fiction from Queens College. The *Long Island Star* awarded her its Pauper Press Award for nonfiction that same year. While enrolled as a graduate student of modern American fiction at the City College of New York, Cade worked as a social worker for the Harlem Welfare Center during 1959-60. She published her second story, "Mississippi Ham Rider," in the summer 1960

Massachusetts Review. In 1961, she studied at the Commedia del'Arte in Milan, Italy, and worked there as a free-lance writer. Between 1962 and 1965, she completed her Master's degree and worked as program director at Colony House in Brooklyn and as the recreational and occupational therapist for Metropolitan Hospital's psychiatric division. During those years she also took various positions as either coordinator or director of local neighborhood programs, such as the Equivalency Program, the Veteran Reentry Program, the Eighth Street Play program sponsored by the Lower Eastside Tenants Association, and the Tutorial Program at the Hamilton Fish Park Branch Library. After receiving her Master's degree Bambara taught at the City College of New York from 1965 to 1969 and served as director/adviser for the Theater of the Black Experience and as adviser for various publications sponsored by the City College SEEK program, such as *Obsidian*, *Onyx*, and *The Paper*. During this same four-year period, more of her stories began to appear in various journals and magazines such as the *Liberator, Prairie Schooner*, and *Redbook*.

Bambara came of age during the 1960s and early 1970s when both the Black cultural nationalist and women's liberation movements were gathering momentum in the United States. She participated in both for a while but soon realized that neither fully addressed the concerns of the African-American woman. Acting upon the advice of the Black scholar Addison Gayle, to whom she complained about this omission, Cade edited *The Black Woman: An Anthology.* This anthology was a first of its kind in the United States. The year it was published, 1970, is now recognized as the beginning of the twentieth-century renaissance of Black women's literature. Toni Morrison's *The Bluest Eye*, Alice Walker's *The Third Life of Grange Copeland*, and Louise Meriwether's *Daddy Was a Number Runner*, first novels for these writers, were published in 1970. In addition, the poets Nikki Giovanni, Sonia Sanchez, and Margaret Walker each published collections of their poetry in 1970. In editing *The Black Woman*, Cade cut across age, class, and occupational barriers to include poetry, short stories, and essays by well-known writers (Nikki Giovanni, Kay Kindsey, Audre Lorde, Alice Walker, and Paule Marshall) and women students in the City College SEEK program to show the world what various Black women were thinking and doing about both the civil rights and the women's movements. In the preface, Bambara, still writing under the name Toni Cade, states that she envisioned the collection as a response to all the male "experts" both Black and white who had been publishing articles and conducting sociological studies on Black women. Even the leading white feminists at that time, Cade felt, were not equipped to understand, much less to explain, the feelings and the situation of the African-American woman. The items included in the anthology vary in their opinions on this matter. Most share some of the same concerns about interpersonal relationships in the Black community (men and women, parents and children), social issues such as quality education and housing for Black Americans, and Black women's personal development. It is evident, however, that at that time these Black women were sharply divided along political lines. Some argued for a radical departure from every known form of Black female behavior, while others cautioned that too many changes would jeopardize a woman's emotional security. These differences notwithstanding, this anthology provided an arena for Black women's opinions to be voiced en masse at a time when it was assumed that all Black people were preoccupied with racial equality. For Cade, the struggle for Black equality in America was important, but not to be obtained at the Black woman's expense.

Toni Cade Bambara taught in the English department at Livingston College in New Jersey in 1969-70. She was promoted to associate professor at Livingston, and in addition to her teaching duties, she worked as the co-adviser for the Harambee dancers, the Malcolm Players, and Sisters in Consciousness. In 1974, she received a plaque from the Livingston College Black community for service.

In 1971, Bambara edited another anthology, entitled *Tales and Stories for Black Folks*. The purpose of this anthology, she explains in the introduction, is to teach young African-Americans the historical value of telling stories. She urges her young readers to take the folktales seriously as lessons on human behavior and as examples of living history. The first section of the collection consists of stories by professional African-American writers such as Langston Hughes, Alice Walker, Pear Crayton, and Ernest Gaines. Bambara's own story "Raymond's Run" is included in this section. The second half of the collection includes an English translation of a fable by the Senegalese Birago Diop and one by the Ghanaian James Aggrey, as well as several selections written by students in a freshman composition course Bambara taught at Livingston College. As with her first anthology, Bambara's decision to include student essays with selections by older professional writers shows her desire to give young writers a chance to make their talents known to a large audience. In addition, such a mixture in *Tales and Stories for Black Folks* helped inspire her intended

audience, African-American high school and college students, to read, to think critically, and to write.

Most of the stories Bambara wrote as Toni Cade between 1959 and 1970 were published in October 1972 in what was to become her most widely read collection: *Gorilla, My Love*. Eight of the fifteen stories in the collection center on young children and adolescents as they move through their neighborhood learning about themselves while responding to their environment. The hallmark of all of Bambara's fiction is her preference for settings outside of the home. The sidewalk, a movie house, a park or athletic field, a local bar, and a community center are some of the locations that recur in Bambara's fiction. Bambara's characters, like those in *Gorilla, My Love*, are rarely at odds with these settings. They move through their immediate neighborhoods comfortably familiar with the people and with each building, street lamp, and fire hydrant they pass. Each character in *Gorilla, My Love* exudes a streetwise sophistication, a confidence in "mother wit," that helps him or her to intimidate immediate rivals.

During the five-year span from 1972 to the publication in 1977 of her second collection of short stories, *The Sea Birds Are Still Alive*, major events took place in Bambara's life that were to have an effect on her writing. She visited Cuba in 1973, where she met with the Federation of Cuban Women. She visited Vietnam in the summer of 1975 as a guest of that nation's Women's Union. Both taught Bambara how effective women's organizations and creative endeavors could be in a political movement. She relocated with her daughter, Karma, to Atlanta, Georgia, in 1974. Concurrent with her teaching duties as writer-in-residence at Spelman College from 1974 to 1977, Bambara became a founding member of the Southern Collective of African-American Writers and the Neighborhood Cultural Arts Center, Inc. She was also director of the Pomoja Writers Guild, a founding member and officer of the Conference Committee on Black South Literature and Art, and an associate/aide for the Institute of the Black World. The effects of Bambara's travels abroad, her relocation to Atlanta, and her work in so many community art groups can be seen in the stories published in *The Sea Birds Are Still Alive* and in *The Salt Eaters*. In both works, Bambara is intent on using her art to convey social and political messages about the welfare of the African-American community. In 1980, Bambara won the American Book Award for *The Salt Eaters*.

During the early 1980s, Toni Cade Bambara and her daughter relocated to Philadelphia, Pennsylvania. She continues to write, work with community organizations, and teach writers' workshops in schools and community centers.

BIBLIOGRAPHY

Byerman, Keith. *Fingering the Jagged Grain: Tradition and Form in Recent Black Fiction* (1985); Chandler, Zala. "Voices Beyond the Veil: An Interview of Toni Cade Bambara and Sonia Sanchez." In *Wild Women in the Whirlwind: Afra-American Culture and the Contemporary Literary Renaissance*, ed. Joanne M. Braxton and Andrée Nicola McLaughlin (1990); *DLB*; Evans, Mari. "Toni Cade Bambara." *Black Women Writers (1950-1980): A Critical Evaluation* (1984); Hull, Gloria. "What It Is I Think She's Doing Anyhow: A Reading of Toni Cade Bambara's *The Salt Eaters*." In *Home Girls: A Black Feminist Anthology*, ed. Barbara Smith (1983); Tate, Claudia. "Toni Cade Bambara." In *Black Women Writers at Work* (1983); Werner, Craig. *Black American Women Novelists: An Annotated Bibliography* (1989).

ALICE A. DECK

BANKS, ANNA DE COSTA
(1869-1930)

By any standard Anna De Costa Banks was an exceptional nurse. Banks was born (September 2, 1869), raised, and educated in Charleston, S.C. She attended Hampton Institute in Virginia, graduating in the first class at Dixie Hospital School of Nursing at Hampton in 1891. Returning to Charleston, she became head nurse of the Hospital and School for Nurses when it opened in 1896. Committed to meeting the health care needs of the Black community, these institutions were also created in response to the denial of staff privileges to Black physicians and the exclusion of Black women from admission to the City Hospital Training School.

From 1903 to 1930, Banks worked for the Ladies Benevolent Society (LBS) as a visiting nurse, caring for the sick poor in their homes. The white ladies of Charleston had hired Banks with some reluctance because she was Black, but they quickly came to appreciate her skill, tender-heartedness, and tact. Banks knew the feelings in Charleston between poor whites and Blacks, and she entered the new field of visiting nursing with some reservation.

She worked among people of both races, but initially her patients were what she described as the poor and ignorant class of white people. Even though the LBS had for at least seventy-five years cared for Black patients, they had done so in a very carefully controlled fashion. Caring for an average of 250 pa-tients annually, Banks cautiously constructed opportunities that allowed her to further extend LBS services to the Black community. Predictably, her efforts proceeded quietly, but by 1910, the growing number of Black patients and physicians served by the Society documented her success.

Despite the demands of her work with the LBS, Banks remained actively involved with the Hospital and School for Nurses. The hospital's patients remained the Black community's most destitute citizens and even though supported by Black churches, businessmen, and the local women's clubs, it was in constant financial crisis. Responding to the desperate need, Banks served as superintendent of the hospital for over twenty years without pay in order to help keep the doors from closing. Beyond caring for the sick, she was also intent on ensuring Black women's opportunities in the newly emerging profession of nursing. During her tenure she educated more than one hundred Black women as nurses.

Through her work with the Black hospital, training school, and the LBS, Banks quietly created an innovative matrix of care for the Black community and simultaneously accustomed the white community to using Black women who were trained as nurses. She pursued her goal by supplying students as the LBS needed them. While the students provided the LBS with flexible and affordable solutions to the demands created by a fluctuating caseload, the money generated through the program provided the hospital with a dependable source of income essential for its survival.

When she died on November 29, 1930, she was honored for her untiring service to her people. Anna De Costa Banks hoped that it would be said of her that "she has done what she could" and it was (Ladies Benevolent Society 1906-11). Her alma mater claimed that no other Hampton graduate had a more vital influence upon his or her community than Anna Banks.

BIBLIOGRAPHY

Banks, Anna De Costa. "The Work of a Small Hospital and Training School in the South." In *Black Women in the Nursing Profession: A Documentary History*, ed. Darlene Clark Hine (1985); Hine, Darlene Clark. *Black Women in White: Racial Conflict and Cooperation in the Nursing Profession, 1890-1950* (1989); The Anna De Costa Banks papers are in the Hampton University Archives, Hampton, Virginia, and at the Waring Historical Library, Medical University of South Carolina, Charleston. The papers of the Ladies Benevolent Society of Charleston are at the South Carolina Historical Society, Charleston.

KAREN BUHLER-WILKERSON

BAPTIST CHURCH

> Black women (and women whose grandmothers were black) are ... the main pillars of those social settlements which we call churches; and they have with small doubt raised three-fourths of our church property. (W.E.B. Du Bois 1918)

Although he does not refer to a specific denomination, this statement by W.E.B. Du Bois aptly describes women in the Black Baptist church, for today, as well as in 1918, women represent a preponderance of its membership, its financial strength, and its missionary force. Indeed, these three characteristics form the basis for understanding how Black Baptist women, in the face of racial and gender discrimination, contributed to the advancement of the Black church and the Black community during the nineteenth and early twentieth centuries.

Baptist women constitute the largest group of Black Christians in America. It is the very presence of women that explains the magnitude of the Black Baptist church. Census data for the early twentieth century reveal that the Black Baptist church formed a microcosm of the Black population in America and included men and women from all social classes and geographic regions. In 1906, Black Baptists made up 61.4 percent of all Black churchgoers. With a membership of 2,261,607, the Black Baptist church had more than four times the members of the second largest denominational body, the African Methodist Episcopal (AME) Church, with its 494,777 members. By 1916, Black Baptists constituted not only the largest Black religious group but the third largest of all religious groups, Black or white, in America; trailing only the Roman Catholic and the Methodist Episcopal churches, Black Baptists numbered 2,938,579 that year. In 1936, Black Baptists continued to constitute the third largest denomination regardless of race. Equally important, census data consistently have shown that Black women make up more than 60 percent of Black Baptist membership. From a numerical standpoint, then, the high proportion of female members underscores their vital presence in empowering the Baptist church.

Women's contributions to the church did not begin in the twentieth century but, rather, took root in the efforts of Black Baptists to establish congregations independent of white control during the late eighteenth and early nineteenth centuries. Although little is recorded about the Black women who participated in this early freedom movement, women certainly were members and financial supporters of those churches founded from the 1750s to 1810 in such places as Mecklenberg, Virginia; Savannah, Georgia; Boston, Massachusetts; and New York City. Mechal Sobel's 1988 study of African-Baptist Christianity during the era of slavery notes instances of women being deaconesses, members of separate women's committees, delegates to associational meetings of both men and women, and active participants in revivals. Yet the autonomous polity of each Baptist church precluded a consistent participation by women. Ample evidence exists to indicate that there were gender proscriptions: women were categorically denied the right to preach; they were excluded from the business meetings of most Black Baptist churches; and, in many instances, women could not sit beside male members during worship, organize into separate women's societies, or even pray publicly.

The Black Baptist church grew tremendously in the years following the Civil War. With the abolition of slavery, Black Baptist women and men expressed their newly won freedom by abandoning the white-controlled churches in which they had been forced to worship. Coming together in Black-controlled churches, Black Baptist women found a spiritual haven for individual communion with God and a public space for schooling, recreation, and organizational meetings. Indeed, women, much more than men, attended church not only for Sunday worship but for a variety of activities that took place throughout the week. For many poor Black women who worked in domestic service, sharecropping, and other forms of menial employment, the church offered the only form of social and organizational life outside the family. In choirs, deaconess boards, and missionary societies, women with little income found personal dignity, developed leadership and organizational skills, and forged programs for their people's advancement. At the level of the individual church as well as at the level of the regional association of churches, commonly called conventions, the Black Baptist church conflated its private, eschatological witness and its public, political stand, thus becoming a catalyst for the transmission of both spiritual and secular ideas to a broad spectrum of Black people.

By means of statewide and other regional conventions, Black Baptist churches allied their efforts, embarking upon programs of racial self-help and self-determination. The ministerial-led movement to unite Black Baptists into conventions was unique, for, unlike the structured network and hierarchy of other denominations, it emerged only because otherwise independent Black Baptist churches voluntarily and freely worked together as race-conscious collectives.

Beginning at the local and state levels, the convention movement grew in momentum between the 1860s and 1890s and culminated with the formation of the National Baptist Convention (NBC) in 1895. However, the restricted participation of women in the ministerial-led conventions led Baptist women to form their own, separate local and state organizations in the 1880s and 1890s and, in 1900, a national auxiliary of the NBC, which by 1903 boasted one million members.

State and national women's conventions offered greater opportunity for effective religious proselytism at home and abroad as well as an arena in which women freely discussed and implemented strategies for racial and gender empowerment. The minutes of Black Baptist women's state conventions attest to the extensive and sacrificial efforts of overwhelmingly low-income women to meet the spiritual, social, and economic needs of Black people, efforts that would have been impossible without their capacity to raise funds. These efforts included visiting homes and reading the Bible, donating clothes and food to the needy, counseling prisoners, caring for the sick, training women in household and parental responsibilities, establishing and supporting orphanages and old folks homes, crusading for temperance, establishing day nurseries and kindergartens, publishing newspapers, instituting vocational training programs, and establishing and/or financing educational institutions.

At a time when southern states had no public facilities at the high school or college level for Black students, late nineteenth- and early twentieth-century women's state conventions worked fervently for the higher education of Black men and women. For this reason, Black Baptist women's conventions often carried the title "educational" as part and parcel of their missionary identity, for example, the Baptist Women's Educational Convention of Kentucky, the Women's Baptist Educational and Missionary Convention of South Carolina, and the Woman's Baptist Missionary and Educational Association of Virginia. Unquestionably, the Black church was the most important institution in the Black community, and it was largely through the organized fund-raising of church women that this claim came to be actualized. In the racist climate of segregation, disfranchisement, and lynching, women's missionary and financial efforts were decisive factors in the Black Baptist church's ability to rally the impoverished masses for the staggering task of building and sustaining self-help institutions.

Women's conventions, notwithstanding their auxiliary relationship to the ministerial-dominated conventions, generated their own distinct dynamism

Mary Cook of Kentucky was prominent in the movement that led to the founding of the National Baptist Convention. In newspaper articles and speeches, she urged women to use their influence in every sphere to achieve suffrage as well as full equality in employment, education, social reform, and church work. [Moorland-Spingarn]

and assertiveness. Women's conventions controlled their own budgets and determined the allocation of funds, and they explicitly denied male participation in any role other than as honorary members. Black women found enormous satisfaction in accomplishing the goals of their conventions and in developing their own individual skills and abilities. In 1888, the president of the Kentucky Baptist group told a predominantly male Baptist audience that the women had learned to delegate authority, to raise points of order, and to transact business as well as men. In 1904, the president of Arkansas Baptist women credited her state association with building the self-confidence of ordinary women regarding their skills and abilities. She explicitly mentioned women's financial contributions and informed Black Baptist ministers: "From a financial standpoint we are prepared to prove that we have given thousands that you would not have, had it not been for the untiring and loyal women in the State." Emboldened by the successes of their separate conventions, Black women also were cognizant of their crucial role in building the denomination as a whole.

The founding and growth of Black Baptist women's societies during the 1880s and 1890s did not occur without gender conflict, however. Ironically, the Black Baptist convention movement that united men and women in the struggle against racial inequality betrayed a masculine bias in its institutional structures and discourses. Tensions arose when male ministers expected women to be silent helpmates. Yet the rising prominence of Black churchwomen and their growing demand for a separate organizational voice during the last two decades of the nineteenth century reflected a heightened gender consciousness

In 1900, at the annual meeting of the National Baptist Convention, Nannie Helen Burroughs delivered a speech entitled "How the Sisters Are Hindered from Helping." It led to the establishment of the Women's Convention. [Moorland-Spingarn]

on the part of women who were no longer content to operate merely within the boundaries of individual churches or silently within ministerial-led state conventions.

Throughout the 1880s and 1890s, Black Baptist women challenged gender proscriptions that thwarted the full utilization of their talents. The debate over women's rights in Arkansas typified that in other states. Ministers argued that separate organizations under the control of women would elicit a desire to rule the men. Some Arkansas ministers contended that women's financial contributions would cease to be under the men's control, whereas others demanded that male officers preside over women's societies—if they were permitted to form. The women of Arkansas responded by stressing their critical importance as a missionary force, insisting that they could better accomplish the work of religiously training the world by uniting as a separate organization. The women claimed their right to be an independent voice in the church on the assumption that they were equally responsible, in proportion to their abilities, as men.

Outstanding leaders such as Virginia W. Broughton of Tennessee and Mary V. Cook of Kentucky turned to the Bible to defend women's rights in the church and the larger society. Broughton, a schoolteacher and zealous missionary, published *Women's Work, as Gleaned from the Women of the Bible* (1904) in order to disclose biblical precedents for gender equality. Her feminist interpretation of the Bible shaped her understanding of women's roles in her own day, and the book summed up the ideas that had marked her public lectures, correspondence, and house-to-house visitations since the 1880s. Broughton led the women of her state in forming Bible bands for the study and interpretation of the Scriptures, and her gender consciousness united Black Baptist women in other states as well, emboldening them to develop their own societies. Traveling throughout the urban and rural areas of Tennessee, Broughton was instrumental in organizing a statewide association of Black Baptist women. She advocated training schools for mothers in order to better the home life of Black people, and she ardently promoted higher education for women.

Mary Cook of Kentucky also appropriated biblical images to prove that God used women in every capacity. During the late 1880s, Cook, a professor at the Black Baptist-owned State University at Louisville (later renamed Simmons University), was the most prominent woman in the ministerial-led convention movement that ultimately led to the founding of the NBC. She urged women to spread their influence in every cause, place, and institution. In newspaper articles and speeches she emphasized woman's suffrage as well as full equality for women in employment, education, social reform, and church work. In a speech given in 1887, Cook praised female teachers, journalists, linguists, and physicians, and she insisted that women must "come from all the professions, from the humble Christian to the expounder of His word; from the obedient citizen to the ruler of the land" (Higginbotham, forthcoming 1993). Both Cook and Broughton noted male resistance to the formation of women's societies; for example, they claimed that ministers and laymen had locked the doors of their churches, refusing to accommodate women's societies. In her autobiography, *Twenty Years as a Missionary* (1907), Broughton even recalled potentially fatal confrontations and physical threats made against women.

Although the Black Baptist convention movement had served the critical role of uniting women and men in the struggle for racial self-determination, it had simultaneously created a separate, gender-based community that reflected and supported women's equality.

In 1900, at the annual meeting of the NBC held in Richmond, Virginia, Nannie Burroughs delivered a speech entitled "How the Sisters Are Hindered from Helping," based on the biblical text, "Ye entered not in yourselves, and them that were entering in ye hindered" (Luke 11:52). Burroughs expressed the discontent and burning zeal of Black Baptist women to work unrestricted as a missionary force for the betterment of society. Burroughs's eloquence triumphed. In response to the motion of the influential NBC officer Lewis G. Jordan, and a second from Charles H. Parrish, the male-led convention approved the establishment of the Women's Convention (WC), Auxiliary to the NBC. It is interesting to note that Burroughs worked as Jordan's secretary at the time, and Parrish was married to the aforementioned Mary V. Cook of Kentucky.

By the close of the Richmond meeting, the women had elected the following officers: S. Willie Layten of Philadelphia, president; Sylvia C. J. Bryant of Atlanta, vice president at large; Nannie H. Burroughs of Washington, D.C., corresponding secretary; Virginia Broughton of Nashville, recording secretary; and Susie C. Foster of Montgomery, Alabama, treasurer. The minutes for 1900 listed twenty-six state vice presidents, including one each from Indian Territory, Oklahoma Territory, and Washington, D.C. The women described their mission as coming to the rescue of the world, and they adopted the motto "The

World for Christ. Women Arise. He Calleth for Thee." The formation of the WC signaled not only a national identity for Black Baptist women but also a Black women's congress, so to speak, where women as delegates from local churches, district associations, and state conventions assembled annually as a national body to discuss and debate issues of common concern, disseminate information to broader female constituencies, and implement nationally supported programs.

In her first open letter to the Black Baptist women of America, S. Willie Layten urged all existing societies to affiliate with the WC, to work closely with the state vice presidents, and to welcome the formation of new societies where none existed at the state and local level. Layten had a long familiarity with the organized work of Black Baptists. Her youth was spent in Memphis, where she acquired her early education and probably her first knowledge of women's missionary activities. After living in California during the late 1880s and early 1890s, Layten moved to Philadelphia in 1894 and became active in religious work and secular social reform. During the first decade of the twentieth century, Layten was a member of the National Association of Colored Women (NACW) and was a leader in the National Urban League and the Association for the Protection of Colored Women.

By the second decade of the twentieth century, WC programs reflected the influence of both Progressive-era reform and Black urbanization. The changing circumstances of employment, housing, and social problems related to the massive migration of Black people from the rural South to the urban North prompted the WC to adopt new methods of mission work. The Baptist women's national organization played an important mediating role in connecting local church and state activities throughout the nation with more sophisticated and changing reform trends. Their organizational networks at the state and national level facilitated a wide dissemination of ideas and expertise for utilization at the local level. Officers of the WC alluded to the educational role of their annual meetings when they referred to them as "institutes" and "schools of methods" for local communities. Through the convention, a national network of communication and cooperation identified women with a particular expertise, collected data, and introduced new methods. The annual meetings of the WC featured papers delivered by physicians, social workers, and civic-improvement activists. Convinced that society and not merely the individual soul was at stake, women in the Black Baptist church involved themselves in the practical work of social salvation—establishing settlement houses, holding forums to discuss industrial problems and public health, creating social service commissions, and working to improve the conditions in city slums. Support for foreign missions constituted another important aspect of the work of the convention. In 1901, the WC contributed money to support Spelman graduate Emma Delaney, who worked as a missionary to Chiradzulu in British Central Africa (now Malawi). In 1902, the women supplied funds to build a brick mission house for her. Through their support of Delaney, the women learned of the harsh consequences of European colonialism on African people. In a visit to America in 1905, Delaney spoke of the need for Black Americans to redeem Africa from colonial rule. In her speech before the WC's annual meeting, she poignantly described the suffering of African people "who were compelled to secure rubber for the Belgium Government at any cost, even the loss of their limbs, if the required quantity of rubber was not brought" (WC Proceedings 1905). During the early decades of the twentieth century, the WC shipped boxes of food and clothing to missionaries in foreign fields, underwrote the educational expenses of African students in the United States, contributed to mission stations in various parts of Africa, and built a hospital in Liberia.

The role of Black Baptist women as a force for missions also entailed the effort to rid American society of the sins of racial and gender discrimination. In this regard, the WC went on record against segregation, lynching, injustice in the courts, the inequitable division of school funds, and barriers to voting rights and equal employment. It supported the civil rights agenda of the National Association for the Advancement of Colored People (NAACP) and invited representatives from that organization to appear at the Baptist women's annual meetings. In 1914, the WC joined forces with the NAACP in a national campaign to end negative stereotyping of Black people in literature, film, textbooks, newspapers, and on the stage. According to their minutes, they also advocated boycotts and written protests to publishers and others who used racial slurs.

Thus the WC afforded Black women an arena in which to transcend narrow social and intellectual confines and become exposed to new places, personalities, and ideas that negated both racist and sexist stereotypes and limitations. At the very time when Booker T. Washington refused to use his influential voice publicly to criticize Black disfranchisement in the South, the leadership of the WC loudly called for suffrage for Black women and men. In 1909, these

Baptist women specified that their political input in state legislatures and the federal government would help improve the living and working conditions of Black people in general and Black women in particular.

Understanding the historic role of Black Baptist women ultimately must evoke recognition of the multivalent character of the Black church itself. The church was not the exclusive voice of a male ministry but the inclusive voice of men and women in dialogue. As the majority of church members, the mainstay of financial support, and the missionary impetus for social change, Black Baptist women were never silent. In the struggle to come into their own voice, they empowered their church, their community, and, not least of all, themselves.

[See also BURROUGHS, NANNIE HELEN.]

BIBLIOGRAPHY

Cook, Mary V. "Work for Baptist Women." In *The Negro Baptist Pulpit*, ed. Edward M. Brawley (1890); Du Bois, W.E.B. *Darkwater* (1918); Harrison, Earl L. *The Dream and the Dreamer* (1956); Higginbotham, Evelyn Brooks. *Righteous Discontent: The Women's Movement in the Black Baptist Church, 1880-1920* (forthcoming 1993); Ross, Mary D. *A Brief Story of the Life and Leadership of Dr. S. Willie Layten* (1987); Sobel, Mechal. *Travelin' On: The Slave Journey to an Afro-Baptist Faith* (1988).

MANUSCRIPT COLLECTIONS

Minutes of Baptist state conventions held between 1880 and 1904, American Baptist Historical Society, Rochester, New York; Nannie Helen Burroughs papers, Library of Congress, Washington, D.C.; Proceedings of the National Baptist Convention and the Woman's Convention, 1900 to 1925, American Baptist Historical Society, Rochester, New York.

EVELYN BROOKS HIGGINBOTHAM

BARNETT, MARGUERITE ROSS (1942-1992)

As a political scientist, Marguerite Ross Barnett had wide-ranging interests, and her writings covered issues from cultural nationalism in India to contemporary Black politics in the United States. As a university administrator, Barnett became noted for the successful development of high-school-to-college transition programs in New York, Missouri, and Houston. As both a scholar and an administrator, she made significant contributions to American education.

Programs for disadvantaged students were the hallmark of Marguerite Ross Barnett's administration when she became the University of Houston's first woman president. [Office of Media Relations, University of Houston]

Born in Charlottesville, Virginia, on May 21, 1942, Marguerite Ross Barnett grew up in Buffalo, New York. She was an only child and was early encouraged in her academic interests. She went to Antioch College and then to the University of Chicago, where she received her M.S. and Ph.D. in political science. Her studies led her to do research in several other countries, including Turkey, England, and India.

Barnett taught at Princeton, Howard, and Columbia, but her real calling was administration. Her first important position in that area was vice-chancellor for academic affairs at the City University of New York (CUNY), a post she held from 1983 to 1986. During her time there she worked to establish a program for high school students from poor families. The purpose of the program was to smooth their transition to college and from college to worthwhile work.

After CUNY, Barnett moved to the University of Missouri-St. Louis. During her tenure there she established a number of new degree programs, doubled the amount of federal research and service grant dollars received, tripled the scholarship support, raised more than $9 million in new donations, and has been credited with the 18 percent increase in enrollment. She repeated her successful program for disadvantaged students at that school and, later, at the University of Houston. The Bridge Program, as it was called, was named the outstanding public school initiative in the country in 1991, receiving the Anderson Medal from the American Council on Education.

Her appointment as president at the University of Houston was groundbreaking in more than one way. She was the first woman to be president of that university and one of the few to lead any school that was not historically a women's college. A parallel situation existed with regard to her race.

Barnett was at Houston for only two years before her death in 1992 of complications from cancer. During that time she earned a reputation for creative cooperation with the business community. She was both a successful fund-raiser and a proponent of the idea that universities should spur economic growth and solve social problems in their communities. In July of 1991 she was the only representative of a university who was named to the President's Commission on Environmental Quality. That commission was formed to explore ways to check environmental destruction without impairing economic development.

Barnett was also the author or editor of five books and forty articles. Her most acclaimed work was *The Politics of Cultural Nationalism in South India* (1976).

SELECTED WORKS BY MARGUERITE ROSS BARNETT

"Educating Youth for the Twenty-first Century," presented at the Missouri Youth 2000 Conference. *Vital Speeches of the Day* (March 15, 1989); *Educational Policy in an Era of Conservative Reform*, coedited with Charles C. Harrington and Phillip V. White (1986); "The New Federalism and the Unfinished Civil Rights Agenda," *Black Law Journal* (1983); "The Congressional Black Caucus: Symbol, Myth, Reality," *Black Scholar* (January 1977); *Public Policy for the Black Community: Strategies and Perspectives*, coedited with James Hefner (1976).

IFE WILLIAMS-ANDOH

BARRETT, EMMA *see*
BARRETT, "SWEET EMMA"

BARRETT, JANIE PORTER
(1865-1948)

Brought up and educated in a white family and looking Caucasian, Janie Porter was urged by her benefactor to go to the North for college and prepare to pass into white society. Had she done so we might now see her name along with Lillian Wald, Jane Addams, and Mary McDowell as founders of the American settlement movement. As it was, she went instead to Hampton Institute, the school for freedpeople, and founded the first social settlement in Virginia, and one of the first in the country for Black people.

Janie Porter was born in Athens, Georgia. Nothing seems to be known about her father; possibly he was white. A white woman in Macon, Georgia, for whom Julia Porter, Janie's mother, worked as housekeeper virtually adopted the child. It was she who urged the fifteen-year-old Janie to go to the North to school. Julia Porter, by contrast, wanted her to maintain her African-American identity, and pushed her to attend Hampton. Although the transition from her sheltered life in Macon was occasionally rough, she graduated from the institute in 1884 and began teaching, first in Georgia and then back at Hampton, where in 1889 she married Harris Barrett, a member of the staff. Walter Besant's novel *All Sorts and Conditions of Men* is said to have been the inspiration for her decision to devote her life to helping the weakest and most vulnerable members of her race.

She began holding weekly meetings for young girls in her home, and the response was so great that in time her husband built another structure to accommodate people of all ages who came for help, training, inspiration, comfort, and advice. This informal institution came to be called the Locust Street Social Settlement. Barrett raised money from northern philanthropists and recruited Hampton students to teach the practical skills they were learning to the people who came to the settlement.

In 1907, Janie Barrett was one of the founders of the Virginia Federation of Colored Women's Clubs, of which she became the first president in 1908. Clubwomen throughout the United States were by that time a major force in what was called the progressive movement. The needs of their community were so glaring that Black clubwomen were tackling serious social problems. Thus it was that the federated Black clubwomen of Virginia, under Barrett's leadership, raised enough money to create a rehabilitation center for Black girls in trouble. In 1915, the Virginia Industrial School for Colored Girls was built on a farm eighteen miles north of Richmond, and the Virginia legislature agreed to provide some support.

After Harris Barrett died, Janie Porter Barrett, whose four children were reaching an age of independence, took over as resident head of the school. She proceeded to make it one of the model schools of its kind in the country, based on the accepted principles of contemporary progressive reform. Barrett's own personality contributed to the atmosphere of trust and hope that visitors noted and other states tried to emulate.

In addition to her remarkable accomplishments at the school, Barrett worked with many groups to develop interracial cooperation in Virginia. Her own school had a biracial board, and she seldom failed to praise the white women who had had the courage to join in the undertaking. She understood how women's voluntary associations could multiply individual effectiveness and made the most of the parallel networks: the white clubwomen and the Black. In 1940, at the age of seventy-five, she retired and returned to live in Hampton for the eight remaining years of her life, honored in Virginia and among social reformers in the North for her work and her example. After her death the school was renamed the Janie Porter Barrett School for Girls.

BIBLIOGRAPHY

Barrett, Janie Porter. "Social Work among Our People," *Proceedings of the Virginia Conference of Charities and Correction* (1911); *DANB*; Daniel, Sadie I. *Women Builders* (1931); Evans, Mrs. Sandidge. "The Locust Street Settlement." In *Lost Landmarks of Old Hampton, Revolutionary War Port Town,* ed. Sandidge Evans (1976); Hall, Winona R. "Janie Porter Barrett, Her Life and Contributions to Social Welfare in Virginia," M.A. thesis, Howard University (1954); *NAW*; Ovington, Mary White. *Portraits in Color* (1927); Whitman, Alden. *American Reformers* (1985).

ANNE FIROR SCOTT

Rejecting suggestions that she pass for white, Janie Porter Barrett became one of the foremost Black organizers in the social settlement movement of the late nineteenth and early twentieth centuries. [Hampton University Archives]

BARRETT, "SWEET EMMA" (1898-1983)

Emma Barrett, also known as "Sweet Emma the Bell Gal," was born March 25, 1898, in New Orleans, Louisiana. Her father, William B. Barrett, was a captain in the Union army during the Civil War. She had one son, Richard Alexis. Barrett's entire career as a pianist and singer was associated with the New Orleans jazz style. Because she disdained giving interviews, many details of her life are unconfirmed. Although the origin of the name "Sweet Emma" is in dispute, she reportedly created it herself, believing that it described her personality. In the 1950s, a Bourbon Street tavern owner gave her a pair of garters with bells. These bells, along with a red beanie inscribed with "The Bell Gal," became a trademark. She was very discreet in discussing her personal affairs and reacted strongly to intrusive individuals. Her distrust in banks was partially the reason she lost her life savings when her house was robbed in 1961. When friends staged a benefit concert and presented her with $1,000, she was robbed again.

In the early 1900s, Barrett played with George McCullum, Sr.'s dance bands and the Original Tuxedo Orchestra, then joined Oscar "Papa" Celestin's band in 1923. Though Barrett was among the many New Orleans musicians who did not read music, she worked with the city's top reading bands, including Bebe Ridgeley's Original Tuxedo Orchestra, Sidney Desvigne's Orchestra, and the Piron-Gaspard Orchestra.

In the decades following, she toured with trumpeter and bandleader Percy Humphrey. Though she refused to travel by airplane, she played distant venues, including Disneyland, the Stork Club in New York, and the Guthrie Theatre in Minneapolis. By 1960, her popularity enabled her to start her own group—one that included some of the musicians whom she had worked with for decades.

In 1961, Barrett substituted for Lester Santiago, in Louis Cottrell's band at the famed Preservation Hall in New Orleans. This concert began an association with Preservation Hall that continued for the remainder of her life. At Preservation Hall she sang songs such as "Just a Closer Walk with Thee," "Won't You Come Home Bill Bailey," and "I Ain't Gonna Give Nobody None of This Jelly Roll." Her energetic approach to playing the piano occasionally damaged the sounding board of the instrument.

During the 1960s Barrett formed an all-star band that included Percy Humphrey, Willie Humphrey, Jim Robinson, Narvin Kimball, and Josiah "Cie"

Frazier. This band recorded two albums, *New Orleans' Sweet Emma and Her Preservation Hall Jazz Band* and *Sweet Emma the Bell Gal and Her New Orleans Jazz Band at Heritage Hall*. She recorded several albums with the Preservation Hall Jazz Band that featured her singing and playing the piano. In the 1960s, Barrett appeared on *The Ed Sullivan Show* and in the motion picture *The Cincinnati Kid*.

A stroke in 1967 paralyzed her left side, but she continued to perform, beating time with her left hand, while providing full right-hand parts. She made frequent television appearances and played at many elite Mardi Gras functions, arriving at performances in her wheelchair. Her last Preservation Hall performance was January 18, 1983, ten days before her death. She died in New Orleans on January 28, 1983.

BIBLIOGRAPHY

Claghorn, Charles E. *Biographical Dictionary of Jazz* (1982); Handy, Antoinette. *Black Women in American Bands and Orchestras* (1981); Pope, John. " 'Sweet Emma' Barrett, Jazz Musician, Is Dead," *New Orleans Times-Picayune* (January 29, 1983); Rose, Al and Edmond Souchon. *New Orleans Jazz: A Family Album* (1978); Slonimsky, Nicolas. *Baker's Biographical Dictionary of Musicians* (1984).

ARTHUR C. DAWKINS

In 1952, Charlotta Bass became the first Black woman to run for vice president of the United States. As the Progressive party candidate, she reserved her most strident attacks for Republican Richard Nixon. Her motto during the campaign also served her well during her longtime editorship of the California Eagle—"*Win or lose, we win by raising the issues.*" *She is shown here in 1943 christening the Liberty Ship* James W. Johnson. *[UPI/Bettmann]*

BASS, CHARLOTTA SPEARS
(1880-1969)

"We offer these candidates as peace candidates," said the candidates committee of the Progressive party in 1952. "We offer them as new hope to an America sick and tired of the corruption, the militarism, the segregations of and discrimination against the Negro people, and the growing unemployment that has been brought about by both Democrats and Republicans." One of the candidates offered was Charlotta Spears Bass, the first Black woman to run for vice president of the United States.

Charlotta Spears was born in October 1880 in South Carolina. She was the sixth of the eleven children of Hiram and Kate Spears. The details of her childhood and education are not known, but in 1900, at age twenty, she left South Carolina to live and work in Providence, Rhode Island. She moved in with her oldest brother and took a job working for the *Providence Watchman*. She remained there for ten years. At the end of that time, she was suffering from exhaustion.

At the suggestion of her doctor, she moved to California to rest. It was to have been a two-year stay, but shortly after arriving, she ignored her doctor's advice and took a part-time job at a newspaper, the *Eagle*. Before her two years in California were over, she had taken over the paper, renaming it the *California Eagle*. A new editor arrived, Joseph Bass, one of the founders of the *Topeka Plaindealer*, and soon the two were married. As managing editor and editor, respectively, Charlotta Spears Bass and her husband set their paper firmly on a course of social and political activism. They vehemently attacked the racial stereotypes and the glorification of the Ku Klux Klan in D. W. Griffith's *The Birth of a Nation*. They defended the Black soldiers of the twenty-fourth infantry who were unjustly sentenced in the Houston riot of 1917. They supported the defendants in the Scottsboro trials.

In 1930, Charlotta Bass helped found the Industrial Business Council, which encouraged Black people to go into business and fought discrimination in hiring and employment practices. She also formed a group to attack housing covenants that denied the right of Black Americans to live wherever they chose.

Joseph Bass died in 1934, and Charlotta Bass continued to run the *California Eagle*. In the years that followed, she became more and more active politically. In 1940, she was western regional director of the political campaign of Wendell Willkie. Three years later, she became the first Black grand jury member for the Los Angeles County Court. In 1945, she ran in the seventh district as a people's candidate for city council. Her platform was progressive, and her campaign united Black organizations in the district. She received wholehearted support from the community, and though her bid was unsuccessful, it was a landmark campaign.

In the postwar United States, there was a plague of oppressive activity in the South, including an increase in Klan activities and, horrifyingly, an outbreak of lynchings. Bass was in the forefront of the battle against these and other outrages. She supported the Hollywood Ten and, during the years of McCarthyism, was accused of un-American activities.

Bass was one of the founders of the Progressive party. She believed that neither of the two traditional parties was committed to working for Black people, so she supported Henry Wallace's candidacy for president in 1948. Although she was now approaching seventy, she began to travel extensively in the service of her growing political concerns. In Prague, she supported the Stockholm Appeal to ban the bomb at the peace committee of the World Congress. She traveled in the Soviet Union and praised its lack of racial discrimination.

In 1950, Bass ran on the Progressive party ticket for the congressional seat from the fourteenth legislative district in California. Again she was unsuccessful, but again she brought attention to important political issues. Her most important campaign came in 1952, when the Progressive party nominated her for vice president of the United States. She campaigned fiercely, reserving her hardest attacks for Republican vice presidential candidate Richard Nixon. Her refrain during the campaign was, "Win or lose, we win by raising the issues." In addition to civil rights and peace, Bass stressed the issue of women's rights, encouraging women to run for political office.

In 1960, Bass published her autobiography, *Forty Years: Memoirs from the Pages of a Newspaper*. She died in Los Angeles in 1969. The causes for which she had fought so hard were now at the forefront in the United States; the issues she had raised were being addressed. She had won.

BIBLIOGRAPHY

EBA; Gill, Gerald R. " 'Win or Lose—We Win': The 1952 Vice Presidential Campaign of Charlotta A. Bass." In *The Afro-American Woman: Struggles and Images*, ed. Sharon Harley and Rosalyn Terborg-Penn (1978); *NA*; *NAW*.

KATHLEEN THOMPSON

BATES, DAISY LEE GATSON (1920-)

Daisy Lee Gatson, journalist, civil rights activist, and major force in the integration of the Little Rock, Arkansas, public schools, was born in 1920 in Huttig, a small town located in the lumbering region of southeast Arkansas. She was raised by her adoptive parents, Orlee and Susie Smith; she never knew her real parents. In the autobiographical sections of *The Long Shadow of Little Rock* (1962), she revealed that as a child she was told that her mother had been ravished and murdered, allegedly by three white men; and her father was forced to flee Huttig for fear of reprisals from whites should he attempt to prosecute the suspects. The Smiths were childless friends of her real parents and agreed to adopt her.

Gatson's relationship with the Smiths was warm and supportive, and she was raised as a somewhat spoiled and willful only child. She was indulged by her loving mother and hard-working, though extremely sensitive father, with whom she enjoyed a close relationship. Daisy Lee Gatson attended the segregated public schools in Huttig, where the Black students were forced to use the worn-out textbooks handed down from the white schools. For Gatson the poor physical condition of the school buildings and facilities for Black children symbolized the inadequacy and injustice of Arkansas's Jim Crow educational system.

When Daisy Gatson was fifteen years old and still in high school, she was introduced to Lucius Christopher Bates, an insurance agent and close friend of her father. L. C. Bates was born in Mississippi, attended segregated county schools, and went on to Wilberforce College, the African Methodist Episcopal (AME) Church-supported school in Ohio, and majored in journalism. Upon graduation, he worked on the *Kansas City Call* in Missouri, but soon lost this position due to the hard times created by the Depression. Mr. Bates turned to selling insurance and was quite successful, but he wanted to return to journalism.

Orlee Smith passed away in 1941. Shortly afterward, L. C. Bates proposed to Daisy Lee Gatson, and she accepted. They were married that year and eventually settled in Little Rock. L. C. soon convinced his wife to join him in a newspaper venture, and the Bateses used their savings to lease a newspaper plant from a church group and to begin a weekly newspaper, the Arkansas *State Press*. Within the first few months the paper reached a circulation of 10,000, and Daisy Bates enrolled in business administration and public relations courses at Shorter College, an AME

school in Little Rock, to learn more about running a business. Initially, the paper was quite successful and attracted a large number of advertisers from the local business community.

With the outbreak of World War II, nearby Camp Robinson was reopened at the request of local businessmen and politicians and was used to train Black soldiers. Soon large numbers of African-American servicemen filled the streets of Little Rock on weekends. Incidents of police brutality involving African-Americans were regularly exposed by the *State Press*, and at times the investigative reporting by the courageous newspaper publishers angered white businessmen in Little Rock, who threatened to withdraw their advertisements. In March 1942, after the *State Press* reported the gruesome details of the killing of a Black soldier by a Little Rock policeman, many advertisements were withdrawn and the Bateses had to double their efforts, working twelve to sixteen hours a day, to keep their enterprise afloat. Gradually, circulation began to increase and within a year the newspaper reached 20,000 readers.

The *State Press* gained a reputation as the independent "voice of the people" and worked for the improvement of the social and economic circumstances of African-Americans throughout the state. In Little Rock, the *State Press* continued to expose police brutality, and eventually it was successful in forcing some changes. Black policemen were hired to patrol the Black neighborhoods, and the state of race relations improved noticeably. By the end of World War II, Daisy Bates believed that Little Rock had gained "a reputation as a liberal southern city" (Bates 1962).

The *State Press* continually had supported the programs and activities of the National Association for the Advancement of Colored People (NAACP) and, in 1952, Daisy Bates accepted the position of president of the Arkansas state conference of NAACP branches. With the U.S. Supreme Court's *Brown* v. *Board of Education* decision on May 17, 1954, the NAACP overturned the legal basis for public school segregation. In Little Rock, public school officials wanted to move slowly on school integration, and Daisy Bates led the Black community's campaign against this policy of gradualism. With assistance and advice from officials in the NAACP national headquarters, Daisy Bates began taking African-American children to be enrolled in all-white public schools. When the children were denied admission, each incident was recorded and later reported in the local newspapers. Under increasing pressure from Black parents and the NAACP, the superintendent of the

In 1957, it took the commitment and planning of the NAACP's Daisy Bates—and 1,000 paratroopers—to get nine Black children into Little Rock's Central High School. She is shown here in New York City in the 1960s supporting "sit-in" students in the South. [Benita Ramsey]

Little Rock Public School District, Virgil Blossom, announced a plan to begin the desegregation process with Central High School in September 1957.

White opponents in Little Rock were outraged and brought litigation to hold or delay the implementation of the plan, all to no avail. In the summer of 1957, Governor Orval Faubus announced his opposition to public school integration and on September 2, the first day of school, ordered units of the Arkansas National Guard to Central High School to prevent the possibility of disorder and violence. NAACP lawyers Wiley Branton and Thurgood Marshall obtained an injunction from the federal courts against the governor's action, but the troops were not removed.

The nine African-American teenagers who were chosen to participate in the integration of Central High School came to be known as the Little Rock Nine. Their activities were planned and coordinated by Daisy Bates, who stood with the children during the ordeal. Violence erupted around Central High School and throughout the city when Elizabeth Eckford, one of the nine students, mistakenly went to the school alone on the morning of September 22, 1957. Her grace under pressure while she was jeered and taunted by white mobs as she tried to enter the school came to symbolize the strength and determination of an entire generation of African-American students.

On the following day, when the police escorted Daisy Bates and the children into the school in secrecy, mob action escalated and they had to be removed because the chief of police could no longer guarantee their safety. The violence continued and the police chief requested the assistance of the U.S. Justice Department. The next day, President Dwight D. Eisenhower federalized all Arkansas National Guard units and sent in 1,000 paratroopers from the 101st Airborne Division to carry out the orders of the federal courts. The following day, September 25, 1957, the paratroopers, under the leadership of Major General Edwin A. Walker, escorted Daisy Bates and the nine students into Central High School. The paratroopers were withdrawn to nearby Camp Robinson on September 30, but Arkansas National Guard units were to remain on patrol at Central High throughout the school year.

On October 31, 1957, the Little Rock city council ordered the arrest of Daisy Bates and other members of the Arkansas NAACP for failure to supply the city clerk's office with information about the NAACP's membership, contributors, and expenditures. At the trial in December 1957, Daisy Bates was convicted and fined $100, plus court costs. The conviction was eventually overturned by the U.S. Supreme Court. Meanwhile, Daisy Bates kept in close contact with the Black students at Central High School and she always accompanied them and their parents to meetings with school officials when incidents occurred. Eventually, white school officials and students learned that anyone who bothered "Daisy Bates's children" would also have to deal with Daisy Bates personally. Her vigilance in the protection and support of her children earned for Daisy Bates the resentment and enmity of most Arkansas whites, and a secure place for herself in twentieth-century African-American history.

The *State Press* was forced to close in 1959, but Daisy Bates remained active on the lecture circuit, in voter registration campaigns, and in community revitalization programs. In 1985, however, the Bateses again began to publish the Arkansas *State Press* and it continues to serve the important social, economic, and political needs of African-Americans in Little Rock. Despite some recent illness, Daisy Bates remains active in a variety of community organizations and is sought by the press, politicians, and the people to provide her unique perspectives on the contemporary problems facing the African-American community.

[*See also* LITTLE ROCK NINE.]

BIBLIOGRAPHY

Bates, Daisy. *The Long Shadow of Little Rock* (1962); Blossom, Virgil T. *It Has Happened Here* (1959); Freyer, Tony. *The Little Rock Crisis: A Constitutional Interpretation* (1984); Huckaby, Elizabeth. *Crisis at Central High School: Little Rock, 1957-58* (1980); Jackoway, Elizabeth. "Taken by Surprise: Little Rock Business Leaders and Desegregation." In *Southern Businessmen and Desegregation*, ed. Elizabeth Jackoway and David Colburn (1982); *New York Times* (September 20-30, 1957); Record, Wilson and Jane C. Record, eds. *Little Rock* (1960); the Daisy Bates papers, which include an oral interview with Daisy Bates, are located at the State Historical Society of Wisconsin, Madison, Wisconsin.

V. P. FRANKLIN

BATSON, FLORA (1864-1906)

Born on April 16, 1864, in Washington, D.C., Flora Batson was one of the most famous Black concert singers of the late nineteenth century, known as "The Double-Voiced Queen of Song" because of her phenomenal baritone to soprano range. Her youth was spent in Providence, Rhode Island, where she made her first public appearances. Although she had already won some recognition in this country and Europe through singing with churches and in programs promoting the temperance movement, she reached the height of her fame with the Bergen Star Company after becoming its star singer in 1885. In 1885, she married Col. John Bergen, the white manager of the company, and their collaboration continued until 1896.

Another phase of Flora Batson's concert career began in 1896 with a new manager, Gerard Millar, a Black basso. The two performed concerts together and sang as a featured duo with the South before the War Company. Batson's last years were spent in Philadelphia, where she was still called upon to perform in concert and in dramatic presentations. Flora Batson was adored by American audiences, who gave her impressive gifts of jewelry that she regularly wore at concerts.

Concert appearances outside the United States included visits to Europe, Great Britain, the Samoan Islands, New Zealand, Australia, India, Fiji, China, and Japan, highlighted by performances for Pope Leo XIII and royalty, such as Queen Victoria of England and Queen Liliuokalani of Hawaii. Flora Batson died in Philadelphia on December 1, 1906.

Flora Batson was known as the "Double-Voiced Queen of Song" when she sang before enthusiastic audiences throughout the United States, Europe, and as far afield as the Samoan Islands. [Schomburg Center]

BIBLIOGRAPHY

BDAAM; Cuney-Hare, Maud. *Negro Musicians and Their Music* (1936); *DANB*.

DORIS EVANS McGINTY

BATTLE, KATHLEEN (1948-)

A soprano with a distinctly sweet and expressive voice, Kathleen Battle was born in Portsmouth, Ohio, and received her B.M. and M.M. degrees at the Cincinnati College-Conservatory. Thomas Schippers was responsible for her debut as the soprano soloist in the German Requiem of Brahms, at Spoleto in 1972. She made her first appearance at the Metropolitan Opera as the Shepherd in Wagner's *Tannhäuser* in 1977, following this as Blonde (*Die Entführung aus dem Serail*), Despina (*Così fan tutte*), Elvira (*L'italiana in Algeri*), Pamina (*Die Zauberflöte*), Rosina (*Il barbiere di Siviglia*), Sophie (*Der Rosenkavalier* and *Werther*), Zdenka (*Arabella*), and Zerlina (*Don Giovanni*). In such soubrette roles, she appeared often with the major opera houses of Europe, and is internationally a frequent soloist and recitalist, moving toward midcareer with an enviable reputation. As a recording artist, her repertoire also includes spirituals, wherein gospel ornamentations enhance the intensity of her interpretations.

BIBLIOGRAPHY

Dyer, Richard. "Battle, Kathleen." In *New Grove Dictionary of Music and Musicians*, ed. Stanley Sadie (1980); Turner, Patricia. *Afro-American Singers: An Index and Preliminary Discography of Opera, Choral Music, and Song* (1977).

DOMINIQUE-RENÉ de LERMA

BEARDEN, BESSYE (c. 1891-1943)

Bessye Bearden was a complete extrovert, an intensely social person whose New York home was the focal point for gatherings of personalities from the varied worlds of politics, journalism, show business, and the arts. Her outgoing personality helped contribute to her formidable achievements as a journalist and community activist.

Bessye Bearden was born in Goldsboro, North Carolina, the daughter of George T. and Carrie G. Banks. Educated in the public schools of Atlantic City, New Jersey, Bessye Banks attended Hartshorn Memorial College in Richmond, Virginia, and graduated from Virginia Normal and Industrial Institute in Petersburg. She also took special courses in journalism at Columbia University.

She married R. Howard Bearden in 1910, and they had one son, the painter Romare Bearden. After living in Charlotte, North Carolina, for several years, they moved to New York City in 1915. For many years Bearden was in charge of the New York office of the E. C. Brown Real Estate Company of Philadelphia. She became the New York news representative for the *Chicago Defender* in 1927 and stayed with the paper until her death in 1943. Bearden was an active member of the Utopia Neighborhood Club, the New York Urban League, and the National Association for the Advancement of Colored People (NAACP). She also served on the executive board of the Harlem Community Council (head of the Widow Pension Bureau) and the executive board of the Citizens Welfare Council of New York. She also was founder and president of the Colored Women's Democratic League and an honorary member of Phi Delta Kappa sorority.

In 1922, Bearden was elected to serve on her local school board, District no. 15 of the Board of Education of the City of New York. She served as secretary for two and a half years. Later, when this board was changed to District no. 12, she was elected chairman. Bearden was a member of Saint Martin's Protestant Episcopal Church and the Independent Order of Saint Luke.

Bearden also was a member of the advisory committee to the Special Assistant on Racial Problems of the Emergency Relief Bureau and was secretary of the Harlem Tuberculosis and Health Committee.

In March 1938, Mary McLeod Bethune invited Bearden "to discuss the part that Negro women and children are playing in the program of the government as it is being administered," and by June 1940 Bearden had been appointed treasurer of the National Council of Negro Women. In September 1940, Bearden was elected chair of the executive board of the Harlem Committee Art Center, and in October of that year she was hostess of the temple of religion at the New York World's Fair.

Bessye Bearden was a multitalented woman who successfully negotiated diverse responsibilities as a woman leader committed to a life of service. She died on September 25, 1943; the *New York Amsterdam News* reported that thousands of people attended her funeral.

BIBLIOGRAPHY

Schomburg Center for Research in Black Culture, The New York Public Library.

JEAN B. HUTSON

BEASLEY, DELILAH LEONTIUM (1872-1934)

Delilah Leontium Beasley stood supreme in challenging education which portrayed the idealism, misconceptions, and contradictions inherent in white America's attitudes toward Black Americans and their proper place in American history. Beasley was a thorough writer and journalist, an intense Black woman with an uncompromising commitment to refute misunderstandings and prove that Black people had made great contributions to the history of California. Her book, *The Negro Trail-Blazers of California*, published in 1919, was nominated for inclusion in the *Guide to the Best Books* because of its great value to students of sociology, and scholars at the University of Califor-

One of the most visible and influential Black female leaders in New York City during the 1920s and 1930s, Bessye Bearden was New York news representative of the Chicago Defender, *among other responsibilities. [Moorland-Spingarn]*

Newspaper columnist Delilah Leontium Beasley chronicled California's early Black settlers in her 1919 book The Negro Trail-Blazers of California. *[Schomburg Center]*

nia at Berkeley found the book to be comprehensive, with a measure of wisdom for all Americans. These labels were well earned.

Delilah Beasley was born on September 9, 1872, in Cincinnati, Ohio. The first child born to Margaret Beasley and her husband, Daniel, Delilah began her writing career at age twelve when she became a "correspondent" for the Cleveland *Gazette*. At age fifteen, she published her first column in the Sunday Cincinnati, Ohio, *Enquirer* under the headline "mosaics."

After moving to California in 1910, Beasley attended lectures on history at Berkeley, but she never registered as a student. Instead, she wrote short essays for presentation at churches.

The experience of researching California history and writing articles as a news contributor for the *Oakland Tribune* affected her whole career. The best known of her works came in 1919, at age forty-seven, with the completion of her one and only classic book, *The Negro Trail-Blazers of California*, which was based on more than eight years of careful research. Her journalistic career began at the *Oakland Tribune* with a weekly Sunday column entitled "Activities among Negroes." As a featured columnist for nearly two

decades, she had an impact far beyond the publication of her column. Through her efforts, the local white press stopped using the expressions "darkie" and "nigger" and began to capitalize the "N" in Negro. She became widely known as an outspoken activist in the struggle for equality for and between the races. She once said that the value of the book lay in its ability to promote understanding between the races. Beasley also used her column as a vehicle for social progress to educate and celebrate Negro History Week and Black art in Oakland.

Beasley died August 18, 1934, at Fairmont Hospital in San Leandro, California. Death was caused by arteriosclerotic heart disease. Her funeral was held at Saint Francis de Sales Catholic Church in Oakland.

Beasley sensed the value of education in developing moral understanding between different peoples. She also has the distinction of being the first person to have presented written proof of the existence of Black Californians.

BIBLIOGRAPHY

Beasley, Delilah L. *The Negro Trail-Blazers of California* (1919), and "Activities among Negroes," *Oakland Tribune* (Sunday editions, 1923-34); Crouchett, Lorraine J. *Delilah Leontium Beasley—Oakland's Crusading Journalist* (1990); Davis, Elizabeth. "Miss Delilah L. Beasley, Historian and Newspaper Writer." In *Lifting as They Climb* (1933); De Witt, Josephine. "Oakland Public Library and America's Tenth Man," *Pacific Bindery Talk* (June 1936); U.S. Census (June 1880).

LORRAINE J. CROUCHETT

BEASLEY, MATHILDA (c. 1833-1903)

Mathilda Beasley made an unsuccessful attempt to establish a convent of Black sisters in Savannah, Georgia. A free woman of color, she was born about 1833 in New Orleans of mixed creole and Native American parentage. Sometime in the 1850s, she married Abraham Beasley, a businessman, restaurant owner, and sometime slave dealer. During Reconstruction he acquired extensive property, including race horses. Although it was against the law, Mathilda taught slaves. After the death of her husband (c. 1878), she gave her property to the Catholic church, stipulating that an orphanage for Black children be established. At some point after 1880, under circumstances that remain unclear, she went to England to become a Franciscan nun.

Born a free woman of color, Mathilda Beasley began a community of Black sisters in Georgia in the late 1880s. She sought in vain to affiliate her community officially to the Franciscan Order. [Georgia Historical Society]

After 1885, Beasley returned to Georgia and began a community of Black sisters, first in Wilkes County and then in Savannah. It is uncertain whether Beasley was a professed Franciscan sister when she returned from England. It is certain that by 1889 she and two other Black women had begun the religious life following the Franciscan Rule. By 1896 the Catholic Directory indicated that there were five sisters and nineteen young orphan girls, all Black, in Savannah.

Mother Beasley sought in vain to affiliate her community officially to the Franciscan Order. From her letters to Mother Katherine Drexel in Philadelphia, the founder of the Sisters of the Blessed Sacrament for Indians and Colored People, we know of her financial needs and her pleas for help in the spiritual formation of her sisters. In the end, she received very little help of any kind. In 1898, the community was suppressed, the orphanage was taken over by the Missionary Franciscan Sisters of the Immaculate Conception, and Mother Beasley retired to a small cottage near Sacred Heart Church, at the time a church for Black Catholics. Here she lived a life of poverty, prayer, and charitable works. On Sunday morning, December 20, 1903, she was found dead in her cottage in an attitude of prayer. Mother Beasley's work was seemingly a failure; her success was her life of holiness and service, a memory that lives on in the Savannah Black community to this day.

BIBLIOGRAPHY

Ahles, Assumpta. *In the Shadow of His Wings* (1977); Dannett, Sylvia. *Profiles of Negro Womanhood* (1964); Davis, Cyprian. *History of Black Catholics in the United States* (1990); Smith, Julia. *Slavery and Rice Culture in Low Country Georgia* (1985). For primary sources, see the archives of the Catholic diocese of Savannah, the Josephite Archives in Baltimore, Maryland, and the Archives of the Sisters of the Blessed Sacrament in Bensalem, Pennsylvania.

CYPRIAN DAVIS, O.S.B.

BEAUTY CULTURE

Since the late nineteenth century, beauty culture has been simultaneously a source of opportunity, self-expression, and controversy for Black women. Work in hairdressing, beauty salons, and door-to-door sales promised economic advancement to Black women, whose job opportunities were extremely limited. At the same time, the new emphasis on appearance and grooming fostered by beauty culture promoted a larger debate about African-American identity, social participation, and cultural modernity. If, on the one hand, beauty culture encouraged a notion of the "New Negro Woman," it simultaneously raised troubling questions about African-Americans' emulation of and assimilation into white culture.

Even before the Civil War, hairdressing and skin care were concerns of Black women. Women in slavery used herbs, berries, and other natural substances to heal, soften, and color the skin. Moreover, a number of enslaved and free women of color worked as

Madam C. J. Walker was the first woman self-made millionaire in the United States. Her Walker Manufacturing Company created a complete line of beauty care products. Hundreds of agents sold the products aggressively throughout the country. [A'Lelia Bundles]

hairdressers for white women, and probably compounded simple pomades and lotions to use on their patrons. By the 1870s, some urban Black women owned hairdressing parlors, manufactured beauty products for sale, and profited in the "hair trade."

It was not until the late nineteenth century, however, that commercial beauty culture took off as part of the more general development of an African-American consumer market. Constrained by poverty and racial discrimination, most Blacks had little spending money for anything beyond the goods essential for survival. Still, the penetration of the market economy into the rural South, a nascent middle class, urban migration, and the growing racial segregation of cities spurred some entrepreneurs to develop businesses serving Black consumers. For African-Americans after the Civil War, grooming, stylishness, and adornment were ideals that signified freedom and respectability. Both Black-owned and white-owned companies responded to these desires with a range of commercial beauty products and services.

Some white-owned firms cultivated the African-American market for cosmetics as early as the 1890s. Patent medicine manufacturers and toiletry goods companies promoted hair tonics to Black Americans through almanacs, trade cards, and newspaper advertisements. Promising to straighten kinky hair and lighten dark skin, these ads blatantly appealed to color prejudices and the desire among some African-Americans for social acceptance. By the 1920s, white-owned firms like Plough and Nadinola had so expanded their marketing that they were the leading advertisers in many African-American newspapers. Highly controversial within the Black community, these companies were at times targeted for protest over their competitive tactics, failure to employ Black workers, and apparent disregard for product safety.

In this same period, a hair and beauty industry emerged that was developed and controlled by African-Americans. Figures such as Anthony Overton, Annie Turnbo Malone, Madam C. J. Walker, and Sarah Spencer Washington were among the most successful African-American entrepreneurs to sell hair tonics, pressing oils, face creams, and other products. Some firms developed out of the drugstore supplies trade or began as small cosmetics companies. Anthony Overton, who by 1916 owned one of the largest African-American businesses in the United States, began his career as a peddler and baking powder manufacturer in 1898. He shifted into cosmetics when his daughter's formula for a face powder proved popular in their local community. Overton sold his High-Brown Face Powder through an army of sales agents who aggressively pushed it into mainstream routes of distribution, making Overton the first African-American to place his products in Woolworth's. Another cosmetics firm, Kashmir Chemical Company, was founded in 1918 by Claude Barnett, head of the Associated Negro Press. Although the company was short-lived, Barnett's advertising for the Nile Queen cosmetics line was particularly ingenious because it targeted the popular interest among Black Americans in Cleopatra and the African origins of Egyptian culture.

Even more significant to the development of African-American beauty culture were the efforts of women entrepreneurs. Beginning around 1900, such pioneers as Annie Turnbo Malone and Madam C. J. Walker created new techniques and products to assure Black women of smooth, manageable hair. These women, who started out with little capital but boundless energy, sold their goods by traveling door to door and teaching women the art of hairdressing. By the 1910s, Malone's Poro products and the Walker System had spread throughout the country, not only in urban areas, but also in the rural South and Midwest; both also exported their goods outside the United States, selling in Africa, Cuba, the West Indies, and Central America. Initially emphasizing hair care products, Malone and Walker began to manufacture skin preparations, including face powders, rouge, creams, and skin lighteners, after World War I.

Beauty culture offered new employment opportunities in a race- and sex-segregated labor market that relegated most Black women to domestic service, laundering, and farm labor. The trade required little capital, was easy to learn, and was in demand. Beauty parlors could be operated cheaply in homes, apartments, and small shops, and hair and skin care products could be purchased cheaply or mixed in the kitchen for use on clients. Because most drugstores, chain stores, and department stores refused to locate in the Black community, door-to-door agents and salon beauticians largely controlled the distribution and sale of the products. In the 1910s and 1920s, thousands of women were trained in different, competing systems of hair and beauty culture. Advertising was generally limited to Black-owned newspapers, although large companies like Poro purchased space in various newspapers throughout the country, achieving a kind of national advertising.

Beauty culture in the early twentieth century was seen as a path toward individual mobility and also as a means of collective economic and social advancement. Both Walker and Malone were known not only for their business acumen but also for their generous

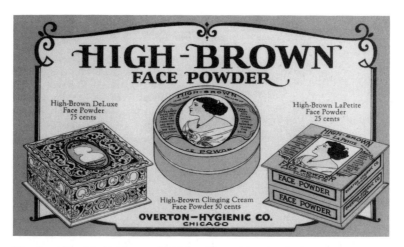

The advertising of the highly successful Overton-Hygienic Company featured light-skinned, refined-looking women and appealed to respectability and gentility. [Lake County (IL) Museum/Curt Teich Postcard Archives]

support of African-American educational, charitable, and civic institutions. Local beauty salons and clubs of cosmetologists similarly emphasized service to the Black community. In the absence of many commercial outlets, female entrepreneurs sought relationships and clientele in women's organizations, Black colleges, and churches. They offered promotions, beauty shows, and product sales to raise needed funds. Moreover, the sales methods they employed—salon operatives and door-to-door agents selling to friends and neighbors—probably enhanced the web of mutual support and assistance integral to Black women's culture. This integration of the industry with aspects of Black community life and politics sets it apart from the white beauty industry.

Aspects of beauty culture, especially hair straightening and skin bleaching, were highly controversial in the Black community. Products with names like Black-No-More and No-Kink (many of which were manufactured by white-owned as well as Black-owned companies) adhered to racist European aesthetic standards. Journalists, politicians, novelists, and others debated the legitimacy and meaning of such practices, relating the question of beauty not only to the definition of female respectability but also to "race consciousness" and Black resistance to white domination. In the eyes of many critics, hair straighteners and skin bleaches signified the emulation of white beauty standards that could only reinforce a degrading sense of physical and psychological inferiority in Black people. Skin bleaching, in particular, repre-

sented an admission of loathing for blackness and denial of African heritage. Others astutely observed a more complicated dynamic at work in African-American appraisals of "good" and "bad" hair and hierarchies of skin colors. Black women with lighter skin and straighter hair, critics like Nannie Burroughs maintained, gained higher-paying jobs in the labor market and fared better socially, especially in marriages to wealthier Black men, who tended to choose women with these characteristics. Obscured in this debate was the degree to which whites—working-class and middle-class, native-born and immigrant—used skin bleaches, hair pullers, and hairpieces to attain certain beauty standards.

African-American beauty culturists replied to this criticism by emphasizing the economic opportunities they produced and the cultural empowerment they offered. They challenged demeaning stereotypes of Black womanhood without explicitly overturning the dominant white aesthetic. White racism had symbolically linked the supposedly natural inferiority and backwardness of Black Americans to an appearance marked by unruly or "kinky" hair, poor grooming, and slovenly dress. The dominant culture's ascription of promiscuity to Black women, in particular, underscored the importance of looking respectable and refined. Thus, hair care and grooming visually signified personal success, cultural modernity, and racial progress. The beauty industry asserted and exploited this view in its advertising. The Madam C. J. Walker Company, for example, ran a full-page newspaper ad in 1928 whose headline announced: "Amazing Progress of Colored Race—Improved Appearance Responsible" (*Oklahoma Eagle*, March 3, 1928).

The African-American beauty industry was hard hit by the Great Depression of the 1930s; many beauty salons closed, sales declined, and women's dominance in the trade eroded. The modern development of the industry, starting in the 1950s with Johnson Products, has been largely controlled by men. In the early decades of the twentieth century, however, African-American beauty culture appealed to women as workers and consumers to take control of their destinies and challenge the stereotypes that limited them. The extraordinary growth of this industry suggests that beauty culture had great meaning for Black women, as they generated new self-definitions and collective responses to decades of abuse, poverty, and discrimination.

[*See also* WALKER, MADAM C. J.]

BIBLIOGRAPHY
Burroughs, Nannie. "Not Color But Character," *Voice of the Negro* (July 1904); *Journal of Negro History.* "Anthony Overton" (July 1947); Peiss, Kathy. "Making Faces: The Cosmetics Industry and the Cultural Construction of Gender, 1890-1930," *Genders* (Spring 1990); Robinson, Gwendolyn. "Class, Race, and Gender: A Transcultural, Theoretical, and Sociohistorical Analysis of Cosmetic Institutions and Practices to 1920," Ph.D. diss. (1984). For archival sources, see Warshaw Collection of Business Americana, National Museum of American History, Smithsonian Institution, Washington, D.C.; Madam C. J. Walker papers, Indiana Historical Society, Indianapolis, Indiana; and Claude A. Barnett papers, Chicago Historical Society, Chicago, Illinois.

KATHY PEISS

BEAVERS, LOUISE (1908-1962)

Film character-actress Louise Beavers was born on March 8, 1908, in Cincinnati, Ohio. In 1913, her family moved to Pasadena, where Beavers spent the rest of her youth.

After graduation from Pasadena High School, she worked in the early 1920s as a maid for silent screen actress Leatrice Joy, a star of many Cecil B. De Mille epics. While working for Joy, Beavers pursued her own dreams of stardom. She appeared briefly

Louise Beavers's role as a slave in the 1927 silent Uncle Tom's Cabin *paved the way for a lifetime of playing mammies, cooks, and maids. Her scenes with Fredi Washington in* Imitation of Life *were said by Thomas Cripps to "transform Hollywood trash into something unique and often powerful." [Donald Bogle]*

as a maid in the 1923 silent *Golddiggers*. During 1923-26 she performed amateur plays with sixteen other young women in a troupe called The Lady Minstrels. Exactly how she got her "big break" in Hollywood remains unclear. She herself gives two different accounts. In one interview (*Philadelphia Tribune*, March 14, 1935), she claimed that an agent from Universal Studios approached her after seeing a Lady Minstrels production. Much later, Beavers wrote in a December 1949 *Negro Digest* article that she was spotted by a representative from Central Casting when she sang solo in an amateur talent show.

However mysterious, Beavers's launch into a movie career was far from glamorous. Her first big role, as a slave in the 1927 silent *Uncle Tom's Cabin*, paved the way for a lifetime of playing mammies, cooks, and maids in over a hundred (mostly forgotten) movies. For most of Beavers's professional life, there were simply no other roles offered to Black actresses. In order to land even these stereotyped parts, Beavers was often forced to speak in unfamiliar southern dialect and to overeat so that she would maintain a mammy-like plumpness.

Even though relegated to the periphery of the screen, Beavers managed to establish a comic presence that became her signature. A famous example of her talent is her portrayal of Pearl, Mae West's sassy maid, in Paramount's 1933 *She Done Him Wrong*. In their scenes together, Beavers provided a sharp foil to West's sultry humor. (In an interesting postscript to the film, the two actresses remained close friends throughout Beavers's life.) Such comedic talent won for Beavers maid roles in comedies like the Jean Harlow vehicle *Bombshell* (1933) and the musical *Holiday Inn* (1942).

As an alternative to sassy Pearl roles, Beavers often played an earnest, God-fearing maid in domestic dramas or tearjerkers. In these films, Beavers's characters proved their absolute devotion to white employers by providing a much-needed miracle cure or wad of money. In *Made for Each Other* (1939), she rescues destitute Carole Lombard and James Stewart. In *The Big Street* (1942), the lucky couple is Lucille Ball and Henry Fonda.

Perhaps the most important of these helpful-maid roles was Beavers's Delilah in the very popular 1934 Universal picture *Imitation of Life*. In the film's plot, single white mother Bea (Claudette Colbert) sells her maid Delilah's pancake recipe and becomes a millionaire. The film received glowing reviews for its sensitive treatment of "race"—meaning that the film portrayed two women of different colors going into business together. The film's critics pointed out that

Delilah was, in fact, just a glorified mammy figure. Nevertheless, one of the film's central images, that of Delilah grinningly holding a griddle, had already firmly entrenched itself in the American cultural psyche. Beavers, who hated pancakes, had finally reached stardom.

Beavers remained active in show business throughout her life. When she could, she diversified her characters. She played a Harlem numbers queen in *Bullets or Ballots* (1936). She acted in two films with all-Black casts: *Life Goes On* (1938) and *Reform School* (1939). She also experimented with different media. In 1935, she appeared in a one-woman show at the Roxy Theatre in New York. In the 1952-53 television season, she played the title role in *Beulah*, a popular ABC series about a sassy maid. She made many more appearances on the small screen in various variety shows. In 1957, she traveled to San Francisco to make her dramatic theater debut in *Praise House*. Her last film, *The Facts of Life*, was released in 1961.

Louise Beavers died of diabetes on October 26, 1962, at Cedars of Lebanon Hospital in Los Angeles. She was survived by her husband LeRoy Moore, whom she married in the late 1950s.

BIBLIOGRAPHY

Bogle, Donald. *Toms, Coons, Mulattoes, Mammies and Bucks: An Interpretive History of Blacks in American Films* (1989); *DANB*; Spradling, Mary Mace. *In Black and White* (1980).

SARAH P. MORRIS

BECROFT, ANNE MARIE (1805-1833)

"In spite of ill health this pious girl rendered herself useful" and "had a very sweet disposition joining with it the firmness necessary to make her respected by children." That diary note, written by Father Nicholas Joubert in 1833, describes one of America's most illustrious women—Anne Marie Becroft. Her accomplishments in education in early nineteenth-century America helped shape Black Catholic history in the United States.

Anne Becroft, the oldest of seven children, was born in 1805 to freeborn William and Sara Becroft. At age four, she began her formal education at the white-operated Potter School in Washington. However, hostilities associated with race and slavery forced her to leave that school in 1812. The following year, she resumed her studies at the New Georgetown School, which was operated by a white widow named

Mary Billing. Becroft studied with Billing until 1820 when the Denmark Vesey Revolt affected Billing's ability to operate the school. It closed because white involvement in the education of Black people was discouraged. That same year, Becroft opened her own school on Georgetown's Dumbarton Street and for eight years operated this small day school for girls, continuing the work of Mary Billing. Then, in 1827, Becroft was invited by the parish priest of Holy Trinity Catholic Church to open a school under the auspices of the church.

Holy Trinity Church was a white church, but as far back as 1787 Black Catholics had been parishioners. Given Becroft's extraordinary abilities as a teacher, it is not surprising that Father J. Van Lommel asked her to begin a day and boarding school for Black girls. With the assistance of the white Visitation nuns, the academy opened on Fayette Street. The tuition, one dollar a month, was paid for thirty-five students who came from well-to-do and poor families in Washington, Virginia, and Maryland. The school remained in Becroft's hands until 1831 when she turned it over to former student, Ellen Simonds, and left to become the ninth nun of the Oblate Sisters of Providence in Baltimore.

On September 8, 1832, Becroft took her habit and a new name, Sister Aloysius; the following year she took her vows. As a teaching Oblate, she instructed her students in arithmetic, English, and embroidery, but her life as a nun was brief. She had been sickly off and on since age fifteen, but in 1833 her health began to deteriorate rapidly. She died on December 16, 1833, and was buried in the Old Cathedral Cemetery in Baltimore.

Anne Becroft was a courageous woman. She brought education and religion to Black females at a time when freedom was a fragile commodity. She lived in a society in which slavery and racism were firmly entrenched, yet even in such a society she was able to stimulate in her students a desire for educational attainment. No stone monument has been erected on behalf of this righteous woman, but her presence continues to be felt in Black history.

BIBLIOGRAPHY

Fitzpatrick, Sandra and Maria R. Goodwin. *The Guide to Black Washington* (1990); Gilliard, John T. *The Catholic Church and the American Negro* (1929), and *Colored Catholics in the United States* (1941); Marrow, Gloria R. "A Narrative of the Founding and Work of the Oblate Sisters of Providence," Master's thesis (1976); *The New Catholic Encyclopedia* (1967); Oblate Archival Materials, Annals of the Oblate Sisters of Providence (1842-77); Sherwood, Grace. *The Oblates Hundred and One Years* (1931); Wanagiris, Sister M. Clare. "Maria Becroft and Black Catholic Education, 1820-1833," Master's thesis (1977); Weatherford, W. D. *American Churches and the Negro from Slave Days to the Present* (1957).

GLORIA MARROW

BENNETT, GWENDOLYN (1902-1981)

"To all Negro youth known and unknown who have a song to sing, a story to tell or a vision for the sons of the earth"—Gwendolyn Bennett wrote these words to dedicate her poem "Usward" to the writers who were showcased at New York's Civic Club gathering on March 21, 1924, spearheaded by Charles S. Johnson, the force behind *Opportunity* and entrepreneur of the New Negro Renaissance, commonly known as the Harlem Renaissance. These writers were the esprit de corps that defined the sentiments of the new expressions in Black literature. The honorees were introduced to white publishers and included Alain Locke, Countee Cullen, Jessie Fauset, Walter White, Helene Johnson, Eric Walrond, and Gwendolyn Bennett. On this occasion Bennett made her debut as a poet and joined with others to energize the New Negro movement.

Bennett was born in Giddings, Texas, on July 8, 1902, the only child of native Texans Joshua Robin and Maime Franke Bennett. Her father was a professional man, a teacher and attorney who had attended Prairie View College in Texas. He was from a large middle-class family, the son of a barber who was proprietor of his own establishment. Her father taught on Indian reservations until the family relocated to Washington, D.C., to escape financial troubles or for some unknown reason. Her mother taught locally in the Black grade schools in Texas. Little is known of her mother's family other than that Bennett's maternal grandmother may have been a member of the Algonquian Blackfoot tribe. The marriage was unstable, and her parents separated and then divorced when Bennett was five or six years old. Realizing that she could not support her daughter adequately on an educator's income, Bennett's mother changed professions from teacher to cosmetologist and manicurist and secured a position in a District of Columbia finishing school for young Caucasian women. After the court granted Bennett's mother custody, mother and daughter settled down comfortably as a single-parent family. However, Bennett's father was incensed that the court awarded custody of his daughter to his

Among Gwendolyn Bennett's many contributions to Black culture during the twentieth century was her column for the Harlem Renaissance magazine Opportunity. *[Moorland-Spingarn]*

former wife and granted him only visitation privileges. He abducted his eight-year-old daughter by pretending to take her to visit a historical site. He fled to various cities and towns in the mid-Atlantic region and subsequently settled in Harrisburg, Pennsylvania, married Marshall Neil Briscoll, also a teacher, and supported his family through janitorial work and odd jobs while hiding out from the family law authorities. Bennett's stepmother was childless but settled into the role of mother as best she knew how. She provided a safe and secure home environment for Bennett, gave her a firm code of morals, values, and ethics, and instilled in her a belief in Christian Science. While employed as a typist for the federal government, Bennett's father passed the Pennsylvania bar examination and relocated his family to Brooklyn, New York, where the three of them settled down as a respectable professional family. Her father died there in 1926.

After her parents divorced, Bennett attended a Black public elementary school in the District and continued her elementary education in Harrisburg

after the abduction. Her secondary education began at Girls' High School in Brooklyn where she was the first Black participant in the literary and drama societies. Though she disliked the rigidity of academics, she wholeheartedly involved herself in extracurricular activities. A poster she designed brought her first prize in a school contest; she wrote lyrics to the class graduation song and wrote the graduation speech. At Girls' High she began to dabble in poetry and expressed an interest in art. These two interests were to chart the course of her life's work—love of the pen and love of the brush. Her high school English teacher, Cordelia Went, and her art teacher were instrumental influences in fueling her creative powers. Bennett graduated from Girls' High in 1921.

The 1920s were a great time to be alive. The ambience of Harlem exerted a magnetic pull that drew Black artists to Harlem's cultural centers. In 1921 Bennett enrolled in Columbia University's Teachers College department of fine arts, but the overt racism discouraged her and after two years she transferred to Pratt Institute, where she studied art and drama. Repeating her performance at Girls' High, she plunged into creative endeavors by writing and playing the lead in the class play. By the time she graduated from Pratt in 1924, she was well on her way to being a recognized artist in Harlem.

Her reputation as a poet and artist helped her to get a faculty position at Howard University in its year-old department of art. However, teaching limited her, confined her, and stifled her creativity. To add to the gloom, the pretentious Washington, D.C., Black cultural society lacked the closeness, genuineness, and love among peers and colleagues that she had embraced in Harlem. Delta Sigma Theta provided a much needed outlet by granting her a $1,000 scholarship to study art abroad. In December 1924, the novelist Dorothy Canfield Fisher presented her with the scholarship award. In June 1925, Bennett went on leave to study art in Paris. She experienced all that Paris had to offer, the cafes, the Louvre, the art galleries, the museums, the musicians, the expatriates, Gertrude Stein, Ernest Hemingway, James Joyce, Konrad Bercovici. She even introduced Paul Robeson and his wife, Essie, a sorority sister, to the Paris scene. Still, she did not know many people and so she plunged into her studies to divert her from the loneliness. She studied art at the Académie Colarossi, Académie Julian, and Ecole de Pantheon, and studied French literature at the Sorbonne. She was proficient in watercolor, pen and ink, and oils, but batik was her forte. She held batik exhibitions in Paris, and the batik collections she shipped to New York to be sold brought her some much needed income. When she was not studying art, she continued to write, yet she longed for Harlem. At the end of the 1926 spring session, she returned home to Harlem to resume her role in the New Negro movement, as an artist and writer.

She became assistant editor of *Opportunity*, the magazine that helped to launch the literary careers of contributors to the Harlem Renaissance. Her literary gossip column "Ebony Flute" kept readers abreast of the Black social scene. Moreover, she served on the editorial board of *Fire!* Though she loved Harlem, she had faculty responsibilities at Howard University; fall came much too quickly and she returned to Washington, D.C., to teach.

Washington, D.C., associates introduced her to Alfred Joseph Jackson, a Morehouse graduate who was an older medical student at Howard. The two fell in love and their romance put Bennett in violation of the school's ethics rule. By fraternizing with a student, Bennett committed the ultimate faux pas. The administration frowned on her behavior but they did not take any action; nevertheless she willingly offered her resignation which the president promptly accepted. While Jackson completed his internship at Freedman's Hospital (now Howard University Hospital), Bennett returned to New York, disguised herself as a Javanese woman, and secured work in a batik factory. She had to be deceptive because white employers had established racist notions about the type of work Black employees should do. Jackson and Bennett were married on April 14, 1928, and he returned to his native Eustis, Florida, to open his medical practice. Bennett did not join him in Florida right away; she taught art education and English at Tennessee A & I College in the summer of 1928. Once again she faced the reality that teaching was not her vocation, and she joined her husband in Eustis.

The marriage was not a blissful one. The couple was plagued by money problems and segregationist attitudes. Bennett tried to supplement their income by working as a Spanish teacher in Eustis's Lake County school for $50 a month, but the meager salary was insufficient. In addition, the absence of the cultural and social scene that Bennett needed to thrive meant she stopped writing. She encouraged Jackson to take the New York medical examination. He passed and the couple moved to Hempstead, Long Island, where Jackson established a successful medical practice for a short time before he became a victim of the effects of the Great Depression and died.

Bennett's major literary activities begin with the New Negro Renaissance and end in 1941, when she became a target of the "red scare." The 1920s proved to be the best times for Bennett when she practiced her crafts of poet, writer of fiction, journalist, reviewer, and scholarly writer. As an artist she held exhibitions and illustrated the covers of the December 1923 and March 1924 *Crisis* magazine and the January 1926, July 1926, and December 1930 covers of *Opportunity*. During the 1930s, she earned her teaching degree from Columbia University and took graduate courses at New York University. This period found her dividing her time among teaching, administration, and community activity. Much of her time was devoted to the Works Progress Administration's Federal Art Project. Under this program she became the director of the Harlem Art Center. The community took a sincere interest in its progress and it became a successful entity under her administration. Renowned Black artist Jacob Lawrence was one of her students. Her tenure as director of the center came to an abrupt halt when she was accused of being a Communist. During the 1940s, she tried to piece together her tattered career by founding the Jefferson School for Democracy and the George Washington Carver School, but the House Un-American Activities Committee targeted these schools and they subsequently closed. In 1940, she married Richard Crosscup, a white Harvard graduate and English teacher who had volunteered his time at the Carver school. She moved with him to Kutztown, Pennsylvania, where they opened an antiques store. He died in January 1980.

Bennett's poetry reflects her love for the literary and the visual, a combination that for her was inseparable. She was the renaissance woman of the New Negro movement. She died in May 1981, having given the Black art world a great gift for over twenty years—herself.

BIBLIOGRAPHY

Daniel, Walter C. and Sandra Y. Govan. "Gwendolyn Bennett." In *Afro-American Writers from the Harlem Renaissance to 1940*, ed. Trudier Harris (1987); Fabre, Michel. *From Harlem to Paris: Black American Writers in France, 1840-1980* (1991); Govan, Sandra Y. "Gwendolyn Bennett: Portrait of an Artist Lost," Ph.D. diss. (1980), and "After the Renaissance: Gwendolyn Bennett and the WPA Years," *MAWA Review* (1988); Perry, Margaret. *Silence to the Drums: A Survey of the Literature of the Harlem Renaissance* (1976); Simcox, Helen Earle, ed. *Dear Dark Faces: Portraits of a People* (1980); Stetson, Erlene, ed. *Black Sister: Poetry by Black American Women, 1746-1980* (1981).

GERRI BATES

BENNETT COLLEGE

Bennett College, one of only two still existing historically Black institutions of higher learning for women, was founded in 1873 as a coeducational school in the basement of Saint Matthew's Methodist Episcopal Church in Greensboro, North Carolina. It was named Bennett Seminary in honor of Lyman Bennett of Troy, New York, who was the school's first large donor. The Freedman's Aid Society took responsibility for the school in 1874, and Reverend Edward O. Thayer, a Wesleyan College alumnus, became its second principal. Thayer left in 1881 to assume the presidency of Clark College in Atlanta. In 1886, an industrial work/domestic science program was begun and a home for women (later named Kent Hall) was built on the Bennett campus under the auspices of the Woman's Home Missionary Society of the Methodist Episcopal Church. In 1889, Reverend Charles N. Grandison became the first African-American president of Bennett and the first Black president of any of the Freeman's Aid Society-funded schools.

In 1926, Bennett became a college for women primarily as a result of the Woman's Home Missionary Society's desire to enlarge its educational programs to include African-American women, a primary objective of the society. After 1926, the society assumed greater responsibility for Bennett College for Women. The retirement of Frank Trigg in 1926 ended the era of coeducation at the institution. David Dallas Jones, a white businessman living in Atlanta, became the first president of Bennett College for Women, where he remained for thirty years, until 1956.

Black women college presidents, even at Black women's colleges, have been extraordinarily rare, which is a reflection of the persistent male control of historically Black institutions in general. When Willa Player became president of Bennett College in 1955, after having served the college in various capacities for twenty-five years, she became the first African-American woman to head a college for Black women. Player, a native of Akron, Ohio, who had earned a Ph.D. from Columbia University, joined the Bennett faculty in 1930 as a teacher of French. In 1952, she became director of admissions and vice president in charge of instruction. During Player's presidency, Bennett gained membership, in 1957, to the Southern Association of Colleges and Schools. She resigned in March 1966 and assumed the position of director of the Division of College Support with the U.S. Office of Education, Department of Health, Education and Welfare. Isaac H. Miller, Jr., succeeded Player as president in September 1966; his father, Isaac H. Miller, Sr., had been dean of Bennett College beginning in 1923. Isaac H. Miller, Jr. was associate professor of biochemistry at Meharry Medical College prior to assuming the Bennett presidency. Following Miller's retirement, a second Black woman, Gloria Randle Scott, then vice president of Clark College, assumed the presidency of Bennett College.

Although the majority of Black women have been educated in coeducational institutions, single-sex colleges for Black women, all of which have been located in the South, have provided unique educational experiences for generations of women who have chosen through the years to attend Bennett, Spelman, Barber-Scotia, Hartshorn, and Houston-Tillotson.

[*See also* EDUCATION.]

BIBLIOGRAPHY

Brawley, James P. *Two Centuries of Methodist Concern: Bondage, Freedom, and Education of Black People* (1974).

BEVERLY GUY-SHEFTALL

BENTLEY, GLADYS (1907-1960)

Lesbian entertainer Gladys Bentley was born in Philadelphia in 1907. When she was a teenager, she ran away from home, as have many gay adolescents who were looking for a world in which they could be themselves. Bentley found her world in the clubs of Harlem. She supported herself by playing the piano and soon developed a reputation for improvising risqué lyrics to the melodies of popular songs. During the 1920s, Bentley adopted her characteristic costume, a white tuxedo and top hat, and headlined at Harry Hansberry's Clam House. The lesbian entertainer soon became a cult star. The intellectual and artistic set of New York—including Langston Hughes and Isamu Noguchi, whose 1929 head of Bentley is illustrated here—found her nightclub act fascinating. Offstage Bentley maintained her image, almost always wearing men's clothing. She was once described

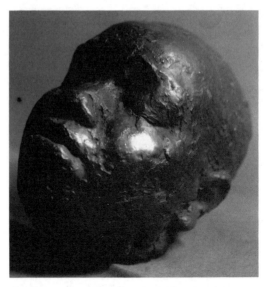

Among the artists and intellectuals who flocked to Harlem to hear risqué musical parodist Gladys Bentley was Isamu Noguchi, whose 1929 bronze head of the lesbian artist is pictured here. [The Isamu Noguchi Foundation, Inc.]

as the person for whom the term "cross-dressing" was invented (though George Sand might have disputed this).

When American society moved into a repressive phase in the late 1940s and the 1950s, Bentley was forced to deny her sexual orientation in order to get work, and she never regained the success she had had earlier in her career. She died in 1960.

KATHLEEN THOMPSON

BERGEN, FLORA BATSON *see* BATSON, FLORA

BERRY, MARY FRANCES (1938-)

Mary Frances Berry is a scholar trained in history and law, a public servant, and a political activist of international renown. She has to her credit impressive firsts, such as being the first African-American woman to serve as chancellor of a major research university and the first African-American woman to

Flamboyant singer Gladys Bentley was once described as the person the term "cross-dressing" was invented for. [Moorland-Spingarn]

hold the post of the nation's chief educational officer. She has taken numerous stands on the basis of principle, but her 1984 suit against President Ronald Reagan to reaffirm the independence of the U.S. Commission on Civil Rights, as well as her sit-in, arrest, and incarceration to protest racial injustice in South Africa, established a place for her in the national and international press. Her place in history, however, has been created not only by prestigious appointments and political activism but also by her contributions as a historian. Berry both writes and makes history.

Mary Frances Berry was born on February 17, 1938, in Nashville, Tennessee, to Frances Southall Berry and George Ford Berry. Throughout her childhood and youth in Tennessee, with her brother, George, Jr., her mother, and later with a stepfather and younger brother, Troy, Berry experienced hardships occasioned by poverty and racial discrimination. Nevertheless, her extraordinary intellect was recognized by Nashville teachers, particularly Minerva Hawkins, who challenged her to overcome obstacles and excel academically. Berry graduated from Nashville's Pearl High School with honors in 1956. Thereafter she worked her way through college and graduate school as a laboratory technician until she had earned a Bachelor of Arts and a Master of Arts at Howard University in Washington, D.C., as well as a Ph.D. in U.S. constitutional history at the University of Michigan in Ann Arbor. Upon receiving her doctorate in 1966, Berry taught at Central Michigan University in Mt. Pleasant while seeking admission to the University of Michigan Law School in order to obtain a J.D. She taught history as an assistant professor of history at Central Michigan University, as an assistant and then an associate professor of history at Eastern Michigan University, and as an associate professor of history at the University of Maryland until she earned her law degree. Concurrently she engaged in antiwar and pro-civil rights activities. In 1970, she accepted an appointment as an adjunct associate professor of history at the University of Michigan in Ann Arbor as well as a full-time appointment as the acting director of Afro-American Studies at the University of Maryland in College Park. She moved to the Maryland-Washington, D.C., area where she has made her home.

Mary Frances Berry's deep personal interest and involvement in the cause of racial justice and the creation of new historical scholarship found expression in her decision to become a member of the Bar in the District of Columbia, in her political activity, in her teaching of African-American and legal history,

Mary Frances Berry became known as "the woman the president couldn't fire" when she successfully sued President Ronald Reagan to retain her position on the U.S. Commission on Civil Rights. [Moorland-Spingarn]

and in her research and writing of the 1970s. While demonstrating for the rights of African-Americans and lobbying for federal enforcement of laws affecting African-Americans, Berry maintained high standards of academic excellence and established an impressive scholarly record. She published *Black Resistance/White Law: A History of Constitutional Racism* in 1971, "Reparations for Freedmen, 1890-1919" in 1972, *Military Necessity and Civil Rights Policy* in 1977, and *Stability, Security, and Continuity: Mr. Justice Burton and Decision-making in the Supreme Court, 1945-1958* in 1978.

Berry also excelled during the 1970s in educational administration. At the University of Maryland she rose from one position of responsibility to another, becoming the director of Afro-American Studies, the interim chairman of the Division of Behavioral and Social Sciences, and the provost of that division. As provost from 1974 to 1976, she became the highest-ranking African-American woman on the College Park campus. When, in 1976, Berry accepted the invitation of the Board of Regents of the University of Colorado to become chancellor of the University of Colorado at Boulder, as well as professor of history and law, she became the first African-American woman to head a major research university, presiding over a student body of 21,000, a faculty of 2,000, and an annual budget of more than $100 million. Berry took a leave of absence from her professorship as well as her chancellorship at Colorado, however, in order to respond to the call of the recently elected President Jimmy Carter. From 1977 to 1980, Berry distinguished herself as assistant secretary for education in the Department of Health, Education and Welfare (HEW), becoming the first African-American woman to serve as the nation's chief educational officer.

Since leaving government, Berry has accomplished much as a scholar, continued her public service, and intensified her political activism. Leaving her posts in the Carter administration and at the University of Colorado, she returned in 1980 to her alma mater, Howard University, for a time teaching legal history in its history department and serving as a senior fellow at the Institute for the Study of Educational Policy. With John Wesley Blassingame, she coauthored, in 1982, *Long Memory*, a history of African-Americans. In 1986, she published *Why the ERA Failed: Politics, Women's Rights, and the Amending Process*, which became the subject of many reviews and debates regarding the Equal Rights Amendment and the women's movement. National recognition of her talents and her contributions to the field of history led in 1987 to Berry's receiving the University of Pennsylvania's distinguished Geraldine R. Segal Professorship in Social Thought as well as a professorship in history. In terms of her professional affiliations, Berry has served as a vice president of the American Historical Association and been elected president of the Organization of American Historians, serving in that capacity for one year beginning in March 1990. Because of her critical analyses, prodigious research, and coverage of timely issues from a historical perspective, she continues to be a sought-after professor, graduate adviser, author, and lecturer.

Combining public service with political activism during the 1980s and early 1990s, Berry has been a member of the U.S. Commission on Civil Rights since her appointment in 1980, and she served from 1980 to 1982 as the commission's vice chairperson. Always emphasizing not only its political autonomy, but also its watchdog role, Berry has come into conflict with presidents Reagan and George Bush because they have wanted the commission to support the conservative policies of their administrations, something Berry cannot do. In 1984, for example, she became known as the woman the president could not fire when she successfully sued President Reagan to retain her position on the commission. Although she has been a minority voice on the commission subsequent to appointments by Reagan and Bush, Berry has continued to be outspoken in the cause of civil rights, stressing the critical nexus between economic and racial justice.

Both in her capacity as a public servant and as a private citizen-political activist, Berry has emphasized the impropriety and immorality of racist policies at home and abroad. With Washington, D.C., delegate to Congress Walter Fauntroy, and TransAfrica executive Randall Robinson, Berry was arrested on November 21, 1984, after holding a sit-in at the South African Embassy. Their sit-in was the catalyst for a series of grass-roots demonstrations, the arrest of thousands of U.S. citizens, and nationwide protests against Reagan's policy with regard to South Africa. It was through such activism that the national Free South Africa movement, of which Berry is a cofounder, had its genesis. Whether in the trenches with other activists such as Jesse Jackson, Roger Wilkins, and Sylvia Hill or doing advocacy history with scholars such as John Hope Franklin for *amicus curiae* briefs in defense of African-Americans' civil rights, Berry has been uncompromising in the struggle for African-American liberation and for justice.

Mary Frances Berry has received numerous honors and awards. She was selected by *Ms.* magazine as one of its 1986 Women of the Year, and she has been awarded honorary doctorates by such institutions as Central Michigan University, Howard University, Oberlin College, Bethune-Cookman College, and the City College of the City University of New York. Numerous organizations have singled her out for special recognition; she is the recipient of the Rosa Parks Award of the Southern Christian Leadership Conference (SCLC), the President's Award of the Congressional Black Caucus Foundation, and not only the Roy Wilkins Civil Rights Award but also the national Image Award of the National Association for the Advancement of Colored People (NAACP).

BIBLIOGRAPHY

Berry, Mary Frances. Papers at the Moorland-Spingarn Research Center, Howard University, Washington, D.C.; Lanker, Brian. *I Dream a World: Portraits of Black Women Who Changed America* (1989); Pinderhughes, Dianne M. "Black Women and National Educational Policy," *Journal of Negro Education* (Summer 1982); Reynolds, Barbara. "The Woman the President Couldn't Fire," *Essence* (October

1984); Smith, Carol Hobson. "Black Female Achievers in Academe," *Journal of Negro Education* (Summer 1982); *WWBA* (1991).

GENNA RAE McNEIL

BESSENT, HATTIE (1926-)

Hattie Bessent, administrator, psychiatric nurse, teacher, author, and researcher, is deputy executive director of the Ethnic/Racial Minority Fellowship Programs of the American Nurses Association (ANA). These programs assist nurses in preparing for doctorates in mental health and related specialties and award fellowships for that purpose.

Hattie Bessent was born on December 26, 1926, in Jacksonville, Florida. Her mother died when Hattie was nine, so her grandmother raised her. Bessent graduated from high school in Jacksonville, Florida. After she earned a B.S. in nursing education from Florida A & M University in 1959, she returned to Jacksonville and became the first African-American nurse to head a psychiatric unit in that city. She also received an M.S. in psychiatric nursing from Indiana University in 1962 and an Ed.D. in the psychological foundations of education from the University of Florida in 1970.

Hattie Bessent has accomplished many firsts for herself, African-Americans, and her profession. She was the first Black nurse in Florida to receive a doctorate, the first Black dean of the Graduate School of Nursing at Vanderbilt University, and the first Black nurse in the South to be inducted into the following honorary organizations: Phi Delta Kappa, Sigma Theta Tau, and Pi Lambda Theta. She also is a member of Delta Sigma Theta sorority.

In addition, in 1977 she was appointed by President Jimmy Carter to the Presidential Task Force for the Friendship Treaty to China and to the Presidential Commission on Mental Health. She received the Distinguished Alumna Award from Florida A & M University in 1980. She also has been awarded the Mary Mahoney Award by the ANA.

As the only minority director on the staff of the ANA, Hattie Bessent has worked tirelessly to ensure that professionals of color, and all nurses, continue to advance their research, clinical, and practice skills. Through her own publications, research, and administrative efforts she has fostered the principles of service —"You must give of yourself in order to be worthy"— that she learned from her grandmother years ago.

CHERYL TAYLOR

BETHUNE, MARY McLEOD (1875-1955)

In October 1941, after Black women had been excluded from membership in the national advisory council of the Women's Interest Section (a female public relations unit in the War Department), Mary McLeod Bethune, the president of the National Council of Negro Women, vigorously challenged the omission. The situation underscored the encompassing nature of racial segregation in the United States in the first half of the twentieth century. Though participation in a women's advisory group was an exceedingly small matter in the country's large defense picture, white decision-makers barred African-American representation. In responding, the superpatriotic Bethune demonstrated the essentials of her leadership. "We cannot accept any excuse that the exclusion of Negro representation was an oversight. . . . We are incensed!" she informed the public and most particularly the Secretary of War (Smith 1980). Concurrently, she maneuvered behind closed doors with influential white supporters, chief among whom was First Lady Eleanor Roosevelt. Bethune's objective was characteristic: to attain a breakthrough opportunity for Black leadership that would lend itself to promoting the general welfare and to assaulting racial discrimination. As usual, Bethune was effective. She established a connection to the War Department via the women's advisory council from which, most notably, she ensured the commissioning of Black officers in the Women's Army Auxiliary Corps when it materialized the following year.

In circumstances common to Black Americans of her generation, the uncommon Mary McLeod Bethune was born on July 10, 1875, near Mayesville, South Carolina, about fifty miles northeast of Columbia. She was the fifteenth of seventeen children. Her parents were Sam and Patsy (McIntosh) McLeod, ex-slaves liberated by the Civil War. Initially it appeared that, despite natural leadership qualities augmented by emulating her iron-willed Christian mother, Mary would become just another poor, rural, uneducated Black girl. At age ten, however, she enrolled in the Trinity Presbyterian Mission School when it opened a few miles from her family's farm. Three years later, through the initiative of her loving teacher and dynamic mentor, Emma Jane Wilson, Mary attended Scotia Seminary, a missionary outpost of northern Presbyterians in Concord, North Carolina. She stayed at this female boarding school from October 1888 to her graduation in May 1894. Scotia's head-heart-hand educational strategy prepared the overwhelming majority of its students to earn a living at teaching other Black Americans—whose slave heritage left them desperate for schooling. Before McLeod began to teach, however, she spent a year at evangelist Dwight Moody's Institute for Home and Foreign Missions in Chicago, an experience that gave her contact with a significant microcosm of the world's people. She had enrolled at the institute to receive training for the African mission field, but the Presbyterian church rejected her application because it declined to support African-American missionaries in Africa. McLeod returned home, therefore, grievously disappointed. Nevertheless, she possessed the experiences, talent, and character for a bright future. She saw herself as God's very own precious child—an equal to any other in the human family. Regardless of the limitations society imposed because she exhibited the physical appearance of her African forebears —kinky-textured hair, flaring nose, full lips, and a coal-black complexion—features that even Black America's middle class disesteemed; regardless of her sex, her rural southern background, and her lingering poverty, this woman believed in God and in herself. More specifically, along with her teaching ability, McLeod possessed a missionary spirit that demanded release. It bubbled over while she taught at Haines Institute in Augusta, Georgia, in 1896-97, and during that same year she organized the Mission Sabbath School for 275 of the city's poorest children. Then McLeod established a mission enterprise in 1902 in Palatka, Florida, a city located about seventy-five miles southwest of Jacksonville. She not only taught children unable to pay tuition but also routinely imparted material goods, encouragement, and the gospel of Jesus Christ to sawmill workers, prisoners, and others in need.

While at the Presbyterians' Kendall Institute in Sumter, South Carolina, McLeod met a store clerk, Albertus Bethune, five years her senior. They married in May 1898, but no long-term conjugal bliss resulted. Bethune pursued a career in Florida—first in Palatka for five years and then in Daytona, about fifty miles to the southeast. Her husband followed her from one location to another, until, though never divorced, the Bethunes separated late in 1907. He returned to his home in Sumter County, South Carolina, where he died in 1918. This experience may have been responsible for her view that marriage and family were only secondary institutions in race advancement.

The Bethunes did have one son. During their first married year in Savannah, Georgia, Albert McLeod Bethune was born on February 3, 1899. Mary was the primary caregiver but Albertus always maintained consistent interest. Their son dropped out of college and failed at several jobs. He died on October 31, 1989. His greatest blessing to his mother was presenting her in 1920 with Albert McLeod Bethune, Jr., her only grandchild. Grandmother Bethune took this first grandchild as her very own, legally adopting him. As an adult with a Master's degree in library science, the younger Albert settled into a rewarding career as a librarian in Daytona Beach at the institution his grandmother had established.

When Bethune moved to Daytona in 1904, it was to start a school. Having previously established an independent mission, she knew the essentials for success. Moreover, she knew she wanted an incarnation of her alma mater, Scotia Seminary. She planned to offer basic academics, a pious religious atmosphere, and training in homemaking and teaching. Around the turn of the century, home training was publicly conceded as the special province of Black female boarding schools. No goal was considered worthier, given the notion that a people could advance only to the extent that women "purified" the home. Accordingly, Bethune planned her school with the idea of educating girls as the keepers of the home. This translated into offering them sewing and cooking, activities subsumed under the rubric "industry." Despite the theoretical foundations of Black girls' schools, in reality most students used whatever skills or knowledge they acquired to earn a living as maids, cooks, seamstresses, and especially teachers.

Though Scotia was the model, Bethune did not intend to imitate it slavishly. Like Emma Wilson's independent Mayesville Educational and Industrial Institute, established in 1892, she planned to have a large farm to feed students and teachers and to generate a cash income. Furthermore, like Haines Institute's Lucy Laney, the era's preeminent Black female founder-educator, she planned to have a kindergarten, a nurse training program, and community outreach.

Few would have predicted the success of these plans when Bethune, on October 3, 1904, launched the Daytona Educational and Industrial Institute from a rented house. According to tradition, she began with "five little girls, a dollar and a half and faith in God" (Smith 1990). Since the material necessities of education were nonexistent, Bethune made do with dry goods boxes for benches, the charred splinters of burned logs for pens, and elderberry juice for ink. In three years, she had achieved enough support to relocate the school to a permanent campus, where the first building was the four-story white frame Faith Hall. In 1910, Bethune bought a farm across the street. Typically she toiled in the fields with her teachers and with students in blue uniforms and white aprons to bring to the kitchen sugarcane syrup, melons, pumpkins, tomatoes, peas, and other food. Yet Bethune's concerns reached beyond her students. She developed several groups and forums to address community issues. None was more important to her than temperance. On September 27, 1905, she and her students mobilized to assure an overwhelming vote to keep Volusia County "dry." In short order, Bethune had become a leader in Daytona's Black community.

In 1912, with a budget of $5,000 for sixty boarding students plus a number of day students, Bethune enjoyed a rush of good fortune that included receiving for an overnight stay the famed Tuskegee educator Booker T. Washington. More important still, she caught the attention of the national Black press. Media exposure was particularly helpful because it presented Bethune with a wider field of potential donors. She needed as many as possible to underwrite a trades cottage for rug weaving, broom making, and other industries as well as a hospital that would train nurses and care for the sick. Both of these facilities became a reality in 1912. Moreover, in that same year Bethune recruited Frances Reynolds Keyser, the superintendent of New York City's White Rose Mission and an executive committee member of the National Association for the Advancement of Colored People (NAACP). Keyser was, in effect, her school's dean and well suited to share the challenges of the Daytona Institute.

Of course, the number one challenge was money. To get it Bethune utilized the well-worn techniques of Black activists: selling chicken dinners, singing for donations, and out-and-out begging. Like other heads of private Black schools, she traveled north to meet America's wealthy philanthropists, but Bethune enjoyed an advantage over most of her fund-raising colleagues: she could find donors in her own front yard as well. The Daytona area enjoyed an ever-expanding economy thanks primarily to its tourist attractions: a near-perfect climate, white sand beaches, and auto racing. Moreover, a core of the white population assisted liberal causes. Bethune routinely solicited from tourists whose names appeared in the local papers. Having trained her students to render Negro spirituals and plantation melodies with great feeling, she marched them into Daytona's prominent hotels to perform. Afterwards, in a magnetic fashion, she pleaded her cause. By 1912, both millionaire winter residents James N. Gamble and Thomas H. White backed her, as did the leading town fathers and mothers. With such benefactors the Daytona Insti-

tute became Florida's center of interracial goodwill. Bethune demanded the respect of all, and all gave it. Yet Daytona was still a southern town, and as the decades unfolded this became clearer than ever.

Nonetheless, having laid solid foundations in the first decade, Bethune's school activities appeared to be headed toward continued success. She attracted large numbers of students and faculty, erected more buildings, and pushed the budget ever upward, so that in 1918 she operated a four-year high school under the banner of the Daytona Normal and Industrial Institute. By April 1920, forty-seven girls had completed the full high-school course, and ten taught in Florida's public schools. In conjunction with her educational work, Bethune took on wide-ranging social service responsibilities, particularly with the Red Cross. She became known throughout the East, and her contacts eventually extended to Washington, D.C. On March 7, 1918, U.S. Vice President Thomas R.

It is often forgotten that the young Mary McLeod planned to be a missionary. This photograph was taken during her year of study at Dwight Moody's Institute for Home and Foreign Missions. [Bethune Museum and Archives]

Marshall spoke to hundreds of eager listeners in the Daytona Institute's new auditorium.

Bethune's tremendous success with her girls' school led to its transformation. In 1923, with more than 300 students and a debt-free physical plant valued at $250,000, it became coeducational; the next year, while promoting its high school, it inaugurated a junior college curriculum. These events occurred under the auspices of the Board of Education for Negroes of the mostly northern Methodist Episcopal Church, which had assumed responsibility for the school. The board wanted to merge Bethune's school with the coeducational Cookman Institute in Jacksonville. The combined institution became Bethune-Cookman College (BCC), named in honor of Mary McLeod Bethune and in recognition of Cookman Institute, founded in 1872 and named for Alfred Cookman, a white New Jersey Methodist minister who had passionately preached social justice and support for Black Americans. The new name epitomized the continuing interracial commitment of Bethune's institution, which was probably the only college of its day to be named specifically to highlight such a commitment.

The merger had practical results as well. Bethune achieved institutional support and college status for her virtually unendowed school just in time. From the mid-1920s onward, the downturn in the economy, the demise of the tradition of individual donors, and the increasing selectivity of philanthropic agencies translated into the closing of many independent Black institutions. Even some colleges affiliated with denominations went under, and most of those that survived did so only barely. This was the case with BCC, which had to close its hospital in 1927. Indeed, the Great Depression started to hit when the Florida land boom collapsed in 1925, and it intensified with two severe hurricanes in subsequent years. Then the bottom fell out with the stock market crash in 1929.

Although she was sometimes given to dramatic hyperbole, when Bethune observed in a February 1935 letter that in the Great Depression "we are passing through the most severe test of our lives," she proclaimed an unadulterated truth. Her hardships as a college president defied exaggeration; but she refused to relinquish the hard-won ground on which she had staked her life. BCC was the only Black college in Florida south of St. Augustine, and had it ceased to exist, many would have lost the chance for college. If white Americans could maintain institutions of higher learning, the indomitable Bethune believed she could do likewise regardless of the handicaps of race, gender, and relative poverty. For this

determination, Bethune paid a high price. In 1933 she canceled all athletic and social affairs, periodically cut the heat off in dormitories, and slashed teacher salaries. Bethune, a champion of vocationalism, even dropped her business course. A facilitator of thousands of scholarships, she withdrew in the middle of the semester the work scholarships essential to many. Consequently, by fives and tens, students "quietly packed up their effects and slipped away " (*Advocate* 1933).

Despite the ordeal of running a college for more than a decade with a gaping insufficiency of funds, throughout this period Bethune presented to the public a positive and inspiring presence. She understood that in fund-raising one had to project optimism, enthusiasm, confidence, and thankfulness. She succeeded in keeping the doors open. Moreover, in 1935, with two new brick buildings, a dining hall, and a science hall, she augmented plant facilities by $80,000. Most important, she steadily raised the caliber of the academic program to comply with accrediting agencies' requirements. In 1934, of the sixty-four students who completed the junior college curriculum, fifty-six concurrently earned state teaching certificates. The next year, in recognition of her standard junior college, the NAACP bestowed on Bethune its annual Spingarn Award, its highest honor.

The year afterward, Bethune's relationship to her college changed. She became in effect a part-time president when she assumed a demanding government job in Washington, D.C., with the National Youth Administration. Under this arrangement of divided priorities, Bethune kept the college functioning by relying on Bertha Loving Mitchell, the secretary-treasurer for business matters, and on James Bond, the academic dean. Yet regardless of this assistance, Bethune had taken upon herself impossible tasks: pursuing national interests while concurrently serving as her school's chief executive. The latter meant nonstop solicitations to individual donors, foundations, and government agencies. Bethune suffered grievously from her colossal burdens. Her health broke in 1940, and months of medical care and recuperation followed.

Despite Bethune's part-time presidency, BCC reflected, as it always had previously, Mary McLeod Bethune. It continued to cultivate better race relations and to emphasize Christian values and practices. Also, it still championed vocationalism—agriculture, secretarial work, cooking, and sewing—in tandem with academics. Symbolizing in 1942 a heightened vocationalism was the addition of a Trades Building for National Defense, a building Bethune had fi-

Mary McLeod Bethune first came to national attention as the director of the Negro Division of the National Youth Administration. She is pictured here (in 1938) in the famous "Black Cabinet" portrait of the Black members of Franklin Delano Roosevelt's administration. [Scurlock Studio]

nanced through her government agency in Washington. Young people trained there for occupations in auto mechanics, masonry, electricity, and tailoring. Academics also enjoyed renewal at BCC. In 1939-40, for example, the school graduated 118 junior college students. The next year it opened a new library and inaugurated the third-year program in teacher education; in 1942 it added the fourth year. Bethune had developed a senior college.

Though accurately reflecting Bethune's vision, the dualism of vocational and collegiate programs would prove unrealistic for the underfunded BCC. Bethune escaped having to choose between them by giving up the presidency on December 15, 1942, because of recurring ill health. At that time she exercised the same control over the school that she had in its beginning, but now the institution boasted total cash receipts of more than $155,000 and a $600,000 physical plant that included a thirty-four-acre campus with fourteen buildings plus a farm.

Although Bethune had become committed to the education of both men and women, her interest in elevating females was so compelling that she found channels beyond her school for achieving this. For many years she worked through the National Association of Colored Women (NACW), America's premier Black women's organization in the first quar-

ter of the twentieth century. Fully controlling a girls' boarding school provided Bethune with an excellent institutional base for NACW's charitable and civic work. Moreover, she benefited from associating with leaders of Daytona's influential Palmetto Club, an affiliate of the General Federation of Women's Clubs, the white counterpart to NACW. She enjoyed the coaching of associate Frances Keyser, the highly respected first president of NACW's Empire State Federation. Given these factors plus her own missionary spirit and aggressiveness, Bethune's ascent in NACW was guaranteed.

Her essential grounding for national leadership occurred during her presidency of the Florida Federation of Colored Women's Clubs (1917-24). Bethune brought to the office the full resources of her school plus her businesslike efficiency manifested in fruitful conventions, a realistic constitution, published minutes, and a respectable periodical. Always she set an inspiring example for club sisters as they confronted great issues. Obviously, the first of these was responding to America's entry into World War I. This Bethune did by promoting canning and preserving food, making articles for soldiers and their families, buying Liberty bonds, and contributing to Red Cross chapters and emergency circles. The second great issue was female enfranchisement. When, in September 1920, the voter rolls opened to women in Daytona in accord with the Nineteenth Amendment to the Constitution, braving the intimidations of the Ku Klux Klan, Bethune registered along with her entire institute faculty and staff and other local Black women attuned to her leadership. A third issue, made all the more urgent due to white supremacists, was forging links with egalitarian-minded white women for the common welfare. Bethune handled this primarily by organizing in 1920 the Southeastern Federation of Colored Women, to which she brought superb organizing and human relations skills and an inspiring presence. Though the scope of this southern aggregation transcended race relations, one of its major triumphs was supplying leadership for the women's general committee of the regional Commission on Interracial Cooperation headquartered in Atlanta.

The most demanding issue Bethune faced stemmed from state conditions relative to a wholesome rehabilitative environment for delinquent Black girls. The state provided accommodations only for adult lawbreakers at the state prison in Raiford. Therefore, the Florida Federation of Colored Women's Clubs established in Ocala an alternative facility for up to twelve residents. On Sunday, September 20,

1921, Bethune opened the new Industrial School with her arm around the first girl committed to the federation's care. From then on she shouldered the responsibility for its efficient operation, which included paying two matrons. A year and a half into operation, the school's needs were compelling enough for President Bethune to write to one matron, "as long as I have a penny I am willing to share it with you. Don't give up" (NACWC 1923). Bethune shared deeply both from her own pocketbook and from renewed financial campaigns. She and the subsequent federation president managed to obtain relief in the late 1920s when the Florida legislature finally appropriated funds for this facility just as it had been doing since 1913 for the Industrial School in Ocala that nurtured white female juvenile delinquents.

In 1924, Bethune achieved the highest office to which a Black woman could then aspire, the presidency of NACW. During her tenure, she turned the organization increasingly beyond itself to the broader society. The National Council of Women of the United States was NACW's primary institutional mechanism for expanded contacts. In 1925, this council of thirty-eight organizations—thirty-seven white and one Black—was the avenue for NACW's partici-

Always interested in world affairs, Mary McLeod Bethune was an adviser to the U.S. delegation at the 1945 founding conference of the United Nations in San Francisco. She is pictured here at the conference with W.E.B. Du Bois (left) and Walter White of the NAACP. [Bethune Museum and Archives]

pation in the International Council of Women at its quinquennial conference, which attracted representatives from thirty-five countries to Washington, D.C. Through unprecedented planning, Bethune had gotten her chief lieutenants from around the country to the meeting and had insisted upon desegregated seating at all events. When this policy was violated on the evening of May 5, 1925, NACW members and other Black Americans walked out. Bethune vented their rage publicly by explaining that it was humiliating to the United States to be segregated in the presence of women from all over the world. The International Council then in earnest ensured open seating. Consequently, Bethune and her members returned to tracking the sixty-four resolutions of the meeting dealing with issues as diverse as approval for the League of Nations and the rights of children. This international meeting whetted Bethune's appetite for foreign travel, and she subsequently visited nine European countries in 1927 as the recognized emissary of African-American women. She observed that other large minorities suffered oppression similar to that of Black Americans and she saw a rose garden in Marseilles, France, with a big black velvet rose growing as luxuriantly as the white rose, the red rose, and all of the others. From that point on, the imagery of humanity as a rose garden became Bethune's unique symbol of universality.

So strong was Bethune's sense of this universality that she espoused a limitless vision for her organization. It could be the equal of any other women's voluntary association. It could be great particularly in relating to people of color around the world and in assuming a position on salient national and international questions. Even before assuming office, Bethune began to nurture the organizational unity and machinery necessary to realize her aspirations. The centerpiece of her program was a national headquarters in Washington, D.C., operated by a full-time paid executive secretary. For this cause she recruited Rebecca Stiles Taylor of Savannah, the talented president of the Georgia Federation of Colored Women, to join her college staff in order to serve as her chief NACW aide.

Obstacles loomed forbiddingly. One was the crunching 1925-28 economy that preceded the Great Depression. NACW possessed relatively little discretionary income, and so economic pressures bombarded it from all sides. Another hurdle was the great schism existing in NACW over the advisability of establishing an independent headquarters. For about a decade, some NACW leaders had supported the Washington, D.C., home of Frederick Douglass, the

nineteenth-century civil rights giant, as a suitable NACW headquarters, and as an incentive for clubwomen to pay for its upkeep. Bethune's position was that NACW members should persist in the noble cause of maintaining the Douglass home but should establish headquarters elsewhere because NACW did not and could not legally own the Douglass property. Bethune's sense of business and awareness of the real possibility of power struggles between the Douglass home trustees and NACW elected officials (even though at times these were the same people) never permitted her to waver in acquiring a building to which NACW held the title. Bethune's view prevailed but always against a powerful undertow of resistance that necessitated superstrenuous efforts such as her visit to twenty-five states in one thirteen-month period. Finally, on July 31, 1928, with more than half the $25,000 mortgage paid, Bethune and NACW proudly opened, with appropriate ceremony, an imposing detached red brick building as the organization's first home. Furthermore, they installed in it a paid secretary. This was the first time that a national Black organization was designed to function in Washington, D.C., in the same way as scores of other national groups.

Had NACW's constitution failed to limit a president to four years in office, Bethune may have stayed on indefinitely. She loved the presidency, though she may have found a prolonged tenure unsuitable. Although NACW had always taken a stand on some public questions directly affecting its membership, it had been basically a decentralized organization responding to local and state self-help projects and, later, national self-help projects—maintaining the Douglass home and establishing a $50,000 scholarship fund. Bethune had attempted to mold it into a unitary body that could forcefully and consistently project itself into a myriad of public issues as the authoritative voice of Black women. Although suited perfectly to the spirit of the equalizing decade for women and the renaissance decade for Black Americans, the imposition of an orientation alien to many members faced rugged opposition in the long run. When the Great Depression dealt a blow to visionary projections, all but the stoutest hearts tended to retreat. The new NACW powers did so with a vengeance, contracting the organization's twenty-two departments covering a broad range of interests down to only two that focused almost exclusively on the Black family.

Bethune, however, could not flinch from her passion for Black women's participation in the mainstream of the body politic and found reinforcement for it in the Depression. When more than 25 percent of Black families were on relief and multitudes more were applying, Bethune longed for Black women to become a channel through which public funds could reach some of them. She wanted Black women to play a substantive role—as did white men and women and Black men—in the governmental process undergirding individual and family survival. Bethune believed that she and her sisters could best assume such activities through an overarching organization that encompassed all existing national women's organizations. To some degree modeled after the National Council of Women, this would be a national council of Black women. It would "cement a spirit of cooperation and unified effort" among women's groups so that they could "speak as one voice and one mind for the highest good of the race" (*Weekly Echo* 1936). Bethune was the perfect creator for this new organization, for she possessed not only its central idea but also the organizational expertise to accomplish it. Moreover, she enjoyed preeminent leadership stature among Black women, as symbolized in the Spingarn Award and through her strong identification with a federal agency. Consequently, on December 5, 1935, in New York's Harlem, thirty representative women of voluntary associations voted the National Council of Negro Women (NCNW) into being. They also made Bethune the president, a position she occupied for almost fourteen years until she relinquished it in November 1949.

Predictably, President Bethune worked wonders with the NCNW machinery. By the end of her tenure the council included twenty-two national women's organizations, including professional and occupational groups, both broadly based and subject-restricted academic sororities, Christian denominational societies, fraternal associations, auxiliaries, and various other aggregations. In addition, NCNW boasted eighty-two local councils and numerous individual life memberships. Bethune left in place noteworthy mechanisms for effective operations such as a debt-free headquarters building in Washington, D.C., a paid executive secretary, and a proud periodical.

Before these assets materialized, however, NCNW proceeded to raise Black women, for the first time ever, to sustained visibility in the nation's capital. Bethune propelled NCNW to the forefront of women's race organizations in the national life of the country through its "Conference on Governmental Cooperation in the Approach to the Problems of Negro Women and Children," held on April 4, 1938, at the Department of the Interior and the White House. Sixty-five of America's most civic-minded

women of African descent met with government personnel to discuss greater Black female integration into social welfare bureaucracies. The conference was a harbinger of what became almost annual visits of NCNW members to the White House—powerful public relations parades projecting a new imagery of Black women as citizens in American democracy.

The 1938 conference also revealed Bethune's basic strategy for advancement, which was to win policy-making and management positions in government for competent Black women. This emphasis upon upper-level employment for the "talented tenth" was to benefit the Black masses. At its first White House conference, NCNW found that Black women and children failed to participate in welfare programs in proportion to their need because of the virtual exclusion of Black women from designing and administering them. Bethune chose to chip away at the era's strong apartheid practices and gender prejudice through conferences, petitions, civil service reform, and other means that would provide greater opportunities for African-American female leadership.

Even though Bethune readily won recognition of her council from First Lady Eleanor Roosevelt, it was only after an episode in 1941 in which the War Department initially barred and then accepted NCNW as a member of its women's advisory council that organized Black women could participate in government programs at a level somewhat approaching that of other women's associations. Like nothing else had, this validated Bethune's concept of gaining power for her constituency through a unified council. With the War Department's acknowledging NCNW as the representative of Black women, the private sector followed suit, as symbolized in the National Council of Women's decision to accept NCNW into membership. As a result, NCNW enjoyed a wider platform from which to promote its fundamental concerns about issues of federal employment, effective enfranchisement, antilynching, and internationalism.

Bethune's determination to involve herself and her organization in international affairs resulted in her participation as an adviser to the U.S. delegation in the 1945 founding conference of the United Nations in San Francisco. By that time the crisis of World War II had so elevated the value of national unity that NCNW had interacted with various government and private agencies to promote the general welfare, as in its sponsorship of the S.S. *Harriet Tubman*, the first Liberty ship to honor a Black woman. In addition, it had devised its own wartime projects. Its greatest pride stemmed from Black women's participation in the military. This had been a priority goal of NCNW and other Black organizations, but one that leading white women's organizations viewed indifferently. The goal was not achieved in all service branches until 1949, when the women's Marine Corps finally admitted a Black applicant. In that year, NCNW pledged to work for more public housing, army desegregation, and President Harry S. Truman's civil rights program.

As the NCNW program in 1949 suggested, Bethune concerned herself with improving the status of all Black Americans regardless of socioeconomic position or gender. In this emphasis, she was most effective in assuming the role of the preeminent race leader at large from 1936 to 1945. From slavery until the recent present, a race leader in white-controlled America could at best win concessions to ameliorate some hardships. More specifically, in New Deal Washington, D.C., a race leader was needed to keep track of Black involvement in proliferating federal programs, to develop recommendations to enhance Black welfare through them, and then to effect contacts to facilitate consideration of the recommendations. Bethune brought sterling qualities and a new political edge to this self-appointed role. She was tied to the leadership of the frontline organizations including the NAACP, the National Urban League, and the Association for the Study of Negro Life and History, and she was held in the highest esteem in Black academia. Moreover, Bethune tackled the problems of African-Americans both intelligently and ardently. She dealt effectively with all types of people, using the language and nuances of diplomacy. She knew how to articulate and dramatize her causes; and she was in her sixties, an age that gave her more distinction than she would have had otherwise in a world of men unaccustomed to women in corridors of political power.

Because Bethune needed a highly trained staff wholeheartedly committed to Black advancement, she organized what became the Federal Council on Negro Affairs, a highly informal network popularly called the Black Cabinet. Composed primarily of New Deal race specialists in September 1939, it consisted of twenty-seven men and three women working mostly in short-term emergency agencies such as the Works Progress Administration (WPA). With generous assistance from Housing Administrator Robert Weaver, Bethune maintained the Black Cabinet with an iron fist inside a velvet glove, a remarkable achievement especially considering that others before her had per-

Ever the world citizen, Mary McLeod Bethune is pictured here with Madame Pandit, India's representative to the United Nations, Ralph Bunche of the United Nations, and President Harry Truman. The occasion is the NCNW's 1949 annual convention, which honored Bethune on her resignation as president. [Bethune Museum and Archives]

Eleanor Roosevelt was one of Mary McLeod Bethune's most visible and vocal champions. This photograph was taken around 1950. [Bethune Museum and Archives]

mitted such an association to falter. The cabinet was newly possible because the government recruited more than a hundred Black managers and administrators for government positions during the Great Depression. These Black Americans collectively constituted the twentieth-century emergence of a Black political presence in Washington, D.C.

The only other prerequisite for at-large leadership was entree into the capital's inner sanctums of power. Even though African-Americans lacked the political and economic clout that would have ensured them hearings on request, arranging such hearings

proved easy for Bethune. She used a personal relationship with Eleanor Roosevelt. Having brought Bethune into government in 1936, Mrs. Roosevelt then extended her carte blanche assistance as long as the Roosevelts lived in the White House. This enabled Bethune to extend her at-large activity a year after leaving government. Mrs. Roosevelt interceded with a wide range of federal officials, including her husband, on Bethune's behalf, and Bethune developed an easygoing friendship with President Franklin Roosevelt. She gave the impression that their relationship was very close—an impression that generally enhanced her status and permitted her to talk with virtually anyone in government. The price Bethune gladly paid for this was loyalty to the Roosevelts, particularly at election time.

With all the factors for at-large leadership in view, Bethune sought to heighten the racial consciousness of the nation but most specifically that of the federal bureaucracy, since it was the institution possessing the greatest power to address Black inequality. In this continuing effort, her most sensational feat was the federally sponsored National Conference on the Problems of the Negro and Negro Youth, held January 6-8, 1937, at the Department of Labor with guest speakers including Eleanor Roosevelt and the Secretaries of Commerce and Agriculture. Bringing together for the first time the Black Cabinet and the most important leaders in African-American life from the NAACP to Bethune's NCNW nucleus, the conference defined the most pressing difficulties of Black Americans in an apartheid culture and outlined the needed government responses. It advanced pragmatic solutions for immediate implementation, advocating a fair share of federal resources to Black citizens within the legally segregated South rather than insisting upon integration.

Framing its deliberations into four categories, the conference developed many recommendations. Some of the most prominent were as follows. Under the category "Security of Life and Equal Protection under the Law," it called for a federal antilynching law, equal access to the ballot in federal elections, and the elimination of segregation and discrimination on interstate carriers. Under "Improved Health and Housing Conditions," it emphasized federal aid to reduce tuberculosis and syphilis among Black Americans, the building of health centers in Black neighborhoods with Black staff, a guarantee to Black veterans that they would have access to veterans' hospitals, insurance of Black involvement as tenants and managers in all federal housing projects, and an end to the total exclusion of Black Americans in the new suburban communities developed through the Resettlement Administration. Under the category "Adequate Educational and Recreational Opportunity," it asked for an equitable share of federal education dollars and recreational and educational centers as integral parts of all public housing projects. The recognition of economics as the preeminent Black issue in the Great Depression evoked a barrage of resolutions, including the provision that Black workers receive the same apprenticeship training as did white workers; the abolition of the practice of requiring a photograph with a civil service application; the

denial of benefits from federal legislation to any union excluding Black Americans; decent wages and standardized norms for domestic workers; the extension of Social Security benefits to domestic and agricultural workers (the areas employing the overwhelming number of Black Americans); and the end of discriminatory employment practices in the army and navy and all branches of the federal government and in all projects receiving federal funds, such as the Tennessee Valley Authority.

No other general Black meeting on civil rights during the Roosevelt administrations generated the interest and publicity of this 1937 conference. It signified not only that Bethune had "gathered everything and everybody under her very ample wing" (Lawson 1937), as one journalist phrased it, but also that she was in the middle of a broad Black consensus and could speak truly as Black America's race representative at large in making the wide-ranging conference report her agenda for leadership. The most prominent formalized channels in which she pursued support for specific conference recommendations included her women's council and youth agency, the President's Special Committee on Farm Tenancy, and the Southern Conference for Human Welfare. Requiring more time and effort still were the numerous private meetings held to advance conference resolutions. Federal acceptance of them was necessary if Black workers were to attain high-echelon government jobs. In this area, with the exception of Black Cabinet members (who were confined chiefly to advising and assisting), Black Americans were virtually unrepresented. For example, in January 1940, only one Black federal judge held court in the United States, and he presided in the Virgin Islands. Race-based discrimination barred more than 13 million Americans from the higher responsibilities of democracy. As Bethune pressed the employment issue, typically with either Franklin or Eleanor Roosevelt, she had in hand lists of positions and names of Black Americans qualified to fill them. Nevertheless, the results she sought had to await the Black Revolution of the 1960s.

As a leader at large, Bethune identified with high visibility programs promising Black advancement outside of government. She even walked the New Negro Alliance's picket line in 1939 to support the hiring of Black clerks in a Washington, D.C., drugstore chain. She joined A. Philip Randolph's march on Washington movement in 1941, and nationwide support for the threatened demonstration led to Roosevelt's most important civil rights action. His Executive Order No. 8802 called for hiring in government and in defense industries without regard to race, and it established the Fair Employment Practices Commission.

Since Bethune was an administration insider and thus required to demonstrate loyalty to the administration, it was fortunate that she firmly believed in both the president and his programs. As the 1937 conference recommendations suggested, she was fully conversant with the glaring shortcomings of the administration's civil rights record and she flatly stated time and again that Black citizens could not be satisfied or complacent. Yet at the same time, she implied that the Republicans offered less than the Democrats and she exhorted her constituency to uphold the administration's efforts for relief, recovery, and reform. As wartime considerations emerged, her commitment to the administration became even greater. She believed that Black Americans must oppose Nazi Germany's Adolf Hitler and that they must support the president's foreign policy. Her concern was consuming enough for her to put aside her other commitments in order to secure, behind closed doors, an all-white training center in Daytona Beach, Florida, for the Women's Army Corps. Aside from the economic vitality it promised her hometown, Bethune must have reasoned that the facility would not be injurious to Black women because they could receive identical training at Fort Des Moines, Iowa. For a Black leader, this action, though unpublicized and controversial, required courage and constituted one measure of Bethune's devotion to country.

For her untiring patriotism and promotion of democratic ideals, Mary McLeod Bethune reaped the wrath of the congressional House Committee on Un-American Activities. In the early 1940s, it branded her a Communist. She suffered grievously from this stigma. Because of it, as late as 1952, she was denied a public school platform in Englewood, New Jersey. A groundswell of public support, however, eventually made her appearance there possible.

Though investing time and energy in at-large activities, Bethune's focus in Washington, D.C., from 1936 to 1943 had to be upon her job in the National Youth Administration (NYA), where she became director of the Negro division. The directorship (which became official in 1939) represented the highest federal appointment held by a Black woman and facilitated her functioning in the agency's upper hierarchy. Behind both the appointment and the agency stood Franklin and Eleanor Roosevelt. They greatly enhanced Bethune's work, as did Aubrey Willis Williams, NYA's sole head administrator, who came to the agency via his deputy directorship in the government's massive Works Progress Administration.

Along with the Civilian Conservation Corps, the NYA was Washington's prescription for enabling youth to weather the Great Depression. During its 1935-44 lifespan, the agency offered young people ages sixteen to twenty-four job placement services and work relief through programs for those both in and out of school. When national defense became the country's preoccupation, NYA concentrated on training youth for war production jobs. During its final year, it transported trained youth when necessary to areas of labor shortages and then housed them temporarily in regional induction centers while they learned the ways of a new community. Through these arrangements Black Americans, and women in particular, found employment in manufacturing as opposed to the agricultural and service sectors. Before budget-cutting imperatives conspired with the agency's powerful opposition—the educational establishment anxious to protect vocational territory and a resurgent Republican bloc determined to stifle New Deal relief—the NYA spent over $685 million on several million youth. Moreover, it firmly established the concept of direct federal assistance to deserving youth both in and out of school—a concept notably revived in the Great Society of the 1960s.

As a dazzling and magnetic personality, Bethune elevated support for the entire NYA program among Black and white citizens. Yet, like most of her Black Cabinet associates, her specific function was to promote equal treatment for Black employees within her agency. Though these young people needed NYA benefits more than any other category of youth, in the racial order of that era they were the least likely to get them. There was no way that proportionate benefits for Black youth could be realized. Nonetheless, with a staff consisting of four successive excellent assistant directors and an extremely competent secretary, Arabella Denniston—who had graduated from the Daytona Institute—Bethune pursued this goal. Her office enabled the NYA to come closer to approximating equity between Black and white benefits than perhaps any other federal entity. Generally, African-American leaders lauded the NYA and worked zealously but unsuccessfully to establish it as a permanent federal institution. In the middle of the Depression, they valued most the work-study grants to students in school; during World War II, NYA shop training and work experience typically were the best available to Black youth.

In the late 1930s, of necessity Bethune crisscrossed the country to realize the full potential of her NYA job, because at that time her agency maintained a decentralized structure permitting state directors

*After President Franklin Roosevelt's death, Mary McLeod Bethune continued to be
actively involved in the affairs of national government. She is shown here with President
Harry Truman and other Black leaders. [Bethune Museum and Archives]*

considerable autonomy. These white directors typically oversaw projects for Black participants that were of lesser complexity and quality than those for whites. Although the white directors and Black participants sometimes divided along racial lines over an issue, Bethune managed to bring the sides together or, regardless of her position, at least to emerge politically unscathed.

Though the virtues of travel were indisputable, Bethune's most concrete contributions to the NYA derived from wielding influence in Washington, D.C. As the agency assumed new programs, she saw to it that Black participants were included in initial phases, as in the Civilian Pilot Training Program (1939-41), through which six Black colleges offered flight instruction. Their programs were foundational to Black pilots in the military. In the agency's established programs, Bethune lobbied for equitable benefits. She pushed for outstanding Black projects, especially ones centered in skilled training for modern manufacturing processes and proportionate job placement services. Wherever possible, Bethune sought to make expenditures equitable. She successfully moved the agency to adopt a policy in 1939 assuring a proportionate distribution of secondary school-aid funds between Black and white students. Moreover, she persuaded the NYA to create a specific resource tai-

lored to the special difficulties Black students faced in higher education: her Special Negro Higher Education Fund advanced funding equality by disbursing $609,930 to 4,119 students over seven years.

Bethune believed that Black involvement in the initial stages of new programs and equity in established programs, both in quality and funding, could all be advanced through placing Black personnel in key positions. She saw Black leadership in every phase of the NYA as translating into greater services to Black youth. She argued that where racism produced dual programs, at least Black Americans should have opportunities for leadership in one of them. In 1941, Bethune's most impressive achievement was to facilitate employment for twenty-seven Black administrative assistants with state NYA directors. Though the effectiveness of these officials varied greatly, they did, in fact, augment benefits for their constituencies.

Through her NYA employment, Bethune reached the zenith of her career. In the years immediately afterward, she focused on her national women's council. Increasingly, she spent less time in the capital in favor of greater involvement in the Daytona community and heightened support for an internationalism that projected the inherent unity of humankind. Moreover, to promote her social and educational ideals, she turned her home into the Mary McLeod Bethune

Foundation. Another highlight of her active retirement was travel. In January 1952, she fulfilled a cherished girlhood dream by visiting Africa. This was occasioned by her official representation of the United States at the inauguration of William Tubman as president of Liberia.

Bethune died of a heart attack in her home of more than fifty years on May 18, 1955.

By any measure, through more than three decades Mary McLeod Bethune was an extraordinary public figure, particularly considering the daunting obstacles to opportunity she faced as a poor, Black, southern female born between America's first and second Reconstructions. In promoting opportunities for young people to obtain an education and employment, and in asserting both personal and organizational equality, she lifted service to others to an exalted high.

Bethune fine-tuned her leadership to the racial climate in which she lived, a climate never characterized by a national commitment to change the subordinate status of African-Americans but one affected greatly by the exigencies of the Great Depression and two world wars. This meant that though Black Americans lacked equal opportunity, they experienced increasing opportunity. Bethune maneuvered at any given time within superimposed restraints that loosened only slightly from the 1910s to the 1950s. In her early years she emphasized the hallmarks of accommodation—vocationalism, self-help, and skillful appeals to influential whites; later she could agitate for higher educational opportunities, government assistance, and full citizenship rights. Though using the program and methods of Booker T. Washington in developing a private school in the South, she found it more difficult than he, even though she had vision, determination, an intuitive understanding of people, and persuasive powers. Because she was a Black woman, she had to work harder to get less. Compared to the financial resources of Washington's Tuskegee Institute, Bethune's school wallowed in poverty. Still, Bethune exercised a level of leadership unavailable to any Black male leader of the era. She led a female constituency into symbolic participation in national affairs. In the 1930s and 1940s, Bethune elevated her women's council to a level approaching that of other national women's organizations in Washington, D.C. She created the image and reality of Black women going to the White House on affairs of state.

In assuming leadership during the New Deal, Bethune's gender posed no handicap. Supported by the Black Cabinet, she confronted influential federal officials and the nation with all issues relative to the status of Black Americans. Always she pursued an array of benefits for all Black Americans. Her forte was facilitating the flow of NYA funds to Black youth for high school and college work-study, vocational training, and job placement. Her most identifiable beneficiaries came from the "talented tenth." At one level, they received essential assistance in paying their higher-education bills from her Special Negro Fund. This was the only financial resource any Black New Dealer controlled. At another level, they secured responsible jobs in the federal establishment, setting precedents for the future that might have been unavailable otherwise. The most notable of these were in the officer cadre of the Women's Army Corps and in the NYA state offices. In the latter, the Black administrative assistants to state directors gave Bethune what amounted to a field staff across the country—another first for a Black New Dealer. So tremendous was her impact that in July 1974 a seventeen-foot bronze statue of her was placed in the District of Columbia public park, a short distance from the Capitol. It was the first statue in the city to portray either a woman or a Black American.

Though long deemed the most influential Black American woman, more recently, a scholarly consensus has emerged ranking Bethune as one of the most important Black Americans in history, along with Frederick Douglass, W.E.B. Du Bois, and Martin Luther King, Jr. Unflinchingly, she championed the democratic values that define the nation. She took personally the well-being of the body politic, particularly in the crisis of two world wars. No less a personage than President Franklin D. Roosevelt viewed Bethune as a great patriot devoted to advancing all Americans. In fact, Bethune's accomplishments were so impressive in relationship to resources, and her interest in people regardless of nationality and locality was so genuine, that any freedom-loving country could feel proud to claim her as its own.

[See also BETHUNE-COOKMAN COLLEGE; EDUCATION; FEMINISM IN THE TWENTIETH CENTURY; JIM CROW LAWS; NATIONAL COUNCIL OF NEGRO WOMEN; SOCIAL WELFARE MOVEMENT.]

BIBLIOGRAPHY

Bennett, Lerone, Jr. "The 50 Most Important Figures in U.S. Black History," *Ebony* (February 1989); Bethune, Mary McLeod. "My Last Will and Testament," *Ebony* (August 1955); Holt, Rackham. *Mary McLeod Bethune* (1964); Knapp, Elizabeth. "Volusia County Recalls: The Day WACS Arrived," *Pelican* (May 16, 1982); Lawson, Edward. "Straight from the Capitol," *Charleston Messenger* (January

23, 1937); Lefall, Dolores C. and Janet I. Sims. "Mary McLeod Bethune—the Educator," *Journal of Negro Education* (Summer 1976); *NAW*; *NBAW*; Peare, Catherine. *Mary McLeod Bethune* (1951); Smith, Elaine M. "Mary McLeod Bethune and the National Youth Administration." In *Clio Was a Woman: Studies in the History of American Women*, ed. Mabel E. Deutrich and Virginia C. Purdy (1980); Taylor, Joseph Earl. "The National Youth Conferences on the Problems of the Negro and Negro Youth 1937 and 1939," Ph.D. diss. (1985); *Weekly Echo* (December 4, 1936).

Bethune's papers can be found in a number of manuscript collections, including: Bethune Foundation and Bethune-Cookman College Archives, Bethune-Cookman College, Daytona Beach, Florida; Amistad Research Center, New Orleans, Louisiana; National Association of Colored Women's Clubs papers, Headquarters, Washington, D.C.; and at Fisk University, Nashville, Tennessee. See also National Council of Negro Women Papers, National Archives for Black Women's History, Washington, D.C.; Eleanor Roosevelt papers and Franklin D. Roosevelt papers, Franklin D. Roosevelt Library, Hyde Park, New York; and National Youth Administration, Record Group 199, National Archives, Washington, D.C.

ELAINE M. SMITH

BETHUNE-COOKMAN COLLEGE

Bethune-Cookman College, a living legacy of Mary McLeod Bethune, is the only historically Black college founded by a Black woman that continues to thrive today.

In 1904, Mary McLeod Bethune went to Daytona Beach, Florida, to respond to the Black community's need for education. The Eastcoast Railway had attracted thousands of Black workers to this coastal community, and their children needed to be educated. A daughter of ex-slaves in South Carolina, Mary Bethune was the answer to their prayers. Along with faith in God, this Black woman had been educated in, and been a teacher at, girls' schools, and she had a missionary zeal to effect change among Black people, especially Black women.

The Daytona Normal and Industrial Institute for Negro Girls began with faith in God, $1.50, and five little girls. Although she was the mother of a son, Bethune had a challenging vision that included the education of female children. Influenced primarily by Lucy Laney of the Haines Institute and Booker T. Washington of the Tuskegee Institute, Bethune's initial curriculum focused on religion and the three Rs. These primary skills were later complemented by vocational training in domestic work, sewing, and

farming. Indeed, Bethune's school reflected the era with its emphasis on traditional female vocational skills, and this emphasis endured throughout Bethune's tenure as president and president emeritus.

When the school merged with the all-male Cookman Institute in Jacksonville, Florida, in 1923, the curriculum broadened to include Cookman's mission of training women for the public school system while training men to preach the gospel. The new school was known as the Daytona Cookman Collegiate Institute until 1933, when it was renamed Bethune-Cookman College. It proved to be a beneficial merger, establishing a source of stable funding by the Methodist Episcopal Church, and providing an infusion of male students while allowing the continuity of traditional female education to remain intact. In fact, the first four-year degree program to be instituted, in 1943, was in teacher education. Thus, at the time of the historic 1954 U.S. Supreme Court decision *Brown* v. *Board of Education*, the primary contribution of Bethune-Cookman College was educating teachers for the mostly segregated public school systems of Florida.

By the time of the merger with Cookman in 1923, the original five girls had increased to several hundred. The male population has increased gradually, however, but the majority of graduates have been female. During World War II, when a decline in enrollment was expected, enrollment actually increased because the number of female students increased. The college survived the war by serving as a training center for women to participate in the wartime economy. In 1944, 111 women passed secretarial training and were placed in various government agencies in Washington, D.C., and other locations throughout the United States and Europe. That same year, sixty-five girls volunteered their services to the college in the production and harvest of food to aid in the war effort. This organization, called the Farmettes, was recognized by the Florida Education Department and touted as a model for other colleges in the state.

No doubt the college received attention and was awarded government contracts during the war because of its president emeritus, Mary McLeod Bethune, who capitalized on her prominence in order to draw public attention to the college. For instance, a forum called the Women for Peace Conference was held on the Bethune-Cookman College campus in 1952. Bethune and Mrs. Samuel Caverts, a theologian and member of the World Council of Churches, cochaired this racially integrated forum on women's and minority rights. Academic freedom, fair employment, and equal political access and participation for women and minority groups in America were among the timeless issues discussed at this historic event, and the list of participants reads like a who's who among women. Representatives of the Young Women's Christian Association (YWCA), the League of Women Voters, the Republican National Committee, the National Council of Women, the National Council of Churches, the National Council of Jewish Women, the Democratic National Committee, and the Women's Bureau of the Department of Labor were among the more than 150 participants. This conference, occurring only three years before her death, demonstrated Bethune's unrelenting desire to achieve equality and sisterhood among women in America.

Today Bethune-Cookman College comprises approximately fifty-two acres and thirty-two buildings and produces graduates in twenty-five major degree programs. Women hold high administrative positions, and female students continue to make up the greater percentage of the more than ten thousand graduates as well as a majority of the international student population, which numbers around twenty-five hundred. Female students are represented not only in the traditional fields of nursing and teaching. They also make up a large percentage of students in nontraditional fields, such as business, engineering, and law. Mary McLeod Bethune's legacy, Bethune-Cookman College, continues to make a difference for women in the world.

BIBLIOGRAPHY

Mary McLeod Bethune Administrative papers, Bethune-Cookman College Administrative Archives; Richard V. Moore Administrative papers, Bethune-Cookman College Administrative Archives; both collections at Bethune-Cookman College, Daytona Beach, Florida.

SHEILA Y. FLEMMING

BIRTH CONTROL MOVEMENT

The fertility rates of African-American women shifted dramatically from the late nineteenth century to World War II. This fertility drop is usually understood by demographers as being the result of natural biological factors, such as general poor health and disease—specifically, venereal disease. Yet there is also evidence that Black women had access to contraceptives and that African-Americans nationwide played an active role in securing contraceptive facilities for their communities.

Bethune-Cookman College is the only historically Black college founded by a woman that continues to thrive today. Its founder, Mary McLeod Bethune, is seen here with the school's choir. [Library of Congress]

The articulation of the African-American birth control debate and the demand for clinics began just prior to the decade of the 1920s, propelled by social and economic changes caused by the great migration of Black southerners to the North. The contraceptive debate linked the consequences of migration to questions of fertility, gender roles, attitudes toward motherhood and the family, sexuality, and, at times, feminism. Birth control use also was discussed in terms of its relation to economics, health, race relations, and racial progress. In turn, this discussion fueled the movement for the establishment of contraceptive clinics.

An important aspect of the contraceptive discussion was its description of birth control as an economic strategy. Migrating families, who left behind the economy of the rural South, used birth control to preserve their new economic independence, as did poor families who remained in the South. Studies of Harlem in this period noted that the low birth rate of urban Black women was deliberate and seen as a way of improving general living conditions by allowing greater opportunity for economic gain. As early as 1919, Chandler Owen, socialist editor of the *Messenger*, began the discussion of the connection between birth rate and economics. He observed that Black slave women, as a result of sexual exploitation by their white overseers, often had twenty or more children, evidence of a pattern of white coercion that continued into the twentieth century with young female sharecroppers having large numbers of children. Owen argued that capitalism, not racism, was primarily culpable; sexual coercion was the result of the need for surplus labor for industry and the military. He argued that birth control use by African-Americans would reduce the possibilities for exploitation and would favorably affect health, housing, food, clothing, and education.

African-American women, however, claimed that racism was indeed a reason for not having children. Racism figured prominently in fiction and poetry written by Black women beginning in 1916 and continuing throughout the 1930s. Writers frequently depicted women who refused to bring children into a racist world and who expressed their outrage at laws that prevented access to birth control information. Angelina Grimké, in a 1919 short story entitled "The Closing Door," described her main character as "an instrument of reproduction," a "colored" woman who was cursed and forced to bring children into the world who later would become victims of lynch mobs.

Racism, sexual exploitation, and impoverishment were negative and enduring facts of life that encouraged Black women to control their birth rate. However, the lively intellectual milieu of the New Negro movement also was responsible for nourishing a host of influential ideas that supported the climate for birth control. Feminism was one of these ideas. Fiction writers in the 1920s often advocated birth control from a feminist perspective. Feminist writer Georgia Douglas Johnson, for example, used both feminist and racial themes in her 1922 poem, "Black Woman," to explain her denial of motherhood: it was because of the "monster men" who inhabited the earth. Nella Larsen, in her 1928 novella *Quicksand*, explored the debilitating physical and emotional problems resulting from excessive childbearing in a society that demanded that women's sexual expression be inextricably linked to marriage and procreation.

The feminism of the New Negro movement encouraged leadership among women in the public sphere, and Black women were the first to begin laying the organizational groundwork for birth control in Harlem. In 1918, the Women's Political Association of Harlem was the very first African-American organization in the nation to advocate birth control. This and later organizations did not see their advocacy of birth control as a panacea but as one aspect of a larger political agenda that later stressed the inclusion of additional health care services, independence from white birth control providers, and a stand against sterilization.

The 1920s also sparked heated debate and disagreement as African-American men and women struggled to define the role of birth control within the African-American community. Black nationalist leader Marcus Garvey, for example, cautioned against racial extinction but did not explicitly condemn the use of birth control until 1934 at the Universal Negro Improvement Association annual convention in Jamaica.

Preventing racial extinction by increasing the Black population was not a concern of other prominent African-American leaders, such as W.E.B. Du Bois. As early as 1902, Du Bois wrote that Black families should have fewer children and that quality, not quantity, was the goal.

Birth control use threatened to alter traditional sexual roles and relationships between men and women; hence, the race suicide argument often was cast in strong antifeminist tones. Dean Kelly Miller of Howard University and journalist J. A. Rogers debated the role of women in the birth control discourse when, in 1925, they publicly expressed differences of opinion concerning the emancipation of Black women. Writing in the *Messenger*, Rogers took Miller to task for saying that Black women had strayed too far from children, kitchen, clothes, and the church. Miller, very aware that Black women had been having fewer children, cautioned against race suicide and argued that the biological function of women was to bear and rear children. Miller's reactionary views were opposed by Rogers, who said that the move of Black women away from domesticity and childbearing was a positive sign.

Other Black leaders supported progressive viewpoints as well. In his 1919 essay "The Damnation of Woman," Du Bois wrote that women must have independence and the right to choose motherhood. In a later essay he described those who would confine women to childbearing as barbarians ("Birth" 1922).

Although birth control was ripe for debate in the 1920s, few clinics operated where African-American women could obtain safe, reliable contraceptives, and women had to count on homemade and folk birth control methods. Although undependable, these remedies were eagerly sought out and regularly used and, to some degree, were effective because fertility rates did in fact decrease. They also were part of the African-American tradition. Contraceptive methods and customs among both Africans and nineteenth-century African-American slaves have been well documented. Folklorists investigating birth control measures in early twentieth-century, southern rural communities have discovered the use of alum water, hot-water douches, getting out of bed immediately after relations to use the slop jar, and withdrawal. As late as 1938, an over-the-counter, one-size diaphragm marketed under the name Lanteen was still being sold in Florida.

In urban areas a very common and distinctive practice among Black women was to place Vaseline and quinine over the uterus; such items were widely available and could be purchased very cheaply in drugstores. Nationwide throughout the 1920s, the Black press was an abundant source of birth control information. The *Pittsburgh Courier*, for example, carried numerous mail-order advertisements for douche powder, suppositories, preventative antiseptics, and vaginal jellies that worked as contraceptives.

The paucity of contraceptive methods was underscored by the acknowledgment that African-American women often resorted to illegal abortion, a practice more widespread in the Black community than is generally presumed. Abortion was commonly cited by Black leaders and professionals as contributing to their race's low birth rates. In the 1920s, the Black press reported numerous cases of abortions that had ended in death or in the arrest of doctors who performed them. Well into the 1940s newspapers across the country carried stories of women who died in efforts to perform abortions on themselves, as well as of many who were left sterile by dangerous abortifacients.

Because the African-American community continued to be plagued by abortion abuse and limited access to safe birth control, it is not surprising that large numbers of women in Harlem gave Margaret Sanger support and encouragement in establishing a birth control clinic. In 1923, the Harlem Community Forum invited Sanger to speak, and in 1925 the Urban League requested that the American Birth Control League establish a clinic in the Columbus Hill section of the city.

Although this clinic proved unsuccessful, another clinic, supported by the Urban League and the Birth Control Clinical Research Bureau, opened a Harlem branch in 1929. This clinic, affiliated with Sanger, had an advisory board of approximately fifteen members, including Harlem-based journalists, physicians, social workers, and ministers. There was little opposition to this clinic by the clergy; in fact, some members of the African-American clergy were among the nation's staunchest supporters of birth control.

Support for birth control clinics by African-American community organizations also was apparent in other locations throughout the country, especially during the 1930s, a period of fast growth and evolution in the birth control movement in general. In Baltimore, for example, a white birth control clinic had begun to see Black patients in 1928; in 1935, the Black community began organizing, and by 1938 the Northwest Center was established, sponsored, and staffed by African-Americans. The Baltimore Urban League played a key role in the clinic's initial organization, and its sponsoring committee was composed of numerous members of the city's Black community, including ministers, physicians, nurses, social workers, teachers, housewives, and labor leaders.

In Richmond, Fredericksburg, and Lynchburg, Virginia, local maternal welfare groups raised funds for expenses and supplies for birth control clinics at Virginia Medical College and Hampton Institute, and they publicized birth control services at city health departments. In West Virginia, the Maternal and Child Health Council, formed in 1938, was the first statewide birth control organization sponsored by African-Americans.

Local clubs and women's organizations often took part in either sponsoring birth control clinics or bringing the topic to the attention of the local community. In New York these included the Inter-Racial Forum of Brooklyn, the Women's Business and Professional

Club of Harlem, the Social Workers Club of Harlem, the Harlem branch of the National Association of Colored Graduate Nurses, the Harlem YWCA, and the Harlem Economic Forum. Down in Oklahoma City, fourteen Black women's clubs sponsored a birth control clinic for Black women that was directed by two Black physicians and one Black clubwoman.

Clinics in other cities were located in African-American community centers and churches. In 1936, in Louisville, Kentucky, a clinic was located in the Episcopal Church for Colored People and operated by an African-American staff. The Cincinnati Committee on Maternal Health reported in 1939 the existence of two African-American clinics staffed by Black physicians and nurses.

In 1939, the Birth Control Federation of America established a Division of Negro Service and sponsored pilot clinics in Nashville, Tennessee, and Berkeley County, South Carolina. The division consisted of a national advisory council of thirty-five Black leaders and a national sponsoring committee of 500 members who coordinated state and local efforts and administrative and field personnel. The project in Nashville was integrated into the public health services in Bethlehem Center, an African-American social service settlement, and at the Fisk University Settlement House. Both clinics were under the direction of Black doctors and nurses. The program also was supplemented by nine African-American public health nurses who made home visits and performed general health services, including birth services. Home visits served the large number of women who worked as domestics and could not attend clinics during the day. In a two-year period, 5,000 home visits were made in Nashville. In South Carolina, clinic sessions providing both medical care and birth control services were held eleven times each month at different locations in the county for rural women, 70 percent of whom were Black women.

By the end of the 1930s, there were nearly 800 birth control clinics throughout the country. Many were staffed, controlled, financed, supported, and patronized by African-Americans. In their debate and community organizing, the African-American community played an active and often independent role in setting the terms of their involvement in the establishment of clinics. Black women, for example, even in rural areas, often insisted upon the inclusion of additional health services with contraceptives and refused to attend clinics that did not employ African-American health professionals. In addition, unlike white birth control advocates who insisted that birth control be dispensed only by individual private physicians, Black health professionals consciously attempted to create a movement that included the participation of all classes of African-Americans in the distribution of contraceptives and in birth control education.

BIBLIOGRAPHY

Bethel, Elizabeth. *Promiseland: A Century of Life in a Negro Community* (1981); Burrill, Mary. "They That Sit in Darkness," *Birth Control Review* (September 1919); Du Bois, W.E.B. "The Work of Negro Women in Society," *Messenger* (February 1902), and *Darkwater: Voices from Within the Veil* (1920), and "Birth," *Crisis* (October 1922); Engerman, Stanley. "Changes in Black Fertility, 1880-1940." In *Family and Population in Nineteenth-Century America*, ed. Tamara K. Hareven and Maris Vinovskis (1978); Farley, Reynolds. *Growth of the Black Population* (1970); Fauset, Jessie. *The Chinaberry Tree* (1931); Gordon, Linda. *Woman's Body, Woman's Right: A Social History of Birth Control in America* (1974); Grimké, Angelina. "The Closing Door," *Birth Control Review* (September 1919); Gutman, Herbert. *The Black Family in Slavery and Freedom, 1750-1925* (1976); Johnson, Georgia Douglas. *Bronze: A Book of Verse* ([1922] 1971); Kiser, Clyde. "The Fertility of Harlem Negroes," *Millbank Memorial Fund Quarterly* (July 1935); Larsen, Nella. *Quicksand and Passing*, ed. Deborah E. McDowell (1986); Lewis, E. S., and N. Louise Young. "Baltimore's Negro Maternal Health Center: How It Was Organized," *Birth Control Review* (May 1938); McFalls, Joseph and George Masnick. "Birth Control and the Fertility of the U.S. Black Population, 1880 to 1980," *Journal of Family History* (Spring 1981); Owen, Chandler. "Women and Children of the South," *Birth Control Review* (September 1919); Puckett, Newbell Niles. *Folk Beliefs of the Southern Negro* (1926); Raper, Arthur. *Preface to Peasantry: A Tale of Two Black Belt Counties* (1936); Reed, James. *From Private Vice to Public Virtue* (1978); Rodrique, Jessie M. "The Black Community and the Birth-Control Movement." In *Passion and Power: Sexuality in History*, ed. Kathy Peiss and Christine Simmons (1989); Rogers, J. A. "The Critic," *Messenger* (April 1925); Weisbord, Robert G. *Genocide? Birth Control and the Black American* (1975).

JESSIE RODRIQUE

BLACK NATIONALISM

When most people, regardless of age, sex, or race, are asked to identify Black nationalists, they mention Marcus Garvey, Malcolm X, or Louis Farrakhan. However, Black women nationalists—Mary Ann Shadd Cary, Audley "Queen Mother" Moore, Amy Jacques Garvey—made significant and underrecognized contributions to the history of the nationalist movement and ideology. Though the publicly acknowledged leaders were African-American men, men and women worked together to define and further nationalist movements.

Black nationalism is the political and social thought as well as the collective strivings of African-Americans seeking political, economic, and cultural autonomy in American society. Arising as a response to institutional and individual racism, as well as the desire for self-determination, Black nationalism is a by-product of slavery and oppression in the Western world. There is a direct correlation between the evolution of Black nationalist expressions and the prevailing political, economic, and social condition of African-Americans.

Encompassing separatism and emigrationism in the late eighteenth and early nineteenth centuries and territorial separatism, emigration, and economic nationalism in the late nineteenth century, the term *Black nationalism* is used interchangeably with *Pan-Africanism* in the contemporary period. Despite its historical and political variances, several features of Black nationalism have remained constant. The primary principle that drives Black nationalism is racial solidarity, whereby African-Americans pursue social change as a racial collective. An extension of this concept is Pan-Africanism, a movement uniting Black people all over the world based on common African ancestry and the common experience of oppression. A second feature of Black nationalism is religious separatism, manifested by the establishment of Black Christian and non-Christian houses of worship. Another focus of Black nationalism is cultural history, a cyclical view of history that promises the reemergence of African greatness in the modern world, at which time the racial pride of all of Africa's descendants will be restored. These three elements are strengthened by the fourth element of self-determination, which provides the autonomy necessary to achieve liberation.

EARLY BLACK NATIONALISM, 1787-1829

Black nationalism has its roots in post-Revolutionary War America. Two of its earliest forms of expression were religious separatism and emigrationism, the former leading to the institutional development of the Black Christian church and the latter sprouting back-to-Africa movements. Separatist development also spearheaded the founding of fraternities and benevolent societies, most notably the Free African Society of Philadelphia. Founded in 1787, this secular society proved to be the parent organization to the African Methodist Episcopal church. The intertwining of secular and sacred themes

in the Black church is rooted in these beginnings, and the Black church grew phenomenally during this period. Several early Black female evangelists, Jarena Lee, Rebecca Cox Jackson, and Julia A. J. Foote, at varied points in their lives, were affiliated with the early Black church.

These women were responsible for the success of many Black churches in reaching and appealing to larger audiences, and they helped generate revenue to keep various Black churches active and viable in the community. Rebecca Cox Jackson, for example, worked with pastors and members of churches to make sure they understood the importance of unity among Black people. When Cox spoke to them, she would tell them that in order for Black churches to be effective and secure in their positions in the community, they had to address the major issues facing Black Americans—civil rights, education, job opportunities, and Black family life.

BLACK NATIONALIST IDEOLOGY AND EXPRESSION, 1829-63

The disparate features of Black nationalism were woven together in a composite ideology from 1829 to 1841. The focus on political equality, antislavery, and nationalist aspirations led Black nationalists to combine both assimilationist and separatist views in a spiritual and political uplift program for members of the Black community. With the publication of Robert Alexander Young's *Ethiopian Manifesto* and David Walker's *Appeal to the Colored Citizens of the World* in 1829, many of the ideas associated with later Black nationalist ideology were expressed. Young's primary argument was that God would send a Black Messiah to spearhead the Black freedom struggle. Walker called for international solidarity uniting embryonic Pan-Africanism with Black nationalist ideology. Walker also advocated violence as a necessary component of the freedom struggle, believing that the superior strength of African-Americans was merely lying dormant until the proper time.

In 1835, in the *Productions of Mrs. Maria W. Stewart*, Stewart defined the role of Black women in the freedom cause. She argued that they must possess morality, obtain an education, develop business acumen, and sustain political activism to restore their dignity and ensure a legacy for the next generation.

Black nationalism produced a stridency in the efforts of its activists. Of particular note was the militancy of Henry Highland Garnet's "Address to the Slaves" in 1843, which reiterated Walker's call for slave resistance. Separatism continued, in the 1830s and 1840s, with the development of all-Black settlements in the Midwest, where African-Americans free from the burdens of white society emphasized their self-reliance. Sarah Woodson Early, who was raised in one of these settlements in Ohio, embraced nationalism and taught in the Black schools in the area.

By the 1850s, the interest in emigrationism was renewed in Black communities. The catalyst for the dramatic upsurge of interest in emigrationism was the passage of the Fugitive Slave Law of 1850. Undoubtedly it was also seen as an answer to the unemployment, disenfranchisement, and segregation that characterized the plight of free African-Americans. Black leaders like Frederick Douglass who were opposed to emigration supported separate institutional development. In its wake, the emigration movement left towns in Ohio and Pennsylvania almost completely emptied of African-Americans as thousands, fugitive and free, fled to Canada. Haiti, the Caribbean, Central and South America, and Africa also all became viable emigration alternatives. To encourage emigrationism, Mary Ann Shadd published *A Plea for Emigration or Notes on Canada West, in Its Moral, Social, and Political Aspect: With Suggestions Respecting Mexico, W. Indies and Vancouvers Island for the Information of Colored Emigrants* (1852). Shadd cited "American oppression" and the "odious Fugitive Slave Law" as the two primary factors necessitating emigration. Shadd had migrated to Canada in 1851. She gained further prominence as a nationalist theorist when she spoke at the 1855 National Emigration Convention, giving what Frederick Douglass called "one of the most convincing and telling speeches in favor of Canadian emigration I ever heard" (Crews 1991).

To explore emigration options, prominent spokespersons such as James T. Holly, Mary Bibb, Martin Delany, and Mary Ann Shadd Cary convened several emigration conventions. Women comprised one-third of the participants of the 1854 National Emigration Convention. Holly reported on Haiti, and Delany, who had recently immigrated to Canada, explored the Niger Valley region in Africa. Mary Bibb and Mary Shadd Cary, both Canadian immigrants, encouraged others to repatriate to Canada. Cary's Canadian weekly, the *Provincial Freeman*, served as one of the official organs of the emigration convention movement. Karen Crews has noted that "most female nationalists did not lecture on emigration. They showed their support by moving, primarily to Canada West and Africa" (Crews 1991). Ultimately, emigration schemes were short-lived and suffered severe financial problems. The Civil War turned the attention of Black nationalists to the antislavery cause.

POST-RECONSTRUCTION, 1879-1915

With the failure of Reconstruction and the rise of white supremacy in the South, most African-Americans revived Black nationalism by choosing to establish separate institutions to gain social and political equality. Others opted for territorial separatism and emigrationism, many responding to southern Jim Crow laws and Ku Klux Klan terrorism by inhabiting all-Black towns away from white society, and others by joining Bishop Henry McNeal Turner, an African Methodist Episcopal minister, in his 1880 Liberian immigration efforts.

But economic nationalism clearly dominated the era. This separate path of economic development placed emphasis on ownership of land, the development of Black businesses, and "buy Black" campaigns, laying an economic foundation in Black communities and at the same time enhancing racial pride.

In the early 1880s, Mary Ann Shadd Cary, now a resident of Washington, D.C., worked with other women through the Colored Women's Progressive Franchise Association to secure suffrage for women, equal job opportunities for women, and more businesses owned and operated by women. Their elaborate plans for accumulating the funds—each member investing one dollar a month—to purchase land and establish agricultural, grocery, dry goods and millinery, and men's clothing store ventures, with Black women having controlling power, did not come to fruition. But their focus on collective economic development was indicative of the main ideological thrust of late nineteenth-century Black nationalism.

This focus on economic development as the key to community self-empowerment was the central idea put forth by Maggie Lena Walker in the early twentieth century. Walker, chief officer of the Independent Order of Saint Luke and president of the Saint Luke Penny Savings Bank, "questioned the fact that while the white community oppressed the black, 'the Negro . . . carries to their bank every dollar he can get his hands upon and then goes back the next day, borrows and then pays the white man to lend him his own money.' . . . Walker considered such behavior racially destructive and believed it necessary to break those ties that kept 'the Negro . . . so wedded to those who oppress him' " (Brown 1989).

A moderate feminist-nationalist movement, the Black women's club movement, was organized in 1896 under the umbrella of the National Association of Colored Women (NACW). The NACW supported collective self-help programs, moral uplift of Black women, social uplift of the masses, and institutional separatism, all contemporary nationalist ideas of the era. Fannie Barrier Williams, Josephine St. Pierre Ruffin, Anna Julia Cooper, Addie Hunton, and others led the organization's fight in challenging the precepts and myths of Black womanhood. In redefining the moral integrity and ethics of Black womanhood, Black women defied the patriarchal system that made them vulnerable to sexual exploitation and debasement in society. Leaders like Ida B. Wells-Barnett, who spearheaded the antilynching crusade, reflected the clubwomen's political independence from either the ideology of Booker T. Washington or that of W.E.B. Du Bois.

CONTEMPORARY NATIONALIST MOVEMENTS, 1916-92

Contemporary nationalist expressions combine Pan-Africanism and economic, religious, and cultural nationalism as sources of Black empowerment. The pervasive nationalist ethos may be attributed to charismatic leadership, nationalist organizations, the independence of African nations, and the worldwide Black liberation struggle. Most certainly, the persistence of racism is a decided factor in its continuance. After W.E.B. Du Bois revived the Pan-African Congress, interest in Pan-Africanism persisted. Certainly Marcus Garvey's multifaceted organization, the Universal Negro Improvement Association (UNIA), transported the nationalist foundation into the twentieth century. With the underpinnings of Pan-Africanism, Garvey wove economic, religious, and cultural nationalism into a comprehensive ideology. His economically based, multi-million-dollar business enterprises sustained the economic development of the Harlem community and enabled many recent migrants from the South and the West Indies to survive. Yet his cultural nationalism, which fostered racial pride and unity through ancestral ties to Africa, was his greatest contribution to the Black masses. Women were noticeable in the economic arm of UNIA, particularly the Black Cross Nurses, who provided the unemployed with food and housing. Despite the lack of an official title, Amy Jacques Garvey was clearly the most influential woman in the Garvey movement, serving as editor of the women's page in the *Negro World*. Henrietta Vinton Davis was one of the founding members of UNIA and used her oratorical talents throughout the Caribbean and Central and South America in the cause of Black liberation. Davis drew large crowds and urged her audiences to understand that being Black should not foster being politically, socially, or economically oppressed. She argued that being Black was a resource by which

Black people could draw the strength and determination they need to fight injustices and remain unified regardless of nationality. Queen Mother Moore also emerged as one of the leaders of the Garvey movement, although she is more widely known as a member of the Communist party and a founder of the Ethiopian Coptic Church in North America and the Universal Association of Ethiopian Women, which protested southern lynching.

The development in the 1930s of Housewives' Leagues and "Don't Buy Where You Can't Work" campaigns represented a continuing form of economic nationalism.

Since the mid-1960s, there has been a proliferation of nationalist organizations on the national, state, and local levels. The Black Panther party achieved national prominence, particularly among Black youth. Founded in 1966, it was an expression of revolutionary nationalism, advocating an overthrow of the capitalist system. Assata Shakur (JoAnne Chesimard) and Angela Davis were both members of the party, although Davis later joined the Che Lumumba Group, an all-Black collective arm of the American Communist party. Claudia Jones and Charlene Mitchell were earlier Black Communists who worked with revolutionary nationalist cadres. Poets Nikki Giovanni and Sonia Sanchez were important in the development of a cultural arm to the nationalist movements.

Other organizations, such as the Republic of New Africa, the Black Political Assembly, and the African Liberation Support Committee, geared their programs of liberation toward the Black masses. The Congress of African Peoples, founded in 1970, emphasizes cultural unity as the vehicle for Black liberation. Most recently, an emerging new field of African women diaspora studies seeks to unite nationalist and African feminist thought in a critical examination of both gender and race in the Americas and Africa.

Black nationalist expression in the 1990s embraces all levels and classes in the Black community, and most individuals adopt and adapt one or more of its various expressions. Coming together in the halls of academe, professional organizations, national organizations, African craft markets in urban cities, student collectives, and neighborhood associations, Black people organize for political and economic empowerment via nationalist channels.

BIBLIOGRAPHY

Bracey, John H., Jr., August Meier, and Elliott Rudwick, eds. *Black Nationalism in America* (1970); Brown, Elsa Barkley. "Womanist Consciousness: Maggie Lena Walker and the Independent Order of Saint Luke," *Signs* (Spring 1989); Carlisle, Rodney. *The Roots of Black Nationalism* (1975); Crews, Karen Yvette. "Mary Ann Shadd Cary and Female Black Nationalism." M.A. thesis, UCLA (1991); Giddings, Paula. *When and Where I Enter: The Impact of Black Women on Race and Sex in America* (1984); Moses, Wilson Jeremiah. *The Golden Age of Black Nationalism, 1850-1925* (1978); Stuckey, Sterling. *The Ideological Origins of Black Nationalism* (1972); Tate, Gayle T. "Black Nationalism: An Angle of Vision," *Western Journal of Black Studies* (Spring 1988), and "A Journey toward Justice: A Portrait of Angela Y. Davis." In *A Celebration of Black Women* (1991), and "Tangled Vines: Ideological Interpretations of Afro-Americans in the Nineteenth Century," Ph.D. diss. (1984); Terborg-Penn, Rosalyn, Andrea Rushing, and Sharon Harley, eds. *Women in Africa and the African Diaspora* (1987); Weisbord, Robert G. *Ebony Kinship: Africa, Africans, and the Afro-American* (1973); Wilmore, Gayraud S. *Black Religion and Black Radicalism* (1983).

GAYLE T. TATE

BLACK PANTHER PARTY

Throughout U.S. history Black women have always participated in political movements within their communities. Although their roles have not been highlighted by the media in the past, Black women have organized as well as participated in the daily functions of various organizations. The Black Panther Party (BPP) was no exception to this rule.

Huey P. Newton and Bobby Seale founded the Black Panther Party in Oakland, California, on October 15, 1966. The organization was established by men and the predominantly male leadership was the focus of media coverage. Nevertheless, women played significant roles within the organization from 1967 until it ceased to function in the early 1980s. Female BPP members held party leadership positions at local levels as well as national levels, delivered speeches at rallies, and participated in the BPP community survival programs (free food, clothing, and health services, among other necessities).

Women who joined the Black Panther Party participated for a variety of reasons. Some women joined to develop their skills in political organization, other women joined to support spouses or significant others who were affiliated with the party, and still others joined to endorse the party's goals.

The three most prominent women at the top of the organization's hierarchy were Kathleen Neal Cleaver, Elaine Brown, and Ericka Huggins. Cleaver was the first woman to hold a national leadership position; she was the communications secretary from 1967 to 1971. Elaine Brown held many positions in the BPP before she became the first and only female chairperson of the party, from 1974 to 1977. Ericka Huggins directed the BPP-initiated Oakland Community School from 1973 to 1981.

The community programs of the BPP, often directed and staffed by female members, included free breakfast for schoolchildren; free medical care, such as sickle cell anemia testing; free transportation to visit relatives in prison and for senior citizens; free shoes and clothing; political education classes; voter registration; petition campaigns for community control of police; and legal aid and advice, among other programs.

Although in doctrine the BPP internal structure allowed for no differential treatment on account of sex, once women joined the party they confronted gender-based discrimination and gender-specific tasks. From 1967 until the party folded, many women encountered sexism, and male chauvinism was an issue within the Panther community. A letter from Eldridge Cleaver to Ericka Huggins appeared in the July 5, 1969, issue of the *Black Panther* (the official party newspaper) addressing the issue: "Women are our other half, they're not our stronger half, they're not our weaker half, but they are our other half and that we sell ourselves out, we sell our children out and we sell our women out when we treat them in any other manner." Despite Cleaver's comments, sexism still continued in the BPP, and beginning in 1969, female members began to voice their displeasure with their treatment in the *Black Panther* and at BPP meetings. They also increased their participation in leadership roles and community activities.

Male chauvinism was not the only issue BPP women faced. Questions of female sexuality and motherhood plagued some women. They complained of being pressured into engaging in sexual activity. Reproduction and birth control were also issues. Many confronted the difficulties of rearing a child and being a full-time political activist. Moreover, mothers who were in the Panthers risked being incarcerated and separated from their children.

Two former female BPP members who experienced the hardships of being a mother and being a full-time political activist are Assata Shakur (formerly JoAnne Chesimard) and Akua Njere (formerly Deborah Johnson). Shakur became pregnant while incarcerated and was separated from her daughter immediately after birth. Shakur's mother raised the child while Shakur was incarcerated. Shakur was emotionally affected by the separation from her daughter and the possible negative effects that such a separation might have on their relationship.

Njere is the mother of the son of Fred Hampton, slain BPP Chairman of the Illinois chapter. Like Shakur, she was also contemplative about the relationship that would develop between her son and herself. For a short period after her son's birth, Njere's mother cared for Fred Hampton, Jr. Meanwhile, Njere attempted to continue full-time participation in the BPP. Njere soon decided that she needed more time to care for her son. Such constraints caused Njere to even consider leaving the Party to avoid jeopardizing her relationship with her son.

The pressures that female members of the BPP faced sometimes caused them to rescind their membership. Since police surveillance and harassment were equally problematic for women and men, female members faced both internal and external pressures. Nevertheless, there were female members who remained politically active in the party.

During its active reign the Black Panther Party leaders instituted many programs that had a lasting effect on Black society and society-at-large. Unquestionably, the female Panther members were an integral part of the creation of this legacy. From their involvement in the community service programs to their national leadership positions, the female Panther members maintained day-to-day functions of the party.

The decline of the BPP was the result of numerous activities and attitude clashes. The intensity of undercover FBI involvement and local police harassment helped to weaken and curtail public interest in the party's activities and members' involvement. The national leadership had also fallen apart over the course of ten years. Throughout this decline, however, large numbers of women sustained the organization's community programs until 1981, when the final Oakland-based program closed.

BIBLIOGRAPHY

Essence (March 1991); Foner, Philip, ed. *The Black Panthers Speak* (1970); Njere, Akua. *My Life with the Black Panther Party* (1991); Seale, Bobby. *Seize the Time: The Story of the Black Panther Party and Huey P. Newton* (1968); Shakur, Assata. *Assata: An Autobiography* (1987).

ANGELA D. BROWN

"BLACK PATTI" *see*
JONES, SISSIERETTA JOYNER

BLACK STUDIES

One of the most significant reforms in American higher education over the past two decades has emerged from the Africana (Black Studies) movement. Africana or Black Studies began as a field of study in the 1960s in the wake of the civil rights movement and in the midst of pervasive campus unrest. From the outset it had both an academic and social mission. Although contemporary Black Studies as an interdisciplinary course of study is a product of the sixties, it draws much of its academic content from earlier times.

Students of the sixties were confronted with an absence or distortion of the Black experience in the higher education curriculum and a sense of cultural alienation generated by the predominantly white colleges and universities they entered. First they demanded Black recognition in the form of an increase in Black faculty and staff, Black programs, more Black students, necessary financial aid, and Black history courses. It quickly became clear that Black history was simply a beginning and that a broader demand would and did emerge for a comprehensive interdisciplinary curriculum with history at its center. From its stormy beginnings, Black Studies has become entrenched in the academy and is showing signs of growth and maturity in its third decade.

While the Black Studies movement addressed some very real inadequacies such as paucity of faculty, absence and distortion of curriculum content, and programmatic resources in the academy, it has not been as responsive in its sensitivity to the unique experiences of women of African descent in America, on the continent, or throughout the diaspora. Today, throughout the country, African-American men and women speak to the existence of racism in Women's Studies and sexism in Black Studies in courses on campuses, in associations, and in scholarly publications. It should be noted, however, that Black women do have a rich legacy in these areas, though they have been numerically smaller as well as reluctant to sing their own praises. Nevertheless, Black women have been actively involved in the initiation, continuity, and development of Black Studies.

Black women students and Black women faculty along with Black women community activists joined with their male peers—their brothers in the struggle—in those protests and other efforts that contributed to the establishment of what is now emerging as the discipline of Africana Studies. Those women, like their male copartners, understood the amazonian tasks before them across the nation, in the accomplishment of meaningful Black Studies with strong academic foundations within higher education. While in a distinct minority, numerous women were founders of Black Studies units at their institutions and, like men, they have provided leadership as program directors or as department chairpersons.

Black women have also been significant as leaders in efforts to professionalize the discipline. They are among those persons who have served in the top leadership positions of the National Council of Black Studies, African Heritage Studies Association, and the Association for the Study of Afro-American Life and History. Bertha Maxwell Reddy (founding president), Delores P. Aldridge (first two-term elected president), and Carlene Young (a president) of the National Council of Black Studies are well known, as is Charshee McIntyre (a president and executive director) of the African Heritage Studies Association. Mary Frances Berry, Darlene Clark Hine, and others may be familiar for their leadership roles with the Association for the Study of Afro-American Life and History. Women such as Vivian Gordon in Virginia and New York, Sonia Stone in North Carolina, and Yolanda Robinson in Ohio, while holding no specific top leadership positions, have been pivotal in establishing Black Studies at their universities and within their major professional organizations.

As relevant as their leadership roles have been, no less significant has been the serious Black Studies scholarship of Black women, much of which has not been simply gender specific. As teachers and research scholars, Black women have been among those at the cutting edge in the development of models and paradigms for Black Studies as well as in the reevaluation of the applicability in the humanities and social sciences of selective research methodologies. They have also blazed new trails in other areas of inquiry within the academy.

A growing number of scholars and administrators are interested in and sensitive to Black women's issues. For example, the Emory University African-American and African Studies program inaugurated the first endowed lecture series in a major private institution in the name of a Black woman. It subsequently created a distinguished chair in the name of that same Black woman. Numerous institutions have followed that lead in recent years.

The affirmation of the need to acknowledge Black heroines and the inclusion of issues of Black women into the Black Studies curriculum does not rest upon a denigration of Eurocentric Women's Studies. Rather, Black women and many Black male scholars in Black Studies maintain that such initiatives are imperative for Black Studies to be truly Black Studies, given that Black women hold up more than one half of the sky for Black people.

Overwhelmingly, against many odds, in the 1970s and 1980s, Black women in Black Studies have maintained their commitment to the dynamics of the emergence of Africana Studies. In the future, the roles of Black women will continue to be critical in professional organizations, program leadership, curriculum development, and scholarship with an increasing focus on linkages with Black women throughout the diaspora.

BIBLIOGRAPHY
Aldridge, Delores P., ed. "New Perspectives on Black Studies," special issue, *Phylon: Review of Race and Culture* (Spring 1988), and "Reflections on Twenty Years in Black Studies," *Word: A Black Culture Journal* (Spring 1991), and "Womanist Issues in Black Studies. Towards Integrating Africana Women into Africana Studies," *The Afrocentric Scholar: Journal of the National Council for Black Studies* (Spring 1992); Anderson, Talmadge, ed. *Black Studies: Theory, Method, and Cultural Perspectives* (1990); Christian, Barbara. *Black Women Novelists: The Development of a Tradition 1892-1976* (1981); Gordon, Vivian V. "The Coming of Age of Black Studies," *Western Journal of Black Studies* (Fall 1981); Harley, Sharon and Rosalyn Terborg-Penn, eds. *The Afro-American Woman: Struggles and Images* (1978); Hull, Gloria T., Patricia Bell Scott, and Barbara Smith, eds. *All the Women Are White, All the Men Are Black But Some of Us Are Brave: Black Women's Studies* (1982); King, William M. "A Comparative History of ASALH, AHSA, and NCBS in the Development of Black Studies," Manuscript (1992); Rodgers-Rose, LaFrances. *The Black Woman* (1980); Steady, Filomina, ed. *The Black Woman Cross-Culturally* (1981); Stewart, James B. "The Field and Function of Black Studies: Toward an Accurate Assessment of the State of Black Studies," National Council for Black Studies (1988); Turner, James E., ed. *The Next Decade: Theoretical and Research Issues* (1984); Young, Carlene, ed. "An Assessment of Black Studies Programs in American Higher Education," special issue, *Journal of Negro Education* (1984), and *Black Experience: Analysis and Synthesis* (1972).

DELORES P. ALDRIDGE

BLACK WOMEN MAYORS' CAUCUS

The Black Women Mayors' Caucus (BWMC) originated at the National Conference of Black Mayors (NCBM) in 1988. The thirteen female mayors in attendance at the first Leadership Institute for Mayors formed the organization in an effort to highlight and enhance the role of Black women mayors, to focus national attention on the needs of Black women elected officials, to expose young women to the challenges of elected office, and to examine issues of particular concern to women. Other issues addressed by the BWMC are child care, the needs of teenaged mothers, and the welfare of Black youth.

As of 1992, sixty-seven Black women mayors nationwide constituted the membership of the BWMC. They represented municipalities in twenty states and the District of Columbia. Mayor Unita Blackwell of Mayersville, Mississippi, chaired the association in 1991, and Mayor Calley Mobley of Alorton, Illinois, in 1992. Active members include Mayor Emma Gresham of Keysville, Georgia, who captured international attention for her leadership in reestablishing municipal government in this predominantly Black town. The staff of the NCBM, along with other organizations, assisted Mayor Gresham and the Concerned Citizens of Keysville in their effort.

The BWMC has annual workshops in conjunction with the meetings of the NCBM. These seminars are designed to improve the leadership and management skills of Black women mayors and to focus on topics affecting women. The first workshop in 1989, "Women Mayors Balancing Family, Career, and Elected Office," focused on enhancing awareness of the issues inherent in the multiple roles of women mayors. The role-model speaker was Yvonne Brathwaite Burke, an attorney and former U.S. representative and California assemblywoman as well as a wife and mother.

The second annual (1990) workshop, "Combatting Sexism in the Work Place through Changes in Language and Attitudes," was led by Dr. Gloria Mixon of Clark Atlanta University. Marion Delaney-Harris, national trainer, led the third annual (1991) workshop, "Breaking Down the Barriers to Non-Traditional Employment." She focused on the obstacles facing women in employment; identified training opportunities for women in nontraditional jobs; provided information on nontraditional occupations for women; examined discrepancies in hiring, wages, and promotions; and provided women mayors with technical assistance for local action.

In addition to these annual workshops, members participate in national forums that focus on women's issues, and the caucus is part of the Women's Agenda. The staff of the NCBM provides technical assistance to the BWMC.

BIBLIOGRAPHY

Center for the American Woman and Politics, Rutgers University; Michelle D. Kourouma, Executive Director, National Conference of Black Mayors.

GRETCHEN E. MACLACHLAN
EDIE C. PEARSON

BLACKWELL, UNITA (1933-)

Unita Blackwell is one of the "extraordinary ordinary" grass-roots leaders of the civil rights movement. Born on March 18, 1933, in Lula, Mississippi, this daughter of sharecroppers rose from poverty in a state that denied Black Americans every basic freedom and became the first Black woman mayor in the history of Mississippi. Elected in 1976 in the town of Mayersville, where she had once been denied the right to vote, Blackwell still stands in the forefront of social and economic change in the state.

Blackwell was drawn into the civil rights movement while a young mother in the early 1960s. When civil rights organizers from outside the state launched voter registration drives in rural Mississippi, she was among the first to step forward. Working with the Student Nonviolent Coordinating Committee (SNCC), whose goal was to develop indigenous leadership, Blackwell registered voters and organized boycotts and citizen participation drives throughout the state; she was arrested and jailed over seventy times. Blackwell initiated several civil rights legislative challenges; among these was the landmark school desegregation suit *Blackwell* v. *Issaquena County Board of Education* (1965-66), which set a historical precedent nationwide in the continuing legal battle for school desegregation. As a founding member of the Mississippi Freedom Democratic Party (MFDP), she was among the delegates to the historic 1964 Democratic National Convention in Atlantic City, New Jersey, where the radically progressive third party challenged the seating of the traditionally all-white Mississippi delegation.

Blackwell's interests in economic development and housing led to cooperative ventures with the National Council of Negro Women and the establishment of home-ownership opportunities for low-income families in the state. Her most successful effort was the incorporation of Mayersville in 1976. Nationally, Blackwell emerged as a prominent speaker on issues involving rural housing and development. As president of the first United States-China People's Friendship Association, she traveled to the Republic of China and exchanged ideas on development. In 1979, she participated in President Jimmy Carter's Energy Summit at Camp David. Blackwell later obtained a Master's degree in regional planning from the University of Massachusetts-Amherst. She was enrolled there based on her abilities, experience, and skills because she had not graduated from high school. She was elected chairperson of the National Conference of Black Mayors in 1989.

Though Unita Blackwell formally received only an eighth-grade education, her philosophy of life, "to educate by doing and being," epitomizes her relentless commitment to social change. Her life and work,

as well as the works of other Black women activists such as Fannie Lou Hamer and Annie Devine, have been a wellspring for principled social action. In 1992 Blackwell received the prestigious MacArthur Foundation Fellowship.

[*See also* MISSISSIPPI FREEDOM DEMOCRATIC PARTY.]

BIBLIOGRAPHY

Blackwell, Unita. Interview, Tom Dent Oral History Collection, Amistad Research Center, Tulane University, New Orleans, Louisiana; Crawford, V. Personal interview with Unita Blackwell, Mayersville, Mississippi (July 25,

The daughter of sharecroppers, Unita Blackwell rose from poverty to become the first Black woman mayor in Mississippi history, elected from the town of Mayersville, where she had once been denied the right to vote. She is shown here receiving the Fannie Lou Hamer Award at the National Conference of Black Mayors convention in 1984. Mayor Johnny L. Ford of Tuskegee, Alabama, and Mayor Riley Owens of Centreville, Illinois, made the presentation. [AP/Wide World Photos]

1986); *Southern Rural Women's Network Newsletter* (January 1983), and *Southern Rural Women's Network Newsletter: Special Economic Development Issue* (June 1983).

VICKI CRAWFORD

BLOUNT, MILDRED E. (1907-1974?)

Mildred E. Blount is considered one of the greatest milliners of all time. She was well known in the fashion world from the 1930s through the 1950s, designing for Hollywood stars and noted personalities.

Mildred Blount was born in October 1907, in Edenton, North Carolina, the youngest of seven children. Her parents died when she was two years old. Blount was raised by various relatives in Philadelphia and other northern cities. Working as an errand girl at Madame Clair's Dress and Hat Shop in New York City, she developed an interest in millinery. Blount and her sister, Clara, a dressmaker, soon opened a shop of their own, designing dresses and hats for wealthy New Yorkers.

In the 1930s Blount was hired by John Frederics' Millinery of New York, where her career escalated. While at Frederics', she created a series of hats based on designs from 1690 through 1900, and the collection was exhibited at the 1939 New York World's Fair. The exhibition resulted in her designing hats for the classic film *Gone with the Wind*. Although Blount rarely received film credit for her designs, she lent her talents to numerous major films including *Back Street, Blood and Sand, Easter Parade,* and *The Lady Is Willing.* Some of her clients were Rosalind Russell, Joan Crawford, Gloria Vanderbilt, Marian Anderson, and many wealthy Black women.

The August 1942 cover of *Ladies' Home Journal* featured one of Blount's hats and, in 1943, she became the first Black American to have her work exhibited at the famous Medcalf's Restaurant in Los Angeles. That same year she was awarded a Rosenwald Fellowship to conduct research on period hats in America. During the late 1940s, she opened her own shop in Beverly Hills. Very little is known about Blount's later years. It has been reported that she died in Los Angeles in 1974.

BIBLIOGRAPHY

Fisk University Special Collections Archives, Nashville, Tennessee; California Afro-American Museum (Los Angeles); Los Angeles County Museum of Art.

KATHY A. PERKINS

BLUES AND JAZZ

Women in general, and African American women in particular, are given short shrift in many discussions and writings on blues and jazz. Fortunately, a growing number of popular music critics, scholars, and culture watchers have begun to change the scene dramatically with their articles, books, and liner notes. Perhaps we owe some of this development to the efforts of the women's movement as it focused on all things female in politics, culture, and the arts. Credit must also be given to the women who sang and played the blues and jazz, because they refused to be silent and fade quietly from the scene.

Women in African American music traditions were actively involved at all levels of music creation and production. These included time-honored roles as praise singers, priests, dancers, and instrumentalists. Since most musical events were community-centered and participatory, women were actively engaged in various ways. They performed as members of age sets, secret societies, choruses, initiates, and as persons with special spiritual powers that could call down the ancestors or other spirits for the benefit of the group. They employed their musical experience and power to heal, to aid in childbirth, to prepare the dead for the spirit world, to soothe a baby with a lullaby that both comforted it and informed it of its ancestry, to celebrate the greatness of warriors and kings, and to elevate toilsome work with lusty rhythms that brought joy. The variations upon these activities depended upon the social organization of a particular group, the environment, and the influence of external forces, such as warfare, religious crusades, trade, commerce, and eventually that most devastating force—the Atlantic slave trade. Early women's music altered as slavers penetrated their villages and ultimately carried them and their kin to the Americas in chains. In these dreadful years, the songs of celebration were transformed into lamentations that were described variously as eerie wails, out-of-tune squalls, and other derogatory terms by European observers in Africa and on the slave ships that carried captives to other lands.

The frequent use of call and response and of improvisatory rhythms and melodies in worksongs described as dull or uninteresting points to the continuing tradition of African music-making that survived in the New World. The spiritual song form derived from these African origins and influenced the sharp expressiveness and content of the blues and, subsequently, jazz. The same mournful expression found in "Sometimes I feel like I'm almost gone, sometimes I feel like I'm almost gone, a long ways from home" is felt in the lines of Ma Rainey's "If I could break these chains, and let my worried heart go free, but it's too late now, the blues has made a slave of me." The ability to capture the deepest personal emotions and frame them in a simple text loaded with metaphors and other figures of speech was the hallmark of the African griots, praise singers, priests, and dirge singers. Singer/creators of the spirituals and blues extended the tradition while incorporating past practices of double entendres, proverbs, and allegories. Thus, a body of poetic literature emerged from the horrors of the slave experience as an everlasting document of the creativity and intelligence of a so-called illiterate people. Freedom and Reconstruction provided the opportunity for further expansion of the musical and poetic output of African American professional and folk musicians. The facts-of-life approach to song-making chronicled the changes that the newly freed Americans experienced—a new brand of oppression as pernicious and deadly as slavery, accompanied by poverty and lack of economic opportunity, natural disaster, white terrorism, poor education, and itinerancy. Onto this scene came the tent shows, minstrel shows, wandering worker/musicians, brass bands, and vaudeville shows at the turn of the twentieth century.

Among the migratory workers seeking jobs in the cities of the Midwest and North also came the audiences for the performers in those shows. For the lumber and turpentine camp workers in the rural South, there was the occasional traveling tent show featuring a blues singer, the first documented being Gertrude Pridgett Rainey, later dubbed Ma Rainey, "Mother of the Blues." For the men and women in the factory and steel towns of the North and Midwest, there were the vaudeville shows and dance halls as well as the local neighborhood saloons and clubs—some too rough for the ordinary customer. In those clubs and halls could be found the upwardly mobile working-class men who sought the company of the "brown and tan" women who worked the dance floors while singing the blues and other popular ballads of the day. This was the setting for the budding careers of singers and musicians such as Alberta Hunter, Lovie Austin, Lillian Hardin Armstrong, and Lucille Hegamin. Their brand and style of blues and jazz were characteristic of the more sophisticated lifestyle of the emerging African American middle class. On the stages of the theaters that featured vaudeville shows we find an interesting development as the blues singers moved to the forefront as featured artists, often backed by highly trained jazz musicians.

Mamie Smith, the first woman to record the blues, in February 1920, set into motion a partnership between blues and jazz that continues today. That collaboration altered for all time the vocal and instrumental styles of the blues and jazz artists as they experimented with new and innovative ways of using the voice and the instrument, sometimes effortlessly interchanging musical lines and roles. Thus, we have the era of wailing trombones, mournful cornets, and shrill clarinets keening like a big voice in the wind. Bessie Smith slid into phrases and attacked her lines as if they were too heavy for her to lift at times, thus adding tension to her lyrics and emotional content. Edith Wilson and Monette Moore took their soprano voices into the clarinet's range to introduce the tremulous quality of a nervous fluttering bird. Later, Billie Holiday, with her inimitable insight, blended the blues and jazz into an unbelievable mélange of sensuous and sometimes painful artistry. In their own ways, the blues queens of the 1920s established an approach to singing and performing that influenced Holiday and nearly every singer who succeeded them. Their theatricality, sense of audience, recognition of their ties to their listeners, and respect for the music are evident in the quality and emotional power of their recordings, which are enjoying renewed popularity among audiences in the United States and abroad.

A brief overview of some of the artists and the venues in which they garnered fame and popularity illustrates how they became influential prototypes in American popular music. Ida Cox, Sara Martin, Bessie Smith, Clara Smith, Rosa Henderson, and the pioneering Ma Rainey and Mamie Smith were stars of the vaudeville stage for nearly a decade during the so-called Jazz Age of the 1920s. Their styles varied considerably. Cox, Bessie and Clara Smith, and Sippie Wallace had big voices that defied the usual definition of a good voice. Yet this very rough-on-the-edges quality was perfectly suited for the verismo required for singing the blues. The new urban experience of the thousands of African Americans who were the mainstays of the vaudeville blues audience was captured by Cox's dry, somewhat hard-edged style. When Bessie sang "Any Woman's Blues," she tapped into the reality of many women who suffered from the ambivalence of a relationship that had a powerful but distressing hold on them. What made Bessie, Ma, Sippie, and Ida unique among most of these women was their superb musicianship, which interacted with the rising and already arrived instrumentalists of the decade. Some of Tommy Ladnier's best cornet work can be found on recordings with Rainey and Wallace. Louis Armstrong and Bessie Smith laid down some lines that eventually influenced horn players and pianists such as Bix Beiderbecke, Mezz Mezzrow, Earl Hines, Thomas "Fats" Waller, Roy Eldridge, Valaida Snow (who was dubbed the female Armstrong), and more recently, Clifford Brown, Dizzy Gillespie, and Marlon Jordan. Composer/pianists Fletcher Henderson, Eddie Heywood, and Clarence Williams surely gained as much from their collaborations with Rainey, Wallace, and Smith as did the singers from their accompaniment and songwriting.

The unexpected success of Noble Sissle and Eubie Blake's 1921 *Shuffle Along* created a demand for dancing and singing talent that attracted some of the brightest stars in the African American community. It also provided a new venue for blues singers who began their careers in the dance halls and social clubs of Chicago and New York. Alberta Hunter, Edith Wilson, Mamie Smith, and Lucille Hegamin met the needs of the so-called sophisticated cabaret and revue audiences who did not wish to mingle with the ordinary Black folk that craved the singing of Ma and Bessie and Ida. The sound of the blues in these clubs and revues, such as Lew Leslie's *Plantation Revue* featuring Florence Mills, provided opportunities for Edith Wilson and Ethel Waters to display their singing and comedic talents. Alberta Hunter carried her sultry brand of blues styling to Europe and gained much admiration for her singing and sleek chic fashions from the rich urbanites in Paris, London, and Copenhagen. Lizzie Miles followed this trend and earned the nickname "La Rose Noir." These women sang a more refined blues that was less graphic in its commentary on the life and struggles of the common folk. Their songs were apt to have risqué lyrics with double entendres that titillated the sensibilities of the mainly white audiences. Yet they were accepted in the Black community as blues singers, members of that exclusive club that had been anointed years earlier by the women who sang in the traveling tent shows—Ma Rainey, Bessie Smith, Trixie Smith, and Bertha "Chippie" Hill.

The country singers, from among whose ranks emerged Bertha Edwards, Ma Rainey, Bobby Cadillac, Lottie Kimbrough, and Lucille Bogan (who was the first blues singer to openly promote the radical feminist line in her "Women Don't Need No Men"), were not as widely recorded, except Rainey. However, they enjoyed the enduring allegiance of the people in the rural South who went to the house parties, picnics, and local joints to dance to their music and commiserate over moonshine, home brew, or bootleg whiskey. They probably maintained a more direct, intimate relationship with their constituencies than

did either the vaudeville city blues women or the cabaret singers. Their lyrics dealt with everything from natural disaster to signifying on no-good men or other women.

Witty lyrics and performances were another art that the blues women and the musicians who performed with them refined. This innovation on the African traditions of call and response interlaced with public signifying is a hallmark of jazz today. Examples of this can be found in Wallace's "Up the Country Blues."

The power of the word juxtaposed with the imitative sounds of nature, trains, funeral dirges, knocks on doors, and other sounds made by the instruments created a visual image for the listener that performers' dramatics elaborated. Rainey coming out of a fake Victrola as she sings her latest blues; Sara Martin hanging onto the curtains because she is so distraught; Wilson rolling her eyes as she mocks other women—these and other devices were a part of the repertoire of many blues singers who recognized that they were the purveyors of the drama of life as the masses of Black folk knew it.

During the blues era, several women participated as composers, arrangers, lyricists, and band members/leaders. The most prolific of these during the 1920s was Lovie Austin, who combined all of the above talents. Her collaboration with Alberta Hunter included "Down Hearted Blues," which Hunter recorded but which was eclipsed by Bessie Smith's version. Austin was the house pianist for Paramount Studios, so she can be heard on the recordings of many of the best blues women, including Hunter. She often recorded with her own group also, the Blues Serenaders, which comprised four to six men. On occasion she traveled on the vaudeville circuit sharing credits with the stars. She continued to compose and record long after the blues decade had ended. According to Sally Placksin, Mary Lou Williams considered Austin better than many of the men of her day and felt that Austin was probably the greatest of any of the women then or now. An assessment of that magnitude from one of the great composer/pianists of the past few decades suggests that Austin was formidable.

Other women who served in the studios as well as on stage as active musicians included the well-known Lillian Armstrong Hardin, pianist/arranger with King Oliver's band when she met her husband, Louis Armstrong. The budding Mary Lou Williams often sat in with Bennie Moten's Kansas City group. They and others were pioneers in the jazz tradition and established the credibility and set the pace for other women who were their peers and their successors. D. Antoinette Handy's *Black Women in American Bands and Orchestras* (1981) is the definitive study of the role and contributions of the many women who suffered the tribulations of sexism but triumphed anyway. They included Savannah Churchill; the young Ella Fitzgerald, who took over Chick Webb's band after his death; Dorothy Donegan, a formidable, powerful, and dynamic pianist; and Valaida Snow, who captivated audiences with her beauty but surprised them with her extraordinary talent as a jazz trumpeter. The epitome of the jazz woman was reflected in the astounding International Sweethearts of Rhythm, led by Anna Mae Winburn. Their rise to fame from the early days as members of the Piney Woods School band in Mississippi is the stuff of which movies are made. This group proved for all time that jazz or, for that matter, music in general, was not a male bastion. Yet their success and popularity were based more on the fact that this was an all-female band. Interestingly, they were not the only all-female group operating during those or subsequent years. Other all-female groups performed throughout the 1930s and early 1940s, but few women were accepted as sidepersons in the swing bands that proliferated during that era. Notable among the many instrumentalists who persevered are outstanding artists such as Melba Liston, trombonist; Dorothy Ashby, harpist; Vi Redd, saxophonist; Shirley Horn, Hazel Scott, Alice Coltrane, and Geri Allen, pianists; Patrice Rushen, percussionist, composer, and bandleader; and Bobbie Humphreys, flutist.

Singers carried the blues into jazz and created an entirely new approach to vocal performance. They raised the question, What is singing? For the jazz singer, just as for the instrumentalist, there were no rules that were sacred. Bend a note, extend a phrase, insert an obbligato, employ a vocalese, or throw away the words and scat in any nonlexical mode that suited the mood of the moment and the flavor of the piece. Ella Fitzgerald, Sarah Vaughan, and Carmen McRae represent the finest in this art form, and they are attended by others who were influenced by them. Maxine Sullivan took smoke and velvet and created a rich vocal tapestry that is still unmatched. She distinguished herself with masterful performances of standards such as "Loch Lomond." Dinah Washington knew the blues as well as she knew her name, but she combined that emotional expressivity with some of the hottest jazz vocals of the 1950s and 1960s. Her album *Dinah Jams* demonstrates her versatility and exceptional musicianship.

Alberta Hunter was among the blues singers who began their careers in the dance halls and social clubs of Chicago and New York. Hunter later achieved success in the chic cabarets of Paris, London, and Copenhagen. [Private Collection]

The rhythm and blues era introduced another group of women blues singers who picked up the tradition of Bessie Smith and Ma Rainey and "jazzed" the tempo and lyrics to fit the dance styles of the day. Ruth Brown, LaVern Baker, Big Maybelle, Big Mama Thornton, Etta James, and others brought to the dance floor an assertive style that had not been heard for many years and that captured the attention of white and Black audiences as the performers shouted or pleaded their case. A new tradition was set and quickly became the hallmark for a generation of younger singers, Aretha Franklin leading the pack. Over the years, Franklin, KoKo Taylor, Denise Lasalle, and other blues specialists used the styles, performance attitude, and perspective of their foremothers, as do their jazz counterparts Anita Baker, Diane Reeves, and Phyllis Hyman.

As we celebrate blues and jazz, we must extend our appreciation and recognition to include the women who contributed to the enhancement, development, and creation of this American art form. Their participation and presence were not as mere decorative appendages but as active innovators and creators of new approaches to sound, melody, rhythm, text, and performance style. They brought a voice that was not previously heard outside the churches or the local community and presented different perspectives and postures when they addressed the makings of the blues. They employed intelligence, wit, and intense sexuality and expressivity when they sang and played. Their collaboration and interaction with their male counterparts changed the music for the better. This they did in spite of the social and sexual politics that prevailed, because they loved the music and its people too much to silently disappear.

[*See also* INTERNATIONAL SWEETHEARTS OF RHYTHM.]

BIBLIOGRAPHY

Albertson, Chris. *Bessie* (1972); Dahl, Linda. *Stormy Weather: The Music and Lives of a Century of Jazz Women* (1984); Epstein, Dena J. *Sinful Tunes and Spirituals: Black Folk Music before the Civil War* (1977); Handy, D. Antoinette. *Black Women in American Bands and Orchestras* (1981); Harrison, Daphne D. *Black Pearls: Blues Queens of the 1920s* (1988), and "The Class Blues and Women Singers." In *The Blackwell Guide to the Blues,* ed. Paul Oliver (1989); Lieb, Sandra. *Mother of the Blues: A Study of Ma Rainey* (1981); Lovell, John. *Black Song: The Forge and the Flame* (1972); Placksin, Sally. *American Women in Jazz: 1900 to the Present* (1982).

SELECTED DISCOGRAPHY

Amtrak Blues: Alberta Hunter (Columbia CK36430); *Bessie Smith, Empty Bed Blues* (Columbia CG 30405); *Best of Mary Lou Williams* (Pablo [S] 2310 856); *The Country Girls! 1927-1935* (Original Jazz Library OJL-6); *Dinah Jams: Dinah Washington* (EmArcy EXPR 1013, reissued on MCR 36000); *Dinah Sings Bessie Smith* (Trip TLP 5556); *Forty Years of Women in Jazz* (Stash STB 001); *Gertrude Ma Rainey, Queen of the Blues 1923-1924* (Biograph BLP 12032); *Hot Snow: Valaida Snow* (Rosetta RR 1305); *I Never Loved a Man the Way I Loved You: Aretha Franklin* (Atlantic SD 8139); *Jailhouse Blues* (Rosetta RR 1316); *"Little" Esther Phillips, The Complete Savoy Recordings* (Savoy Jazz SJL 2258); *Maxine Sullivan & Earl Hines Live at the Overseas Press Club* (Chiaroscura DHI 107); *Mean Mothers* (Rosetta RR 1300); *Off the Record: Koko Taylor* (Chess CH 9263); *Sarah Vaughan & Dizzy Gillespie* (Zone 17); *Super Sister* (Rosetta RR); *Tell Mama: Etta James* (Chess MCA CH 9269); *Women Don't Need No Men: Lucille Bogan* (Agram Blues AB 2005); *Women in Jazz, vol. 1: All-Women Groups* (Stash ST 111); *Women in Jazz, vol. 2: Pianists* (Stash ST 112); *Women in Jazz, vol. 3: Swingtime to Modern* (Stash ST 113); *Women of the Blues* (RCA Victor Vintage Series LPV 534); *Women's Railroad Blues* (Rosetta RR 1301); *Young Alberta Hunter* (Stash SJ 123).

SELECTED FILMS RELATING TO WOMEN IN BLUES AND JAZZ

Alberta Hunter Live (Proud to Be Black video); *Aretha Franklin: Queen of Soul* (Proud to Be Black video); *Billie Holiday: Long Night of Lady Day* (Proud to Be Black video); *Caldonia (Louis Jordan with Young Billie Holiday)* (AM videos); *Ella Fitzgerald in Concert* (AM videos); *St. Louis Blues (Bessie Smith)* (AM videos); *Sarah Vaughan Live from Monterey* (Proud to Be Black video); *Sippie (Wallace)* (AM videos); *Wild Women Don't Have the Blues* (California Newsreel video).

DAPHNE DUVAL HARRISON

BOLDEN, DOROTHY LEE (1923-)

Using the knowledge of her years doing domestic work and her experiences as a community activist, in 1968 Dorothy Lee Bolden organized the National Domestic Workers Union, which successfully improved the wages and working conditions of domestic workers in Atlanta and served as an ongoing model for those in other cities.

Dorothy Lee Bolden was born on October 13, 1923, in Atlanta, the daughter of Raymond Bolden, a chauffeur, and Georgia Mae Patterson, a cook who had migrated to Atlanta from Madison, Georgia. She received her formal education through the ninth grade at E. P. Johnson Elementary School and David T. Howard High School in Atlanta.

At age three, Bolden was blinded after a fall that damaged her optical nerve. Her sight returned between the ages of seven and nine, and during this period, her work life began. She took her first job in 1930 washing diapers after school for $1.25 per week. At age twelve, she cleaned house for $1.50 per week for a Jewish family that, according to Bolden, was kosher and hung her bread "outside the door in a sugar sack" on holidays.

In 1941, Bolden married Frank Smith, whom she referred to later as "just a good looking man coming." Within a short period of time, the couple divorced and Bolden married Abram Thompson. Bolden is the mother of six children.

Over the years Bolden was employed in a variety of jobs. She worked at the Greyhound bus station, Linen Supply Company, Railroad Express, and Sears Roebuck. She would regularly quit these jobs after a brief tenure and do domestic work, then take on another job with a company in order to pay into Social Security. According to Bolden, "I would quit when I got ready and take a domestic job because of the excitement of going." She worked as a maid from

1930 until 1968. At one time in her career, she was jailed for allegedly talking back to an employer. According to Bolden, "They said I was 'mental' because I talked back. No one had ever talked as nasty to me as she did. I was in jail for five days."

In the 1960s, Bolden was involved in the civil rights movement with her neighbor, Dr. Martin Luther King, Jr. In 1964, when the Atlanta School Board decided to move the eighth grade out of her community to a condemned school building downtown, she organized a boycott and protest demanding equal and quality education. As a result of these efforts, the board built a modern school in her neighborhood.

Well aware of the working conditions and problems facing fellow workers in private households, in 1964 she began plans for an organization that would work to improve the wages and working conditions of maids. The legal minimum wage set by the U.S. government at the time was $1.25 per hour, but African-American maids in Atlanta were earning $3.50 to $5.00 a day for twelve to thirteen hours of work.

The organizing techniques Bolden learned during the skirmish with the school board were to serve her well when she attempted to organize Atlanta's maids. As a result of her community involvement, Bolden was well known to many Atlanta citizens. Further, during bus rides with other maids over the years, she had heard their complaints about "no money, no respect, and long hours." She was also encouraged by King in her organizing efforts.

In 1968, Bolden asked representatives of organized labor for support and direction. They advised her to assemble a meeting of at least ten women. Within a few months, after several hundred women gathered, organized labor responded. Instead of affiliating with the AFL-CIO, the group decided to create a new union, the National Domestic Workers Union. In September 1968, Bolden was elected president.

Under Bolden's charismatic leadership, the group received a charter, and membership increased. As a result of the group's efforts, wages increased and working conditions improved; maids received $13.50 to $15.00 per day plus carfare. Members were taught to work out their problems with their employers. In time the organization gained clout because of its cohesiveness, evangelical spirit, and community involvement. As president, Bolden was recognized as a major community leader.

During the 1970s, Bolden was consulted by presidents Richard Nixon, Gerald Ford, and Jimmy Carter on issues regarding workers, and she received many local, state, and national appointments. From 1972 to 1976, she served as a member of the advisory committee in the Department of Health, Education and Welfare to Secretary Elliot L. Richardson. In 1975, she was appointed to the Georgia Commission on the Status of Women by Governor George Busbee. She also spent considerable energy organizing domestic workers in other cities.

In 1980, negative publicity surrounding a federal grand jury investigation of the National Domestic Workers Emergency Assistance Fund served to undermine the growth of the organization. An audit of the organization's books revealed that more money had been spent than was allocated by grants funding the group. The investigation found, however, that Bolden had supplemented federal funds with personal monies in order to carry out the organization's programs.

The main goals of the National Domestic Workers Union have been to develop training programs for maids and create a nonprofit employee service to provide job placement and counseling for its members. As president of the group, Bolden spends her days providing social services to her clients and placing eligible applicants in domestic jobs. According to Bolden, "God put me here to help other people."

[See also NATIONAL DOMESTIC WORKERS UNION.]

BIBLIOGRAPHY
Laker, Barbara. "The Fighter," *Atlanta Constitution* (January 6, 1983); Bolden, Dorothy Lee. Personal interviews (September 15, 1982; February 1, 1983; and November 11 and 13, 1991). Records of the National Domestic Workers Union can be found in the Southern Labor Archives, Georgia State University, and at the organization's office, Atlanta.

DOROTHY COWSER YANCY

BOLIN, JANE MATHILDA (1908-)

Judge Jane Bolin's view of her job upon her appointment to the Domestic Relations Court of the City of New York in 1939 was that she was a judge for the whole city and for all children who are in trouble. She was the first Black woman judge in the United States. Other notable firsts in her life have included being the first Black woman to be admitted to the Association of the Bar of the City of New York in the 1940s.

Jane Mathilda Bolin was born in Poughkeepsie, New York, on April 11, 1908, to Gaius C. and Mathilda Bolin. She received her elementary and second-

When he appointed her to the Domestic Relations Court of New York City in 1939, Mayor Fiorello LaGuardia made Jane Bolin the first Black woman judge in the United States, praising her for her broad sympathy for human suffering. [Library of Congress]

ary education in the public school system and attended Wellesley College. She graduated from Wellesley in 1928 and was named a "Wellesley Scholar," an honor reserved for the twenty women with the highest scholastic standing in their class. She went on to graduate from Yale University Law School in 1931, becoming the first Black woman ever to have done so.

Upon her admission to the New York Bar in 1932, Bolin began her career as an attorney in her father and brother's law firm in Poughkeepsie, New York. She married attorney Ralph E. Mizelle in 1933 and worked as his law partner until 1937. It was during this time that she ran for public office. In the 1936 election, she was the unsuccessful Republican candidate for the state assembly seat from New York's seventeenth district.

On April 7, 1937, Bolin was assigned as assistant corporate counsel in New York City's law department. She felt that in her new office and position her biggest job was to educate private employers to give African-Americans jobs without discrimination, according to their qualifications.

Perhaps the most important day in Bolin's career came on July 22, 1939. On that date, Bolin was appointed as Justice of the Domestic Relations Court of New York by Mayor Fiorello LaGuardia. She was responsible for bringing citywide attention, in the 1940s, to the ways in which private schools and child care institutions in New York City discriminated against children because of race or color. Bolin remained a justice when the court was reorganized to become the New York Family Court in 1962.

During her first ten years on the bench, Judge Bolin was never reversed by the higher courts. When asked why he had originally selected Bolin, Mayor LaGuardia explained that she had common sense, patience, courtesy, and a broad sympathy for human suffering. Judge Bolin remained on the bench for over forty years, retiring on December 31, 1978. In recognition of her work on the bench, Bolin received honorary LL.D. degrees from Williams College, Morgan State College, Tuskegee Institute, Hampton Institute and Western College for Women.

Throughout her career, Judge Bolin remained active in the New York community. She served on the board of the New York Urban League, the New York branch of the National Association for the Advancement of Colored People, the Harlem Tuberculosis Committee, the legislative committee of the United Neighborhood Houses, and the Harlem Lawyers' Association, and she was a member of the New York County Lawyers Association. A woman ahead of her time, Judge Bolin retained her maiden name and is reported to have said it sounded strange to be addressed by her married name. She was cited for distinguished achievement and the improvement of race relations in 1939 in a nationwide poll conducted by the Schomburg Collection of the New York Public Library.

Bolin's first husband, Ralph E. Mizelle, died in September 1944. Bolin's only child, Yorke Bolin Mizelle, was born on July 22, 1941. Bolin married Reverend Walter P. Offutt, Jr., in November 1951, and was widowed a second time when Offutt died on October 7, 1974.

Since her retirement, Bolin has practiced family law as a consultant and has done volunteer tutoring in math and reading for public school children. Friends describe her as a "fighter," and a "courageous, nononsense, hard worker who never shirked an assignment" (*New York Times* 1978). Judge Bolin describes herself as determined to wage a fight for racial justice.

BIBLIOGRAPHY

Klemesrud, Judy. "For a Remarkable Judge, a Reluctant Retirement," *New York Times* (December 1978); Wellesley College Alumni Association. Clipping file.

WENDY BROWN

BONDS, MARGARET ALLISON RICHARDSON (1913-1972)

Margaret Bonds was born on March 3, 1913, in Chicago, Illinois. Her mother, Estella C. Bonds, was a church organist as well as her first teacher. Their home was frequented by young pianists, singers, violinists, and composers such as Will Marion Cook and Florence B. Price. It was a natural environment to nurture her own talents as both singer and composer.

As a high school student, Bonds studied with William L. Dawson and Florence Price. She received a Bachelor of Music and a Master of Music from Northwestern University in Evanston, Illinois, and continued graduate studies at the Juilliard School of Music in New York City.

She was the recipient of a Rosenwald Fellowship, a Roy Harris Scholarship, a National Association of Negro Musicians Award, and a Rodman Wanamaker Award. During her illustrious career she taught at the American Theatre Wing and she performed with several orchestras, including the Woman's Symphony, the New York City Symphony, and the Scranton (Pennsylvania) Philharmonic, and she was the first Black guest soloist with the Chicago Symphony at the Chicago World's Fair in 1933. From 1968 to 1972 she worked with the inner-city Cultural Center in Los Angeles and she also served as music director for several musical theater institutions in New York.

Bonds composed music for the theater as well as ballets, orchestral works, art songs, popular songs, spirituals, and piano pieces. Her works for piano and orchestra are programmatic, and each depicts her sense of ethnic identity through the use of jazz harmonies, spiritual materials, and social themes. Leontyne Price commissioned and recorded many of her arrangements of spirituals.

Margaret Bonds died in Los Angeles, California, on April 26, 1972.

[*See also* COMPOSERS.]

The first Black guest soloist with the Chicago Symphony Orchestra, Margaret Bonds was also a noted composer, many of whose arrangements of spirituals were commissioned and recorded by Leontyne Price. [Schomburg Center]

BIBLIOGRAPHY

Ammer, Christine. *Unsung: A History of Women in American Music* (1980); Berry, Lemuel, Jr. *Biographical Dictionary of Black Musicians and Music Educators* (1978); Bonds, Margaret. "A Reminiscence." In *The Afro-American in Music and Art—International Library of Afro-American Life and History*, ed. Lindsay Patterson (1976); Cohen, Aaron I. *International Encyclopedia of Women Composers* (1981); Harris, C. C., Jr. "Three Schools of Black Choral Composers and Arrangers, 1900-1970," *Choral Journal* (1974); Hitchcock, H. Wiley and Stanley Sadie. *The New Grove Dictionary of American Music* (1986); Obituary, *Variety* (May 10, 1972); Roach, Hildred. *Black American Music: Past and Present* (1984); Southern, Eileen. *The Music of Black Americans: A History* (1983); Spencer, Jon Michael. *As the Black School Sings* (1987); Stern, Susan. *Women Composers: A Handbook* (1978); Thomas, A. J. "A Study of the Selected Masses of Twentieth-Century Black Composers: Margaret Bonds, Robert Ray, George Walker and David Baker," Ph.D. diss. (1983); White, Evelyn Davidson. *Choral Music by Afro-American Composers: A Selected Annotated Bibliography* (1981); Williams, Ora. *American Black Women in the Arts and Sciences: A Bibliographic Survey* (1978); Programs of Margaret Bonds's concert performances can be found in the vertical file clippings of the Special Collections and Archives Division of Atlanta University's Robert W. Woodruff Library.

SANDRA CANNON SCOTT

BONNER, MARITA (1899-1971)

"On Being Young—a Woman—and Colored," a 1925 essay written by Marita Bonner and published in *Crisis*, embodies her concern for the deplorable conditions that Black Americans endure, particularly Black women. In this essay, Bonner speaks of the constraints placed on Black women, emphasizing that females should seek husbands they can look up to without looking down on themselves. She also suggests that Black women are doubly victimized by those who devalue their race and gender. Bonner advises young Black women to avoid bitterness and, instead, to quietly outthink their oppressors.

Publishing between world wars, from 1925 to 1941, in two leading magazines, *Opportunity* and *Crisis*, essayist, playwright, and short-story writer Marita Bonner treated a host of themes including miscegenation, the tragic mulatto, generational conflicts, European definitions of female respectability, dreams deferred, the destructiveness of the urban environment, racial revolution in America, infidelity, southern decadence, class bias, and interracial ties.

One of four children, Marita Bonner was born on June 16, 1899, in Boston to Joseph Andrew and Mary Anne (Noel) Bonner. Educated locally, Bonner attended Brookline High School before entering Radcliffe College, where she studied English and comparative literature between 1918 and 1922. While in college, Bonner began teaching at a local high school. After graduation, she taught school in Bluefield, West Virginia, and then in Washington, D.C., for eight years, where she became friends with Georgia Douglas Johnson, Langston Hughes, May Miller, Countee Cullen, Alain Locke, Jessie Fauset, S. Randolph Edmonds, Willis Richardson, and Jean Toomer.

Between 1922 and 1930, Bonner linked herself to the "S" Salon, a group of writers who met weekly at Georgia Douglas Johnson's home. She was nurtured and encouraged to write by this cadre of writers who became major figures of the Black Renaissance that occurred in urban areas such as Harlem, Chicago, and Washington, D.C. It was during this period that she published two essays that captured the spirit of the Black Renaissance. In addition to "On Being Young—a Woman—and Colored," which won first place in the *Crisis* literary contest of 1925, Bonner published "The Young Blood Hungers" (*Crisis*, 1928), which resonates with the warning of violence to come as a result of poor race relations in America.

Bonner wrote several noteworthy experimental plays during her years in Washington, D.C., including *The Pot Maker* (*Opportunity*, 1927), which levels an indictment against infidelity; *The Purple Flower* (*Crisis*, 1928), which calls for a bloody revolution to temper racism; and *Exit—An Illusion* (*Crisis*, 1929), which deals with the complications of mixed ancestry.

After marrying Rhode Island native and Brown University graduate William Almy Occomy in 1930, she moved to Chicago, where she raised three children, William Almy, Jr., Warwick Gale Noel, and Marita Joyce, who helped to recover her mother's texts in *Frye Street and Environs: The Collected Works of Marita Bonner Occomy* (1987).

Bonner concentrated exclusively on developing her craft in fiction in the 1930s, a choice that led to her winning several first- and second-place literary prizes offered by *Crisis* and *Opportunity*. The fictitious, multiethnic Frye Street of Chicago is the setting of her short stories. Preoccupied with the destructiveness of the urban environment, her Chicago stories deal with class and color demarcations, poverty, and poor housing. Some of Bonner's stories written in the early 1930s may have influenced Richard Wright, who knew Bonner and her work. Bonner's "Tin Can" (*Opportunity*, 1933) resembles in its plot Wright's *Native Son* (1940).

Although Bonner rarely wrote after 1941, she continued to teach periodically during the forty-one years she lived in Chicago, including working with mentally handicapped persons. She died on December 6, 1971, of injuries sustained in a fire in her Chicago apartment.

Marita Bonner's major literary contribution is her characterization of the urban environment as a corrupting force. Her portraits of elite Black Chicagoans and their poor counterparts reflect the negative impact of the urban environment on human dignity. Her characters belong to a lost world that cramps people in substandard housing, turns middle-class African-Americans against recently immigrated, uneducated southerners, and allows homeless and other poor people to die unattended. Bonner's mark is no small one, considering that she frequently captured literary prizes and served as a role model to aspiring writers who looked to her innovative craft. Educated at one of the finest universities in America, Bonner rejected prescriptive roles. By balancing a writing career with family responsibilities and teaching, Marita Bonner exemplified the lessons of her first published work, "On Being Young—a Woman—and Colored."

BIBLIOGRAPHY

AAW2; Brown-Guillory, Elizabeth, ed. *Wines in the Wilderness: Plays by African American Women from the Harlem Renaissance to the Present* (1990); Flynn, Joyce and Joyce Occomy Stricklin, eds. *Frye Street and Environs: The Collected Works of Marita Bonner Occomy* (1987); Isaacs, Diane. "Marita Bonner." In *The Harlem Renaissance: A Dictionary for the Era*, ed. Bruce Kellner (1984).

ELIZABETH BROWN-GUILLORY

BOONE, EVA ROBERTA COLES (1880-1902)

Wives who accompanied their husbands to Africa were designated as assistant missionaries and were engaged in so-called women's work. Such was the case for Eva Boone. Eva Roberta Coles was born on January 8, 1880, in Charlottesville, Virginia. In May 1899, she graduated from Hartshorn Memorial College (Richmond, Virginia; later merged into Virginia Union University), which had been established

One of Eva Boone's most difficult missionary tasks was teaching sewing to African women; they viewed it as "men's work." [Sylvia M. Jacobs]

to train young Black women as teachers and in the domestic arts.

Coles taught in Charlottesville for a short time before marrying Clinton C. Boone on January 16, 1901. Coles probably met Boone in Richmond while he was a student at Richmond Theological Seminary (now Virginia Union University).

The couple traveled to Africa in April 1901, under the auspices of the American Baptist Missionary Union (ABMU, now the American Baptist Churches in the U.S.A.) in cooperation with the Lott Carey Baptist Foreign Mission Convention (after 1902 the Lott Carey Baptist Home and Foreign Mission Convention of the United States). They were stationed at Palabala, Congo (now Zaire), the oldest station in Africa of the ABMU, which they reached on May 24, 1901.

Although Clinton Boone was the officially appointed missionary, his wife was also expected to perform mission duties. Consequently, Eva Boone took charge of the kindergarten class in the mission day school where thirty to forty children attended daily. She organized a sewing group among forty reluctant African women who saw sewing as men's work. In addition, since women missionaries often dispensed first aid, Boone sometimes administered medical treatment. However, after several weeks of illness, brought on by a poisonous bite, Eva Boone died at Palabala on December 8, 1902, only twenty-two years old.

BIBLIOGRAPHY

Annual Report of the American Baptist Missionary Union (1905-1906); Boone, Clinton C. *Congo as I Saw It* (1927), and *Liberia as I Know It* (1929); Freeman, Edward A. *The Epoch of Negro Baptists and the Foreign Mission Board* (1953).

SYLVIA M. JACOBS

BOOZE, MARY CORDELIA MONTGOMERY (1877-c. 1948)

Mary Cordelia Montgomery Booze was an African-American clubwoman, civic leader, and Republican National Committee member. Born at Brierfield (Davis Bend, Mississippi), the antebellum home of Confederate President Jefferson Davis, she was one of the twelve children of former slaves Isaiah T. and Martha Robb Montgomery.

From childhood, she experienced material comfort and family connections such as few Black Mississippians could imagine. Her paternal grandfather, Benjamin Montgomery, and his sons briefly owned the vast Davis plantation (4,000 acres), and he was one of the largest cotton producers in Mississippi and the state's first Black public officeholder. Her father won fame as town builder, businessman, state Republican leader, and close political ally of Booker T. Washington. In 1887, following the loss of their Davis Bend properties, her parents moved to Mound Bayou, the all-Black Bolivar County agricultural colony founded and dominated by her father.

She attended high school and completed two years of college at Straight University in New Orleans and then found employment as her father's bookkeeper and instructor at Mound Bayou Normal Institute. In 1901, she married Eugene P. Booze, a prosperous Clarksdale businessman. The couple had two children and lived briefly in Colorado Springs, Colorado, before returning to Mound Bayou in 1909. Together they acquired extensive agricultural interests; he became a business partner of her father, and she turned to what she often called "race building."

Mary Montgomery Booze was the town example of Black achievement. In 1924, she became the first Black woman elected to the Republican National Committee, a position she held for two decades. Victimized by the racial and gender values of her time and place, her political life was often plagued by controversy—including allegations that she violated social taboos by both dancing and dining with Herbert Hoover in 1928. With fellow "Black and Tan" leaders she helped deny a "lily-white" takeover of the state Republican organization. She also numbered among Mississippi clubwomen who quietly agitated for more equitable distribution of public services to Black Americans. Although she moved to New York City following the unsolved murder of her husband in 1939, she continued to represent Mississippi on the Republican National Committee until 1948.

BIBLIOGRAPHY

Hermann, Janet Sharp. *The Pursuit of a Dream* (1981); McMillen, Neil R. *Dark Journey: Black Mississippians in the Age of Jim Crow* (1989); Redding, Saunders. *No Day of Triumph* (1942); the Benjamin T. Montgomery Family papers are in the Library of Congress, Washington, D.C.

NEIL R. McMILLAN

BOWEN, CORNELIA (1858-1934)

"One could feel the impact of her dedication and commitment. It was here that my outlook on, and commitment to, life began to take shape. It was here that I began to dream dreams of the life I wanted to live." This brief comment demonstrates the lifelong impression that was made on Solomon Seay (1991), a Montgomery civil rights leader, by Cornelia Bowen, his teacher and principal, whose life was dedicated to the education of Black youth.

Cornelia Bowen was born into slavery in 1858, on Col. William Bowen's plantation home in Macon County, Alabama. She attended Tuskegee Institute, where she was a member of the first graduating class in 1885. Upon graduation, she was named principal of Tuskegee Institute's Children's House. While on a fund-raising tour in the New England area in 1888, Washington telegraphed Bowen with a request that she start a school in the vicinity of Mt. Meigs, Alabama. Toward that end and with the use of funds provided by E. N. Pierce of Plainville, Connecticut, Bowen purchased land and began an industrial school known as the Mt. Meigs Institute. After the state assumed control of the school in the early 1900s, Bowen remained on the board of trustees.

Bowen continued her own education by attending Teachers College at Columbia University and Queen Margaret College in Glasgow, Scotland, among other institutions of higher learning. She also served as an officer of many organizations, including the Alabama State Teachers Association, the Colored Women's Federation of the State of Alabama, and the National Association of Colored Women. After a life of stressing the importance of education, Cornelia Bowen died in 1934.

BIBLIOGRAPHY

Gray, Jerome A., Joe L. Reed, and Norman W. Walton. *History of the Alabama State Teachers Association* (1987); Harlan, Louis R., ed. *Booker T. Washington Papers* (1972); Lerner, Gerda. "Early Community Work of Black Club Women," *Journal of Negro History* (April 1974); *The National Encyclopedia of the Colored Race* (1919); Seay, Solomon S., Sr. *I Was There by the Grace of God* (1991); Thompson, B. S., Sr. *A Century of Negro Progress in Montgomery City and County* (1963); Washington, Booker T. *Up from Slavery* ([1901] 1963).

SANDRA BEHEL

BOWEN, RUTH (1924-)

Ruth Bowen is president of Queen Booking Corporation, once the largest Black-owned talent clearinghouse in the world. Born in Danville, Virginia, on September 13, 1924, the product of an interracial marriage between her Black/French mother and her father, who was an English-born Irishman, Ruth never was made to feel inferior growing up with three older white half sisters.

She attended New York University for two years prior to her 1944 marriage to Billy Bowen, one of the original Ink Spots, a group renowned as one of the first Black acts to break the racial barrier of the 1950s. They remained married until his death in 1982.

Managing her husband's business affairs provided Bowen with much of the background and practical business experience that led to her long and successful career in the entertainment business. Bowen spent a great deal of time traveling with the Ink Spots in the 1940s and 1950s, during which time she learned first-hand about racism and the treatment of African-Americans as second-class citizens. Although the Ink Spots were a big act, after World War II there were still hotels that would not rent rooms to them. In an interview she stated that on one such occasion, "Arrangements had been made for us to stay in a guest house in Salt Lake City," Bowen recalls. "When we pulled up I said, 'I'm not staying here.' Billy asked where were we going to stay. I said, 'Take me to the best hotel in the city.' . . . I left Billy and Harold Francis, the piano player, in the car, and scared to death I marched into the hotel and asked for two rooms," Bowen continued. "When the bellboy went to the car to get the luggage and Billy and Harold, I knew it was over. But there were no problems, and we spent the night in the best hotel in Salt Lake City."

Major Robinson, a nationally syndicated columnist, introduced Bowen to Dinah Washington in 1945, and Bowen became Washington's press secretary in 1946. Soon Washington began urging Bowen to assume personal management responsibilities for her because of the rampant exploitation that she faced as a performer.

In 1959, Bowen opened up her business, Queen Artists, with an initial investment of $500. The office was so small that her staff of four "had to back in and out," according to Bowen. Before long, Queen Artists began handling the press and bookings for Earl Bostic, Johnny Lytle, Kenny Burrell, and the Basin Street East nightclub. The number of clients grew, and the staff increased to thirty. By 1969, Queen Booking Corporation had become the largest Black-owned entertainment agency in the world. The more than 100 acts handled by Queen Booking ran the gamut from individual singers to soul-rock groups to gospel choirs to comedians. The most famous single performers included Sammy Davis, Jr., Aretha Franklin, and Ray Charles.

Among the other popular acts handled by Queen Booking were the Drifters, Harold Melvin and the Bluenotes, Patti LaBelle and the Blue Belles, Curtis Mayfield and the Impressions, Gladys Knight and the Pips, the Isley Brothers, Kool and the Gang, the Dells, the ChiLites, the O'Jays, Teddy Pendergrass, Smokey Robinson, Bobby Womack, Marvin Gaye, Ike and Tina Turner, the Four Tops, the Marvelettes, Dee Dee Warwick, the Delfonics, the Staple Singers, the Stylistics, Barbara Mason, Ben E. King, Al Green, Tavares, the Reverend James Cleveland, Shirley Caesar, the Mighty Clouds of Joy, Andrae Crouch, Clara Ward, Richard Pryor, Slappy White, Willie Tyler, and Stu Gilliam.

BIBLIOGRAPHY

Information provided in personal interviews with Ruth Bowen.

REGINA JONES

BOWLES, EVA DEL VAKIA
(1875-1943)

As white and colored women we must understand each other, we must think and work and plan together, for upon all of us rests the responsibility of the girlhood of our nation. (Olcott 1919)

Eva del Vakia Bowles, longtime Secretary for Colored Work for the Young Women's Christian Association (YWCA) National Board, can be credited as the architect of race relations in the largest multiracial movement for women in the twentieth century. During the period of the nation's most stringent segregation policies and practices, while she was in charge of work with Black women in the YWCA, Bowles supervised an enormous increase in local and national Black staff as well as in services to Black women.

She was born in Albany, Athens County, Ohio, on January 24, 1875, the eldest of three children. Her parents, John Hawkes Bowles and Mary Jane (Porter) Bowles, were native Ohioans. Her grandfather, John R. Bowles, served as chaplain of the all-Black, Fifty-Fifth Massachusetts Infantry during the Civil War and later became the first Black teacher hired by the Ohio Public School Fund. Her father taught school in Marietta, Ohio, but quit when he realized that his employment could be used to rationalize segregated education for Black children. The family then moved to Columbus, where he became the first Black postal clerk for the Railway Mail Service.

After completing high school in Columbus, Bowles attended a local business college and took summer courses at Ohio State University. Later she attended the Columbia University School of Philanthropy. She began her working career as the first Black faculty member at Chandler Normal School in Lexington, Kentucky, and, later, on the faculties of St. Augustine's School in Raleigh, North Carolina, and St. Paul's Normal and Industrial Institute in Lawrenceville, Virginia. In 1905, she was called to New York to work as secretary of the Colored Young Women's Christian Association (later the famous 137th Street YWCA in Harlem). With this position she became the first Black YWCA secretary.

In 1913, after a short assignment as a caseworker in her hometown, Bowles was invited to return to New York as secretary of the newly formed YWCA National Board Subcommittee for Colored Work. Under her careful and cautious leadership, the sub-

committee, which was responsible for work among Black women in cities, evolved to departmental status with a full staff. However, she maintained what she called "a vision of a truly interracial movement" and fought vigorously any notion of a permanent "colored department." In her view, while Black women should be responsible for decision-making for their own constituency, it was equally important that they should be in "constant conference with the white women of the Central Association" (Olcott 1919). Thus, she supported the idea that there should be only one association in a city, with branches to serve Black women.

As a secretary under the YWCA's War Work Council during World War I, Bowles supervised the expansion of service to Black women and girls from sixteen branches and centers at the beginning of the war to the establishment of recreation and industrial centers in over forty-five cities. To accomplish this, she involved many prominent local and national Black clubwomen. Asserting that "the War [gave] opportunity for the colored woman to prove her ability for leadership," Bowles used the influence of these women to press for more equitable representation on local boards and committees (Olcott 1919). President Theodore Roosevelt was so impressed with the magnitude and quality of Bowles's work during the war that he designated $4,000 of his Nobel Peace Prize award to be disbursed as she designated.

After the war, Bowles concentrated on moving the national association to more active work on race relations. Immediately after the war, when Black southern leaders threatened to leave the association because of their displeasure with what they felt was a governance structure that "could go no faster than the white women ... would permit," she was able to mediate the situation by having the national board appoint Black women to the regional field committees as well as to field staffs (Association Records 1920). She also led an effort to have the national board sponsor meetings and conventions only in facilities where all participants could be accommodated. In her international work, she was an advocate for increased work with Black women in Africa and in the Caribbean. She also served as an important liaison between the association and such organizations as the National Urban League, the National Interracial Conference, the American Interracial Peace Committee, the National Association for the Advancement of Colored People (NAACP), the National League of Women Voters, the Commission of Church and Race Relations of the Federal Council of Churches, and her own denominational Episcopalian women's interracial organization.

When the national board reorganized its staff in 1931, the "colored department" was phased out and Black staff were assigned to the organization's three main divisions. While this move was greeted by Bowles as a real achievement in an interracial setup, she resigned from her position in 1932. According to biographer Clarice Winn Davis, Bowles's objective "to have Negro women share fully and equally in all activities" was not fulfilled as she had hoped. Rather, Bowles protested that, in effect, the reorganization "diminish[ed] participation of Negroes in the policy making of the Association" (*DANB*).

Following Bowles's retirement from the YWCA National Board staff, she briefly filled an executive position with the National Colored Merchants Association, sponsored by the National Business League. She returned to Ohio and served as acting secretary for the West End Branch of the YWCA in Cincinnati from January 1934 until June 1935. During the 1940 presidential campaign, she was a Harlem organizer for the Wendell Willkie Republicans. She died of complications from cancer while visiting a niece in Richmond, Virginia, on June 14, 1943. She is buried in the Bowles family plot in Columbus, Ohio, where she resided in her final years.

BIBLIOGRAPHY

Association Records. YWCA, Richmond, Virginia (1920); Bell, Juliet O. and Helen J. Wilkins. "Interracial Practices in Community Y.W.C.A.s" (1944); Bowles, Eva D. "The Colored Girls in Our Midst," *Association Monthly* (December 1917), and "Negro Women and the Y.W.C.A.," *Women's International Quarterly* (October 1919), and "The YWCA and Racial Understanding," *Woman's Press* (September 1929); Calkins, Gladys Gilkey. "The Negro in the Young Women's Christian Association," M.A. thesis (1960); *DANB*; Jones, Adrienne Lash. "Struggle among the Saints: Black Women in the YWCA, 1870-1920," Paper (1991); *NAW*; Obituaries, *Woman's Press* (September 1943), and *Norfolk Journal and Guide* (June 19, 1943); Olcott, Jane. "The Growth of Our Colored Work," *Association Monthly* (November 1919), and *The Work of Colored Women* (1919), and "History of Colored Work . . . 1907-1920," typescript (1920); Speer, Emma Bailey. "Eva del Vakia Bowles," *Woman's Press* (July 1932); YWCA National Board Archives. *War Work Bulletin* (December 28, 1917, and December 6, 1918); YWCA National Board personnel files and association records.

ADRIENNE LASH JONES

BOWMAN, LAURA (1881-1957)

"No history of the Negro in the twentieth-century theatre can be complete without the name of Laura Bowman," whose fifty-year career spanned stage, screen, and radio (Johnson 1933). The daughter of a Dutch mother and a mulatto father, Laura Bradford was born on October 3, 1881, in Quincy, Illinois, but was raised in Cincinnati, Ohio. She began singing as a youngster in church choirs, but her professional career began as a chorus girl in *In Dahomey* (1902), starring the legendary comic team of Bert Williams and George Walker. Bowman had married Henry Ward Bowman, a railroad porter, in 1898, but had left him after only a few years of marriage.

In 1903, the cast of *In Dahomey* sailed from New York to London where they gave a command performance at Buckingham Palace at the ninth birthday party for the Prince of Wales. After the first company of *In Dahomey* broke up in London, Bowman and Pete Hampton, an executive and star of *In Dahomey* who had fallen in love with her, formed a quartet called the Darktown Entertainers, featuring William Garland, tenor; Fred Douglas, bass; Pete Hampton, baritone; and Bowman, soprano. Bowman and Hampton had a common-law marriage. The Darktown Entertainers sang a variety of songs, and Bowman performed several character sketches in costume. These characterizations proved to be good training for her later work on the dramatic stage.

After the Darktown Entertainers disbanded, Bowman and Hampton performed as a duo in Switzerland, Moscow, Budapest, and England. When the English government ordered all foreigners home, the couple returned to New York, and Hampton and Bowman toured the East Coast performing their act. Shortly afterward, however, Hampton died.

In 1916, Bowman joined the celebrated Lafayette Players, Harlem's most successful stock acting troupe. At her first rehearsal she met Sidney Kirkpatrick. After appearing in numerous shows at the Lafayette, Bowman and Kirkpatrick left the company, married, and formed an act. They played along the East Coast before moving to Indianapolis, Kirkpatrick's home town. Racial restrictions were so severe for Black performers in Indianapolis that they billed themselves as a modern Hawaiian duet in order to work. Because the couple was fair-skinned, they were able to play in theaters where neither Black performers nor patrons were allowed.

In 1923, Bowman and Kirkpatrick returned to New York where she played the part of Aunt Nancy in Willis Richardson's *The Chip Woman's Fortune*, the first drama by a Black author to reach Broadway. After *Chip Woman* closed, the couple worked in the Indianapolis area again before rejoining the Lafayette Players. In February 1928, Bowman played Josephine, Mose's wife, in *Meek Mose*, written by actor Frank Wilson (who had played the title role in *Porgy*). The show ran for thirty-two performances at the Princess Theatre in New York. *Meek Mose* received mixed reviews, but Bowman's acting was praised.

In August 1928, Bowman and Kirkpatrick moved to Los Angeles with the Lafayette Players. After the group disbanded in 1930 (they later reunited in 1932 before disbanding permanently), they became members of the Hall Singers and sang in the films *Check and Double Check* with Amos and Andy and *Dixiana* with Bebe Daniels (both 1930).

Bowman returned to New York, where she appeared as a servant in *Sentinels* (1931). Virtually all the critics panned the play but cited Bowman as giving an excellent performance. Four months later, Bowman was back on Broadway in *The Tree* (1932). This drama about lynching in the North also was panned by the critics, but Bowman's work was again enthusiastically received. After more than twenty-five years in show business, Bowman had finally begun to establish herself as a dramatic actress on the professional stage. Although the shows were short-lived and her roles were stereotyped, she had had two Broadway openings within six months, quite an accomplishment at the time.

In 1932, Bowman appeared on the screen in *Ten Minutes to Live*, produced by Oscar Micheaux, a Black film pioneer. The couple then went back to performing their act, but shortly thereafter, Kirkpatrick died in Harlem Hospital of a heart attack, and Bowman was once again left a widow. A few weeks later, however, in February 1933, she appeared in *Louisiana*. Written by Black author Augustus Smith, *Louisiana* opened at the Majestic Theatre in Brooklyn before moving to the 48th Street Theatre. For the most part the reviews were unfavorable, except for Bowman's.

After Kirkpatrick's death, Bowman began to drink heavily at a bar in Harlem frequented by theater people. While there, she met her fourth husband, LeRoi Antoine. Antoine, a Haitian who had aspirations of becoming an opera singer, was twenty-three years her junior. She called him "my boy," and many of her friends called her a "cradle snatcher" (Antoine 1961). Nonetheless, after knowing each other for only a short time, Bowman and Antoine got married, and Bowman's drinking problem improved.

At the end of 1933, Bowman returned to Broadway in *Jezebel*, with film star Miriam Hopkins playing the title role and Bowman playing Mammy Winnie. Her notices were good. During the 1930s, Bowman worked with Helen Hayes on the radio program *New Penny Show* as well as on other radio programs, including *Stella Dallas, John's Other Wife, Pepper Young's Family, The O'Neills, Pretty Kitty Kelly,* and *The Southernaires*. During that time, Bowman could be heard on some radio show nearly every day. Also, in 1934 Bowman recreated the role of Aunt Hagar in *Drums of Voodoo*, the film version of *Louisiana*. The following year, she was seen in Oscar Micheaux's *Lem Hawkin's Confession* (1935).

Returning to drama, Bowman played Miranda, a servant, in Sophie Treadwell's *Plumes in the Dust* (1936) at the 46th Street Theatre in New York. Pauline Myers, one of Bowman's students, played Lou, another servant. In 1938, she appeared in the landmark production of *Conjur* at the Saint Felix Theatre in Brooklyn playing Parthenia, the Conjur Woman. A new play about religion and superstition, *Conjur* featured an all-Black cast, which was considered bold in Brooklyn theatrical circles. Also in 1938, Bowman was seen in Oscar Micheaux's *God's Stepchildren*.

During the early part of 1939, Bowman was on Broadway in *Please, Mrs. Garibaldi* playing Endora, servant to an Italian-American family. The show closed after only four performances. Antoine had co-starred in *Voodoo Fire*, produced by Warner Brothers and starring Floyd Gibbons, and when he decided to pursue a film career, the couple moved to Los Angeles. They were disappointed by Hollywood, but fortunately, Bowman still had a film contract, and in 1940 she appeared as Dr. Helen Jackson in *Son of Ingagi*. Written by Spencer Williams, this film is significant as the first all-Black horror film. Also in 1940, she was seen on the screen in *The Notorious Elinor Lee* with Edna Mae Harris and Robert Earl Jones. In order to make ends meet, Bowman organized an amateur theater troupe and taught acting. Earlier, in Harlem, she had opened the National Art School, where she taught acting.

Bowman returned to New York in 1946 to perform in *Jeb*, a play about a World War II veteran, starring Ossie Davis. Ruby Dee played his sweetheart, and Bowman played his mother. Her weekly salary was $250. *Jeb* received mixed reviews and the show ran for only nine performances. Immediately following the closing of *Jeb*, Bowman, Ossie Davis, and Ruby Dee were cast in one of the touring companies of *Anna Lucasta*, Abram Hill's adaptation of Philip

Yordan's play about a Polish family. Bowman played Theresa, the role created by Georgia Burke on Broadway. She also performed with the Broadway cast.

Theresa was Bowman's last role. After a paralyzing stroke she retired from the stage. For seven years she had been Antoine's benefactor; now he took care of her. Although she had earned a considerable amount of money, she now was destitute. Confined to her bed, Bowman expressed bittersweet feelings about her life in show business: "I must say that my fifty years in the theatre have been most colorful . . . but, nevertheless, I have paid a price for my fifty years" (Antoine 1961).

On March 29, 1957, at the age of seventy-six, Bowman died in Los Angeles. Her obituary in the March 31, 1957, *New York Times* is a testament to her determination and talent: "It was said of Miss Bowman that she had played in about every country that had a theatre."

By performing on the stage, in film, and on radio, Bowman was able to sustain a career that lasted a half century. It was her flexibility, the ability to move from one area of show business to another, that enabled her to keep working. The problems of race relations in America during the period were reflected in the roles she was permitted to play. When she made the transition from a very successful career on the musical stage to drama, the majority of her roles, which were written by white authors, were as servants. Despite the negative implications, however, both Black and white critics agree that Bowman brought a certain dignity to every role she played.

A charter member of the Negro Actors Guild, Bowman often spoke out against the ill treatment of Black characters and Black performers, yet in order to earn a living, she, like some of her contemporaries, continued to play the parts that were available to her. In so doing she helped keep a Black presence on Broadway. Moreover, by utilizing the paths open to her, she helped find new gateways through which other Black women have since entered. Because of her perseverance, Bowman was among the first group of Black women to become respected dramatic actresses on the Broadway stage, establishing herself as a role model for the contemporary Black dramatic actress.

Through her association with the Lafayette Players and her own shows (she hired other Black actors, singers, and dancers), Bowman also helped foster and develop Black theater. In addition to organizing amateur acting troupes, she taught some of the Black actors of the 1930s and 1940s, and by helping to provide trained talent, she made a contribution to mainstream American theater. Thus, although she never had the opportunity to reach her full potential, Bowman, like some of her contemporaries, not only survived, but flourished.

BIBLIOGRAPHY

Amsterdam News, "Calls New Play Morbid Drama" (Review of *The Tree*, April 20, 1932); Antoine, LeRoi. *Achievement: The Life of Laura Bowman* (1961); Atkinson, Brooks. "Sentinel," *New York Times* (December 26, 1931), and "The Tree," *New York Times* (April 13, 1932), and "Conjur," *New York Times* (November 1, 1938); Black Theatre Scrapbook. Schomburg Center for Research in Black Culture, The New York Public Library, New York City; *Jezebel* Scrapbook. Billy Rose Theatre Collection, The New York Public Library for the Performing Arts, New York City; Johnson, Dido. "The Truly Startling Story of Laura Bowman," *Daily Citizen* (December 30, 1933); Klotman, Phyllis. *Frame by Frame* (1979); Mackey, Garland. "Former Local Girl Stars in 'Drums of Voodoo,' " *Washington Tribune* (February 1, 1934); Mantle, Burns. "Gods of Vengeance and '*Louisiana*,' " *Daily News* (New York) (March 1, 1933); *New York Post*, "Conjur" clippings (November 1, 1938); Rigdon, Walter, ed. *Biographical Encyclopedia and Who's Who of the American Theatre* (1966); Sampson, Henry T. *Blacks in Blackface: A Sourcebook on Early Black Musical Shows* (1980); Tanner, Jo A. *Dusky Maidens: the Odyssey of the Early Black Dramatic Actress* (1992); and personal interview with Dick Campbell (May 7, 1990); *Variety*, "Jeb" (February 13, 1946).

JO A. TANNER

BOWMAN, SISTER THEA (1937-1990)

Sister Thea Bowman, singer, dancer, liturgist, educator, evangelist, prophet—all these roles were embodied in one exuberant woman who was able to find the common thread that interweaves people of all races, colors, and creeds. She spent her life preaching the Good News as a woman, a Black American, and a Franciscan Sister. Sister Thea saw herself as a "pilgrim in the journey looking for home," often lamenting, "sometimes I feel like a motherless child." Yet she never doubted she was "God's child—somebody special," adding, "we are all beautiful children of God." Called to share her gift—her song and story, her life—in the end, she envisioned herself not as dying but as "going home like a shooting star."

Sister Thea (Bertha) Bowman was born December 29, 1937, in Yazoo City, Mississippi, the daughter of Dr. Theon Edward and Mary Esther (Coleman) Bowman. She grew up in Canton, Mississippi, where her father had located his medical practice. At the age of nine she became a member of the Catholic Church. Because her parents were not satisfied with the quality of education given their only child in the local public school, the Bowmans enrolled her in Holy Child Jesus School in Canton, staffed by the Franciscan Sisters of Perpetual Adoration from La Crosse, Wisconsin.

When she was fifteen, Bertha decided to enter the community of Sisters who had taught her. At her reception into the novitiate in 1956, she received the name Sister Thea. She was the first and only Black member of that religious community—a challenge to both Sister Thea and to the community to look at and accept racial differences.

Sister Thea earned her undergraduate degree in English from Viterbo College, La Crosse, as well as a Master's degree and a doctorate in English literature and linguistics from the Catholic University of America in Washington, D.C. As a graduate student she taught the first class in Black literature at the university.

Sister Thea's teaching career included students at all levels—elementary, secondary, and college. She

Franciscan nun Sister Thea Bowman was a strong Black voice in the Catholic Church of the 1980s, speaking widely for intercultural awareness and directing the Hallelujah Singers. [Franciscan Sisters of Perpetual Adoration]

taught at Holy Child Jesus High School in her hometown of Canton during the 1960s. From 1971 to 1978, Sister Thea taught English at Viterbo College and became head of the English department. During these years she had a profound influence on her students not only as a teacher of English but also as one who prized her own Black culture and its values. To enhance these values she founded and directed the Hallelujah Singers, a choir with a repertoire of spirituals in the tradition of the Black South. This group performed throughout the United States.

During her years at Viterbo College, Sister Thea also reached out to the city of La Crosse and the surrounding area by conducting intercultural workshops for elementary school children, introducing them not only to the customs and values of different races and cultures but also to persons for whom these values and cultures had special meaning.

In 1978, she accepted the invitation of Bishop Joseph Brunini of Jackson, Mississippi, to become the consultant for intercultural awareness for the diocese. She lived in Canton to help her parents, whose health was failing. She also joined the faculty of the Black Catholic Studies Institute at Xavier University, New Orleans, Louisiana. Sister Thea's efforts were not limited to building community between Black and white people; her sensitivity extended to Native Americans, Hispanics, and Asian Americans.

Her work in promoting intercultural awareness brought her to the attention of the nation and, in May 1987, CBS television aired a *60 Minutes* segment about her. Since 1984, however, Sister Thea had battled cancer. Confined to a wheelchair by 1988, she continued a rigorous schedule of travel and appearances. To share her message beyond those she could contact personally, she wrote and edited a number of books. She was also the lead singer on an album of spirituals cut with a group of friends, *Sister Thea: Songs of My People* (1989). Other tapes by and about Sister Thea, both audio and video, plus a book by Sister Christian Koontz, RSM, a good friend from graduate school, have also been published.

In the course of a distinguished career as an evangelist and teacher, Sister Thea Bowman received many honors recognizing her contributions to humanity. In 1982, she received the first La Crosse Diocese Justice and Peace Award. On March 26, 1989, in a surprise presentation, she received four awards: one from former President Ronald Reagan, one from Secretary of Education William Bennett, another from Wisconsin Congressman Steve Gunderson, and one from Wisconsin Governor

Tommy G. Thompson. They said in part: "You are, in a single word, an inspiration. You draw potential from our inner beings . . . make us aware of gifts we never knew we possessed . . . and, most importantly, through your ministry of joy, enable us to improve the quality of our lives and those we touch every day." In January 1989, she was the first recipient of the Sister Thea Bowman Justice Award from Bishop Topel Ministries in Spokane, Washington. Sister Thea also received numerous honorary doctorates from colleges and universities in the United States, including the prestigious Laetare Award from Notre Dame University.

Two years before her death she received the American Cancer Society's Courage Award in a ceremony in the Rose Garden of the White House. Two weeks before her death, Sister Thea granted an interview to Patrice J. Touhy for *U.S. Catholic* in which she stated: "I've always prayed for the grace to live until I die." She died on March 30, 1990. Her prayer was answered.

BIBLIOGRAPHY

Bauer, Pam. "Invitation to Sing," *Extension* (January 1984); Bookser-Feister, John. "We Are All Children of God," *Extension* (April/May 1989); "Sister Thea Teaches Cultural Awareness," *Cornerstone* (August 1985), and "I Am Beautiful, You Are Beautiful: Thea Bowman's Ministry of Joy," *St. Anthony Messenger* (July 1985); Bowman, Sister Thea, FSPA. "Making a Joyful Noise," *CUA Magazine* (Winter 1990), and "Justice, Power, and Praise." In *Liturgy and Social Justice*, ed. Mark Searle (1980), and *Songs of My People: Compilation of Favorite Spirituals* (1989), and "Black History and Culture, 1880-1987," *U.S. Catholic Historian* (1988), and "Black Spirituality," *Extension* (March-April 1987), and "Spirituality: Soul of the People." In *Tell It Like It Is—A Black Catholic Perspective on Christian Education*, ed. National Black Sisters Conference (1983), and "Simple Ways to Work toward Intercultural Awareness," *Momentum* (February 1983); Bowman, Sister Thea, ed. *Ministry in Black Rural Contexts: Sharing the Good News with Blacks in the Rural South* (1987), and *Families: Black and Catholic, Catholic and Black* (1985); Donnelly, Mary Queen. "Nun Brings Black Roots into Church," *Xavier Gold* (Spring 1989); Ford, Reverend John, SS. Funeral Homily for Sister Thea, Saint Mary's Catholic Church, Jackson, Mississippi (April 3, 1990); Giaimo, Donna William, FSP. "A Song in Her Soul," *The Family* (February 1989); Taylor, Fabvienen. "Let Me Live Till I Die: Interview with S. Thea Bowman," *Praying* (November-December 1989); Touhy, Patrice. "Sister Thea Bowman: On the Road to Glory," *U.S. Catholic* (June 1990).

SISTER MARY GSCHWIND

BOWSER, MARY ELIZABETH
(b. c. 1840s)

Jefferson Davis, during the years of the Civil War, made the fatal error of underestimating the power—and the intelligence—of a Black woman. As a result, military plans discussed in his dining room unerringly, for a time, made their way into Ulysses S. Grant's hands.

The immediate agent of this dazzling piece of espionage was Mary Elizabeth Bowser. She was born on a plantation outside Richmond, Virginia, as a slave; the owners were the Van Lew family. When John Van Lew died in 1851, however, the abolitionist women of his family freed all of his slaves. They are reported even to have bought and then freed the members of their servants' families who lived in other households. Bowser remained at the Van Lew home as a servant, along with another former slave, named Nelson. Nelson, who went North with her after the fall of Richmond many years later, may have been her father. In the meantime, however, the Van Lew family sent Bowser to Philadelphia to receive an education, and she was there at the beginning of the Civil War.

Elizabeth Van Lew, the daughter of the family, was a strong Union sympathizer. For the first few months of the war, she nursed Union soldiers in Libby Prison. Later, her activities became more daring. She became a spy. Feigning weakness of the mind, she allowed herself to be called "Crazy Bet" in order to avert suspicion from herself. Then she began to aid prisoners escaping from Libby Prison by hiding them in a secret room in her house. While they were there, the prisoners would tell her everything they had been able to learn by listening to their guards while in the Confederate prison. Van Lew wrote down the information in cipher code and sent it through the lines to Grant, General Benjamin J. Butler, and other Union officers.

Van Lew's ardor did not stop there. She decided that she should have an intelligence agent in Jefferson Davis's own home. She sent for Bowser to come back to Richmond. Bowser did, and she soon became a servant in the Confederate White House. Like Van Lew, Bowser pretended to have a mental deficiency. She was therefore disregarded while her sharp wits garnered information from the Davises' conversations with their guests. She also read dispatches as she dusted, and carried all this information home with her in her head. Back at the Van Lew home each night, she recited from memory everything she had learned, and Van Lew put it into code.

The coded messages were carried to the Union officers in a variety of ways. A Black servant of Van Lew's—an old man—went from Richmond to the Van Lew farm for provisions every day. He carried a pass that allowed him to make the journey. The story goes that one egg in each batch of provisions was a dummy and that messages were carried in that egg. Another servant, a Black seamstress who worked for a family named Carrington, carried the materials of her trade between the homes of Union sympathizers. Cipher messages were worked into her dress patterns.

Elizabeth Bowser recorded much of this espionage activity in a diary. That diary is now owned by a Black family in Richmond that has never allowed it to be published or even read by outsiders.

BIBLIOGRAPHY

Bailey, James H. "Crazy Bet, Union Spy," *Virginia Cavalcade* (Spring 1952); Dannett, Sylvia G. L. *Profiles of Negro Womanhood* (1964); Lebsock, Suzanne. *A Share of Honor: Virginia Women 1600-1945* (1987); *NAW*; *News Leader* (Richmond) (October 16, 1977); Rywell, Martin, ed. *Afro-American Encyclopedia* (1974).

KATHLEEN THOMPSON

BOYNTON, AMELIA (1911-)

Amelia Boynton (Amelia Platts Boynton Billups Robinson) was perhaps the most important local leader of the civil rights movement in Alabama's western Black Belt. Primarily through her efforts, the Dallas County Voters League sponsored and sustained the voting rights demonstrations in Selma organized by the Student Nonviolent Coordinating Committee (SNCC) in 1963 and 1964. When those demonstrations were halted by a state court injunction, Boynton personally induced Martin Luther King, Jr. to come to Selma in 1965 to revive them and thereafter played a central role in generating local support for King's initiatives. As a result, it would probably not be too much to call her the mother of the Voting Rights Act.

Amelia Boynton was born Amelia Platts on August 18, 1911, the daughter of George G. and Anna Eliza (Hicks) Platts of Savannah, Georgia, where George Platts worked as a carpenter and operated a woodyard. She graduated from Tuskegee Institute in 1927 and in 1930 went to Selma as the county's Black home demonstration agent for the U.S. Department of Agriculture. In Selma she worked with Samuel William ("S.W.") Boynton, the county's Black agricultural agent, and soon became an enthusiastic

assistant in his vigorous efforts to secure economic and political advancement for Dallas County's impoverished Black tenant farmers and sharecroppers. In 1936, Boynton left his wife to marry Amelia. The two became leading figures in the Dallas County branch of the National Association for the Advancement of Colored People (NAACP) and in the Black Dallas County Voters League. As a result, they fell under intense pressure from white segregationists. Amelia's marriage had forced her to give up her position as a home demonstration agent, and she had opened an employment agency. In 1952, S. W. Boynton resigned his government job and together they entered the real estate and insurance business, hoping that if neither of them held a public position the harassment might decline; but, in fact, particularly after they testified at a hearing of the U.S. Civil Rights Commission in Montgomery in 1958, segregationist pressure greatly increased. At the end of 1961, S. W. Boynton was hospitalized with a heart condition, and he remained in the hospital until his death on May 13, 1963, whereupon Amelia Boynton immediately took up his cause. Throughout the 1960s she remained one of the most active and uncompromising Black leaders in Alabama. She was an unsuccessful candidate for the Democratic nomination for a seat in the U.S. House of Representatives in 1964, running against the incumbent, Kenneth Roberts. She also was the candidate of the Black National Democratic Party of Alabama for probate judge of Dallas County in 1972 and for state senator in 1974, in both cases also unsuccessfully.

In 1970, she married Robert W. Billups, who died in a boating accident in 1975. In 1976, she married James Robinson and moved to his home in Tuskegee, where she continues to reside. Robinson died in 1988. In recent years Boynton has become a devoted follower of Lyndon La Rouche, whose Schiller Institute in Washington, D.C., published a second, revised and expanded edition of her autobiography, *Bridge across Jordan*, originally published in 1979.

Amelia and S. W. Boynton had two sons, S. William Boynton, Jr., and Bruce C. Boynton. Bruce Boynton, a graduate of Howard University law school, is Dallas County Attorney. In 1960, he was the appellant in the U.S. Supreme Court decision *Boynton* v. *Virginia*, which forbade racial segregation in bus terminal facilities. William Boynton, Jr., is a postal employee and restaurant manager in Philadelphia.

BIBLIOGRAPHY

Boynton, Amelia P. *Bridge across Jordan* ([1979] 1991); Fager, Charles E. *Selma, 1965* (1974); Garrow, David J.

Bearing the Cross: Martin Luther King, Jr., and the Southern Christian Leadership Conference (1986), and *Protest at Selma: Martin Luther King, Jr., and the Voting Rights Act of 1965* (1978).

J. MILLS THORNTON, III

Kramarz), *Journal of Mathematics Analysis and Applications* (April 1981), and "Black Women Mathematicians: In Short Supply," *Sage* (Fall 1989); *CBWA*.

PATRICIA CLARK KENSCHAFT

BOZEMAN, SYLVIA TRIMBLE (1947-)

Dr. Sylvia Trimble Bozeman has been a dynamic leader of the national mathematical community as chairperson of the Spelman College Mathematics Department, member of the Board of Governors of the Mathematical Association of America (MAA), and vice president of the National Association of Mathematicians. She cochairs the MAA Committee on Minority Participation in Mathematics, which oversees Strengthening Underrepresented Minority Mathematics Achievement.

In 1988, Dr. Bozeman received both the White House Initiative Faculty Award for Excellence in Science and Technology and the Tenneco United Negro College Fund Award for Excellence in Teaching. In 1980, she was named "Outstanding Young Woman of America." She has published in the mathematical field of functional analysis and recently turned to research in image processing, supported by the National Aeronautics and Space Administration. Previous research was supported through grants from the Army Research Office and the National Science Foundation.

In 1968, she received a B.S. degree in mathematics from Alabama A & M University in Huntsville. She was vice president of the student government and second in her 200-member class. In January 1970, she received an M.A. from Vanderbilt University, where she continued her graduate studies. After a year as an instructor in the Upward Bound program of Tennessee State University in Nashville and a year on leave, she joined the faculty of Spelman College, where she is now a full professor. During three years of study leave, she earned a Ph.D. degree in mathematics from Emory University, awarded in August 1980.

Sylvia Trimble was born on August 1, 1947, in Camp Hill, Alabama, to Horance E. Trimble, Sr., and Robbie Jones Trimble. She and her husband, Robert E. Bozeman, a professor of mathematics at Morehouse College, have a daughter and a son.

BIBLIOGRAPHY

Bozeman, Sylvia. "Approximating Eigenfunctions of Fredholm Operators in Banach Spaces" (with Luis

BRAGG, JANET HARMON WATERFORD (1907-)

I'm not afraid of tomorrow because I've seen yesterday, and today is beautiful. (Janet Harmon Bragg, 1991)

Janet Harmon Bragg simultaneously and successfully pursued two careers, one in the more traditional field of nursing and one in a field reticent to accept either African-Americans or women, aviation. Janet Harmon was born on March 24, 1907, to Cordia (Batts) and Samuel Harmon in Griffin, Georgia, about thirty miles south of Atlanta. She was the youngest of seven children. Her maternal grandmother was a full Cherokee, and her maternal grandfather, Oss Batts, was a freed slave of Spanish descent.

Janet Harmon completed her primary education in Griffin and her secondary education in Fort Valley, Georgia. Always independent, she broke with family tradition and attended Spelman College in Atlanta rather than Tuskegee Institute. She graduated from Spelman with an R.N. degree, fulfilling her childhood ambition of becoming a nurse. Soon after graduation she moved to Rockford, Illinois, to live with an older sister. She worked as a supervising nurse at Wilson Hospital and attended night school at Loyola University, receiving a graduate certificate in public health administration.

Janet Harmon married Evans Waterford, but the two divorced after five years, citing incompatibility. After the divorce, she worked for a dentist, a general practitioner, and an eye, ear, nose, and throat specialist while doing graduate work in pediatric nursing at the Cook County Hospital School of Nursing. By 1933, she was a health inspector for Metropolitan Burial Insurance Company, which became the Chicago Metropolitan Insurance Company. In 1951, she married Sumner Bragg, a supervisor whom she had met earlier at Metropolitan. Sumner, a graduate of Fisk University and an accomplished athlete, had majored in sociology and later studied hospital administration at Northwestern University. The couple later established two nursing homes in the Hyde Park area for elderly Black people.

159

After passing her flight exam, Janet Bragg was turned down for her pilot's license because the Alabama examiner had "never given a colored girl a commercial license and don't intend to." Bragg went to Illinois, got her license, and became a leading proponent of Black aviation. [Elizabeth Freydberg]

Janet Harmon Bragg's pursuit of aviation was inspired by a roadside billboard that read, "Birds learn to fly. Why can't you?" Although Chicago was the center of aviation in the 1930s, Bragg could not gain admission to an aviation school there because Black Americans were considered mentally and physically incapable of piloting airplanes. Eventually she registered in the inaugural class of the Aeronautical University, founded by Cornelius R. Coffey and John C. Robinson, two Black men who had graduated from Chicago's Curtiss Wright School of Aeronautics in 1928. Both men had been initially denied admission because of their race, but the school relented after the men, who were automobile mechanics, threatened the school with a lawsuit endorsed by their employer, Emil Mack, president of Elmwood Park Motors. In spite of relentless harassment, Coffey and Robinson graduated with distinction in 1928,

after which the school enlisted them as instructors with a mandate that they recruit African-Americans. Bragg was the only woman during the first semester in this segregated class of twenty-seven students. The class increased to thirty-two during the second semester, including four more women. The students were taught airplane construction, the function and operation of the airplane engine, and airplane safety inspection.

Although the classes were coeducational, the men initially harassed Bragg during her first semester by refusing to lend her tools to complete her assignments and by preventing her from working on the airplanes. Since she had remained financially independent by continuing to work as a nurse, she was able to buy her own tools, which her fellow students soon wanted to borrow. The antagonism was also lessened through Janet's demonstrated mechanical competence and by the presence of four more women during the second semester. In 1933, after this group built an airport and hangar together in Robins, Illinois, Bragg bought the first airplane and shared it in return for maintenance of the aircraft.

The Coffey School of Aeronautics at Harlem Airport in Chicago was the site of the first Civilian Pilot Training Program (CPTP) for Black aviators. Pilots who completed basic training at Harlem were sent to Tuskegee for advanced training. Charles Johnson and Bragg established an additional coeducational, interracial flight school at Harlem Airport for potential pilots who were ineligible for Coffey's CPTP school.

Bragg continued to meet opposition in her pursuit of a career in commercial and military aviation. During World War II, she applied in 1943 to work with the Women's Auxiliary Service Pilots (WASPs), transporting military aircraft across the country and to England. Her application was accepted, but during an interview, Ethel Sheehy, vice president of the Ninety-Nines and a Women's Flying Training Detachment executive officer, told her that she did not know what to do with a Black woman and that she would refer the case to her superior, Jacqueline Cochran. Bragg, undaunted, forwarded a letter of interest to Cochran, the Army Air Force's director of women pilots in Washington, D.C., and received a reply validating Sheehy's statement. Although she was well educated, a registered nurse, and a licensed pilot with her own airplane, Bragg was rejected because of her race.

Emboldened by this dismissal, Bragg went to Tuskegee, where Black male pilots were enrolled in the CPTP, to earn her commercial and instrument certificates. She held a private pilot's license, had already completed theory courses, and had passed the written exam for a commercial license, but Chicago's inclement weather had delayed her flight test. In Alabama, however, Bragg was denied certification by a white examiner, the only person with the authority to license pilots in that region. Although she had unequivocally passed her flight exam, she was denied her license because no Black woman had ever been given a commercial license, and the examiner refused to pass her. Imbued with even more conviction to earn her commercial pilot's license, Bragg returned to Chicago, took the flight test at Palwaukee Airport, and picked up her license at Chicago Municipal Airport (now Midway Airport) within a week.

Bragg once again attempted to serve her country after reading an article in the *Chicago Tribune* summoning 60,000 or more nurses for the military nurse corps. Upon application, however, she was told that the quota for Black nurses was filled.

Bragg continued to fly as a hobby and encouraged others to pursue careers in aviation. During the 1920s and 1930s, she wrote a weekly column, "Negro in Aviation," in the *Chicago Defender* and reported the exploits of Col. John C. Robinson, a Black American aviator in charge of the Imperial Ethiopian Air Forces in Addis Ababa under Emperor Haile Selassie. She also reminded her readers that the late Bessie Coleman had inspired African-Americans to engage in aviation, and she rallied them to continue where Coleman left off.

Janet Harmon Bragg was a founding and charter member of the Challenger Air Pilots Association (1931), a national organization of Black American aviators, inspired by the legacy of Bessie Coleman, which constructed its first airstrip in the Black township of Robins, Illinois, in 1933—the Chicago airports were off limits to African-Americans at that time. She was a founding member of the National Airmen's Association of America, an organization that has sent representatives across the United States to visit Black colleges and universities and to inspire interest in and inform students about aviation. Bragg, along with Willa Brown, Cornelius Coffey, and Dale White, was among a group of Black pilots who flew the first memorial flight over Coleman's grave in 1935, a commemoration that continues today.

Janet Harmon Bragg has only recently begun to receive acknowledgments, awards, and honors for her tireless efforts in promoting aviation careers among youth. In June 1991, she was inducted into the International Forest of Friendship. Most notably, in 1984, she received an award from the Civil Rights Division

of the Federal Aviation Administration (FAA) acknowledging her as a pioneer and Black female aviator and aircraft owner and as a charter member of the National Airmen's Association of America and honoring her for her role in establishing a place for Black people in American aviation. In 1985, Bragg received the Bishop Wright Air Industry Award (created by Wilton Wright, the father of Orville and Wilbur Wright) for outstanding contributions to aviation. Bragg has also received awards from the Tuskegee Airmen and from the Chicago Graduate Nurses Association.

Janet Harmon Bragg lives in Tucson, Arizona, where she frequently speaks at churches, libraries, and schools to encourage youngsters to consider aviation as a career choice. She is also an active member of the Tuskegee Airmen's Association, Habitat for Humanity, and the Tucson Urban League.

BIBLIOGRAPHY

Freydberg, Elizabeth Hadley. Personal interviews with Janet Harmon Bragg (April 1988 and March 1991).

ELIZABETH HADLEY FREYDBERG

BRAGG, LINDA BROWN *see* BROWN, LINDA BEATRICE

BRANDON, BARBARA (1958-)

Cartoonist Barbara Brandon was born in 1958 in the Bushwick section of Brooklyn, the youngest of three children of Brumsic Brandon, Jr. Her father was the creator of the comic strip "Luther," which first

The first Black female cartoonist to be syndicated in the mainstream white press, Barbara Brandon is carrying on a family tradition. Her father, Brumsic Brandon, Jr., created the comic strip "Luther." [Edward Keating/NYT Pictures]

Barbara Brandon's cartoon strip "Where I'm Coming From" features nine "girls" with diverse lives and points of view, talking about life from a Black perspective. ["Where I'm Coming From" copyright 1991 Barbara Brandon. Dist. by Universal Press Syndicate. Reprinted with permission. All rights reserved.]

appeared in the late 1960s. The strip, which was about an inner-city Black child, ran for seventeen years.

Brandon was brought up in New Cassel, Long Island, and attended Syracuse University, where she studied illustration. After graduation, she applied for a job at *Elan*, a magazine for Black women. The editor wanted a comic strip to run regularly in the magazine and Brandon created "Where I'm Coming From." When the magazine went out of business before the strip was published, she took it to *Essence*. They said no to the strip but yes to Brandon, hiring her as a beauty and fashion writer.

In 1988, however, the *Detroit Free Press* asked Brandon's father if he knew of any Black cartoonists. Brandon got out her strip , and it began appearing in the *Free Press* in 1989 and was acquired by Universal Press Syndicate in 1991. Brandon thereby became the first Black female cartoonist to be syndicated in the mainstream white press. (Jackie Ormes was syndicated in Black-owned newspapers beginning in the 1930s.) Not thrilled to be the "first Black woman" anything in the last decade of the twentieth century, Brandon was nevertheless happy to get a larger audience for her increasingly political cartoons. "Where I'm Coming From" features nine Black "girls" with diverse lives and perspectives.

BIBLIOGRAPHY

Jet, "Barbara Brandon Is First Black Female Cartoonist Nationally Syndicated" (August 26, 1991); Jones, Lisa. "Girls on the Strip," *Village Voice* (March 10, 1992); Linden, Amy. "Barbara Brandon: A Comic Strip about Us," *Essence* (March 1990); Rule, Sheila. "The 'Girls' Talking, with a Black Perspective," *New York Times* (July 19, 1992).

KATHLEEN THOMPSON

BRAUN, CAROL MOSELEY (1947-)

When she ran in 1992 for the Democratic nomination for the U.S. Senate from Illinois, Carol Moseley Braun could afford only one television commercial. The morning after she won the primary, she no longer had to buy time to get on television. First she did ABC's *Good Morning America.* Then she was on NBC's *Today* and *First Thing in the Morning.* At noon, she was interviewed on the Chicago midday news, and later in the day she was on CNN. Her nomination was making history.

Carol Moseley Braun is the first African-American woman nominated for a Senate seat by a major political party. Her election would make her only the second African-American elected to the Senate since

Reconstruction. (The first was Edward W. Brooke of Massachusetts, elected in 1966.) In a sense, those two facts played a significant part in her campaign. Braun was part of the wave of women who won elections all over the country after the 1991 confirmation hearings of U.S. Supreme Court justice Clarence Thomas. Her nomination, therefore, was a sign of the anger of the public and its determination to elect public officials who would genuinely represent them. It would be a mistake, however, to attribute her win—over incumbent Alan Dixon and millionaire Al Hofeld—solely to circumstance. Carol Moseley Braun had the record to back up her bid.

Carol Moseley was born in Chicago, Illinois, on August 16, 1947, the daughter of a Chicago police officer. She attended public schools, including Parker High School, and the University of Illinois at Chicago. She received her law degree from the University of Chicago and worked for three years as a prosecutor in the U.S. Attorney's office. Her success as a prosecutor won her the U.S. Attorney General's Special Achievement Award.

In 1978, she ran for, and was elected to, the Illinois House of Representatives. She quickly earned a reputation as a skilled legislator, one who could forge coalitions and get things done. From 1980 to 1987, she was the chief sponsor of every school funding bill that affected the city of Chicago. In 1985, she was chief sponsor of the Urban School Improvement Act, which created parents' councils in Chicago schools. She also sponsored a bill that allowed public aid recipients to go to college without losing their benefits. After two terms, she became the first woman and the first Black American to serve as assistant majority leader in the Illinois house. She was legislative floor leader for the late Mayor Harold Washington and sponsored bills to ban discrimination in housing and private clubs.

For each of her ten years in the legislature, she received the Best Legislator Award given by the Independent Voters of Illinois-Independent Precinct Organization (IVI-IPO). In 1987, Braun left the house and ran for the office of Cook County Recorder of Deeds. She was elected, becoming the first woman

The first Black woman to be nominated by a major party to run for the U.S. Senate, Carol Moseley Braun received the "Best Legislator Award" for each of the ten years she was a member of the Illinois legislature. She is shown here with fellow democrat Bill Clinton. [AP/ Wide World Photos]

and the first Black American to hold executive office in Cook County government.

This was the woman who went up against Dixon, the man who had never been defeated, and she did it because she was mad—just like millions of other women and men in the country. She was quoted in the *New York Times* as saying that the Clarence Thomas hearings shattered her view of the Senate as "a Valhalla where decisions were made by serious men—instead we saw they were just garden-variety politicians making bad speeches."

There was more to her campaign, however, than just a good record and a good head of steam. The *Chicago Tribune*, a conservative newspaper, reported the morning after the primary that "Braun earned her victory through determination, an honest message, and a confidence in her ability to win that not many others shared. . . . Braun remained open and positive as she talked about the nation's problems and her ideas for solving them." Even columnist Mike Royko—who is anything but a feminist or a conciliator—wrote in a column mourning the defeat of Dixon, "But the good news is that he was beaten by someone who will probably make an excellent senator."

[Editor's note: She was elected senator November 3, 1992.]

BIBLIOGRAPHY

Chicago Sun-Times, "Braun's Historic Win Was Well-Earned One" (March 19, 1992); Fountain, John W. "Braun Already a Pioneer, Experts Say," *Chicago Tribune* (March 19, 1992); McNamee, Tom. "It's a Magic Morning," *Chicago Sun-Times* (March 19, 1992); *New York Times*, "Legacy of Anita Hill" (March 22, 1992); Royko, Mike. "Braun Still Has a Long Way to Go," *Chicago Tribune* (March 19, 1992).

KATHLEEN THOMPSON

BRENT, LINDA *see* JACOBS, HARRIET ANN

BRICE, CAROL (1918-1985)

Carol Brice was born on April 16, 1918, in Sedalia, North Carolina, to a highly musical family. The Brice Trio, with which she was active from 1932, included her brothers Eugene and Jonathan, each of whom had his own individual career. She studied at the Palmer Memorial Institute in her home town and Talladega

In addition to a long career in musical theater, Carol Brice (on right) also distinguished herself as a classical singer and was one of the earliest Black classical singers to record extensively. [Moorland-Spingarn]

College in Alabama before enrolling at New York's Juilliard School of Music, during which period she began a long career on the musical stage with *The Hot Mikado* (alongside Bill "Bojangles" Robinson).

Prior to becoming the first Black musician to win the Walter Naumburg Award (1943), she was soloist at St. George's Episcopal Church in New York, where Harry Burleigh had enjoyed a prodigiously long tenure as baritone soloist. In 1944, she presented her debut recital as contralto at Town Hall, and appeared on network television the next year. Few Black singers of her generation had access to the American opera stage. Her career was initially confined to musical theater, in works by Harold Arlen, Jerome Kern, and George Gershwin, although she was cast as the Voodoo Princess in Clarence Cameron White's *Ouanga* in 1956. In the 1970s she was active with the Volksoper in Vienna, returning to the United States in 1974 with her husband, expatriate baritone Thomas Carey, to serve on the faculty of the University of Oklahoma where together they established a regional opera company. She died on February 15, 1985, in Norman, Oklahoma.

With Marian Anderson, she was one of the earliest Black classical singers to record extensively. In addition to those works she performed on stage, her recorded repertoire included arias and Lieder by Bach, Beethoven, Carpenter, Dett, Falla, Franz, and Mahler.

BIBLIOGRAPHY

BDAAM; de Lerma, Dominique-René. "Brice, Carol (Lovette Hawkins)." *The New Grove Dictionary of Music and Musicians*, ed. Stanley Sadie (1980); Turner, Patricia. *Afro-American Singers: An Index and Preliminary Discography of Opera, Choral Music, and Song* (1977).

DOMINIQUE-RENÉ de LERMA

BRICKTOP (ADA SMITH)
(1894-1984)

Ada Beatrice Queen Victoria Louise Virginia Smith ("Bricktop"), vaudevillian, saloon entertainer, international host, and nightclub owner, was born August 14, 1894 in Alderson, West Virginia. Ada Smith was the youngest of four children born to Thomas and Hattie Thompson Smith. After her father's death (c. 1898), Ada's mother moved the family to Chicago, where she ran rooming houses and worked as a maid. Ada Smith attended Keith School.

Smith's stage debut, at four or five years old, was as Harry in *Uncle Tom's Cabin* at Chicago's Haymarket

In the Paris of the 1920s and 1930s, Bricktop's was the place to find royalty, from the Prince of Wales to the great Duke Ellington. Ada "Bricktop" Smith performed herself and presented such entertainers as Mabel Mercer. [Library of Congress]

Theatre. At age fourteen, after persistent appearances at the stage door of the Pekin Theatre, she acquired a job in the chorus. A diligent truant officer, however, ended the job ten days later.

At age sixteen, Smith toured the Theater Owners' Booking Association (TOBA) and Pantage vaudeville circuits with entertainers such as Miller and Lyles, McCabe's Georgia Troubadours, Ten Georgia Campers, the Kinky-Doo Trio, and the Oma Crosby Trio. Barron Wilkins, the owner of Barron's Exclusive Club in New York City, gave her the name "Bricktop." The name referred to her flaming red hair and freckles.

By the time Smith was twenty, she was entrenched in a life style that included traveling, performing, and living in a wide variety of locations throughout the United States and foreign countries. Smith's work and adventures took her from Chicago to San Francisco, Vancouver to New York. At Barron's Exclusive Club in Harlem, she convinced the owner to hire Elmer Snowden's Washingtonians, a band that included Duke Ellington.

Her first performance in Paris, France, was in 1924 when she replaced Florence Jones at the nightclub Le Grand Duc. It was during this period that Smith's ability as an entertainer combined with her skills as a host. She caught the attention of the rich and famous, notably F. Scott Fitzgerald and Cole Porter, with whom she became friends. Porter wrote the song "Miss Otis Regrets She's Unable to Lunch Today" for her. She soon began hosting and entertaining at private parties for the wealthy, as well as benefits for various charities.

In 1926, Smith's involvement with Paris nightclubs became more vigorous. She opened and closed The Music Box and Le Grand Duc. She later opened a club she called Bricktop's that featured American music and a high society clientele. Among her distinguished guests, who often performed unannounced, were Jascha Heifetz, Duke Ellington, Noel Coward, the Prince of Wales, and Paul Robeson. She and Josephine Baker became friends during this time.

Smith married musician Peter Duconge in 1929. Two years later, she moved Bricktop's in Paris to 66 Rue Pigalle, with Mabel Mercer as the main attraction. Business thrived until the mid-1930s, when an economic depression hit Paris. Smith separated from her husband in 1932, though they never divorced. From 1938 to 1939 she did radio broadcasts for the French government, but as World War II approached, she returned to the United States, urged to do so by the Duchess of Windsor and Lady Mendl.

She returned to New York, where her attempts with nightclub enterprises were not as successful as some of her previous undertakings. Between 1943 and 1951 she opened and closed nightclubs in Mexico City, Paris, and Rome. Continuing to name many of the clubs Bricktop's, she was usually successful in attracting international celebrities.

"So Long Baby," her only recording, was done in 1972 with Cy Coleman. Afterwards, she performed occasionally in nightclubs and at charity events. She had a heart attack in 1975, but continued to perform into the early 1980s. Ada "Bricktop" Smith's autobiography, *Bricktop*, written with James Haskins and published in 1983, appeared in print just months before her death. She died on January 31, 1984, in New York City.

BIBLIOGRAPHY

Hentoff, Nat and Nat Shapiro. *Hear Me Talkin' to Ya* (1966); *Newsweek* (February 13, 1984); Smith, Ada and James Haskins. *Bricktop* (1983); *Time* (February 13, 1984).

ARTHUR C. DAWKINS

BRIGGS, MARTHA B. (1838-1889)

University faculty member and public school administrator Martha B. Briggs is noteworthy for her service in the preparation of schoolteachers in the nation's capital. As a member of the Normal and Preparatory Department of Howard University, 1873-79, principal of Miner Normal School, 1879-83, and principal of the Normal Department of Howard University, from 1883 until her death in March 1889, Briggs participated in efforts at the District of Columbia public schools and at Howard University to prepare men and women to teach. These new teachers taught not only in the District but also in schools in the South—serving in the latter almost as young missionaries.

Martha B. Briggs was born of John and Fannie Bassett Briggs in New Bedford, Massachusetts. She was educated in that New England town and first taught there in her father's home. Briggs left New Bedford for Easton, Maryland, and then in 1869 moved to Washington, D.C. She remained in the District for the next twenty years.

With four years' experience as teacher and principal in the Washington, D.C., public schools, Briggs left the public school system in 1873 to begin her career at Howard University.

The Howard University *Catalogue*, 1873-74, records the Normal Department Faculty and identifies Martha B. Briggs as "Instructor in Normal Department." Briggs is identified in later years as an "Instructor in Mathematics."

The performance of Martha B. Briggs at Howard University as an instructor in the Normal Department for the six-year period 1873-79 drew the attention of the public school leadership. When the board of trustees for the District of Columbia assumed authority over Miner Normal School in 1879 and sought a principal for that institution, the board offered the position to Briggs and she accepted.

Assuming leadership of the institution that had been inaugurated by Myrtilla Miner in December 1851, Martha B. Briggs was praised at the conclusion of her first year. In June 1880, Briggs received the commendation of the board: "We express the belief and hope that the Miner Normal School, whose first year has proved so successful under the earnest and faithful charge of its principal, Miss Martha B. Briggs, will eventually not only supply the colored schools of the District with educated and earnest teachers, but that it will in a measure contribute to supply the demand of the South for colored teachers for the colored race."

Miner Normal—often officially recorded as Washington Normal School No. 2—was a relatively new school building. Miner had been built in 1876 by the trustees of the Miner Fund Board, a legal institution flowing from the creation in 1863 by the U.S. Congress of the "Institute for the Education of Colored Youth." In addition, the Miner Fund Board's financial support for the Normal Department of Howard University in 1871 resulted in Myrtilla Miner Hall (a dormitory for girls at Howard).

Because of illness in 1883, Briggs elected to end her service as Miner Normal School Principal and returned to Howard University's Normal Department. The *Catalogue* records her as "Principal of the Normal Department."

Briggs died March 28, 1889, at the age of fifty. The District of Columbia Certificate of Death records the cause of death as a tumor. Over the years since her death, the District of Columbia Board of Education named two elementary schools in her honor. Both have subsequently been demolished. However, Briggs's contributions to the preparation of teachers have been more permanently enshrined in the history of Miner Normal School. By Act of Congress in 1930, it became Miner Teachers College. Housed in a Georgian structure still standing at 2565 Georgia Avenue N.W., this building served Miner Normal School (1913-29), Miner Teachers College (1929-55), and the District of Columbia Teachers College (1955-77), and today it houses some of the teacher preparation programs of the University of the District of Columbia.

Martha B. Briggs was returned to New Bedford, Massachusetts, her birthplace, for her burial. A memorial to her life and service was held by the Bethel Literary and Historical Association. Furthermore, Howard University memorialized her with a tablet placed in the wall of Andrew Rankin Chapel on the campus. In its March 1934 Founder's Day program, Miner Teachers College celebrated her service as the third principal of Miner Normal School.

BIBLIOGRAPHY
Dyson, Walter. *Howard University—The Capstone of Negro Education* (1941).

PAUL P. COOKE

BRIGGS-HALL, LOUISE EVANS *see* EVANS, LOUISE

BRITTON, MARY E.

M.D., elocutionist, teacher, journalist, and metaphysician Mary E. Britton was prominent among nineteenth-century Black women leaders in the South whose work and writings advanced the causes of both racial and sexual liberation. She was born in Lexington, Kentucky, to Henry and Laura Britton. Her birth date is unknown. An exceptionally bright child who loved reading, she excelled in the primary and secondary schools she attended in Lexington, which were run, for the most part, by the American Missionary Association. In order to give their children the best college education available in the state, the Brittons moved to Berea, where Mary attended Berea College from 1869 to 1874. Before her graduation, in

One of the most prolific journalists among Black women of the nineteenth century, Mary E. Britton was also a physician and an early proponent of alternative medicine. [Schomburg Center]

March of 1874, her father died, and four months later, in July, her mother died.

To support herself, Mary became a schoolteacher, working for a short time in Chilesburg, Kentucky, before accepting a position, in 1876, with the Lexington public schools, where she gained recognition for her brilliance as a teacher, her talents as an elocutionist (often ranked with Hallie Q. Brown), and her accomplishments as a journalist.

It is as a journalist that Britton earned her place in the annals of Black women's history. She was considered one of the leading women journalists of the nineteenth century, writing for a number of newspapers, among them the *Courant*, the *Cleveland Gazette*, the *Lexington Herald*, the *Indianapolis World*, the *Cincinnati Commercial*, and the *Ivy*. Using the pen name "Meb" or "Aunt Peggy" (the latter only for a column devoted to the interests of children), Britton wrote passionately about racial discrimination, woman's suffrage, temperance, abstinence from tobacco, the influence of teachers and preachers on the morals of youth, and health.

Britton continued her education at the American Missionary Medical College in Chicago, from which she graduated in 1903, and at Battle Creek Sanitarium, which was famous at the time. She was a specialist in hydrotherapy, electrotherapy, and massage. She believed in metaphysics and in phrenology and, as a devout Seventh-Day Adventist, in vegetarianism. During her life, she was one of the most loved, respected, and honored Black women in Kentucky and a very visible and prominent Black woman leader in the nation.

BIBLIOGRAPHY

Boris, Joseph, ed. *Who's Who in Colored America* (1927); Harris, Lawrence. *The Negro Population of Lexington in the Professions, Business, Education, and Religion* (1907); Johnson, William D. *Biographical Sketches of Prominent Negro Men and Women of Kentucky* (1897); Majors, Monroe. *Noted Negro Women: Their Triumphs and Activities* (1893); Penn, Irvine Garland. *The Afro-American Press and Its Editors* (1891); Scruggs, Lawson A. *Women of Distinction: Remarkable in Works and Invincible in Character* (1893).

GLORIA WADE-GAYLES

BROOKS, GWENDOLYN (1917-)

A poem is a search for understanding, and a poet is a seeker of understanding. In that sense, and in every other, Gwendolyn Brooks is one of the finest contemporary poets. At a time when the American poetry establishment is looking for a voice, Brooks's finely tuned but thoroughly accessible poetry seems every year more valuable.

Gwendolyn Elizabeth Brooks was born on June 17, 1917, in Topeka, Kansas, to David Anderson Brooks and Keziah Corinne Wims Brooks. Her mother's family lived in Topeka and her mother returned there for a few weeks to give birth, but Brooks is a Chicago poet. As a child, she went to. Chicago schools and played in Chicago streets. She began composing poetry when she was seven and recording it in notebooks when she was eleven, nurtured by loving parents who imbued her with a love of songs, stories, and learning.

During her otherwise isolating adolescence (she attended predominantly white high schools), Brooks found a connection with other poets. That T. S. Eliot, Ezra Pound, and Wallace Stevens were white men was of much less importance than that they were poets, that they shared with her this thing that *was* life—writing poems. Then, at sixteen, Brooks met Langston Hughes, who read her poetry and encouraged her. His enthusiasm for her work was of tremendous importance to the young poet.

After graduating from high school, Brooks went to Woodrow Wilson Junior College for two years. Two years after that, she met Henry Lowington Blakely II. They were married not long after they met and are still, though they separated from 1969 to 1973.

In 1941, Brooks's development as a poet received another boost when Inez Cunningham Stark presented a class on modern poetry at the South Side Community Art Center. Brooks experienced the stimulation of talk and criticism and sharing with other writers. Two years later she received an award at the Midwestern Writers' Conference. That award led indirectly to the publication of her first book of poetry, *A Street in Bronzeville*. The reviews were highly favorable, and the book brought Brooks to the attention of other Black writers. She also received Guggenheim fellowships in 1946 and 1947 and grants from the American Academy of Arts and Letters and the National Institute of Arts and Letters in 1946.

Her next book, *Annie Allen*, won the Pulitzer Prize for poetry in 1950. Brooks was the first Black person, man or woman, to receive the award in any category. Her autobiographical novel, *Maud Martha*, was published in 1953 and, in 1956, her first book of children's poetry, *Bronzeville Boys and Girls*, appeared.

The Bean Eaters, a collection of poetry that appeared in 1960, speaks in powerful, moving, and sometimes bitterly ironic language of the lives of

The first Black person to receive the Pulitzer Prize, poet Gwendolyn Brooks speaks with simple eloquence of the human condition. [Schomburg Center]

among the crowded, violent, hate-and-anger-filled inhabitants of the building. Hortense Spillers calls the Brooks who wrote *In the Mecca* "Gwendolyn the terrible."

With *Riot*, in 1969, Brooks began publishing exclusively with Black presses. She also began, as she put it, to "*clarify* my language. I want these poems to be free. I want them to be direct without sacrificing the kinds of music, the picturemaking I've always been interested in." This focus on clarity and simplifying is, in part, a way of reaching out to an ever larger audience of Black readers. It also reflects a maturing that can be seen in the great lyric poets of our language. Simplicity in poetry usually comes late in a poet's life, when confidence is at its height.

In *Family Pictures* (1970), Brooks's natural optimism begins to reemerge. Though never blind to the pain of the Black experience, Brooks has only rarely reflected its darkest aspects. A certain belief in the positive possibilities of the human condition can probably be expected in a woman who had a happy childhood, who shares a strong lifelong love relationship, who has found fulfillment as an artist in a lifetime of creative work, and who, in the words of her daughter Nora, "opens places for people—new doorways and mindpaths."

BIBLIOGRAPHY

CBWA; *EBA*; McLendon, Jacquelyn. "Gwendolyn Brooks." In *African-American Writers*, ed. Lea Baechler and A. Walton Litz (1991); *NA*; *NBAW*; Pryse, Marjorie and Hortense Spillers. *Conjuring: Black Women, Fiction, and Literary Tradition* (1985); *WWBA* (1992).

KATHLEEN THOMPSON

Black people. Its poems are often anthologized in high school and college literature texts and are among the classics of American poetry. In 1968, Brooks was named Poet Laureate of Illinois, succeeding Carl Sandburg. She began conducting poetry contests for young people with prize money she often provided herself, and poetry workshops, including at least one for the Chicago gang the Blackstone Rangers. She also toured extensively, reading her poetry at schools and prisons, libraries and bookstores.

In the late 1960s, a change in Black consciousness was happening in America, and Gwendolyn Brooks let it carry her further along on her poetic path. Her 1968 book, *In the Mecca*, contains a long narrative poem interrupted by ballads and ballad-like interpolations. Set in the old Mecca Building in Chicago, it details a mother's search for a lost child

BROOKS, HALLIE BEACHEM (1907-1985)

"Nobody's going to rain on my parade, including me," was Hallie Beachem Brooks's response when asked if her retirement from Atlanta University after forty-seven years of service would be tearful. Brooks retired on May 13, 1977, having served the university, the library science profession, and the community with distinction.

Hallie Beachem Brooks was born in West Baden, Indiana, on October 9, 1907, the daughter of Hal and Mary Lucy Beachem. After graduating from Shortridge High School in Indianapolis, she earned an A.B. at Butler University, a B.L.S. degree at the Columbia University School of Library Service, and a

Master's degree at the University of Chicago. She studied an additional year at the University of Chicago, where she completed course work toward a doctorate in library science, aided by grants from the Carnegie Corporation and the General Education Board. In 1936, she married Frederic Victor Brooks.

Brooks's entire professional career was spent in the field of librarianship. In 1930, President John Hope of Atlanta University recruited her, then a public librarian in Indianapolis, to organize library services for the university's new Laboratory High School. The high school was closed in 1941, and after serving as director of Field Services to Schools and Libraries in thirteen southern states financed by a grant from the Carnegie Corporation of New York, Brooks was appointed to the faculty of the Atlanta University School of Library Science, which had been established the previous year. During her long association with Atlanta University, she also served as acting dean of the library school and as chairperson of every committee in the school. She was a member of Beta Phi Mu, the international honorary fraternity for library and information science, and, in 1983, was awarded the status of professor-emerita of Atlanta University.

Brooks held offices or committee memberships in the American Library Association, the Association for Library and Information Science Education, the Southern Library Association, the Georgia Library Association, and the Metropolitan Atlanta Association.

Brooks's knowledge of the art of bookmaking was extensive. In 1948, she published a *Panoramic Chart of the Manuscript Period in Bookmaking*, which is still used in graduate library schools throughout the United States and Canada. In addition, she authored numerous articles on reading and communications. She died October 10, 1985.

BIBLIOGRAPHY

Atlanta University Bulletin (July 1977); Manuscript collection, Robert W. Woodruff Library, Clark Atlanta University, Atlanta, Georgia.

ARTHUR C. GUNN

BROTHERHOOD OF SLEEPING CAR PORTERS *see* INTERNATIONAL LADIES' AUXILIARY

BROUGHTON, VIRGINIA W. *see* BAPTIST CHURCH

BROWN, ANNE WIGGINS (1915-)

Had it not been for Anne Wiggins Brown, George Gershwin's folk opera of the African-American experience might have come to be known by its original title, *Porgy*. To make it into a star vehicle for Brown, Gershwin revised the work and retitled it *Porgy and Bess*.

Currently a citizen of Norway, Anne Wiggins Brown was born to Dr. Harry F. Brown and Mary Wiggins Brown in Baltimore, Maryland, in 1915. At an early age she was obsessed with being a star on the stage, although she realized that Blacks were cast only as servants or in degrading comic roles. Her mother, recognizing this extraordinary talent who was now all of seven years old, attempted to enroll Anne in a local private Catholic school, where the prodigious child caused great excitement among the nuns. When school officials discovered that the family was not Spanish, but Black, however, Anne was denied admission even though her father was a prominent Baltimore physician. She was to encounter the same discrimination a few years later at the now famous Peabody School of Music, currently located in Baltimore, Maryland.

Not to be discouraged, Brown always kept her dream of becoming a star in the forefront of her numerous activities, which included plays and musicals in which she sang everything from Bach to blues.

Her talent captured the attention of Constance Black, wife of the owner of the *Baltimore Sun*. After having presented Anne in numerous private performances, Black encouraged the young Brown to enter the Juilliard School of Music.

Brown's vocal teacher at Juilliard was Lucia Dunham. As a result of entering many competitions, Anne won the prestigious Margaret McGill Scholarship. She then attracted the attention of George Gershwin and auditioned for him. Still wanting to become a "serious" singer, she auditioned with the typical Western European repertoire. He requested of her an unaccompanied rendition of the spiritual "City Called Heaven," since the spiritual was more akin to the idioms of his forthcoming opera, *Porgy*. This spiritual was soon to become internationally known as one of her signature selections.

Having found his "perfect" Bess, Gershwin worked closely with Brown. He not only rewrote act three of the opera in order to have Bess sing the lullaby "Summertime" but changed the title of the opera to *Porgy and Bess*, so that Brown would share equal billing with the promising young Black baritone Todd Duncan.

The much anticipated premiere of the opera took place at New York's Alvin Theatre on October 10, 1935. The event was met with mixed critical reviews; however, the critic Olin Downs had much respect and praise for the two lead voices, Brown and Duncan. Anne Brown, now twenty, had achieved her dream.

The opera, which had a run of 123 performances, was not a financial success but did embark upon a national tour. Brown married, for the second time, to Jacob Petit. Her first marriage, to Floard Howard, which ended in divorce, occurred while she was a student at Juilliard. To Dr. and Mrs. Petit was born her first child, Paula.

In 1942, she returned to Broadway in a more upbeat version of *Porgy and Bess*. This version proved to be more successful financially.

Feeling her career a bit stagnant, Brown embarked upon a concert career. Upon the expiration of her contract with *Porgy and Bess*, and declining the lead in Oscar Hammerstein's new musical, *Carmen Jones*, Brown was to be managed by Albert Morini. She successfully toured the United States, Canada, and Europe. Her performance with the Robin Hood Dell Orchestra in Philadelphia broke, at that time, all attendance records. However, her most celebrated

performances between 1942 and 1948 were the appearances at Carnegie Hall and with the Los Angeles Philharmonic.

Brown's 1948 European tour, especially the performance in Norway, was extremely well received. Divorced from her second husband, she was married to Norwegian ski jumper Thorleif Schkelderup. Along with raising a family, she continued to perform in Europe, South America, and Asia. She was not to return to America for twenty years. Although now an adopted Norwegian, she had never forgotten her racial struggles during her formative years in America. Always a civil rights advocate, Anne Brown in 1935 led the *Porgy and Bess* cast in protest when they learned that the performances at the National Theatre in Washington, D.C., were to be before segregated audiences. The theater relented in its segregation policies for these performances; however, the general policy of segregation was not to change for another twenty years.

During a 1953 tour in Europe, Anne Brown developed respiratory problems. Consequently, she did not quite achieve her new goal as an Italian opera diva. She did continue to study and sing. Upon her return to Norway, she was diagnosed as asthmatic. This condition ended her singing career, but she continued to teach. Still one of the most sought-after teachers in Norway, her celebrated students include actress Liv Ullmann and jazz singer Karen Krog. Her

Creator of the role of Bess in George Gershwin's Porgy and Bess, *Anne Brown led cast protests to desegregate audiences for the show at the National Theatre in Washington, D.C. Here she is seen christening the S.S.* Frederick Douglass. *[Schomburg Center]*

time is spent with her family of two daughters and four grandchildren.

Anne Brown has been the subject of a Norwegian television documentary and authored a best-selling autobiography, *Sang Fra Frossen Gren*.

BIBLIOGRAPHY

Brown, Anne Wiggins. Personal interview.

J. WELDON NORRIS

BROWN, CHARLOTTE HAWKINS (1883-1961)

Charlotte Hawkins Brown was committed to good manners, and she made sure that students at her school, Palmer Memorial Institute, were carefully drilled in the proper social graces. But her interest in manners and education was coupled with a fierce determination to fight for civil rights and not to accept injustice quietly. This too she conveyed to both her students and to clubwomen, Black and white, throughout the South. Brown was a major force in the educational and club work of early twentieth-century African-American women. Born Lottie Hawkins on June 11, 1883, in Henderson, North Carolina, she was the daughter of Caroline Frances Hawkins and Edmund H. Hight. Her grandmother, Rebecca, was a descendant of the English navigator John D. Hawkins and worked as a housemaid on the Hawkins plantation.

Caroline Hawkins, who had received an education in the elementary department of Shaw University, was determined that her daughter and her son, Mingo, should have opportunities for a better life. So when young Lottie was seven years old, the family moved to Cambridge, Massachusetts. The family, in this case, consisted of nineteen people, including cousins and aunts and Caroline's new husband, Nelson Willis.

In Cambridge, the Willises operated a hand laundry, boarded Harvard students, and took care of infants in their home. Lottie Hawkins went to the Allston Grammar School and became friends with the children of Henry Wadsworth Longfellow. At twelve, she organized a kindergarten in the Sunday school of the Union Baptist Church. She excelled in her schoolwork and, when she went on to Cambridge English High School, she cultivated a talent in art by sketching her classmates.

It was when she was about to graduate that fate stepped in for the first time. She decided that her white organdy graduation dress called for a silk slip and took a job caring for two babies in order to pay for it. She was pushing a baby carriage and reading Virgil in her Latin book when she was spotted by Alice Freeman Palmer. Palmer, second president of Wellesley College, was impressed by the girl's intelligence and determination. She would enter Hawkins's life again shortly.

Besides the slip, Lottie Hawkins felt there was one other prerequisite for her graduation—a more dignified name. She became Charlotte Eugenia. She wanted very much to go to Radcliffe College, but her mother was firmly against it, insisting that she ought to go directly into teaching. They compromised, agreeing on the State Normal School at Salem. In the catalogue for that institution, Hawkins saw that Alice Freeman Palmer was a member of the board that supervised normal schools for the state and she wrote to her asking for a recommendation. Palmer wrote back, offering to pay for the young woman's education.

Hawkins was in her second year at Salem when fate stepped in again. On her way home to visit, she met a stranger on a train, a field secretary of the American Missionary Association (AMA). The AMA was a group of white New Yorkers who provided schools for Black children in the South. When the secretary straightaway offered Hawkins a job, she accepted immediately and left Salem before graduation. She had long believed that her purpose in life was to go back to the South and use her education to benefit her people.

When the AMA gave her a choice between a thriving school in Orlando, Florida, and a one-room school in rural North Carolina, Hawkins did not hesitate. Soon she was stepping off another train in McLeansville, North Carolina. The school was in Sedalia, four miles away. It was housed in a dilapidated country church. Hawkins's quarters were an attic room above the parsonage. If she had wanted a challenge, she had it. There were fifty children in Hawkins's first class. Most of them were so poor that she spent almost all of her salary buying them clothing and school supplies. Then the AMA informed her that they were closing the school, along with all the other schools in their network that were being operated by one or two teachers. The decision was a blow to the people of Sedalia, and one they were not willing to accept. They urged Hawkins to stay and open another school. Hawkins agreed. She was now nineteen years old.

The community gave her fifteen acres of land, and the minister of the Bethany Congregational Church donated an old building that had once housed a blacksmith shop. It was Hawkins's job, however, to find money. So she gave music recitals and recitations at New England resorts. She talked to Alice Freeman Palmer—who died before she was able to help as she had promised—and to Palmer's friends, who gave her the money she needed to begin. Hawkins named the school the Alice Freeman Palmer Memorial Institute.

In the years that followed, Hawkins was administrator, teacher, and fund-raiser. She also continued her own education, taking classes in the summer at Harvard, where she met Edmund S. Brown. She and Brown were married in 1911, and he joined her in Sedalia. He taught and administered the boys' dormitory at Palmer Memorial for about a year before taking a teaching job in South Carolina. The marriage ended in 1915; but Charlotte Hawkins Brown was not alone. She reared her brother Mingo's three daughters, after their mother died, and the four children of her young aunt, Ella Brice, who was away from home a great deal pursuing her career in music. All seven children graduated from Palmer Memorial.

Brown continued to expand the school, initiated interracial cultural activities in the community, and became an active clubwoman. She was a founding member of the National Council of Negro Women and served as president of the North Carolina State Federation of Negro Women's Clubs and the North Carolina Teachers Association. She was the first African-American woman chosen for membership in the Twentieth Century Club of Boston. She also served on the national board of the YWCA. During all this, she took courses at a number of universities and had a modest career as an author.

In 1941, Brown's *The Correct Thing to Do, to Say, and to Wear* was published, and she became known as the "First Lady of Social Graces." Some, less charitably, called her a "social dictator." She wrote many articles and short stories as well, the most famous of which was "Mammy: An Appeal to the Heart of the South" (1919).

Brown was an impassioned advocate of civil rights. She was proud of the number of times she was ejected from Pullman berths and first-class railway seats in the South and she refused categorically to ride freight elevators in New York City buildings. Brown became a key figure in the southern interracial women's movement as it developed in the 1920s. In fact, her speech at a 1920 interracial meeting in Memphis, in which she detailed the everyday examples of disrespect which Black women regularly endured from southern white men and women and challenged the Christian principles of the white female delegates, was one of the

Charlotte Hawkins Brown was only nineteen years old when she founded the Palmer Memorial Institute at the beginning of the twentieth century. She retired over fifty years later, with generations of students in her debt. She is shown here with a bust of Alice Freeman Palmer, her mentor, for whom the institute is named.

key moments in the difficult struggle to create a working relationship between Black and white women. She spoke out against lynching, publicly stating that colored women were insulted by white men a thousand times more than the opposite.

Brown retired as president of Palmer in 1952. She remained an active member of the board of directors and director of finances, however, until 1955. She died in 1961, just a decade before Palmer was forced to close because of financial problems.

[*See also* NATIONAL COUNCIL OF NEGRO WOMEN.]

BIBLIOGRAPHY
CBWA; DANB; EBA; Hunter, Tera. "The Correct Thing: Charlotte Hawkins Brown and the Palmer Institute," *Southern Exposure* (September/October 1983); *NAW;*

NBAW; Smith, Sandra N. and Earle H. West. "Charlotte Hawkins Brown." In *Black Women in American History: The Twentieth Century*, ed. Darlene Clark Hine (1990).

KATHLEEN THOMPSON

BROWN, CLEO PATRA (1909-)

Cleo Patra Brown has had two careers in music, one in the 1920s, 1930s, and 1940s as a jazz pianist, and the other, beginning in the 1970s, in religious music. She was born on December 8, 1909, in Meridian, Mississippi. She began studying piano at four. As a youngster, and daughter of a Baptist minister, she played in her father's church and continued her music studies when her family moved to Chicago in 1919.

Cleo's older brother, Everett, was also a pianist—but of a different breed. He played ragtime and boogie woogie in Chicago nightclubs. Although her parents were strict about her style of playing, she managed to learn the style from her brother. Envious of her brother's artistic freedom and better pay, she ran away from home and got married.

She toured briefly with a traveling orchestra at fourteen, before returning to Chicago. During the 1920s, she performed in Chicago's clubs and on select radio stations. In 1935, she replaced Fats Waller on his New York radio series and began recording shortly thereafter.

With the exception of a brief illness in the 1940s, Cleo Brown played regularly until 1953. She is credited with popularizing the "eight-beat-to-the-bar" (Placksin 1982) style of playing when she remade Pine Top Smith's "Boogie Woogie" classic. Despite her popularity, she recorded only twenty-four tracks during her career, eighteen of those during the year 1935-36.

Cleo Brown retired from music in 1953 and took up nursing. In 1973, she switched careers again to return to music—but this time she played religious and inspirational tunes under the name C. Patra Brown.

In 1979, C. Patra Brown had a weekly feature on a radio station in Denver, Colorado, playing religious melodies. She still resides in Denver and plays the piano for a Seventh-Day Adventist Church.

BIBLIOGRAPHY

Carr, I., D. Fairweather, and B. Priestley. *Jazz: The Essential Companion* (1988); Dahl, Linda. *Stormy Weather: The Music and Lives of a Century of Jazzwomen* (1984); Handy, D. Antoinette. *Black Women in American Bands and Orchestras* (1981); Placksin, Sally. *American Women in Jazz 1900 to the Present: Their Words, Lives, and Music* (1982); Sampson, Henry T. *Blacks in Blackface: A Source Book on Early Black Musical Shows* (1980).

SELECTED DISCOGRAPHY

Mama Don't Want No Peas an' Rice an' Coconut Oil, Women In Jazz: Pianists ST-112 (1978); *Kings & Queens of Ivory, Vol. 1*, MCA Jazz Heritage Series 1329 (1980).

PAULETTE WALKER

BROWN, DOROTHY LAVINIA (1919-)

"Men said that a woman wasn't able to stand up to five years of training in surgery. . . . I tried to be . . . not hard, but durable. . . . I am a fighter who learned how to get along with the male ego" (*Afro-American* 1953). Dorothy Lavinia Brown, the first Black female surgeon to become a fellow of the American College of Surgeons, learned to fight for what she wanted from a very early age. Born in Troy, New York, she was placed in an orphanage at the age of five months by her mother, Edna Brown. She did not meet her father, Kevin Thomas Brown, until she was well into adulthood. The orphanage, where Brown remained until the age of twelve, was a predominantly white institution. Brown later recalled that she was one of only a handful of Black children in a "sea of white faces" (*Ebony* 1958). Even so, it was the only home she knew, and she was reasonably happy there.

Just before her thirteenth birthday, Brown's mother reentered her life for a brief period. Fearful that her daughter would be placed in service, Edna Brown took Dorothy out of the orphanage, but by that time mother and daughter were strangers. Brown ran away from home on five separate occasions, each time returning to the Troy orphanage. Finally, at the age of fifteen, determined to get a high school education, Brown ran away again and enrolled at Troy High School. She had no place to stay and no one to live with, but the principal of the school found an appropriate living situation for the determined teenager, who was placed in the custody of foster parents, Mr. and Mrs. S. W. Redmon.

With the Redmons, Dorothy found the security, support, and stability that had thus far eluded her, and they had a significant influence on her. The Redmons considered Brown a daughter and passed along to her their Christian values and outlook. It was these values, Brown professed much later, that helped her come to terms with a growing bitterness toward white society. Ultimately she found a way to forgive oppression without relinquishing her own self-esteem and dignity.

After Brown graduated from high school, the Troy Methodist Women nominated her for a scholarship to Bennett College in Greensboro, North Carolina, and in 1937, in the midst of the Great Depression, she made her first trip south. After a shaky start, she graduated second in her class from Bennett. Fortunately, it was not until many years later that she learned Bennett administrators had advised the Troy Methodist Women that they should persuade Brown not to return for a second year because she was not Bennett material.

Since the age of five, when her tonsils were removed, Brown had harbored a desire to be a doctor, and when World War II made it possible for more women to gain acceptance into medical schools, she took advantage of the opportunity. She entered Meharry Medical College in 1944 and earned an M.D. four years later. After a year's internship at Harlem Hospital, Brown began a five-year residency in surgery at Meharry and Hubbard Hospital. Her decision to pursue surgery was met with almost universal resistance. But Brown persisted to become a fellow of the American College of Surgeons and to be appointed chief of surgery at Nashville's Riverside Hospital, a position she held from 1957 until 1983.

If her achievements were limited to her success as a physician and surgeon, Brown's life would be noteworthy, but she has been a pathbreaker in other areas as well. For example, she became the first single woman in Tennessee to adopt a child, after a young, unmarried patient begged her to adopt her newborn daughter. Brown's love for children, and her desire to help a child just as the Redmons had helped her, prompted her to begin the process. In 1956, Brown legally adopted her daughter, Lola.

In 1966, Brown was approached to run for a seat in the Tennessee state legislature when it became apparent that redistricting would make it possible to elect a Black candidate. When she won, Brown became the first Black woman to serve in the state legislature. Initially she indicated that she probably would return to her medical practice after two years, but it soon became clear that good planning would make it possible for her to accommodate her many roles as physician, surgeon, teacher, mother, and legislator, and she began to rethink her early decision to limit herself to one term. However, following a bitter losing battle over her sponsorship of an expanded abortion rights bill, which she claimed would have saved the lives of many Tennessee women, Brown resigned her seat and returned full time to her medical practice, her teaching career, and to caring for her daughter.

Dorothy Lavinia Brown continues to live in Nashville where she is an active teacher and physician as well as a national and international lecturer. Now a grandmother, she is an outstanding role model for those who remain undaunted by circumstance.

BIBLIOGRAPHY

"Bachelor Mother," *Ebony* (September 1958); *CBWA*; Innes, Doris F., ed. *Profiles in Black: Biographical Sketches of 100 Living Black Unsung Heroes* (1976); "Meharry Gets Woman Chief of Surgery," *Afro-American* (July 25, 1953); Organ, Claude H. and Margaret M. Kosiba. *A Century of Black Surgeons: The U.S.A. Experience* (1987); "A Surgeon Goes to Legislature," *Washington Post* (June 4, 1967).

CHRISTINE A. LUNARDINI

BROWN, ELAINE (1943-)

The image of the Black Panther Party (BPP) most often perpetuated is a masculine one, but women were central to all aspects of the BPP's development. One of these women, Elaine Brown, held the BPP's highest position, chairperson, during the difficult and transitional years of the early 1970s.

Elaine Brown was born March 3, 1943, in Philadelphia, Pennsylvania, and grew up singing in the junior and adult choirs at the Jones Tabernacle African Methodist Episcopal Church in North Philadelphia. Brown, raised by her mother and grandmother, attended the Philadelphia High School for Girls and upon graduation entered Temple University as a prelaw candidate. Brown later attended the Philadelphia Conservatory of Music, the University of California at Los Angeles, and Mills College in Oakland, California.

When Brown left Temple University in 1965 she moved to Los Angeles, California. In 1967, she began to volunteer as a piano teacher for children in the Jordon Downs projects in Watts. This experience contributed to her ultimate decision to serve the Black community via the Black Panther Party (BPP).

Brown was involved in several political organizations key to the Black Movement before joining the BPP in April 1968. She began a Black Student Union newsletter at the University of California at Los Angeles and helped to organize the Southern California College Black Student Alliance.

Elaine Brown became BPP deputy minister of information of the Los Angeles chapter in 1969, and was elevated to minister of information in 1971. By 1974 Brown was chairperson of the BPP, the highest leadership position within the BPP ever held by a woman. Under Elaine Brown's leadership the BPP became an influential political force in Oakland. Strong BPP voter registration activities helped Oakland's first Black mayor, Lionel Wilson, to be elected in 1977.

In 1973 and 1976, Brown campaigned unsuccessfully for an Oakland City Council position. In each of her campaigns for city government positions Brown's platform was based on establishing social programs for Black and poor people and forging a link between the lawmaking bodies and the community. Perhaps the height of Elaine Brown's political involvement in national politics was in April 1976 when she was chosen as a delegate to the Democratic party's national convention.

Brown was a board member of several political organizations while she was chairperson of the BPP. She was executive director and chairperson of the board of the Executive Opportunities Corporation (EOC), a nonprofit corporation that operated the Oakland Community School and the Community Learning Center. In addition, Brown was a member of the board of directors of the Oakland Community Housing Corporation, whose responsibility it was to allocate funds for replacement housing for the poor.

Elaine Brown left the BPP in November 1977. During the early 1970s she gave birth to her daughter, Ericka. In 1977, they moved to Los Angeles, where Brown focused on her singing and songwriting career. She had already released two albums: *Seize the Time* in 1969 and *Until We're Free* in 1973, the latter recorded on the Motown label. Several songs on each album were based on Brown's experiences while a member of the BPP.

More recently Elaine Brown has worked as a paralegal and as a freelance writer for *Essence*. She published her autobiography, *A Taste of Power*, in 1992.

[*See also* BLACK PANTHER PARTY.]

BIBLIOGRAPHY

Anthony, Earl. *Spitting in the Wind: The True Story Behind the Violent Legacy of the Black Panther Party* (1990); *Black Panther Intercommunal News Service* (1971-77); *Essence* (December 1988); Hampton, Henry. *Voices of Freedom* (1990).

ANGELA D. BROWN

BROWN, HALLIE QUINN
(c. 1845-1949)

"Full citizenship must be given the colored woman because she needs the ballot for her protection and that of her children." So said Hallie Quinn Brown, a charismatic public speaker, teacher, and civil and women's rights advocate. Brown was born on March 10, 1845(?) in Pittsburgh, the fifth of six children of Thomas Arthur Brown and Frances June (Scroggins) Brown. A former slave from Frederick County, Maryland, Thomas had purchased his freedom in 1834. Frances, a native of Winchester County, Virginia, was freed by her white grandfather, who was her owner and a former officer in the American Revolution. At the time of Hallie's birth, her father was a steward and express agent on riverboats traveling from Pittsburgh to New Orleans. He owned a considerable amount of real estate prior to the Civil War, and worked actively with the Underground Railroad in assisting fugitive slaves to freedom.

Thomas Brown moved with his family to Chatham, Ontario, in 1864 because of his wife's poor health and began farming. Hallie's education began in Canada from 1864 to 1870. Later, the Brown family moved to Wilberforce, Ohio, where they built a house, Homewood Cottage, so that Hallie and her brother could attend Wilberforce University, an African Methodist Episcopal (AME) Church institution. Brown received a Bachelor's degree in 1873. She later studied at the Chautauqua Lecture School and graduated in 1886 as salutatorian of her class. In 1890, she was awarded an honorary M.S. She received an honorary doctorate in law from Wilberforce University in 1936.

Brown's first position as a teacher was in South Carolina, where she taught children and adults from various plantations to read. She later took charge of a school on the Sonora plantation in Mississippi and held teaching positions in the city public schools of Yazoo, Mississippi, and Columbia, South Carolina. In 1875, she returned to Ohio, where she taught in the Dayton public school system for four years. From 1885 to 1887, Brown was dean of Allen University in Columbia and administered a night school for adults. From 1892 to 1893, she served as dean of women at Tuskegee Institute, under the leadership of Booker T. Washington, to whom she had been introduced a decade before. Then, in 1893, she accepted an appointment as professor of elocution at Wilberforce University. While teaching at Wilberforce, Brown performed and traveled with the Wilberforce Concert Company (later known as the Stewart Company).

In 1894, she began a five-year sojourn in Europe. She lectured for the British Women's Temperance Association and was made a member of the Royal Geographical Society in Edinburgh. In London, Brown was a speaker at the Third Biennial Convention of the World's Woman's Christian Temperance Union in 1895 and a representative to the International Congress of Women in 1897. She also gave a command performance for King George and Queen Mary and was a dinner guest of the Princess of Wales. After she returned to the United States, she again began teaching elocution at Wilberforce in 1906. In 1910, she returned to Europe as a representative to the Woman's Missionary Society of the African Methodist Conference held in Edinburgh. For the next seven months, she raised funds for Wilberforce in England. After returning from her European travels, she was a longtime instructor in the English department and a member of the board of trustees at Wilberforce.

Brown was one of the first to become interested in the formation of Black women's clubs. In her club work, she supported the cause of woman suffrage, which she first espoused while a student at Wilberforce when she heard Susan B. Anthony speak. She was an organizer and crusader in the Women's Christian Temperance Union movement. In 1893, her attempt to stimulate a national organization of Black women brought into being the Colored Woman's League of Washington, D.C., a forerunner of the National Association of Colored Women. She founded the Neighborhood Club in Wilberforce and was president of the Ohio Federation of Colored Women's Clubs from 1905 to 1912.

Brown served as president of the National Association of Colored Women from 1920 to 1924. During her presidency, two major programs were initiated: the preservation of the Frederick Douglass Home in Washington, D.C., and the establishment of a scholarship fund for the higher education of women. Brown was chairperson of the scholarship committee for many years, and eventually the fund was named the Hallie Q. Brown Scholarship Loan Fund in her honor.

Brown was a speaker for state, local, and national campaigns in Ohio, Pennsylvania, Illinois, and Missouri. During the 1920s she was vice president of the Ohio Council of Republican Women. In 1924, she spoke at the Republican National Convention in Cleveland and afterward was director of Colored Women's Activities at the Republican national cam-

The Hallie Q. Brown Library at Wilberforce University contains records of the life of a most remarkable woman. The lady principal of Tuskegee Institute traveled the world in support of civil rights, feminism, and temperance. Brown is seen here (at left center) at the library's dedication. [Moorland-Spingarn]

paign headquarters in Chicago. Brown was instrumental in securing the support of the National Association of Colored Women for the presidency of Warren G. Harding. Skilled at uniting women on all fronts, she also organized women to "render aid in the battle waged against lynch law and mobocracy and plead for Federal interference in eradicating evils" (Wesley 1984).

In May 1925, she delivered a scathing speech against discrimination in the seating of Black Americans at the All-American Music Festival of the International Council of Women, which was held in Washington, D.C. Brown declared in her protest that unless the policy of segregation was changed, all Black performers in the program would withdraw. She maintained that it was a gathering of women of the world, wherein color was irrelevant. The policy was not changed, but her speech was so powerful that all Black performers as well as audience members boycotted the proceedings.

Brown's published writings include *Bits and Odds: A Choice Selection of Recitations* (1880), *First Lessons in Public Speaking* (1920), *The Beautiful: A Story of Slavery* (1924), *Tales My Father Told* (1925), *Our Women: Past, Present, and Future* (1925), *Homespun Heroines and Other Women of Distinction* (1926), and *Ten Pictures of Pioneers of Wilberforce* (1937).

Hallie Quinn Brown died of coronary thrombosis on September 16, 1949, in Wilberforce. She was buried in the family plot in nearby Massie's Creek Cemetery. Two buildings serve as a memorial to this outstanding woman: the Hallie Quinn Brown Community House (St. Paul, Minnesota) and the Hallie Q. Brown Memorial Library (Wilberforce).

BIBLIOGRAPHY

DANB; Daniel, Sadie Iola. *Women Builders*, 2nd ed. (1970); Majors, Monroe A. *Noted Negro Women: Their Triumphs and Activities* (1893); *NAW*; Roses, Lorraine Elena and Ruth Elizabeth Randolph. *Harlem Renaissance and Beyond* (1990); Wesley, Charles Harris. *The History of the National Association of Colored Women's Clubs: A Legacy of Service* (1984). The Hallie Q. Brown Memorial Library of Central State University, Wilberforce, Ohio, houses the unpublished papers of Brown.

VIVIAN NJERI FISHER

BROWN, LETITIA WOODS (1915-1976)

As one of her colleagues once wrote, "Those who knew her soon learned never to name her to a committee unless one intended to take care of business. One learned never to engage her in conversation unless ready for real talk" (French 1980). Letitia Woods Brown was a historian committed to being an educator.

Born in Tuskegee, Alabama, in 1915, she received her B.A. in 1935 from the Tuskegee Institute, where both parents had been teachers. After receiving that degree, she taught in the segregated school system of Macon County, Alabama, and then went to Ohio State University, where she received an M.A. in 1937, after which she returned to teaching, accepting appointments at Tuskegee Institute and Lemoyne-Owen College in Memphis, Tennessee. She decided again to return to graduate school, at Harvard University, where she received her Ph.D. in 1966. While pursuing her doctorate, Brown taught at Howard University and later became a full professor of history in the American Studies Department at George Washington University, both in Washington, D.C. Her writings include *Free Negroes in the District of Columbia, 1790-1846*, published by Oxford University Press in 1972, and for the National Portrait Gallery she coauthored "Washington from Banneker to Douglass, 1791-1870" as well as other articles about the history of Black Americans in Washington, D.C. Active in professional organizations, she served 1971-73 on a restructuring committee formed to reorganize the American Historical Association, and her tenure as a senior Fulbright Lecturer in Australia led to collaborations with foreign scholars through the American Studies Association. Her commitment to school-age children was evidenced by her involvement in the National Assessment for Educational Progress.

Toward the end of her life, Brown became a prime advocate for the creation of an oral history project on Black women, which was organized by the Schlesinger Library. Letitia Woods Brown died in August 1976, in Washington, D.C. Her memorial service was held at the National Cathedral.

In 1983, the Association of Black Women Historians established the Letitia Woods Brown Memorial Publication Prizes to honor excellence in scholarship by or about Black women.

BIBLIOGRAPHY

French, Roderick S. "Letitia Woods Brown, 1915-1976," Columbia Historical Society, Washington, D.C. (1980).

NORALEE FRANKEL

BROWN, LINDA BEATRICE (1939-)

"Yes, I am an African-American writer. Yes, I am a woman writer. Yes, I am an American writer, but I am also none of these," Linda Beatrice Brown said in a 1989 interview. "[M]y concerns are that the struggle for social equality go forward. . . . My concerns are global, and I think we start with what's immediate." The interview concluded with a modest request: "That I might not be put in niches is probably the thing I would like to ask the most."

In fact, it is hard to put Brown in niches. Although she places her fiction writing first, she was first published as a poet, and she acknowledges that her fiction is often like poetry. Her public life has similar intersections. Although she has been a college teacher most of her adult life and has spoken on campuses and participated in academic conferences all over the country, she has remained committed to the community beyond the academy, serving, for example, on boards and committees for her church, the North Carolina Writers Network, and the Black Child Development Institute, and speaking in schools and communities throughout the state of North Carolina.

Linda Beatrice Brown was born in Akron, Ohio, on March 14, 1939, to Raymond and Edith Player Brown. In spite of being raised in the North, Brown feels that her life has been greatly influenced by her mother's childhood in Mississippi, before her father took the family to Ohio in order to escape southern racism. Brown went south to Bennett College in Greensboro, North Carolina. There she heard Langston Hughes and Sterling Brown. As a junior she wrote what would be her first published poem, "Precocious Curiosity," which appeared in the 1962 collection *Beyond the Blues* (edited by Rosey Pool).

Her first book, *A Love Song to Black Men* (1974), which includes poems written over more than a decade, reflects the experimental forms, the celebration of being Black, the outrage at injustice and racism, and the vitality and humor—albeit sardonic—associated with the Black poets who emerged out of the 1960s. Although many of the poems are directed outward, in others the voice is lyrical and quiet. One recognizes the dual impulses of personal spirituality and public responsibility that continue to motivate her life and her art. The appearance of *Love Song* placed Brown within a national community of Black writers whose works continue to sustain her. Her poems have since appeared in such publications as *The Black Scholar, Encore, Ebony, Jr.*, and *Cricket, A Magazine for Children*. The 1980s marked Brown's debut as a fiction writer.

Novelist Linda Beatrice Brown, author of Rainbow Roun Mah Shoulder *(1984), is also a poet and a teacher.* [M. H. Brookhart]

Stories that a close friend at Bennett told her about growing up in Greensboro and about a local woman the friend had known became the stimulus for Brown's first novel, *Rainbow Roun Mah Shoulder* (1984). The manuscript of *Rainbow Roun Mah Shoulder* was the unanimous choice for first prize in a literary contest sponsored by the North Carolina Cultural Arts Coalition and Carolina Wren Press. After *Rainbow* was published by Carolina Wren Press in 1984, the National Endowment for the Arts selected the novel as one of a few titles to represent new American writing in international book exhibits. In 1989, Ballantine issued an edition, essentially the same but with some additions. *Rainbow* tells the story of Rebecca Florice, a woman who must balance mystical healing powers with a complex personal life within the racist southern setting of Greensboro from the 1920s to the 1950s.

A Woodrow Wilson Teaching Fellow at Case Western Reserve University, Brown received her M.A. in English literature in 1962. She held a teaching fellowship at Kent State University from 1962 to 1964. In 1967 and 1969, she and Harold Bragg, whom she had married in 1962, had their two children, Christopher and Willa. From 1970 to 1986, Brown served on the English faculty of the Residential College of the University of North Carolina at Greensboro. She earned a Ph.D., with specialties in creative writing and Black literature, from Union Graduate School in Cincinnati in 1980. During her dissertation year she held a fellowship from the National Fellowships Fund. Since 1986, she has held a faculty position at Guilford College in Greensboro, where she teaches African-American literature and creative writing.

Since the 1989 edition of *Rainbow*, the author has gone by her birth name, Linda Beatrice Brown, rather than Linda Brown Bragg. Now married to the artist Vandorn Hinnant, she is at work on her second novel, *Story Temple Greene*.

BIBLIOGRAPHY

Brookhart, Mary Hughes. "As Had Been Ordained: Spiritual Daughters of the Black American South." In *The Female Tradition in Southern Literature*, ed. Carol Manning (in press); Brown, Linda Beatrice. *Rainbow Roun Mah Shoulder* ([1984] 1989); "Interview with Linda Brown." Unpublished transcripts of videotaped interviews for the series *Talk about Writing: Portraits of North Carolina Writers* (1989); Smith, Virginia W. and Brian J. Benson. "An Interview with Linda Brown Bragg," *College Language Association Journal* (September 1976).

SELECTED WRITINGS BY LINDA BROWN (BRAGG)

A Love Song to Black Men (1974); "And This They Have Done to Their Own," *The Black Scholar* (June 1975); "In the Overtime," *The Black Scholar* (May 1976); "Dream" and "My Sisters Speak to Me," *The Black Scholar* (November/ December 1978); "Last Fling for Mr. J," "I Want to Make the Drums Talk Again," "Stripping," "The Mask God," "Only Death Can Tell Us Whom We Truly Love," "You Play It on the Edge." In *A Living Culture in Durham*, ed. Judy Hogan (1987).

MARY BROOKHART

BROWN, LINDA CAROL (1943-)

Linda Brown was born in 1943, the daughter of Oliver and Leola Brown. In 1950 her father joined in the National Association for the Advancement of Colored People's (NAACP) test case to integrate the schools of Topeka, Kansas. In September 1950, Oliver Brown, a welder for the Atchison, Topeka and Santa Fe railroad and a lay minister, attempted to enroll his seven-year-old daughter, Linda, in the school closest to their home, the all-white Sumner School. In the lawsuit that followed, Oliver Brown, on behalf of his daughter Linda, became the "named plaintiff" in *Brown* v. *Board of Education* (1954), the landmark case that held unconstitutional laws enforcing segregation in public schools. In the U.S. Supreme Court, Thurgood Marshall successfully argued this case on behalf of the NAACP.

Because she was a child, Linda Brown took no part in the case; she did not even testify in court. But Oliver Brown did testify, explaining that his daughter had to travel an hour and twenty minutes to school each day, walking across a hazardous railroad yard before reaching her bus stop. Her school was more than a mile from her home, but the Sumner School, which her white playmates attended, was only seven blocks away. Because the decision was not handed down until after Linda had completed grammar school, Linda Brown did not attend integrated schools until junior high, but her younger sister, Cheryl, began school at the previously segregated Sumner School.

As an adult, Linda Brown Smith, a divorced mother of two, was a more active plaintiff. In 1979, she filed suit to reopen the Brown litigation on behalf of her two children, who were attending schools that were segregated, not by statute but because of housing patterns and a combination of two child-placement policies. In response to the Supreme Court's decision in *Brown*, Topeka began to assign children to the schools nearest their homes, but in 1978 the city modified this procedure by implementing a so-called open enrollment policy, which allowed parents to register their children in virtually any school if they did not like their neighborhood school, and by 1979 residential housing patterns had led to segregated schools. (Ironically, had either, or both, systems been in place in 1954, Linda Brown would have attended the Sumner School, and no desegregation case would have been initiated in Topeka.) The new case was not argued until 1986, by which time Linda Brown Smith had remarried and become Linda Brown Buckner. She was now litigating not on behalf of her children but on behalf of her grandson, who was attending the predominantly Black neighborhood school. In 1987, a federal judge in Topeka threw out the new suit, but in 1989 the Tenth Circuit Court of Appeals reversed that ruling, finding "persuasive evidence that the school system has not met its duty to desegregate" and ruling that the city had failed to "actively strive to dismantle the system that existed" prior to the 1954 *Brown* decision. However, in 1992, in a case ironically called *Board of Education* v. *Brown*, the U.S. Supreme Court ordered the court of appeals to reassess its ruling. At the time of this writing, the litigation has not been concluded.

Linda Brown Buckner is a Head Start teacher and community activist who has lectured on desegregation and taken part in various symposia on the original *Brown* case. She co-founded, with her two sisters, Terry Brown Tyler and Cheryl Brown Henderson, the Brown Foundation for Educational Equity, Excellence, and Research, which was organized to provide scholarships to minority students planning a career in education.

BIBLIOGRAPHY

Campbell, Linda P. "High Court Orders Topeka School Case Review," *Chicago Tribune* (April 21, 1992); Flaherty, Francis J. "Thirty Years after 'All Deliberate Speed,' " *National Law Journal* (May 4, 1984); Kluger, Richard. *Simple Justice* (1975); Lever, Robert. " 'Brown': Is It a Promise Unfulfilled," *National Law Journal* (November 3, 1986); Robbins, William. "Historic Battleground, Old Battle: School Bias," *New York Times* (December 22, 1989).

PAUL FINKELMAN

The refusal of the Sumner School in 1951 to admit then nine-year-old Linda Brown led to the historic U.S. Supreme Court case Brown v. *Board of Education. The adult Brown posed in front of the school in 1964, ten years after the court's decision outlawing school segregation. She has since been a plaintiff in segregation cases on behalf of both her children and grandson. [AP/Wide World Photos]*

BROWN, LUCY HUGHES (1863-1911)

Lucy Hughes Brown, founder of the Cannon Hospital and Training School for Nurses, felt strongly the need for total commitment by the individual to the nursing profession. As associate editor of the *Hospital Herald: A Journal Devoted to Hospital Work, Nurse Training, and Domestic and Public Hygiene,* Brown wrote the following in the October 1899 issue: "She who has not first considered the matter from every standpoint should not enter the field of nursing."

Lucy Hughes Brown was born in North Carolina in April 1863. She attended Scotia Seminary and graduated in 1885. After graduating from the Woman's Medical College of Pennsylvania in 1894, she returned to her home state of North Carolina, where she practiced for two years. In 1896, Brown moved to Charleston, South Carolina, where she became the first African-American woman physician in the state. Her practice was reported to have been thriving and successful.

In 1897, she was instrumental in founding the Cannon Hospital and Training School for Nurses; it later became known as the McClennan-Banks Hospital. In addition to her position as head of the nursing program at Cannon Hospital, Brown was also editor of the *Hospital Herald* and secretary of the Cannon Hospital Association.

In 1904, her health was failing rapidly, and so she retired from her practice. She died on June 26, 1911. She was survived by her husband, Reverend David Brown, and one daughter.

BIBLIOGRAPHY
Brown, Lucy Hughes. Black Women Physicians Collection and Special Collection on Women in Medicine, Medical College of Pennsylvania, Philadelphia.

MARGARET JERRIDO

BROWN, MARY LOUISE (b. 1868)

Mary Louise Brown came from a family whose members were as talented and eager as she to take advantage of post-Civil War educational and career opportunities. Brown taught school while attending evening medical classes at the Howard University medical department and graduated from that program in 1898. In a move that was extraordinary for her time, Brown traveled to Edinburgh, Scotland, for postgraduate training. For more than twenty-five years

she contributed her services to the Black community as both a teacher and a physician.

Her father, the Reverend John Mifflin Brown, a bishop in the African Methodist Episcopal (AME) Church, had entered the Howard medical school program soon after it opened but failed to graduate because of frequent reassignments to southern cities, where he established several Black colleges. Brown's three brothers completed their professional education at Howard. One brother, John Mifflin Brown, followed a career similar to her own. He studied medicine at Howard between 1877 and 1881 and then settled in Kansas to practice medicine. Another brother became a minister; the third, a teacher.

BIBLIOGRAPHY
Brown, Sara W. "Colored Women Physicians," *Southern Workman* (December 1923); District of Columbia, Board of Education Personnel Records; Lamb, Daniel S., ed. *Howard University Medical Department: A Historical, Biographical, and Statistical Souvenir* (1900); *Polk's Directory of the District of Columbia* (1907-30).

GLORIA MOLDOW

BROWN, RUTH (1928-)

Crowned "the fabulous Miss Rhythm" by legendary vocalist Frankie Laine, Ruth Brown recorded such hits as "Teardrops from My Eyes," the million-seller "5-10-15 Hours," "Mambo Baby," and "Mama He Treats Your Daughter Mean," all for Atlantic Records. Born in January 1928 in Portsmouth, Virginia, the oldest of eight children, Ruth Brown has seen it all. With five number-one and two dozen top-ten hits on the rhythm and blues charts during the 1950s, Miss Rhythm sold so many records for Atlantic that the fledgling company was dubbed "the house that Ruth built."

Ruth Brown first performed professionally in 1947, but she made her debut singing spirituals as a teenager in the Baptist church choir of her mother and the Methodist church choir of her father, eschewing the blues because her father thought of it as "the devil's music." As a girl, Brown's primary exposure was to white, popular music and country and western. After she was exposed to so-called race records in late 1940, however, she won amateur night at the famed Apollo Theatre in New York by singing the ballad "It Could Happen to You." She began singing with Lucky Millinder's renowned band in 1948, but her first real professional experience came from touring with big bands in the South during World War II and as a pop singer for United Service Organizations (USO) shows in 1950. The circumstances under which the performers of that day had to perform in the South were less than optimum, yet sharecroppers and farmers alike shared in the rhythmic and lyrical expressions of her music. Brown has noted that "the music came out of a very trying period; a period where people were fighting for self-esteem, for dignity and equal rights ... that was the struggle" (Ruth Brown, personal interview, 1991). While touring in the South she went to jail more than once in protest of Jim Crow laws but continued to sing fervently in the musical tradition borne out of true living experience.

After listening to recordings of Billie Holiday that her uncle had brought from New York, Brown began to shape her vocal style to encompass the blues-tinged sounds she grew to love. When finally she was convinced to switch to rhythm and blues in the late 1940s, her career skyrocketed. She recorded more than eighty songs for Atlantic Records, consistently topping the rhythm and blues charts with hits like "So Long," "Oh What a Dream," and many others. In the late 1950s, she shared star billing at the Apollo Theatre with many greats, including Miles Davis and Thelonious Monk.

Attracting white audiences through her performances in promoter Alan Freed's rock 'n' roll shows in 1956, Brown hit the pop charts the following year with her first crossover hit, "Lucky Lips," and continued that success in 1958 with "This Little Girl's Gone Rockin'," "Jack o' Diamonds," "I Don't Know," "Don't Deceive Me," and "Shake a Hand." Brown left Atlantic Records in 1962 and moved to Philips Records. Two years later, after a few minor hits, she went into semiretirement in order to raise her family, often working under a pseudonym as a domestic worker and bus driver to make ends meet.

Following a ten-year hiatus, Brown reemerged on the music scene with stints at Hollywood's Cinegrill and Michael's Pub in New York. In 1988, she appeared in Atlantic Records's Fortieth Anniversary Celebration at Madison Square Garden. Her work as Motor Mouth Mabel in John Waters's feature film *Hairspray* (1987) introduced her to yet another new audience. She received both a Tony Award and a Keeping the Blues Alive Award in 1989 for the best performance by a leading actress in a musical for her role in the critically acclaimed Broadway show *Black and Blue*. She received a Grammy Award (1989) for her album *Blues on Broadway* and also was awarded the Rhythm and Blues Foundation Career Achievement Award in November 1989 for her contributions as a

During the 1950s, singer Ruth Brown sold so many records for Atlantic Records that the fledgling company was dubbed "the house that Ruth built." [Schomburg Center]

trailblazer in the development of rhythm and blues. In 1990, Brown became host of National Public Radio's weekly syndicated program, *BluesStage*. She also has appeared in a documentary entitled *That Rhythm, Those Blues* (1988), funded, in part, by the National Endowment for the Arts, and has performed to standing-room-only audiences internationally.

Ruth Brown continues to live in New York City where she is involved in several television and theater projects.

BIBLIOGRAPHY

Clarke, Donald. *The Penguin Encyclopedia of Popular Music* (1989); Deffaa, Chip. "I'll Come Back Some Day—Ruth Brown," *Living Blues* (July/August 1990); Feather, Leonard. "Ruth Brown's Battle Royal," *Los Angeles Times Calendar* (June 3, 1988); George, Nelson. *The Death of Rhythm and Blues* (1989); Hirshey, Gerri. *Nowhere to Run* (1984); Jenkins, Suzan E. Personal interview with Ruth Brown. Smithsonian Folklife Festival (July 1991);

McGarvey, Seamus. "This Little Girl's Gone Rockin'— Ruth Brown Part 1," *Juke Blues* (Winter 1989/90); Shaw, Arnold. *Honkers and Shouters* (1978); Whitburn, Joel. *Top R&B Singles 1942-1988* (1988).

SUZAN E. JENKINS

BROWN, SARA WINIFRED (b. 1870)

Sara Winifred Brown, a founder of the College Alumnae Club and assistant principal of the District of Columbia Normal School, was a member of Washington's elite professional community. In 1894, while a teacher of English in the District of Columbia Normal School, Brown took a leave of absence to earn a B.S. from Cornell University. Upon her return to Washington in 1897, she taught science at the prestigious M Street School and enrolled in the Howard University medical department, from which she later graduated. While advancing in her career as an educator, Brown took advanced courses in pathology and physiology at Howard and maintained a part-time medical practice for twenty-five years.

In 1910, with a group of friends, including Mary Church Terrell, a graduate of Oberlin College and the first woman trustee of the District of Columbia Board of Education, Brown founded the College Alumnae Club. Although technically eligible for membership in the predominantly white Association of Collegiate Alumnae (ACA) because she was an alumna of Cornell, Brown contributed her efforts to the segregated society to enable graduates of Howard and other "colored colleges" who were denied membership in the ACA to enjoy the benefits of professional affiliation.

BIBLIOGRAPHY

Brown, Sara W. "Colored Women Physicians," *Southern Workman* (December 1923); District of Columbia, Board of Education Personnel Records; *Journal of the College Alumnae Club of Washington, Twenty-Fifth Anniversary* (1935); Lamb, Daniel S., ed. *Howard University Medical Department: A Historical, Biographical, and Statistical Souvenir* (1900); *Polk's Directory of the District of Columbia* (1907-30); *Polk's Medical and Surgical Register of the United States and Canada* (1886-1920).

GLORIA MOLDOW

BROWN, WILLA BEATRICE (1906-1992)

Willa Beatrice Brown, pioneer aviator, was born on January 22, 1906, to Rev. and Mrs. Eric B. Brown in Glasgow, Kentucky. She was reared and educated in Indiana.

A pioneer aviator, Willa Brown and her husband trained Black pilots throughout the Depression at the Harlem Airport in Chicago. In 1939, she was a cofounder of the National Airmen's Association of America. [Elizabeth Freydberg]

Brown, an exceptional student, attended elementary schools in Indianapolis and Terre Haute, Indiana. She graduated from Sarah Scott Junior High School in 1920 and from Wiley High School in 1923, after which she attended Indiana State Teachers College where she received her B.A. in 1927. She earned an M.B.A. in 1937 from Northwestern University in Evanston, Illinois.

After Brown had completed her traditional education, she pursued her interest in aviation. Following Bessie Coleman's example, Brown also enlisted the assistance of *Chicago Defender* editor Robert Abbott when she embarked upon her career in aviation. During the early 1930s Abbott financed tours by African-American aviators to African-American colleges and universities for the purpose of encouraging young people to get involved in aviation. He also lobbied Congress to include African-Americans in federally sponsored aviation programs. Brown enrolled in the Aeronautical University in Chicago, earning a Master Mechanic certificate in 1935. She studied with Cornelius Coffey, certified flight instructor and an expert aviation and engine mechanic, and earned her private pilot's license on June 22, 1938, passing her exam with a near-perfect score of 96 percent. Brown received her Civil Aeronautics Administration (CAA) ground school instructor's rating in 1940.

After a short-lived marriage to Wilbur Hardaway, an alderman in Gary, Indiana, Brown later married Coffey, and together they established the Coffey School of Aeronautics, where they trained Black pilots throughout the Depression at the Harlem Airport in Chicago. Brown handled administrative and promotional responsibilities as well as teaching. An activist for racial equality, Brown exercised her position as president of the Chicago branch of the National Airmen's Association of America to petition the United States government to integrate African-Americans into the U.S. Army Air Corps and to include African-Americans in the Civilian Pilot Training Program (CPTP), a government-funded aviation training program designed to prepare a reserve supply of civilian pilots who could be called upon in the event of a national emergency. The United States military forces were segregated, African-Americans were not permitted to enlist in the Air Corps, and there was no indication that the government would award contracts for the training of African-American pilots. Brown also promoted the efforts of Chauncey Spencer (son of Anne Spencer, poet and Virginia's literary salon queen of the Harlem Renaissance) and Dale

White, two licensed pilots and members of the association who flew from Chicago to Washington in an antiquated airplane and lobbied for African-American inclusion in the CPTP.

Their efforts met fruition when, in 1939, legislation based on the separate-but-equal policy was adopted by Congress, authorizing African-Americans to be admitted in the civilian flight training programs. Although the majority of the government contracts were awarded to ten Black colleges (Agricultural & Technical College; Delaware State College; Hampton Institute; Howard University; Lincoln University, Missouri; Lincoln University, Pennsylvania; North Carolina A & T; Tuskegee Institute; Virginia State College for Negroes; and West Virginia State College), Brown was awarded contracts to train African-American pilots at the Coffey School of Aeronautics in a noncollege unit. She became the coordinator for the CPTP in Chicago.

In addition to training some of the most celebrated African-American pilots of World War II (several went on to become members of the celebrated Tuskegee Airmen) under the CPTP, together Brown and Coffey paved the way for integration of the aviation industry as they trained both Black and white American pilots. Brown was promoted to the rank·of lieutenant, becoming the first African-American officer in the Civil Air Patrol. She was a member of the Federal Aviation Administration's (FAA) Women's Advisory Board, and by 1943 she was the only woman in the United States concurrently holding a mechanic's license and a commercial license, and the presidency of a large aviation corporation.

Willa Beatrice Brown's achievements are numerous. She founded the National Airmen's Association of America (1939), along with Cornelius R. Coffey and Enoch P. Waters, Jr., and served as national secretary. She taught aviation subjects for the Works Progress Administration (WPA) Adult Education Program during 1939-40, was selected by the U.S. Army Air Corps and the CAA to conduct experiments for the admission of Black aviators into the U.S. Army Air Corps in 1940, and served as ground school instructor for the CAA during 1940. She was director of the Coffey School of Aeronautics, aviation mechanic's instructor for the Chicago Board of Education during 1940-41, president of the Pioneer (Chicago) branch of the National Airmen's Association of America for 1940-41, and vice president of the Aeronautical Association of Negro Schools in 1941.

Willa Beatrice Brown died in July 1992.

BIBLIOGRAPHY

Collins, Kathleen and Elizabeth Hadley Freydberg. Personal interview with Willa Brown (January 12, 1985); Dixon, Walter T., Jr. *The Negro in Aviation* (1950); Downs, Karl E. "Willa B. Brown: Vivacious Aviatrix." In his *Meet the Negro* (1943); Freydberg, Elizabeth Hadley. Personal interview with Willa Brown (March 1988); Rose, Robert A. *Lonely Eagles: The Story of America's Black Air Force in World War II* (1976); U.S. Department of Transportation, Federal Aviation Administration. *The Afro-American Airman in World War II* (1971); Waters, Enoch P. "Little Air Show Became a National Crusade." In his *American Diary: A Personal History of the Black Press* (1987).

ELIZABETH HADLEY FREYDBERG

One of the first two Black women to receive doctorates in mathematics, Marjorie Lee Browne worked for thirty years to build the mathematics department at North Carolina Central University. [Patricia Kenschaft]

BROWNE, MARJORIE LEE
(1914-1979)

"I always, always, *always* liked mathematics! . . . As far back as I can remember, I liked mathematics because it was a lonely subject. I do have plenty of friends, and I talk with them for hours at a time. But I also like to be alone, and mathematics is something I can do completely alone" (Browne 1979).

As one of the first two Black women to earn a doctorate in mathematics (the other is Evelyn Granville), Marjorie Lee Browne had plenty of opportunity to act, as well as think, alone. She taught at North Carolina Central University (NCCU) from 1949 to 1979, and for twenty-five years was the only person in the department with a Ph.D. in mathematics. Under her leadership NCCU became the first predominantly Black institution to be awarded a National Science Foundation grant for a summer institute for secondary teachers; she directed the mathematics section of these institutes for thirteen years.

Browne was the principal writer of a successful proposal to IBM for $60,000 to fund the first electronic digital computer at NCCU for academic computing. In 1960 and 1961, she directed the installation of this computer laboratory. In 1969, she obtained the first Shell Grant to give awards to outstanding students in her department, a program that continued for over ten years.

Marjorie Lee was born on September 9, 1914, in Memphis, Tennessee, to Mary Taylor Lee and Lawrence Johnson Lee, a railway postal clerk. Marjorie's mother died before her second birthday, and her father remarried. Her father had attended college for two years and excelled at mental arithmetic. He shared his love of mathematics with his children and kept up

with them as they earned undergraduate degrees in mathematics.

After attending public schools in Memphis, Marjorie Lee was sent to LeMoyne High School, a private high school, and then attended Howard University. While in high school she won the Memphis city women's tennis singles championship, and in college she sang in the Howard University choir. In 1935, she graduated cum laude.

She taught for a short while at Gilbert Academy in New Orleans; then, after earning an M.S. in mathematics from the University of Michigan in 1939, she joined the faculty of Wiley College in Marshall, Texas, and began working on her doctorate during summers in Michigan. In 1947, she became a teaching fellow at the University of Michigan, and in 1949 she earned a doctorate in mathematics.

She won a Ford Foundation fellowship to study combinatorial topology at Cambridge University in 1952-53, and that year she also traveled throughout western Europe. During 1958-59, she was a National Science Foundation Faculty Fellow studying numerical analysis and computing at the University of California at Los Angeles, and she traveled in Mexico. She won a similar fellowship for the 1965-66 year, when she studied differential topology at Columbia University.

In 1975, four years before her retirement, Dr. Browne was the first recipient of the W. W. Rankin Memorial Award for Excellence in Mathematics Education, given by the North Carolina Council of Teachers of Mathematics. The award states, "She pioneered in the Mathematics Section of the North Carolina Teachers Association, helping to pave the way for integrated organizations."

Marjorie Browne had a lively personal and professional life. During her final years, she used her own money to provide financial aid to many gifted young people so they could pursue their educations. She helped many students—some of whom came to her with less than adequate preparation—to pursue the study of mathematics to the completion of the Ph.D. degree. Browne died of a heart attack on October 19, 1979.

BIBLIOGRAPHY

American Mathematical Monthly. "A Note on Classical Groups" (August 1955); Browne, Marjorie Lee. Personal interview (October 1979); Kenschaft, Patricia C. "Marjorie Lee Browne: In Memoriam," *Newsletter of the Association for Women in Mathematics* (1980).

PATRICIA CLARK KENSCHAFT

A member of the Black elite in Washington, D.C., Josephine Bruce occupied a conspicuous place in the Black social life of the city and was identified with numerous enterprises designed to promote the welfare of Blacks. [Moorland-Spingarn]

BRUCE, JOSEPHINE BEALL WILLSON (1853-1923)

"The new found pleasure in doing something really worthwhile is quite sufficient as a motive power to keep things going," Josephine Beall Willson Bruce declared in 1904 in an enthusiastic report regarding the activities of the National Association of Colored Women, an organization in which she figured prominently for more than a decade. Born in Philadelphia on October 29, 1853, and reared in Cleveland, Ohio, Josephine Willson was the daughter of Dr. Joseph Willson, a dentist and writer, and Elizabeth Harnett Willson, a talented musician. After graduating from Cleveland's Central High School in 1871 and completing a teacher training course, she joined the faculty of one of the city's racially integrated elementary schools, reputedly the first Black teacher to receive such an appointment.

In 1878, Willson married Blanche K. Bruce, a Mississippi senator. Following a six-month wedding trip to Europe, the couple settled in Washington, D.C., where their only child, Roscoe Conkling Bruce, was born in 1879. In addition to assisting her husband in the advancement of his political career and being largely responsible for the rearing of their son, she occupied a conspicuous place in the social life of Washington's Black elite and was identified with numerous enterprises designed to promote the welfare of Black Americans. Though reared an Episcopalian, she later transferred her membership to the Congregational church and joined her husband and others in organizing the University Park Congregational

Temple in Washington, D.C., in 1896. A strong advocate of industrial education for the Black masses, she persistently argued that education, both industrial and liberal, was essential for overcoming obstacles in the path of Black progress. Following the death of her husband, she served as lady principal of Booker T. Washington's Tuskegee Institute from 1899 to 1902. Devoting herself primarily to "direct teaching in morals and manners" at Tuskegee, she served as a role model for the women students there, most of whom were from the rural South. After she left Tuskegee, she lived for a time in Josephine, Mississippi (a town and post office named in her honor), and managed her family's cotton plantations. Despite her claims that rural life was superior to life in the crowded cities, she returned to Washington, D.C., in 1906 when her Harvard-educated son became assistant superintendent in charge of the district's Black schools.

An early leader in the club movement among Black women, she was a founder of the Booklovers' Club and the Colored Woman's League, both in Washington, D.C., and the National Association of Colored Women (NACW). She held high offices in the latter organization until 1906, when a controversy over her light complexion precluded her election to the presidency. Though less prominent in the NACW thereafter, she remained active in the Women's Christian Temperance Union, World Purity Federation, and the National Association for the Advancement of Colored People. Always in demand as a public speaker, she consistently stressed the stewardship role of educated Black Americans toward the less fortunate of the race.

Josephine Bruce spent the last few months of her life in Kimball, West Virginia, where her son had become a school principal. She died there on February 15, 1923, at the age of seventy. By her direction, her sizeable estate was to be used to finance the higher education of her three grandchildren.

BIBLIOGRAPHY

Bruce, Josephine B. "The Farmer and the City," *Voice of the Negro* (June 1904), and "What Has Education Done for Colored Women," *Voice of the Negro* (July 1904), and "The Afterglow of the Women's Convention," *Voice of the Negro* (November 1904); Gatewood, Willard B. *Aristocrats of Color: The Black Elite, 1880-1920* (1990). Blanche K. Bruce's papers are in the manuscript division of the Library of Congress, Washington, D.C.; the papers of Roscoe Conkling Bruce are at the Moorland-Spingarn Research Center, Howard University, Washington, D.C.

WILLARD B. GATEWOOD

BRUNSON, DOROTHY *see* RADIO

BRYANT, HAZEL JOAN (1939-1983)

Hazel Joan Bryant, actress, opera singer, director, and playwright, became one of the most prominent visionaries and producers off Broadway as executive director of the Richard Allen Center for Culture and Art (RACCA) from 1969 to 1983. Born September 8, 1939, to African Methodist Episcopal Bishop Harrison James Bryant and Edith Holland Bryant, the third of six children in their Zanesville, Ohio, home, her childhood was dominated by the excitement of religious rituals and church functions. Her musical talents, nurtured in the church, were refined at the Peabody Preparatory School of Music, Oberlin College and Conservatory of Music, and the Mozarteum School of Music. She studied acting with Stella Adler and Harold Clurman and did graduate study in theater administration at Columbia University.

Prior to her years as a director/playwright/producer, she was a working performer. In 1962, she toured Europe with Robert Shaw. On Broadway, she appeared in *Funny Girl* as Emma and with Barbra Streisand, *A Taste of Honey* as Helen, *Hair* as Sheila, and *Lost in the Stars* as Irina. She toured Europe performing in operas in such roles as Mimi in *La bohème*, Bess in *Porgy and Bess*, Fiordiligi in *Così fan tutte*, Tosca in *Tosca*, and Butterfly in *Madama Butterfly*.

She established the Afro-American Total Theatre in 1968, initially to produce musicals and operas, but later to stage one-act plays and eventually full-length plays. In 1974-75 the name was changed to the Richard Allen Center for Culture and Art, commemorating the founder of the Methodist tradition of her childhood. RACCA produced over 200 performances highlighted by numerous special events, spearheaded by Bryant. In 1971, she developed a special youth project in South America. As a result, RACCA was endorsed by the Bishop's Council as the cultural arm of the AME Church. She was the cofounder of the Lincoln Center Street Theatre Festival (1971-81) with Mical Whitaker and Geraldine Fitzgerald. She produced the first Black Theatre Festival USA in the summer of 1979, featuring ten Black theater companies from around the country to celebrate RACCA's tenth anniversary. She produced the first International Black Theatre Festival in the summer of 1980, featuring companies from Africa, London, the Caribbean, and the United States. In 1982, she launched the Holland Limited Touring Company (named after her mother) and took Langston Hughes's *Black Nativity* to the Vatican in Rome for Pope John Paul II. She wrote several plays that were produced by RACCA: *Circles, Star,* and *Making It.* In 1978, the RACCA production of *Long Day's Journey into Night* was presented at the Public Theatre, and in 1982, it appeared on television starring Ruby Dee and Earle Hyman. It won ACE awards for best production and for best actress (Ruby Dee).

RACCA received numerous AUDELCO (Audience Development Committee) Award nominations for its productions. Hazel Bryant received the Mayor's Award of Honor for outstanding contributions to the arts in 1978 and a special citation from the governor of New York for the Black Theatre Festival in 1979. Her spirit was summarized in the words of Mical Whitaker, former artistic director of RACCA, who said, "She was a visionary who was always thinking of new things to do and getting new things done."

BIBLIOGRAPHY

Bryant, Hazel. Personal interview (March 20, 1980); Whitaker, Mical. Personal interview (October 28, 1991).

LINDA NORFLETT

BULLOCK, CARRIE E. (d. 1961)

Carrie E. Bullock, a Black nurse who graduated from Scotia Seminary Normal Department in Concord, North Carolina, is best known for her relentless work with the Chicago Visiting Nurse Association for Black people. Very little is known of Bullock's formative years. Upon completion of her nurse's training, Bullock took a job at the Provident Hospital of Chicago in June 1909. She worked at this institution for nineteen years. During this time she also served as the assistant supervisor and then supervisor of the Chicago Visiting Nurse Association. The National Association of Colored Graduate Nurses (NACGN) met in Chicago in 1923 due to Bullock's efforts. It was reportedly the largest and most successful meeting ever held by that organization. During this meeting Bullock was elected vice president of the NACGN. From this position Bullock worked tirelessly to promote the ideas of the organization. The association's official publication, the *National News Bulletin,* was published monthly, and Bullock served as its managing editor (for how long is unknown). In 1927, Bullock

was elected president of the association at the Philadelphia meeting.

Bullock's role in the NACGN has marked her as an important figure in the overall evolution of Black nursing organizations. As she stated at one point in her life, "I try to practice the golden rule; I believe we get out of the world what we put into it. I wish sincerely to be just to others, and I am truly humble" (Thoms 1985).

[*See also* NATIONAL ASSOCIATION OF COLORED GRADUATE NURSES; NURSING.]

BIBLIOGRAPHY

Hine, Darlene Clark. *Black Women in White: Racial Conflict and Cooperation in the Nursing Profession, 1890-1950* (1989); *National News Bulletin.* "Nursing Portrait: Carrie E. Bullock" (June 1936); Thoms, Adah B. *Pathfinders: A History of the Progress of Colored Graduate Nurses* ([1929] 1985).

FELIX ARMFIELD

BUMBRY, GRACE (1937-)

Grace Bumbry, the self-described "shy, very shy girl" from St. Louis, Missouri, achieved international acclaim in roles that established her as one of the outstanding operatic divas and concert artists of the twentieth century. She was born on January 4, 1937, to Benjamin and Melzia Bumbry, who recognized early her unique musical talents. She studied piano with her mother from the age of seven and joined her musical family in choirs at the Union Memorial United Methodist Church, where she was a soloist by age eleven. She sang in vocal ensembles at Sumner High School, directed by Kenneth Billups, who tutored her in voice and influenced her early career development. She received scholarships from the National Association of Negro Musicians. She was inspired by Marian Anderson, for whom she sang at the age of seventeen; impressed by her "magnificent voice of great beauty," Anderson called her to the attention of Sol Hurok, whose roster of artists she later joined. She studied at Boston University; at Northwestern University, where she became the student and protégé of Lotte Lehmann, the German-born operatic legend, who encouraged her to pursue a career in opera; and at the Music Academy of the West. She studied with Pierre Bernac and with Armand Tokatyan. Lehmann presented her in a solo recital in 1958 in a performance that received critical acclaim.

Bumbry made her operatic debut with the Paris Opera Company as Amneris in Verdi's *Aida* in 1960 and made operatic history in 1961 as the first Black performer at the Bayreuth Festival when she sang the role of Venus in Wagner's *Tannhäuser*; she made her American debut in 1963 at the Chicago Lyric Opera in the same role and her Metropolitan Opera debut in 1965 in Verdi's *Don Carlo*. Her leading roles include Verdi's *Macbeth*, *Nabucco*, and *Ernani*; Strauss's *Salome*; Janacek's *Jenufa*; Ponchielli's *La Gioconda*; Donizetti's *Roberto Devereux*; Mascagni's *Cavalleria Rusticana*; Meyerbeer's *L'Africaine*; and Gershwin's *Porgy and Bess*. She sang in the world's leading opera houses and concert halls and in a 1962 command performance at the White House. Recordings of opera, lieder, and oratorio document the extent to which she succeeded in performing repertoires that covered the range of her rich and powerful voice.

She lives in Basel, Switzerland, with her husband, Polish-German tenor Erwin Jaekel.

BIBLIOGRAPHY

BDAAM; Slonimsky, Nicolas, ed. *Baker's Biographical Dictionary of Musicians* (1978); Story, Rosalyn M. *And So I Sing: African American Divas of Opera and Concert* (1990).

REBECCA T. CUREAU

BURKE, SELMA HORTENSE (1900-)

I shaped my destiny early with the clay of North Carolina rivers. I loved to make the whitewash for my mother, and I was excited at the imprints of the clay and the malleability of the material. (Spady 1983)

One of the chores assigned to the Burke children every Saturday was whitewashing the fireplaces with a wash made of local clay. Selma Hortense Burke discovered early that this clay could be molded into shapes that delighted her. Her varied career as a teacher, arts administrator, model, and nurse has been one of distinction and achievement, but it is her work as a sculptor that is the most memorable achievement. Working with a variety of woods, marbles, and stones, Burke infuses her figures with expressiveness, heroism, and power. She has consistently focused on the human figure, from the earliest clay figurines she created as a young artist to a statue she completed in the late 1970s of Martin Luther King, Jr.

Born December 31, 1900, in Mooresville, North Carolina, one of ten children of Neal Burke and Mary

Sculptor Selma Burke gained fame in 1945 when she created a plaque honoring Franklin Delano Roosevelt for the Recorder of Deeds Building. Her portrait profile of FDR probably served as the model for the Roosevelt dime. She is shown here with Eleanor Roosevelt at the dedication ceremony for the plaque. [Moorland-Spingarn]

Jackson Burke, her introduction to and appreciation for the arts came early in her life. Her artistic interest was fostered by her father, a Methodist minister, who traveled throughout the world as a chef on several sea lines. Neal Burke's globe trotting landed him in South America, the Caribbean, Africa, and Europe, and he collected artifacts and fine art objects made in these various countries. Moreover, two paternal uncles who had graduated from Hood Theological Seminary traveled to Africa as missionaries during the late nineteenth century. As part of their mandate to teach Christianity to the Africans, they took the carved religious figures and masks and placed them in trunks rather than disposing of them. Upon their deaths, these artifacts and other personal belongings were returned to the Mooresville home. African sculpture, therefore, became one of Burke's first references to art and the first objects that she duplicated. "I have known African art all of my life," she has explained. "At a time when this sculpture was misunderstood and laughed at, my family had the attitude that these were beautiful objects" (Burke 1970).

Mooresville had only an elementary school for Black children, and Burke was sent to the Nannie Burroughs School for Girls in Washington, D.C. Her attendance at Burroughs was brief, however, because "at Burroughs there was no encouragement for the arts. If you wore your silk-ribbed stockings, patent leather Mary Janes, and gloves, you were a lady. I wanted to be a lady and an artist" (Trescott 1975).

When Burke was fourteen, William Arial, a white educator and superintendent of schools, took her into his home for tutoring. Arial, constantly battling some of the townspeople over his befriending a Black child, became the first of Burke's patrons. The young aspiring artist had to travel to Winston-Salem (nearly fifty miles away) to obtain a high school education. She attended the Slater Normal and Industrial School (now Winston-Salem State University) where she studied with Frances and Jack Atkins and Lester Granger. Although her mother, an educator and homemaker (who lived to be 103) did not discourage her from pursuing the arts (her maternal grandmother was a painter), she insisted that Selma get a practical education. So Burke pursued a nursing career at the St. Agnes School of Nursing (under the auspices of St. Augustine College, Raleigh, North Carolina), becoming a registered nurse in 1924.

In 1925, Burke moved to Philadelphia, where some of her relatives resided. To earn a living, the young artist practiced nursing in the area for two years. In 1927, Pennsylvania passed a law prohibiting nurses from giving anesthesia to patients. This inter-

President Franklin Roosevelt agreed to sit for Selma Burke's plaque honoring him. She later remarked that she was "so imbued with the greatness of the man that my first seven studies of him were so idealized they were not good."
[Tritobia Benjamin]

ruption of the range of services she could perform prompted Burke the following year to enroll in the Woman's Medical College, where a family friend was the president. There she specialized in operating room techniques to expand her nursing training. While at the college, Burke rekindled a relationship with Durant Woodward, a lifelong friend from childhood. They were married in 1928. Tragically, however, Woodward, a mortician by profession, died of blood poisoning after only eleven months of marriage. A woman of great determination and purpose, Burke completed her extended course work at the medical college. Upon the recommendation of the president of the college, Burke in 1929 became the private nurse of an heiress to the Otis Elevator business. She remained in her service for four years.

After the stock market crashed in 1929, the 1930s presented problems of epidemic proportions for most Americans. Employed throughout these turbulent years, however, Burke was unscathed by the Great Depression. Tom Sieg, writing in the Winston-Salem *Sentinel* (September 24, 1983), characterized those years as follows:

[Selma Burke] ended up working for a charmingly crazy white woman, a Cooper, of the family for which Cooperstown, New York, was named. The woman turned out to be affectionate, generous, and very rich. By the time her employer died four years later, Miss Burke had a fantastic wardrobe, had become a regular at the Metropolitan Opera and Carnegie Hall, and had an acquaintance with royalty—and a nest egg.

Selma Burke was able to remain afloat during the Depression years while many of her colleagues succumbed to economic deprivation. Nursing sustained her financially, but it was not the profession she desired for life.

Seeking professional direction and study in sculpture, Burke went to New York City in 1935. To earn money when she first arrived, the artist took a job modeling at Sarah Lawrence College, while continuing her work in sculpture. Burke soon met Claude McKay (1890-1948), writer, author, a major figure in the Harlem Renaissance, and coeditor of the nation's outstanding avant-garde literary and political publication, the *Liberator*. Burke respected his accomplishments and his knowledge of European and African arts. Their relationship, though stormy, widened her circle of friends: Eugene O'Neill, Langston Hughes, Max Eastman, Sinclair Lewis, James Weldon Johnson, Rosamund Johnson, and Ethel Waters, among others.

Burke immersed herself in work. She won a scholarship to Columbia University and a $1,500 Julius Rosenwald Award for a paper on sculpting materials. Further recognition came in 1936 with a Boehler Foundation Award.

In 1938, Burke went to Europe and spent nearly a year in France, Germany, and Austria gathering fresh material and experiences while improving her craftsmanship. In Vienna, Austria, she studied ceramics with Povolney, and in Paris, the cultural capital of Europe, she studied the human figure with Aristide Maillol, a major influence in early twentieth-century sculpture.

Feeling confident of her abilities, Burke resolved to obtain a professional degree in sculpture. She returned to Columbia University to work as an assistant to Oronzio Maldarelli, a well-known sculptor, and

Burke's quasi-classical leanings gave way to experimentation. Realizing that a creative insight could alter a composition in progress, she often used inexpensive materials. "It is very inspiring to release a figure from a piece of stone or wood," Burke declared. "Very often I look at a piece of stone or wood for a year or longer. Sometimes I will have completed the piece mentally before attacking the material" (Burke 1970).

The years at Columbia nurtured many meaningful relationships. Margo Einstein, daughter of Albert Einstein, was one of her classmates and a lifelong friend. Her visits to their home throughout the years, and the Einsteins' quiet support, encouraged Burke's aspirations as a sculptor. She graduated with an M.F.A. in 1941. In November of that year Burke exhibited at the McMillen Galleries in New York City with classic compositions.

When World War II broke out, Burke joined the navy and drove a truck at the Brooklyn Navy Yard, because, as she said, "I felt that during the war artists should get out of their studios" (Burke 1970). Then she injured her back and was hospitalized. It was during her hospitalization that she heard of the national competition sponsored by the Fine Arts Commission in Washington, D.C., to create a profile portrait of Franklin Delano Roosevelt. Burke entered the competition and was awarded the commission in 1943.

Expected to create the profile from photographs, Burke researched newspapers and library records for such an image. Finding no photographs in profile (all were in full or three-quarter view), she wrote to the president requesting a sitting to make sketches of him. He gave her an appointment for February 22, 1944.

Burke produced several sketches of the president on a roll of brown paper. Recalling the first two meetings with President Roosevelt, Burke remarked that she had been "so imbued with the greatness of the man that my first seven studies of him were so idealized they were not good." She explained that the president had been very gracious in his conversation with her concerning her work, and that she told him, on her second visit, that she wanted this work "to be the best piece of sculpture I had ever done" (*New York Times*, July 25, 1945).

The 3'6" by 2'6" bronze plaque depicting Roosevelt in profile listed the four freedoms: freedom from want, freedom from fear, freedom of worship, and freedom of speech. The freedoms were placed at the top of the plaque. It was installed at the then-new Recorder of Deeds Building in Washington, D.C.

Prior to its installation, however, approval was sought from Eleanor Roosevelt and members of the Fine Arts Commission.

On March 10, 1945, the president's wife visited Burke's studio to view the final draft. As she studied the plaque, Eleanor Roosevelt commented on the youthfulness of her husband and the height of his head. Burke explained, "I have not done it for today but for tomorrow and tomorrow. Five hundred years from now America and all the world will want to look on our president, not as he was for the few months before he died, but as we saw him for most of the time he was with us—strong, so full of life, and with that wonderful look of going forward" (Spady 1983). Asked if she would like to visit with the president again, Burke accepted an appointment on April 20; however, the president died, at Warm Springs, Georgia, on April 12, 1945. No further changes were made before the plaque's installation.

President Harry S. Truman spoke at the ceremonies on September 24, 1945. The plaque was unveiled by Frederick Weaver, great-grandson of Frederick Douglass, statesman, orator, and first Black American to be recorder of deeds. After a celebratory whirlwind around Washington, D.C., Burke and members of her family returned to their homes the following day. As Burke recalled, "My mother was very proud of my achievements—she felt that I had delivered the Burkes from the cotton patch to the White House" (Burke 1970).

Much controversy has surfaced in recent years as to whether Burke's profile of Roosevelt on the plaque was used directly by the Bureau of the Mint of the U.S. Treasury for the Roosevelt dime. Few artists had had the opportunity of a private sitting with President Roosevelt during his lifetime, and Burke's profile had been evaluated as a good likeness of him. It is quite possible that John R. Sinnock, chief engraver at the Mint in 1945, credited with the design of the Roosevelt dime, consulted the Burke profile in his research, as it was the most recent rendering created from life. Burke's head of Roosevelt expresses a kind of hauteur that suggests, as she stated, "the going forwardness that we needed at that time. I wanted to inject the feeling of pride and a positive direction" (Burke 1970). Sinnock, possibly seeking approval from Eleanor Roosevelt, who felt that in Burke's profile the president's head was too high, lowered Roosevelt's head for the design on the dime. The J. S. initials that appear on the truncation of the neck, however, confirm the artist and the designer of the coin. Artistically, the dime portrait is (with a few detail changes in the arrangement of FDR's hair) a mirror image of the

plaque. Moreover, according to the National Archives and Records Administration of the Franklin D. Roosevelt Library in Hyde Park, New York, the source of the Roosevelt image on the coin was the "sculpture of FDR done by Selma Burke" (Roosevelt papers).

Determined that young minds would not be discouraged for lack of training or an outlet to express their artistry, Burke taught in numerous school systems, workshops, and studios. Her work at the Harlem Art Center in New York City touched the lives of many now famous and nationally recognized African-American artists (Robert Blackburn, Jacob Lawrence, Ernest Crichlow). Under the supervision of sculptor Augusta Savage (1892-1962), Burke taught classes in sculpture. Located at Lenox Avenue and 125th Street as a unit of the federally sponsored Works Progress Administration (WPA) program, courses were offered in drawing, painting, sculpture, lithography, etching, and photography. Burke also conducted sculpture workshops and art clinics under the auspices of the Friends Council on Education. She taught or lectured at numerous other institutions throughout her long career. Chief among them are the St. George's

Selma Burke's bust of Mary McLeod Bethune is one of several she made of Black leaders. [National Archives]

School in New York City; Old Solebury School in Bucks County, Pennsylvania; Friends Charter School in Pennsylvania; Swarthmore College; and the Pittsburgh School District.

Selma Burke married Herman Kobbe in October 1949. Marriage to the famous architect, author of *Housing and Regional Planning*, and a former candidate for lieutenant governor of New York (1934) meant a more public life for the artist. The couple moved in the 1950s to New Hope, Pennsylvania, long recognized as an artists' colony, home to writers, musicians, and visual artists. Burke became an intricate part of the Bucks County community. She was an active member of the local chamber of commerce, chairperson of the sculpture committee (Doylestown, Pennsylvania), and a member of the Bucks County Arts Council. Her success with this organization led to many years of hard work and dedication to the Pennsylvania Council on the Arts. As a member of this august body, Burke served three years under Governor William W. Scranton, four years under Governor Raymond P. Schaefer, and five years under Governor Milton Schapp. Selma Burke Day was proclaimed in Pittsburgh on June 20, 1975, by Governor Schapp in recognition of her statewide contributions to the arts.

With a strong sense of purpose and a desire to return something to the community, Burke opened the Selma Burke Art Center in Pittsburgh (1968-81). Located at 6118 Penn Circle South, the center was developed to answer the community's growing artistic needs. Offering studio classes both day and night in drawing, painting, ceramics, sculpture, visual communication, television production, and puppetry, it became an integral part of the Pittsburgh community. A full range of services included exhibitions by professional artists (group and one-person), concerts, lectures, demonstrations, and films. The theme of the center, "a place to grow and a place to show," was implemented and sustained through a variety of educational programs.

During her years as an arts administrator, Burke also served as a consultant to the A. W. Mellon Foundation in Pittsburgh. Throughout the decades of the 1950s, 1960s, and 1970s, Burke continued to exhibit in groups and one-woman shows and to teach at a variety of schools and art studios.

Her awards and honors are numerous and include: honorary doctorate in fine arts from the Moore College of Art, Philadelphia, Pennsylvania, 1979; honorary doctorate of humane letters, Winston-Salem State University, North Carolina, 1979; Ambassador of Bucks County, Central Bucks County Chamber of Commerce, 1979; Award for Outstanding Achievement in the Visual Arts, Women's Caucus for Art, presented by President Jimmy Carter, Washington, D.C., 1979; Bucks County Council on the Arts Citation, 1979; honorary doctorate of fine arts, University of North Carolina, Chapel Hill, 1977; honorary doctorate, Livingston College, Salisbury, North Carolina, 1955; fellowship, Yaddo Foundation, 1955.

Her works are represented in many private and public collections, including Atlanta University; Bethune-Cookman College, Daytona Beach, Florida; Dry Dock Savings Bank, New York City; Gulf Oil Company, Pittsburgh; Hill Center House, Pittsburgh; Holy Rosary Church, Pittsburgh; Howard University Gallery of Art, Washington, D.C.; Jamaica High School, Long Island, New York; John Brown Association, Lake Placid, New York; Johnson C. Smith University, Charlotte, North Carolina; Livingston College Library, Salisbury, North Carolina; Mooresville Public Library, Mooresville, North Carolina; Museum of Modern Art, Miami, Florida; National Archives, Washington, D.C.; Scattergood School, West Branch, Iowa; United States Armory, New York City; and Winston-Salem State University, Winston-Salem, North Carolina.

In the early 1980s, Burke retired from an active life as a sculptor, consultant, and arts administrator and returned to her New Hope, Pennsylvania, home.

BIBLIOGRAPHY

Bontemps, Arna Alexander, ed. *Forever Free: Art by African-American Women 1862-1980* (1980); Burke, Selma Hortense. Personal interview, Pittsburgh, Pennsylvania (March 21, 1970); Cederholm, Theresa Dickason, comp. and ed. *Afro-American Artists: A Biobibliographical Dictionary* (1973); Davis, John P. *American Negro Reference Book* (1966); Dover, Cedric. *American Negro Art* (1960); Driskell, David C. *Two Centuries of Black American Art* (1976), and *Hidden Heritage: Afro-American Art, 1800-1950* (1985); *Ebony*, "Selma Burke" (March 1947); Folliard, Edward T. "Truman Praises Roosevelt Ideals at Plaque Unveiling," *Washington Post* (September 15, 1945); Lewis, Samella. *Art: African-American* (1978); Locke, Alain. *Negro Art: Past and Present* ([1940] 1968); Logan, Charles. "The Forgotten Roosevelt," *Coinage* (November 1978); *New York Amsterdam News*, "Interracial Marriage" (October 8, 1949); Porter, James A. *Modern Negro Art* ([1943] 1969), and "Negro Artists Gain Recognition after Long Battle." In *The Negro in Music and Art*, ed. Lindsay Patterson (1967); President Franklin Roosevelt papers. Franklin and Eleanor Roosevelt Foundation, Hyde Park, New York; Spady, James G. "Three to the Universe: Selma Burke, Roy DeCarava, Tom Feelings." In *9 to the Universe, Black Artists*, ed. Black History Museum Committee (1983); Trescott, Jackie. "Sculptor Selma Burke: A Life of Art, for Art," *Washington*

Post (March 17, 1975); Yeoman, R. F., ed. *Guide Book to U.S. Coins* (1991).

TRITOBIA HAYES BENJAMIN

BURKE, YVONNE BRAITHWAITE (1932-)

Yvonne Braithwaite Burke was the first Black woman from California to serve in the U.S. House of Representatives. Before she was elected in 1972, she established an impressive record in state politics. Her national career was disappointing, however, cut short after only three terms.

Born in Los Angeles on October 5, 1932, Yvonne Watson received a J.D. degree from the University of Southern California in 1956. She worked for the Los Angeles Police Commission and in 1965 served on the commission that investigated the Watts riot. The next year she was elected as a Democrat to the California State Assembly. During six years as a legislator, she helped pass tenants' rights legislation and child health care bills, and also was active in the League of Women Voters. In 1972, she reached a national audience as official co-chair of the Democratic party convention in Miami. When she ran for the U.S. House from Los Angeles, prominent Black Americans and feminists across the country endorsed her campaign.

She won easily, taking 64 percent of the vote. During the campaign she married businessman William A. Burke, and in 1973, she had a daughter, Autumn Roxanne. Burke predicted that her daughter might one day become president, but she herself found service in the House of Representatives frustrating. She was named to the Appropriations Committee, and in 1976 she became chair of the Congressional Black Caucus, but she was unable to get any major legislation passed in the areas of child care, housing, or education.

Burke abruptly resigned her seat in 1978, citing the difficulty of having an impact on such a large assembly, but personal reasons also figured in her decision. She was exhausted from six years of commuting (her husband remained in Los Angeles). Furthermore, many politicians believed her husband's involvement in a bankrupt corporation under federal investigation was a serious liability. She ran instead for California Attorney General but lost to Republican George Deukmejian; she then served as a Los Angeles County supervisor. Since 1981, she has practiced law in California and has served on the boards of corporations, banks, and public institutions, including the University of California Board of Regents. Throughout her public life Burke has received numerous awards and honors, yet her record is somewhat bittersweet because she was unable to build upon her extraordinary early accomplishments to make a lasting impact on national politics.

BIBLIOGRAPHY

EBA; Fosburgh, Lacey. "Women's Status: A Key Factor in Race by Rep. Burke," *New York Times* (May 13, 1978); Hunter, Marjorie. "Democratic Rules Panel Backs Sweeping Changes," *New York Times* (June 25, 1972); *NA*; Papers of the League of Women Voters of Los Angeles, 1920-80, Urban Archives Center, California State University, Northridge; Turner, Wallace. "California Democrats Suffer Losses as Gov. Brown Coasts to a Victory," *New York Times* (November 9, 1978); *Who's Who among American Women* (1991); *WWBA* (1990).

JOAN E. CASHIN

Her commitment to issues that concern Blacks and women helped Yvonne Braithwaite Burke become the first Black woman from California to serve in the U.S. House of Representatives. [Moorland-Spingarn]

BURKS, MARY FAIR (d. 1991)

Mary Fair Burks, an English professor and scholar of African-American literature, was the founder and first president of the Women's Political Council, the grass-roots organization that initiated and helped lead the year-long Montgomery, Alabama, bus boycott (1955-56).

As an adolescent growing up in Montgomery during the 1930s, she defied the Jim Crow system by insisting on using white-only elevators, rest rooms, and other facilities in what she later called "my own private guerrilla warfare" (Burks 1990). At eighteen she earned her B.A. in English literature at Alabama State College in Montgomery. A year later, after receiving an M.A. in the same field from the University of Michigan, she returned to Montgomery to teach English at the Alabama State Laboratory High School and then taught at the college. She married the high school principal, a former professor of hers. In the late 1940s Burks became head of the Alabama State College English Department. She later earned her doctorate in education at Columbia University.

In 1949, Burks created the Women's Political Council, an organization of Black professional women, to address racial problems in Montgomery. The council was "the outgrowth of scars I suffered as a result of racism," she recalled, the immediate impetus having been a personal experience of racist treatment by city police (Burks 1990). Although it focused initially on voter registration and citizenship education programs, in the early 1950s the council began to lobby city officials about the mistreatment of Black passengers on city buses. In December 1955, after the arrest of Rosa Parks, the council launched the bus boycott that it had long discussed. Burks, Jo Ann Robinson, and other council leaders played a crucial role in sustaining the boycott until segregated seating was abolished by Federal Court decisions a year later.

In 1960, Burks resigned from Alabama State College after several professors were fired for civil rights activity. She accepted a position at the University of Maryland, Eastern Shore, where she taught literature until her retirement in 1986. Her wide-ranging literary scholarship included articles on contemporary Black writers such as Toni Morrison. She won teaching awards and numerous professional honors and fellowships, and she did postgraduate study at Harvard University, Oxford University, the Sorbonne, and other leading universities. A longtime resident of Salisbury, Maryland, she continued her civic activism in such areas as coordinating hospital volunteers, serving on the Maryland Arts Council, and founding two African-American historical societies.

Burks died on July 21, 1991. Her only child, Nathaniel W. Burks, is a physician in San Diego, California.

[*See also* MONTGOMERY BUS BOYCOTT; WOMEN'S POLITICAL COUNCIL, MONTGOMERY, ALABAMA.]

Mary Fair Burks founded and was first president of the Women's Political Council, the grass-roots organization that initiated and helped lead the Montgomery, Alabama, bus boycott of 1955-56.

BIBLIOGRAPHY

Burks, Mary Fair. "Trailblazers: Women in the Montgomery Bus Boycott," in *Women in the Civil Rights Movement: Trailblazers and Torchbearers, 1941-1965*, ed. Vicki L. Crawford, Jacqueline Anne Rouse, and Barbara Woods (1990); *Daily Times*, Obituary (July 25, 1991).

STEWART BURNS

BURRELL, MARY E. CARY
(1863-c. 1920)

We have not been working long, but I believe we have wrought well, and I hope we will merit at the end of our day the Master's well done thou good and faithful servant enter thou into the joys of thy Lord. (Women's Baptist Missionary and Educational Association of Virginia 1910)

Mary E. Cary Burrell, along with many African-American women, labored faithfully to improve the lot of Black women in the late nineteenth- and early twentieth-century United States. The work done by Burrell and others indicates the important role Black women played in the attempts to advance African-Americans everywhere. Mary E. Burrell was a tireless and willing activist who worked to improve the material, educational, medical, and social well-being of Black people in both Virginia and New Jersey.

Mary E. Cary was born in 1863, the daughter of slave parents, in Richmond, Virginia. Educated in the public schools of Richmond, Cary graduated from the Richmond High and Normal School in 1883. She taught in the local schools for the next two years, after which she married William P. Burrell, an active participant in numerous benevolent associations including the Grand Fountain, United Order of True Reformers. The Burrells had two sons.

Mary Burrell joined the True Reformers in 1885 and became intricately involved in its work. She became the first female canvasser for the organization, its first bank clerk, president of the Rosebud Board of Managers, and treasurer of the Rosebud Nursery Convention of the Southern Grand Division, organizing several Fountain and Rosebud chapters during her tenure.

As an active participant in church activities, Mary Burrell was a leading force in the Women's Baptist Missionary and Educational Association of Virginia as chairman of the executive board. This organization aimed to "spread the light of Christian intelligence among the masses." To accomplish this goal the association established educational institutions throughout Virginia staffed by "a mighty army of intelligent and consecrated teachers" who were to "develop the noblest ideas and highest character" in Black youth (Buford 1910).

In 1907, various Black women's clubs in Virginia organized a State Federation of Colored Women's Clubs headed by Janie Porter Barrett of Hampton. This organization was an outgrowth of the Hampton Negro Conference and the general movement among Black women to organize. The avowed purpose of the Virginia federation was to encourage cooperation among Black women in order to elevate the home, moral, and civil life of Black people in Virginia. Specifically, the Virginia Federation attempted to secure funding for an Industrial Home School for wayward girls. Mary E. Burrell became the Virginia federation's secretary.

Mary Burrell's activities encompassed more than moral and spiritual uplift. She was a prominent force in the activities of the Richmond Hospital. As was the case in so many Black communities throughout the Jim Crow South, Richmond's African-American community developed institutions to provide vital services inaccessible to Blacks in the wider community. The women's auxiliary to the hospital was organized on November 5, 1902, in order to help maintain the charity ward. Burrell was secretary of the auxiliary's Executive Board.

In 1913, Burrell joined the increasing numbers of Black Americans who trekked northward. Migrating to Newark, New Jersey, she did not abandon her efforts on behalf of others. For example, Burrell operated a soldier's canteen during World War I. This operation was part of the Women's Volunteer Service League's efforts to have a building that provided both the canteen and a rest house for Black soldiers and sailors. In addition, this house became a training ground for Black women in various trades. For her efforts, the government conferred on Burrell the distinguished service badge.

When the war ended, Burrell continued in her life of service as a member of the executive board of the Newark branch of the National Association for the Advancement of Colored People, and she headed the home economics department of the National Association of Colored Women. She also worked for her local federation as chairman of the legislative department of the Federation of Colored Women's Clubs of New Jersey. Truly, Mary E. Burrell "wrought well . . . thou good and faithful servant."

BIBLIOGRAPHY

Brown, Hallie Quinn. *Homespun Heroines and Other Women of Distinction* (1926); Buford, Ada E., comp. *Proceedings of the 10th Annual Session of the Women's Baptist Missionary and Educational Association of Virginia* (1910); Burrell, W. P. and D. E. Johnson, Sr. *Twenty-Five Years History, Grand Fountain, U.O.T.R.* (1909); *Crisis* (December 1918); Dannett, Sylvia G. L. *Profiles of Negro Womanhood* (1964); Hunton, Addie W. "Women's Clubs: State Conventions," *Crisis* (September 1911); Milholland, Mrs. John E. "Talks about Women," *Crisis* (February 1911);

Neverdon-Morton, Cynthia. *Afro-American Women of the South and the Advancement of the Race, 1895-1925* (1989); "Richmond Hospital," (Richmond) *Dispatch* (January 1, 1903); *Richmond Planet* (November 15, 1902); *Richmond Planet* (December 6, 20, 1902); Salem, Dorothy. *To Better Our World: Black Women in Organized Reform, 1890-1920* (1990); *Southern Workman,* "Federation of Colored Women" (August 1911).

MICHAEL HUCLES

BURRILL, MARY P. (c. 1884-1946)

The September 1919 issue of *Birth Control Review*, a monthly periodical that agitated for the birth control rights of women, was a special issue on "The Negroes' Need for Birth Control, as Seen by Themselves." To this issue, Mary Burrill contributed *They That Sit in Darkness,* one of her two known published plays. Possibly the first feminist play written by a Black woman, *They That Sit in Darkness* informs us that every woman should have access to birth control. The play also emphasizes the importance of acquiring an education to improve Black America. Burrill's other work, *Aftermath,* was published the same year in another periodical, the *Liberator,* and was produced during the 1920s by the Krigwa Players of New York City. *Aftermath* focuses on a decorated Black soldier returning home from World War I, only to discover that his father has been lynched and burned. Although these are her only two available plays, she was known to have written others.

Burrill holds an important place in theater history because she was one of the earliest Black women to promote social change through plays that chronicle the plight of Black Americans realistically.

The daughter of John H. and Clara E. Burrill, Mary P. Burrill was born and raised in Washington, D.C., where she graduated in 1901 from the famous M Street School (later Dunbar High School). Burrill attended Emerson College of Oratory (later Emerson University) and received a diploma in 1904. She returned to Emerson in 1929 and earned a Bachelor of Literary Interpretation degree. While at Emerson, she revised *They That Sit in Darkness* and renamed it *Unto the Third and Fourth Generation.*

Burrill had a reputation as an outstanding teacher and directed numerous productions throughout Washington, D.C. She spent most of her career at Dunbar High School, where she taught English, speech, and dramatics. During Burrill's years at Dunbar High School, she inspired many students, among them Willis Richardson, who became the first Black dramatist on Broadway, and May Miller, who became the most published Black female playwright of the 1920s and 1930s.

During the 1920s, Burrill was well known throughout the District for her directing of classical plays. She served as director of the Washington, D.C., Conservatory of Music School of Expression from 1907 to 1911 and taught elocution, public speaking, and dramatics there. Upon her retirement from Dunbar High in 1944, Burrill moved to New England. She died on March 13, 1946.

BIBLIOGRAPHY

Dunbar High School Archives, Washington, D.C.; Emerson College Archives, Boston, Massachusetts; Hundley, Mary Gibson. *The Dunbar Story 1870-1955* (1965); Miller, May. Personal interview (1988).

KATHY A. PERKINS

BURROUGHS, MARGARET TAYLOR GOSS (1917-)

For several decades, writer, artist, educator, museologist, organizer, and social activist Margaret Taylor Goss Burroughs has used a variety of media to describe, teach, preserve, and enhance humane values in general and the Black experience in particular. Her feelings are best expressed in these lines from perhaps her most famous poem, "What Shall I Tell My Children Who Are Black?":

> I have drunk deeply of late from the fountain
> Of my black culture, sat at the knee and learned
> From Mother Africa, discovered the truth of my
>   heritage,
> The truth, so often obscured and omitted.
> And I find I have much to say to my black children.
> I will lift up their heads in proud blackness
> With the story of their fathers and fathers'
>   Fathers.

Although this multitalented woman has been involved in educational and artistic activities all over the world, a great deal of her efforts have taken place in the city of Chicago, where she has been a decided cultural influence.

Margaret Burroughs taught art in Chicago for several decades at the elementary, secondary, and college levels. Her writings include three books for children and two volumes of poetry. Her works of art represent several forms, from *Still Life Oil on Canvas*, a painting from the 1940s, to *Black Queen*, a bronze sculpture done in 1968. Many consider her most significant contribution to be the founding, in 1961, of the Ebony Museum of African-American History (later the DuSable Museum of African-American History and Art). This institution, which was established on Chicago's South Side, was named after the Black Haitian trader Jean Baptiste Point DuŞable, the city's first permanent resident. Founding a museum of Black culture and naming it after a Black man whom several have tried to write out of the history of Chicago is typical of Margaret Burroughs's lifelong mission to restore to Black people a greater sense of their culture and heritage.

Born in Saint Rose, Louisiana, on November 1, 1917, Margaret Taylor migrated to Chicago with her family at a young age. Like many other Black southerners of that era, her parents, Alexander and Octavia Taylor, left the South to seek a better life.

Margaret Taylor availed herself of many of the educational opportunities that Chicago had to offer. She graduated from Englewood High School in 1933 and from Chicago Teachers College (now Chicago State University) in 1937. Later, she studied at the prestigious Art Institute of Chicago, where she was awarded a Bachelor of Fine Arts in 1944 and a Master of Fine Arts in 1948.

In 1939, she married Bernard Goss, an artist who had graduated from the University of Iowa in 1935 and studied at the Art Institute of Chicago from 1935 to 1937. His painting *Always the Dirty Work* was included in an exhibit at Hull House along with the work of other Black artists. Both Margaret and Bernard were active in the Chicago arts community. The couple had a daughter named Gayle.

During the first half of the 1940s Margaret Taylor Goss taught art in elementary school while developing her own skills as an artist. One of her works during this period was an egg tempera on board entitled *I've Been in Some Big Towns*. She divorced Goss and joined the faculty of DuSable High School, where she would teach art for more than twenty years (1946–69). In 1947, she published her first book, a children's book called *Jasper, the Drummin' Boy*.

On December 23, 1949, she married Charles Gordon Burroughs, who was to be an active and supportive participant in her many endeavors. During the following years she was extremely productive, both as a writer and as an artist. She wrote two more children's books: *Did You Feed My Cow? Rhymes and Games from City Streets and Country Lanes* (1955) and

The DuSable Museum of African-American History, one of Chicago's most distinctive and distinguished cultural institutions, was founded by poet and artist Margaret Burroughs, with her husband, Charles. She is seen here receiving a lithographic portrait of Fannie Lou Hamer. [Schomburg Center]

Whip Me Whop Me Pudding and Other Stories of Riley Rabbit and His Fabulous Friends (1966).

Burroughs's artwork has covered an impressive range of media. She painted a watercolor, *Ribbon Man, Mexico City Market*, after a year of study at the Institute of Painting and Sculpture in Mexico. Some of her other works include *Insect*, an oil painting (1963); pen and ink sketches from the march on Washington (1963); *Head*, a marble sculpture (1965); and two bronzes in 1968, *Black Queen* and *Head*. Burroughs's art has been exhibited widely, from the South Side Community Center of Chicago to the Studio Museum in Harlem to the Soviet Union. Her works also have been reproduced in numerous newspapers and magazines, such as *Arts in Society*, *Connoisseur*, *Art News*, and the Boston *Globe*. In 1962, *Freedomways* featured four of her prints depicting Black historical figures and integrated scenes: *Sojourner Truth*, *Playground Peace*, *Riding Together*, and *Crispus Attucks*.

In 1961, with the help of her husband, Charles, Burroughs founded in their South Side Chicago home the Ebony Museum of African-American History. The purpose of the museum was to provide a cultural resource that would make the art, history, and literature of the Black experience available to the community. Later named the DuSable Museum of African-American History, the institution was eventually relocated to Washington Park, where the City of Chicago had donated property. In early 1991, the museum was awarded a Build Illinois appropriation, and later in the year preparations were made to add a new $3 million wing. Margaret Burroughs served as executive director of the DuSable Museum from its founding in 1961 until 1984 and since then has been director emeritus.

At the end of the 1960s, Burroughs was both an inspiration for and a major participant in the Black cultural movement. In 1967, she and Broadside Press publisher Dudley Randall edited *For Malcolm: Poems on the Life and Death of Malcolm X*, an anthology of poems by many celebrated Black writers and cultural leaders, including Mari Evans, Robert Hayden, Etheridge Knight, Margaret Walker, Amiri Baraka, Sonia Sanchez, and Burroughs herself, whose contribution is "Brother Freedom." In 1968, Burroughs published a volume of her own poems, *What Shall I Tell My Children Who Are Black?* The title poem portrays the psychological damage of racism:

> What shall I tell my children who are black
> Of what it means to be a captive in this dark skin.
> What shall I tell my dear one, fruit of my womb,
> Of how beautiful they are when everywhere they
> turn
> They are faced with abhorrence of everything that
> is black.
> Villains are black with black hearts.
> A black cow gives no milk.
> A black hen lays no eggs.
> Bad news comes bordered in black,
> black is evil. . . .

Some poems, such as "Lines to Blood Brothers and Sisters," "The Beauty of Black," "Proem on Africa," and "Message to Soul Sisters," carry a Black cultural theme. "Open Letter to Black Youth of Alabama and Other Places" continues her message of Black pride and addresses an anonymous piece, included in the book's preface, that was written by a student at Alabama Agricultural and Mechanical College during an appearance by Burroughs as a guest lecturer at the Second Negro Writers Conference in 1966:

> Dear Black Young People:
> Recently, I had the pleasure of being a guest on the
> Campus of Alabama
> A. & M. and your Second Writers Conference. On
> seeing
> My "Natural" or
> "Afro" hairdo, I noted that some of you students
> Seemed to go into a state of
> shock. Later someone asked the questions: "Why
> is she wearing her hair
> like that? Doesn't she know it looks a mess? What
> is she trying to prove?" . . .

> I am wearing my hair like this to let the
> world know that I am opposed to
> the position of second-class citizenship which
> black people have been
> consigned to in this country. Further, I wear
> it this way as a reminder to
> black people that they should be proud of their
> own beauty and their heritage
> both in Africa and the New World. . . .

Other poems in this volume carry more personal messages: "Apology to My Little Daughter for Apparent Neglect," "Lines for My Mother," and "Memorial for My Father," which reflects folk traditions from African-American culture as well as renders a vivid portrait:

> My father was good at telling ghost stories.
> He told us one about the time when
> He was cook for a levee gang and whenever
> He went into the cooks' shanty, how the skillets
> And pots had been moved from the stove with
> Not a soul around. He had seen many spirits
> And ghosts, having been born with a veil over
> His eyes

In 1970, she published a second volume of poetry, *Africa, My Africa!*, after she had traveled to that continent. The verses provide emotional and descriptive chronicles of her visit. The poem, "On My Return Home" begins as follows:

> I am home now
> At last I've linked the circle round
> For so long homeless
> Now my own hearth found
> I, who was
> So forcibly removed am now returning
> To gather parts of me that were left behind
> In Africa, my sacred lands
> And best beloved ancestral lands.

Other poems in this volume, such as "From the Portal at Legon," "Elmina," and "The Women of Ghana," examine many topics, including the devastation of slavery, the richness of African history and culture, the beauty of African women, and African daily life. Moreover, the ironic intrusion of Western culture into African life is described in "Of Mercedes Benzes and the Big Coke" and "The Fetish Princess," whose business is so good that she owns the only Mercedes in town and, following her seances, "She herself is transformed by the TV magic."

In 1968, Burroughs taught African and African-American art history at the Art Institute of Chicago. The following year she became a professor of humanities at Kennedy-King Community College, where she was a member of the faculty until 1979.

Margaret Burroughs continues to be a dynamic civic and cultural leader. Since the mid-1980s, for example, she has served on the board of the Chicago Park District. Numerous awards and honors have been issued in recognition of her achievements, including a Doctorate of Humane Letters from Lewis University in Illinois and other honorary degrees from Chicago State University, Columbia College, and the Art Institute of Chicago. Mayor Harold Washington declared February 1, 1986, Dr. Margaret Burroughs Day in Chicago. In 1991, Senator Paul Simon of Illinois, inspired by an article in the Chicago *Sun-Times*, read into the Senate Congressional Record "What Shall I Tell My Children Who Are Black?," which concludes as follows:

I must find the truth of heritage for myself
And pass it on to them. In years to come I believe
Because I have armed them with the truth,
My children.
And their children's children will venerate me.
For it is the truth that will make us free!

BIBLIOGRAPHY

DLB; Hedgepeth, Chester M. *Twentieth Century African American Writers and Artists* (1991); Igoe, Lynn Moody. *250 Years of Afro-American Art* (1981); Lewis, Samella S. *Art: African American* (1978); Lewis, Samella S. and Ruth G. Waddy. *Black Artists on Art* (1971); Metzger, Linda, ed. *Black Writers: A Selection of Sketches from Contemporary Authors* (1989); Woods, Alfred L. "The Many Faces of Margaret," *Chicago Sun-Times* (March 1991).

SELECTED WRITINGS BY MARGARET TAYLOR GOSS BURROUGHS

Africa, My Africa! (1970); *Did You Feed My Cow? Rhymes and Games from City Streets and Country Lanes* (1955); *For Malcolm: Poems on the Life and the Death of Malcolm X*, ed.

Dudley Randall and Margaret G. Burroughs (1967); *Jasper, the Drummin' Boy* (1947); *What Shall I Tell My Children Who Are Black?* (1968); *Whip Me Whop Me Pudding and Other Stories of Riley Rabbit and His Fabulous Friends* (1966).

ROSEMARY STEVENSON

BURROUGHS, NANNIE HELEN (1879-1961)

Nannie Helen Burroughs was only twenty-one years old when she became a national leader, catapulted to fame after presenting the speech "How the Sisters Are Hindered from Helping" at the annual conference of the National Baptist Convention (NBC) in Richmond, Virginia, in 1900. Her outspoken eloquence articulated the righteous discontent of women in the Black Baptist church and served as a catalyst for the formation of the largest Black women's organization in America—the Woman's Convention Auxiliary to the NBC. Some called her an upstart because she led the organization in the struggle for women's rights, antilynching laws, desegregation, and industrial education for Black women and girls. Most people, however, considered her an organizational genius—a religious leader, educator, clubwoman, political organizer, and civil rights activist all in one. At the helm of the Woman's Convention (WC) for more than six decades, Burroughs remained a tireless and intrepid champion of Black pride and women's rights.

Burroughs was born on May 2, 1879, in Orange, Virginia, to John and Jennie (Poindexter) Burroughs. Her paternal grandfather, who was known during the slave era as Lija the slave carpenter, had been able to buy his own freedom. Her father, John Burroughs, attended the Richmond Institute (renamed Virginia Union University) and afterwards became an itinerant preacher. Her mother was born a slave in Orange County. Burroughs described her mother as an independent type who, without her husband, took her two daughters (Burroughs's sister died in childhood) to Washington, D.C., in order to find employment for herself and schools for her children. Burroughs and her mother lived in the home of her mother's older sister, Cordelia Mercer.

Nannie Burroughs attended public schools in the District of Columbia and considered her education at the Colored High School (later called M Street High and still later renamed Dunbar High) to have been a glorious experience. She identified Black women teachers such as Mary Church Terrell and Anna J. Cooper as important role models during her formative years. Her oratorical talents were nurtured in the literary society of her high school and especially in the Black Baptist church. A member of the Nineteenth Street Baptist Church in Washington, D.C., Burroughs noted the interest of her pastor, Rev. Walter H. Brooks (1851-1945), in the young people of the church. Race conscious and active in the formation of the NBC during the 1880s and 1890s, Brooks encouraged Burroughs in church programs when she was a girl, and he remained her mentor and friend throughout his life.

Yet Burroughs's future greatness also was influenced by a disappointment she experienced soon after graduation from high school. Her domestic science teacher failed to keep her promise to ask that Burroughs become her assistant, a position Burroughs sorely wanted. (Some published accounts assert that Burroughs sought the position of domestic science teacher, but her own handwritten notes state otherwise.) It was suggested to Burroughs that her dark skin color and her lack of social pull had thwarted her being chosen for the appointment, but whether or not this was true, Burroughs later confessed that "the die was cast [to] beat and ignore both until death." This early disappointment inspired a zeal to provide opportunities for Black women of low income and social status. Her goal of empowering women in the Black Baptist church and her dream of establishing a training school for women and girls grew directly out of her determination to fight injustice.

Undaunted, Burroughs sought work outside of the Washington, D.C., area. In 1896, she wrote to Booker T. Washington with the hope of acquiring a job as a typist and stenographer at Tuskegee Institute. Unable to get work at Tuskegee, she finally found clerical work in Philadelphia at the office of the *Christian Banner*. During her stay in Philadelphia she met Rev. Lewis G. Jordan, pastor of the city's Union Baptist Church and an officer of the Foreign Mission Board of the NBC. Burroughs worked on a part-time basis for Jordan in order to supplement her income from the *Banner*, but she later moved to Louisville, Kentucky, when Jordan relocated there. While in Louisville, Burroughs won acclaim in the local press for organizing a women's industrial club. A harbinger of her future educational work, the Louisville club offered evening classes in bookkeeping, sewing, cooking, typing, and other vocational skills.

During her years in Louisville, Burroughs traveled to the Richmond Convention and delivered her historic speech, "How the Sisters Are Hindered from Helping." Her dynamic presence at the NBC annual meeting in 1900, coupled with the long-standing ef-

forts of Black Baptist women to form a national organization, culminated not only in the birth of the WC but also in the election of Burroughs as its corresponding secretary. Her youthful energy, resourcefulness, and speaking abilities assured the growth of the newly formed convention. During her first year in office, Burroughs reported having worked 365 days, traveled 22,125 miles, delivered 215 speeches, organized 12 societies, written 9,235 letters, and received 4,820 letters. In 1903, Burroughs reported that the WC represented nearly one million Black Baptist women; by 1907, she boasted 1.5 million. Burroughs tried to systematize the work of women's state and local societies by publishing the handbook *What to Do and How to Do It*, and by distributing uniform record books and bookkeeping advice. In 1908, she conceived of National Woman's Day and inaugurated its annual celebration in local churches as an expression of sisterhood and as a means of garnering financial support for the WC. That same year she wrote *The Slabtown District Convention*, a humorous play that continues to be reprinted and performed.

Never married, Burroughs devoted her energies to a variety of causes, but her life's work clearly was rooted in the religious and educational work of the WC. Despite her at times stormy relationship with the ministerial-led NBC, Burroughs maintained the love and loyalty of the women. They elected her corresponding secretary year after year between 1900 and 1948. In 1948, she was voted president of the WC, a position she held until her death on May 20, 1961. Under Burroughs's long and illustrious leadership, the WC provided a deliberate arena for Black women to address freely their religious, political, and social concerns.

On the lecture circuit, in the press, and in her speeches to the WC, Burroughs boldly denounced lynching, segregation, employment discrimination, and African colonialism. Her verbal attacks were coupled with calls to action. During World War I, her militant demands for racial equality and her strong criticism of President Woodrow Wilson's silence on lynching led to her being placed under government surveillance. Her uncompromising stand on racial equality included a woman's right to vote and equal economic opportunity.

Challenging Black churches to educate their female members about their political rights and responsibilities, Burroughs stressed the importance of woman's suffrage for both racial and gender advancement. Black women voters, she argued, would oppose candidates who supported segregation, job discrimination, and southern disfranchisement. In articles in the secular and religious press, Burroughs also disclosed her strong feminist convictions when she referred to woman's suffrage as a safeguard against male dominance and sexual abuse. In August 1915, in the *Crisis*, magazine of the National Association for the Advancement of Colored People (NAACP), Burroughs emphasized that the vote would help Black women "reckon with men who place no value on her virtue." Nor did she hesitate to condemn those Black men who quietly accepted the South's policy of Black disfranchisement. She called for a united leadership that would "neither compromise nor sell out." In her report to the WC in 1912, she threatened: "If women cannot vote, they should make it very uncomfortable for the men who have the ballot but do not know its value."

As a clubwoman, Burroughs joined with other women in the National Association of Colored Women (NACW) to promote the political mobilization of Black women after the ratification of the Nineteenth Amendment. Also during the 1920s, Burroughs became actively involved in partisan party politics. At that time, the great majority of Black voters were loyal to the Republican party, identifying it with the party of Abraham Lincoln and the abolition of slavery. Most Black voters identified the Democratic party, on the other hand, with segregation and disfranchisement. At the same time, ever growing numbers of Black southerners were migrating to northern cities where racist voting restrictions no longer dominated the political landscape. Realizing the potential of Black women voters to augment the Black electorate, Burroughs and other clubwomen founded the National League of Republican Colored Women in 1924. Burroughs was elected the league's president; other officers included such notables as Daisy Lampkin of Pennsylvania, treasurer and chairman of the executive committee; Mary Church Terrell of the District of Columbia, treasurer; and Elizabeth Ross Haynes, parliamentarian. Like Burroughs, the other officers were well known for their visibility in numerous organizations such as the NACW, the NAACP, and the Urban League.

Burroughs's oratorical abilities made her particularly attractive to the Republican high command. She was placed on the party's national speakers' bureau and was highly sought after during the presidential races of the 1920s. On January 12-14, 1927, Burroughs represented the league at a conference sponsored by the women's division of the Republican National Committee. She was one of three Black women along with eighty-two white

women from thirty-three states invited to the conference for a discussion of such topics as women's political roles, problems of organizing and fund-raising, and overcoming differences among Republican women. With the inauguration of Herbert Hoover as president in 1928, Burroughs was appointed to chair a fact-finding commission on housing. The commission was composed of outstanding Black scholars and community leaders such as the sociologist Charles S. Johnson of Fisk University, the architect Moses McKissick of Nashville, and clubwoman and political activist Daisy Lampkin of Pittsburgh. Research conducted by this group was published in the book-length study *Negro Housing: Report of the Committee on Negro Housing* (1932).

An articulate and vocal Black leader, Nannie Helen Burroughs was the founder and longtime president of the National Training School for Women and Girls in Washington, D.C. [Library of Congress]

Burroughs so linked her religious and political ideals that she saw the Black church as a critical vehicle for the political education and mobilization of the masses of working-class Black women. At election time, Burroughs frequently addressed church congregations, soliciting support for candidates. Her political visibility was eclipsed in the 1930s, however, by the ascendancy of Franklin Roosevelt and the New Deal. Burroughs continued to support the Republican party despite her periodic frustration with its racial policies and the shifting allegiance of the majority of Black voters to the Democrats. Although her direct influence in electoral politics waned considerably from its highpoint in the 1920s and early 1930s, Burroughs maintained a wide following in the Black community. Her popularity continued beyond the 1930s because of her public statements on Black pride and racial self-help and because of her participation in a diverse array of religious and secular organizations, some of which included Baptist and other ecumenical groups, the NAACP, the Association for the Study of Negro Life and History, and the Commission on Interracial Cooperation.

Perhaps Burroughs's most challenging achievement was the National Training School for Women and Girls, which, founded in 1909, continues to operate. (It was renamed the Nannie Helen Burroughs School in 1964 and today serves elementary school children.) As early as 1901, Burroughs introduced the idea of founding a school to the fledgling WC, and on October 19, 1909, the National Training School, with Burroughs as president, opened its doors to thirty-five students. In the school's first twenty-five years, more than 2,000 women from across the United States and from Africa and the Caribbean matriculated at the high school and junior college levels. Burroughs dubbed her institution the "school of the three B's" because of the importance she placed on the Bible, bath, and broom as tools for race advancement. The school's first motto, "Work, Support Thyself, to Thine Own Powers Appeal," captured Burroughs's valorization of work as a central tenet of racial pride and self-help. In a similar vein, the later motto, "We Specialize in the Wholly Impossible," stressed Burroughs's belief in the need of Black women to be self-sufficient wage earners.

The school offered missionary training as well as an industrial curriculum that prepared women for jobs as cooks, laundresses, chambermaids, ladies' maids, nurses, housekeepers, dressmakers, stenographers, bookkeepers, and clerks. Although the school emphasized domestic service, its industrial training curriculum also prepared Black women to seek work outside the realm of traditional female employment by offering courses in printing, barbering, and shoe repair. Like Booker T. Washington in her pragmatic approach to the reality of job discrimination, and in her belief in the primacy of industrial rather than liberal arts education for the masses, Burroughs extolled all forms of honest labor, no matter how menial. "Don't scorn labor nor look with contempt upon the laborer," she once said. "Those who encourage Negro women to loaf, rather than work at service for a living are enemies to the race" (WC Proceedings 1915). Indeed, Burroughs sought to professionalize domestic service and to redefine the work identities of Black women as skilled workers rather than incompetent menials.

In 1920, Burroughs launched the short-lived National Association of Wage Earners in order to improve the living and working conditions of domestic servants. Burroughs spoke ardently in defense of domestics, and repudiated policies that treated them differently from other unskilled workers. That same year, for instance, the federal government recommended a minimum wage for laundresses that was two dollars less than that for other unskilled laborers. Sensitive to the fact that most laundresses were Black women, Burroughs wrote to Archibald Grimké, then president of the Washington, D.C., branch of the NAACP, in hopes of organizing a broad-based demand for a decent living wage.

Through her speeches and press releases, Burroughs became a familiar voice among Black Americans of all classes and regions. Her eloquent and dynamic voice commanded many followers, ranging from uneducated domestic servants to Harvard-trained educators such as Carter G. Woodson. Rev. Earl L. Harrison, in his 1956 biography of Burroughs, recalled her impact on him when he heard her speak in a rural and remote part of Texas. Seeing her for the first time, and admiring her spellbinding style, Harrison recalled, "I shall not forget that day, when the young woman from Washington, D.C., charmed the old and the young with her logic, wit and wisdom. She made us country folk proud. We had not seen or heard such gift displayed in a Negro woman."

In the final analysis, Burroughs's appeal rested in her commitment to overcome what seemed to be wholly impossible. She fervently believed that self-esteem and self-determination developed independent of race, gender, and income. Although she acknowledged the damaging effects of institutional racism, she believed that achievement ultimately was a question of individual will and effort. Burroughs decried the abridgement of her people's civil and political rights but exalted the resultant rise of Black-owned businesses and other expressions of racial self-help. Submission to the Jim Crow laws, she asserted in 1905, denied Black Americans civil equality but never human dignity: "Men and women are not made on trains and on streetcars. If in our homes there is implanted in the hearts of our children, of our young men and of our young women the thought they are what they are, not by environment, but of themselves, this effort to teach a lesson of inferiority will be futile" (WC Proceedings 1905).

At the same time, she demanded that Black people fight in season and out of season for equal justice. In 1933, she told an overflowing audience of young people at the Bethel African Methodist Episcopal (AME) Church that Black people must give notice to the world that they were willing to die for their rights. In the apocalyptic language of the Old Testament, she admonished her listeners not to wait for a deliverer: "We must arise and go over Jordan. We can take the promised land." For decades, she supported the NAACP's crusade against racial discrimination and violence by advocating boycotts, petitions, prayer vigils, and other forms of protest. In 1934, she insisted that Black Americans fight for their rights with "ballots and dollars" rather than "begging the white race for mercy." She proclaimed in the Black press that "It is no evidence of Christianity to have people mock you and spit on you and defeat the future of your children. It is a mark of cowardice." She was equally militant in her attacks against sexism: "We must have a glorified womanhood that can look any man in the face—white, red, yellow, brown, or black—and tell of the nobility of character within black womanhood" (Brooks 1988).

When Nannie Helen Burroughs died on May 20, 1961, at the age of eighty-two, Mary O. Ross, who would soon take Burroughs's place as president of the WC, exclaimed that "womankind has lost a conquering heroine." The *Afro-American* reported that 5,500 people came to the Nineteenth Street Baptist Church to pay their last respects. Nannie Helen Burroughs, by her life's example and her teachings, laid a strong foundation upon which to build a more just and equitable America.

[*See also* BAPTIST CHURCH; EDUCATION; NATIONAL TRAINING SCHOOL FOR WOMEN AND GIRLS; RELIGION.]

BIBLIOGRAPHY

Nannie Helen Burroughs papers, Library of Congress, Washington, D.C.; Barnett (Higginbotham), Evelyn Brooks. "Nannie Burroughs and the Education of Black Women." In *The Afro-American Woman: Struggles and Images*, ed. Sharon Harley and Rosalyn Terborg-Penn (1978); Brooks (Higginbotham), Evelyn. "Religion, Politics, and Gender: The Leadership of Nannie Helen Burroughs," *Journal of Religious Thought* (Winter-Spring 1988); *DANB*; Dodson, Jualynne E., and Cheryl Townsend Gilkes. "Something Within: Social Change and Collective Endurance in the Sacred World of Black Christian Women." In *Women and Religion in America, volume 3: 1900-1968*, ed. Rosemary Radford Ruether and Rosemary Skinner Keller (1986); Harrison, Earl L. *The Dream and the Dreamer* (1956); Higginbotham, Evelyn Brooks. "In Politics to Stay: Black Women Leaders and Party Politics during the 1920s." In *Women, Politics and Change*, ed. Louise Tilly and Patricia Gurin (1990), and *Righteous Discontent: The Women's Movement in the Black Baptist Church, 1880-1920* (1993); *NAW*; Proceedings of the Annual Sessions of the National Baptist Convention and Women's Convention, 1900-1925, American Baptist Historical Society, Rochester, New York.

EVELYN BROOKS HIGGINBOTHAM

BUSH, ANITA (c. 1883-1974)

Speaking in an interview about the opening of the Lafayette Players, Anita Bush once said, "I laugh whenever I hear myself called 'The Little Mother of Drama.' No one will ever know what labor pains were borne by me the week before the first show opened." It was in November 1915 that this young, determined Black performer finally brought her long-held dream to reality: a Black dramatic stock company that would perform serious, nonmusical theater for Black audiences. Bush was convinced that Black performers could be just as good at legitimate drama as their white counterparts, that singing and dancing were not the only threatical realms in which Black people could excel. Except for the short-lived African Grove Theatre, founded in the 1800s, few Black performers had ventured into the domain of serious acting. Anita Bush was to change the face of legitimate theater in America.

Brought up in New York, the daughter of a popular tailor who catered to show business folk, Black and white, Bush early came into contact with the profession that was to shape her life and the lives of so many other Black performers. In a 1969 interview, she spoke of "falling in love with grease paint, costumes, backstage, drama," and she "married" herself to them for life.

Anita Bush was only sixteen when she secured her parents' reluctant permission to join the company of

Bert Williams and George W. Walker, although she considered herself very untalented musically. When her concerned father asked Williams why he wanted Anita to join his troupe, Williams gallantly assured him that she "would make a pretty picture on stage." Bush remained with the famous team until they discontinued their association and Williams went on to greater fame with the Ziegfeld Follies.

In 1915, driven by the constant dream of forming a group of actors to perform in serious drama, Bush gathered some of Harlem's favorite performers and began what at first was called the Anita Bush Players, a name the group retained until they moved to the Lafayette Theatre from the Lincoln Theatre in December of that year. Shortly thereafter, they began to be advertised in newspapers as The Lafayette Players, and the name stayed with the troupe throughout its seventeen-year existence.

The newly formed company consisted of such Harlem luminaries as Charles Gilpin, Dooley Wilson, Andrew Bishop, and Carlotta Freeman, who, prior to joining the group, had never performed professionally. The Lafayette Players introduced legitimate theater to more than twenty-five cities across America. Performing more than 250 dramas never presented by a completely Black group, either before or since, the Players became a virtual training ground for more than 300 Black performers before they disbanded permanently in 1932. Bush herself starred with the Players for several years and then, in 1921, co-starred with Lawrence Chenault in the first all-Black Western movie, *The Crimson Skull*. Later, in 1936, Bush was featured in the Works Progress Administration (WPA) Federal Theatre Project's *Swing It*.

During her long and varied career, Anita Bush was given credit for initiating the professional careers of more than fifty successful Black performers. She died in February 1974 at the age of ninety-one knowing that her dream had been the seed that blossomed and changed the face of Black theater forever.

[*See also* THEATER.]

BIBLIOGRAPHY

Thompson, Sister Francesca. "Final Curtain for Anita Bush," *Black World* (July 1974), and "The Lafayette Players: 1915-1932," Ph.D. diss. (1972).

SISTER FRANCESCA THOMPSON

The Lafayette Players, founded by actress Anita Bush, was one of the first Black theater groups to perform serious, nonmusical theater. For seventeen years the Players brought quality legitimate theater to Black audiences. Shown here is a scene from Girl at the Fort, *featuring Anita Bush, Edward Thompson, Andrew Bishop, Dooley Wilson, and two unidentified actors. [Sister Francesca Thompson]*

BUTCHER, MARGARET JUST
(1913-)

When one hears the name Margaret Just Butcher, it is usually in conjunction with Alain Locke, for she completed what was to have been his "magnus opus." Before his death in 1954, Alain Locke turned over his research materials to Margaret, the brilliant daughter of one of his best friends. *The Negro in American Culture* (1956, 1971), which historically yet topically traces "the folk and formal contributions" of the Negro to American culture, is an important African-American reference text that is often cited in discussions of artists Edward Bannister and Meta Warwick Fuller. Yet *The Negro in American Culture* is not Margaret Just Butcher's sole accomplishment; she was also an educational and political activist.

Born April 28, 1913, in Washington, D.C., Margaret was the oldest of the three children of Ernest Everett Just, the famed cell biologist and first recipient of the Spingarn Medal, and Ethel Highwarden, daughter of one of the first Black female graduates of Oberlin College. Margaret's brilliance and preference for the humanities were recognized even in her early years. Her educational training included attending school in Naples, Italy, when she accompanied her father to Europe in 1927, Emerson College, and Boston University where she received her Ph.D. in 1947.

The influence of her parents, both educators, is evident in Margaret Just Butcher's choice of a profession. As an English professor, she taught at Virginia Union University (1935-36), in the Washington, D.C., public schools (1937-41), at Howard University (1942-55), and at Federal City College (1971-82). Her interest in the humanities also took her abroad—as a Fulbright visiting professor in France (1949-50), as the Director of the English Language Training Institute in Casablanca (1960-65), and as Assistant Cultural Affairs Officer of the U.S. Embassy in Paris (1968).

While teaching was her primary profession, Butcher made inroads as a reformer in education and politics. From 1953 to 1956, she served on the board of education for the Washington, D.C., schools during the time the school system was to be integrated, and was the only board member who fought for equality in integration. Butcher became well known in the District for her scathing criticisms of the board, and her challenges were often reported in the newspapers. She was honored in 1955 by Lambda Kappa Mu "for her militant fight for integration of education." Butcher was also active in the political arena: she served as a member of the National Civil Defense Advisory Council in 1952 (replacing Mary McLeod Bethune); she was a special educational consultant to the National Association for the Advancement of Colored People during 1954-55 (assisting Thurgood Marshall); and she was elected as the District's delegate to the Democratic party's national convention in 1956 and 1960.

Margaret Just was married for a short time to Stanton L. Wormley (the precise dates are unknown); they had one daughter, Sheryl Everett. In 1949, she married James W. Butcher; they divorced ten years later. Margaret Just Butcher currently resides in Washington, D.C.

BIBLIOGRAPHY

BABB; *Black Dispatch*, "Member of School Board Cited for Accomplishments" (December 4, 1955); Margaret Just Butcher. *The Negro in American Culture* ([1956] 1971); Lenwood Davis. *Black Artists in the United States: An Annotated Bibliography of Books, Articles and Dissertations on Black Artists, 1779-1979* (1980); *EBA*; *LBAA*; Charlotte Lytle, ed. *Index to Selected Periodicals by and about Negroes, 1950-1959* (1961); Gerri Majors with Doris E. Saunders. *Black Society* (1976); Kenneth R. Manning. *Black Apollo of Science: The Life of Ernest Everett Just* (1983); *Washington Afro-American*, "Dr. Butcher on Defense Council" (June 17, 1952); Information about Margaret Just Butcher is on file at the Moorland-Spingarn Research Center, Howard University, Washington, D.C.

PAULA C. BARNES

BUTLER, LAURETTA GREEN
(1881-1952)

Lauretta Green Butler relinquished a professional music career to devote her life to training children to perform for the stage. Lauretta Green was born November 6, 1881, in Los Angeles, California. She was one of three children born to Joseph and Amanda Shelton Green. She married Charles Butler, of whom very little is known.

Butler began her musical career as a church pianist. For several years she performed with many of the best Black orchestras in the country. Inspired by a children's production she saw in Chicago, Butler returned to Los Angeles and opened the first Black professional dance studio for children. A great lover of children, Butler realized that with proper training she could develop the latent talent not only in precocious youngsters but also in those considered to be without ability or aptitude.

The Butler Dance Studio opened in 1916 for children from two years old to teenagers. At the studio, the students learned dancing, singing, and mime along with strong discipline. In 1917, Butler presented her first Kiddie Minstrel Review, which established her as the foremost producer of children's acts. The Butler Studio became an established tradition and institution in Los Angeles until the late 1940s. Around 1923, the Kiddie Minstrel Review was renamed the Kiddie Review, and the use of blackface makeup was eliminated.

Butler trained many of the young people, directed productions, played piano, and conducted the orchestra for performances. The "Butler Kids" were in constant demand to perform for major social events, nightclubs, military bases, and the movie industry. The children were highlighted in numerous Black films of the 1930s and 1940s. While the Butler Studio was primarily established for Black children, many white children were trained by Butler, including cast members from *The Little Rascals* and *Our Gang*.

Butler also trained many young Black legendary stars for the stage and screen such as Dorothy and Vivian Dandridge, the great dancing team of Ananias and James Berry, and Jimmie and Freddy Moultrie.

Butler, who never had any children of her own, adopted several during her lifetime. She inspired other Black professionals to open schools for young people, but none equaled the success of the Butler Studio.

BIBLIOGRAPHY

Interviews with former Butler Kids Nettie Jeter and Eugene "Sunshine Sammy" Jackson in summer of 1988; Interview with Leni A. Sovenson in 1991; Butler Dance Studio. Program and clipping file. Private collection, Nettie Jeter, Los Angeles, California.

KATHY A. PERKINS

BUTLER, OCTAVIA E. (1947-)

Octavia E. Butler is the first African-American woman to gain popularity and critical acclaim as a major science fiction writer. The author of nine novels and numerous short stories, she has won two of science fiction's most prestigious awards, the Nebula and the Hugo.

Butler's novels include *Patternmaster* (1976), *Survivor* (1978), *Mind of My Mind* (1977), *Kindred* (1979), *Wild Seed* (1980), *Clay's Ark* (1984), *Dawn* (1987), *Adulthood Rites* (1988), and *Imago* (1989). Her other writings include "Speech Sounds," a short story that won a Hugo Award in 1984, and the novelette, "Bloodchild," which won a 1984 Nebula Award and a 1985 Hugo.

An enthusiastic reader, Butler constantly researches new developments in biology, genetics, and the physical sciences, as well as keeps up with current events. In her stories, however, character development, human relationships, and social concerns predominate over intergalactic hardware. A substantial portion of her writing features Black women who find the strength to cope with bigotry, persecution, and pain as well as efforts to keep them in their place.

Born in Pasadena, California, on June 22, 1947, Octavia Estelle Butler was the only child of a maid and a shoeshine man. A sensitive, introspective young girl, she became interested in science fiction after being turned off by the standard reading fare of elementary schools. In an essay entitled "Why I Write," she explains: "When I discovered that my first-grade teacher expected me to be content with Dick and Jane, I asked my mother if I could have a library card. From the day she took me to get one, I was a regular at the fairy tale shelves. I also explored, read anything else that looked interesting, got hooked on horse stories for a while, then discovered science fiction" (Butler n.d.).

Although fascinated by the literature of science fiction, she was somewhat disconcerted by the fact that Black characters were rare in the genre. Moreover, she was disturbed by the stereotypical images of women, and found that most science fiction writing emphasized ideas and machinery over character development. As early as age thirteen Butler was producing stories that, she later concluded, had been heavily influenced by the white-male-oriented science fiction stories she had read.

As an adult, Butler continued to write. After graduating from Pasadena City College, she attended California State University in Los Angeles, but she credits several nonacademic programs for helping her perfect her craft. Two of the most helpful were the Open Door Program of the Screen Writers Guild of America, West (1969-70) and the Clarion Science Fiction Writers Workshop (1970). With the resolve shown by some of her characters, she continued to write in spite of rejection by publishers, financial hardship, and discouragment from family and friends who advised her to get a "real" job. Her obstinacy was later vindicated, however. In 1971, as a result of her participation in the Clarion workshop, one of her short stories, "Crossover," appeared in the Clarion anthology. Five years later, her first novel was published by Doubleday.

Five of Butler's first six novels (*Patternmaster, Mind of My Mind, Survivor, Wild Seed,* and *Clay's Ark*) were part of her patternist series. A prominent figure in this series is Doro, a 4,000-year-old Nubian whose mentally linked descendants form the "pattern." Doro is a "psychic vampire" who takes over other people's bodies at will and uses terror to control his progeny in the pattern. Butler admits in "Why I Write" that there is a connection between herself and this frightening character: "I have a running character named Doro in my patternist novels. Sometimes I can see all too clearly the part of myself from which he was created. Writers, too, are a species of vampires —happily nonlethal, usually harmless, but constantly acquiring bits and pieces of other people's lives" (Butler n.d.).

Patternmaster, the first novel in the patternist saga, describes the struggle between two brothers to inherit control of the pattern from their dying father, the Patternmaster Royal. Coransee, the elder son, is a brutal man who controls with force, in contrast to his younger brother, Teray, who relies more on his mental powers. In his struggle to defeat his brother, as well as to prevail against attacks by the bestial Clayarks, Teray obtains essential support from Amber, a Black woman with healing powers and a strong sense of her own independence. Set in the future, this novel goes far beyond a struggle between good and evil. It also comments on society's class structure, the struggle between brute force and cerebral powers, and the role of women.

Mind of My Mind takes place in Los Angeles and concerns the devastating struggle between the brutal and powerful Doro and his mentally linked community in the pattern led by his daughter, Mary. Unlike Doro, who is compelled to kill and take over other people's bodies, Mary takes over other people's minds by linking them to hers in the pattern. The author provides the following information about how the development of this character relates to Butler's chilling insight into human behavior: "I deliberately made . . . Mary Larkin my opposite. She was small, lighter-skinned, feisty, and eventually very powerful. . . . But Mary Larkin didn't handle power very well. I suspect that most people, given sudden power, would have trouble with it. . . . Their careless public utterances may become policy before they realize it. Their pride can become something other people die for. I let this happen to Mary in *Mind of My Mind* after watching it happen in the real world, in the White House every four years" (Butler n.d.).

Eventually Mary becomes wiser in her use of power and finally is able to summon the collective strength of her telepathic community in order to defeat Doro and free the pattern from his malevolent control. Another interesting character in this novel is Mary's grandmother, Emma, whose past is compellingly revealed in one of Butler's subsequent novels, *Wild Seed.*

The patternist novel following *Mind of My Mind* is *Survivor,* which is set in the future. It describes the efforts of Alanna, an Afro-Asian "wild child," to survive amid many ongoing conflicts, including one on earth between the telepathic Patternists and the diseased inferior creatures, the Clayarks. On another planet, an ongoing struggle is being waged by two rival groups of the furry Kohns. In this novel, which examines prejudice based on caste and color, Alanna is forced to mate with a Kohn creature but is able to overcome many difficult situations by her willingness to adapt to an alien environment.

The fourth patternist novel, *Wild Seed,* is a historical saga that incorporates a great deal of the Black experience, including slavery. Set in several centuries in the past in Africa and America, this story chronicles the relationship between Doro, the Nubian psychic vampire in *Mind of My Mind,* and the African healer, Anyanwu, who appeared as Emma in that same story. Doro forces many people under his control to participate in breeding projects in order to produce Patternists who will be under his control. Anyanwu, a powerful healer who has the ability to alter her own form, is Doro's lover and at other times struggles against his terrifying activities.

The final novel in the patternist series is *Clay's Ark,* in which the Black astronaut Eli, the sole survivor of a trip into space, returns to earth infected with, and involuntarily spreads, the clayark disease, which spawns a debased race of mutants called the Clayarks, who have plagued the Patternists throughout several earlier novels.

Butler's 1979 novel, *Kindred,* is a deviation from the patternist theme prevalent in her other novels. Dana, a Black woman in twentieth-century Los Angeles, is summoned back in time to an antebellum Maryland plantation in order to save the life of the plantation owner's son. Dana is compelled to save the life of this reckless and obnoxious white boy because he is destined to impregnate a Black woman with a child who is to become Dana's ancestor. Her travel back into another era is especially perilous because during much of this time she must be disguised as a slave and learn firsthand the brutalities of slavery.

Butler's award-winning novelette "Bloodchild" offers an intriguing exploration of a reversal of gender roles. In this story, males are used for pregnancy and reproduction.

Butler's most recent novels, *Dawn, Adulthood Rites,* and *Imago,* are part of her Xenogenesis trilogy, a series that examines efforts by the human race to survive both a devastating war on earth and the gene-swapping activities of extraterrestrials. Much of the story is centered around a Black woman, Lilith Iyapo, and her son, Akin, who is the offspring of Lilith, an Asian father, and an extraterrestrial. The alien being who is the third element in the propagation process is one of the Oankali, the race that has captured human survivors of the war on earth and has forced them to breed and exchange genes with them. As a result, both the humans and the Oankali will undergo genetic transformation. One of the observations made by the extraterrestrials is that humans have the contradictory characteristics of being both intelligent and hierarchical. The second characteristic, which results in prejudice, class divisions, and conflict, makes it almost inevitable that humankind will eventually destroy itself even without the interference of aliens.

Octavia Butler resides in Los Angeles where, in addition to writing, she volunteers her time as a literacy instructor. Her intense intellectual and emotional involvement in the human experience, as well as her keen powers of observation, continues to be an integral part of her storytelling. As she reveals in the conclusion to her essay "Why I Write," "I began to write consciously, deliberately, about people who were afraid and who functioned in spite of their fear. People who failed sometimes and were not destroyed. . . . Every story I write adds to me a little, changes me a little, forces me to reexamine an attitude or belief, causes me to research and learn, helps me to understand people and grow. . . . Every story I create creates me. I write to create myself."

BIBLIOGRAPHY

"Black Women and the Science Fiction Genre: *Black Scholar* Interview with Octavia Butler," *Black Scholar* (March-April 1986); Butler, Octavia E. "Why I Write," Unpublished paper (n.d.); *DLB*; Govan, Sandra Y. "Connections, Links, and Extended Networks: Patterns in Octavia Butler's Science Fiction," *Black American Literature Forum* (Summer 1984); Metzger, Linda, ed. *Black Writers: A Selection of Sketches from Contemporary Authors* (1989); Salvaggio, Ruth. "Octavia E. Butler." In *Suzy McKee Charness, Octavia Butler, Joan D. Vinge,* ed. Marleen S. Barr et al. (1986).

SELECTED WORKS BY OCTAVIA E. BUTLER

Adulthood Rites: Xenogenesis (1988); "Bloodchild," *Isaac Asimov's Science Fiction Magazine* (June 1984); *Clay's Ark* (1984); *Dawn: Xenogenesis* (1987); *Imago: Xenogenesis* (1989);

Kindred (1979); *Mind of My Mind* (1977); *Patternmaster* (1976); "Speech Sounds," *Isaac Asimov's Science Fiction Magazine* (December 1983); *Survivor* (1978); *Wild Seed* (1979).

ROSEMARY STEVENSON

BUTLER, SELENA SLOAN (1872?-1964)

Whenever life around Selena Sloan Butler was uncertain, she simply took affairs into her own hands. When there was no kindergarten for her son to attend, she created one. When there was no support organization for his public school, she founded one. When there were no community organizations for Black women to work through, she banded with others and established them. And later, when her husband died, she simply packed up and moved on. Her efforts, particularly on behalf of school children, have been recognized in her designation as one of the founders of modern-day Parent-Teachers Associations.

Selena Butler never revealed much information about her early life; only a few facts are known. She was born Selena Sloan in Thomasville, Georgia, on January 4, 1872(?), to Winnie Williams, a woman of African and Indian descent, and William Sloan, a white man. Her father took care of her, her elder sister, and her mother, but he did not reside with them. Selena's mother died while Selena was still young; she may have lived a short time with her married sister.

Selena received elementary school training from missionaries in Thomas County and was sponsored for admission to Spelman Seminary (later Spelman College) in Atlanta, Georgia, by her mother's minister. After six years of schooling, at age sixteen, she graduated. After matriculating, she began a career teaching English and elocution, first in Atlanta and then in Florida. While teaching in Atlanta she met and later married Henry Rutherford Butler, destined to be one of Atlanta's finest and foremost Black doctors. They traveled together to Boston, where Henry went to medical school at Harvard and she studied oratory at Emerson School. In 1895, the couple returned to Atlanta.

When Butler's son, Henry Rutherford, Jr., was born, she began her lifelong involvement in parent-teacher associations. There was no preschool teacher in her neighborhood, so she set up a kindergarten in her own living room. When Henry went to public school, she followed a supportive course by establishing the first Black parent-teacher association in the country at Yonge Street School. From this small beginning, Butler went on to establish an association at the state level (1920), and then, six years later, at the national level (1926). The National Congress of Colored Parents and Teachers maintained a good relationship with the white national Parent-Teacher Association organization because Butler made every effort to see that the policies and programs of both organizations were coordinated. The Black association serviced primarily the southern states, where there were the largest concentrations of racially segregated schools. When the two organizations were joined nationally, after Butler's death, Butler was elevated to national founder status along with two white women, Alice McLellan Birney (also from Georgia) and Phoebe Hearst.

Selena Butler was an active clubwoman in arenas other than education. She served as a delegate to the founding convention of the National Association of Colored Women, the first president of the Georgia Federation of Colored Women's Clubs, and a member of the Georgia Commission on Interracial Cooperation. In addition, the Chautauqua Circle, the premiere Black women's social organization in Atlanta, claimed her as a member, as did the Ruth Chapter of the Order of the Eastern Star. She maintained her interest and activity in the Eastern Star long after she left Atlanta.

In 1931, when her husband died, she moved with her son to England. Her son also pursued a career in medicine and had studied, as his father had, at Harvard. Unlike his father, however, Henry Rutherford, Jr., felt no particular loyalty to the South. Lightskinned, educated, articulate, sophisticated, and polished in manner, Butler's son voiced a deep-seated denunciation of the South's racial constrictions with his own permanent exile from home. World War II forced Dr. Butler to leave England. He and his mother moved to Fort Huachaca in Arizona, where he served in the army hospital. At the same hospital, Butler organized the first Gray Lady Corps for Black women.

When Dr. Butler married and moved to California, Butler returned to Atlanta, where she kept up an active community service career until 1953. Some late-life health problems required her retirement from strenuous activity, and she moved in 1953 to Los Angeles to live with her son and daughter-in-law. She died in 1964 in Los Angeles, but she is buried in Atlanta next to her husband in Oakland Cemetery.

During her lifetime Butler was recognized for her philanthropic and charitable service, especially in the field of child welfare. The Lord Mayor of London, the American Red Cross, Spelman College, and President Herbert Hoover, all honored her in some way. Her portrait hangs in the State Capitol of Georgia and Atlanta named a park after her, which sits next door to the Henry Rutherford Butler Elementary School, formerly the Yonge Street School, where her first PTA was founded.

BIBLIOGRAPHY

Obituaries, *Atlanta Daily World* (October 8 and 10, 1964); Papers of the Chautauqua Circle, Woodruff Library, Clark-Atlanta University, Atlanta, Georgia; National PTA publications; Rutherford, Henry, Jr. Personal interview; Selena Sloan Butler File, Spelman College Archives, Atlanta, Georgia.

DARLENE ROTH

BYRD, FLOSSIE M. (1927-)

Flossie M. Byrd's more than four decades of outstanding teaching and leadership in home economics led to her selection as recipient of the Distinguished Service Award from the American Home Economics Association in 1990, and to her induction into the Gallery of Distinction for Agricultural and Home Economics Graduates at Florida A & M University. She has taught at Florida A & M University, Oregon State University, and Prairie View A & M University, where she is now vice president for academic affairs. Byrd holds an M.Ed. from Pennsylvania State University and a Ph.D. from Cornell University. She has also studied at Trinity University, Pepperdine University, and the University of Southern California.

Born to John and Elizabeth Byrd in Sarasota, Florida, on August 8, 1927, she served as president of the National Council of Administrators of Home Economics, 1971-72, cochair of the Home Economics Commission of the National Association of State Universities and Land Grant Colleges, 1966-69, chair of the Southern Region of Home Economics Administrators, 1978-79, vice president of the American Home Economics Association, 1985-87, and president of the Association of Administrators of Home Economics, 1981-83. She has published articles in the *Journal of Home Economics* and contributed chapters to books and edited volumes. More than $800,000 of funding for home economics research was garnered by Byrd while she was professor and dean of home economics at Prairie View, 1964-87. Since 1987, she has received grants for more than $2 million for Title III projects.

BIBLIOGRAPHY

Houston Post. "Dr. Byrd Is Selected as Dean at PV" (September 28, 1964); *Jet.* "Prairie View Gets New Academic Affairs VEEP" (July 1, 1991); *Texas Advocate.* "At PVAMU Flossie Byrd Wins Award" (August 28, 1990).

JEWEL LIMAR PRESTAGE

C

CABLE, MARY ELLEN (1881-1944)

African-American educator, director of practice teaching, principal, supervising principal, clubwoman, and civil rights activist, Mary Ellen Cable was born and raised in Leavenworth, Kansas.

She graduated from Leavenworth Teachers' Normal School in the late 1890s. After graduation she taught elementary school for a brief time in Topeka, Kansas, where she met her husband, George Cable, at that time also a teacher. The couple moved to Indianapolis by 1900, where George accepted a position at the post office and Mary began her forty years of service with the Indianapolis Public School System. Cable further enhanced her education skills and abilities through study at the University of Chicago, Columbia University in New York, and the Indiana University Extension at Indianapolis. In 1903-5, Cable successfully oversaw the Black community's elementary school vegetable garden project, which ultimately prompted residents in surrounding neighborhoods to plant gardens and improve property upkeep.

In 1916-17, with the support of several Black women's clubs, Cable instituted the first "fresh air" classroom for Black tuberculous children at Public School 24. During her tenure as director of practice teaching, the Indianapolis School Board certified sixty-one much-needed African-American teachers.

Mary Cable was also an active member of various social and civic groups, among them Bethel African Methodist Episcopal Church, Browning Literary Society, and Sigma Gamma Rose sorority. In 1912, as president of the Colored Women's Civic Club, a local philanthropic group, Cable provided the impetus for organizing the local chapter of the National Association for the Advancement of Colored People (NAACP)—its most western branch at that time. She served as Indiana's first NAACP president, and for the first thirteen months all other officers and members of the executive board were clubwomen. In 1913, finding themselves overwhelmed by family, club, and NAACP responsibilities, the women petitioned the Black community's men—"who have more time"—to shoulder the burden of leadership.

BIBLIOGRAPHY

Crisis (July, October 1912; April 1915); Ferguson, Earline Rae. "The Woman's Improvement Club of Indianapolis: Black Women Pioneers in Tuberculosis Work, 1903-1938," *Indiana Magazine of History* (September 1988); *Indianapolis News.* Obituary (September 19, 1944); Letter from Mary Cable in National Association for the Advancement of Colored People Manuscript Collection, Library of Congress, Washington, D.C.

EARLINE RAE FERGUSON

CADE, TONI *see*
BAMBARA, TONI CADE

CADORIA, SHERIAN GRACE (1940-)

In 1985, when Sherian Grace Cadoria was promoted to brigadier general, she was the first Black woman in the regular U.S. Army to achieve this rank and the second Black female in history to earn the honor. The year Cadoria made first lieutenant and became a platoon officer in Company B of the Women's Army Corps Training Battalion at Ft. McClellan, Alabama, a series of events occurred that had a major impact on U.S. history. The year was 1963. During that year violence threatened the core of America as racism sparked riots around the country and President John F. Kennedy was assassinated. The feminist movement emerged with Betty Friedan's *Feminine Mystique*. The death of civil rights activist Medgar Evers and the unprecedented march on Washington, where Dr. Martin Luther King, Jr., gave his "I Have a Dream" speech, renewed widespread support for the Black revolution. Meanwhile, not far from Ft. McClellan, Governor George Wallace bodily blocked a Black student from entering the University of Alabama.

Throughout the turbulent 1960s, while the United States waged war at home and abroad, Sherian Cadoria fought a personal battle that would eventually take her to the top. The military, perhaps more than any other institution, was a male dominion. Although initially Cadoria was in the Women's Army Corps (where racism was prevalent), after the women's corps was dissolved in 1978 she moved into the male-dominated corps. She excelled as an executive officer in Europe, during a tour in Vietnam, at the U.S. Army Command and General Staff College, and as a regional commander of a criminal investigation division in Maryland.

Born January 26, 1940, the Marksville, Louisiana, native also had career-building assignments in military schools such as the Adjutant General School (advance course) and U.S. Army War College. She received a B.S. in Business Education from Southern University and A & M College in Baton Rouge, Louisiana (1961) and an M.A. in social work from the University of Oklahoma in Norman (1974).

From 1985 to 1987, General Cadoria, as director of Manpower and Personnel, J-1, Organization of the Joint Chiefs of Staff, in Washington, D.C., was responsible for the placement of personnel in all branches of the armed services, including the army, air force, navy, marines, and reserve components.

After a successful campaign against double discrimination—racism and sexism—Cadoria retired from military service in 1990. Her outstanding military record was signified by the Defense Superior Service Medal, the Distinguished Service Medal, the Bronze Star with two oak leaf clusters, a Meritorious Service Medal with an oak leaf cluster, an Air Medal, the Joint Chiefs of Staff Identification Badge, and an Army Commendation Medal with three oak leaf clusters.

BIBLIOGRAPHY

Army records. General Officer Management Office, Headquarters, Department of the U.S. Army, Washington, D.C.; *Essence*, "Women in the Military" (April 1990).

LINDA ROCHELLE LANE

CAESAR, SHIRLEY (1938-)

"Baby Shirley, the gospel singer," as she was called by the age of ten, has had three incarnations in gospel music. At age twelve she was traveling throughout the Carolinas and Virginia as soloist for the one-legged preacher Leroy Johnson; by age twenty she was one of the leaders of the Chicago-based gospel group, the Caravans; and by age thirty-two, two years before the death of Mahalia Jackson, she was dubbed "Queen of Gospel."

Caesar was born on October 13, 1938, in Durham, North Carolina, to James and Hannah Caesar. Her father, known as "Big Jim," was legendary throughout the Carolinas as the powerful lead singer of the gospel quartet the Just Come Four. Caesar observed the quartet in rehearsals and by age ten was singing solos in their concerts. Her life was changed in 1950, however, when her father died in his sleep and she was left to care for her invalid mother. She began appearing in solo concerts, and at twelve years old joined the troupe of the evangelist Reverend Leroy Johnson. She appeared regularly on his television show out of Portsmouth, Virginia, in 1950 and in November 1951 made her first recording for the Federal label, "I'd Rather Have Jesus." From age fourteen to eighteen, she traveled alone throughout the South on bus and train, appearing in solo concerts, and often arriving home with only a few minutes before she was to attend classes. After graduation from high school, she enrolled at North Carolina College in Durham (now

North Carolina Central University), pursuing a major in business education.

In 1958, while a student at North Carolina State, she attended a concert by the Caravans, a female gospel group, and was so impressed that she wanted to become a member. With the help of gospel singer Dorothy Love Coates, leader of the Original Gospel Harmonettes of Birmingham, Alabama, Caesar was granted an audition. The audition was successful, and after she withdrew from college, she was immediately taken into the group. The three members of the Caravans each had distinctive singing styles: the leader, Albertina Walker, was known for her ability to stand "flat-footed" and sing the old hymns with wrenching sincerity and coloraturalike embellishments; Inez Andrews, known as the "High Priestess of Gospel," was a contralto with a three-octave range who could shatter glass with her powerful, high-pitched screams; and Sarah McKissick was a soft-voiced gospel ballad singer. Caesar brought a unique quality to the Caravans, for her style was one of energy, percussive attacks, explosive releases, and a florid treatment of melodic lines. Though Caesar was a Baptist, she had adopted the practice of Sanctified singers of dramatizing songs; she would act out each of her solos, often moving into the auditorium to shake hands with members of the congregation.

She made her first recording with the Caravans in 1958 and, from the first session, scored success with "I've Been Running for Jesus a Long Time, and I'm Not Tired Yet." The song was set to a lively tempo, and in performances, Caesar would run down the aisles each time the word "running" appeared in the chorus. She found her true style, however, with the 1961 recording of "Hallelujah, It's Done." During the choruses of the song, Caesar began ad-libbing in the style of the African-American folk preacher and found that she possessed a special gift for adding text to the song to illustrate important points. She cultivated this technique, called "song and sermonette," a device created by Mother Willie Mae Ford Smith and developed by Edna Gallmon Cooke. This device was to become her trademark in later years, both in her singing and as an evangelist, which she became in 1961.

She scored tremendous success with her 1962 recording of "I Won't Be Back," dramatizing the song by walking through the auditorium, looking for a door by which to leave, and at the end leaving the auditorium and remaining outside for a short period of time. "Sweeping through the City" was the next big hit for Caesar; during the performance she would mimic sweeping the floor.

Caesar left the Caravans in 1966 and organized her own group, the Caesar Singers. It was with this group that she discovered her ability to generate excitement through her "mother" songs. Her first big hit with these songs was a 1969 ten-minute "song and sermonette" entitled, "Don't Drive Your Mama Away." The song recounts the story of a mother with two sons, one of whom leaves home while the other remains, completes college, and marries. Tired of her mother-in-law's old-fashioned ways, the successful son's socialite wife commits her to a senior citizens' home, but the wayward brother returns home to tell his brother that if he drives his mother away, he will surely need her someday. The African-American sense of family was touched by this rescue of the mother, and the song became a huge success. It was followed by "No Charge" in 1978, the story of a small child who, when asked by his mother to do chores after school, submits a list of his charges for such work. The mother responds by stating that for carrying the child for nine months, for breast feeding him when he was a baby, for washing and ironing his clothes, for cleaning his room, and for praying for him each night, there would be no charge.

In 1980, Caesar garnered a crossover audience with her recording of "Faded Roses," set to country-and-western accompaniment, which again tells the story of a wayward child. On this occasion, a mother dies without the opportunity to say goodbye to a son who has not contacted her since he moved to Germany. His sisters notify him of her death, but by the time of his arrival at the cemetery, the roses on her grave have faded. Besides her poignant "mother" songs, Caesar is lauded for her standard "house-rocking" songs, such as "This Joy I Have, the World Didn't Give to Me." In such songs she elects a fast or medium tempo, sings at the very top of her range, uses abundant embellishments, adds extra notes, scoops, and growls to the melody, and executes her runs and shouts for Jesus.

Caesar currently makes her home in Durham, performing around 150 concerts each year in addition to a few reunion concerts with the Caravans. In 1984, she returned to college at Shaw University in Raleigh and earned a bachelor's degree in business education. She served on the Durham City Council from 1987 until 1991; is the pastor of the Mount Calvary Word of Faith Church in Raleigh, one of the sixty churches of the Mount Calvary Holy Churches of America, of which her husband, Harold I. Williams, is the presiding bishop; and is the founder and president of Shirley Caesar Outreach Ministries, an organization providing emergency funds, food, clothing, and shelter for the needy. She is the recipient of an honorary doctor of humane letters degree from Shaw University.

Caesar won a Grammy Award, for her 1971 recording of "Put Your Hand in the Hand of the Man." In addition to winning the Grammy for gospel in 1971, she has been nominated eleven times, winning five more Grammys. Out of ten nominations for the Dove Award for Gospel, she has won six, as well as five Stellar Gospel awards and two NAACP Image awards and has been inducted into the Gospel Music Hall of Fame.

BIBLIOGRAPHY

American Gospel Magazine, "Shirley Caesar: Queen of Gospel" (March/April 1992); Heilbut, Anthony. *The Gospel Sound—Good News and Bad Times* (1985).

HORACE CLARENCE BOYER

CALLOWAY, BLANCHE (1902-1978)

Blanche Calloway was a consummate entertainer who carved out a remarkable career despite race and gender discrimination.

Born on February 9, 1902, to Eulalia and Cabell Calloway, Jr., in Baltimore, Maryland, Blanche was the oldest of six children. Her father was a lawyer, and her mother was a teacher and organist at the Presbyterian church, where young Blanche sang in the church choir.

In 1921, Oma Crosby and her five Cubanolas, a song-and-dance show, passed through Baltimore. A young married woman at the time, Blanche auditioned, won a part in the show, and left town as a Cubanola. Her husband followed but, not being in the business, did not stay long. The act went to New York, and Blanche landed a job singing in the wings in *Shuffle Along*, a Broadway revue. Before the show closed, she sang in front of the chorus line as a soubrette.

Later Calloway appeared in *Plantation Days* in Chicago. Traveling with the show to Baltimore, she came home to find her brother Cab playing drums with a local band. She took him back to Chicago with her and enrolled him in school with the aim of helping him follow their father's footsteps into law. Cab dropped out of school, however, and became an entertainer himself, famous for the "hi-de-ho."

Blanche Calloway performed as a regular at the Sunset Cafe, a haven for jazz musicians such as Louis Armstrong and Earl Hines. While doing vocals with her brother's band, she was noticed by the manager of

the Pearl Theater in Philadelphia, who suggested that she front her own band. Calloway became the first woman in the country to lead an all-male band. Beginning in 1931, for thirteen years she toured with "The 12 Clouds of Joy," singing, conducting, and dancing in a particularly energetic acrobatic style.

Eventually the difficulties of life on the road and the unrelenting pressures of racism made Calloway decide to leave the band. That same year, 1944, she remarried and settled in Washington, D.C., where she managed the Crystal Caverns. Later she moved to Philadelphia and managed the Jim Jam nightclub. She became deeply involved in civil rights and other political activities and took the significant financial risk of managing Ruth Brown, a brown-skinned singer, at a time when even light-skinned women such as Calloway herself sometimes dusted white flour on their faces to get jobs.

After moving once more, to Miami, Florida, Calloway became the first woman disc jockey on American radio. Later, as hostess of her own daily show, *News, Views and Interviews*, she interviewed many of her former show business colleagues. Her career in radio lasted twenty years. Calloway was also founder and president of Afram House, Inc., a mail-order cosmetics firm that reportedly was the first of its kind in the nation to be both Black-owned and Black-operated.

In about 1972, Calloway's health began to fail, and after the death of her fourth husband, she returned to Baltimore. She died on December 16, 1978, at the age of seventy-six.

BIBLIOGRAPHY

Arnett, Earl. "The Other 'Hi-de-ho' Blanche Calloway, 76, Still Young," *Baltimore Morning Sun* (August 12, 1978); "Blanche Calloway Jones, 1st Female Bandleader, Cab's Sister, Dies in Md.," *Jet* (January 4, 1979); "Blanche Calloway Jones, the Queen of 'Hi-de-ho,'" *Washington Post* (December 19, 1978); Calloway, Cab. *Of Minnie the Moocher and Me* (1976); Foundation for Research in the Afro-American Creative Arts. *The Black Perspective in Music* (1979); "It Was Like Old Days for Calloways," *Baltimore Afro-American* (August 19, 1978); "Remembering Blanche Calloway," *Baltimore Afro-American* (December 23, 1978); Smith, Linell. "Again, the Toe Taps, the Memories Stir and Blanche Calloway Sings," *Baltimore Evening Sun* (August 11, 1978); "A Visit with Blanche and Cab Calloway," videorecording, Waxter Center for Senior Citizens, Commission on Aging/Retirement Education (1978). Interviews with Bernice Calloway Monroe, Baltimore (November 29, 1991), and Camay Calloway Murphy, Baltimore (December 6, 1991).

MARGARET D. PAGAN

CAMPBELL, LUCIE E. (1885-1963)

Lucie E. Campbell once said, "Teaching is my vocation, music is my avocation." She taught American history and English in the public schools of Memphis for fifty-five years, retiring in 1954. Concurrently, she was music director of the Sunday School and Baptist Young People's Union Congress of the National Baptist Convention for forty-seven years, from 1916 until her death. As music director she exerted great influence over the dissemination, growth, and development of African-American religious music in Black Baptist churches nationwide. She has been called "the great song composer of the National Baptist Convention."

Campbell was born on April 30, 1885, in Duck Hill, Mississippi, the youngest of eleven children of Burrell and Isabella Wilkerson Campbell, both of whom were former slaves. Burrell Campbell died before his daughter was two years old, and Isabella moved the family to Memphis, where Lucie was educated. After graduating from Kortrecht High School in 1899 as class valedictorian, she was assigned to teach at her alma mater, later named Booker T. Washington High School, where she remained until her retirement. She received a bachelor of arts degree from Rust College, in Holly Springs, Mississippi, in 1927, and a master of science degree from Tennessee State University in 1951.

Campbell was essentially a self-taught musician. She possessed an outstanding contralto voice and began playing piano and organ at the Metropolitan Baptist Church in Memphis, where in 1909 she began teaching the young people's choirs. By 1904, she had organized and was made president of the Music Club, a local affiliate of the National Federation of Colored Musicians.

In 1916, she was made music director of the Sunday School and Baptist Young People's Union Congress. In this position, she was responsible for helping to create and maintain an atmosphere of optimism and religious fervor at the annual sessions in order to keep the organization intact and discourage churches from defecting to the convention that had split from the parent body in 1915. For these meetings, she organized and directed 1,000-voice choirs; composed songs; wrote and staged original musicales and pageants, such as *Ethiopia at the Bar of Justice;* and selected soloists and organized ensembles to provide music. She was a member of the Music Committee that compiled hymn books for the denomination, such as *Golden Gems, Inspirational Melodies, Spirituals Triumphant,* and *Gospel Pearls.* Compiled in

the 1920s, these books contain such Campbell songs as "Something Within" (1919), "He Understands, He'll Say 'Well Done'" (©1950), "Heavenly Sunshine" (1923), and "The King's Highway" (1923).

The songs she wrote in the 1920s, 1930s, and early 1940s are considered outstanding examples of gospel hymn writing; the texts are full of imagery and the melodies are memorable. By the mid-1940s she began to compose in the new gospel music style of the Chicago School of Mahalia Jackson, Roberta Martin, and Thomas A. Dorsey. Her compositions in the new genre included "Jesus Gave Me Water" (1946), "There Is a Fountain" (1948), "When I Get Home" (1948), and "Footprints of Jesus" (1949). She wrote anthems, such as "Praise the Lord" (1946), which sold a record 30,000 copies, and songs for liturgical use, such as "This Is the Day the Lord Has Made" (1947), for Christmas and Easter.

She was a dynamic orator and rivaled the famous Nannie Helen Burroughs in popularity as a sought-after Woman's Day speaker. Also like Burroughs, she was frequently at odds with ministers who resented her forceful manner. Her positions of leadership included president of the Tennessee Education Congress (1941), the first woman to hold the office; vice president of the American Teachers Association (1944); member of the National Education Association's National Policy Planning Commission (1946); and president of the Women's Convention, Auxiliary of the Tennessee State Regular Baptist Missionary and Education Convention (1948).

Campbell composed approximately eighty songs, some of which have been lost. She did not copyright her music until 1950, having given much of it to the Baptist denomination. Today her songs are heard more frequently at the Grand Ole Opry in Nashville than at Baptist conventions and congresses, but contemporary singers such as Take Six are taking an interest in her output.

On January 14, 1960, she married the Reverend C. R. Williams in Memphis after a forty-year courtship and moved to Nashville. Following a testimonial in her honor given at the Sunday School and Baptist Training Union Congress in Denver in June 1962, she became ill. She died at Riverside Hospital in Nashville on January 3, 1963.

BIBLIOGRAPHY

Bradley, J. Robert. "Miss Lucie: The Legacy of the Woman and Her Music," *National Baptist Voice* (April 1979-80); George, Luvenia A. "Lucie E. Campbell: Baptist Composer and Educator," *Black Perspective in Music* (Spring

1987), and *Lucie E. Campbell and the Enduring Tradition of Gospel Hymnody* (1983); Hamilton, G. P. *The Bright Side of Memphis* (1908); *In the Upper Room: The Stars of Faith Sing the Songs of Lucie Campbell.* Sony (1960?); Stratton-Dobbins, Sharon. "Gospel Music in Memphis: The Black Church's Heritage," *Tri-State Defender* (February 16, 1980).

LUVENIA A. GEORGE

CARLISLE, UNA MAE (1915-1956)

Una Mae Carlisle was born on December 26, 1915, in Xenia, Ohio, of American Indian and Black parentage. She started singing at three and studied piano as a child.

In 1932, at the age of seventeen, she worked at a Cincinnati radio station. Fats Waller heard her play and asked her to join his band. She had intended to make a career of singing, but the opportunity to play piano with Fats Waller was too compelling to decline.

She left Fats Waller's band in 1934 to audition for the Cotton Club in New York, then rejoined him four years later to sing on his album *I Can't Give You Anything but Love* (1939).

In the late 1930s, Carlisle performed solo and recorded in Europe. She worked with the *Blackbirds* stage show during their European tour in 1938. She worked in clubs and the film industry in France, and she operated her own club in Montmartre, studying music at the Sorbonne.

When World War II began, she returned to the United States and recorded for Blue Bird Records (*Walkin' by the River* [1940] and *I See a Million People* [1941]). She became a popular nightclub performer and had her own radio show in the late 1940s and early 1950s.

In 1940, Carlisle performed with Her Jam Band, with Slam Stewart (bass), Benny Carter (trumpet), and Zutty Singleton (drums). She recorded with tenor saxophonist Bob Chester and with Don Redman.

She became ill in 1954 and retired. She died two years later, on November 7, 1956, in New York City.

BIBLIOGRAPHY
Dahl, Linda. *Stormy Weather: The Music and Lives of a Century of Jazzwomen* (1984); Handy, D. Antoinette. *Black Women in American Bands and Orchestras* (1981); Placksin, Sally. *American Women in Jazz 1900 to the Present: Their Words, Lives, and Music* (1982); Sampson, Henry T. *Blacks in Blackface: A Source Book on Early Black Musical Shows* (1980).

SELECTED DISCOGRAPHY
Walkin' by the River, Bluebird Records-11033 (1940); *I See a Million People*, Bluebird Records-11181 (1941).

PAULETTE WALKER

In the late 1940s and early 1950s, singer and piano player Una Mae Carlisle had a popular radio show. A protégé of Fats Waller, Carlisle at one time operated her own nightclub in Montmartre in Paris. [Schomburg Center]

CARNEGIE, MARY ELIZABETH LANCASTER (1916-)

Mary Elizabeth Lancaster did not grow up with dreams of becoming a nurse. Her career came about more by chance than by choice; yet she has made a lasting mark on the profession of nursing and the history of Black women in it.

Born on April 19, 1916, in Baltimore, Maryland, Mary Elizabeth Lancaster was the daughter of Adeline Beatrice Swann and John Oliver Lancaster. After her parents were divorced, Mary Elizabeth lived most of the time with her aunt and uncle in Washington, D.C., because her mother was unable to care for her. While still quite young, she began working after school and on weekends at a whites-only cafeteria, the Allies Inn.

After graduating from Dunbar High School, Lancaster left Washington for New York. Ready and willing for either work or further education, she found opportunity for neither. Then a cousin suggested that she try nursing. Lancaster applied to Lincoln Hospital School for Nurses and then returned to Washington and the steam table at the Allies Inn. In July 1934, Lancaster received a letter notifying her that she had been accepted to Lincoln.

During training she discovered a genuine enjoyment in her work as well as a flair for it. She also developed an interest in organizing and activism. She was chosen to serve as a hostess at the 1936 convention of the National Association of Colored Graduate Nurses, an event which encouraged Lancaster's growing interest in the fight to gain professional acceptance and equality for Black professional nurses.

After Lincoln, Lancaster went to West Virginia State College, where she received a B.A. in sociology in 1942. In 1943, while assistant director of nursing at Hampton University, she established the first Black baccalaureate program in nursing in Virginia. In December of 1944, she married Eric Carnegie. They divorced in 1954. In 1945, she became the first dean of the school of nursing at Florida A&M University in Tallahassee. She also became active in the battle that Black professional nurses were waging to become members of the Florida State Nurses' Association. Eventually she became the first Black American to be elected to the board of that or any other state association.

Over the years, Mary Elizabeth Carnegie earned a number of other degrees and awards, including a doctorate in public administration from New York University in 1972. From the early 1950s on, she held editorial positions on a number of nursing journals, traveled extensively as a consultant, and in 1986 published the book *The Path We Tread: Blacks in Nursing 1854-1984.* A second edition of the book (in preparation) will extend coverage to 1990.

BIBLIOGRAPHY

Carnegie, Mary Elizabeth. Personal interview (August 31, 1991 and August 18, 1992); *CBWA*; Rowland, H. S. *The Nurses Almanac* (1978); Tomes, Evelyn and A. Delores Nicholson. *Black Nursing Pioneers, Leaders, and Organizers, 1770-1980* (1979); Vance, Connie. "A Group Profile of Contemporary Influentials in American Nursing," Ph.D. diss. (1977).

MARIE MOSLEY

A leader in the fight to gain professional acceptance and equality for Black professional nurses, Mary Elizabeth Carnegie was the first Black to be elected to the board of a state nurses' association.

CARROLL, DIAHANN (1935-)

For Diahann Carroll, as for many other Black entertainers, success has sometimes been a two-edged sword, giving her notoriety in the mainstream but separating her from her roots. She once complained that she was a Black woman with a white image. Although she has achieved some success, her career has been hampered by the limited opportunities available to Black actresses both on stage and screen. However, as her tell-all memoir, *Diahann: An Autobiography* (1986), makes clear, her career aspirations were frustrated by marital struggles and rocky romances.

Carol Diann Johnson was born on July 17, 1935, and raised in Harlem and the Bronx by her mother

Actress and singer Diahann Carroll has achieved success in nightclubs and on film, television, and the Broadway stage, but has had to struggle against the perception that she is a Black woman with a white image. [Schomburg Center]

and father, who was a subway conductor. Pretty and talented, at ten she won a Metropolitan Opera scholarship, and at fourteen she won first prize on *Arthur Godfrey's Talent Scouts*, for which she began using the name Diahann Carroll. As a teen she attended New York's High School of Music and Art, and by the time she graduated she was working steadily as a model for *Ebony, Jet*, and *Sepia* magazines.

She studied psychology briefly at New York University, but she left when she won the costarring role of Ottilie in Truman Capote and Harold Arlen's Broadway musical, *House of Flowers* (1954), directed by Peter Brook. Although the show closed in the face of unusually strong Broadway competition, Carroll's singing and acting won her a small role in *Carmen Jones* (1954). She then studied acting with Lee Strasberg and spent a number of years as a nightclub singer in New York and other major entertainment centers; she also recorded several albums influenced by Frank Sinatra's singing.

In 1956, she married Monte Kay, a white casting agent, and in 1960 gave birth to a daughter, Suzanne. A long-term romance with Sidney Poitier, whom she met while playing the small role of Marie in the 1959 film *Porgy and Bess*, eventually destroyed the marriage.

In the early 1960s, Carroll continued to sing and play supporting film parts, but her most important role was the lead in Richard Rodgers's Broadway musical *No Strings* (1962). This story of a doomed interracial romance ran for more than a year and won Carroll a Tony Award. When Hollywood then promised the lead in the film version to a Eurasian actress, Carroll created a minor scandal by complaining to the press of the film industry's racism; the film was, in fact, never made. (In 1965, Rodgers was said to be at work on another Broadway musical for Carroll, but it never materialized.)

By the mid-1960s, Carroll was a frequent guest on television talk shows, and in 1968, in *Julia*, she became the first Black star of a television situation comedy. This slick, popular, and generally unimaginative show, produced by Hal Kanter, ran for three seasons; Carroll played a single mother, the widow of an American who had died in the Vietnam War. She gained a tremendous viewership, but the change in her image—from glamorous to maternal—later diluted her nightclub success.

In 1972, Carroll was briefly engaged to the television interviewer David Frost, then unexpectedly married Freddie Glusman, a white Las Vegas shopowner. Their stormy marriage lasted only four months and ended with Carroll's charges of physical abuse by Glusman.

In 1974, Carroll starred in what is generally considered her best film, *Claudine*, directed by John Berry and costarring James Earl Jones. Her uncharacteristically gritty portrayal of a single welfare mother garnered her an Academy Award nomination as Best Actress.

In 1976, she married Robert DeLeon, an editor of *Jet* magazine and a dozen years her junior, and largely abandoned her career. DeLeon died in a car crash.

After DeLeon's death, Carroll devoted herself completely to rebuilding her career, beginning all

over again as a nightclub singer. Finally, in the late 1970s and early 1980s, she earned major roles in the TV specials *Roots: The Next Generation* (1979) and *I Know Why the Caged Bird Sings* (1979), and the Broadway drama *Agnes of God* (1982).

For several seasons beginning in 1984, Carroll played the unscrupulous Dominique Deveraux on TV's *Dynasty*. She considered this introduction to prime-time audiences of a Black character as vicious as her white counterparts to be a high point of her career. "I wanted," as she later put it, "to be the first Black bitch on television" (Carroll and Firestone 1986).

In 1987, Carroll married Vic Damone, a white singer. She now makes frequent appearances as the mother of Whitley Guilbert (played by Jasmine Guy) on the television situation comedy *A Different World*.

[*See also* TELEVISION.]

BIBLIOGRAPHY

Aros, Richard A. *An Actor's Guide to the Talkies: 1965 through 1974* (1977); Carroll, Diahann and Ross Firestone. *Diahann: An Autobiography* (1986); Clipping file on Diahann Carroll, Billy Rose Theatre Collection, The New York Public Library for the Performing Arts, New York City; Oliviero, Jeffrey. *Motion Picture Players' Credits* (1991).

MAJOR WORK

House of Flowers, musical play (1954); *Carmen Jones*, film (1954); *Best Foot Forward*, album (1958); *Diahann Carroll Sings Harold Arlen Songs*, album (1958); *Porgy and Bess*, film (1959); *Fun Life*, album (1961); *Aimez-Vous Brahms?*, film (1961); *Goodbye Again*, film (1961); *Paris Blues*, film (1961); *No Strings*, musical play (1962); *Hurry Sundown*, film (1967); *The Split*, film (1968); *Julia*, television series (1968-71); *Claudine*, film (1974); *Diahann Carroll*, album (1974); *Same Time Next Year*, play (1975); *Death Scream*, television film (1975); *Roots: The Next Generation*, television miniseries (1979); *I Know Why the Caged Bird Sings*, television film (1979); *Sister, Sister*, television film (1979); *Agnes of God*, play (1982); *Dynasty*, television series (1984-88); *A Different World*, television series (1988-).

PAUL NADLER

CARROLL, VINNETTE (1922-)

Vinnette Carroll drew national attention in 1972 when she became one of the first Black women to direct a production on Broadway. Carroll was born March 11, 1922, in New York City but spent much of her childhood in the West Indies. Before turning to the theater, she was a clinical psychologist. She re-

It would be difficult to name a theatrical honor that has not been awarded to actress/director Vinnette Carroll. Her productions, including Don't Bother Me, I Can't Cope *and* Your Arms Too Short to Box with God, *have won three Tonys, an Emmy, an Obie, and dozens of other awards. [Schomburg Center]*

ceived a B.A. in 1944 from Long Island University and an M.A. in 1946 from New York University.

As founder and artistic director of New York City's Urban Arts Corps (UAC) in 1967, Carroll was instrumental in beginning the careers of many of today's leading performers. Her original works combine music, dance, and the spoken word and have thrilled audiences around the world. She directed the Broadway hits *Don't Bother Me, I Can't Cope* (1972) and *Your Arms Too Short to Box with God* (1976), and *When Hell Freezes Over I'll Skate* (1979), performed at Lincoln Center and on national public television. Through UAC, Carroll developed many works that reached major audiences. She has also acted and directed for stage, film, and television throughout the world. Among her many honors are three Tony Award nominations, an Emmy Award, an Obie Award, the National Association for the Advancement of Colored People Image Award, the Los Angeles Drama Critics Circle Award, the New York Outer Critics

Circle Award, and induction into the Black Filmmakers Hall of Fame.

Her work continues as the producing artistic director of the Vinnette Carroll Repertory Company in Fort Lauderdale, Florida.

BIBLIOGRAPHY

Carroll, Vinnette. Personal interviews (1990, 1991); *DBT*; Mapp, Edward. *Directory of Blacks in the Performing Arts* (1978); Mitchell, Loften. *Voices of the Black Theatre* (1975); Williams, Mance. *Black Theatre in the 1960s and 1970s* (1985).

KATHY A. PERKINS

CARTER, BETTY (1930-)

Born Lillie Mae Jones on May 16, 1930, in Flint, Michigan, Betty Carter has used several other stage names, including Lorraine Carter and Betty Bebop (coined by Lionel Hampton). Carter studied piano and, as a teenager, began working as a singer in clubs in Detroit, where she grew up; she also sat in with visiting artists such as Dizzy Gillespie and Charlie Parker. From 1948 to 1951, she toured with and wrote several arrangements for Hampton and made her recording debut. She accompanied Hampton to New York in 1951 and thereafter worked in various nightclubs and theaters, including the Apollo, and toured with other bands. She toured with Ray Charles (1960-63) and visited Japan (1963), London (1964), and France (1968).

After she married in the mid-1960s, Carter went into a brief retirement in order to raise her children. She returned to the stage with her own trio in 1969 and her own recording company, Bet-Car Productions, in 1971. Since 1969, Carter has worked with several young, virtually unknown, but talented pianists such as John Hicks, Danny Mixon, Mulgrew Miller, and Benny Green. Simultaneously, she has expanded her musical palette to include a part in Howard Moore's musical *Don't Call Me Man* (1975), and to sing with string orchestras conducted by David Amram in New York (1982) and Boston (1983).

Betty Carter's style was initially inspired by Billie Holiday and Sarah Vaughan but is now more instrumentally than vocally focused. It is common to hear melodic fragmentation of text and melodies as well as reharmonization of harmonies. Carter appears to feel that the audience knows a given tune and that it would therefore be redundant for her to restate the specific musical elements of that tune throughout each performance. Her approach to singing also includes a myriad of horn sounds, vocal effects, an excellent ear, and a strong sense of harmony and rhythm. Betty Carter is a jazz singer's singer.

BIBLIOGRAPHY

Hollenberg, D. "Betty Carter," *Downbeat* (1977); Joans, T. "Betty Carter," *Coda* (1976); Kernfield, Berry. "Betty Carter." In *New Grove Dictionary of Jazz* (1988); Kuhl, C. "Betty Carter: Interview," *Cadence* (1985); Locke, G. "Betty Carter: In Her Own Sweet Way," *The Wire* (1986); McLarney, B. "Betty Carter: The 'In' Singer," *Downbeat* (1966); Nolan, H. "Betty Carter's Declaration of Independence," *Downbeat* (1976); Van Rooven, B. and P. Brodowski. "Betty's Groove," *Jazz Forum* (1979).

SELECTED DISCOGRAPHY

Meet Betty Carter and Ray Bryant. Epic 3202 (1955); *Modern Sound of Betty Carter*. ABC-Paramount 363 (1960); *Ray Charles and Betty Carter*. ABC-Paramount 385 (1961); *Round Midnight*. ATCO 33-152 (1963); *Finally Betty Carter*. Roulette 5000 (1969); *Betty Carter Album*. Verve 835682-1 (1972); *Now It's My Turn*. Roulette 5005 (1976); *Audience, Whatever Happened to Love*. BET-CAR 1004 (1982); *Audience with Betty Carter*. Reissue; 2-Verve 8-35684-1 (1988); *Look What I Got*. Verve 835661-1 (1988); *Droppin' Things*. Verve 843991 (1990).

EDDIE S. MEADOWS

CARTER, EUNICE HUNTON
(1899-1970)

The appointment of Eunice Hunton Carter as the first Black woman district attorney in the State of New York made her one of the "twenty against the underworld," as special prosecutor Thomas E. Dewey called his prosecution team. Carter's work on theories about organized crime triggered the biggest organized crime prosecution in the nation's history in New York City in the late 1930s.

Eunice Hunton was born in Atlanta, Georgia, on July 16, 1899, to William A. Hunton and Addie Waites. She attended Smith College in Northampton, Massachusetts, and graduated *cum laude* with both a Bachelor's and a Master's degree in 1921. She attended Fordham School of Law, graduated in 1931, and was admitted to practice law in New York in 1934. After a short time in private practice, she began work in the district attorney's office in 1935.

Carter was hired by New York County District Attorney William C. Dodge to handle primarily low-level criminal prosecutions, many of them prostitution cases. After handling several prostitution cases, she

began to suspect the links of prostitution with the underworld. She began to note that defendants told nearly identical stories, that all of the women were represented by the same law firms, and that if they were fined, the same bondsmen would appear with the money. Based largely on her research, special prosecutor Dewey ordered a major raid of more than eighty houses of prostitution. Information from the raid provided Carter with enough details on the prostitution racket to convict the top Mafia leader in New York. Dewey, who subsequently was appointed New York County District Attorney, chose Carter to head

"Twenty against the underworld" was Thomas E. Dewey's name for his crack prosecution team, which included Eunice Hunton Carter, the first Black woman district attorney in the State of New York. [National Archives]

the Special Sessions Bureau where she supervised more than fourteen thousand criminal cases each year.

Carter remained with the district attorney's office until 1945 and then returned to private practice. Her other professional achievements include being a consultant to the United Nations and International Council of Women; vice president of the National Council of Women of the U.S. YWCA; member of the U.S. National Committee of Educational, Scientific and Cultural Organizations; trustee and chairman of the National Council of Negro Women; and a member of the American Association of University Women.

Hunter married Lisle C. Carter and had one son, Lisle Carter, Jr. She died on January 25, 1970.

BIBLIOGRAPHY

New York Times, Obituary (January 26, 1970); Morello, Karen. *The Woman Lawyer in America: 1638 to the Present* (1986).

WENDY BROWN

CARY, MARY ANN SHADD
(1823-1893)

In the winter of 1856, upon receiving the news that antislavery agents were roaming through Canada, Mary Ann Shadd Cary began to write. She objected to those who, begging on behalf of the fugitive slaves who had fled to Canada, took advantage of antislavery sentiment. Feeling a moral right and duty, she became single-minded in her efforts to expose them. She charged that "begging agents" were "wending their way from Canada to the States in unprecedented numbers." "Bees gather honey in the summer," she wrote, "but beggars harvest in the winter." In typically blunt language, Cary preached integrationism, self-reliance, and independence among Black Canadians during the 1850s. A pillar of zeal, she helped found the newspaper known as the *Provincial Freeman* as an instrument for transforming Black refugees into model citizens. What she wrote, as the first Black North American female editor, publisher, and investigative reporter, marked the beginning of a fierce argument over how to manage the ex-slaves.

Born in Wilmington, Delaware, on October 9, 1823, Mary Ann Shadd was the first of thirteen children of prominent free Black parents, Harriet and Abraham Shadd. Her father was a leader in the Underground Railroad movement and a subscription agent for William Lloyd Garrison's *Liberator*. In her childhood Shadd developed an abiding sympathy for the slave, an assiduous understanding of the issues, and a penchant for lively debate. When she was ten years old, she and her family moved to West Chester, Pennsylvania, where Mary Shadd spent the next six years in a Quaker school. Feeling sufficiently educated to open a school for Black children in Wilmington, she returned there in 1840. A few years later, she also secured teaching appointments in New York City and Norristown, Pennsylvania.

Following the passage of the 1850 Fugitive Slave Law, Mary and her brother, Isaac, joined the Black exodus from the United States to Windsor, Canada. During this time, Shadd established an integrated school in Canada West supported by the American Missionary Association, met the abolitionists Henry and Mary Bibb, and became embroiled in a dispute with them that helped to launch her biting, vituperative campaign against unscrupulous antislavery agents.

Shadd first published her account of the values of self-reliance in 1849, in a pamphlet entitled "Hints to the Colored People of North America." Three years later, in 1852, she published "Notes on Canada West," a forty-four-page pamphlet which promoted Black immigration to Canada. Hundreds of miles away, people read Shadd's reports of crop yield, terrain, climate, soil, timber, and the virtues of integrated churches and schools. She rallied their attention with statistical and tangible evidence of Canada's glory. By marshaling primary evidence as she did, Mary Ann Shadd became the first Black female to develop and utilize a database for propaganda purposes. She carefully crafted "Notes on Canada West" to stop the ugly stories about the region that southern slaveholders circulated to thwart Black immigration.

In 1853, Shadd declared it was time to counter the programs of the Bibbs, Josiah Henson, John Scoble, and other leaders who advocated the moral, social, physical, intellectual, and political elevation of the ex-slaves through the Refugee Home Society, a separatist organization that used agents to secure funds, clothing, and land for the fugitive slaves. Shadd considered the techniques of these men, especially begging, to be a threat to her goal of an integrated, self-sufficient society for the Black fugitives, one free of any tincture of inferiority, floundering, or failure. Shadd's attacks appeared in the *Provincial Freeman*, cofounded by editor Samuel Ringgold Ward, a traveling agent for the Anti-Slavery Society of Canada. In fact, Mary Ann Shadd [Cary] edited the paper.

Once embarked on her mission, Shadd Cary became unshakable in exposing the malfeasance of the "begging agents," using the *Provincial Freeman* as a vehicle for revealing misconduct and for examining how much money was collected and what was done with it. By nineteenth-century norms, Shadd Cary's caustic, jolting language seemed ill-suited to a woman. She used phrases such as "gall and wormwood," "moral pest," "petty despot," "superannuated ministers," "nest of unclean birds," "moral monsters," and "priest-ridden people," in order to keep her ideas before the public. Shadd Cary also attacked Black folk religion in her firm, abrasive style, arguing that it retarded Black moral and social development.

Mary Ann Shadd married Thomas F. Cary of Toronto in 1856, three years after the first issue of the *Provincial Freeman*. They lived in Chatham, Canada, until his death in 1860. They had two children: a daughter, Sarah, and a son, Linton. Spurred on by a worsening economic situation for Black Canadians and the financial demise of her paper in 1859, Cary continued to teach in Chatham until 1863, when she returned to the United States. During the Civil War she became a Union army recruiting officer and, through contact with Martin Robinson Delaney, developed an interest in Black nationalism. Later, with experience as an organizer of a Black regiment, Cary settled in Washington, D.C., where she opened a school for Black children and attended the Howard University Law School. Considered the first Black woman lawyer in the United States, Cary received her degree in 1870.

Soon after her graduation, she opened a law office in Washington, D.C., and renewed her political activism by challenging the House of Representatives Judiciary Committee for the right to vote. She won her case and became one of the few women to vote in federal elections during the Reconstruction period. She also vigorously campaigned for women's rights through the Colored Women's Progressive Franchise Association, which she organized in 1880. She exhorted Black women to address their own specific political and economic condition and to fight for equal rights and opportunities. Cary died in 1893.

Whether Cary's efforts to promote change were successful is difficult to determine. Like most ideologues, she gave advice to humanity, but failed to see that her bulldozer bluntness alienated people. Yet she fought against begging as a way of life and thus contributed, however ideologically, to a Black American movement toward economic independence. Ironically, Cary's adamance ultimately diminished her ability to implement her ideas throughout her life. Nonetheless, as an influential Black leader and as a remarkable pioneering journalist, she continued to

Not since Ralph Waldo Emerson had a writer spoken so eloquently for self-reliance as Mary Ann Shadd Cary. Her virulent attacks against antislavery "begging agents" shocked nineteenth-century society, both Black and white. [Moorland-Spingarn]

live by her paper's motto, "Self-reliance Is the Fine Road to Independence."

[*See also* ABOLITION; COLORED WOMEN'S PROGRESSIVE FRANCHISE ASSOCIATION.]

BIBLIOGRAPHY

Bearden, Jim and Linda Jean Butler. *Shadd: The Life and Times of Mary Ann Shadd* (1971); Delaney, Martin R. *The Condition, Elevation, Emigration, and Destiny of the Colored People of the United States* (1968); Giddings, Paula. *When and Where I Enter: The Impact of Black Women on Race and Sex in America* (1984); Lerner, Gerda, ed. *Black Women in White America: A Documentary History* (1973); *North Star* (June 8, 1848); *Provincial Freeman* (1854-59); Ripley, C. Peter. *The Black Abolitionist Papers: Canada, 1830-1865* (1986); Silverman, Jason. *Unwelcome Guests: Canada West's Response to American Fugitive Slaves, 1800-1865* (1985); *Voice of the Fugitive* (1851-52); Ward, Samuel Ringgold. *Autobiography of a Fugitive Negro* (1965); Winks, Robin. *The Blacks in Canada* (1971); Woodson, Carter G. *The Negro in Our History* (1932).

MANUSCRIPT COLLECTIONS

The Black Abolitionist Papers: microfilm edition, ed. C. Peter Ripley (1986); Mary Ann Shadd Cary papers.

Manuscript Division, Moorland-Spingarn Research Center, Howard University. Washington, D.C.; Mary Ann Shadd Cary. Pre-Confederation Section, Manuscript Division, Public Archives of Canada. Ottawa, Ontario, Canada.

CAROLYN CALLOWAY-THOMAS

CATHOLIC CHURCH

O, write my name. / O, write my name. / O, write my name. . . . / Write my name when-a you get home / Yes, write my name in the book of life. . . . / The angels in the heav'n going to write my name. (Spiritual—Underground Railroad)

Within the history of women in America, Black Catholic women occupy a unique place, but one that has been ignored or portrayed in distorted ways. Their triple burden and challenge—that of being woman, Black, and Catholic—has required them to cope with realities affecting their essential humanity. The history of their perseverance and faith extends hundreds of years in both Africa and America.

PRE-CIVIL WAR

Black Catholic women have been an active and persistent presence in the long struggle for freedom and justice in America and within the American Catholic church; however, they have been portrayed from a male (both Black and white) perspective. Nonetheless, selected public records and church documents reveal fascinating glimpses of their lives.

The most substantial Catholic settlement was in Maryland, a proprietary colony founded in 1632 and settled by English Jesuits. Along with Catholic laymen, these Jesuits bought, kept, and sold Black slaves. Perhaps as early as 1634 or 1635, Reverend Andrew White brought two mulattos into the province, Matthias de Sousa and Francisco, who had been taken aboard the *Ark* and the *Dove* in the port at Barbados Island. Since Jesuit policy was to catechize and baptize all slaves, a substantial number of slaves became Catholic.

Early mention of a Black woman in a Catholic setting appears in a 1656 description of St. John's Manor, Maryland, which housed the seat of government in St. Mary's County. A notice for a court case, *Attorney General* v. *Overzee*, states that "a pear tree stood near the dwelling house. A Negro woman was not a witness since she stayed in the quartering house [servant's quarters]."

The development of a single-crop tobacco economy in Maryland relied on slavery. As the slave population increased, laws were promulgated to regulate the slave community. The law of 1664 made Black people slaves for life, enslaved white women who married slaves, and made their children slaves for life. Though the law was repealed in 1681, a number of mulatto children had already been enslaved. Even many years later, descendants of mixed unions, including Black Catholic women, had to sue for their freedom. In 1771, Mary and William Butler, grandchildren of a Negro slave and a free white Irish Catholic woman named Eleanor, commonly called "Irish Nell," sued for their freedom in a Maryland court. They secured their liberty in a lower court, only to have the case reversed by the Court of Appeals. Sixteen years later, their daughter, also named Mary, initiated another suit and won.

By the late 1790s, the population of Black Catholic women increased with the immigration of Catholics from Haiti. Among those who settled in Baltimore were free mulatto women, including the highly educated Elizabeth Lange. With several companions, she opened a school in her home for Black children. In 1829, these women, with the support of the Sulpician priests, established the first religious community of Black women in America. They became known as the Oblate Sisters of Providence.

One of the women who joined this community was Anne Marie Becroft, a free Black woman from Washington, D.C. In 1820, at the age of fifteen, she had opened a school in Georgetown for Black girls. Deciding to join the Oblate Sisters in 1831, she placed the school in the care of a former pupil, Ellen Symonds.

The Sulpician Archives in Baltimore contain a most remarkable document: *Journal of the Commencement of the Proceedings of the Society of Coloured People: With the Approbation of the Most Rev. Archb. Samuel and the Rector of the Cathedral, Rev. H. B. Coskery*. This journal of Black Catholics living in Baltimore, Maryland, provides a vivid portrait of the spiritual life of over 250 men and women. An alphabetical listing of the members shows approximately 170 female names. Officers included Mary Holland, first counselor; Elizabeth Berry, third counselor; and Mary Howard, fourth counselor. Land records show that some of the female members owned their own homes. Their listed occupations were domestic, such as washers and ironers.

The entries of the weekly sessions and monthly council meetings indicate that the group met from 1843 until 1845 in Calvert Hall in the basement of the Baltimore Cathedral. Monthly dues for each member were 6¼ cents. A detailed report of their prayer life includes descriptions of singing, the lending library, their financial status, and provisions for the needy. The group held masses for members who died. In March 1844 Harriet Queen died, followed in August by Lucy Butler, who left $21 to the Society and $21 to the Cathedral. The journal records document the activities of a group of Black Catholics in the antebellum period who nurtured a distinctive community within the Catholic church.

The oldest Black Catholic community was established in 1784 in St. Augustine, Florida (Davis 1990). In return for military service and conversion to the Catholic faith, slaves who had fled plantations in the Carolinas and Georgia were promised their freedom. They built the fortified town of Gracia Real de Santa Teresa de Mose. Excavations have yielded artifacts including gun flints, buckles, thimbles, buttons, clay pipes, bowls, and even a handmade St. Christopher medal.

Black Catholics lived in the Louisiana territory probably as early as 1724, when the French *Code Noir* established the laws governing slavery there. Early Catholic missionaries in the territory owned slaves and profited from their labor. Some Black Catholics were able to establish their own communities. Isle Breville, an area on the Cane River in what is now northern Louisiana, became home to one such community. Coincoin, a slave woman with the French name of Marie Thérèse, was born in Natchitoches in 1742. In 1767, she became the concubine of a French merchant, Claude Metoyer. She bore him seven children who were baptized. After purchasing Coincoin and their children in 1778, Metoyer emancipated Coincoin and the last son. He gave her and the children sixty-eight acres. By diligent work, the family had a thriving business of tobacco, indigo, and bear grease by 1793, and Coincoin purchased the freedom of the rest of her children. She died in 1816. Her son Augustin became head of the Black Catholic community. He constructed one of the world's oldest Black Catholic churches, St. Augustine, in 1829.

By the beginning of the nineteenth century, the practice of concubinage between well-to-do men and free women of culture was well established, especially in New Orleans. From this milieu of "genteel immorality" emerged Henriette Delille, founder of the second Black religious congregation in America in 1842.

In California, eleven families founded the community of Nuestra Senora de Los Angeles in 1781. Half the adults were Black, two were Spanish, and the rest were Native Americans. All were Catholic.

By the mid-nineteenth century, other Black Catholic communities had grown up in Alabama, Maryland, and South Carolina. Small settlements could be found in Kentucky; Mobile, Alabama; Savannah, Georgia; St. Louis, Missouri; Philadelphia, Pennsylvania; Baltimore, Maryland; Chicago, Illinois; and New York. Black women lived in all of these communities, but church registers acknowledged them in different ways. Many slaves or indentured servants remained unnamed, some were listed with only a first name under "property of . . . ," while "free people of color" were listed with both a first and last name.

POST-CIVIL WAR TO THE 1990s

After the Civil War, Black Catholics formed separate parishes, began societies to assist the needy in their communities, and held national lay congresses. Women played supporting roles in these endeavors. By the early 1900s, an urgent need for educational resources became apparent. Through the Federation of Colored Catholics led by Dr. Thomas W. Turner, a biology professor at Hampton Institute in Virginia, appeals were made to every level of the hierarchy for Catholic education.

In many areas, the Catholic schools were the only means of providing an education for Black people. Black Catholic women, serving as religious sisters and laity, staffed most of these schools. In 1910 in Lafayette, Louisiana, Eleanora Figaro, a graduate of St. Paul's School in Lafayette, gathered eighteen children in a shed and began the first Catholic school for Black children in that part of the state. She taught at Sacred Heart School for forty-two years. In 1949, Figaro became the first Black woman to receive the Papal honor "Pro Ecclesia et Pontifice."

In 1924, after much delay, the Cardinal Gibbons Institute opened in Ridge, Maryland, with Victor Daniel as principal and Constance Daniel, his wife, as assistant principal. Both were Black Catholics and graduates of Tuskegee Institute. Their school provided academic, vocational, and religious instruction to Black students, male and female, from across the United States. Extension courses in agriculture, home economics, and health were also available to Black Catholic families. Because of financial difficulties, the institute closed in 1933, but it reopened in 1936 and operated until 1967.

By the 1940s and 1950s, Catholic individuals and groups had begun to organize interracial efforts to combat the serious social and economic problems of that time. Many Black women volunteered in the houses of hospitality in the Catholic Worker Movement, begun by Dorothy Day in 1933. Helen Caldwell

Day, a young Black Catholic, helped at the New York House. In 1950, she returned to her home in Memphis, Tennessee, and began an interracial house of hospitality. Her autobiography, *Color Ebony*, describes her spiritual journey as a Black woman in a racist and sexist society.

Black women were highly visible and extremely vocal as staff workers and volunteers in the Friendship House Apostolate, an interracial organization founded by Catherine de Hueck in Harlem in 1938. The group used lectures and articles in the house newsletter to confront and change the institutional racism within the Church. One of the staff workers in this New York "settlement type" house was a young Black writer, Ellen Tarry. She and a white associate went to Chicago in 1942 to start a Friendship House following race riots there. As in houses in Washington, D.C., Portland, Oregon, and Shreveport, Louisiana, many Black women were on the staff or served as volunteers. Ellen Tarry is the author of *The Third Door: The Autobiography of an American Negro Woman* (1955) and *The Other Toussaint: A Post-Revolutionary Black* (1981).

A small group of Catholic women began the interracial *Caritas* in New Orleans in 1950. Six years later, Eunice Royal, a young Black woman from Napoleonville, Louisiana, joined. With only three permanent members, including Eunice Royal, and many supporters, *Caritas* continues to do parish and community work in Louisiana, Guatemala, and Africa.

Since their inception in the 1930s, Catholic Interracial Councils have included Black women. One particularly active member in both the Jersey City, New Jersey, and Washington, D.C., chapters was Dr. Lena Edwards, a devout Catholic who strongly and effectively protested racism and sexism wherever she encountered it. A wife, mother of six, medical doctor, educator, and missionary to migrant workers in Texas, she received many honors, including the Medal of Freedom.

With the advent of the civil rights movement and Vatican II, momentous changes occurred in the United States and in the Catholic church. Black Catholic women actively participated, and many assumed leadership roles.

With the advent of the Black Power movement, Black Catholic men and women formed national organizations of clergy, sisters, and lay persons. In November 1969, the National Conference of Catholic Bishops approved the establishment of the National Office for Black Catholics. Another national organization, the National Association of Black Catholic

Administrators, was founded in 1976. Delores Morgan, an early organizer of the Office of Black Catholics in Syracuse, New York, served as the first woman president of the association.

Numerous women have played prominent roles in diocesan offices for Black Catholics. A secretariat for Black Catholics was established in 1973 in Washington, D.C., where the Black Catholic population approximated 80,000. Its first director was Cynthia Roberson. Of the five offices for Black Catholics existing in the early 1970s, the Washington, D.C., office was the first to be headed by a Black woman.

In 1987, the National Black Catholic Congress met in Washington, D.C., at the Catholic University of America. Theresa Wilson Favors of Baltimore, Maryland, served as the first director of the Black Catholic Congress. Many delegates were women and seven of the twelve major speakers were women, including keynote speaker Sr. Francesca Thompson. Sr. Thea Bowman, whose extraordinary ministry was documented on television's *60 Minutes*, addressed the topic of "History and Culture." She greatly enhanced the times of prayer with her remarkable songs.

Women have also played major roles in enhancing the Catholic church with liturgy reflecting the African roots of Black Catholics. The first Rejoice! Conference on Black Catholic Liturgy was held in 1984, following a series of meetings convened in 1983 by Jacqueline Wilson, Executive Director of the Office of Black Catholics in Washington, D.C. Wilson also served as a regional coordinator for the National Black Catholic Congress. At a special Rejoice! Conference in Rome in 1989, Dr. Diana Hayes spoke on "Tracings of an American Theology: A Black Catholic Perspective." Currently at Georgetown University, Hayes earned her Ph.D. and S.T.D. degrees at the Catholic University of Louvain in Belgium. She is the first Black Catholic lay woman to receive these highest degrees in Catholic theology. Sr. Eva M. Lumas, also a presenter at the Rejoice! Conference in Rome, is a distinguished lecturer, educator, and leader in Catholic religious education. Other leading Black Catholic theologians in the United States who are women include Sisters Jamie Phelps, Toinette Eugene, and Sean Copeland.

Black women have begun to assume increasingly significant positions within the Catholic church. The nation's first Black nun to head a parish, Sr. Cora Billings, was installed as a pastor in Richmond, Virginia, on September 23, 1990. In the Archdiocese of New York, Delores Grier was appointed Vice Chancellor for Community Relations in 1985. On the national level, Beverly Carroll became the executive director for Black Catholics in the National Conference of Catholic Bishops in 1989.

On the threshold of the twenty-first century, Black Catholic women enhance the rich legacy of commitment to their freedom and their faith. They will continue to do so.

[*See also* BEASLEY, MATHILDA; BECROFT, ANNE MARIE; COINCOIN; NATIONAL BLACK SISTERS' CONFERENCE; OBLATE SISTERS OF PROVIDENCE.]

BIBLIOGRAPHY

Berlin, Ira. *Slaves Without Masters: The Free Negro in the Antebellum South* (1974); Braxton, Rev. Edward. "The National Black Catholic Congress of 1987: An Event of the Century," *The Josephine Harvest* (Summer 1987); Butler, Loretta M. "A History of Catholic Elementary Education of Negroes in the Diocese of Lafayette, Louisiana," Ph.D. diss. (1963); Davis, Cyprian, O.S.B. *The History of Black Catholics in the United States* (1990); Day, Helen Caldwell. *Color, Ebony* (1951); Doherty, Catherine de Houeck. *Friendship House* (1946); Hennessy, James. *American Catholics: A History of the Roman Catholic Community in the United States* (1981); *Journal of the Holy Family.* R. G. 42, Box 2, Sulpician Archives, Baltimore, Maryland; Scally, Mary Anthony. *Mother, Medicine, and Mercy: The Story of a Black Woman Doctor* (1979); Sherwood, Grace H. *The Oblates' One Hundred and One Years* (1931); Stone, Gary Wheeler. "St. John's: Archeological Questions and Answers," *Maryland Historical Magazine* (Summer 1974); Tarry, Ellen. *The Other Toussaint: A Post-Revolutionary Black* (1981), and *The Third Door: The Autobiography of an American Negro Woman* (1955); Warnagiris, Sr. M. Clare. "Maria Becraft and Black Catholic Education (1827-1832)," M.A. thesis, Morgan State College (1974).

LORETTA M. BUTLER

CATLETT, ELIZABETH (1919-)

I don't have anything against men but, since I am a woman, I know more about women and I know how they feel. Many artists are always doing men. I think that somebody ought to do women. Artists do work with women, with the beauty of their bodies and the refinement of middle-class women, but I think there is a need to express something about the working-class Black woman and that's what I do. (Catlett, in Lewis 1984)

Sculptor and printmaker Elizabeth Catlett is an important figure in U.S. and Mexican art. Catlett's careful balance of dynamic form and content in both two- and three-dimensional works, and the acclaim that she has earned over a fifty-year period, firmly establish her contribution to the history of modern art. As a figurative artist, Catlett assimilates influences of modernist, social realist, expressionist, African, and pre-Hispanic styles into visual forms that imaginatively depict the human experience in subject matter ranging from heroic to ordinary characters and events. Though her stylistic influences have varied over the years, increasingly moving from realism toward abstraction, the work itself consistently adheres to perceptual reality. Preeminent in that reality is the theme of human dignity, a quality that Catlett interprets with penetrating emotional depth in both plastic and graphic form.

Catlett was born in 1919 in Washington, D.C., where she grew up during a period of overt segregation and oppression. She was the youngest of three children who were raised by their widowed mother, Mary Carson Catlett. John Catlett, Elizabeth's father, died shortly before she was born. He had been a math professor at Tuskegee Institute and in the public school system in Washington, D.C. Mary Carson Catlett and the children lived in a middle-class neighborhood in their own home, built by her father-in-law. Elizabeth Catlett recalls that they were "the poor cousins" within an extended family that included a famous surgeon; yet even so, they maintained a middle-class social standing because of their kinship ties (Lewis 1984). Catlett's mother supported her children with her job as a truant officer. As a young child, Elizabeth was inspired by both of her parents. Her mother encouraged Catlett to draw and paint and provided her with "materials, a place to work, and time apart" (Rubinstein 1990). Her late father inspired Catlett through his history, including his artistic accomplishments in playing violin, mandolin, and piano, and in writing music and carving wood.

Catlett's formal education began at Lucretia Mott Elementary School in Washington, D.C., and continued at Dunbar High School where she received encouragement in art and graduated in 1933 with academic honors. Upon graduating from high school, she participated in entrance examinations for one week at Carnegie Institute of Technology in Pittsburgh, but was rejected in spite of her competitive art works. She overheard one of the teachers at the school say to another, "It's too bad she's a Negro, isn't it?" (Fax 1971).

She began her formal study of art in 1933 at Howard University, where Catlett studied with monumental figures in the history of African-American art.

At Howard, Catlett studied drawing and painting with painter/art historian James Porter, author of *Modern Negro Art* (1943). She studied printmaking and crafts with leading printmaker James L. Wells, and design with leading painter Lois Mailou Jones. Catlett was exposed to the preeminent philosopher Alain Locke, author of *The New Negro* (1925), who encouraged Black artists to turn to the ancestral arts of Africa for inspiration. Locke was a collector of African art, the influence of which is evident in Catlett's work. Catlett also was exposed to African art and classes in Western art in the art gallery of Howard University.

Catlett's education at Howard provided her with mentors and lifelong friends. She remembers, for example, how Porter "allowed her to spend time in his library and talked to her at length about life and art" (Rubinstein 1990). Porter also encouraged Catlett to become involved with the Federal Art Project of the Works Progress Administration (WPA), a government program structured during the Great Depression by the Roosevelt administration to provide jobs by employing artists to produce art for public buildings. Catlett followed Porter's advice. In fact, it was through her involvement with the federal project that Catlett realized she lacked the necessary technique to paint a mural as she had planned. Research for the mural project introduced Catlett to the Mexican muralists who influenced her later work. Through Howard, Catlett had acquired a foundation in drawing, painting, design, and woodcuts, and an appreciation of African, African-American, Mexican, and European art. She earned a B.S. in art, graduating cum laude in 1937.

For the next year Catlett taught art at the high school level and supervised art programs at eight elementary schools in Durham, North Carolina. During this time, she protested salary inequities of Black teachers (salaries were equivalent to about half that of European-American teachers), and made plans to attend graduate school at the University of Iowa. There she studied with leading regionalist painter Grant Wood.

Catlett enrolled in the art department at the University of Iowa in 1938. Working under Wood's tutelage, Catlett expanded her styles and media while deepening her thoughts about art and its purpose. (Wood is also known for his work in interior design, stained glass, and carpentry.) Wood encouraged his students to paint what they knew. Reflecting on Wood's influence, Catlett noted, "That is probably why I do more work on Black women than on any other single subject" (Shaw 1974). Catlett completed

her M.F.A. in 1940, the first student to do so. Catlett's thesis piece was a mother and child figure that was carved in limestone; the work won the first place award in sculpture in the American Negro Exposition in Chicago the following year.

In summer 1940, Catlett got a summer teaching job at Prairie View College in Texas. From fall 1940 to 1942, she headed the art department at Dillard University in New Orleans. During summer 1941, Catlett studied ceramics at the Art Institute in Chicago and worked at the South Side Community Art Center, an active cultural center established during the WPA. Catlett interacted with Charles White, a painter and printmaker who worked in the realist tradition and became a major figure in African-American art. They married the same year and went to New Orleans, where Catlett taught another year at Dillard. The couple then went to Hampton Institute in Virginia for six months; Catlett taught and White painted a mural. They finally settled in New York City in 1942.

Catlett studied privately with French sculptor Ossip Zadkine, beginning in 1943. During that year she also studied lithography at the Art Students League. As Catlett expanded her techniques, she directed an alternative community school, the George Washington Carver School, where she taught for two years, from 1944 to 1946. Catlett was awarded a Julius Rosenwald Fellowship for 1945-46, an event that marked a turning point in the artist's life. The award was renewed in 1946-47, and in 1946 Catlett and White visited Mexico together and worked with Taller de Grafica Popular (TGP), a collective of socially involved printmakers, an experience that had an important influence on the lives and works of both artists. Their marriage, however, failed and they soon returned to the United States to get a divorce.

Catlett subsequently returned to Mexico and became immersed in professional and social activities as she continued her work with TGP. She also studied pre-Hispanic ceramic techniques with Mexican artist Francisco Zuniga at Esmeralda, Escuela de Pintura y Escultura. Between 1946 and 1947, she completed her graphic series on the "Negro Woman" for which she had received the fellowship. This significant body of work consisted of fifteen linocuts that were characterized by black linear rhythms that dramatically configured monumental real-type (as opposed to stereotype) images of Black women. Her selection of and approach to her subjects uniquely inscribed convincing personalities, a quality that was rarely evident in American prints or painting depicting Black women up to that time. Later identified as Afrofemcentrist (or Afro-female-centered), the series was exhibited at the Barnett-Aden Gallery in Washington, D.C., in 1947-48 and introduced Catlett to the public as an emerging professional artist. Its subjects and style evoked thoughts and emotions that suggested Catlett's empathy for humanity, her womanist/feminist proclivities, and her public voice for Black women. It was a voice that challenged the oppression of all people of color, especially women. Subsequently, her position challenged the oppression of all women, though emphasizing women of color.

In 1947, Catlett married Mexican painter Francisco Mora, with whom she had three sons, Francisco, Juan, and David. Catlett and Mora continued to work with TGP until 1966. However, in 1956, Catlett returned in part to sculpture, studying woodcarving with José L. Ruiz at Esmeralda, Escuela de Pintura y Escultura. In 1958, she became a professor of sculpture in the National School of Fine Arts at the Universidad Nacional Autonoma de Mexico, and in 1959, she became head of the sculpture department, remaining in that position until her retirement in 1976.

While expanding both her personal and professional responsibilities, Catlett remained politically active in Mexico. "Red-baiting" had marked her as an undesirable in the United States, a development that influenced her to become a Mexican citizen. With the change in citizenship, however, Catlett could not travel in the United States. Her inability to enter the country attracted the attention of younger Black American artists, politicians, museum directors, religious leaders, and others who wrote letters in her support to the U.S. State Department. Her status as an "undesirable" was finally changed in 1974.

Catlett's command of a variety of materials reveals her unusual versatility. She produces three-dimensional forms in marble, limestone, bronze, terracotta, and various types of wood, and two-dimensional works in linocut and lithography printmaking processes. Whether a geometricized sculptural representation of a Black woman subject or an expressionist print on the theme of oppression, each work reveals a delicate balance of clarity, inventiveness, and philosophical conviction. The human figure remains prominent in this regard. In sculptural form (portrait bust, singular figure, or group figure), the representatives of the human subject calls attention to the beauty, character, and circumstance of specific or symbolic individuals. In graphic form, it expressively stimulates thought about social, cultural, historical, and/or political conditions.

Choosing to sculpt or print Black and Mexican subjects, particularly women, Catlett depicts maternity, love, elderly wisdom, youthful beauty, feminine beauty-character, male and female leadership, work, female bonding, and identity, among other concerns. Her styles range from realism to semi-abstraction, and she sees form and meaning as inextricably bound.

Catlett's commissioned works are located in public spaces in the United States and Mexico; they include *Olmec Bather*, a ten-foot bronze at the National Politechnical Institute in Mexico (1966); *Phillis Wheatley*, a life-size bronze at Jackson State College in Mississippi (1973); *Louis Armstrong*, a ten-foot bronze in New Orleans (1975-76, presented at the U.S. bicentennial celebration); *Students Aspire*, a twenty-four-foot bronze relief on the Chemical Engineering Building at Howard University (1978); *Torres Bodet* and *Vasconcelor*, two life-size bronzes for the Secretary of Education in Mexico (1981); a thirty-six-foot-by-ten-foot bronze bas relief entitled *The People of Atlanta* for the New City Hall in Atlanta (1989-91); and *Mother and Child*, a nineteen-inch black marble carving for Colgate Palmolive (1992).

Catlett's prints are in important collections as well. Both her prints and sculpture are represented in major collections in the following institutions: Atlanta University in Georgia, Cleveland Museum of Art in Ohio, Fisk University in Tennessee, Hampton University in Virginia, High Museum in Atlanta, Library of Congress in Washington, D.C., Metropolitan Museum of Art in New York, Museo de Arte Moderno in Mexico City, Narodniko Musea in Prague, National Museum of American Art in Washington, D.C., New Orleans Museum of Art, Schomburg Center for Research in Black Culture in New York City, University of Iowa, and the Studio Museum in Harlem, among others.

The commissions and collections in African-American, European-American, and Mexican institutions indicate Catlett's general historical importance. However, she is particularly important in the history of African-American art because of her representation in pioneering African-American exhibitions, including "Evolution of Afro-American Artists, 1800-1950" (New York, 1967); "Two Centuries of Black American Art" (Los Angeles County Museum of Art, 1976-77); "Forever Free: Art by African American Women, 1862-1980" (Normal, Illinois, 1980); and "National Black Arts Festival" (Atlanta, 1988), among others. Given the few existing texts on African-American art, those exhibitions and their catalogue texts serve as important documents of the history of African-American art.

As her subjects and commissions might imply, Catlett has consistently made her works available to various communities in different domains of life. Her works are shown in major museums internationally and locally. They are found on Black college campuses and in offices of community organizations. From Catlett's perspective, exhibiting in a community church or social club is as important as exhibiting in a museum or gallery, and this is the message that she has passed on to younger Black artists. Her historic lecture, "The Negro People and American Art at Mid-Century," delivered at the National Conference on Negro Artists (NCA) on April 1, 1961, contained this message of social commitment. Catlett presented ideas that synthesized the populist ideology of TGP, cultural nationalist ideology, and activist positions of the civil rights movement. She encouraged an art of communication and emphasized the necessity of Black artists to exhibit in Black community spaces. Catlett said: "Let us take our painting and prints and sculpture not only to Atlanta University, to the art galleries, and to patrons of the arts who have money to buy them; let us exhibit where Negro people meet—in the churches, in the schools and universities, in the associations and clubs and trade unions. Then let us seek inspiration in the Negro people—a principal and never-ending source" (Lewis 1984). These words were consistent with the thought that she conveyed to art historian/artist (and her former student) Samella Lewis in the late 1970s as she noted, "Art must be realistic for me, whether sculpture or printmaking, I have always wanted my art to service my people—to reflect us, to relate to us, to stimulate us, to make us aware of our potential. . . . We have to create an art for liberation and for life" (Lewis 1984).

BIBLIOGRAPHY

Catlett, Elizabeth. "The Role of the Black Artist," *Black Scholar* (June 1975); Coleman, Floyd. *A Courtyard Apart: The Art of Elizabeth Catlett and Francisco Mora* (exhibition catalogue) (1990); Crawford, Marc. "My Art Speaks for Both My Peoples," *Ebony* (January 1970); Fax, Elton. *Seventeen Black Artists* (1971); Gedeon, Lucinda H. "Elizabeth Catlett, Francisco Mora, and David Mora Catlett: A Family in the Tradition of the Arts." In *Selected Essays: Art and Artists from the Harlem Renaissance to the 1980s* (1988); Gouma-Peterson, Thalia. "Elizabeth Catlett: The Power of Human Feeling in Art," *Women's Journal* (Spring-Summer 1983); Lewis, Samella. *Art: African American* (1990), and *The Art of Elizabeth Catlett* (1984); Rubinstein, Charlotte. *American Women Sculptors* (1990); Shaw, Sharon. "Elizabeth Catlett Mora—Making Art Like the Blues," *Washington Star-News* (December 1974); Tesfagiorgis, Freida High W. "Afrofemcentrism: The Art of Elizabeth Catlett and Faith Ringgold," *Sage* (Spring 1987), and personal interview with Elizabeth Catlett (March 23, 1992).

FREIDA HIGH W. TESFAGIORGIS

CHAMP, DOROTHY *see* BAHA'I FAITH

CHASE-RIBOUD, BARBARA DEWAYNE (D'ASHNASH TOSI) (1939-)

The name Barbara Chase-Riboud stirs as much controversy as that of Sally Hemings, the protagonist of her first and best-selling novel of the same name. The historical romance *Sally Hemings* (1979) is Chase-Riboud's re-creation of the alleged liaison between the third president of the United States, Thomas Jefferson, and his slave mistress of thirty-eight years, which purports a legacy of seven children. Chase-Riboud found herself as sensationalized in 1979 in newspapers such as the *Chicago Tribune*, the *Washington Post*, and the *New York Times* as Sally Hemings was in 1802, the year the story created such furor in American publications such as the *Richmond Recorder*. Chase-Riboud was caught amid the clamor of an outraged public who found it impossible to digest the idea of a president's intimate involvement in miscegenation and of a legion of Jefferson historians who repudiated the relationship in their own biographies. Yet, besides rekindling the historical controversy, Chase-Riboud created a not only compelling but sensitive account of the widely circulated story, and her novel won the Janet Heidinger Kafka Prize in 1979 for the best novel by an American woman.

She is also the author of two other novels and two books of poetry and has been accorded international acclaim for her sculptures and drawings. The novel *Valide* (1986) is a saga of the 1802 kidnapping and enslavement of an American Creole girl by Algerian pirates. Paradoxically, the girl, Naksh-i-dil, rises to the pinnacle of power to become the Valide, or Queen Mother, of an ancient harem in the Ottoman Empire, while still a slave to the sultan. In *Echo of Lions* (1989), Chase-Riboud recasts the story of the African slave Joseph Cinqué (Sengbe Pieh), who was seized in an illegal slave trade, imprisoned for organizing a revolt on the slave ship, and later acquitted after a Supreme Court defense by former president John Quincy

Adams. Chase-Riboud's first book of poetry, *From Memphis to Peking* (1974), reflects her visits to Egypt as a college student and as the first American woman to visit post-revolutionary Peking. Her second book of poetry, *Portrait of a Nude Woman as Cleopatra* (1987), is a gracefully sensuous rendition of the Antony and Cleopatra story in sonnet form, inspired by a Rembrandt drawing.

The nurturing that ultimately led to Chase-Riboud's reputation as a visual artist began during her early years in Philadelphia. The only child of Charles Edward, a building contractor, and Vivian May West, a medical assistant, Chase-Riboud was deemed artistically gifted and was immersed in cultural activities, such as classical piano, poetry writing, dancing, sculpting, and drawing, prior to entering high school. She later earned a bachelor of fine arts degree from Temple University's Tyler Art School (1957), a John Hay Whitney Fellowship for study at the American Academy in Rome (1957), and a master of fine arts degree from Yale University (1960).

Her artistic pursuits eventually took her to Paris, where she met and married photojournalist Marc Edward Riboud on December 25, 1961. They had two sons, David and Alexis. The marriage ended in divorce, and Chase-Riboud subsequently married art expert, broker, and historian Sergio Tosi in 1981.

During her early years in Paris, Chase-Riboud began a sculpting career that spans a twenty-five-year period and is replete with honors, awards, and a multitude of art exhibits in Europe. She received a National Endowment for the Arts Fellowship and the first prize in the New York City Subway Competition for architecture in 1973 and a U.S. State Department traveling grant in 1975. She was named the Academic of Italy with a gold medal for sculpture and drawing in 1978, and in 1981 she received an honorary doctorate of arts and humanities from Temple University.

BIBLIOGRAPHY

CA; Cohen, Roger. "Judge Says Copyright Covers Writer's Ideas of a Jefferson Affair," *New York Times* (August 15, 1991); *DLB*; McHenry, Susan. " 'Sally Hemings': A Key to Our National Identity—A Conversation with Barbara Chase-Riboud," *Ms.* (October 1980); McMurray, Kristin. "A New Black Novelist Explores Thomas Jefferson's Love Affair with a Beautiful Slave," *People* (October 8, 1979); Russell, John. Review of *Sally Hemings*, *New York Times* (September 5, 1979); Simmons, Charity. "Thomas Jefferson: Intimate History, Public Debate," *Chicago Tribune* (July 3, 1979); Trescott, Jacqueline. "The Hemings Affair: The Black Novelist and Jefferson's Mistress," *Washington Post* (June 15, 1979); *WWBA* (1991).

B. J. BOLDEN

Outrage and controversy greeted the publication of Barbara Chase-Riboud's 1979 historical romance Sally Hemings. *The compelling and sensitive novel is based on the widely accepted story of Thomas Jefferson's thirty-eight-year relationship with his slave mistress. [Schomburg Center]*

CHILDRESS, ALICE (1920-)

Playwright, novelist, actress, essayist, columnist, lecturer, and theater consultant, Alice Childress has never been flattered by the litany of firsts that have been used to refer to her works. She believes that when people have been barred from something for so long, it seems ironic to emphasize the "first." Childress, instead, looks to the day when she will be the fiftieth or one-hundredth African-American artist to accomplish something. Long regarded as a champion for the masses of poor people in America, Childress writes about the disparity between rich and poor, underscoring that racism and sexism are added burdens forced upon people of color. A reticent and private person, Childress boldly speaks out in her works against an American government that either exploits or ignores poor people in the name of capitalism. One of Childress's strongest convictions is that Black authors must explore and include Black history in their writings. Her sagacity and commitment to preserving Black culture and history are evident in her refusal to tell lies about Black people, even at the expense of Broadway options.

Alice Childress was born on October 12, 1920, in Charleston, South Carolina. When she was five, she moved to Harlem to live with her grandmother, Eliza Campbell, who reared her after her parents divorced. Although Childress grew up very poor, she was enriched by her grandmother's love, patience, and appreciation for the arts. It was her grandmother who taught her the art of storytelling and who took her to museums, art galleries, and Wednesday night testimonials at Salem Church in Harlem. Childress's inspiration for writing came from these testimonials because in them she heard the troubles of many poor people.

Childress attended Public School 81, the Julia Ward Howe Junior High School, and, for three years,

Attacking stereotypes and institutional racism, Alice Childress's plays have shaken up audiences and the American theater for four decades. Her Trouble in Mind *was the first play by a Black woman ever to receive an Obie. [Schomburg Center]*

Wadleigh High School, which she left when her grandmother and mother died in the late 1930s. Mostly self-taught, Childress remembers discovering the public library as a youngster and voraciously reading two books a day. She took on a series of odd jobs in the 1940s to support herself and her daughter, Jean, from her first marriage. Childress worked as assistant machinist, photo retoucher, domestic worker, salesperson, and insurance agent, all jobs that kept her in close contact with the working-class people that she characterizes in her works.

Childress began her writing career in the 1940s. In 1943, she began an eleven-year association with the American Negro Theater, where she studied acting, performed in Broadway productions, directed, and served on the board of directors. One of Childress's major accomplishments during her tenure with the American Negro Theater was initiating in the early 1950s advanced, guaranteed pay for union off-Broadway contracts in New York City. Childress benefited from this effort because her *Just a Little Simple* (1950) and *Gold through the Trees* (1952) became the first plays by a Black woman to be professionally produced, that is, performed by unionized actors.

Since 1949, Childress has written more than a dozen plays, including *Florence* (1949); *Wedding Band: A Love Hate Story in Black and White* (1966), televised on ABC in 1974; *Wine in the Wilderness* (1969), produced on National Educational Television in 1969; *Mojo: A Black Love Story* (1970); and *Moms* (1987). Her plays attack institutional racism and stereotyped roles assigned to African-Americans.

Childress became the first Black woman ever to receive an Obie Award, for the off-Broadway production of *Trouble in Mind* (1955), a play about white directors who know little about Black life yet insist on presenting stereotypes. Running for ninety-one performances at the Greenwich Mews Theatre, Childress's two-act drama drew rave reviews and generated interest from commercial backers. *Trouble in Mind* was scheduled for a Broadway production in April 1957 but was withdrawn by Childress because of changes required by the director.

Childress also has written several novels, including *Like One of the Family: Conversations from a Domestic's Life* (1937); *A Hero Ain't Nothin' but a Sandwich* (1973), which was adapted as a motion picture; *A Short Walk* (1979); *Rainbow Jordan* (1981); and *Those Other People* (1990). Her novels, like her plays, portray poor people who struggle to survive in capitalist America. She incorporates Black history in her novels in order to inform Black children of the heroic lives that paved the way for them to succeed. *Like One of the Family* is a collection of vignettes in which the maid enlightens her employers about their shortcomings. An exceptional novel, *A Short Walk* chronicles Garveyism and the Black experience through the 1960s. *A Hero Ain't Nothin' but a Sandwich*, *Rainbow Jordan*, and *Those Other People* are novels for adolescents and deal with sexuality, drugs, and growing up in a homophobic society.

Childress's innovativeness has garnered her several major awards and honors, including writer-in-residence at the MacDowell Colony; featured author in a BBC panel discussion on "The Negro in the American Theater"; a Rockefeller grant administered through the New Dramatists and the John Golden Fund for Playwrights; and a Harvard appointment to the Radcliffe Institute for Independent Study (now Mary Ingraham Bunting Institute), from which she received a graduate medal. Noted American authors Lillian Hellman and Tillie Olsen were instrumental in recommending Childress to Radcliffe. During her stay at Radcliffe, she wrote *Wedding Band* (1966), a play that deals with interracial love and the objections raised by members of both races.

Alice Childress has written for the stage consecutively for over four decades, and she remains a major link in the development of African-American theater. Lorraine Hansberry, who would later author the 1959 Broadway success *A Raisin in the Sun*, wrote the 1950 review of Childress's play *Florence* in Paul Robeson's *Freedom* magazine, evidence of the impact Childress's work would have on future generations of Black dramatists. She is a master craftsperson whose deft handling of language aligns her with America's most brilliant authors.

Childress married professional musician and music teacher Nathan Woodward on July 17, 1957. Her daughter Jean died in 1990. Childress currently lives on Long Island, New York, where she is writing her memoirs and working on her sixth novel.

BIBLIOGRAPHY

Brown-Guillory, Elizabeth. "Alice Childress: A Pioneering Spirit," *Sage: A Scholarly Journal on Black Women* (Spring 1987), and *Their Place on the Stage: Black Women Playwrights in America* (1988); Brown-Guillory, Elizabeth, ed. *Wines in the Wilderness: Plays by African American Women from the Harlem Renaissance to the Present* (1990); *Contemporary Literary Criticism* (1980); *DLB*; Peterson, Bernard. *Contemporary Black Playwrights and Their Plays* (1988).

ELIZABETH BROWN-GUILLORY

CHINN, MAY EDWARD (1896-1980)

May Edward Chinn, physician, was born in Great Barrington, Massachusetts, in 1896, the only child of William Lafayette Chinn, a slave who had escaped to freedom at the age of eleven from the Chinn (Cheyne) plantation in Virginia, and his wife, who had been born on a Chickahominy Indian reservation near Norfolk, Virginia.

When May was three years old, her family moved to New York. Her mother, wishing to protect her from the distress caused by her father's alcoholism and determined that her daughter would receive a good education, sent her, at the age of five or six, to boarding school at the Bordentown Manual Training and Industrial School. Forced to leave school when she developed osteomyelitis, May went to live with her mother on the Tarrytown estate of the Tiffanys, a wealthy white family. Though her mother was working for the family, Chinn recalls having been raised as one of the Tiffany children: dining with them, studying the classics with them, attending concerts with them as would any child in the house.

It was through her exposure to music while living on the Tiffany estate that Chinn's musical gifts were first nurtured. When she and her mother returned to New York after the Tiffany estate had been sold, Chinn attended grammar school and took piano lessons. When she dropped out of high school she gave piano lessons to kindergarten children. Eventually, with encouragement from her mother, Chinn took and passed a high school equivalency exam. She entered Columbia University's Teachers College in 1917. After her first year, she changed her major from music to science and graduated in 1921. While still in college, she played and sang in concerts around New York, accompanying such celebrated performers as Paul Robeson and singing for soldiers under the auspices of the United Service Organizations.

In 1926, Chinn became the first Negro (the designation that she preferred) woman to obtain a medical degree from Bellevue Hospital Medical College. She went on to become the first Negro woman to hold an internship at Harlem Hospital and the first woman physician to ride with the ambulance crew of the Harlem Hospital on emergency calls. In 1928, she joined the ranks of a group of Black doctors who practiced in the Edgecombe Sanitarium, an alternative establishment to the predominantly white New York hospital system. She received a Master's degree in public health from Columbia University in 1933.

Well known by the end of her career for her work in the early detection and diagnosis of cancer, she was

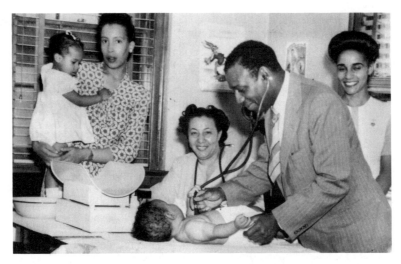

In 1928, physician May Edward Chinn joined with other Black doctors to practice in the Edgecombe Sanitarium as an alternative to the predominantly white and white-oriented New York hospital system. In the 1970s, after her retirement from the Strang Clinic at the age of eighty-one, the inexhaustible Chinn continued to work in three day-care centers in Harlem. [Moorland-Spingarn]

on staff at the Strang Clinic until her retirement at the age of eighty-one, after which she continued her work in three day-care centers in Harlem. She was a member of the U.S. surgeon general's advisory commission on urban affairs, and she received an honorary doctor of science degree from Columbia University in 1980.

BIBLIOGRAPHY

Dammond, Ellen Craft. Interview with May Edward Chinn, M.D., *Black Women Oral History Project*, Schlesinger Library, Radcliffe College (1979).

SUSAN SHIFRIN

CHISHOLM, SHIRLEY (1924–)

Shirley Chisholm, the first Black woman to be elected to the U.S. House of Representatives, was born Shirley Anita Saint Hill in 1924 in the Bedford-Stuyvesant section of Brooklyn, New York. Her parents, both natives of Barbados, had left the island during the famines of the 1920s for a better life in the United States. When Chisholm was four years old, she and her sisters were taken to live on her grandmother's farm in Barbados. During the six years that Chisholm lived in Barbados, her grandmother became one of the major influences in her life and her first Black female role model.

When Chisholm returned to Brooklyn, she excelled in her academic work at a public high school and was offered scholarships to both Vassar and Oberlin colleges. Because of financial constraints, she chose instead to remain close to home and attend Brooklyn College. She decided upon a career in teaching, which was one of the few occupations open to educated Black women in the 1940s. After her graduation in 1946, she took evening classes at Columbia University toward a Master's degree in early childhood education while she also worked during the day as a teacher's aide. During this period she married Conrad Chisholm, also a native of the West Indies.

It was during this time that Chisholm first became seriously involved in politics through her local political organization, the Seventeenth Assembly District Democratic Club. As she described it in her first autobiography, *Unbought and Unbossed* (1970), it was through her involvement with this club that Chisholm began to perceive the lack of power of both Black people and women in regular Democratic party politics in Bedford-Stuyvesant. Black residents were by far the majority group in the district, but there were no prominent Black elected officials, and Black concerns often were ignored by the people in power. Also, although women were the main organizers of the fund-raising committee, their opinions on concrete political matters were not solicited and, when offered, often were ignored.

Chisholm eventually joined the Bedford-Stuyvesant Political League, an alternative to the regular all-white Democratic machine, led by Mac Holder, a local politico concerned with electing Black leaders in the community. In 1960, however, after a period of inactivity in politics as a result of a falling-out with Holder, Chisholm and several others formed another alternative organization, the Unity Democratic Club, with the explicit purpose of challenging the regular political machine by running Black candidates for all elected positions. It was through this organization that Chisholm herself ran as a candidate for New York State Assembly in 1964—and won. For four years she was the only woman and one of only eight Black representatives in the Assembly.

In 1968, using the slogan "Unbought and Unbossed," Chisholm ran against James Farmer, former leader of the Congress of Racial Equality

(CORE), for the seat in the newly formed Twelfth Congressional District of Brooklyn, which included Bedford-Stuyvesant. The race would have made history no matter what the outcome, for either way Brooklyn would have had its first Black member of Congress. However, Chisholm's overwhelming victory made her the first Black woman ever to be elected to the House of Representatives. She remained in the House for fourteen years, during which time she was a staunch advocate for many diverse progressive issues, most prominently civil rights and women's liberation issues. Chisholm was an early member of the National Organization for Women (NOW), a founder of the National Women's Political Caucus, and a spokesperson for the National Abortion Rights Action League (NARAL).

In 1972, Chisholm attempted to coalesce her various potential constituencies into a potent force for change when she became the first African-American to make a bid for the presidential nomination of the Democratic party. In spite of a lack of money,

Unbought and unbossed, Shirley Chisholm made political history in 1972 when she made the first serious bid by a woman for the presidential nomination of a major party. She is shown here with National Council of Negro Women president Dorothy Height. [Bethune Museum and Archives]

organization, and serious consideration from either the press or her male opponents, Chisholm remained in the race until the convention, where she captured more than 150 votes on the first ballot. The experience was a watershed event in her political life. In her second autobiography, *The Good Fight* (1973), which concentrated solely on her run for the presidency, she described her disappointment and hurt at the coolness her candidacy received from both Black male-led and white female-led organizations.

Shirley Chisholm retired from the House in 1983 and has since remained outside the political arena, although she made a show of support for Jesse Jackson in both his 1984 and 1988 presidential campaigns. She has spent most of her time speaking at functions and on college campuses throughout the country and occasionally teaching (she was a guest lecturer at Mount Holyoke College in 1985). She and her second husband live in upstate New York.

BIBLIOGRAPHY

Chisholm, Shirley. *The Good Fight* (1973), and *Unbought and Unbossed* (1970).

LISA WOZNICA

CHURCH OF GOD IN CHRIST

The Church of God in Christ (COGIC) is the Pentecostal denomination with the largest and most elaborately organized Women's Convention. Possibly the largest Pentecostal denomination in the United States and the seventh largest African-American Christian church, the COGIC was originally founded in 1895 as a Holiness church. It is currently the largest among those called the Sanctified church. Like other Holiness and Pentecostal denominations, the church emphasizes sanctification as a believer's experience subsequent to or separate from salvation or justification. Bishop Charles Harrison Mason, a Baptist minister in the Mount Helm Baptist Association of Lexington, Mississippi, founded the church along with C. P. Jones, after a conflict with other association members. Upon hearing of the Azuza Street revival of 1906, Mason and Jones sent several elders to observe and evaluate the revival and its doctrine. Adoption of Pentecostal doctrine led to conflict between Mason and Jones that resulted in Mason's retaining the church's charter and Jones's founding the Church of God in Christ (Holiness).

Women's work and the Women's Convention are central to the history of the Church of God in Christ. Since Bishop Mason believed women should govern other women, he appointed a women's "overseer" (or national supervisor or National Mother), Mother Lizzie Woods Roberson. In addition to her organizing, she was a noted revivalist, evangelist, and founder of congregations. Mother Lillian Brooks Coffey was the second head of what was called the Women's Department. She pioneered a more elaborate women's organizational structure, founding several new organizations within the convention and connecting the Women's Convention with the mainstream of African-American women's organizations, such as the National Association of Colored Women and the National Council of Negro Women, through her friendship with Mary McLeod Bethune. Another noted leader of the church, Dr. Arenia C. Mallory, was responsible for the church's academy becoming an accredited junior college. Although official church doctrine does not permit the ordination of women to the offices of elder, pastor, or bishop, women may "teach the gospel to others" and may "have charge of a church in the absence of the pastor." In spite of these restrictions, the autonomy of the Women's Convention has enabled it to encourage the development of national evangelists, women who teach the gospel who have conducted revivals successfully in at least seven states, and whose public speaking is indistinguishable from the most exemplary "preaching." Bishops within the church also have ordained women to charges outside of the denomination, such as military chaplaincies. The Women's Convention meets annually in May.

BIBLIOGRAPHY

Church of God in Christ. *Official Manual with the Doctrines and Discipline of the Church of God in Christ* (1973); Cornelius, Lucille. *The Pioneer History of the Church of God in Christ* (1975); Dodson, Jualynne E. and Cheryl Townsend Gilkes. "Something Within: Social Change and Collective Endurance in the Sacred World of Black Christian Women." In *Women and Religion in America: Volume Three—The Twentieth Century*, ed. Rosemary Radford Ruether and Rosemary Skinner Keller (1986); Gilkes, Cheryl Townsend. "Together and in Harness: Women's Traditions in the Sanctified Church," *Signs* (Summer 1985), and "The Roles of Church and Community Mothers: Ambivalent American Sexism or Fragmented African Familyhood?" *Journal of Feminist Studies in Religion* (Fall 1986), and "The Role of Women in the Sanctified Church," *Journal of Religious Thought* (1986).

CHERYL TOWNSEND GILKES

CIVIL RIGHTS MOVEMENT

The role of African-American women in the civil rights movement has come under increasing attention over the past decade. Sociologists and historians have begun to examine in greater detail the organizations, social movements, and social networks as well as the individuals that gave birth to the civil rights protest and mobilization in the 1950s and 1960s. Previous research has tended to focus only on the period of highly visible direct confrontation and conflict that succeeded the 1954 *Brown* v. *Board of Education* decision and which prompted the legislation of the 1950s and 1960s and the ensuing executive orders, overlooking the specific roles that individuals, particularly women, had in the movement.

Although eras, organizations, types of action, or types of politics are not completely distinguished by gender, important differences in values, and in organizational roles, can be found between women and their involvement in the civil rights movement and men and their roles and direction in the civil rights movement. First, women laid the foundation for and built the organizational infrastructure that was used to conduct legal challenges, boycotts, voter registration, and other direct actions, including the most intense phases of the campaign that led to the passage of civil rights legislation. Men, however, were more likely to speak for Black organizations that existed and to interact with the external forces with whom they were in competition, namely the white political and economic leadership of the town, state, or nation. It is clear that these roles and their limitations were not acceptable to many women of the community, but a few women, such as Gloria Richardson, were, within the confines of these roles, able to participate in all phases of the movement. Second, some women approached the types of norms and values that the organizations emphasized from a more collective perspective; that is, they were more likely to emphasize the benefits of actions for the entire community, and they were more likely to subordinate their own individual achievement or goals to that of the larger community.

AFRICAN-AMERICAN ORGANIZATIONS

Political freedom has come with the increasing ability of African-Americans to develop and manage their lives through the creation and evolution of organizations capable of focusing on goals that challenged racial hierarchy, bargained with political leaders, mobilized the masses of the Black population, and competed with the racial status quo. These organizations have had, and currently have, a variety of meanings inside the Black community; the form necessarily varies with the status of its members. When they were slaves, unfree, or freed people, but in no cases citizens before 1870, when citizenship was conferred and recognized after the Civil War, or subsequently removed in combined de jure and de facto form at the turn of the century, organizations, especially political ones, took on very different forms. The issue of citizenship and its recognition placed extremely tight constraints around the evolution of political and social organizations. The racially hierarchical nature of the society virtually required separate Black organizations. Secret, camouflaged, multifunctional organizations became a necessity as a defense against routine attacks by the state and private citizens. Given the scarcity of a population with education, economic standing, and physical or social mobility, the same people often served in several different organizations. Black organizations often mix substantive policy focus and specific tasks while continuing to address issues of great complexity, ideologically and organizationally.

Historically, the form in which Black organizational life most often appeared was in connection to, within, or sponsored by a church. The church itself often served as the umbrella for a great deal of organizational activity, presided over by the minister. Ministers often also served in leadership roles in "secular" organizations; social or secular organizations often met in and were sheltered by churches, or were organized by ministers and other church members. Religious institutions thus had and continue to have a powerful influence in Black life. In some organizations their religious leadership is determined by and they are part of a more hierarchically organized denomination, while in others the church members themselves identify a minister and determine their governing structure. Almost all, however, have a formally developed system of authority in which religious, economic, and social decisions are presided over by the religious leader of the congregation, who is in all but a very few instances male.

The organization of the community, the exploration of spirituality whether in the oral tradition of the sermon or through examination of the written word in the Bible, was over the last two centuries taken on and dominated by men. Most of this had not changed significantly by the mid-twentieth century despite the fact that the day-to-day work and basic developmental activities were carried out by the women of the community.

Ella Baker, a crucial figure in the National Association for the Advancement of Colored People (NAACP), the Southern Christian Leadership Conference (SCLC), and the Student Nonviolent Coordinating Committee (SNCC), once observed: "All of the churches depended, in terms of things taking place, on women, not men. Men didn't do the things that had to be done, and you had a large number of women who were involved in the bus boycott. They [the women] were the people who kept the spirit going and the young people" (Payne 1989). This contrasted directly with the control of final decision-making and formal authority in the hands of men that Baker reported in the SCLC's failure to appoint her as its executive director even though she had been central to the organization's development and existence: "I knew from the beginning that as a woman, an older woman, in a group of ministers who are accustomed to having women largely as supporters, there was no place for me to have come into a leadership role" (Mueller 1990). After Septima Clark had developed the SCLC's citizenship schools throughout the South, which Andrew Young commended as the base for the civil rights movement, she became a member of the organization's executive board, which prompted Ralph D. Abernathy's opposition. This pattern of failure to recognize or acknowledge the important roles women played plagued women throughout the history of the civil rights movement.

Although Black women were directly involved in the day-to-day development of the civil rights movement, they were instrumental in other ways as well. The clubwomen's movement, the activities of sororities and clubs of women in cities in the South and the North at the turn of the last century, helped create the organizational and strategic foundations for the civil rights movement and political mobilization efforts over a half century later. The women who founded and joined Delta Sigma Theta and Alpha Kappa Alpha sororities, the National Association of Colored Women (NACW), the National Council of Negro Women, the Alpha Suffrage Club in Chicago, local Parent-Teacher Associations, the Independent Order of St. Luke in Richmond, and the Young Women's Christian Association (YWCA) also founded local chapters of the NAACP and the Urban League in cities and towns throughout the South. They and their successors in the middle of the century connected their social clubs, professional organizations, political groups, neighborhood associations, and churches into the Montgomery Improvement Association, the Alabama Christian Movement for Human

Rights, the SCLC, the United Defense League (Baton Rouge, Louisiana), and many other local groups that challenged the racial status quo on a community-wide basis. Ida B. Wells-Barnett, Daisy Bates, Mary Fair Burks, Fannie Lou Hamer, Diane Nash, Rosa Parks, Jo Ann Gibson Robinson, Modjeska Simkins, and Maggie Lena Walker are only a few of the women who created and extended organizational networks into many parts of the country that had been economically and politically subordinated.

INDIVIDUAL v. COLLECTIVE

A second area of involvement concerns the values incorporated within, conveyed by, and represented in the character of the organizational structure of these groups. This is a complicated, subtle, and indirect area because of the requirements of submerging and camouflaging African core values in order to ensure the collective survival of the group and its values. There is a complex and dense interaction of and competition between values of Blackness, negritude, or racial identity, that is, "the illuminated creativity produced and reproduced in the eternal fires of black rebellion," and "blanqueamiento," the "somatic, *cultural*, or ethnic lightening to become increasingly acceptable to those classified and self-identified as 'white'" (Whitten and Torres 1992).

Values such as egalitarianism and collectivism, which can be associated with Blackness or identification with communal values in the African-American community, were more strongly emphasized by some of the women activists and were incorporated into their organizational behavior. The form the Black church assumed, the men, and the roles they played within these organizations were more compatible with hierarchy and individualism. This brought them greater respect within the African-American community, but it also brought them closer to the norms, values, and institutional structures present in white society.

There was a shift from collective, community-based political meetings involving men, women, and children who participated and voted in the early post-Civil War years, to small closed meetings by the end of the century in which only a few men participated. Ella Baker remembered "the world of her childhood as a kind of 'family socialism,' a world in which food and tools and homes were shared, where informal adoption of children was taken for granted, a world with a minimal sense of social hierarchy" (Payne 1989). In her organizational life she valued "group-centered leadership rather than leader-centered groups"; and she argued that "Strong people don't need strong leaders" (Payne 1989). This put her at odds with the hierarchically structured NAACP, which used its large membership (which she had helped build in the 1940s) to finance its legal campaign but did not allow it to be activated for locally specific purposes. This same philosophy deepened the disagreements between Baker and the SCLC that were generated by her gender—a woman among male ministers; it was only when college student involvement in the civil rights movement began that she was able to put these beliefs into practice.

Baker was not alone in her communal memory of and approach to Black communities. The willingness of so many women to involve themselves deeply and completely in the social, political, religious, and organizational work in their communities, actually to create networks and literacy and health care where there had been too little, represented a highly communal and collective commitment. Alice Dunbar-Nelson, Mabel K. Staupers, Ida B. Wells-Barnett, Lugenia Burns Hope, Maggie Lena Walker, and others were often active in many different organizations simultaneously. The civil rights movement was the mobilization of a network of organizations, what Aldon Morris calls an "organization of organizations" (Morris 1984), rooted in community life, to challenge the racial status quo. Its ultimate success will be based on the mass mobilization of the entire African-American community.

BIBLIOGRAPHY

Barnett, Marguerite Ross and James A. Hefner. *Public Policy for the Black Community: Strategies and Perspectives* (1976); Brock, Annette K. "Gloria Richardson and the Cambridge Movement." In *Women in the Civil Rights Movement: Trailblazers and Torchbearers, 1941-1965*, ed. Vicki L. Crawford, Jacqueline Anne Rouse, and Barbara Woods (1990); Brown, Cynthia Stokes. *Ready from Within: Septima Clark and the Civil Rights Movement* (1986); Brown, Elsa Barkley. "Womanist Consciousness: Maggie Lena Walker and the Independent Order of Saint Luke," *Signs* (1989), and "To Catch the Vision of Freedom: Reconstructing Southern Black Women's Political History 1865-1885," Colloquium paper, Afro-American Studies and Research Program, University of Illinois, Urbana-Champaign (March 26, 1992); Burks, Mary Fair. "Trailblazers: Women in the Montgomery Bus Boycott." In *Women in the Civil Rights Movement: Trailblazers and Torchbearers, 1941-1965*, ed. Vicki L. Crawford, Jacqueline Anne Rouse, and Barbara Woods (1990); Clark, Septima. *Echo in My Soul* (1962); Crawford, Vicki. "Beyond the Human Self: Grassroots Activists in the Mississippi Civil Rights Movement." In *Women in the Civil Rights Movement: Trailblazers and Torchbearers, 1941-1965*, ed. Vicki L. Crawford, Jacqueline Anne Rouse, and Barbara Woods, eds. *Women in the Civil Rights Movement:*

Trailblazers and Torchbearers, 1941-1965 (1990); Garrow, David, ed. *The Montgomery Bus Boycott and the Women Who Started It: The Memoir of Jo Ann Gibson Robinson* (1987); Hamilton, Charles V. *The Black Preacher in America* (1972); Hine, Darlene Clark, ed. *Black Women in United States History* (1990); Littlefield, Valinda W. "A Yearly Contract with Everybody and His Brother: Durham County, North Carolina, Black Female Public High School Teachers 1885-1927," unpublished manuscript (1992); Locke, Mamie E. "Is This America? Fannie Lou Hamer and the Mississippi Freedom Democratic Party." In *Women in the Civil Rights Movement: Trailblazers and Torchbearers, 1941-1965*, ed. Vicki L. Crawford, Jacqueline Anne Rouse, and Barbara Woods (1990); McFadden, Grace Jordan. "Septima P. Clark and the Struggle for Human Rights." In *Women in the Civil Rights Movement: Trailblazers and Torchbearers, 1941-1965*, ed. Vicki L. Crawford, Jacqueline Anne Rouse, and Barbara Woods (1990); Morris, Aldon. *The Origins of the Civil Rights Movement: Black Communities Organizing for Change* (1984); Mueller, Carol. "Ella Baker and the Origins of 'Participatory Democracy.'" In *Women in the Civil Rights Movement: Trailblazers and Torchbearers, 1941-1965*, ed. Vicki L. Crawford, Jacqueline Anne Rouse, and Barbara Woods (1990); *NBAW*; Payne, Charles. "Men Led, But Women Organized: Movement Participation of Women in the Mississippi Delta." In *Women in the Civil Rights Movement: Trailblazers and Torchbearers, 1941-1965*, ed. Vicki L. Crawford, Jacqueline Anne Rouse, and Barbara Woods (1990), and "Ella Baker and Models of Social Change," *Signs* (1989); Pinderhughes, Dianne M. "The Role of African American Political Organizations in the Mobilization of Voters." In *From Exclusion to Inclusion: The Long Struggle for African American Political Power*, ed. Ralph C. Gomes and Linda Faye Williams (1992); Whitten, Norman E., Jr. and Arlene Torres. "Blackness in the Americas," *Report on the Americas: The Black Americas 1492-1992* (February 1992); Whitten, Norman E., Jr. and Arlene Torres, eds. *Blackness in Latin America and the Caribbean: Social Dynamics and Cultural Transformations* (1992).

DIANNE M. PINDERHUGHES

CIVIL WAR AND RECONSTRUCTION

The emancipation of slaves was unquestionably the single most significant event in the history of African-American women within the United States. This dramatic shift in legal status for the majority of women of African descent within the country—a shift precipitated by war and followed by sectional and political crises that continued throughout much of the century—marked a new era. Although most ex-slaves were given "nothing but freedom," and although most African-American women found "freedom" had different meanings for men and women, this momentous occasion had a permanent impact on the future of Black women in America.

Guns were fired at Fort Sumter, South Carolina, in April 1861, and within months the North and South were mobilized for battle. Southern states declared their independence and formed a Confederacy, while the North waged a fight to preserve the Union. African-Americans in the United States were affected dramatically by the war's outbreak, with nearly four million slaves residing almost entirely within the Confederate states. Only 11 percent of the Black population within the country was free, and a third of the South was Black. In addition, the majority of slaves on plantations were women; therefore, the central economic unit within the South and the institution most under siege during wartime sheltered a female majority. The urban Black population—slave and free—contained a surplus of women as well. However, evidence indicates that the small holdings of slaves in rural areas—the majority of southern slaveholders—were primarily male dominated. The portrait in Toni Morrison's novel *Beloved* (1987) of Sethe's Sweet Home, with one woman slave and several male slaves held by a single master on a small farm, was typical if not statistically average.

The typical experience of the majority of those held in bondage was the plantation, where slaves

The harsh fieldwork of Black women working during Reconstruction may have seemed identical to the labor of slave women, but to emancipated African-Americans, the opportunity to contribute to the family economy—their own, rather than a master's—symbolized freedom. [New-York Historical Society]

resided in units of twenty or more on one estate. The war threatened to fundamentally disrupt this system. First, masters and able-bodied men might enlist, leaving many plantations without male supervision. Second, many plantation mistresses left alone felt alienated and vulnerable. Third, the chaos of war created both opportunities and disadvantages for slaves left behind on estates.

The war could turn power relations upside down on the homefront. Kate McClure, a plantation mistress left behind in Union County, South Carolina, banned Maybery, the overseer hired by her husband, from entering her household. She deputized a slave, Jeff, and admitted him into her home, since she trusted her slaves more than the white man left in charge. Her resistance to the overseer's authority and her discovery of his coercive sexual relationship with a slave named Susan forced Maybery to flee the plantation. Alliances between mistresses and slaves were rarely documented during wartime, but glimmers of these bonds remain nonetheless.

A large body of anecdotal evidence was supplied by plantation owners to demonstrate the loyalty, and by implication contentment, of slaves within the Confederacy. Much of this evidence is based on recollection, consisting of highly exaggerated and perhaps fictionalized accounts meant to repudiate the cause of Yankee invaders. Slave women were reported to have cooperated in efforts to protect supplies from Yankee requisitioning. Yet there is an equal body of evidence within the records of planters as well as documents preserved by the Union army to show that flight and "Confederate treason" (also known as "Union heroism") equally typified the wartime experience of slaves.

Slaves fleeing behind federal lines provided the Union with a public relations coup as well as a dilemma. Why were slaves escaping slavery if it was the pleasant paternalistic system owners painted? But beyond the abstract, what was the army to do with these hundreds, and soon thousands, who sought refuge from the Confederacy? General Benjamin Butler classified the runaway slaves as "contrabands"—the enemy's property—appropriating them for Union use. When slaves appeared in droves at Fortress Monroe, having deserted their posts building Confederate fortifications, Butler put the runaways to work finishing a bakehouse for his troops. Congress formally ratified this policy with the First Confiscation Act in 1862, prohibiting the return of runaways to their masters, which had been a practice of some Union officers. Further, with the Second Confiscation Act of 1862, all slaves were granted their freedom when they fled the South for federal protection, except for those owned by masters in the border states who remained loyal to the Union.

This gave many slave families the opportunity to escape to freedom and to remain together. Mary Barbour recalled her family's flight: "We snook out o' de house an' long de woods path, pappy totin' one of de twins an' holding me by de han' an' mammy carryin' de odder two." Barbour's family later joined with Union soldiers, and her father became a bootmaker for the troops. Some "contrabands" suffered harassment from former owners. One former slave reported that her mistress "begged an' cried," claiming, "General dese han's never was in dough—I never made a cake o' bread in my life; please let me have my cook." General Grant refused to intercede, maintaining that the cook was free to go, but she "can do as she likes about it."

Former slave Eliza Sparks remembered a lost Union soldier seeking guidance while she was nursing her child. She directed him to his destination, and he pulled out some money from his pocket, admired her child, and asked his name. He said, "Well, you sure have a purty baby. Buy him something with this; an' thankee fo' de direction. Goodbye Mrs. Sparks." Sparks recalled the incident clearly because it was the first time she was addressed as "Mrs.," and she remarked, "Now, what do you think of dat? Dey all call me 'Mrs. Sparks'!"

These charitable acts—granting ex-slaves the dignity they deserved—were uncommon. Most slaves were aware that Union soldiers were not fighting against slavery but merely for pay. The abolitionist paper, the *Liberator*, reported a ghastly incident in August 1862: "Four soldiers went to the house of two colored men, (father and son-in-law). Two of them seized a colored woman in the front yard, each in turn gratifying his brutal lusts while the other stood guard with sword and pistol." Despite this and other examples of outrages, most slaves, freedpeople, and free African-Americans saw the Union cause as their own. Further, after the Emancipation Proclamation on January 1, 1863, the fight to preserve the Union was transformed into a battle against slavery. Black men enthusiastically enlisted for this cause.

African-American soldiers suffered enormous hardship and deprivations in their battle for society's recognition of their manhood. First, many were rejected by those who saw the war as "a white man's war." But Black participants volunteered, most notably in Massachusetts, where the first two northern regiments were formed. Also, during the fall of 1863, over 20,000 ex-slaves were recruited in the Mississippi Valley alone. Although African-Americans were less than 1 percent of the North's population, by the war's end over 180,000 African-Americans had served in the Union army. Perhaps the most famous African-American who volunteered to serve the Union was Harriet Tubman. Born a slave in Maryland, Tubman had earned fame as a conductor on the Underground Railroad, and with the outbreak of war, she redoubled her efforts to liberate the slaves, serving as nurse, scout, and spy for the Union army. Acting on information gathered during Tubman's secret missions, Colonel James Montgomery, commander of the Second Carolina Volunteers, was able to lead several successful raids on ammunition depots, supply warehouses, and other valuable Confederate strongholds along the Combahee River. Although the Confederacy put a steep price on Tubman's head, fame was her only reward, as she received less than $200 from the army during her three years of service.

Army service was an enormous sacrifice for the African-Americans who enlisted. Offered discriminatory pay and treatment, they suffered disproportionate death rates as well. Whereas one in twelve white soldiers in the Union army died of disease during the war, one in five Black soldiers succumbed. Combat deaths proved equally gruesome: at Milliken's Bend, one Black regiment lost almost 45 percent of its men. The slaughter at Fort Wagner, the executions at Fort Pillow, and the inequalities of pay and conditions wore on the Black soldier. One African-American complained in 1863: "It is rettin that a man can not Serve two master but it Seems that the Collored population has got two a rebel master and a union master. They both want our Servises one wants us to make Cotton and Sugar and Sell it and keep the money the union masters wants us to fight the battles under white officers and injoy both the money and the union."

Besides the burdens on Black soldiers, the wives and families they left behind shared in the suffering. Black women were suddenly thrown into economic chaos by a male relative's war service, as Jane Welcome complained to President Lincoln in her letter of November 21, 1864: "Mr. Abaraham lincon I wont to knw sir if you please wether I can have my son relest from the arme he is all the subport I have now his father is Dead and his brother that wase all the help that I had he has bean wonded twise he has not had nothing to send me yet." The reply was curt: "The interests of the service will not permit that your request be granted." Husbands and fathers at the front were sometimes wounded by news from home, especially the tribulations of loved ones left behind in slavery. One Missouri wife confided: "They are treating me worse and worse every day. Our child cries for you. Send me some money as soon as you can for me and my child are almost naked." The destruction of family harmony and the fears of wives and mothers wreaked havoc within the Black community, slave and free.

Wartime provided Black women—especially slaves—with new opportunities. Unlike white women, who were experiencing male work roles and taking on male responsibilities for the first time in unprecedented numbers in the fully mobilized Confederacy, slave women always had been forced to shoulder equal burdens in the productive plantation work force. The absence of white male rule and the increasing fears of white women on many plantations put slaves in better bargaining positions. Many African-Americans on plantations took advantage of this situation. They voted with their feet, and the Sea Islands of South Carolina and other areas deserted by Confederate planters became pioneering communities of ex-slaves where education, family farms, and civil rights became a part of the landscape for African-Americans within the occupied South.

The majority stayed behind—recalcitrant, rebellious, and, in the end, an effective fifth column. Historians credit the failure of nerve and the failure of rule in the plantation South as undermining Confederate independence, and they document women's roles in disrupting plantation work patterns and, in some cases, initiating work stoppages or strikes in the fields. These and other activities by Black women behind the lines disheartened plantation mistresses at a minimum, and at a maximum prevented them from maintaining discipline and productivity, key factors within the Confederate master plan.

Whatever the causes of defeat, the advent of Emancipation marked the beginning of the end of slavery. Surrender on April 9, 1865, was only the formal recognition of the loss of Confederate control. Maryland had abolished slavery in 1864 and Missouri followed in 1865. One Kentucky mother tried to take advantage of a congressional law that allowed families of Black soldiers their freedom. After she took her children away to Lexington during March 1865, she was accosted by her master's son-in-law, "who told me that if I did not go back with him he would shoot me. He drew a pistol on me as he made this threat. I could offer no resistance as he constantly kept the pistol pointed at me." She was forced to return to her owner's home and the son-in-law kept her seven-year-old as hostage. However, within two weeks of

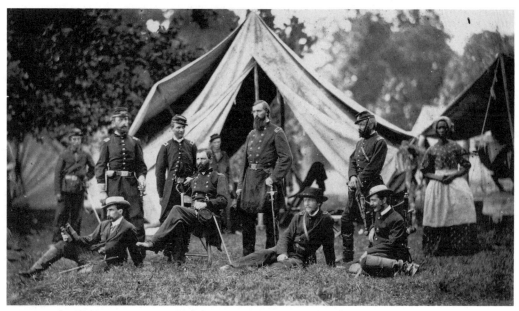

During the war, runaway slaves were classified by the Union forces as "contraband"—enemy property—and were put to work by the Union forces. This contraband camp woman served the officers of the Fifth Army Corps Headquarters at Harrison's Landing, James River, Virginia. [National Archives]

her appeal to the Freedmen's Bureau, General Robert E. Lee laid down his sword at Appomattox.

The jubilation at war's end was celebrated by most slaves in intense, dramatic fashion. Most ex-slaves interviewed by the Works Progress Administration during the 1930s recalled the momentous occasion of Union victory. The mother of author Paul Laurence Dunbar, Mathilda Dunbar, recounted her story: "I was in the kitchen getting breakfast. The word came—'All darkies are free.' I never finished breakfast! I ran 'round and 'round the kitchen, hitting my head against the wall, clapping my hands and crying 'Freedom! freedom! freedom! Rejoice, freedom has come!' Oh, how we sang and shouted that day!" (Sterling 1984). Thousands of similar celebrations echoed throughout the country, in both North and South, as Black households expressed jubilation. Maggie Lawson recounted a scene on her plantation: "Caddy threw down that hoe, she marched herself up to the big house, then, she looked around and found the mistress. She went over to the mistress, she flipped up her dress and told the white woman to do something. She said it mean and ugly. This is what she said. 'Kiss my ass'!" (Sterling 1984).

Many women, freed from the domestic tyranny of abusive mistresses, celebrated in ways calculated to offend former owners. Using dress and fashion as weapons, many freedwomen in the postwar South paraded in finery, often clothing liberated from their mistress's wardrobe. One ex-slave remembered with exasperation his wife's demand that the master's bed be dragged into their cabin, even though the massive piece of furniture occupied the entire floor space so the couple could not walk around inside their home. The freedwoman cherished this symbol of her personal liberation, as she could now sleep in the bed that she had made for almost half a century. Some women who worked as laundresses in the aftermath of the war refused the demeaning chores slavery had required, such as cleaning menstrual rags, even for pay.

Indeed, freedom had dramatically different meanings for slave men and women, although they shared common assumptions about its advantages. The passage of the Thirteenth Amendment in December 1865 abolished slavery. But the Fourteenth Amendment (introduced in 1866 and ratified in July 1868) extended citizenship rights only to males of the former slave class; this was reinforced by the Fifteenth Amendment, introduced in 1869 and ratified in 1870. By federal statute, Black women would be subjected to the same unequal status as white women. Nevertheless, freedwomen gratefully embraced the new laws of the land intended to protect Black civil rights: the right to work, the right to marry, the right to raise a family, and many other basic principles denied under slave law. Southern legislators, Freedmen's Bureau agents, and freedpeople themselves tried to untangle the snarl of status conflict during the wake of the war during the complex era of Reconstruction.

Freedwomen, deprived of alternatives, sought assistance from the Freedmen's Bureau when children were unlawfully apprenticed, when white employers drove them off the land without compensation for their labor, when husbands deserted a family, or when destitution and desperation pushed them to seek governmental intervention. Looking at the petitions for relief in one Alabama county in 1867, almost 90 percent of the petitioning households were without adult males. Mothers were most severely affected by adversity, since they were responsible for the care and feeding of children, and planters hiring hands discriminated against women with children.

Emancipation created few opportunities for Black women within the political economy. Nevertheless, many ex-slaves seized the opportunity to express themselves. This culture of articulation pioneered a new role for individual and collective African-American female identity. First, former slaveowners and most whites wanted to enforce "silence," to muzzle an increasingly outspoken Black female presence within the conquered South. In case after case cited in the Freedmen's Bureau records, whites would threaten, beat, and in some cases kill African-American women for their bold resistance to oppression. In Clinch County, Georgia, Viney Scarlett was arrested and given sixty-five lashes for using abusive language to a white woman. This revealed a bleak and abusive double standard. An article in a Black newspaper in Augusta questioned, "Why is it that the wives and daughters of freedmen, though they be chaste as ice, and pay the same fare that white people do on railways, are put into filthy freight cars and compelled to submit to all kinds of vulgar and insulting language?" (Clinton and Silber 1992). Black leaders vehemently objected to women's ejection from the "ladies car" and protested the use of the term "colored females," demanding the appellation "ladies." Freedpeople did not seek social status—the niceties of ladyhood were irrelevant—but racial dignity and personal integrity were central to African-American campaigns. Ex-slaves sought protection of women and, by extension, all persons of

In 1862, the First Confiscation Act prohibited the return of runaway slaves to their masters, and the Second Confiscation Act granted slaves their freedom when they fled the South for federal protection, unless they were owned by masters in border states who remained loyal to the Union. This photograph shows a school for the runaways, or contrabands. [National Archives]

These refugee quarters were located in Hilton Head, South Carolina. [National Archives]

African descent who were handicapped by the racism that continued to poison southern society.

Both Black men and women suffered dehumanization as victims of the ridicule, caricature, and eventual violence that white racists promoted. The exact nature and impact of abuse varied, most acutely in matters of sexual violence. Slave women were subject to harassment, coercion, abuse, and rape, practices that did not end with Emancipation. Some planters attempted to reinstitute liaisons with their former slave concubines. Women workers in the fields, forced to labor on plantations, found themselves vulnerable to sexual threats by white supervisors. A climate of intimidation and violence prevented Black men from retaliation against white aggressors. Further, increasing numbers of white southern males, frustrated by postwar economic gloom and blaming ex-slaves, joined in the crusade to "redeem" and to restore white supremacy in the South.

Some of these campaigns involved hooded nighttime raids, lynching, and the sexual violation of African-American women. For example, in Louisiana during the fall of 1868, the Freedmen's Bureau compiled a massive record of complaints of violence under the heading, "Murders and Outrages." By October, over 100 freedpeople were reported dead, and terrorism against African-Americans was on the rise. One agent in Claiborne Parish confided that nine or ten men, armed and disguised, had beaten and "ravished" a woman, but "the freedpeople will not divulge anything for fear of death." In another chilling example, the wife of George Band was hanged on a tree by the Ku Klux Klan before they "hacked her to death with knives" (Clinton and Silber 1992). Band was able to surprise these terrorists with his Winchester rifle and

kill fourteen of the murderers, but was forced to flee his home to save his life. The conquered Confederates did not so much surrender as take the war home.

Unfortunately for southern Black women, Reconstruction escalated the degree of violence, especially sexual violation, to which they might be subjected. Slave women were prey to the abuses of their owners, but with Emancipation white men as a race rather than slaveowners as a class viewed sexual trespass as a privilege, a right that might reinstitute white supremacy. A white character in Jean Toomer's *Cane* fantasizes that he rapes a Black woman, Louisa: "He went in as a master should and took her. Direct, honest, bold." Although Louisa meets him regularly for consensual sex, the white man rages: "None of this sneaking that he had to go through now. The contrast was repulsive to him. His family had lost ground." African-American women struggled against this tide of violence and resentment, seeking respectability as a shield in increasingly perilous times.

Despite the perils, Reconstruction was a period during which institutions that had been invisible during slavery emerged, namely, the church, marriage, kinship ties and fraternal networks, and the exchange of goods and services. African-American women were in the forefront of movements for education. Southern Black women teachers, like Mary S. Peake and Susie King Taylor (who was a laundress and a nurse during her war service), and African-American women from the North (celebrated by W.E.B. Du Bois as the "tenth crusade"), like Charlotte Forten, worked together to make the next generation better prepared to enjoy the freedom that had been thrust upon them. Black southern women were central to building the cooperatives, burial societies, and savings and loan associations established in the wake of the war. The groundswell of self-help organizations that blossomed in devastated southern towns and cities sustained African-American migrants fleeing harsh conditions in the countryside. The bulwark of the Black community, the Black church, was nurtured by women members whose charity and good works filled every corner of the South. Finally, women banded together to plant the seeds for the club movement that would flourish by the century's end. Through these bonds of Black womanhood, mighty strides were made. Gains were even more impressive when measured against the overwhelming odds stacked against freedpeople during Reconstruction.

Black working women tried to use collective bargaining as a defense against worsening economic conditions. In Mississippi in June 1866, "the Washerwomen of Jackson" addressed the mayor of the city in the daily paper, petitioning for better and uniform wages: $1.50 a day for washing, $15 per month for family washing, and $10 per month for individuals. African-American women in towns and cities wanted recognition of their invaluable labor, especially as domestic servants in white households, to improve or empower their weak roles in the southern economy. Their ability to negotiate diminished considerably in rural areas, where hundreds of thousands of poor Black women had little or no opportunity to improve deteriorating economic lots. By 1870 eight out of ten Black children remained illiterate. Southern state legislatures were preparing to write into law Jim Crow practices enforcing segregation, which began in Tennessee in 1881. The withdrawal of federal troops from the South in 1877 signaled a halt of African-American gains, and dreams slipped away along with Yankee guardians.

White backlash decreased Black hopes of a steady path to permanent progress. Rather, the march to equality would be marked by obstacles, detours, and detainment along the way, even after the great signpost of freedom that had accompanied the Civil War. African-American women would nevertheless continue the course, journeying forward on the path begun by their foremothers, down the road to a better life for those who would follow.

BIBLIOGRAPHY

Berlin, Ira, et al., eds. *Freedom: A Documentary History of Emancipation, 1861-1867* (1982); Clinton, Catherine, and Nina Silber, ed. *Divided Houses: Gender and the Civil War* (1992); Foner, Eric. *Reconstruction: America's Unfinished Revolution* (1988); Jones, Jacqueline. *Labor of Love, Labor of Sorrow: Black Women, Work, and the Family from Slavery to the Present* (1985); Quarles, Benjamin. *The Negro in the Civil War* (1969); Schwalm, Leslie. "The Meaning of Freedom:

This store for freed people was located in Beaufort, South Carolina, in 1864.
[National Archives]

African-American Women and Their Transition from Slavery to Freedom in Lowcountry South Carolina," Ph.D. diss. (1991); Sterling, Dorothy, ed. *We Are Your Sisters: Black Women in the Nineteenth Century* (1984); Stevenson, Brenda, ed. *The Journals of Charlotte Forten Grimké* (1988); Taylor, Susie King. *A Black Woman's Civil War Memoirs*, ed. Patricia W. Romero (1988).

CATHERINE CLINTON

CLARK, SEPTIMA POINSETTE (1898-1987)

From the Sea Islands of South Carolina to urban and rural areas throughout the Southeast, Septima Poinsette Clark's citizenship schools galvanized local citizens who transformed the social, political, economic, and cultural issues of the United States. She was born on May 3, 1898, in Charleston, South Carolina, the daughter of Peter Poinsette, who was born a slave on the Joel Poinsette Plantation, and Victoria Warren Anderson Poinsette, who was born free in Charleston and spent her early years in Haiti. Her mother boasted that her Haitian upbringing better prepared her for the racist United States society. Her mother's dignified and assertive attitude and her father's gentle and nonviolent composure gave Clark the characteristics to work in the South during the civil rights era. She stressed, "When I went to Mississippi and Texas and places like that, I had a feeling that his non-violence helped me to work with people and her haughtiness helped me to stay. We had a lot of harassment from the KKK and the White Citizen's Council in Tuscaloosa, Alabama and Grenada and Natchez, Mississippi" (McFadden 1980).

Clark's parents instilled in their eight children the importance of education. She attended Avery Institute in Charleston. The liberal arts school was founded in 1865 through the joint effort of philanthropist Charles Avery and the American Missionary Association. In 1916, she completed the twelfth grade at Avery, took the state examination, and received the Licentiate of Instruction that enabled her to teach in rural areas. African-Americans were not allowed to teach in the public schools of Charleston. Her first teaching job was on John's Island, South Carolina, where she remained until 1919. It was here that her dedication to service and citizenship education commenced. John's Island had dismal economic, social, and health conditions in 1916. Septima Poinsette lived in an attic room with no inside toilet. Workers signed contracts and were employed in tasks on large plantations. Women carried their children to the fields and placed them in boxes at the end of the row where they were working. A "sugar tit"—lard and sugar—was placed in the babies' mouths to squelch crying. A health problem began as a result of the flies and mosquitoes that bit the babies, often causing malaria. Poinsette observed that many babies failed to "reach the second summer." These conditions motivated her to assist in bringing health reforms to the Sea Islands. Conducting workshops on health issues was a segment of citizenship education.

Her work on John's Island prepared her for confronting unequal teachers' salaries and unequal teaching facilities. Her school, the Promiseland School, was made of logs with clay in the cracks. It had no glass windows, only a shutter that was closed when the wind was high. The chimney heated the children who sat in the front. The benches were without backs, and the children learned to read and write kneeling on the floor. The building was creosoted black. It had two teachers and 132 children; Poinsette was a teaching principal. Together they received $60. Across the road in a whitewashed building was a white teacher with three students. She was paid $85. The discrepancy cemented Poinsette's resolve to become a provocateur for the equalization of teachers' salaries.

Septima Poinsette [Clark] taught at Avery Institute from 1919 to 1921. While there, she joined nationally renowned artist Edwin Harelston and former Reconstruction congressman Thomas E. Miller in their drive to collect 10,000 signatures to demonstrate to the South Carolina legislature that all African-Americans in South Carolina, regardless of their economic status, believed that Black teachers should be allowed to teach in Charleston's public schools. An affirmative law was passed in 1920. Clark was only twenty-two years old, but she felt this to be her first effort to establish for Negro citizens what she firmly believed to be their God given rights. She was now known as an advocate for equal rights.

Septima P. Clark faced housing discrimination following the death of her husband, Nerie Clark, who succumbed to kidney failure in December 1925. They had married in May 1920 and had two children. The first, a daughter, died within a month of her birth. Their second child was Nerie Clark, Jr. Following her husband's death, Clark lived in Hickory, North Carolina; Payton, Ohio; and John's Island, South Carolina (1927-29), until settling in Columbia, South Carolina, where she remained until 1946. In 1935, she sent her son to Hickory, North Carolina, to live with his paternal grandparents because she was not financially able to support him and most boarding-houses did not allow children. A positive result of the separation was that she had the freedom to pursue her studies, receiving her B.A. from Benedict College in 1942 and her M.A. from Hampton Institute in 1945. In 1937, she studied at Atlanta University with the eminent scholar W.E.B. Du Bois. Du Bois's lectures on racism and segregation helped Clark understand the link between protest and education and assured her that dedication to the eradication of segregation was a noble pursuit. His endeavors toward excellence and scholarly research enhanced her documentation of events as well as her commitment to writing. This became very vivid as she reported the successes of citizenship schools throughout the South.

While living in Columbia Clark worked to converge the social and political reforms of African-American organizations. Unity was strength. She affiliated with the Federated Women's Club of South Carolina, the Columbia Young Women's Christian Association (Black component), the Palmetto Education Association, and the National Association for the Advancement of Colored People (NAACP). She strongly endorsed the overall mission of the South Carolina Conference of Branches of the NAACP: "To insure the political, educational, social and economic equality of minority group citizens to remove all barriers of racial discrimination through democratic processes."

In Columbia she taught in the elementary department of Booker T. Washington School. On the same corridor was civil rights leader Modjeska M. Simkins, who taught algebra in the mathematics department. They and others joined Booker T. Washington principal J. Andrew Simmons, South Carolina NAACP attorney Harold Bloulware, and NAACP counsel Thurgood Marshall in preparing a court case for the equalization of teachers' salaries. Clark openly worked against some of the people who were directing the system for which she worked. One man, C. A. Johnson, Superintendent of Negro Schools, thought that it was foolish for teachers to bring the salary issue to the courts. Equalization of teachers' salaries became a law in 1945 as a result of the Viola Duvall class action suit. Federal District Judge J. Waties Waring rendered the decision. Clark returned to Charleston in 1947 in order to aid her ailing mother. She taught school and actively participated in civil rights activities, serving as membership chairperson of the local NAACP.

The South Carolina NAACP in the 1940s was a major force in eradicating unjust laws in the Palmetto State. Because of its challenge to the status quo, the association suffered the wrath of relentless politicians. In 1945, it had been successful in the Viola Duvall case. The same year it had been instrumental in the case of *John H. Wrighten* v. *the University of South Carolina.* Wrighten's denial of entry to the University of South Carolina law school prompted the establishment of a law school at South Carolina State College. In 1947, in *Elmore* v. *Rice*, the South Carolina NAACP helped break the "whites only" membership barrier to the Democratic party, which denied African-Americans the right to vote in primary elections. *Briggs* v. *Elliott* (Clarendon County, S.C.) was one of the test cases that led to *Brown* v. *Board of Education*, outlawing segregation in public schools. The South Carolina NAACP had become more radical and confrontational.

On April 19, 1956, the South Carolina legislature passed a law stipulating that no city employee could affiliate with any civil rights organization. The law was an attempt to minimize the effectiveness of the NAACP. Septima P. Clark was dismissed from her teaching job when she refused to quit the NAACP and to stop her activities to protest the "affiliation statute." She was fifty-eight years old and had been teaching for forty years. She lost not only her job but also her retirement benefits. From 1956 to 1976 she confronted the system that dismissed her until she received annual stipends to restore her retirement monies.

Myles Horton, director of Highlander Folk School in Monteagle, Tennessee, recruited her as director of workshops. Clark had attended workshops at Highlander and was inspired by its humanistic, biracial approach to solving the nation's problems. She mobilized Highlander to support the social programs of people such as Esau Jenkins of John's Island, South Carolina, and Rosa Parks of Montgomery, Alabama. Rosa Parks was sent a scholarship to attend workshops at Highlander. She gained knowledge of civil disobedience, which sparked her defiance of segregation statutes in Montgomery, Alabama, leading to the Montgomery bus boycott of 1955. With the assistance of Myles Horton and the expertise of Septima P. Clark and Bernice Robinson, who later directed citizenship schools on John's Island, Jenkins opened a night school for adults in 1956 which became the prototype for citizenship schools that emerged throughout the South.

Literacy training and democratic empowerment were among the goals of the citizenship schools. Between 1956 and 1961, Clark traveled throughout the South working in citizenship education, teaching people to write their names, balance check books,

Septima Poinsette Clark's citizenship schools emphasized citizenship training, literacy, and domestic empowerment. Clark is seen here, at center, with Rosa Parks (left) and Leona McCauley (right), the mother of Rosa Parks, at Highlander Folk School in December 1956. [Highlander Folk School]

vote in elections, and write letters. Millions of people were direct recipients. Seven hundred teachers working in the schools and thousands of people were registered to vote. Septima P. Clark helped transform the southern political system.

In 1961 she joined the Southern Christian Leadership Conference (SCLC) as director of education and teaching. This position paralleled her work at Highlander, focusing on citizenship training, voting, and literacy. At sixty-three years of age, the "grand lady of civil rights" traveled throughout the South directing citizenship schools. She faced the wrath of the KKK and the White Citizen's Council, observed beatings, harassment, shootings, and killings. She stood her ground and never lost sight of her mission—social, economic, educational, and political parity for all citizens. By 1963 she was concerned that many states were dissolving their citizenship schools because of the lack of follow-up. Many, she felt, preferred the dramatic impact of direct action over the daily routine that came with genuine citizenship education. She observed that follow-up and dedicated service were essential for the continuation of her life's quest of citizenship education. Clark maintained, nonetheless, that citizenship schools had a powerful impact

not only in the quest for civil rights but for women's rights as well.

In her later years Clark revealed that women such as Ella Baker and Rosa Parks had never received their rightful place in the civil rights movement. Even Clark's position on the executive board of the SCLC was questioned because she was a woman. She credited Martin Luther King, Jr., with being one of the few civil rights leaders who viewed women as equal to men. A great amount of work was done by women, but they seldom received the notoriety.

The citizenship schools of the SCLC enhanced social and political progress in eleven Deep South states. After departing from the SCLC, Clark conducted workshops for the American Field Service, raised money for scholarships, organized day care facilities, and remained a spokesperson for civil rights. In 1975, she was elected to the Charleston School Board. In 1978, the College of Charleston awarded her an Honorary Doctorate of Humane Letters. In 1979, President Jimmy Carter presented her with a Living Legacy Award. A section of the Charleston Highway is named in her honor. In 1982, she received the Order of the Palmetto, South Carolina's highest award.

Septima Poinsette Clark, political activist, educational reformer, proponent of citizenship education, and civil rights crusader, died December 15, 1987, in Charleston, South Carolina.

[See also HIGHLANDER FOLK SCHOOL.]

BIBLIOGRAPHY

Clark, Septima Poinsette. "Citizenship and Gospel," *Journal of Black Studies* (June 1980), and *Echo in My Soul* (1962); Heyes, Sam. "Civil Rights Hero Gets Recognition—Decades Overdue," *Atlanta Constitution* (May 21, 1987); Hughes, C. Alvin. "A New Agenda for the South: The Role and Influence of the Highlander Folk School, 1953-1961," *Phylon* (September 1985); McFadden, Grace Jordan. *The Oral Recollections of Septima P. Clark* (1980), and "Septima P. Clark and the Struggle for Human Rights." In *Women in the Civil Rights Movement*, ed. Vicki Crawford, Jacqueline Anne Rouse, and Barbara Woods (1990); Papers of Septima P. Clark. College of Charleston, Robert Scott Small Library, Charleston, South Carolina; Yarbrough, Tinsley E. *A Passion for Justice: J. Waties Waring and Civil Rights* (1987).

GRACE JORDAN McFADDEN

CLEAVER, KATHLEEN NEAL
(1945-)

Kathleen Cleaver held one of the highest positions in the Black Panther Party in 1960s and worked to build an international base for the party; today she teaches law.

Kathleen Neal Cleaver was born May 13, 1945, in Dallas, Texas, the first child of Dr. Ernest Neal and Juette Johnson Neal. At the time of her birth her father was on the faculty at Wiley College. Shortly thereafter her father joined the foreign service and Cleaver spent her childhood and teen years abroad, spending time in New Delhi, the Philippines, Liberia, and Sierra Leone.

An honor student, she graduated in 1963 from the George School, a Quaker boarding school, outside of Philadelphia. Cleaver entered Oberlin College, transferred to Barnard College, and dropped out in 1966 to join the Student Nonviolent Coordinating Committee (SNCC).

Cleaver began in the New York office then moved to the organization's headquarters in Atlanta in January 1967, where she was secretary of SNCC's campus program. While organizing a Black students' conference in Nashville in the spring of 1967 she met Eldridge Cleaver, then Black Panther Party (BPP)

Minister of Information. They married on December 27, 1967.

Kathleen Cleaver left SNCC in November 1967 to join the BPP in San Francisco, an organization more radical and confrontational than SNCC. She became a member of the Party's central committee, the highest decision-making body, and served as national communications secretary.

Cleaver was the first woman included in the central committee. She delivered speeches across the country and organized the "Free Huey" campaigns (rousing support for the jailed minister of defense of the BPP, Huey Newton) in 1968. She campaigned, unsuccessfully, on the Peace and Freedom party independent ticket in the 1968 election.

In June 1969, Kathleen Cleaver joined her husband in exile in Algeria where they established an international branch of the BPP. Shortly after her arrival she gave birth to a son, Maceo. A second child, a daughter, Jojuyounghi, was born in 1970 in North Korea.

The international branch of the BPP was expelled from the national organization in 1971. Kathleen Cleaver and a new group of former Panthers initiated the Revolutionary People's Communications Network, which she promoted both nationally and abroad.

In 1975 Kathleen Cleaver returned to the United States after her husband surrendered to U.S. authorities. She lived in California with her family until 1981. Later that year she and her children moved to New Haven, Connecticut, where she completed a Bachelor's degree in history at Yale University. In 1988 she graduated from Yale Law School and joined the New York City law firm of Cravath, Swaine and Moore.

Cleaver divorced Eldridge Cleaver and, in 1991, moved to Philadelphia, Pennsylvania, where she became a law clerk in the Third District Court of Appeals. In 1992, Cleaver began teaching law at Emory University in Atlanta, Georgia.

[See also BLACK PANTHER PARTY.]

BIBLIOGRAPHY

Anthony, Earl. *Picking up the Gun: A Report on the Black Panthers* (1970); *Black Panther Intercommunal News Service* (1968-71); *Black Scholar* (December 1971); *Ebony* (March 1988); *Essence* (May 1970); Cleaver, Kathleen Neal. Interview (November 1991); Marine, Gene. *The Black Panthers* (1969); Rout, Kathleen. *Eldridge Cleaver* (1991).

ANGELA D. BROWN

CLIFF, MICHELLE (1946-)

Michelle Cliff, poet, novelist, and essayist, was born on November 2, 1946, in Kingston, Jamaica. From age three to ten she lived in New York City, where she maintained her American citizenship. Returning to Jamaica, she attended private girls' schools, where the severity of intraracial violence with its color/caste system of privilege and condemnation converged with the omnipresent colonial past to mark her indelibly. These lines of light and dark, alienation and acceptance, confinement and escape, retribution and complacency, mark all of her writing. In her writing, characters are often portrayed as ghosts among the living who try to sort out the "Jamaica I" (or spiritual "I") from the "I and I" (or the personal "I"). Cliff left Jamaica to complete her education in London, where she received an A.B. from Wagner College in 1969 and a Master's degree in philosophy from the Warburg Institute in 1974.

Cliff's writing clearly reflects her work as a reporter, researcher, editor, historian, and teacher—jobs she has held in the public sphere. Her writing can be spare and cryptic, intermingling patois and Standard English. Although her works contain historical detail, they always return to the autobiographical. Her interest in the British colonial history of Jamaica as well as the American colonial history of slavery can both be considered autobiographical due to her dual citizenship.

Her first novel, *Abeng* (1984), expresses the themes of alienation, colonialism, and color consciousness that inform all her work. The background for the characters Clare and Zoe are first outlined in her autobiographical essay "If I Could Write This in Fire, I Would Write It in Fire." In that essay, as in the novel, the privileges of class and almost white skin lead one woman away from Jamaica to education and success, while the other, Zoe, remains on the island, trapped by poverty and her dark skin. *Abeng* also recalls the essay's response to colonialism: "We are here because you were there."

No Telephone to Heaven (1987) is about Clare Savage's return to her grandmother's land. The novel weaves back and forth in time from Clare's first leaving Jamaica with her parents to her return to her grandmother's farm, which has fallen into ruination. This novel pursues the subject of immigration and passing, with its attendant humiliation and conflated images of loss. If one passes for white, Black culture is lost; if one passes for Black, privilege is lost. First, there is the loss of Jamaica as motherland; next, the loss of the grandmother in Jamaica while the Savage family is exiled in New York; then the loss of the mother who, unable to bear American racism, departs for Jamaica, where she dies, separated from her husband and their eldest daughter, Clare. When Clare realizes that she has lost her father, ironically named Boy Savage, to assimilation and an Italian-American lover, she departs for London and more education. There she confronts her British colonial past from a different perspective and finally flees to Jamaica.

Cliff's most recent novel, *Bodies of Water* (1990), continues the journey motif as characters involve themselves in various kinds of crossings. Having described her writing as "fabulous," "mythic," and "insane," Cliff exposes these tendencies in *Bodies of Water*. Although the novel can be read as individual short stories, characters reappear in different stories, forming networks that tie together the entire work. *Bodies of Water* fictionalizes history, weaving it into myth, legend, and folklore. The title story brings together ghosts from Jess Dillon's past who serve as guides to help her understand her present aloneness, exile, speechlessness, and silence. Cliff parallels the supposed madness of an old woman bereft of her lover with her memories of her brother's forced treatments for homosexuality. Homosexuality serves as a metaphor for a split consciousness in which a person is colonized by his or her other. In this way, *Bodies of Water* recalls *No Telephone to Heaven* and Harry/Harriet's dictum: "Cyan [can't] live split. Not in this world."

Cliff's other books, *Claiming an Identity They Taught Me to Despise* (1980) and *The Land of Look Behind* (1985), reveal her skill as an essayist and poet. She describes *Claiming an Identity*, a collection of prose and poetry, as an expression of her heritage and status in the world: "halfway between Africa and England, patriot and expatriate, White and Black" ("Journey into Speech"). She sees the book as an "honest self-portrait of who I was at the time. . . . Someone . . . who wrote from a feminist consciousness and a rapidly evolving consciousness of colonialism, and a knowledge of self-hatred." In pursuing her craft, Cliff follows the advice of Clare's mother in *No Telephone to Heaven*: "Make something of yourself, and someday help your people."

BIBLIOGRAPHY

Cliff, Michelle. "A Journey into Speech." In *Multi-Cultural Literacy: Opening the American Mind*, ed. Rick Simonson and Scott Walker (1988), and "If I Could Write This in Fire, I Would Write This in Fire." In *Homegirls*, ed. Barbara Smith (1983); Cliff, Michelle, ed. *The Winner Names the Age: A Collection of Writing by Lillian Smith*

(1978); Dejanikus, Tacie and Loie Hayes. "An Interview with Michelle Cliff," *Off Our Backs* (June 1981).

YVONNE FONTENEAU

CLIFTON, LUCILLE (1936-)

Lucille Clifton says plainly: "I am a woman and I write from that experience. I am a Black woman and I write from that experience. I do not feel inhibited or bound by what I am. That does not mean that I have never had bad scenes relating to being Black and/or a woman, it means that other people's craziness has not managed to make me crazy. At least not in their way because I try very hard not to close my eye to my own craziness nor to my family's, my sex's, nor my race's" (Evans 1984).

This statement is an apt introduction to Clifton's writing, both for adults and for young people. She is one of the most prolific writers of picture books created out of an African-American consciousness and experience. She is also a 1980 Pulitzer Prize nominee for *Two-Headed Woman*, one of her poetry collections for adults. Always, she writes about the totality of who she is—an African-American woman who is a parent, a teacher, a daughter, a writer, a member of a kin group and a community.

The daughter of Thelma Moore Sayles and Samuel L. Sayles, Sr., Thelma Lucille Sayles was born in Depew, New York, on June 27, 1936. At seventeen, she entered Howard University, where she held a full scholarship and majored in drama. Leaving there after two years (1953-55), she attended Fredonia State Teachers College in New York. She met Ishmael Reed in a writers' group and he showed her poems to Langston Hughes, who included a few pieces in his anthology *Poetry of the Negro*. She met her husband, Fred Clifton, through this group. They were married in 1958.

Lucille Clifton worked as a claims clerk for the New York State Division of Employment in Buffalo (1958-60). From 1969 through 1971, she was a literature assistant for the U.S. Office of Education in Washington, D.C. It was during this period that her writing began to attract attention. In 1969 she was the recipient of the Young Men's and Young Women's Hebrew Association (YM-YWHA) Poetry Center (New York City) Discovery Award, and she won the first of her several National Endowment for the Arts grants (also 1970, 1972). Her first book of poems, *Good Times*, was published in 1969 by Random House

and chosen by the *New York Times* as one of the ten best books of the year.

When her first book appeared, Lucille Clifton was thirty-three years old and the mother of six children under the age of ten: Sidney, Fredrica, Channing, Gillian, Graham, and Alexia. During the following year, 1970, she published her first book for children, *Some of the Days of Everett Anderson*. This book was influenced by her experiences with her own family, and when her husband died, she explored the stages of mourning in *Everett Anderson's Goodbye* (1983).

Everett has gone on to be the main character in six more books to date, and he is an important character for a host of reasons. Through him, Clifton explores the meanings of the word/concept "black" as used in our culture and language. At bedtime in *Some of the Days*, she wrote, " 'Afraid of the dark / is afraid of Mom / and Daddy / and Papa / and Cousin Tom. / I'd be a silly / as I could be / afraid of the dark / is afraid of me!' / Says ebony / Everett / Anderson." Through Everett, Clifton depicts a child who clearly has been raised in an African-American household. At age seven, during September in *Everett Anderson's Year* (1974), he asserts frankly: "I already know where Africa is / and I already know how to count to ten and / I went to school every day last year / why do I have to go again?" For Everett and his mother, knowledge of Africa is just as fundamental as the skill of counting. His sense of self and identity is secure, and this is evident to any reader. This fact, for the young Black reader, functions as a stabilizing and assuring force. For the white reader, it should merely accentuate the characterization. In fact, there are white and other non-Black characters in Clifton's children's books, but Everett Anderson's voice is an especially powerful and memorable one.

For her contribution to changing the face of American children's literature, as well as for her poetry and nonfiction, various organizations have honored Lucille Clifton over the years. Between 1972 and 1976, she served as a visiting writer at Columbia University School of the Arts and as poet-in-residence at Coppin State College in Baltimore. From 1979 through 1982, she was Poet Laureate for the State of Maryland. She was a visiting writer at George Washington University from 1982 to 1983. In 1980, the same year as her Pulitzer Prize nomination, she won the Juniper Prize. In 1974, Clifton's *Don't You Remember* was named a Coretta Scott King Honor Book by the American Library Association. This is one of the most prestigious awards given in the world of children's literature, annually honoring the most distinguished books published by African-American writers and illustrators. Clifton, along with other recipients of this honor, deem it their honor, and in many cases their responsibility, to speak to African-American young people.

One of Clifton's main concerns in writing for children is that such work needs to portray and sustain the African-American community. In *The Black BC's* (1970) she says, "B is for Books / where readers find / treasures for the heart / and mind," and then later, "Y is for Youth / if any man / or men can save us / the young folk can." The relationship between Black children's literature and the larger African-American literary canon is, in a literary, sociological, and historical sense, that literacy has always been a treasure chest for Black Americans.

This concern with writing, with books, with literacy, is just one link between Clifton's children's and adult literature. She also explores issues such as physical appearances, religion, and spirituality in the Black community.

Clifton's concern with the dialogue between the child and the adult is evident not only within her children's literature, but also between her children's and adult writing. Her girl characters talk about the virtues of good hair as opposed to natural hair and in "Homage to my hair" in *Two-Headed Woman* (1980), her adult voice tells us that her hair has the ability to "jump and dance." By exploring issues such as physical beauty, the significance of names, and the meaning of freedom throughout her children's and adult literature, she creates a dialogue between the young and the mature. She is concerned, always, with continuities within communities and across generations. *Generations: A Memoir* (1976) is one of Clifton's most acclaimed books, and in it she appeals to readers with the power of her own family's history/mythology.

Lucille Clifton has been a member of various organizations: International PEN, Authors' Guild of Authors' League of America, Maryland State Committee for Black Art and Culture, and the Windsor Hills Association. Yet her most enduring membership is the one she holds in the African-American community. This is a community whose experience she chronicles, interprets, and celebrates. Knowing the value of all that is positive, she tells us in *Good Times* (1969) to "think about the good times." In *Good News about the Earth* (1972), writing of the positive, the negative, and the love, she tells us to "pass it on."

Lucille Clifton now lives in California where she is a tenured professor at the University of California, Santa Cruz.

BIBLIOGRAPHY

Bain, Virginia, Patricia Clements and Isobel Grundy, eds. *The Feminist Companion to Literature in English: Women Writers from the Middle Ages to the Present* (1990); *CA*; *Children's Literature Review* (1981); *Dictionary of American Poets Since WW II* (1978); *DLB*; Evans, Mari, ed. *Black Women Writers, 1950-1980* (1984); Holtze, Sally Holmes, ed. *Fifth Book of Junior Authors and Illustrators* (1988); *Twentieth-Century Children's Writers* (1989).

SELECTED WORKS BY LUCILLE CLIFTON

For adults: *Good Times* (1969); *Good News about the Earth: New Poems* (1972); *An Ordinary Woman* (1974); *Generations: A Memoir* (1976); *Two-Headed Woman* (1980); *Next: New Poems* (1987). For young people: *Some of the Days of Everett Anderson* (1970); *The Black BC's* (1970); *All Us Come Cross the Water* (1973); *The Times They Used to Be* (1974, 1976); *Everett Anderson's Year* (1974); *Don't You Remember* (1974); *The Lucky Stone* (1979); *Everett Anderson's Goodbye* (1983).

DIANNE JOHNSON-FEELINGS

CLINTON, MARIE CLAY *see* NORTH CAROLINA FEDERATION OF COLORED WOMEN'S CLUBS

COACHMAN, ALICE (1921-)

Alice Coachman's reign over high jump competition in the United States began in 1939 when she won her first national championship. The first Black woman Olympic champion demonstrated exemplary determination, and her dominance of the high bar was unparalleled. For nearly a decade, her opponents knew they would finish no better than second.

Alice Coachman (Davis) was born on November 9, 1921, in Albany, Georgia, to Fred and Evelyn Jackson Coachman. In an era when few girls entered high-performance sport, Coachman's interest in the high jump began when she attended a boys' track and field meet. Intrigued with the sport, she began jumping over ropes. She left Albany for the first time at age sixteen to enter a meet at Tuskegee Institute in Alabama. Officials began rewriting the record books when Coachman, without shoes, broke the high school and collegiate high jump records. Coach Cleve Abbott of Tuskegee invited her to train with his team during the summer of 1939. Preparatory school students and collegians comprised Tuskegee's track and field teams.

After lengthy family debate, Coachman gained the approval of her parents and enrolled at Tuskegee Preparatory School.

Coachman's stellar performance at national Amateur Athletic Union meets contributed to Tuskegee Institute's reputation as a power in women's track and field. From 1941 to 1948, she won three 100-meter dash titles, finished second in that event three times, ran on two championship relay teams, and won five 50-meter dash titles. On four occasions she won the national individual high-point title. While competing for Tuskegee and in her senior year at Albany State College, Coachman won a dozen national indoor and outdoor high jump titles and was named to five All-American teams. She also excelled in basketball at both schools and was an All-American guard at Tuskegee.

During the 1948 Olympic trials at the Brown University stadium, Coachman eclipsed the American high jump record by an inch and a half. In spite of back pain, she cleared the bar at 5 feet 4¾ inches and secured a place on the Olympic team. On the eve of the Olympic high jump competition at the London Olympics, Coach Catherine Meyer reminded Coachman that she was the only American woman who had a chance of winning a medal. Upon entering the stadium, Coachman concentrated more on Meyer's words than on the 65,000 spectators. During the final moments of the high jump, all other events had ceased and the crowd was enthralled with the duel between Coachman and Dorothy Tyler of Great Britain. Both jumpers were credited with a new Olympic record of 5 feet 6¼ inches, but Coachman had fewer misses and was awarded the gold medal. The first Black woman Olympic champion concluded her sterling competitive career.

After graduating from Albany State College with a major in home economics and a minor in science, Coachman began teaching physical education. Her background in nutrition, science, and sports was put to use at South Carolina State College, Albany State College, and Tuskegee High School. Her son, Richmond, and her daughter, Evelyn, were versatile athletes. Now retired, she currently resides with her second husband, Frank Davis, in Tuskegee, Alabama.

Coachman competed when society at large did not embrace sportswomen and excelled in international sports during an era of limited fanfare. She was a pioneer who competed because she loved sports. She has been inducted into eight halls of fame, including the National Track and Field Hall of Fame, the Georgia Sports Hall of Fame, and the Albany Sports Hall of Fame.

BIBLIOGRAPHY

Chicago Tribune. "Tuskegee Girl Beats Stella Walsh in Track" (July 1, 1945); Davis, Alice Coachman. Telephone interview; Lacy, Sam. "Tuskegee Girls Win National AAU Track and Field Championships in Landslide," *Baltimore Afro-American* (April 15, 1944); Meyer, Catherine D. "Women's Track and Field Report of Committee Chairman," *Report of the United States Olympic Committee 1948 Games XIV Olympiad, London, England* (1948); *New York Times.* "Three Events Won by Stella Walsh" (August 16, 1943).

PAULA WELCH

COATES, DOROTHY McGRIFF LOVE (1928-)

Dorothy Love Coates is one of the protean gospel talents, celebrated as a singer, group leader, composer, and arranger. She was born Dorothy McGriff on January 30, 1928, in Birmingham, Alabama. After her father, a minister, abandoned his wife and six children, McGriff quit school to support her mother. Her verbal fluency and political acumen were such that she could have become a social force, another Rosa Parks. Instead, she applied her talents to gospel music. She became the piano accompanist for several local choirs and in the mid-1940s formed the Royal Gospel Singers. Composed of McGriff; her sisters, Ruth and Jessie McGriff; her brother, Fred McGriff; and three friends, the Royals were the first gospel group to have their own radio program in Birmingham. During the week McGriff worked standard menial jobs, but on weekends she performed as a soloist, inspired by Queen C. Anderson and Mahalia Jackson.

In 1946, Coates married Willie Love, a quartet luminary who sang for years with the Fairfield Four. Her second husband, Carl Coates, was another quartet veteran who sang bass for the Sensational Nightingales. In 1947, she brought a quartet drive to the Original Gospel Harmonettes, Birmingham's top gospel group, with whom she toured for more than twenty years, becoming a gospel legend.

Coates never had a majestic voice, but her irresistible rhythms and singularly impassioned delivery more than compensated. She seemed to be made up of raw energy, but her intelligence was never in doubt. She was not only an animated performer, but also an astonishing lyricist. She began by interpolating original verses into other composers' songs, but the response convinced her to start writing full time. She has composed a dozen standards, including "That's Enough," "He's Right on Time," "You Must Be Born Again," "Come on in the House," "I Won't Let Go," and "You've Been Good to Me."

Deeply committed to the civil rights movement, Coates spoke about the problems of segregation, a particularly insidious condition for an itinerant performer in the 1950s. Like her idol, composer W. Herbert Brewster, she intends her songs to work doubly, as encouragement to worldly political advancement and as meditative or testifying "rave-ups."

Coates now travels with an ensemble that includes her sister, Lillian McGriff Caffey, and her daughter, Carletta Coates. In recent years she has appeared at the New York and New Orleans jazz festivals, at New York's Central Park Summer Stage, and in Germany and Switzerland. In 1990, she appeared in *The Long Walk Home*, a film about civil rights starring Whoopi Goldberg and Sissy Spacek.

[*See also* GOSPEL MUSIC.]

BIBLIOGRAPHY

Heilbut, Anthony. *The Gospel Sound: Good News and Bad Times* (1985).

DISCOGRAPHY

Best of Dorothy Love Coates and the Original Gospel Harmonettes (n.d.); *Get on Board* (1992); *Stars of the Gospel Highway* (1989); *The Great Gospel Women* (1992).

ANTHONY HEILBUT

COBB, JEWELL PLUMMER (1924-)

Jewell Plummer Cobb has achieved an impressive record as educator, administrator, and author, and done it all with grace and style.

Born to an upper-middle-class family in Chicago in 1924, Jewell Plummer had parents who could scarcely have been better role models. Her father, Frank V. Plummer, one of the founders of Alpha Phi Alpha fraternity when he was at Cornell University, began practicing medicine in Chicago in 1923 and served that city's Black population for many years. Her mother, Carriebel Cole Plummer, was a teacher of dance who had studied at Sargeants, a physical education college affiliated with Harvard. Among her parents' friends were historian Carter G. Woodson, poet Arna Bontemps, and anthropologist Allison Davis.

Young Jewell Plummer attended Chicago's primarily segregated public schools, but her education was supplemented by her parents' remarkable library

and trips to New York City for cultural events. She was an honor student throughout her elementary and high school years and became interested in biology when she was a sophomore. After graduation, she attended the University of Michigan.

In her second year at Michigan, she decided to transfer to Talladega College in Alabama. She graduated with a major in biology in 1941 and went on to New York University. In 1950, she completed work on her Ph.D. in cell physiology and began a career in research. Her primary area of concentration was pigment cell research, dealing especially with melanin. She did particularly important work investigating melanoma, tumors on the skin that usually are malignant. She did research at the Cancer Research Foundation with Dorothy Walker Jones that involved studying the effects of cancer chemotherapy drugs on human tumors that the two women grew in culture in the laboratory.

In 1954, Jewell Plummer married Roy Paul Cobb and, three years later, had a son, Roy Jonathan. After a time at the University of Illinois College of Medicine, she joined the faculty of Sarah Lawrence College in 1960. There she taught, carried on her research, and became dean of the college. She and Roy Cobb were divorced in 1967. In 1969, she became dean of Connecticut College and professor of zoology. It was not until she became dean of Douglass College in 1976 that she finally gave up her research.

While at Connecticut College, she founded a privately funded premedical and predental program for minority students. That program has served as a model for similar programs at twenty other colleges, but it was dropped by Connecticut College after Cobb left.

In 1981, Cobb became president of California State University at Fullerton. While she was there, she accomplished a great deal for the school and the community. She established, for example, the first privately funded gerontology center in Orange County. She created an opportunity program for ethnic students. She also built an apartment complex for students, transforming the former commuter campus into a residential school. That complex was named in her honor.

In 1990, at the age of sixty-six, Cobb became Trustee Professor at California State College in Los Angeles. She is working with a consortium of six colleges whose goal is to encourage minority students to enter the fields of science and engineering. The group hopes to get corporate funding to replace federal grants and fellowships that are rapidly disappearing. They are also working on a more personal level with individual students to remedy any deficiencies in their educational backgrounds.

The recipient of many honorary doctorates and other awards, Cobb has published extensively. The majority of her publications are scientific in nature, but several deal with issues concerning women and minorities. One of her best known is an article, "Filters for Women in Science," published in the *Annals of the New York Academy of Sciences* (1979). In it, she draws a parallel between the process of achieving success in the sciences and a filter, such as that used in a laboratory. For women, she says, the filter is much finer than for men. Fortunately for women and other minorities in the sciences, Jewell Plummer Cobb focuses on locating talent, not filtering it out.

BIBLIOGRAPHY

NBAW; Press, Jacques Cattell. *Leaders in Education* (1974); *Who's Who in America* (1979); *Who's Who of American Women* (1980).

KATHLEEN THOMPSON

COINCOIN (1742-1816)

I have conceded to my slave Thérèse the privilege of being sold by me, with her mulatto son Joseph Maurice, age nine years, to her mother, Marie Thérèse, free Negress, for the sum of seven hundred dollars. (Marie St. Denis, 1790)

These words, from a French colonial document created in 1790, personify the life, character, and times of an extraordinary woman. The place was Opelousas, Louisiana. The seller was an acerbic, politically prominent Frenchwoman whose family had, for generations, held this Black family in slavery. The buyer was a forty-eight-year-old freedwoman of the upriver post of Natchitoches, who had traversed 120 miles of forests and bayous to buy the freedom of this one child. This she would do again and again, in one direction or another, until virtually all of her offspring were free. The unstinting labor, determination, and family cohesiveness that shaped her life would inspire generations to come. Building upon her efforts, the dynasty she spawned would represent outstanding wealth, education, and political clout in the pre-Civil War South.

While most eighteenth-century American Blacks were enslaved for life, some managed to acquire free-

dom. A small number used their skills and acumen to earn a comfortable living and even wealth. Of those who prospered, few were women. Although slave females were more likely to win manumission, via sexual favors, they had less potential to prosper in free society. Coincoin was, in most respects, an exception. Born at Natchitoches about August 24, 1742, as the child of imported slave parents, she was given the French name Marie Thérèse at baptism. For the rest of her life, however, she was more commonly known by the African name her parents called her, Coincoin, a name given to second-born daughters by those who spoke the Glidzi dialect of the Ewe people of Western Africa. Her family's master was the founder of the post, the chevalier and commandant Louis Juchereau de St. Denis. In the span of her childhood, Coincoin would pass to his widow, their son, and then their daughter. The last transfer was a fortunate one, for Marie de Nieges de St. Denis—wife of a political defector from Mexico named Antonio Bermudez y de Soto—was a spirited and unconventional woman who defied the colony's law by renting her young female slave to a bachelor in need of a housekeeper.

For two decades, Coincoin lived with the French merchant Claude Thomas Pierre Metoyer as his servant and his mistress, bearing him ten children. Amid a clerical battle to end their "scandalous alliance" and the threat of a court-ordered sale of Coincoin away from the post, Metoyer purchased her and freed her, together with the "infant at her breast." The first six children she had borne him remained in slavery, as did five others to whom she had given birth before her union with Metoyer. For eight additional years she remained with the Frenchman, bearing three more freeborn infants—and burying two of them.

In 1786, Coincoin and Metoyer parted. On the eve of taking a legal wife, he gave to Coincoin a small plot of land and promised an annuity of 120 piasters to support those children already free. At age forty-four, after fifteen childbirths, she began to build a life for herself and her offspring. She planted tobacco and indigo, raised cattle and turkeys, and trapped bear for their marketable grease and hides. By 1794 she qualified, financially and otherwise, to apply for a land grant from the Spanish government. On the 800 arpents (about 640 acres) of piney woods granted to her a dozen or so miles from her homestead, she set up a *vacharie*—a cattle range—hiring a Spaniard to oversee her herd and raise the corn and other crops necessary to meet the grant requirements of the government.

The manner in which Coincoin used her profits speaks eloquently of her values. Eschewing the comforts that money could bring, she set out to manumit those still-enslaved children. Her eldest daughter, in 1786, cost her only 300 piasters—Marie Louise had been crippled in a gunshot accident—yet even that sum represented nearly three years of the annuity that was to support her family. Over the next decade, Coincoin tracked down her enslaved children and grandchildren, from the downriver post of Opelousas to the Mexican outpost of Nacogdoches, Texas; most of their masters consented to the sale—some for cash, some on credit. Only one daughter was unattainable; yet, by sundry means, the grandchildren in this family line were freed over the next two decades.

At the age of sixty, Coincoin renegotiated her annuity agreement with Metoyer. Two of the six slave children she had borne him had been manumitted by him at their marriage. In return for the freedom of the last four, she agreed to forfeit the annual payments that would have provided security in her old age. In the interim Coincoin herself became a slaveowner, for the same reasons that motivated other contemporaries—a need for labor. Before her death in 1816, at the age of seventy-four, she had become the mistress of sixteen slaves and a thousand arpents of land—no small fortune for a male or female of any color in the late-eighteenth and early-nineteenth centuries.

Yet it was not material accomplishments that made Coincoin a notable historical figure. A few other slave and free Black women did as much and more. It was, instead, the enduring inspiration of her example that enshrined her memory and her legacy in Louisiana lore. Building upon the foundation Coincoin laid for them, her offspring—indomitable and ingenious—developed a highly effective economic and social network based on kin loyalty and mutual assistance. Maximizing the legal rights available in their society, they built an agricultural empire on Isle Brevelle in Louisiana's Red River Valley. As the largest slaveowning family of color in the United States, their peak holdings included nearly 20,000 acres of land, 500 slaves, and a dozen plantation manor houses. Their self-contained, Catholic-inspired community centered around their own school and their own church—allegedly the only nonwhite church in America to operate a white mission. The degree to which their success was based on the labors of their less-fortunate Black slaves remains a debatable point. Local lore insists they were kind masters, and extant records do document numerous manumissions by them. In retrospect, the era in which they lived limited the choices they might have made; and whatever their exploitations, they were cut from the same economic cloth that motivates all business people, indus-

trialists, or planters whose society is underpinned more by social class than by color.

Contrary to the belief that few genealogical records exist on early Black families, there have been found many records to piece together this slave-born family. Her parents, François and Françoise, had been legally married at Natchitoches on December 26, 1735. There, they produced eleven children, whose stories are told in dozens of church records, lawsuits, property inventories, wills, and deeds. Some would earn their freedom, others would not. Coincoin's own children were as follows: Marie Louise, baptized September 8, 1759; Thérèse, baptized September 24, 1761; Françoise, baptized July 8, 1763, never manumitted; Nicolas Chiquito, born c. 1764-65, died April 12, 1850; Nicolas Augustin, born January 22, 1768, died December 18, 1856, after amassing an estate that exceeded $140,000; Marie Suzanne Metoyer, born January 22, 1768, died July 28, 1838, leaving an estate valued at $61,000; Louis Metoyer, born c. 1770, died March 11, 1832, leaving an estate valued at $132,000; Pierre Metoyer, born c. 1772, died June 25, 1833, leaving $19,969 to his heirs—in addition to plantations already given them; Dominique Metoyer, born c. 1774, died c. 1840, leaving $42,405 in addition to donations already made to his seventeen children; Marie Eulalie Metoyer, born January 15, 1776, died 1783-1801; Joseph Antoine Metoyer, born January 26, 1778, died October 9, 1838; Marie Françoise Rosalie Metoyer, born December 9, 1780, died before 1783; Pierre Toussaint Metoyer, born c. 1782, died February 17, 1863; and François Metoyer, born September 26, 1784; died after 1841.

The changes wrought by Civil War, emancipation, reconstruction, and industrialization, as well as the intensified racism and segregation of the late-nineteenth and early-twentieth centuries, destroyed the world that Coincoin and her offspring built. Amid new social and economic conditions, younger generations dispersed to other parts of the nation, developing migratory patterns of import to sociologists and historians. Yet, many descendants still remain on family lands, their culture still centered around the values that Coincoin taught. The Church of St. Augustin still stands, named for Coincoin's eldest Metoyer son and dominated by a life-sized oil of him, made in his patriarchal years. Nearby stands Melrose Plantation—the only reasonably intact estate grounds to survive the ravaging of their forgotten empire; in 1975, it was declared a National Historic Landmark. This world that Coincoin created on Isle Brevelle, has, in the twentieth century, become fabled through the work of such Louisiana folk-writers as Lyle Saxon,

François Mignon, and Harnett Kane, as well as the more recent studies of sociological, historical, and genealogical scholars.

BIBLIOGRAPHY

Mills, Gary B. *The Forgotten People: Cane River's Creoles of Color* (1976); Mills, Gary B. and Elizabeth S. "Slaves and Masters: The Louisiana Metoyers," *National Genealogical Society Quarterly* (September 1982), and *Melrose* (1974); Woods, Frances Jerome. *Marginality and Identity: A Colored Creole Family through Ten Generations* (1972).

GARY B. MILLS

COLE, JOHNNETTA BETSCH (1936-)

Johnnetta Betsch Cole is the seventh president of Spelman College, the oldest college for Black women in the United States; she is the first Black woman to serve as president since the college's founding in 1881. She was born October 19, 1936, in Jacksonville, Florida. Her maternal great-grandfather, Abraham Lincoln Lewis, co-founded the Afro-American Life Insurance Company of Jacksonville in 1901.

Her father, John Betsch, Sr., worked for Atlanta Life Insurance Company but later joined his wife's family's business. Her mother, Mary Frances Lewis Betsch, an educator and graduate of Wilberforce University in Ohio, taught English and was registrar at Edward Waters College in Jacksonville before joining the family insurance business after her husband's death.

When Cole was appointed president of Spelman on April 5, 1987, she was professor of anthropology and director of the Latin American and Caribbean Studies Program at Hunter College of the City University of New York; previously she had been associate provost for undergraduate education at the University of Massachusetts at Amherst.

In her acceptance statement, Cole said she envisioned Spelman under her leadership as a "renown[ed] center for scholarship by and about Black women" as well as a place where "Black women leaders of the world are nurtured, trained, and developed." She indicated that "scholars, teachers, artists, policy analysts, and community leaders will turn to Spelman for comprehensive information on the rich and diverse history, struggles, conditions, and accomplishments of Black women."

The historic appointment of Cole as the first African-American woman to head Spelman was sig-

In accepting her historic appointment as the first African-American woman to head Spelman College, Johnnetta Cole described her vision of Spelman as a place where "Black women leaders of the world are nurtured, trained, and developed." Here she speaks with students on campus. [Spelman College]

nificant also because for the first time in its history the college was to be headed by a president with an explicitly Black feminist vision. In her first statement to the Spelman community, Cole alluded to the essence of her work prior to becoming president: "I have *consciously* lived and studied, taught and written, as an African-American woman. The issues of race and gender have been central in my life, in my work as an anthropologist, and in my community activities. There is a fundamental question at the base of the work that I do: how can people of color, poor people, and women become full, productive, and equal members of the society in which they live?"

Shortly after coming to the campus, Cole donned the affectionate title of "sister president," a label she gave herself in her first published interview as president, which was alluded to in the October 1987 issue of *Ms.* A year later, during her November 8, 1988 inauguration, Cole announced that a historic gift of $20 million had been made to the college by Bill and Camille Cosby.

Cole spent her formative years in Jacksonville and, in 1952, at age fifteen, entered Fisk University in Nashville, Tennessee, under its early admissions program. After only a year at Fisk, she left to join her older sister, Marvyne Betsch, at Oberlin College in Oberlin, Ohio. During her first year at Oberlin (1953), Johnnetta Betsch took a class on racial and cultural minorities; taught by George Eaton Simpson, the class inspired her to major in sociology and to pursue a career in anthropology. After graduating from Oberlin in 1957, she went to Northwestern University to pursue a Master's degree in anthropology, which she received in 1959. In 1967 she was awarded the Ph.D. in anthropology at Northwestern after studying under noted anthropologists Melville J. Herskovits and Paul J. Bohannan.

Following appointments at the University of California at Los Angeles and at Washington State University in Pullman, Washington, Cole joined the faculty of the University of Massachusetts at Amherst, where she remained for thirteen years. She went to Hunter College in 1983, first as Russell Sage Visiting Professor and then as a tenured professor of anthropology. She also has held visiting appointments at Oberlin and Williams College in Williamstown, Massachusetts.

Cole's scholarly research and writing have been in the areas of cultural anthropology, African-American studies, and women's studies. She is especially interested in systems of inequality based on race, gender, and class, and in the Pan-African world of the United States, the Caribbean, and Africa. Her major publications include *All American Women: Lines That Divide, Ties That Bind* (1986), *Anthropology for the Eighties: Introductory Readings* (1982), and *Anthropology for the Nineties* (1988). She has researched female-headed households in New York City, the lives of Caribbean women, racial and gender inequality in Cuba, and economic issues in Liberia. She is former president of both the Association of Black Anthropologists and the International Women's Anthropology Conference.

During her first marriage to economist Robert Cole, she had three sons; currently she is married to Arthur Robinson III.

BIBLIOGRAPHY

Giddings, Paula. "A Conversation with Johnnetta Betsch Cole," *Sage* (Fall 1988); McHenry, Susan. "Sister President," *Ms.* (October 1987).

BEVERLY GUY-SHEFTALL

COLE, REBECCA J. (1846-1922)

Rebecca J. Cole was born on March 16, 1846, in Philadelphia, Pennsylvania. She was the second Black woman physician and the first Black woman to graduate from the Woman's Medical College of Pennsylvania.

Cole completed her secondary education in Philadelphia at the Institute for Colored Youth (ICY), now Cheyney University. While at ICY, she received a $10 prize for "excellence in classics and mathematics, and for diligence in study, punctuality of attendance, and good conduct" (Institute for Colored Youth 1862). She graduated from ICY in 1863.

Cole received her medical degree from the Woman's Medical College in 1867 and eventually moved to New York, where she was appointed resident physician at the New York Infirmary for Women and Children, a hospital entirely owned and operated by women physicians. Elizabeth Blackwell, the first American woman physician to receive a medical degree, described Cole as an intelligent young Black physician who performed her duties with tact and care. Impressed by her work, Blackwell assigned Cole to the post of sanitary visitor, a position in which she visited families in slum neighborhoods and instructed them in family hygiene and in infant and prenatal care.

After practicing medicine in Columbia, South Carolina, for a short time, Cole returned to Philadelphia and opened an office in the South Philadelphia section of the city. In 1873, with the assistance of fellow physician Charlotte Abbey, Cole started a Women's Directory Center to provide medical and legal services to destitute women and children.

Cole practiced medicine for fifty years. She died in Philadelphia on August 14, 1922.

[See also PHYSICIANS, NINETEENTH CENTURY.]

BIBLIOGRAPHY

Cole, Rebecca. Black Women Physicians Collection and Special Collection on Women in Medicine, Medical College of Pennsylvania, Philadelphia; Institute for Colored Youth. Annual Report (1862), and Report of the Board of Managers (1859); Kerr, Laura. Doctor Elizabeth (1946).

BRENDA GALLOWAY-WRIGHT

COLEMAN, BESSIE (1896-1926)

I knew we had no aviators, neither men nor women, and I knew the Race needed to be represented along this most important line, so I thought it my duty to risk my life to learn aviation and to encourage flying among men and women of our Race who are so far behind the white Race in this modern study. (Bessie Coleman, 1921)

Elizabeth (Bessie) Coleman, aviator, barnstormer, parachutist, and activist, was born in Atlanta, Texas, on January 20, 1896, the twelfth of thirteen children. Her mother, Susan Coleman, was an African-American. Her father, George Coleman, was three-quarters Choctaw Indian and one-quarter African. While Bessie was still a toddler, the Coleman family moved to Waxahachie, Texas, an agricultural and trade center that produced cotton, grain, and cattle. The town was about thirty miles south of Dallas and was recognized as the cotton capital of the West. Here, the Coleman family made a living from picking cotton. George Coleman built a three-room house on a quarter acre of land, but by the time Bessie was seven years old, he had returned to Choctaw country in Oklahoma. Susan Coleman continued to raise nine children alone as she also continued to harvest in the fields, pick cotton, and do domestic work to make ends meet. When the children became old enough, usually about age eight, they too went to work in the cotton fields to supplement the Coleman family income. Recognizing Bessie's excellent mathematical skills, Susan

Coleman exempted her daughter from working in the cotton fields and assigned her the family bookkeeping responsibilities.

The Colemans were religious Baptists, and each child was expected to demonstrate literacy skills by reading aloud from the Bible every evening. When Bessie was old enough to take in laundry, her mother permitted her to save her earnings for her college education. She was enrolled in the elementary division of the Colored Agricultural and Normal University in Langston, Oklahoma. The school was popularly known as Langston and was named for the great-uncle of poet Langston Hughes. After graduating from high school, Coleman attended the teachers college for one year until her finances were depleted.

Coleman, like many African-Americans of the period, migrated to Chicago, where two of her brothers lived, sometime between 1915 and 1917. Just as she had avoided the backbreaking work of cotton picking in Texas, she also eschewed conventional women's labor in Chicago—she sought neither domestic nor factory work, the prevalent occupations of African-American women migrants of the day. She took manicuring classes at the Burnham's School of Beauty Culture and obtained a job as a manicurist in the White Sox barbershop. In the masculine environment of her workplace Coleman listened to men who had returned from World War I, including her brother Johnny, discuss the war and the fledgling field of aviation. Coleman developed an intense interest in aviation, quit her job as manicurist, and focused her attention on becoming an aviator. Because Coleman was an African-American woman, her initial pursuit of a formal education in aviation met with rejection from the administration of newly established aviation schools in the United States. These schools were conforming to Jim Crow laws that stipulated separation between the races.

Upon advice from Robert Abbott (1870-1940), founder and editor of the Chicago Defender, and with financial support from him and Jesse Binga, founder and president of the Binga State Bank—both African-American philanthropists—in 1920, Coleman temporarily eluded this discrimination by registering in an aviation school located in France. She specialized in parachuting and stunt flying, and upon completion of her program of study, she received the first international pilot's license granted to an American aviator from the Fédération Aeronautique Internationale, on June 15, 1921. Armed with a license that allowed her to fly in any part of the world, she returned to the United States as a barnstormer.

After Coleman received recognition as a top-flight barnstormer from predominantly white audiences and press in the northern and midwestern regional air shows, she concentrated her performances in the South toward primarily African-American audiences. Many of her southern appearances were at circuses, carnivals, and county fairs on the Theatre Owners and Booking Association (TOBA) circuit, which also included Black theaters where documentary film footage of Coleman's achievements in Europe were shown between acts. She lectured at African-American schools, churches, and recreation facilities in an attempt to encourage African-Americans to become involved in aviation and to raise money to launch an aviation training school for African-Americans.

Although Coleman needed larger sums of money to establish her aviation school, she would not compromise her integrity. She refused to perform in her childhood town at the Waxahachie airport until the authorities desegregated the audience. In March 1926, she turned down the Orlando Chamber of Commerce when she learned that African-Americans would be excluded from her performance. Although the white businessmen relented, Coleman did not agree to perform until "the Jim Crow order had been revoked and aviators had been sent up to drop placards letting the members of our Race know they could come into the field" (Kriz n.d.).

Shortly after the Orlando engagement Coleman was hired by the Negro Welfare League in Jacksonville, Florida, to perform at their annual First of May Field Day. Coleman had trouble, however, locating an airplane in Florida because local dealers would not sell, rent, or loan an airplane to an African-American. She summoned William D. Wills, her white mechanic in Dallas, Texas, to fly a plane to her in Jacksonville for the performance. During a dress rehearsal, Coleman was catapulted out of the airplane at about 2,000 feet when the plane somersaulted in several revolutions; she was not wearing a seatbelt or a parachute. Every bone in her body was crushed by the impact.

In spite of her untimely death, Coleman influenced other African-Americans to pursue aviation as a profession. Several generations of African-American pilots still honor her during an annual memorial service by flying over her gravesite and dropping a wreath. In Atchison, Kansas—Amelia Earhart's birthplace and location of the International Forest of Friendship, which honors pilots from around the world—Coleman's achievements are commemorated by a plaque bearing her name.

BIBLIOGRAPHY

CBWA; Ebony, "They Take to the Sky: Group of Midwest Women Follow Path Blazed by Pioneer Bessie Coleman" (May 1977); Hardesty, Von and Dominick Pisano. *Black Wings: The American Black in Aviation* (1983); Kriz, Marjorie. "Bessie Coleman, Aviation Pioneer," *U.S. Department of Transportation News* (n.d.), and "They Had Another Dream: Blacks Took to the Air Early," *U.S. Department of Transportation News* (1980); Sampson, Henry T. *Blacks in Blackface: A Source Book on Early Black Musical Shows* (1980); Waters, Enoch P. *American Diary: A Personal History of the Black Press* (1987).

ELIZABETH HADLEY FREYDBERG

One of hundreds of Black aviators encouraged by Chicago Defender *publisher Robert Abbott, Bessie Coleman had to travel to France to receive her training. But she enjoyed a spectacular career in the United States as a barnstormer in air shows for circuses, carnivals, and fairs until she died when she fell from a plane at the age of thirty. [Elizabeth Freydberg]*

COLLINS, CARDISS ROBERTSON (1931-)

Cardiss Robertson was born on September 24, 1931, in St. Louis, Missouri, the only child of Finley and Rosia Mae Cardiss Robertson. Her father was a laborer, and her mother was a nurse. When she was ten years old, the family moved to Detroit, Michigan, where she attended Bishop and Lincoln elementary schools. Upon graduation from Detroit's High School of Commerce, she moved to Chicago to find a job.

After hand-tying mattress springs and working as a stenographer for a carnival equipment company, Robertson found a job as a secretary with the Illinois Department of Revenue and enrolled in night school. Her studies in accounting at Northwestern University led to her promotion to accountant and then to auditor. At about this time, she met George Washington Collins. They were married in 1958, when she was twenty-seven. They had one son. When her husband ran for political office, Cardiss Collins became involved in his career. She worked in his campaigns

Cardiss Collins of Illinois was the first African-American and the first woman to be appointed Democratic whip-at-large in the U.S. House of Representatives, as well as the first woman chair of the Congressional Black Caucus. [Office of Representative Collins]

and later became politically active herself, representing the Democratic party as a committeewoman.

After serving as alderman, George Collins ran for and won the office of U.S. Representative from Illinois's sixth district. He remained in close contact with his constituency and his family, flying back from Washington, D.C., to Chicago nearly every weekend. On one of those flights, his airplane crashed into a residential area near the Chicago airport, and he was killed. Mayor Richard Daley immediately offered to support Cardiss Collins in a bid for her husband's vacant seat in Congress. With the encouragement of her son, she decided to make the attempt to carry on her husband's work.

Collins won the election by a comfortable margin and began her new career on June 5, 1973. Two years after she first took office, she became the first Black American and the first woman to be appointed Democratic whip-at-large. Not long after that, she repeated both "firsts" as chair of the House Government Operations Subcommittee on Manpower and Housing.

In 1979, Collins became chair of the Congressional Black Caucus. She was the first woman to hold that position. She was determined to unify the seventeen members of the caucus, giving them more power in Congress. Her skills in dealing with people helped her achieve that goal, and she was highly praised as both forceful and tactful.

Standing together became a greater and greater necessity as legislation was proposed that would move the country further from the goals that had been set during President Lyndon Johnson's War on Poverty. As Collins said to her fellow caucus members, "We're going to have to be in there fighting for butter, because they're going to give everything to guns." She also warned that attempts would be made to roll back gains in civil rights, and they were. Still, under her leadership the caucus helped defeat an antibusing amendment to the constitution, monitored the 1980 census to protect minorities, and pushed for economic sanctions against apartheid governments in Africa.

While serving on a number of important congressional committees, Collins has been a strong defender of civil rights. She was a critic of administration policies during the Reagan era and has battled discriminatory hiring practices in the private sector. She has had the full support of her constituency. Every time she has run for reelection, she has won decisively. In 1988, she was unopposed. Her district, which is 55 percent Black, 22 percent foreign-born, and 17 percent Hispanic, knows that she will represent them with integrity and defend them with courage.

BIBLIOGRAPHY

CBWA; EBA; Ebony, "Our New Men in the House" (January 1981); NA; NBAW; Women in Congress, 1917-1990 (1991); WWBA (1992).

KATHLEEN THOMPSON

Years before she became the first Black prima ballerina in the Metropolitan Opera, Janet Collins was offered a position with the Ballets Russes de Monte Carlo on the condition that she paint her skin white. To her eternal credit, she refused. [Moorland-Spingarn]

COLLINS, JANET (1923-)

Janet Collins is known as the first Black prima ballerina in America to perform in a major ballet company. Collins was born in 1923 in New Orleans and moved to Los Angeles, California, as a young girl. She attended Los Angeles City College and the Los Angeles Art Center School. Collins was also an accomplished painter, which helped her finance her move to New York to pursue her dance career.

Collins was in the initial tour of the Katherine Dunham dance troupe in Los Angeles. She auditioned for the Ballets Russes de Monte Carlo but was rejected on the basis of her skin color. However, she was offered a chance to perform with the company if she would paint her skin white; she refused. Collins received a Rosenwald Fellowship to study classic, Hebrew, and Negro dances. In 1949, she made her New York City debut in a solo concert. From 1950 to 1951, Collins was lead dancer in Cole Porter's musical *Out of This World* for which she won the Donaldson Award. She then joined the corps de ballet of the Metropolitan Opera in 1951. The following year she went on to become prima ballerina. Collins was a professor at the School of American Ballet in New York. She is now retired, living in Seattle, Washington, and pursuing her painting.

BIBLIOGRAPHY

Cohen-Stratyner, Naomi. *Biographical Dictionary of Dance* (1982); *EBA*; Long, Richard. *The Black Tradition in American Concert Dance* (1990); *NA*; Toppin, Edgar A. *A Biographical History of Blacks in America since 1528* (1971); Willis, John. *Dance World* (1967, 1976).

KARIAMU WELSH ASANTE

COLLINS, MARVA N. (1936-)

"When we create a positive environment for our students, we can see some miraculous things happen." This is the view of Marva N. Collins, an innovative Black educator of national reputation who concentrates her interests in teaching as well as in creating and implementing progressive educational concepts. After nineteen years of experience with the methods and policies of the Chicago public schools, Collins found herself openly challenging a system that failed to educate all children with equal vigor and reasonable success. By 1975, she realized that her dissatisfaction could not be remedied with a large, impersonal, and politicized school system of nearly a half million children who were predominantly nonwhite. Consequently she established the Westside Preparatory School, an alternative educational institution for Black children on Chicago's neglected and maligned West Side.

Marva Nettles Collins was born on August 31, 1936, in Monroeville, Alabama. She "grew up in a very nurtured background." She had much support for her own education: "If you went to college in Alabama, you were a celebrity. The minister had you stand in church and all the people would give you a quarter or fifty cents, what they could. You didn't get into trouble because in your mind's eye you could see all these people caring about you, depending on you" (Lanker 1989). It was the same supportive and demanding environment that Collins sought to create for Black children in Chicago.

Attaining her goal required traits that Collins possesses in abundance: a strong will, dedication to the highest principles of teaching, an abiding love for the young students whose future she embraced, and full confidence in her ability to move forward from critic to builder. Her greatest obstacle was financing, which she provided herself from personal funds and loans. Even today she disdains any financing from federal or corporate sources that might inhibit her independence. Collins has critics, but she also has legions of supporters whose recognition of her successes influenced Presidents Ronald Reagan and George Bush, successively, to offer her an appointment as U.S. Secretary of Education; she declined each time. Collins also received the attention of the national media when she was featured on *60 Minutes* and was the subject of a television movie.

In her role as builder, Collins refined, blended, and implemented traditional as well as progressive teaching concepts and methods at Westside Prep. National interest in her demonstrated success convinced some Ohio parents to seek her assistance in creating an alternative school in Cincinnati, which opened in 1990 as the Marva Collins Preparatory School. In 1991, the state of Oklahoma invited Collins to design a training program for its staff to show what can be accomplished academically with youngsters who often are written off by mainstream school systems as ineducable.

Collins's success at Westside Prep depended, first, on creating an environment that was conducive to learning and bringing out to the greatest measure every child's intellectual potential and, second, on assembling a teaching staff with broad liberal arts training, a dedication to teaching, and a love of children. Students are accepted from throughout Chicago,

with the preponderance coming from the city's West Side Black neighborhoods. Contrary to some of the criticism, there has never been an exclusionary admissions policy based on previous academic performance, economic status, or behavioral problems. The miracle of Westside Prep has rested on heavy doses of time-tested basics such as phonics, memorization, reading aloud, exposure to foreign languages, and exercises in critical thinking—all undergirded by the use of interdisciplinary materials that range from the classics to modern thought. Further, Collins structured her school so that students attend four clusters of classes that are formed without regard to age differences, rather than in the standard nine grade levels (K-8) found in most elementary schools. At present, the miracle continues as Collins encourages her pupils to say goodbye to failure.

BIBLIOGRAPHY
Collins, Marva N. *Ordinary Children, Extraordinary Teachers* (1992), and *The Marva Collins Method: A Manual for Educating and Motivating Your Child* (n.d.), and "Relighting the Candles of Excellence across America," Westside Preparatory School brochure; Lanker, Brian. *I Dream a World* (1989).

CHRISTOPHER R. REED

COLORED FEMALES' FREE PRODUCE SOCIETY

No, dear lady, none for me?
Though squeamish some may think it,
West India sugar spoils my tea;
I cannot, dare not, drink it.
(Gertrude, *Genius of Universal Emancipation* 1831)

Organized to boycott the products of slave labor, the Colored Females' Free Produce Society sought to overthrow the economic power of slavery, one bolt of cotton and one teaspoon of sugar at a time. A union of Black women, Philadelphia's Colored Females' Free Produce Society joined contemporary Free Produce unions, such as the Colored Free Produce Society, Philadelphia Free Cotton Society, and the Free Produce Society of Philadelphia, dedicated to promoting the manufacture and marketing of goods produced entirely by free labor.

The minutes of a regular organizational meeting on January 24, 1831, at the Bethel Church in Philadelphia provide the clearest picture of the membership of the Colored Females' Free Produce Society. After a reading of the society's constitution, the members elected President Judith James, Vice President Susannah Cork, Treasurer Hester Burr, and Secretary Laetitia Rowley. The Committee of Correspondence included Priscilla Wilkins, Rebecca Hutchins, Mary Benjamin, Sarah White, Pleasant Lloyd, Lydia Lecompt, Elizabeth Baker, Martha Holcombe, Maria Potts, and Hannah Alexander. Raising the consciousness of members and the wider community, the society fought the direct and indirect economic contributions that consumers made to slavery in the nominally free states. Such discussion allowed the public refutation of the argument that slave produce boycotts would ultimately hurt the position of slaves.

Supported by Frederick Douglass and others in the abolition movement, the Colored Females' Free Produce Society and groups in the Free Produce movement supplied access to nonslave produce merchants and goods to its members—sometimes in as much as fifty-pound bags of free sugar at a time—to send a moral and economic message to the community at large. Influential members of the community, male and female, Black and white, formed associations as part of a larger effort to overthrow slavery.

The Free Produce Movement was, like the majority of abolition organizations, segregated by both race and sex in the early 1830s. It provided, however, a launching platform for the growing prominence of Black women political activists such as Frances E. W. Harper and Grace Douglass, one of the vice presidents of the Anti-Slavery Convention of American Women held in 1837. Free Produce women activists encouraged other women, Black and white, to suffer the deprivation of slave-produced cotton, rice, sugar, molasses, tobacco, and other goods to break the stranglehold of slavery-based economics on the markets of the free states. Encouraging the advertising and patronizing of shops and suppliers of freely produced goods strengthened the effects of the boycott.

Fostered primarily in areas of Quaker concentration, like Philadelphia and Wilmington, Delaware, the greatest impact of the Free Produce Movement was more moral than financial. From an unsweetened cup of tea, to a coarser calico, to a platform for Black female activism and an eventual integration of the abolition movement, the Colored Females' Free Produce Society brought the spirit of the cause home.

BIBLIOGRAPHY
CBWA; *Genius of Universal Emancipation, or American Anti-Slavery Journal, and Register of News* (July 4, 14; August 11; September 15, 1827. March 8, 1828. January; February; April; May; July 1831); Quarles, Benjamin. *Black Abolitionists* (1969); Sterling, Dorothy, ed. *The World Turned Upside Down: The Anti-Slavery Convention of American Women Held in New York City May 9-12, 1837* (1987).

SUSAN A. TAYLOR

COLORED WOMEN'S PROGRESSIVE FRANCHISE ASSOCIATION

The Colored Women's Progressive Franchise Association was organized by Mary Ann Shadd Cary in Washington, D.C., on February 9, 1880. The first meeting was held at Mount Pisgah Chapel and presided over by the church's pastor, Rev. Joseph Nichols. The chief purpose of the organization was to assert the equal rights of women. Toward that goal, the association set forth a twenty-point program, the chief objective of which was gaining the ballot for women. The association sought to assert the equal rights of women not only by gaining the right to vote, but also by working to expand the number of occupations available to women, to establish newspapers under the control of Black women, and to support only those newspapers that supported equal rights for all. The association also tried to improve the situation of the entire community by supporting home missionaries and training programs for youth, establishing a job bank and labor bureau for the unemployed, developing leadership among the masses, and establishing a company that would help small businesses get started. Another important objective was the establishment of banks and stores for the community.

Thus, the women of the Colored Women's Progressive Franchise Association worked not only to gain the franchise for women; they also took responsibility for the well-being of their own community.

[*See also* CARY, MARY ANN SHADD.]

BIBLIOGRAPHY
Cary, Mary Ann Shadd. "Colored Women's Progressive Franchise Association." Mary Ann Shadd Cary Papers, Moorland-Spingarn Research Center, Howard University, Washington, D.C.

ALLISON JOLLY

COLTRANE, ALICE (1937-)

Alice Coltrane describes her music as an endeavor to create a feeling of spiritual perfection. As a pianist, organist, harpist, vibraphonist, and composer, she epitomizes a tradition of great Black musicians who have elected to pursue their art outside the confines of the commercial industry. Coltrane is perhaps best known as a member of the John Coltrane ensemble, arguably the premier avant-garde jazz group of the 1960s. Since the early 1970s her performances of secular music have been limited to infrequent benefit concerts in Japan, Holland, Poland, London, and New York, although she occasionally has recorded religious music with other jazz musicians.

Born Alice McLeod on August 27, 1937, in Detroit, Michigan, she is the mother of four children: one daughter, Michelle, and three sons, Ravi, Oranyan, and John, Jr. (who died in an automobile accident in 1982). Coltrane descends from a family of musicians. Her mother, Anna, played piano and sang in the church choir, and her mother's brother, Ernie Farrow, was a professional jazz bassist. Alice McLeod began piano study when she was seven and later studied organ and music theory privately. Her development into an accomplished pianist and organist was influenced early on by Earl "Bud" Powell and Thelonious Monk.

She launched her professional career when she joined the Terry Gibbs Quartet in 1960; prior to that she gained experience with other groups led by Kenny Burrell, Johnny Griffin, Lucky Thompson, and Yusef Lateef. In 1963, she married John Coltrane; she joined his group in 1965. After her husband's death in 1967, she continued to record and tour with her own groups until she settled in Woodland Hills, California, in the early 1970s. Among those touring with her as members of her groups were, at various times, saxophonists Pharoah Sanders, Archie Shepp, Joe Henderson, Frank Lowe, and Carlos Ward; bassists Cecil McBee and Jimmy Garrison; and drummers Rashied Ali, Ben Riley, and Roy Haynes. In 1975, following a journey to India to pursue spiritual studies, Alice Coltrane received a Sanskrit name, Turiyasangitananda, and founded the Vedantic Center.

Coltrane has displayed a wide range of musical interests throughout her career. For instance, she has recorded with Laura Nyro, the Rascals, and other pop groups but also has performed excerpts from Stravinsky's *Firebird Suite*. In 1987, she led a quartet, which included her sons, in a tribute to John Coltrane at New York's Cathedral of Saint John the Divine. She continues to play devotional music on her organ

Through her music, Alice Coltrane endeavors to achieve a feeling of spiritual perfection: "To me, to bring music to an exalted transcendental level was the reason for the engagement with music in the first place." [Schomburg Center]

at home and occasionally practices classical music on her Steinway concert grand piano.

Alice Coltrane's current musical orientation may be best captured by her own words: "Avant-garde music is very highly technical music, but I saw instrumental music elevated to a higher plateau, where it was no longer avant-garde, but was spiritual, or devotional, music. To me, to bring music to an exalted transcendental level was the reason for the engagement with music in the first place" (Rivelli and Levin 1970).

BIBLIOGRAPHY

BDAAM; Berendt, J. E. "Alice Coltrane," *Jazz Forum* (1972); Claghorn, Charles Eugene. *Biographical Dictionary of Jazz* (1982); Cole, Bill. *John Coltrane* (1976); Feather, Leonard and Ira Gitter. *Encyclopedia of Jazz in the Seventies* (1976); Jost, Ekkehard. *Free Jazz* (1981); Kernfeld, Barry, ed. *The New Grove Dictionary of Jazz* (1988); Leonard, Neil. *Jazz Myth and Religion* (1987); Lerner, David. "Alice Coltrane: Jazz Pianist, Inspirational Organist," *Keyboard* (1982); Rivelli, P. "Alice Coltrane Interview." In *Black Giants*, ed. P. Rivelli and R. Levin (1970); Simpkins, Cuthbert Ormond. *Coltrane: A Biography* (1975); Thomas, J. C. *Chasin' the Trane* (1975); Turiyasangitananda (Alice Coltrane). *Monument Eternal* (1977), and *Endless Wisdom* (1979); Wild, David. *The Recordings of John Coltrane: A Discography* (1979-90); Wilmer, Valerie. *As Serious as Your Life* (1980).

DISCOGRAPHY

Coltrane Live at the Village Vanguard Again!, Impulse 9124 (1966); *John Coltrane: Concert in Japan*, Impulse AS-9246-2; MCA 2-4135 (1966); *John Coltrane: Infinity*, Impulse 9225 (1966); *John Coltrane: Live in Japan*, Impulse CD GRD-4-102 (1966); *Terry Gibbs Plays Jewish Melodies in Jazztime*, Mercury 60812 (1966); *John Coltrane: Expression*, Impulse A9120 (1967); *The Mastery of John Coltrane*, vol. 3, Impulse IA-9360; MCA 29031 (1967); *Monastic Trio*, Impulse 9156 (1968); *Huntington Ashram Monastery*, Impulse 9185 (1969); *John Coltrane: Cosmic Music*, Impulse 9148; MCA 29025 (1970); *Ptah the El Daoud*, Impulse 9196 (1970); *The Rascals: Peaceful World*, Columbia G 30462 (1970); *Journey in Satchidananda*, Impulse 9203 (1971); *Laura Nyro: Xmas & the Beads of Sweat*, Columbia PC-30259 (1971); *Universal Consciousness*, Impulse 9210 (1971); *World Galaxy*, Impulse AS-9218 (1971); *Lord of Lords*, Impulse 9224 (1972); *Joe Henderson: The Elements*, Milestone/Fantasy M-9053 (1973); *Carlos Santana: Illuminations*, Columbia PC-32900 (1974); *Radha-Krsna Nama Sankirtana*, Warner Bros. BS 2986 (1977); *Transcendence*, Warner Bros. BS 3077 (1977); *Transfiguration*, Warner Bros. 3218 (1978).

TOMMY LOTT

COMBAHEE RIVER COLLECTIVE

In 1974, it took a great deal of courage for Black women to assert that they were Black feminists. Most African-Americans considered the mere act of addressing sexual political issues to be divisive—an attack upon the Black community and especially upon Black men. It was in January 1974, however, that the first meeting of the Combahee River Collective took place in Roxbury, Massachusetts.

The Collective began as the Boston chapter of the National Black Feminist Organization, which had held its founding conference in New York City in November 1973. In the summer of 1975, Collective members decided to become an independent organization. They took the name of the river in South Carolina where Harriet Tubman, during the Civil War, had led the only military campaign in U.S. history that was planned by a woman and that resulted in the freeing of more than 750 slaves.

Like many feminist groups during that period, the Collective's first objective was consciousness raising. By early 1975, meetings were being held at the Cambridge Women's Center and were open to any Black woman who wanted to attend. Black women who believed that sexual oppression did indeed affect Black women and that sexism as well as racism, class oppression, and homophobia needed to be confronted

directly through political action were usually isolated from each other at the same time that they were likely to be ostracized for their views by other members of the Black community. Throughout its existence, the Collective served the important function of connecting Black feminists to each other, both locally in the Boston area and eventually nationally.

During the process of consciousness raising, Collective members began to define Black women's issues from a Black feminist multi-issued perspective. They also had the opportunity to share, examine, and heal some of the specific pain they faced as a result of being Black women in a white male-dominated society.

By the time the Collective decided to become an autonomous organization, it also had made a commitment to radical political activism. In *The Combahee River Collective Statement*, written in 1977, members stated: "The most general statement of our politics at the present time would be that we are actively committed to struggling against racial, sexual, heterosexual, and class oppression, and see as our particular task the development of integrated analysis and practice based upon the fact that the major systems of oppression are interlocking." The Collective also defined itself as anticapitalist, socialist, and revolutionary.

During the six years of its existence, members worked on a variety of issues that affected Black women, including sterilization abuse, reproductive freedom, and violence against women. The Collective also worked with women in prison, actively supported the growth of Black women's art and culture, and was in the forefront of confronting racism in the women's movement. The Collective often worked in coalition with other women of color, with white feminists, and with progressive men. Membership in the Collective was open to Black women of all sexual orientations. Black lesbians, however, often provided the Collective's leadership during an era when many heterosexual Black women were reluctant to address feminist issues or did not want to work with open lesbians. One of the Collective's major achievements was to initiate a series of seven Black feminist retreats beginning in 1977. The retreats, held in various locations on the East Coast, provided an opportunity for Black feminist activists from other cities to meet each other and to engage in critical political dialogue.

The Collective's ability to integrate the politics of race, sex, and class and to build links among various communities culminated in 1979. After twelve Black women were murdered in Boston during a four-month period, Collective members wrote and distributed tens of thousands of copies of a pamphlet, originally entitled "Twelve Black Women: Why Did They Die?" that analyzed the murders as sexual as well as racial violence. They also played a crucial role in the many groups and coalitions that arose in response to the murders.

The Combahee River Collective made a major contribution to the growth of Black feminism in the United States. It was one of the earliest groups to assert the legitimacy of Black women's opposition to sexual exploitation and oppression. Its widely circulated *Combahee River Collective Statement* helped to lay the foundation for feminists of color organizing in the 1980s and 1990s. The Collective also played a key role in raising the issue of homophobia in the Black community and in initiating communication among Black women of different sexual orientations. The Collective's historical legacy continues in the contemporary organizing efforts of radical women of color.

BIBLIOGRAPHY

Combahee River Collective. *The Combahee River Collective Statement* ([1977] 1986), and "Twelve Black Women: Why Did They Die?" (1979); Delacoste, Frederique and Felice Newman, eds. *Fight Back: Feminist Resistance to Male Violence* (1981).

BARBARA SMITH

COMPOSERS

For more than one hundred years Black American women trained in the Western musical tradition have been creating music. Although they have not received the recognition afforded male composers, these women have expressed themselves through musical composition. The types of composition have been varied: solo songs, choral works, chamber works (for a variety of combinations), symphonies, and operas. The records indicate that Black women composers in this tradition have been active from the late 1800s to the present.

One early Black woman composer was Amanda Ira Christina Elizabeth Aldridge (1866-1956), daughter of the first internationally recognized Black actor/singer, Ira Aldridge. She was born in London, England, and studied at the Royal College of Music there. She was also a vocal student of the famous white singer Jenny Lind. Aldridge wrote several compositions, including several dances and a dance suite.

Other early Black women composers include Lucie Campbell (1885-1963), composer of many gospel songs, and Florence Price (1888-1953), the first Black woman to receive international recognition as a composer. Born in Little Rock, Arkansas, Price spent most of her life in Chicago. Her works include four symphonies (one of which was performed by the Chicago Symphony at the 1933 World's Fair), concerti, solo works for piano and/or voice, and choral works. Her compositions show the influence of the post-romantic styles of most of her New England Conservatory of Music teachers. Eva Jessye (1895-1992) was a Kansas-born composer and choral conductor who was selected by George Gershwin to direct the chorus in his folk opera, *Porgy and Bess.* Jessye arranged spirituals for choruses and wrote several choral works, including a folk oratorio, *Paradise Lost and Regained.* Loretta Manggrum (b. 1896) was a late-blooming composer from Ohio who earned her undergraduate degree in music from Ohio State University when she was fifty-five years old. The first Black student at the Conservatory of Music at Cincinnati, Manggrum received her Master's degree at age fifty-seven and also became the first Black member of the American Organ Guild. She wrote seven sacred cantatas for choir with piano, organ, or orchestral accompaniment, and other shorter works that are classified as classical religious music.

Undine Smith Moore (1905-), a Virginian, is representative of the Black women composers born in the early twentieth century. She was educated at Fisk University (Bachelor's degree), Columbia University Teachers College in New York (Master's degree), and at the Juilliard School of Music and other institutions in New York. Moore wrote a variety of compositions, including *Scenes from the Life of a Martyr*, a cantata, and *Afro-American Suite*, a work for flute, cello, and piano. She is especially known for her many choral works, both original pieces and arrangements of spirituals.

Other early twentieth-century Black women composers are Shirley Graham Du Bois (1896-1977), born in Indiana, who was a musician and writer. The second wife of W.E.B. Du Bois, her compositions include a children's opera, *Little Black Sambo*, and an opera called *Tom-Toms.* Oklahoma-born composer and music educator Evelyn LaRue Pittman (1910-) studied composition in France with Nadia Boulanger. She had been recommended by her graduate composition teacher, Harrison Kerr of the University of Oklahoma, where she received her Master's degree. Although she is also known for her choral arrangements of spirituals, her major works were operas or music dramas. She was intensely interested in teaching Black history through music. Her book for children, *Rich Heritage*, includes biographical sketches and songs about famous Black Americans, and two of her music dramas are based on Black historical figures: *Freedom Child* (Dr. Martin Luther King, Jr.) and *Jim Noble* (the Black man responsible for moving the Oklahoma State seal from Guthrie to Oklahoma City, changing the capital city). Mary Lou Williams (1910-1981), born in Georgia, is best known as a jazz pianist. She began composing early in her career and contributed a great number of works. She wrote jazz pieces for piano and other instruments as well as for larger ensembles, such as *Zodiac Suite*, a piece for orchestra and piano performed by the New York Philharmonic in Carnegie Hall in 1946. Other jazz works include *Mary Lou's Mass*, hymns, and other pieces composed for religious worship services.

Margaret Bonds (1913-1972), a student of Florence B. Price and William Dawson, was born in Chicago. She received her Bachelor's and Master's degrees from Northwestern University in Evanston, Illinois. Bonds had a compositional style showing the influence of both the blues and jazz. Her association with most of the Black musicians, artists, and poets of her time had a decided effect on her musical expression. One of her well-known works is *Ballad of the Brown King*, a Christmas cantata that focuses on one of the three wise men. The libretto is by her lifelong friend, Black poet Langston Hughes. Another second-generation Black American woman composer is Oklahoma-born Zenobia Powell-Perry (1914-). She studied with William Dawson of Tuskegee Institute, where she received her Bachelor's degree. She later became a student of French composer Darius Milhaud while he was in the United States. She also received degrees from Northern Colorado University and Wyoming University. Perry's works include art songs, orchestral and band works, chamber music for a variety of combinations, and a music drama, *Tawawa House*.

Black women composers born since 1920 include Julia Amanda Perry (1924-1979), a Lexington, Kentucky, native who grew up in Akron, Ohio. She received her Bachelor's and Master's degrees from Westminster Choir College in Princeton, New Jersey, and studied composition with Luigi Dallapiccola in Italy and Nadia Boulanger in France. Her works combine various compositional techniques and are characterized by a liberal use of dissonance and unconventional harmonies. Her works include arrangements of spirituals, choral works, art songs, symphonies, operas, and chamber works for a variety

of instrumental and vocal combinations. Her recorded works include the chamber piece *Homunculus C.F.* for percussion, harp, and piano; *A Short Piece for Orchestra*; and *Stabat Mater* for contralto and string orchestra or string quartet.

Lena Johnson McLin (1928-) was born in Atlanta but has spent most of her adult life in Chicago. The niece of Thomas A. Dorsey, "Father of Gospel Music," and a Spelman College graduate, McLin studied composition in Atlanta with Leonora Brown and Willis Lawrence James. She studied composition and electronic music at Roosevelt University in Chicago and received her Master's degree from the American Conservatory of Music. Her works show a variety of influences, including rock, gospel, and dissonant styles. Her compositions include cantatas, masses, spirituals (solo and choral arrangements), gospel songs, choral anthems, art songs, operas, soul

Although Philippa Duke Schuyler is best known as a concert pianist, she began composing music at age three and continued to do so until her tragic death in 1967. [Schomburg Center]

songs, and electronic music. One of her works is the cantata *Free at Last*, described as a portrait of Dr. Martin Luther King, Jr., written for solo voices, chorus, narrator, and piano.

Betty Jackson King (1928-) was born in Chicago and received her Bachelor's and Master's degrees from Roosevelt University there. She is best known for her choral works, especially her arrangements of spirituals. Philippa Duke Schuyler (1931-1967) is best known as a concert pianist, but her compositions date back to 1935, when she was only three years old. She wrote for piano, orchestra, string quartet, chorus and orchestra, and voice and piano. Not long after her tragic death in a helicopter crash in Vietnam, her *Niles Fantasia* (*The Nile Fantasy*) for piano and orchestra had its American premiere at New York's Town Hall. Delaware native Dorothy Rudd Moore (1940-) studied with Mark Fax at Howard University in Washington, D.C., where she received her Bachelor's degree. She also studied with Nadia Boulanger in Paris and Fontainebleau, France, and with Chou Wenchung in New York City. Her works have been performed in Europe, South America, Asia, and the United States. Moore has written symphonies, chamber music, instrumental works, works for voice, and operas, including the opera *Frederick Douglass*, which premiered in 1985 in New York City.

Micki Grant (1941-) is a Chicago-born composer of stage works, the best known being *Don't Bother Me, I Can't Cope*. Jeraldine Saunders Herbison (1941-), a composer and music educator born in Virginia, received her undergraduate degree from Virginia State University, where she studied with Undine Smith Moore. She has written for string orchestra, string quartet, and cello and piano, and has composed ballets, choral and instrumental works, and themes for television shows.

BIBLIOGRAPHY

Abdul, Raoul. *Blacks in Classical Music* (1977); *BDAAM*; Goldsmith, Diane. "Undine Smith Moore: Classical Composer of Life's Sweet Song," *Virginia-Pilot* (February 16, 1984); Green, Mildred Denby. *Black Women Composers: A Genesis* (1983); Handy, D. Antoinette. *Black Women in American Bands and Orchestras* (1981); Hayes, Anthony. "Jeraldine S. Herbison," Unpublished manuscript (1991); Mroczek, Patricia. "A Woman and Her Music: From Nickelodeons to the Library of Congress," *Quest* (1988); Roach, Hildred. *Black American Music: Past and Present* (1985); Wakefield, Tony. "Zenobia Powell-Perry, Composer," Unpublished manuscript (1991).

MILDRED DENBY GREEN

CONCERT MUSIC

In the decade before the Emancipation there were talented Black performers giving concerts. Many of these performers were women, and most of these women were singers. One, said to have so beautiful and graceful a vocal sound that she was called the "Black Swan," was Elizabeth Taylor Greenfield, the first Black American concert singer. After her debut in Buffalo, New York, in 1851, she toured the United States. A few years later she studied in and toured England and gave a command performance for Queen Victoria. Returning to the United States, she had a relatively short concert career, retired from the stage, and opened a studio in Philadelphia where she taught singing. She also formed an opera troupe that provided opportunities for other Black musicians.

Among the Black women instrumentalists who performed as early as the 1890s was Myrtle Hart, a pianist and harpist who played at the British exhibit at Chicago's 1893 World's Fair.

Outstanding Black women singers from the period following the Emancipation include soprano Anna M. Hyers and her sister, contralto Emma L. Hyers. Their debut in Sacramento, California, won them great critical praise and, after touring widely in the western and northern areas of the country, they formed a touring company. In her travels abroad, Marie Smith Selika—known as the "Queen of Staccato" and also as Madame Selika (a name taken from the leading female character in Meyerbeer's *L'Africaine*)—performed for Queen Victoria. Soprano Matilda Sissieretta Jones, called "Black Patti" after Italian singer Adelina Patti, sang in Europe, Asia, and Africa and gave command performances for royalty and, in America, for President Benjamin Harrison. Flora Batson toured throughout the world; she was called the "Double-Voiced Queen of Song" because of her tremendously wide vocal range.

As opportunities for developing other musical talents grew at the turn of the century, the number of Black women concert performers expanded beyond the world of vocal music. Hazel Harrison, the first Black woman concert pianist, won acclaim both in America and abroad. Helen Hagan was the first Black pianist to earn the Bachelor of Music degree from Yale University. She toured extensively until the 1930s, when she began a teaching career in Black colleges.

Outstanding Black women singers of this time included Florence Cole Talbert (McCleave), the first Black woman to sing the title role in *Aida*; Lillian Evanti, one of the first Black Americans to sing opera abroad; Abbie Mitchell, celebrated singer and actress,

Anna M. Hyers (shown here) and her sister, Emma, were the first Black women to gain success on the American stage. This talented operatic team emerged in the early 1870s and then toured nationally for several seasons in a series of concerts. The Hyers Sisters were exceptional also because they dared to deviate from the stereotypes of the era. [Moorland-Spingarn]

member of the original cast of Gershwin's *Porgy and Bess*, and wife of Will Marion Cook; Caterina Jarboro, who sang with opera companies in Europe and America; Anne Brown, who was the original Bess in Gershwin's folk opera and had an extensive concert career; and Etta Moten, who concertized widely, sang the role of Bess, and worked in musicals, films, radio, and television.

One of the most famous Black women musicians of this century is the internationally recognized contralto Marian Anderson. Told by conductor Arturo Toscanini that hers was a voice one hears once in a century, Anderson enjoyed a long and illustrious concert career until she retired in 1965.

Black women who were active as concert musicians from the 1940s through the 1960s included Dorothy Maynor, soprano, who toured widely in the

United States and abroad and founded a school of the arts for children in Harlem after her retirement; Camilla Williams, who sang with the New York City Opera; Mattiwilda Dobbs, who won international recognition in the opera world (her debut at the Metropolitan Opera in 1956 followed Marian Anderson's by one year); Carol Brice, contralto, who was called the "new" Marian Anderson; and Margaret Bonds, pianist and composer, who cultivated and promoted Black expression in her works and used the verses of Black poets (most notably her lifelong friend Langston Hughes) in her vocal works.

Pianist Philippa Duke Schuyler, a child prodigy, performed extensively, composed, and served as a correspondent in Vietnam, where she died tragically in a helicopter crash. Natalie Hinderas, who promoted the music of Black Americans in her piano concerts, successfully combined a performing career with a professorship at Temple University in Pennsylvania; she also performed on television and made several recordings. Composer and conductor Julia Perry's European tour in the late 1950s as an orchestral conductor was acclaimed by critics. As a composer she used an eclectic musical language, and her style extended from the moderately dissonant, standard harmonic expression of her first works to the more dissonant, unorthodox harmonies of the later ones.

From the 1960s to the 1990s an even larger number of Black women musicians came upon the scene. Following Marian Anderson's 1955 debut at the Metropolitan Opera House, several Black women have served as principal singers there and with other opera companies. Most notable among the many divas of international fame are Leontyne Price, Grace Bumbry, Shirley Verrett, Martina Arroyo, Leona Mitchell, Betty Allen, and Hilda Harris.

Leontyne Price began performing in the early 1950s, when she appeared in revivals of *Four Saints in Three Acts* and *Porgy and Bess*. She performed in several televised operas, including the title role in Puccini's *Tosca* on NBC-TV in 1955, but it was not until 1961 that she made her Metropolitan debut. Grace Bumbry was the first Black singer to perform a major role at the Bayreuth Festival in Germany, singing Venus in Wagner's *Tannhäuser* in 1961, following her Paris debut in 1960. She made her American debut in Chicago in 1963 and her Met debut in 1965. Shirley Verrett's Met debut came three years later, following her 1967 debut at London's Covent Garden.

Betty Allen, mezzo-soprano, made her concert debut at New York's Town Hall in 1958. Leonard Bernstein, impressed with her performance at the Berkshire Music Festival, invited her to sing in his *Jeremiah Symphony*. She toured widely in the United States and abroad and has recorded extensively. Hilda Harris, also a mezzo-soprano, made her concert debut at Carnegie Hall. She toured extensively at home and in Europe as a recitalist and performed in oratorios and with symphony orchestras. At St. Gallen in Switzerland she made her operatic debut in the title role of Bizet's *Carmen* and subsequently sang with several opera companies in America and abroad. She joined the New York City Opera in 1974 and made her Metropolitan Opera House debut three years later.

Black women concert singers perform worldwide, and many are also developing careers as recording artists. Jessye Norman, considered one of the world's finest sopranos, has concertized abroad and throughout the United States. In 1989, she was selected to sing the French national anthem for the bicentennial of the French Revolution. For a number of years she sang with the Deutsche Oper in Berlin and with other European companies before she eventually changed the focus of her career to the concert stage.

More Black women concert musicians have been performing outside the vocal realm since the 1970s. As opportunities have opened up, more Black women musicians have ventured into the areas of conducting, composition, and instrumental music as full-time endeavors. At one time musicians interested in these areas were associated with an educational institution as a main source of livelihood.

Black women instrumentalists include D. Antoinette Handy (Miller), concert flutist, who has played in orchestras in Paris and Geneva as well as in the United States. She toured Germany and America with Trio Pro Viva, a group she founded, whose programs feature the music of Black composers. Frances Walker, pianist, has performed widely in Europe, the West Indies, and America and has recorded works by Black composers for Orion Records. As a member of the New World Ensemble, she toured New York colleges. Gail Hightower, bassoonist, has performed with symphonies in the United States and Italy and founded the Universal Symphony in 1978 in New York.

Others include Nina Kennedy, pianist, who has performed with several symphony orchestras and concertized widely, and Frances Cole, harpsichordist, pianist, and violinist. Cole performed music from the seventeenth to the twentieth centuries, including jazz, and received rave reviews from critics.

BIBLIOGRAPHY

Abdul, Raoul. *Blacks in Classical Music* (1977); *BDAAM*; Cuney-Hare, Maude. *Negro Musicians and Their Music* ([1936] 1974); Green, Mildred Denby. *Black Women Composers: A Genesis* (1983); Handy, D. Antoinette. *Black Women in American Bands and Orchestras* (1981); Long, Richard A. *Black Americana* (1985); Roach, Hildred. *Black American Music: Past and Present* (1985); Seidman, Peter. "Eva Jessye," *Black Perspective in Music* (1990); Southern, Eileen. *The Music of Black Americans: A History* (1983).

MILDRED DENBY GREEN

CONGRESS OF RACIAL EQUALITY *see* MARYLAND FREEDOM UNION

COOK, CORALIE see
BAHA'I FAITH

COOK, MARY see
BAPTIST CHURCH

COOKE, ANNE (REID) (1907-)

In 1949, the Howard Players of Howard University became the first American undergraduate group to be invited by the U.S. State Department and a foreign government to perform abroad. This historic event was spearheaded by Dr. Anne Cooke. Anne Cooke was known for nearly four decades as an innovative director and educator in theater. Throughout her career, she developed and maintained professional standards in the theater programs on predominantly Black campuses such as Howard University, Spelman College, and Atlanta University. Cooke was born Anna Margaret on October 6, 1907, in Washington, D.C., but she spent her early years in the Midwest. She is the daughter of Mr. and Mrs. William W. Cooke. She received her A.B. from Oberlin College in 1928. Cooke also studied at Columbia University, American Academy of Dramatic Arts, and Chicago Art Theatre. Cooke was a recipient of Fulbright, Rosenwald, and Rockefeller Fellowships. She received her Ph.D. in theater from Yale University in 1943, making her possibly the first Black American to receive such a degree. During her time at Yale, Cooke had an opportunity to work with film director Otto Preminger. Through Preminger, Cooke was able to gain experience as a director during the early years of television.

In 1928, Cooke became director of dramatics at Spelman College. In 1934, she organized and directed the Atlanta University Summer Theatre, a dramatic organization comprised of Atlanta University, Morehouse College, and Spelman College students. This organization gained a reputation for excellence in dramatics. Cooke brought in the best and brightest Black theater educators and professional actors to work with the students. Major white designers would also lend their expertise to the program. Students from around the country converged on Atlanta to work under Cooke. For many years, the summer theater was the only place in the country where Black American students were afforded an op-

portunity to have a concentrated professional theater experience.

In 1942, Cooke left Spelman to become director of the Communications Center at Hampton Institute. From 1942 to 1958, she organized and chaired Howard University's first Drama Department, making it the premiere Black institution for drama. Cooke brought international acclaim to the Howard Players when the group traveled to Norway and other Scandinavian countries.

In 1958, Cooke married sociologist and author Ira De A. Reid. While her husband was on the faculty of Haverford College, Cooke was active in campus and community drama in Haverford. After the death of her husband in 1968, Cooke became a professor of drama at the University of Maryland, where she retired.

[See also THEATER.]

BIBLIOGRAPHY
Cooke, Anne. Personal interviews (1984, 1988); Read, Florence Matilda. *The Story of Spelman College* (1961).

MANUSCRIPT COLLECTIONS
Howard University Channing Pollock Archives, Theatre Collection, Washington, D.C.; Moorland-Spingarn Research Center, Manuscript Division, Howard University, Washington, D.C.; Atlanta University Archives, Manuscript Division, Atlanta, Georgia; Spelman College Archives including *The Messenger*, Theatre Collection, Atlanta, Georgia; Rockefeller General Education Board Archives, Manuscript and Recipients' File Divisions, Rockefeller University, North Tarrytown, New York.

KATHY A. PERKINS

COOPER, ANNA JULIA HAYWOOD (1858-1964)

"Not the boys less, but the girls more," wrote Anna J. Cooper in her collection of writings and essays, *A Voice from the South by a Black Woman of the South* (1892). Marked by an unusual maturity and mental aptitude, Cooper said that "not far from . . . kindergarten age" she had decided to be a teacher. Her early and unbridled passion for learning and the belief that women were equipped to follow intellectual pursuits carried Cooper from the then-ungraded St. Augustine's Normal School and Collegiate Institute in Raleigh, North Carolina, to the Sorbonne in Paris. During this more than fifty-year sojourn in pursuit of her dream, she also earned A.B. (1884) and

Anna Julia Cooper's book A Voice from the South by a Black Woman of the South *(1892) has been called the first Black feminist publication. [Scurlock Studio]*

blossomed. Years later, however, as president of Frelinghuysen, Cooper touchingly honored her mother by naming one small department of the struggling institution the Hannah Stanley Opportunity School. As Cooper wrote about her mother, "mother . . . sacrificed and toiled to give me advantages that she had never enjoyed herself." Of her father, Cooper later wrote that beyond the act of procreation she owed him nothing.

Cooper entered St. Augustine's in 1867. There she coached or tutored other students, some of whom were years beyond her tender age of nine. About a decade later, when she protested the exclusion of young women from higher courses scheduled only for ministerial studies and, therefore, only for men, Cooper met her future husband. From Nassau, British West Indies, George A. G. Cooper was an Episcopal theology student and St. Augustine's new Greek teacher. Although George was nearly fourteen years her senior, teacher and pupil developed a friendship, which later developed into love. They were married on June 21, 1877. With shared career goals, the couple worked tirelessly to achieve them during the two years they were married. George died on September 27, 1879, just two months after becoming the second Black ordained clergyman in the Protestant Episcopal Church in North Carolina.

At age twenty-one, Cooper was alone. Not one to complain about adversities, the young widow stoically continued the pursuit of her goals. Denied a modest increase in her thirty-dollar-a-month teaching salary, she left St. Augustine's in the fall of 1881 for Oberlin, Ohio. The previous summer she had written to James Harris Fairchild, president of Oberlin College, saying "for a long time, I earnestly desired to take an advanced course in some superior Northern college, but could not . . . for lack of means."

Considering its enviable reputation for liberal thought and superior scholarship, Cooper believed that admission to Oberlin was an important step in her long quest for higher education. Unlike most young women students of the time, Cooper—along with Mary Eliza Church (Terrell) and Ida A. Gibbs (Hunt)—took the four-year "gentlemen's course." The trio graduated from Oberlin in 1884, following Mary Jane Patterson (1862) as the first Black women to complete a four-year course of study from an accredited American college.

While at Oberlin, Cooper began to see herself as a defender of her race and an advocate for Black women. Personal successes and achievements aside, she remained sensitive to the plight and needs of oppressed peoples and was encouraged to be a free

M.A. (1887) degrees from Oberlin College, was principal of the M Street High School in Washington, D.C. (1902-6), and, in 1929, became the second president of Frelinghuysen University, in Washington, D.C. Best known as an educator, Cooper also was a feminist, human rights advocate, distinguished scholar, essayist, author, lecturer, and vital force in the late nineteenth-century Black woman's club movement.

The daughter of a slave woman, Hannah Stanley, and her master, George Washington Haywood of Raleigh, Cooper was born Annie Julia Haywood on August 10, 1858. Hired out as a nursemaid for Charles Busbee (later a successful lawyer), Hannah named the infant girl for Charles's mother. No one in her own home was literate, so probably it was in the Busbee home that young Annie's love for books and learning thinker and the voice of unheard southern Black women. Her interaction with faculty members and peers, whose sound scholarship and intelligence reinforced her own views, helped Cooper prepare for her lifelong work. The first member of her family to go beyond the primary grades, Cooper left Oberlin eager to serve those who were unserved. Confident, poised, self-assured, and armed with an A.B., she felt ready to address the inequities and indignities that Black women like her mother had experienced in slavery and in the post-Civil War South.

Cooper postponed for a year her planned return to Raleigh in order to teach at Wilberforce College in Ohio. As a devout and lifelong Episcopalian, Cooper had many contacts in the national Black church community. At Wilberforce she met Bishop Benjamin W. Arnett, a noted cleric of the African Methodist Episcopal (AME) Church. Cooper admired Arnett for his support of the cause of Black women, and Arnett later wrote a favorable introduction to *A Voice from the South*. Also among her supporters were clergymen Alexander Crummell, Francis J. Grimké, and Walter H. Brooks. Later, she befriended Alexander Walters, a bishop in the AME Zion Church and head of the National Negro-American Political League. All social activists, these men worked to help those who, in Cooper's words, "were stuck at the bottom" (Cooper [1892] 1969). In each of them she found a brother's sympathy for the difficult and adverse situation of Black women.

As in her life experiences, Cooper forthrightly addressed critical issues in her writings. Not given to expediency or vagueness, she never avoided tough situations or difficult decisions. She used cogent arguments to persuade others of the importance and correctness of the causes she embraced. Although some people found her to be difficult, intractable, and blunt, St. Augustine's principal John E. C. Smedes described her in 1881 as "a woman of unusual culture and intelligence, and of unfeigned zeal and piety." Cooper, he said, had decided to "be better qualified to take part in the great work going forward in the South for the . . . education of its colored people."

After a year as head of the modern languages department at Wilberforce, Cooper returned to Raleigh to deal with urgent family matters. (In 1880-81, she had purchased a modest dwelling for her mother from Richard Battle, a member of the prominent Haywood clan.) For the next two years Cooper taught mathematics, Greek, and Latin at St. Augustine's, began outreach extension programs under the school's aegis, and helped found a Sunday school and a mission guild. As a member of the North Carolina

Teacher's Association, she involved herself with critical education issues, and in signing the group's report to the state legislature, she was very outspoken about the failure of lawmakers to appropriate "reasonable and just provisions for the training of . . . colored youth" (*The Southland* 1891).

In 1887, Washington, D.C.'s first Black Superintendent of Colored Schools, inspired by high praise from people at Oberlin, invited Cooper to join the faculty of M Street (now Paul Laurence Dunbar) High School. Not completely unknown in Washington, Cooper boarded with the Rev. Alexander Crummell and his wife. Already living with the Crummells were Oberlin graduates Mary Jane Patterson, also from Raleigh, and her sister, Channie, Mary Eliza Church (Terrell), Ida Gibbs (Hunt), and, later, Gibbs's sister, Harriet Gibbs Marshall. Cooper quickly joined with them and others to work for social progress, allying herself with groups that addressed issues important to the national Black community. Battles won in Washington often had broad implications for Black Americans across the nation, and Cooper worked unstintingly to present a more positive image of her race.

The decade of the 1890s was an important period in the fostering of Black intellectual and political thought. In the vanguard of the struggle for human rights, Cooper and the groups with whom she was associated promoted opportunities for academic excellence for Black youth; built groups and clubs of learning and culture for Black women; defended the honor of, and demanded respect for, the reputations and views of Black people; and effectively articulated their needs, hopes, and aspirations. To these efforts Cooper and her colleagues brought more than a half-century of commitment to, and activism in, antislavery groups, abolitionist societies, women's rights groups, literary and self-improvement clubs, and benevolent organizations. Some, like Cooper, had published and lectured on circuits such as Chautauqua. Known for her learning, modesty, and culture, Cooper herself was recognized as an "inspiring lecturer and leader" (Hutchinson 1981).

As spokeswomen for their race, Anna Cooper, Fannie Barrier Williams, and Fanny Jackson Coppin were invited in 1893 to address a special meeting of the Women's Congress in Chicago. This international gathering of women was held to coincide with the World's Columbian Exposition, in order to insure a large audience and wide press coverage. A special session addressing the theme "The Intellectual Progress of Colored Women of the United States since Emancipation" was held to give Black women a hearing before an international body of white women. Cooper's thesis was a subject she often addressed, "The Needs and Status of Black Women." A platform guest who was deeply moved by what he had heard, Frederick Douglass rose to make impromptu remarks. In closing he said, "When I hear such speeches . . . from our women—*our women*—I feel a sense of gratitude to Almighty God that I have lived to see what I now see" (*World's Congress of Representative Women* 1894).

Cooper was the only woman elected to membership in the esoteric American Negro Academy, founded in 1897 by Alexander Crummell. Among its select members were W.E.B. Du Bois, Kelly Miller, Jesse E. Moorland, Arthur A. Schomburg, and Carter G. Woodson. This late nineteenth-century Black think tank had among its objectives "the publication of scholarly work and the defense of the Negro against vicious assault." At the first Pan-African Conference in London's Westminster Hall in 1900, Cooper and Anna H. Jones of Missouri were the only two Black women to address the international gathering of African, Afro-Caribbean, and Afro-American descendants. Cooper's address, "The Negro Problem in America," was to have been published in the conference report but has not been found. An official U.S. delegate and elected member of the executive committee, Cooper also served on a committee that drafted a memorial to Queen Victoria, which also addressed the issue of apartheid. Concisely and poignantly, the conferees appealed for immediate relief from "acts of injustice directed against Her Majesty's subjects in South Africa" (Hutchinson 1981).

Cooper followed this heady experience with a trip to France to tour the Paris Exposition. Among egalitarians and Black expatriates, and accompanied by Du Bois, Cooper visited the Social Economy Building's Negro Pavilion, which housed the Exposition des Nègres d'Amérique. Mounted by the Library of Congress and first displayed at M Street High School, the exhibit featured the Black community of Washington, D.C.

Revitalized by her involvement in the Pan-African Conference, Cooper returned home to her teaching duties. Although she had been asked to serve on the planning committee for the next gathering, to be held in Boston in 1902, this conference did not materialize. The conference's cancellation may have been linked to monitoring by the U.S. State and War departments of Black activists in Puerto Rico, the Philippines, and Cuba, where a Negro revolution was rumored in 1900-1901. The Interior Department's Bureau of Insular Affairs compiled files (captioned

"Negro") about the militancy of Black islanders. These so-called investigations were followed by a second occupation of Cuba and American civil-military rule there from 1906 to 1909.

When Robert H. Terrell resigned as principal of M Street High School on December 31, 1901, to become the District of Columbia's first Black municipal judge, Cooper, who had taught math and science at the school since 1887, succeeded him, becoming the second Black female principal in the school's history. Others who had served in the post were Mary Jane Patterson, Richard T. Greener, Francis L. Cardozo, and Winfield Scott Montgomery. Cooper began her new duties on January 2, 1902. At the time, M Street was the only high school in the nation to offer a diverse curriculum that prepared Black students for either industry or college, including the Ivy League schools. Under Cooper's leadership the school became a showcase for the best and brightest, and Cooper and her faculty used their alumni contacts to get scholarships for worthy pupils. When Father Felix Klein of the Catholic Institute of Paris visited the school in 1903 and observed a Latin class being taught by Cooper herself, he found it incredible that a terrible race problem existed in the United States. However, Cooper's leadership and the school's college preparatory work were not to go unchallenged.

The 1904-5 school year was one of turmoil, as allegations of insubordination and personal impropriety by Cooper and rumors of student misconduct circulated around the city. Cooper was the fulcrum of what was called the M Street High School controversy. Community opinion—whether for or against her—depended largely on so-called revelations in the local press. The *Washington Post* reported in 1905 that the controversy began with an address to M Street students by W.E.B. Du Bois in the winter of 1902-3. His remark that there was "a tendency throughout the country to restrict the curriculum of colored schools" sent shock waves through the city school system. Cooper's chief antagonist was her supervisor, Percy M. Hughes, director of Washington's high schools. Despite the school board's promise to conduct a speedy inquiry, it dragged through inconclusive evidence for months.

Finally, in October 1906, the board decided not to reappoint Cooper; school board member Mary Church Terrell, part of the Oberlin trio, and her husband, Judge Robert H. Terrell, were silent about the board's reasons and actions. The tendency of Congress to meddle in the affairs of the District of Columbia cannot be ignored as a factor in Cooper's dismissal, but some people suspected the influence of

Booker T. Washington and the so-called Tuskegee machine. Amid the recurring debate over vocational training (Washington's position) versus classical education (the position of Du Bois), Cooper left Washington, D.C., proud of M Street's record, now recognized as a creditable college preparatory high school whose students merited admission even into Ivy League colleges. Cooper taught at Lincoln University in Missouri for four years and then returned to Washington, D.C., to teach Latin again at the school she had formerly led.

Tough-minded and tenacious, Cooper would meet new and diverse challenges. She bought a home, made extensive repairs, and became guardian to five great-nieces and nephews, aged six months to twelve years. It was a strenuous challenge at any age, but Cooper, then in her fifties, persevered. In 1911, while pursuing a Ph.D., she attended summer sessions at "La Guilde" in Paris. From 1915 to 1917, she attended summer classes at Columbia University and later took extension courses there. Sponsored by Father Klein, she applied to the Sorbonne in 1923. When that school accepted her Columbia credits, she studied for many hours at the Library of Congress and then traveled to France to meet dissertation requirements; this, of course, was before teachers were allowed sabbatical leave.

On March 23, 1925, Cooper became the fourth African-American woman to earn a Ph.D. (preceded by Georgiana R. Simpson, Eva B. Dykes, and Sadie T. M. Alexander). Cooper's dissertation, "The Attitude of France toward Slavery during the Revolu-

In 1901, Anna Julia Cooper became the second Black female principal in the history of the famous M Street High School in Washington, D.C. She succeeded Robert H. Terrell. A life-long educator and leader, she received her Ph.D. from the Sorbonne at the age of sixty-six. She is shown here on the veranda of her Washington, D.C., home. [Scurlock Studio]

Frelinghuysen University was dedicated to providing an education to adult "colored working people." Anna Julia Cooper was its second president and fought valiantly for the school's survival. [Scurlock Studio]

tion," was indicative of her broad knowledge, sound scholarship, and continued interest in pan-Africanism (Gabel 1982). At the age of sixty-six, she had completed her journey from slavery to the Sorbonne; her dream had become a reality. On December 29, 1925, William Tindall, a D.C. commissioner, awarded her the degree at Howard University's Rankin Chapel in a ceremony sponsored by the Xi Omega chapter of the Alpha Kappa Alpha sorority.

Frelinghuysen University was founded in Washington, D.C., in 1907 by Jesse Lawson. This nontraditional group of schools was to be a beacon of hope for "colored working people," and Cooper was installed as its second president on June 15, 1930. There were serious problems, however. Frelinghuysen had no permanent building or endowment; tuition alone paid teachers' stipends; and university trustees seemed unable to overcome old management disputes. Recurring exigencies forced Cooper, at great sacrifice, to move some academic programs into her home at 201 T Street, N.W. She neither charged rent nor accepted a salary. Instead, she chartered the

Hannah Stanley Opportunity School, which was annexed to the university but had a self-governing board of trustees charged to protect the school and Cooper's property from any threat of dissolution that the university might face. A 1933 codicil to Cooper's will devoted her property *"in perpetuo* to [the] Education of Colored Adults."

Frelinghuysen lost its charter in 1937 and no longer awarded degrees. The Washington, D.C. Board of Education, the only agency that could independently recognize it as a university, refused to do so. The university's trustees urged Cooper to make a public appeal for funds needed in order to upgrade Frelinghuysen and attract a stronger faculty. Feeling that such an appeal would be an unfair burden on the very community the institution was founded to serve, she refused. Instead, at age seventy-nine, Cooper sought a job with the Works Progress Administration's Office of Education but was not hired. She then tried to sell her property in Raleigh. The U.S. District Court upheld the school superintendent's decision not to accredit Frelinghuysen's law school, a disastrous ruling for the university. With just a few students enrolled, Cooper remained in a largely ceremonial role. In about 1940, the university became the Frelinghuysen Group of Schools for Colored Working People, and Cooper became its registrar.

The death of her great-niece and namesake, Annie Cooper Haywood Beckwith, of pneumonia in 1939 hastened Cooper's decline. Beckwith was six months old in 1915 when Anna Cooper became her guardian. After refusing to yield to most adversities, she had rested her hope for Frelinghuysen's future in Annie; now that hope was gone. Her post-Frelinghuysen endeavors were anticlimactic. In 1951, she privately published *Personal Recollections of the Grimké Family and the Life and Writings of Charlotte Forten Grimké.* In her book, Cooper told about the lives of the Grimkés, who were also slave descendants. She lived many more years—mostly with her memories—and spoke of other books she wished to write, but her failing health did not permit her to do so.

Anna J. Cooper was a versatile woman whose cogent ideas and diversity of thought are best demonstrated in her published works, lectures, poems, and miscellaneous writings. A consummate teacher, she ranked high among her peers. She was a feminist and a stoic activist in the struggle for the betterment of Black people. A much sought-after speaker, she was outspoken on such subjects as racism, the status of Black women, and educational systems that failed to consider the needs of Black and female students. Continuing to seek solutions to vexing problems, she addressed diverse themes, including "College Extension for Working People," "Modern Education," "The Negro Dialect," "A Problem in American Education: Loss of Speech through Isolation," and "Legislative Measures Concerning Slavery in the U.S." Cooper's commitment to education and organizational work left scant time for her personal life. She did not retire from her active career as an educator until her eighty-fourth year.

At the age of 105, Cooper died peacefully at her Washington, D.C., home on Thursday, February 27, 1964. She asked only to be remembered as "somebody's teacher on vacation . . . resting for the Fall opening" (Hutchinson 1981). After a simple service at St. Augustine's College Chapel, she was buried in Raleigh, North Carolina on Wednesday, March 4, 1964.

BIBLIOGRAPHY

A. J. Cooper papers. Moorland-Spingarn Research Center, Howard University, Washington, D.C.; Brown,

Hallie Q., compiler. *Homespun Heroines and Other Women of Distinction* ([1926] 1971); Cooper, Anna J. *A Voice from the South by a Black Woman of the South* ([1892] 1969), and "College Extension for Working People," *Journal of the Alumnae Club,* Oberlin College Archives, Washington, D.C. (n.d.); Franklin, John Hope. *The Free Negro in North Carolina, 1790-1860* (1943); Gabel, Leona C. *From Slavery to the Sorbonne and Beyond: The Life and Writings of Anna J. Cooper* (1982); Giddings, Paula. *When and Where I Enter: The Impact of Black Women on Race and Sex in America* (1984); Harley, Sharon and Rosalyn Terborg-Penn, eds. *The Afro-American Woman: Struggles and Images* (1978); Hutchinson, Louise Daniel. *Anna J. Cooper: A Voice from the South* (1981); Lerner, Gerda, ed. *Black Women in White America: A Documentary History* (1973); Loewenberg, Bert James and Ruth Bogin, eds. *Black Women in Nineteenth-Century American Life: Their Words, Their Thoughts, Their Feelings* (1976); Majors, Monroe A. *Noted Negro Women: Their Triumphs and Activities* ([1893] 1971); *NAW* (1980); Sterling, Dorothy, ed. *We Are Your Sisters: Black Women in the Nineteenth Century* (1984); *World's Congress of Representative Women* (1894).

LOUISE DANIEL HUTCHINSON

COPPIN, FANNY JACKSON (1837-1913)

When Fanny Jackson became principal of Philadelphia's Institute for Colored Youth, she held the highest educational appointment of any Black woman in the nation at the time. While most of Fanny Jackson's attention, before and after her marriage, was given to the institute, Jackson Coppin was also active in the African Methodist Episcopal Church, the National Association of Colored Women, and, in later life, as a missionary to Africa.

Fanny Jackson Coppin was born a slave in Washington, D.C., in 1837. Her freedom was bought during her early childhood by a devoted aunt, Sarah Orr. Jackson moved to New Bedford, Massachusetts, and, by the early 1850s, to Newport, Rhode Island, to live with relatives. While in Newport, Jackson worked as a domestic in the home of George Henry Calvert, great-grandson of Lord Baltimore, settler of Maryland. Calvert's wife, Mary, was a descendant of Mary, Queen of Scots. With the money earned at the Calverts', Jackson was able to hire a tutor for one hour a day for three days a week. She worked for the Calverts for six years, and during her last year of employment with the couple Jackson attended the segregated public schools of Newport. In 1859, she attended Rhode Island State Normal School in Bristol.

In 1860, Jackson enrolled in the Ladies Department of Oberlin College in Ohio. She was assisted financially by her aunt Sarah, a scholarship from Bishop Daniel Payne of the African Methodist Episcopal (AME) Church, and scholarship aid from Oberlin. Jackson also worked while a student at Oberlin and graduated in 1865 with an A.B., the second African-American woman to do so. While at Oberlin, Jackson was active in all facets of college life. Her outstanding reputation as a teacher resulted in her being chosen as a student teacher of the preparatory department at Oberlin—the first African-American to achieve such an honor. Also, during her senior year, she was chosen as class poet.

In addition to Jackson's activities on campus at Oberlin College, she was also involved in an array of community events. For example, in 1863 Jackson opened an evening school for freedpeople who were migrating into Oberlin. The classes were highly successful and received favorable press coverage in both local and abolitionist newspapers. As a result of the publicity Jackson received for establishing the evening school for freedpeople, and for her outstanding academic record at Oberlin, she was well known throughout the Black communities of the nation when she graduated in 1865.

After leaving Oberlin in 1865, Jackson was appointed principal of the female department at the prestigious Institute for Colored Youth (ICY) in Philadelphia. The institute was a classical high school founded by the Society of Friends in 1837. The school included a preparatory department, girls' and boys' high school departments, and a teacher training course. By 1869, when her principal, Ebenezer Bassett, was appointed U.S. minister of Haiti, Jackson was appointed to take his place. This was a significant appointment; Jackson was the first Black woman to head an institution of higher learning in the nation.

The institute was located within the heart of the Philadelphia African-American community, near the historic Mother Bethel AME Church. The *Christian Recorder*, the newspaper of the AME Church, frequently publicized the institute's and Jackson's activities. In addition, Jackson wrote children's stories and a woman's column for the paper.

In 1881, at the age of forty-four, Jackson married Levi Jenkins Coppin, an AME minister at least fifteen years her junior. They maintained a commuting relationship for the first three years of their marriage. Levi Coppin pastored a church in Baltimore and commuted to Philadelphia while Fanny Coppin remained as principal of the institute. When it became apparent that Fanny Coppin was not going to leave her position at the institute, Reverend Coppin transferred to a small church in Philadelphia in 1884. Fanny Coppin's marriage coincided with a huge campaign she headed to establish an industrial department at the institute. By the 1880s, Black Americans were shut out of the growing number of technical and industrial positions in Philadelphia. Fanny Coppin was adamant that Black Americans should open their own schools to prepare themselves for these new avenues of employment.

After a decade of fund-raising, the industrial department at the institute opened in January 1889. The new department did not meet the expectations that Coppin had for the school to offer advanced technical courses. However, the department did offer training in carpentry, bricklaying, shoemaking, printing, plastering, millinery, dressmaking, and cooking. The department was the first trade school for African-Americans in Philadelphia. The school was in great demand; the department was flooded with applications, and a waiting list of hundreds was maintained throughout its existence.

After her marriage, Coppin joined the AME Church. She was elected president of the local Women's Mite Missionary and later became national president of the Women's Home and Foreign Missionary Society of the AME Church. In 1888, she represented the organization at the Centenary of Missions Conference in London.

Fanny Jackson Coppin was politically active throughout her life. Although women could not vote during her lifetime, she viewed the franchise as being as important for women as for men. She often spoke at political rallies and most often was the only woman on the program. Coppin was elected one of the vice presidents of the National Association of Colored Women (NACW). She also served as a member of the board of managers for the Home for Aged and Infirmed Colored People in Philadelphia for over thirty years (1881-1913).

By the turn of the century, the years of activity began to take a toll on Coppin's health. She had spent endless hours working at the institute and had earnestly tried to find employment and housing for her students and other African-Americans in Philadelphia. Her speaking engagements were numerous, and her involvement with civil and religious activities was endless. In 1896, she became ill with pleurisy and was confined to her home. She never fully recovered, and in 1901 she announced her retirement as principal of the institute effective June 1902.

Fanny Jackson Coppin was extremely private concerning her personal affairs. She made only one brief mention of her marriage to Levi Coppin in her auto-biography, *Reminiscences of School Life and Hints on Teaching* (1913). However, from all indications, the Coppins' marriage was a close one, and Levi Coppin seemed genuinely proud to be married to such a distinguished and well-regarded woman. He often spoke of her with deep respect, admiration, and appreciation.

Although Coppin was devoted to the institute, during the summers she often traveled with her husband for the AME Church. After Levi Coppin graduated from the Philadelphia Episcopal Divinity School in 1887, he was appointed editor of the *AME Review*, a prestigious position within the AME Church. He maintained this position from 1888 until 1896, when he was appointed pastor of Mother Bethel, where he remained until 1900. He was then elected bishop of the Fourteenth Episcopal District in South Africa.

After her retirement from the institute in 1902, Coppin accompanied her husband to Cape Town, South Africa. Because of her poor health and her age, many in the Philadelphia community feared she would not survive the trip. Prior to the couple's departure, testimonials were given in Fanny Coppin's honor. Newspapers reported that audiences were overflowing at each occasion. Gifts and money were given, and Coppin was deeply touched by this outpouring of affection from the community and her former students.

The Coppins arrived in Cape Town in December 1902. They traveled into the interior country. As many feared, the trip affected Fanny Coppin's health. She experienced fainting spells but then recovered and devoted her stay to developing missions among the women of the country. Her impact on the women of the country was profound. At the AME school in Cape Town named Wilberforce Institute, the African missions raised $10,000 to build the Fanny Jackson Coppin Girls Hall as a symbol of their appreciation of her efforts on their behalf.

Spending only a year in South Africa, the Coppins left in December 1903. After visiting several European countries, they arrived in the United States in spring 1904. Levi Coppin was then appointed bishop to the Seventh Episcopal District of the AME Church, which encompassed South Carolina and Alabama. Fanny Coppin traveled to South Carolina with her husband. However, the South African trip had increased her health problems. By 1905, she was so physically weak that the remaining eight years of her life were spent primarily confined to her Philadelphia home on Nineteenth and Bainbridge streets.

A brilliant teacher and a daring innovator in Black education, Fanny Jackson Coppin advocated vocational training many years before Booker T. Washington while maintaining, as he did not, a firm commitment to the importance of liberal arts in Black education. [Schomburg Center]

On January 21, 1913, Fanny Jackson Coppin died at her home in Philadelphia. Thousands, many of whom traveled from cities and towns from around the country, filled Mother Bethel AME Church for her funeral. Following the funeral, memorial services were conducted in Washington, D.C., Baltimore, and Philadelphia.

Known as a champion of the poor, Fanny Jackson Coppin was a captivating speaker who never spoke with notes. Throughout her life she attempted to make education available to all Black Americans.

Coppin State College in Baltimore, Maryland, is named in her honor.

[*See also* EDUCATION; INSTITUTE FOR COLORED YOUTH.]

BIBLIOGRAPHY

Coppin, Fanny Jackson. *Reminiscences of School Life, and Hints on Teaching* (1913); Coppin, Levi Jenkins. *Unwritten History* (1968); *DANB*; *NAW*; *NBAW*; Perkins, Linda M. *Fanny Jackson Coppin and the Institute for Colored Youth, 1865-1902* (1987); Fanny Jackson Coppin's papers are in the Oberlin College Archives, Oberlin, Ohio, and at the Friends Historical Library, Swarthmore College, Swarthmore, Pennsylvania.

LINDA M. PERKINS

COSTON, JULIA RINGWOOD

The vibrations of our silent suffering are not
ineffective. They touch and communicate. They
awaken interest and kindle sympathies. (Majors
1893)

Julia Ringwood Coston was concerned about the
long-suffering and hopeless endurance of Black women
in the South, and she argued that press editorials
could be effective in protesting their barbarous treatment. She supported women writers because she felt
they had broad appeal and were excellent role models
for young girls. She deplored the absence of Black
topics in ladies' fashion magazines of the 1890s and
so, in 1891, she edited and published the pioneering
Ringwood's Afro-American Journal of Fashion. In various departments edited by Black women, the journal
contained illustrations of the latest Paris fashions,
fashion articles, biographical sketches of prominent
Black women and promising young ladies, instructive

*Love stories and the latest Paris fashions took their place beside
biographical sketches of prominent Black women in the pages of*
Ringwood's Afro-American Journal of Fashion, *edited and
published by pioneer journalist Julia Ringwood Coston.*
[Schomburg Center]

messages to women and their daughters, witty passages, and love stories. It was then the only illustrated
journal for Black women in the world. From 1893 to
1895, she published a second journal, *Ringwood's Home
Magazine.* Coston was a pioneer among the Black
periodical press publishers in the United States. She
distinguished herself as a journalist and addressed the
interests of Black women of her day.

Julia Ringwood was named for Ringwood Farm
in Warrenton, Virginia, where she was born. Her
birth date is unknown. While an infant, she moved to
Washington, D.C. She was educated in the public
schools and had almost completed school when her
mother's health failed and she had to withdraw. She
became governess for the family of a general in the
U.S. Army while continuing her studies. In spring
1886, Julia Ringwood married William Hilary Coston,
a student at Yale University and later a minister. They
had two children—a daughter, Julia R., born in 1888,
and a son, W. H. born in 1890.

In 1884, William Hilary Coston had published
an eighty-four-page pamphlet, *A Freeman and Yet a
Slave.* The work was expanded and published in book
form in Chatham, Ontario, in 1888, two years after
the Costons married. The Costons settled in Cleveland, Ohio, where William Coston was pastor of
Saint Andrew's Episcopal Church. His tenure there
was fairly short, for he was deposed on May 14, 1894
(the reasons are unknown). Husband and wife were
mutually supportive of each other's work: Julia Coston
met household responsibilities as well as those of the
church's congregation, while William Coston encouraged her in her writings and offered wisdom and
guidance from his own experiences as a writer. Since
white journals ignored Black interests and excluded
Black faces and Black themes, Coston was spurred to
found *Ringwood's Afro-American Journal of Fashion* in
1891. The subscription rate was $1.25 per year.

The initial edition noted the journal's aim "to
satisfy the common desire among us for an illustrated
journal of our own ladies" (Scruggs 1893). It immediately appealed to its audience and received high praise
from many subscribers and from other publications.
Sarah G. Jones wrote on March 1, 1892, that she was
pleased with the journal and noted that men and
women of considerable literary ability who were unknown beyond the locality in which they lived should
"not be encouraged to remain in obscurity" (Majors
1893). She believed that the journal should make
their works known.

Mary Church Terrell, author, women's rights
and civil rights activist of Washington, D.C., edited

the biographical section of the first issue and immediately brought distinction and stature to the journal. Departments within the publication included "Plain Talk to Our Girls," edited by journalist Susie I. Lankford Shorter; "Art Department," edited by journalist Adina White; and "Literary Department," edited by journalist M. E. Lambert. Later women who were in charge of the departments were referred to as associate editors and managed their respective departments with ability and literary tact. Victoria Earle Matthews, a social worker and free-lance writer for leading Black newspapers, wrote on May 22, 1892, in praise of the journal. She wished Coston "positive and permanent success in establishing it." She said, "it is so pure, so womanly—positively agreeable in every feature as reading for private home, instruction, and guidance" (Majors 1893).

Bishop Theodore Holly of Haiti received a sample copy of the journal and noted with pleasure its contents as well as "the peculiar characteristics of its engravings." *Ringwood's Journal* was the first ladies' fashion journal in Haiti—a Black country. Bishop Holly marveled that it was introduced "by a lady of our race" (Majors 1893).

An unnamed friend wrote of Julia Ringwood Coston's femininity and modesty. She called Coston a lovable woman whose primary concern was to serve the highest interests of women at that time. She wanted to give them modest publicity to highlight their lives and present them as role models for "our growing womanhood" (Scruggs 1893).

Julia Ringwood Coston's life after 1895 is undocumented. Although there was a circulation of thousands of copies monthly of both journals, no copy of either is known to exist. William Hilary Coston wrote other works and was still publishing in 1899 when he issued the *Spanish-American War Volunteer: Ninth U.S. Volunteer Infantry Roster, Biographies, Cuban Sketches*. Julia Ringwood Coston was one of several Black women journalists of the nineteenth century and is known primarily for her work as editor and publisher of the world's first fashion magazine for Black women. It was popularly received not only for its fashions but also because it celebrated Black women and girls through biographical sketches and timely articles that addressed matters of interest to Black women and their families.

BIBLIOGRAPHY

Ayer Directory of Newspapers and Periodicals (1892, 1893-94, 1895); Bragg, George Freeman, Jr. *History of the Afro-American Group of the Episcopal Church* (1922); Bullock, Penelope L. *The Afro-American Periodical Press: 1838-1909* (1981); *DANB*; Majors, Monroe A. *Noted Negro Women: Their Triumphs and Activities* (1893); *NBAW*; Scruggs, Lawson Andrew. *Women of Distinction: Remarkable in Works and Invincible in Character* (1893).

JESSIE CARNEY SMITH

COTTEN, ELIZABETH "LIBBA" (c. 1895-1987)

Born around January 1895, in Chapel Hill, North Carolina, "Libba" Cotten became interested in music as a child. She began playing her brother's banjo and guitar shortly after the turn of the century and taught herself to tune and play them left-handed (upside-down). Cotten came of age at a particularly rich time in the history of southern rural music. The just emerging blues, along with the large body of fiddle/banjo dance tunes, minstrel show songs, ballads, and religious songs, formed her repertoire.

Chapel Hill was her home until the early 1940s, when she joined the great migration northward, settling in Washington, D.C. Cotten eventually became the housekeeper for the famed ethnomusicologist Charles Seeger, whose family discovered her talents and diverse storehouse of songs. In the late 1950s, during the beginning of the "folk revival," Cotten slowly began a professional music career. She eventually became a regular performer at folk festivals throughout the United States and Canada, and she was identified with the country dance tune, "Freight Train." During this period Cotten recorded three albums for Folkways Records and one for Arhoolie Records, which featured her broad repertoire.

Cotten continued performing into the early 1980s as one of the few Black women on the folk music circuit. She eventually received awards from the National Endowment for the Arts as well as a 1984 Grammy Award for *Elizabeth Cotten Live!* Washington, D.C., remained her home until she moved to Syracuse, New York, to be closer to relatives. She died there on June 29, 1987.

BIBLIOGRAPHY

BWW; Coy, Carol. "Elizabeth Cotten," *Folk Scene* (April 1974); Seeger, Mike. "Freight Train and Other North Carolina Folk Songs and Tunes," *Smithsonian/Folkways Records*. SF 40009 (1989).

KIP LORNELL

The strains of "Freight Train" performed left-handed on Elizabeth Cotten's (upside-down) guitar were a familiar sound at folk festivals around the country from the late 1950s through the early 1980s. [Schomburg Center]

COTTON, DOROTHY FOREMAN (1931-)

One of the few women officers of the Southern Christian Leadership Conference (SCLC), Dorothy Cotton spearheaded efforts during the civil rights movement to create educational programs in the South.

Dorothy Lee Foreman was born in 1931 in Goldsboro, North Carolina. After her mother's death in 1934, she and her three sisters, Effie Mae, Dazzelle, and Annie Margaret, were raised by their father, Claude Daniel Foreman, a tobacco factory worker. Cotton remained with her father until leaving to attend Shaw University in Raleigh, where she supported herself by working as housekeeper for the university president. When her employer took the presidency of Virginia State College in Petersburg, Virginia, Foreman transferred to that institution and graduated with a degree in English and library science. Shortly after graduation she married a college acquaintance,

George Cotton. She then enrolled at Boston University, where she received her Master's degree in speech therapy in 1960.

While completing work for her master's, Cotton became active in the civil rights movement that was spreading throughout the South. Her involvement in protest activities began after she joined the Gillfield Baptist Church in Petersburg and became a protégé of the church's minister, the Rev. Wyatt T. Walker, who also chaired the local chapter of the National Association for the Advancement of Colored People (NAACP). Cotton helped Walker organize a protest against the segregation policies of the Petersburg Public Library and also participated in sit-ins at a local segregated lunch counter. As a member of the Petersburg Improvement Association, Cotton taught student sit-in protesters about direct-action tactics.

In 1960, Martin Luther King, Jr., recruited Walker to become SCLC's executive director, and in September of that year Cotton moved to Atlanta to join Walker's administrative team. During the next few years she worked closely with King and other SCLC leaders, including Ralph Abernathy and Andrew Young, to orchestrate the organization's expanding protest activities, from the Freedom Rides of 1961 and voter registration drives to the Poor People's Campaign of 1968. In 1963, she became a director of SCLC's Citizenship Education Program, a Highlander Folk School program taken over by SCLC when Tennessee authorities halted the school's operations. The SCLC program sought to increase literacy among Black southerners in order to encourage them to register to vote and to participate in the political life of their communities. The program also trained local leaders in the tenets of nonviolent protest. Using the text of the U.S. Constitution, the Bill of Rights, and the Fourteenth Amendment, Cotton taught Black southerners not only how to read but also to understand the rights embodied in citizenship. She traveled across the South with Young and Septima Clark of the Highlander Folk School, recruiting participants for the training program. A talented singer, Cotton also led programs featuring freedom songs from the southern struggle.

Although Cotton was a laywoman among the male clergymen who predominated in SCLC leadership, her role was not limited. She became one of King's closest confidants and her presence in SCLC's inner circle put her at the forefront of the southern civil rights movement as a planner, coordinator, and demonstration leader.

After King's assassination in 1968, Cotton continued her work at SCLC, watching the organization suffer internal turmoil until she left in 1972. A year later she became director of the federal Child Development/Head Start program in Jefferson County, Alabama. From 1975 to 1978, she worked at the Bureau of Human Services of the City of Atlanta. In 1978, she accepted the invitation of former movement associate John Lewis to become southeastern regional director for ACTION, the federal agency for volunteer programs. After leaving ACTION in 1981, she worked briefly at the Martin Luther King, Jr., Center for Non-Violent Social Change in Atlanta. After more than two decades of intense involvement in civil rights activities, Cotton left Atlanta in 1982 for Cornell University, where she served as director of student activities. In May 1991, she left Cornell to conduct seminars on leadership development and social change.

BIBLIOGRAPHY

Branch, Taylor. *Parting the Waters: America in the King Years, 1954-63* (1988); Carson, Clayborne. Interview with Dorothy F. Cotton at the Martin Luther King, Jr., Papers Project, Stanford University (June 24-26, 1991); Cotton, Dorothy F. "CEP: Challenge to the 'New Education,'" *Freedomways* (Winter 1969); Fairclough, Adam. *To Redeem the Soul of America: The Southern Christian Leadership Conference and Martin Luther King, Jr.* (1987); Garrow, David J. *Bearing the Cross: Martin Luther King, Jr., and the Southern Christian Leadership Conference* (1986); Raines, Howell. "Aides Feud Threatens Rights Group Started by Dr. King," *New York Times* (April 8, 1979).

CLAYBORNE CARSON
STEPHANIE BROOKINS

COUVENT, MARIE BERNARD
(c. 1757-1837)

The oldest continuously existing Black Catholic school in the United States came into being because, even before public education came to New Orleans, a former slave, Marie Bernard Couvent, provided in her will for the "establishment of a free school for orphans of color."

The Widow Couvent, as she came to be known, was born in Guinea, West Africa, and brought to San Domingue where she was enslaved at such an early age that she had no memory of her father and mother. When she died in New Orleans on June 29, 1837, a free Black woman speaking a French-derived language, her age was given as eighty. That would mean that the year of her birth was probably 1757. Not much is known about her except that she eventually obtained her freedom, established residency in the Marigny district of New Orleans, and at some time married a free Black man, Gabriel Bernard Couvent. Her husband's death preceded hers by eight years, and he left her the property that she donated for the establishment of a free school for free orphans of color living in Faubourg Marigny. (The present-day boundaries of Marigny are the Mississippi River, St. Claude Avenue, Esplanade Avenue, and Franklin Avenue.)

Madame Couvent dictated her will in 1832 and provided biographical information about herself in the document, which is written in French. A translation of a portion of the will states: "I bequeath and order that my land at the corner of Grand Hommes (Dauphine) and Union (Touro) Streets be dedicated and used in perpetuity for the establishment of a free school for orphans of color of the Faubourg Marigny. This said school is to be operated under the direction of Reverend Father Manehault . . . or under the supervision of his successors in office."

Henry Fletcher, a free man of color, was named executor. He did not implement the terms of the will within a reasonable time, and the estate was dwindling. Finally, a group of free men of color brought him to court and requested an accounting. These men were leading members of the community of free people of color living in the city. Among them were Emilien Brule, Adolphe Duhart, Nelson Fouche, François Lacroix, and Barthelemy Rey. They succeeded in establishing the school in 1848; however its student population consisted of more than indigent orphans, as its name suggested. L'Institution Catholique des Orphelins Indigens attracted students from a broad base and included a faculty of notable members of the city. One of its principals was Armand Lanusse, compiler of *Les Cenelles*, the first poetry anthology published by an African-American in this country. Lanusse became principal in 1852.

The Couvent School, as it was popularly known in local circles, not only attracted an excellent faculty and board, it was also destined to include among its alumni many of the leading citizens among the *gens de couleur libres* and their descendants. Ernest N. Morial, the first African-American mayor of New Orleans, was among the school's alumni. Still in existence and believed to be the oldest continuing Black Catholic school in the country, the school is now known as Holy Redeemer School. Two blocks away is a public school named in honor of Madame Couvent, but the school her will caused to come into existence still bears testimony to her piety and generosity. She dic-

tated her will eight years before public education came to New Orleans, and even then it excluded people of color.

The Widow Couvent is buried in historic St. Louis Cemetery Number 2, Square 3, in New Orleans. Her grave may still be visited, and her will may be read in the Louisiana division of the New Orleans Public Library.

BIBLIOGRAPHY

Christian, Marcus B. "Dream of an African Ex-Slave," *Louisiana Weekly* (February 12, 1938): Desdunes, Rodolphe L. *Nos Hommes et Notre Histoire* (Our History and Our People), trans. and ed. Sister Dorothea Olga McCants ([1911] 1973); Meyer, Robert. *Names over New Orleans Public Schools* (1975); Recorder of Wills. Book of Wills, 1837-42. Microfilm, Louisiana division, New Orleans Public Library; Rousseve, Charles B. *The Negro in Louisiana* ([1937] 1970).

FLORENCE BORDERS

COX, IDA (1896-1967)

Ida Cox sang the blues in minstrel shows, vaudeville, nightclubs, and on records during the heyday of blues recording in the 1920s. She was born Ida Prather on February 25, 1896, in Toccoa, Georgia, and received her early musical training in the church. Her theatrical career began in her teens, when she ran away to join White & Clark's Black & Tan Minstrels, at first performing "Topsy" roles in blackface. For the next decade she traveled as a singer with some of the best minstrel troupes of the day, including the Rabbit Foot Minstrels, Silas Green from New Orleans, and the Florida Cotton Blossom Minstrels. During this period she married Adler Cox, whose name she kept throughout her career, although she remarried twice.

She began recording for Paramount Records in 1923, and by 1929 she had made over forty records. On her recordings, Cox sang in classic blues style, often accompanied by a pianist or by a small jazz combo. Her most frequent accompanists were Lovie Austin, a pianist and arranger for Paramount, and Jesse Crump, who became her third husband.

During the height of her popularity in the 1920s she toured extensively, playing theaters and clubs in major cities with major jazz figures, among them Ferdinand "Jelly Roll" Morton and "King" Joe Oliver. When the Great Depression hit, Cox produced her own shows, *Raisin Cain* and *Darktown Scandals*, and took them on the road. In 1934, billed as "The Sepia Mae West," she appeared with Bessie Smith at the Apollo Theatre in New York in the *Fan Waves Revue*. When impresario John Hammond put together his second "From Spirituals to Swing" concert at Carnegie Hall in 1939, with the intention of introducing Black music to a white highbrow audience, Ida Cox was on the program.

After 1929, Cox did not record again until 1939, when she made recordings for John Hammond with a group of jazz greats billed as her "All-Star Orchestra." These were issued on the Vocalion and Okeh labels. Cox continued to tour until she suffered a stroke in 1945, but she came out of retirement in 1961 to record an album, *Blues for Rampart Street*, on the Riverside label. She spent her final years living with her daughter in Knoxville, Tennessee, where she died of cancer on November 10, 1967.

Ida Cox was a blues queen in every way. Her shows were always high-class, and though she is remembered as imperious and demanding, she was a good manager and a fair employer. She combined glamour and sophistication with a singing style both sultry and emotionally appealing. She performed and recorded many of her own songs, and though she was, in the words of Lovie Austin, "always a lady," her lyrics are often salty, laced with sexual allusions and sly humor directed at men. Her song "Wild Women Don't Have the Blues" has become a feminist anthem among modern blues lovers, a situation "Miss Ida" would probably have appreciated.

BIBLIOGRAPHY

Albertson, Chris. Liner notes to Cox, Ida. *Blues Ain't Nothing Else But . . . .* Milestone MLP 2015; *BDAAM*; *BWW*; Harrison, Daphne Duval. *Black Pearls: Blues Queens of the 1920s* (1988); Hitchcock, H. Wiley and Stanley Sadie, eds. *The New Grove Dictionary of American Music* (1986); *New York Times*, "Ida Cox Is Dead; Blues Singer, 78" (November 12, 1967); Placksin, Sally. *American Women in Jazz, 1900 to the Present: Their Words, Lives and Music* (1982); Reitz, Rosetta. Liner notes to Cox, Ida. *Wild Women Don't Have the Blues*. Rosetta Records RR 1304; Stewart-Baxter, Derrick. *Ma Rainey and the Classic Blues Singers* (1970).

SELECTED DISCOGRAPHY

Blues Ain't Nothing Else But . . . . Milestone MLP 2015 (1971); *Wild Women Don't Have the Blues*. Rosetta Records RR 1304 (1981) (previously issued as *Blues for Rampart Street*, Riverside 374 [1961]).

SUZANNE FLANDREAU

COX, MINNIE M. GEDDINGS (1869-1933)

Minnie M. Geddings Cox was one of America's most significant citizens and a role model—as an educator, government worker, businesswoman, and homemaker—for Blacks throughout the United States.

Minnie Geddings was one of two daughters born to former slaves, William and Mary Geddings of Lexington, Mississippi. She was born in 1869. The Geddingses owned a restaurant and used their money to send Minnie to Fisk University. She graduated with a teacher's certificate and began to teach public school in Lexington and later taught in Indianola, Mississippi.

Minnie Cox was widely known because of her appointment as postmistress of Indianola. Although she had been appointed by President Benjamin Harrison in 1891, it was her reappointment on May 22, 1897, that was controversial. President William McKinley reappointed Cox at a time when white racists wanted Black Americans eliminated from leadership positions. In 1902, white protestors in Indianola claimed that Cox's reappointment permitted "nigger domination." To protect Black citizens, Cox, a peaceful and religious Methodist, offered her resignation. It was refused by President Theodore Roosevelt who, in order to show support for Black Americans, suspended postal service in Indianola. However, white supremacists did succeed in displacing Cox temporarily. In January 1903, Cox left Indianola but returned a year later, after the controversy had faded. The controversy surrounding her appointment brought her national attention, placed her in the company of notable leaders such as Booker T. Washington and Theodore Roosevelt, and forced Indianola and racism into the national news.

Minnie Cox had married Wayne Wellington Cox on October 31, 1889. They had a daughter, Ethel Grant Cox. The Coxes became successful business people. They were farmers and owned considerable agricultural holdings in Indianola. They organized the Delta Penny Savings Bank of Indianola, which attracted both Black and white depositors, as well as the Beneficial Life Insurance Company to serve the Black community specifically. Minnie Cox was the secretary and treasurer of the insurance company. Even though white citizens had objected to her as postmistress, she constructed her home in the white residential district and continued to interact with all of the citizens of Indianola.

During the 1920s, Minnie Cox left Indianola. She lived in Memphis, Tennessee, before moving to

Rockford, Illinois, with her second husband, George Key Hamilton, whom she married on July 2, 1925. On August 31, 1933, she died in Rockford, Illinois. Throughout her life, Cox was politically active, supporting the Republican party while promoting national awareness of racism. She founded business enterprises, provided jobs for others, and advocated pride, progress, and justice during a period of negrophobia.

BIBLIOGRAPHY
As to the Nigger. H. D. Money Campaign Committee. Indianola, Mississippi (1903); *Atlanta Constitution* (January 5, 6, 7; May 26; June 29; August 13, 29, 1903); Bishop, Joseph B. "The Negro and Public Office," *International Quarterly* (1903); Burkett, R. K., N. H. Burkett, and H. L. Gates, eds. *Black Biography, 1790-1950: A Cumulative Index* (1991); *Cleveland Gazette* (January 18, 31; February 6, 7, 15, 1903); Gatewood, Willard B. "Theodore Roosevelt and the Indianola Affair," *Journal of Negro History* (January 1968); *Greenwood Commonwealth* (October 17, 24, 31, 1902; January 10, 24, 31; February 28; March 14; April 18; May 10; June 27; July 18, 1903); *Indianola Enterprise* (January 1, 1902-December 31, 1903); *The Indianola, Mississippi Post Office Incident to the Race Question: Speech of Honorable H. D. Money of Mississippi in the Senate of the United States* (1903); *Jackson Evening News* (January 5, 6, 7; April 15, 1903); *Literary Digest,* "Negro Appointment in the South" (December 6, 1903); *Literary Digest,* "Southern Press on the Indianola Incident" (January 17, 1903); Lopez, Clara. "James K. Vardaman and the Negro: The Foundation of Mississippi's Racial Policy," *Southern Quarterly* (1965); McMillen, Neil R. *Dark Journey* (1989); *Nation,* "The Nation vs. Indianola" (January 29, 1903); *New York Times* (January 3, 6, 1903; January 28, 1904); *Public Opinion,* "Negro Officials in the South" (January 15, 1903); Scheiner, M. Seth. "President Theodore Roosevelt and the Negro, 1901-1908," *Journal of Negro History* (July 1962); U.S. House of Representatives. *Resignation of the Postmaster at Indianola, Mississippi* (1903); *Washington Evening Star* (January 5, 6, 7, 17; February 17, 1903).

VALERIE GRIM

CRAFT, ELLEN (1826-1891)

Ellen Craft was born in 1826 in Clinton, Georgia, to Major James Smith, a cotton planter and slaveholder, and his house slave, Maria. Craft was given as a gift to Smith's daughter, Eliza, and was moved to Macon in 1837; there she met and later married a fellow slave, William, in 1846. Two years later the young couple fled in what is regarded as the most dramatic escape from slavery ever recorded. Since she was quadroon, she dressed as a slave master

who was traveling to Philadelphia for medical reasons; William acted as her valet. The couple settled in Boston, and Craft established herself as a seamstress. However, their freedom was threatened after the passage of the Fugitive Slave Act in 1850, when slave-catchers tried to return them to Georgia. That November, the couple fled Boston for the safety of England, where they spent the next nineteen years.

In England the Crafts attended an agricultural school established by Lady Byron in Ockham, Surrey. After completing their course of study, they purchased a home in Hammersmith, London, and Craft continued to work as a seamstress. They were active on the antislavery lecture circuit and were members of the executive committee of the London Emancipation Committee. Craft also worked to raise funds for southern freedmen and to establish a school for girls in Sierra Leone. Their five children—Charles, Ellen, William, Jr., Brougham, and Alfred—were born in England.

The Crafts returned to the United States in 1869. Two years later they purchased Woodville plantation in Ways Station, Georgia, where they grew cotton and rice and where Ellen Craft ran a school for local children. Constantly rising debts, opposition from local white farmers, and an inability to raise needed capital worked against them. When Ellen Craft died in 1891, the school had been closed for some time, and the plantation was struggling to make ends meet.

BIBLIOGRAPHY
Blackett, R.J.M. *Beating against the Barriers: Biographical Essays in Nineteenth-Century Afro-American History* (1986); Craft, William. *Running a Thousand Miles for Freedom* (1860); Sterling, Dorothy. *Black Foremothers: Three Lives* (1979); Still, William. *The Underground Rail Road* (1872).

RICHARD J. M. BLACKETT

CRUMPLER, REBECCA LEE (b. 1833)

"I early conceived a liking for and sought every opportunity to be in a position to relieve the suffering of others." These are the words of the first Black woman to receive a medical degree in the United States.

Born in Richmond, Virginia, in 1833, Rebecca Lee was raised in Pennsylvania by her aunt, who served as a doctor to her community. Influenced by her aunt, Lee sought every opportunity to help others. Between 1852 and 1860, she worked as a nurse in Massachusetts. Then, upon the recommendations of her employers, she entered the New England Female Medical College in Boston and in March 1864 became the first and only Black woman to obtain the Doctress of Medicine degree from that school.

After graduating, Lee practiced in Boston, but at the end of the Civil War she moved her practice to Richmond, Virginia, where she worked with newly freed people. After years of a successful practice in Richmond, she moved back to Boston and, in 1883, published *A Book of Medical Discourses in Two Parts*. Based on Crumpler's personal journals, the book offered advice to women on how to provide medical care to their children and themselves.

Rebecca Lee Crumpler is an inspiration not only because she opened the doors of the medical profession to Black women but also because she devoted her life's work to the study of diseases affecting women and children.

BIBLIOGRAPHY

Sammons, Vivian Ovelton. *Blacks in Science and Medicine* (1990); Waite, Frederick C. *History of the New England Female Medical College, 1848-1874* (1950).

ALLISON JOLLY

CUMMINGS, IDA REBECCA (1867-1958)

Ida Rebecca Cummings, educator, organization leader, and clubwoman, was born on March 17, 1867, in Baltimore, Maryland. Her father, Henry Cummings, was a hotel chef who also owned a catering business. Her mother, Eliza Davage Cummings, descended from free African-Americans, operated a boarding-house at the family residence.

Cummings was reared in an atmosphere that promoted education, Black unity, and community service. The family's church, Metropolitan Methodist, which was formerly a station on the Underground Railroad, offered literacy classes prior to the establishment, in 1867, of Black public schools in Baltimore. While most African-Americans were uneducated laborers, many of Cummings's family members were clergymen, civil servants, and educators. Cummings's brother, one of the first Black graduates of the University of Maryland Law School, was, in 1890, the first African-American elected to the Baltimore City Council. Her aunt, Charlotte Davage, was for many years president of the Colored Young Women's Christian Association (YWCA). A dormitory at Morgan State University is named for her mother, Eliza

Among the many philanthropies of Ida Rebecca Cummings was the Colored Empty Stockings and Fresh Air Circle. For four decades, the Circle provided Christmas gifts and summers in the country for Black children from poor families.

Cummings, in recognition of her fund-raising efforts for the school.

The Oblate Sisters of Providence, an order of Black nuns, were Cummings's first teachers. She later enrolled in Baltimore's only public school for African-Americans. Cummings attended Hampton Institute in Virginia; Morgan State College in Maryland, where she earned a bachelor of arts degree in 1922; and Columbia University.

By 1900 Cummings was teaching in primary school. She then completed specialized courses in Baltimore and Chicago and became Baltimore's first kindergarten teacher. Affectionately called "Miss Ida" by her students, Cummings taught for thirty-seven years.

Cummings participated in organizations that worked to improve housing, health care, and education for poor children. She founded the Frances E. W. Harper Temple of Elks and served for twenty-nine years as Daughter Ruler. She was the Elks' state director of the Department of Education and the national chairman of the Child Welfare Department. A board member of Maryland's Cheltenham School for Boys, she also served as a trustee of Bennett College, as the first woman trustee of Morgan State College, and as president of the Republican Women's League.

In 1904, Cummings, her mother, and other members of the Colored YWCA established the Colored Empty Stocking and Fresh Air Circle. The women provided Christmas stockings to children who would otherwise have had no gifts. Also, in order to expose city children to a healthier environment during the summer, the group paid for their board in the homes of rural families. Cummings was president of the Circle for most of its approximately forty years of existence. The group regularly solicited funds from Black organizations, and white merchants made occasional contributions. Under Cummings's leadership the Circle purchased a farm and built a camp staffed by volunteers. Between 1904 and 1907, more than 5,000 children benefited from Circle efforts.

From 1912 to 1914 Cummings was corresponding secretary of the National Association of Colored Women and chairperson of the planning committee for its annual convention, held in Baltimore in 1916. During this convention, which featured symposia on antilynching and women's suffrage, Cummings was elected vice president.

Cummings died in Baltimore on November 8, 1958. Her will included bequests to the schools and organizations she had supported during her lifetime.

BIBLIOGRAPHY
Baltimore Afro-American (July 29, 1905; July 22, August 12, 1916; September 8, 1917; November 10, 15, 22, 1958); *Baltimore Evening Sun* (November 10, 1958); Chappelle, Suzanne Ellery Greene, Jean H. Baker, Dean R. Esslinger, Whitman Ridgway, Jean Russo, Constance Schulz, and Gregory Stiverson. *Maryland: A History of Its People* (1986); Coleman, Robert. *The First Colored Professional, Clerical, Skilled and Business Directory of Baltimore City* (1918, 1921, 1936, 1941); Cummings, Harry Sythe, Jr. Personal interview (November 5, 1991); Dorcas, Louise Cummings. Personal interview (November 5, 1991); Greene, Suzanne Ellery. "Black Republicans on the Baltimore City Council, 1890-1931," *Maryland Historical Magazine* (September 1979); Neverdon-Morton, Cynthia. *Afro-American Women of the South and the Advancement of the Race, 1895-1925* (1989); Paul, William George. "The Shadow of Equality: The Negro in Baltimore 1864-1911," Ph.D. diss. (1972); Reid, Ira De A. *The Negro Community in Baltimore* (1934); Wesley, Charles Harris. *The History of the National Association of Colored Women's Clubs* (1984); Wilson, Edward N. *The History of Morgan State College: A Century of Purpose in Action 1867-1967* (1975).

DONNA HOLLIE

D

DAFFIN, SALLIE *see*
FREEDMEN'S EDUCATION

DANCE

The story of Black women in dance is the story of generations of dancers whose gestures, feelings, and concepts have been handed down from one group of women to another, from one time in history to another. The generations overlap, of course, and the earliest generations continue to impact upon the collective consciousness of the African-American cultural heritage. These women often gave without recognition and created without demanding attention. In their forced powerlessness, they gave voice to dance, poignant articulation to movement, and the result of the process they began was a panoply of Black talents who would change the American artistic community with the strength, beauty, and power of their dances.

The first, silent generation of dancers laid the foundation by maintaining a connection and intimacy with the earth, dancing under a full moon, remembering the power of ritual in Africa, marking moments for remembrance. They danced whenever there was birth, marriage, or death; and even if they wished for the latter, dance helped to affirm life and the possibility of a better life. The first generation

was able to infuse the various religions of the New World with their eclectic heritages, representing a myriad of African ethnic groups. Because of these women, dance found a permanent home in the churches and temples of Black people. Although it survived in a synthesized form that represented hundreds of cultures, it belonged to the women, who were the keepers of the traditions. It was their task to ensure continuity and they did.

The second, anonymous generation reveals itself in the literature of African-Americans who through epic memory recall the pain of enslavement and the role of music and dance in the alleviation of that pain. Arna Bontemps in his novel *Black Thunder* (1968) writes about Juba, the dancer who is being beaten for her participation in a slave uprising. "A crowd of frightened Blacks materialized in the dusk. They followed at a safe distance, the whites of their eyes, the palms of their hands, their rounded white mouths, distinct in the shadows." Later they sent up a soft, dove-like lamentation, "Pray Massa, Pray. Oh Pray, Massa Pray." With each lash of the whip as it went into Juba's flesh, the crowd moaned "Pray massa pray" or "Lord a mercy." It has been suggested that African-American dance traditions grew out of the moans, groans, and movement of the enslaved Africans.

The third, minstrel generation began to shape a more formal tradition in dance from the time, in

1891, that *The Creole Show* introduced African-American women to the stage. The women were often caricatures of themselves as they sang and danced, becoming objects of pleasure and even ridicule. Still, they drew from their cultural traditions. While they made fun of themselves to survive, their movements told another story, the real story, and provided a poignant juxtaposition of different realities—theirs and the white man's.

The dance steps of the minstrel shows spoke of past legacies and cultural traditions. They at once empowered women in the chorus lines and featured solo female dancers. The traditional dances of the American South were no longer "ring shout," "juba," and "bambouche." Instead, Black women would shimmy and shake, ball the jack, and sashay from side to side as they grew in confidence. The images of free-wheeling, sensuous Black women at first transfixed America and ultimately transformed American dance.

The musical theater, the fourth, generation emerged in 1892. That year, the character of Topsy, played by Jennie Chapman, danced in Harriet Beecher Stowe's *Uncle Tom's Cabin*. A chorus danced behind her. In 1899, the musical *The New Creole Show* introduced a line of sixteen young women dancing and singing in a chorus. The finale was the "Cakewalk," danced by the beautiful Miss Dora Dean, who was the first Black woman to wear thousand-dollar costumes.

The women in the musical generation came from the chorus line in the early 1920s to take front and center stage in such musicals as *Hallelujah*, *In the Heart of Dixie*, and *Shuffle Along*, which launched Josephine Baker's career. These musicals, with their integration of music, dance, and song, helped to shape the American theater and gave the country and the world the incomparable Ethel Waters, Adelaide Hall, and Florence Mills. All of them had distinguished careers that took different directions, but all of them became known first as dancers. Josephine Baker went on to become a legend and a symbol for several generations to come.

Social dances were still being created at this time, and Cora La Redd did much to popularize a social dance called "trucking." Florence Mills, a cakewalk dance champion who won many dancing competitions, went on to several other musicals after *Shuffle Along* including, in 1924, *Dixie to Broadway*. She traveled to London and Paris after the Harlem opening of *Blackbirds*, in which she also appeared, but died suddenly in 1927. Adele Bush stepped in for her in the 1928 edition of *Blackbirds*.

A transitional performer, Ethel Waters bridged the gap between the musical theater generation and the heritage generation. In 1928, she danced and sang in the musical revue *Africana*. The revue reflected Black Americans' need to make an artistic connection between themselves and Africa. It was the beginning of many such expressions as other generations of Black women dancers emerged.

The fifth, the heritage generation marked a conscious change for Black women in dance. The Harlem Renaissance, World War I, the Garvey movement, and the World War II era dramatically combined to alter opportunities for women in dance. Edna Guy, in 1931, was featured with Hemsley Winfield in what was known as "the First Negro Dance Recital in America." The same year, Katherine Dunham founded the Negro Dance Group in Chicago. In 1932, anthropologist, writer, and folklorist Zora Neale Hurston wrote a play that featured Bahamian dancers.

Once new opportunities appeared, Black women began to emerge as a dynamic force in concert dance. Katherine Dunham starred in the ballet *La Guiablesse* by Ruth Page. Edna Guy continued to have recitals, and in 1938, the Sierra Leonean Asadata Dafora choreographed *Kunguru*, whose cast included the then unknown actress Esther Rolle as a dancer. Dunham choreographed her first version of *L'Ag'Ya*, and America was introduced to the Trinidadian dancer and teacher Beryl McBurnie, who affected generations of African-American and Caribbean dancers. Lavinia Williams, who was born in Philadelphia and danced with the Katherine Dunham Company, devoted her career to Haitian dance and went on to found and direct the Haiti Academy of Classic and Folklore Dance in 1954. Ruth Page, Agnes De Mille, and Helen Tamiris were among the prominent white choreographers who worked with Black dancers and themes.

From 1939 to 1950, Pearl Primus and Katherine Dunham dominated the dance scene, creating protest dances to decry oppression and racism. "Strange Fruit," a poem set to music and sung by Billie Holiday, was choreographed by Pearl Primus to express her outrage and pain at lynching. Dunham opened the Katherine Dunham School of Arts and Research in 1943 and strengthened her artistic and intellectual vision in a war-weary country. These two women exemplify Black women who are artistically talented, creatively courageous, and unafraid to take their culture and heritage to masses of American people.

The sixth, the concert dance generation introduced Janet Collins and Carmen DeLavallade to the world. Both dancers hailed from California and had studied with Lester Horton. They represented a new wave of Black female dancers in that they were exclusively oriented to ballet and modern dance. In fact, they did not necessarily consider themselves specifically Black dancers, although both had opportunities to work in the heritage genre. Collins, for example, worked with Katherine Dunham in California, and DeLavallade worked in the Broadway musical *House of Flowers*. Also among this first wave of concert dancers were Mary Hinkson and Matt Turney, both graduates of the University of Wisconsin. They joined the Martha Graham Dance Company in 1951, the year that Collins became the first Black prima ballerina at the Metropolitan Opera.

Primus and Dunham continued their work, both having trained in modern and ballet dance traditions, and both took their shows on international tours, including long stays in Africa and Haiti.

John Butler choreographed *Portrait of Billie* in 1961 for Carmen DeLavallade, the first of many collaborations between white choreographers and Black dancers in the concert dance genre. Agnes De Mille choreographed *The Four Marys* with newcomer Judith Jamison in 1965. The following year, Jamison joined Alvin Ailey's company. In no time, the great Black choreographer and the great Black dancer catapulted each other to international fame. Alvin Ailey helped to give the world not only Judith Jamison, but also dancers and teachers like Thelma Hill and Ella Moore. In 1969, the Dance Theatre of Harlem was founded after the death of Dr. Martin Luther King, Jr. It gave us another prima ballerina, Virginia Johnson, who redefined the image of a Black ballerina and helped to shape Black ballet.

Sara Yarborough was signed by the Harkness Ballet in 1958 and went on to dance with the Alvin Ailey American Dance Theater in the reconstruction of Pearl Primus's works *Fanga* and *Wedding Dance*, in which Yarborough played the bride. Yarborough distinguished herself in Donald McKayle's ballet *Rainbow 'Round My Shoulder* and in a work by Alvin Ailey, *A Lark Ascending*.

The seventh, the Black Renaissance generation was affected by and affected the 1960s cultural revolution. This generation—an extension of the heritage generation with the skills and savvy of the concert dance generation—sought to make statements that were bold, sometimes inflammatory, and always expressively and unapologetically Black.

Dianne McIntyre started her company, Sounds in Motion, in 1971. Kariamu Welsh started the Black Dance Workshop, later to become known as Kariamu and Company, in Buffalo, New York, in 1970. Judith

Jamison expressed the feelings of millions of Black women when she danced Ailey's *Cry* in 1971. Sara Yarborough, Sylvia Waters, Consuelo Atlas, and Carole Johnson all emerged in this generation to dance and lay new artistic and aesthetic foundations. Dyane Harvey, Mickey Davidson, Frances Hare, Yvonne James, Loretta Abbott, Donna Woods, Thea Nerissa Barnes, and Bernadette Jennings were all dancers making a statement about themselves as Black women in America. In the tradition of Mary Hinkson and Matt Turney, Thea Barnes danced with the Martha Graham Company after leaving the Alvin Ailey American Dance Theater. Donna Woods inherited the legacy of Judith Jamison in the Alvin Ailey American Dance Theater. And so the tradition continued.

In the Black Renaissance period, several women who were empowered by the self-determination of the era used regional arenas to make a national impact. Joan Myers Brown founded Philadanco in Philadelphia. Geraldyne Blunden founded the Dayton Contemporary Dance Theater in Dayton, Ohio. Cleo Parker founded the Cleo Parker Dance Company of Denver, Colorado, and Lulu Washington founded the L.A. Contemporary Dance Theater in Los Angeles, California. These companies funneled dancers to the national companies, most notably the Alvin Ailey American Dance Theater and the Dance Theatre of Harlem. The acceptance of dancers from the regional dance companies into the national companies was an affirmation of the skills and artistic visions of these artistic directors.

When Judith Jamison became choreographer and artistic director of the Alvin Ailey American Dance Theater, a transition began to the eighth generation, the generation of continuity and innovation. The women of this generation dance all the styles—mixing, matching, and synthesizing them into whatever speaks for the dancer. This generation is unafraid either to be themselves or to draw on the traditions of the past and antiquity. They are Africans, they are Black, they are women, and they are human, and that composition can look like anything in the dance.

JaWolle Willa Jo Zollar, choreographing for her company Urban Bush Women, translates "Song of Lawino," an African classical poem by the late Ugandan poet Okot p'Bitek, into a statement about change and humanity. Blondell Cummings, in her *Chicken Soup*, invokes the image and memory of grandmothers and evokes warmth and laughter. Judith Jamison, in her work *Ancestral Divinations*, makes a point about who she and her sisters are. Eva Golson is lyrical, fragile in her strength, and so full of music that all her works sing. Dianne McIntyre, alone or with her company, makes her connections, whether they be in the historical ballet *Up North* or in her opera about the writer Zora Neale Hurston.

McIntyre closes the circle for Black women in dance because, as she moves forward, she looks back at the classic and traditional African-American dance forms that the silent and anonymous generations helped to bring to the floor. She unabashedly weaves those movements into her work, creating a tapestry of voices, some loud, some quiet, some fighting, some a sacred dance in a strange land.

Eight generations of Black women in dance and there are many more to come. They come daring to be, daring to confront, willing to share, willing to expose, and they keep coming. They dance the rituals of young women, they know the secret dances of mature women, and they dance the dances of birth, death, enslavement, celebration, and victory.

Black women danced the "Ring Shout" dance and kept the spirit. They danced the Cakewalk, Charleston, and Lindy hop and changed the rhythms of America. They danced "A Luta Continua" and "A Change Is Gonna Come I Know." When Malcolm and Martin were killed, they danced a slow moanful dance that threatened to raise Nzingha, our ancient warrior dancer, for daring to destroy our princes. Keepers of the dance, of the culture, and ultimately of the people, Black women in their movement bear witness to a life force that is diverse, dynamic, fluid, and spiritual. Since antiquity, dance has been a part of who Black women are.

BIBLIOGRAPHY

Clarke, Mary and David Vaughn, eds. *The Encyclopedia of Dance and Ballet* (1977); Cohen-Stratyner, Naomi. *Biographical Dictionary of Dance* (1982); *EBA*; Emery, Lynne Fauley. *Black Dance in the United States from 1619 to Today* (1988); Goodman, Saul. "Dancers You Should Know," *Dance Magazine* (1964); Long, Richard. *The Black Tradition in American Concert Dance* (1990); McDonagh, Don. *The Complete Guide to Modern Dance* (1976); *NA*; *NWAT*; Patterson, Lindsay, ed. *Anthology of the Afro-American in the Theatre: A Critical Approach* (1978); Rollins, Charlemae. *Negro Entertainers of Stage, Screen, and T.V.* (1967); Thorpe, Edward. *Black Dance* (1990); Toppin, Edgar A. *A Biographical History of Blacks in America since 1528* (1971); *WA*; Willis, John. *Dance World* (1967, 1976); *WWBA* (1990).

KARIAMU WELSH ASANTE

DANCE COMPANIES, ARTISTIC DIRECTORS

The tradition of Black women as artistic directors of dance companies is over sixty years old. It started when Edna Guy cofounded the New Negro Art Theater Dance Company in 1931 with Hemsley Winfield. Katherine Dunham and Pearl Primus are premier Black artistic directors of twentieth-century dance companies. Both choreographers are now in their sixth decade of creative work. These women have created a tradition that encourages artists to choreograph out of their ethnic traditions and they have empowered women to articulate, express, and determine their artistic and creative aspirations. Dunham and Primus stand at the forefront of the movement of Black artistic directors and they continue to guide by example and inspire by their works.

Judith Jamison (born 1944 in Philadelphia, Pennsylvania), is a renowned dancer and choreographer who studied with Marion Cuyget, Nadia Chilkovsky, and Joan Kerr in Philadelphia. Jamison was selected by the late Alvin Ailey himself as his successor and artistic director of the Alvin Ailey American Dance Theater. The Alvin Ailey American Dance Theater is one of the largest, most popular, and most prestigious dance companies in America. Jamison's image symbolized for a generation of Black women that Black people could indeed be beautiful and talented. In her characterizations of Black women in such ballets as *Cry* and *Revelations*, choreographed by Ailey, she danced the history of Black women in America.

Ella Moore is a former Ailey dancer and codirector (with her husband, Charles Moore) of the Charles Moore Dance Theater, founded in 1974. After the death of her husband in 1985, Moore took over the artistic directorship of the company. Moore has directed the company to new artistic visions and challenges and the company has maintained a healthy and viable existence under her artistic stewardship.

Dianne McIntyre was born in Cleveland, Ohio, in 1946 and studied dance at the Karamu House in Cleveland. She has been artistic director of Sounds in Motion, the dance company she created in 1972. McIntyre has also choreographed for other companies, as well as Broadway and off-Broadway shows, including the Alvin Ailey American Dance Theater and Avery Brooks's one-man show *Paul Robeson*. McIntyre has also collaborated with playwright Ntozake Shange on *Spell #7, Boogie Woogie Landscapes,* and *The Great McDaddy*. Her dance company, Sounds in Motion, exemplifies her personal vision of the fusion and interrelatedness of music and movement in Black dance.

Amania Payne of Muntu Dance Company in Chicago, Illinois, and Ferne Caulker Bronson, artistic director of Kho-Thi Dance Company in Milwaukee, Wisconsin, are two prominent artistic directors of their own African dance companies. Both women have helped to document, choreograph, and institutionalize the art of African dance in America for the concert stage and in the dance studio.

Joan Myers Brown has been the artistic director of Philadanco in Philadelphia for over twenty years. Under Brown's direction, Philadanco has given the dance world such prominent dancers as Deborah Chase and Danielle Gee, both of whom now dance with the Alvin Ailey American Dance Theater. Joan Myers Brown's high technical standards and commitment to keeping Black dancers and choreographers employed made her company a haven for aspiring and professional Black dancers and choreographers. Brown's school, training company, and professional company all attest to her vision of a viable and self-supporting Black dance company.

Geraldyne Blunden, artistic director of the Dayton Contemporary Dance Company; Cleo Parker, artistic director of the Cleo Parker Dance Company in Denver, Colorado; Lulu Washington, artistic director of the Los Angeles Contemporary Dance Theater; and Nanette Bearden (wife of the late collage artist Romare Bearden) of the Nanette Bearden Contemporary Dance Theater, headquartered in New York City, are all major forces in their individual communities and the larger dance community.

Artists like JaWolle Willa Jo Zollar, artistic director of Urban Bush Women (an all-women dance company committed to the performance of African and African-American dance forms in a holistic context), extend the vision of Black dance and Black women in America. Zollar received her B.A. in dance from the University of Missouri and her M.F.A. from Florida State University. She studied with Diane McIntyre and went on to create her now famous *Lifeforce I*, *Girlfriends*, and *The Magician*. Like McIntyre, Zollar collaborates with poets, drummers, and folk artists. BeBe Miller, artistic director of the BeBe Miller Dance Company, is an African-American who leads a predominantly white dance company. Miller has been daring in her expressions of her sensibility and sensitivity as a feminist and humanist. Her vision is complementary to the vision of her colleagues who share her commitment to justice and equality for all women. Blondell Cummings is the artistic director of Blondell Cummings, an essentially solo enterprise. Cummings is not only a dance soloist but also an improvisation and performance artist.

All of the artistic directors mentioned have distinguished themselves first as dancers, then as choreographers, and finally as artistic directors of companies in a continuity of traditions. Katherine Dunham and Pearl Primus continue to have an impact on dance in America. Their dynamic and fluid legacies have yet to be completed and remain a challenge for dancers, choreographers, and artistic directors who want to continue the legacy into the twenty-first century. Judith Jamison honors their challenge to Black women.

BIBLIOGRAPHY

Emory, Lynne Fauley. *Black Dance in the United States from 1619 to Today* (1988); Long, Richard. *The Black Tradition in American Concert Dance* (1990); McDonagh, Don. *The Complete Guide to Modern Dance* (1976).

KARIAMU WELSH ASANTE

DANDRIDGE, DOROTHY (1922-1965)

Dorothy Dandridge was one of the most acclaimed actresses of her time, yet Hollywood producers' inability or unwillingness to see past race meant she was often without acting roles unless the part called for the stereotypically exotic, sexual Black temptress. Dandridge always rose above stereotypes, even when playing the temptress. Her story lies in both the brilliance of her talent and in Hollywood's willingness to squander such brilliance.

Dorothy Dandridge was born on November 9, 1922, in Cleveland, Ohio. Her father, Cyril Dandridge, was a cabinetmaker and minister. Her mother, Ruby, was an aspiring actress. They separated shortly before Dandridge was born. When she was still a young child, she performed with her older sister, Vivian, in an act called the Wonder Kids. They toured all over the country, not in vaudeville, but in Baptist churches, singing, dancing, acting in skits written by their mother, and doing acrobatics. At the end of the act, the children would stand on stage and answer personal questions about their lives as performers. Dandridge blamed those question sessions for her aversion to interviews later in life, remembering them as painful and difficult.

She also remembered a time when her father followed and found them. "I remember one night when I was about three," she said in a 1962 *Ebony* interview, "and Vivian and I were sleeping, and Mother had to put both of us up in the attic so our father wouldn't find us. He was looking for us to take us away, and Mother didn't want this, so she hid us. I remember that horror because I wanted so desperately to see him. I just wanted to know what he was like."

In the early 1930s, Dandridge and her mother and sister moved to Los Angeles. Ruby found work on radio and television, eventually appearing in such films as *Tish, Cabin in the Sky,* and *My Wild Irish Rose.* She also became a regular on the radio and television show *Beulah* and, later, *Father of the Bride.* Her daughters joined with a third girl, Etta Jones, and changed their stage name to the Dandridge Sisters. When Dorothy Dandridge was sixteen, the three went to New York and performed at the Cotton Club, often appearing on the same bill with Cab Calloway, W. C.

Dorothy Dandridge was a prodigiously talented and charismatic actress who was forced into a destructive stereotype that wasted her talent and, eventually, her life. Her first important film role was as a southern schoolteacher in Bright Road *(1953), in which she costarred with Harry Belafonte. [National Archives]*

Handy, and Bill ("Bojangles") Robinson. While there, she met her father for the first time.

The Dandridge Sisters debuted in Hollywood in a short turn near the end of the Marx Brothers film *A Day at the Races.* Soon after the film was made, the trio split up. In 1941 and 1942, Dandridge appeared several times in the 1940s' version of the music video, the musical film short. Her appearances included the classic Mills Brothers *Paper Doll,* in which she appeared as the paper doll each Mills brother wanted to "call my own." She also played bit parts in *Lady from Louisiana, Sun Valley Serenade, Bahama Passage, Drums of the Congo,* and *Hit Parade of 1943.*

In 1942, Dandridge married Harold Nicholas, one of the famous dancing Nicholas Brothers, and had a child. For about six years after the child was born, she remained at home and supported her husband in his bid for a movie career. However, the child, Harolyn, was discovered to be severely brain-damaged and was eventually institutionalized. The marriage ended in divorce.

At this point, Dandridge singlemindedly set out to become an actress. Her first step was to begin supporting herself by singing. She appeared with the Desi Arnaz Band at the Macombo in 1951 and, in 1952, at La Vie en Rose. That New York nightclub was just about to close when she opened there. She sold out for two weeks, stayed on for fourteen more, and saved the club from bankruptcy. *Theatre Arts* magazine referred to her act as "vocalized sex appeal." When she returned a year later, she had toned down that aspect of her performance, hoping to be taken more seriously.

In the meantime, Dandridge had been spending every penny she earned singing on trying to develop an acting career. Her life was a round of auditions, lessons of all kinds, and singing performances. In 1953, she made her first important step toward an acting career when she was cast opposite Harry Belafonte in the film *Bright Road.* She played a southern schoolteacher. It was a good film, and Dandridge made her mark, but she almost missed out on her biggest screen opportunity because of her class and dignity. Otto Preminger was not going to let her read for the title role in his Black musical *Carmen Jones* (1954) because he thought she was too "regal." However, by appearing at an interview with him dressed for the part in skirt and low-cut blouse with tousled hair, she snared the role.

Dandridge's performance in the film, an adaptation of Bizet's opera *Carmen,* was dazzling. *Life* put her on its cover, and the critics went wild. *Time* said she "holds the eye—like a match burning steadily in a

tornado." Comparing her role with the one she played in *Bright Road, Newsweek* said, "The range between the two parts suggests that she is one of the outstanding dramatic actresses of the screen." She won an Academy Award nomination, the first for a Black woman in the category of Best Actress, and she was suddenly an international star. She would not make another film for three years.

When Dandridge finally appeared in front of the camera again, it was in the first of a series of films in which she played opposite white actors. Hollywood did not really know what to do with her. A 1966 article in *Ebony* summed up the situation. Dandridge was a leading lady, it pointed out, and that was the problem. "Except for Harry Belafonte and the quietly but brilliantly rising Sidney Poitier, there were no prominent Negro romantic male leads about. Besides, a Negro male can be made a star without becoming a leading man. He may play a variety of roles not involving romance. *But a leading lady such as Dorothy had to set male hormones sizzling*" (emphasis added).

So Dandridge was relegated to temptress roles in films such as *The Decks Ran Red* (1958), *Tamango* (1959), and *Malaga* (1962). Her love scenes were played with white men who were not allowed to kiss her for fear of alienating southern theater owners and audiences. The situation was reminiscent of the career of Chinese actress Anna May Wong, who, in order to avoid an interracial happy ending, died in every single one of her films.

In 1959, Dandridge was cast as Bess in the film version of *Porgy and Bess.* The only real improvement on her past few films was that now she was tempting Black men instead of white men. The cast was a virtual duplication of that in *Carmen Jones*—Dandridge, Pearl Bailey, Brock Peters, Roy Glenn, and Diahann Carroll. The major substitution was Sidney Poitier for Harry Belafonte, who had flatly refused to do the film on the grounds that it was an insult to Black people. (Poitier tried to refuse but was coerced.) The major addition was Sammy Davis, Jr. Again, Dandridge rose above her material. She won the Golden Globe Award for best actress in a musical.

Dandridge made two more films, but her film career was essentially over. When Rouben Mamoulian was selected to direct *Cleopatra,* he told Dandridge that he wanted her for the part. "You won't have the guts to go through with it," she said. "They are going to talk you out of it." Of course, they did. The role of the greatest Black temptress in history went to violet-eyed Elizabeth Taylor. (Mamoulian himself was fired from the film soon after shooting began.)

During the late 1950s, Dandridge was linked romantically with Peter Lawford, Otto Preminger, and many others. Dandridge was the first Hollywood celebrity to sue the magazine *Confidential*, when it printed an article accusing her of an affair in Reno with a musician. Then, in 1959, she satisfied all of the speculation about her personal life when she married white nightclub owner Jack Denison and revealed that they had been seeing each other secretly for four years.

In 1962, Dandridge divorced Denison and, five months later, declared bankruptcy. In 1959, her income had been $250,000; in 1963, it was less than $40,000. She was no longer able to pay for the private institutionalization of her daughter, who was suddenly deposited, disoriented and violent, at her home. She was eventually transferred to a state institution.

Dandridge was on the rebound from her problems in late 1965. She had a huge success in a nightclub engagement in New Mexico and was contracted to open in New York at Basin Street East. She signed contracts for two films with Mexican producer Raul Fernandez for $100,000. She had been hired to do an American western for $25,000. She was finishing up her autobiography, for which she had an eager publisher. Then, on September 4, she was found dead in her apartment from an overdose of an antidepressant. The drug, Tofranil, is not one that causes drowsiness or forgetfulness, making an accident unlikely.

Dorothy Dandridge was a fine actress with a wide range who was forced into a destructive stereotype for reasons of race and gender. Her talents were wasted because she was a woman and because she was Black.

BIBLIOGRAPHY

BAFT; Bogle, Donald. *Brown Sugar* (1980); *DANB*; *Ebony*, "Ill-fated Star Defies Scrutiny Even in Death" (March 1966), and "The Private Life of Dorothy Dandridge" (June 1962); Katz, Ephraim. *The Film Encyclopedia* (1979); *NBAW*; *Theatre Arts*, "Bright Road for Dorothy" (May 1953); Truitt, Evelyn Mack. *Who Was Who on Screen* (1974); *Who's Who in Hollywood, 1900-1976* (1976).

KATHLEEN THOMPSON

DANNER, MARGARET ESSIE (1915-)

"I want no more humility," says Margaret Danner in her poem "Passive Resistance." It exemplifies an often-repeated theme in her work, the quiet, reflective strain of protest characteristic of her poetry.

Through both her writing and her community work, Danner was a force in the 1960s Black arts movement.

Margaret Essie Danner was born on January 12, 1915, in Pryorsburg, Kentucky. Her family moved to Chicago, where she attended Englewood High School. From there she went on to Loyola, Roosevelt, and Northwestern universities. Her poet mentors during her school years were Paul Engle and Karl Shapiro. In 1945, she won second place in the poetry workshop of the Midwestern Writers Conference.

In 1951, Danner went to work for *Poetry: The Magazine of Verse* as an editorial assistant. A series of four of her poems was published in the magazine that same year, winning her a John Hay Whitney fellowship. In 1955, she became the first Black assistant editor of the publication. In 1960, Danner's first collection of poetry, *Impressions of African Art Forms*, appeared. It expressed Danner's absorbing interest in African materials and was well received by critics.

In 1961, Danner went to Detroit to become poet-in-residence at Wayne State University. Her time in Detroit was particularly fulfilling for her, largely because of her work in the community. She persuaded the minister of Detroit's King Solomon Church, Dr. Boone, to allow her to turn an empty parish house into a community arts center. She named the center Boone House to honor the minister's contribution. A number of other poets helped Danner, including Dudley Randall, Robert Hayden, and Naomi Long Madgett. In a poem called "Boone House," she referred to it as "a sun made of shade" and "a balm to those struggling through creativity's strident, summer, city heat." Danner and the center helped make Detroit a focus of the Black arts movement of the 1960s.

In 1963, *To Flower Poems* was published, and in 1966 Danner and Dudley Randall collaborated on a volume called *Poem Counterpoem*. This unusual work contained, on each set of facing pages, one poem by Danner and one by Randall, each pair on a single subject. In the same year, Danner made her first visit to Africa. While there, she read her poetry at the World Exposition of Negro Arts in Dakar, Senegal.

Iron Lace appeared in 1968, and from 1968 to 1969 Danner was poet-in-residence at Virginia Union University in Richmond. While there, she edited two anthologies of student poetry. In 1973, she was one of eighteen Black women poets invited to read at the Phillis Wheatley Poetry Festival at Jackson State College. *The Down of a Thistle* was published in 1976. It is filled with African imagery and contains a strong note of protest.

Margaret Essie Danner is married to Otto Cunningham and has one child, Naomi. Her grandson, Sterling Washington, Jr., inspired what Danner calls the "muffin poems."

BIBLIOGRAPHY

CBWA; DLB; EBA; NA; NBAW; Negro History Bulletin, "Margaret Danner" (October 1962); WWBA (1992).

KATHLEEN THOMPSON

DASH, JULIE (1952-)

"I like telling stories and controlling worlds. In my world, black women can do anything. They ride horses and fly from trapezes; they are in the future as well as in the past" (NYTimes BioServ, February 12, 1992). It is this vision of Black women that independent filmmaker Julie Dash is bringing to the screen in her series of films portraying Black women in the United States throughout the twentieth and into the twenty-first century. This series began in 1983 with the film short Illusions and was continued with 1991's feature-length Daughters of the Dust.

Illusions, the most critically acclaimed of Dash's films, examines the roles of Black women in the film industry. Two Black women occupy differing spaces in wartime (1942) Hollywood: one has become a studio executive while passing for white; the other is a behind-the-scenes singer, dubbing the voices of the white starlets on the screen. Both illustrate how the film industry specifically and society in general conspire to keep Black women both voiceless and invisible. In 1985, Dash received the Black American Film Society award for Illusions. The thirty-four-minute film, nominated for a 1988 cable ACE Award in Art Direction, was named Best Film of the Decade by the Black Filmmaker Foundation in 1989.

Also critically acclaimed is Daughters of the Dust, set in 1902 on the South Carolina Sea Island of Ibo Landing. Depicting the changes, conflicts, and nostalgia of the women of the Peazant family as they prepare to migrate North, it is, according to Dash, about "the fear of going away from home and not being able to come back, the fear of abandoning one's culture" (Thomas 1992). Primarily funded with grants from the Public Broadcasting System series American Playhouse, Daughters was shot in Super 35mm on Agfa-Gevaert film rather than Kodak because, according to Dash, Black people film better on Agfa. "Extravagantly poetic from beginning to end" (Kauffman 1992), Daughters and co-producer/director of pho-

tography Arthur Jafa were honored with the Best Cinematography Award at the 1991 Sundance Film Festival in Utah, where the film premiered. The screenplay, written by Dash, is primarily in Gullah patois with only occasional subtitles, which adds to the poetry of the film. Despite the successful premiere of Daughters, this aspect of the dialogue hampered its distribution, as studio executives and distribution companies decided there was neither a market nor an audience for a film that they considered inaccessible. Kino International finally assumed the task of marketing the film nationally, and in July 1992 it was televised nationally on PBS's American Playhouse.

Dash, as producer, writer, and director of Daughters, has been touted as the first African-American woman to make a feature-length film enjoying national release. However, Dash simply joined the ranks of a number of Black female creative forces both within and without the Hollywood structure. Madeline Anderson's 1970 documentary, I Am Somebody, is one of the earliest known works by a Black female filmmaker. Kathleen Collins's Losing Ground (1982) marked both Collins as the first African-American woman to direct a feature-length film and the film as the first Black independent to portray a Black woman professional as protagonist. More recently, Euzhan Palcy, a young African-American woman from Martinique, directed two major films from her own screenplays: the French Sugar Cane Alley (1984) and 1989's A Dry White Season. Season, backed by Metro-Goldwyn-Mayer, featured a budget eleven times the size of that of Daughters as well as such stars as Marlon Brando and Donald Sutherland from the U.S. and Zakes Mokae from South Africa.

While a graduate student at the University of California at Los Angeles (UCLA), Dash developed Diary of an African Nun (1977), based on a short story by Alice Walker. It won a Directors Guild Award for a student film at the Los Angeles Film Exposition. In 1978, she conceived and directed Four Women, prints of which, along with Illusions, are archived at Indiana University and at Clark-Atlanta University in Atlanta. An experimental dance film, Four Women received a Gold Medal for Women in Film at the 1978 Miami International Film Festival. Dash completed the feature-length screenplay Enemy of the Sun as the youngest fellow at the American Film Institute. She has worked with the Atlanta-based National Black Women's Health Project on a series of videotapes, in 1987 directing Breaking the Silence: On Reproductive Rights as well as producing, directing, and editing Preventing Cancer. Dash has been awarded a Fulbright

Fellowship to work in London on a screenplay with Maureen Blackwood of the Black British film collective Sankofa.

Born and raised in New York City, Dash began studying film in 1969 at the Studio Museum of Harlem. Graduating in 1974 from the City College of New York with a B.A. in film production, she also studied at the American Film Institute in Los Angeles, and did graduate work at UCLA. Her film production company, Geechee Girls, is based out of Atlanta, where she lives with her daughter, N'Zinga.

BIBLIOGRAPHY

Boyd, Valerie. "*Daughters of the Dust,*" *American Visions* (February 1991); Chambers, Veronica. "Women Right Now," *Glamour* (March 1992); Chan, Vera. "The Dust of History," *Mother Jones* (November/December 1990); "Daughters of the Dust," press release, Kino International Corporation, New York City (1991); Davis, Zeinabu Irene. "Daughters of the Dust," *Black Film Review* (1990); Hartman, S. V. and Farah Jasmine Griffin. "Are You as Colored as That Negro?: The Politics of Being Seen in Julie Dash's *Illusions,*" *Black American Literature Forum* (Summer 1991); Hoban, Phoebe. "A Building Dust Storm," *New York* (March 30, 1992); Kauffman, Stanley. Review of *Daughters of the Dust, New Republic* (February 10, 1992); Klotman, Phyllis Rauch, ed. *Screenplays of the African American Experience* (1991); Kuhn, Annette, ed. *Women in Film: An International Guide* (1990); *New York Times Biographical Service* (February 12, 1992); Reid, Mark A. "Dialogic Modes of Representing Africa(s): Womanist Film," *Black American Literature Forum* (Summer 1991); Southgate, Martha. "Women in Film," *Essence* (October 1989); Tate, Greg. "Favorite Daughters: Julie Dash Films Gullah Country," *Village Voice* (April 12, 1988); Taubin, Amy. "Exile and Cunning," *Village Voice* (January 13, 1987); Thomas, Deborah. "Julie Dash," *Essence* (February 1992).

VIDEO AND FILMOGRAPHY

Passing Through, assistant sound (1973); *Working Models of Success*, producer (1974); *Sylvia*, production manager (1975); *Diary of an African Nun*, director (1977); *Four Women*, director (1978); *My Brother's Wedding*, first assistant director (1983); *Illusions*, producer, writer, director (1983); *Preventing Cancer*, producer, director, editor (1987); *Breaking the Silence: On Reproductive Rights*, director (1987); *We Are Mothers Too Early . . .* (1987); *Daughters of the Dust*, producer, writer, director (1991).

N. H GOODALL

DAVIDSON, OLIVIA AMERICA (1854-1889)

The daughter of an ex-slave father and a freeborn mother, Olivia Davidson taught in Ohio, Mississippi, and Tennessee before helping to build Tuskegee Institute with her peer and later her husband, Booker T. Washington. In "The Story of My Life and Work," Washington wrote, "The success of the school, especially during the first half dozen years of its existence, was due more to Miss Davidson than any one else."

Six siblings welcomed Davidson's birth on June 11, 1854, and she in turn welcomed the births of three others. Her father, Elias, had been a slave of Joseph Davidson, whose family participated in the Scot-Irish migration into Virginia by way of Pennsylvania. Her mother, Eliza Webb, is thought to have been one of two daughters of Elizabeth Webb, a "free colored" woman recorded in the Tazewell County, Virginia, census of 1830.

The Elias Davidson family migrated to southern Ohio around 1857, pushed by the intolerance directed against mulattoes in the upper South. They settled for a time in Ironton Village, where Elias died a few years later. Eliza then took her family farther north into Ohio, settling in turn in Albany and Athens.

Davidson started school in Ironton Village, where a school for Black children opened in 1857. The Enterprise Academy, owned and controlled by Black educators, opened in Albany in 1864 and most likely was the pull that led the family to move there. Albany, where several Oberlin College graduates had settled, was the scene of strong antislavery sentiment and the site of three routes of the Underground Railroad. As a teenager Davidson knew and interacted with Oberlin College liberals and Black activists connected with the academy. Later she was exposed to the dynamics of an ever-changing urban area when she lived for a time with her sister, Mary, and Mary's husband, Noah Elliott, at Gallipolis, a river town.

Davidson started teaching at the age of sixteen. She taught for two years in Ohio and then followed a sister to Mississippi to teach freed people and their children. She ran a school at Spencer, Mississippi, which was no more than a flag stop on the railroad. In 1886, she addressed the members of the Alabama State Teachers' Association on the topic "How Shall We Make the Women of Our Race Stronger?" In Davidson's view, which she stated in a speech before the Alabama State Teachers' Association, the way to improve the situation for Black Americans was to work with the girls, who were the "hope of the race."

Olivia America Davidson's story is an example of the missing woman in history. Although she is not recognized as such, she was one of the cofounders of Tuskegee Institute. Her husband, Booker T. Washington, attributed the early success of the school "more to Miss Davidson than anyone else." [Schomburg Center]

She did this in part by talking about the lives of noble women.

After two years in Mississippi, Davidson accepted employment in Memphis, Tennessee. Her four-year tenure in the Memphis Public School system overlapped with one of the worst financial periods in the city's history of education. Otherwise, however, Davidson was in an exciting environment. She was caught up in the argument in favor of Black teachers teaching at Black schools, and she worked for a superintendent who introduced advanced teaching and curriculum changes. Her work in Memphis came to an end as a result of the 1878 yellow fever epidemic; she might have died had she not been in Ohio for a summer break when the epidemic broke out. Davidson wrote to Memphis, offering her services as a nurse, but was advised instead to spend the time studying at the Hampton Normal and Agricultural Institute in Hampton, Virginia.

Davidson enrolled in Hampton's senior class in the fall of 1878 with a scholarship paid for by Mrs. Rutherford B. Hayes. She graduated the following May and delivered one of the commencement essays, entitled "Decision of Character." Booker T. Washington, class of 1875, was the postgraduate speaker at the ceremony. While at Hampton, Davidson was brought to the attention of benefactress Mary Hemenway, who financed two years of study for her at the Framingham (Massachusetts) State Normal School. Once again, she earned a spot on the graduation program, speaking on the topic "Work among the Freedmen." After spending only a few months back at Hampton, Davidson left for Tuskegee, where she served the public roles of teacher, curriculum specialist, principal, fund-raiser, and builder as well as the private roles of confidant, wife, and mother.

Davidson was very ill when she left Framingham and returned to Hampton, the first indication that she was in failing health. Then, after about three years of intense activity at Tuskegee, she became very ill again and was forced into inactivity for about a year. During that same year, Washington's first wife, Fannie Smith, died, and he and Davidson wed on August 11, 1886. Davidson, who became stepmother to Washington's daughter, Portia, gave birth to two sons, Booker, Jr., born May 29, 1887, and Ernest Davidson, born February 6, 1889.

A few days after Ernest's birth, the Washington home caught fire. Washington himself was away. Davidson's exposure to the early morning chill after she and the baby had been carried out of the house further weakened Davidson's physical condition, and she never recovered. She was taken for medical attention, first to Montgomery and then to Boston, where she died on May 9, 1889, at Massachusetts General Hospital. Washington wrote in a letter to his mentor, General Samuel C. Armstrong, that "Few will ever know what she has done for Tuskegee and for me." Similarly, an unknown writer in *Southern Letters* wrote of Davidson that "in her great earnestness she made the mistake of thinking too little about her own health."

Davidson's story is another example of the missing woman in history, for although she is not recognized as such, she was one of the co-founders of an institution that continues to thrive today. The history of what is now Tuskegee University is not complete without an appreciation of the vast contributions made to its development by Olivia A. Davidson.

BIBLIOGRAPHY

Athens Messenger, "Famed Negro Educator Wed Here: Records Incomplete" (August 24, 1969); Brieger, James F., comp. *Hometown Mississippi* (1980); Catalogue of the Hampton Normal and Agricultural Institute, for the Academic Year 1878-79 (1879); "Constitution of the Albany Enterprise Academy" (1864). Circular in Ohio University Archives, Athens, Ohio; Davidson, Joseph. Last Will and Testament. West Virginia Historic Records Survey, Box 87, West Virginia University, Morgantown, West Virginia; Davidson, Olivia A. "Olivia Davidson to Eleanor Jameson Williams Baker, September 6, 1884." In *The Booker T. Washington Papers, Volume 2, 1860-89*, ed. Louis R. Harlan (1972), and "How Shall We Make the Women of Our Race Stronger?" In *The Booker T. Washington Papers, Volume 2, 1860-89*, ed. Louis R. Harlan (1972); Dorsey, Carolyn A. "The Pre-Hampton Years of Olivia A. Davidson," *The Hampton Review* (Fall 1988), and "Despite Poor Health: Olivia Davidson Washington's Story," *Sage: A Scholarly Journal on Black Women* (Fall 1985); Harlan, Louis R. *Booker T. Washington: The Making of a Black Leader, 1856-1901* (1972); Harlan, Louis R., ed. *The Booker T. Washington Papers, Volume 2, 1860-89* (1972), and *The Booker T. Washington Papers, Volume 5, 1889-95* (1974); Hilliard, David Moss. *The Development of Public Education in Memphis, Tennessee, 1848-1945* (1946); Hunter, Wilma King. "Three Women at Tuskegee, 1882-1925: The Wives of Booker T. Washington," *Journal of Ethnic Studies* (September 1976); Majors, Monroe A. "Mrs. Olivia Davidson Washington: Educator, Financier and Christian Martyr." In *Noted Negro Women: Their Triumphs and Activities* (1893); Marshall, James Fowle Baldwin. "Mrs. Olivia D. Washington," *Christian Register* (June 6, 1889); Mossell, Mrs. N. F. *The Work of the Afro-American Woman* ([1894] 1988); Phillips, Sarah A. Letter to Carolyn Dorsey (July 3, 1980), and letter to Connie Perdreau (September 26, 1977); Russell, John H. *The Free Negro in Virginia, 1619-1856* (1913); Schreiner-Yantis, Netti. "The Davidson Family: A Case Study in Research in Tazewell County." Netti Schreiner-Yantis Archives of the Pioneers of Tazewell County, Springfield, Virginia (1973), and *1830 Census, Tazewell County, Virginia* (1971); Siebert, Wilbur H. *The Mysteries of Ohio's Underground Railroads* (1951); *Southern Letters*, "Mrs. Olivia Davidson Washington and the Training of the Colored Girls" (August 1890); *Southern Workman*, "A Crown of Life" (July 1889); *Southern Workman*, "Anniversary Exercises at Hampton Institute" (June 1889); *Southern Workman*, "Olivia A. Davidson to Friend" (March 1879); State Centennial Educational Committee. Historical sketches of public schools in cities, villages, and townships of the state of Ohio, Columbus, Ohio (1876); Stewart, Ruth Ann. *Portia: The Life of Portia Washington Pittman, the Daughter of Booker T. Washington* (1977); Tribe, Ivan M. "The Development of a Rural Community, Albany, Ohio, 1840-1880," M.A. thesis (1967), and "Rise and Decline of Private Academies in Albany, Ohio," *Ohio History* (Summer 1969); U.S. Bureau of the Census, Seventh Census of the United States (1850), and Eighth Census of the United States (1860), and Ninth Census of the United States (1870); Washington, Booker T. "The Story of My Life and Work." In *The Booker T. Washington Papers, Volume 1: The Autobiographical Writings*, ed. Louis R. Harlan (1972), and "Booker T. Washington to Samuel Chapman Armstrong, April 21, 1889." In *The Booker T. Washington Papers, Volume 1: The Autobiographical Writings*, ed. Louis R. Harlan (1972); Williamson, Joel. *New People: Miscegenation and Mulattoes in the United States* (1980).

CAROLYN DORSEY

DAVIS, ANGELA (1944-)

Shouts of "Free Angela" echoed across the early 1970s, and a California college professor became an icon of the counterculture. She was fierce, brilliant, and uncompromising.

Angela Davis was born on January 26, 1944, in Birmingham, Alabama, the youngest child of B. Frank and Sallye E. Davis. Her mother was a schoolteacher, and her father had been one until, because teachers' salaries were so low, he gave it up to buy a gas station. The family was comfortable financially, living in a middle-class area in Birmingham. Davis's mother taught her reading, writing, and arithmetic before she entered school.

Not all of Davis's classmates were so economically advantaged as she was. She early saw children who had no warm clothing or money for lunch and became highly conscious of social differences. In the segregated schools Davis attended, there were teachers who went out of their way to teach Black history and instill a sense of Black heritage, but there were also school buildings near to falling down and textbooks long out of date. She became aware of the messages Black children were being sent by their teachers and others around them. If their parents were poor, the system told them, it was because they did not work hard enough, were not bright enough, did not have enough determination. Davis ferociously resented these messages and believed they were undermining a whole generation.

As Davis became angrier and more dissatisfied with the life around her, she found support at home. Her mother had been politically active since college, and her grandmother worked to instill a sense of outrage over the injustices suffered by African-Americans. While still in elementary school, Davis participated with her mother in civil rights demonstrations. In high school she was one of the organizers

On July 4, 1974, Angela Davis addressed a rally of 5,000 people who marched through downtown Raleigh, North Carolina, to the Capitol Building to protest the North Carolina death penalty. The demonstration was sponsored by the National Alliance against Racist and Political Repression. [UPI/Bettmann]

of interracial study groups that were disbanded by the police. At the age of fifteen, Davis moved to New York to attend a progressive private school, the Elizabeth Irwin High School. Her tuition was paid by a scholarship from the American Friends Service Committee and she lived with the family of Episcopal minister William Howard Melish.

Elizabeth Irwin High School was the proverbial "hotbed of radicals." Many of the teachers had been blacklisted from the public schools for their leftist political beliefs. Davis was ripe for radicalizing herself and soon joined Advance, a Marxist-Leninist group. She also worked hard to overcome the quality of her early education before she entered Brandeis University in Waltham, Massachusetts. At Brandeis, Davis excelled academically. She spent her junior year at the Sorbonne. In Paris, Davis met with political activity on an intense level. Among her fellow

students were Algerians who were involved in the struggle against French colonialism.

In 1963, four girls whom Davis had known were killed when a Birmingham church was bombed, and her radicalism developed deeply personal roots. Then, in her senior year, she began to study under the philosopher Herbert Marcuse. Marcuse's analysis of modern history and his belief in the responsibility of the individual to rebel had a profound effect on Davis. She graduated from Brandeis in 1965 with a degree in French and went on to study philosophy in Europe. In Frankfurt, at Goethe University, she became a member of a socialist student group that was demonstrating against the Vietnam War. By 1967, she had resolved to return to the United States, to study again under Marcuse, who was now at the University of California at San Diego. She became active again in the civil rights movement.

In 1967, she went to Los Angeles for a workshop sponsored by the Student Nonviolent Coordinating Committee (SNCC). There she met Kendra and Franklin Alexander, who were active in SNCC, the Black Panthers, and the Communist party. The next year, she moved to Los Angeles to work with the Alexanders. However, various aspects of these radical groups disturbed her, especially the sexism. Finally, she made a choice that would drastically change her life: she joined the Communist party. In 1969, she made a pilgrimage to Cuba.

Having completed her Master's degree and "all-but-the-dissertation" on her doctorate in philosophy, Davis was hired, in 1969, to teach philosophy at the University of California at Los Angeles. She was a popular teacher, but that did not help her when her membership in the Communist party was revealed. The students and administration of the university stood behind her, but the California board of regents and Governor Ronald Reagan fired her.

Davis challenged the dismissal in court and won. She was reinstated, but her classes were monitored, and the board of regents was determined to find a way to get rid of her.

Davis became more and more involved in work with the Black Panthers, especially with prison inmates, whom she considered prisoners of class war. Then two Marxist inmates of Soledad Prison organized a revolutionary cell in the prison. One of the inmates, W. L. Nolen, was killed by a guard while involved in a fistfight with two other prisoners. The other, George Jackson, was indicted for murder when a white guard was found murdered. Davis became fervently involved in the cause of the "Soledad Brothers." Her speeches in their defense were enough, along with her lack of a doctorate, for the board of regents to deny her a new contract.

That was only the beginning. George Jackson, with whom Davis had developed a strong emotional involvement, was killed by guards during an alleged escape attempt—after all charges against him had been dropped. His brother, Jonathan, went to the Marin County Courthouse, where a San Quentin inmate was on trial for stabbing another prisoner, took hostages, and tried to make a getaway. Before he could do so, two prisoners, a judge, and Jackson himself were killed.

Jackson had taken the guns he used in the rescue attempt from Davis's home. Though the guns had been purchased by Davis because of threats on her life, and though they were registered, a federal warrant was issued for her arrest. She did not wait to be served with the warrant; she went underground. On August 18, 1970, the brilliant middle-class professor of philosophy whose crime consisted of owning guns used in a crime was placed on the Federal Bureau of Investigation's ten-most-wanted list. She was charged by California with kidnapping, conspiracy, and murder. After two months, she was found in New York, extradited to California, and put in jail without bail.

The "Free Angela" movement erupted. The slogan appeared on urban walls, on bumper stickers, and in newspapers. Her face appeared on posters and on T-shirts. Singer Aretha Franklin offered to pay her bail, saying, "I'm going to set Angela free ... not because I believe in communism but because she's a Black woman who wants freedom for all Black people." On February 23, 1972, she was released on $102,000 bail and, at her trial, she was acquitted of all charges. Ronald Reagan and the board of regents voted that she would never again teach at a university supported by the state of California.

The defense committee set up for Angela Davis was renamed the National Alliance against Racism and Political Repression, with Davis as cochair. Its purpose was to help in the defense of political cases. The majority of those defended have been Blacks and Hispanics.

In recent years, Davis has written and lectured extensively and remained politically active, running for vice-president of the United States in 1980 and 1984 on the Communist party ticket. Her books include *If They Come in the Morning* (1971), *Women, Race, and Class* (1983), *Women, Culture, and Politics* (1989), and the best-selling *Angela Davis: An Autobiography* (1988).

BIBLIOGRAPHY

Abbot, D. "Revolution by Other Means," *New Statesman* (August 14, 1987); Buhle, Mary Jo, Paul Buhle, and Dan Georgakas. *Encyclopedia of the American Left* (1990); *CBWA*; Davis, Angela. *Angela Davis: An Autobiography* (1988); *EBA*; *NBAW*; *WWBA* (1992).

KATHLEEN THOMPSON

DAVIS, ELIZABETH LINDSAY
(b. 1855)

Much of what we currently know about the early club work of African-American women is due to the commitment of Elizabeth Lindsay Davis, not only to building the women's clubs but also to documenting their history. Elizabeth Lindsay, the eldest daughter of Thomas and Sophia Lindsay, was born in Peoria

County, Illinois, in 1855. At the age of ten, she enrolled in the Bureau County High School in Pinceton, Illinois. She was one of three Black students to graduate from the institution. She used her teaching skills in several schools throughout the midwest—Keokuk, Iowa; Quincy, Illinois; New Albany, Indiana—and in Louisville, Kentucky. When she married William H. Davis of Frederick, Maryland, in 1885, she discontinued teaching to do club work.

Davis ardently believed in reform and social uplift. She believed that elite Black women should be at the forefront of the reform movement. Thus, she organized the Chicago Phyllis Wheatley Women's Club in 1896 and served as president for twenty-eight years. This club, in 1908, opened the Phyllis Wheatley Home for young Black females who needed a safe place to live. The Home provided living accommodations, recreation, and an employment bureau. It also

Committed reformer Elizabeth Lindsay Davis founded and served for twenty-eight years as president of Chicago's Phyllis Wheatley Women's Club. [Schomburg Center]

operated a club program and classes in domestic arts. The home and its activities were solely managed and supported by the Black community.

Davis was also a member of the Ida B. Wells Club, the Woman's City Club, the Chicago Forum League of Women Voters, the Woman's Aid, the Giles Charity Club, the E.L.D. Study Club, and the Service Club. In 1918, the Elizabeth Lindsay Charity Club was organized in her honor. The club provided legal counsel, educational facilities, medical aid, food, and clothing to the thousands of southern Black migrants seeking economic opportunity in Chicago.

Her long involvement in the National Association of Colored Women—she was national organizer from 1901 to 1906 and from 1912 to 1916—led to her success as state organizer and president (1910-12) of the Illinois Federation of Colored Women's Clubs. Under her presidency, the federation endorsed the National Association for the Advancement of Colored People and pushed for the ballot for women.

Davis's documentation of the women's club movement in *The Story of The Illinois Federation of Colored Women's Clubs* (1922) is the first record of women's clubs in the state. Her *Lifting as They Climb* (1933) is the first national history of the club movement. A committed reformer and active clubwoman, Davis helped build and document the reform agenda for Black Americans throughout the last decade of the nineteenth century and the first decades of the twentieth century.

BIBLIOGRAPHY

Dannett, Sylvia G. L. *Profiles of Negro Womanhood* (1964); Davis, Elizabeth Lindsay. *Lifting as They Climb* (1933), and *The Story of The Illinois Federation of Colored Women's Clubs* (1922).

WANDA HENDRICKS

DAVIS, FRANCES ELLIOTT
(1882-1965)

Frances Elliott Davis rose above much adversity to become the first Black nurse officially recognized by the American Red Cross.

Born in 1882 in Knoxville, Tennessee, "Fannie" had a white mother and a father of mixed Cherokee and Black American ancestry. Fannie's mother, Emma Elliott, was ousted from her family as a result of having given birth to her. Emma Elliott spent the last five years of her ailing life in the mountains of Tennessee and, in 1887, died of tuberculosis, leaving her five-year-old daughter to the orphanage society. Fannie Elliott lived with numerous families throughout Tennessee, North Carolina, and Pennsylvania, and developed a desire to care for others. The last family that young Fannie Elliott stayed with was the Vickerses, a Black family who took her to Pittsburgh, Pennsylvania. Mr. Vickers took Elliott in as a servant, forcing her to provide for herself financially. A wealthy jewelry store owner in Pittsburgh, Joseph Allison Reed, and his wife offered Elliott domestic employment in their home. The Reeds grew fond of Elliott and became her greatest patrons throughout her academic and professional life.

Fannie Elliott received teacher training at Knoxville College, from which she graduated in 1907, but a career in nursing was her lifelong dream.

Elliott pursued this career in 1910 by entering the Freedmen's Hospital Training School in Washington, D.C. Graduating in 1912, she then did three years of private duty work in Washington, D.C. Nurse Elliott then decided to apply to the American Red Cross. She was informed that in order to do Red Cross work she would need further training in public health or rural nursing. She completed the necessary training in one year at Columbia University and received her first call to duty with the Red Cross in July 1917 in Jackson, Tennessee. Nurse Elliott was initially denied official recognition by the Red Cross because it had not begun to enroll "colored" nurses. A few days after the initial notice in 1919, however, she received a package that contained the Red Cross nurse's pin. Inscribed on the back of the pin was 1A. The "A" indicated that she was a "colored" nurse. It was not until after World War II that the Red Cross discontinued this practice.

Fannie Elliott Davis thereafter spent her life as a public and private duty nurse, organizing at Detroit's Dunbar Hospital the first training school in the state of Michigan for Black nurses, and later working for the Detroit Nurses Association and the Detroit Department of Health. She devoted her private life to her husband William A. Davis (whom she married on December 24, 1921) and a host of friends and relatives. Nurse Davis never lived to receive the recognition to be given her by the American Red Cross in 1965. Fannie Elliott Davis died shortly before, in May of that year, in Mount Clemens, Michigan.

She had belonged to numerous organizations, including the Freedmen's Hospital Alumnae Association, the National Association of Colored Graduate Nurses, the American Red Cross, the National Organization for Public Health Nursing, the League of Nursing Education, the Detroit District and Michigan State Nurses' Association, and the American Nurses' Association.

BIBLIOGRAPHY

Hine, Darlene Clark. *Black Women in White: Racial Conflict and Cooperation in the Nursing Profession, 1890-1950* (1989); Pitrone, Jean Maddern. *Trailblazer: Negro Nurse in the American Red Cross* (1969); Thoms, Adah B. *Pathfinders: A History of the Progress of Colored Graduate Nurses* (1929).

FELIX ARMFIELD

DAVIS, HENRIETTA VINTON (1860-1941)

Marcus Garvey described Henrietta Vinton Davis as the "greatest woman of the Negro race today" (*Negro World*, May 1, 1920). One of the most illustrious Black actresses of the turn of the century in the United States, she became famous internationally as a leader in the Garvey movement.

Born in Baltimore in 1860, Davis was the daughter of Mansfield Vinton Davis, a musician, and Mary Ann Johnson Davis. She taught school in Maryland and Louisiana and in 1878 became the first Black woman to be employed in the Office of the Recorder of Deeds in Washington, D.C., where she worked as an assistant to Frederick Douglass. Douglass encouraged her commitment to a dramatic career and introduced her debut performance in Washington, D.C., in April 1883. Over the next decade she traveled widely as an elocutionist, attracting audiences with her rendering of works by Shakespeare, Dunbar, and others. In 1884, she married Thomas Symmons, a Detroit theatrical producer who became her manager, but the marriage and business relationship dissolved by 1893 after he was arrested for domestic violence. After years of performing without winning a place in an established Shakespearean company—despite glowing reviews of her talent—Davis established her own company in Chicago in 1893. She produced works by William Edgar Easton (*Dessalines, Christophe*) and collaborated with New York journalist John E. Bruce in the writing of *Our Old Kentucky Home*, a Civil War drama. She traveled to the Caribbean on tour with singer Nonie Bailey Hardy in 1912-13 and managed the Covent Garden Theater in Kingston, Jamaica.

Her experience and connections in Jamaica, along with her friendship with Garvey supporters John E. Bruce and Florence Bruce, attracted her to the Universal Negro Improvement Association (UNIA) as

Marcus Garvey called her the "greatest woman of the Negro race today" when Henrietta Vinton put the power of her reputation as a highly acclaimed actress behind the Universal Negro Improvement Association in 1917. [Schomburg Center]

the young Marcus Garvey began to reformulate it in Harlem in 1917 and 1918. The then-obscure Garvey relied on her to draw huge crowds in cities where she had gained a reputation as an actress. She became the UNIA International Organizer and was indispensable in building the movement, touring tirelessly with Garvey in the early years and chairing key mass meetings at Carnegie Hall, Madison Square Garden, and the UNIA's Liberty Hall. She was one of the founding directors of the UNIA's Black Star Line, and later, an organizer for the Black Cross Navigation and Trading Company, traveling on organizational tours of the Caribbean aboard UNIA ships. Long the only woman among the slate of central UNIA officers, she became Fourth Assistant President General in 1922. She was the only woman in the UNIA delegation that met with President C.D.B. King in Liberia in 1924 and in the committee that delivered petitions to President Coolidge later the same year. During Garvey's incarceration (1925-27), she handled UNIA affairs in British Honduras, and after Garvey's release and deportation, she was his senior administrator in Jamaica, directing UNIA affairs there in his absences. In August 1929, she became secretary general of Garvey's splinter group, the UNIA of the World, and continued to chair meetings, direct pageants, and

assist in the organization's administration and with Garvey's *Blackman* newspaper. She became increasingly alienated from Garvey and by 1932 had become the First Assistant President General of the competing UNIA Incorporated, headquartered in New York. In 1934 Davis became the first (and only) woman to be elected President General of that rival organization. She died in Washington, D.C., November 23, 1941, after a long illness.

Davis succeeded grandly in converting her experience as an actress-elocutionist into a powerful political career as an orator and organizer. Her renunciation of the racial discrimination she experienced as an actress fueled the fervor with which she dedicated herself to nationalist politics, especially to the hope of freedom and self-actualization for Black people through the redemption of Africa. Her long years of personal dedication to Garvey, however, ended in disillusionment, illness, and relative poverty, and despite her many achievements and popularity, little note was made of her death at the time.

[*See also* UNIVERSAL NEGRO IMPROVEMENT ASSOCIATION.]

BIBLIOGRAPHY

Bair, Barbara. "True Women, Real Men: Gender, Ideology, and Social Roles in the Garvey Movement." In *Gendered Domains: Beyond the Public-Private Dichotomy in Women's History*, ed. Susan Reverby and Dorothy O. Helly (1992); John E. Bruce papers. Schomburg Center for Research in Black Culture, New York Public Library, New York; Hill, Errol. *Shakespeare in Sable: A History of Black Shakespearean Actors* (1984), and "Henrietta Vinton Davis." In *Women in the American Theatre*, ed. Helen Chinoy and Linda Jenkins (1981); Hill, Robert A., et al., eds. *The Marcus Garvey and Universal Negro Improvement Association Papers*. 7 vols. (1983-1990); Seraile, William. "Henrietta Vinton Davis and the Garvey Movement," *Afro-Americans in New York Life and History* (July 1983).

BARBARA BAIR

DAVIS, HILDA ANDREA (1905-)

Accompanying the senior class photo and résumé of Hilda Andrea Davis in the 1925 Howard University yearbook is the caption "Prexy," a diminutive for president. This inscription, as well as the activities listed, prophetically capsulize the career of a distinguished educator and organizational leader. A dean of women, professor of English, mental health administrator, and leader of educational, women's, civic, and religious organizations, Davis has waged a struggle for race and sex equality throughout the twentieth century.

Born to Louis Alexander and Ruth Gertrude Cooke Davis on May 24, 1905, in Washington, D.C., Hilda Davis was the fourth child in a family of eight daughters—Ruth Olivette, Henrietta Josephine, Charlotte Isabelle, Rhoda Alexandra, Thalia Annazean, Norma Eugene, Jean-Marie—and one son, Louis Alexander. During her youth, the family household briefly included a white foster child, Virginia McKay. The extended family included two sets of grandparents, three aunts, and six uncles. Her paternal uncle, Benjamin Oliver Davis, Sr., became the nation's first Black general of the regular army.

Davis attended public schools in the District of Columbia, graduating in 1921 from Dunbar High School at age sixteen. First in the family to enroll in a four-year university, she earned a Bachelor's degree magna cum laude in English and Latin from Howard University in 1925. Always eager for more education, she later earned a Master's degree in English from Radcliffe College in 1932 and a Doctorate in Human Development from the University of Chicago in 1953.

For nearly twenty-six years, Davis was a teacher and advocate for women's concerns in historically Black institutions. She was director of girls' activities, teacher of English and Latin, and registrar at Palmer Memorial Institute, Sedalia, North Carolina, from 1925 to 1931; dean of women and assistant professor of English at Shaw University, Raleigh, North Carolina, from 1932 to 1935; and dean of women and professor of English at Talladega College, Talladega, Alabama, from 1936 to 1952. Like most early deans of women, she was the principal guardian of women's interests and, at both Shaw and Talladega, the sole woman administrator in the president's cabinet.

In 1952, after sixteen years at Talladega, Davis left the field of higher education, resigning in protest when the college's first Black president, Arthur Douglass Gray, tried to displace her through reassignment. She accepted an administrative post in the Delaware State Mental Health Department in Delaware City and remained there for eleven years. Returning to education in 1965, she broke the color barrier as the first Black educator to be awarded a full-time faculty contract at the University of Delaware in Newark. Upon leaving the university in 1970, she accepted a faculty appointment at Wilmington College in New Castle, Delaware. She retired in 1977.

Coupled with Davis's lifetime of service to higher education has been a similar commitment to progressive organizations. Since her undergraduate days, Davis has nurtured and provided leadership to nu-

merous groups. Among these are Delta Sigma Theta Sorority, Inc., for which she served as president of the Alpha Chapter during the 1924-25 term and as chair of the National Projects Committee from 1963 to 1967. In 1938, she became the second elected president of the Association of Deans of Women and Advisers to Girls in Negro Schools after the death of its founder, Lucy Diggs Slowe. By creating stability and engendering self-confidence, Davis rescued the organization from despair and dissolution. She provided similar leadership for the National Association of College Women as its acting president from 1939 to 1945 and from 1957 to 1961. She was the only person elected to the presidency for two non-consecutive terms.

An unwavering integrationist, Davis was among the earliest Black members of the American Association of University Women, the National Association for Women in Education (formerly the National Association of Deans of Women), and the Society of Companions of the Holy Cross, an Episcopalian women's group. In addition to fighting racial barriers, she challenged sex prejudice and religious traditions to become the first woman senior warden of the Episcopalian Diocese of Delaware.

For her contributions to higher education and progressive organizations, Davis has garnered many honors, including induction into the Delaware Women's Hall of Fame, 1986; the Medal of Distinction from the University of Delaware, 1987; and an honorary doctorate from Trinity College, Washington, D.C., 1989. In addition, she received citations for outstanding service from the Wilmington, Delaware chapter of the Talladega College Alumni and the Wilmington Alumnae Chapter of Delta Sigma Theta Sorority, Inc., both in 1981. Scholarships and awards in her name have been established by the National Association for Women in Education, *Sage: A Scholarly Journal on Black Women*, Wilmington College, and the National Association of University Women (formerly the National Association of College Women). In 1988, the Young Women's Christian Association (YWCA) of New Castle County, Delaware, dedicated the new Hilda A. Davis Residence, designed to house women in need, as a public symbol of Davis's commitment and generosity.

Davis currently resides in Newark, Delaware, where she remains active in regional and national organizations.

BIBLIOGRAPHY

Brett, Ruth, Edna M. Calhoun, Lucille J. Piggott, Hilda A. Davis, and Patricia Bell-Scott. "Our Living

History: Reminiscences of Black Participation in NAWDAC," *Journal of the National Association for Women Deans, Administrators, and Counselors* (1979); Davis, Hilda A. Personal interviews (1988-91); Davis, Hilda A. and Patricia Bell-Scott. "The Association of Deans of Women and Advisors to Girls in Negro Schools, 1929-1954: A Brief Oral History," *Sage: A Scholarly Journal on Black Women* (1990); *NBAW* (1992).

PATRICIA BELL-SCOTT

DAWSON, MARY LUCINDA CARDWELL (1894-1962)

Mary Lucinda Cardwell Dawson, opera director, emerged during the 1950s as a noted leader in the field of music in the United States. She opened the Cardwell Dawson School of Music in Pittsburgh, Pennsylvania, c. 1926 and was a well-known choral director in Pennsylvania for more than twenty years. She served as the tenth president of the National Association of Negro Musicians (NANM) from 1939 to 1941 and founded the National Negro Opera Company (NNOC) in 1941-42.

Mary Lucinda Cardwell was born February 14, 1894, in Madison, North Carolina, to James A. and Elizabeth Cardwell. She was the oldest of six children—two brothers and three sisters—several of whom were active in music. The family moved to Homestead, Pennsylvania, where Dawson attended local schools and began her early training in piano. In 1925, Dawson graduated from the New England Conservatory of Music, then continued her studies at Chicago Musical College and the Metropolitan Opera Studio, training in organ, voice, staging, and opera technique. She studied choral music under Arthur Hubbard, Clara Huhn, and Harvey Gaul, and opera technique under Vincent Sorey and Clayton Gilbert.

She married Walter Dawson c. 1926 and they moved to Pittsburgh. There she started the Mary Cardwell Dawson School of Music, which became one of the most highly regarded private schools in the East. The Cardwell Dawson Choir won the Pittsburgh *Sun-Telegraph*'s Harvey Gaul Award for musical excellence in 1937 and 1938 and performed at the New York World's Fair in 1939. Meanwhile, Dawson performed recitals as a pianist and singer throughout Pennsylvania and in Washington, D.C., and Chicago. In 1941, the Dawsons moved to Washington.

As a direct outgrowth of her work as president of NANM, Dawson founded NNOC to provide opportunities for trained Black singers to perform. The company's first production, Verdi's *Aida*, was staged in Pittsburgh during the twenty-first annual NANM convention in 1941. The leading roles were sung by LaJulia Rhea, Napoleon Reed, Nellie Dobson Plante, William Franklin, Shelby Nichols, Reginald Burrus, and Thelma Wade Brown; Frederick Vajda staged the opera and conducted the orchestra. The NNOC received its first charter from the State of Illinois, where *Aida* was restaged on October 10-11, 1942. Dawson started opera guilds in Chicago, Pittsburgh, Washington, D.C., and New York to assist in subsequent productions of *La Traviata*, *Faust*, *Aida*, and *Ouanga*. The latter, written by Black composer Clarence Cameron White, had its premiere in a concert performance at the Metropolitan Opera House on May 27, 1956, conducted by Henri Elkan, and several more performances were sung the following September at Carnegie Hall. The NNOC presented staged operas with orchestra from 1941 to 1956; between 1946 and 1961 the company performed an operatic version of *The Ordering of Moses* by Nathaniel Dett. The National Negro Opera Foundation was formed by Dawson in 1950-51 to provide a broader cultural and national base for the company's activity. However, from its inception NNOC was constantly in debt, and Dawson and her husband often used personal funds to underwrite the financial costs of productions.

Although NNOC used both Black and white musicians and technical staff in its productions, Dawson accomplished her goal of giving talented Black singers opportunities denied them by white companies. Singers such as Camilla Williams, Muriel Rahn, Robert McFerrin, LaJulia Rhea, Lillian Evanti, and Carol Brice gained valuable experience as leading NNOC soloists. The company had the support of many national figures, including Eleanor Roosevelt, Mary McLeod Bethune, Marian Anderson, and W. C. Handy. NNOC became a member of both the national council of the Metropolitan Opera Association and the Central Opera Services.

In 1961, Dawson was appointed to President John F. Kennedy's National Committee on Music. She also held memberships in Delta Sigma Theta Sorority, the National Council of Negro Women, the National Association of Colored Women, and the National Association of Negro Business and Professional Women's Clubs.

Following a visit to Chicago in July 1961, Dawson became ill and on March 19, 1962, she died of a heart attack in Washington, D.C. She was one of a cadre of Black women who assumed positions of national importance at mid-century and was praised for her determination to provide artistic and cultural opportunities for musically talented Black Americans.

BIBLIOGRAPHY

BDAAM; *The Call*, Obituary (March 3, 1962); Lewis, Ellistine P. (Holly). Interview with Barbara Edwards Lee, niece of M. C. Dawson (October 1, 1991); Mary Cardwell Dawson papers are at the Library of Congress, Washington, D.C.

ELLISTINE P. LEWIS

DAY, CAROLINE STEWART BOND
(b. 1889)

"I should state at the outset," stated anthropologist Caroline Bond Day about the interracial families she studied in the early 1930s, "that however the achievements of this group may seem to argue for the advantages of race-crossing, it is my firm belief that Negroes who are of unmixed blood are just as capable of achievement . . . as those who are mixed" (Day 1932). Day herself was a light-skinned woman of Black, Native American, and white ancestry, and that personal history may well have prompted her scientific curiosity about others who shared a similar heritage.

The daughter of Georgia and Moses Stewart, Caroline was born in Montgomery, Alabama, in 1889. The family lived in Boston for several years, but after her father's death Caroline and her widowed mother moved to Tuskegee, Alabama, where Georgia taught. Following her mother's remarriage, Caroline took the name of her new stepfather, John Bond. The Bonds subsequently lived in Birmingham, Selma, and then Washington, D.C., and the family was completed by the birth of a half-sister and half-brother.

Caroline earned a Bachelor's degree from Atlanta University. A few years later, when she wanted to pursue graduate study, Radcliffe College of Harvard University refused to accept all of her Atlanta University credits. She went to Radcliffe for two additional years of undergraduate study, earning a second Bachelor's degree in 1919. Following World War I, she worked briefly in New York City in relief and support services for Black soldiers and their families. She then served with the Young Women's Christian Association (YWCA); taught at Prairie View College in Texas, where she married another teacher, Aaron Day; and became an instructor of English, drama,

and anthropology at Atlanta University. She also wrote short stories, essays, poetry, and plays, and her work appeared in magazines and anthologies.

In 1927, Day received the funding needed to pursue her long-delayed studies and was admitted to Harvard's graduate school of anthropology. For several years she collected material for a multigenerational study about interracial families, but she was frequently debilitated by recurring problems from a rheumatic heart condition. Day was probably the first person of African-American ancestry to earn a higher degree in anthropology when she acquired an M.A. in 1932. That same year, Harvard University's Peabody Museum of Archeology and Ethnology published her master's thesis, *A Study of Some Negro-White Families in the United States*.

Day's work goes beyond the physical anthropology that was her central academic focus. She touches on complex political, socioeconomic, and historical issues as well. The study includes descriptions of skin color, anthropomorphic measurements, hair samples, and numerous photographs of interracial families—sometimes going back as far as five generations. It has provided scholars with details about the lives of hundreds of individuals but has been criticized by some later anthropologists for its unsophisticated methodology.

Day's poor health necessitated a more sedentary life, and with the exception of intermittent teaching assignments and some unpublished writings, she went into semi-retirement following the publication of her book. She lived with her husband in Durham, North Carolina, where he had become an executive with North Carolina Mutual Life Insurance Company. The Days adopted a teenaged son, and most of her remaining time was spent with her family. She died in the late 1940s from complications from her chronic heart condition.

BIBLIOGRAPHY

Day, Caroline. "A Fairy Tale." In *Readings from Negro Authors for Schools and Colleges*, ed. Otelia Cromwell (1931), *Crisis* (October 1917), and *A Study of Some Negro-White Families in the United States* (1932); Ross, Hubert B. "Caroline Bond Day: Pioneer Black Female Anthropologist." Paper presented to the American Anthropological Association (November 1983). Some of Day's private papers are in the possession of Adele Logan Alexander.

ADELE LOGAN ALEXANDER

DEARING, JUDY (1940-)

Judy Dearing has designed costumes for over a dozen Broadway productions, including *For Colored Girls Who Have Considered Suicide/When the Rainbow Is Enuf*, *Checkmates*, *The Babe*, *The Mighty Gents*, and *Once on This Island*. One of the few Black female designers on Broadway, Dearing has inspired many young women to pursue a career in costume design.

Judy Elizabeth Dearing was born February 28, 1940, in New York City to Charles and Elizabeth Dearing. One of six children, she attended City College of New York and the Sapho School of Design. Her earliest stage designs were for dance, for such choreographers as Alvin Ailey, Rod Rodgers, and Donald McKayle. She was inspired to design for theater by actors Bill Duke and Garrett Morris.

In 1974, Dearing designed her first Broadway production, *What the Wine-Sellers Buy*. The next year, she became a member of United Scenic Artists Association (USAA). Her other major credits include *A Soldier's Play* for the Negro Ensemble Company and *The Dance and the Railroad* for the New York Shakespeare Festival. Dearing has designed throughout the country for regional theaters and has taught on numerous university campuses.

Her many awards include seven Audience Development Committee (AUDELCO) Awards, a Tony Award nomination, National Association for the Advancement of Colored People Image Award, and an Obie. In 1970, Dearing married choreographer/dancer John Parks. They have one daughter.

BIBLIOGRAPHY

Dearing, Judy. Personal interview (August 1991); *Essence* (January 1990); Designers' Files, Billy Rose Theatre Collection. The New York Public Library for the Performing Arts, New York City.

KATHY A. PERKINS

DEE, RUBY (1924-)

The history of Black actors in American film has often been one of exploitation and repression. In theater, it has been one of careful isolation from the mainstream. Among the handful of actors who have risen above that condition by sheer intelligence, dignity, and determination is Ruby Dee.

Born Ruby Ann Wallace on October 27, 1924, in Cleveland, Ohio, she was the third of four children of Marshall and Emma Benson Wallace. When Ruby was an infant, the family moved to New York City

and settled in Harlem. Her mother, who was a schoolteacher, was determined that her children should escape the ghetto that area was fast becoming. She saw that they studied literature and music, and in the evenings the family read aloud to one another from the poetry of Longfellow, Wordsworth, and Paul Laurence Dunbar.

By the time she was in her teens, Ruby Dee—the name she adopted when she went onstage—was also adept at art and was submitting poetry to the *New York Amsterdam News*, a Black weekly newspaper. During this time she first became involved in political activity as well. She spoke at a mass meeting protesting the cancellation of a federally funded music program, the result of which had been the suicide of a teacher whose job had ended.

After high school, Dee went to Hunter College, where she majored in French and Spanish and began to study acting. She also joined the American Negro Theater (ANT), a Harlem group founded by playwright/director Abram Hill. From 1941 to 1943, Dee appeared in a variety of ANT productions. In December 1943, she made her Broadway debut as a native girl in a drama entitled *South Pacific*. It was a

Ruby Dee's performances as an actress have been marked by a dignity and humanity that reflect the values she stands for in the Black community and in the dramatic community at large. She has often worked with her husband, actor-writer-director Ossie Davis. [Moorland-Spingarn]

walk-on role, but just three years later she was back in a principal role in the play *Jeb*, the story of a Black World War II veteran. Ossie Davis, whom she married two years later, played the lead.

In 1944 and again in 1947, Dee played the title role in touring productions of a Black adaptation of *Anna Lucasta* that appeared first at ANT and then on Broadway. The play drew national attention to many of its actors. In 1946, Dee appeared in her first film, *Love in Syncopation*.

In 1953, through friends she had made while protesting the treatment of Julius and Ethel Rosenberg, Dee received a role in *The World of Sholem Aleichem*. She credits that production with changing her consciousness about theater and about the universality of oppression.

During the late 1940s and the 1950s, Dee appeared frequently in both plays and films, including *The Jackie Robinson Story*, in which she played the great baseball player's wife. She also worked in radio, performing the title role in the serial *Nora Drake*, a non-Black part. In 1959, on Broadway, she created the role of Ruth Younger in *A Raisin in the Sun*, by Lorraine Hansberry, a play that has been called perhaps the most important event in the history of modern Black theater. Two years later she played Ruth in the film version of the play. Sidney Poitier played her brother, the lead male role. It was the fifth time the two had played opposite each other.

In earlier films, both Dee and Poitier had been forced to play sexless, self-effacing stoics. In *Raisin*, they broke that mold for themselves and others. Dee made another break from her "Negro June Allyson" image when she appeared in her husband's satirical play *Purlie Victorious* that same year. (It was later made into a film entitled *Gone Are the Days* and musicalized as *Purlie*.) In 1965, she became the first Black actress to appear in major roles at the American Shakespeare Festival at Stratford, Connecticut, playing Kate in *The Taming of the Shrew* and Cordelia in *King Lear*.

A year later, Dee won the Drama Desk Award for her performance in the lead role in Alice Childress's prize-winning play *Wedding Band*. Widely acclaimed and financially successful, the work focuses on an interracial love affair. In 1974, a televised version again starred Dee. In the meantime she appeared in Athol Fugard's *Boesman and Lena*, for which she won an Obie in 1971.

Dee's performances in such films as *The Balcony*, *The Incident*, *Uptight*, *Black Girl*, and *Buck and the Preacher* gained her a reputation for powerful, honest, and highly skilled performances. In 1974, however,

frustrated by the attitudes and actions of those in power in Hollywood, Dee took a break from films to work with her husband on the radio series *Ossie Davis and Ruby Dee Hour*. The series lasted until 1976, but Dee did not return to films until 1982, when she starred in *Cat People*.

In 1989, Dee appeared in Spike Lee's critically and historically important film *Do the Right Thing*. Her portrayal was marked by a dignity and humanity that reflect the values she stands for in the Black community and in the dramatic community at large.

Since the 1960s, Dee has appeared regularly on television in prestigious dramas, in nighttime soap operas, in historical treatments of Black heroines such as Harriet Tubman, and in police and detective dramas. In 1981, Dee and Davis had their own series on PBS, *With Ossie and Ruby*. In 1983, she played Mary Tyrone in an all-Black televised production of Eugene O'Neill's *Long Day's Journey into Night*. In 1991, she won an Emmy Award as Outstanding Supporting Actress in a Miniseries or Special for her performance in *Decoration Day*, an NBC Hallmark Hall of Fame production.

Dee has also long been politically active. Following the 1963 church bombing in Montgomery, Alabama, and the assassination of President John F. Kennedy, Dee and Davis mounted a campaign encouraging people to donate to the promotion of civil rights instead of buying Christmas presents. They have consistently supported and lent their names to leaders such as Martin Luther King, Jr., Bayard Rustin, and A. Philip Randolph. Dee regularly performs at benefits and serves on national committees. She has also established a scholarship for young women entering the field of drama.

Finally, Ruby Dee has written a number of books, including two volumes of poetry, *Glow Child and Other Poems* and *My One Good Nerve*, and two children's stories, *Two Ways to Count to Ten* and *Tower to Heaven*.

There have been a number of "First Ladies of the American Theater," distinguished actresses who have inspired respect and admiration in their audiences and among their co-workers over a lifetime. Ruby Dee belongs among their ranks.

BIBLIOGRAPHY

BAFT; "The Big Picture," *Us* (August 21, 1989); Bogle, Donald. *Toms, Coons, Mulattoes, Mammies, and Bucks* (1973); *Current Biography* (1970); *CBWA*; Fax, Elton C. *Contemporary Black Leaders* (1970); Hill, Michael. "Story of Black Folklorist Well Told on MPT," *Baltimore Sun* (February 14, 1990); Korman, K. "Do the Right Thing: Video Film Review," *Video* (February 1990); Lanker, Brian. *I Dream a World:*

Portraits of Black Women Who Changed America (1989); Mapp, Edward. *Directory of Blacks in the Performing Arts* (1990); Raffin, D. "What Christmas Means to Me," *Good Housekeeping* (December 1990); "Ruby Dee in 'Cat People,' " Baltimore *Afro-American* (April 3, 1982); Suggs, Donald. "Standing Still," *Village Voice* (June 20, 1989); Sweeney, Louise. "Melting Stage Stereotypes," *Christian Science Monitor* (November 21, 1989), and "Three Love Stories," *Ebony* (February 1988).

MARGARET D. PAGAN

DeFRANTZ, ANITA (1952-)

An outspoken advocate of social reform through athletics, Anita DeFrantz has been among the most powerful women in the area of sports organization. A bronze medalist in the Olympics of 1976, she was born in Philadelphia in October 1952. Shortly thereafter, her family moved to Indianapolis where her father ran a local Young Men's Christian Association. She had undertaken little in the way of athletic training prior to becoming a student at Connecticut College, where she was first introduced to the sport of rowing. DeFrantz competed officially for the first time in 1975, the same year she began law school at the University of Pennsylvania, located near Vesper Boat Club, an outstanding location for women's rowing. Already determined to prepare for Olympic competition, she maintained a six-day-a-week training schedule, and at the Montreal Olympics in 1976 received a third-place award in the first eight-member women's rowing competition ever to be included in the games. She went on to become U.S. national champion in eight-member competition, two-time national champion in two-member competition, and three-time national champion in the four-member category.

Receiving her law degree in 1977 from the University of Pennsylvania, she devoted herself to training in preparation for the 1980 Olympics. When President Jimmy Carter called for a U.S. boycott of the Moscow competition in response to the Soviet invasion of Afghanistan, DeFrantz quickly voiced opposition. After filing a suit against the U.S. Olympic Committee (USOC) in response to the boycott, she retired from competition in 1981. She received the 1980 Olympic Order medal for lifetime contributions to the sport, given by the International Olympic Committee. Bearing the torch in the 1984 Los Angeles Olympics, DeFrantz was second in charge of the USOC Olympic village. She also served on the Athletes' Advisory Council, the President's Council on Physical Fitness, the Los Angeles Organizing Committee on Physical Fitness, and the Los Angeles Organizing Committee for the 1984 competition. An advocate of athletes' rights and other reforms, DeFrantz in 1988 became the first Black woman to serve on the ninety-member International Olympic Committee, and she subsequently served as president of the Amateur Athletic Foundation of Los Angeles.

BIBLIOGRAPHY

Ashe, Arthur. *A Hard Road to Glory, Since 1946* (1988); *Chicago Tribune*, "A Sporting Chance" (September 4, 1988); *Los Angeles Times*, "She Offers a Sporting Proposal" (December 17, 1989); Reich, Kenneth. *Making It Happen: Peter Ueberroth and the 1984 Olympics* (1986); Ueberroth, Peter. *Made in America: His Own Story* (1985).

JOHN L. GODWIN

An advocate of athletes' rights, Anita DeFrantz was the first Black woman to serve on the ninety-member International Olympic Committee. At the 1976 Summer Olympics in Montreal, she and her teammates won the bronze medal in the first eight-member women's rowing competition ever included in the games. [Amateur Athletic Foundation, Los Angeles]

DELANEY, EMMA BERTHA (1871-1922)

In an address delivered before she left for Africa, entitled "Why I Go as a Foreign Missionary," Emma Delaney discussed her interest in mission work: "At the age of thirteen . . . I united with the [Baptist] church, and the spirit of missions increased. After entering Spelman Seminary and spending twelve years there, where our duty to God and humanity, both at home and abroad, is daily set forth, the mere desire for this work was changed to duty and a longing for the work that nothing else would satisfy" (Martin 1984).

Emma Bertha Delaney (or DeLaney) was born in Fernandina Beach, Florida, on January 3, 1871. She graduated from Spelman Seminary (now Spelman College) in Atlanta, Georgia, in 1894, the missionary training course in 1896, and nurse training in 1900. After graduation she worked for several years as a boarding school supervisor at Florida Institute (Live Oak).

On January 15, 1902, Delaney sailed for Africa and was stationed at Chiradzulu, in Nyasaland (Malawi). Delaney was sent out by the National Baptist Convention (today the National Baptist Convention, U.S.A., Inc.) and supported by the Baptist women of Florida. Schools were built on the mission station and she taught there. Moreover, Delaney was influential in establishing a women's society and weekly sewing classes for girls. Certainly she was responsible for arousing interest among African-American women in African mission work. After four years in Nyasaland Delaney left the Providence Industrial Mission in 1906.

Because the British government denied her permission to reenter Nyasaland, Delaney transferred to Liberia in 1912. She selected a spot near Monrovia, secured a grant of twenty acres of land from the Liberian government, and built the Suehn Industrial Mission. Delaney became the first principal of Suehn Industrial Academy, which was built at Suehn Mission and became a model for industrial centers.

In 1920 Delaney returned to the United States. She died of what was known as hematuric fever on October 7, 1922, at her mother's home in Fernandina Beach, Florida.

[*See also* BAPTIST CHURCH.]

BIBLIOGRAPHY

Adams, C. C. and Marshall A. Talley. *Negro Baptists and Foreign Missions* (1944); Freeman, Edward A. *The Epoch of Negro Baptists and the Foreign Mission Board* (1951); Jordan, Lewis Garnett. *In Our Stead: Facts about Foreign Missions* (1913), and *Negro Baptist History, U.S.A.* (1930); Martin, Sandy D. *Black Baptists and African Missions: The Origins of a Movement, 1880-1915* (1989), and "Spelman's Emma B. DeLaney and the African Mission," *Journal of Religious Thought* (Spring-Summer 1984); Read, Florence Matilda. *The Story of Spelman College* (1961).

SYLVIA M. JACOBS

Dedicated missionary Emma Delaney, founder of the Suehn Industrial Mission in Liberia, greatly increased the interest of African-American women in mission work in Africa. [Sylvia Jacobs]

DELANEY, SARA "SADIE" MARIE JOHNSON (1889-1958)

Sara "Sadie" Marie Johnson Delaney was for thirty-four years the chief librarian (1924-58) of the

U.S. Veterans Administration Hospital in Tuskegee, Alabama. Known for her determination, energy, and magnetism, Delaney became an outstanding practitioner of bibliotherapy in the twentieth century. Delaney defined bibliotherapy as "the treatment of a patient through selected reading." She began providing library services to thousands of physically and mentally disabled patients in a small enclave in the South, but knowledge of and need for her work spread, leading to worldwide recognition for her practice of bibliotherapy.

Born on February 26, 1889, in Rochester, New York, to James and Julia Frances Hawkins Johnson, she attended City College of New York, 1919-20, and received a certificate from the New York Public Library School. She married Edward Louis Peterson in 1906. In 1907, they had a daughter, Grace Hooks, at present a retired social worker in Tuskegee. Her

marriage ended in divorce in 1921, and in 1928 she married Rudicel Delaney of Jetersville, Virginia.

Sadie Johnson Peterson began her professional career at the 135th Street Branch of the New York Public Library in 1920. She lived in the Strivers' Row section of Harlem. As the neighborhood changed from native-born and European whites to African-Americans migrating from other parts of the country, the library responded by hiring "colored assistants," according to its 1920 annual report. In this post, she was in the thick of the literary, artistic, and social ferment of Harlem in the 1920s. She worked with children and the blind (learning Braille and Moonpoint, another system of embossed writing), and arranged many concerts, art exhibitions, and lectures, at which figures such as W.E.B. Du Bois and James Weldon Johnson spoke in 1921-23. She left New York in December 1923 after accepting a posi-

A dynamic woman who believed profoundly in the healing power of books, Sadie Delaney served for thirty-four years as chief librarian of the U.S. Veterans Administration Hospital in Tuskegee, Alabama. She did pioneering work in what she called bibliotherapy, "the treatment of a patient through selected reading." [Schomburg Center]

tion as librarian at the Veterans Administration Hospital in Tuskegee.

She opened the veterans' library two days after she arrived, on January 3, 1924, with one table and 200 books. At year's end she had acquired larger quarters filled with plants, maps, photographs, and 4,000 books; she also set up a library for the medical staff. As the years went on she established a literary society, unique in veterans' hospitals, and she encouraged discussion groups. Through these activities and consultations with doctors and psychiatrists, she pioneered her empirical practice of bibliotherapy. Although books were recognized as healing devices by the Greeks, the word *bibliotherapy* was not coined until 1919, and the American Library Association (ALA) did not have a committee on bibliotherapy until 1939. Delaney used bibliotherapy with patients maimed in body and mind from both World War I and the pervasive racism of the time in order to reunite them with a broad community of ideas and to add significance to their experience. Her methods served as the model for other hospital librarians and students.

Sadie Johnson Delaney also was active in national and international professional organizations, representing American hospital librarians in Rome in 1934 and serving as councillor for the ALA's Hospital Library Division in 1946-51. She held memberships in, among others, the National Council of Negro Women, the Tuskegee Women's Club, and the New York National Association for the Advancement of Colored People, where she served seven years on the advisory board.

For her pioneering work as a bibliotherapist, Delaney was cited over fifty times in library, medical, and Black publications. She was named Woman of the Year in 1948 (Iota Phi Lambda), in 1949 (Zeta Phi Beta), and in 1950 (National Urban League). Atlanta University bestowed an honorary doctorate on Delaney in 1950. She died on May 4, 1958, in Tuskegee. The Alabama Library Association inducted her into its Roll of Honor in 1982.

BIBLIOGRAPHY

Bauer, Henry C. "Seasoned to Taste," *Wilson Library Bulletin* (February 1955); Cantrell, Clyde H. "Sadie P. Delaney: Bibliotherapist and Librarian," *Southeastern Librarian* (Fall 1956); *Christian Science Monitor*, "Librarian Hailed as Pioneer" (August 28, 1957); Delaney, Sadie Peterson. "The Library: A Factor in Negro Education," *Messenger* (July 1923); Jones, Virginia Lacy. "Delaney, Sadie Peterson (1889-1959 [*sic*])." In *Dictionary of American Library Biography* (1978); *Look Magazine*, "Look Applauds" (September 26, 1950); Oppenheim, Gladys. "Bibliotherapy—A New Word for Your Vocabulary," *Cape Times* (January 15, 1938); Roosevelt, Eleanor. "My Day," *New York Post* (January 18, 1957); Sprague, Morteza D. "Dr. Sadie Peterson Delaney: Great Humanitarian," *Service* (June 1951).

MANUSCRIPT COLLECTIONS

Sadie Johnson Delaney's papers are in the Schomburg Center for Research in Black Culture, New York City; and Archives, Tuskegee University, Tuskegee, Alabama.

BETTY K. GUBERT

DeLAVALLADE, CARMEN (1931-)

Carmen DeLavallade was born in Los Angeles, California, on March 6, 1931. She was a protégé of the late modern dance pioneer Lester Horton, and she came to be known as a "total" dancer who was equally at home in ballet, modern, or theatrical dancing. DeLavallade could also sing and act, which contributed to her reputation as a well-rounded performer.

She began her dancing career with the Horton Dance Theater in 1950 in the role of Salome in Horton's ballet *The Face of Violence*. Since then, she has been featured with the Metropolitan Opera Ballet, the Boston Ballet, the Alvin Ailey American Dance Theater, and her own company. DeLavallade is best known for her interpretation of West Indian dances choreographed by her husband, Geoffrey Holder, a renowned dancer, choreographer, and artist. Carmen DeLavallade is also known for her work with choreographers John Butler and Glen Tetley.

She danced in four films, *Lydia Bailey* (1952), *Demetrius and the Gladiators* (1954), *The Egyptian* (1954), and *Carmen Jones* (1955). The choreographer for *Carmen Jones* was Herbert Ross, who cast DeLavallade in *House of Flowers* (1954), a Broadway production that also featured Alvin Ailey and Geoffrey Holder. DeLavallade also starred in several television productions including Duke Ellington's *A Drum Is a Woman* and Gian Carlo Menotti's Christmas Opera *Amahl and the Night Visitors*. From 1956 to 1958, DeLavallade appeared as a prima ballerina with the Metropolitan Opera Ballet in several productions including *Aida* and *Samson et Dalila*. The film *Odds against Tomorrow* (1959), starring Harry Belafonte, featured DeLavallade in her first acting role. DeLavallade danced the role of Bess in a ten-minute ballet sequence adapted from *Porgy and Bess* and presented on CBS on January 15, 1961.

Carmen DeLavallade has taught at the Yale School of Drama in New Haven, Connecticut, and has choreographed several of the theater's productions.

BIBLIOGRAPHY

Clarke, Mary and David Vaughan, eds. *The Encyclopedia of Dance and Ballet* (1977); Cohen-Stratyner, Naomi. *Biographical Dictionary of Dance* (1982); *EBA*; Emery, Lynne Fauley. *Black Dance in the United States from 1619 to Today* (1988); Goodman, Saul. "Dancers You Should Know," *Dance Magazine* (1964); Long, Richard. *The Black Tradition in American Concert Dance* (1990); McDonagh, Don. *The Complete Guide to Modern Dance* (1976); Moritz, Charles, ed. *Current Biography Yearbook*; *NA*; *NWAT*; Rollins, Charlemae. *Negro Entertainers of Stage, Screen, and T.V.* (1967); Thorpe, Edward. *Black Dance* (1990); Toppin, Edgar A. *A Biographical History of Blacks in America since 1528* (1971); Willis, John, ed. *Dance World* (1967, 1976); *WWBA* (1990).

KARIAMU WELSH ASANTE

Best known for her interpretation of West Indian dances by her husband, Geoffrey Holder, Carmen DeLavallade has had a wide-ranging career, appearing in films such as the acclaimed Carmen Jones, *on television in Duke Ellington's* A Drum Is a Woman *and Gian Carlo Menotti's* Amahl and the Night Visitors, *on Broadway in* House of Flowers, *and at the Metropolitan Opera as a prima ballerina in* Aida *and* Samson et Dalila. *[Schomburg Center]*

DELILLE, HENRIETTA *see* SISTERS OF THE HOLY FAMILY

DELTA SIGMA THETA SORORITY

On a winter morning in 1913, twenty-two young women of African-American descent were set to march in one of the most important woman's suffrage demonstrations in U.S. history. The date was March 4, the eve of Woodrow Wilson's presidential inauguration in Washington, D.C., and the women, students at Howard University, a liberal arts college founded after the Civil War to educate former slaves, raised their Delta Sigma Theta banner in anticipation. The contingent was to be led by an honorary member of the student organization, Mary Church Terrell, then fifty years old and a revered role model for younger women of the Progressive era.

The suffrage march, organized by the militant Congressional Union (later the Woman's party), drew some 5,000 participants and marked the suffrage movement's coming of age. As the first public activity of the sorority, the march also marked an important development in the history of the Black fraternal movement in general, and Delta Sigma Theta sorority in particular.

Delta had been incorporated as an official sorority on Howard's campus almost two months before, on January 13. It was the fifth such organization in the country, following three Black Greek fraternities: Alpha Phi Alpha (1906), Kappa Alpha Psi, and Omega Psi Phi (1911), and one sorority, Alpha Kappa Alpha (1908). In addition to fostering scholarship and social bonds among its members, these organizations symbolized the right of Black students to pursue a liberal arts education at a time when such studies were deemed to be either beyond the intellectual reach of, or impractical for, the growing number of Black students, especially Black women, seeking higher education. For Delta specifically, founded at a time when the exigencies of woman's suffrage converged with the new movement toward race reform, as characterized by the creation of the National Association for the Advancement of Colored People in 1909 and the National Urban League in 1911, it was inevitable that their mandate would include political concerns.

In subsequent decades, Delta Sigma Theta grew, and its focus evolved as the sorority responded to both external and internal developments. For example, the sorority's tremendous growth during the 1920s was spurred both by the increasing number of Black students in both Black and white universities and by the racist backlash that accompanied their attendance in predominantly white schools. On many white campuses, the sorority house was not only a social center but also an important refuge for Black students who were allowed to matriculate but not permitted to live in university dorms or participate in other interracial activities. This shaped the traditional programs of the sorority, which included bringing well-known activists to speak on campus and raising scholarship funds. By 1930, the sorority included graduate chapters and was established in every region of the country.

The 1930s saw a rise in the academic level of Black land grant colleges in the South and their subsequent inclusion in the sorority movement. This, and the crisis of the Great Depression, spurred programs designed to reach out to those with fewer economic resources. In 1937, for example, Delta's National Library Project provided a bookmobile, or traveling library, to several states in the South. In the late 1940s, when gains made by Black women during World War II were threatened, Delta's Jobs Analysis and Opportunities Project helped nonprofessional women find training and employment. In 1947, the Detroit chapter purchased the Delta Home for Girls, which provided an alternative to juvenile detention homes.

The 1950s and 1960s were characterized by international outreach and involvement in the civil rights movement. In 1950, Delta established its first non-North American chapter in Haiti; ten years later it would establish its first African chapter in Liberia. In 1961, the sorority raised funds to equip a maternity wing of the Njorge Mungai Hospital in rural Kenya. On the heels of its support for Daisy Bates, leader of the Little Rock, Arkansas, school desegregation struggle of 1957, Delta established the Social Action Commission to provide information and direction on current civil rights issues. In addition to financial support for movement activities, the national office embarked on successful lobbying efforts that culminated in the passage of the Civil Rights Act and the Voting Rights Act of 1964 and 1965, respectively.

In the 1970s, Delta emphasized sorority support for the arts with the establishment of the National Arts and Letters Committee, which produced a full-length feature film, *Countdown at Kusini*, in 1976. Subsequent national initiatives included the establishment of a revolving distinguished endowed professor's chair awarded to Black colleges; "summit" calls to action around the issues of inner-city youth, Black families, and Black single mothers; and

educational and informational projects concerning the Black diaspora.

From its first chapter comprising twenty-two members in 1913, Delta Sigma Theta has grown to include more than 125,000 women and 750 chapters in the United States, Africa, and the Caribbean.

BIBLIOGRAPHY

Giddings, Paula. *In Search of Sisterhood* (1988); Vroman, Mary Elizabeth. *Shaped to Its Purpose: Delta Sigma Theta—The First Fifty Years* (1964).

PAULA GIDDINGS

DENNING, BERNADINE NEWSOM (1930-)

Bernadine Newsom Denning was born August 17, 1930, in Detroit, Michigan, one of three children of William Charles Newsom and Evelyn T. (Pembrook) Newsom. Her family lived in a low-income public housing project until after her graduation from college. She developed an interest in athletics at an early age, learning to swim at eight. She became a swimming instructor at sixteen at the Black branch of the Detroit Young Women's Christian Association and later worked as a lifeguard and swimming instructor to help pay her college expenses. After graduation from Northeastern High School in Detroit in 1947, she attended Michigan State Normal College in Ypsilanti, relying on scholarships and work to pay expenses. She graduated in 1951 with a B.S. in physical education and taught in the Detroit public schools from 1951 to 1959. In 1956, she married Blaine Denning, a professional athlete with the Harlem Globetrotters and the Baltimore Bullets who later worked as a businessman, youth counselor, and owner of rental homes. They had one son, Blaine Denning, Jr.

From 1959 to 1972, Denning was administrator of a variety of programs in the Detroit public schools. Starting her graduate study in the 1950s, she received the Ed.D. in curriculum development from Wayne State University in 1970. In the 1970s, she held administrative positions at the University of Michigan and was also an assistant professor of education. In 1975, she was named director of the Civil Rights Office for the Detroit public school system. The quality of her work in this office brought her an appointment in 1977 as director of the Office of Revenue Sharing for the United States Department of the Treasury. Over 39,000 state and local governments relied on this office to receive a share of the federal taxes collected. As the third director of this office, she administered a fund of $9 billion and enforced civil rights laws prohibiting federal funds from going to any unit practicing racial discrimination. Denning received high praise in this position.

Returning to Detroit in 1979, she became executive director of the School-Community Relations department for the Detroit public schools until her retirement in 1985. She served as director of the Human Relations Department for the city of Detroit from 1986 to 1987, before becoming an educational consultant. By 1989, she had founded and become president of DMP Associates, an interracial consulting firm emphasizing education and leadership training. She has exercised leadership in a wide variety of civic and social affairs and received numerous awards.

BIBLIOGRAPHY

"Dr. Bernadine Newsom Denning: Office of Revenue Sharing," *Ebony* (August 1977); *NBAW*; Sprating, Cassandra. "Bernadine N. Denning," *Essence* (June 1981).

DE WITT S. DYKES, JR.

DENVER, COLORADO, CLUB MOVEMENT

There is evidence that Black women in Denver were organizing as early as 1885. From the limited information available, it appears that these early clubs represented broader interests than did those formed after the turn of the century. Even the names of the clubs serve to indicate a shift in interest—from the Colored Ladies' Legal Rights Association, the Colored Women's Republican Club, and the Woman's League, all formed prior to 1900, to Pond Lily Art Club, Taka Art and Literary Club, Book Lovers' Club, and Carnation Art Club, established after 1900. This shift corresponds with broader ideological shifts occurring among Black intellectuals during the late nineteenth century. The earlier emphasis on agitation for equal political, economic, and social rights for African Americans was gradually replaced with an emphasis on preparation for equal rights. Self-help, self-improvement, and racial unity became the dominant themes of the day.

The leaders of the women's club movement came from the relatively small but prosperous middle-class segment of Denver's Black community. Many were recent immigrants from larger urban areas who had been exposed to and recognized the potential of women's club efforts in helping the less fortunate within the race.

Elizabeth Piper Ensley was one such person. She had studied abroad during the 1870s, and upon returning to the United States had established a circulating library in Boston, where she became a public school teacher. She married Horwell N. Ensley in 1882, and the Ensleys moved to Denver in the early 1890s, where she quickly became active in club work. She was one of the founding members of the Woman's League, which was organized in 1894, and served as Denver's correspondent to the *Woman's Era*, the official journal of the National Association of Colored Women. In 1904, she founded the Colorado Association of Colored Women's Clubs. Support for this group had begun to form as early as 1896, when Ida DePriest, another early club mover, suggested the possibility of such an organization to the national association.

DePriest was also a member of the Woman's League, serving as corresponding secretary in 1895-96. She appears to have been most often linked with political activities, working through the Colored Women's Republican Club of Denver. This club had, according to the *Denver Times* (March 28, 1901), accomplished "more telling work in the last two campaigns than any other colored organization in the state." Ensley, DePriest, and others like them established the foundation upon which countless Black women in later years based their club work.

When Ensley issued a call for the formation of a state association in the early spring of 1904, only one of the eight responding clubs—the Woman's League—was from Denver; by 1908 there were twelve Denver clubs represented. That year the City Federation of Denver, which represented from twelve to fifteen clubs, joined the state association. While the state association engaged in a variety of activities during its early years—from sponsoring mothers' meetings, providing assistance to various churches throughout the state, and contributing to the National Association for the Advancement of Colored People antilynching fund as well as to the war effort—its major accomplishment was supporting the Colored Orphanage and Old Folks' Home in Pueblo. Support included raising and donating not only money but also food, clothing, and shoes (in 1913 alone, seventy-six pairs of shoes were given to the orphanage).

At least twenty-two federated clubs in Denver were organized between 1900 and 1925. Some of the clubs existed for only a short time while others merged with stronger clubs. Four of the twenty-two clubs are still in existence: Pond Lily Art and Literary Club (1901), Taka Art and Literary Club (1903), Carnation Art, Literary, and Charity Club (1903), and the Self-Improvement Club (1906). These four clubs are part of an association that established a day nursery in 1916 which still exists today.

Black women organized because many were concerned with self- and community improvement. External forces may have brought about club formation, as in the case of the Pond Lily Club, organized by the then sixteen-year-old Augustavia Young (Stewart). Young had become incensed over a local newspaper article which had made derogatory comments about Black women, and she decided to form a club of young women who could help dispel the negative stereotypes about women of color.

These early clubwomen were primarily married with children, had completed high school, and were employed outside the home in occupations ranging from elocutionists and musicians, seamstresses and milliners, to domestics and laundresses. The major indication that many of the early members were employed is the fact that meetings for all clubs were held on weekdays—domestics and laundresses rarely had Saturdays off. Most important, they were Christian women who were committed to "up-lift work."

The activities of the clubs included efforts to improve the members' skills in arts, crafts, and music; encourage literary and intellectual development; help the poor and needy in both individual cases and through more formalized giving such as contributing to the Red Cross; assist the community's many attempts to combat discrimination; work with children to encourage higher health and educational standards; sponsor mothers' meetings, girls' clubs, and (always!) fund-raising activities.

[See also NEGRO WOMEN'S CLUB HOME, DENVER.]

BIBLIOGRAPHY

Atkins, James T. "The James T. Atkins Collection," Colorado State Historical Society, Denver, Colorado; *Denver Times* (March 28, 1901); Dickson, Lynda F. "African-American Women's Clubs in Denver: 1890-1925," *Essays and Monographs in Colorado History* (1991); "Federation of Colored Women's Clubs in Colorado." Minutes of annual state association meetings, 1904-50. Western History Collection, Denver Public Library, Denver, Colorado; National Association of Colored Women's Clubs, Inc. *A History of the Club Movement among the Colored Women of the United States of America* ([1902] 1978); State Association of Colored Women's Clubs. Minutes for annual meetings, 1904-10. Dorothy Reaves, Denver, Colorado; *Woman's Era* (1894).

LYNDA F. DICKSON

THE DEPRESSION

When times get hard, people work harder to survive. During the 1930s, the triple responsibilities of Black women—earning cash through paid employment; caring for their families and friends by stretching meager resources with their unwaged labor (housework); and building community and social change with voluntary labor in churches, clubs, and political organizations—increased as they fought off the ravages of the worst economic cataclysm of the twentieth century. Hard times were nothing new to Black women. What was new about the Great Depression was that it shook the whole country so deeply that the people at the bottom of the economy could not rely upon old coping mechanisms; the crisis undermined their efficacy and other women beat them to the punch. As one unemployed Black woman concluded, "You can't get no job no more like you used to. I used to have a new job before I was let out from the old" (Women's Bureau, Bulletin no. 139). Women's double day of paid employment, in addition to the emotional and physical labor of housework and relationships, assured that Black women shouldered a heavy load during the 1930s.

While the Great Depression devastated the United States, its specific impact on Black communities depended on their particular circumstances. In 1930, more than three-quarters of Black people (78.7 percent) lived in the South; a small majority still lived in the rural South (53.8 percent). Many African-Americans lived in small southern cities and towns, but northern metropolises provided homes to more Black people than did large southern cities; New York, Chicago, and Philadelphia all had far larger Black populations than the border cities of Baltimore and Washington, D.C., or New Orleans, Birmingham, and Atlanta, the largest African-American concentrations in the South. Of the 20.3 percent of the Black population who lived in the North and Midwest, the large majority had moved there during the Great Migration. Whether Black women resided on a cotton plantation or in Harlem, whether they were recent immigrants from the Caribbean, new or long-time urban dwellers, they sustained far higher rates of unemployment than white women and men, and often higher rates than Black men as well. Race and gender guaranteed many commonalities among Black women's experiences, but differences of urbanization, region, ethnicity, migration, and immigration, as well as class distinctions, determined the survival strategies that might be available to them.

Almost 40 percent of Black women and girls ten years old and older were in the labor force in 1929. Black women had long been far more likely to hold jobs than were white women; high unemployment and low wages for Black men, coupled with the availability of work for Black women, ensured their high rate of employment, but they had few choices of jobs. Two occupations—agriculture (26.9 percent) and cleaning other women's homes and caring for their families (35.8 percent)—employed almost two-thirds of Black women wage earners. Even in cities, where jobs were more diverse and opportunities more abundant, domestic and commercial service occupations (including hairdressers, laundry operatives, home laundresses, cooks, waitresses, janitors, and chambermaids, as well as household servants) accounted for about three-quarters of Black women's employment. Hard physical labor, low wages, and harsh working conditions characterized service occupations; northern service workers earned from $10 to $15 weekly, southern service employees far less. Agricultural workers, whether tenant farmers, sharecroppers, small landowners, or wage laborers, endured hard physical labor, braved the elements, attuned their hours to the crops, and often earned no wages; family shares of the sale of cotton, tobacco, or other crops purchased supplies for the following season and the minimum goods that could not be produced at home. Only 5 percent of Black women held manufacturing jobs; in the Durham, North Carolina, tobacco factories, Black women earned from $6.50 to $8 weekly, but because stemming tobacco was seasonal labor, they earned less than $400 annually. Fewer than 5 percent of employed Black women worked in white-collar professional, sales, and clerical occupations; fewer than 200,000 of the almost two million employed Black women worked anywhere except in fields, kitchens, and commercial service jobs. Black and white women shared the experience of sex-segregated occupations, but white women dominated the better, so-called female jobs; 69.6 percent of employed white women worked in manufacturing, sales, clerical, and professional jobs, compared to only 10.3 percent of employed Black women.

The Depression hit Black women hard and fast. By January 1931, more than a quarter of Black women had lost their jobs in every city with a substantial Black population, regardless of region. Their

The Depression of the 1930s was especially hard on Black women. They were frequently at the bottom of the economic ladder and had family and community responsibilities as well. This woman had her picture taken by one of the several government photographic teams of the 1930s. She is simply described as a "rural widow." [National Archives]

proportion of joblessness, as high as 68.9 percent in Detroit, was far higher than that of white women—whose unemployment rate was never more than 19 percent in those cities—and was the same as or higher than that of Black men. Typically, employers shortened hours and cut wages before they laid off workers; restaurant employees worked short shifts, housewives cut back dayworkers from a day to a half-day weekly, or changed a weekly job to a biweekly job. Unemployment and underemployment hit Black women more harshly and more rapidly than they affected either Black men or white women, because Black women's location in the occupational structure was more vulnerable. Black women felt the hardest pinch because middle-class and well-to-do white families and businesses, feeling strapped themselves, contracted their budgets by cutting out household help and reducing their patronage of commercial establishments such as hotels, restaurants, and laundries. Furthermore, employers practiced discriminatory policies, laying off Black women before white women when they found it necessary to cut their staffs.

Throughout the decade, unemployment was consistently highest in manufacturing, a white-male-dominated sphere, and thus sex segregation of occupations provided protection to women, whose jobs were mostly outside the sphere of production; sex segregation protected white women more than Black women, however. Black women who had managed to escape the service sector by finding factory work were particularly vulnerable to job loss. Black women lost almost half their jobs in the tobacco

Although New Deal reforms are credited with saving the country during the Depression, much of the legislation that most affected labor had no effect on many Black workers of both sexes. The Social Security Act, for example, did not apply to the majority of Black women because its provisions excluded agricultural and domestic workers. Here, a Black woman is counseled by a Social Security representative. [National Archives]

industry over the decade, and although white women also lost jobs, in 1940 they held a larger share of all tobacco jobs than they had held in 1930. Both the clothing and the food industries added women workers during the 1930s, but the jobs went to white women; Black women's employment fell substantially in both industries.

The situation of white-collar workers hinged on their employers. Black-owned businesses depended on the patronage of the Black community for their survival; as cash became ever more scarce, small businesses failed and larger businesses cut their staffs. Thus, small entrepreneurs, self-employed professionals, and clerical workers at Black insurance companies lost jobs and businesses; some professionals supplemented their regular occupations with makeshift jobs to provide income. In conrast, schoolteachers, who accounted for more than half of all Black female white-collar workers, were public employees. Some suffered extreme hardships, as some school boards defaulted on salaries that were already far lower than those paid to their white counterparts. They did, however, usually maintain their jobs in segregated school systems in the South. However, white-collar workers who competed with white women lost work. Graduate nurses, for example, suffered pay cuts and loss of jobs as the nursing profession remained segregated; fewer Black people could afford health care, and Black-run hospitals relied on the cheap labor of student nurses. Yet by 1940, the number of Black women in white collars, including professionals, salespersons, proprietors, managers, and clerical workers, had increased slightly, from 88,457 to 97,300, from 4.8 percent to 6.1 percent of employed Black women. A tiny number of Black women earned good money during the 1930s; riding trains from coast to coast, Mahalia Jackson, for example, earned as much as $50 a week singing gospel songs in Black churches.

The major strategy of unemployed women of all races and from all occupations was downward mobility. Schoolteachers became secreatries, clerical workers took waitress positions, waitresses moved into laundries. Women from every occupational realm, as well as women without labor-force experience and women who had been at home for years, all compted for jobs. They especially competed for household employment because everyone assumed that any woman could do domestic work. In this buyers' market, not only unemployment and increased competition, but also the racial preferences of employers, contributed to Black women's loss of jobs. For example, a Chicago domestic worker found what appeared to be a good job in 1932, paying $15 a week

These New York City children were part of a Federal Music Project rhythm band in 1938.
[Moorland-Spingarn]

and room and board. She helped her employer move into a new home, cleaned the house, and arranged the furniture. She recounted, "Then she hired a white maid after I had done the heavy work" (Women's Bureau, Bulletin no. 139). When the National Industrial Recovery Act (NIRA) mandated minimum wages, many industrial and service employers laid off Black workers and replaced them with white workers rather than pay both races the same rate.

When unemployment and competition both increased, because Black women were already on the lowest rung of the ladder of occupational desirability, they had no lower rung to which they could move defensively when they lost their regular jobs. Consequently, many Black women, especially domestic workers, particularly older women, were forced out of employment entirely. The number and proportion of Black women who were employed fell significantly between 1929 and 1940, while white women gained both numbers and share of total female employment over the decade. The employment rate for Black women fifteen and older dropped from 43.3 percent to 33.5 percent; 160,000 fewer Black women had paid jobs despite the continued growth of the population.

At the same time, the number of employed white women increased by more than a million, although their employment rate declined slightly, from 22.9 percent to 21.8 percent. Black women's structural location in the sex- and race-segregated labor force; the policies of employers, who preferred to retain or hire white women rather than Black; and the increased competition for jobs, including white women's applications for so-called Negro jobs which they previously would not have considered—all contributed to the high rates of unemployment that Black women sustained.

The displacement of Black workers by white was not unique to the Great Depression; for several decades commercial laundries, for example, had been displacing Black women in two ways; they replaced Black home laundresses and they employed more white women than Black. During the 1930s, Black women continued to lose employment in the laundry business in both of these ways. Commercial laundries continued to grow, Black washerwomen continued to lose work to them, and the numbers fell even further. Within laundries, Black women lost both numbers and proportion of jobs, while white women gained both numbers and proportion of jobs.

By 1940, nationally, regionally, and in specific cities Black women still suffered higher unemployment rates than white workers of either gender, but they were more likely to be employed than Black men, proving once again the adage that Black women could find work more easily than their brothers and husbands. Near the end of the Depression, Black unemployment was higher in the Northeast and north central states than in the South. Southern Black workers had recovered more jobs than had their northern cousins. While white women and men replaced Black workers in the 1920s and early 1930s despite white southern traditions concerning race- and gender-appropriate jobs, as the employment outlook improved, these long-standing white southern beliefs had reasserted themselves as white workers returned to segregated jobs and some "Negro jobs" were once again relegated to Black women and men. In addition to their higher unemployment rates everywhere in the nation, Black women and men were more likely than white workers both to have become discouraged and to have dropped out of the labor force entirely.

Given high unemployment rates for both Black men and women Black women created a set of job strategies to survive. Some women held on to and even found new jobs in the sectors that already employed them, although these jobs generally offered lower pay and worse conditions than had been true in the 1920s. Women worked harder for less pay simply because they had to do so in order to survive. Black women had pioneered the move away from live-in housework to daywork earlier in the century, but in desperation some returned to live-in jobs, sometimes receiving only room and board. Despite hard times, because wages for housework fell so precipitously, some housewife/employers and even women who could never before afford household help did hire dayworkers. In northern cities such as New York, Philadelphia, and Chicago, so-called slave markets were established in white neighborhoods where Black women gathered at street corners and white housewives came by to bargain with them for a day's work. While many Black women condemned the indignity of being judged and rejected in public, others believed that this practice allowed them a modicum of control over their working conditions.

Another Depression-era makeshift strategy to earn money was petty entrepreneurial activity. Urban Black women bought or produced a small stock of goods that they peddled from door to door: dresses, cleanser, peanuts, home-baked treats. Yet this strategy could

not support a woman, much less her family. Likewise, the underground economy provided work in the numbers game, prostitution, the manufacture and sale of alcohol, and crime. A Chicago woman who "wrote policies" (gambled or played the numbers game) was often arrested and was ashamed of her job, but it ensured that her child graduated from high school. In that city alone, 5,000 people were employed by the policy business during the 1930s. These alternative strategies enabled some women to survive, but they fell far short of the mark of regular, legal employment that paid a living wage.

For agricultural workers, the majority of rural women, the Depression hit hard whether they were landowners or tenants, and fewer than one-tenth of Black agriculturalists owned their land in 1930. For rural southerners, falling agricultural prices and the boll weevil had ensured widespread poverty throughout the 1920s, but in the 1930s agricultural prices, especially for cotton, the largest crop employing Black people, plummeted. The New Deal further impoverished Black farm workers; the Agricultural Adjustment Act (AAA) compensated planters for growing less in order to raise the price of cotton; while landowners were supposed to share their payments with their tenants, they rarely did so. White planters needed fewer Black families to grow smaller crops and they evicted many Black tenants and sharecroppers; those who remained received a smaller income because the crop was smaller. Some landowners used their cash subsidies to purchase machinery and employed hired hands seasonally, as needed, forcing formerly year-round tenants to find other living arrangements. The number of Black women and men employed in agriculture, whether as owners, wage laborers, or sharecroppers, fell sharply; Black women's agricultural employment dropped 50 percent over the decade, while Black men's agricultural employment dropped by almost 20 percent.

Displaced agriculturalists survived, using a variety of strategies. Some moved into town and sought town jobs, some moved to the North, some became migrant agricultural workers. Often they moved from place to place, from job to job, depending on seasons, circumstances, and the support of their kin. Some rural women did daywork and took in laundry, moving back and forth between town and country, staying with a relative in town when there was no fieldwork. Rural dwellers poured into towns and cities in the North and South, searching for jobs, but some urbanites returned to the country, knowing that, at a bare minimum, they could eat there. The net result of movement during the decade was only a small increase in the proportion of northern residents. Yet there were differences between the migratory patterns of Black women and men; between 1935 and 1940 women were more likely than men to move to cities and towns, and men were more likely to move to rural areas.

The New Deal's recognition of public responsibility for economic well-being produced mixed results in Black communities. Although New Deal reforms have been credited with saving the country during the Depression, much of the legislation which most directly affected labor had no effect or a negative impact on Black workers of both sexes. The AAA enabled landowners to displace Black agricultural workers, and employers fired Black employees rather than pay equal wages to both races, as mandated by the National Recovery Administration (NRA). Three of the most comprehensive pieces of labor legislation did not apply to the majority of Black women because they excluded agricultural and domestic workers: the NRA, which set minimum wages and maximum hours; its successor, the Fair Labor Standards Act; and the Social Security Act with its provisions for old age and unemployment insurance. Furthermore, the NRA legalized a lower minimum wage in the South; Black communities referred to it as the Negro Removal Act and Negro Run Around. As a Black woman from Columbia, South Carolina, wrote to President Roosevelt in 1933, "I would like very much to know why they insisted on us signing those Cards if it did not apply to us" (National Archives). The economic gap between Black and white grew even larger, because so many Black workers were excluded from the minimal protections which this legislation offered.

Still, New Deal programs that provided direct relief or government-sponsored jobs offered a boon to some Black communities; given their lopsided share of unemployment, a larger proportion of Black individuals and families were eligible for New Deal relief and work programs. Relief benefits varied by region; in northern cities, where Black unemployment was highest, relief checks were also higher and Black and white relief clients received equal amounts. In 1938, general relief and Aid to Dependent Children (ADC) benefits ranged between $20 and $40 monthly in northeastern and midwestern states; in the South ben-

New Deal work programs attempted to alleviate misery by putting poor people to work on worthwhile projects. The Civilian Conservation Corps, a public works project intended to promote environmental conservation and to build good citizens through disciplined outdoor labor, was operated under the army's control. This Yancyville, North Carolina, couple is inspecting their son's discharge papers from the corps in 1940. [National Archives]

efits were less than $20 monthly; in 1941 the average relief family in Mississippi received $3 for an entire month. Southern Black recipients usually received lower relief allotments than their white neighbors, despite the fact that they paid the same prices for goods and services. About half of urban northern Black families received relief in the mid-1930s, three or four times the rate of white families in the same areas. In the South, the proportions of Black people receiving relief compared with whites declined with the size of the population. In cities, about twice as many Black families as white received relief payments, and in smaller towns and villages, the proportions of Black and white receiving relief were much closer to each other. In the rural South, poor whites were more likely to receive relief than were poor Blacks, and in many rural places the only relief available to poverty-stricken Black families was federal surplus food.

Deciding to apply for relief was not an easy decision; their inability to support themselves and the necessity of asking for what they saw as charity was humiliating to most women. A Chicago widow explained, "If I could get a job even for room and board I wouldn't be asking for relief" (Women's Bureau, Bulletin no. 139). Even when they received payments equal to those of white clients, Black women had to endure the racist judgments of social workers about their morality, mental and physical health, occupational histories, and inability to find work. After families or individuals received certification for relief, they nevertheless had to demonstrate their neediness continually. Relief provided a small margin of survival, but added another responsibility to women's load: negotiating public bureaucracies to acquire benefits. As the Depression lengthened, people began to expect that relief was a responsibility of government and to criticize its shortcomings and low cash payments. One unemployed Chicago woman told an investigator, "The relief just makes you live like a dog! How can anyone make out on $12 a month for rent, light, heat, and gas?" (National Archives).

New Deal work programs such as the Works Progress Administration (WPA) were quite popular in Black communities, for they provided jobs; occasionally Black people were hired for work to which they had had little previous access, and sometimes WPA jobs paid higher wages than Black women and men were able to command in the private economy. Sexist and racist presumptions abounded in the WPA, however. Women often could not secure WPA jobs because eligibility was limited to heads of household. Black women who were determined to be eligible received assignments primarily in sex- and race-segregated domestic work. Yet to most women, work was preferable to relief. Regional wage differentials applied; in 1935 minimum WPA monthly wages started at $19 in many southern states, but at $40 in New York and Illinois, and $45 in Washington, D.C. Considering that a woman living outside of a family and on relief in Chicago received a monthly maximum payment of $23, working for the WPA was financially far superior to receiving a relief check. Black women were especially interested in getting jobs in WPA sewing rooms, where they constructed clothing for distribution to relief clients. Higher pay, the ability to escape a white woman's kitchen, and the opportunity to gain a skill by working on electric sewing machines made the WPA sewing room a desirable goal for unemployed Black women. Small numbers also worked in clerical and teaching positions or as artists and writers. In addition to the jobs the WPA provided to individuals, its projects aided Black communities in other ways. WPA literacy classes, for example, taught 400,000 Black people during the 1930s.

Not all women were employed, but virtually all women did housework, and their scrimping, stretching, and saving grew ever more important as cash grew more scarce. Housework took up the slack of unemployment suffered by household members. Rural women had not, for the most part, moved very far into the cash economy by 1929; their diet of fatback, beans, molasses, and corn bread was supplemented with the vegetables, fruit, fish, and meat that their families grew, gathered, hunted, and raised. They built fires, carried water, boiled laundry, sewed garments and bedding, and provided daily necessities with their labor. The form of rural women's housework changed little during the Depression, although the women doubtless worked even harder.

While subsistence labor was routine for most rural Black women, city dwellers purchased more of the necessities of life. During the 1920s, urban Black women, especially in the North, lived in a consumer economy, paying cash for housing, food, clothing, utilities, and recreation; they were able to escape the most physically demanding tasks of housework. Urban women returned to a country-style way of living in the city during the 1930s; when they had less cash, they invested their labor instead. Where space was available, women planted gardens and canned the surplus. They returned to making their own clothes and to repairing and making over old clothing, investing time and energy but little money. When they could not pay the rent or when they were evicted, they moved into less desirable housing. A cheaper house or apartment meant fewer conveniences: stove heat rather than a coal furnace, kerosene lamps instead of electricity, no running water, cold water only, shared toilets. Lacking access to utilities that helped them to create cleanliness and comfort, women's physical labor increased as their pocketbooks shrank; they boiled water on the stove top for baths, dishes, and laundry and they hauled coal and ashes up and down flights of steps. Southern urban dwellers were far less likely to live in modern housing equipped with amenities such as electricity, gas lines, indoor plumbing, and hot and cold running water, but as their incomes shrank, they, too, moved into poorer housing that required more labor to make it habitable. Regardless of region and rural/urban status, moving into less desirable housing was a common Depression practice, following eviction or in search of cheaper rent or a better landlord. Some women moved several times yearly. Uprooting a household and then carrying on housework and family life under more difficult circumstances was one more addition to women's labor.

Familial cooperation became increasingly necessary for survival, but as poverty deepened, families changed and tensions increased. Black women's Depression stories are full of both cooperation and conflict. Both marriage and birth rates declined during the 1930s as couples consciously postponed getting married and limited the number of children they brought into the world. Douching was the preferred method of contraception, but condoms, diaphragms, folk methods, and abortions also contributed to lowering the birth rate. Households grew larger, adding kin and nonkin in order to share meager resources among a greater number of persons; and women cared for the emotional as well as practical needs of ever-changing households. Cooperation extended over many miles. Northern mothers sent their children to the South to mothers, sisters, or aunts; assured that kin would care for their children, they could take any available work, even the hated live-in jobs, without the constraints of children's daily needs, and they could send money south. Cooperation stretched far beyond blood lines; friends extended a welcome to one another when they could; older women living alone in the North were more likely to receive assistance, especially a place to live and meals, from friends than from kin.

Conflict increased along with cooperation. Some marriages could not withstand the increased tensions of unemployment and deepening poverty, as men, women, or both lost jobs. Some men jumped freight trains to look for work elsewhere or simply deserted their families in their shame over their joblessness,

Not all Black women were employed outside the home, but virtually all of them did housework, whose value increased as cash became scarcer during the Depression. They built fires, carried water, tended gardens, boiled laundry, sewed garments and bedding, and provided daily necessities with their labor. [National Archives]

creating female-headed families. Some women blamed men for their unemployment, men blamed themselves, and both were angry that women could find work when men could not. The loss of women's wages was critical; their income had meant the difference between survival and eviction, between food and hunger. Consequently, although the divorce rate fell, because divorce was too expensive, separations and desertions increased. Familial tensions were not confined to marriages, however, as older women often discovered that they could not rely upon their adult children for assistance when lack of jobs and poor health made them dependent. In Chicago, for example, close to 6,000 Black women living outside of families were receiving relief in 1937; a combination of unemployment, old age, ill health, the end of marriages, and the inability of other kin to support them left these women with no other recourse except relief.

For agricultural workers, the majority of rural women, the Depression hit hard. In the 1930s, agricultural prices, especially for cotton, the largest crop employing Black people, plummeted. As white landowners evicted many Black tenants and sharecroppers, Black agricultural employment fell sharply. [National Archives]

Women's waged and unwaged labor and a few federal programs were among the most important practical coping methods of the Black community during the 1930s. Political activism and spirituality also contributed significantly to people's survival. Black churches provided community, solace, a belief in better times by and by, but only rarely could they provide substantial material aid. On a worldly plane, Black women were active participants and leaders in unions and strikes, organizing the unemployed and relief recipients, and in Left-wing and civil rights organizations. They worked in racially and/or sexually integrated and separate organizations. Not all of their efforts bore immediate fruit, but they challenged unendurable conditions. A domestic worker from New Rochelle, New York, wrote to President Roosevelt in 1933, "If this depression keep on we will die under the strain" (National Archives). Activism offered the possibility of social change, rather than acceptance of mental as well as material depression.

Despite the fact that few Black women worked in sectors that were organized by Congress of Industrial Organizations (CIO) unions in the 1930s, they played an active role in union campaigns and strikes. Women in the Alabama Share Croppers Union participated in cotton pickers' strikes in the early 1930s and joined eighty women's auxiliaries disguised as Sewing Clubs. In many cities domestics attempted to organize themselves, a singularly difficult task given that they lacked workplace connections with one another. Although their attempts usually culminated in failure, they left a legacy that lived into other eras. Laundries also attempted to unionize. Small numbers of organized women participated in strikes of the International Ladies' Garment Workers Union (ILGWU); others struck independently, such as the nutpickers of St.

Louis, 1,400 of whom, Black and white, were organized into the Food Workers' Industrial Union in 1933. Hundreds of tobacco stemmers successfully struck Richmond plants in 1937 and received picket-line support from white ILGWU members. Black women participated in the organization of men in the steel and auto industries through women's auxiliaries.

Black women's efforts to challenge the Depression, racism, and sexism spread far broader than the union movement. They worked for change through their sororities, professional organizations, the National Association for the Advancement of Colored People, and the Urban League. They also played significant roles in both mainstream and Left-wing politics. Black women joined the Communist party in rural Alabama, in Harlem, and in places in between, attracted not only by its activism on behalf of the unemployed, workers, and Blacks, but also by its defense of the Scottsboro Boys. They demanded better treatment by relief agencies, joined Unemployed Councils, and helped evicted families move their possessions back into their homes. From a different political perspective, Mary McLeod Bethune, a former president of the National Association of Colored Women, led the founding of the National Council of Negro Women (NCNW) in 1935, which brought prominent educated Black women to political attention when the NCNW sponsored a White House conference in 1938. While the public leadership of many activist organizations appeared to be exclusively male, not only did Black women play many behind-the-scenes roles, but the most well-known Black activist of the 1930s, Mary McLeod Bethune, became the director of minority group affairs in the National Youth Administration and leader of the unofficial Black cabinet.

BIBLIOGRAPHY

Aptheker, Herbert. *A Documentary History of the Negro People in the United States* (1973, 1974); Blackwelder, Julia Kirk. *Women of the Depression: Caste and Culture in San Antonio, 1929-1939* (1984); Bureau of the Census. *Fifteenth Census, Population* (1930), and *Sixteenth Census, Population* (1940); Clegg, Brenda Faye. "Black Female Domestics during the Great Depression in New York City, 1930-1940," Ph.D. diss. (1983); Cohen, Lizabeth. *Making a New Deal: Industrial Workers in Chicago, 1919-1939* (1990); Drake, St. Clair and Horace R. Cayton. *Black Metropolis: A Study of Negro Life in a Northern City* ([1945] 1970); Foner, Philip S. *Women and the American Labor Movement from World War I to the Present* (1980); Helmbold, Lois Rita. "Beyond the Family Economy: Black and White Working-Class Women during the Great Depression," *Feminist Studies* (Fall 1987), and "Downward Occupational Mobility during the Great Depression: Urban Black and White Working Class Women," *Labor History* (Spring 1988), and *Making Choices, Making Do: Survival Strategies of Black and White Working Class Women during the Great Depression* (forthcoming); Howard, Donald S. *The WPA and Federal Relief Policy* ([1943] 1973); Janiewski, Dolores E. *Sisterhood Denied: Race, Gender, and Class in a New South Community* (1985); Johnson, Charles S. *Growing Up in the Black Belt: Negro Youth in the Rural South* ([1941] 1967), and *Shadow of the Plantation* (1934); Jones, Beverly W. "Race, Sex, and Class: Black Female Tobacco Workers in Durham, North Carolina, 1920-1940, and the Development of Female Consciousness," *Feminist Studies* (Fall 1984); Jones, Jacqueline. *Labor of Love, Labor of Sorrow: Black Women, Work, and the Family from Slavery to the Present* (1985); Kelley, Robin D. G. *Hammer and Hoe: Alabama Communists during the Great Depression* (1990); Lewis, Earl. *In Their Own Interests: Race, Class, and Power in Twentieth-Century Norfolk, Virginia* (1991); Mebane, Mary. *Mary* (1981); Myrdal, Gunnar. *An American Dilemma* ([1944] 1964); Naison, Mark. *Communists in Harlem during the Depression* (1983); National Archives, Washington, D.C. Record Group 86, Records of the Women's Bureau. Record Group 9, Records of the National Recovery Administration; Palmer, Phyllis. *Domesticity and Dirt: Housewives and Domestic Servants in the United States, 1920-1945* (1989); Powdermaker, Hortense. *After Freedom: A Cultural Study in the Deep South* (1939); Raper, Arthur F. *Preface to Peasantry: A Tale of Two Black Belt Counties* ([1936] 1974); Rodrique, Jessie M. "The Black Community and the Birth-Control Movement," in *Unequal Sisters: A Multicultural Reader in U.S. Women's History*, ed. Ellen Carol DuBois and Vicki L. Ruiz (1990); Simonson, Thordis, ed. *You May Plow Here: The Narrative of Sara Brooks* (1986); Sterner, Richard. *The Negro's Share: A Study of Income, Consumption, Housing, and Public Assistance* (1943); Wolters, Raymond. *Negroes and the Great Depression: The Problem of Economic Recovery* (1970); Women's Bureau, Department of Labor (1929-1939). Numerous Women's Bureau publications of the 1930s deal, in part, with Black women, including studies on particular occupations that employed Black women and on particular localities where Black women lived. Only two bulletins focus exclusively on Black women. Bulletin no. 70, *Negro Women in Industry in 15 States* (1929) and Bulletin no. 165, *The Negro Woman Worker* (1938).

LOIS RITA HELMBOLD

DePRIEST, IDA *see* DENVER, COLORADO, CLUB MOVEMENT

DERRICOTTE, JULIETTE
(1897-1931)

Juliette Derricotte's sincere wish for all humankind was that everyone should be free of the debilitating effects of repression and discrimination. She knew that working together in harmony could be achieved despite differences and difficulties, and her career as a Young Women's Christian Association (YWCA) official, and later as a college dean of women, provided the means to work for the realization of this ideal.

Born in Athens, Georgia, on April 1, 1897, Juliette Derricotte was the fifth of nine children born to Isaac and Laura Hardwick Derricotte. She grew up in Athens and became aware at an early age of the racial conventions of a small southern town in the early 1900s. This knowledge was crucial in forging her determination to fight discrimination.

After completing public schooling in Athens, Derricotte went to Talladega College in Alabama. Here she was a popular and active student, a member of the debating team, and president of the campus YWCA. As she planned student activities, made speeches, and mediated disputes, her leadership potential began to emerge. It was during these formative years that she came to believe she should work toward her ideals.

She graduated from Talladega in 1918 and enrolled in the national YWCA training school in New York City. That fall she was made secretary of the national student council of the YWCA, a post she held for eleven years. In this position she worked with student groups around the country, bringing ideas, building leadership, and pioneering the work methods and organizational structure that made the council an interracial fellowship. Through the warmth and forcefulness of her personality she succeeded in making people understand each other in the most practical manner.

In 1924, as a member of the general committee of the World's Student Christian Federation, she attended a meeting in England to discuss the responsibilities of Christian students in the world. Four years later she was one of the American delegates to the committee's Mysore, India, conference. She remained for seven weeks, living in student hostels, mission schools, and Indian homes, and she came to understand the worldwide extent of discrimination and its various and complex forms. She came to realize that the general committee, with over ninety delegates from around the world, was a microcosm of what was possible among people. Coming home from the Mysore conference, she stopped in China and Japan for meetings with students. Summing it all up, she wrote: "My head whirls, but now and again I remember 'that there is so much more to know than I am accustomed to knowing, and so much more to love than I am accustomed to loving' " (Derricotte 1929).

In 1927, she received a Master's degree in religious education from Columbia University, and from 1929 to 1931 she was the only woman trustee of Talladega College, her alma mater. Feeling a special call to participate in the education of Black Southerners, she resigned from the YWCA in 1927 and went to Fisk University as its dean of women. In November 1931, she decided to drive to Athens to visit her mother. Making the trip with her were three Fisk students from Georgia. After stopping for lunch in Chattanooga, they headed south to Atlanta, with Derricotte driving. About a mile outside Dalton, Georgia, their car collided with that of a white couple. The details of the accident have never been known. Derricotte and one student were seriously injured, and the two other students were treated and released. As the local tax-supported hospital did not admit Black patients, Derricotte and the student were taken to the home of a Black woman who had beds available for the care of Black patients. The student died during the night, and Derricotte was driven by ambulance to Chattanooga's Walden Hospital, where she died the next day, November 7, 1931. Many in the Black community attributed her death to the segregationist policies which kept her from getting immediate hospital care.

Perhaps Juliette Derricotte is best remembered for her death and the national outrage it caused. However, her contributions remain. At a time when race relations in the United States were eroding, she had an uncompromised vision of the universality of human dignity and a just future for her own people. Memorial services were held all over the country. Her friend Howard Thurman delivered the eulogy at the service held in her hometown, reading her haunting words from the Mysore conference.

BIBLIOGRAPHY

Cuthbert, Marion V. *Juliette Derricotte* (1933); *DANB*; Derricotte, Juliette. "The Student Conference at Mysore, India," *Crisis* (August 1929); Du Bois, W.E.B. "Dalton, Georgia," *Crisis* (March 1932); Fisk University Library. Thomas Elsa Jones papers. Nashville, Tennessee; Jeanness, Mary. *Twelve Negro Americans* (1936); *NBAW*; White, Walter. *New York Herald Tribune* (December 31, 1931);

Wygal, Winifred. "Juliette Derricotte, Her Character and Martyrdom: An Interpretation," *Crisis* (March 1932).

JEAN CAZORT

DeVEAUX, ALEXIS (1948-)

I'm trying to explore with greater concentration the black woman and her love ... woman in relation to her eros, her sexuality. Where is she in relation to that? Is it a place of beauty for her, a place of harmony, conflict, change, antagonism? What does it have to do with her sense of herself as a political person? Where is she going? That's where I'm going in my writing.

Love dominates Alexis DeVeaux's writings, and expressions of Black women's love are her forte. She feels a sense of responsibility to foster positive images of Black women in literature. She sees no distinction between herself and her creative craft, for she wants her writings to have unity with the lives of Black women globally.

She ideally perceives "herstory" as having sameness with "ourstory" because an incident in one Black life is compounded into occurrences in all Black lives. DeVeaux comes to the writer's table with a mission; the page and the words are the tools she uses to deliver her message about Black women as three-dimensional human beings. Her own words sum up the ethos of this prolific writer: "I want to explore her questions, strengths, concerns, madnesses, love, evils, weaknesses, lack of love, pain, and growth. Her perversities and her moralities" (Washington 1980). She explores the depths of these inquiries through essays, fiction, drama, poetry, and art.

Reluctant to reveal intimate details of family life, DeVeaux has revealed little information except that she was born to Mae DeVeaux and Richard Hill in New York City on September 24, 1948, and that she has sisters and brothers. Her writing emerged from a desire to improve communication with her mother, whose own mother died when she was very young. DeVeaux participated in an independent study program at Empire State College of the State University of New York (SUNY), from which she received a B.A. in 1976.

DeVeaux's background in Harlem and the South Bronx perhaps prepared her to break barriers, exceed parameters, and soar to new heights in literature. She is streetwise—all too familiar with the anguish, de-spair, poverty, and pain of a contemporary urban environment. In many ways, she is caught up in a 1960s time warp, still emulating the Broadside Press poets of that time in her application of language. She rebels against standard conventions through her use of Black English, all lowercase letters, choppy syntax, slang, street language, and African cultural ties. The spirit of rebellion reigns within her. She champions the cause of the Black underclass, forcing the reader to come to grips with a much neglected and ignored subculture that will never conform to the dictates of a white dominant culture but is determined to define its own Black aesthetics.

DeVeaux worked as an assistant instructor in English for the WIN Program of the New York Urban League (1969); a creative writing instructor for New York City's Frederick Douglass Creative Arts Center (1971); a community worker for the Bronx Office of Probations (1972); and a reading and creative writing instructor for Project Create (1973). She later commuted north to New Haven's Coeur de l'Unicorne Gallery where her paintings were exhibited. In the same year that she received her B.A., she became a regular contributor to *Essence* and a freelance writer (1976). She was guest lecturer at Livingston College (Rutgers University) in 1975 and was also a speaker in Paule Marshall's graduate seminar in writing at Columbia University. DeVeaux continues to write and teach in the New York City area.

She has been honored with first prize in Black Creation's National Fiction Contest (1972); the Best Production Award, Westchester Community College Drama Festival (1973); and the Art Books for Children Award from the Brooklyn Museum (1974 and 1975).

DeVeaux has numerous publications to her credit. *Na-Ni* (1973) is a juvenile book set in Harlem. *Spirits in the Streets* (1973) is a poetic prose narrative (illustrated by DeVeaux) that captures in microcosm the 1970s Harlem world of raw lives and sensibilities. *Li Chen/Second Daughter First Son* (1975) is a prose poem. *Don't Explain: A Song of Billie Holiday* (1980) is a biographical prose poem on the life of the jazz singer. Selections from it appeared in *Essence*. *Adventures of the Dread Sisters* (1982) is an independently published comic book. This publication was followed by *Blue Heat: A Portfolio of Poems and Drawings* (1985). *An Enchanted Hair Tale* (1987) is a juvenile book about a character named Sudan who must learn to appreciate the enchantment of his strange-looking hair.

DeVeaux continues her penchant for freeing Black life and Black love from the restrictions of Euro-Western realism through her periodical publications.

Her short fiction examines the reality of Black life in America's largest city. "Remember Him a Outlaw" (*Black Creation* 1972, *Midnight Birds* 1980) tells the story of Uncle Willie through the eyes of his favorite niece, Lexie. Uncle Willie is a survivor on the streets of Harlem whose life is ultimately snuffed out by the mean streets. To the casual observer, he appears to be an outlaw, but to the knowledgeable and the wise, he is an outcast. "The Riddles of Egypt Brownstone" (*Nimrod* 1977, *Essence* 1978, *Midnight Birds* 1980) deals with the young girl Egypt's handling of two sexual encounters as she matures into womanhood, one initiated by her mother's boyfriend and the other by her lesbian French teacher. The riddle of Egypt, literally and figuratively, engulfs the entire story: What has a mother who is a father who has a Negro female child that the twentieth century has tattooed illegitimate? Egypt's solving of the riddle points to proud ancient African-Egyptian icons, but her present situation deems the solution a paradox.

DeVeaux's political essays take on a neo-Africanist perspective and exhibit her views of the move toward a Black feminism. In "Zimbabwe: Woman Fire" (*Essence* 1981), she chronicles the contributions of Zimbabwean women to the struggle for independence and the role they played in the establishment of Mugabe as leader and president of the country. She is disillusioned by the subservient positions that women had to assume in a male-dominated society after the struggle was over. "South Africa: Listening for the News" (*Essence* 1982) voices her abhorrence of the system of apartheid in South Africa and the dislike of the U.S. alliance with the white-rule government. "Blood Ties" (*Essence* 1983), which was inspired by a trip to Haiti in the summer of 1975 where she witnessed first hand the enormous poverty that plagues the tiny island, attacks with a vengeance the government of Haiti and its chief demagogues, "Papa Doc" and "Baby Doc" Duvalier.

"Sister Love" (*Essence* 1983), a prose poem, is an example of the extremes to which DeVeaux will go to discover the ways women love and to bridge the gaps between women and between their struggles. Through this prose poetry, she brings into the mainstream the theme of Black lesbian love and implores the reading public, especially women, to be receptive to lesbians and to her own lesbianism. She envisions a world that is not dominated by race, sex, and class, where one can be free to develop relationships devoid of labels.

Her published poetry includes "The Sisters" (*Conditions* 1979, *Home Girls* 1983); "Poems" (*Hoo-Doo* 1980); "Madeleine's Dreads" (*Iowa Review* 1981, *Extended Outlooks* 1982); "And do you love me" (*Open*

Places 1982); "French Doors: A Vignette" (*Open Places* 1982, *Confirmation* 1983); and "Poems" (*Sunbury* 1984). She also has published in *Encore, 2 Poetry Magazine, Black Box*, and the *New Haven Advocate*.

DeVeaux has made an impact in drama as well. She sees the production of her first play as a turning point in her career. *Circles* (1973) is a one-act play about a young Black woman who breaks the chains that bind her to home in order to pursue her professional career and realize her dream. The play was performed by the Frederick Douglass Players at the Frederick Douglass Creative Arts Center and by the same group at Westchester Community College's Drama Festival. It was televised by California's KCET-TV's (1976) *Visions*, a program directed by Maya Angelou. Deveaux the playwright explores the sexual needs of Black women through art and introduces the theme of gay love. In the two-act play *The Tapestry* (1976), Jet, the young Black woman law student, must probe her inner self to determine how much to retain of the baggage accumulated in her upbringing. This play was performed by the West Coast Black Repertory Theater (1976) and New York City's Quaigh Theater (1977). Televised productions were shown on KCET-TV's (1976) *Visions*. Public readings were done by Frank Silvera's Writers' Workshop. *A Season to Unravel* (1979) is a one-act Freudian drama whose setting is within the psyche of the leading character. The Negro Ensemble Company premiered this play at New York City's St. Mark's Playhouse (1979).

The one-act dream fantasy *A Little Play* (1972) and the one-act *Whip Cream* (1973) were performed by the Young People's Workshop of All Soul's Church (1973) in Harlem. *The Fox Street War* (1979) is a full-length drama about Black women occupying an apartment complex who use the power of voodoo to persuade the owner to improve living conditions. DeVeaux's drama and poetry also have been performed in Greenhaven Prison, the Brooklyn Academy of Music, Cathedral of Saint John the Divine, Empire State College, and Riverside Church. Her work has been broadcast on radio stations WBAI, WNYC, WRVR, and WVLR and televised on WABC's *Like It Is* and WTTG's *Panorama* in Washington, D.C., and shown at the INPUT Public Television Conference in Milan, Italy, in March 1978.

DeVeaux continues in the tradition of the activist-artist. The artist and the art are one inseparable, seamless fiber. She is a spirit in the street, a true echo of the underrepresented underclass who also have stories to unfold. DeVeaux is the catalyst through which the stories surface; she foregrounds Black women's experiences to propel her onward, upward, and usward.

BIBLIOGRAPHY

Baraka, Amiri and Amina Baraka. *Confirmation: An Anthology of African-American Women* (1983); Cooper, Jane, et al. *Extended Outlooks: The Iowa Review Collection of Contemporary Women Writers* (1982); *DLB*; Smith, Barbara, ed. *Home Girls: A Black Feminist Anthology* (1983); Tate, Claudia. *Black Women Writers at Work* (1983); Washington, Mary Helen, ed. *Midnight Birds: Stories of Contemporary Black Women Writers* (1980); Wilkerson, Margaret B., ed. *9 Plays by Black Women* (1986).

GERRI BATES

DEVINE, ANNIE BELLE ROBINSON (c. 1912-)

Veteran civil rights activists agree that there would not have been a movement in Madison County, Mississippi, had it not been for the work of Annie Belle Robinson Devine.

Raised in the rural town of Canton, Annie Devine grew up during the most oppressive years in the segregated South. When the civil rights movement gained momentum in the early 1960s, all of Mississippi was dead set against change; any efforts to challenge the status quo were met by violence and intimidation. At the request of Anne Moody, who later wrote *Coming of Age in Mississippi* (1968), Annie Devine attended a meeting of the Congress of Racial Equality (CORE). This was the turning point of her life. At fifty, she committed herself to the Black freedom struggle, joining the cadre of fearless local leaders who risked their lives for social change.

As a churchwoman, independent insurance agent, and mother, Devine was highly respected in Canton. As an older adult in the community, Devine propelled civil rights organizing throughout the state. Working through CORE, she made an invaluable contribution in launching voter registration and in the political education of Mississippi's Black voters. In 1964, along with her close friends Fannie Lou Hamer and Victoria Gray, she helped to organize the Mississippi Freedom Democratic Party (MFDP). As an alternative to the illegally elected, all-white state Democratic party, the MFDP challenged the seating of the state delegation to the Democratic National Convention in Atlantic City, New Jersey. In a history-making precedent, Annie Devine was among the sixty-eight elected representatives to champion the cause of justice.

Annie Devine continues to live in Canton, where her lifetime commitment to social change is still being realized through community leadership and activism.

[*See also* MISSISSIPPI FREEDOM DEMO-CRATIC PARTY.]

BIBLIOGRAPHY

Crawford, Vicki. Personal interview with Annie Belle Robinson Devine, Jackson, Mississippi (March 1985); Dent, Tom. "Annie Devine Remembers," *Freedomways* (Second Quarter 1982); McLemore, Leslie Burl. "The Mississippi Freedom Democratic Party: A Case Study of Grassroots Politics," Ph.D. diss. (1971).

VICKI CRAWFORD

DICKENS, HELEN OCTAVIA (1909-)

Helen Octavia Dickens stands proud and imposing among African-American women physicians.

She was born to Charles and Daisy Jane Dickens on February 21, 1909, in Dayton, Ohio. Her father was a former slave who had legally changed his name after meeting the writer Charles Dickens.

As a child, after seeing a visiting nurse and watching a physician who came into her home to care for family members, Helen decided to become a physician. Helen's father died when she was eight years old, and it was her mother who prodded, encouraged, and supported her educational efforts. After graduating from high school, Helen lived with her mother's aunt, a college-educated woman who also encouraged her. She graduated from Roosevelt High School and then attended Crane Junior College, Chicago, Illinois. She went on to graduate from the University of Illinois with an M.D. in 1933.

Helen Dickens married Purvis Sinclair Henderson, a pediatric neurosurgeon, in 1943. They had two children: Jayne and Norman Sinclair. Her husband died early in their marriage, and she raised the children with the help of her mother, who came to live with her, and a long-time female friend who became a live-in helper.

Dickens and her husband had settled in Philadelphia, where she established an obstetrics and gynecology practice. She worked extensively on the issues of teenage pregnancy prevention, the necessity of Pap smears, and the recruitment of minority students into the health care field. During her practicing years, she was affiliated with Mercy Douglass Hospital (now defunct), the Medical College of Pennsylvania, and the University of Pennsylvania, where she is the associate dean of minority affairs and a professor of obstetrics and gynecology.

In her long career, many awards and honors have been bestowed upon her, including the Gimbel Award, the Distinguished Daughters of Pennsylvania Award, and admittance as a Fellow of the American College of Surgeons. She is a member of the American Medical Association, American Medical Women's Association, Links Inc., and the Delta Sigma Theta sorority.

BIBLIOGRAPHY

Dickens, Helen O. Black Women Physicians Collection and Special Collection on Women in Medicine, Medical College of Pennsylvania, Philadelphia.

MARGARET JERRIDO

As a doctor with an obstetrics and gynecology practice, Helen Octavia Dickens worked extensively on the issues of teenage pregnancy prevention, the necessity of Pap smears, and the recruitment of minority students into the health care field. [Medical College of Pennsylvania]

DICKSON, AMANDA AMERICA (EUBANKS, TOOMER) (1849-1893)

Amanda America Dickson, a slave-aristocrat, was born on November 21, 1849, on the plantation of her father, the famous white agricultural reformer David Dickson of Hancock County, Georgia. Her birth resulted from the rape of her slave mother, Julia Frances Lewis-Dickson, when Julia was twelve years old. At the time, David Dickson was forty and the wealthiest planter in the county. Amanda Dickson spent her childhood and adolescence in the house of her white grandmother and owner, Elizabeth Dickson, where she learned to read, write, and play the piano—the survival skills of a young lady, but not normally the opportunities of a slave. According to the Lewis-Dickson family oral history, David Dickson doted on Amanda America, and Julia Dickson quite openly became his concubine and housekeeper.

In 1866, Amanda Dickson married her white first cousin Charles Eubanks, a recently returned Civil War veteran. The union produced two sons: Julian Henry Dickson (1866-1937) married Eva Walton, the daughter of George Walton, and Charles Green Dickson (1870-1900?) married Kate Holsey, the daughter of Bishop Lucius and Harriet Holsey.

By 1870, Amanda Dickson had returned to her father's plantation and reclaimed her name of birth. From 1876 to 1878, she left her father's plantation and her mother's domain to attend the Normal School of Atlanta University. In the winter of 1885, David Dickson died leaving the bulk of his estate, which the executors appraised at $307,000 (including 17,000 acres of land in Hancock and Washington counties), to Amanda Dickson and her children. In his will Dickson stated that the administration of his estate was to be left to the sound judgment and unlimited discretion of Amanda America Dickson without interference from any quarter, including any husband that she might have. A host of David Dickson's white relatives immediately contested the will, but the Hancock County Superior Court ruled in favor of Amanda Dickson and her sons in November 1885. The disgruntled relatives then appealed to the Georgia Supreme Court, which in 1887 upheld the lower court decision, stating that whatever rights and privileges belonged to a white concubine, or to a bastard white woman and her children, belonged to a "colored" woman and her children and the "rights of each race were controlled and governed by the same enactments on principles of law."

Prior to the Supreme Court decision, Amanda Dickson purchased a large house at 452 Telfair Street,

Born the slave of her planter father, Amanda America Dickson became one of the wealthiest women in Augusta, Georgia, when the Georgia Supreme Court upheld her right to inherit under his will in 1885. Her life reflected the power of family and class to erode the boundaries of race in the nineteenth-century South. [Joan Jackson]

in the wealthiest section of the then integrated city of Augusta, Georgia. By the time the courts settled the Dickson Will Case, as it came to be called, she had firmly ensconced herself in this new home decorated with Brussels carpets, oil paintings, and books. While white Georgians were establishing apartheid as the ruling social order in the public sphere, members of the Dickson family went about their private lives. On July 14, 1892, Amanda America Dickson married Nathan Toomer of Perry, Georgia. Toomer had been born the son of a slave woman named Kit and one of the prominent white Toomer brothers who had migrated from North Carolina to Houston County, Georgia, in the 1850s. In his youth Nathan Toomer served as the personal servant of Col. Henry Toomer and in that position learned the manners of class. The census of 1870 lists Nathan Toomer as worth more than all of the other freedmen in Houston County combined ($30,000). Toomer and Dickson's marriage lasted until she died on July 11, 1893, of neurasthenia or nervous exhaustion. Shortly thereafter, Nathan Toomer married Nina Pinchback and became the father of the Harlem Renaissance author Jean Toomer (*Cane*, 1923).

Amanda America Dickson's life reflects the power of family and class to erode the boundaries of race in the nineteenth-century South.

BIBLIOGRAPHY

Leslie, Virginia Kent Anderson. *Woman of Color, Daughter of Privilege: Amanda America Dickson, 1849-1893* (1993), and "A Mulatto Lady in Nineteenth-Century Georgia: Amanda America Dickson, 1849-1893," unpublished manuscript (1992), and "Amanda America Dickson," *Mind and Nature* (January 1984).

KENT A. LESLIE

DIGGS, ELLEN IRENE (1906-)

Anthropologist Ellen Irene Diggs is best known for her research on Afro-Latin American culture and society, and the history of the African diaspora. Diggs was born in 1906 in Monmouth, Illinois, a small college town located in the state's agricultural belt near the Iowa border. She was raised in the supportive environment of an industrious but poor working-class nuclear Black family. At a very young age, Irene Diggs became aware of and disturbed by poverty, social inequality, and inequitable wages.

Diggs's family saw education as a way to improve oneself and as a means to upward social mobility.

Graduating at the top of her high school class, Irene Diggs spent one year at local Monmouth College before transferring to the University of Minnesota. She received her B.A. in economics and anthropology from the University of Minnesota in 1928. Soon after her graduation, Diggs moved to Atlanta and enrolled in the graduate school at Atlanta University, a historically Black institution. There, she studied under the foremost Black scholar of the day, W.E.B. Du Bois. Diggs received Atlanta University's first master's degree in sociology in 1933.

For the next eleven years, Irene Diggs remained at Atlanta University, serving as Du Bois's research associate. With Du Bois, Diggs founded the journal *Phylon: A Review of Race and Culture*. During this period, Diggs developed an interest in the African diaspora and African historiography. Her research focused on the contributions of peoples of African descent in the physical, cultural, and social construction of the Americas, as well as on the continent of Africa.

In 1942, following an exciting summer holiday in Cuba, Irene Diggs decided to leave Atlanta and return to the Caribbean. As a Roosevelt Fellow of the Institute of International Education at the University of Havana, Irene Diggs began her research on Afro-Cuban culture. From 1942 to 1944, Diggs traveled throughout Cuba studying the impact and continuities of African cultural elements in Cuban society. Her mentor was the distinguished Cuban ethnographer Fernañdo Ortiz. In 1944, Irene Diggs was awarded a doctorate from the University of Havana.

After the end of World War II, Irene Diggs spent a year in Montevideo, Uruguay, doing archival and participant observation fieldwork on the African presence in the Plantine region of Uruguay and Argentina. Shortly after her return from South America, she joined the faculty of Morgan State College. For twenty-nine years, Diggs was a member of the department of sociology and anthropology, retiring in 1976. She was a prominent teacher and taught sociology to countless students, fifteen hours per week and seven courses per year.

Diggs also produced numerous articles, reviews, and lengthy monographs on the African-diaspora cultures and histories and African history that appeared in the *Crisis, Phylon: A Current Bibliography on African Affairs, Negro History Bulletin*, and the *American Anthropologist*. Irene Diggs has been honored with the Distinguished Alumni Award from Monmouth College and a Lifetime Achievement Award from the Association of Black Anthropologists.

SELECTED WRITINGS BY IRENE DIGGS
Black Chronology: From 4000 B.C. to the Abolition of the Slave Trade (1983); "The Biological and Cultural Impact of Blacks on the United States," *Phylon* (June 1980); "The Socio-Anthropological Background of Africans and Their Descendents in South America," *Black History Museum Newsletter* (1978); "Tribute to William Edward Burghardt Du Bois," *Freedom Ways* (Winter 1965).

A. LYNN BOLLES

DIXON, LUCILLE (1923-)

Classical and jazz bassist, orchestra manager, and artistic activist, Lucille Dixon has devoted much of her life to providing opportunities for young Black musicians to achieve orchestral playing experience.

Dixon was born in Harlem on February 23, 1923, the daughter of a Baptist minister. In her early years she studied piano with Carmen Shepperd and played for her father's church services, earning fifty cents each Sunday. At Wadleigh High School she began to study the bass viol and was encouraged to audition for the All-City High School Orchestra, which performed at various sites around New York City. After she passed the audition and was accepted into the orchestra, arrangements were made for scholarship study with New York Philharmonic bassist Fred Zimmerman.

Dixon's participation in various other symphonic groups began in 1941 with the National Youth Administration Orchestra, an organization that served as the country's clearinghouse for symphony orchestras. From 1960 to 1964 she played with the National Orchestral Association and, in 1964-65, with the Boston Women's Symphony. In 1965, she was a founding member of the Symphony of the New World and became its manager in April 1972. This organization provided valuable performing experience for young Black musicians whose opportunities were few.

Because Dixon was not exempt from the racial discrimination experienced by most Black classical musicians, she became active as a jazz bassist, beginning with a two-year tenure with Earl Hines from 1943 to 1945. However, needing more flexibility than Hines's rigorous touring schedule allowed, she formed her own band, the Lucille Dixon Orchestra. This group remained together from 1946 to 1960 and included at various times such luminaries as Tyree Glenn, James Taft Jordan, Buddy Tate, Sonny Payne, Bill Smith, and George Matthews.

Lucille Dixon has performed and recorded with some of the greatest names in the music industry, including Ella Fitzgerald, Johnny Hartman, Sarah Vaughan, Billy Daniels, Earl Coleman, Tony Bennett, Dinah Washington, Vincentico Valdez, Machito, Joe Franklin, Georgia Gibbs, Frank Sinatra, Jan Peerce, Billie Holiday, and Eubie Blake.

BIBLIOGRAPHY

Handy, D. Antoinette. "Conversations with Lucille Dixon Manager of a Symphony Orchestra" (Fall 1975). Foundation for Research in Afro-American Arts, Cambria Heights, New York.

CAROL YAMPOLSKY

DIXON, SHARON PRATT *see* KELLY, SHARON PRATT

DOBBS, MATTIWILDA (1925-)

Mattiwilda Dobbs is an internationally renowned coloratura soprano who has the distinction of being the second Black woman to sing with the Metropolitan Opera Company. She was born in Atlanta, Georgia, on July 11, 1925. One of six daughters of Irene Thompson and John Wesley Dobbs, she grew up in Atlanta, starting piano study at age seven and singing in the First Congregational Church choir. She earned a B.A. from Spelman College in 1946, where she studied voice with Naomi Maise and Willis James. Continuing her education in New York, she attended Columbia University Teachers College (M.A., 1948, in Spanish language and literature) and studied voice privately with Lotte Leonard (1946-50). She also studied at the Mannes Music School (1948-49), at the Berkshire Music Festival at Tanglewood (1950), and with Pierre Bernac in Paris (1950-52). During this period she won the Marian Anderson Award (1947) and the John Hay Whitney Fellowship (1950-52).

Mattiwilda Dobbs's career opportunities surged when she won first prize in the International Music Competition held in Geneva, Switzerland, in 1950. She studied with Lola Rodriguez de Aragon in Madrid in the next year and began to concertize under the management of Sol Hurok. She embarked upon a highly successful series of recitals and appearances with orchestras in European capitals. Her first operatic success occurred during the Holland Festival of 1952 in Stravinsky's *Le Rossignol* and was followed by

The American operatic career of Mattiwilda Dobbs was given great impetus by her highly successful tour of European capitals in the 1950s. [Schomburg Center]

appearances in other celebrated opera houses such as La Scala in Milan (1953) and the Royal Opera House at Covent Garden (1954) where she sang a command performance for the British royal family and the king and queen of Sweden (1954). She was decorated with the Order of the North Star by King Gustaf VI of Sweden. In one way, 1954 was a tragic year for the singer, for her husband of one year, Louis Rodriguez, died four days before the historic Covent Garden performance.

However, in 1954, American audiences gave Dobbs full recognition in the wake of the critical acclaim accorded her Town Hall appearance as Zerbinetta in the Little Orchestra Society performance of the Strauss opera *Ariadne auf Naxos* (Hermann Scherchen, director). Her American operatic debut as the Queen of Shemakha in Rimsky-Korsakov's *Le Coq d'Or* took place in the San Francisco Opera House (1955) and in the next year she appeared at New York's Metropolitan Opera as Gilda in Verdi's *Rigoletto* (November 9, 1956), following Marian Anderson and Robert McFerrin as pioneer Black singers with that organization.

Dobbs married journalist Bengt Janzen of Sweden in 1957 and, in 1959, settled in Stockholm, continuing to perform in Europe, America, Australia, and Israel as recitalist and as opera singer. She returned to the United States and taught on the faculty of several American institutions including Spelman College, the University of Texas at Austin, and the University of Illinois. She retired from a position as Professor of Voice at Howard University in 1991, after a tenure of fifteen years. In 1989, she was elected a member of the Metropolitan Opera Association National Board. She made several recordings of operas and art songs.

BIBLIOGRAPHY

BDAAM; Dobbs, Mattiwilda. Personal interview (1991); Hitchcock, Wiley and Stanley Sadie, eds. *New Grove Dictionary of American Music* (1986); Story, Rosalyn M. *And So I Sing* (1990); *WWBA*.

DORIS EVANS McGINTY

DOMESTIC WORKERS IN THE NORTH

The presence of African-American domestic workers in the North dates from very early colonial days, and discrimination against those workers goes back nearly as far.

According to the colonial records of New Netherlands and New Sweden, many free African-Americans worked as servants in the earliest American settlements. When those settlements passed to the

English in 1664, regulations were made restricting Black workers because of the complaints made by competing whites. In the eighteenth century, records show that colonies such as New Jersey, New York, and Connecticut adopted statutes restricting African-American domestic workers because of opposition from white citizens. By 1800, Philadelphia reported that more than one-tenth of its population was "a large coterie of negroes largely working as servants."

After the American Revolution, many African-Americans worked as servants in the new states, and some employers tried to attract others from the South to relieve the servant shortage. The number of free, nonsouthern African-Americans in the country remained low, however, because they encountered the mark of caste and employers with a repugnance to them.

In about 1840, a massive immigration of Europeans into the United States further reduced the employment of African-Americans in domestic work, and by 1850 that employment had nearly ceased. In the late 1850s, the internationally recognized stereotype of the United States servant was the young immigrant girl, most often Irish. Three-fourths of the servants in the North were white by the Civil War period, and in many urban centers European immigrant servants outnumbered African-Americans ten to one.

Prosperity following the Civil War greatly increased the demand for servants, and there was a strong movement to get affluent white employers to hire newly freed slaves. The movement was spearheaded by charitable agencies and was supported by the federal government, which was willing to pay transportation costs from the South and, if things did not work out, back again. Even employment agencies tried to place freed slaves, but white employers did not budge. They wanted white servants and were unwilling to accept any others. Only about 6,000 African-Americans found work in the North.

In the 1870s, the situation began gradually to change. Factory work was increasingly available, and now virtually no native-born whites were willing to do domestic work. Moreover, immigrants also began pouring into the factories instead of the pantries. By 1900 there was a serious shortage of domestic workers throughout the North.

In the meantime, the situation for African-Americans in the South was creating a people economically reliant on those whom they had served as slaves. The federal government failed miserably in carrying to its economic conclusion the process of emancipation. As a result, African-Americans developed survival strategies based on family and community. Women were at the center of these strategies and the early employment of the young was important for the African-American family's survival. Helping to support the family was a primary task for each woman by the time she was seven years old. Her first assignment was usually to care for the younger children while older women did other work. After a period of tutelage with her mother (or another adult female family member), she went out to work. By the age of nine, she had usually been placed with a white family near her home as a live-in servant. She cleaned, cared for children, and assisted white housewives with other household work.

From about 1870 to the turn of the century, African-American families in the South lived in terrible poverty or barely scraped by as sharecropping farmers, with income supplemented by domestic work. When landlords began to demand a fixed cash rent instead of a crop share, the Black population shifted dramatically. The migration north of about 200,000 African-Americans from 1870 to 1910 was dwarfed by the surge of more than a million people who moved north looking for improved living and working conditions from 1910 to 1920. Between 1916 and 1921, the number of women who left the South exceeded the number of women who had left in the preceding forty years. The migration alarmed southern landowners, who attempted to coerce their labor force into remaining, using violence and intimidation. Their tactics backfired, and even more African-Americans went north in search of respect and a better life.

The family's culturally sustaining processes—not simply its survival needs—timed and directed the migration of its young women. Their journey north was the result of extensive family deliberation. By the time young women left home, the family had usually gone to great lengths to prepare and protect them.

In the North, young Black women found only the domestic jobs that had been vacated by white workers in their rush to the factories. The few nondomestic positions available to African-American women went to northern women who were already established in the community. The southern women lived with kin who helped them adjust to urban life and find work. In overwhelming numbers they became household workers, and these domestic servants from the South not only numerically dominated domestic service in the first two and a half decades of the twentieth century; they also altered the characteristics of domestic service in the North.

They were usually hired as live-in servants and soon learned that their primary task was to serve the mistress of the house, not just to complete assigned tasks, which was a departure from the way they had worked in southern households. In the North, the home was the white mistress's stage. Task assignments and directions given to the staff were perceived as evidences of power. Again unlike southern employers, northern employers required the wearing of uniforms, which symbolized the subservient role of the worker. The young women were also isolated from the rest of the African-American community by their live-in status and their long hours. Thus domestic work was oppressive and undesirable. Those who were forced to do it looked always to the day when they could leave it.

The way out was often through "penny savers clubs." All over the North, women domestics who had been born in the rural South associated themselves with these mutual benefit associations. The clubs sponsored social gatherings, provided sickness and/or death benefits to members, and allowed their members to save against the time when they would be able to escape from live-in service. When a woman had saved enough money to maintain herself and help her rural kin, she began to look for the coveted "day work."

For Black women in search of autonomy, the laundress was a critical figure. She was a non-live-in servant role model, and she was also able to identify households that were seeking the services of women on a live-out basis. She served as an informal employment agent.

The household day worker had working conditions the live-in could not but envy. She had fixed working hours, the opportunity to set her own priorities for tasks, and no isolation from her community. The day worker quickly shed her uniform. She carried work clothing in "freedom bags," wearing her own clothes to and from work to show that she was her own person and that her life was a series of personal choices rather than predetermined imperatives.

By 1925, the growth in the number of African-American women domestics was a national phenomenon. The majority of these household servants did not live in the homes of their employers. In the three largest cities—New York, Chicago, and Philadelphia—the total number of servants declined by 25 percent, but the percentage of African-American women in that occupation increased significantly. They were one-fifth of all domestics in New York and Chicago and more than one-half in Philadelphia. In

Pittsburgh, 90 percent of African-American women worked as day workers, washerwomen, or live-in servants. Around the country more than 80 percent of women not working on rural farms were maids, cooks, or washerwomen. They averaged about $5 per week in the North, and this was more than five times what they were paid in the rural South. Few African-American women who migrated to the "benevolent" North from 1900 to 1950 escaped the drudgery and low pay of domestic service.

During the Depression, the situation deteriorated greatly. White women who had lost their jobs in factories began to compete for domestic work and were generally preferred. Many African-American women were forced to stand on street corners and offer their housecleaning services for ten to twenty cents an hour. Some women received only transportation costs, old clothing, or lunch for a day's work. The national and state welfare policies that were instituted to alleviate Depression suffering did not affect most household workers. Domestics were excluded from Social Security benefits.

When World War II started, nearly 64 percent of African-American working women were in institutional or private household service employment, compared with 16 percent of working white women. During the war, white politicians and businessmen yielded to pressure from civil rights groups to open employment of other kinds to these women. President Roosevelt, prompted by the threat of a demonstration in Washington, issued Executive Order No. 8802, which outlawed discriminatory practices by defense contractors. With the establishment of the Committee on Fair Employment Practices to investigate discrimination, employers slowly and grudgingly lowered the barriers against African-American women in industrial employment. As a result, the proportion of machine operators increased from 4 to 17 percent, and 6 percent of African-American women were employed in clerical or sales jobs. About 13 percent worked as professionals or semiprofessionals. The effect on domestic workers was to put them, for the first time, in a decent bargaining position. Because other options were open, the supply of domestics was low. African-American household workers could demand higher wages and better working conditions.

When the war ended, men, both African-American and white, returned to the labor market, and women were encouraged to leave the factories and offices. White women, as Betty Friedan has pointed out, were encouraged to go home to take care of families and to keep their houses clean; African-

American women, on the other hand, were encouraged to go to the white people's houses to take care of white families and keep white people's houses clean. Government and private agencies developed projects to encourage the return of African-American women to domestic service.

In the 1950s, women in domestic service still did not receive the benefits of national worker legislation—minimum wage laws, unemployment compensation, Social Security benefits. Workers did their best to organize to improve their situation, however. They tried to keep wages at the relatively high wartime rate. They tried to set uniform standards for hourly pay and employment requirements and to improve the overall working conditions of domestics. No one group was successful for very long. They had little or no support from either government agencies or labor unions.

The same is true today. For domestic servants in the North, the records reveal the many ways race and gender intersect to restrict job opportunities and possibilities for improvement. In the last half of the twentieth century, the individual actions of women's associations have not halted the process of marginalization that still engulfs domestic servants. For African-American domestics, a long life of work is still the corollary of a long day of work.

BIBLIOGRAPHY

Clark-Lewis, Elizabeth. *The Shift from Live-in Servant to Daywork* (1985); Giddings, Paula. *When and Where I Enter: The Impact of Black Women on Race and Sex in America* (1984); Higginbotham, A. Leon. *In the Matter of Color* (1980); Jones, Jacqueline. *Labor of Love, Labor of Sorrow* (1986); Katzman, David. *Seven Days a Week* (1978); Sutherland, Donald. *Americans and Their Servants* (1981).

ELIZABETH CLARK-LEWIS

DOMESTIC WORKERS IN THE SOUTH

An exchange between a runaway slave woman and a former female slaveholder in Sherley Anne Williams's novel *Dessa Rose* (1986), challenges one of American culture's most deep-seated stereotypes about women of African descent. Rufel, the slave mistress, conjured memories of her Mammy, donning the requisite bandanna wrapped around her head, as the unerringly dutiful and subservient slave. "Mammy ain't nobody name, not they real one," exclaimed the protagonist, Dessa, incensed by Rufel's apparent ignorance of the person behind the romanticized figure, a person who had a name and a life of her own. Rufel's image of Mammy continues to shape what many white Americans think about Black women, especially domestic workers. Yet it is an image that dismisses the rich and complex history of Black women laborers.

The formative period in the development of wage household labor in the South falls between 1861, marking the transition from slave to free labor, and 1920, the end of the Great Migration and the era of World War I. African-Americans' heightened expectations of freedom during the Civil War translated into increased conflict with their masters over fundamental issues that prefigured the post-Civil War struggle between wage laborers and employers. Masters frequently remarked on changed dispositions and displays of defiance as slaves tried to shape the emergent context of freedom and articulate their desire for autonomy, respect, and just compensation in seemingly minor domestic disputes.

Most African-Americans remained in the rural South and continued to perform agricultural work after emancipation; but women migrated to southern cities in disproportionate numbers as they were pushed off farms and plantations that demanded male labor or family units. They filled jobs performing the same kind of work many had held as slaves in the Big House. Virtually every occupation was closed to them except as cooks, general maids, child-nurses, and laundresses. More specialized positions were available as chambermaids, kitchen helpers, or pastry cooks. A relatively small number found other work as seamstresses, midwives, nurses, and teachers. Most Black women in the urban South could expect to enter domestic service between the ages of ten and sixteen and remain within it throughout their entire lives. Domestic work and Black women were virtually synonymous in the region that stigmatized so-called menial labor and assigned it almost exclusively to one race. Black women not only contributed to the physical maintenance of white households, their presence became a vaunted emblem of white supremacy.

Despite the occupational confinement of the majority, African-American women exercised some choice in selecting certain kinds of domestic jobs. Positions as child-nurses tended to attract younger and single women. Laundresses were usually married, older, and women with children. They constituted the largest proportion of domestic workers, especially in large cities where the total numbers significantly exceeded those employed in smaller towns and rural areas. Women with families took in washing because it gave

them greater independence and versatility. Washerwomen picked up dirty bundles from their patrons on Monday and performed the labor in their own homes throughout the week, which not only allowed them to perform their housework and child care intermittently, it also encouraged them to work together in communal spaces within their neighborhoods. Women often gathered to wash clothes in backyards or common wells and streams, which fostered informal networks of reciprocity. The practical value of this support system was realized at critical moments when there was a need to spread vital news or share resources.

Cooks, child-nurses, and maids tended to work in relative isolation in most white households that employed only one or a few domestic workers. Still, one of the most distinguishing characteristics of domestic service in the South was that workers lived in their own homes. In order to maximize the distance between slavery and freedom, most African-American women refused to live with their employers. White southerners' ambivalence about close contact with Black servants and the residential proximity of the races before the emergence of formal segregation made the live-out arrangement convenient for bosses as well.

A major benefit of live-out arrangements was that southern domestics could actively participate in the creation of community institutions, escaping some of the atomization that has characterized domestic labor throughout the world. Laundresses blended the sustaining of family with the sustaining of neighborhood in their daily activities, but cooks, maids, and child-nurses also contributed toward the common good.

Domestics widely participated in two of the most important institutions in African-American communities—the church and the benevolent society. Churches provided a multitude of spiritual and social functions as they buttressed collective self-help efforts, fostered leadership development opportunities, sanctioned moral standards, and promoted education and political awareness. Mutual aid organizations such as the Daughters of Friendship, the Sisters of Love, and the Daughters of Liberty cropped up throughout the region after emancipation, with some able to trace their antebellum roots. They provided benefits to the sick, infirm, unemployed, widowed, and orphaned, as well as provided opportunities for trade association, and political and social expression. Domestic workers participated in such institutions and activities even if that meant giving short shrift to their wage work. Their dedication and willingness to take time off created friction with employers. Benevolent societies bolstered the ability of individual wage earners to quit spontaneously and provided a surreptitious mechanism for exacting justice against unfair and unscrupulous bosses through informal boycotts.

Workers and employers disagreed about many issues, with disputes over wages topping the list. Household laborers toiled long hours, often twelve-hour days every day of the week, yet they were compensated poorly for their arduous exertions. Their incomes, especially in cities that were disproportionately female, sometimes provided the sole financial resources for their families. Low wages made domestic labor available to a broad spectrum of the white population, permitting even some poor white workers to afford laundresses. Paltry wages certainly diminished Black women's living standards, but the complete denial of cash wages could wreak even greater havoc. Many employers readily engaged in questionable practices that bilked workers of their rightful earnings. At the end of the week or month, for example, a domestic might discover exorbitant deductions from her wages, for breaking household objects or committing behavioral infractions, that left her in debt.

Compensation in the form of food, as a supplement to wages, was a practice routinely acceptable to both workers and employers. "Pan-toting" or taking away table scraps and pantry goods from employers' homes evolved as a customary expectation, but it became more controversial in the early twentieth century. Domestic workers sometimes appropriated foodstuffs beyond the limitations imposed by employers or without their consent. African-American women stressed the inequitable wage structure and the importance of pan-toting in making ends meet. Employers grew increasingly disgruntled with what they perceived as theft that burdened their expenses.

Conflicts between employers and workers were not easily resolved. When negotiations degenerated and Black women could not obtain the proper redress, they developed a variety of overt and covert methods to demonstrate their grievances and seek justice. Quitting, for example, proved to be a vexing way to deny employers unmitigated control. The ease with which Black women moved from job to job became a popular complaint for employers bemoaning the perpetual so-called servant problem.

Strikes were rare but profound expressions of household workers' opposition to oppression. Washerwomen, taking advantage of their relative autonomy, led the vanguard of such mobilizations. They organized strikes in Jackson, Mississippi, in 1866; Galveston, Texas, in 1877; and Atlanta, Georgia, in

1881. Household workers in Norfolk, Virginia, joined a strike with tobacco stemmers and waitresses in 1917. The demand for self-regulation—the ability to maintain control over their occupation—loomed large throughout these strikes. The strikers galvanized wide support among other African-Americans by canvassing their neighborhoods and knocking on doors, conducting mass meetings, and building on infrastructures previously established. They sent petitions to local officials and newspapers to argue their cases and demonstrated remarkable resilience and skill in the face of the considerable forces marshalled against them. Ad hoc organizations usually drove these occasions of open rebellion, though most dissent was sustained outside the boundaries of conventional trade unions. Even secret societies created for other expressed purposes sometimes transformed themselves on the spur of the moment to carry out work-related resistance. Domestic workers also joined the Knights of Labor in both separate and mixed-trade assemblies during its heyday in the late 1880s. In 1920, several local domestic workers' unions in southern cities were affiliated with the American Federation of Labor.

Public debates about household labor were not confined to moments of large-scale insurgency. White middle-class reformers carried on lively debates, especially in newspapers, about the need to create a more acquiescent, chaste, and cheaper work force. Rarely were the needs and voices of the laborers themselves taken into consideration. Black middle-class reformers often intervened through such networks as the National Association of Colored Women, even if frequently limited by the class biases that inspired their mission to "uplift" the "degraded" masses. Yet many of the local Black women's clubs not only involved working-class women but also advocated fairer distribution of public resources and they adopted programs to meet pressing needs of domestic workers for housing, child-care, health, and education. Less sympathetic voices of the white elite more often prevailed as they suggested and enacted reform measures that were quite draconian in intention and scope. White political candidates, municipal authorities, reformers, and health-care providers broadcast images of Black domestics as perils to public safety and health that required containment. Though employers hired household laborers to perform rather intimate tasks, they scapegoated the outsiders in their midst as the agents of germs and diseases such as tuberculosis. Whiteness was associated with purity and cleanliness, blackness with pollution and dirt, according to this view. Solutions as severe as reviving the institution of slavery, subjecting all domestics to bodily inspections, and home-site surveillance of washerwomen's personal surroundings were not unknown. Social control reached a peak during the period of World War I as labor conflicts intensified. "Work or fight" laws, originally instituted to compel able-bodied men to obtain gainful employment or serve in the armed forces, were used against Black domestics in the South. African-American women were forced to perform domestic labor against their will or face jail, fines, or vigilante violence at the very moment that jobs became available in areas that had been previously barred to them.

African-American women exercised the ultimate protest in response to the multitude of repression they encountered. The mounting pressures during the war period only compounded the social, political, and economic discrimination they had already endured. New opportunities became available during this period as European immigrants returned to their home countries and northern industries recruited more workers to meet the demands of war production. Between 1914 and 1920 at least one-half million Black southerners moved to the North. African-American women had entered the urban South in the 1860s hopeful of their future as free people, but by 1920 domestic workers were desperate to get out of the land of Jim Crow.

[See also MAMMY.]

BIBLIOGRAPHY

"Condition of the Negro in Various Cities," *Bulletin of the Department of Labor* (May 1897); Federal Writers Project Papers. Southern Historical Collection, University of North Carolina, Chapel Hill; Fleming, Walter L. "The Servant Problem in a Black Belt Village," *Sewanee Review* (January 1905); Goldin, Claudia. "Female Labor Force Participation: The Origin of Black and White Differences, 1870 and 1880," *Journal of Economic History* (March 1977); Hill, Joseph A. *Women in Gainful Occupations, 1870 to 1920: A Study of the Trend of Recent Changes in the Numbers, Occupational Distribution, and Family Relationship of Women Reported in the Census as Following a Gainful Occupation* (1929); Hunter, Tera W. "Household Workers in the Making: Afro-American Women in Atlanta and the New South, 1861 to 1920," Ph.D. diss. (1990); Janiewski, Dolores. *Sisterhood Denied: Race, Gender, and Class in a New South Community* (1985); Jones, Jacqueline. *Labor of Love, Labor of Sorrow: Black Women, Work, and the Family from Slavery to the Present* (1985); Katzman, David. *Seven Days a Week: Women and Domestic Service in Industrializing America* (1978); Lerner, Gerda, ed. *Black Women in White America: A Documentary History* (1972); A Negro Nurse. "More Slavery at the South," *Independent* (January 25, 1912); Northen, William J. "Tuberculosis among Negroes," *Journal of the Southern Medical Association* (October 1909); Rabinowitz, Howard N. *Race Relations in the Urban South, 1865-1890* (1978); Rachleff, Peter. *Black Labor in the South: Richmond, Virginia, 1865-1890* (1984); Reed, Ruth. *The Negro Women of Gainesville, Georgia* (1921); Reiff, Janice L., Michel R. Dahlin, and Daniel Scott Smith. "Rural Push and Urban Pull: Work and Family Experiences of Older Black Women in Southern Cities, 1880-1900," *Journal of Social History* (Summer 1983); Sterling, Dorothy, ed. *We Are Your Sisters: Black Women in the Nineteenth Century* (1984); Sutherland, Daniel. *Americans and Their Servants: Domestic Service in the United States from 1800-1920* (1981); White, Deborah. *Ar'n't I a Woman? Female Slaves in the Plantation South* (1985); White, Walter F. " 'Work or Fight' in the South," *New Republic* (March 1, 1919); Williams, Sherley Anne. *Dessa Rose* (1986).

TERA HUNTER

DONEGAN, DOROTHY (1922-)

Educated hands moving across the keys as if controlled by some manic force, legs kicking out gleefully at the pedals, eyes shut tight, coif glistening with perspiration: this is a portrait of Dorothy Donegan when she is thoroughly caught up in the muse. Records do not do her justice. Her spirit is not easily captured in a recording studio, and she must be seen in order to be properly appreciated and believed. Although steeped in the classics, Donegan inevitably chose jazz, the art of improvisers, because no page of notated music could possibly harness her talents and interests. Honored as a Jazz Master by the National Endowment for the Arts, she has been caught up in the muse since the tender age of six.

A native of the South Side of Chicago, one of the crucibles of African-American culture, Donegan began her musical odyssey almost from the moment she entered Willard Elementary School, and her parents enrolled her in piano lessons at the studio of Alfred Simms. Her interest in music accelerated greatly when she entered the famous DuSable High School, coming under the tough and learned tutelage of Captain Walter Dyett. Known for encouraging a raft of celebrated jazz musicians, Dyett practiced a kind of tough musical love that gave Donegan the boost she needed.

Donegan's first professional job was playing with the Bob Tinsley Band at the age of seventeen. From there she got a job playing solo at a downtown grill. In 1942 the owner of one of the grills where she worked presented the twenty-year-old Donegan at Orchestra Hall in a concert featuring a winning mix of jazz, boogie-woogie, and European classical mu-

Hands moving across the keys as if controlled by some manic force, legs kicking out gleefully at the pedals, coif glistening with perspiration, Dorothy Donegan becomes thoroughly caught up in the music when she performs. Here she entertains Black troops during World War II. [Moorland-Spingarn]

sic. Donegan was the first jazz pianist to take the stage at Orchestra Hall, a venue previously graced only by classical talents such as Vladimir Horowitz.

That 1942 concert proved to be a portent of the future, as Donegan has gone on to a rich, globe-trotting career that often finds her straddling disparate musical spheres. Fluent in the classics as well as jazz, she truly belongs to that special class of orchestral jazz piano playing occupied by such masters as Art Tatum, Erroll Garner, and Oscar Peterson.

BIBLIOGRAPHY

Travis, Dempsey J. *An Autobiography of Black Jazz* (1983).

WILLARD JENKINS

DOUGLAS, MARION (1920-)

"Io mangio dove voglio. Eh! Tu! . . . Va te ne!" ("I'll eat where I want. As for you, beat it!") European child star Marion Douglas snapped to bewildered Atlantans who had introduced her to Jim Crow practices. Marion Douglas had performed on the stages of Switzerland, France, and Italy in her father's *Louis Douglas Revue*; her father had choreographed on Broadway and in Paris for Josephine Baker; her grandparents, ragtime composer Will Marion Cook and the legendary singer Abbie Mitchell, had performed for royalty; and Uncle Mercer Cook was the head of French at Spelman College. No monolingual backwater plebe was going to tell *her* where she could or could not dine.

Marion Douglas, also known as "Maranantha Quick," was born Abbie Louise Douglas in 1920 in North Marylebone, England. She grew up between the world wars touring Europe with her parents, based in Italy and Germany. Billed as an acrobatic dancer, she performed matinees with the revue while at the same time attending school in Catholic convents. With the rise of Mussolini and Hitler, her father decided that the family should return to the United States and that she should become educated as a Black American woman at Spelman College. With greater fluency in French and Italian than in

English and no knowledge of racism, Douglas arrived in Atlanta in 1937. Her interest in languages and theater became her means of coping with the "unreality" of life around her.

Her work with the Atlanta Repertory Players at Spelman and the Hampton Institute's Summer Theatre program under the direction of Owen Dodson gave her a dramatic outlet for her frustration with America in 1938. She performed in *Les précieuses ridicules* in French, and in 1941 she played several roles, including the Countess in a noted performance of *The Cherry Orchard* and major parts in *Tovarich, Cyrano de Bergerac,* and racial plays *Outward Bound* and *Elijah's Ravens.*

The most noted role of her career was as Ophelia in Dodson's historic 1945 production of *Hamlet* at the Hampton Institute. Gordon Heath, who played the lead, recalls in his autobiography that Dodson felt she had over-researched the part, exclaiming, "Oh, how I hate *thinking* actors!" In spite of her excessive industry, Heath wrote, "Marion was still the best Ophelia I ever saw."

Before *Hamlet,* she had already been working on the New York stage. In the 1945 season, she played the part of Sophie Baines in *A Young American,* produced by the Blackfriars Guild, an off-Broadway troupe that performed plays with Catholic and racial themes. In this play she worked with a young Black actor and fellow Dodson pupil who was to become a prolific filmmaker, William Greaves. In 1982 and 1985, Douglas had cameo roles in his two award-winning films commissioned by the National Park Service: *Frederick Douglass: An American Life* and *Booker T. Washington: The Life and Legacy.* Maintaining contact with the theater throughout her life, she worked in *Uncle Vanya* in 1984 as well as *The Threepenny Opera* and *The Confidential Clerk* at the Cynthia Belgrave Studio Theater in Brooklyn.

When not on stage, Marion Douglas has been an educator, teaching French in the New York City public school system since the 1950s. Always committed to the theater, she designed a program for teaching languages to children through drama. In the late 1960s, she directed the Children's Theater at the Harlem School of the Arts, where she introduced and wrote Black-centered material for the program. From 1971 until 1983, she set drama aside to investigate mysticism and tour as a psychic.

Late in life Douglas stated her career objectives: "To express and create through humor; to enhance the vitality of life, and to communicate the mature outlook of age as a desirable achievement." She has continued to pursue these goals, working in Jesse Jackson's 1988 presidential campaign and serving on the New York State Committee on Multicultural Education. Although modest about her contribution to the theater, she offers the unique perspective of a Black American who grew up in Europe and has touched a wide network of dramatists and educators.

BIBLIOGRAPHY

Douglas, Marion. Oral history tapes, Hatch-Billops Collection, New York (1988, 1992); Heath, Gordon. *Autobiography* (forthcoming); Hill, Errol. *Shakespeare in Sable* (1984).

DAVID A. GOLDFARB

DOUGLASS, ANNA MURRAY
(c. 1813-1882)

"Anna Murray-Douglass" was how Rosetta Douglass Sprague referred to her mother in a reminiscence that tells almost all that is known about the first wife of Frederick Douglass. Determined to give the woman an identity separate from that of her husband, Sprague did not have an easy task. Of all the American women eclipsed by famous, articulate husbands, few have been shadowed more totally than Anna Murray Douglass. Like Deborah Franklin (Mrs. Benjamin Franklin), she was married to a successful, self-taught man who announced himself to the world with a famous autobiography that says virtually nothing about his wife.

Anna Murray was born, probably in 1813, near the town of Denton in remote, interior Caroline County on Maryland's eastern shore. Her parents, Mary and Bambarra Murray, were manumitted a month before she was born, so she was born free, the eighth of twelve children. At seventeen she, like many free Black people and ex-slaves, emigrated from her rural home to find work in the growing city of Baltimore. Perhaps she worked in a cookshop with her mother; it is known that a Mary Murray owned one in 1836. She did work as a domestic servant for at least two white families.

The free black community in Baltimore was growing rapidly in the 1830s, and accompanying its active churches were self-improvement societies that provided both intellectual stimulation and opportunities for social meetings. At one of these socials Murray reportedly met Frederick Bailey, a young (five years her junior) caulker in one of Baltimore's many shipyards. Still a slave, Bailey had already tried to escape to the North; caught, he had been lucky enough not to have been sold South but instead was sent to Baltimore. Given the chance, Murray helped him make good on a second escape attempt. With her money he bought a train ticket; dressed in sailor's clothing that she had made for him and carrying another seaman's papers, Bailey traveled through Maryland and Delaware into the free North.

Murray followed him to New York, where they were married by Rev. James W. C. Pennington, another former slave from the Eastern Shore. Assisted along the way by members of the Underground Railroad, Mr. and Mrs. Frederick Johnson, as they now called themselves, traveled to New Bedford, Massachusetts, a prosperous whaling port dominated by Quakers who had made the town perhaps the safest haven in the nation for runaway slaves. In New Bedford they adopted the name Douglass that was to be theirs for the rest of their lives.

Frederick was barred, because of his race, from practicing his skill as a caulker, but the two made a satisfactory living doing unskilled labor. The family might well have remained obscurely settled in New Bedford had Frederick not heard William Lloyd Garrison preach the powerful doctrine of abolition. In 1841, in a famous speech heard by Garrison and Wendell Phillips, Frederick began his great career as an antislavery orator, and Anna Murray Douglass's life was forever altered.

With their first two children, Rosetta, born in 1838, and Lewis Henry, born in 1840, the Douglasses moved to Lynn, Massachusetts, another antislavery town and one closer to the Boston headquarters of the American Anti-Slavery Society. Employed by the society to travel as a speaker for abolition, Frederick often was absent from home, sometimes for months. In 1845-46 he was in Great Britain for more than a year, leaving Anna Douglass to care for the growing family, which now included Charles Remond, born in 1844. Douglass also was also left with the need to provide for expenses not covered by Frederick's slim salary. She sewed shoes at home on a piece-work basis and smarted under the humiliation of having checks sent by white benefactresses.

Frederick's career advanced, as author of the successful *Narrative of the Life of Frederick Douglass* (1845) and as editor of *North Star*, a Rochester, New York, antislavery newspaper. In 1847, Frederick moved the family to Rochester and himself into an increasingly elegant circle of acquaintances, many of them white. The gulf between husband and wife widened. Rosetta, growing up a sensitive young woman, tried to bridge the gulf between her worldly, famous father and her housebound mother. Douglass, however, determin-

ing that she could never match Frederick intellectually, never achieved more than a rudimentary ability to read; perhaps her unwillingness to learn signified a defiance of her husband and his fame. The maintenance of a well-run household and, even more, a love of gardening seemed most to sustain Douglass.

Perhaps the worst indignity that Douglass had to endure was visits by curious, elegant white callers to the family home. In letters describing such visits, during which Douglass appears to have greeted people at the door and then retreated to the kitchen, these guests often betrayed appalling racial assessments of their hostess. Douglass can hardly have escaped noticing such attitudes.

In 1860, while her husband was again in England, the youngest child and Douglass's namesake died at age seven. Anna Douglass seems never to have overcome the loss; beginning in her late forties, her health began to deteriorate, although it is not clear exactly what her medical problems were. Following a stroke, Anna Murray Douglass died on August 4, 1882, at her final home, Cedar Hill, a lovely country house across the Anacostia River from Washington, D.C. Her body was carried to the Mount Hope Cemetery in Rochester, where her daughter Annie was buried and where her husband of forty-four years later would be interred.

Although in many ways it seems that Frederick Douglass was insensitive to the needs of his wife and often caused her to feel isolated, he never abandoned the marriage. His letters at the time of her death reveal intense grief, and in the following year (well before he remarried) he appears to have suffered a breakdown, recovering only after much attention from his friends, children, and grandchildren.

In writing her reminiscence, Rosetta Douglass Sprague was determined to have the world pay her mother the attention she deserved, and it was Rosetta's four surviving daughters (together with their cousin Joseph Douglass, a concert violinist) who best paid her that attention. All four granddaughters were active early in the twentieth century in the movement to establish organizations in which they, as women, could achieve an autonomy denied their grandmother.

BIBLIOGRAPHY
McFeely, William S. *Frederick Douglass* (1991); Quarles, Benjamin. *Frederick Douglass* (1968); Sprague, Rosetta Douglass. "Anna Murray-Douglass—My Mother as I Recall Her," *Journal of Negro History* (January 1923).

WILLIAM S. McFEELY

DOUGLASS, FREDERICK

As the preeminent African-American leader of his time, Frederick Douglass (1818-1895) has come to personify his people's nineteenth-century passage from slavery to freedom. His gripping life story of self-made achievement against seemingly insuperable odds served then, as now, as an object lesson in how his oppressed people might succeed, individually and collectively. Douglass saw himself as an exemplar and symbol, as well as a leader, and the dominant thread in subsequent writing about him has relied heavily—arguably too heavily—on the self-image Douglass carefully constructed. Devised principally via his three autobiographies—*Narrative of the Life of Frederick Douglass, an American Slave, Written by Himself* (1845); *My Bondage and My Freedom* (1855); and *Life and Times of Frederick Douglass* (first published in 1881; revised in 1892)—the heroic image shines brightly.

A closer look at both the autobiographical Douglass and the historical Douglass, however, reveals a far more complicated and fascinating figure than the unproblematic figure so common in popular portrayals. Perhaps nowhere is the Douglass legend more provocative than in his views on and relationships with Black women. Any attempt to sort through this complex aspect of his life and legacy must confront head-on the thorny issues of gender and race and their intersections. The pivotal issues for him were identity and destiny—Who am I? Who can I become? For Douglass—a mulatto slave with a Black slave mother and a white slave-owner father—these issues were never simple. Rather, they were a lifelong contest on a field constrained by ideologies and practices of race, class, and gender.

Black women were powerful influences throughout Douglass's life. From his grandmother Betsey Bailey, mother Harriet Bailey, wife Anna Murray, and daughters Rosetta and Annie, to colleagues Harriet Tubman, Sojourner Truth, Frances E. W. Harper, Mary Church Terrell, and Ida Wells-Barnett, Douglass came to know Black women well. As a slave and as a free man, he saw his personal destiny and that of all Black men as inextricably tied to that of Black women (and children). Douglass accepted the prevailing nineteenth-century belief that women were the guardians of the related values of home, virtue, morality, and culture. Similarly, he accepted the common belief that the status of Black women was a key barometer of the status of African-Americans as a people. In other words, Black elevation depended upon the uplift of Black women as much as Black men. Ultimately, of course, the elevation struggle was a collective enterprise.

Not surprisingly, therefore, Douglass pointed to the oppression of Black women, slave and free, as especially cogent evidence of the heinous nature of racism. Notably in his autobiographies, he portrayed the sufferings of slave women as representative of slavery's irredeemable evilness. The beatings and rapes of Black women by white men were particularly abhorrent. Slavery, he maintained, had sanctioned the brutalization of Black women by white people, especially white men. It had also rationalized the paradoxical de-feminization and sexualization of Black women: they were alleged to be both far less (if at all) feminine than white women and sexually loose. Douglass vigorously attacked these vicious slanders against Black women, offering a view of them as enduring against tremendous odds to maintain their dignity and virtue as women. Such moving witness and support for Black women substantiated his reputation as a valiant spokesman for Black women and men. A vital component of his leadership, then, was to expose the oppression African-Americans—in this instance women—endured as a way to enhance both understanding and amelioration of that oppression.

Douglass's autobiographies, notably the earlier two, discuss his relationships with his mother, Harriet, and his grandmother Betsey in some detail. Although he spent precious little time with his mother, those interactions etched an indelible impression of strong maternal affection under duress. He spent considerably more of his early years under the indulgent care of his grandmother. Although the overall characterization of these relationships is touching and warm, clearly the very young Douglass sought a maternal relationship through a series of subsequent relationships with white women, like Lucretia Auld (his half sister) and his mistress, Sophia Auld. Notwithstanding the projection in his autobiographies of a loving Black mother and Black grandmother, there is also the reality of a stunted biological maternal tie and of a deep personal disappointment owing to his early abandonment by both of them (due to circumstances beyond their control).

His wife, Anna, received far scantier autobiographical treatment, partially owing most likely to traditional Victorian concerns with domestic propriety. Still, Anna played a crucial role in his ascension to success. Not only did she, a free African-American, help him with his escape to freedom in 1838, but she assumed primary responsibility for caring for their three sons—Charles Remond, Frederick, Jr., and Lewis Henry—as well as daughters Rosetta and Annie. She also created a domestic refuge that proved crucial for her increasingly famous husband. Even though her private accomplishments have been vastly overshadowed by her husband's public ones, the former contributed powerfully to the latter.

Nineteenth-century public life was predominantly male. Black spokeswomen like Maria W. Stewart, Sojourner Truth, and Frances E. W. Harper braved a tough and ubiquitous public sexism compounded by racism and class prejudice. Given this severely circumscribed public platform, it was both necessary and inevitable that male leaders like Douglass would try their best to articulate the particular concerns and perspectives of Black women. To an extent, they succeeded. In light of the qualitatively distinctive experiences of Black women, however, Black male leaders could not speak fully and wholly authoritatively for Black women. As a result, an unfortunate consequence of this male-dominated leadership was to overshadow further Black women's voices, notably those, like Sojourner Truth's, undaunted by the likes of Douglass.

Douglass, like so many male leaders, saw his leadership in humanist terms, which, he suggested, transcended gender, race, and class. He employed his considerable talents as an orator, abolitionist, newspaper editor, social reformer, and politician to promote struggles that he believed would benefit all. Operating as a gadfly or "Jeremiah," he endeavored vigilantly to help his country realize its better and truer self. Even as a race leader, he envisioned the ideals for which he battled—freedom, equality, justice—as subverting racial or political nationalism, economic inequality, and patriarchy. American society, he hoped, would one day reflect a composite nationality where differences of race/ethnicity—and by implication gender and class—would be meaningless. His belief in capitalist success, reflecting his own amazing personal confirmation of the American self-made success mythology, revealed a traditional faith in the fundamental soundness of the system, provided it was made actually open and accessible to all on an equal basis.

As a supporter of the contemporary women's movement and the woman suffrage movement in particular, Douglass pioneered an uncommon commitment to and insight into women's struggle for freedom and equality. From his pivotal support for Elizabeth Cady Stanton's proposal at the 1848 Seneca Falls Convention to push for woman suffrage, to the morning of the last day of his life when he attended a women's rights convention, he lent his singularly powerful voice to the nineteenth-century feminist struggle. While an avid supporter of women's rights,

Douglass understood that a woman was her own best advocate. Consequently, he listened to women's concerns and voices and tried to follow their lead in the struggle. In his support for the Fifteenth Amendment enfranchising Black men but not women—Black or white—however, he made it clear that he saw the problems of race and Black manhood as superseding in importance the issue of feminism. To Sojourner Truth's argument that his position reinforced Black male privilege at the expense of Black women, he could only reply that Black women suffered more because of racism than sexism. Obviously there were limitations to his feminism. For example, like that of most of his female and male feminist contemporaries, his feminism left virtually intact the ideology of home and domesticity as women's sphere. Indeed, this inability to see how, why, and to what effect domestic conventions structured and reinforced woman's oppression was pervasive.

Another vital component of Douglass's public vision and leadership, extending ideologically beyond the barriers of gender, race, and class, was his concept of the American nation. He believed deeply in the central nineteenth-century constellation of ideals basic to the young nation: democracy, republicanism, progress, optimism, and egalitarianism. As for so many African-Americans before and after him, for Douglass, America's highest and best ideals, exemplified by the revolutionary struggle, were vital as both inspiration and argument. Activists like Douglass thus necessarily embraced Black women in their ultimate visions of republican democracy and political equality, while giving strategic and tactical primacy to the struggle to enfranchise Black men. The onward march of progress compelled optimism regarding the prospects for women's elevation generally and Black women's elevation specifically. The primary focus of Douglass's reformist philosophy was his profound, unceasing commitment to agitation and resistance. That American women finally achieved the ballot in 1920 through the Nineteenth Amendment would seem to support his faith.

Thus it is clear that as a family member, a local and national community leader, and the principal race spokesman of his generation, Douglass was quite sensitive to Black women's travails and triumphs, their hopes and dreams. Likewise, Douglass's leadership and rhetoric often spoke insightfully to Black women's historical experience. It is also clear that as the personification of nineteenth-century Black manhood, self-made success, middle-class respectability, and his people's liberation quest, his relationships with and views of Black women were not unproblematic. A critical part of the dilemma has been the traditional projection—by Douglass, Black leaders, African-Americans generally, and almost all scholars until recently—of the African-American experience as prototypically male. The conflation of the nineteenth-century slave and free African-American sojourn with that of "representative" men like Douglass has obscured that of "representative" women like Sojourner Truth. The common tendency to see Douglass's life and thought as singularly significant buttresses this problem. A more accurate historical portrait drawing upon a multiplicity of lives and a range of thought must center on the gender dimension.

For example, how are scholars to interpret Douglass's second marriage, to Helen Pitts, a white woman? Many African-Americans, especially Black women, at the time of that celebrated wedding and since have seen this marriage as an attack on racial integrity, race unity, and Black female beauty. In other words, these critics interpreted the marriage as evidence that Douglass wished to escape the race. Douglass, on the other hand, presented the union as evidence that he and his new wife had risen above the debilitating strictures of race prejudice and racialism.

In a related vein, shortly after escaping to freedom, Douglass dropped the name his mother gave him and assumed a new one modeled on a character from a Sir Walter Scott novel. In a sense this renaming signified, as Deborah McDowell has argued, an erasure of his mother and both the racial and feminine selves she represented. Similarly, Douglass's discussion of the victimization of Black women and the correlative objectification of both their bodies and their sexuality transpires principally in the arena of male (white and Black) power and desire. Once again, Black women's voices are silenced, their experiences subordinated.

These gendered interpretations force us to deepen our examination of an exceedingly complex individual. Why is it, furthermore, that women generally and Black women especially are increasingly marginalized in his post-emancipation autobiographical writings? How does this square with his feminism and his race leadership? For one thing, this pattern is consistent with his belief that the concerns of race and manhood were more important than those of feminism. Put another way, for him, ultimately, the concerns of Black men were more crucial than those of Black women.

The critical analysis of Douglass's views of Black women in no way diminishes the value and importance of his considerable struggles and achievements, particularly those on behalf of Black women. Just the opposite: it helps us to situate historically those struggles and achievements—his "greatness"—in a more measured and insightful way. Only by acknowledging and analyzing the gendered reality of his leadership and thought can we begin to comprehend fully the meaning of that leadership and thought for women and men, Black and white.

[See also SPRAGUE, FREDERICKA DOUGLASS AND ROSABELLE DOUGLASS.]

BIBLIOGRAPHY

Andrews, William L., ed. *Critical Essays on Frederick Douglass* (1991); Blassingame, John W., et al., eds. *The Frederick Douglass Papers* (1979); Douglass, Frederick. *Life and Times of Frederick Douglass: Written by Himself* ([1881] 1962), and *My Bondage and My Freedom* ([1855] 1969), and *Narrative of the Life of Frederick Douglass, An American Slave, Written by Himself* ([1845] 1968); Foner, Philip S. *Frederick Douglass: A Biography* (1950), and *The Life and Writings of Frederick Douglass* (1950, 1975); Foner, Philip S., ed. *Frederick Douglass on Women's Rights* (1976); Franchot, Jenny. "The Punishment of Esther: Frederick Douglass and the Construction of the Feminine." In *Frederick Douglass: New Literary and Historical Essays*, ed. Eric J. Sundquist (1990); McDowell, Deborah E. "In the First Place: Making Frederick Douglass and the Afro-American Narrative Tradition." In *Critical Essays on Frederick Douglass*, ed. William L. Andrews (1991); McFeely, William S. *Frederick Douglass* (1990); Martin, Waldo E., Jr. "Frederick Douglass: Humanist as Race Leader." In *Black Leaders of the Nineteenth Century*, ed. Leon Litwack and August Meier (1988), and *The Mind of Frederick Douglass* (1984); Preston, Dickson J. *Young Frederick Douglass: The Maryland Years* (1980); Quarles, Benjamin. *Frederick Douglass* ([1948] 1968); Sundquist, Eric J., ed. *Frederick Douglass: New Literary and Historical Essays* (1990); Walker, Peter F. *Moral Choices: Memory, Desire, and Imagination in Nineteenth-Century Abolition* (1978).

WALDO E. MARTIN, JR.

DOUGLASS, SARAH MAPPS (1806-1882)

Sarah Mapps Douglass served Black society as an educator and abolitionist. Born into a prominent free Black family in Philadelphia on September 9, 1806, she was reared in comfortable circumstances and was educated by private tutoring. Her family background was one of commercial success and cultural awareness. Her maternal grandfather, Cyrus Bustill, a Quaker, owned a bakeshop and, after his retirement, ran a school. He was also an early member of the Free

African Society, the first Black benevolent association. Her mother ran a "Quaker millinery store," and her father helped found the First African Presbyterian Church of Philadelphia.

As a young woman, Douglass joined the Philadelphia Female Anti-Slavery Society, of which her mother had been a founder. In 1838 the society assumed the financial support of a school for Black children that she had opened. Her associates and close friends in the society were the Forten sisters, daughters of wealthy Black shipbuilder James Forten, and the Quakers Lucretia Mott and Sarah and Angelina Grimké. The latter were the daughters of a slaveowning justice of the South Carolina Supreme Court and the only white southern women to become active antislavery agents. The lifelong friendship between Douglass and the Grimké sisters was remarkable for their time. The letters of Douglass to the sisters

Anna Murray Douglass lived her adult life in the shadow of her husband, Frederick. All four of her granddaughters were active early in the twentieth century in the movement to establish organizations in which they, as women, could achieve an autonomy denied their grandmother. [Moorland-Spingarn]

reveal her intelligence, abolitionist commitment, and sensitivity.

Douglass provided the Grimké sisters with support and personal testimony in their challenge of discrimination within the Quaker Meeting. Douglass described her indignation when white Quakers were prevented from sitting next to her during meeting. Her mother had been kept from membership; when she attended the funeral of a Quaker she was made to walk behind the carriages with two Black servant boys. The information Douglass provided to Sarah Grimké was incorporated into a British pamphlet published in 1840 and widely distributed in the United States and in England.

Douglass's friendships, as well as her activities, were quite controversial. When Douglass and her mother attended Angelina's wedding, the Philadelphia press expressed outrage, calling the event an intolerable incident of "amalgamation." Two days later a mob burned down the newly built headquarters of the Pennsylvania Anti-Slavery Society and set fire to the Shelter for Colored Orphans.

Though Philadelphia Quakers did not end discrimination for several decades, Douglass remained a member of the Society. In 1853 she became a teacher and later an administrator of the Institute for Colored Youth, a Quaker-supported school where she trained many teachers for the public schools until her retirement in 1877. She married Reverend William Douglass in 1855; he died in 1861. After the Civil War, she was vice chairman of the Women's Pennsylvania Branch of the American Freedmen's Aid Commission. She died in Philadelphia in 1882.

[*See also* FREE BLACK WOMEN IN THE ANTEBELLUM NORTH; QUAKERS.]

BIBLIOGRAPHY

Barnes, Gilbert H. and Dwight L. Dumond, eds. *Letters of Theodore Dwight Weld, Angelina Grimké Weld and Sarah Grimké* (1934); Bustill, Anna. "The Bustill Family," *Journal of Negro History* (October 1925); Cadbury, Henry J. "Negro Membership in the Society of Friends," *Journal of Negro History* (April 1936); Drake, Thomas E. *Quakers and Slavery in America* (1950); Grimké, Sarah. Letter "on the subject of prejudice against color amongst the Soc. of Friends in the U.S." (April 10, 1839), Weston papers, Boston Public Library; Lerner, Gerda. *The Grimké Sisters from South Carolina* (1967); Letters of Sarah Grimké to Sarah Douglass in Gratz Collection, Historical Society of Pennsylvania, Philadelphia, and in the New-York Historical Society; Letters of Sarah Grimké to Sarah Douglass in Sarah Grimké Personal File. Library of Congress, Washington, D.C.; Letters from Douglass to Sarah Grimké in Theodore Wight Weld Collection, William Clements Library, University of Michigan, Ann Arbor; Minutes of Board of Managers, Institute for Colored Youth, 1837-65, Arch Street Center, Society of Friends, Philadelphia; Minutes of the Philadelphia Female Anti-Slavery Society, 1833-39, 1848-67, Historical Society of Pennsylvania; *NAW*.

GERDA LERNER

DOUROUX, MARGARET PLEASANT (1941-)

"Gospel music is energy. Whereas you can sing a hymn academically, gospel music demands a soul kind of deliverance. The energy is what gives gospel its character" (Douroux 1987). Because of her sensitivity to and understanding of both the technical and spiritual characteristics of different religious music genres, Margaret Jean Pleasant Douroux (composer, arranger, and publisher of gospel music, hymns, anthems, and spirituals) has been able to write more than 115 sacred songs.

Born March 21, 1941, in Los Angeles, Douroux is the daughter of Los Angeles gospel pioneer Earl Amos Pleasant (1918-1974) and music teacher Olga Williams Pleasant (b. 1920). Douroux and her husband, Donald Douroux, are the parents of one daughter, Mardoné Patrice Douroux, who is studying to become a legal secretary and preschool teacher.

During the three years that Douroux attended Southern University (Baton Rouge, Louisiana) in the 1960s, she was actively involved in the civil rights movement sit-ins and later became the West Coast music director for Operation PUSH (People United to Save Humanity). Douroux received her B.A. degree in music from California State University, Los Angeles. Her Master's degrees in education and educational psychology were earned at the University of Southern California. She received a doctorate in educational psychology from the University of Beverly Hills. During her thirteen-year career in the Los Angeles school system, she served as elementary teacher, guidance counselor, and psychologist.

Douroux acquired much of her religious music training from working in her father's church (Mount Moriah Baptist Church) where she was greatly influenced by contacts with Los Angeles gospel musicians Thurston Gilbert Frazier and Gwendolyn Lightner. In recent years, she has served as choir director for various television shows—including *227* starring Marla Gibbs, and Billy Graham's twenty-fifth anniversary special. Since the late 1970s she has served as minister of music at Greater New Bethel Baptist Church.

"Gospel music is energy." The energetic Margaret Douroux has composed more than one hundred sacred songs. In 1981, she founded the Heritage Music Foundation, whose mission is to establish a gospel music hall of fame and museum complex. [J. C. DjeDje]

Also, she regularly conducts gospel music workshops around the United States. Several of Douroux's compositions have become standards in various hymn books and religious communities: "Give Me a Clean Heart" (1968), "I'm Glad" (1970), "What Shall I Render" (1975), "The Lord Is Speaking" (1976), "He Decided to Die" (1976), "Trees" (1979), and "Follow Jesus" (1981). Songs that have won awards or been recorded and featured in special projects include "God Is Not Dead" (The Mighty Clouds of Joy won a Grammy Award for Best Gospel Performance with this song) and "I'm Glad" (Nikki Giovanni used this song as background music for a recording of poetry). In addition, several songs have been featured on recordings by James Cleveland and his Gospel Music Workshop of America as well as by other established gospel musicians (e.g., Shirley Caesar, Clay Evans).

Not only have a number of music awards been presented to Douroux—the Best Song Award (James

Cleveland and the Gospel Music Workshop of America), the Music Accomplishment Award (A Corporation for Christ Church News), and the Gospel Academy Award (Daviticus)—she has also received a host of proclamations and official tributes from cities around the country. She is the founder and president of her own publishing company (Rev. Earl A. Pleasant Publishing Company); has made three recordings—*Revival from the Mount* (1970), *The Way of the Word* (1982), and *Signs of the Advent* (1987); and is the author of several publications: *About My Father's Business* (1977), *Christian Principles That Motivate and Enhance Education among Black Children* (1979), *Why I Sing* (1983), and *Find the Kingdom* (1985).

In 1981, Douroux established the Heritage Music Foundation, an organization whose mission is to build Gospel House in Los Angeles (a monument, hall of fame, and museum complex that would be devoted to the nurturing and preservation of gospel music). Country music has the Grand Ole Opry and Western classical music has Carnegie Hall, and Douroux believes that gospel music should be recognized and supported in a comparable manner.

BIBLIOGRAPHY

DjeDje, Jacqueline Cogdell. "Gospel Music in the Los Angeles Black Community: A Historical Overview," *Black Music Research Journal* (Spring 1989); Douroux, Margaret Pleasant. Interviews (October 7, 1987, and November 25, 1991).

DISCOGRAPHY
Revival from the Mount, K-CAL Productions (1970); *The Way of the Word*, Greater New Bethel Baptist Church, LBR-001 (1982); *Signs of the Advent*, Pleasant Publishing, PP-001 (1987).

JACQUELINE COGDELL DJEDJE

DOVE, RITA (1952-)

Rita Dove says that she tried to "string moments as beads on a necklace" in the making of the Pulitzer Prize-winning poetry collection *Thomas and Beulah* (1985). The inspiration for this volume came from a story about her grandfather told to Dove by her grandmother. The poems grew over the course of five years, starting with the poem "Dusting," which is one of the key pieces in the "Beulah" section but which appeared in 1983 in the volume entitled *Museum*. *Thomas and Beulah* is divided into two sections: Part One, "Mandolin," is devoted to the grandfather; Part Two, "Canary in Bloom," is devoted to the grandmother.

Dove gathered background material for *Thomas and Beulah* by talking to her mother, by reading Works Progress Administration texts on the state of Ohio, by exploring the significance of Black migration from the agrarian South to the industrial North (especially to Akron, Ohio), and by listening to older blues recordings from Lightnin' Hopkins to Billie Holiday. This historical information was distilled into the fictional story of Dove's grandparents' lives. Dove won the Pulitzer Prize for poetry for *Thomas and Beulah*, the first Black woman to win this award since Gwendolyn Brooks received it in 1950.

In addition to *Thomas and Beulah*, Dove has published three volumes of poetry and a collection of short stories. *The Yellow House on the Corner*, published in 1980, relates the experiences of "The Bird Frau," maddened by war, who "went inside, fed the parakeet, / broke its neck." The judiciousness of tone and feeling in this poem about the German woman is matched in the poem "The Abduction," about "Solomon Northrup / from Saratoga Springs, free papers in my pocket, violin / under arm, my new friends Brown and Hamilton by my side" who, participating with his "friends" in a carnival act, "woke and found [himself] alone, in darkness and in chains."

The poems in *The Yellow House* seem more "domestic" than those in *Museum*, published in 1983. These poems have an exotic flair, retelling ancient myths, religious legends, and stories about faraway lands. One of the loveliest selections, "Tou Wan Speaks to Her Husband, Liu Sheng," describes the tomb Tou Wan constructs for her dead mate: "I will build you a house / of limited chambers / but it shall last / forever: four rooms / hewn in the side of stone / for you, my / only conqueror." Rita Dove's most recent collection of poetry, *Grace Notes*, was published in 1989. Her volume of short stories, *Fifth Sunday*, appeared in 1985. Probably the best known of the stories in the collection is "The Spray Paint King," a poignant tale about a mixed-blood Black and German youth who, with a decidedly contemporary touch, spray paints the ancient walls of the buildings in the city of Cologne. "The First Suite" (a complex story about a traveling puppeteer who performs for elementary school children), from a novel in progress, was published in the fall 1986 issue of *Black American Literature Forum*.

Rita Dove was born in Akron, Ohio, in 1952. She earned a B.A. from Miami University in Oxford, Ohio, in 1973 and an M.F.A. from the University of Iowa in 1977. She has taught at Arizona State University and

Pulitzer Prize-winning poet Rita Dove writes of Black lives with controlled power and delicacy. [Schomburg Center]

now teaches creative writing at the University of Virginia. She was writer-in-residence at Tuskegee Institute in Tuskegee, Alabama, in 1982 and recipient of a Guggenheim Fellowship in 1983. She is a Fulbright scholar and holds important editorial positions on journals such as *Callaloo*, *Gettysburg Review*, and *TriQuarterly*. Dove is married to Fred Viebahn, a German novelist; they have a daughter, Aviva.

BIBLIOGRAPHY

CA; Giddings, Paula. "Word Star," *Essence* (August 1987); Hall, Sharon K., ed. *Contemporary Literary Criticism* (1988); McDowell, Robert. "The Assembling Vision of Rita Dove," *Callaloo* (Winter 1986); McKinney, Rhoda E. "Introducing Pulitzer Prize-Winning Poet, Rita Dove," *Ebony* (October 1987); Rampersad, Arnold. "The Poems of Rita Dove," *Callaloo* (Winter 1986); Rubin, Stan Savel, and Earl G. Ingersoll. "A Conversation with Rita Dove," *Black American Literature Forum* (Fall 1986); Schneider, Steven. "Coming Home: An Interview with Rita Dove," *Iowa Review* (Fall 1989); *Who's Who in Writers, Editors and Poets*, ed. Curt Johnson (1989-90).

CAROLYN MITCHELL

DRANES, ARIZONA JUANITA
(c. 1905-c. 1960)

With a unique combination blues and gospel style born out of her Texas Church of God in Christ background, Arizona Dranes had a successful, though short-lived, recording and touring career. One of the first women to enter the field of professional gospel singing, a field previously dominated by male quartets, her piano and vocal style influenced generations of gospel musicians.

Arizona Juanita Dranes was born blind to a poor, highly religious family. The exact date of her birth is unknown but was probably around 1905. After learning the piano in her early teen years, Dranes played at Church of God in Christ (COGIC) prayer meetings in and around her hometown of Dallas, Texas. The Reverend Samuel Crouch, of the Fort Worth COGIC, alerted the Okeh Record Company of Dranes's talent and, in 1926, Okeh's Richard M. Jones heard her in Fort Worth. In May of that same year Dranes received an invitation to make a test recording at Okeh's studios in Chicago.

Dranes's first records from Okeh, including two piano solos which appear to be almost straight blues and her trademark barrel house piano sanctified singing numbers, sold well from the start. Given a staff writer's contract with Okeh, Dranes earned $25 "per issued side, nothing for unissued work" (Shaw), and $3 a day to cover living expenses in Chicago. Her contract also called for her to receive a 25 percent royalty on her compositions when other artists recorded them, but Dranes never received any income from royalties.

Dranes continued to perform at church gatherings in Chicago to plug her recordings for Okeh, and in COGIC meetings throughout the Bible Belt. Traveling primarily throughout Tennessee, Texas, and Oklahoma, Dranes frequently fell ill and wrote many letters to Okeh requesting an advance on her next recording session. This second session did not improve her financial situation, since the man who supervised her recording dates stole her earnings. Though this man was fired, relations between her and the record company suffered, and her health continued to deteriorate, so that throughout 1927 she was physically unable to attend scheduled recording sessions.

After the July 1928 session, relations grew increasingly strained. There were disputes about payments due to Dranes and other musicians at the session. The following winter, Dranes, still ill, requested another advance. This final session never came to be. Her last letter, from Oklahoma City, indicated that she had recovered, and requested a new Victrola for which she would repay the company as soon as she began working. After this February 1929 letter, there is no more record of Dranes, though she is thought to have died around 1960. Dranes's distinctive style, a mixture of secular, ragtime/boogie piano playing and high-pitched nasal religious singing was known to thousands who had heard her in person or through her recordings. Her piano and/or singing style influenced such gospel luminaries as Clara Ward, Rosetta Tharpe, and Ernestine Washington.

Her 1926-28 Okeh recordings have been reissued by Herwin Records, and include "In That Day," "I Shall Wear a Crown," "He Is My Story," "My Soul Is a Witness for the Lord," and "I'm Going Home on the Morning Train."

BIBLIOGRAPHY

Heilbut, Anthony. *The Gospel Sound—Good News and Bad Times* (1985); Shaw, Malcolm. Liner notes to *Arizona Dranes 1926-1928 Barrel House Piano with Sanctified Singing*, Herwin Records 210; Southern, Eileen. *The Greenwood Encyclopedia of Music: Biographical Dictionary of Afro-American and African Musicians* (1982).

N. H GOODALL

DRUMGOLD, KATE

Kate Drumgold was born into the Old Virginia system of slavery and had blossomed into a young girl by the time of the Civil War. Her date of birth cannot be determined because official birth records were not maintained on most enslaved African Americans, but certainly her childhood was lived out under slavery. Her autobiographical narrative, *A Slave Girl's Story*, published in 1898, indicates that she was one of seventeen daughters in the Drumgold family; her only brother died as a teenager when he was sent by his owner to fight in the Civil War. Both the war and slavery severely fractured the family, separating young Drumgold from her mother, father, and siblings. She wrote: "My dear mother had a dear husband that she was sold from also . . . he waited a while and then he found him another wife."

After the Civil War, Drumgold was reunited with her mother and sisters, but not with her father and brother. In 1865, the family of women migrated north to Brooklyn, New York, where she wrote her *Story* in

spite of frequent bouts with serious illness. The book begins with a reflection on her life under slavery and then documents her life after emancipation up to 1897. Her prose exhibits a rigorous, almost puritanical self-discipline and is filled with praise and tributes to God as being the source of her religious, educational, and teaching accomplishments:

> God be praised for the way he has led me since I was three years old until this day, for it was his hand that taught me to remember all those long years. I have in my mind the time at the old home when they put me on the fine dressing table in front of the large mirror, while the Rev. Mr. Walker baptized me in the name of the Father and the Son and the Holy Ghost.

Drumgold spent many years traveling, spreading the gospel, and converting African-Americans to Christianity; she even studied for three years and eight months at Wayland Seminary in Washington, D.C.

Published writing by African-Americans was rare in the late 1800s, but many former slaves wrote impassioned autobiographies espousing the abolition of slavery, encouraging the education of African-Americans, and exhorting self-disciplined piety among African-Americans. Drumgold's text speaks directly to the latter two. On education, she wrote:

> I made up my mind that I would die to see my people taught. I was willing to prepare to die for my people, for I could not rest till my people were educated.

On religion:

> If we should fail to give Him the honor due there would a curse come to us as a race, for remember those of olden times were of the same descent of our people, and some of those that God honored most were of the Ethiopians.

Although Drumgold's discourse on slavery is brief, her reflections on how it severed her family can be viewed as having an antislavery theme. Given that the continuing themes of racism, educational advancement, and a spiritual way of life are evident in the modern autobiographies of African-Americans, Drumgold can be viewed as a foremother of this tradition as well as a nineteenth-century African-American literary pioneer.

BIBLIOGRAPHY

Drumgold, Kate. *A Slave Girl's Story* (1898).

TOMIKA DePRIEST

DU BOIS, SHIRLEY GRAHAM (1896-1977)

When Shirley Graham wrote in a 1933 *Crisis* essay, "Black man's music has become America's music. It will not die," she summed up one of her life's ambitions: to bring to the foreground the many accomplishments of African-Americans in every field. One of Graham's concerns was that African-Americans would eventually abandon their spirituals, with their unique rhythms and haunting melodies. In an effort to preserve Black music, she became the first African-American woman to write and produce an all-Black opera, *Tom-Toms: An Epic of Music and the Negro* (1932). This was just one successful effort in a lifetime devoted to the preservation of Black history and culture.

Professional writer, composer, conductor, playwright, and director, Shirley Lola Graham was born on November 11, 1896, on a farm near Evansville, Indiana, to Reverend David Andrew Graham and Etta Bell Graham. Graham and her four brothers were encouraged by their father, a Methodist missionary, to discover Black culture and music and to work to uplift the race. Shortly after graduating from Lewis and Clark High School in Spokane, Washington, Graham married Shadrach T. McCanns in 1921. McCanns died three years later, leaving her with two children, Robert and David.

In 1935, she completed a Master's degree in music history from Oberlin College, after studying music at the Sorbonne in 1926 and at Howard University in Washington, D.C., and Morgan State University in Baltimore in 1929-32.

During her first year at Oberlin, Graham converted her play *Tom-Toms* into an opera, which was produced by the Cleveland Opera Company in 1932. Drawing national media attention because of the monumental cast of 500 and the novelty of a Black female composer, librettist, and dramatist, the opera played to a house of 10,000 on the first night and 15,000 for the second and final performance. Tracing African music through the United States, *Tom-Toms* began a trend that popularized musicals and dance concerts based upon African and West Indian themes.

Dancers like Katherine Dunham and Asadata Dafora became prominent on the heels of Graham's successful production of an opera that generated mass appeal.

With the success of her opera, Graham chose to develop her craft as a dramatist. She accepted a position in 1936 as director of the Black division of the Chicago Federal Theatre Project, a job that allowed her to combine her expertise in music with theater. Between 1938 and 1940, Graham studied at the Yale Drama School, where she wrote and produced five plays: *Dust to Earth, I Gotta Home, It's Mornin', Track Thirteen,* and *Elijah's Raven.* Most notable is *It's Mornin',* which centers on a Black slave woman who kills her teenaged daughter to protect her from a lecherous master. At the end of the decade, Graham worked on a doctorate in English and education at New York University.

Feeling a need to record Black progress, Graham published thirteen book-length biographies between 1944 and 1976, including *Paul Robeson: Citizen of the World* (1946), *There Was Once a Slave: The Heroic Story of Frederick Douglass* (1947), *The Story of Phillis Wheatley* (1949), *Booker T. Washington: Educator of Hand, Head, and Heart* (1955), and *A Political History of W.E.B. Du Bois* (1976).

Graham had corresponded with W.E.B. Du Bois since 1936, seeking advice and job opportunities. They married in 1951 and together worked for justice and world peace. Her efforts to end discrimination against Black soldiers and other civil rights activities in the 1940s had prompted her dismissal from her job as director of the Young Women's Christian Association-United Service Organizations. Her activism in Ghana led the U.S. government to hold Graham suspect. After her husband's death in Ghana in 1963, she was denied entry to the United States on the basis of alleged un-American activities. She lived in Cairo, Egypt, for several years before being invited by the Chinese government to take up residence. She died in Beijing.

Shirley Graham Du Bois lived up to her commitment to uplift the Black race. Evidence of success in her several simultaneous careers came in the form of prestigious awards, including a Julius Rosenwald fellowship in 1938-40, a Guggenheim fellowship in 1945-47, the Julian Messner Award in 1946, the Anisfield-Wolf Award in 1949, and the National Institute of Arts and Letters Award in 1950. She also was a founding editor of *Freedomways,* a journal of Black literature and culture. Her aim was to preserve Black history and culture, and she succeeded from the mammoth production of *Tom-Toms* to working for world peace with a home base in China.

[*See also* COMPOSERS.]

BIBLIOGRAPHY

Brown-Guillory, Elizabeth, ed. *Wines in the Wilderness: Plays by African-American Women from the Harlem Renaissance to the Present* (1990); *CA*; *Current Biography* (1946); Perkins, Kathy A. "The Unknown Career of Shirley Graham," *Freedomways* (1985).

ELIZABETH BROWN-GUILLORY

DU BOIS, W.E.B.

W.E.B. Du Bois (1868-1963), a central figure in launching the modern Black and African liberation movements, was a scholar, novelist, poet, and activist of extraordinary range and energy. He made several very particular contributions toward the emancipation of Black women. He was a supporter of woman suffrage, women's reproductive freedom, and women's economic independence from men. He also condemned the sexual abuse of Black women, valued and celebrated the work of Black women, and positioned himself as a key ally in the struggle to integrate the predominantly white woman suffrage movement.

Du Bois's most important book (from a woman-centered perspective) is *Darkwater* (1920), in particular his essay "The Damnation of Women." Here he described what he called the "unendurable paradox" of women's position in society: "The world wants healthy babies and intelligent workers. Today we refuse to allow the combination and force thousands of intelligent workers to go childless at a horrible expenditure of moral force, or we damn them if they break our idiotic conventions. Only at the sacrifice of intelligence and the chance to do their best work can the majority of modern women bear children. This is the damnation of women." Du Bois proposed solutions that bear a striking similarity to contemporary feminist demands: "The future woman must have a life work and economic independence. She must have knowledge. She must have the right to motherhood at her own discretion."

Further exploring the issue of women's emancipation, Du Bois observed in this same essay that he could clearly recall four women from his childhood: "My mother, cousin Inez, Emma, and Ide Fuller. They represented the problem of the widow, the wife, the maiden, and the outcast." He continued: "They existed not for themselves, but for men; they were named after men to whom they were related and not after the fashion of their own souls. They were not beings, they were relations."

In focusing on the special suffering of Black women under slavery, Du Bois condemned the white world for "its wanton and continued and persistent insulting of Black womanhood which it sought and seeks to prostitute to its lust." Likewise, he contributed a crucial insight about the position of Black women within the slave community. Du Bois asserted that because Black women had been forced to labor in the fields alongside Black men, and had suffered the same brutality and punishments, the community had experienced an equality between women and men unknown to their white counterparts. "Our women in black," Du Bois wrote, "had their freedom contemptuously thrust upon them." Du Bois saw this history as both "fearful and glorious." The abuse caused terrible suffering and produced "the haunting prostitute, the brawler, and the beast of burden." However, "it also has given the world an efficient womanhood" of courage and strength that is now in a position to give leadership to the whole struggle for women's emancipation and "have a vast influence on the thought and action of the land."

Consistent with these views Du Bois featured women in the *Crisis*, the publication of the National Association for the Advancement of Colored People (NAACP), which he edited from 1910 to 1934. For example, he campaigned for woman suffrage. Among his reasons was the fact that any "reopening of the problem of voting must inevitably be a discussion of the right of Black folk to vote in America and Africa. . . . Votes for women mean votes for Black women" (Du Bois 1920). Similarly, in 1912 Du Bois was keynote speaker at the National American Woman Suffrage Association's (NAWSA) convention. Here he appealed to the white delegates to admit Black women into their ranks as full and equal members, and to support the enfranchisement of Black people in the South. Likewise, in his "Men of the Month" column in the *Crisis* reporting on community leaders, Du Bois frequently included women. Typical was his report of the appointment of Coralie F. Cook to the Board of Education in Washington, D.C.; or his mention of Mrs. Ella E. Ryan of Tacoma, Washington, who was the Black editor of the *Forum*, a newspaper with an almost entirely white readership that took a strong stand against segregation and racism; or the tribute to the Black educator Hallie Quinn Brown: "Of all the present forces among colored women she is perhaps the strongest and most far-reaching" (*Crisis* 1914).

Du Bois corresponded with many Black women activists, artists, writers, poets, and novelists, encouraging their work, featuring pieces in the *Crisis*, and sometimes providing financial assistance. For example, there are letters between him and Mary Church Terrell, Ida B. Wells-Barnett, Jessie Fauset, Zora Neale Hurston, Lorraine Hansberry, and Augusta Savage. Savage was to become an extraordinary sculptor and teacher, and it was Du Bois who raised the money to send her to Paris where she was able to study with Auguste Rodin. Occasionally women were critical of Du Bois. For example, Wells-Barnett disagreed with Du Bois's decision to abandon the all-Black Niagara movement he had founded in 1905 and join instead the interracial founders of the NAACP. She was then very disappointed when he subsequently failed to invite her to its founding convention, an invitation she eventually secured. Most of all in these letters, however, and in his writing and research, one sees the extent to which Du Bois honored, and valued, indeed almost venerated, Black women.

Du Bois's two novels, *The Quest of the Silver Fleece* (1911) and *Dark Princess* (1928), feature women as at least co-equal with men in action and vision. In *Quest*, a story set in and around a swamp in Toomsville, Alabama, in the post-Reconstruction period, the main figure is a Black girl, Zora. The novel is a celebration of her birth into womanhood. In presenting her strength, intelligence, and beauty, Du Bois envisions the rebirth of a people. *Dark Princess* features an Indian princess in liaison with a Black medical student inspiring a world uprising of colored peoples. Of it, Du Bois wrote: "*Dark Princess* is a story of the great movement of the darker races for self-expression and self-determination" (Du Bois 1928). In this he presaged the history of the national liberation movements of this century. Widely reviewed, critics found Du Bois too much of a romanticist. Still, Alice Dunbar-Nelson commented that she found *Dark Princess* to be a gripping tale that, once begun, she could not put down. She pronounced it to be "completely and eminently soul satisfying" (Dunbar-Nelson 1928).

W.E.B. Du Bois was one of the most significant supporters of Black women of his day, and he leaves us a legacy of invaluable research and insightful analysis.

[*See also* BLACK NATIONALISM.]

BIBLIOGRAPHY

Aptheker, Bettina. *Woman's Legacy: Essays on Race, Sex, and Class in American History* (1982); *Crisis* (June 1912; September 1912; April 1913; August 1914); Du Bois, W.E.B. *Correspondence*, 3 vols., ed. Herbert Aptheker (1973, 1976, 1978), and *Darkwater, Voices from Within the Veil* ([1920] 1969), and *Dark Princess, a Romance*, ed. Herbert Aptheker ([1928] 1974), and *Efforts for Social Betterment among Negro Americans* ([1909] 1968), and "The Freedom of Womanhood." In W.E.B. Du Bois, *The Gift of Black Folk*, ed. Herbert Aptheker ([1924] 1975), and *The Philadelphia Negro*, ed. Herbert Aptheker ([1899] 1978), and *The Quest of the Silver Fleece*, ed. Herbert Aptheker ([1911] 1974); Du Bois, W.E.B., ed. *The Negro American Family* ([1908] 1968), and *The Negro Church* ([1903] 1968); Dunbar-Nelson, Alice. "As in a Looking Glass," *Washington Eagle* (May 11, 1928); Yellin, Jean Fagan. "Du Bois's *Crisis* and Woman's Suffrage," *Massachusetts Review* (Spring 1973).

BETTINA APTHEKER

DUNBAR-NELSON, ALICE RUTH MOORE (1875-1935)

If Alice Ruth Moore had not married Paul Laurence Dunbar, she probably would not have attracted quite as much historical attention. Yet with or without the Dunbar name, she is a figure worthy of notice. With a life spanning the postbellum South to the Great Depression North, her story is uniquely representative of Black women in the United States during this pivotal time. Moreover, she commands consideration for her many-faceted racial activism, clubwoman endeavors, passionate sexuality, vibrant and contradictory personality, and her achievements as a multigenre author whose work helped to maintain and extend the tradition of African-American women's writing.

Alice Ruth Moore was born July 19, 1875, in New Orleans, Louisiana. Her mother, Patricia Moore, was an ex-slave turned seamstress and was of Black and American Indian ancestry. Her father, Joseph Moore (who never lived with the family), was a seaman from whom she received some Caucasian blood. Her reddish-auburn hair and light skin helped her in Creole society and allowed her to occasionally pass for white in order to imbibe the high culture of operas, bathing spas, and museums in a segregated country intent on racial exclusion. Because of her appearance, Dunbar-Nelson struggled throughout her life with intraracial color prejudice and her own corresponding ambivalence about dark-skinned Black people.

Moore completed a public school education and the two-year teachers' program at Straight College (now Dillard University) in 1892. In addition to her work as a teacher, she was bookkeeper and stenographer for a large Black printing firm. She also studied art and music (playing the piano and cello); acted in amateur theatricals; wrote the "Woman's Column" for the *Journal of the Lodge*, a fraternal newspaper; served as president of the local literary society; and was active in her Protestant Episcopal church. In 1895, when she was only twenty years old, she published her first book, *Violets and Other Tales*, a potpourri of short stories, sketches, essays, reviews, and poetry that augured her future success. Modestly presented in a tone of ladylike authorship, brief and impressionistic pieces about history, books, the city, romantic themes, and the status of women show the youthful writer trying out the voices and strategies that she used in later years.

Moore began teaching school in Brooklyn, New York, in 1897 and conducting various academic and manual training classes at Victoria Earle Matthews's White Rose Mission (later White Rose Home for Girls) in Harlem. In her work with what she described as "the toughest, most God-forsaken hoodlums you ever saw," her size (she was six feet tall and had a robust physique) was a great advantage.

On March 8, 1898, she married the celebrated Black dialect poet Paul Laurence Dunbar, who had begun an increasingly warm correspondence with her in 1895 after seeing one of her poems and her picture in a Boston magazine. From the beginning, their romance was crossed by familial tension and disapproval, temperamental differences and moodiness, Paul Dunbar's medically induced addiction to alcohol and heroin tablets, Alice Dunbar's controlling tendencies, and their inability to have a child. Still, their correspondence reveals their abiding passion for each other, and for the three years they were together (making their home in Washington, D.C., where he was employed at the Library of Congress), they were a glittering couple. When Paul Dunbar died on February 9, 1906, Alice Dunbar received recognition as his wife, and her lifelong career as his widow was officially launched. This auxiliary identity often eclipsed her own important accomplishments, but it paradoxically gave her much-needed income and visibility.

As the lesser-known, female half of the Dunbar writing duo, Alice Dunbar probably benefited from her professional association with her husband. Shortly after they married, his agent, Paul Reynolds, began marketing her short fiction to the leading magazines of the day. In 1899, Paul Dunbar's publisher (Dodd, Mead and Company) brought out her *The Goodness of St. Rocque and Other Stories*, as the companion volume to his *Poems of Cabin and Field*. These stories, more

fully developed than those in *Violets*, are set firmly in New Orleans and fruitfully utilize the Creole history and distinctive culture of the city. The reviewer for the *Pittsburgh Christian Advocate* (December 21, 1899) regarded it as a collection of "delightful Creole stories, all bright and full of the true Creole air of easy-going ... brief and pleasing, instinct with the passion and romance of the people who will ever be associated with such names as Bayou Teche and Lake Pontchartrain." However, their superficial brightness is belied by deeper themes of sadness, loss, death, and oppression. In the title story, the tall, dark heroine, Manuela, resorts to a voodoo madam and the Catholic Saint Rocque to vanquish her petite blue-eyed blonde rival for the attentions of Théophile. It is replete with Old World Creole traditions, emphasizing family, formality, and a closed society.

In other stories—which either went unpublished or found outlets in Black publications—Alice Dunbar frankly confronted race/racism and the problems of the Black Creole, adding the popular turn-of-the-century motifs of "passing" and "the color line" to her equally in vogue local color regionalism. "The Pearl in the Oyster," published in the *Southern Workman* (August 1902), chronicles the fall of Auguste Picou, a fair Creole with a Black grandfather, who rejects his Negro friends and neighbors to pass as a white politician. Another series of tenement stories mined her settlement house experience. Set on New York City's Lower East Side, the protagonists are Irish ghetto youth whose hard lives are sympathetically illuminated. Still other works—such as "Elisabeth" and "Ellen Fenton"—explore the psyche of ordinary (white) post-Victorian women. Alice Dunbar also tried her hand at novels (attempting two during this period and two near the end of her career) and, later, popular pulp fiction, but was not successful in these genres. Cumulatively speaking, in the stories that occupied her during these heyday years with Paul Laurence Dunbar, Alice Dunbar skirted the prevalent Black fictional stereotypes of tragic mulatto and happy slave by a variety of interesting means that can be regarded, in retrospect, as her contribution to the newly developing tradition of the short story, especially among Black and Black female writers.

By the fall of 1902, Alice Dunbar was established in Wilmington, Delaware (joined there by her mother and her sister—who had separated from her husband and brought with her four small children). Until 1902, when she was in effect fired for her independent behavior and political activities, she worked at the Howard High School as teacher, then head, of English and drawing, supplementing classroom duties with supervisory responsibilities, fund-raising, playwrighting, and directing. She furthered her own education with special study of English, education, and psychology at Cornell University, Columbia University, and the University of Pennsylvania, while overseeing seven summer sessions for in-service teachers at State College for Colored Students (now Delaware State College). A portion of her Cornell University Master's thesis on the influence of Milton on Wordsworth was published in the respected scholarly journal *Modern Language Notes* in April 1909.

Following relationships with her principal, Edwina B. Kruse, and perhaps others, Dunbar-Nelson made a secret marriage to Henry Arthur Callis, Jr., on January 19, 1910. Later a medical doctor and

Author and activist Alice Dunbar-Nelson published not only poetry and short stories, but also drama, scholarly literary criticism, and journalism. [Schomburg Center]

founder of Alpha Phi Alpha fraternity, he was a fellow teacher at Howard High School, twelve years her junior. Six years after, on April 20, 1916, she formed a more lasting union with Robert J. Nelson, a journalist from Harrisburg, Pennsylvania, widowed with two young children. Their two households merged into an economic and extended family unit, and calm, practical, race-conscious "Bobbo," as he was called, became a quiet blessing she enjoyed for the rest of her life. Together, they published the *Wilmington Advocate* newspaper from 1920 to 1922 and actively participated in the tumultuous politics of Delaware. She served on the state Republican Committee and directed campaign activities among Black women (1920), was a member of the prestigious delegation that presented Black concerns to President Warren G. Harding at the White House (1921), and headed the Delaware Crusaders for the Dyer Anti-Lynching Bill (1922). In World War I-related work, she organized a much-publicized Flag Day parade, formed a local chapter of the Circle for Negro War Relief, and toured the South as field representative of the Woman's Committee of the Council of National Defense (1918). As a noted feminist and clubwoman, she was field organizer for the Middle Atlantic states in the fight for women's suffrage (1915). Together with colleagues from the Federation of Colored Women, she founded the Industrial School for Colored Girls in Marshallton, Delaware, where she functioned as teacher and parole officer from 1924 to 1928.

Just as her personal activities during this period were oriented toward concrete projects, her writing, too, was nonbelletristic, more utilitarian. She edited *Masterpieces of Negro Eloquence* (1914) and *The Dunbar Speaker and Entertainer* (1920), volumes that reflect both the honored place of oratory in African-American culture and her own extensive experience as a noted platform speaker. She wrote formal speeches and contributed articles on Louisiana, Delaware, and war work to the *Journal of Negro History* (1916-17), the *Messenger* (1924), and Emmett J. Scott's (with whom she had a romantic liaison) *Official History of the American Negro in the World War* (1919), respectively. *Mine Eyes Have Seen* (1918), her one-act war propaganda play, was printed and staged. Until she died, Dunbar-Nelson maintained an interest in drama, occasionally writing various kinds of dramatic pieces and trying her hand at screenplays (she was an avid fan of movies and the theater).

Though she was forty-five years old in 1920 and clearly not one of the brash young voices, Dunbar-Nelson participated in the literary upsurge of the Harlem Renaissance. She received recognition as an older, but still active contemporary; attended the numerous race meetings and conferences, rubbing shoulders with the likes of W.E.B. Du Bois, Bessye Bearden, Carter G. Woodson, Mary Church Terrell, and Georgia Douglas Johnson; and wrote and published her poetry, which has served more than any other of her writings to keep her name alive. Her sonnet "Violets," which first appeared in the August 1917 *Crisis* magazine, has become her signature poem. It begins: "I had not thought of violets of late, / The wild, shy kind that springs beneath your feet / In wistful April days, when lovers mate / And wander through the fields in raptures sweet." Though her gifts as a writer were more discursive than poetic, Dunbar-Nelson was a fairly good poet who was particularly competent in rhymed and metered forms, and at her best when she combined these forms with traditional, yet sincerely felt, lyric subjects.

She made shining contributions, however, in the genre of print journalism. The intellect, wit, protest, sassiness, iconoclasm, racial pride, feminism, and humor—in short, all those qualities which marked her as a personality—that do not appear in her canonical writings and fictional heroines are wonderfully evident in her newspaper columns. A male commentator in the 1927 *Opportunity* magazine declared that "there are few better column conductors of her sex on any newspaper. I should like to see her on some influential daily where her unmistakable talents would be allowed full exercise." Drawing on her lifelong experience as reporter, editor, and publisher, Dunbar-Nelson wrote "From a Woman's Point of View," later "Une Femme Dit" for the Pittsburgh *Courier* from February 20 to September 18, 1926; "As in a Looking Glass" for the Washington *Eagle* from 1926 to 1930; and "So It Seems—to Alice Dunbar Nelson" again for the *Courier*, from January to May 1930.

Dunbar-Nelson's most singular contribution to the field of Black women's literature may ultimately prove to be the diary she kept in 1921 and between 1926 and 1931. Discovered in her papers and published in 1984, it is one of only two existing full-length diaries written by a nineteenth-century African-American woman (the other being Charlotte Forten's journal). Kept with effort and in a sophisticated but not self-consciously artsy style, it illuminates areas of crucial concern, such as work, family, sexuality, health, money, and writing. In its pages, for example, can be found documentation for the existence of an active Black lesbian network and for Dunbar-Nelson's own romantic involvement with at least three prominent women.

The 1920s were exciting professionally for Dunbar-Nelson because of her position as executive secretary of the American Inter-Racial Peace Committee from 1928 to 1931. Instituted by the Quakers to further racial understanding and international peace, the committee's work gave her an opportunity to use her fame and skills in unique and largely rewarding public ways, traveling and speaking widely, staging large festivals and programs, and managing the functioning of the committee.

In January 1932, Robert was finally given the political sinecure he had worked hard to gain. After his appointment to the Pennsylvania State Athletic (Boxing) Commission, Dunbar-Nelson was at last able to realize her dreams of owning a well-appointed home (in Philadelphia) and enjoying financial security. Playing the roles of philanthropic society matron, patron of the arts, racial activist, and seasoned politico, she lived her remaining years in a manner that graciously befitted the life which had gone before. She died of coronary complications at the University of Pennsylvania hospital on September 18, 1935.

[*See also* JOURNALISM.]

BIBLIOGRAPHY

Hull, Gloria T. *Color, Sex, and Poetry: Three Women Writers of the Harlem Renaissance* (1987); Hull, Gloria T., ed. *Give Us Each Day: The Diary of Alice Dunbar-Nelson* (1984), and *The Works of Alice Dunbar-Nelson* (1988); Williams, R. Ora. *An Alice Dunbar-Nelson Reader* (1979), and "Works by and about Alice Ruth (Moore) Dunbar-Nelson: A Bibliography," *CLA Journal* (March 1976); the Alice Dunbar-Nelson papers are at Morris Library, University of Delaware, Newark, Delaware.

GLORIA T. HULL

DUNCAN, SARA J. HATCHER (b. 1869)

Through her work on behalf of missions, Sara J. Hatcher Duncan became an important force in the late nineteenth and early twentieth centuries in the African Methodist Episcopal Church.

Sara J. Hatcher was born in 1869 in Cahaba, Alabama, the youngest of four children. Her father, S. George Hatcher, was an ex-slave who earned his living in the grocery and liquor retail business. Sara's mother, Eliza English, of mulatto heritage, was George's first wife and died one year and one month after Sara's birth.

Sara was raised as one of five foster children and spent her early life helping her grandfather with his postal clerk duties in Cahaba. Jordan Hatcher had received the position of postmaster after the Civil War and encouraged Sara's assistance. She attended public school and continued her education at Presbyterian Knox Academy at Selma, Alabama.

In 1889, Sara married Robert H. Duncan of Rome, Georgia. Her active involvement in church work began early in her youth and continued after she was married. In 1897, she was appointed general superintendent of the Women's Home and Foreign Missionary Society of the African Methodist Episcopal (AME) Church. This was the second and specifically southern women's society of the church and had been created in 1893 in spite of resistance from most of the all-male hierarchy.

Duncan's accomplishments represented ideals of womanhood for African Methodist church women, particularly southern women. She was born into a known Alabama family and was well educated, and she was a member of a prominent congregation in her town. A licensed schoolteacher, she married a respected African-American businessman and was foster mother to at least two children. In addition to the prestigious national position Duncan held in her denomination, she also founded a missionary newspaper, *Missionary Searchlight*, that was adopted by the church. She wrote *Progressive Missions in the South* (1906). She was active in almost every civic and social organization of African-Americans in Alabama and was conferred an honorary M.A. by Alabama A&M College.

BIBLIOGRAPHY

Wright, Richard R. *Centennial Encyclopedia of the African Methodist Episcopal Church* (1916).

JUALYNNE E. DODSON

DUNHAM, KATHERINE (1909-)

Katherine Dunham, an artist of many talents, is best known as a popular and widely acclaimed dancer who, with her troupe, performed on stages throughout the world in the 1940s and 1950s, choreographing Caribbean, African, and African-American movement for diverse audiences. Her concerts were visually and kinesthetically exciting and appealing; they were also based on a profound understanding of the peoples and cultures represented as well as on a keen knowledge of social values and human psychology. Her achievements as anthropologist, teacher, and social activist are less well known.

By her own account, in her autobiography, *A Touch of Innocence* (1959), Dunham was born on June 22, 1909, in Chicago. The family lived in Glen Ellyn, a white suburb of Chicago. Katherine's mother, Fanny June (Taylor), was an accomplished woman of French-Canadian and Indian ancestry. She died when Katherine was young. Katherine's father, Albert, Sr.,

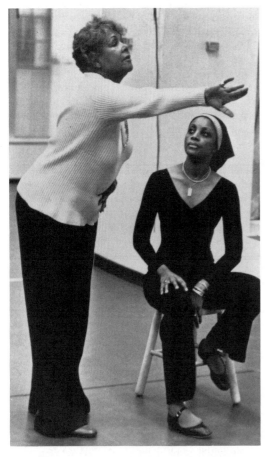

When the great dancer, choreographer, and teacher Katherine Dunham researched the dances of the Maroon peoples of Jamaica, she so won their trust that they accepted her as one of the "lost peoples" of Africa. Her work with the Children's Workshop in East St. Louis inspired a former gang member to credit her with saving his life. This charismatic figure has incalculably enriched the world of dance, opened communication between cultures, and served the Black community of the present and future. [Schomburg Center]

of Malagasy and West African descent, left Katherine and Albert, Jr., her brother, with aunts in Chicago while he traveled as a salesman.

Katherine's father subsequently remarried and his family moved to Joliet, Illinois, where he ran a dry-cleaning business. Albert, Sr., was an embittered man and conflicts between her father, brother, and stepmother caused the young Katherine to seek solace in her own life of imagination. She attended Joliet High School, where she was active in athletics and joined the Terpsichorean (dance) club. She continued her education at Joliet Junior College, where she took lessons in dance. Albert, Jr., persuaded her to apply for admission to the University of Chicago where he was studying philosophy. She was accepted, and she was able to support her education by giving dance lessons and by working as an assistant librarian (Dunham 1946; Beckford 1979).

In Chicago, Dunham studied modern dance and ballet and joined with a member of the Chicago Civic Opera Company to establish a Black dance group, later the Chicago Negro School of Ballet. Her troupe performed at the Chicago Beaux Arts Ball in 1931 and Ruth Page invited her to appear as a solo lead in *La Guiablesse* (1934), based on Martinique folklore, at the Chicago Civic Opera Theater. Dunham also appeared in one of the productions of the Cube Theater, co-founded by her brother. There she met Langston Hughes, St. Clair Drake, W. C. Handy, and dramatists Ruth Attaway and Canada Lee.

At the University of Chicago, she was attracted to anthropology through a course with Robert Redfield, who stressed the importance of dance as a part of social and ceremonial life. She chose to do fieldwork in the Caribbean, where she could study the forms and functions of African-based ritual dance as well as the role of dance in popular culture. She prepared for her fieldwork with Melville Herskovits, who had published numerous works on African and Haitian societies.

Dunham impressed psychologist Erich Fromm and sociologist Charles Johnson with her accomplishments. They recommended that she be invited to present her fieldwork plans before the board of the Julius Rosenwald Foundation. During her presentation, she startled the board members by demonstrating the different dance styles she planned to investigate. Moved by her resolve and enthusiasm, they decided to support her research. She received a Guggenheim Award in 1937 to pursue her investigation of dance in Haiti, Jamaica, Martinique, and Trinidad.

Journeying to Jamaica, she visited the Maroon peoples of Accompong. She succeeded in viewing the

Koromantee, a war dance with sacred and political meaning. The Maroon peoples' decision to allow her to see the dance signaled their acceptance of her as one of the "lost peoples" of Africa, whose mission was to instruct her people in their heritage (Dunham 1946). Her abilities were further demonstrated in Haiti, where she was initiated into the Vaudun and performed in the public dance after the secret ritual. Since her first visit to Haiti in 1935, she has maintained a lifelong relationship with the people and culture of Haiti and has participated in the Vaudun up to the highest level, that of "seer." An avowed mystic, she has demonstrated the power of dance and an open spirit to heal and transform lives.

To complete her Ph.D., Dunham wrote a thesis, "Dances of Haiti," which was later published in Spanish, French, and English (1947, 1957, 1983). Subsequently, she chose to present her cultural knowledge through dance, although she continued in her relationship to the academic world, giving lecture-demonstrations at Yale, University of Chicago, the Royal Anthropological Society of London, and the Anthropological Societies of Paris and Rio de Janeiro. She also held academic positions, as Visiting Professor at Case Western Reserve University and Artist in Residence at Southern Illinois University at Carbondale and the University of California at Berkeley, as well as University Professor and Professor Emerita at Southern Illinois University at Edwardsville.

Dunham's social conscience and political awareness were heightened through her association with political and cultural leaders in Haiti, such as Dumarsais Estimé, president of the Republic (1946-50), and Dr. Jean Price-Mars, anthropologist and cultural nationalist; but she had challenged racism even as a child. She and her family had encountered discrimination in the white community of Glen Ellyn, where in grade school she had refused to sing a song that was degrading to African-Americans, and where she had faced the "color barrier" when she worked as a librarian. She felt that her brother, a brilliant philosophy student of Alfred North Whitehead, never received recognition commensurate with his abilities. Dunham saw these aspects of her personal history as part of a heritage of colonialism and slavery, in which Africans and peoples of African descent were oppressed and exploited for purposes of power and profit. In her career, she expressed her social convictions through her art, promoting understanding and respect for African-based cultural expression as well as fostering self-esteem and creativity among her students.

A scholar as well as a performer, Katherine Dunham wrote a Ph.D. thesis on the dances of Haiti that was published in Spanish, French, and English. [Moorland-Spingarn]

Throughout her career, Dunham has taken controversial stands, working with the National Association for the Advancement of Colored People and the Urban League to end segregation in accommodations and audiences in the cities in which the Dunham troupe performed. In one city she announced after a performance that she would not return until the audience was integrated. In Brazil, the strong criticism and embarrassment that occurred when the Dunham troupe was not allowed to stay in a hotel led to the first public accommodations act in that country. While on an international tour she presented the ballet *Southland* (which dramatized a lynching) during the sensitive period following the lynching of Emmett Till in Mississippi, despite pressure by the U.S. State Department to stop the performance.

Dunham founded her first professional dance company in 1939, performing in Chicago and New York; at first, she subsidized her company through federal support projects that were a part of President Roosevelt's New Deal program; she produced and choreographed the ballet *L'Ag'Ya*, based on martial arts of Martinique, for the Federal Theatre Project. Later the company appeared at the Windsor Theatre in New York and in the Broadway production *Cabin in the Sky* (1940), in which Dunham worked with George Balanchine on choreography. They went on tour with the musical in 1940-41, closing in Los Angeles. In 1942, Dunham appeared in *Star-Spangled Rhythm*, a wartime film to raise morale. She choreographed and appeared with her troupe in several other movies during 1942-43, then toured the United States in her *Tropical Revue* with impresario Sol Hurok. During a Boston appearance, the troupe's performance of "Rites de Passage," a serious treatment of sexuality in a non-Western context, was censored.

While working for the Federal Theatre Project, Dunham met and married John Pratt, a costume and set designer, who continued to design her productions until his death in 1986. Their daughter, Marie Christine, was adopted in 1951. A designer, she resides in Rome.

In 1943, the Katherine Dunham School of Arts and Research opened in New York. Students studied theater arts, dance, literature, and world cultures as a part of their training as artists. In addition to members of the Dunham troupe, other well-known artists such as Marlon Brando, Arthur Mitchell, and James Dean studied there. Some members of her dance troupe went on to establish international reputations in their own right, including Talley Beatty, Eartha Kitt, and Archie Savage. The Katherine Dunham troupe appeared in concerts, touring the United States, Canada, Europe, Asia, and Latin America between 1940 and 1963. Dunham continued to conduct anthropological investigations throughout this time, taking dancers into the villages and neighborhoods where she obtained her movements and ideas for choreography, so that they could become knowledgeable about the cultural and social contexts of the dances they performed.

After its early years, the Katherine Dunham troupe was entirely self-supporting. Audiences were transported by performances; psychiatrists sent patients to them as a part of therapy, and people often came to her dressing room with tears in their eyes. During a postwar London performance of *Shango*, representing a Haitian war god, the audience screamed in empathetic response to the presentation. The last performance of the Dunham company was at the Apollo Theatre in 1965.

Although she considered herself a teacher and choreographer rather than a dancer and favored ensemble over solo dancing, Katherine Dunham was an extremely popular and critically acclaimed performer. In Europe, hat styles and spring fashion collections were named the "Dunham line" and "Caribbean Rhapsody"; the Chiroteque Française made a bronze cast of her feet. Alvin Ailey commented that the interior meaning of his work *Masekela Language* is that all of the women are Katherine Dunham in some aspect of her performance (Terry 1969).

From 1965 to 1967, Dunham was in Senegal, representing the United States at the Festival of Black Arts in Dakar and training the National Ballet of Senegal. When she returned to the United States, she moved to East St. Louis to develop the Performing Arts Training Center of Southern Illinois University. Through the center, Dunham has encouraged an appreciation for cultural heritage by bringing in artists and scholars from Haiti, Brazil, Senegal, and elsewhere. In the Children's Workshop, students learn Creole, African languages, and folk arts including music, stories, and dance from representatives of African, Latin American, and Caribbean cultures. Through Dunham technique, the children learn discipline and develop balance and grace; they develop respect for themselves and for others. Nearby is the Katherine Dunham Museum, which houses artifacts and art objects from Dunham's world travels.

Katherine Dunham has published a number of works in addition to those already mentioned. *Island Possessed* (1969) is an account of her ongoing relationship with the people of Haiti; *Kasamance* is a fictional work based in Senegal. She has published many articles on her philosophy of dance and of life; she is at present engaged in writing her memoirs. She has won many awards, including the Kennedy Center Award (1983), the Albert Schweitzer Music Award (1979), the *Dance Magazine* Award (1968), and the University of Chicago Alumni Professional Achievement Award (1968), as well as numerous honorary degrees. In 1986 she received the Distinguished Service Award of the American Anthropological Society. She has received numerous medals and citations from the government of Haiti.

[*See also* DANCE COMPANIES, ARTISTIC DIRECTORS.]

BIBLIOGRAPHY

Aschenbrenner, Joyce. *Katherine Dunham: Reflections on Social and Political Aspects of Afro-American Dance* (1981); *AWW*; *BABB*; Beckford, Ruth. *Katherine Dunham: A Biography* (1979); *BI*; *BW*; *CA*; Dunham, Katherine. *Journey to Accompong* (1946), and *A Touch of Innocence* (1959); *IWW*; *NYTBS*; Terry, Walter. Interview with Alvin Ailey. Billy Rose Theatre Collection, The New York Public Library for the Performing Arts, New York City (1969); *WWBA*; *WWCA*.

SELECTED PERFORMANCES AND CHOREOGRAPHY BY KATHERINE DUNHAM

1931: *Negro Rhapsody*. Choreographer, performer. Chicago Beaux Arts Ball; 1934: *La Guiablesse*. Performer. Chicago Civic Opera; 1937: *Primitive Rhythms*. Choreographer, performer. Goodman Theater, Chicago; 1939: *Tropics; Le Jazz Hot*. Choreographer, performer. Windsor Theatre, New York; 1940-41: *Cabin in the Sky*. Choreographer (with Balanchine), performer. New York and U.S. tour; 1943-44: *Tropical Review*. Choreographer, performer. Martin Beck Theater, New York and U.S. tour; 1945: *Carib Song*. Choreographer, performer. 54th St. Theater, New York; 1947: *Windy City*. Choreographer, performer. Great Northern Theater, Chicago; 1946-48: *Bal Negre*. Choreographer, performer. Belasco Theater, New York and U.S. tour, Mexico, and transcontinental tours; 1950-60: *Caribbean Rhapsody*. Choreographer, performer. Tours in Europe, Latin America, Far East, Middle East; 1962-63: *Bamboche*. Choreographer, performer. New York and U.S. tour; 1964: *Aida*. Choreographer. Metropolitan Opera, New York; 1972: *Treemonisha*. Choreographer. Atlanta, and Wolftrap Park, Virginia; 1980: *Divine Drumbeats*. Choreographer. WNET Television, New York; Dunham has also choreographed and/or appeared in a number of films, including *Stormy Weather* (1943), *Green Mansions* (1958), and *The Bible* (1964).

JOYCE ASCHENBRENNER

DUNLAP, ETHEL TREW

Ethel Trew Dunlap was a prolific contributor to the "Poetry of the People" column of the *Negro World*. This weekly newspaper was founded in Harlem in 1918 by the Jamaican Black nationalist Marcus Garvey (1887-1940). It was the official organ of his Universal Negro Improvement Association (UNIA), founded in 1916. Discussing issues affecting Black men and women in the United States, glorifying Africa, and commenting on the rise of Islam and political issues in the Muslim world, Ethel Trew Dunlap's poetry contributed to and reflected the UNIA's efforts to create a consciousness of the ties among people of African descent around the world.

Little is known of Dunlap's birth and childhood except that she may have been born in the South and was of mixed parentage. In 1921, when her poetry first appeared in the *Negro World*, she was writing from Chicago. At the end of that year she wrote a few poems in Danville, Illinois, where she stopped briefly before continuing on to Los Angeles, California, where she settled until sometime in 1923 and where a rela-

tive, Eva Trew, also lived. Dunlap may have been affiliated with the UNIA branch in Los Angeles. In 1925, she sent in her poems from Watts, California. Although information on her life is scarce, her poetry is interesting and captivating and the subjects on which she writes inform us about Dunlap, a Garveyite woman of mixed ethnic descent.

From 1921 to 1925, Dunlap contributed close to one hundred poems to the *Negro World*, most of which were written in 1921 and 1922. During those years her verses focused primarily on African-Americans and issues relating to them. She often wrote about historical events such as the Tulsa Riot (1919), the Tulsa Fire, and the Dyer Bill (1921), and about social practices such as southern peonage and lynching. Toward the end of 1921, she wrote several pieces that reflect her strong attachment to the Black Belt of Chicago, an area where descendants of Africans were concentrated. Some of her rhyming compositions are tributes to noted bards such as Claude McKay and J. R. Ralph Casimir and to social and political figures, including Garvey, Henrietta Vinton Davis, J. M. Smith, who was president of the Los Angeles chapter of the UNIA, and J. D. Gibson, surgeon general of the UNIA. Much of her poetry espouses Garvey's mission to rescue and redeem Africans from the grip of Europe and to lead "four million strong" across the water back to their rightful homeland.

Whatever the subject of her poems, they show Dunlap's clear identification with her African roots. This is apparent in two series of verses. In the earlier series, she speaks in the first person as if she is of African ancestry. In the later one, the biblical character Ephraim figures as a symbol representing the "Negro race." She glorifies Africa and yearns for her return to the continent's bosom. On rare occasions there is ambivalence: at times she speaks of herself as a child of freedom who loves the slave and sometimes she speaks as if she herself is a slave.

From 1923 to 1925 Dunlap wrote only thirteen poems, few of which are related to African-American issues. Instead, they reflect an increasingly favorable and positive stance toward Islam and an awareness of events taking place in some parts of the Muslim world. In 1923, in addition to a poem extolling the Nile River, she dedicated "Progress" to a Sheikh Ahmed Din and expressed the notions that Christianity and Islam are at war but the better of the two is the one which will give "storm-tossed souls" rest and that Islam is a force of progress. In "Tolerance" she exhorted Christians to revere Muhammad, Zoroaster, and Buddha and to love Muslims. That year the *Negro World* reported on the spread of Islam in Africa, its benefits to Black people in general, and the growing interest among African-Americans in Islam.

In 1924, two of Dunlap's four poems dealt with racial matters. Of the remaining two, one is in praise of Zaghlul Pasha, an Egyptian nationalist whose name repeatedly appeared in *Negro World* articles on Egypt's occupation by the British. The other, entitled "Voices from Arabia," is a vision of scenes from the account of Moses, Jethro, and Zipporia.

In 1925, the last year in which her poetry appeared in the *Negro World*, three of six poems she contributed show partiality toward Islam and question Christianity and the deeds of Christian conquerors in Muslim lands. In them, she conveys the message that Islam will be triumphant in the world, that humankind will marvel in its splendor, and she urges rapprochement between Christians and Muslims. Her poem "El Islam's Call" questions Christianity and manifests a degree of knowledge about Muslim religious culture and its history that suggests she contemplated converting or in fact became a Muslim. Whatever the case, the *Negro World* provides no concrete answers.

Her poetry struck a chord in the hearts of several of her readers, and many expressed their satisfaction in rhyming lines addressed to her. She and J. R. Ralph Casimir, a Dominican poet, correspondent for the *Negro World*, and a lifelong Garveyite, were mutual admirers who each composed poetry in praise of the other that was published in the *Negro World* and in Casimir's anthology, *Farewell* (1971). Most important, however, is that Garvey, a believer in art for the people and art for the cause, approved of her verses and invited her to read a few poems at Liberty Hall in Harlem (the date is unknown). Moreover, Garvey wrote her a letter of recommendation to facilitate future sales of a small collection of her poetry, which she intended to compile and for which she was requesting financial contributions. In 1923, she supposedly collected $10 for her book; however, the book was not published because of the controversy surrounding Garvey's impending trial.

Nothing more is known about Ethel Trew Dunlap's life following her contributions to the *Negro World*.

BIBLIOGRAPHY

Casimir, J. R. Ralph. *Farewell (And Other Poems)* (1971); Dunlap, Ethel Trew. Letters to J. R. Ralph Casimir (January 19, 1922; March 21, 1922; September 20, 1923), J. R. Ralph Casimir papers, Schomburg Center for Research in Black Culture, New York City; Hill, Robert, ed. *The*

Marcus Garvey and Universal Negro Improvement Association Papers (1986, 1989); Martin, Tony. *Literary Garveyism: Garvey, Black Arts, and the Harlem Renaissance* (1983); *Negro World* (1921-25).

AMAL MUHAMMAD

DUNNIGAN, ALICE ALLISON (1906-1983)

Alice Allison Dunnigan, educator and journalist, had to struggle for her education, for jobs, and for economic and professional security. In the end, it was struggle and determination that allowed her to break through a major journalistic barrier and become the first African-American woman to obtain congressional and White House press credentials.

Alice Allison was born to a tobacco-growing sharecropper, Willie Allison, and a laundress, Lena Pittman Allison, near Russellville, in Logan County, Kentucky, on April 27, 1906. A passion for learning framed her early life: "I always wanted to go to school, even when I was only three or four years old. . . . When I had to stay home, I cried all day" (Hill 1991). Allison's faithfulness paid off. She graduated as valedictorian from the county's Black high school.

Following graduation, Allison resolved to attend Kentucky State College in Frankfort, one of the state's two publicly supported Black colleges. Her parents, especially her father, dismissed the notion, until a dentist, one of the area's few Black professionals, intervened and persuaded the Allisons to give their daughter a chance. Alice Allison supplemented her family's financial support by working in the college dining hall. In 1926, despite poor health and intermittent elementary school teaching, Allison completed the intermediate teachers' training course, which qualified her to teach in the state's elementary and secondary public schools.

That fall she began teaching in a one-room school in rural Todd County. There she met and married her first husband, Walter Dickinson, a sharecropper, who she quickly discovered did not intend for his wife to continue teaching. She was equally determined not to work in the fields and take in laundry. They divorced in 1930 and she married Charles Dunnigan, a childhood friend, a year later. He fathered her only child, Robert William Dunnigan. This marriage also ended in divorce, though not until her son was an adult. After Dunnigan completed her undergraduate degree in 1932 at West Kentucky Industrial College

In 1948, Alice Dunnigan became the first Black woman journalist to travel with a president, joining Harry S. Truman on his famous cross-country campaign trip. [Rodger Streitmatter]

in Paducah, she taught for ten years in Logan County schools.

Despite her training, Alice Dunnigan found it hard to make ends meet on a teacher's salary. In 1942, tired of the economic struggle and of the humiliating summer jobs available to her in Russellville, Dunnigan took a federal civil service examination and headed to Washington, D.C. There she found that, as in Kentucky, jobs were not distributed or promotions

awarded without regard to race. By the end of World War II, she had advanced from entry-level clerk to first-rung professional in the Office of Price Administration, but with the war's end the government scaled down its operation and Dunnigan soon found herself unemployed.

Her job search, even with the aid of a government placement office, met with one disappointment after another, each in Dunnigan's opinion tied to race discrimination. Dunnigan turned hopefully to journalism. While teaching in Russellville, she had gained some experience by writing for several of the state's Black newspapers, including the *Owensburg Enterprise* and the *Louisville Defender*. In 1946, she applied to the Associated Negro Press (ANP) for a position as the news service's Washington, D.C., correspondent. Claude Barnett, ANP's founder and director, rejected Dunnigan's application for correspondent, but offered her employment on a space-rate basis, rather than pay her a salary. Dunnigan, desperate for a job and hopeful that she might eventually impress Barnett, accepted his terms—$5 per column of a thousand words.

From the beginning, her relationship with Barnett and the ANP proved frustrating, and she often felt that she and the ANP worked at cross purposes. It was practically impossible to support herself in Washington, D.C., as a piecework journalist and Dunnigan engaged in a more or less continuous battle to establish and protect her professional standing. Notwithstanding formidable barriers, Dunnigan managed to obtain congressional and White House press credentials. As a White House correspondent, in one of the highlights of her career, she accompanied Harry Truman's 1948 campaign train from Washington, D.C., to California.

In 1960, Dunnigan left the ANP to work on the Kennedy-Johnson campaign. Vice-President Lyndon Johnson rewarded her efforts the following year by appointing Dunnigan as a consultant to the president's Committee on Equal Employment Opportunity. She continued working for the Equal Employment Opportunity Commission, established by the Civil Rights Act of 1964, and later became a Department of Labor information specialist. By her own analysis, with the changing political tides signaled by the 1968 election of Richard Nixon, her opportunities for retention as a federal employee receded and she turned back to various writing projects. Among them, she published a massive autobiography in 1974, and a rambling history of African-Americans in her native state in 1982. Alice Dunnigan died in Washington, D.C., on May 6, 1983.

BIBLIOGRAPHY

Dunnigan, Alice Allison. *A Black Woman's Experience—From School House to White House* (1974), and *The Fascinating Story of Black Kentuckians: Their Heritage and Traditions* (1982); Hill, Ruth Edmonds. "Interview with Alice Allison Dunnigan," *Black Women Oral History Project* (1991); *NBAW*; the Claude A. Barnett papers are at the Chicago Historical Society, Chicago, Illinois; and the Alice Allison Dunnigan papers are at the Moorland-Spingarn Research Center, Howard University, Washington, D.C.

V. A. SHADRON

DUSTER, ALFREDA BARNETT (1904-1983)

Alfreda Barnett Duster will be remembered most for her successful resurrection of the works of her mother, Ida B. Wells-Barnett, from the dustbins of American history. Although the city of Chicago had named a public housing project for Wells-Barnett before World War II, outside the city limits only a handful of scholars had ever heard of her. For nearly thirty years, Duster painstakingly researched and edited an early first draft of her mother's moving autobiography, then cajoled a score of publishers before one finally agreed to publish it. Wells-Barnett now occupies an increasingly prominent place in history.

As the youngest daughter of Ida B. Wells-Barnett, from early childhood Alfreda had watched public life and the perpetual spotlight of notoriety consume much of her mother's energies. Even into her early teens, she was a constant companion at civic club meetings and public lectures, where her mother was much in demand. For the first half of her life, Duster avoided public life and laid no claim to her mother's legacy. Yet a series of forces moved her more and more onto the public stage, where she slowly emerged as an important public figure in her own right.

Alfreda Barnett was born on September 3, 1904, the daughter of Ferdinand L. Barnett and Ida B. Wells. Barnett was one of the first African-American attorneys in Chicago in 1878 and the founder and publisher of the first Black newspaper in the city, the *Conservator*. Wells is credited with pioneering investigative journalism and arousing the conscience of the nation to stop mob lynchings of African-Americans. Alfreda therefore grew up in a household with a strong tradition of public service to the Black community.

Alfreda attended Douglass Elementary School and Wendell Phillips High School on Chicago's South Side, then went on to earn a bachelor of philosophy degree from the University of Chicago in 1924. One of only four African-Americans in her class, she would later reminisce about how she, a very talented swimmer and tennis player, was not allowed to play tennis or swim on campus. (Some forty years later, as a member of the Women's Board of the University of Chicago, she would monitor and influence policies to reduce gender and race discrimination.)

Alfreda then worked in her father's law offices, where, through her brother, Herman (also an attorney), she met and on July 9, 1925, married Benjamin Cecil Duster of Mount Vernon, Indiana. Although a graduate of Indiana State Normal School, Ben Duster never pursued a career in education. During the trying years of the Great Depression, he withdrew from the world, seldom holding steady employment. Nev-

ertheless determined to raise a family and provide a nurturing home environment, the couple had five children. In 1945, Ben Duster died suddenly at the age of fifty-four, leaving Alfreda with the task of rearing the children, at that time ranging in age from nine to eighteen.

Having no savings, after the death of her husband Duster joined the staff of the Southside Community Committee, an organization that sponsored youth programs ranging from entertainment activities to work with probation and parole officers. She supple-

Alfreda Duster is best remembered for her successful resurrection of the works of her mother, Ida B. Wells-Barnett, from the dustbins of history. In this 1917 Barnett family portrait, she is shown as a young woman standing beside her mother. The family members are: (standing) Hulette D. Barnett (wife of Albert G. Barnett), Herman Kohlsaat Barnett, Ferdinand L. Barnett, Jr., Ida B. Barnett, Jr., Charles Aked Barnett, Alfreda M. Barnett, and Albert G. Barnett; (seated) Ferdinand L. Barnett, Sr., Beatrice Barnett, Audrey Barnett, Ida B. Wells-Barnett; (foreground) Hulette E. Barnett, Florence B. Barnett; the four little girls are the children of Albert and Hulette Barnett. [The Joseph Regenstein Library, The University of Chicago]

mented her meager earnings of approximately $150 per month by using her clerical skills to fill out income tax forms for neighbors and friends and take on typing and mimeographing work for ministers and students. She routinely worked many hours into the night at such tasks.

Living in an environment hardly conducive to her children's academic achievement, she characteristically turned her adversity to advantage. She involved the children in helping perform her clerical tasks by assembling, stapling, and stamping, meanwhile employing a potpourri of home-based academic achievement strategies, such as word games and mathematical problems. She was a forceful presence in the Parent-Teacher Association (PTA), often serving as president, and in 1950 she became the first Black woman to receive the PTA's Mother of the Year Award in Chicago.

Eventually she was able to send all five children to college and see them become president of the National Association of Minority Enterprise Small Business Investment Corporation (Benjamin); architect and architectural engineer and participating associate at Skidmore, Owings & Merrill (Charles); Commonwealth Edison executive and member of the cabinet of Governor Thompson as director of business and economic development for the state of Illinois (Donald); special education administrator for Los Angeles County (Alfreda Duster Ferrell); and professor of sociology and director of the Institute for the Study of Social Change at the University of California, Berkeley (Troy).

The remarkable feat of successful child rearing in these unlikely circumstances was only one of her careers. Slowly, Duster found herself moving more and more into a public life. It was during this period that Duster worked late at night on her favorite personal project, completing her mother's unfinished autobiography. For the next quarter century, on weekends and during vacations, she followed leads to Mississippi and Tennessee, buttressing the facts with her own skillful research and carefully re-editing the early draft. When she felt it was ready for publication, initially she had difficulty interesting a publisher in the project, but events of the 1960s led to demands for a fuller history of the Reconstruction era. Finally, in 1970, under the editorship of John Hope Franklin, the University of Chicago Press published *Crusade for Justice: The Autobiography of Ida B. Wells*, edited and with an introduction by Alfreda B. Duster.

Upon publication of the book, Duster began a decade of public speaking at universities and other public forums around the country. Much like her mother before her, she helped increase the consciousness of students and faculty alike about the economic and political strategies that were at the core of the "crusade for justice."

With the resurgence of interest in the life of Wells-Barnett, the book has been used as a standard reference work in classrooms and libraries across the country and in Europe. It was the basis of a Public Broadcasting Service (PBS) television documentary in 1989 and later served as a catalyst for the U.S. Postal Service's issuance of a commemorative stamp in early 1990, called Black Heritage U.S.A.

Duster likewise produced a legacy of her own. In 1973, the University of Chicago Alumni Association awarded her its prestigious Citation for Public Service. In 1978, for her life's work and public service, she was awarded a doctorate of humane letters by Chicago State University. She died the grandmother of fifteen and the grande dame of a distinguished family, who had helped rekindle and rejoin the legacy of Ida B. Wells-Barnett.

BIBLIOGRAPHY

Duster, Alfreda M. Black Women's Oral History Project interview. Schlesinger Library, Radcliffe College, Cambridge, Massachusetts.

TROY DUSTER

DYKES, EVA BEATRICE (1893-1986)

Eva Beatrice Dykes devoted her early life to acquiring impeccable academic credentials. A pioneer and model of academic excellence, Dr. Dykes served the Black community throughout her life, using her knowledge to educate thousands of young Black people. Born in Washington, D.C., in 1893, Dykes was one of three Black women to receive their Ph.D. degrees in 1921, the first Black women to earn doctorates.

Dykes graduated from Howard University with a B.A. in English (summa cum laude) in 1914. She entered Radcliffe College in 1916 earning a second B.A. (magna cum laude) in 1917, and was elected to Phi Beta Kappa. She received her M.A. degree in English in 1918 and a Ph.D. in English Philology in 1921.

In 1929, after teaching at Dunbar High School in Washington, D.C., for eight years, she became associate professor of English at Howard University. Dykes moved to Oakwood College in Huntsville, Alabama, in 1946 to head the English department,

Longtime head of the English Department at Oakwood College in Huntsville, Alabama, Eva Beatrice Dykes was one of the first three Black women to earn a Ph.D. [Moorland-Spingarn]

and in 1958 she chaired the accreditation quest committee. In 1978, in appreciation of her contributions, Oakwood College named its new library the Eva Beatrice Dykes Library.

A dedicated teacher, author, and scholar, Eva Beatrice Dykes held her students to the same standards of achievement she demanded of herself. When she died in 1986, Eva Dykes left an enduring legacy of excellence and service.

BIBLIOGRAPHY

Bathurst, Dana. *Eva B. Dykes: A Star to Show the Way* (n.d.); *CBWA* (1982); Dykes, Eva B. Interview with Merce Tate. Schlesinger Library, Radcliffe College, Cambridge, Massachusetts (November 30–December 1, 1977); Rivers, Gertrude B. "The Negro in English Romantic Thought," *Journal of Negro History* (July 1942); Strong, Mary Louise. "Readings from Negro Authors," *Journal of Negro History* (July 1932); Williams, DeWitt S. *She Fulfilled the Impossible Dream: The Story of Eva B. Dykes* (1985).

SELECTED WORKS BY EVA BEATRICE DYKES

"Black Gods of the Metropolis," *Journal of Negro History* (July 1944); "Higher Education of Negroes," *Crisis* (July 1921); "My Lord What a Morning," *Journal of Negro History* (January 1957); *The Negro in English Romantic Thought: or A Study of Sympathy for the Oppressed* (1942); "The Poetry of the Civil War," *Negro History Bulletin* (February 1944); *Readings from Negro Authors for High Schools and Colleges*, ed. Eva B. Dykes, Otellia Cromwell, and Lorenzo Dow Turner (1931); "Rising above Color," *Journal of Negro History* (April 1944); "Three Negro Publishers," *Negro History Bulletin* (January 1943); "William Cullen Bryant: Apostle of Freedom," *Negro History Bulletin* (November 1942).

CATHERINE JOHNSON

E

EARLEY, CHARITY ADAMS (1918-)

In military jargon, "riding point" means being at the very front of an advance guard; it is a position of responsibility and vulnerability. Charity Adams "rode point" during World War II as the first Black commissioned officer in the Women's Army Auxiliary Corps (WAAC; renamed Women's Army Corps [WAC]), and she commanded the only organization of Black women to serve overseas during that war. Her determined leadership gave Black women the opportunity to serve their country. When she left the army with the rank of lieutenant colonel—the highest possible rank except for WAC commander—Charity Adams went from serving her country to serving her community. She flourished equally in both capacities.

Charity Adams was no stranger to discipline before entering the WAC. Born on December 5, 1918, in Kittrell, North Carolina, she was the daughter of Reverend Eugene Adams and Charity A. Adams. Her parents, a minister and a teacher, expected exemplary behavior and educational achievements from their four children, and Charity, the oldest, set an example for her siblings by graduating from high school as valedictorian. She earned a scholarship to Wilberforce University in Ohio and, after graduating in 1938, became a math and science teacher in the Columbia, South Carolina, segregated school system.

In 1942, the dean of women at Wilberforce recommended her for the Women's Army Auxiliary Corps. After completing the necessary applications, she was selected for membership in the first officer-candidate class. After training at Fort Des Moines, she was commissioned on August 29, 1942.

Having experienced segregation in the South, Major Adams was determined to gain respect in the segregated army. While she was in command of the 6888th Central Postal Directory Battalion in Europe, a general reviewing her troops found fault, and when she protested he responded by saying that he would find a white junior officer to show her how to do her job. She replied, "Over my dead body, sir," and he promised a court martial. When Major Adams and her staff began filing court-martial charges against the general for violating policy that forbade racial "emphasis" in any verbal or written commands, reports, or any type of communications between personnel, the general dropped his charges. On other occasions, Major Adams organized boycotts of segregated recreational facilities and military housing in Europe.

After leaving the army in 1946, she completed the requirements for a Master's degree in vocational psychology at Ohio State University. She then worked as a registration officer for the Veterans Administration and as educational director at Miller Music Academy, both in Cleveland; as director of student personnel at Tennessee A & I University in Nashville; and as di-

After World War II, Charity Adams Earley (saluting, right), the first Black commissioned officer in the Women's Army Auxiliary Corps, continued to serve her country by serving her community. [Charity Adams]

rector of student personnel and assistant professor of education at Georgia State College in Savannah. In 1949, she married Stanley A. Earley, Jr., a medical student at the University of Zurich, and moved with him to Switzerland. After gaining proficiency in German, she began taking courses at the University of Zurich and the Jungian Institute of Analytical Psychology.

After the Earleys' return to the United States and the birth of two children, Stanley and Judith, Earley became involved in community affairs. She served on committees, task forces, and corporate boards encompassing all areas of human and social services, civic affairs, education, and business, from the United Way to the Black Leadership Development Program to the Dayton Power and Light Company board of directors. In 1982, she was honored by the Smithsonian Institution in a salute to 110 of the most important women in Black history. Also in that year, the Atlanta chapter of the National Association for the Advancement of Colored People (NAACP) presented her with the Walter White Award for her pioneering service in the military. In 1989, her book, *One Woman's Army: A Black Officer Remembers the WAC*, was published, and she was a guest on the National Public Radio program, *Morning Edition*. In 1991, she was awarded an honorary doctorate in humanities by Wilberforce University and an honorary doctorate in humane letters by the University of Dayton. Upon her retirement from the Dayton Power and Light board of directors, a scholarship at Wilberforce University was established in her honor.

Earley and her husband currently make their home in Dayton, Ohio. Their son is a senior budget analyst for the city of Dayton, and their daughter works for the Department of Publications at the University of Southern California.

Charity Adams Earley entered an army segregated by both race and gender during World War II. By 1992, the fiftieth anniversary of women's membership in the military, those barriers were broken down, largely due to the efforts of Charity Adams Earley and her peers.

BIBLIOGRAPHY

Earley, Charity. *One Woman's Army* (1989), and personal interviews.

MAUREEN CREAMER

EARLY, SARAH JANE WOODSON (1825-1907)

Sarah Jane Woodson was born to Thomas and Jemimma Woodson in Chillicothe, Ohio, on November 15, 1825. As a pioneer Black-feminist-nationalist, she served the Black community through her involvement in the early woman's movement, the

The first Black woman to serve on the faculty of an American university, Sarah Jane Woodson Early was hired by Wilberforce University in 1859. In 1865, the school named her its Preceptress of English and Latin and Lady Principal and Matron. [Schomburg Center]

African Methodist Episcopal Church, and a variety of Black educational institutions.

In 1856, Woodson earned an L.B. degree from Oberlin College, becoming one of the first Black women to obtain a college degree. From 1859 to 1860, while employed by Wilberforce University, she became the first Black woman college faculty member. She taught in many of Ohio's Black community schools and served as principal of the Black public school in Xenia, Ohio, 1860-61. In 1865, she was appointed Wilberforce University's "Preceptress of English and Latin and Lady Principal and Matron."

In 1868, Woodson left Wilberforce to teach at a school for Black girls run by the Freedman's Bureau in Hillsborough, North Carolina. On September 24, 1868, she married Rev. Jordan W. Early, a pioneer in the AME Church movement. While continuing to teach in Black schools throughout the South, Sarah Early participated in her husband's ministry. She led prayer meetings, taught Sunday school, and ministered to the sick. In 1894, she chronicled her husband's life in *The Life and Labors of Rev. J. W. Early*.

Sarah Jane Woodson Early preached and practiced her belief that the Black woman's role in racial uplift and moral reform was crucial. Beginning in 1888, she was appointed Superintendent of the Colored Division of the Women's Christian Temperance Union (WCTU). She remained active in the WCTU as a public lecturer as long as her health allowed. She died of heart disease on August 15, 1907.

BIBLIOGRAPHY

Lawson, Ellen NicKenzie and Marlene D. Merrill. *The Three Sarahs: Documents of Antebellum Black College Women* (1984).

CATHERINE JOHNSON

EDELMAN, MARIAN WRIGHT (1939-)

In the past, legally protecting children meant little more than limiting the number of hours they could spend running a loom or working in a field. Marian Wright Edelman was one of those who changed that, redefining and defending the rights of children everywhere.

Marian Wright was born on June 6, 1939, in Bennettsville, South Carolina. Her parents, Arthur Jerome Wright and Maggie Leola Bowen Wright, instilled in their five children the belief that serving their community was one of life's highest duties.

Marian went to Marlboro Training High School and then on to Spelman College in Atlanta, Georgia. The traveling overseas that she did while still a student changed Edelman's perspective on the world. "After a year's freedom as a person," she said, "I wasn't prepared to go back to a segregated existence."

Wright was back in the United States for her senior year. It was 1960 and civil rights demonstrations were beginning all over the South. When she participated in a sit-in in Atlanta, she was among fourteen students who were arrested. Soon she had decided to forego graduate studies in Russian and become a lawyer. She graduated as valedictorian from Spelman and entered Yale University Law School as a John Hay Whitney Fellow. Her civil rights activities continued. She went to Mississippi to work on voter

registration in 1963 and, after graduation, returned as one of the first two National Association for the Advancement of Colored People Legal Defense and Education interns. She opened a law office, became the first Black woman to pass the bar in Mississippi, got demonstrating students out of jail, and was put in jail herself. She also became involved in several school desegregation cases and served on the board of the Child Development Group of Mississippi, which represented one of the largest Head Start programs in the country.

In 1968, Wright went to Washington, D.C., on a Field Foundation grant and started the Washington Research Project. Her goal was to find out how new and existing laws could be made to work for the poor. Shortly after Robert Kennedy was shot, Wright married Peter Edelman, who had been a legislative assistant to Kennedy; she and Edelman had met in Mississippi. Though she moved with her husband to Boston in 1971 and became director of the Harvard University Center for Law and Education, Marian Wright Edelman regularly flew back to Washington so that she could remain at the helm of the Washington Research Project, which developed into the Children's Defense Fund (CDF). The CDF quickly became the nation's most effective advocate for children and Edelman, as its dedicated director, became known as "the children's crusader." One of the CDF's largest campaigns was against teenage pregnancy, but it has also been active in all areas of children's health, child care, youth employment, social service, child welfare, and adoption.

In 1979, Edelman returned with her husband to Washington, D.C. In 1980, she became chair of the board of trustees of Spelman. She was the first Black and the second woman to hold that position. She has also served on the boards of a wide variety of organizations that are involved in children's welfare, including the Carnegie Council on Children, the March of Dimes, and the United Nations International Children's Emergency Fund (UNICEF) Committee. Her activities are not limited to her work for children. She was also the first Black woman elected to the Yale University Corporation and has served on the boards of a large number of influential political organizations.

Edelman has been called an unusual and effective lobbyist and has communicated her message eloquently and with passion in many arenas. Her books include *Children Out of School in America*, *Portrait of Inequality: Black and White Children in America*, and *A Letter to My Children and Yours*. She was a MacArthur Foundation Fellow in 1985 and has received honor-

Known as "the children's crusader," Marian Wright Edelman is director of the Children's Defense Fund. She has been a powerful voice in the struggle to improve the world for future generations. [Rick Reinhard]

The Children's Defense Fund, the nation's most effective advocate for children, is active in the areas of children's health, child care, employment, social service, child welfare, and adoption. This is the fund's logo. [Children's Defense Fund]

ary degrees from more than thirty universities. She has been throughout her career a powerful voice in the struggle to improve the world for generations to come.

BIBLIOGRAPHY

CBWA; EBA; NBAW; WWBA.

KATHLEEN THOMPSON

EDMONDS, HELEN GRAY (1911-)

Helen Gray Edmonds is a distinguished historian, educator, political activist, and teacher whose contributions to the study of history have been recognized by numerous universities. Her philosophy of education is a traditional one. It seeks to equip students with the essential tools of a holistic education, one that includes all areas of history, not just African-American history.

Helen Gray Edmonds was born in Lawrenceville, Virginia, on December 3, 1911, to John Edward Edmonds and Ann Williams. Her education started at St. Paul's High School and St. Paul's College. "My mother and father inspired us all," Edmonds once said in an interview. "There was never a moment in our family that higher education wasn't stressed." After attending the Lawrenceville schools, she entered Morgan State College and earned a B.A. in

history in 1933. Edmonds furthered her education at Ohio State University, receiving an M.A. in history in 1938 and a Ph.D. in history in 1946. In 1954-55, she did post-doctoral research in the area of modern European history at the University of Heidelberg, Germany.

Edmonds has taught at Virginia Theological Seminary College, St. Paul's College, and North Carolina College, now North Carolina Central University (NCCU) in Durham. She spent much of her career at NCCU as chair of the history department and dean of the graduate school, and from 1983 to 1991 was a member of the university's board of trustees. Edmonds has been the recipient of numerous professional awards, including the Award of Scholarly Distinction from the American Historical Association. Her books

Distinguished historian Helen Gray Edmonds helped make history herself when she seconded Dwight D. Eisenhower's nomination for reelection at the 1956 Republican National Convention.

include *Black Faces in High Places* (1971) and *The Negro in Fusion Politics in North Carolina, 1894-1901* (1973). Many of her articles have been published in professional journals.

In the political arena, Edmonds seconded the nomination of President Dwight David Eisenhower for reelection in 1956. She served as a special emissary for President Eisenhower in Liberia and as an alternate delegate to the United Nations. Edmonds also has been active in the Black community, serving as president of Links, Inc., a national service organization.

Helen Gray Edmonds is a giant in the field of history, who has always sought to achieve a sense of balance in her teaching and writing.

BIBLIOGRAPHY

Durham Morning Herald, "Dr. Helen Edmonds Honored by American Historical Association" (January 19, 1989), and "Dr. Helen Edmonds: Teaching and Making History" (April 5, 1981); *Durham Sun*, "Historian Receives National Award" (September 10, 1982); *News and Observer*, "Retired NCCU Historian Receives Scholar Award" (January 19, 1989); *WWBA* (1977-78).

BEVERLY JONES

EDUCATION

The quest for equal access to education for both women and African-Americans has been a long and difficult one. Both groups have historically been portrayed as intellectually inferior and childlike compared to white men. Consequently, education for all women and for African-American men suffered serious neglect. During the late eighteenth and early nineteenth centuries, the prevailing view of most of American society was that neither women nor African-American men should be educated beyond what was appropriate to their different and inferior roles in society.

ANTEBELLUM ERA

While enslaved African-Americans in the South were legally barred from learning to read prior to Emancipation, free African-Americans in the North had some nominal opportunities for schooling. This was one of the few freedoms they could enjoy, since in many northern states free African-Americans were barred from voting, testifying in court, carrying arms, traveling freely, pursuing certain occupations, and obtaining an equal education. Free African-Americans in the South faced even greater restrictions. They could be sold back into slavery without a certificate of freedom and their right to assembly was restricted. Frequently, a "respectable" white person was required to attend any gathering of free African-Americans.

White women of this era were expected to adhere to the image of idealized womanhood referred to as the "cult of true womanhood" by historian Barbara Welter. This idealized image stressed piety, purity, submissiveness, and domesticity for women. Literature of this period described women's natural fragility. Innocence and modesty were key attributes of the "true woman." Central to the development of this new and perfect woman was the commitment to white women's education that emerged during the early decades of the nineteenth century. Female seminaries flourished throughout this period and offered curricula to correspond to society's expectation of women.

This notion of "true womanhood," of course, did not include African-American women. They could not be viewed as fragile or delicate since they frequently did the same work as slave men. Further, the question of purity in relation to African-American women was also a moot one since African-American women were frequently victims of sexual assaults by overseers and masters, and since they were required to mate with slave men to increase the slave population.

The image of African-American women as subhuman was made clear when Prudence Crandall, a white Quaker school teacher, opened a "genteel female seminary" for women of the prosperous village of Canterbury, Connecticut, in 1831, and in 1833 admitted as one of its students an African-American. This action resulted in most of the white parents withdrawing their daughters. The public ridicule and condemnation that Crandall received prompted her to open a seminary solely for African-American women.

Crandall advertised in the abolitionist newspaper the *Liberator* for her new "High school for young colored Ladies and Misses" (Foner and Pacheco 1984). The references to African-American women as "ladies and misses"—titles reserved for white women—were highly inflammatory to white citizens. Fifteen African-American young women from Philadelphia, Boston, New York, Providence, and Connecticut responded to the ad and enrolled in the boarding school in April 1833. Outraged, the town authorities instituted a law that prohibited the teaching of any out-of-state Black students. A series of events resulted in the demise of the school: the town's members refused to supply food to the school and

Anna Julia Cooper dedicated her life to the education of Blacks. She served as principal of Washington, D.C.'s famous M Street High School and as the president of the city's Frelinghuysen University, an institution dedicated to providing an education to adult "colored working people." [Moorland-Spingarn]

threatened to prosecute the Black students as vagrants and paupers; windows of the school were broken; the water well was polluted; and finally Crandall was arrested for harboring out-of-state African-Americans and the school was burned down.

Despite the efforts of Crandall, most attempts to educate African-Americans were through their own efforts. As early as 1793, a slave, Catherine Ferguson, purchased her freedom in New York and took forty-eight Black and white children from an almshouse and opened Katy Ferguson's School for the Poor. The same year, the Committee for Improving the Condition of Free Blacks in Pennsylvania opened a school and recommended an African-American woman as teacher.

Unlike white society, where men and women lived in separate spheres, African-Americans did not experience sex segregation in their education. Because education had been denied both African-American men and women, it was perceived as being important for the entire race rather than for a specific sex. It was not uncommon for African-American families to relocate to areas where their daughters and sons could receive a better education. For example, when Blanche Harris was denied admission to a white female seminary in Michigan, her entire family moved to Oberlin, Ohio, where she and her four brothers and her sister could receive a good education.

Harris graduated from the Ladies' Department at Oberlin College in 1860 and her sister graduated ten years later. Similarly, the parents of Mary Jane Patterson, who was the first African-American woman to earn a college degree (Oberlin, 1862), moved to Ohio from North Carolina in the 1850s to educate their children. Four of the Patterson children graduated from Oberlin College (three of them daughters).

Education within the African-American community extended beyond the classroom and was augmented by the formation of literary and educational societies. Philadelphia was the leader in the number of such organizations for both men and women. For example, in 1834, a group of African-American women organized the Female Literary Society of Philadelphia. This group's preamble voiced the prevailing ethos of African-Americans during this period, that education was for the improvement of the race and not merely for individual accomplishments. It stated that it was their duty as:

> daughters of a despised race, to use our utmost endeavors to enlighten the understanding, to cultivate the talents entrusted to our keeping, that by so doing, we may in a great measure, break down the strong barrier of prejudice, and raise ourselves to an equality with those of our

fellow beings, who differ from us in complexion. (*Liberator* 1831)

The women of this literary society submitted unsigned poems, essays, and short stories to be critiqued by one another. Their works were frequently published in the abolitionist newspaper the *Liberator*. During a period when women of the larger society were universally ridiculed for educational aspirations, within the Black community, African-American women received encouragement and praise for their educational efforts.

Obtaining a secondary education was difficult for both African-American women and men prior to the Civil War. Thus, the founding in 1829 of St. Frances Academy of Rome in Baltimore, a boarding school, was an important event for the race. The school was founded by the Oblate Order, a group of French-educated Black nuns. Most of the women were from prosperous families. One of the nuns, Elizabeth Lange, who became the First Superior of the Order and head of the school, had operated a free school for poor Black children in her home prior to the opening of St. Frances. Classes were offered in both French and Spanish. Because the St. Frances Academy was the only secondary institution available to African-American females, the school was well known. Girls from all over the country and Canada attended the academy. To preserve their native language, the Sisters conducted classes at the academy on alternate days completely in French. By 1865, the school was coed and known simply as the St. Frances Academy.

Other institutions emerged during this period as well. The Institute for Colored Youth in Philadelphia was established in 1852 by the Society of Friends as the first coeducational classical high school, and the Normal School for Colored Girls was founded by a white woman, Myrtilla Miner, in the District of Columbia. These institutions produced some of the first formally trained African-American teachers in the North prior to Emancipation.

Although most opportunities for the education of African-Americans were in the North prior to the Civil War, many clandestine schools existed in the South during this period. For example, numerous such schools were reported in Savannah, Georgia. Julian Froumountaine, a Black woman from Santo Domingo, openly conducted a free school for African-Americans in that city as early as 1819, and she continued to teach secretly after the 1830s when such activity became illegal in the South. Another Black woman, known only as Miss DeaVeaux, opened an underground school in 1838 and operated it for over twenty-five years without the knowledge of local whites. There were similar schools in other areas of the South as well. In Natchez, Mississippi, slave Milla Granson learned to read and write from her master's children and then she taught hundreds of slaves to read and write in what they termed Milla's midnight school because the classes were held after midnight. These educational activities reveal not only the importance that African-Americans of this era placed on education but also demonstrate the risk that they took to obtain it. Having been deprived of education, many Black women sought after the Civil War to become educators of their race.

One such example is Fanny Jackson Coppin. Born a slave in 1837 in the District of Columbia, her freedom was purchased by the time she was twelve by a devoted aunt. She was sent to New Bedford, Massachusetts, and later to Newport, Rhode Island, to live with relatives where it was believed her educational opportunities would be greater. Surrounded by the numerous Black self-help and literary groups, as a young girl Coppin decided "to get an education and help my people" (Perkins 1987). While working as a domestic in Newport, she was allowed by her employers to hire a tutor for one hour, three days a week. She later attended the segregated schools of Newport and by 1859 had completed the normal course at the Rhode Island State Normal School. She continued her education by enrolling in Oberlin College in Ohio in 1860, the only institution in the nation that admitted both Black Americans and white women into the same program with white men. Coppin obtained financial assistance from Bishop Daniel Payne of the African Methodist Episcopal Church.

Coppin excelled at Oberlin and she graduated with a baccalaureate degree in 1865, becoming one of the earliest Black women to obtain a college degree. She spent her entire professional career as principal of the Institute for Colored Youth in Philadelphia.

Bound together by a common sorrow, Black women and men, whether free or slave, were intricately linked. Viewed by society as neither humans nor citizens, they had to work together to "uplift" the race. This effort required the contributions of both men and women. Consequently, as the Black community sought to obtain whatever education was available to them during this period, the education of women was included.

EMANCIPATION AND RECONSTRUCTION

With the end of legal slavery, African-Americans immediately sought to obtain the education denied them in bondage. Numerous studies have recounted the efforts former slaves made to become literate. Black scholar W.E.B. Du Bois reported in his 1901 study of the Negro Common School that two years after the Civil War fewer than 100,000 African-American children were in schools in the South. However, the demand for literacy was so great that by 1900, more than 1.5 million were enrolled.

It is well known that several thousand northern white female teachers journeyed to the South during and after the Civil War to teach in private schools established by an array of missionary and religious organizations, and by the federal government's Freedman's Bureau. It is less well known that Black women played a crucial role in the massive task of educating the newly emancipated slaves. When the American Missionary Association (AMA), the largest of the organizations to establish schools in the South for African-Americans, arrived to open a school in Fortress Monroe, Virginia, in 1861, it found the prosperous Black woman Mary S. Peake already teaching. Her school became the first AMA school in the South. Many of the African-American women educated in the North prior to Emancipation migrated South to teach.

These private elementary and secondary institutions (along with Black colleges established in the South in the decades following the Civil War) educated the bulk of the earliest African-American teachers. Over 70 percent of the teacher training took place in these private Black institutions. The white South was so hostile to the education of African-Americans that Du Bois reported that between 1900 and 1910 the number of Black students attending publicly financed common schools had in some places decreased.

Most Black colleges in the South were overwhelmingly devoted to preparatory and secondary education in the nineteenth century. Consequently, most Black women and men obtained their collegiate training during this period from predominantly white institutions. Du Bois reported in his 1900 study of Black college graduates that a total of 252 women compared to 2,272 men had obtained baccalaureate degrees. Of this number 65 had graduated from Oberlin College. Only 22 of the 156 graduates of Black colleges by 1900 were women.

This great disparity in educational achievement led some African-American women to become concerned and question this disturbing trend. In a book entitled *A Voice from the South*, published in 1892, Oberlin graduate and educator Anna Julia Cooper addressed the issue of growing sexism within the Black community and the limited educational oppor-

It is well known that thousands of white women journeyed to the South during and after the Civil War to teach newly emancipated slaves. It is less well known that Black women also played a crucial role in the massive task of educating freed people. This is a schoolroom circa 1902. [Library of Congress]

tunities for African-American women. She wrote, "I fear the majority of colored men do not yet think it worthwhile that women aspire to higher education. . . . Let money be raised and scholarships be founded in our colleges and universities for self-supporting worthy young women."

During the 1890s, African-American women became increasingly concerned about issues specific to women and children of the race and organized the National Association of Colored Women in 1895. Education, job opportunities, protection from sexual assaults by white men in the South, and defense of the character of African-American women were the primary focus of this group. With Black women concerned about the special plight of African-American girls and the growing population of single Black women in the nation, numerous attempts were made to establish schools exclusively for Black women.

Among the first African-American women to establish such a school was Lucy Laney. Born free in Georgia in 1854, Laney attended the schools of the American Missionary Association and in 1873 she graduated from the first normal class of Atlanta University. With the assistance of the Presbyterian Board of Missions, in 1886 Laney founded the Haines Normal and Industrial Institute in Augusta, Georgia. Laney had hoped that Haines would be a girls' school, but the need for a high school for both boys and girls resulted in the institution's becoming coed, though most of the students were girls.

Likewise, Mary McLeod Bethune, who became a renowned educator and leader within the African-American community, was inspired by Lucy Laney to establish a school for Black girls. Bethune taught at Haines for one year and later moved to Daytona Beach, Florida, where she opened the Daytona Normal and Industrial School for Negro Girls in 1904. Although Bethune intended it to be for females only, her own son attended from the first day the school was opened. As with Laney's Haines Institute, the need for education was so great that single-sex institutions were a luxury the Black community could not afford. At Bethune's school, within two years, boys showed up at the school. However, it was not until 1923 that a formal merger took place with the Cookman Institute for Boys, creating Bethune-Cookman College. It was not until 1943, however, that this institution awarded baccalaureate degrees.

Nannie Burroughs, a graduate of M Street High School in Washington, D.C., founded the National Training School for Women and Girls in 1909 in the nation's capital. A prominent churchwoman in the Baptist Church, Burroughs's school was initially funded by the National Baptist Women's Convention, an auxiliary to the men's convention. Burroughs was a devotee of Booker T. Washington and her school's emphasis was on "Christian womanhood" and vocational training. Sewing, home economics, practical and home nursing, bookkeeping, shorthand, typing, gardening, laundering, interior design, printing, shoe repairing, and barbering were taught. The school closed with Burroughs's death in 1961.

TWENTIETH CENTURY

Few four-year institutions existed solely for Black women in the twentieth century. The best known are Spelman College in Atlanta, Georgia, and Bennett College in Greensboro, North Carolina. Spelman College was established in 1881 by two white New England women and Bennett College was established in 1873 by the Methodist Episcopal Church as a coeducational institution. It became a women's college in 1926.

Despite the few efforts at single-sex education for Black girls and women, coeducation was the norm for Black education. As college departments in Black colleges slowly grew, so did the number of women enrolled. Du Bois reported that 23 percent of the college students of Howard, Atlanta, Fisk, and Shaw in the year 1898-99 were women. However, by 1910 Black women graduates annually slightly outnumbered Black male college graduates. This trend continued throughout the century and, except for the decade of the 1920s, African-American women annually earned more college degrees than Black men every year.

The reasons for the great disparity in the numbers of African-American women and men with college degrees are complicated. Although women outnumbered men nationally in high school attendance in general in the twentieth century, Black women did so at numbers greater than the national average. For example, public high school enrollment figures by race and gender for fifteen southern cities in 1915 show that while white women represented 56 percent of all white high school students, African-American women represented 66 percent of Black students attending high schools within the same cities.

The disenfranchisement of Black men after Reconstruction and the fact that Black men could not obtain employment commensurate with their educational experiences resulted in Black families educating daughters disproportionately to men in the twentieth century. Teachers were critically needed in the developing school systems in the South and employment was virtually guaranteed to any minimally trained

Although there were a few efforts at single-sex education for Black girls and women, coeducation was the norm for Black education. Here, students in a Tuskegee Institute history class learn the story of Pocahontas. [Library of Congress]

person. While the salaries in the Black public schools of the South were abysmal, the work was highly respectable and desperately needed. In the twentieth century, teaching was increasingly viewed as primarily women's work and so Black women were overrepresented in the student bodies of the state land-grant teacher training colleges. Of the 14,028 Black students admitted to the seventeen Black land-grant colleges in 1928, 64 percent of those admitted by high school certificate were women and 73 percent admitted by examination were women.

Although Black men taught at percentages higher than white men, as other employment opportunities opened to them they abandoned the teaching profession. For example, the 1930 census reported that 45,672 Black women were schoolteachers, compared with 8,767 Black men. A 1938 study of Black college graduates indicated that 71 percent of Black elementary school teachers and 63 percent of Black high school teachers were women. Despite these figures, few Black women were represented in leadership positions within these schools. Only one in fifteen high school principals was female and one in every five elementary school principals was female.

These data were disturbing to Lucy Diggs Slowe, the first Black female dean at Howard University (1922-37). In a survey Slowe conducted in 1931 of 153 first-year women at Howard University concerning their careers, 90 percent indicated that they aspired to teach—particularly at one of the leading Black liberal arts institutions. Noting a trend in Black women's limited career choices, Slowe wrote an article in 1933 entitled "Higher Education of Negro Women." Repeating concerns voiced by Anna Julia Cooper three decades earlier, Slowe pointed out the varied career opportunities for Black men but the limited areas of education and social work for Black women. Surveying four coeducational Black colleges, Slowe discovered that Black women received little in courses, activities, or role models that prepared them for leadership. Although leadership was expected of educated Black Americans, Slowe charged that Black colleges perpetuated a conservative view of women that limited their leadership growth. Black women were expected to serve and not lead.

Unlike academic white women—who were shut out of faculty positions at most coeducational institutions except in traditional female disciplines and were virtually unemployable at all-male institutions—Black women were represented on the faculties and staffs of most campuses that employed Black Americans. The need was so great for trained Black faculty that barring women from such positions due to gender bias would have been difficult. Though white elites dominated the college presidencies of many of the elite private Black colleges well into the twentieth century, Black land-grant institutions had African-American presidents from the beginning. In addition, most students at these institutions were women. Yet a woman has never been president of one of these institutions.

Three private colleges for Black women have had women as presidents. In 1955, Willa Player became president of the private Bennett College, making her the first Black female president of a college since Bethune founded Bethune College. The appointment in 1987 of Johnnetta Cole as the first Black woman president of Spelman College was another such historic event.

CONCLUSION

Motivated by the notion of "race uplift," Black women throughout the nineteenth century sought an education to be of service to their race. By the beginning of the twentieth century, Black women began to organize to challenge prevailing racist assumptions about their moral conduct. Unfortunately, as they were founded, Black colleges established rigid rules and regulations concerning the social conduct of their female students, which had the effect of reinforcing the notion that Black women were wild, untamed, and needed constant surveillance. As Jeanne Noble writes: "Her [the African-American woman's] education in many instances appears to have been based on a philosophy which implied that she was weak and immoral and that at best she should be made fit to rear her children and keep house for her husband" (Noble 1956).

Despite these discouragements, throughout the early twentieth century the need for teachers of Black students resulted in thousands of Black women attending normal and teachers' colleges. Despite the fact that by the 1950s, twice as many Black women as Black men were college graduates, few Black women obtained advanced or professional degrees. This was directly related to Black women's overrepresentation in teacher training colleges with curricula that stressed domestic training at the expense of courses required as preparation for graduate schools. Even at Black liberal arts colleges, as Lucy Diggs Slowe's research suggested, Black female students seldom considered professions other than teaching.

A 1946 survey of Black American holders of doctorates and professional degrees indicated that 381 African-Americans had earned such degrees since 1876—but only forty-five were women. Of the top five institutions that had awarded baccalaureate degrees to the Black Ph.D.s, two were male institutions—Lincoln University in Pennsylvania and Morehouse College in Atlanta, Georgia. The other three—Howard, Fisk, and Virginia Union—were institutions with strong liberal arts and professional schools that enrolled large numbers of men. None of the teacher-training institutions or Black state land-grant colleges, where women were heavily concentrated, ranked among even the top twenty baccalaureate-producing institutions. Overwhelmingly, the Black women who received doctorates were graduates of white undergraduate institutions where they had taken liberal arts courses compatible with graduate training.

Despite a long and impressive history of African-American women's educational attainments—given the enormous obstacles—women are finally and slowly beginning to see their achievements rewarded with positions of leadership. Du Bois, early in the twentieth century, recognized the extraordinary sacrifices and contributions made by African-American women on behalf of their race. He also noted their lack of recognition by most men of the race. In his 1920 publication *Darkwater: Voices from within the Veil*, he noted that "after the [Civil] war, the sacrifice of Negro women for freedom and uplift [was] one of the finest chapters in their history." He went on to say that while the men of the race received more press and praise for their accomplishments, women's achievements had been more impressive: "As I look about me today in this veiled world of mine, despite the noisier and more spectacular advance of my brothers, I instinctively feel and know that it is the five million women of my race who really count." Pointing out that Black women were the foundation of the public schools, settlement houses, and churches within the African-American communities of the nation and that Blacks had more than $1 billion in accumulated property and goods, Du Bois wrote, "who shall say how much of it has been wrung from the hearts of servant girls and washerwomen and women toilers in the fields?"

The dawn of the twenty-first century brings with it the hope and expectation that African-American women's educational attainments and aspirations will be acknowledged and rewarded at last.

BIBLIOGRAPHY

Anderson, James D. *The Education of Blacks in the South, 1860-1935* (1988); Barnett, Evelyn Brooks. "Nannie Burroughs and the Education of Black Women." In *The Afro-American Woman: Struggles and Images,* ed. Sharon Harley and Rosalyn Terborg-Penn (1978); Berlin, Ira. *Slaves without Masters: The Free Negro in the Antebellum South* (1974); Bracey, John H., et al., eds. *Free Blacks in America, 1800-1860* (1971); Cooper, Anna Julia. *A Voice from the South* (1892); Du Bois, W.E.B. *The College Bred Negro* (1900), and *Darkwater: Voices from within the Veil* (1920), and *The Negro Common School* (1901); Foner, Philip S. and Josephine F. Pacheco. *Three Who Dared: Prudence Crandall, Margaret Douglass, Myrtila Miner—Champions of Antebellum Black Education* (1984); Greene, Harry Washington. *Holders of Doctorates among American Negroes* (1946); Henle, Ellen and Marlene Merrill. "Antebellum Black Coeds at Oberlin College," *Women's Studies Newsletter* (Spring 1979); Johnson, Charles S. *The Negro College Graduate* (1969); *Liberator* (December 3, 1831); Litwack, Leon F. *North of Slavery: The Negro in the Free States, 1790-1860* (1961); Noble, Jeanne. *The Negro College Woman's College Education* (1956); Peare, Catherine Owens. *Mary McLeod Bethune: A Biography* (1964); Perkins, Linda M. *Fanny Jackson Coppin and the Institute for Colored Youth* (1987); Sherwood, Grace H. *The Oblates' Hundred and One Years* (1931); Slowe, Lucy. "Higher Education of Negro Woman," *Journal of Negro Education* (1933); Woodson, Carter G. *The African Background Outlined: or Handbook for the Study of the Negro* ([1936] 1968); Wright, Richard R., Jr. *The Negro in Pennsylvania: A Study in Economic History* (1912).

LINDA M. PERKINS

EDWARDS, LENA FRANCES (1900-1986)

In 1964, President Lyndon B. Johnson awarded Lena Frances Edwards, M.D., the Presidential Medal of Freedom, the highest civilian award for service. No other obstetrician-gynecologist has ever received this honor. Given Lena Frances Edwards's dedication to her profession and devotion to providing medical services to migrant workers and other low-income women, it is understandable that she was singled out.

Lena Edwards was born in Washington, D.C., on September 17, 1900, to Marie Coakley Edwards and Thomas Edwards. She was the valedictorian of her 1917 Dunbar High School class. She began her career in community practice in 1924 upon graduation from Howard University College of Medicine. Skillful attendance at home deliveries established her reputation in obstetrics.

In 1931, Edwards was appointed to the first medical staff of the Margaret Hague Maternity Hospital in

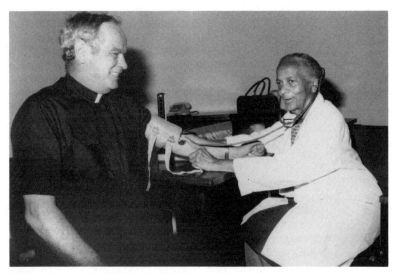

Dr. Lena Frances Edwards was honored as a "Living Legend" by Howard University's medical alumni in 1984. For her dedication to the medical profession and her devotion to providing medical services to migrant workers and other low-income women, she received the Presidential Medal of Freedom in 1964.

Jersey City, New Jersey. She served as assistant gynecologist until 1945, when the color and gender bars were lifted and she was allowed an opportunity for specialized training. Late in life she revealed that it had been the departmental secretary who had exposed the availability of positions and embarrassed the chairman into accepting her. In 1948, she passed the oral examination of the American Board of Obstetrics and Gynecology. Dr. Edwards's biography recounts that she was rebuffed by the medical establishment upon return to her still segregated native Washington, D.C. However, by the time she was forty-eight she was one of the first African-American women certified in the specialty. For three decades, in part because of Edwards, the Hague Hospital was among the leading clinical centers in the country, renowned for research on the hypertensive conditions of pregnancy. Indeed, the first issue of volume one of the hospital's *Bulletin* contains a description of a patient under her care.

In 1954, after many years at the Hague Hospital, Dr. Edwards returned to Howard University as a faculty member. Then, in 1959, she redefined her course in midlife. A devout Roman Catholic, she subsidized the founding of Our Lady of Guadeloupe Maternity Clinic in Hereford, Texas. She provided medical services for migrant workers at the clinic. It was this work for which President Lyndon B. Johnson awarded her the Presidential Medal of Freedom.

Dr. Edwards returned to New Jersey in 1965. Her efforts to introduce Pap smear screening to low-income women were recognized in 1973 by an award presented by Dr. LaSalle D. Lefall, the cancer surgeon who became the first African-American president of the American Cancer Society.

Dr. Edwards endowed a scholarship fund at Howard University for students interested in family medicine. In 1984, the medical alumni association honored her as a "Living Legend." She received honorary doctorates from St. Peter's College in Jersey City and the University of Portland.

Lena Edwards died on December 3, 1986. She had married a medical school classmate, Dr. Keith Madison. They had six children. Among them, Edward Madison and Marie Madison Metoyer are practicing physicians. She was also survived by sons Paul, John, and Thomas, and daughter Genevieve, sixteen grandchildren, and six great-grandchildren.

BIBLIOGRAPHY

Alexander, Leslie. Obituary. *Journal of National Medical Association* (July 1987), and "Lena Edwards—Pioneering Black Physician," *Washington Post* (October 27, 1985), and "Monthly Staff Conference, Feb. 2, 1948: Case Report and Discussion of a Maternal Death," *Bulletin of the Margaret Hague Maternity Hospital* (March 1948); Knapp, Sally. *Women Doctors Today* (1947); Scally, S. M. Anthony. *Medicine, Motherhood and Mercy: The Story of a Black Woman Doctor* (1979).

DEBORAH SMITH

ELAW, ZILPHA (b. c. 1790)

As an itinerant evangelist, Zilpha Elaw's life was characterized by an intense journey toward spiritual empowerment, a need to define herself as a Black woman in a racist society, and psychological wholeness through preaching the word of God. Born around 1790 just outside Philadelphia, Zilpha was one of three children who survived childbirth. At twelve years of age, following her mother's death in childbirth with her twenty-second child, she was placed by her father in service to a Quaker family, where she remained until she was eighteen years old.

Coming from a pious home where God's praises were joyously sung, she found the silent devotion of Quakers unsettling and was drawn, instead, to the emotional appeal of the evangelical Protestants proselytizing in the area. During a period of frustration shortly after her placement in the Quaker home and, undoubtedly, grief over the loss of her father only one and a half years after her mother's death, Zilpha began having visionary experiences. In the initial instance, Jesus came to her as an apparition, with arms opened to receive her, while she was performing one of her chores, milking a cow. As with most Black women evangelists of that time period, her religious conversion followed this vision around 1804. Visionary experiences, for most Black women evangelists, served not only to transform their lives but allowed them to criticize the existing social order, particularly slavery, racism, and sexism. Following subsequent visionary experiences that were to last throughout her life, she joined a Methodist Episcopal Society near Philadelphia in 1808.

In 1810, Zilpha married Joseph Elaw and moved to Burlington, New Jersey, where Joseph had found employment. A daughter was born to the couple soon thereafter. Because Joseph had been expelled from the Methodist Episcopal Society and encouraged Zilpha to renounce her religion, her religious zeal strained their marriage. In 1817, during a week-long camp meeting and intense religious revival, Elaw fell into a trance. Recovering from this trance, Elaw believed that she had received sanctification of her soul from God. Encouraged by other women, Elaw gave her first public exhortation at the meeting and, following a second camp meeting, became an exhorter in the Burlington area. This sort of sanctification experience of being totally in harmony with the Divine Will enabled women to withstand societal criticism for their nontraditional ministerial roles.

Elaw's husband died in 1823, and she and her daughter were forced to labor as domestics. Incensed by the racial prejudice that allowed only white children to attend public schools, she opened a school for Black children sometime later but closed it after two years, believing the Lord had called her to start her evangelical ministry.

Soon, Elaw was on the itinerant ministry circuit and became the preaching partner of Jarena Lee, the first Black woman evangelist of record, for a time in western Pennsylvania. Elaw never preached under the auspices of any religious denomination but relied for guidance upon her inner sense of spirituality. In 1828, Elaw displayed her courage by preaching in Washington, D.C., and the slaveholding states of Maryland and Virginia to both Black and white converts. Repulsed by both slavery and racial prejudice, Elaw denounced in her messages the abominations of both. She also sought to justify, according to the Scriptures, her right to preach. Her ministry was largely confined to the northeastern and mid-Atlantic region of the country until 1840. In that year, believing that God had ordained her for a greater undertaking, Elaw went to central England, where she recorded in her memoirs that she preached over a thousand sermons on the word of God and enjoyed great success. Her memoirs close in 1845, when she writes of her plans to return home from England.

BIBLIOGRAPHY

Elaw, Zilpha. "Memoirs of the Life, Religious Experience, Ministerial Travels, and Labours of Mrs. Zilpha Elaw: An American Female of Colour." In *Sisters of the Spirit: Three Black Women's Autobiographies of the Nineteenth Century*, ed. William L. Andrews ([1846] 1986).

GAYLE T. TATE

ELDRIDGE, ELLEANOR
(1784-c. 1845)

A skilled businesswoman and amateur lawyer, Elleanor Eldridge labored industriously to become respected in the Black community. She excelled in her crafts and business ventures, and as an amateur lawyer she assisted her brother, George, in securing an acquittal of charges that he "horsewhipped and otherwise barbarously treated a man on the highway."

Elleanor Eldridge was born on March 27, 1784, in Warwick, Rhode Island. Her father, Robin Eldridge, was an African who was captured with his entire family and brought to America on a slave ship. Her mother, Hannah Prophet, was a Native American. Eldridge was born free in part because of the bill enacted in 1784 that called for gradual emancipation.

Robin Eldridge and two of his brothers had fought in the American Revolution. They were promised their freedom and two hundred acres of land apiece for their service. When the war ended they were pronounced free, but because they had been paid in worthless Old Continental currency, they were unable to take possession of their lands.

Eldridge was the youngest of seven daughters, only five of whom lived to maturity. After her mother died when she was ten years old, Eldridge was invited to live with the family of Joseph Baker, for whom her mother had worked as a laundress. Despite the protest of her father, she accepted, receiving wages of twenty-five cents a week, and remained for six years. During these years with the Baker family, she became skilled in spinning, weaving, arithmetic, and all types of housework. She was considered a fully accomplished weaver by the age of fourteen and made carpets and bedspreads, among other things. At the age of sixteen, she went to work for Captain Benjamin Green and his family, first as a spinner and later as a dairy worker, making cheeses recognized as of "premium quality."

After Eldridge's father died when she was nineteen, she traveled 180 miles to Adams, Massachusetts, where her aunt helped her to obtain letters of administration of her father's estate. When she returned to Warwick, she settled the estate and went back to work for Captain Green, where she remained until his death in 1812. She then returned home to live with her oldest sister, Lettise.

Eldridge and her sister went into business, doing weaving, nursing, and soap making. Eldridge was so successful that she purchased a lot and built a house, which she rented out for forty dollars a year. After three years, she was persuaded by another sister to come to Providence, where she resided for almost twenty years.

She continued various business ventures, and by 1822 her painting and wallpapering business was such a success that she had saved $600. She purchased a lot and built a house costing $1,700, with an addition on the east side for herself and on the west side for a tenant. She borrowed $240 at ten percent interest in order to purchase two more lots. She agreed to renew the note annually and to purchase a house for $2,000 with a down payment of $500, the balance to be paid within four years. After she contracted typhoid fever in September 1831, it was reported that she died and so the holder of the note for $240 filed an attachment to her property. When she returned to Providence from visiting friends in Massachusetts she discovered that all of her property had been auctioned off to pay the note. Friends persuaded her to enter a lawsuit before the Court of Common Pleas in January 1837 for trespass and ejectment because the sale at auction had not been legally advertised and she had not been notified. Although she lost the lawsuit, her conduct during the legal proceedings won her the admiration and respect of friends and neighbors. Eldridge was entitled, however, to recover her property after payment of $2,700 since there was no record of advertisement.

The Memoirs of Elleanor Eldridge was first published in 1838, one of the few narratives of the life of a free Black woman.

BIBLIOGRAPHY

DANB; Dannett, Sylvia G. *Profiles of Negro Womanhood, 1619-1900* (1964); Greene, Frances Whipple, ed. *Memoirs of Elleanor Eldridge* (1838); Loewenberg, Bert James and Ruth Bogin, eds. *Black Women in Nineteenth-Century American Life* (1976); Sterling, Dorothy, ed. *We Are Your Sisters: Black Women in the Nineteenth Century* (1984).

VIVIAN NJERI FISHER

ELGIN, ELLEN *see* INVENTORS

ELLIOTT, DAISY (1919-)

For almost twenty years, Daisy Elliott served as an elected official in the State of Michigan, first as a delegate to the Michigan Constitutional Convention, and then as a member of the Michigan State Legislature. In these capacities she successfully engineered constitutional and legislative provisions that significantly expanded the civil rights laws of the state.

Daisy Elizabeth Lenoir Elliott was born on November 26, 1919, in Filbert, West Virginia, the sixth of eight children of Robert Lenoir and Daisy (Dorum) Lenoir. Coal mining provided Robert with regular employment that allowed reliable but modest support for his family's needs. Daisy (Dorum) Lenoir was a homemaker who created a positive environment for her children's development. When Daisy was quite young, the family moved to Beckley, West Virginia, where Daisy attended school, graduating from Stratton High School in 1936. A few months after her graduation at seventeen, Daisy married Robert Elliott, a carpenter. They had one child, Doris Mae Elliott, in 1938. In the early 1940s, Daisy and Robert Elliott moved to Detroit hoping to find wartime factory work and Daisy did work as a riveter and inspector in California before returning to Detroit. In 1947, Daisy and Robert divorced; in 1964, Daisy married Charles Bowers, who worked in the Detroit Department of Transportation. Daisy added to her education by attending college classes both in Detroit and in California but without completing a formal degree. She did complete a course of study and graduate from the Detroit Institute of Commerce in 1950. In the 1950s, she sold real estate and worked in a Michigan Secretary of State branch office, rising to the position of assistant manager.

For many years, Daisy Elliott had longed for greater social and economic opportunities for Black men and women. Her World War II experiences convinced her that pressure from private civic groups and labor unions, combined with federal government orders against job discrimination, could bring needed changes. She resolved to enter politics to serve as a catalyst for these changes. In addition to her activities with several civic organizations, Elliott became active in the Michigan Democratic party and also sought election to the Michigan State Legislature. From 1957 to 1959, she was president of the Michigan Federal Democratic Clubs and in 1961, she won election to the Michigan Constitutional Convention, in which she played a key role on civil rights issues. Elliott was instrumental in establishing the Michigan Civil Rights Commission as part of the new Michigan Constitution, the first time a state had included such an agency in its constitution. The commission's authority allows it to investigate charges of discrimination based on race, religion, color, or national origin and to enforce antidiscrimination laws. Elected to the Michigan State Legislature in 1962, she served through 1978 and was reelected again in 1980 and served through 1982. Elliott played a significant role in the legislature, serving for several terms as chair of such important committees as Constitutional Revisions and Labor and sponsoring valuable reform legislation. More than eighty laws which she sponsored or cosponsored were enacted by the legislature, including the Elliott-Larsen Civil Rights Act of 1977, often cited as the most comprehensive state civil rights law in the United States. It added prohibitions against discrimination based on sex, weight, height, age, or marital status and increased the amount of damages the Civil Rights Commission could award.

In 1982, Elliott's electoral district was combined with the district of another Black female representative, requiring two incumbents to oppose each other. Four months before the August primary election, Elliott was charged with knowingly driving a stolen car. News stories led to her defeat in the primary. Elliott maintained her innocence, claiming she bought the car legally at a car dealership, but she was convicted. Claiming that she was "set up" because powerful people wanted her out of the state legislature, Elliott appealed the conviction, but was not able to overturn it.

BIBLIOGRAPHY

Detroit Free Press. "Civil Rights Commission Turns 25" (November 27, 1989); *Detroit News.* "Rights Bill Is Daisy's Triumph" (March 10, 1977); *Ebony.* "Black Power in State Government" (April 1972); *Michigan Chronicle.* "Daisy Elliott Says She Was 'Set-Up' " (November 20, 1982); *NBAW.*

DE WITT S. DYKES, JR.

ELLIS, EFFIE O'NEAL (1913-)

In 1970, when Effie O'Neal Ellis assumed the position of special assistant for health services to the American Medical Association (AMA), she became the first Black woman physician to hold an administrative post or executive office with the AMA. That same year, the National Medical Association bestowed upon Ellis its prestigious Trailblazer Award.

Effie O'Neal Ellis was born in Harkinsville, Georgia, on June 15, 1913. She was the daughter of Joshua P. and Althea (Hamilton) O'Neal. A bright and talented student, Effie received an A.B. with honors from Spelman College in 1933 and a Master's degree in biology from Atlanta University in 1935. In June 1935, she married Arthur W. Ellis.

During her graduate study at Atlanta University, Effie O'Neal received a grant to study diseases and parasites in Puerto Rico. During her stay, she noted the numerous health problems faced by poor people in ghettos and economically depressed rural areas and the need for more physicians and better health care

facilities. These observations convinced her to become a physician.

O'Neal was admitted to the University of Illinois College of Medicine where she graduated, on June 16, 1950, fifth in her class. She was among twenty-three of 160 medical students to graduate with honors.

From 1950 to 1951, O'Neal served her internship at the University of Illinois Hospital, followed by her residency in pediatrics at the Massachusetts General Hospital from 1951 to 1952. She was awarded a postdoctoral fellowship to study heart trouble in children at Johns Hopkins University School of Medicine from 1952 to 1953. She was also appointed staff physician at Johns Hopkins from July 1951 to June 1953 and again from July 1956 to July 1957.

On March 23, 1953, she married James D. Solomon, a doctor from Meharry College in Tennessee who had a Ph.D. from the University of Illinois. Solomon was appointed to the staff of the Elizabeth Hospital in Washington, D.C., in 1953, where he remained until his retirement in 1983.

From 1953 to 1961, she served as director of medical education and the house pediatrician at Provident Hospital in Baltimore, Maryland. She then held a post as director of maternal and child health for the Ohio State Department of Health in Columbus, Ohio, from 1961 to 1965.

She traveled all over the United States speaking to various medical establishments and community and educational groups. She stressed the importance of family planning and prenatal and postnatal care for families in poor communities. In order to influence policy decisions, she served in numerous capacities for the federal government, including an appointment as chairwoman for a panel at the White House conferences on food and nutrition (1969); as the first regional commissioner for social and rehabilitation services; and as regional medical director for the U.S. Department of Health, Education and Welfare Children's Bureau.

From 1970 to 1975 she served in her post as special assistant for health services to the AMA.

She is a member of the National Medical Association, the American Public Welfare Association, the American Association for Maternal and Child Health, Alpha Omega Alpha and Delta Sigma Theta sororities.

Among her many honors, she is an honorary fellow of the School Health Association.

Effie O'Neal Ellis currently resides in Chicago, Illinois.

BIBLIOGRAPHY

Ellis, Effie O'Neal. Black Women Physicians Collection and Special Collection on Women in Medicine, Medical College of Pennsylvania, Philadelphia; Baltimore *Evening Bulletin* (February 12, 1952); *Who's Who of American Women* (1975).

BRENDA GALLOWAY-WRIGHT

ELLIS, EVELYN (1894-1958)

Evelyn Ellis was an accomplished actress whose career spanned some thirty-five years on stage, television, and the big screen. From her beginnings with the famous Lafayette Theater to her work in major motion pictures, directed by such venerable directors as Orson Welles, Ellis performed a wide variety of roles with realism and finesse.

Evelyn Ellis was born on February 2, 1894, in Boston. Little is known about her childhood and education, but her stage career began in 1919 in a production of *Othello* by the celebrated Lafayette Theater in Harlem. Shortly thereafter she was given parts in several Broadway shows, including Nan Bagby Stephen's *Roseanne*. In 1927, she won critical praise in the role of Lucy Bell Dorsey in *Goat Alley*, a play about life in the slums of Washington, D.C. That same year she performed to even greater acclaim as Bess in the hit show *Porgy*, forerunner of George and Ira Gershwin's *Porgy and Bess*.

Ellis's career was greatly affected by the Great Depression, as work for performers dried up across the country, but in 1937 she made her comeback as director of Dorothy Hailparn's comedy *Horse Play*, a production financed by the federal government's Negro Theater program through the renowned Works Projects Administration (WPA). In 1941, Ellis played the part of Hannah Thomas in Orson Welles's impressive staging of Richard Wright's *Native Son*; the following year she again played the role in another, equally acclaimed production. A succession of successful performances followed, first in 1945, as a housekeeper in *Deep Are the Roots*, and then in 1951, as Della in *The Royal Family*. In 1950, Ellis directed and acted in an all-Black production of *Tobacco Road*, staged by the Negro Drama Group.

Her last Broadway show was William Stuckey's *Touchstone* in 1953, but by that time her television and movie career was growing. She had played the part of Bessie in Orson Welles's film *The Lady from Shanghai*, in 1948, and in 1953 Ellis took on the role of Mrs. Barrow, the fighter's mother, in *The Joe Louis Story*.

Also in 1953, Ellis made her final film appearance, playing a dignified maid in *Interrupted Melody*, starring Eleanor Parker and Glenn Ford.

Evelyn Ellis died in the Will Rogers Memorial Hospital in Saranac Lake, New York, on June 5, 1958.

BIBLIOGRAPHY

CBWA; McGill, Raymond D., ed. *Notable Names in the American Theatre* (1976); Nash, Jay Robert and Stanley Ralph Ross. *The Motion Picture Guide: 1927-1983* (1986); *NBAW*; *New York Times*, "Evelyn Ellis," obituary (June 6, 1958), and *New York Times Film Reviews* (various volumes published between 1920 and 1970), and *New York Times Theater Reviews* (various volumes published between 1920 and 1970).

FENELLA MACFARLANE

EMPIRE STATE FEDERATION OF WOMEN'S CLUBS, INC.

> May our Federation stand!
> Ever staunch and true,
> Loyal to the grandest aims,
> Thus we will renew
> Every effort to uplift
> Then will good ensue
> As we are climbing together.

Like tightly woven cloth, the women of the Empire State Federation of Women's Clubs, Inc., have held together for nearly nine decades. Keeping in tune with their federation song, these bold Black clubwomen have never stopped climbing together in their effort to champion the causes of women and children in New York State.

The federation, a coalition of various Black women's organizations in New York, still stands strong with seventeen active clubs in five regions: Albany, Buffalo, New York City, Hudson, and Westchester. The federation is affiliated with the Northeastern Federation of Women's Clubs, Inc., and the National Association of Colored Women's Clubs, Inc.

The organization had its inception in 1908 at the White Rose Home, a home for girls in New York City. The moving force behind its founding was Alice Wiley Seay of Brooklyn. The original mission of the federation was to advance the political, social, and economic work and experiences among girls and women and to care for abolitionist and ex-slave Harriet Tubman and her home in Auburn. After Tubman's death in 1913, however, the federation continued its mission of protecting the rights of women and children by promoting educational opportunities and interracial understanding among all people.

In its infancy, the federation was composed primarily of organizations located within New York City and Buffalo. However, when Maria C. Lawton, newspaper reporter, orator, and politician, started to organize for the federation in 1912, clubs in the Hudson River and central regions of New York joined, and through Lawton's efforts membership substantially increased. In the 1920s there were 103 clubs, several of which were ladies' usher groups from various churches that later withdrew to join a new national ushers' league.

The federation can be credited with a long list of accomplishments. In the 1920s it supported a young girl in South Africa. In 1933 it formed the Empire State Association of Youth Clubs, Inc., which exists today as a branch of the federation with five active youth clubs. In 1937, the federation erected a tombstone over the grave of Harriet Tubman.

At the federation's thirty-fifth annual convention in Auburn, a letter was drafted to President Franklin D. Roosevelt that indicates the federation's dedication to civil rights: "We further urge you, Mr. President, to take a resolute stand and use your full executive power to include, unreservedly, Negroes in all branches of the armed forces so that our nation shall truly be one nation indivisible with liberty and justice for all." During World War II the federation held panel discussions on various issues such as the integration of Black women into war-time employment.

The federation also has sustained, and continues to support, service projects such as homes for unwed mothers and two scholarship funds, the Victoria Earle and the Hallie Q. Brown scholarships. In 1974, the Federation dedicated its sixty-sixth annual convention to Tubman and made a pilgrimage to her home.

In a recent interview, Beuenia Brown, current president of the federation, summarized the secret of the organization's success by saying, "We are holding onto a rich legacy, and, most importantly, we have determination and faith."

BIBLIOGRAPHY

Brown, Beuenia. Telephone interview (December 2, 1991); Empire State Federation of Women's Clubs papers, 1938-90, Library Archives, State University of New York at Albany.

NANCY DAWSON

ENNIS, ETHEL LLEWELLYN
(1932-)

Pianist, jazz vocalist, and bandleader Ethel Llewellyn Ennis was born November 28, 1932, in Baltimore, Maryland. Her mother, Bell, was a housewife, and her father, Andrew, was a barber. Before she expressed an interest in music, Ethel was shaped and nurtured by the strong moral and religious values of her family, especially by her mother and grandmother, "Honey" Elizabeth Small.

Versatile song stylist Ethel Ennis, whose first job was playing the piano at her church's Sunday school, sang at President Richard Nixon's second inauguration. [Schomburg Center]

Ennis's musical interest surfaced in the second grade. She started playing piano at age seven. Her first job as a pianist was playing for her church Sunday school at fifty cents a week. By the age of fifteen, Ennis was surrounded and influenced by rhythm and blues. She listened to R&B artists like LaVern Baker, Hadda Brooks, Savannah Churchill, Camille Howard, and Rose Murphy. Additionally, Ennis was influenced by tunes like "I'm Tired Crying over You," by Ella Johnson, "Fine Brown Frame," by Nellie Lutcher, and "Please Don't Freeze on Me," by Ruth Brown.

In the late 1940s, Ennis joined a jazz octet led by Abraham Riley, where she honed both her piano and vocal skills. It was during this period that Ennis met and collaborated with William Everhart to write a rock 'n' roll composition entitled "Little Boy" (published and produced by Savoy in 1950). The song was recorded by several artists, including Little Richard. Also in 1950, she entered and won the *It's High Time* talent show, her first exposure on local television (WAAM). The prize for winning was an all-expense-paid trip to Philadelphia to appear on the *Paul Whiteman Teen-Age TV Show*. After high school graduation (1950), Ennis's musical career began to blossom. By day, she studied shorthand and typing; at night, she performed with an R&B group called the Tilters, the JoJo Jones Ensemble, and at clubs like the Red Fox (Baltimore), the Apollo Theatre (Harlem), the Village Vanguard (New York), the Red Onion (Aspen, Colorado), and the Astor Club (London), to name a few. In addition, she performed with Benny Goodman, sang for eight years on *The Arthur Godfrey Show*, and made numerous additional TV appearances, nightclub appearances, and recordings.

Despite a bad first marriage (to Jacques Leeds), Ennis married again. Her second husband was Earl Arnett. Ennis's strong moral and religious values catapulted her to significant musical heights. Her style is imbued with influences from Billie Holiday, Sarah Vaughan, and Dinah Washington. In her vocal stylings, one can hear a flair for humor, impersonations of Holiday, Vaughan, and Washington, equal competence whether singing a ballad or up-tempo composition, and the ability to personalize her lyrics. Ennis also has the ability to fit diverse musical situations, whether singing at Richard Nixon's second inauguration or on *The Arthur Godfrey Show*, or performing with her trio. Ethel Ennis is a national treasure of African-American music.

BIBLIOGRAPHY

Kravetz, Sallie. *Ethel Ennis: The Reluctant Jazz Star* (1984).

DISCOGRAPHY

Ethel Ennis Sings Lullabys for Losers, Jubilee (1955) (5 reissues, most recent on Columbia Nippon in 1977); *Change of Scenery*, Capitol T941 (1957); *Have You Forgotten*, Capitol T1078 (1958); *Once Again, Ethel Ennis*, RCA LPM2862, LSP2862 (1964); *This Is Ethel Ennis*, RCA LPM2786, LSP2786 (1964); *Ethel Ennis, My Kind of Waltztime*, RCA LPM2986, LSP2986 (1965); *Eyes for You/Ethel Ennis*, RCA LPM2984, LSP2984 (1965); *Ethel Ennis, God Bless the Child*, RCA (1973) (Camden reissue 1973 and 1980, ACL10157); *Ten Sides of Ethel Ennis*, BASF BB25121 (1973); *Ethel Ennis*, RCA ENE3113 (1980); *Once Again* (originally on RCA), Fresh Sound NDCD74663 (1984).

EDDIE S. MEADOWS

ENSLEY, ELIZABETH *see* DENVER, COLORADO, CLUB MOVEMENT

ENTREPRENEURS IN ANTEBELLUM AMERICA

By 1860, 11 percent of the African-American population (which numbered 4,488,000) were free. At that time, 15 percent of free Black women were dressmakers and hairdressers, including women who owned their own businesses; 5 percent operated boarding houses or small shops; and the remaining 80 percent were laundresses and domestics, including day workers and those in service. From the colonial period until well into the twentieth century, a preponderance of African-American women worked in domestic service, performing the occupational tasks of housecleaning, child care, washing and ironing, cooking, sewing, and nursing.

The commercial activities of Black women—slave and free, North and South—as they developed in the three-to-four-decade period before the Civil War had their origins in colonial America, for, although acculturation shaped the form and structure of enterprises developed by African-American women, their initial economic activities in household production and management, farming, and marketing were derived primarily from the commercial activities of women in West and West Central Africa. Precolonial African women participated in the economy in three major areas, as household managers, food and clothing producers, and market brokers and traders. The household was the basic production and economic unit, and few traditional African households were entirely self-sufficient. Consequently, marketing was prominent among the commercial activities conducted by African women, who were experts in trade, merchandising, and barter. In addition to skills in farming, household management and allocation of resources, food production and preparation, child care, and midwifery, African women were proficient in textiles, weaving, dyeing, quilt-making, basketry, pottery-making, and pharmacopeia. The economic activities of African women who became victims of the trans-Atlantic slave trade survived in the Americas and provided a foundation for subsequent economic activities developed by African-American women. Even the mutual aid societies founded by Black Americans, including women, represented an extension of the African cultural pattern of consanguineous cooperative enterprise and the pooling and sharing of resources.

Reviewing the economic activities of African women in America from the colonial period to the development of a new nation provides a basis on which to establish the foundation of business activities of African-American women. During the two-century period from 1619 to 1819, African gender-based labor activities were transformed into various economic activities, which found expression in the commercial enterprises of antebellum African-American women. However, although African women were involved in many areas of the colonial economy, few escaped the harsh, unyielding forced labor demands of farm work, or field drudgery, either then or in antebellum America. Indeed, the farming skills of African women provided the basis for their initial economic activity in the colonies as market women. Selling produce from their gardens not only enabled them to participate in the colonial economy, their inimitable market skills enabled them to dominate this sector of the economy in the South. One traveler's account notes the success of African-American women in urban markets in South Carolina and Louisiana: "The market places are filled with Negro women selling fruits and vegetables. . . . They have control of the markets in New Orleans [and] bring their products to the market very neatly." Other Black women served as commodities brokers of farm produce, purchasing fruits, vegetables, and poultry in rural areas, then transporting them to town markets and selling them at wholesale prices to market women and vendors and hustlers who retailed these commodities.

Although agricultural work was foremost, domestic service also was extracted from slave women, both in town and country. An eighteenth-century South Carolina newspaper advertisement emphasized the household skills of a slave woman up for sale, noting that she could "milk very well, wash and iron, dress victuals and do anything that is necessary to be done in the house." Expertise in cooking and baking provided a base for Black women to establish restaurants, catering houses, and bakeries. Often these women began as vendors or hucksters, then opened a stall in the market and used their profits to establish a shop, either by renting or purchasing property. The carefully planned marketing of domestic services also provided earnings that led to the establishment of business enterprises. Loren Schweninger has reported on the business activities of a slave called Sally (1790-1849) who was allowed to hire out her own time as a cleaning woman. Using her savings, Sally rented a house in the Nashville business district and established a laundry and cleaning business while also manufacturing soap for sale.

In some cases, mistresses deeded property to their former slaves, and this provided the basis for the establishment of rooming houses, inns, restaurants, and cleaning establishments. According to Suzanne Lebsock, Amelia Gallé of Petersburg was proprietor of a bath house that she had managed for years before inheriting the business in 1819 from her former slaveowner. Other manumitted slave women with skills as seamstresses, dressmakers, and milliners opened shops on property acquired from former owners. In this way, they changed from being managers to being entrepreneurs.

Most business enterprises developed by Black men and women were located in towns and cities, although there were Black women in agricultural areas who owned and managed plantations or commercial farms. According to Gary Mills, Marie Therez of Louisiana (1747-1816), a slave until she was forty-six, used her business skills to establish a 12,000-acre cotton plantation worked by more than 200 slaves whom *she* purchased. Paradoxically, as Marie Therez purchased slaves for plantation labor she also used her business profits to buy both children and grandchildren from slavery.

More common were the commercial farm activities of slave-born Lucy McWorter (1771-1870), whose freedom was purchased in 1817 by her slave entrepreneur husband, Free Frank. Lucy lived on both the Kentucky and Illinois frontiers, and her farm households manufactured cloth goods produced by spinning, weaving, and knitting as well as candle- and soap-making. Food-processing activities included butter- and cheese-making as well as vegetable and fruit canning. The collection and sale of bees' honey and wax also were profitable farm commercial enterprises, as was poultry raising. On the Illinois frontier, where Lucy lived after 1830, a traveler noted that farm wives could "raise three or four hundred fowls, besides geese, ducks, and turkeys, in a season." Lucy's earnings, added to those of her Illinois town-founder husband, enabled them to buy freedom for sixteen family members.

One cannot underestimate the societal and economic forces that motivated Black women to participate in commercial activities. For slave women, freedom was paramount. After paying their owner to allow them to hire out their own time, they saved the remaining profits and invested them in freedom. Successful self-purchasers invariably were entrepreneurs, slaves who hired out their own time and established enterprises. Often slave women entrepreneurs were specialists in gender-based occupations, such as the home health care service enterprise established in Petersburg by Jane Minor before she was manumitted in 1825. Using her skills in nursing, and her knowledge of the pharmacopeia of folk medicine, Minor used profits from this enterprise to free sixteen women and children from slavery. An apprentice she freed became a cupper and leecher specialist who kept records of her business receipts in an account book.

For the free Black woman, the economic imperative also was critical. In urban areas of the antebellum South, Black women outnumbered Black men. Establishing a business often provided the only means by which a Black woman, as the self-supporting head of her household, could provide for her family beyond subsistence. A few women assumed control of a business after their husband's death, but earning a livelihood was difficult for most antebellum Black women. Some resorted to illegal activities by establishing ordinaries, taverns, or grog shops, often concocting their own brew, another proscribed activity. A few women succeeded as madames, owning houses of prostitution, or as proprietors of luxury boarding houses. San Francisco's famous Mammy [Mary Ellen] Pleasant used investment tips from her prominent clients to enhance her wealth, which she then used to support abolitionist causes, including John Brown's raid at Harpers Ferry, Virginia, in 1859.

Several sources provide information on the antebellum business activities of Black women. Occupations and businesses were listed in city directories and traveler guides, and Black-owned newspapers carried business advertisements. However, although municipal censuses often included the occupations of city residents, they seldom indicated whether the individual was an employee or an em-

ployer; nor does the 1850 federal manuscript census, the first to list specific occupations, always make that distinction even though both the census and state and county tax records indicate the value of property. Because vendors were required to pay municipal licenses and fees, these records indicate the market activities of Black women, as do municipal ordinances and state laws that proscribed the participation of Black entrepreneurs in certain occupations.

Some business advertisements seem quite modern, such as the following for an antebellum Black business woman who was both a hairdresser and shop owner: "Mrs. Sarah A. Tillman, fancy hair braider, in all branches as BRACELETS, EAR-RINGS, WATCH GUARDS, FINGER RINGS, CHARMS." A dressmaker placed the following ad in an antebellum Black newspaper: "fashionable DRESS MAKING, SHIRT MAKING, EMBROIDERING, AND QUILTING. . . . Ladies' and children's dresses cut and made in the most fashionable style and warranted to fit."

In the areas of merchandising, health and beauty aids, and catering and dressmaking, several antebellum Black women achieved local, regional, and national recognition for their business successes. A prominent New Orleans merchant, Madame Cecee McCarty, owned a depot in Plaquemines Parish that provided a base for merchandising her goods outside New Orleans. Madame McCarty sold imported goods, using her thirty-two slaves as a traveling sales force, and by 1848 was worth more than $155,000. In the health and beauty aids sector, the Remond sisters, Cecilia, Maritcha, and Caroline, operated an exclusive hair salon for Black women in Salem, Massachusetts. Their business interests included the largest wig factory in that state, and they also manufactured a popular medicated hair tonic, which they sold wholesale and retail, both locally and through the mail-order distribution side of their business. The Remond family was prominent in abolitionist circles as well as in the Salem business community. Their mother, Nancy, controlled the catering trade in Salem and also ran a small, exclusive restaurant.

Only the commercial activities of Elizabeth Keckley (1818-1907), as the dressmaker of Mary Todd Lincoln, wife of Abraham Lincoln, have been given wide historic recognition. Keckley's business success was due to her expertise as a dress designer; her Washington, D.C., dress shop employed twenty seamstresses. Keckley's skills eventually enabled her to purchase her freedom from slavery.

Within the broad context of the term *entrepreneur*, generally defined as an individual with the ability to make unusual amounts of money using commonly available resources, antebellum Black businesswomen were indeed entrepreneurs, for their business activities were characterized by ingenuity, creativity, and innovativeness. Given that almost 90 percent of the antebellum Black population were slaves and, therefore, that antebellum Black women participated in business while having to contend with slavery, racism, and sexism, these women no doubt had developed a formidable business acumen. Their successes can be measured to some extent by the amount of property they owned and by the business profits they earned, which, in turn, enabled them to purchase freedom.

BIBLIOGRAPHY

Lebsock, Suzanne. *The Free Women of Petersburg: Status and Culture in a Southern Town, 1784-1860* (1984); Mills, Gary. "Coincoin: An Eighteenth-Century 'Liberated' Woman," *Journal of Southern History* (1976); Schweninger, Loren. "A Slave Family in the Ante Bellum South," *Journal of Negro History* (1975); Sterling, Dorothy, ed. *We Are Your Sisters: Black Women in the Nineteenth Century* (1984); Walker, Juliet E. K. *Black Business in American History* (forthcoming), and *Free Frank: A Black Pioneer on the Antebellum Frontier* (1983), and "Racism, Slavery, and Free Enterprise: Black Entrepreneurship in the United States before the Civil War," *Business History Review* (Autumn 1986).

JULIET E. K. WALKER

EPPS, ROSELYN PAYNE (1930-)

A strong advocate for medical service for poor people, Roselyn Epps has been a practicing pediatrician, teacher, administrator, and organizational leader. The first Black woman to serve as president of the American Medical Women's Association (AMWA), in 1990-91, Roselyn Payne was born in Little Rock, Arkansas, in December 1930. She matriculated at Howard University, receiving her B.S. in 1951 and her M.D. in 1955.

She served her internship and residency at Freedmen's Hospital, where she was chief resident. Later she obtained her M.P.H. from Johns Hopkins University and her M.A. from the American University in 1981. During the 1970s, Epps served in various medical capacities in the government of the District of Columbia. Since 1981, she has been a professor of pediatrics and child health at Howard University medical school. From 1981 to 1985, Epps was project director for the Project to Consolidate Health Services for High Risk Young People. From 1985 to

1988, she was director of the Know Your Body Health Project.

Roselyn Epps has served as an international consultant for the World Bank, the U.N. Fund for Population, and the U.S. Department of Health and Human Services. She is a fellow of the American Academy of Pediatrics and has served as an officer of many organizations, including the National Medical Association, American Public Health Association, and American Medical Association.

Roselyn Payne Epps is married to Charles E. Epps, Jr., professor of orthopedic surgery and the dean of Howard University College of Medicine. They have four children.

BIBLIOGRAPHY

Epps, Roselyn. "Cultural Diversity and the Future of Medicine," *Journal of the American Medical Women's Association* (1991), and "Freedom to Practice, Freedom to Speak," *Journal of the American Medical Women's Association* (1991).

SUSAN SHIFRIN

A practicing pediatrician, Roselyn Payne Epps is also an advocate for medical service for the poor, as well as a teacher, administrator, and organizational leader. [Medical College of Pennsylvania]

ESSENCE MAGAZINE

Debuting in May 1970, *Essence* was not the first national periodical aimed primarily at Black women, but it has been the most successful in terms of circulation and longevity. In fact, *Essence* might be viewed as the contemporary fulfillment of Julia Ringwood Coston's dream in the 1890s when she founded both *Ringwood's Afro-American Journal of Fashion* and *Ringwood's Home Magazine* to provide fashion news and highlight the accomplishments of Black women. In the interim, a number of publications have been aimed at Black women; some of them, such as *Woman's Era* and *National Notes*, were associated with organizations, and others, such as *Elegant* (founded 1963), *Designs for Gracious Living* (founded 1964), and *New Lady* (founded 1966), attempted to survive on advertisements and general subscriptions. But, after twenty-two years of publication, *Essence* is probably the longest continuously published periodical targeted toward Black women and not associated with an organization.

Essence was developed by a group of young African-American men: advertising salesman Jonathan Blount, printing expert Cecil Hollingsworth, financial planner Ed Lewis, and insurance salesman Clarence Smith, also known as the Hollingsworth Group. Although the magazine was begun as a "Black" venture, with a full-time staff of twenty-six (twenty-four of whom were African-American) including photographer/writer Gordon Parks as editorial director, *Essence* received much of its support from white patrons. With encouragement from the Wall Street brokerage firm of Shearson, Hammill & Co.; technical advice from Time-Life, *Newsweek*, *Psychology Today*, *New York*, and CBS; advance publicity from *Time*, *Newsweek*, and NBC's *Today* show; and the financial support of Chase Manhattan, Morgan Guaranty, and First National City banks, and Playboy Enterprises, *Essence* began with an initial operating budget of $1.5 million, enough to sustain two years of publication and thus a degree of financial stability unprecedented for a Black woman's periodical.

This financial stability no doubt ensured the magazine's survival, as the first years were plagued with problems of distribution, funding, control, editorial authority, and focus or direction. Eighty percent of the copies of the first issue went unsold, in part due to distribution problems. More than a year passed before sales picked up significantly, and it was not until 1976 that the magazine began operating in the black. Advertising was initially hard to come by as the traditional advertisers in white women's magazines, the health, beauty, and fashion industries, were reportedly unreceptive to the idea of targeting a Black female consumer. *Essence*, therefore, focused on automobile manufacturers and cigarette companies. The latter, having just been banned from television advertising and trying to develop a Black market, accounted for a substantial portion of advertising revenues. Disputes in 1971 over a $250,000 investment from *Playboy* magazine led to Blount severing his connections with the publication. After a brief 1977 legal battle with Parks, Blount, and Hollingsworth, Lewis and Smith retained control; today Lewis is Publisher and Chief Executive and Smith is President.

Marketed toward African-American women, *Essence* has continuously dealt with the standard women's journalism issues such as health, beauty, fashion, female and male relationships, diet and nutrition, and family matters. It is also credited with being a forerunner in the field of career advice to women. Born at the height of the "Black is Beautiful" and "Black Power through Black Capitalism" movements, *Essence* was a product of the contradictions within the Black community; focus and audience were central problems. Gordon Parks suggested the ambivalent nature of *Essence*'s mission when he said, "The black woman should be able to get anything she wants out of this magazine.... And that goes from militancy to her place in the nation and in the white world" (*Newsweek* 1970).

During the first year, the editorial control and editorial focus of *Essence* were relatively unclear, as three editors-in-chief came and went. Bernadette Carey worked in the initial stages of development but left before the first issue; Ruth Ross returned to her former position at *Newsweek* after editing the first issue, citing lack of editorial authority as the reason for her departure. The first issue, with Ross as editor-in-chief, contained twenty pages of high fashion, including six pages of "bangles and baubles of jewelry against a background of body stockings and black skin" (*Time* 1970), and a cover story on "Five Shades of Militancy;" which included Rosa Parks and Kathleen Cleaver. This was a difficult balance, and in an article in *Newsweek* following the first issue of *Essence*, publisher Jonathan Blount stated, "This is a woman's service magazine, not a *Ramparts*. . . . But we're a communications vehicle that can change detested images into meaningful ones" (*Newsweek* 1970). Blount thus pointed the magazine more toward woman's service, and less toward politics, but emphasized that in being a woman's service periodical that changed the images of Black women, it would be performing a political function. Revamping the

By far the most successful magazine ever published for Black women, Essence *has a circulation of over 800,000. The first issue, whose cover is reproduced above, was published in May 1970.* [Essence]

second issue with new editor-in-chief Ida Lewis, executive editor Barbara Kerr, one of the few Euro-Americans on the staff, suggested that the approach would be "more woman, less black" (*Time* 1970). But political issues were not eliminated; one of the articles during the first year focused on "Cornell: Black Students in Crisis," and was a sympathetic portrayal of the Black student movement.

Under the direction of its third editor-in-chief, Marcia Ann Gillespie beginning in 1971, *Essence* evolved into a service magazine with a social conscience. Fashion features and advertisements represent women of differing ages, body types, facial features, skin color, and personal and political styles; *Essence* models have not always conformed to white standards of beauty. Feature articles have dealt with topics such as child rearing, careers, politics, war, religion, and racism. Controversial topics such as lesbianism and color consciousness within the Black community have not been avoided. In addition, the works of major African-American writers and poets have appeared over the years, including Maya Angelou, Toni Cade Bambara, Gayl Jones, Nikki Giovanni, June Jordan, Ntozake Shange, and Alice Walker. Since 1981 under the editorship of Susan L. Taylor, *Essence* has reached out to African-American male readers as well, with an annual issue on men and a monthly column by men called "Brothers" that has dealt with such issues as fathering, abortion rights, the Gulf War, sexism, and physical abuse.

Over the years, *Essence* has sought to celebrate and project positive images of African-American women. Unlike other African-American magazines such as *Jet* and *Ebony*, *Essence* addresses African-American women directly and is filled with both glamour and reality. And unlike *New Lady*, a woman's service periodical begun in 1966, *Essence* is better produced. Another reflection of its times, *Essence* emerged at a time when the civil rights struggles had widened job opportunities in publishing houses and national journals, and *Essence* could then draw on a small core of experienced Black women: Carey came from *Vogue*; Ross from *Newsweek*; Lewis from ten successful years of freelance writing for *Life*, *L'Express*, and a number of French publications; Gillespie from Time-Life Books and *Life* magazine. By 1980, when Gillespie left, *Essence* had fulfilled another mission, developing its own talent; the new editor-in-chief, Daryl Royster Alexander, came from within. Susan Taylor, who assumed the helm in 1981, had been with the magazine for ten years, first as a freelance editor and then as fashion and beauty editor.

Essence has a place not only in Black journalism history but also in women's journalism in general, as a pioneer. Started at a time when the basic fare in women's journalism was the domestically oriented *Family Circle* or the high fashion *Vogue*, in its early years *Essence* was often accused of imitating white women's fashion magazines. Now it is recognized as a forerunner of those magazines which took seriously women's whole lives—in the home, in the workplace, in the social and political world. Other, predominantly white, magazines oriented toward career women have emerged since 1970, but *Essence* was there in the beginning.

Although, as Bonnie Allen wrote, *Essence* may have been "created to satisfy 12 million upwardly mobile/poverty-stricken, man-hungry/lesbian, hippie/Muslim/revolutionary Black women" (Allen 1980), former editor Marcia Ann Gillespie noted the difficulty in being "the only" Black women's magazine, maintaining that the magazine must be careful "not to fall prey to the notion of being all things to all Black women all the time" (Gillespie 1976). Nevertheless, *Essence* seeks to reflect the broad and diverse African-American community, and with a current circulation of over 800,000, mainly among African-American women and men, it appears to be a commercial success.

BIBLIOGRAPHY

Allen, Bonnie. "*Essence* and Other Thoughts on the '70's," *Essence* (May 1980); *Black Enterprise*, "On the Move" (July 1981); Dullea, Georgia. "*Essence* Marks 15 Years of Serving Black Women," *New York Times* (April 5, 1985); *Ebony*, "Speaking of People" (August 1977); Edwards, Audrey. "The Essence of Sweet Success," *Black Enterprise* (June 1980); *Essence*, "Essence Goes to . . . Hollywood . . . For Days," (October 1974); Fraser, C. Gerald. "Ousted *Essence* Magazine Chief Accuses Playboy," *New York Times* (May 6, 1971); Gillespie, Marcia. "Getting Down," *Essence* (May 1976; June 1977); Katz, Bill and Linda Sternberg Katz. *Magazines for Libraries* (1992); Kennedy, Shawn. "In Essence, A Celebration of Black Women," *New York Times* (May 7, 1990); *New York Times*. "*Essence* Control Contested" (April 20, 1977), and "*Essence* Plans for Growth" (June 5, 1980), and "The Fight for *Essence*" (April 19, 1977); *Newsweek*. "Meaningful Images" (May 11, 1970); Smith, Jessie Carney. "Julia Ringwood Coston" (in this volume); Stewart, Ted. "Glorifying Black Women," *Sepia* (July 1975); *Time*. "Black Venture" (May 4, 1970); Wilson, Clint C., II. *Black Journalists in Paradox: Historical Perspectives and Current Dilemmas* (1991); Wolseley, Roland E. *The Black Press U.S.A.* (1971).

JAMIE HART
ELSA BARKLEY BROWN

EVANS, LOUISE (1921-)

During the 1940s, when opportunities for Black Americans and particularly women were rare behind the scenes in theater, Louise Evans achieved distinction as a costume, scenic, and lighting designer. Evans also became the first Black woman to be admitted into the prestigious United Scenic Artists Association (USAA) in 1952.

Born in St. Louis, Missouri, on March 29, 1921, Louise Evans was one of three children born to Alexander E. and Johncie Hunter Evans. She attended Northwestern University (1940-42) to study children's theater and directing. As a director, Evans believed it was important to know the design side of theater, and she took several design courses. After two years at Northwestern, Evans transferred to the Art Institute of Chicago to study at the Goodman Theatre, where she specialized in design. At Goodman, Evans worked on numerous productions as a designer of costumes, scenery, and lighting, as well as the lighting technician and property manager. Evans also directed and designed with the Chicago Negro Art Theatre and served as director of drama with the Chicago Park District.

In 1946, Evans moved to New York to pursue a professional career as a designer. She designed and worked as the technical director for the Broadway Stock Company in Milford, Pennsylvania. In New York City, she designed for off-Broadway productions, particularly at the Equity Library Theatre. Evans also worked with the American Negro Theatre during the late 1940s, where she met her actor husband, Austin Briggs-Hall. They were married in 1948 and had two sons. They were later divorced. In 1962, Evans gave up her career in theater and is now a nun with the Third Order of Carmelites.

BIBLIOGRAPHY

Evans, Louise. Personal interviews (1982, 1983, 1984, 1988, 1991); Billy Rose Theatre Collection, The New York Public Library for the Performing Arts, New York City.

KATHY A. PERKINS

EVANS, MATILDA ARABELLA (1872-1935)

Matilda Arabella Evans was the first woman licensed to practice medicine in South Carolina. In her years of practice, she developed a model public school health testing program and founded a free health maintenance clinic, a hospital and training school, and a statewide health association.

Evans was born on May 13, 1872, in Aiken, South Carolina. Her parents were Anderson and Harriet Evans. Her maternal grandmother, Edith Corley, was the daughter of Henry and Julia Willis, who came from Pennsylvania.

Evans enrolled in the Schofield Industrial School in Aiken, South Carolina. The school was established in 1868 under the auspices of the Pennsylvania Farmers Relief Association to provide instruction to young Black men and women.

At the urging of Martha Schofield, Evans enrolled in Oberlin College. Within three months she

The first woman licensed to practice medicine in South Carolina, Matilda Arabella Evans was active in community health and public school health issues, creating model testing programs and establishing a free public clinic, hospital and training school, and a statewide health association. [Medical College of Pennsylvania]

had won a scholarship to cover her tuition. To cover her other expenses she held a job as a waitress during the school year and canned fruit in the summer months. She attended Oberlin College from 1887 to 1891. Three months before her scheduled graduation, she dropped out of school to pursue a career in medicine. She taught briefly at the Haines Institute in Augusta, Georgia, and the Schofield School before enrolling at the Woman's Medical College of Pennsylvania in 1893.

Evans graduated from the Woman's Medical College in 1897 and returned to South Carolina to set up practice. She became a very successful surgeon who attracted both Black and white patients. Her clientele grew so large that she opened her home as a hospital.

With the permission of South Carolina school authorities, Evans examined the health of Black school children. She discovered that many of the children suffered from numerous ailments, including dental decay, bad tonsils, ringworm, and other diseases. As a result of her findings, the school district established a permanent examination program within the public school system of South Carolina.

Evans was the founder of the Columbia Clinic Association in Columbia, South Carolina. The clinic was based on public health facilities in Durham, North Carolina, Philadelphia, and New York City that Evans had visited. The aim of the clinic was to teach families proper health maintenance while providing a variety of health services. All services at the clinic were provided free of charge.

In 1901, Evans established the Taylor Lane Hospital and Training School in Columbia. Although the city's population was 50 percent Black, Taylor Lane Hospital was the only Black hospital in the city. Evans gave up her private practice to work at the hospital. In addition to the services it provided Black patients, the hospital proved to be an excellent training ground for Black doctors and nurses.

Evans was not only a physician but also a great educator and humanitarian. She established the Negro Health Association of South Carolina to educate South Carolinians on proper health care procedures. She also provided recreation for underprivileged boys and formed swimming classes.

Evans received numerous honors and awards. She was given a commission from the National Council for Defense. She was elected president of the Palmetto State Medical Society and was vice president of the National Medical Association. During World War I, she was appointed a member of the Volunteer Medical Service Corps.

Matilda Arabella Evans died at her home in Columbia, South Carolina, on November 17, 1935.

BIBLIOGRAPHY

Caldwell, A. B., ed. *History of the American Negro* (1919); *CBWA*; Evans, Matilda Arabella. Black Women Physicians and Special Collection on Women in Medicine, Medical College of Pennsylvania, Philadelphia; Lerner, Gerda, ed. *Black Women in White America* (1972); Schofield School. Annual Report (1882); Woman's Medical College of Pennsylvania. Faculty minutes (September 15, 1895).

BRENDA GALLOWAY-WRIGHT

Lyric soprano Lillian Evans Evanti scored international successes in Europe, the United States, and the Caribbean. She is seen here with her son. [Scurlock Studio]

EVANTI, LILLIAN EVANS
(1890-1967)

Lillian Evans was born in Washington, D.C., on August 12, 1890. She was the daughter of Anne Brooks and Bruce Evans, M.D. A lyric soprano, she was the first Black American to sing opera with an organized company in Europe. As a protégé of Lulu Vere Childers, she studied at the Howard University School of Music, graduating in 1917. The name Evanti was a combination of her maiden name and the last name of Roy Tibbs, a Howard University professor of music whom she married. Five years of study and performance beginning in 1925 included voice lessons with Mme. Ritter-Ciampi in Paris and Rosa Storchio in Italy and acting lessons with M. Gaston Dupins. Her most notable performances in Italy and France were at the Casino Theatre in Nice, France (1925), and at the Trianon Lyrique in Paris (1927) in the lead role in *Lakmé* by Delibes. After her return to Washington, D.C., Evanti made her Town Hall debut in 1932 and gave recitals throughout the United States, Europe, and the Caribbean.

Lillian Evanti was honored by an invitation to sing at the White House for President and Mrs. Roosevelt in 1934, and she won critical acclaim for her performance as Violetta in the National Negro Opera Company production of Verdi's *La Traviata* in Washington, D.C. (1943). She was sent by the State Department to Argentina and Brazil with Arturo Toscanini and the NBC Orchestra as a goodwill ambassador in 1940. One of her compositions, *Himno Panamericano* (1941), was well received in Latin American countries. Lillian Evanti died in Washington, D.C., on December 6, 1967.

BIBLIOGRAPHY

BDAAM; Evanti, Lillian Evans. Unpublished Autobiography, Evans-Tibbs Collection, personal collection, Washington, D.C.; Story, Rosalyn M. *And So I Sing* (1990).

DORIS EVANS McGINTY

In 1925, *lyric soprano Lillian Evans Evanti (shown here in costume, circa 1924) was forced to go to France for her operatic debut, but in 1943 she sang Violetta in* La Traviata *with the National Negro Opera Company in Washington, D.C. [Scurlock Studio]*

EVERS, MYRLIE *see*
WILLIAMS, MYRLIE BEASLEY
EVERS

F

FASHION INDUSTRY

From the earliest days of this country, Black women have been pivotal in the creation of fashion images for women in the United States. Initially behind the scenes and unacknowledged as seamstresses and designers, it was not until the mid-twentieth century that Black women came into the spotlight as both models and designers. Within the Black community, the major determinants of fashion have been community-based fashion shows that began with those sponsored by neighborhood churches or clubs, displaying local talent and shaping local tastes, and that now include the Ebony Fashion Fair, the world's largest traveling fashion show. Black women have had a continuous impact on how all women dress and look; but, as with other industries, there has been a struggle to be recognized.

SEAMSTRESSES AND DESIGNERS

The Black Fashion Museum, founded in Harlem in 1979 by Lois Alexander (who also founded a school, the Harlem Institute of Fashion, in 1966), seeks to celebrate the work of Black designers, male and female. It especially showcases Black seamstresses and dressmakers within the community, the history of whose work in the United States reaches back to slavery.

Large plantations often had slave seamstresses and slaves who did nothing but embroider the white family's wardrobe. For those whose owners allowed them to buy their freedom, dressmaking was a sometimes viable way to make money. Elizabeth Keckley (1818-1907) was a slave who bought her freedom through profits on her seamstressing; she eventually designed for the elite in Washington, D.C., who competed for her services. Choosing to design for Mary Todd Lincoln, Keckley became so embroiled in backstage White House phenomena that she was able to write *Behind the Scenes, or 30 Years a Slave, and 4 Years in the White House* (1868). Keckley's most famous design, Mary Todd Lincoln's inaugural ball gown, is in the Smithsonian Institution and a re-creation is exhibited at the Black Fashion Museum.

Other Black dressmakers/designers have been equally creative, if not as renowned. For instance, in the late nineteenth and early twentieth centuries, Fanny Criss (c. 1866-1942) designed for wealthy white women in Richmond, Virginia. That city's Valentine Museum has in its collection several of Criss's designs, including a white wool Second-Day (wedding reception) dress from 1896. Since dressmaking was a primary occupation of Black women in many cities of the late nineteenth century (especially Charleston, New Orleans, and Louisville), there were no doubt many Fanny Crisses who are now unknown to us but who were hard at work designing and creating the fashion images of the white elite. Criss continued her career in New York City after moving there around 1918.

With the emergence of ready-made clothing, some Black women set up small but successful shops where they adapted illustrations from *Vogue* and *Harper's Bazaar* for the women in their communities; others operated more informally but nonetheless developed regular clientele for their dressmaking. Church and community socials were their advertising venues. Mamie Garvin, a twenty-five-year-old South Carolina schoolteacher, spent the summer of 1913 in Boston with two other young women. Together they opened

a sewing room at home. . . . Very few if any of the neighborhood ladies could afford to buy the dresses *Vogue* magazine advertised, but they did have the taste for them, and some of them had enough money to buy nice material and the various trimmings. I knew how to make patterns and get the most up-to-date lines. Ellestine and Myrtle knew how to do everything else, so we got busy copying the expensive dresses we found in *Vogue*.

Our "factory" was Ellestine's bedroom, which overlooked Wallpole Street, a well-traveled street in Roxbury. We made a display out of magazines and made a big sign for the window: "Parisian Vogue." A lady passing by would come up to see what we were working on; the next thing you know, here she comes back with an order. Or Miss so-and-so would appear in church wearing a suit we made; Wednesday or Thursday, Miss such-and-such wants one like it (but not *just* like it, of course). The word got out quickly that we were stylish girls who knew all about clothes . . . and soon we had more business than we knew what to do with. . . . Each of us got to the point where we specialized in a certain part of the job. (Fields 1983)

Similarly, but less formally, in the mid-1950s in Louisville, Kentucky, two sisters, high school students Gwendolyn and Natalie Brown, acquired a reputation within their church and neighborhood for not only the quality of their work but also the currentness of their designs. Denied the opportunity to shop in fashionable white department stores, Black middle- and upper-class women throughout the South sought ways to obtain the current fashions without traveling to stores in the North and Midwest. These sisters were two of thousands of women throughout the South who provided that opportunity. Going at night to the deserted downtown streets, one, an artist, would draw the fashions in the white department store windows and then fashion patterns for them; the other, a skilled dressmaker, would create these in a

range of colors and fabrics. Wearing their creations in church attracted their first clients and after that, as their clothes were seen and their skills admired, their client base grew. Some clients ordered entire vacation and seasonal wardrobes, including coats. Neither sister pursued designing or dressmaking as a career after high school and college, but these skills did provide them with needed funds throughout their school years. More significantly, they provided women within their community with access to the latest styles at a reasonable cost, and without fear of potential humiliation upon entering a predominantly white fashion environment.

Within the early twentieth-century white community, word-of-mouth was also the primary means of acquiring clientele. If a socialite was complimented for her wardrobe, her seamstress/designer could hope to be recommended to others. Ann Lowe (born 1899) gained her reputation in just such a way. The granddaughter, daughter, and niece of experienced seamstresses, Lowe began her career when, as a teenager, she completed the inaugural ball gown for the wife of an Alabama governor (a work begun by her mother). Soon all the wealthy Alabama society/debutante/political women were requesting Lowe's services. This was at the time of the great Northern migration, and at age sixteen, she moved to New York. There she enrolled in a design school that admitted her but requested she place her sewing table in the hall outside the classroom, away from the white students. Within a year, Lowe had opened her own dressmaking shop on Madison Avenue with clients such as the Astors and Rockefellers. Though her designs were featured nationally on the covers of fashion magazines and women's magazines, her name was not well known outside of debutante circles until the 1953 wedding of Jacqueline Bouvier and John Fitzgerald Kennedy. Ann Lowe designed the mother-of-the-bride and bridesmaids dresses, as well as the bridal gown. At last she was acknowledged as a designer as well as a dressmaker/seamstress, an artist as well as a craftsperson.

Similarly, milliner Mildred Blount's talents went without public recognition, despite the fact that she designed for Joan Crawford, Gloria Vanderbilt, and other society and Hollywood women. Her creations adorned the casts of *Gone with the Wind, Easter Parade*, and *Back Street*, and her hats were featured on the cover of *Ladies' Home Journal* (August 1942). She and other Black women designed for Hollywood for more than half a century before, in 1972, Hollywood acknowledged that history. That year, Elizabeth Courtney became the first Black woman to be nominated for an Academy Award in Costume Design (*Lady Sings the Blues*). Today, Parsons School of Design graduate Therese Rogers designs for Hollywood and singing stars, while Olympic medalist Florence Griffith Joyner designs her own line of workout apparel.

Today's Black women designers now work within a global community. Tracy Reese, whose 1987 business venture failed two years later because of production problems despite orders from Bergdorf Goodman, Barneys, and Ann Taylor, has been the primary designer for the Japan-based Magaschonni collection since 1990. Beverly Olivace is central to the New York Designer Network, which cultivates new and rising stars within the design world, while Shirley Gibson's one-woman design firm in Brooklyn, KurKur is Wearable Art, features tie-dyes, batiks, and hand-painted fabrics. Barbara Bates's Chicago-based leather and suede company caters to specialty boutiques and private clients, while Philadelphia-based Yvonne O'Gara retails affordably priced separates in department stores across the country. Similarly, Sandy Baker's hand-crafted jewelry company (f. 1986) finds distribution in department stores nationwide, while Coreen Simpson's highly theatrical (not to mention expensive) jewelry must be custom-made. Many young Black women designers are apprenticing in Europe and Japan with companies that have nurtured brilliant Black male designers such as the late Willi Smith and Patrick Kelly.

FASHION SHOWS

Mainstream fashion shows, as dominated by whites in the United States and Europe as the rest of the fashion industry, have fluctuated from private showings by dressmakers to exclusive boutique showings to the present spectacle of runway shows. The runway fashion show system—private, trendy, and based outside of the United States—has historically employed Black models earlier and in greater numbers than modeling venues such as retail catalogues, print and television advertising, and the editorial pages in fashion and women's magazines.

Dorothea Towles, a Texarkana, Texas, native, graduated with a degree in biology from Wiley College (Marshall, Texas) and a masters in education from the University of California, Los Angeles. Deciding not to continue teaching, she attended charm school in Los Angeles, and in 1949 joined her sister, concert pianist Lois Towles, in Europe, where she promptly began runway and showroom modeling for Dior and Italian designer Schiaparelli. Her work in Dior's showroom, and Dior's prominence in post-World War II European fashion trends, promoted

opportunities for other light-skinned Black models of the era. Towles became the first Black woman to earn her living entirely as a professional model.

In the late 1960s and early 1970s, the Black is Beautiful philosophy became increasingly commercial; high fashion responded by manufacturing dashikis, afro-wigs, and so-called ethnic fashions. Since then, darker, statuesque, "exotic" Black women (exemplified by Naomi Sims in 1967 and Iman in 1987) have been in vogue on European runways. The most blatant example of this was by Parisian designer Givenchy, whose 1978 fall collection was dramatically presented with models all of whom were darker-skinned women, including then-newcomer Mounia, wearing earth tones and jungle prints.

Throughout the 1980s and 1990s, few light-skinned models have attained runway success in Europe. In the United States, however, Gail O'Neil and Sonia Cole have been featured in shows by various U.S. designers. The relative success of Black women on the runway can be attributed in large part to the notion of high fashion, which calls for the exotic and something to gawk at, *not* identify with. This is in direct contrast to the purpose of print and especially television modeling, which seek to have the consumer identify with the model.

High fashion and high tech designer shows aside, community-based shows—as common a fund-raiser as bake sales or talent shows—historically have had a greater influence on the fashions that Black women buy and wear. In these shows Black women see how the creations featured in *Vogue* can be adapted to their own figures, lifestyles, and bank accounts. Whether styling in their Sunday-go-to-meeting best or twirling down makeshift runways, these shows have been rooted in certain constant and influential elements in the community: churches, historically Black colleges, clubs and benevolent societies, and sororities. In the mid-1950s, for instance, Dorothea Towles toured the country with clothes she had acquired as a runway model in Europe, holding fashion shows for Black colleges and Alpha Kappa Alpha Sorority. Forty years later, she still produces benefit fashion shows, but her one-woman productions are now overshadowed by the world's largest traveling fashion show, the Ebony Fashion Fair.

When, in 1956, Jessie C. Dent (wife of the then-president of Dillard University) asked the Chicago-based Johnson Publishing Company to sponsor a fund-raiser for a New Orleans hospital, the response was so positive that two years later Freda DeKnight, *Ebony*'s food and fashion editor, organized the first tour of ten cities with four models. In 1963,

Eunice W. Johnson (secretary-treasurer of Johnson Publishing Company and wife of *Ebony* publisher John Johnson) began producing and directing the tour. In three decades, the Fashion Fair expanded to include nearly two hundred cities in the United States, Canada, and the Caribbean. The show remains distinctive for its drama, production quality, and musical coordination; for featuring the creations of several dozen new and established designers rather than one or two; and for its community base. The Ebony Fashion Fair is sponsored in each city by local sorority, NAACP, and Links chapters, and proceeds benefit the United Negro College Fund, Thurgood Marshall Scholarship Fund, National Urban League, and other charitable causes. Eunice Johnson's viewing, selecting, and buying of ensembles for a Black fashion show (as opposed to, for instance, borrowing the clothes from stores, models, or designers) is a far cry from the days when fashion houses refused to allow *Ebony*, *Jet*, *Sepia*, and other Black publications to photograph their collections. To get around this prohibition in the 1940s and 1950s, Dorothea Towles borrowed several of the designs she modeled during the week, notified Black publications of her weekend personal schedule, and allowed photographers to follow her around as she tried to wear all the clothes. When these magazines published their candid shots ostensibly of her social schedule, they would, obviously, also have pictures of the latest designs. White designers' reluctance to market to a Black audience was another factor in restricting Black women's opportunities in print and television modeling.

MODELS

If Black women designers and runway models faced obstacles, those seeking a career in print and television modeling have had an even more difficult time. Acceptance in this arena of the fashion industry meant redefining the United States'—indeed, the entire Western world's—notions of beauty. While stage and screen women, such as Lena Horne, Dorothy Dandridge, Eartha Kitt, and Cicely Tyson, all revolutionized the world of beauty in some way or another, there have been hundreds of Black women over the years struggling voicelessly to revise our image. Black models persevered and pioneered—moving from "posing as a servant in an ad" (Summers 1987) to modeling Christian Dior ensembles to hawking Virginia Slims cigarettes.

Among the women who transformed our image is Dorothea Towles. Returning to the United States in the mid-1950s from her success as a runway model in Europe, Towles was rejected by white agencies and

photographers, but she remained a top model in Black publications and advertisements aimed at Black consumers. Eventually, at the height of her career, Towles was a primary spokeswoman for Chesterfield cigarettes.

Towles's contemporaries included Sara(h) Lou Harris, a North Carolinian who became the first Black model in the New York buyers' fashion show. Like Towles, Harris was a former schoolteacher and was featured in cigarette advertisements (posters for Lucky Strike). Harris did not model full-time; instead she proved her versatility by dancing and acting (she toured Europe with a USO troupe, performing in *Shuffle Along*), singing (she began in night and supper clubs in New York City in 1958), and being a disc jockey (she hosted a radio program with her husband, Buddy Bowser). Harris appeared on the cover of national Black publications, including *Jet*, *Ebony*, *Tan*, and *Hue*, at least thirty times over the course of her modeling career.

Towles's and Harris's successes were relatively small, however, when compared to the meteoric rise of Detroit native Donyale Luna. The first African-American model to appear on the cover of a mainstream fashion magazine (*Harper's Bazaar*, 1964), Luna commanded top fees, equal to and sometimes surpassing those of her white counterparts, before moving to Europe to embark on an acting career. Luna, whose fair skin photographed white, at once upheld and refuted traditional notions and stereotypes of Black and white women, and beauty.

In 1985, Paris-based *Elle* launched its U.S. version, becoming the first white fashion magazine in the U.S. to use Black women with some consistency throughout its editorial pages. Despite this breakthrough, models with darker skin have never been completely accepted in publications and advertisements geared toward white consumers. These models have, however, occasionally found niches in Black advertising. The top model in 1970, for instance, was Pat Evans, a dark-skinned woman who had shaved her head completely. (After her 1972 denouncement of racism in the industry, published in *Essence*, Evans's career suffered significantly.) Other dark-skinned models, such as Naomi Sims, Iman, and Naomi Campbell, have been able to use their success as European runway models to break into U.S. print modeling.

"The blond, blue-eyed ideal is out, diversity is in, and the concept of beauty is growing as wide as the world," announced *Time* after Mary Xinh Nguyen, a Vietnamese-American from California, was named Revlon's Most Unforgettable Woman of 1989 (Scott 1989). Indeed, the presence of women of color has been growing in the clothing and cosmetic industries, in part due to the concept of a "global village" and the remarkable success of clothing and perfume manufacturer Luciano Benetton's long-running "United Colors of Benetton" campaign (launched in 1984). When Revlon created its short-lived Polished Ambers line of cosmetics in 1981, Iman was chosen as its spokeswoman; today, Karen Alexander, Stacey Lowe, and Aya Thorngren are featured in print ads for Cover Girl cosmetics. Other modeling venues, including catalogue and product endorsements, remain all but closed to Black models, however. A broad spectrum of industries rely on pleasant, smiling faces on billboards, television screens, and magazine pages to lure us into buying automobiles, household appliances, and food products. Models who started in this arena, such as Jayne Kennedy in the early 1980s and Kara Young (best known for her Victoria's Secret catalogue modeling) in the early 1990s, find that youth, fair skin, light eyes and hair, in addition to natural photogeneity and vitality, are the main contributors to their success. In advertising, such characteristics are considered especially wholesome and all-American, producing one of two desired results: allowing the consumer to identify with the model or allowing the model to blend into the woodwork, in which case the consumer focuses on the product rather than the model. A notable exception has been the tobacco industry, which since the early 1970s has targeted a Black consumer market through magazine ads (particularly in *Essence* and *Jet*), billboards, and point-of-sale advertising. Such luminaries as Naomi Sims, Beverly Johnson, and Iman have proclaimed "You've come a long way, baby" while brandishing a Virginia Slims.

Contemporary Black models have received their start in a variety of ways. Gail O'Neil was stopped on her way to work as a sales marketing representative for Xerox Corporation, while Tracee Ross won *Star Search*'s modeling contest (a syndicated television talent competition). Karen Alexander, the woman who in 1987 and again in 1988 broke *Sports Illustrated*'s swimsuit edition color barrier, contacted agent after agent (including Eileen Ford, John Casablancas, and Bethann Hardison) before she was finally signed by Pauline Bernatchez of the Legends Agency. Many models turned their careers into further opportunities: Whitney Houston went from being a *Seventeen* cover girl to being a Grammy Award-winning pop singer (aided by her mother, Cissy Houston, and aunt Dionne Warwick); Diahann Carroll and Cicely Tyson became renowned actresses. Others, including runway models Mounia and Iman, have been at the top of

their fields for over a decade. Still others, the majority of Black models, have started big, only to have their career growth stunted. Suzette Charles, the former Miss America who assumed Vanessa Williams's reign, has been unable to launch her much-sought-after singing and acting career, and, as a model, is most frequently seen as a model in advertisements for Modern Wig Designs. Jayne Kennedy, a household name throughout the 1980s, moved from modeling to sports broadcasting before settling into concentrating on her husband and family, while some breakthrough models, most notably Billie Blair and Donyale Luna, suffered tragic descents into drug addiction and, for Luna, suicide. Blair, who took a break from modeling in 1986, has recovered from her addiction and now lectures on body awareness, beauty, health, and fitness, in addition to modeling.

THE FASHION BUSINESS

Even as opportunities in front of the camera, on the runway, and in international fashion houses are slowly beginning to broaden, opportunities for Black businesswomen in fashion remain limited. Those few Black women who have broken through the barriers have been successful. Clementine LeTouze, for instance, is a New York native residing in Paris, where she works as a press attaché for major design houses and trendy boutiques.

Bethann Hardison, former runway model and booking agent for Click, founded her own agency in 1985. One of the fastest-growing modeling agencies in New York City, Bethann Management is frequently called when advertisers want to add multiculturalism to their image. Hardison's success can be attributed in part to her history in the fashion industry and her desire to learn every aspect of a historically dangerous business for women. Bethann Management's most successful predecessor, the Grace Del Marco Modeling Agency, was headed by Ophelia DeVore. DeVore began running the agency in 1947, ultimately guiding the careers of Helen Williams, a part-time print model, and Avis McCarther, a full-time television commercial model. Other pioneering Black women agents included Valaida M. Walker, who directed Wendy's Models in Philadelphia, and Elaina Brooks, who headed the American Model Agency in New York. Brooks, a former model, helped Madelyn Sanders become one of the first Black models to appear in a television commercial (for Chock full o' Nuts), and pushed for the use of Black male and Black female models.

Helen Williams, who distinguished herself as the first brown-skinned (not light-skinned) model to achieve national prominence when she was featured in "the sepia version of white ads" (Summers 1987) for Noxema, Modess, and Budweiser, began in the industry in 1954 as an artist for Pagano Studios, the second largest commercial photography studio in New York City. Even after becoming a successful model, Williams continued at Pagano as a stylist, coordinating models, wardrobe, and props for advertisements.

The most notable Black woman behind the scenes in the fashion business is Naomi Sims (b. 1949). The fashion model who set the industry on end with her "authoritative ebony" beauty (Summers 1987) and unflappable poise made history as the first Black woman to appear on the covers of *Ladies' Home Journal* (1968) and *Life* (1969), then quit the business in 1973, at the age of twenty-three. Frustrated with the wigs and make-up given her for photo shoots, Sims eventually created the Naomi Sims Collection of wigs and hair pieces for women of color. She wrote four books: *How to Be a Top Model* (1979), *All about Success for the Black Woman* (1982), *All about Hair Care for the Black Woman* (1982), and *All about Health and Beauty for the Black Woman* (1986). Sims continued her jaunt on the other side of the camera with the 1987 creation of the Naomi Sims Skin Care Collection, a thirteen-product line that took ten years to develop. Her success, as well as that of a handful of other start-up cosmetics companies founded by women of color (e.g., Juin Rachele Cosmetics, directly distributed, founded in Houston in 1986; Gazelle International, based in Paris, founded in 1983 by Georgia native Patricia A. French), continues to inspire Black women entrepreneurs.

Overall, the fashion industry has been slow to accept Black beauty and Black talent. When it has acknowledged Black talent, it has focused on male designers. When it has accepted Black beauty, it has alternated between Black women adhering to European standards of beauty on the one hand and an exotic, fantasy image on the other. As U.S. consumer markets and the work force become predominantly people of color, as demographics in the United States and the world politically and economically continue to shift, and as the concept of the global village becomes increasingly fashionable, the industry will be forced to widen the opportunities already staked out by Black women pioneers.

[*See also* BEAUTY CULTURE.]

BIBLIOGRAPHY

Banik, Sheila. "Cutting on the Bias," *Black Enterprise* (July 1981); Brandon, Barbara. "Making of a Star: Gail O'Neil," *Essence* (January 1987); Brown, Elsa Barkley. Personal interview (September 1992); Campbell, Roy. "Working It!," *Essence* (September 1992); Darden, Norma Jean. "Harlem's Fashion Museum," *Essence* (November 1979); Darnton, Nina. "The Rainbow Coalition," *Newsweek* (July 13, 1992); *Ebony*. "Ebony Fashion Fair Celebrates 33rd Anniversary" (April 1991), and "Have Black Models Really Made It?" (May 1970), and "New Beauties versus Old" (March 1954); Edmond, Alfred, Jr. "Battle of the Vanities," *Black Enterprise* (March 1989); *Essence*. "Black Beauty at the Couture" (December 1991), and "How the Top Models Stay on Course" (January 1987), and "Top Women Designers" (July 1990), and "Works of Art to Wear" (October 1990); Fields, Mamie Garvin with Karen Fields. *Lemon Swamp and Other Places: A Carolina Memoir* (1983); *Glamour*. "The New Top Models" (May 1989); Gregory, Deborah. "They Shoot Models, Don't They," *Essence* (April 1991); Hartman, Rose. "Bethann: Then and Now," *Essence* (January 1987); *Hue*. "Model Turns Singer" (February 1958); *Jet*. "Singer Whitney Houston a Model of Success" (July 16, 1990); Jones, Jacqueline. *Labor of Love, Labor of Sorrow: Black Women, Work, and the Family from Slavery to the Present* (1985); Lurie, Diana. "Naomi," *Ladies' Home Journal* (November 1968); Milano, Carol. "Small-Budget Start-Ups," *Essence* (October 1989); Murray, James. *To Find an Image: Black Films from Uncle Tom to Superfly* (1973); *Newsweek*. "A Collection That Spans the Centuries" (July 13, 1992); Norwich, William. "Role Model," *Vogue* (November 1991); Perkins, Kathy A. "Mildred E. Blount" (in this volume); Scott, Sophfronia. "It's a Small World after All," *Time* (September 25, 1989); Shield, Jody. "Hype and Hoopla Have Been the Hallmarks of Fashion Shows since They Were Created in the 1800s," *Vogue* (March 1991); Summers, Barbara. "Model Firsts: Pioneers in Black Beauty," *Essence* (January 1987), and "The Modeling Industry: Our Story," *Essence* (January 1987); Taylor, Peggy Ann. "Mounia!" *Essence* (January 1987); Valentine Museum, Fannie Criss Vertical File. Richmond, Virginia; Whigham, Marjorie. "Self-Renewal: Billie Blair's Story," *Essence* (January 1987); Williams, Etta Rebecca. "Fannie Criss: Turn of the Century Dressmaker," *Richmond Quarterly* (Spring 1982).

N. H GOODALL

FAUSET, CRYSTAL BIRD
(1894-1965)

Crystal Bird Fauset was the first African-American woman to be elected to a state house of representatives. She was born in 1894 to Benjamin O. and Portia E. (Lovett) Bird in Princess Anne, Maryland, but was raised in Boston by her maternal aunt, Lucy Groves. There she attended public schools and was considered an outstanding student. Later in life Fauset maintained that her social and political conscience was shaped by her experiences as a child in Boston. She went on to Teachers College, Columbia University, where she earned a B.S. (1931).

Upon graduation Crystal Bird worked as a social worker and administrator of Negro affairs for the Young Women's Christian Association in New York City and Philadelphia. In 1933, she was named executive secretary for the Institute of Race Relations at Swarthmore College. While serving in that position, she became convinced of the necessity of political action for economic change. In 1935, after marrying author and educator Arthur Huff Fauset, she became director of Negro women's activities for the Democratic National Committee. Through that position she established numerous political contacts and was appointed in 1936 as an assistant personnel director in the Philadelphia office of the Works Progress Administration (WPA).

In 1938, the leadership of Philadelphia's local Democratic party organization asked Fauset to run for a seat in the Pennsylvania House of Representatives from the Eighteenth District in Philadelphia, and she accepted. Upon election in November 1938, she became the first African-American woman ever to achieve such a position. She remained in the legislature only one year, however, before accepting an appointment in November 1939 to the Pennsylvania WPA as assistant director in charge of education and recreational programs. She remained in that position until 1941, when, with the assistance of Eleanor Roosevelt, a close friend, she was appointed as the special consultant on Negro affairs in the Office of Civilian Affairs in Washington, D.C.

By 1944, however, Fauset had become disappointed with the Democratic party because of its handling of Black Americans in the war effort, and she announced her support of Governor Thomas E. Dewey's bid for the Republican presidential nomination. After meeting with Dewey and other Republican leaders, she became an advisor to the Republican National Committee's division on Negro affairs.

Fauset held a number of other important posts during her distinguished career. For a time she was chair of the Philadelphia Negro Women's Democratic League and served on the board of trustees of Cheyney State Teachers College. In 1963, Philadelphia Mayor James Tate appointed her to the board of directors of the Small Business Opportunities Corporation.

Fauset suffered a heart attack and died in Philadelphia on Sunday, March 27, 1965. She believed that wide economic gaps between human beings interfered with human relationships and she spent most of

Crystal Bird Fauset, who believed in going to the heart of the economic situation through political action, was the first Black woman to be elected to a state legislature. [National Archives]

her life attempting to close those economic gaps to improve the quality of human life.

BIBLIOGRAPHY

Aptheker, Herbert, ed. *A Documentary History of the Negro People in the United States, 1910-1932* (1932); Franklin, V. P. *The Education of Black Philadelphia, the Social and Educational History of a Minority Community 1900-1950* (1979); *NA*; *Philadelphia Inquirer* (November 13, 1938; December 21, 1938; February 14, 1939; October 17, 1939; November 3, 1939; July 11, 1940; September 15, 1940; July 12, 1944; September 8, 10, 21, 1944; January 20, 1945); *Philadelphia Tribune* (March 30, 1965); Westbrook, C. H., ed. *The Pennsylvania Manual* (1940).

V. P. FRANKLIN

FAUSET, JESSIE REDMON (1882-1961)

"Nothing . . . has ever been farther from my thought than writing to establish a thesis," Jessie Fauset stated flatly in the foreword to her novel *The Chinaberry Tree* (1931). She was not only introducing her third novel, but also defending her first two novels, *There Is Confusion* (1924) and *Plum Bun* (1929), against the criticism that they presented thesis-ridden, middle-class Black characters in the service of racial uplift. Fauset's foreword pointed quite specifically to race as the driving force behind her fiction: "Colored people have been the subjects which I have chosen for my novels partly because they are the ones I know best, partly because of all the other separate groups which constitute the American cosmogony none of them, to me, seems to be naturally endowed with the stuff of which chronicles may be made." Throughout her career the condition of Black people in America was to be the subject of her writings.

Fauset's insistence, however, that being "a Negro in America posits a dramatic situation" waiting for a writer "to interpret [the elements] with fidelity" included two terms, Negro and American, inextricably linked in her own interpretative strategy. Her overt connection of the two terms contributed in part to the negative criticism of her fiction as reactionary that persisted into the second half of the twentieth century with critics such as Robert Bone, who labeled her one of "the Rear Guard," old-fashioned writers of the Harlem Renaissance. The focus on her texts as dated novels of manners obscured her modern treatment of gender roles, female socialization, and sexism, a treatment that recent critics such as Carolyn Sylvander have identified in reevaluating Fauset's woman-centered fiction.

As a committed writer of poetry, essays, reviews, and fiction during the Harlem Renaissance of the 1920s and early 1930s, Fauset did have a thesis influencing her literary production. Her conviction was that in order to combat racism, white Americans had to be educated about the realities, rather than the exoticism, of Black American life, and Black Americans had to be represented in their home life and personal relations as similar to white Americans. In her foreword to *The Chinaberry Tree*, she discussed her conception of "the colored American who is not being pressed too hard by the Furies of Prejudice, Ignorance and Economic Injustice" as "not so very different from any other American, just distinctive." In establishing "the colored American" as having "wholesome respect for family and education and labor and the fruits of labor," Fauset emphasized the terms of her comparison: "the dark American ... wears his [or her] joy and rue very much as does the white American. He [or she] may wear it with some differences but it is the same joy and the same rue." Fauset remained faithful to this vision of Black Americans throughout her career, yet all of her writings show her keen awareness of the racism and sexism

often beneath the surface in the cultural and literary politics of the 1920s and 1930s.

Jessie Redmon Fauset's formative years shaped her specific brand of race consciousness and her awareness of the contradictions often apparent in being both Black and American that informed her writing. Born in Camden County, New Jersey, on April 26, 1882, she was the youngest daughter of seven children of Annie Seamon and Reverend Redmon Fauset, an African Methodist Episcopal minister who crusaded for racial justice in his community outside of Philadelphia. Her family was cultured and refined, but never financially secure. Placing a high value on education for the upward mobility of Black people, her parents inspired Fauset to succeed in the Philadelphia public schools, but they also prepared her for the certain impact of racism upon her achievements. An honors student at the High School for Girls, she applied to Bryn Mawr, a women's college that was not prepared to admit a Black woman and instead initiated a scholarship for her at Cornell University. There, as a student of classical languages, Fauset continued her record of academic achievement and was elected to Phi Beta Kappa.

Despite an impressive undergraduate record and a 1905 Baccalaureate degree, she did not find the world of work hospitable. Throughout her life, her talents and interests rarely matched the limited employment options available to an African-American and a female. Fauset was unable to secure a teaching post with the segregated Philadelphia public schools, but she was both resourceful and determined. After a brief tenure in the Baltimore school system, Fauset moved to Washington, D.C., to teach French and Latin at the M Street High School (later renamed Paul Laurence Dunbar High). While teaching, Fauset completed an M.A. in French at the University of Pennsylvania. Although a popular and well-respected member of the M Street faculty, she desired a greater use of her talents than teaching allowed, and in 1919 she received an offer for more challenging work from the *Crisis*, whose editor, W.E.B. Du Bois, had recognized Fauset as the ideal candidate for the new position of literary editor on the basis of both her educational background and her creative writing, which she had begun contributing to *Crisis* in 1912.

The position in New York with *Crisis*, the official publication of the National Association for the Advancement of Colored People (NAACP), propelled Fauset into a literary career and into a mentoring role for Black writers. At the beginning of her editorial work, Fauset persuaded Du Bois that the arts, and creative writing in particular, could be a force in racial uplift. Left to pursue her own direction at the magazine, she placed a greater emphasis on poetry and fiction by cultivating the talents of young writers, such as Claude McKay, Jean Toomer, Countee Cullen, George Schuyler, Arna Bontemps, and Langston Hughes, who later recognized her contribution as an enabling force by calling her a "midwife" to the emerging literary renaissance in New York. From her arrival in 1919 to her departure in 1926, Fauset was the astute guiding spirit behind *Crisis* and its movement into the forefront of literary and racial modernism. With this cultural work, she secured a significant place for herself in African-American literary history.

Not only did Fauset serve as a literary editor, she also shaped a cultural agenda for the *Crisis*, an agenda that centrally involved the youth of the race. She envisioned a march of racial progress in which succeeding generations would distance Black people from the negative societal constructions of inferiority resulting from enslavement. In 1920 and 1921, she directed her energies toward realizing an NAACP monthly magazine for children, *The Brownies' Book*. Although Du Bois was its founder, Fauset was its functional editor, and she stated in the magazine's introduction that she was designing a format to "teach Universal Love and Brotherhood for all the little folks—black and brown, yellow and white." She herself wrote numerous children's articles, stories, poems, biographies, and plays, in addition to soliciting and publishing pieces by a number of aspiring authors, such as Nella Larsen, who would become prominent during the Harlem Renaissance.

Fauset turned to writing novels in 1922 when she recognized that Black authors should take control of their representation in fiction. Begun in response to white novelist T. S. Stribling's *Birthright* (1922), her first novel, *There Is Confusion*, appeared in 1924, the eve of the most productive period of the Harlem or New Negro Renaissance. Both racial identity and racial heritage were central discourses in the cultural movement that gave rise to a new generation of Black artists and intellectuals. Fauset's novel explored both discourses in rendering the lives of three interconnected characters, Joanna Marshall, Peter Bye, and Maggie Ellersley, who survive racial discrimination and transcend class divisions during the early decades of the twentieth century.

Ambitious and industrious, Joanna is the daughter of a successful caterer whose ascent from slavery in Virginia anchors his faith in the American Dream of financial success and class mobility for his children. Shiftless and irresponsible, Peter is the son of a freeborn father who descends the socioeconomic ladder and leaves a legacy of despair. Dependent and opportunistic, Maggie is the daughter of a poor laundress who attempts to teach the value of an honest, self-supporting existence.

The three youths initially misread their access routes to productive adulthoods and misunderstand the impact of racial barriers on their lives, but all three come to terms with themselves, with racism and sexism in American society, and with their own potential for transforming the future. Their experiences in combating marginality and attaining visibility in a multifaceted urban environment reflect Fauset's faith in motivation, work, and discipline as correctives to stereotypical views of Black persons, as well as her recognition of the difficulty of public or personal achievement for people of color, particularly women.

Although praised by critics such as Du Bois and William Stanley Braithwaite, anxious for positive representations of Black men and women, *There Is Confusion* did not propel Fauset into the forefront of the New Negro movement. But her limited success inspired her to concentrate on writing fiction. After studying in France and traveling in Europe during 1925, she resigned from the *Crisis* in 1926. Unable to break the color bar in the New York publishing industry, she could not obtain a job as a publisher's reader despite her graduate education, fluency in foreign languages, and experience in editing. Nor could she secure employment with a New York foundation or as a social secretary ("in a private family, preferably for a woman," as she wrote to Joel Spingarn of the NAACP, whose help she sought in finding positions that would allow her more time to write).

Fauset's second novel, *Plum Bun: A Novel without a Moral*, was published in 1929, two years after she had returned to teaching French at Junior High School No. 136 and later at DeWitt Clinton High School. While full-time teaching slowed her writing, the greater difficulty Fauset faced was finding a publisher. The publisher of her first novel, Boni and Liveright, refused the *Plum Bun* manuscript; following rejections from Alfred A. Knopf and other major New York publishing firms actively seeking New Negro books, Fauset secured an acceptance from a small company, Frederick A. Stokes, who remained committed to publishing Fauset's novels despite the mixed reviews.

Fauset's personal experiences as an independent, educated, and well-traveled woman who because of her race and gender encountered social and cultural forces restricting her personal development and limiting her career choices influenced her themes in

Plum Bun. In a satiric exposition of seductive fairy tale and romance plots for Black women, Fauset creates a racialized female *bildungsroman* divided into five sections: "Home," "Market," "Plum Bun," "Home Again," and "Market Is Done." The five

Jessie Redmon Fauset began writing novels in order to take control of the representation of Black characters in fiction; her four novels use passing as white as a metaphor to represent the arbitrariness and destructiveness of racism. As literary editor of the Crisis, *she fostered the work of many young writers prominent in the Harlem Renaissance, including Claude McKay, Jean Toomer, Countee Cullen, Arna Bontemps, and Langston Hughes. [Schomburg Center]*

correspond to the parts of a nursery rhyme provided as epigraph ("To Market, to market / To buy a Plum Bun; / Home again, Home again, / Market is done."), and they serve to underscore the destructiveness of adhering to a fairy-tale marriage plot when the social constructions of race and the cultural inequities of gender render the Black female a powerless commodity.

Angela Murray, the fair-skinned protagonist, understands the restrictions placed on her ambitions not simply because she is a Black person but also because she is a woman. Discerning that "men had a better time of it than women, coloured men than coloured women, white men than white women," Angela decides to emancipate herself from the bottom half of the racial hierarchy. After the death of her parents, she leaves her darker-skinned sister Virginia in Philadelphia and moves to New York, where, as Angela Mory, she passes for white. In her dual efforts to become an artist and to marry a white man, Angela seeks not only "freedom and independence," but also "power and protection." Though she recognizes the arbitrariness of color in racial designations and the irony of racism directed toward a white-skinned Black person, she does not recognize that her own romantic idealization of marriage invests color with a substantive reality and allows for the white male's exercise of power over her.

Ultimately, Angela relinquishes subordination to men by empowering herself through her painting and her job as a designer. In realigning her priorities, she achieves self-actualization that contributes to her reclaiming her racial identity and affirming her heritage. Yet, in storybook fashion, she receives the reward of a true love, Anthony Cross, whom she is preparing to marry as the novel ends. Coincidentally, at the age of forty-seven and just as *Plum Bun* appeared, Fauset herself married insurance executive Herbert Hill.

Her third novel, *The Chinaberry Tree: A Novel of American Life*, was introduced in 1931 by white novelist Zona Gale. Gale attempted to alleviate claims that Fauset's Black characters were unbelievable: "there is in America a great group of Negroes of education and substance who are living lives of quiet interests and pursuits, quite unconnected with white folk save as these are casually met." Fauset herself stated that as a girl of fifteen, she had actually heard the story that became the basis of first a short story, "Double Trouble," and then the novel *The Chinaberry Tree.*

The plot centers on the women of the Strange family. Aunt Sal Strange has been excluded from the Black community of Red Brook, New Jersey, because of her love relationship with the white Colonel Halloway. Laurentine, the product of Sal's union with the Colonel, grows up well provided for but isolated in the white house bought by her father, after she learns from a playmate that she has bad blood. Judy Strange, Sal's sister, nurtures Laurentine out of her retreat, but she departs Red Brook after an affair with Sylvester Forten. Melissa Paul, Judy's daughter, arrives from Philadelphia to live with her relatives whom she sees as lacking respectability. The tension in the household mounts over issues of legitimacy and conventionality; Melissa feels superior to Laurentine, as well as to Sal, and Laurentine resents reminders of her birth outside of wedlock. Melissa's own origins are revealed dramatically when she discovers that Malory Forten, the Red Brook youth who shares her views and values and whom she plans to marry, is her half-brother.

In examining attitudes within the Black community toward miscegenation, class pretensions, extramarital and interracial relationships, Fauset attempted to break new ground in her fiction and to represent a revision of the constructs stratifying Black people. She positioned social conventions and communal expectations against the grain of meaningful human relationships. In defiance of arbitrary values and rules, her characters come to accept the integrity of human life and the basic equality of all living people. As Dr. Stephen Denleigh remarks in *The Chinaberry Tree*, "Biology transcends society!" His response is to Laurentine's confession of her illegitimacy, a condition that he dismisses: "The facts of life, birth, and death are more important than the rules of the living, marriage, law, the sanction of the church or man." Denleigh's dismissal of the relevancy of legitimacy in determining an individual's significance nullifies one of the measures of social status overvalued by the newly emergent Black middle class. That Denleigh and Laurentine marry argues for a reintegration of the Black community and for a transformation of its restrictive attitudes.

Fauset's last novel, *Comedy: American Style*, was published in 1933, when the more intense activity of the Harlem Renaissance was over, and this text may be her satiric response to the elevation of color among its more vocal participants. Olivia Blanchard Carey, the central figure in the text, is a self-hating, deluded woman who despises Black people ostensibly because they are victims, vulnerable to injury, and discriminated against in American society. Unable to accept herself as Black, she has an all-consuming need to be herself, though she ultimately achieves her desire to pass for white and to escape the confines of American

society. Olivia's psychology is not fully revealed; this failure is especially noticeable in the early section of the text, which focuses primarily on Olivia's mother, Janet Blanchard, and her efforts to survive after the death of her husband Lee, and her subsequent happy marriage to Ralph Blake. While Janet is class conscious, all three are secure in their racial identity and are strong supporters of their race. Olivia completely escapes their influence during her formative years.

Olivia's husband, Christopher Carey, a Harvard-trained physician, does not share her obsession with color. He and their first two children, Teresa and Christopher, are light enough to satisfy Olivia's fantasies, but the third child, Oliver, is brown-skinned like Olivia's own father. While the entire family suffers because of her mania, Oliver commits suicide when he realizes the cause of his mother's aversion to him. Even Teresa, who pleases her mother by marrying outside the race, is miserable in her loveless union to a Frenchman who refuses to acknowledge her mother. Only Christopher, who marries Phebe Grant (blond, blue-eyed, working-class, and proudly Black), manages to survive his mother's obsessions and to build a productive life.

In all four of her novels, Fauset used passing as white as a means of representing the arbitrariness and destructiveness of racial constructions in the United States. Her particular concerns with the impact of race on women and the limitations placed on Black women by their own communities were often masked in complicated, unwieldy plots culminating in happy marriages. Because her fictional strategy relied upon the anticipation of change within social institutions, her critiques of race, gender, and class ideologies were circuitous, and her messages of female emancipation, development, autonomy, and empowerment were coded. Fauset died in 1961, before the current decoding and revaluation of her fiction began. Read now with fresh critical tools, her texts reveal the determined effort of a woman writer to tell the stories of Black Americans that, while not always successful or popular, demand articulation and attention.

BIBLIOGRAPHY
AAW2; *AAWW*; Bone, Robert. *The Negro Novel in America* (1958); Braithwaite, William Stanley. "The Novels of Jessie Fauset." In *The Black Novelist*, ed. Robert Hemenway (1970); Davis, Arthur. *From the Dark Tower: Afro-American Writers 1900 to 1960* (1974); Davis, Thadious M. "Foreword" to *There Is Confusion* by Jessie Redmon Fauset (1989); Fauset, Jessie. *The Chinaberry Tree* (1931), and *Comedy: American Style* (1933), and *Plum Bun* (1929), and *There Is Confusion* (1924); Hughes, Langston. *The Big Sea* (1940); Lewis, David Levering. *When Harlem Was in Vogue*

(1981); McDowell, Deborah. "The Neglected Dimension of Jessie Redmon Fauset." In *Conjuring: Black Women, Fiction, and Literary Theory*, ed. Marjorie Pryse and Hortense Spillers (1985); Perry, Margaret. *Silence to the Drums: A Survey of the Literature of the Harlem Renaissance* (1976); Sims, Janet. "Jessie Redmon Fauset (1882-1961): A Selected Annotated Bibliography," *Black American Literature Forum* (Winter 1980); Singh, Amritjit. *The Novels of the Harlem Renaissance: Twelve Black Writers, 1923-1933* (1976); Starkey, Marion. "Jessie Fauset," *Southern Workman* (May 1932); Sylvander, Carolyn Wedin. *Jessie Fauset, Black American Author* (1981); Wall, Cheryl. "Jessie Redmon Fauset (1882-1961)." In *The Gender of Modernism*, ed. Bonnie Kime Scott (1990); Watson, Carole McAlpine. *Prologue: The Novels of Black American Women, 1891-1965* (1985).

THADIOUS M. DAVIS

FEARING, MARIA (1838-1937)

At the age of fifty-six, with less than a high school education, Maria Fearing applied to the executive committee of Foreign Missions of the Southern Presbyterian Church (now Presbyterian Church in the United States) for an appointment as a missionary. Fearing had vowed as a young girl that she would go to Africa. The executive committee refused to subsidize her because of her advanced age. Undaunted, Fearing sold her home in Anniston, Alabama, took her savings and $100 pledged by the women of the Congregational Church in Talladega, Alabama, and for two years paid her own way as a missionary. Eventually, on October 7, 1896, the Southern Presbyterian Church appointed Fearing as a regularly stationed and salaried missionary.

Maria Fearing was born a slave on July 26, 1838, in Gainesville, Alabama. She completed the ninth grade at Talladega College (Talladega, Alabama) and taught at a rural school in Anniston. She later returned to Talladega College and worked in the boarding department. In 1894, Stillman College (Tuscaloosa, Alabama) graduate William Sheppard, who was on furlough from the Presbyterian Congo Mission, spoke at Talladega and appealed for missionary volunteers.

Fearing sailed to the Congo Free State (now Zaire) on May 26, 1894. She was stationed at the Luebo station. There she founded and directed the Pantops Home for Girls until 1915. In addition to her activities with the home, Fearing taught in the mission day school and Sunday School and worked with women in surrounding villages.

Fearing took a furlough in 1915 but because of her age, she did not return to Africa. She died in Gainesville, Alabama, on May 23, 1937.

BIBLIOGRAPHY
Jacobs, Sylvia M. "Their 'Special Mission': Afro-American Women as Missionaries in the Congo." In *Black Americans and the Missionary Movement in Africa*, ed. Sylvia M. Jacobs (1982); Timmons, Sarah Lee, ed. *Glorious Living, Informal Sketches of Seven Missionaries of the Presbyterian Church, U.S.* (1937).

SYLVIA M. JACOBS

FEDERAL WRITERS PROJECT SLAVE NARRATIVES

The Federal Writers Project Slave Narratives constitute a valuable source of information on the history of Black women. Consisting of the transcripts of interviews conducted in the late 1930s with thousands of elderly Black women and men throughout the former Confederate (and other) states, the narratives are in readily accessible, published form. This material provides our fullest picture of the institution of slavery as seen through the eyes of the people who lived under it.

The narratives are the result of a Federal Writers Project (FWP) program initiated at the state level and, in 1936-38, conducted under the auspices of the Works Progress Administration (WPA), a New Deal agency with central offices in Washington, D.C. The purposes of the project were to provide employment for out-of-work writers and to record the memories of former slaves who by that time were quite advanced in age. In the 1970s, editor George P. Rawick collected and compiled transcripts that were scattered throughout the nation. Published in 1972-73, series 1 and 2 (nineteen volumes) of the narratives include an introduction written by Rawick, more than 2,000 interviews from the Library of Congress Rare Book Room, plus two volumes of interviews sponsored by Fisk University in the early 1930s. Supplementary series 1 (twelve volumes) followed in 1978 and includes interview transcripts discovered in the Archive of Folk Song at the Library of Congress as well as material from several southern university libraries and state archive collections, most notably the Mississippi interviews. Supplementary series 2, published in 1979 (ten volumes), consists primarily of Texas narratives located at the Barker Texas History Center at the University of Texas in Austin. The

Virginia narratives are available in a separate volume edited by Charles L. Perdue, Jr., Thomas E. Barden, and Robert K. Phillips entitled *Weevils in the Wheat: Interviews with Virginia Ex-Slaves* (1980).

The narratives are an essential historical source for several reasons. They provide a necessary corrective to accounts of slavery based on the exclusive use of the record books, diaries, and correspondence of slaveholding men and women during the late antebellum period. Also, the interview material covers a wide variety of topics related to slavery, from the material well-being of Black people on southern plantations to the sexual division of labor in the fields and in the big house, from techniques of slave resistance to the creation of an African-American culture in the slave quarters. Of special relevance to the history of women are the former slaves' comments on family relations, child-rearing techniques, the role of women as spiritual leaders in the community, sexual abuse by white men, and relations with white women of the master class.

Moreover, material in the narratives covers not only the period of slavery from approximately 1830 to 1861 but also the Civil War years and Reconstruction (encounters with Yankees, family reconstitution after emancipation, emergence of sharecropping); family histories in the late nineteenth century (life in the rural South, the resourcefulness of landless households); and the struggles of elderly Black women during the Great Depression. Finally, the narratives provide much useful information on slavery as a multiracial institution, involving persons of Native American, African, and Anglo descent, and on the routine, forced separation of slave family members despite the claims of paternalistic planters to the contrary.

Still, the social context under which the interviews took place, and the fact that they later underwent an editing process, limits their usefulness as a historical source. With the exception of the interviews conducted in Virginia and Florida, most were carried out by middle-class white people (usually women). The interviewees, all of whom were elderly Black men and women, tended to abide by the age-old southern code of racial etiquette in response to the questions, some of which were insulting ("Were newborn slave babies good looking?" "Have you been happier in slavery or free?" "Did slaves mind being called nigger?") and later were recorded in so-called Negro dialect, embellished with the condescending comments of the interviewers. In the process of editing the original transcripts, some state FWP employees actually softened comments that were critical of slavery in an effort to emphasize the alleged humaneness of the institution. Also, because most of the informants were over eighty years old at the time of the interview, their memories of slavery had been shaped many years before, primarily by their childhood experiences, and, in some cases, by family oral traditions. Because the interviews were conducted during the Depression, many informants were suffering from severe physical and material deprivation, and their responses sometimes reveal a certain wistfulness for times past when, whether accurately or not, they remembered having enough food to eat. In addition, some were under the misconception that interviewers were in a position to increase their meager pension or welfare checks. In his book *Slavery Remembered* (1979), Paul Escott examines different responses to similar questions based on the race of the interviewer. All these factors helped shape not only the interviews but also the final transcripts found in FWP files.

In an effort to achieve a balanced assessment of a limited number of interviews, *Weevils in the Wheat* includes background information on the Virginia narratives as well as duplicate transcripts of the interviews. The editors also present a history of the Virginia project and the book that resulted from it, *The Negro in Virginia* (1940). Appendices record, for example, the race of interviewers, the birth year and residence of the informants, dates of interviews conducted by each FWP worker, and all 333 questions listed in a sample questionnaire sent out from the Washington WPA office to state officials. This material helps the historian evaluate the gender and racial dynamics between Black and white men and women involved in the interviewing process, and it also provides insight into the work of the middle-class southern Black women who helped administer the project and who derived their living, however briefly, from their contributions to it.

BIBLIOGRAPHY

Bailey, David. "A Divided Prism: Two Sources of Black Testimony on Slavery," *Journal of Southern History* (August 1980); Blassingame, John W. "Using the Testimony of Ex-Slaves: Approaches and Problems," *Journal of Southern History* (November 1975); Escott, Paul D. *Slavery Remembered: A Record of Twentieth-Century Slave Narratives* (1979); Goodson, Martia Graham. "An Introductory Essay and Subject Index to Selected Interviews from the Slave Narrative Collection," Ph.D. diss. (1977); Jacobs, Donald M. *Index to the American Slave* (1981); Perdue, Charles L., Jr., Thomas E. Barden, and Robert K. Phillips. *Weevils in the Wheat: Interviews with Virginia Ex-Slaves* (1980); Rawick, George P., ed. *The American Slave: A Composite Autobiography* (1972, 1978, 1979); Social Science Institute, Fisk University.

Unwritten History of Slavery: Autobiographical Accounts of Negro Ex-Slaves (1945); Woodward, C. Vann. "History from Slave Sources," *American Historical Review* (April 1974).

JACQUELINE JONES

FEMINISM IN THE TWENTIETH CENTURY

"Shall it any longer be said of the daughters of Africa, they have no ambition, they have no force?" asked Maria W. Stewart in 1831. "By no means," she answered. "Let every female heart become united" (Richardson 1987). Stewart's call for Black women's unity, like that offered by other prominent nineteenth-century Black feminists such as Sojourner Truth, Mary Ann Shadd Cary, Harriet Tubman, and Lucy C. Laney, marked the origins of Black feminism in the United States. These nineteenth-century Black women laid the intellectual and political cornerstone of Black feminism, but African-American women in the twentieth century brought Black feminism as a political movement, and Black feminist thought as its intellectual voice and vision, to full fruition.

WHAT IS BLACK FEMINISM?

Black feminism originated in the lived experiences that enslaved African women brought with them to the United States in the eighteenth and early nineteenth centuries. African women were socialized to be independent, self-reliant, and resourceful. While this African feminism was modified by slavery, being enslaved also encouraged Black women to maintain these key elements of their African self-definitions as women.

Black feminism is the process of self-conscious struggle which empowers women and men to realize a humanistic vision of community. African-American women's experiences with work and family during slavery and after Emancipation led them to develop a specific perspective on the relationship between multiple types of oppression. Black women experienced not just racism, but sexism, classism, and other forms of oppression. This struggle in turn fostered a broader, more humanistic view of community that encouraged each individual to develop his or her own individual, unique human potential. Such a community is based on notions of fairness, equality, and justice for all human beings, not just African-American women. Black feminism's fundamental goal of creating a humanistic vision of community is more comprehensive than that of other social action movements. For example, unlike the women's movement in the United States, Black feminism has not striven solely to secure equal rights for women with men, because gaining equal rights with Black men would not necessarily lead to liberation for African-American women. Instead, Black feminism encompasses a comprehensive, anti-sexist, anti-racist, and anti-elitist perspective on social change. Black feminism is a means for human empowerment rather than an end in and of itself.

CORE THEMES IN BLACK FEMINISM

Since its inception in the early 1800s, Black feminism has reflected a uniformity of theme and philosophical outlook. Despite differences of age, sexual orientation, ethnicity, and region of the country, all Black women share the universal experience of being African-American women in a society that denigrates women of African descent. This commonality of experience suggests that certain characteristic themes will shape Black women's thought and activism. Contemporary Black feminist scholars' efforts to reclaim a longstanding yet suppressed Black feminist intellectual tradition reveal Black women's historical attention to four core themes—the legacy of struggle, the search for voice, the interdependence of thought and action, and the significance of empowerment in everyday life.

One core theme has been the legacy of struggle against racism, sexism, and social class exploitation. Despite heterogeneity among African-American women, this legacy has fostered a heightened consciousness among Black women intellectuals about the importance of thinking inclusively about how race, class, and gender shape Black women's lives. The legacy of struggle against racism, sexism, and classism is a common thread binding African-American women regardless of historical era, age, social class, or sexual orientation.

This legacy of struggle and its resulting humanistic vision differentiate Black feminism from historical expressions of white feminism in the United States. While middle-class white feminists condemn the restrictions of affluence, the majority of Black women struggle against the oppression of racism and poverty. As a result, Black feminists' central concern has been the transformation of societal relations based on race, class, and gender.

The search for voice or the refusal of Black women to remain silenced comprises a second core theme of Black feminism. In order to exploit Black women, dominant groups have developed controlling images or stereotypes claiming that Black women are inferior. Because they justify Black women's oppression, four interrelated controlling images of Black women—the mammy, the matriarch, the welfare mother, and the jezebel—reflect the dominant group's interest in maintaining Black women's subordination. Challenging these stereotypes has been an essential part of the search for voice.

Black women's lives are a series of negotiations aimed at reconciling the contradictions of their own internally defined images of self as Black women with these controlling images. Much Black feminist thought reflects this search for a self-defined voice that expresses a Black feminist standpoint. Being labeled "Black women" makes African-American women especially visible and exposes them to the negative treatment afforded Black women as a group. From their experiences, Black women have developed a unique vision and voice that many have used as a source of strength. The controlling images of Black women are so negative that they require resistance if Black women are to have any positive self-images. For African-American women, the search for voice emerges from the struggle to reject controlling images and embrace knowledge essential to their survival.

Another core theme is the impossibility of separating intellectual inquiry from political activism. This theme of the interdependence of thought and action stresses the connections between Black women's ideas and their actions. Historically, Black feminism has merged the two by espousing a both/and orientation that views thought and action as a part of the same process. This both/and orientation grows from Black women's experiences living as both African-Americans and women, and, in many cases, in poverty. It is this interrelationship between thought and action that allows Black women to see the connections among concrete experiences with oppression, to develop a self-defined voice concerning those experiences, and to enact the resistance that can follow.

The last core theme is empowerment in the context of everyday life. Black feminism cannot challenge race, gender, and class oppression without empowering Black women to take action in everyday life. Black feminist thought sees Black women's oppression and their resistance to oppression as inextricably linked. Thus, oppression responds to human action. Black feminist thought views the world as a dynamic place where the goal is not merely to survive or fit in, but as a place where Black women feel ownership and accountability. The very existence of Black feminism suggests that Black women always have a choice and the power to act, no matter how bleak a situation may appear to be. It also shows that although the empowerment of individual Black women is important, only

collective action can effectively eradicate longstanding political, social, and economic inequalities.

Empowerment for African-American women involves a variety of strategies. Empowerment occurs when a formerly silent Black mother in the inner city complains to school officials about her child's treatment. Empowerment happens when Black women take organized political action through churches, sororities, community advocacy groups, civil rights organizations, and unions. Black feminism can incorporate a variety of political strategies to bring about a more humanistic and just community. The program is not built into the philosophy itself. Instead, the adage "make a way out of no way" captures the range of actual strategies pursued by African-American women to empower themselves and others.

Despite the overall consistency of thematic expression, Black feminism has not been expressed in the same way across different historical periods. Black feminism in the twentieth century can be divided into three major periods, namely, Laying the Foundation (1890-1920), a period when Black women organized a national political movement and first articulated Black feminist thought; Working for Change (1920-60), a period when Black women advanced the humanistic vision in Black feminist thought primarily within African-American communities; and Contemporary Black Feminism (1960-present), a period when Black feminism as a political movement and Black feminist thought as its intellectual voice emerge. Each period has its own specific set of historical issues, distinctive organizational and institutional locations, and a resulting unique expression of the core themes of Black feminist thought.

LAYING THE FOUNDATION, 1890-1920

During the period 1890-1920, African-American women organized on the national level, aiming to "lift as we climb." The growth of Jim Crow segregation in schools, employment, political life, and public accommodations heralded deteriorating conditions in the South and fostered a mass migration to cities of the North. This increasing urbanization created African-American communities that could support a range of ideas and organizations.

Politically, women struggled for suffrage and African-Americans demanded political and civil rights, an end to the terrorism of lynching, and adequate standards of living. Spurred on by these catalysts, middle-class Black women began to organize on a local level to undertake educational, philanthropic, and welfare activities. Black women's clubs were founded in a number of cities. The growth of Black urban communities and the urgent needs of the poor gave rise to a national Black women's club movement.

The National Federation of Afro-American Women was founded in 1896 and elected Margaret Murray Washington as its president. The National League of Colored Women was founded in Washington, D.C., in 1892. Together, these two organizations represented over 100 local Black women's clubs. After their merger into the National Association of Colored Women (NACW) in 1896, Mary Church Terrell was elected president. The NACW became a unifying force, an authoritative voice in defense of Black womanhood.

The Black women's club movement was both an activist and intellectual endeavor. The leadership of this national organization worked not only to eliminate Black women's oppression but also to produce analyses of Black women's oppression. The work of these Black feminist intellectuals was influenced by the four core themes of Black feminism, particularly the merger of action and theory. The activities of early twentieth-century Black women such as Ida B. Wells, Fannie Barrier Williams, Mary Church Terrell, Anna Julia Cooper, and others illustrate the Black feminist tradition of merging intellectual work with activism. These women produced analyses of subjects as diverse as the struggle for education, sexual politics and violence, race pride, racial prejudice, the importance of Black women collectively defining Black womanhood, and inclusion in white women's organizations. Since the vast majority of African-American women in the early twentieth century were burdened both by long hours in either agricultural or domestic work and by shouldering the responsibilities of caring for families, they had little time to engage in either theorizing or organizing. The activities of the clubwomen on behalf of all African-American women, and not just those of the middle class, remain noteworthy.

African-American women in the Black women's club movement did not identify themselves as Black feminists. Ida B. Wells, Mary Church Terrell, and Anna Julia Cooper were much closer to Sojourner Truth's perspective—"I suppose I am about the only colored woman that goes about to speak for the rights of the colored women" (Lerner 1972)—than to that of today's Black feminists. Yet they did construct and shape Black feminism as a political movement and Black feminist thought as its intellectual voice and vision.

To lay the foundation for Black feminism, Black women leaders challenged Black women to reject the negative images of Black womanhood so prominent in their times. Anna Julia Cooper, a Black woman born into slavery, recipient of a master's degree from Oberlin College in 1884, granted a Ph.D. in Latin from the Sorbonne in Paris, spent the bulk of her life as an educator. In her book, *A Voice from the South*, she described Black women's legacy of struggle against racism and sexism by protesting Black women's vulnerability to sexual violence:

> I would beg . . . to add my plea for the Colored Girls of the South:—that large, bright, promising fatally beautiful class . . . so full of promise and possibilities, yet so sure of destruction; often without a father to whom they dare apply the loving term, often without a stronger brother to espouse their cause and defend their honor with his life's blood; in the midst of pitfalls and snares, waylaid by the lower classes of white men, with no shelter, no protection.

Refusing to be silenced, Fannie Barrier Williams, the first Black woman admitted to the Women's Club of Chicago and organizer of the first training school for Black women in Chicago, championed the power of self-definition at the turn of the century, a period of heightened racial repression. Williams viewed the Black woman not as a defenseless victim but as a strong-willed resistor: "As meanly as she is thought of; hindered as she is in all directions, she is always doing something of merit and credit that is not expected of her." She saw the Black woman as "irrepressible. She is insulted, but she holds up her head; she is scorned, but she proudly demands respect. . . . The most interesting girl of this country is the Colored girl" (Washington 1987).

In their writings and teachings, early twentieth-century Black feminists urged Black women to forge their own self-definitions and to be independent and self-reliant. Through their actions in building a powerful national Black women's club movement, they championed the utility of Black women's relationships with one another in providing a community for Black women's activism and self-determination. They analyzed why Black women had such hard lives, and they empowered Black women to make changes in their daily lives. This fusion of theory and activism is characteristic of Black feminism, becoming the foundation on which subsequent Black women were able to work for change.

WORKING FOR CHANGE, 1920-60

The Great Depression, the New Deal, World War II, and the civil rights movement all brought sweeping changes in African-American community structures and corresponding shifts in the organizational bases for Black feminism. Heightened de jure segregation in the South and de facto segregation in the North during this period meant that most African-American women lived in highly segregated environments. Since the majority of Black women worked in domestic service, their contact with white people, especially white women, afforded few opportunities for interracial contact among equals. Until the resurgence of national organizing in the civil rights movement of the 1960s, the decline of the Black women's club movement in the 1920s left the majority of Black women with few options to participate in national political movements.

The period from 1920 to 1960 seemingly lacked a self-conscious Black feminist movement that both identified itself as such and that explicitly advanced the core themes of Black feminism. However, racism during the 1930s through the 1950s was so pervasive that Black women advanced a Black feminist agenda primarily through existing Black organizations. High labor force participation coupled with substantial family responsibilities meant that most African-American women during this period had little time or inclination to participate in organizations designed exclusively to address issues unique to Black women. By far the largest number of African-American women either worked within existing Black organizations, such as churches or local self-help groups, or participated in Black political movements to ensure that Black women and men alike would be treated with dignity. Thus, while they lacked the overarching organizational structure of a strong, national Black women's organization expressing a Black women's position, Black women's activism to work for change generally occurred in the context of fostering local Black community development.

Those women who engaged in political activities such as starting schools or organizations typically aimed at building Black community institutions. While some organizations were designed to address issues unique to African-American women, the majority aimed to serve both women and men. This choice does not make Black women less feminist—instead, it represents the feminism inherent in Black women's humanistic vision of community. Instead of just talking about inequality between women and men, these women built institutions based on Black feminist principles. In keeping with the Black feminist core theme of the fusion of theory and action, their feminism was embedded in their actions. By working on behalf of everyone, they were in effect working for Black women.

Mary McLeod Bethune's work reflects the complexity of how Black women of this period saw their special mission of working for Black women. Elected president of NACW in 1924, Bethune continued efforts to acquire a federal antilynching bill, help rural women and those in industry, train clerks and typists, and support the rights of Black women globally. Bethune's effort to build the Daytona School for Girls into the coeducational liberal arts school Bethune-Cookman College demonstrate her efforts to foster Black community development and offer a glimpse of how many Black women worked for change during this period. Still, Bethune's noteworthy influence on national politics foreshadowed the actions of Black women in the contemporary period. Her life marks the transition from the foundation-laying activities of early twentieth-century Black feminists to the broad-based activities characterizing contemporary Black feminists.

Black women worked on behalf of the core themes of Black feminist thought although they rarely described their work in these terms. Each core theme wove through Black women's political work and much of everyday life. For example, Black women working in the civil rights movement during the 1950s advanced the humanistic vision of community in Black feminist thought. Women like Fannie Lou Hamer, Rosa Parks, Ella Baker, and Septima Clark were tireless workers for Black community development. Since it came out of church groups, the movement was carried largely by women. Many rural Black women showed extreme courage. "Dyin' is all right," said Mary Dora Jones, who was told that her house would be burned down if she continued to let civil rights workers stay in her home. "Ain't but one thing 'bout dyin'. That's make sho' you right, 'cause you gon' die anyway" (Giddings 1984). Similar views were expressed by Fannie Lou Hamer, the daughter of sharecroppers and a Mississippi civil rights activist. "The only thing they could do to me was kill me, and it seemed like they'd been trying to do that a little bit at a time ever since I could remember," observed Hamer (Giddings 1984). Women like Jones and Hamer did not call themselves "Black feminists"—this naming occurred in a later period—but they clearly lived the core themes of Black feminism through their actions.

The search for voice and the refusal to be silenced pervade the words and actions of a range of women throughout this period. For example, Jones, Hamer, and numerous women in the civil rights struggle used their voices to challenge white racism. Other women fostered a Black feminist agenda by refusing to be silenced, even within the context of Black-controlled organizations. Black feminist activist Pauli Murray was president of the 1944 class at the Howard University School of Law. Since she was also the only woman, she did not receive the same privileges as her Black male classmates. This discovery, remembers Murray, "aroused an incipient feminism in me long before I knew the meaning of the term 'feminism' " (Murray 1987).

In other cases, Black women acquired wide-ranging influence within Black organizations and used their status to advance women's issues. For example, in the 1920s, Amy Jacques Garvey's women's page in the *Negro World*, the newspaper of the Universal Negro Improvement Association, took a strong women's rights position. As Paula Giddings notes, "while she held no specific office, it would have been hard to find anyone with greater influence in the UNIA, save for Marcus Garvey himself " (Giddings 1984).

The refusal to be silenced was not confined to women in political movements. Zora Neale Hurston's work, especially her widely read 1937 novel, *Their Eyes Were Watching God*, aimed to give voice to Black women's issues through fiction. By placing Black women's issues in the center of their work, other Black women writers of this period—including Ann Petry in *The Street* (1946), Gwendolyn Brooks in *Maud Martha* (1953), and Lorraine Hansberry in *A Raisin in the Sun* (1959)—explored a Black woman's standpoint as something framed by both Blackness and womanhood.

A Black feminist emphasis on the importance of empowerment in the context of everyday life finds expression in multiple locations during this period. For example, Ella Baker, a major figure in the civil rights movement who worked closely with students, believed that teaching people how to be self-reliant fosters more empowerment than teaching them how to follow. Baker recounts how she nurtured the empowerment of student civil rights workers: "I never intervened between the struggles if I could avoid it. Most of the youngsters had been trained to believe in or to follow adults if they could. I felt they ought to have a chance to learn to think things through and to make the decisions" (Cantarow 1980). Ella Baker and Septima Clark were particularly consistent in forwarding a humanistic vision of community through their leadership styles.

CONTEMPORARY BLACK FEMINISM, 1960-PRESENT

The fundamental distinguishing feature of contemporary Black feminism is the self-conscious voicing of Black feminist perspectives. Though turn-of-the-century Black women laid the organizational framework of institutions and ideas on which subsequent Black women built, until recently African-American women neither called themselves Black feminists nor identified what they were doing as working on behalf of Black feminism. They worked on behalf of Black women and advanced a Black feminist agenda, but they refused to be categorized as solely advancing the special interests of any one group. In contrast, the contemporary period is characterized by the emergence of a broad-based movement that encompasses both traditional humanistic approaches and issues unique to Black women. Contemporary Black feminism embraces the key contributions of the two prior periods, namely, articulating a Black women's agenda and building an organizational base to advance core themes of Black feminism. Contemporary Black feminism expresses and gives voice to this long-standing, preexisting intellectual and political movement.

Contemporary Black feminism advances the same core themes as its predecessors but does so from very different institutional locations and with a very different voice. Two major trends of the last thirty years fostered these changes. First, increasing social-class stratification among Black women led to a much larger pool of women available to think about and work on behalf of Black feminist concerns. Black women graduated from high schools and colleges in record numbers, and they broadened their traditional placement in domestic service to include jobs previously unavailable, especially placement in academic institutions. The emergence of a sizable group of literate middle-class Black women meant that Black feminist thought as the intellectual component of Black feminism could be more readily advanced. This does not mean that only middle-class Black women embrace Black feminism. Rather, differential access to resources shapes Black women's abilities to bring Black feminism to voice.

Second, Black women's growing sense of disenchantment with the racism in the women's movement and the sexism in the civil rights and Black Nationalist movements led to a growing focus on Black women's concerns. Specifically, Black women in male-controlled nationalist organizations became increasingly unwilling to trade their silence for an ill-defined unity. Similarly, the narrow scope of the early phase of the contemporary women's movement—expressing the concerns of white middle-class women—held little appeal. African-American women perceived that neither Black organizations nor white feminist groups fully spoke for them. Thus emerged the need to develop a distinctive Black feminist agenda that built on the core themes long guiding Black women's actions yet simultaneously spoke to issues specific to African-American women.

Contemporary Black feminism dates to the efforts of numerous trailblazing African-American women in the 1970s who stated Black women's concerns as women. While these far-reaching efforts did not constitute a Black feminist agenda per se, they did contain the powerful precursors of one. Toni Cade [Bambara]'s publication of *The Black Woman: An Anthology* in 1970 marked the beginnings of a Black feminist agenda. The Black women in her anthology raise many issues still being explored today. For example, Frances Beale's article "Double Jeopardy: To Be Black and Female" provides a summary of race, class, and gender as interconnected oppressions. Several works of fiction also served to articulate Black feminist thought. Ntozake Shange's 1975 choreopoem *For Colored Girls Who Have Considered Suicide/ When the Rainbow Is Enuf*, Toni Morrison's 1970 novel *The Bluest Eye*, and Alice Walker's 1976 novel *Meridian* all raise issues specific to Black women that have significance beyond Black women. Echoing *Tomorrow's Tomorrow*, Joyce Ladner's groundbreaking 1972 study of Black adolescent girls, social science researchers like Bonnie Thornton Dill, LaFrances Rodgers-Rose, and Cheryl Townsend Gilkes centered their work on the lives of African-American women. Historians, including Jeanne Noble, Sharon Harley, Rosalyn Terborg-Penn, Darlene Clark Hine, and Elsa Barkley Brown, showed a willingness to ground their research in the lives and experiences of African-American women. Paula Giddings's *When and Where I Enter: The Impact of Black Women on Race and Sex in America* (1984) provided an especially important synthesis of African-American women's history. Political figures were increasingly willing to discuss their politics in the race-, class-, and gender-specific Black feminist framework. For example, Shirley Chisholm's 1970 autobiography, *Unbought and Unbossed*, resonates with the core themes of Black feminist thought.

Many Black writers and scholars took the ideas first expressed in these diverse sources during the 1970s and began to hone them into Black feminist theory. During the 1980s, African-American women developed Black feminist thought by emphasizing the unique concerns of African-American women and explicitly exploring the core themes in Black feminist thought. Noteworthy examples of important contemporary works include Angela Davis's 1981 book on African-American women's political economy, *Women, Race and Class*; bell hooks's 1981 analysis of Black women and feminism, *Ain't I a Woman*; the groundbreaking essay by the Combahee River Collective, "A Black Feminist Statement," published in 1982; Alice Walker's *In Search of Our Mothers' Gardens* in 1983; Barbara Smith's 1983 anthology of Black women's writings, *Home Girls: A Black Feminist Anthology*, dealing with the overlooked issue of Black lesbianism; Audre Lorde's important collection of essays *Sister Outsider*, published in 1984; the works of Black feminist literary critics, like Barbara Christian's 1985 *Black Feminist Criticism, Perspectives on Black Women Writers* and Hazel Carby's 1987 *Reconstructing Womanhood*; June Jordan's collections of political essays, *Civil Wars* in 1981 and *On Call* in 1985; and Filomina Chioma Steady's 1987 essay on "African Feminism: A Worldwide Perspective." These works spoke to Black women inside and outside academia who were developing Black feminist thought.

By the 1980s, the many decades spent building Black feminism as a political movement and expressing its vision through Black feminist thought grew into a broad-based Black women's movement located in a variety of organizational settings and expressing various interpretations of Black feminism. While they choose multiple strategies, African-American women of all types typically ground their actions in the core themes of Black feminism.

Contemporary Black feminism finds a home in multiple organizational settings. First, many Black women belong to and remain active in traditional Black women's organizations such as churches, sororities, and Black women's clubs and local organizations. Others remain active in organizations devoted to Black community development such as the National Association for the Advancement of Colored People and the Urban League.

Second, this period marks the formation of new Black women's organizations. Some are housed within professional associations, such as the Association of Black Women Historians. Others represent Black women organized to focus on specific issues. For example, the National Black Feminist Organization, founded in 1973, explicitly addressed the concerns of Black women. The National Coalition of 100 Black Women, founded in 1981, focuses on voter registration and mobilization.

Third, Black feminist intellectuals in academia have used their writings and teachings as a vehicle for the spread of Black feminism. *All the Women Are White, All the Blacks Are Men, But Some of Us Are Brave*, a 1982 anthology edited by Gloria T. Hull, Patricia Bell Scott, and Barbara Smith, was devoted to legitimizing Black women's studies as a serious area of intellectual inquiry, and it offered a road map for Black women academicians laboring to develop Black feminist thought. Other works devoted to developing Black women's studies and Black feminist thought include *Black Womanist Ethics* by Katie Geneva Cannon (1988), *Talking Back: Thinking Feminist, Thinking Black* by bell hooks (1989), *Women, Culture, and Politics* by Angela Davis (1989), *Black Feminist Thought: Knowledge, Consciousness and the Politics of Empowerment* by Patricia Hill Collins (1990), and *Invisibility Blues* by Michele Wallace (1990).

Fourth, Black feminists have become actively involved in the women's movement and have begun to influence its purpose and direction. National women's organizations such as the National Organization for Women and the National Women's Studies Association are increasing efforts to grapple with race and class in their push for gender equality.

Fifth, Black women who have acquired recognition or leadership positions in organizations and institutions that do not appear to be dealing directly with Black women's issues have often used their positions to advance Black feminist agendas. For example, during her tenure as the national head of Planned Parenthood, Faye Wattleton typically did not identify herself as being a Black feminist but did advance programs perceived by many to be highly beneficial for Black women. Bernice Johnson Reagon's work in African and African-American culture at the Smithsonian Institution attends to Black women as creators of culture. Marian Wright Edelman's founding and astute stewardship of the Children's Defense Fund, one of the most respected advocacy organizations in Washington, D.C., offers a similar example. Wattleton, Reagon, and Edelman tap a legacy of struggle wherein challenging the interconnectedness of race, class, and gender is a central tenet. Black women musicians like the six vocalists and one signer in Sweet Honey In The Rock, and emerging Black female rappers like Sister Souljah and Queen Latifah, demonstrate a willingness to raise their voices in song about Black feminism.

Moreover, many Black women who have been successfully elected to public office, such as Shirley Chisholm and Cardiss Collins, or who hold other governmental positions, such as Eleanor Holmes Norton, Mary Frances Berry, and Patricia Roberts Harris, have used their positions to advance a Black women's vision of a humanistic community.

Unlike prior periods, Black feminism as a political movement and Black feminist thought as its intellectual voice and vision find multiple expression in diverse organizational settings. As the community of African-American women has grown more heterogeneous, so has the expression of Black feminism. Thus, the foundation laid by early Black feminists has supported and nurtured the complex and growing movement of today.

BIBLIOGRAPHY

Brooks, Gwendolyn. *Maud Martha* (1953); Brown, Cynthia Stokes, ed. *Ready from Within: Septima Clark and the Civil Rights Movement* (1986); Cade, Toni, ed. *The Black Woman: An Anthology* (1970); Cannon, Katie Geneva. *Black Womanist Ethics* (1988); Cantarow, Ellen. *Moving the Mountain* (1980); Carby, Hazel. *Reconstructing Womanhood: The Emergence of the Afro-American Woman Novelist* (1987); CBWA; Chisholm, Shirley. *Unbought and Unbossed* (1970); Christian, Barbara. *Black Feminist Criticism, Perspectives on Black Women Writers* (1985); Collins, Patricia Hill. *Black Feminist Thought: Knowledge, Consciousness and the Politics of Empowerment* (1990); The Combahee River Collective. "A Black Feminist Statement." In *But Some of Us Are Brave*, ed. Gloria T. Hull, Patricia Bell Scott, and Barbara Smith (1982); Cooper, Anna Julia. *A Voice from the South; By a Black Woman of the South* ([1892] 1988); Davis, Angela. *Women, Race and Class* (1981), and *Women, Culture, and Politics* (1989); Dill, Bonnie Thornton. "The Dialectics of Black Womanhood," *Signs* (Spring 1979); Duster, Alfreda M., ed. *Crusade for Justice: The Autobiography of Ida B. Wells* (1970); Giddings, Paula. *When and Where I Enter: The Impact of Black Women on Race and Sex in America* (1984); Gilkes, Cheryl Townsend. " 'Holding Back the Ocean with a Broom': Black Women and Community Work." In *The Black Woman*, ed. LaFrances Rodgers-Rose (1980); Guy-Sheftall, Beverly. "Remembering Sojourner Truth: On Black Feminism," *Catalyst* (Fall 1986); Hansberry, Lorraine. *A Raisin in the Sun* (1959), and *To Be Young, Gifted, and Black* (1969); Harley, Sharon and Rosalyn Terborg-Penn, eds. *The Afro-American Woman: Struggles and Images* (1978); hooks, bell. *Ain't I a Woman: Black Women and Feminism* (1981), and *Talking Back: Thinking Feminist, Thinking Black* (1989); Hull, Gloria T., Patricia Bell Scott, and Barbara Smith, eds. *All the Women Are White, All the Blacks Are Men, But Some of Us Are Brave* (1982); Hurston, Zora Neale. *Their Eyes Were Watching God* ([1937] 1969); Jordan, June. *Civil Wars* (1981), and *On Call* (1985); Ladner, Joyce. *Tomorrow's Tomorrow* (1972); Lerner, Gerda, ed. *Black Women in White America: A Documentary History* (1972); Lorde, Audre. *Sister Outsider* (1984); McDowell, Deborah E. "New Directions for a Black Feminist Criticism." In *New Feminist Criticism*, ed. Elaine Showalter (1985); Morrison, Toni. *The Bluest Eye* (1970); Murray, Pauli. "The Liberation of Black Women." In *Voices of the New Feminism*, ed. Mary Lou Thompson (1970), and *Song in a Weary Throat: An American Pilgrimage* (1987); Naylor, Gloria. *The Women of Brewster Place* (1980); Noble, Jeanne. *Beautiful, Also, Are the Souls of My Black Sisters: A History of the Black Woman in America* (1978);

Petry, Ann. *The Street* (1946); Reagon, Bernice Johnson. "Coalition Politics: Turning the Century." In *Home Girls: A Black Feminist Anthology*, ed. Barbara Smith (1983), and "African Diaspora Women: The Making of Cultural Workers." In *Women in Africa and the African Diaspora*, ed. Rosalyn Terborg-Penn, Sharon Harley, and Andrea Benton Rushing (1978); Richardson, Marilyn, ed. *America's First Black Woman Political Writer* (1987); Shange, Ntozake. *For Colored Girls Who Have Considered Suicide/When the Rainbow Is Enuf* (1975); Steady, Filomina Chioma. "African Feminism: A Worldwide Perspective." In *Women in Africa and the African Diaspora*, ed. Rosalyn Terborg-Penn, Sharon Harley, and Andrea Benton Rushing (1987); Walker, Alice. *Meridian* (1976), and *The Color Purple* (1982), and *In Search of Our Mothers' Gardens* (1983); Wallace, Michele. *Invisibility Blues* (1990); Washington, Mary Helen, ed. *Invented Lives: Narratives of Black Women, 1860-1960* (1987); White, E. Frances. "Listening to the Voices of Black Feminism," *Radical America* (1984). Special thanks to Patrice L. Dickerson for research assistance and for drafting part of this article.

PATRICIA HILL COLLINS

FEREBEE, DOROTHY CELESTE BOULDING (1898-1980)

Born in Norfolk, Virginia, in 1898, Dorothy Boulding was the daughter of Benjamin Richard and Florence Ruffin Boulding. She came from a family that included eight lawyers but no physicians. While her childhood friends were playing with toys she would seek out and minister to injured birds and small dogs. Her adult physician activities included teaching, directing a university health service, and directing a mobile health clinic which served patients who otherwise would have received no medical care.

Dorothy attended and graduated from Simmons College in Boston and pursued her medical education at nearby Tufts University School of Medicine. After graduating from Tufts in 1924, she went on to do her internship at Freedmen's Hospital in Washington, D.C. Freedmen's was one of the few hospitals that were owned and staffed by African-Americans. Boulding completed her training, remained in Washington, D.C., and set up practice. She immediately became involved with numerous organizations and activities in Washington and nationally. In 1925, she joined the faculty of Howard University Medical School, and in 1949 she was appointed director of Howard's health services, a post she held until her retirement in 1968. She was the founding president of the Women's Institute, an organization that serves community groups, educational institutions, associa-

tions, industry, corporations, government agencies, nonprofit organizations, and individuals.

Dorothy Boulding married Claude Thurston Ferebee, a dentist and instructor in the Howard University College of Dentistry, in 1930. The next year twins were born to them: a daughter named after Dorothy and a son named after Claude.

In 1934, Ferebee gained national prominence when she was appointed medical director of the Mississippi Health Project, sponsored by the Alpha Kappa Alpha sorority. In this position, she directed the activities of mobile field units in neglected rural areas of Mississippi for seven years.

Active in the National Council of Negro Women (NCNW), she served as its second president from 1949 to 1953, following Mary McLeod Bethune. As NCNW president she worked toward expanding its programs aimed at eliminating discrimination against

A graduate of the Tufts University School of Medicine, Dorothy Ferebee gained national prominence in 1935 as the medical director of the Mississippi Health Project, which sent mobile health units into neglected rural areas of the state. Ferebee served as president of the National Council of Negro Women from 1949 to 1953. She is seen here (right) with two other NCNW presidents, Dorothy Height (center) and Vivian Carter Mason (left). [Bethune Museum and Archives]

Black Americans and women in health care education, housing, and the armed forces. She also proposed that the NCNW be active in expanding basic civil rights such as voting, fair employment, and education. Although she had the formidable task of following Bethune in this position, she was able to lead the NCNW ably while also carrying on a full-time job.

She was a member of the American College Health Association, the National Medical Association, the American Association of University Women, and the National Council of Negro Women, to name a few.

Dorothy Boulding Ferebee died on September 14, 1980.

[See also ALPHA KAPPA ALPHA SORORITY; NATIONAL COUNCIL OF NEGRO WOMEN.]

BIBLIOGRAPHY
Ferebee, Dorothy Boulding. Black Women Physicians and Special Collection on Women in Medicine, Medical College of Pennsylvania, Philadelphia.

MARGARET JERRIDO

FERGUSON, CATHERINE (KATY) (c. 1774-1854)

Catherine Williams was born on a schooner, in about 1774, as her mother was being transported from Virginia to her new slaveowner in New York. Her mother was sold again when Katy was eight years old, but before their separation her mother had taught Katy the scriptures. Katy was allowed to attend church services, but she was not taught to read and write. Reverend John M. Mason, Murray Street Church, encouraged her and admitted her as a member.

At sixteen, she was purchased by an abolitionist sympathizer who gave her half of her $200 purchase price in exchange for one year's work. A merchant, Divee Bethume, helped her obtain the other half. At eighteen, a free woman, she married a man named Ferguson. She had two children who died in infancy, and her husband died soon after.

In 1793, Ferguson began an integrated Sunday school in her home. From her impoverished neighborhood and the almshouse she gathered forty-eight children (twenty of them white) who did not have parents able to care for them. She taught them scripture and how to care for themselves, and found them homes; some she took into her home.

Word of Ferguson's school and home placement of children reached Dr. Mason. He visited and invited Ferguson to move her activities to the basement of his new church. He provided her with assistants to teach secular courses along with her teaching the scriptures. For the next forty years, Ferguson supervised the education and welfare services offered at the integrated Murray Street Sabbath School.

Ferguson's school was New York's first Sunday school. She began it with no knowledge of the Sunday school started by Robert Raikes in England in 1780; it was entirely her own inspiration, and she supported it with her own funds. She worked as a caterer for the parties of wealthy white families, and she was also in demand for cleaning fine laces and other delicate materials. She died of cholera in 1854 in New York. Her last words were "All is well."

Ferguson's contributions to integrated/spiritual education and child welfare services on behalf of the poor were recognized by New York City. In 1920, the city opened the Katy Ferguson Home for unwed mothers, which was described as the only one of its kind for Black women in the country.

BIBLIOGRAPHY
American Tract Society. *Katy Ferguson: Or What a Poor Colored Woman May Do* (n.d.); Brown, Hallie Quinn, ed. *Homespun Heroines and Other Women of Distinction* (1926); Clark, William E. "The Katy Ferguson Home," *Southern Workman* (December 1923); Ellison, Ralph W. "Katy Ferguson." Typed notes for biographical sketches for "Negroes of New York," ed. Chase B. Cumberbatch (1938-41); Hodges, George W. *Early Negro Church Life in New York* (1945); Lossing, Benson J. *Eminent Americans* (1881); Loewenberg, Bert James and Ruth Bogin, eds. *Black Women in Nineteenth Century American Life: Their Words, Their Thoughts, Their Feelings* (1976); Reasons, George, and Sam Patrick. *They Had a Dream* (1969).

AUDREYE JOHNSON

FIELDS, MAMIE ELIZABETH GARVIN (1888-1987)

"I will *never* do it" was a favorite phrase of Mamie Elizabeth Garvin Fields whenever she spoke of the unwritten rules and customs of the Jim Crow order in South Carolina. In 1909, she began her professional career by disregarding the custom that African-Americans present applications for teaching positions through the mayor's butler and, instead, presented her credentials in person to the superintendent of education in Charleston. To widespread astonishment, she got her first position, in a one-room school at Humbert Wood on John's Island in rural Charleston County. Testing the unwritten rules and

In 1909, Mamie Garvin Fields began her professional career as an educator by flaunting the unwritten Jim Crow custom that Black persons seeking teaching positions should present their applications to the mayor's butler—Garvin instead presented her credentials directly to the superintendent of schools in Charleston, South Carolina, and was hired! In 1982, she published a memoir, Lemon Swamp and Other Places: A Carolina Memoir, *with her granddaughter, Karen Fields (left). [Wendell Johnson]*

contesting the written ones are concerns to which Fields returned often in speeches before the many civic, religious, and fraternal organizations to which she belonged and in her autobiography, *Lemon Swamp and Other Places: A Carolina Memoir* (1982).

Born in Charleston on August 13, 1888, and already rebellious by 1895, when South Carolina enacted its Jim Crow constitution, she claimed to have acquired "race pride" from her father, George Washington Garvin, a self-employed carpenter who made it possible for her mother, Rebecca Bellinger Garvin, never to "work *out*"; from her mother, who placed her education and energy at the service of church and community; from her father's father, Hannibal Garvin, who farmed independently after the Civil War on property near Bamberg, South Carolina, where he had previously been a slave; and from Middleton and Bellinger kin whose education during slavery in clandestine schools prepared them for leadership after the Civil War. She began her education at the age of three in a private school operated by her cousin, Anna Eliza Izzard (who was in the first graduating class of Avery Normal Institute in Charleston), continued at the Robert Gould Shaw School, and earned a teach-

ing certificate at Claflin University in 1908, boldly claiming her first job the following year.

In 1914, she married Robert Lucas Fields, a craftsman in brick and mortar and an active member of the first union local in South Carolina, Chapter No. 1 of the International Bricklayers, Masons, and Plasterers Union. The couple lived briefly in Charlotte, North Carolina, before returning to Charleston in 1917. They had two sons, Robert Lionel, who became an architect in Washington, D.C., and Alfred Benjamin, who became a social worker in Charleston. The family moved to New York City in 1923 but soon returned to Charleston.

In 1926, Fields returned to full-time work in rural Charleston County as head teacher of the Society Corner School on James Island. She and one assistant instructed 120 children ages six to eighteen in the daytime and at night conducted classes for adults, ranging from reading to canning. She established a "diet kitchen" at the school that was the forerunner of cafeterias in other Charleston County schools. During the Great Depression her kitchen also served some 200 neighbors daily. Her other projects at the time included work in conjunction with Mary McLeod Bethune's effort to gain National Youth Act projects for Black youth and supplementary programs for the school through the Works Progress Administration (WPA). During World War II, she was appointed to the Selective Service Commission and joined a group that organized United Service Organizations (USO) facilities in Charleston for Black soldiers. She retired from teaching in 1943.

Inspired in the 1920s by women like Mary Church Terrell, who lectured in Charleston about women's duty to organize and promote social uplift, Fields founded the Modern Priscilla Club, which eventually affiliated with the Federation of Colored Women's Clubs. Through simultaneous involvement with the Charleston Interracial Committee, she joined volunteers summoned by Susie Dart Butler to help conduct the urban surveys that laid the basis for public housing built in the city between 1936 and 1941. In the 1940s and 1950s, Fields served two terms as president of the state Federation of Women's Clubs and one term as statistician of the national federation. In the mid-1960s, she was resident director of the state federation's Marion Birnie Wilkinson Home for Girls. In 1969, Fields took the lead in organizing the first public day-care center in Charleston; a center built in 1979 at the Sol Legare Homes bears her name. She was a member of Centenary United Methodist Church, the National Association for the Advancement of Colored People (NAACP), the Young Women's Christian Association (YWCA), and the Order of the Eastern Star for many years; and in the 1960s she became a member of the League of Women Voters, the Council of Democratic Women, and the South Carolina Council on Aging (which in 1972 named her Outstanding Senior Citizen of the Year).

BIBLIOGRAPHY

Fields, Mamie Garvin, with Karen E. Fields. "Lala," *Facing South* (May 1980), and "No. 7 Short Court," *Southern Exposure* (December 1980); McDowell, Elsa F. "Mamie Fields Honored," *Evening Post* (Charleston, June 7, 1979); Newby, I. A. *Black Carolinians: A History of Blacks in South Carolina from 1895 to 1968* (1973).

KAREN E. FIELDS

FILM

The history of Black women's images in film has been characterized by a constant tension between an overwhelmingly white Hollywood and a largely male independent scene, both situations representing the dual oppression faced by Black women in American society as a whole and in the Black community in particular. However, in spite of the stereotypical images and the negative roles, Black actresses have asserted their own personalities and etched a unique role in America's film industry.

During the era of the silent movie, D. W. Griffith's *The Birth of a Nation* (1915) recounted the Civil War and Reconstruction through the eyes of white southerners. In this extremely racist but highly acclaimed picture, Griffith's heroes were the Ku Klux Klan; his targets were the "great Black threat" and the reforms instituted by the victorious northerners. Centering around a romantic tale involving white characters, Griffith's film included Black characters only for atmosphere and as an excuse for the anger and fear entrenched in the white southern mentality. In his portrayal of Black characters, Griffith borrowed old stereotypes from sentimental novels, popular poetry, and music. Just as the popular American culture had painted Black people as either contented slaves or sexually charged, violent bucks, *Birth of a Nation* injected these stock characters into its depiction of southern life. The loyal and nurturing mammy raises the white family's children as if they were her own, and she fights to protect her white masters from annihilation at the hands of the northerners. The tragic mulatto mistress of a white southerner nervously ponders her allegiance to both her white and her Black ancestry. Meanwhile, the Black bucks in the film threaten to dishonor and rape all southern white women. Every one of Griffith's Black characters was extremely sketchy and two-dimensional. Furthermore, the roles were played not by Black actors and actresses but by white actors in blackface. Thus, the long-standing racism of the film industry is evident in one of its first feature films, and one of its foremost films on the issue of race in America, *Birth of a Nation*.

As the motion picture industry developed, Black women were portrayed as either benignly and stoically content and loyal to their white masters or troubled and confused by a mixed heritage and insecure about their beauty and sexual attraction. Laden with the rhythm and happiness that supposedly were characteristic of the entire Black community, *Hallelujah* (1929), with one of the first all-Black casts in Hollywood, offered the first tragic mulatto in talking pictures. The heroine, played by Nina Mae McKinney, systematically upset the lives of each of the white characters and the equilibrium of the film as a whole as she stumbled innocently and sexily through the film. The underlying message was that blood mixing was the main cause of the confusion in American society.

Even though the very first Black characters in Hollywood were portrayed by white actors and actresses in blackface, individual Black women received numerous memorable roles in the early days of motion pictures. *Imitation of Life* (1934) featured outstanding performances by Louise Beavers as the mammy figure, Aunt Delilah, and Fredi Washington as Peola, the tragic mulatto daughter. Although it

The first Black characters in film were portrayed by white actors in blackface. However, talented Black women did eventually win major roles in Hollywood films. Among the most memorable early performances by Black actresses was that of Fredi Washington as the tragic mulatto, Peola, in 1934's Imitation of Life. *[Scurlock Studio]*

Hollywood's difficulties in dealing with Black talents are exemplified by the experience of Lena Horne (left). After giving her a seven-year contract, Metro-Goldwyn-Mayer cast her in only one speaking role, in the all-Black film Cabin in the Sky *(1943), which also featured Eddie "Rochester" Anderson and Ethel Waters. Horne's other appearances in the studio's films were in musical numbers that could easily be edited out of prints of the film, for showing in southern theaters. [Donald Bogle]*

reinforced America's conventional views of Black women as sexless matriarchs and guilt-ridden, troubled mulattos, the movie explored the tensions within the Black community with respect to white society for one of the first times on film. Furthermore, the two actresses extended their characters beyond the stereotypes of a pancake-flipping Aunt Delilah and a confusedly passing Peola. Both Beavers and Washington articulated the frustrations associated with race and color in America through their sophisticated and sensitive characterizations.

Also during the 1930s, white audiences received Hattie McDaniel with unprecedented acclaim. As Mammy in *Gone with the Wind* (1939), McDaniel's portrayal exemplified every loud, but nurturing, as-

pect of the stereotypical mammy character. Rivaling the fiery temperament of Vivien Leigh's Scarlett O'Hara, McDaniel's tough, even hostile, rendition of the Black maid and nanny, as well as her large physical size, reinforced traditional images of Black women in the minds of white Americans. The strength of the Black matriarch traditionally had been used to excuse white America's maltreatment of her and her inferior position in American society, but McDaniel brought a personal dignity to the role that gave audiences the sense that she did not ascribe to the inferior position that Hollywood had reserved for Black performers. Indeed, in 1939 McDaniel won the Academy Award for best supporting actress for her work in *Gone with the Wind*, the first Black person to be recognized by the Motion Picture Academy and the only Black actress to receive an Oscar until Whoopi Goldberg's 1990 Academy Award for her supporting role in *Ghost*.

In the 1940s and 1950s, America witnessed the emergence of the prototypical Black starlet, who, as a singer or dancer, usually crossed over from another medium into film. A trend in Hollywood toward glamour and social sophistication encouraged the emergence of sex symbols such as Lena Horne and Hazel Scott. Without a hint of crude ethnicity, Horne

By the 1970s, the mainstream film industry was beginning to present more frequent, positive images of Blacks on screen. Among the best films of this type was Sounder *(1972), in which Cicely Tyson played the wife and mother in a sharecropper family that included son Kevin Hooks. [Donald Bogle]*

mirrored the styles of white starlets as she became the first Black woman to secure a long-term contract at a major Hollywood studio (Metro-Goldwyn-Mayer). Following in the tradition of glamorous Black movie stars, Dorothy Dandridge expanded the tragic mulatto role in her work as well as in her life. In *Carmen Jones* (1954), Dandridge proved to be the first Black film phenomenon. Her talent and beauty were larger than life, and she was one of the first Black women to appear on the cover of *Life* magazine. However, just as the typical tragic mulatto faced a society that could not handle her presence, Dandridge herself daily confronted a movie industry that repeatedly offered her substandard roles. Professional frustrations as well as personal problems and insecurities led to her untimely death in 1965 from an overdose of antidepressants. She was only forty-three.

As the political climate grew more radical in the 1960s, the Black image in films changed to reflect racial and social realism in American society. The increasingly militant Black population no longer seemed interested in the high-society starlets of the 1950s. A more urban, defiant flavor pervaded Black films. Toward the end of the 1960s and into the early 1970s, Black independent filmmakers created a new genre to appeal to militant and nationalistic audiences. These films, including *Sweet Sweetback's Baadasssss Song* (1971), *Shaft* (1971), and *Superfly* (1972), featured tough Black male heroes who defied whitey at every turn. To compensate for years of silly and asexual Black male characters, these "blaxploitation" pictures celebrated the strong sexuality of Black men. Not surprisingly, women, Black as well as white, were merely trophies for the new Black male hero as they had been for white male heroes. After the male-oriented films gained a popular audience within the Black community, however, similar films with Black heroines emerged. These films featured tough, hypersexual Black women who fought the system on behalf of the Black community. The raunchy sexuality of these films, although negating the male-dominated sexuality of the earlier blaxploitation films, did not improve the stereotypical image of Black women as exotically oversexed. However, these films did gain a following in the resurgent women's movement, as exemplified by Pam Grier, one of the cult stars of this genre, who was featured on the cover of *Ms.* magazine.

Just as Black women began to assert themselves in the blaxploitation realm, they also made a quieter impact on the film industry through their roles in the sensitive, romantic movies that were returning to the screen. During the early 1970s, Black film audiences found an increasing number of characters to whom they could relate, as filmmakers, in and out of Hollywood, explored the situations of Black America independent of white America as well as Black familial and sexual relationships. In the rural setting for *Sounder* (1972), Cicely Tyson reconstructed the strong Black mother image in the context of her own family and her own community. Likewise, Diahann Carroll, with her role in *Claudine* (1974), portrayed a Black ghetto mother as she dealt with tensions within Black society and between Black and white people in general. Both films reinforced the notion that Black Americans have lives of their own apart from mainstream America.

Also during the 1970s, the film industry, the same institution that had denied many talented Black actresses a place among America's Hollywood elite, ironically became a forum for exposing the hardships of Black women in entertainment. The ghetto-girl-makes-it-big story line showcased the talent and perseverance of Black entertainers. In grand melodramatic fashion, Diana Ross, in *Lady Sings the Blues* (1972), traced the rags-to-riches story of Billie Holiday's career. Not only did Ross examine the pitfalls of the entertainment industry with respect to Black women in this film, she also used it as a vehicle to her own superstardom. The films *Mahogany* and *Sparkle* followed close behind, and each detailed the rise of a poor girl to stardom.

As the 1970s drew to a close, the interest in Black-oriented films dwindled, and many Black artists suddenly found themselves out of work. However, because Black-oriented television shows, such as *The Jeffersons*, *Good Times*, and *What's Happenin'*, were on the rise, the presence of Black characters in film was not missed as much as it otherwise would have been. While Hollywood largely ignored Black themes in the 1980s, a few individual projects did explore the voice of Black women in America. Although directed by a white director, Steven Spielberg, *The Color Purple* (1985), an adaptation of Alice Walker's powerful book, showcased the strengths of Black women and the talents of several Black actresses. This important film examined the sisterhood and solidarity of Black women under the dual oppression of racism in white society and sexism in the Black community in the rural South. Likewise, Black director Spike Lee has refused to reinforce two-dimensional stereotypes in his own films, in which he unfolds complex characters and relationships at every turn. In *She's Gotta Have It* (1986), Nola Darling, played by Tracy Camila Johns, juggles three male suitors, yet Lee makes no moral judgment about her character. This truthful exposure of relationships and personalities without a character judgment liberates Black female characters and actresses from quick and convenient stereotypes.

Although the images of Black women in film have greatly improved since the stock characters of *Birth of a Nation*, and even though opportunities for Black actresses have substantially increased, the history of Black women in film exposes a delicate balance between a racially and sexually biased movie business on the one hand and Black women's efforts to succeed in it on the other. Ultimately, the history of struggle for Black women in film must inform and correct the biases of the film industry and of American society as a whole.

BIBLIOGRAPHY

BAFT; Bogle, Donald. *Brown Sugar: Eighty Years of America's Black Female Superstars* (1980); Gulliver, Adelaide C., ed. *Black Images in Films: Stereotyping and Self-Perception as Viewed by Black Actresses* (1974); Mapp, Edward. "Black Women in Films," *Black Scholar* (March-April 1973); Stephens, Lenora C. "Black Women in Film," *Southern Quarterly* (Spring-Summer 1981); Taylor, Clyde. "Shooting the Black Woman," *Black Collegian* (May-June 1979).

SHIRLEY E. THOMPSON

Refused admission to the University of Oklahoma Law School in 1946 because of her race, Ada Sipuel Fisher was named to the university's Board of Regents in 1992. [University of Oklahoma News Services]

FISHER, ADA LOIS SIPUEL (1924-)

Ada Lois Sipuel was an honors graduate of all-Black Oklahoma State College for Negroes (now Langston University) and the first African-American woman to attend an all-white law school in the South.

The daughter of a minister, Ada Lois Sipuel was born on February 8, 1924, in Chickasha, Oklahoma. Her brother had planned to challenge the segregationist policies of the University of Oklahoma but instead went to Howard University Law School, in part because he did not want to delay his career further by protracted litigation, having already been delayed by serving in World War II. Ada, who was younger and who had been in college during the war, was willing to delay her legal career in order to challenge segregation.

In 1946, Sipuel applied for admission to the University of Oklahoma Law School. She was denied admission because of her race, and a lengthy court battle ensued. The Supreme Court ruled in 1948 that the state of Oklahoma must provide instruction for Blacks equal to that given whites. Unfortunately, since this decision did not invalidate segregated education, the regents created the Langston University School of Law located at the state capital. Further legal action was necessary to prove that this law school was inferior to the University of Oklahoma law school. Finally in the summer of 1949, Sipuel was admitted to the University of Oklahoma law school.

By the time the law school allowed her to register, the semester had already begun. She had married Warren W. Fisher, and was pregnant with the first of her two children. The law school gave her a special chair marked "colored" and roped off from the rest of the class. Her classmates and teachers welcomed her, however, sharing their notes, studying with her, and helping her catch up on the material she had missed. Although she was forced to eat in a separate chained-off and guarded area of the law school cafeteria, she recalled many years later that white students crawled under the chain and ate with her when guards were not around. Adding to these circumstances, and the usual difficulties of law school, was the added pressure of the lawsuit. "I knew the eyes of Oklahoma and the nation were on me," she said in an interview years later. Her lawsuit and tuition were supported by hundreds of small donations, and she believed she "owed it to those people to make it."

After graduating from the law school in 1951, Fisher earned a Master's degree, also from the previously all-white university. In 1952, she began practicing law in her hometown of Chickasha, and as early as 1954 she represented a client before the Oklahoma Supreme Court. In 1957, she joined the faculty at Langston University, where she served as chair of the social sciences department and later as assistant vice president for academic affairs. In 1988, she became counsel to Automations Research Systems, Ltd., in Alexandria, Virginia. That same year, the Oklahoma Legislative Black Caucus honored her on the fortieth anniversary of the U.S. Supreme Court's decision in *Sipuel* v. *Board of Regents of the University of Oklahoma*. In 1974 and 1975, she served on the Advisory Committee on Civil Rights for the Oklahoma Regents for Higher Education. Throughout her career she was active in civil rights organizations, serving the Urban League, the National Association for the Advancement of Colored People (NAACP), and the American Civil Liberties Union (ACLU). In 1992, Oklahoma Governor David Walters appointed her to the Board of Regents of the University of Oklahoma, which, she noted in an interview, "completes a forty-five-year cycle." She plans to bring "a new dimension to university policies. Having suffered severely from bigotry and racial discrimination as a student, I am sensitive to that kind of thing."

[*See also SIPUEL* v. *BOARD OF REGENTS.*]

BIBLIOGRAPHY

Gannett News Service (April 29, 1992); Kluger, Richard. *Simple Justice* (1975); *New York Times* (June 5, 1992); United Press International (May 2, 1988); *WWBA* (1992-93).

PAUL FINKELMAN

FISHER, RUTH ANNA (1886-1975)

Ruth Anna Fisher was a researcher and manuscript archivist for the Library of Congress from 1928 to 1956 and supervised the compilation of documents relating to American history in British archives. Born in Lorain, Ohio, on March 15, 1886, into the family of realtor David Crockett Fisher, she graduated from Oberlin College in 1906. She then taught at Tuskegee Institute but was fired by Booker T. Washington because she refused to cooperate with his philosophy of industrial education and would not teach Sunday school.

After teaching in Lorain and Indianapolis and working with a recreation center in New York, Fisher was sent by patrons to study in England. When she finished her program at the London School of Economics, she began work as a researcher with American historian J. Franklin Jameson, director of historical research for the Carnegie Institute of Washington, D.C. His research project included making copies of documents relating to American history in British repositories. Fisher soon became supervisor of this "foreign copying" project, reproducing documents in the Public Record Office, the British Museum, and the libraries of the House of Lords and the House of Commons, as well as various other repositories. She continued in that role when Jameson became chief of the Division of Manuscripts at the Library of Congress.

In 1940, when London was bombed, Fisher's apartment was destroyed and she returned to the United States. After another three-year stint in London, she returned to the United States to work in the Library of Congress preparing calendars of the British documents she had accumulated. She retired in 1956 and died in late January 1975.

BIBLIOGRAPHY

Evening Star, Obituary (January 30, 1975); Fisher, Ruth Anna and William Lloyd Fox, eds. *J. Franklin Jameson: A Tribute* (1965); Jameson, J. Franklin. Papers, Manuscript Division, Library of Congress, Washington, D.C.; Library of Congress Archives, Manuscript Division, Library of Congress, Washington, D.C.; Render, Sylvia Lyons. "Afro-American Women: The Outstanding and the Obscure," *Quarterly Journal of the Library of Congress* (October 1975); *Washington Post*, Obituary (January 31, 1975).

DEBRA NEWMAN HAM

FISK JUBILEE SINGERS

Wherever they have gone, they have proclaimed to the hearts of men in a most effective way, and with unmeasurable logic, the brotherhood of the race. (Marsh 1969)

This great tribute introduces us to the original Fisk Jubilee Singers. These singers were a band of emancipated slaves who toured to raise money for Fisk University and to introduce the world to the beauty of the songs of a people. These songs told of an unvoiced longing for a truer world, where people were free from rejection, disappointment, and sorrow.

The Fisk Jubilee Singers were led by George L. White, a man of vision and purpose, who began training a group of young people in 1866. From this band of singers, he organized the original Jubilee Singers composed of four Black men and five Black women, so that they could sing for the world as they had sung for him. The five women in the original group were Ella Sheppard, Maggie L. Porter, Minnie Tate, Jennie Jackson, and Eliza Walker.

Ella Sheppard was born into slavery in February 1851. Rescued from slavery by her father at an early age, she found her way to Fisk School in Nashville, Tennessee, when she was thirteen. Her musical ability greatly developed both as a singer and a pianist, and she eventually served as pianist for the Jubilee Singers.

Maggie Porter lived in slavery for twelve years. She was born on February 24, 1853, in Lebanon, Tennessee, and later moved to a plantation in Nashville. At thirteen, having attained freedom, she entered Fisk School. Her vocal ability soon won her the role of Queen Esther in the cantata *Esther.* She continued vocal instruction there and joined the Jubilee Singers.

Minnie Tate was the youngest of the Jubilee Singers. Born in Nashville in 1857 to free parents, she entered Fisk School to pursue musical training. Minnie Tate had been taught from infancy by her mother, who, having received educational training, opened her home to teach other Black children.

Jennie Jackson was born free. Her grandfather was a slave and the body servant of General Andrew Jackson. After several years of work, she began singing at Fisk School and became a member of the Jubilee Singers. She enrolled in Fisk School in 1866.

Eliza Walker was born into slavery near Nashville in 1857. Her freedom came with the release of her mother from slavery. In 1866, at the age of nine, she entered Fisk School and sang with the group until 1870.

This photograph of the renowned Fisk Jubilee Singers was taken in 1882, when three of the five original women members were still performing. They are, seated at left and center, Ella Sheppard and Maggie L. Porter, and, standing at far right, Jennie Jackson. [Moorland-Spingarn]

In 1871, the Jubilee Singers began a successful singing tour to save Fisk School from imminent closing due to financial difficulties. They toured the United States and England, Scotland, Ireland, Holland, and Switzerland, bringing back $50,000 to save Fisk School and found Fisk University.

BIBLIOGRAPHY

Du Bois, W.E.B. *The Souls of Black Folks* (1961); Marsh, J.B.T. *The Jubilee Singers: With Their Songs* (1969); Pike, G. D. *The Jubilee Singers, and Their Campaign for Twenty Thousand Dollars* (1873); Special collections, Fisk University Library and Media Center, Fisk University, Nashville, Tennessee.

CATHERINE KING CLARK

FITZGERALD, ELLA (1918-)

After being orphaned at an early age, Ella Fitzgerald, the "First Lady of Jazz," spent most of her formative years in Yonkers, New York, where she began to nurture her musical interest while attending that city's public schools.

In 1934, she won the legendary Apollo Theatre's amateur contest; the prize was a week's work with the theater's band, whose director was seminal big band drummer William "Chick" Webb. The Baltimore-born Webb was so impressed with the aspiring vocalist that he immediately asked her to join his group. Her association with Webb led to two of Fitzgerald's most memorable recordings: "A-tisket, A-tasket" (1938) and "Undecided" (1939). After Webb's death in 1939, Fitzgerald assumed directorship of the band, which she continued for three years.

Following her stint with Webb and his band, Fitzgerald embarked upon a solo career, most notably with the sponsorship of renowned jazz impresario Norman Granz, whose Jazz at the Philharmonic tours introduced the singer to immensely appreciative audiences in the United States, South America, the Orient, and Europe. She also dabbled in motion pictures, with notable cameo appearances in *St. Louis Blues* (1958) and *Let No Man Write My Epitaph* (1960).

In 1956, Fitzgerald signed with Granz's Verve record label and, with the aid of late arranger Nelson Riddle, produced a string of what many critics and fans have deemed definitive readings of songs by George and Ira Gershwin, Johnny Mercer, and Richard Rodgers and Lorenz Hart, among others. Her association with Granz continued into the 1960s, as did her notable recordings with jazz greats such as

The first lady of jazz, Ella Fitzgerald turned scat singing into a fine art. [Schomburg Center]

Duke Ellington, Louis Armstrong, Oscar Peterson, and Count Basie. More recently she has collaborated with guitarist Joe Pass on a series of classic duet sessions for Granz's Pablo label.

Fitzgerald received her first Grammy Award in 1980. She also has been honored by countless organizations for her contributions to the American art form of jazz and has long been considered by many to be the ultimate jazz vocalist. Her artistry incorporates a stunning technical range, including a dazzling command—perhaps the most dazzling of any artist to date—of what has come to be known as scat singing.

Although age and bouts of illness have diminished her once-astounding technical faculties, Fitzgerald, like other legendary jazz artists, has learned the deceptive art of distilling a composition's melodic and emotional essence into a comparatively minimalistic series of musical gestures. She is capable of great jazz singing even while simply meandering her way through a composition's theme.

BIBLIOGRAPHY

BDAAM; Colin, S. *The Life and Times of Ella Fitzgerald* (1986); Feather, L. "Ella Today (and Yesterday Too),"

Downbeat (1965); Pleasants, H. *The Great American Popular Singers* (1974).

DISCOGRAPHY

For discographies, see Colin, Sid. *Ella: The Life and Times of Ella Fitzgerald* (1986); Nolden, Rainer. *Ella Fitzgerald: ihr Leben, ihre Musik, ihre Schallplatten* (1986).

REUBEN JACKSON

FLACK, ROBERTA (1940-)

Would she have been missed had it not been for the 1971 movie *Play Misty for Me?* Maybe not, but the inclusion of her 1969 love song "The First Time Ever I Saw Your Face" in that film made Roberta Flack a household name and a gold-record winner in 1972. The success of her single "Killing Me Softly" quickly followed in 1973, and she has been dazzling our ears ever since.

Born in 1940 in Black Mountain, North Carolina, Flack grew up in Arlington, Virginia. She played the piano by ear at age four and began lessons at age nine. Later, while teaching music in Washington,

After her recording of "The First Time Ever I Saw Your Face" was featured in Play Misty for Me, *Roberta Flack became a gold-record winner and a household name. [Schomburg Center]*

D.C., she moonlighted by accompanying opera singers on the piano. When her own singing began to attract crowds at a local Washington eatery, the owner built a showcase room for her called Roberta's. Jazz pianist Les McCann heard her there and brought her to the attention of Atlantic Records.

Known for her intense, yet soft, singing style, Flack presents a sharp contrast to the gospel-inflected style epitomized by Aretha Franklin in the late 1960s and early 1970s. Her ability to cover, or restyle, songs by other artists so that they take on new meaning and new life makes Flack more of an artist than a mere pop singer. For example, her versions of "To Love Somebody," originally released by the Bee Gees, and "Bridge Over Troubled Water," a Simon and Garfunkel hit, are vastly different from the originals.

Roberta Flack's most recent album is *Set the Night to Music*, released in 1991—the title song was a top ten hit.

BIBLIOGRAPHY

Morse, Charles and Anne Morse. *Roberta Flack* (1975).

ARTHUR J. JOHNSON

FLEETWOOD, SARA IREDELL (1849-1908)

Sara Iredell Fleetwood, an educator and clubwoman, is best known for her involvement in the early Black women's professional nursing movement. A native of Pennsylvania, Sara Iredell was born in April 1849. She remained active in the Black community of Washington, D.C., until her death on February 1, 1908, at the age of fifty-eight.

A graduate of the Institute for Colored Youth in Philadelphia, Iredell attended Oberlin College, as did several other Black activist women at the turn of the twentieth century. After her graduation from Oberlin, where she was classified as a "pupil-teacher," Iredell began her teaching career in the Frederick, Maryland, public schools. Her dissatisfaction with the low pay and the treatment of Black teachers there prompted her to seek a teaching position in the District of Columbia public schools for Blacks. After a brief stint as a teacher, Sara Iredell Fleetwood devoted most of her adult professional life to the field of nursing.

In 1896, Fleetwood graduated in the first class of the Freedmen's Hospital Nursing Training School. Upon completing the nursing program, Fleetwood joined many of her fellow classmates in becoming a private nurse in Washington, D.C. After the resignation of Sara C. Ebersole and then that of her immediate successor, in February 1901 Sara I. Fleetwood was appointed by the surgeon-in-chief, Dr. Austin M. Curtis, as the first Black superintendent of the hospital's nursing training school. In August of that same year, Fleetwood was reappointed by the new surgeon-in-chief, Dr. William A. Warfield, and given the title of Directress of Nurses for Freedmen's Hospital. In 1904, Fleetwood resigned at the insistence of Warfield. According to W. Calvin Chase of the Washington *Bee*, her resignation was the result of a personal conflict with Warfield.

Her pioneer role as a Black nurses' leader and educator extended beyond and after her years as a hospital administrator. Her interest in promoting the nursing profession and, in particular, greater Black participation in the health care field led her to organize the Freedmen's Nurses Association. In May 1904, she attended the seventh annual convention of the Nurses Association Alumnae of the United States as a delegate from the Freedmen's Association.

In recognition of her pioneer role in the nursing profession, Fleetwood became, in March 1907, the first and only Black female appointed to the newly formed Nurses Examining Board of the District of Columbia. One of the chief responsibilities of the board was to certify registered nurses. Of the five women appointed, Fleetwood received the shortest term, ending in June 1907. She appealed to the District of Columbia commissioners to appoint as her replacement on the board someone who would represent the interests of Freedmen's Hospital in particular and the Black community in general.

Her professional life overlapped with her active community role in the areas of Black health and child care. As one of the nine original incorporators of a pioneer Black women's club, the Colored Women's League of the District of Columbia (formed in 1892 and incorporated in 1894), she concentrated on Black family issues and health care. As did other educated league members, Fleetwood spoke at various public forums about various league projects and activities, ranging from day nurseries for working mothers and kindergarten work to alley sanitation. "Motherhood—Its Relations to Race Development" was the title of her paper at the March 1891 meeting of the Bethel Literary and Historical Association. The 1898 annual report of the Colored Women's League included a testimonial to Fleetwood and her work as chairperson of the Mother's Meeting committee of the league, in which she focused on child care and parenting training for mothers.

Fleetwood, along with another prominent league member, Anna E. Murray, represented the Colored Women's League at the 1898 Congress of Mothers. Three years earlier, she was one of the league's delegates to the 1895 triennial meeting of the predominantly white National Council of Women.

Fleetwood combined her active civic and professional life with her responsibilities as a wife and mother. Like Sara, her husband, Civil War hero Christian A. Fleetwood, whom she married in 1869, was an active member of the Washington Black community. Together they had one daughter, Edith, who continued the family tradition of community service. The family resided for many years on Spruce Street in the northwest neighborhood of LeDroit Park. Originally an all-white neighborhood, it soon became home to a large enclave of Black professionals.

Sara Iredell Fleetwood symbolized the Black professional woman of her day in that she was equally dedicated to her professional nursing career and to the Black women's clubs she joined. It was important to these educated, middle-class women to bring the value of their education and training to the persons they identified as the less fortunate members of their race.

BIBLIOGRAPHY

Colored Woman's League of Washington, D.C. Constitution and By-Laws (1896), and *Fifth Annual Report, June 30, 1898*, Mary Church Terrell papers, Library of Congress, Washington, D.C., and the Terrell papers, Moorland-Spingarn Research Center, Howard University, Washington, D.C.; *DANB*; Christian A. Fleetwood papers, Library of Congress, Washington, D.C.

SHARON HARLEY

FLEMING, LOUISE "LULU" CECILIA (1862-1899)

On January 10, 1886, Lulu Fleming became the first Black woman to be appointed and commissioned for career missionary service by the Woman's Baptist Foreign Missionary Society of the West, an auxiliary of the American Baptist Missionary Union (now American Baptist Churches in the U.S.A.). Louise (Lulu was a nickname) Cecilia Fleming was born a slave in Hibernia, Clay County, Florida, on January 28, 1862. She attended Shaw University (Raleigh, North Carolina), graduating as class valedictorian on May 27, 1885.

Born into slavery, Louise "Lulu" Fleming courageously served her African heritage as a medical missionary in the Congo in the late 1880s and early 1890s. [Sylvia Jacobs]

Fleming set sail from the United States on March 17, 1887, stopped in Europe on the way to the field, and reached Palabala, Congo (now Zaire) on May 16 of that year. Fleming taught the primary classes and the upper English classes. In a report to Dr. J. W. Murdock of the American Baptist Historical Society in 1888 she lamented: "All our converts thus far are men. Oh, how I long to see the women reached."

Fleming returned to the United States in 1891 to regain her health. While on furlough she studied medicine, first entering Shaw University's Leonard Medical School and then in 1895 completing the full course at the Woman's Medical College of Philadelphia (now known as the Medical College of Pennsylvania). Fleming was transferred to the Woman's Baptist Foreign Missionary Society, which had headquarters in the East.

On October 2, 1895, Fleming again sailed from the United States and was stationed at Irebu in the Upper Congo where she worked as a medical missionary. In 1898, when the Irebu station was closed,

she was reassigned to the Bolengi station. Fleming was stricken with what was known as African sleeping sickness before the end of her second term and so she reluctantly returned to the United States; she died in Philadelphia on June 20, 1899.

BIBLIOGRAPHY

Baptist Missionary Magazine (1888, 1889, 1899); "Biographical Digest of Lulu Cecilia Fleming." International Ministries, American Baptist Churches in the U.S.A. (unpublished paper, n.d.); Jacobs, Sylvia M. "Afro-American Women Missionaries Confront the African Way of Life." In *Women in Africa and the African Diaspora*, ed. Rosalyn Terborg-Penn, Sharon Harley, and Andrea Benton Rushing (1987); Jennings, Ray. "Zaire Missionary Pioneer—Lulu Cecelia Fleming, M.D., 1862-1899." International Ministries, American Baptist Churches in the U.S.A. (pamphlet, n.d.); *Missionary Review of the World* (1888); *Woman's Baptist Foreign Missionary Society of the West* (1887, 1888, 1890, 1891).

SYLVIA M. JACOBS

FLORENCE, VIRGINIA PROCTOR POWELL (1903-1991)

The first African-American woman to receive professional training in librarianship in the United States, Virginia Proctor Powell was born to Socrates Edward Powell and Caroline Elizabeth Proctor Powell on October 1, 1903, in Wilkinsburg, Pennsylvania. Her early education was in the public schools of Wilkinsburg. Following the death of both parents, she moved to Pittsburgh to live with an aunt. A 1915 graduate of Pittsburgh's Fifth Avenue High School, Powell received a Bachelor's degree in English literature from Oberlin College in 1919.

Following her graduation from Oberlin, Powell worked for a brief time in St. Paul, Minnesota, as a secretary in the Girl Reserves of the Colored Girls Work Section of the Young Women's Christian Association (YWCA). After a year, she returned to Pittsburgh to work in her aunt's beauty parlor. She sought a teaching position in the Pittsburgh public school system, but because the schools had no African-American employees, she was forced to consider other professional options or continue to work in her aunt's salon.

Her fiancé, Charles Florence, introduced Powell to the notion of a career in librarianship. Aware of her love of children and books, Charles obtained the necessary applications for the Carnegie Library School. She was admitted to the school in 1922 and completed the course of study within one year. How-ever, because school officials were uncertain about placement of their first African-American graduate, she did not receive her diploma until several years later.

She began her professional career with the New York Public Library in 1923 and continued there until 1927. In that year she became the first African-American to take and pass the New York high school librarian's examination and was appointed librarian at the Seward High School in Brooklyn. She re-mained in that position until 1931.

Following her marriage to Charles in 1931, Flo-rence spent the next eight years as the "First Lady" of Lincoln University in Jefferson City, Missouri, where her husband served as president. When the couple moved back East in 1938, Florence returned to librarianship. Charles became chairman of the En-glish department at Virginia Union University in

The first African-American woman to receive professional training in librarianship in the United States, Virginia Florence graduated from Oberlin College in 1919, the year this photograph was taken, and then attended Carnegie Library School. [Arthur C. Gunn]

Richmond, and Florence was librarian at Cardoza High School in Washington, D.C., until 1945. Fol-lowing a five-year period of recuperation from illness, Florence became librarian at Richmond's Maggie L. Walker Senior High School until her retirement in 1965. Widowed in 1974, Florence lived her remain-ing years in Richmond.

BIBLIOGRAPHY

Florence, Virginia Proctor Powell. Personal interview (June 1982); Gunn, Arthur C. "The Struggle of Virginia Proctor Powell Florence," *American Libraries* (February 1989).

ARTHUR C. GUNN

FOOTE, JULIA A. J. (1823-1900)

"Redeemed! redeemed! glory! glory!" Shouting these words, fifteen-year-old Julia Foote sprang from her bed where she had lain semiconscious for twenty hours. Fearing eternal damnation, she had fainted while listening to her minister's powerful sermon on sin and redemption. In this semiconscious state, she heard voices singing, "This Is the New Song." She awakened joyful, peaceful, and redeemed. This mo-ment of conversion launched her personal commitment to Christian righteousness and evange-lism as it emboldened her to confront family, friends, and Black ministers who challenged her right to preach a message of Christian salvation.

Born in Schenectady, New York, in 1823, the fourth child of former slaves, Julia was raised in a Christian household as a member of the African Meth-odist Episcopal (AME) Church in Albany, New York. Her conversion transformed her into an assertive dis-ciple for her religion, and she studied to improve her reading and speaking abilities to enhance her Chris-tian mission. Although her Christian self-affirmation and struggles for self-improvement empowered her with a sense of autonomy and individuality, they placed her in conflict with the prescribed behavior for women in the nineteenth century. In her commitment to proclaim her own salvation and her unyielding deter-mination to preach, Julia defied her parents. After her marriage to George Foote in 1841, she defied him as well. Even under the threat of excommunication, she defied her minister, Reverend Jehiel C. Beman, of the AME church in Boston.

From the 1840s through the 1870s, Foote trav-eled throughout New York, New England, and the mid-Atlantic states, and as far as Cincinnati, Detroit, and Canada, preaching the doctrine of sanctification—the belief that the soul can be purified of and liberated from sin, thus providing for a more perfect union with Christ, not only in death, but in life. Her thirty years of itinerant evangelism were sporadically interrupted by the illnesses and deaths of her father, mother, and husband.

Although nothing is known of her activities during the 1880s and 1890s, she became a missionary for the African Methodist Episcopal Zion Church, the first ordained deacon in 1894, and the second woman to be ordained an elder in the church.

Julia Foote's willingness to defy the conventions of Christian female propriety sanctioned her condemnation of all forms of evil and sin, including gender discrimination, racism, and slavery. Julia Foote's story is one of self-determination, individualism, and self-affirmation, ordained not by secular authority but by God.

BIBLIOGRAPHY

Andrews, William L., ed. *Sisters of the Spirit: Three Black Women's Autobiographies of the Nineteenth Century* (1986); Foote, Julia A. J. *A Brand Plucked from the Fire* (1879).

LILLIE JOHNSON EDWARDS

FORD, JUSTINA LAURENA CARTER (1871-1952)

Justina Ford was the first African-American woman physician in the Denver, Colorado, area.

Born on January 22, 1871, in Knoxville, Illinois, Justina grew up in Galesburg, Illinois. Her mother was a nurse, and she was the seventh child in the family. She would not play with her siblings unless they played hospital and she was the doctor.

Following her graduation in 1899 from the Hering Medical School in Chicago, Illinois, she directed a hospital in Normal, Alabama, for two years. Then she moved to Denver in 1902. She applied for her license and found the authorities reluctant to grant it to her because she was an African-American woman. However, she did get her license and set up her practice. Still, the medical community was slow to recognize her abilities. Ford was not accepted into membership by the Denver Medical Society, the Colorado Medical Society, or the American Medical Association until very late in her life.

Specializing in obstetrics, gynecology, and pediatrics, she came to be known as the "baby doctor."

Because Denver General Hospital would not take Black patients or physicians, Ford took her practice door-to-door. A stern and brisk-mannered woman, Ford was known for her unique system of delivering and providing the best care for mother and baby in the home. She delivered over 7,000 babies before, during, and after World War II. Her patients came from many ethnic groups including Hispanic, Native American, Chinese, Greek, Japanese, African-American, and white cultures. Transportation to her patients progressed from horse and buggy to taxicabs. She finally purchased a car and hired a relative to drive her. When her car came into a neighborhood it was a sure sign that someone was having a baby.

Justina married Reverend Ford early in her career. She remarried after her first husband's death, but she continued to be known as Dr. Ford. Her second husband was Alfred Allen.

She succeeded in being admitted as a staff member of the Denver General Hospital, the same hospital that refused her services early in her career. Moreover, her home and office have been relocated, renovated, and reopened as the permanent headquarters of the Black American West Museum in Denver, Colorado. It is also used as a community meeting place.

She died at the age of eighty-one in October 1952.

BIBLIOGRAPHY

Gallegos, Magdalena. "Dr. Justina Ford: Her Medical Legacy Continues" (n.d.). In Black Women Physicians Collection and Special Collection on Women in Medicine, Medical College of Pennsylvania, Philadelphia; *Urban Spectrum* (September 1988).

MARGARET JERRIDO

FORSYTHE, RUBY MIDDLETON (1905-1992)

Ruby Middleton was born in 1905 in Charleston, South Carolina, the daughter of Lewis Burns Middleton and Marthenia E. Middleton. She received her earliest education from Mrs. Seward Montgomery. She attended Charleston's prominent Black private school, Avery Normal Institute. After she received her licentiate of instruction certificate in 1921 from Avery, she embarked on a teaching career in South Carolina's low country that would span seven decades.

She taught for one year under the supervision of Charlotte Ross at Laing School in Mt. Pleasant, South Carolina. From 1924 until 1938, she taught in the North Charleston schools. In 1928, she married the Reverend William Essex Forsythe, an Episcopalian minister at Holy Cross-Faith Memorial Church and School on Pawley's Island and at St. Cyprian's Church in Georgetown, South Carolina. In 1938, at the age of 34, Ruby Forsythe began teaching at the one-room private school on the island, the only educational facility available to Black people on the island. Pawley's Island—like most of South Carolina's Sea Islands—was overwhelmingly Black, largely isolated, impoverished, and neglected until a bridge was built in the relatively recent past. When Forsythe's one-room wooden school and adjacent church burned, they were rebuilt. When the bridge and a highway were built, the school was moved to make room for the road.

In the mid-1950s, Ruby Forsythe attended South Carolina State College and earned a Bachelor's degree in education by 1956. In 1988, the historically Black institution awarded her an honorary doctorate in education. The Forsythes had one son, Burns Maynard Forsythe, a Howard University graduate and school administrator in Mt. Pleasant, South Carolina, who is married and has five children. In 1974, the Reverend William Forsythe died. Ruby Middleton Forsythe continued to teach at Holy Cross-Faith Memorial School until she retired in 1991. Never one to coddle her charges, she did not hesitate to resort to corporal punishment. She acknowledged that "I use the strap." In more eloquent words she summed up her legacy to education and to the people of the island where she labored for much of the twentieth century by affirming that she sowed "the best seed into whatever soil we come into contact with, watching the growth, and the reproduction of the product sent forth." She died in Mt. Pleasant, South Carolina, on May 29, 1992.

BIBLIOGRAPHY

Gatling, Holly. "State's 'Hero,' " *The State* (June 30, 1987); Ryan, Michael. "Mrs. Ruby's One-Room School Is Still Going Strong," *Parade Magazine* (January 25, 1987).

WILLIAM C. HINE

FORTEN, CHARLOTTE L. *see* GRIMKÉ, CHARLOTTE L. FORTEN

FORTEN SISTERS

MARGARETTA FORTEN (c. 1815-1875)

Dual careers as an educator and an abolitionist gave Margaretta Forten an uncommon life for a nineteenth-century Black woman. During the 1840s she taught in a school operated by Sarah Mapps Douglass before opening her own private grammar school equipped with boarding facilities in 1850. In 1859, her school had an enrollment of ten scholars. Margaretta's antislavery career closely paralleled the thirty-six-year existence of the Philadelphia Female Anti-Slavery Society. In December 1833, Margaretta, her mother, and two sisters became charter members of this pioneering women's group. She was one of fourteen women selected to draft the Society's constitution.

From 1833 to 1870, Margaretta helped to chart the Society's agenda. She served as recording secretary in 1833, and then during 1836 she was elected treasurer to assist Esther Moore, the Society's president. At the end of that year, Margaretta reported a treasury balance of $114.81. Reelected to a second term as treasurer in 1837, she served with the new president, Sarah Pugh. Margaretta frequently sat on the Society's policy-making board of managers. Periodically, she represented her group at meetings of the Pennsylvania State Anti-Slavery Society. On January 16, 1837, for example, Margaretta and four others traveled to a state meeting in Harrisburg as official delegates of the Philadelphia Female Anti-Slavery Society.

Margaretta combined office holding with extensive committee work. She served on the Society's membership committee, the education committee, the annual antislavery fair committee, and the petition campaign committee. During Margaretta's tenure, the education committee was involved in many activities, including donating books to Black schools. As one of several fair coordinators in 1856, Margaretta reported a profit of over $1,700.

Margaretta Forten was also involved in charitable activities. In June 1841, she joined Sarah Pugh and four others to spearhead the Society's collection of money for the widow of slain abolitionist Elijah P. Lovejoy. Similarly, in 1856, Margaretta forwarded $25 she had collected to Massachusetts. Those funds were used to build a home for abolitionist William Lloyd Garrison and his family. During November 1863, Margaretta advocated women's rights when she joined Society members Louisa Keller and others in securing signatures for a Women's National League petition.

After almost four decades of involvement in the antislavery crusade, Margaretta Forten offered a resolution at the last meeting of the Philadelphia Female Anti-Slavery Society in 1870. Acknowledging the newly ratified post-Civil War constitutional amendments, Margaretta's resolution announced the triumph of liberty and celebrated her Society's labors in that noble cause.

While her sisters, Harriet and Sarah Louisa, married and raised children, Margaretta remained single and lived in the Forten family home on Lombard Street in Philadelphia. After the death of her father, James Forten, Sr., in 1842, Margaretta resided with her mother and younger brothers, Thomas Francis Willing Forten and William Deas Forten. Margaretta Forten died on January 28, 1875.

SARAH LOUISA FORTEN PURVIS (1814-1883)

Beginning with its January 29, 1831, issue, the *Liberator* newspaper published Sarah Forten's antislavery views. Writing under the pen names of Ada and Magawisca, Sarah, then only seventeen years old, challenged the institution of slavery with such creative works as "The Slave Girl's Address to Her Mother," "The Abuse of Liberty," and "The Slave." Her poems and essays poignantly described the humanity of the bondsmen while attacking the hypocrisy of slavery in a nation founded on the concept of individual liberty. At the conclusion of one essay, Sarah invoked the image of divine intervention on behalf of slaves when she wrote, "He, that Great Spirit, who created all men free and equal . . . He is just, and his anger will not always slumber. He will wipe the tear from Ethiopia's eye; He will shake the tree of liberty, and its blossoms shall spread over the earth" ("The Abuse of Liberty" 1831).

Two years after her debut as an antislavery author, Sarah joined her mother and two sisters as a charter member of the Philadelphia Female Anti-Slavery Society. Like her siblings, she remained a member throughout the Society's thirty-six-year existence. Sarah assumed leadership positions on a number of important committees. In May 1835, she joined with Angelina Grimké and eight others to promote the moral and intellectual improvement of Philadelphia's Black residents. One emphasis of the committee was to improve educational opportunities for children. From 1835 until February 1838, she also worked on the Society's petition campaign to end slavery in the District of Columbia. Sarah's primary responsibility was to secure petition signatures in

Columbia County, Pennsylvania. During February and March 1837, U.S. Congressman James Harper and U.S. Senator Samuel McKean acknowledged receipt of the Society's numerous petitions.

Because abolitionists often encountered difficulty renting halls to hold their meetings, antislavery groups in and around Philadelphia proposed erecting their own building. During December 1836, Sarah joined Lucretia Mott and eight others to spearhead this effort on behalf of the Society. In January 1837, the building committee recommended that the Society purchase twenty-five shares at $5 per share, and Pennsylvania Hall was completed a year later. Their triumph proved short-lived, however, when an angry mob of proslavery sympathizers burned the hall to the ground on the evening of May 17, 1838.

As a member of the Society's board of managers, Sarah helped to make policy. During her tenure on the board from 1836 to 1838, the Philadelphia Female Anti-Slavery Society initiated its support for the Philadelphia Vigilant Committee, a group that assisted slaves fleeing southern states.

Throughout her antislavery career, Sarah maintained a close friendship with Angelina Grimké. Besides serving together on several committees, they wrote to one another. On April 15, 1837, Sarah wrote to Angelina concerning the upcoming Antislavery Convention of American Women to be held the following month in New York City. Sarah and her sisters were traveling from Philadelphia to attend the gathering. Sarah thanked Angelina for offering to arrange lodging in New York, but told her that the Forten women had accepted an invitation to stay at the home of Reverend Peter Williams, pastor of the African Methodist Episcopal Zion Church.

In 1838, Sarah married Joseph Purvis. Six years earlier Sarah's sister Harriet had become the bride of Robert Purvis, Joseph's older brother. By all accounts, Sarah and Joseph enjoyed a happy marriage. The couple had several children. Her duties as a wife and mother and her residence outside of Philadelphia curtailed Sarah's antislavery activities for several years. However, she did not abandon the emancipation crusade. During the 1860s, Sarah worked with the antislavery fair committees alongside her sisters, Margaretta and Harriet.

Joseph Purvis died in January 1857; he was forty-four years old. Sometime after the death of her husband, Sarah and her children moved to the Forten family home on Lombard Street in Philadelphia. The 1880 census lists Sarah as a widow living with her daughter and son, Anne and William Purvis. Other family members residing in the home during the 1880s were Sarah's mother, Charlotte Forten, and her two younger brothers, William Deas Forten and Thomas Francis Willing Forten.

HARRIET D. FORTEN PURVIS (1810-1875)

During a tour of the United States in November 1852, English abolitionist Sallie Holley visited the Byberry, Pennsylvania, home of Harriet and Robert Purvis and recorded her impressions. Holley remarked that "his wife is very lady-like in manners and conversation; something of the ease and blandness of a southern lady. The style of living here is quite uncommonly rich and elegant" (Chapwick 1899). The lady-like wife to whom Holley referred was Harriet Purvis, the eldest daughter of abolitionists James Forten, Sr., and Charlotte Forten. When Sallie Holley met Harriet and Robert in 1852, the couple had been married for twenty years and were the parents of five children, Robert, Jr., Charles Burleigh, Henry, Harriet, and Emily.

Harriet Purvis, like her mother and two sisters, Margaretta and Sarah Louisa, was a charter member of the Philadelphia Female Anti-Slavery Society. Harriet's energies went primarily to this group and the Pennsylvania State Anti-Slavery Society. She was active in the Female Society for nearly all of its thirty-six years of existence. Harriet frequently cochaired the antislavery fairs, an annual fund-raising event. Besides helping to organize and manage the fairs, Harriet also helped devise the strategy to make these events successful. In February 1841, for example, she and Sarah Mapps Douglass were members of a group that evaluated the profitability of the previous fair activity.

Harriet viewed the antislavery fairs as important events. In 1861, and with the start of the Civil War, Harriet urged the Society to hold a fair even though the fair committee was smaller because of increased war efforts. Harriet's arguments proved persuasive, and the members voted to proceed with the annual event. In time, Harriet had additional assistance from her daughter, Harriet Purvis, Jr., who joined the fair committee from 1866 through 1868.

As a skilled seamstress, Harriet served on the Philadelphia Female Society's sewing committee, charged with the responsibility of establishing a sewing school in an economically disadvantaged section of the city. On June 23, 1842, the committee reported that they had located a room for the school, which had been donated rent free, and they had engaged a sewing teacher.

On numerous occasions, Harriet represented the Philadelphia Female Anti-Slavery Society as a delegate to other group meetings. In 1838 and 1839, Harriet was one of the Society's delegates to the Antislavery Convention of American Women. Also in 1839, she and nine others attended the Free Produce Convention on behalf of their Society. The antislavery convention delegates pledged themselves to secure free labor products, especially cotton goods, for the Philadelphia area. During May 1841, Harriet and her husband attended the Pennsylvania State Anti-Slavery Society convention where Harriet represented the Female Society during the proceedings.

Besides her role as an antislavery delegate, Harriet's connections in abolitionist circles gave her an array of prominent friends and acquaintances. William Lloyd Garrison, Sallie Holley, Angelina Grimké, and many others frequented the Purvis home. Harriet also knew Boston abolitionist Sarah Parker Remond. On December 10, 1857, Harriet introduced Remond to the Female Society, and Remond then addressed the group on her emancipation efforts in Ohio. On another occasion, during the post-Civil War era, Harriet accompanied Frances Ellen Watkins Harper, a Black author, and the Reverend Francis S. Cardozo of South Carolina to a state antislavery meeting.

Harriet also lectured on civil rights topics. On September 13, 1866, she spoke to the Female Society in support of Black suffrage. During the speech Harriet denounced the practice of segregating Black passengers on Philadelphia's railroad cars. She urged the Society's committee on railroads as well as the citizens of Philadelphia to correct this injustice. Harriet then reminded her audience of the sentiments of Judge Pitkin, a Republican from Louisiana who believed that it would be difficult to outlaw segregation.

Aside from her public activities, relatively little is known about Harriet's personal life. Evidence suggests that her forty-three-year marriage to Robert Purvis was an equal partnership. Robert encouraged and even assisted Harriet in pursuing a public life dedicated to the causes of abolition and civil rights. From the time of their marriage in 1832, this couple worked as an effective team. While raising a family, they also attended antislavery meetings, lectured, and raised funds to further the emancipation crusade. As a wife, mother, antislavery activist, lecturer, and hostess, Harriet seems to have successfully combined a public career with the more traditional roles set aside for women of her era.

[See also ABOLITION MOVEMENT.]

BIBLIOGRAPHY

Bacon, Benjamin C. *Statistics of the Colored People of Philadelphia* (1859); Barnes, Gilbert H. and Dwight L.

Dumond, eds. *The Letters of Theodore Weld, Angelina Grimké and Sarah Grimké, 1824-1840* (1931); *Cemetery Records of Philadelphia, Pennsylvania* (1803-60); Chapwick, John White, ed. *A Life for Liberty: Anti-Slavery and Other Letters of Sallie Holley* (1899); "Constitution of the Philadelphia Female Anti-Slavery Society," Historical Society of Pennsylvania (December 14, 1833); "Estate of Administration for Margaretta Forten." Filed by William D. Forten, Philadelphia City Hall (February 25, 1876); *The History of Pennsylvania Hall which Was Destroyed by a Mob on the 17 of May 1838* (1838); *Liberator* (January 29, March 26, 1831; April 16, 1831); "Minutes of the Philadelphia Female Anti-Slavery Society," Historical Society of Pennsylvania (1833-70); *National Anti-Slavery Standard* (November 4, 1854); *Proceedings of the Third Anti-Slavery Convention of American Women Held in Philadelphia* (1839); Putnam, Caroline E., and Sarah Cassey Smith, et al. Letter to Wendell Phillips. William Lloyd Garrison papers, Massachusetts Historical Society (November 1, 1856); Sumler-Lewis, Janice L. "The Forten-Purvis Women of Philadelphia and the American Anti-Slavery Crusade," *Journal of Negro History* (Winter 1981-82).

JANICE SUMLER-EDMOND

FORTH, ELIZABETH DENISON (LISETTE) (d. 1866)

Ironies abound in African-American history. Surely one of the most ironic accounts concerns the ex-slave Elizabeth Denison Forth, who bequeathed her fortune to be used to build a church in one of the most exclusive white communities in the country. The daughter of slaves Peter and Hannah Denison, Elizabeth, known as Lisette, was a slave in the Michigan Territory when Congress passed the Northwest Ordinance of 1787 prohibiting slavery in the territory, which would eventually become the states of Michigan, Ohio, Illinois, Indiana, and Wisconsin. When their owner, William Tucker, died on March 7, 1805, he stipulated in his will that Peter and Hannah were to receive their freedom upon the death of his wife, Catherine. Their eight children, however, were bequeathed to his sons. Thus the antislavery provisions of the Northwest Ordinance had little effect on the children's status.

A suit for the Denison children's freedom failed when Judge Augustus B. Woodward ruled on September 23, 1807, that the Northwest Ordinance applied only to new slaves, not to existing ones, in accordance with Jay's Treaty of 1794. Lisette and her brother Scipio escaped, with the aid of white friends, into Canada. The exact date of their return to the

Michigan Territory is not known, but by the early 1820s Lisette was working as a domestic in the Solomon Sibley household in Detroit.

Having saved her meager earnings and perhaps with the advice of her wealthy employer, Lisette bought four lots, totaling 48.5 acres, on April 21, 1825, in Pontiac, Michigan. On September 25, 1827, she married Scipio Forth, according to records of Saint Paul's Protestant Episcopal Church in Detroit. The records do not reveal the exact date of his death, but apparently within three years, Lisette became a widow.

In 1830, she joined the John Biddle household as a domestic servant. Continuing to invest her earnings, during the 1830s Lisette acquired stock in the steamboat *Michigan* and twenty shares of Farmers and Mechanics' Bank stock. Her investments proved profitable. On May 25, 1837, Lisette bought a lot in Detroit, paying the mortgage off in installments. In 1854, Lisette was living in her own home on the edge of the business section of old Detroit. After journeying to Paris in 1855 to attend to the ailing Mrs. Biddle, she returned to Detroit a year later, where she remained until her death on August 7, 1866.

In her final will Lisette left the bulk of her estate "to be used in the erection of a 'Fine Chapel for the use of the Protestant Episcopal Church' of which I am a communicant." She prefaced this rather unusual bequest with the following:

> Having long felt the inadequacy of the provisions made for the poor in our houses of worship, and knowing from sad experience that many devout believers, and humble followers of the lowly Jesus, are excluded from those courts, where the rich and the poor should meet together, shut out from those holy services by the mammon of unrighteousness, from that very church which declares the widow's mite to be more acceptable in the sight of the Lord than the careless offerings of those who give of their "abundance" and wishing to do all in my power as far as God has given me the means to offer to the poor man and the stranger "wine and milk without price and without cost."

Lisette's estate amounted to approximately $1,500. In 1867, with the aid of the bequest, Saint James Chapel was built on Grosse Ile, Michigan.

BIBLIOGRAPHY
Ebony, "Ex-slave's Dream Builds White Church: Freed Woman Contributed First Thousand Dollars towards

Ex-slave Elizabeth Denison Forth, known as Lisette, stipulated in her will that her fortune be used to build a church. With the aid of the bequest, the Protestant Episcopal Church established Saint James Chapel, in Gross Ile, Michigan. [Burton Historical Collection, Detroit Public Library]

Exclusive Detroit Church" (May 1959); Swan, Isabella E. *Lisette* (1965).

DARLENE CLARK HINE

FOSTER, AUTHERINE JUANITA LUCY (1929-)

Her ambition to have the best education she could get led her into a nightmare and into history.

Autherine Juanita Lucy was born on October 5, 1929, in Shiloh, Alabama, the daughter of Minnie Hosea Lucy and Milton Cornelius Lucy, a farmer. One of ten children, she went to the public schools of Shiloh through junior high school. She also helped her family work in the cotton fields and raise watermelon, sweet potatoes, and peanuts. For high school, she went to Linden Academy, graduating in 1947.

Lucy's undergraduate college years were spent at Selma University in Selma, Alabama, and at all-Black Miles College in Fairfield, Alabama, where she met Hugh L. Foster, whom she would later marry. She graduated from Miles with a B.A. in English in 1952. The next decision Lucy made changed her life drastically. She decided to go to graduate school at the University of Alabama. She was not naive; she knew that getting into the school would be a struggle and she prepared for it. With a friend who shared her ambition, she approached the National Association for the Advancement of Colored People (NAACP) for help. Thurgood Marshall, Constance Baker Motley, and Arthur Shores were assigned to be her attorneys. While they started laying the groundwork

for her case, she worked as a secretary, among other jobs. Court action began in July 1953.

"If I graduated from the University of Alabama," she said in a recent interview, explaining her determination, "I would have had people coming and calling me for a job. I did expect to find isolation . . . I thought I could survive that. But I did not expect it to go as far as it did."

It is probable that no one expected things to go that far. On June 29, 1955, the NAACP secured a court order restraining the university from rejecting Lucy and her friend based upon race. The University

After three and a half years of court action and the efforts of attorneys including Thurgood Marshall (right), the NAACP succeeded in forcing the University of Alabama to enroll Autherine Lucy as its first Black student in 1956. NAACP executive secretary Roy Wilkins is at left. [Library of Congress]

Autherine Lucy, left, became the first Black student at the University of Alabama in 1956. Thirty-six years after she was threatened and assaulted by rioters—and subsequently expelled—she received a master's degree from the school, alongside her daughter, Grazia Foster, who earned a bachelor's degree the same year. [Mike Clemmer]

of Alabama was thereby forced to admit them. Two days later, the court amended the order to apply to all other African-American students seeking admission to the university. On February 3, 1956, twenty-six-year-old Lucy enrolled as a graduate student in library science. (Her friend had reconsidered the situation.)

That is when the nightmare began. On the third day of classes, Autherine Lucy faced mobs of students, townspeople, and even groups from out of state. "There were students behind me saying, 'Let's kill her! Let's kill her!'" she said. The mobs threw eggs at her and tried to block her way. A police escort was needed to get her to her classes, and even from within the classroom, she could hear the crowds chanting.

That evening, Lucy was suspended from the university. The university's board stated that the action was taken for her safety and that of the other students. The NAACP lawyers did not accept the suspension, however. They filed a contempt of court suit against the university, accusing the administrators of acting in support of the white mob. Unfortunately, they were unable to support these

charges and were forced to withdraw them. The suit was used as justification for expelling Lucy from the school.

In the days and months that followed, Lucy was invited to study at several European universities at no charge, but she declined. "I didn't know whom to hate," she said. "It felt somewhat like you were not really a human being. But had it not been for some at the university, my life might not have been spared at all."

For some time after her expulsion, Lucy could not find work as a teacher. She was simply too controversial. In the spring of 1956, she moved to Texas and married her college sweetheart, the Reverend Hugh Foster. They had five children, and eventually, she was hired as a teacher. The Fosters lived in Texas for seventeen years, returning in 1974 to Alabama, where she worked as a substitute teacher. During this time, she maintained her interest in civil rights, speaking periodically at meetings.

Then, in 1988, two professors at the University of Alabama invited her to speak to a class, telling students about her experience more than thirty years before. One of the questions she was asked was, "Did you ever try to re-enroll?" Foster said that she hadn't, but that she might consider it. Several faculty members heard about her statement and began working to get the university to overturn her expulsion. In April of that year, the board officially did so.

A year later, Autherine Lucy Foster entered the University of Alabama to earn a master's degree in elementary education. Her daughter, Grazia, enrolled at about the same time, as an undergraduate majoring in corporate finance. In the spring of 1992, they both received degrees.

BIBLIOGRAPHY

The New York Times (February 4, 1956; March 4, 1956; April 26, 1992); *Ebony* (November 1988).

TIYA MILES

FOX, LILLIAN THOMAS (1866-1917)

Black journalist, clubwoman, and civic leader, Lillian Thomas was born in Chicago in 1866 to the Reverend Byrd Parker, pastor of Quinn African Methodist Episcopal (AME) Church, and Jane Janette Thomas, a schoolteacher. Lillian Thomas was raised in Oshkosh, Wisconsin, until moving to Indianapolis in the early 1880s. She began writing at an early age and by the late 1880s achieved national recognition through her work as a reporter and correspondence editor for the *Freeman*, a nationally prominent Black newspaper.

In 1893, Lillian Thomas married James E. Fox, a Jamaican merchant tailor in Pensacola, Florida. That year he relocated his business to Indianapolis, and Lillian retired from the *Freeman*. Although she curtailed her formal work commitment, Fox continued her involvement in community organizations. She also gained national prominence as a public speaker on numerous speaking tours in the Midwest and South for various political and religious organizations as well as at conventions of the Afro-American Council, the Negro business league, the Anti-Lynching League, the Atlanta Congress of Colored Women at the 1895 National Exposition, and the National Association of Colored Women.

After separating from her husband, Fox returned to her writing career. In 1900, the *Indianapolis News* hired her as the first Black journalist to write a news column regularly appearing in any Indiana newspaper. For fourteen years she used her contacts with the white community and her position at the *News* to

further the social and political agendas of various groups within the Black community. A superb organizer, Fox was founder and member of community organizations, among them Bethel AME Literary Society; the Woman's Improvement Club, which provided health care to Black tuberculosis patients; and the Indiana State Federation of Colored Women's Clubs.

BIBLIOGRAPHY

Adams, Cyrus Field. "The Afro-American Council: The Story of Its Organization—What It Stands For—Its Personnel," *Colored American* (1903); Ferguson, Earline Rae. "Lillian Thomas Fox: Indianapolis Journalist and Community Leader," *Black History News and Notes* (May 1987); Hine, Darlene Clark. *When the Truth Is Told: A History of Black Women's Culture and Community in Indiana, 1875-1950* (1981); Wesley, Charles Harris. *The History of the National Association of Colored Women's Clubs: A Legacy of Service* (1984).

EARLINE RAE FERGUSON

FRANCISCAN HANDMAIDS OF THE MOST PURE HEART OF MARY

The Franciscan Handmaids of the Most Pure Heart of Mary is a religious congregation of women in the Catholic church that was founded by a French priest and a Black woman. In 1916 Ignatius Lissner, a priest of the Society of African Missions working among the Black population of Georgia, sought to establish a community of Black sisters to teach Black children in the Catholic schools. Because the Georgia legislature was considering legislation to prohibit white sisters from teaching Black children, Black sisters for the Black children became a necessity.

As superior of the Society of African Missions, which had been charged with the spiritual care of Black Catholics in Georgia, Lissner found a strong and capable leader in Elizabeth Barbara Williams. Williams was working for the Sisters of Notre Dame de Namur when she met Lissner and accepted his invitation. Lissner had the plans and the permission for a new congregation; Williams had the charisma, the courage, and the inspiration to found the congregation and to sustain it.

Elizabeth Barbara Williams was born February 7, 1868, in Baton Rouge, Louisiana. She received her education from the Religious of the Sacred Heart and the Sisters of the Holy Family, a Black religious community with its motherhouse in New Orleans. In

1887, at the age of 19, she joined a community of Black sisters in Convent, Louisiana, who followed the Franciscan Rule. It was disbanded at the beginning of the twentieth century. Later, Elizabeth Williams became a novice for a short while with another congregation of Black sisters, the Oblate Sisters of Providence, in Baltimore.

She was working as a receptionist at Trinity College in Washington, D.C., when she agreed to join Lissner in the founding of a community of Black religious women. As founding superior of the community she took her vows in 1916, taking Theodore as her religious name. The community was established in 1917.

Growth was slow and difficult. The threatened legislation to ban white religious sisters from the education of Black children did not materialize. This left the Black sisters without a mission save for one school. Father Lissner, unable to continue his work in Georgia, left Mother Theodore with the major responsibilities. In 1922, she moved the Handmaids from Savannah to Harlem in New York City. From the beginning, the sisters operated a day nursery to serve the needs of the working parents of Harlem and a soup kitchen for the indigent. Service to the poor and the education of children was their new mission. In 1929, Mother Theodore joined the congregation to the Franciscan Order, and it became known as the Franciscan Handmaids of the Most Pure Heart of Mary. On July 14, 1931, Mother Theodore died.

Primarily a community of Black sisters, its membership has included women from the Caribbean and the Virgin Islands. In 1991, the community numbered thirty-three members engaged mainly in educational and social work. The motherhouse is in Harlem with a novitiate and summer camp on Staten Island and a mission in South Carolina.

BIBLIOGRAPHY

The New Catholic Encyclopedia (1967-79); Davis, Cyprian. *History of Black Catholics in the United States* (1990).

CYPRIAN DAVIS, O.S.B.

FRANKLIN, ARETHA (1942-)

In her 1967 recording of "Respect," Aretha Franklin transformed Otis Redding's mixed appeal for civil and sexual rights into a compelling demand for the equality of Black women. Cast in a crucible of vernacular musical styles that evoked images of the Black experience, "Respect" resonated with a moral certitude embodying contemporary notions of soul. That the song's feminist message would exceed the confines of race and gender owed to the profundity of Franklin's singing and to the enabling power of African-American performance; that her soulful declaration would at times take a secondary position to trivializations about her personal life, dress, and business dealings underscored the disrespect that she and other Black musical figures consistently have endured.

As was true with so many performers in the soul and rhythm-and-blues genres, Franklin's formative musical education took place in the Black church. Born on March 25, 1942, in Memphis, Tennessee, she moved with her parents and siblings first to Buffalo, then to Detroit, where her father, the Reverend C. L. Franklin, would become famous as an evangelist and pastor of the New Bethel Baptist Church. Performing and recording locally in New Bethel's gospel choir (Chess Records 1956) and appearing on the gospel circuit as the featured soloist with her father's evangelical troupe, Franklin literally grew up in the music profession at a time when gospel had begun to reach beyond the boundaries of the church and into the popular realm. Models who inspired her to pursue her teenage avocation as a career included her mother, Barbara Siggers Franklin, a gospel singer who had left the family in 1948, and three women who were national successes and her closest mentors, Clara Ward, Mahalia Jackson, and Dinah Washington, all family friends. With encouragement from pop-gospel star Sam Cooke and guidance from another family friend, jazz bass player Major Holley, Franklin directed her ambition toward the contexts of mainstream popular music and jazz.

In 1960 she moved to New York, where with Holley's help she auditioned with John Hammond, the Columbia Records executive who had overseen the recording careers of Count Basie, Billie Holiday, and other major jazz artists. Under contract with Columbia from 1960 to 1966, Franklin recorded ten albums, beginning with a jazz-oriented mixture (accompanied by a group led by Ray Bryant) seemingly crafted in the image of Holiday's style and presence. When Franklin failed to secure a major following, Columbia assigned her to other producers, who introduced lush accompaniments and a repertory of standards and novelties that led her even further from the stylistic drama of the Black church. Although she earned a respectable following among nightclub audiences—notably for *Unforgettable* (1964), a recorded tribute to Dinah Washington following Washington's death—Franklin gained only marginal national success; she was limited by the conventions of a style that had foundered in the wake of an emerging rock-pop style.

The turning point in her career came in 1966 when Franklin signed with Atlantic Records, one of the premier labels specializing in Black rhythm and blues. Collaborating with producer Jerry Wexler, she recrafted her popular style against the background of gospel and blues, replacing Columbia's studio orchestrations with the rough-and-ready accompaniment of a white soul band from Muscle Shoals, Alabama. Her initial Atlantic LP, *I Never Loved a Man (the Way I Loved You)* (1967) was an immediate popular success, generating two number-one hit singles, "I Never" and "Respect." Remarkably, the latter not only capped *Billboard* magazine's rhythm-and-blues chart but also crossed over to earn the top position in the white-oriented pop category.

Franklin's next albums—especially *Lady Soul* (1968) and its singles, "Chain of Fools" and "(Sweet Sweet Baby) Since You've Been Gone"—established her as the dominant presence in Black popular music; she was the new "Queen of Soul."

Record releases from the early 1970s, moreover, reflected efforts to widen stylistic scope and audience by attenuating the soul sound without lessening personal artistry. *Live at the Fillmore West* (1971), crafted for a white rock audience, highlighted previous hits and popular songs accompanied by a soul band led by King Curtis. *Young, Gifted and Black* (1971), a deeply introspective, autobiographical portrait, also sought a broadly popular audience. Here Franklin provided a series of deeply moving performances despite lackluster accompaniment and frequently insipid arrangements. The capstone of the early Atlantic period was *Amazing Grace* (1972), a live performance that marked her return to the traditional gospel setting. Featuring accompaniment by the Rev. Mr. James Cleveland and the Southern California Community Choir, the album represented a watershed moment in musical intersections of sacred and secular, arcane and popular, Black and white.

What made all of these recordings so compelling, so profoundly moving, was Franklin's ability to materialize a character, a way of being, summed up in the purposely vague term *soul*. Mixing themes of love, sex, struggle, joy, pain, and affirmation, Franklin succeeded by crafting profound images out of the seemingly mundane, everyday experiences of ordinary life. Her recorded performances of "Respect," "A Natural Woman," and "Do Right Woman" acknowledged inadequacy as they celebrated perseverance, granted

fallibility as they voiced optimism and hope. These messages were powerful because they were sung with such conviction by a singer whose voice evoked human qualities of rightness and integrity at a time of dynamic struggle. They were her vocalized symbols of the African-American experience, of resistance, of affirmation, of celebration—symbols enhanced by the down-home, down-to-earth certainty of her blues and gospel accompaniments. For white audiences, moreover, Franklin's message carried similar depth of meaning, and her crossover appeal spoke positively about the successes of a musical-based racial dialogue during a period of extreme contentiousness and misunderstanding.

However, the condescending portraits to which Franklin was subjected during moments of personal difficulty showed how her successes could easily be undermined. Notable among these negative representations were commentaries on her love life, judgments about her embrace of African style and dress, and a 1968 *Time* feature that deteriorated into a silly comparison of soulful and not-so-soulful historical figures.

The immortal Aretha Franklin demanded R-E-S-P-E-C-T in 1967. [Schomburg Center]

After the extraordinary creative and popular successes of the late 1960s and early 1970s, Franklin seemed unable to sustain the energy and vibrancy that so enlivened her initial Atlantic recordings. As civil rights activities declined, soul music correspondingly lost much of its captivating power, and Franklin herself began to move whimsically from style to style. From 1974 to 1979 she recorded a series of albums with various producers, and despite some success from her collaborations with Curtis Mayfield, *Sparkle* (1976) and *Almighty Fire* (1978), none seemed to measure up to her earlier dramatic achievements. Significantly, while the limited appeal of these records may have said more about the evanescence of popularity than about the limits of her creative talents, commentators rarely sought to contextualize or explain. Even her biographer worked from the assumption that popularity defined value, as he cast her so-called decline as a reflection of poor judgment in the studio and on stage as well as of unfortunate choices in style and dress.

The reality of declining economic success did, however, have tangible effects, leading to a break with Atlantic Records in 1980. From Atlantic she switched to Clive Davis's Arista label. That move, staged publicly as the comeback of the soul diva, helped to revive her distinctive sound within the disco inflections of the era. Despite an extended legal dispute with Arista, Franklin gained considerably from the label's marketing powers, which capitalized on her stature as the grand figure of Black pop. An appearance in the film *The Blues Brothers* (1980) and collaborations with major rock artists—George Michael and Annie Lennox on the album *Who's Zoomin' Who?* (1985) and Keith Richards as coproducer of *Aretha* (1986)—renewed her appeal among interracial youth audiences. The collaboration with Lennox, "Sisters Are Doin' It for Themselves" (*Who's Zoomin' Who?*), became something of an interracial feminist anthem in rock and rhythm-and-blues circles.

By the late 1980s, Franklin had reemerged in mainstream markets, this time symbolically as the voice of liberation when "Respect" was heard on the soundtrack of CBS's prime-time television show *Murphy Brown*.

BIBLIOGRAPHY

Bego, Mark. *Aretha Franklin, the Queen of Soul* (1989); Hodenfield, Chris. "Reassessing Aretha," *Rolling Stone* (May 23, 1974); Sanders, Charles L. "Aretha: A Close-up Look at Sister Superstar," *Ebony* (December 1971); *Time*, "Lady Soul: Singing It Like It Is" (June 28, 1968); Welding, Pete. "Aretha Franklin," *Downbeat* (September 28, 1961).

DISCOGRAPHY

For a discography, see Bego, Mark. *Aretha Franklin, the Queen of Soul* (1989).

RONALD M. RADANO

FRANKLIN, MARTHA MINERVA (1870-1968)

Prior to the founding of the National Association of Colored Graduate Nurses (NACGN) in 1908, Black women were outcasts in the nursing profession. Martha Minerva Franklin resolved to change the status of Black nurses and so founded the NACGN.

Born on October 29, 1870, in New Milford, Connecticut, to Henry J. Franklin and Mary E. Gauson Franklin, Martha graduated from Meriden Public High School in 1890. Five years later she entered the Woman's Hospital Training School for Nurses in Philadelphia, one of the few Black women to have access to such a nursing program. The vast majority of nursing schools either severely restricted or prohibited the admission of Black women. This widespread system of racial discrimination and exclusion propelled many African-Americans to found a separate Black network of health care institutions and nurse training schools.

The sole Black student in her class, Franklin received her diploma in December 1897. She found employment as a private-duty nurse, hospital staff or public health nursing seldom being available to Black nurses. Franklin worked for a while in Meriden and then in New Haven.

As a graduate nurse, she was confronted by the unjust treatment of Black nurses. The denial of admission to hospital nursing schools limited the number of Black trained nurses, and those few who did graduate were denied membership in the American Nurses' Association (ANA) since membership in a state nurses' association was a prerequisite to membership in the ANA, and all southern state associations barred Black women.

In fall 1906, Franklin launched an investigation of the status of Black graduate nurses. She discovered widespread dissatisfaction among Black nurses, coupled with an eagerness to improve themselves professionally. Franklin and the Black nurses who responded to her survey recognized the need to unite in order to promote racial integration and to achieve greater acceptance within their profession.

Adah Belle Samuels Thoms, president of the Lincoln Hospital School of Nursing Alumnae

Association, responded to one of the 1,500 letters Franklin wrote. Thoms invited Franklin and interested nurses to meet in New York City as guests of the association. In August 1908, fifty-two nurses attended a meeting chaired by Franklin. During the three-day conference, the participants reached a consensus about the need to form a permanent professional organization. Out of this meeting emerged the National Association of Colored Graduate Nurses, with twenty-six charter members. In light of her initiative and leadership, the group unanimously elected Franklin president. She was re-elected in 1909. When she declined to serve a third term, the members designated her honorary president for life and made her the NACGN's permanent historian.

During the 1920s, Franklin relocated to New York City. She enrolled in a six-month postgraduate course at Lincoln Hospital, became a registered nurse, and found employment as a nurse in the New York City public school system. Considering education a life-long pursuit, at the age of fifty-eight, she studied at the Teachers College of Columbia University in the Department of Practical Arts, now the Department of Nursing Education. She died on September 26, 1968.

BIBLIOGRAPHY

Hine, Darlene Clark. *Black Women in White: Racial Conflict and Cooperation in the Nursing Profession, 1890-1950* (1989); Staupers, Mabel K. *No Time for Prejudice: The Story of the Integration of Negroes in Nursing in the United States* (1961); Thoms, Adah B. *Pathfinders: A History of the Progress of Colored Graduate Nurses* (1929).

DARLENE CLARK HINE

FREE BLACK WOMEN IN THE ANTEBELLUM NORTH

Freedom held important advantages for African-American women. Although almost all of them worked for wages in service employment and remained socially and economically vulnerable, most were able to establish a rich and secure family and community life scarcely possible in bondage.

By the turn of the nineteenth century, slavery was rapidly becoming an exclusively southern institution. Conditions of climate and soil ensured that most regions of the North would never support the plantation agriculture most conducive to large slaveholdings. Thus, the economic power of northern slaveholders was not sufficient to cushion them from antislavery

attack. Starting with Vermont in 1777 all northern states abolished slavery either outright or through plans of gradual emancipation. Within two generations only 1,100 slaves remained in a northern population of over 170,000 Black Americans. On the eve of the Civil War the number of northern slaves had dropped to eighteen.

African-American women accounted for slightly more than half of all free Black people during this period but they were not evenly distributed throughout the Black population. In frontier areas of the West, like California, there were many more Black men than women, but in the northeastern and north central regions, Black women held a numeric advantage, especially in urban areas. Northern Black women, who in slavery lived on farms or in small settlements, used their new freedom of mobility to migrate to the larger cities. Jobs were more readily available there and substantial numbers of Black people settled into emerging African-American urban communities.

The work lives of most African-American women did not change appreciably in freedom. They remained full-time domestic workers in white households. In nineteenth-century Philadelphia, New York, and Boston, two-thirds of Black women were service workers. Yet the general work title "servant" often obscured the variety of jobs that these women did. The largest group performed traditional household work, cleaning, washing, and cooking. Many provided child care for white families and a few performed more specialized services like dressmaking and gourmet cooking. The nature of work often depended upon the social and economic status of the employer and carried with it significant social and economic meaning for the worker. To work in the home of a family of power was to have potential access to influence. Such a position might make a woman important to her friends and neighbors.

The establishment of Black institutions also provided work opportunities for women. Early African-American schools founded in many cities were staffed by white reformers. Elie Neau, a white New Yorker, founded the first slave school in British North America in New York at the Trinity Church in 1704. Other schools were established by Puritans in New England and by Quakers in Philadelphia and other towns in Pennsylvania and New Jersey. From the beginning, however, Black women played important roles as classroom aids in some of the early schools and as teachers in many of the later ones. Eleanor Harris was the first teacher of her race in Philadelphia, and Sarah Dorsey and Margaretta Forten were among those who followed in her footsteps. In the early 1830s, Sarah Mapps Douglass returned from New York City, where she had been a teacher, to open a school for Black girls in her native Philadelphia. Hers was, at the time, the only high school for Black girls in the nation. Douglass took the bold step of teaching science to her female students and later, after taking courses in medicine at the Female Medical College of Pennsylvania and at Pennsylvania Medical University, she traveled widely lecturing to Black women.

Throughout the North in the early decades of the nineteenth century, Black women provided and even supervised the education of Black girls and, less frequently, Black boys as well. These were far more desirable jobs than domestic service, but they were few and required education far beyond the reach of most free Black women of the period. Thus they remained the province of the small Black middle class that developed during this era.

For most, domestic work was one of the only respectable jobs available, but Black women were vulnerable to sexual harassment at the hands of male employers who held considerable power over them. In some areas, periodic shortages of domestic workers provided leverage to Black women in their dealings with white male employers, but in most cases these women were financially imperiled and largely unprotected by law.

For Black women unable to secure a living through more respectable employment, prostitution remained a job of last resort. In New York's Five Points districts, along Philadelphia's Delaware waterfront, or in Boston's North End, desperate women, Black and white, found men willing to compensate them for sexual favors.

Whatever work Black women undertook, it was sure to affect other aspects of their lives. No less than other women in the nineteenth century they were influenced by the societal expectations of gender roles. American women were instructed through their families, churches, schools, and popular culture to assume dependent, subordinate, supportive postures in their society. Theirs was the domain of the home, the responsibility of the moral maintenance of the family, and the role of helpmate to their husbands. These ideals were contradictory to the realities of all poor women's lives but they were especially so for Black women, many of whom were poor and all of whom were limited by the restrictions of a society that circumscribed opportunities according to race.

The issue of race complicated the issue of gender in the lives of African-American women. Because slavery was no respecter of gender, female slaves were

protected by neither traditional Western assumptions about feminine frailty, nor presumptions about their emotional delicacy. When heavy fieldwork was required and Black males were not available in sufficient numbers to perform such labor, female slaves were field hands. Moreover, the obedience, humility, and dependency demanded of male slaves deprived Black men of the traditional privileges accorded men in American society. They were expected to exhibit "male qualities" of physical strength and "female qualities" of subordination, not only to their masters but also to all white people.

If slavery sought to defeminize Black women and emasculate Black men, most believed that freedom should reestablish traditional gender roles. As free Black communities took form in the early nineteenth century, this message appeared in the sermons of Black ministers, in the expectations of family life, and even in the pages of Black newspapers. The socializing agencies of Black society instructed Black women and men in the gender expectations of America.

The economic realities of Black life frustrated all African-Americans but posed special problems for Black women. Forced to work long hours at inadequately compensated employment, women also were expected to fulfill the duties of wife and mother for their own families. Society implicitly recognized the full-time nature of housework and child care in its expectation that such work might be done by domestic staff, yet women were expected to perform such tasks in addition to their full-time compensated employment. Such expectations burdened not only Black women but also all working-class women. In the nineteenth century, however, most married white women did not work full time outside their homes, and traditionally white women moved out of the work force after marriage. Racial discrimination limited job and income possibilities for Black males so that Black women were likely to remain employed after marriage. Thus they faced the double burden of work inside and outside of the household. Still, their situation was even more complex.

There were some white women who also worked long hours at poorly compensated employment and they, like their Black counterparts, generally faced an additional work burden at home. There was, however, one important difference. Whereas white women might be expected to do double duty because of gender expectations, Black women were charged with such duty as part of their special responsibility to their race. If Black men were to be true men by predominating in the family, Black women must be true women by subordinating themselves to their husbands' will and wishes. Such beliefs put women in particularly difficult situations, as in the case of Chloe Spears who, with her husband, Cesar, operated a boardinghouse in nineteenth-century Boston. In addition, Chloe did domestic work for a prominent Boston family. During the day, while she was at work, Cesar saw to the cooking and other duties associated with the boardinghouse. When Chloe returned in the evening, he retired and turned the operation over to her while he rested. At this point, what had been seen as work during the day became housework at night, fit not for the man of the house, but for the housewife.

Thus, after working all day at her day-job, Chloe cooked dinner for her family and the boarders and cleaned the house. Then, in order to make extra money she took in washing, another job fit for women, which she did at night, setting up lines in her room for drying the clothes. She slept a few hours while the clothes dried, then ironed them, and prepared breakfast for the household before going off to work for the day.

It was important that Cesar not be expected to participate in the housework, for that was not man's work, and both Cesar and Chloe had an obligation to uphold every Black man's manhood as a part of their duty to the freedom and manhood of the race, a duty reinforced by the teachings of almost every authority in Black society. This was one of the ways that race complicated Black life. Yet, in some ways Black women benefited from their critical economic roles in Black society. Despite the custom and law in American society that husbands controlled the family finances, Chloe did not routinely place her wages under Cesar's management. Instead, she controlled her own money and, when at one point she decided to acquire an unfurnished house, Cesar was surprised that she had the $700 needed for the purchase. In fact, the only reason he became involved in the acquisition was the law that would not allow a married woman to buy a house in her name. Chloe's independence in financial matters was limited not by the customs or admonitions of Black society but by laws that limited all women in American society.

This independence extended to many areas of life, giving Black women certain advantages within their communities not provided to women in the broader American society. Whereas white women, in theory at least, were restricted to the private sphere of home and children, Black women were allowed, even expected, to take part in the public arena of community politics. Not only did they organize their own gender-separate organizations, as did white women, but also they joined with Black men to work for the common political and social goals of the abolition of slavery and the improvement of the conditions of life for free Black Americans. Whether in the cause of education, temperance, community service, civil rights, antislavery, or the Underground Railroad, Black women were central actors.

Mary Ann Shadd Cary of Philadelphia and later of Canada, Sojourner Truth of New York State, Maria Stewart of Boston, and Ellen Craft who escaped from slavery in Georgia were among the many Black women who, with the full support of Black men, traveled the nation speaking out against slavery and in favor of racial justice. These and other Black women, like Sarah Remond of Boston, also journeyed to Europe in the cause of freedom to be received by the royalty of the Old World. Theirs was not the retiring role of the traditional nineteenth-century female ideal. In the female antislavery societies, the less formal vigilance groups that sheltered and defended fugitive slaves, and the literary societies that placed the issues of freedom and justice before the public for discussion and debate, Black women were among the leaders.

Yet these women paid a price for this expanded role. Although they traveled the globe as cosmopolitan representatives of their race, they were nevertheless expected to perform the housewife's duties in addition to those of the public figure. For Black women, any service they provided to the community was service in addition to that they provided to their families—it was a second job. To the extent that they took on full-time responsibilities in the public sphere, it was with the assistance of other Black women. Mary Ann Shadd Cary's sister assisted with the care of Cary's children while she was on the road speaking for antislavery. Ellen Craft had no children for whom she was responsible while she worked for the cause. Zilpha Elaw, an itinerant minister, relied on relatives to care for her daughter in her absence. Whereas Black men like Frederick Douglass, William Wells Brown, and Charles Lennox Remond could rely on their wives to shoulder the day-to-day responsibilities of family while they tended to their careers in the protest movement, female reformers relied on surrogate wives, most often female relatives.

The domestic expectations of married women sometimes encouraged Black women to postpone marriage, allowing time to establish public careers first. Sarah Mapps Douglass remained single until well into middle age. Some Black women refused to marry because they found few Black men capable of supporting them. One consequence of the limited occupational opportunities for Black men was the disproportionate number of single Black females and female-headed Black families, ranging as high as one-third of free Black families in the antebellum North. Yet this situation, like most others for African-Americans at the time, was more complex than its surface appearance. One important reason for the absence of Black men from Black families was their high death rate, brought about by the dangerous jobs that they were often forced to take and the high mortality rate among poor people generally in U.S. society.

Furthermore, the jobs open to Black men often required them to be away from home for long periods of time. Jobs like seaman and boatman, in port cities of the North, generally accounted for the largest proportion of Black male employment. Whereas white sailors often dropped out of the profession as they got older and married, Black men generally remained at sea even after marriage, as it was one of the only steady sources of work available to them. This forced Black women to shoulder enormous burdens for the family while their men were at sea for months or years at a time. The absence of a father from a Black family was most often a consequence of death or the adjustment to a racially constricted job market—not generally of the preference of Black men and women.

The lives of free Black women in the antebellum North were thus exacerbated by economic and social forces that were often beyond their control. Race complicated gender, forcing Black women and men to make adjustments in their relationships and their expectations of one another. Under these circumstances, Black women experienced some benefits but most often bore a special burden.

BIBLIOGRAPHY

Berlin, Ira. *Slaves Without Masters: The Free Negro in the Antebellum South* (1974); Curry, Leonard P. *The Free Black in Urban America, 1800-1850: The Shadow of the Dream* (1981); Gutman, Herbert G. *The Black Family in Slavery and Freedom, 1750-1925* (1976); Harley, Sharon and Rosalyn Terborg-Penn, eds. *The Afro-American Woman: Struggles and Images* (1978); Hine, Darlene Clark. *Black Women in American History* (1990); Horton, James Oliver and Lois E. Horton. *Black Bostonians: Family Life and Community Struggle in the Antebellum North* (1979); Horton, James Oliver. *Free People of Color: Interior Issues in African American Community* (1992), and "Freedom's Yoke: Gender Conventions among Antebellum Free Blacks," *Feminist Studies* (Spring 1986); Hull, Gloria T., Patricia Bell Scott, and Barbara Smith, eds. *All the Women Are White, All the Blacks Are Men, But Some of Us Are Brave: Black Women's Studies* (1982); Jones, Jacqueline. *Labor of Love, Labor of Sorrow: Black Women, Work, and the Family from Slavery to the Present* (1985); Lerner, Gerda, ed. *Black Women in White America: A Documentary History* (1973); Loewenberg, Bert James and Ruth Bogin, eds. *Black Women in Nineteenth-Century American Life: Their Words, Their Thoughts, Their Feelings* (1976); Sterling, Dorothy, ed. *We Are Your Sisters: Black Women in the Nineteenth Century* (1984).

JAMES O. HORTON

FREE BLACK WOMEN IN THE ANTEBELLUM SOUTH

Long before the Thirteenth Amendment to the U.S. Constitution, ratified in 1865, declared free millions of women, men, and children who had long been enslaved throughout the American South, hundreds of thousands of black, brown, and tan people already lived outside the bounds of slavery. In fact, by 1860, more than 260,000 free people of color lived in the South and had either personally experienced slavery or had at least one African antecedent who had been enslaved. Freedom was rare, however, and it was both limited and costly. Although more than 260,000 free people of color resided in the South at the outbreak of the Civil War, they constituted a small minority compared to the 8 million white people and the 4 million slaves who lived there as well. Of the small percentage of nonwhite southerners who enjoyed some degree of freedom, a majority (53 percent) were women. The preference that freedom afforded women was no accident. It was, in part, an expression of the division between the productive and reproductive roles of slave women and men. How those women, once free, defined their lives can be understood only within the framework of the relations of race, class, and gender in the region.

The experiences and identities of free women of color directly reflected the South's system of slavery, a system that changed over time and place. During the formative years of the colonial period, when slave codes were not yet established, many Africans who had been brought to the South lived and worked not as free white people but not exactly as slaves, either. As the seventeenth century drew to a close, however, and as white southerners increasingly committed themselves to Black slave labor, fewer and fewer displaced Africans were able to attain, or maintain, their nonslave status. Thus, most women who found themselves enslaved during the final years of the seventeenth century remained enslaved into the eighteenth century.

The natural-rights ideologies championed during the American Revolution provided opportunities for circumscribed freedom to most people who had been enslaved in New England and the mid-Atlantic region, but even such limited freedom was not extended to slaves in the South. Although a few southern slaveholders took the revolutionary ideals to heart and emancipated some slaves, the overwhelming number of people of African ancestry remained in bondage following the revolution. Southern slaveholders staunchly defended their constitutionally confirmed right to own people as if they were property. In their minds, property rights far outweighed any slave's presumed right to personal liberty. The first federal census of 1790 confirms the southern commitment to slavery. Of the nearly 700,000 Africans and their descendants who lived in the South, only slightly more than 32,000 were not enslaved.

At the end of the eighteenth century, and early into the nineteenth century, the free nonwhite population of the South increased as a result of several factors. A trend toward manumission in the Upper South—Maryland, Delaware, Kentucky, Virginia, Tennessee, and even North Carolina—began to redefine the character of the community of free people of color living there. Revolutionary ideology did influence a slave's chances for freedom in the Upper South, but, for the most part, the increase was more a consequence of the declining viability of a plantation economy in the region than of any broad-based ideological change. Slaveholders in the Upper South found that it was cheaper to hire workers—Black or white—than to buy and support slaves. In addition, fugitive slaves often disappeared into the anonymous and transient ferment of port cities such as Baltimore or the sparsely populated countryside—thus swelling the region's free nonwhite population.

Slaveholders in the Lower South—Alabama, Georgia, Louisiana, Mississippi, and South Carolina—were less tolerant of the fledgling abolitionist movement than were slaveholders in the Upper South and, thus, were less likely to manumit their slaves. Of primary importance, however, was the fact that slavery remained a viable, productive labor system in the Lower South, one that encouraged slaveholders to maintain full hegemony and rigid control over the slave population. Most of the increase in the number of free people of color in the Lower South resulted from natural increases as well as the influx of tens of thousands of free nonwhite refugees from Santo Domingo in the wake of the slave revolution and thousands more who suddenly found themselves on U.S. soil as a result of the Louisiana Purchase of 1803 and the Adams-Onis Treaty of 1820 through which Spain ceded Florida to the United States.

White southerners, especially in the Lower South, who felt threatened by the increasing number of free people of color and the growing abolitionist movement in the North, began to close, even more securely, the already narrow gateways to freedom. Between 1810 and 1860, southern states strengthened their laws to preclude any further increases in the number of free people of color, and through expulsion, emigration, or reenslavement schemes they even attempted to eliminate the free population entirely.

Of course, nonslave status never guaranteed real freedom or equality for those who had moved out of slavery. Free people of color knew that in southern society race was presumed to signify condition and that their collective existence challenged the inherent assumptions of that world. Freedom made them few promises. Instead, it alternately confirmed the legal advantages that distinguished their condition from that of slaves, while, at the same time, it reinforced the racial stigma that bound them to slaves. Finding themselves neither enslaved nor wholly free, free people of color recognized that they were anomalous to the social, economic, and legal realities of the slave system. They were a group apart from both Black slaves and free whites.

Personal liberty was not only tenuous for these free people of color; it was relative as well. Among other things, gender influenced freedom. Because the legal status of a child always followed that of the mother, a daughter or son of a slave woman was inescapably defined as a slave, whereas the child of a free woman—be she Black, white, or Native American—was always free, regardless of the father's status. Thus, the child of a free man of color and a slave woman remained the property of her owner. Therefore, the slaveowner who manumitted a male slave freed only one individual, but if a slaveowner freed a woman, all of her future offspring and, as a matter of course, the entire female line also would be free. For this reason, manumitting a female slave had a long-term, multiple effect on the Black population, slave and free, as well as social, economic, and demographic implications that far outweighed the consequences of freeing a man.

Despite such implications, women were more likely to be freed than men, primarily because the white population viewed women as less threatening to the social order. Slave women seemed less frightening than men, who were feared for their physical strength and for their presumed ability—and tendency—to foment rebellion. Therefore, slaveholders considered women of color who lived outside the boundaries of slavery less of a potential social threat than men and, thus, were more likely to allow women their freedom through will, deed, self-purchase, or legislative act.

In addition, most former slaves were urban dwellers, and most nonwhite urban dwellers in the South were women. The predominance of women in the urban slave population was the product of a twofold phenomenon. First, urban slaveholders feared the proximity of large numbers of male slaves. Riots and violence, as well as the relative freedom that urban slaves experienced in comparison to plantation slaves, encouraged urban slaveowners to limit the number of men in the urban slave population. Second, urban slaveholders were less likely to manumit men, and they sought greater control over those who already were free. Southern legislatures enacted laws specifically designed to curtail the number and autonomy of free men of color. Urban occupational patterns also contributed to the predominance of women among that population, as a large number of women were needed to perform the countless domestic chores of the urban environment.

A recognizable and coherent community appears to have provided protection and social opportunities for free women of color in the cities, community support systems such as churches and benevolent societies that generally were not available to free women of color in rural areas of the South. Indeed, the advantage of living in urban areas is reflected in the total number of free people of color who lived in cities. For instance, in 1860, while approximately 85 percent of the white and 95 percent of the slave population lived in the countryside, more than 72 percent of free people of color lived in cities, the majority of whom were women.

Urban slave women sometimes managed to purchase their own freedom as well as freedom for their children. A portion of the urban free nonwhite population had been freed from plantation slavery, but most who managed to achieve their freedom did so in an urban setting, in such cities as the nation's capital, Baltimore, Richmond, Charleston, Savannah, Mobile, and New Orleans.

The character of urban slavery also advanced the opportunity for freedom. Slaves in the cities often worked and lived away from their owners, who were paid a regular weekly or monthly sum from their wages. Therefore, slave women who managed to establish lives beyond the direct day-to-day influence of their owners were more likely to be able to save money toward purchasing their freedom, at least in those jurisdictions where self-purchase remained an option. However, few slave women actually were able to accumulate enough money for that purpose, even in an urban setting.

Slave women were more likely to secure their freedom through familial relationships. Some mothers and grandmothers worked their entire lives to purchase the freedom of their children and grandchildren, while fathers and husbands sometimes purchased the rights to their daughters or wives for the purpose of manumitting them. On rare occasions, men who were still enslaved worked to free the women they loved at the expense of their own freedom, but most men who manumitted women already were free themselves. Free men of color who were legally married to slave women (in the few jurisdictions that allowed slaves to marry), or who cohabited with them, and even white men who were committed to their de facto wives and their racially mixed offspring sometimes negotiated their freedom.

Women also were somewhat more likely to be freed by masters or mistresses for sentimental reasons. Slave women who served as domestics, cooks, nurses, and nannies formed relationships with their owners that demonstrated at best love and caring and at worst fear and hatred. Such relationships, however complicated, sometimes resulted in freedom for those women who lived most intimately with their owners and who therefore had greater opportunity to negotiate the terms of their emancipation. Also, some white slaveowners manumitted elderly servants who were no longer economically productive.

Access to freedom, as well as its conditions and limitations, also differed by region. Because plantation slavery had become a less viable economic institution in the Upper South by the early nineteenth century, owners in that region were less likely to hold as tightly to their slaves as were slaveholders in the Deep South. Also, more slave women in the Upper South enjoyed quasi-freedom—living as if they were free without going through the process of legal manumission—than did slave women in the Lower South, and others were likely to achieve their freedom when they or their owners chose to test it.

Notwithstanding considerable inflexibility toward emancipation, one part of the Lower South nonetheless accommodated the most thriving population of free people of color in the slave states. These were the racially mixed descendants of African, French, and Spanish settlers of colonial Louisiana and Florida who identified themselves as free Creoles of color. Louisiana's Creoles of color became U.S. residents following the 1803 Louisiana Purchase. Then, in 1812 and 1821, the Creoles of color in Spanish west Florida joined their Louisiana counterparts. By 1860, the approximately 20,000 Creoles of color who lived in Louisiana, southern Alabama and Mississippi, and northwest Florida were distinct from both slaves and whites. Unlike many of the free people of color elsewhere in the South, who were viewed by their white neighbors as slaves without masters, free Creoles considered themselves, and were acknowledged by the dominant white population as well as by slaves as, an intermediate caste. Consequently, Creoles of color occupied a special status in their communities. Unlike their counterparts in the rest of the South, free Creole women and men of color, for the most part, were socially and legally recognized as free citizens. The law protected their legal status, and members of the white community, to whom they often were related, ensured their social standing.

Throughout most of the antebellum period, free Creole women of color, and free Creole men, retained the right to buy and sell property, including slaves. They were able to marry, sue in court, and acquire an education—until both fear of slave uprisings and paranoia drove white leaders to limit their freedom. Increasingly after 1850, white politicians in Louisiana, Alabama, and Florida passed laws forbidding free people of color to transact business without white guardians. As a result, many free Creoles of color left the region for France, Cuba, even Mexico, where they hoped to find a racial climate that was similar to the one they formerly had known along the Gulf Coast. Despite the hardships confronting those who chose to remain, however, most educated their children and worshipped without interference.

Creole women of color celebrated and protected their distinct crosscultural heritage, and as mothers they transmitted that special heritage to their children. Because of their unique social identity, free Creoles of color were closely tied to both their Creole white and their Black slave kin and neighbors. As part of an intermediate caste, however, free Creoles of color usually segregated themselves into communities where they spoke only French or Spanish and remained true to the Roman Catholicism that the early settlers had brought with them to the New World.

The Catholic Church itself reinforced the special identity of the Creoles of color. Viewing itself as the moral protector of women, the church continued to support Creole women of color even as racism deepened through the antebellum South. From the early days of settlement, the Catholic Church had educated free women of color; consequently, while many white southerners remained uneducated, many Creole women of color received some formal education. The

skills of reading, writing, ciphering, and sewing that the church taught these women, while at the same time imparting religious doctrine, reinforced what their mothers and grandmothers had told them about the social roles of women. Thus, free Creole women of color instructed their daughters as to the proper behavior of daughters, sisters, wives, and mothers, roles that had been established by both African and Western traditions.

Beyond the Gulf Coast region, however, most free women of color in the rural plantation South lived in areas where they were always a small minority. In spite of their apparent isolation and small number, however, these women knew themselves to be the daughters, sisters, wives, and mothers who anchored family and community networks. In Georgia's plantation belt, for example, free people of color made up only about one-half of 1 percent of the total population, but, their number notwithstanding, they were firmly linked to one another by extended interlocking families characterized by conjugal, sanguinal, and co-residential ties.

In addition, as was the case with many free Creoles, free people of color in the plantation belt maintained familial links with white southerners. Strict social sanctions that sought to control the sexuality of white women suppressed all but a few liaisons between slave, or free, men of color and white women. Public outrage aimed at the white women and free or slave men of color who became parents of racially mixed children was so severe that few entered into such alliances. If discovered, the white woman would have been ostracized, and any man of color could expect to be brutally punished. Thus, although such liaisons did occur, they were rare, or at least very secretive. Nonetheless, a few free people of color in the antebellum South did have white mothers.

No such censures applied to slave, or free, women of color who bore the children of white men, or who even cohabited with them. Laws forbade such relationships, but law enforcement agents, and the community in general, usually ignored liaisons between women of color and white men. For one thing, free women of color often lived in white households or worked side by side with white men who could easily exploit them sexually. The social and legal institution of slavery, which assigned ownership of slave women's bodies to their owners, officially denied slave women the right to reject any sexual overtures and, by extension, also denied the presumption of virtue to free women of color, who often had to deal with the sexual advances of white men. Such advances were often unsought and unwelcome, but few free women of color had the resources to avoid them.

Even those free women of color who willingly cohabited with white men were marginalized by laws that prohibited interracial marriage, and their children were penalized as well. These laws were almost always adhered to by religious and civil authorities, who refused to sanctify or legitimize unions between white men and free women of color. Even when such marriages were performed, courts usually failed to recognize them, leaving the women and their children to vie with white relatives for their share of a de facto husband and father's affections and financial assets. On the other hand, many free women of color had spouses and other close friends and relatives within the slave community. Because the child of a free woman assumed its mother's more favored status, an enslaved spouse did not endanger the freedom of that woman's offspring. In spite of links with both the free white and the enslaved Black communities, the preferred alliances clearly were those that tied the small number of free families of color to one another.

Free people of color who lived in the Lower South often clustered together in enclaves where they formed tight-knit communities. The Cane River region of Louisiana and Chastang Bluff and Mon Luis Island in Alabama are examples of rural communities where free people of color lived in the majority and were able to enjoy their separate status. However, even in regions such as Georgia's rural plantation belt, where free people of color constituted only a small percentage of the population, they were not scattered like isolated grains of sand across a landscape of plantations worked by slaves and owned by hostile white planters. Rather, they usually lived near one another in small towns or on adjoining farms. They formed loose neighborhood clusters in which they could maintain small but protective and nurturing communities of women, men, and children who shared the everyday rituals of life with similarly situated friends and relatives.

In addition to family and community networks, free women of color identified themselves through their work. A few were comfortably situated, but most had to work to provide, or at least supplement, their family's income. Slave women never benefited from the gender conventions associated with white women. For instance, they usually worked as field hands alongside Black men. On the other hand, gender conventions frequently defined the work of free women of color, who more often performed work that was an extension of the domestic sphere. Some were household servants while others were spinners, weavers, or dressmakers; still others worked as independent farmers, often raising both crops and animals and toiling at rigorous physical labor just like men.

Women who hoped to strengthen their position in the free community worked diligently to accumulate property, and a few were astute businesswomen. Home ownership not only offered free women of color a place to house their families; it also extended their economic and political security. Some free women of color centered their work within their households, turning their homes into boardinghouses or devoting domestic space to seamstressing, laundering, or even baking goods to peddle.

A few free women of color even owned slaves, many of whom were female and some of whom were relatives. A free woman of color might own her mother, sister, or even her children, whom statute or local authorities forbade her to manumit. Other free women of color, however, like white slaveholders, owned slaves for economic reasons, and because they generally needed slaves who shared or supplemented their own skills, they usually owned other women.

Many free women of color were permitted to own property and transact business with few restrictions until the early to mid-nineteenth century, when state laws began to heap insult on injury by limiting their political, social, and economic independence. These new laws, designed to restrict the autonomy of free people of color, pertained to both women and men. In many jurisdictions, free people of color had to register annually in county courthouses. They were required to acquire and maintain legal guardians and usually could transact business only through those guardians. Many occupations were closed to them, and they often bore an unequal tax burden. Most jurisdictions considered them residents but denied them the rights of citizenship. Few southern states allowed free people of color to pursue an education, and, for the most part, criminal codes placed free people of color on the same footing as slaves.

Of course, all women, including free women of color, lacked many of the rights extended to white men. In most jurisdictions, married free women of color, like married white women, were denied the right to own property and control their children; their rights, as defined by common or civil law, were subsumed by their husbands. However, if they were widowed or remained unmarried, they retained rights to both property and their children. Notwithstanding the idealization of marriage and the prevalent domestic model that defined women within the household as wives and mothers—entirely dependent on men who were supposed to support and protect them—many free women of color remained unmarried and thereby maintained a fair amount of control over their own lives, and over their own children and real property as well. Because free people of color could enter into contracts only through the agency of a white person, and because marriage is a contract, there is some question as to whether marriages between free people of color would have been recognized in most jurisdictions. Many free women of color probably stayed single because they could not marry, however, not because they chose to remain single.

In some respects, the day-to-day experiences of free women of color changed little after general emancipation. Most of these women celebrated when they saw friends and family members freed, but a few regretted the loss of their own slaves. Yet even as their lives changed very little in mundane ways, nothing prepared them for the great social changes that would take place as a result of the Civil War. Freedom—the status that had distanced free women of color from female slaves—was no longer unique. Some free women of color struggled against all odds to maintain what had been a relatively prestigious social position. Threatened by increasing racism in the white community, and the possibility of submersion into the larger group of former slaves, many members of this group tried to maintain their distinct identity, but they were not generally successful.

After the war, the dominant society defined everyone who was nonwhite, free persons of color as well as freedpeople, as Black, and African-Americans quickly began to coalesce into a new, all-inclusive community. That community was not without its own social and economic diversity and stratification, however. In many cases, those who had been free prior to general emancipation—often usually because of nothing more than good fortune—gravitated toward the top of the newly emerging nonwhite community. Prior to emancipation, many of them had enjoyed the advantages of owning property, getting an education, participating in business, and having close relationships with white people. In a disproportionate number of cases, these people parlayed such advantages into positions in the upper echelon of their new community—however oppressed that community might be. Thus, during Reconstruction former free people of color became the nucleus of a nascent African-American middle class.

BIBLIOGRAPHY

Alexander, Adele Logan. *Ambiguous Lives: Free Women of Color in Rural Georgia, 1789-1879* (1991); Berlin, Ira. *Slaves without Masters: The Free Negro in the Antebellum South* (1972); Brown, Letitia Woods. *Free Negroes in the District of Columbia, 1790-1846* (1972); Curry, Leonard P. *The Free Black in Urban America, 1800-1850* (1981); Davis, Angela Y. *Women, Race, and Class* (1981); Desdunes, Rodolphe. *Our People and Our Heritage* (1971); Dominguez, Virginia R. *White by Definition: Social Stratification in Creole Louisiana* (1986); Everette, Donald E. "The Free Persons of Color in New Orleans, 1803-1865," Ph.D. diss. (1952); Fields, Barbara Jeanne. *Slavery and Freedom on the Middle Ground: Maryland during the Nineteenth Century* (1985); Flanders, Ralph B. "The Free Negro in Ante-Bellum Georgia," *North Carolina Historical Review* (July 1932); Foner, Laura. "The Free People of Color in Louisiana and St. Domingue: A Comparative Portrait of Two Three-Caste Slave Societies," *Journal of Social History* (1970); Frazier, E. Franklin. *The Negro Family in the United States* ([1939] 1951); Gatewood, Willard B. *Aristocrats of Color: The Black Elite, 1880-1920* (1990); Gould, Virginia Meacham. "In Full Enjoyment of Their Freedom: The Free Women of Color of New Orleans, Mobile, and Pensacola, 1769-1860," Ph.D. diss. (1991); Gutman, Herbert B. G. *The Black Family in Slavery and Freedom, 1750-1925* (1976); Harris, J. William. *Plain Folk and Gentry in a Slave Society: White Liberty and Black Slavery in Augusta's Hinterlands* (1985); Johnson, Michael P. and James L. Roark. *Black Masters: A Free Family of Color in the Old South* (1984), and "Strategies of Survival: Free Negro Families and the Problem of Slavery." In *In Joy and in Sorrow: Women, Family, and Marriage in the Victorian South, 1830-1900*, ed. Carol Bleser (1991); Jones, Jacqueline. *Labor of Love, Labor of Sorrow: Black Women, Work, and the Family from Slavery to the Present* (1985); Lebsock, Suzanne. *The Free Women of Petersburg: Status and Culture in a Southern Town, 1784-1860* (1984); Mills, Gary B. *The Forgotten People: Cane River's Creoles of Color* (1977), and "Miscegenation and the Free Negro in Antebellum Anglo-Alabama: A Reexamination of Southern Race Relations," *The Journal of American History* (June 1981); Nordmann, Christopher. "The Free Negroes in Mobile County, Alabama," Ph.D. diss. (1990); Rankin, David C. "The Forgotten People: Free People of Color in New Orleans, 1850-1870," Ph.D. diss. (1976); Schafer, Judith K. "Open and Notorious Concubinage: The Emancipation of Slave Mistresses by Will and the Supreme Court in Antebellum Louisiana," *Louisiana History* (September 1987); Schweninger, Loren. "Property-Owning Free African-American Women in the South, 1800-1870," *Journal of Women's History* (Winter 1991); Sterkx, H. E. *The Free Negro in Antebellum Louisiana* (1972); Sweat, Edward Forrest. "The Free Negro in Antebellum Georgia," Ph.D. diss. (1957); Wallenstein, Peter. *Slave South to New South* (1987); West-Stahl, Annie Lee. "Free Negroes in Antebellum Louisiana," *Louisiana Historical Quarterly* (1942); Whitten, David O. *A Black Sugar Planter in Antebellum Louisiana* (1981); Wikramanayake, Marina. *A World in Shadow: Free Negroes in South Carolina* (1973); Williamson, Joel. *New People: Miscegenation and Mulattoes in the United States* (1980);

Woods, Sister Frances Jerome. *Marginality and Identity: A Colored Creole Family through Ten Generations* (1951); Woodson, Carter G. *Free Negro Heads of Families in the United States, 1830, together with a Brief Treatment of the Free Negro* (1925).

ADELE LOGAN ALEXANDER
VIRGINIA GOULD

FREEDMEN'S EDUCATION

Black schoolmistresses who taught contrabands (escaped slaves) and freedmen during the Civil War rightly considered themselves pioneers. A freedwoman from Alexandria, Virginia, named Mary Chase established the first day school for contrabands on September 1, 1861. Later that month, American Missionary Association (AMA) representative, Lewis C. Lockwood, engaged Mary Peake, an educated free Black woman already instructing slaves around Hampton, Virginia, to begin classes behind federal lines near Fortress Monroe. Reverend Lockwood soon added other free and freed women, followed shortly by a small contingent of educated Black northerners. Farther south, Charlotte Forten represented the Pennsylvania Freedman's Relief Association at Port Royal, South Carolina, and the Union naval commander on St. Simon's Island, Georgia, asked Susie, a fourteen-year-old refugee secretly educated in Savannah, to teach the island's children. Over the next decade, Black educators increased from a mere handful to more than half the teachers reported by the Freedmen's Bureau. Many were women, ranging from barely literate ex-slaves to highly cultured graduates of northern colleges, from obscure monitors and assistants to veteran antislavery crusaders like Forten, Harriet Jacobs, and Ellen Craft. Often overshadowed by white teachers and the comparatively high percentage of Black male educators, women of color nevertheless figured prominently in freedmen's education throughout the history of the movement.

Born Mary Smith Kelsey at Norfolk, Mary Peake had attended a select school taught by a Black woman in Alexandria and, afterward, a school managed by whites. During her ten-year stay she obtained a good English education as well as training in needlework and dressmaking. Back in the Norfolk area Peake sewed for a living but also proselytized for the First Baptist Church, aided the poor and sick through her Daughters of Zion, and taught slaves around Hampton until the Confederates burned the town. In the contraband school, she impressed Lockwood with her blending of secular and religious instruction. "What an impression for good would be made upon the rising generation," he urged in a tract published soon after her premature death, "were this course universally pursued!" (Morris 1981). Mary Peake died of tuberculosis on February 22, 1862.

By 1864, the AMA employed at least five Black women from the North in the Norfolk area and gave partial support to several local people. Blanche Harris, Clara C. Duncan, and Sara G. Stanley came from Oberlin College, and Mary Watson was a graduate of the Rhode Island Normal School. Later, when William H. Woodbury attempted to enlist an all-Black staff in Norfolk, the white superintendent chose Harris and Duncan and added Sallie L. Daffin and Edmonia Highgate, who had left a higher-paying position as principal of a Black school in Binghamton, New York, to be a pioneer in raising freedmen "up to the stature of manhood and womanhood in 'Christ Jesus' " (AMAA 1864). All considered themselves particularly well qualified for missionary work among Black southerners. Sara Stanley, originally from New Bern, North Carolina, had pursued the literary course of studies at Oberlin College between 1852 and 1854 and taught in Cleveland. "I myself am a Colored woman," she informed the AMA, "bound to that ignorant, degraded, long enslaved race, by ties of love and consanguinity: they are socially and politically 'my people' " (AMAA 1864). However much whites might sympathize with the former slaves, Sallie Daffin insisted, "none can so fully experience the strength of their needs, nor understand the means necessary to relieve them as we who are identified with them" (AMAA 1864, 1865).

Illness and allegations that an all-Black school was necessary because the races could not work together prematurely ended Woodbury's plan. The teachers nevertheless continued their extensive relief and educational activities. Even after heart trouble forced Harris to take what she hoped was a temporary leave of absence, the principal planned to work for her "benighted and long-oppressed race" back home in Oberlin. Sallie Daffin replaced another teacher on leave. For a salary of $15 per month she taught day, evening, and Sunday schools; visited Black families; aided the sick and wounded; and assisted the teacher at a hospital across from the mission house.

Between 1861 and 1866, aid societies supported Black teachers in the District of Columbia, Virginia, Maryland, the Carolinas, Georgia, Kentucky, Louisiana, and Mississippi. On the South Carolina Sea Islands, Charlotte Forten quickly dispelled doubts among the plantation women and became one of Port

Royal's most respected teachers. The product of a well-known abolitionist family from Philadelphia, this sophisticated young mulatto had graduated from grammar and normal schools in Salem, Massachusetts, and taught in the North before the war. After receiving assurances that Edward L. Pierce, the lawyer in charge of the free-labor experiment, did not oppose the use of Black missionaries and teachers, Forten worked harmoniously with most white colleagues, although she was critical of superintendents who seemed strongly prejudiced against the freedmen. She, in direct contrast, appreciated the culture of the Black islanders. Forten's journal provides an intimate glimpse into her approach. Less than two months after President Abraham Lincoln issued the Preliminary Emancipation Proclamation, she wrote, "We ... commenced teaching the children 'John Brown,' which they entered into eagerly. I felt too the full significance of that song being sung here in S[outh] C[arolina] by little negro children, by those whom he—the glorious old man—died to save. Miss [Laura] T[owne] told them about him." Three days later: "Talked to the children about the noble Toussaint. They listened very attentively. It is well that they sh'ld know what one of their own color c'ld do for his race. I long to inspire them with courage and ambition (of a noble sort) and high purpose" (Forten 1961).

While still a student in Massachusetts, Forten shared the common abolitionist faith that knowledge would break down the barriers of prejudice and oppression. Freedmen's schools offered an opportunity to prove it. "There is," Sallie Daffin thought, "abundant evidence of an increasing desire on the part of our people to become educated; and I hesitate not to affirm that if we have the same advantages afforded us as the whites, we will convince those who deny the fact that we are inferior to none" (AMAA, Virginia, 1864, 1865).

White abolitionist Lydia Maria Child included selections from Forten and Harriet Jacobs in *The Freedmen's Book* (1865), compiled to encourage Black people by "honorable examples of men of their own color, and to convey moral instruction in a simple, attractive form." Along with selections by or about Toussaint L'Ouverture, Benjamin Banneker, Phillis Wheatley, James Forten, Peter Williams, William and Ellen Craft, Frederick Douglass, and Frances E. W. Harper, the author published extracts from Jacobs's *Incidents in the Life of a Slave Girl*, which Child had edited. An agent for Philadelphia and New York Quakers, Jacobs and her daughter had established a school in Alexandria under New England Freedmen's Aid Society teacher Virginia Lawton, a

young, well-educated Black woman and the granddaughter of a fashionable Boston caterer. Born in 1813 in Edenton, North Carolina, Harriet Jacobs had learned to read and sew from her first mistress. Fleeing to Boston in 1842, she enrolled her daughter, Louisa, at an abolitionist boarding school in Clinton, New York. "I ask nothing," Harriet Jacobs said of her autobiographical narrative to a Quaker friend. "I have placed myself before you to be judged as a woman whether I deserve your pity or contempt—I have another object in view—it is to come to you just as I am a poor Slave Mother." Child informed readers that the fugitive slave who had written *Incidents* under the pseudonym Linda Brent "is an esteemed friend of mine, and I introduce this portion of her story here to illustrate the power of character over circumstances. She has an intense sympathy for those who are still suffering in the bondage from which she escaped. She has devoted all her energies to the poor refugees in our camps, comforting the afflicted, nursing the sick and teaching the children" (Child 1865).

In addition to the primarily white associations, Black leaders organized their own schools. As early as the Colored National Convention of 1853, William J. Wilson, William Whipper, and Charles B. Ray had argued that "the force of circumstances compels the regulation of schools by us to supply a deficiency produced by our conditions; that it should be our special aim to so direct instructors, regulate books and libraries; in fine, the whole process to meet entirely our particular exigencies" (Morris 1981). Extending this philosophy into the 1860s, Wilson, formerly principal of Brooklyn's Black Public School No. 1, employed his wife and daughter at an AMA school in Washington and later insisted on hiring only Black persons. On a larger scale, the African Civilization Society maintained all-Black systems. Both cooperated with the AMA but commissioned only Black teachers "to prove the complete fitness of the educated negro ... to teach and lead his own race." In Georgia the top bureau school official supported two successive self-help organizations—the Savannah Educational Association and Capt. J. E. Bryant's politically oriented Georgia Educational Association.

In the year and a half immediately after the war, the number of Black teachers increased substantially. Freedmen in North Carolina had started a number of private institutions, and AMA agent Samuel S. Ashley proposed to staff self-supporting plantation schools with local residents. In South Carolina, statistics through the end of 1865 showed twenty-four of seventy-six regularly reporting teachers, and most of those on the plantations were persons of color. At

Charleston, where free Black people had established their own schools during the antebellum period, the AMA, the New England Freedmen's Aid Society, and Old School Presbyterians all employed Black teachers. The headmaster of the AMA's Saxton School was Francis L. Cardozo, a native of the port city who had studied at the University of Glasgow, the United Presbyterian Church's seminary in Edinburgh, and the London School of Theology. On his sectionally and racially mixed staff, he employed several local teachers from leading free Black families. The New England society supported thirty northern teachers along with seventy assistants, forty-five southern white teachers, and twenty-five local Black educators, reasoning that native educators would encourage sectional cooperation. The Presbyterian Zion school under Reverend M. Van Horne from New Jersey maintained an entirely Black teaching force of thirteen. "Although the Southern people seem generally opposed to the education of the negroes," a *Harper's Weekly* (December 15, 1866) artist noted after visiting the school, "if they must have it, they prefer to see colored people in charge of their own race to having Northern whites as teachers."

Under the same assistant commissioner as South Carolina, Georgia schools listed forty-three Black teachers of a total of sixty-nine. Savannah's Black community, according to John W. Alvord's first bureau inspection report, undertook teaching and expenses themselves, "receiving from white friends only advice and encouragement." In New Orleans, Alvord visited a self-supporting school for the "common class of families" taught by educated Black men. The inspector believed it would bear comparison to any ordinary school in the North: "Not only good reading and spelling were heard, but lessons at the black-board in arithmetic, recitations in geography and English grammar. Very creditable specimens of writing were shown, and all the older classes could read or recite as fluently in French as in English." The city's free Black elite also maintained six select pay schools where a "better class" attended. Six months later, after Gen. Nathaniel Banks's school was suspended, "large numbers of private schools were started, most of them of inferior grade, and usually taught by colored persons." In Kentucky and Tennessee, Black educators maintained numerous private schools at Louisville, Nashville, Memphis, and Knoxville. While Florida had far fewer schools of any kind, in Tallahassee, Alvord found five taught by Black preachers and one run by an educated mulatto woman committed to making ladies of her students. The future bureau educational superintendent estimated there were at least 500 such native schools in various stages of advancement throughout the South: "Some young man, some woman, or old preacher in cellar, or shed, or corner of a negro meeting-house, with the alphabet in hand, or a torn spelling-book, is their teacher" (Freedmen's Bureau [1868, 1870] 1980).

The most advanced freedmen's schools employing Black teachers were in New Orleans and Charleston, both known for their educated free Black communities. Through the efforts of the Brown Fellowship Society, the Minors Moralist Society, and leaders like Thomas S. Bonneau and Daniel Alexander Payne, Charleston residents had maintained schools of their own since the early nineteenth century. Despite antiliteracy laws, some continued through the war. Mary Weston, for example, having been educated by her father, the prosperous mulatto Jacob Weston, just before the war began a class of forty or fifty free Black girls in her home. Under an antiliteracy law, she was arrested twice but allowed to continue classes for free Black women on condition that no slaves be admitted and that a white person should always be present during school hours. As first assistant in Saxton's normal school, Weston continued teaching many of her old pupils.

The *Charleston Daily News* described Saxton as "the *recherché* seminary to which all the aristocracy send their children." A quarter of the students had been free before the war, and in staffing the facility Thomas and Francis Cardozo drew their native teachers primarily from this "aristocracy of color." Both brothers had attended local private schools before leaving South Carolina to complete their education. Thomas studied in New York and was teaching in Flushing before becoming superintendent of the AMA mission. Although critical of inexperienced native teachers, he was able to fill his positions with northerners of both races and a few free Black teachers. Most of the southern appointees were from prominent families in the area. Mary Weston was twenty-six and a member of the Episcopal Church. In private moments she wrote poetry. Her cousin William Weston at thirty-one was a pious, strictly temperate man, a diligent student who aspired to the ministry. Formerly a bookkeeper for S. & P. Weston Tailors on Queen Street, he had been educated in the common branches and such advanced subjects as logic, rhetoric, algebra, geometry, surveying, astronomy, Greek, and Latin. Frances Rollin, one of five socially prominent sisters from Columbia, had attended Philadelphia's Institute for Colored Youth. She was active in women's rights, wrote a biography of Martin Delany, and later married Black legislator William J.

Whipper. Margaret Sasportas came from a family headed by a mulatto butcher who in 1860 owned $6,700 in real estate and five slaves. Amelia Shrewsbury was the sister of Henry L. Shrewsbury, a bureau instructor who represented Chesterfield County in the state constitutional convention of 1868 and sat in the state legislature.

When Thomas Cardozo resigned over charges that he had seduced a young female student in Flushing while still married, his brother Francis would have preferred all, or nearly all, northern teachers, thinking it better "that no colored persons should engage in this work ... than to have such as would only disgrace the cause, and retard the progress of their own people" (Morris 1981). Limited by financial constraints, however, the new principal selected one southern white woman; reappointed Frances Rollin, Mary Weston, Amelia Shrewsbury, and William Weston; and added other local teachers in less responsible positions, where they could learn from their white fellow laborers. Denying rumors that he wanted no more Black teachers from the North, Francis Cardozo also hired his sister and brother-in-law—Mr. and Mrs. C. C. McKinney—and Amanda Wall, the sister of John Mercer Langston and wife of O.S.B. Wall, a prosperous Oberlin merchant then on Rufus Saxton's bureau staff. C. C. McKinney had worked in schools in both Charleston and Cleveland, and just before returning to South Carolina the couple was teaching in Thomas Cardozo's old school in Flushing. By the fall of 1886, Saxton was divided about evenly between northern and local teachers. Francis Cardozo at this early date was already developing a normal school for free Black students eager to become teachers and proposed establishing a college in two or three years.

Cardozo's system did have its critics among the northern white staff. Sarah W. Stansbury, the primary principal, clashed with native Black instructors over their teaching methods and criticized the school's focus on "freeman's children, many of whom *owned slaves* before the war." When Cardozo forced her out, she transferred to a school where the students were all ex-slaves, telling the AMA, "This is more like missionary work than any I have done since coming here" (AMAA, South Carolina, 1866). Jane A. Van Allen had the same objection. "I wish to do all I can for the *suffering* of any class," she assured the field secretary, "but I am not willing to labor or beg for the 'free browns,' in a manner that will help to make the difference between them & the freed people, even greater than it was in slavery" (AMAA, South Carolina, 1867). Claiming Van Allen was incompetent

physically and intellectually, by temper and disposition, Cardozo removed her.

At Zion, according to *Harper's Weekly* illustrator A. R. Waud, the Black staff had to accommodate "a harder set among its pupils, in some cases the refuse of other schools." This delayed Zion's progress for some time, Waud told readers, but the school was exhibiting steady improvement. "The children were apparently very obedient and attentive to their teachers, and out of eight hundred and fifty scholars enrolled had an average daily attendance of seven hundred and twenty" (*Harper's Weekly*, December 15, 1866). Shaw Memorial School, managed by the New England Freedmen's Aid Society, reported that 90 percent of its students, and 80 percent of those in advanced classes, were former slaves. Bureau state superintendent Reuben Tomlinson found it interesting "that among the most distinguished scholars in these classes, those who were formerly slaves rank equally with those who were free and had received some instruction before and during the war" (Drago 1990).

While not as prolific as Charleston or New Orleans, Savannah produced its share of native teachers. Susie King learned to read and write in a secret school taught by Mary Woodhouse, a free widow, assisted by her teenaged daughter. At the school for over two years, King completed her studies with a series of white tutors, learning enough to teach fellow contrabands on St. Simon's Island and Black troops in her husband's regiment. Between 1865 and the fall of 1868, King helped support her family by conducting pay schools in Savannah and Liberty County until competition from the AMA's Beach Institute forced the ex-slave back into domestic work. Among other private teachers in the city, Lucinda Jackson held classes near King's home on South Broad Street, and Catharine Deveaux had been teaching since 1834. Eluding detection for over a quarter-century, the elderly Deveaux, according to John W. Alvord, was "instrumental, under God, of aiding in the education of many colored persons, who scattered here and there through the south, are now able to contribute somewhat towards the general elevation of the newly-emancipated race" (Freedmen's Bureau 1980).

American Missionary Association superintendent William T. Richardson was surprised to find so much intelligence among Savannah's freedmen. In January 1865, he reported that several showed a competence for teaching and were in the employ of the AMA. About the same time the Savannah Educational Association (SEA) opened its first schools under teachers selected by Alvord, Reverend Mansfield French, and Methodist Episcopal missionary James D. Lynch.

Over the next six months, attendance increased to 700, and the board started schools on plantations as far upriver as Augusta. Although the SEA's Black leadership impressed some as "men of real ability and intelligence," they failed to gain essential support from AMA officials who doubted the board's ability to manage freedmen's schools on its own. By March 1866, all SEA teachers had left the organization and were seeking employment elsewhere.

Such strict insistence on conventional qualifications prompted charges that both leading aid organizations opposed using Black teachers. Black southerners exerted pressure on the AMA institutions from primary schools to universities, whereas criticism of the American Freedmen's Union Commission came mainly from antislavery veterans opposed to the whole freedmen's aid concept. Indeed, frustrated in attempts to recruit through the society at Hartford, Connecticut, or the Institute for Colored Youth, so respected an abolitionist as J. Miller McKim found himself answering criticism from the editor of the *National Anti-Slavery Standard* that the commission refused to employ competent Black teachers in its schools.

Most officials agreed that even literate freedmen lacked the experience and management ability needed in first-class schools. With qualified teachers of either race in short supply, however, societies sometimes employed poorly trained applicants as temporary expedients or assigned them to small towns and plantations where the prejudice against Black teachers would be less than against northern teachers. For a New England Freedmen's Aid Society educator at Charlottesville, appointing freedwoman Isabella Gibbons was an experiment in how a newly freed slave would adapt to her new vocation. Although Black southerners were frequently criticized for their teaching methods and discipline, Gibbons equaled Anna Gardner's sanguine expectations, especially in organizing the school and governing it without resorting to severe punishment. Gibbons and other former slaves commonly continued their own education while teaching. Mary Chadwick, who knew she needed to learn more than her letters and how to read a little, served as a student monitor at the AMA's Washburn Seminary in Beaufort, South Carolina, before becoming a primary teacher. Usually aware of their deficiencies, inexperienced Black teachers still considered themselves qualified to educate freedmen. "I know that my education is poor," northerner Mary Still conceded in defending her Sea Islands school. "This circumstance I regret. But it is ample (having age and experience) to teach in the first stages of civilization."

A visitor to the school agreed, informing AMA superintendent Samuel Hunt, "She is not the thorough teacher some are and lacks very much in government, yet I am confident her scholars are making fair progress" (AMAA, South Carolina, 1866).

Northern schoolmistresses coming south faced racial discrimination and threats of violence. En route down the Mississippi to Vicksburg, two young Black women, after the first meal, were excluded from the cabin and turned out of their staterooms. Francis Cardozo protested bitterly in 1866 that Black instructors traveling on Arthur Leary's steamers between New York and Charleston were not only charged more than their white colleagues but were required to ride in steerage. Cardozo's sister, accompanied by another woman teacher, refused to accept these conditions and booked passage with another company. The same year, the *Freedmen's Record* reported that Louisa and Harriet Jacobs, then working in Georgia, were thrown off a boat bound for New York when first-class passengers discovered Louisa had "colored blood in her veins." The editors hoped this instance of southern arrogance against their esteemed friends would be followed up and the right of citizens on public conveyances secured. Threats and violence were too frequent to be ignored. At Vermillionville, Louisiana, 200 miles from the nearest military protection, whites threatened to burn Edmonia Highgate's school and residence and twice fired shots into her room.

Although white and Black teachers usually worked well together, some of the Black women claimed they were not treated as equals. In December 1865, Mary Weston objected that a National Freedman's Relief Association teacher was getting $50 a month compared with $25 for her and Frances Rollin. Cardozo recommended that the AMA raise their salaries to $35, but he spoke too late to prevent Rollin's resignation in favor of a better-paying position. From Natchez, Blanche Harris charged the AMA failed to provide Black instructors with space for their classes. More disturbing, Harris claimed Reverend Sela G. Wright as an economy measure wanted her to move into the mission house, where she would room with two of the domestics and take her meals apart from the white missionaries. Having already informed the teachers that he and Palmer Litts could not associate with them as they did in Oberlin, Wright warned of threats to mob the home if northern educators practiced social equality. Harris, however, encouraged by the Black citizens she consulted, rejected the offer, setting off a dispute that seriously weakened the association's influence and destroyed Wright's usefulness in Natchez. A student at Oberlin from 1835 to 1837, Wright, according to John Bardwell, was heavily influenced by popular sentiment to do things that prejudiced Black teachers against him, and they in turn did things that annoyed him. Bardwell, who had known Wright for two decades, reported that Harris and Pauline Freeman "have not worked in with the other teachers as kindly as they might & and ought to have done, tho' I think they were in the first instance sin[n]ed against" (AMAA, Mississippi, 1867). The next school year, Harris accepted a commission from the Friends Freedmen's Association to teach in Hillsboro, North Carolina.

A similar incident occurred in Wilmington when AMA educator Samuel Ashley contended that mixed households would encourage southern charges of complete social equality and create an intolerable situation for white missionaries. After a tense year in which Sallie Daffin lived in the mission home, Ashley agreed to rehire the veteran teacher only if she would board with a Black family, insisting he had too much regard for her to make her miserable. Daffin declined the commission.

Many white educators at the other end of the spectrum objected to accommodating in race relations. Martha Kellogg, who did not wish to be identified in Ashley's policy of "non-association with the colored people on the same social terms," asked to be transferred out of his district. About the same time, Julia Shearman warned the AMA from Augusta, Georgia, that discrimination was creating a gulf between missionaries and freedmen. Unless teachers established closer social relations, Black southerners would soon distrust everything white: "When they learn that white Republicans have cared for them only to gain their votes & deny them the suffrage where those votes are not an indispensable necessity—when they perceive that their white leaders in the South have an unconquerable aversion to color & that even white missionaries cannot brook to eat with them—then we shall lose influence" (AMAA, Georgia, 1867).

Occasional instances of racial intermarriage within the educational program tested the limits of this egalitarianism. When George Putnam refused to allow Sara Stanley to marry a white man in the teachers' home at Mobile, Stanley was surprised and indignant. The disappointed instructor denied that a quiet and unostentatious marriage would cause talk or injure anyone. Her appeal to AMA secretary J. R. Shipherd countered "the injury Mr. P. purposes doing me would be far greater than any injury caused to others by a contrary course. Something is due me in the matter as

a woman simply" (AMAA, Alabama, 1868). In a follow-up letter, Stanley informed Shipherd that field secretary Edward P. Smith had offered to perform the ceremony himself if necessary. Rather than confront the sensitive issue, however, Shipherd invoked a rule that no teacher could be married until her resignation was accepted.

Educators of both races were equally critical of caste distinctions. While principal of the Frederick Douglass School in New Orleans, Edmonia Highgate blamed the elite class, mostly creoles, who did not in the least identify with the freedmen or their interests. "Nor need we wonder," she added pointedly in a letter to the AMA, "when we remember that many of them were formerly slaveholders. You know the peculiar institution cared little for the Ethnology of its supporters" (AMAA, Louisiana, 1866). At the Freedmen's Village in Arlington, Virginia, Sarah C. Greenbrier quickly earned a reputation for identifying with whites. Unable to find an acceptable place to live in the village, she explained: "Although I am willing to do any thing in my power for the good of these people and although I have one eight[h] of African blood cursing through my veins I am none the more willing to go into all kinds of places to board where there are no conveniences than the purest Anglo Saxon that ever lived." Such statements make it clear why the superintendent claimed, "Miss Greenbrier is *white*—at least so in her *feelings* and *prejudices*" (AMAA, Virginia, 1867).

Toward the end of 1866, the accelerated pace of social and political change led the Freedmen's Bureau and aid societies to step up efforts for training Black teachers as part of an expanded emphasis on adult and female education. More than most northern or southern observers, bureau general superintendent John W. Alvord understood the importance of the Black family even in slavery. In his third semiannual report, the superintendent proposed a wider, more general educational program: instruction in civil affairs; the improvement of home life and the family condition; encouragement of industry, thrift, and the accumulation of property; and the establishment of families in homesteads. The following year Alvord called for girls' departments in the higher schools and female seminaries. In a statement reminiscent of Harriet Jacobs's contention that slavery was far more terrible for women, the superintendent admonished:

> Both sexes were bereft of all true culture—cultured rather in whatever could corrupt and demoralize—but womanly virtues were wholly ignored; the female as a slave was crushed

literally. She was driven from domestic life to the fields, to bear burdens fit only for the beast. She was bereft of social position, and abandoned to become the subject and victim of grossest passion. Every surrounding influence forced her back to the stupor and brutality of the savage state. There was no binding matrimony, no family sacredness, nothing which could be called *home* in slavery; and the wonder is, that after two hundred years of such influence, any trace of feminine delicacy remains, or that girls, the offspring and imitators of such mothers, are aught but degraded (Freedmen's Bureau 1980).

Over the next three years, Commissioner O. O. Howard allotted $407,752 to twenty advanced institutions, and by 1871 there were eleven colleges and universities and sixty-one normal schools for Black students. According to bureau statistics, the percentage of Black teachers increased from 33 percent in 1867 to 53 percent in 1869. Proportions varied from state to state. In Kentucky, where freed people preferred Black teachers, percentages stayed around 80 percent. North Carolina, Louisiana, and Florida normally reported figures above half, whereas South Carolina, Alabama, and Georgia rarely rose above 35 percent. Other states fell somewhere in between. The underlying figures included many student assistants and poorly educated private instructors, but the trend was unmistakable.

Educators continued to recruit heavily from northern institutions; Oberlin College and the Institute for Colored Youth especially received more requests than they could handle. The Friends Freedmen's Association kept up an extended correspondence with Oberlin when filling positions at Hillsboro, North Carolina, and answering General Samuel Chapman Armstrong's request for Black teachers on the Peninsula. For Hillsboro the association selected Sarah Jane Woodson, a product of Oberlin's literary course, who taught until forced by her mother's illness to return to Ohio. Encountering difficulties finding competent Black teachers, officials in Philadelphia turned to the antislavery college for volunteers. After some confusion over white candidates assumed to be Black, the teachers' committee diverted Blanche Harris from Virginia to Hillsboro and appointed as associate teacher Robert G. Fitzgerald, a native of New Castle County, Delaware, who had been educated at a Quaker school in Wilmington, the Institute for Colored Youth, Ashmun Institute, and Lincoln University. The Presbyterian church's Committee on Freedmen, in its attempt to cultivate Black ministers

and teachers, encouraged Lincoln students to spend their summer vacations working in the South. Many, including Francis and Archibald Grimké and William F. Brooks, answered the call. By the middle of 1868, Black students represented 55 percent of the committee's missionary teachers. Late in the bureau program, the committee also added several experienced women teachers, assigning Blanche Harris and Sallie Daffin to Knoxville and supporting Amelia Shrewsbury in Charleston.

The AMA, gradually coming to the conclusion that Black missionaries and teachers could accomplish more among their race than northerners, between 1867 and 1870 expanded its proportion from 6 percent to 20 percent. The bulk of the AMA's increase was made up of southerners. Reflecting a growing emphasis on teacher training, the ratio of southern to northern Black educators rose from just over one-half to two-thirds. More than a third of these were products of the association's normal schools and classes. Its Black counterpart, the African Civilization Society, by 1868 had expanded beyond the District of Columbia, Virginia, and Maryland into the Carolinas, Georgia, Mississippi, and Louisiana.

Freedmen's textbooks published by both factions of the American Tract Society provided a detailed plan for undoing the adverse effects of slavery and recasting southern Black society in the northern mold. Often underestimating the extent of the damage, authors advised young and adult pupils on character, sexual morality, marriage, the family, education, the home, and work. Isaac W. Brinckerhoff tied many of these elements together in a passage from his *Advice to Freedmen*:

> All the members of your family have heretofore been accustomed to work in the field, or at some other labor. The father, mother, and children together have toiled the livelong day. At present this cannot perhaps be changed. It is to be hoped, however, that the time will come when the wife and mother will be able to devote her whole time and attention to family and household duties, to the care of the house, keeping it tidy and clean, and to the training of her children for usefulness and happiness. In this case the support of the family will rest on the husband and father.

The African Civilization Society adapted the approach to its own agenda. Freedmen needed precepts illustrated in "living epistles," advised Amos G. Beman, who was affiliated with both the society and the AMA. Pupils in the society's schools, according to Rufus Perry, "are pursuing such studies as are generally pursued in common schools, with such variations as seem best to accelerate the scholar's fitness for practical life." More specifically, students were taught "to have a very clear idea of the personal responsibilities attending their new relation to society, and fully to understand the state of FREEDOM is the state of SELF-RELIANCE" (Morris 1981).

Black teachers added a new dimension to the bureau program, reinforcing the broader emphasis on good citizenship, morality, education, industry, and advancement as keys to equal rights while providing their own perspective on race and Reconstruction. In the process they became symbols of the potential for improvement and self-help. With the bureau and aid societies cutting back on primary education in the last year of the government program, Black teachers for the first time outnumbered white colleagues 1,321 to 1,251. Students from Howard, Fisk, Claflin, Atlanta, Central Tennessee College, Richmond Normal and High School, Cardozo's Avery Institute, and Emerson Institute in Mobile supplied an increasing number of teachers for freedmen's schools. At Hampton Normal and Agricultural Institute, Samuel Chapman Armstrong applied an industrial model to counteract the pupils' poverty, "depraved tastes and habits," and "their servile want of respect." These institutions and their products, Alvord correctly concluded, were the most promising results of freedmen's education: "Many hundreds of teachers and leading minds have already been sent forth . . . to commence a life work, and make their mark upon the coming generation. These hundreds will be followed by thousands" (Freedmen's Bureau 1980).

BIBLIOGRAPHY

American Missionary Association Archives (AMAA), Amistad Research Center, Tulane University, New Orleans, Louisiana; Child, Lydia Maria, ed. *Freedmen's Book* [1865]. Reprinted in Morris (1980); De Boer, Clara Merritt. "The Role of Afro-Americans in the Origin and Work of the American Missionary Association, 1839-1877," Ph.D. diss. (1973); Drago, Edmund L. *Initiative, Paternalism, and Race Relations: Charleston's Avery Normal Institute* (1990); Forten, Charlotte L. *The Journal of Charlotte L. Forten: A Free Negro in the Slave Era*, ed. Ray Allen Billington (1961); *Freedmen's Schools and Textbooks*, 12 vols. ([1864-70] 1980); Jacobs, Harriet A. [Linda Brent]. *Incidents in the Life of a Slave Girl, Written by Herself* (1861), ed. Jean Fagan Yellin (1987); Litwack, Leon F. *Been in the Storm So Long: The Aftermath of Slavery* (1979); Morris, Robert C. *Freedmen's Schools and Textbooks*, 12 vols. ([1864-70] 1980), and *Reading, 'Riting and Reconstruction: The Education of Freedmen in the South, 1861-1870* (1981); U.S. Bureau of Refugees, Freedmen, and Abandoned Lands (Freedmen's Bureau). Semi-annual reports on schools for freedmen, 1866-70 [1868, 1870]. Reprinted in Morris (1980).

ROBERT C. MORRIS

[Editors' note: The editors believe that the word *freedpeople* should be used to refer to newly freed slaves, rather than the traditional word *freedmen*.]

FREEMAN, ELIZABETH "MUM BETT" (c. 1744-1829)

"I heard that paper read yesterday, that says, 'all men are born equal, and that every man has a right to freedom.' I am not a dumb critter; won't the law give me my freedom?" So in 1781 Elizabeth Freeman, an enslaved Black woman also known as Mum Bett or Mumbet, with the assistance of counsel, entered a Massachusetts court to demand her freedom.

Despite her enslavement, Elizabeth Freeman, an illiterate Black woman, was able to secure legal counsel and provide him with a legal theory for her case. Freeman, through her counsel, filed a writ of replevin alleging that Colonel Ashley and his son were illegally detaining her and a Black male co-petitioner named Brom. The writ declared that the enslavement of Freeman and Brom violated a provision of the newly enacted 1780 state constitution which declared that all men are born free and equal. The state court granted their freedom.

Historians overlook or marginalize Freeman's contribution, citing instead the cases of two Black men, Quok Walker and Nathaniel Jennison, initiated and decided after Freeman's. However, Elizabeth Freeman's contribution is significant because, unlike other freedom suits based on individual circumstances or technicalities and designed to secure freedom only for the petitioner, the legal theory set forth in her suit had the potential to free not just the petitioners, but all enslaved Blacks in Massachusetts. Clearly this was Elizabeth Freeman's intent since she later told people that she was moved to sue after taking a blow from her physically abusive mistress that was intended for her sister. Thus, Freeman was suing for her freedom and her sister's as well.

Freeman's suit was the first freedom suit to use a state constitution as the basis to challenge chattel slavery. In addition, her suit resulted in the first court decision construing a state constitutional provision as inconsistent with the institution of slavery. Unfortunately, neither Freeman's suit nor Quok Walker's resulted in the complete emancipation of enslaved Blacks in the state.

BIBLIOGRAPHY

"Brom and Bett versus Ashley." Court Files, Suffolk 1192, no. 159966 (May 1779-October 1, 1783); "Brom and Bett versus Ashley." Supreme Judicial Court, 1781-1782, Massachusetts; Kaplan, Sidney. *The Black Presence in the Era of the American Revolution, 1770-1800* (1973); Litwack, Leon F. *North of Slavery* (1961); Moore, George H. *Notes on the History of Slavery in Massachusetts* ([1866] 1968); Rosenthal, James M. "Free Soil in Berkshire County," *New England Quarterly* (1937); Sedgwick, Catherine. "Slavery in New England," *Bentley's Miscellany* (1853); Williams, George W. *History of the Negro Race in America, 1619-1900* ([1883] 1968); Zilversmit, Arthur. "Quok Walker, Mumbet, and the Abolition of Slavery in Massachusetts," *William and Mary Quarterly* (1968).

TAUNYA LOVELL BANKS

FULLER, META VAUX WARRICK
(1877-1968)

Meta Vaux Warrick Fuller was one of America's first studio sculptors of African-American ancestry. Called "elegantly Victorian" and "deeply spiritual," Fuller was, according to contemporary W.E.B. Du Bois, one of those persons of ability and genius whom "accidents of education and opportunity had raised on a tidal wave of chance" (*Crisis* 1926).

Meta Vaux Warrick was born in Philadelphia on June 9, 1877, the daughter of William H. Warrick, Jr., a master barber, and Emma (Jones) Warrick, a wigmaker and hairdresser. Ten years younger than her brother William and sister Blanche, Meta was one of three surviving children of the Warricks. A sister, Virginia, died before Meta was born.

As a child, Warrick had been intrigued with the activities of her sister, Blanche, an art student. Outings with her father to the Philadelphia Academy of Fine Arts sharpened this interest.

In primary school, her own facility in art emerged. In high school she was one of those selected to attend J. Liberty Tadd's art school once a week for special training. Little is known of Warrick's record at Tadd's; however, a small woodcarving of hers was among the school's exhibits at the World's Columbian Exposition in Chicago in 1893.

After graduating from high school, Warrick applied for and received a three-year scholarship to the Pennsylvania Museum School for the Industrial Arts, where she studied from 1894 to 1897. One of the conditions of that scholarship was to produce a work of art for the school. Thus, in 1897, she executed *Procession of the Arts and Crafts*, a bas-relief composed of thirty-seven medieval figures. The relief won a prize as one of the year's best works.

In 1897, the Pennsylvania Museum School granted her a postgraduate scholarship to continue her studies in sculpture. Sculpture proved to be her strength and her vivid imagination her gift. Like many artists, theater, music, and mythology inspired her, but the subjects she chose to interpret tended to be sensational: *Medusa*, with "hanging jaw, beads of gore, and eyes staring from their sockets" (O'Donnell 1907); *Gestar*, portrayed in the dead of winter in order to show that romanticism could not exist in a cold and sterile environment, just as intellect proved insubstantial without spiritual content; and *Siegfried Slaying the Dragon* and the *Three Daughters of the Rhine*, inspired by Wagner's *Ring of the Nibelungs*. The latter diploma piece won a prize for modeling at her graduation exhibit in 1898. However, it was *Crucifixion of Christ in Anguish* that evoked the most comment. Some observers objected to so tormented a Christ. Warrick's reply combined the intellectual with the spiritual: "If the Savior did not suffer, wherein lay the sacrifice?" (Porter 1969). Generally, those evaluating her work viewed it positively; though perhaps too much toward the sensational in art, its handling was "masculine." Her boldness convinced many that she should continue her studies in Paris.

In September 1899, Warrick sailed for Europe. She arrived in England and spent a month with a friend of her mother, Harriet Loudin, whose husband, Frederick, was director of the touring Fisk Jubilee Singers. She then went to Paris, where a friend of her uncle, painter Henry Ossawa Tanner, had agreed to act as her guardian.

When she arrived at the Paris railway station on October 26, Tanner was not there to meet her. Consequently, she went alone to the American Girls Club, a hostel for young women studying in Paris. Warrick was horrified to discover that she could not stay there because of her race. However, with the help of Henry Tanner and the club's director she found a room in a small hotel. The club's director also introduced Warrick to American sculptor Augustus Saint-Gaudens. During one of her many visits to his studio, he recommended that she not begin sculpting immediately but take drawing instead. He also suggested teachers, aiding Warrick's search, made more difficult by inadequate finances. Therefore, for the first year she studied drawing, visited museums, and attended lectures at the Académie des Beaux-Arts; but by the summer of 1900, she was sculpting from live models.

The Paris Universal Exposition was held in 1900 and attracted a number of Black Americans, some who had come specifically to participate in the exposition. Among those with whom Warrick toured the fair were exposition commissioner Thomas J. Calloway; agent Andrew F. Hilyer, an employee of the U.S. Department of the Interior and his wife, Mamie, an accomplished pianist; Alonzo Herndon; Adrian McNeal Herndon, who taught at Atlanta University and was recognized as a talented actress; and Professor W.E.B. Du Bois of Atlanta University. Before leaving Paris, Du Bois suggested that Warrick specialize in African-American subjects. For her part, Warrick was unwilling to limit herself in this way. In the fall, she enrolled at the Académie Colarossi, where she continued to be guided by French sculptors.

In the summer of 1901, a fellow student at Colarossi arranged a meeting with Auguste Rodin at his home in Meudon. Warrick carried an example of her sculpture, *The Man Eating His Heart*, hoping that the quality of this work would convince the artist to accept her as his student. Rodin examined the statuette and was impressed: "Mademoiselle, you are a sculptor, you have the sense of form" (O'Donnell 1907). Even so, Rodin had too many students and could not add another, but he promised to come to Paris often and criticize her sculpture.

Warrick's creations become more daring in theme and execution. One of her aims had always been to explore the psychology of human emotions, a belief in the function of art that she shared with Rodin. Under his tutelage, she learned to execute such ideas with greater force. She refused to limit herself to subjects that were merely aesthetically pleasing, never avoiding portrayals because they were ugly or abhorrent.

Actually, Warrick used such imagery to make a philosophical point. The importance of duty was the theme of *Man Carrying a Dead Comrade*. The plight of the wise man who, despite his wisdom, is unable to alleviate human suffering is symbolized by *The Wretched*. The artist celebrated the 1902 Victor Hugo Centennial with a portrayal of Hugo's *Laughing Man*. The protagonist's face had been altered to resemble a grotesque mask. His mouth opened to his ears. His ears folded over his eyes. His shapeless nose heightened the effect of it all. No one could look upon this face without laughter and derision. Warrick's intention, however, was not to shock the public. She lived in an era when African-Americans were portrayed as slow, lazy dullards with saucer eyes, thick lips, and wide grins: "Sambo" was the national jester. Although Warrick did not wish to specialize in African-American types, being Black undoubtedly affected her world view. Like contemporary Paul Laurence Dunbar, she protested such stereotypes, but she did so indirectly by commenting on the Black experience within the context of generally accepted visual images—in this instance, cloaked in the allegory of Hugo's *Laughing Man*.

During her last year in Paris, Warrick began holding private exhibitions and, under Rodin's sponsorship, began receiving attention. The "delicate sculptor of horrors," as the press called her, was the only American artist asked to join several French artists in a Paris exhibit (O'Donnell 1907). There she displayed her *Head of John the Baptist* and *The Impenitent Thief on the Cross*. Patron of such innovators as Aubrey Beardsley, Mary Cassatt, and Henri de Toulouse-Lautrec, S. Bing sponsored a one-woman show for her at his gallery, L'Art Nouveau.

In October 1902, Warrick returned to the United States and to her native city, Philadelphia. She set up a studio and continued to work but soon discovered that local art dealers were not interested in her sculpture. They claimed that they did not buy domestic pieces, but they ignored the Paris pieces as well. Warrick was convinced that the real issue was her color. She found a more appreciative public in Black Philadelphia. The more she became reinvolved in Black social and intellectual life, the more African-American themes shared a place with European thematic influences in her sculpture. *Two-Step* and *The Comedian* (song-and-dance-man George Walker) are examples of this transitional period. Warrick held exhibits in her studio. She also accepted invitations from community organizations and, periodically, from local art schools to contribute to their art shows.

The greater part of Warrick's patronage was local, but in 1907, upon the recommendation of Thomas Calloway, she received a commission to produce a set of tableaux for the Negro pavilion at the Jamestown Tercentennial Exposition. Her dioramas were composed of 150 figures representing Black progress since the arrival of the first Africans at Jamestown in 1619. For this effort, she won a gold medal. Furthermore, she gained prominence as the first Black woman artist to receive a federal commission.

At the turn of the century, many women did not believe it was possible to combine career and marriage. Meta Warrick was not one of these women. On February 3, 1909, she married Dr. Solomon C. Fuller. Born in Liberia, Fuller was a director of the pathology lab at Westborough State Hospital and a neurologist at Massachusetts State Hospital. The Fullers moved to 31 Warren Road, Framingham, Massachusetts, into a home Dr. Fuller had built. Meta, as her contribution, provided a frieze for the fireplace, *The Four Seasons.*

Before moving to Framingham, Meta Warrick Fuller had left her tools and sculpture in a Philadelphia warehouse, with the intention of having them shipped to her later. In 1910, a fire in that warehouse destroyed sixteen years of work done in Philadelphia and Paris. Fuller was devastated and lost the urge to continue sculpting. Instead, she concentrated on her role as wife and mother. Between 1910 and 1916, she gave birth to three children—Solomon, Jr., William Thomas, and Perry.

In 1913, W.E.B Du Bois, then editor of the *Crisis,* asked Fuller to reproduce *Man Eating His Heart* for the New York celebration of the Emancipation Proclamation's fiftieth anniversary. Inasmuch as this was one of the pieces lost in the fire, Fuller thought that recreating it would be too painful. Instead, she provided *Spirit of Emancipation,* a three-figured group standing eight feet in height. Fuller's emancipation piece was unlike any other of its genre. There were no discarded whips or chains, no grateful freedmen kneeling before a paternalistic Lincoln. Fuller had also not chosen to favor the female figure with Caucasian features, indicating her heightened race consciousness.

For Meta Fuller, taking up the chisel to create *Spirit of Emancipation* was the beginning of fifty prolific years of work. She turned from the grotesque of her youth and became more interested in realism and African-American themes. The change was in style rather than in substance: she did not abdicate her role as a social observer and advocate. For example, in 1915, she contributed a medallion to be sold in support of Framingham's Equal Suffrage League. Between 1914 and 1921, she dealt with a variety of issues stemming from American anxieties over the world at war—nativism, the atrocities of war, and the search for peace. Increasing violence against Black Americans during this period resulted in two antilynching pieces in 1917, one based on the infamous Mary Turner case, which Walter White investigated for the National Association for the Advancement of Colored People (NAACP). Hoping to inspire Black youth to rise above troubled times, Fuller created a relief for Atlanta, Georgia's, Black Young Men's Christian Association depicting a boy rising from a kneeling position to meet the morning sun. Indeed, Fuller did perceive a new level of race consciousness and pride taking shape among African-Americans. Consequently, when asked to provide a sculpture for the New York City "Making of America" Festival in

1921, she responded with *Ethiopia Awakening.* She used an Egyptian motif to represent Americans of African descent, unwinding the bandages of their past, looking at life expectantly but unafraid. It was a compelling symbol of the Black renaissance.

For most of this period, Fuller's attic had been her studio, but an increasing lack of space and Dr. Fuller's concern that dust in so confined an area would ruin her health made working there impractical. Consequently, in 1929, the artist designed and had a studio built on the shore of Larned's Pond, a short distance from her home. This improved setting allowed her to begin teaching as well as creating and exhibiting new works.

In the 1930s, Fuller's popularity grew. She exhibited at local libraries and churches and at the Boston Art Club. Her association with the Harmon Foundation, established in New York City to showcase the works of young Black artists, was both as juror and exhibitor. Fuller's most appealing sculptures during this decade were rooted in African-American culture—*Water Boy,* based on a folksong; *Richard B. Harrison as "De Lawd"* in the popular play *The Green Pastures;* and *The Talking Skull,* derived from a folktale with African roots. During the 1930s and into the 1940s, Fuller maintained meaningful links with African-America.

In 1950, Meta Fuller gave up her studio to care for her husband. Dr. Fuller died in 1953. During this time she too was ill with tuberculosis and entered a sanitarium, where she remained until 1956. Later that year, Fuller went to the Palmer Institute in Sedalia, North Carolina, in order to do a portrait of its founder, Charlotte Hawkins Brown. In 1957, the National Council of Negro Women in Washington, D.C., commissioned her to model heads and hands for dolls representing ten notable Black women.

In March 1961, Meta Fuller, age eighty-four, was one of three artists honored in the "New Vistas in American Art" exhibit, celebrating Howard University's new art building. Fuller donated several works, including *Richard B. Harrison,* to the university.

Advanced age did not dull the sculptor's creativity. Framingham Union Hospital, where her husband had practiced, commissioned Fuller to design a plaque depicting working doctors and nurses. The local women's club requested sculpture for the Framingham Center Library. The result was unveiled in 1964—*Storytime,* a mother reading to her children.

During the 1960s, Fuller contributed to the civil rights movement by donating the proceeds of art sales to the cause and by producing symbols of the era. *The*

Crucifixion was her reaction to the death of four little girls in the bombing of the Sixteenth Street Baptist Church in Birmingham, Alabama, on September 15, 1963. *The Good Shepherd* was dedicated to the clergymen who marched with Martin Luther King, Jr., across the Edmund Pettus Bridge on March 9, 1965.

On Wednesday, March 18, 1968, Meta Vaux Warrick Fuller died at the age of ninety. Her funeral was held at Saint Andrew's Episcopal Church in Framingham. Afterward, her body was cremated and her ashes scattered in Vineyard Haven Sound, Massachusetts, as she had requested.

An artist whose career spanned over seventy years, Fuller was versatile and productive. At times she was a literary sculptor, at other times a creator of portraiture, and because she believed her artistic gifts were God-given, she created at least one piece of religious art a year in thanks. Her real significance, however, was in her depiction of African-American subjects. Although she once declared that she would not specialize in African-American types, Fuller was among the first artists to employ Black visual aesthetics in her portrayal of African-Americans. As such, she was an important precursor of the Harlem Renaissance, but, more than that, within those seventy years she presented a haunting chronicle of the Black experience within the context of the American experience.

[*See also* THEATER.]

BIBLIOGRAPHY

Crisis (October 1926); *DANB*; Kerr, Judith N. "God-given Work: The Life and Times of Meta Vaux Warrick Fuller," Ph.D. diss. (1986), and personal interview with Solomon C. Fuller, Jr. (November 29, 1976), and personal interview with Harriet Fuller (November 20, 1976); Murray, Freedman H. M. *Emancipation and the Freed in American Sculpture* (1916); O'Donnell, William. "Meta Vaux Warrick, Author of Horrors," *World Today* (November 1907); Porter, James. *Modern Negro Art* ([1943] 1969).

JUDITH N. KERR

G

GAFFORD, ALICE TAYLOR (1886-1981)

I love to paint. It nourishes my soul as food nourishes the body. If I create something beautiful which enriches the lives of others, then my art serves a dual purpose. (Louis 1971)

Alice Taylor Gafford spent twenty-five years in the nursing profession before deciding to attend Otis Art Institute in 1935 at the age of forty-nine. She was born on August 15, 1886. One of ten children of Benjamin and Alice Armstead Taylor, she was the only one to show any interest in art even though her mother was a "Sunday painter" who had won a blue ribbon at an international exposition.

Shortly after she graduated from the Otis Art Institute, Gafford attracted the attention of the critics when she was awarded second prize for one of her paintings at the Stendahl Gallery on Wilshire Boulevard in Los Angeles. A few years later, A. Atwater Kent, a noted New York collector, purchased one of Gafford's still-life paintings at the Biltmore Galleries. Art critic Arthur Millier published a photograph of this Gafford painting in the *Los Angeles Times* with the caption, "art thrill of the week."

Alice Gafford added a third career to her list when she entered the University of California at Los Angeles (UCLA) in 1951 to earn a teaching certificate in art. She then taught art to adults in the Los Angeles county schools for five years before retiring to devote all of her time to her creative work. Today, some of her former students are accomplished artists and teachers.

From a group of five hundred artists who submitted their work for the Sixth Annual Southern California Exhibition in 1968, Alice Gafford was among the seventy-nine artists selected to participate by New York critic Clement Greenberg. Later, Gafford's *The Tea Party* was added to the collection of the Long Beach Museum.

On her eighty-first birthday, Gafford was commissioned to paint the portraits of twelve famous Black Americans for the Family Savings Bank gallery.

Alice Gafford played a prominent role in the founding and development of various pioneer art groups, including the Val Verde Art and Hobby Show that now bears her name (the Alice Gafford Art and Hobby Show). She received more than twenty-five awards from the League of Allied Arts, the National Association of College Women, and city, county, and state legislative bodies.

She died on October 27, 1981. She was buried in the Los Angeles National Cemetery next to her husband, Louis Sherman Gafford, whom she married in 1928.

Nurse Alice Taylor Gafford found it was never too late when she enrolled in art school at the age of forty-nine and became a respected figure in the world of art. [Miriam Matthews]

BIBLIOGRAPHY

Jackson, Verna. "Alice Taylor Gafford," *Black Art, An International Quarterly* (January 15, 1979); Louis, Semella S. and Ruth Waddy, eds. *Black Artists on Art* (1971); Matthews, Miriam. Personal interviews with Alice Taylor Gafford; Memorial Service Announcement, Los Angeles (1981).

MIRIAM MATTHEWS

GAINES, IRENE McCOY (1892-1964)

Irene McCoy Gaines, noted Chicago social worker, prominent community, political, civil, children's, and woman's rights activist, and nationally known clubwoman, was born in Ocala, Florida, the daughter of Charles and Mamie Ellis McCoy, but grew up in Chicago. She graduated from Fisk University and studied social service administration at the University of Chicago (1918-21) and Loyola University (1935-37). In 1914, she married Harris B. Gaines, a Chicago lawyer and Illinois legislator (1929-41). They had two children, Charles, born in 1922, and Harris, born in 1924.

Her social service career began during World War I in the Girl's Work Division of the War Camp Community Service. During World War II, she served in the Women's Division of the Illinois War Council. From the 1920s until 1947, when she retired as a social worker, Gaines held positions in Chicago's juvenile court, the Black Young Women's Christian Association (YWCA), the Urban League, the Cook County Bureau of Public Welfare, and the Parkway Community House.

Gaines was president of the Illinois Federation of Republican Colored Women's Clubs from 1924 to 1935 and in 1940 became the first Black woman to run for the office of Illinois state representative. In 1936, she helped found the Chicago Council of Negro Organizations, and in 1941 she led Chicagoans in a march on Washington to protest employment discrimination. From 1952 to 1958, Gaines was president of the National Association of Colored Women. Her platform—Unitedly We Work for a Better World—reflected her interest in international peace and human rights. Gaines also was active in the National Association for the Advancement of Colored People (NAACP), Sigma Gamma Rho, Order of the Eastern Star, and the National Association of College Women.

BIBLIOGRAPHY

NAW; *NBAW*; Wesley, Charles Harris, *The History of the National Association of Colored Women's Clubs, Inc.: A Legacy of Service* (1984); *WWCA*; *Who's Who of American Women* (1950).

COLLECTIONS

Irene McCoy Gaines Collection, Chicago Historical Society, Chicago, Illinois; Irene McCoy Gaines Collection, University of Illinois at Urbana-Champaign, Urbana, Illinois.

JULIET E. K. WALKER

Dedicated social worker Irene Gaines led fellow Chicagoans on one of the earliest marches to protest discrimination in employment, in Washington, D.C., in 1941. [Schomburg Center]

GAINES-SHELTON, RUTH (b. 1872)

Ruth Gaines-Shelton was a grandmother at the time she won $40 for her play *The Church Fight*, published in *Crisis* in May 1926. Her play, a comedy, pokes fun at the internal squabbles that parishioners engage in when they are not sufficiently preoccupied with spiritual matters or social action. There is a critical edge in Gaines-Shelton's naming of two of her characters, Sister Sapphira and Brother Ananias, after biblical namesakes who deceptively withheld money and lied in an attempt to cheat their local church. Sources reveal that Gaines-Shelton wrote many other plays, but it is unclear whether the manuscripts, presumably unpublished, survive. Some of her other plays were *Aunt Hagar's Children, The Church Mouse, Gena, the Lost Child, Lord Earlington's Broken Vow, Mr. Church*, and *Parson Dewdrop's Bride*.

The daughter of an AME Church minister, the Reverend George W. Gaines, and his wife, Elizabeth Gaines, Ruth was born on April 8, 1872, in Glasgow, Missouri. Her mother died when Ruth was small, and Ruth assisted her father with church work as he di-

rected the building of the Old Bethel AME Church on Dearborn Street in Chicago. She attended Wilberforce University in Ohio, graduating in 1895, and she taught school in Montgomery, Missouri, until she married William Obern Shelton in 1898. Gaines-Shelton continued to write plays while raising her three children.

Gaines-Shelton's work, like that of other playwrights of her time, is significant because it documents the creative activities of Black women within their own communities during an era when most other avenues of opportunity were closed to them.

BIBLIOGRAPHY

Hatch, James V., and Omanii Abdullah. *Black Playwrights, 1823-1977: An Annotated Bibliography of Plays* (1977); Hatch, James V. and Ted Shine, eds. *Black Theatre U.S.A.: Forty-Five Plays by Black Americans, 1847-1974* (1974); Kellner, Bruce. *The Harlem Renaissance: A Historical Dictionary for the Era* (1984); Roses, Lorraine Elena, and Ruth E. Randolph. *Harlem Renaissance and Beyond* (1990).

LORRAINE ELENA ROSES

GANNETT, DEBORAH SAMPSON (1760-1827)

The back of the tombstone reads, "Deborah Sampson Gannett, Robert Shurtleff, The Female Soldier: 1781-1783." Dressed in men's clothing and using a man's name, Deborah Sampson served for over a year in the Continental Army. Her legacy is one of heroism and adventure as a Revolutionary War soldier.

Deborah Sampson was the daughter of Jonathan and Deborah (Bradford) Sampson. She was born in Plymouth, Massachusetts, on December 17, 1760. One of six children, she could trace her ancestry back to old Pilgrim stock. Her mother's lineage was traced to Governor William Bradford, and Miles Standish and John Alden were among her father's ancestors. Despite their illustrious background, the Sampsons were not wealthy people. As a means to provide a better life for his family, Jonathan Sampson decided to become a sailor. Most likely as a result of a storm or shipwreck at sea, he disappeared and was never seen or heard from again. Deborah Bradford Sampson found herself unable to find work that would allow her to take care of them.

Due to financial difficulties, young Deborah went to live initially with a cousin. Upon the death of her cousin, when Deborah was about eight years old, she went to live with a pastor's wife, with whom she remained for approximately two years. She was then bound out as a servant in the home of Benjamin Thomas of Middleborough, where she remained until age eighteen. She was able to acquire skills in many of the domestic arts associated with expectations about women, becoming generally adept as a cook and a seamstress. Deborah Sampson, owing in large part to her tall and well-proportioned physique, also plowed the fields, fed the farm animals, and did other chores usually done by men, including carpentry.

Sampson had the advantage of part-time attendance at the Middleborough public school. In time, much of her reading centered on the major issues of her day: the quarrel between Britain and the colonies, the vexing concern about Britain's financial problems, and the hateful regard for the taxes imposed on the colonies by Britain. The venturesome young woman continually busied herself not only with female undertakings but also with her avid interest in colonial and British politics. When Deborah Sampson was twenty-one and the war was still being fought, she began to entertain the idea of active involvement in the colonial army.

From her work in the local school district, Sampson had accrued a sum of $12, which she used for purchasing materials for a man's suit. From this time on, she worked diligently to present herself as a man. On May 20, 1782, disguised in men's clothing and using the alias Robert Shurtleff (or Shirtliff or Shirtlieff), she enlisted as a volunteer in the Continental forces. She was mustered into the service by Captain Eliphalet Thorp, at Worcester, on May 23, 1782, and served in Captain George Webb's company, Colonel Shepard's (later Colonel Jackson's) Fourth Massachusetts Regiment until discharged by General Knox at West Point on October 23, 1783.

During the battle at Tarrytown, Sampson was seriously wounded but was afraid to go to a hospital lest her sex be discovered. However, four months later, she was shot through the shoulder. As a consequence of this injury and exposure to extremely cold weather, she developed brain fever. While hospitalized, Dr. Barnabas Binney of Philadelphia, the attending physician, discovered that she was female, but he did not divulge her secret.

After her discharge, Deborah returned to her native New England in November 1783, where she resided with an uncle in Sharon, Massachusetts. She resumed female attire and settled into the community life of Sharon. It was there that she met a farmer by

the name of Benjamin Gannett, whom she married on April 7, 1784. They had three children: Earl Bradford, Mary, and Patience; they adopted a fourth, Susannah Shepherd, whose mother had died in childbirth.

Eventually Deborah Sampson's sojourn as Robert Shurtleff in the Continental army began to attract attention. In the late 1790s Herman Mann published a fascinating account of what many regard as a much romanticized biography of Sampson under the title *The Female Review*.

Beginning with her appearance at the Federal Street Theatre in Boston on March 22, 1802, Deborah Sampson Gannett adapted the lecture written for her by Mann to her own liking and toured several New England towns where she told of her Revolutionary War experience. She was awarded a pension by the state of Massachusetts. On March 11, 1805, she was listed among those receiving pension payments from the United States government.

Deborah Sampson Gannett died on April 29, 1827. She is buried in Rockridge Cemetery in Sharon, Massachusetts. Her decision to serve in the Continental army represents an intense patriotism, and her life as a soldier in the Continental army dramatically refutes the pervasive belief that women cannot serve admirably in combat.

Deborah Sampson Gannett's life exemplifies the Black experience, wherein there are many heroes and heroines. While it is generally accepted that Deborah was a Black American, there are those who question the authenticity of this claim.

BIBLIOGRAPHY

Ellet, Elizabeth F. *The Eminent and Heroic Women of America* (1974); Forbes, Esther. *Paul Revere and the World He Lived In* (1942); Gannett, Deborah. *An Address at the Federal Street Theatre, Boston* (1802); Gannett, Michael R. *Gannett Descendants of Matthew and Hannah Gannett* (1976); Hart, James D. *The Oxford Companion to American Literature* (1983); Mann, Herman. *The Female Review: Life of Deborah Sampson* ([1797] 1866); *Massachusetts Soldiers and Sailors of the Revolutionary War: A Compilation from the Archives Prepared and Published by the Secretary of the Commonwealth* (1896-1906); *The National Cyclopedia of American Biography* (1983); *NAW*; Niles, Hezekiah. *Principles and Acts of the Revolution in America* (1822); Stickley, Julia Ward. "The Records of Deborah Sampson Gannett, Woman Soldier of the American Revolution," *Prologue: The Journal of the National Archives* (Winter 1972).

LARRY MARTIN

GARNET, SARAH S. T. (1831-1911)

Sarah Smith Tompkins Garnet spent fifty-six years as an educator. She began as a teacher's assistant at the age of fourteen and by 1854 she was teaching in the African Free School in Williamsburgh, Brooklyn. In 1863, she was the first Black woman appointed principal of a public school (Grammar School No. 80 and later No. 81) in the borough of Manhattan. She was a principal until 1900. Prominent contemporary educators include Catherine Thompson Clow, Maritcha Remond Lyons, and Florence T. Ray.

Born on July 31, 1831, Minsarah (known as Sarah) was the oldest of ten children of Sylvanus and Annie (Springstead) Smith. Both her father and her mother were descendants of Long Island Native Americans and Black Americans. Sylvanus Smith was a landowner, successful farmer, and pork merchant in Weeksville, the oldest Black community in Brooklyn.

Sarah was first married to James Tompkins, an Episcopal minister, until his death in the late 1860s. Her second marriage, to Henry Highland Garnet in 1879, a Presbyterian minister, abolitionist, and diplomat, lasted only a few years. He died of an asthma attack in Liberia on February 13, 1882.

Principal Garnet devoted her life to a crusade against discrimination in education and civil rights. She was active in the National Vigilance Committee and the Women's Loyal Union Club, and she was a founder of the Equal Suffrage League, one of the earliest equal rights organizations in Brooklyn. A member of the National Association of Colored Women, she was superintendent of its suffrage department.

In July 1911, Garnet and her sister, Dr. Susan Smith McKinney Steward, were delegates to the first Universal Races Congress in London, England. Upon their return, the Equal Suffrage League held a reception in Garnet's honor that was attended by W.E.B. Du Bois and other distinguished guests. Sarah S. T. Garnet died suddenly on September 17, 1911, of arteriosclerosis at her Brooklyn home at 748 Hancock Street. She is buried in Brooklyn's Green-Wood Cemetery.

BIBLIOGRAPHY

Davis, Russell. *Black Americans in Cleveland* (1972); Hunter, Jane Edna. *A Nickel and a Prayer* (1941); Jones, Adrienne Lash. *Jane Edna Hunter: A Case Study of Black Leadership, 1905-1950* (1989); Kusmer, Kenneth. *A Ghetto Takes Shape: Black Cleveland, 1870-1930* (1978); Western Reserve Historical Society. Manuscript Collections: Phillis Wheatley, Jane Edna Hunter, and Young Women's Christian Association, Cleveland, Ohio.

FLORIS BARNETT CASH

GARRISON, MEMPHIS TENNESSEE (1890-1988)

When asked about her unique name, Memphis Tennessee Garrison once answered that her mother had never been to Biloxi, Mississippi. Born in McDowell County, West Virginia, on March 4, 1890, Garrison died in Huntington, West Virginia, on July 25, 1988. The youngest of two children of former slaves, Wesley Carter, a coal miner, and Cassie Thomas Carter, she grew up in the coal fields of southern West Virginia. After receiving her elementary education in the segregated public schools, she earned a B.A. with honors from Bluefield State College in West Virginia and pursued advanced study at Ohio State University in Columbus. Twenty-five years after the historic 1963 march on Washington, she received the governor's Living the Dream Award for distinguished service to West Virginia and the nation.

In 1908, she launched her public school teaching career in McDowell County, where she taught until her retirement in the early 1950s. She later recalled that she had wanted to be a lawyer, but her mother could not afford the required training. Memphis Carter married Melvin Garrison, a coal miner, but they had no children. If they had, it is likely that her teaching career would have been cut short because, as elsewhere, West Virginia openly discouraged the employment of married teachers with children.

Garrison not only completed a distinguished career as a public schoolteacher, she also influenced the political life of the region. As secretary of the Gary, McDowell County, branch of the National Association for the Advancement of Colored People, her activities covered a broad range of local, regional, and national projects. In addition to local campaigns against racial inequality before the law, she spearheaded the national Christmas seal campaign during the late 1920s and early 1930s. Under the motto, Merry Christmas and Justice for All, the Christmas seal campaign generated widespread support for the NAACP and netted substantial sums for the national office.

Until her death in 1988, Garrison continued to serve the state and nation. She served as the first woman president of the West Virginia State Teachers' Association, 1929-30; treasurer of the NAACP West Virginia State Conference for twenty-two years; NAACP national field secretary, 1956-59; national vice president of the NAACP board of directors, 1964-66; member of the West Virginia Human Rights Commission, 1963-66; and member of President Lyndon B. Johnson's National Citizens Committee on Community Relations, 1964. For her distinguished public service, Garrison received numerous awards and honors, including the NAACP's Madam C. J. Walker Gold Medal Award, 1929; the T. G. Nutter Award for outstanding achievement and service in the field of civil rights, 1959; the NAACP Distinguished Service Award, 1969; and an honorary doctorate of humanities, Marshall University in Huntington, West Virginia, 1970.

Although Garrison was recognized for fighting racial injustice, her activities demonstrated a keen interest in equity across gender and class lines. Despite her professional training, Garrison retained close ties with the Black coal-mining working class. In two very illuminating essays about Black Americans in southern West Virginia, she exhibited an unusual sensitivity to the ideas, aspirations, and grievances of Black voters. During the 1920s, Garrison challenged the gender distribution of power within the McDowell County Colored Republican Organization, which often held the balance of power in West Virginia politics. The career of Memphis Tennessee Garrison takes on added significance because the southern Appalachian mountains are often perceived as isolated from the main currents of American history. Her contributions deepen our understanding of life in the Mountain State, link Black West Virginians to a national Black community, and highlight the interplay of class, race, and gender in American society.

BIBLIOGRAPHY

Johnson, D. "Memphis Tennessee Garrison: The Real Gains of a Life, 1890-1988," *Beacon Digest* (August 30-September 7, 1988); Lewis, Ronald L. *Black Coal Miners in America: Race, Class and Community Conflict, 1780-1980* (1987); Maurer, B. B., ed. *Mountain Heritage* (1980); Trotter, Joe William, Jr. *Coal, Class, and Color: Blacks in Southern West Virginia, 1915-1932* (1990); Trotter, Joe William, Jr., and Ancella Radford Bickley. *Honoring Our Past: Proceedings of the First Two Conferences on West Virginia's Black History* (1991); Turner, William H. "Special Issue: Blacks in Appalachia," *Appalachian Heritage: A Magazine of Southern Appalachian Life and Culture* (1991); Turner, William H. and Edward J. Cabbell, eds. *Blacks in Appalachia* (1985).

JOE W. TROTTER
H. LARUE TROTTER

GARRISON, ZINA (1963-)

It was a historic moment. In the 1990 Wimbledon women's singles final, Martina Navratilova won her ninth singles title, a record held by no other person, when she defeated Zina Garrison, the first Black woman to play on Wimbledon's center court since 1958, when Althea Gibson won her second of two Wimbledon crowns. Making history, or being first, has been a rather common occurrence for professional tennis player Zina Garrison.

Zina Garrison, the youngest of seven children, was born on November 16, 1963, in Houston, Texas, to Mary and Ulysses Garrison. Her father died before she was a year old, and she was raised by her mother, who worked as an aide in a nursing home. When Zina was ten, she began playing tennis at the local public park courts where she received instruction from the coach. After a few months he was impressed with her talent and entered her in local tournaments; she did well. By the time she was sixteen, she was playing in national tournaments. She and Lori McNeal, another Black player from the Houston public courts, won the 1979 National Hard Court Doubles Championship for sixteen and under. The next year, 1980, Garrison won the National Girls Sixteen Singles Championship and, with McNeal, three national junior doubles titles. In 1981, at seventeen, she was the first Black player to win the junior singles championship at Wimbledon. She also won the junior singles title at the U.S. Open. As a result of these wins, the U.S. Olympic Committee named her top female amateur athlete in tennis, she received the Junior of the Year Award from the International Tennis Federation, and she was awarded the Girl's Sportsmanship Trophy by the U.S. Tennis Association. Washington, D.C., proclaimed January 6, 1982, Zina Garrison Day. She turned professional and was ranked sixteenth in the world at the end of 1982.

In her ten years as a professional tennis player, Garrison has won many championships and millions of dollars in prize money. She has been a member of the Federation Cup team and captain of the Wightman Cup team (1988). Zina Garrison was a member of the 1988 U.S. Olympic tennis team—the first team since 1924 to compete in the Olympic games. At the games, held in Seoul, Korea, she won the gold medal with Pam Shriver in doubles and a bronze medal in singles.

Another historic moment for Garrison occurred at the U.S. Open in 1989, when she defeated Chris Evert 7-6, 6-2, during the last tournament of Evert's career. Garrison has also had big wins over Martina Navratilova and Steffi Graf, both champion players. Ranked among the top ten women tennis players 1983-91, at one time she was ranked number four in the world.

Zina Garrison married Willard Jackson, a Houston businessman, in 1989. She is a role model for Black youngsters and often gives clinics and talks in inner-city areas.

Zina Garrison is one of the top professional tennis players in the world and, as such, is the number one Black player, the best since Althea Gibson. Popular among the professionals, she is said to be one of the few players who applaud their opponents when they make a good shot. A determined competitor, her ultimate goal is to win a Grand Slam title.

BIBLIOGRAPHY

Cunningham, Kim. "Think of England," *World Tennis* (July 1988); Emery, David, ed. *Who's Who in International Tennis* (1983); Flink, Steve. "Wilander and the Surprise Open," *World Tennis* (November 1988); Moore, Kenny, and J. E. Vader. "Living a Dream," *Sports Illustrated* (November 27, 1989); *The Official United States Tennis Association Yearbook and Tennis Guide with the Official Rules 1991* (1990); Young, Josh. "Zina's Zenith," *Women's Sports and Fitness* (May/June 1990).

JOANNA DAVENPORT

GARVEY, AMY ASHWOOD
(1897-1969)

Amy Ashwood Garvey sometimes claimed to have cofounded Marcus Garvey's Universal Negro Improvement Association (UNIA), the most successful Pan-African mass movement ever. What can be asserted with more confidence is that she may have been the first member, apart from Garvey himself.

Born in 1897 in Port Antonio, Jamaica, Amy was seventeen years old when she met Marcus Garvey after his return to Jamaica, just days earlier, from four years of wandering in Latin America and Europe. The UNIA was formed shortly after their meeting.

Amy became "lady secretary" of the new association, whose objectives included the uplift of the African race locally and internationally. She also became ro-

mantically involved with Garvey, and within the next year or so, they became engaged. Throughout the UNIA's first year, Amy accompanied Garvey on organizational trips around the island and figured prominently in the association's activities. She took part in UNIA-sponsored debates, read poetry at UNIA literary events, helped feed the poor, and visited the sick.

Sometime before Garvey left Jamaica for the United States in 1916, Amy left for Panama. In 1918, she joined Garvey in New York. By this time the UNIA was poised for its spectacular take-off into Pan-African acclaim. Amy plunged once more into the work of the association. She traveled across the country with Marcus, helped with the UNIA's new organ, the *Negro World*, and in 1919 became an official of the newly launched Black Star Line Steamship Corporation. In October 1919 she apparently helped save Garvey's life (the facts are disputed) from a would-be assassin's bullet.

Amy and Marcus were married on Christmas Day 1919, in the presence of several thousand UNIA members and well-wishers. The marriage was on the rocks within a few months. Marcus accused his wife of infidelity, excessive drinking, and financial dishonesty; she accused him of infidelity and lack of political

Amy Ashwood Garvey sometimes claimed to have cofounded Marcus Garvey's Universal Negro Improvement Association; in any case, she was certainly its first member, apart from Garvey himself. After her divorce from Garvey in 1922, she maintained a deep and active interest in Pan-Africanism. [Schomburg Center]

correctness. Several suits for annulment, divorce, separation, alimony, and bigamy were brought by one or the other party over the next six years. In the midst of these suits and countersuits, Marcus obtained a divorce in Missouri in 1922 and almost immediately married Amy Jacques. Jacques had been a close friend and roommate of Ashwood's and had been chief bridesmaid at Ashwood and Garvey's wedding. As Garvey's private secretary, she had accompanied the newlyweds on their honeymoon to Canada.

An excellent public speaker and, to a certain degree, a good organizer, Amy Ashwood Garvey had a deep interest in Pan-African affairs, quite independent of Garvey's. These characteristics shaped the rest of her life.

In London in 1924, she worked with several prominent West Africans in founding a Nigerian Progress Union. Back in the United States in 1926, she collaborated with the Trinidad-born calypsonian Sam Manning on the musical comedies *Brown Sugar*, *Hey Hey*, and *Black Magic*. She and Manning took a musical revue on tour in the Caribbean in 1929.

Between 1935 and 1938, Amy again found herself at the center of Pan-African activity. Her restaurant in the West End of London became the gathering place for such famous Pan-Africanists as George Padmore and C.L.R. James of Trinidad and Jomo Kenyatta of Kenya. She was an active participant in their political activities.

In Jamaica in the early 1940s, she founded a short-lived political party and attempted to establish a School of Domestic Science. By now her peripatetic lifestyle was firmly established, and her endless wanderings would continue to the end of her life. In New York in 1944 she was active in the campaign to elect Adam Clayton Powell, Jr., to the U.S. Congress. She also came under Federal Bureau of Investigation surveillance for her association with left-wing activists and others such as Paul Robeson suspected of Communist leanings.

She found herself at the center of Pan-African activity once more in 1945 when, together with the elder statesman of the movement, W.E.B. Du Bois, she chaired the opening session of the famous Fifth Pan-African Conference in Manchester, England. George Padmore and Kwame Nkrumah of Ghana were the organizers.

She lived in West Africa from 1946 to 1949. In Liberia she became a close friend of President W.V.S. Tubman. In Ghana she was able to trace her ancestry back to Ashanti, in a manner remarkably similar to that recounted by Alex Haley in *Roots* decades later.

During the 1950s, her time was divided among England, the Caribbean, and West Africa again. Her interest in women's issues, developing for a long time, now competed with Pan-Africanism for the focus of her attention. She lectured to women's groups and encouraged women to organize in a 1953 tour of the Caribbean. In London in this period she organized a community center and was active in the aftermath of the Notting Hill race riots of 1958.

Amy spent the early 1960s in West Africa, where she tried her hand at a series of unsuccessful business ventures in Ghana and Liberia. The rest of the decade was spent in England, Trinidad, the United States, and Jamaica. She was in England in 1964 when Garvey's body was returned to Jamaica amid much pomp and ceremony. (He had died in England in 1940.) She participated officially in the ceremonies in London marking the occasion. In the United States in 1967 she was feted by the Black Power generation, who had rediscovered Garvey and were in the process of elevating him to fame and honor once more.

She died in Jamaica in 1969, still dreaming of new business ventures and political activities.

Amy Ashwood Garvey was an engaging woman who was able to engender fierce loyalty in the few friends she made. Her encounter with Garvey was both a blessing and a curse. Garvey and the UNIA presented her with a moment of great glory. The encounter also condemned her to live in the shadow of the man and his organization for the rest of her life. Whether indulging in recrimination over her years with Garvey or basking in the reverence bestowed upon her in later years as wife of the fallen hero, she could not and would not divorce herself from the defining experience of her life.

BIBLIOGRAPHY

Martin, Tony. *Amy Ashwood Garvey: Pan-Africanist, Feminist, and Wife No. 1* (forthcoming), and "Amy Ashwood Garvey: Wife No. 1," *Jamaica Journal* (August-October 1987).

TONY MARTIN

GARVEY, AMY EUPHEMIA JACQUES (1896-1973)

Journalist, Pan-Africanist, and historian, Amy Euphemia Jacques Garvey was a key figure in the Universal Negro Improvement Association (UNIA) and in establishing a record for later generations of the UNIA and its founder, Marcus Garvey. Amy

Euphemia Jacques Garvey was the second wife of Marcus Mosiah Garvey, founder of the UNIA. Amy Jacques was born in Kingston, Jamaica, December 31, 1896, and educated at Wolmers Girls' School. Her parents, Charlotte and George Samuel Jacques, were also formally educated and owned valued property; the Jacques family's heritage was rooted in the Jamaican middle class. Plagued by ill health due to recurring bouts with malaria, Amy Jacques was in need of a cooler climate and in 1917 migrated to the United States. She became affiliated with the UNIA in 1918 and served as Marcus Garvey's private secretary and office manager at the UNIA headquarters in New York. She married Marcus Garvey, July 27, 1922, in Baltimore, Maryland.

During Marcus Garvey's incarceration for alleged mail fraud, Amy Jacques Garvey's three-tiered (writer, spokesperson, and archivist) activist nature evolved. She served as the editor of the woman's page column "Our Women and What They Think" in the *Negro World*, the UNIA's weekly newspaper published in New York. Amy Jacques Garvey's editorials demonstrated her political commitment to the doctrines of Pan-Africanism and also her belief that women should be active within their communities even, to some extent, at the sacrifice of self. As the liaison between Marcus Garvey and UNIA officials, and secretary-treasurer of both the Marcus Garvey Freedom and Protection Fund and the Marcus Garvey Committee of Justice, Amy Jacques Garvey traveled across the United States and spoke on Marcus Garvey's behalf in the campaign to secure his release from prison. Amy Jacques Garvey's uncompromising attitude toward organizational efficiency made her a controversial figure within the UNIA. Nonetheless, she was able to keep meticulous records on Marcus Garvey and the UNIA in the midst of this flurry.

Upon Marcus Garvey's release from Tombs Atlanta Penitentiary on November 26, 1927, and his subsequent deportation from the United States, he and Amy returned to Jamaica. In Jamaica, Amy gave birth to her two children, Marcus Garvey, Jr. (1930) and Julius Winston Garvey (1933). After Marcus Garvey's death on June 19, 1940, Amy Jacques Garvey continued to serve the UNIA. Her books *The Philosophy and Opinions of Marcus Garvey*, published in two volumes (1923, 1925), *Garvey and Garveyism* (1963), and *Black Power in America* (1968) helped to stimulate a rebirth of interest in Garveyism. As a result, there has been a growth of historical scholarship focusing on the activities of Marcus Garvey and the UNIA. Amy Jacques Garvey was awarded a Musgrave Medal in 1971 in Jamaica for her distinguished contribu-

Married to Marcus Garvey in 1922, Amy Jacques Garvey carried on his work with the UNIA during his imprisonment. Her writings on Garvey helped to stimulate a rebirth of interest in Garveyism. She is shown here studying a bust of Garvey in Jamaica, West Indies, in 1956. [Schomburg Center]

tions on the philosophy of Garveyism. On July 25, 1973, Amy Jacques Garvey died at University Hospital of the West Indies in Jamaica.

BIBLIOGRAPHY

Amy Jacques Garvey papers. Marcus Garvey Memorial Collection. Fisk University, Nashville, Tennessee; Hill, Robert, ed. *The Marcus Garvey and Universal Negro Improvement Association Papers* (1983-90); Lewis, Ida. "Mrs. Garvey Talks with Ida Lewis," *Encore* (May 1973); Lewis, Rupert and Maureen Warner Lewis. "Amy Jacques Garvey," *Jamaican Journal* (1987); Matthews, Mark. "Our Women and What They Think: Amy Garvey and the Negro World," *Black Scholar* (May-June 1979); Reed, Beverly. "Amy Garvey—Black, Beautiful and Free," *Ebony* (June 1971); Smith, Honor Ford. "Women and the Garvey Movement in Jamaica." In *Garvey: His Work and Impact*, ed. Rupert Lewis and Patrick Bryan (1988).

ULA TAYLOR

GARVEY, MARCUS *see*
UNIVERSAL NEGRO
IMPROVEMENT ASSOCIATION

GAUDIN, JULIETTE *see*
SISTERS OF THE HOLY FAMILY

GIBSON, ALTHEA (1927-)

Althea Gibson was the first person to break the color barrier in professional tennis. Gibson's 1950 integration of tennis occurred within the same time frame as baseball's inclusion of Jackie Robinson into major league baseball. Perhaps Gibson's achievements are even more remarkable than Robinson's since they occurred in an upper-class sport, seldom played by African-Americans, and also since her pursuit of athletic excellence was unconventional for Black women and women in general during this era. It was Gibson's driving desire to excel, as described in her biography, *I Always Wanted to Be Somebody* (1958), that cast her in the fateful position as the first Black woman in modern professional sports.

Althea Gibson was born on August 25, 1927, in Silver, South Carolina, the oldest of five children of Daniel and Annie Gibson. When Althea was three, her father pulled up his sharecropper roots and moved the family to New York City. In Harlem, Gibson developed a "tough kid on the block" image, which would manifest itself in adulthood in the competitive qualities of mental toughness and determination. Truancy from school and her flight from home and relatives brought Gibson in touch with the Society for the Prevention of Cruelty to Children. She then acquired a license to work, but after moving from job to job she lapsed into welfare dependence. Gibson's athletic ability stood out among other youth, and she drew attention to her aptitude by winning the Police Athletic League and Parks Department paddle tennis competitions.

Musician Buddy Walker recognized her talent, purchased rackets, and took her to the Harlem River Tennis Courts. Shortly thereafter, the prestigious Harlem Cosmopolitan Tennis Club took up a collection to provide her with membership and tennis lessons. Gibson got her start in 1942 by winning the girls' singles New York State tournament sponsored by the all-Black American Tennis Association (ATA).

The Cosmopolitan Club then sent her on to the ATA nationals, where she lost in the girls' singles finals. Gibson consecutively won the 1944 and 1945 girls' tournaments. At age eighteen she played in the women's 1946 ATA nationals and lost to Roumania Peters in the finals.

Friends played an important role in the direction of Gibson's life. Boxer Sugar Ray Robinson was one of her most supportive friends. Gibson's big break was to occur when Hubert A. Eaton of Wilmington,

Althea Gibson rose from childhood brawling in the streets of New York to the fabled courts of Wimbledon, integrating the women's singles tennis tournament in 1951. In 1957, she won the singles title. [National Archives]

Althea Gibson's autobiography is entitled I Always Wanted to Be Somebody. *She succeeded. The first Black woman to reach the top ranks of professional tennis, she has also served as a role model to generations of children and young people. She is shown here giving pointers to an aspiring (and clearly admiring) young tennis player. [National Archives]*

North Carolina, and Robert W. Johnson of Lynchburg, Virginia, offered her a home, secondary schooling, tennis instruction, and the encouragement and support to realize her potential. As a consequence of their interest in her, she graduated from Williston Industrial High School in South Carolina, learned to get along in a variety of social settings, acquired self-discipline and self-respect, and won the ATA women's singles ten years in a row (1947-56), thus establishing herself as the best Black woman tennis player.

In 1949, Gibson was invited to play in the desegregated National Indoor Championships, where she lost in the quarterfinals. In 1950, while in her freshman year at Florida Agricultural and Mechanical University, she reached the finals before being defeated. It then appeared that political intervention would keep Gibson out of the segregated grass court invitationals, but her break came in July 1950 when tennis champion Alice Marble declared in the magazine *American Lawn Tennis*, "She is not being judged by the yardstick of ability but by the fact that her pigmentation is somewhat different." Largely due to Marble's influence, the Orange Lawn Tennis Club in

New Jersey issued Gibson an invitation. This led to a long-awaited invitation to the 1950 national championships at Forest Hills, where she lost to Louise Brough in the second round. Gibson entered Wimbledon in 1951 and thus became the first African-American to play in this exclusive international tournament. After disappointing tournament performances in 1951, 1952, and 1953 and a two-year stint as a physical education teacher at Lincoln University in Missouri, she accepted an invitation from the State Department to represent U.S. tennis on a team tour of Southeast Asia. The tour instilled self-confidence in Gibson, and the quality of her tennis improved. She proceeded to win the Indian and Asiatic women's singles titles and other European tournaments at the conclusion of the Asian tour. In 1956, although the Wimbledon singles title was to elude Gibson, who lost in the first round to Shirley Fry, she went on to win the Wimbledon doubles championship with her partner, Angela Buxton.

Ranked second in the United States, after Shirley Fry, Gibson again faltered before Fry at Forest Hills in 1956. Gibson then won pre-tournament championships in England before the 1957 Wimbledon championship. She was ready for her third Wimbledon attempt. Seeded first, her game fell into place, and she played Darlene Hard, another American, in the finals. Gibson won the singles title at Wimbledon, 6-3, 6-2. Thereafter, teamed with Darlene Hard, she continued winning by taking the doubles title at Wimbledon. The tough-minded kid from Harlem succeeded at doing what no other Black woman had accomplished before or since—winning the Wimbledon championship. Gibson's tennis accomplishments continued. She won the national clay court and Forest Hills singles titles in 1957, and in 1958 she returned to Wimbledon to win yet another singles and doubles championship.

Gibson retired from professional tennis in 1959. She played exhibition tennis on tour with the Harlem Globetrotters, appeared in *The Horse Soldiers* (1959) with John Wayne and William Holden, and played professional golf from 1963 to 1967. In later years she served as program director for a racquet club and a parks commission in New Jersey. A few of her honors have included Associated Press Woman Athlete of the Year, 1957-58; Lawn Tennis Hall of Fame; and Black Athletes Hall of Fame. Althea Gibson remains the benchmark by which other Black women measure their achievement in the sport of tennis.

BIBLIOGRAPHY

Ashe, Arthur R., Jr. *A Hard Road to Glory: A History of the African-American Athlete, 1919-1945* (1988); Candee, Marjorie Dent, ed. *Current Biography Yearbook* (1957); Dawson, Alice. "Matches to Remember: Women of the U.S. Open," *Women's Sports and Fitness* (August 1985); *EBA*; Henderson, Edwin B., et al. *The Black Athlete: Emergence and Arrival* (1976); King, Billie Jean. *We Have Come a Long Way: A Story of Women's Tennis* (1988); *NA*; *NBAW*; Reynolds, Quentin. "Long Road to the Center Court," *Saturday Review* (November 29, 1958); Smith, Margaret Chase and H. Paul Jeffers. *Gallant Women* (1968); *Who's Who of American Women* (1991); *WWBA* (1992).

JUDITH GEORGE

GILBERT, ARTISHIA GARCIA
(b. 1869)

Artishia Gilbert, the first Black woman to pass the medical boards and register as a physician in Kentucky, had an extraordinary educational career. The daughter of an itinerant miner, she graduated in 1885, at the age of sixteen, from the State Normal and Theological Institute and then earned a B.A. from the

State University of Kentucky. Three years later, in 1892, Gilbert completed her M.A. at that school and went on to earn a medical degree from the Louisville National Medical College, even while she traveled and lectured extensively for the Baptist Educational Convention.

Seeking further training, she moved to Washington, D.C., and entered the medical program at Howard University, from which she graduated in 1897. Shortly thereafter, she married John Wilkerson, a Louisville lawyer, and accepted a position as teaching assistant in obstetrics at the State University of Kentucky. She served also as superintendent of the Red Cross Sanitarium and on the board of Orphans Home in Louisville.

BIBLIOGRAPHY

Brown, Sara W. "Colored Women Physicians," *The Southern Workman* (December 1923); District of Columbia, Board of Education Personnel Records; *Journal of the College Alumnae Club of Washington, Twenty-Fifth Anniversary* (1935); Lamb, Daniel S., ed. *Howard University Medical Department: A Historical, Biographical, and Statistical Souvenir* (1900); Maher, Frank L. *Who's Who of the Colored Race* (1915); Majors, Monroe. *Noted Negro Women* (1893); *Polk's Directory of the District of Columbia* (1907-30); *Polk's Medical and Surgical Register of the United States and Canada* (1886-1920); Scruggs, Lawson A. *Women of Distinction* (1893).

GLORIA MOLDOW

GILMER, GLORIA

Dr. Gloria Gilmer is one of the very few people familiar with the levels of mathematics education from nursery school to the Ph.D. level. A dynamic innovator, she is president of Math-Tech, a corporation (established 1984) in Milwaukee, Wisconsin, that translates research findings into effective programs of mathematics education, especially for women and minorities.

Since 1985, she has chaired both the International Study Group on Ethno-mathematics and the Committee on Opportunities in Mathematics for Underrepresented Minorities. The latter is a joint endeavor of three scholarly societies that together organized a series of national conferences. "Making Mathematics Work for Minorities," as these were titled in 1989 and 1990, included six regional conferences and a national conference, for which Gilmer served on the steering committee.

Mathematics educator and president of Math-Tech, Gloria Gilmer utilizes her warmth and humor, as well as her intellect, to improve the working relationship between mathematics and Black women. [Patricia Kenschaft]

She was the first Black female (1980-82) on the board of governors of the Mathematical Association of America (MAA); thereafter, the board decided to appoint and continue appointing a governor-at-large for minorities. During the same years she was national director of the MAA speakers' program, "Blacks and Mathematics." From 1981 to 1985, she chaired an MAA panel on remediation.

Always exploring varied ways of learning and teaching mathematics, Gilmer gave a speech on worldwide developments in ethnomathematics at the Sixth International Congress on Mathematical Education in Budapest, Hungary, in July 1988. She was a member of the U.S. mathematics delegation to the People's Republic of China in 1983 and of the mathematics educators' study tour of the Soviet Union in 1988.

Gilmer was a research associate with the U.S. Department of Education (1981-84) and is a former mathematician in exterior ballistics with the U.S. Army at Aberdeen Proving Grounds. She has served on the mathematics faculties of six traditionally Black

institutions of higher education and taught mathematics at the Milwaukee Area Technical College (1965-79) and in the Milwaukee public schools (1959-65).

Born in Baltimore, Maryland, to Mittie and James Ford, she holds B.S. and M.A. degrees in mathematics from Morgan State University and the University of Pennsylvania, respectively. Her Ph.D. in curriculum and instruction is from Marquette University. Gilmer married and had two children. Her son is a lawyer and her daughter, who holds an M.B.A., is vice president of Math-Tech.

Without Gloria Gilmer's energetic and imaginative contributions, the U.S. mathematics community would be far less diverse and welcoming. For example, it was she who suggested skits dramatizing micro-inequities to facilitate mathematicians' self-examination; hundreds of mathematicians have flocked to these skits and discussed them widely. Her lively humor and warm compassion complement her visionary perspective and her commitment to social change.

BIBLIOGRAPHY

Gilmer, Gloria. "Socio-Cultural Influence on Learning." In *American Perspectives on the Fifth International Congress on Mathematical Education* (1985), and "Computers in the Remedial Mathematics Curriculum." In *Computers and Mathematics*, ed. David Smith et al. (1988), and "An Interview with Clarence Stephens," *Undergraduate Mathematics Education Trends* (May 1990), and "Developing African-Americans in Mathematics: An Interview with Abdulalim Abdullah Shabazz," *Undergraduate Mathematics Education Trends* (January 1992).

PATRICIA CLARK KENSCHAFT

GIOVANNI, NIKKI (1943-)

Nikki Giovanni emerged on the artistic and political scene as one of the New Black Poets, who became popular in the 1960s. The outspokenness of her style and her message earned her extraordinary public acclaim, which she continues to enjoy. Her first poems were militant calls to armed action for all Black people who desired freedom from racism and injustice in America. Her writing and her political activities, however, were large, clear reflections of her commitment to end oppression and her allegiance to the emerging civil rights movement.

One of the best examples of Nikki Giovanni's militant poems is "The True Import of Present Dialogue, Black vs. Negro," which appeared in her first collection, a self-published volume entitled *Black Feeling, Black Talk* (1967). The poem begins, "nigger / Can you kill / Can you kill / Can a nigger kill / Can a nigger kill a honkie." The shock value in the opening lines continues as the poem names the enemies of Black people and Giovanni writes, "We ain't got to prove we can die / We got to prove we can kill." Of equal importance in the poem is Giovanni's attention to Black attitudes of inferiority, which also have to be killed. She writes, "Can you kill the nigger / in you / Can you make your nigger mind / die / Can you kill your nigger mind / And free your Black hands to / strangle." Part of the structural innovativeness of the poem is its repetition of the rhetorical question "can you kill?," which eventually reads not as a question but as an imperative.

Two poems from Nikki Giovanni's early work foreshadow her later thematic focus. One, "Seduction," from *Black Feeling, Black Talk*, pictures the poetic persona taking time out from making revolution for making love. She disrobes her lover, but he is preoccupied with the momentum of the political movement and seems oblivious to her actions until the last four lines, when the poet writes, "then you'll notice / your state of undress / and knowing you you'll just say / 'Nikki, isn't this counterrevolutionary'?" "Nikki Rosa," probably the most anthologized of Giovanni's poems, is a lovely, accessible poem that reveals the human complexities of traditional Black life. Focusing on childhood memories, the verses show the alternate side to Giovanni's militant political consciousness. "Nikki Rosa" first appeared in *Black Judgement*, published by Broadside Press in 1968. *Black Judgement* was combined with *Black Feeling, Black Talk* and published by William Morrow in 1970.

"Nikki Rosa" and "Seduction" are poems that suggest the nonviolent and personal direction of Giovanni's subsequent work. Her later work rejects the violence, and Eugene Redmond points out that the new poetry charts her "rite of passage toward womanhood." Paula Giddings writes that by "the early seventies, the Black movement was in disarray. . . . Giovanni, however, could still maintain an appeal across ideological lines." Giddings suggests that young people who missed the "heroic age of the SNCC (Student Nonviolent Coordinating Committee) successes in the South, or the urgency which inspired them" were drawn to the personal qualities in Giovanni's poetry. Giddings astutely observes that older people also like her, finding her "precocious persona . . . more mischievous than 'bad,' " prob-

ably getting "vicarious pleasure from her sharp-tongued defense of the race" (Giddings 1984).

Nikki Giovanni (named Yolande Cornelia after her mother) was born in Knoxville, Tennessee, on June 7, 1943, to Gus and Yolande Giovanni. Her parents, who met while students at Knoxville College, relocated to Wyoming, Ohio, a suburb of Cincinnati, when Nikki was very young. The younger of two daughters, Nikki had an independent, assertive, courageous temperament that was apparent early; these qualities also defined the temperament of her maternal grandmother, Louvenia Watson, with whom Nikki lived during her sophomore and junior years of high school. Louvenia Watson probably reinforced these attributes in Nikki, who would manifest them not only in her personal life but also in her poetry and prose.

Giovanni entered Fisk University in September 1960, when she was seventeen years old. Given the political viewpoint in her subsequent writing, it is interesting to note that she supported Barry Goldwater, an extreme right-wing Republican, who was campaigning to be president of the United States. Though Giovanni was conservative and middle class, Fisk (traditionally respected for educating the children of middle-class Blacks) did not appeal to her; she did not get along with the dean of women and left the campus without permission to spend Thanksgiving in Knoxville with her grandmother. She was placed on probation upon her return and was later suspended when her "attitude" did not improve.

Nikki Giovanni returned to Fisk University in 1964, graduating magna cum laude in February 1967 with honors in history. She took part in the Fisk Writers Workshop, directed by the distinguished author John O. Killens, who influenced her writing and her politics. Her change in political consciousness is marked by the fact that she was responsible for getting SNCC reinstated on Fisk's campus. In June of 1967, Giovanni planned the first Cincinnati Black Arts Festival; she helped show the links between art and culture and became a major figure in the movement to foster Black awareness in the city. Giovanni's political activities caused concern in her parents, who saw no professional future in her organizational work. Her response was to enroll in graduate school. She received a Ford Foundation grant and attended the University of Pennsylvania School of Social Work but later entered the School of Fine Arts at Columbia University. As an assistant professor of English, she taught in the SEEK Program at Queens College of the City University of New York.

Nikki Giovanni's work has been criticized as unpredictable and uneven; similar critiques are often also leveled against her as a person. Eugene Redmond's observation that the range of her work represents her rite of passage into womanhood is very important since life is fluid and Giovanni's poetry and prose reflect normal personal and intellectual change. In an interview with Claudia Tate, the editor of *Black Women Writers at Work* (1983), Giovanni says that she does not reread her prose because she does not want to be trapped by what she has previously said. The comment provides partial insight into Giovanni's aesthetic philosophy, since she does not believe that "life is inherently coherent." She continues, "If I never contradict myself then I'm either not thinking or I'm conciliating positions and, therefore, not growing." These thoughts are important clues to the often controversial positions that Giovanni has taken since she first emerged on the literary scene.

Nikki Giovanni's poetic transition from militant revolutionary to a more "balanced" perspective is evident in the poem "Revolutionary Dreams" from her 1970 collection *Re-Creation*, published by Broadside Press. She writes, "i used to dream militant / dreams of taking / over america . . . / i even used to think i'd be the one / to stop the riot and negotiate the peace / then i awoke and dug / that if i dreamed natural / dreams of being a natural / woman doing what a woman / does when she's natural / i would have a revolution." The poem echoes Aretha Franklin's version of the song "Natural Woman," and the sexual implications of Giovanni's words are obvious; yet there is something to be said for the latent political interpretation of the poem: "revolutionizing" oneself before attempting to change the world. Her subsequent volumes of poetry, *My House* (1972), *The Women and the Men* (1972), *Cotton Candy on a Rainy Day* (1978), and *Those Who Ride the Night Winds* (1983), continue the introspective personal tone that began in *Re-Creation*.

Giovanni's volumes of children's poetry are delightful, and her prose works are scrappy, thought-provoking texts that present brilliant observations of the social, cultural, and political scene in contemporary America. *Spin a Soft Black Song: Poems for Children* (1971), *Ego-Tripping and Other Poems for Young People* (1973), and *Vacation Time: Poems for Children* (1980) are collections written by Nikki Giovanni for children. One of the best and most widely known of Giovanni's verses, the title poem in the volume *Ego-Tripping*, begins, "I was born in the congo / I walked to the fertile crescent and built / the sphinx / I designed a pyramid so tough that a star /

that only glows every one hundred years falls / into the center giving divine perfect light / I am bad." The poem continues by celebrating and mythologizing the power of ancient Black people whose civilizations have been misrepresented in history. It ends with these lines: "I am so hip even my errors are correct / I sailed west to reach east and had to round off / the earth as I went. . . . I am so perfect so divine so ethereal so surreal / I cannot be comprehended / except by my permission / I mean . . . I . . . can fly / like a bird in the sky." The theme of flying back to Africa is central to Black folklore, but Giovanni gives it a contemporary spin by telling of African magnificence at a time when Blacks were struggling to know themselves in the context of their African past.

Nikki Giovanni's poetry reflects not only her personal history but also the shifting nature of the Black experience in America. [Schomburg Center]

Gemini: An Extended Autobiographical Statement on My First Twenty-Five Years at Being a Black Poet (1971), composed of autobiographical essays—some previously published—contains much of Giovanni's earliest prose. It provides selective glimpses of the feisty Nikki, including the four year old "protecting" her older sister, Gary, and the young woman giving birth to Tommy. Though the publication of essays on the first twenty-five years of one's life might seem presumptuous, the collection is refreshingly opinionated and honest and was nominated for a National Book Award. Giovanni's importance as a young writer is underscored by two texts that record her conversations with her Black literary foreparents. *A Poetic Equation: Conversations between Nikki Giovanni and Margaret Walker* (1974) and *A Dialogue: James Baldwin and Nikki Giovanni* (1973) are especially valuable not only because of the collaboration with the older writers but also for the extraordinary documentation of the evolution of Black artistic and aesthetic thinking from one generation to another. Nikki Giovanni's most recent collection of essays, *Sacred Cows and Other Edibles* (1988), is full of comfortable, casual observations as well as insightful commentary on the seemingly unchanging nature of social and political conditions in America.

Most interesting, given her life as a writer, Giovanni says, "There will never be a poem that will free mankind." Her belief is that writers preach to the saved, rarely changing people's minds. Giovanni's early writings make excellent sense if we accept her idea that art is potentially dangerous because it is egalitarian. Though her personal and political decisions might not be those of others, she has moved beyond the rhetoric of the 1960s, understanding that militant words are not sufficient to make lasting political change. She reiterates her point: "Writing is not who I am, it's what I do." If readers allow Nikki Giovanni her right to change, given her belief that life itself is fluid and incoherent, they will find her current work an accurate measure of American and Black American life in the last years of the twentieth century.

BIBLIOGRAPHY

American Women Writers: A Critical Reference Guide from Colonial Times to the Present, ed. James Page (1977); *DLB*; Elder, Arlene. "A *MELUS* Interview: Nikki Giovanni," *MELUS: The Journal of the Society for the Study of the Multi-Ethnic Literature of the United States* (Winter 1982); Giddings, Paula. "Nikki Giovanni: Taking a Chance on Feelings." In *Black Women Writers (1950-1980): A Critical Evaluation*, ed. Mari Evans (1984); Giovanni, Nikki. "An Answer to Some Questions on How I Write: In Three Parts." In *Black Women Writers (1950-1980): A Critical Evaluation*, ed. Mari Evans (1984); Giovanni, Nikki, ed. *Night Comes Softly: An Anthology of Black Female Voices* (1970); Harris, William J. "Sweet Essence of Possibility: The Poetry of Nikki Giovanni." In *Black Women Writers (1950-1980): A Critical Evaluation*, ed. Mari Evans (1984); Lee, Don L. *Dynamite Voices I: Black Poets of the 1960s* (1971); Loyd, Dennis. "Contemporary Poets." In *Literature of Tennessee*, ed. Ray Willbanks (1984); Redmond, Eugene. "Festivals and Funerals." In his *Drumvoices: The Mission of Afro-American Poetry, a Critical History* (1976).

DISCOGRAPHY

Truth Is on Its Way, Right-On Records (1971); *Like a Ripple on a Pond*, NikTom (1973); *The Way I Feel*, Atlantic Records (1974); *Legacies*, Folkways Records (1976); *The Reason I Like Chocolate*, Folkways Records (1976); *Cotton Candy on a Rainy Day*, Folkways Records (1978).

CAROLYN MITCHELL

GLEASON, ELIZA ATKINS (1909-)

Eliza Atkins Gleason, librarian and educator, was the first dean of the School of Library Service at Clark Atlanta University (formerly Atlanta University) and the architect of a library education program that trained more than 90 percent of all African-American librarians in the United States. She was born in Winston-Salem, North Carolina, on December 15, 1909, to Simon Green Atkins and Oleona Pegram Atkins.

Following graduation Phi Beta Kappa from Fisk University in 1930, Gleason received a B.S. from the library school of the University of Illinois in 1931. In 1936, she received an M.A. in library science from the University of California at Berkeley. She studied at the University of Chicago Graduate Library School and in 1940 became the first African-American to receive a doctorate in library science. She married Maurice F. Gleason, a physician, in 1937.

Gleason's professional career was distinguished, varied, and productive. Between 1931 and 1936, she held positions at Louisville Municipal College and Fisk University. From 1936 to 1937, she was director of libraries at Talladega College, where she became aware of the lack of public library services for African-Americans throughout the South. Because of this concern, she opened the college library resources to Black citizens in the surrounding communities. Her interest in the availability of public libraries to African-Americans is reflected in her dissertation, "The Southern Negro and the Public Library."

Following her tenure as dean of the School of Library Service at Atlanta University from 1940 to 1946, Gleason moved to Chicago. In 1953, she became head of the reference department of the Wilson Junior College Library. From 1953 to 1954, she was associate professor and head of the reference department of the Chicago Teachers College Library. She returned to library education in 1954 as associate professor of library science at Illinois Teachers College, serving until 1963. From 1964 to 1967, she was assistant librarian at John Crerar Library. She served as professor of library science at the Illinois Institute of Technology from 1967 to 1970, when she became assistant chief librarian in charge of regional centers of the Chicago Public Library. During the 1974-75 academic year, Gleason was professor of library science at Northern Illinois University.

Active in professional associations, Gleason served as the first African-American member on the American Library Association Council (ALA) from 1942 to 1946. In 1964, she received the Fisk University Alumni Award for outstanding accomplishments.

In addition to writing *The Southern Negro and the Public Library: A Study of the Government and Administration of Public Library Service to Negroes in the South* (1941), she authored *A History of the Fisk University Library* (1936) and numerous journal articles.

In the fall of 1978, Gleason was appointed executive director of the Chicago Black United Fund. Retired, she continues to make her home in Chicago.

BIBLIOGRAPHY

Gleason, Eliza Atkins. Manuscript collection, Clark Atlanta University, Atlanta, Georgia; Wedgeworth, Robert, ed. *ALA World Encyclopedia of Library and Information Services* (1980).

ARTHUR C. GUNN

GLENN, LULA MAE HYMES (1917-)

One of Tuskegee Institute's leading track stars of the 1930s, Lula Mae Hymes Glenn was born in Newman, Georgia, on March 5, 1917. She belonged to the era of segregation when even the most outstanding Black women athletes might go virtually unnoticed. With Glenn's participation, Tuskegee became the first Black team to win the National Amateur Athletic Union (NAAU) championship in the first fourteen years of the competition. Years of effort to build up the women's athletic program at Tuskegee under coach Amelia C. Roberts led to the 1937 Tuskegee

victory at the women's track and field championship sponsored by the NAAU. The star of the Trenton, New Jersey, competition was Lula Hymes, who took first place in the long jump with a 17' 8½" jump. She also took second place in the 50-meter dash and second place in the 400-meter relay, along with three other participants.

In 1938, the Tuskegee women's team again won the NAAU women's track and field championship, with Hymes as the high-point winner in the 100-meter dash and the broad jump. In the 1939 nationals, Glenn set a new American record with an 18' 1½" jump in the running broad jump competition. She married Miles Alfonso Glenn that same year.

Glenn was the first all-around star for the Tuskegee women's team and continued to be a leading figure until 1941. In the years since, Tuskegee Institute has continued to field a leading women's team in the track and field competition.

BIBLIOGRAPHY

Ashe, Arthur, Jr. *A Hard Road to Glory: A History of the African-American Athlete, 1919-1945* (1988); *EBA*; Hickok, Ralph. *New Encyclopedia of Sports* (1977); Levy, Gayle. Personal interview (August 4, 1992).

JOHN L. GODWIN

GOLDBERG, WHOOPI (1949-)

Whoopi Goldberg will tell anyone who will listen that she is not a comedienne. Indeed, her talents as an actress are recognized to go far beyond the limits of what that term might seem to imply. Still, if Goldberg's career is historically significant for Black women, it is because she is funny.

Born in 1949 in a New York City housing project, Goldberg has worked hard to keep her real name a secret. She received a Catholic education and started acting at the age of eight at the Helena Rubinstein Children's Theatre at the Hudson Guild. She spent her childhood and adolescence watching old movies and television comedy and then, dropping out of high school, became an active part of the counter-culture during the 1960s. While participating in civil rights marches and demonstrations, she performed in the choruses of *Hair, Jesus Christ Superstar*, and *Pippin*. She was married for a short time and has a daughter from that marriage, Alexandrea Martin.

In 1974, a series of circumstances took Goldberg to San Diego, where she became a founding member of the San Diego Repertory Theatre, joined an

Whoopi Goldberg's glowing humor and humanity have won the name she created a permanent place in entertainment history. She is shown here in the 1986 film Jumpin' Jack Flash. *[Donald Bogle]*

improvisational comedy troupe called Spontaneous Combustion, and created her name. Six years later, with an impressive theatrical and stand-up resume behind her, she moved to Berkeley. There she continued to work on her comedy while supporting herself and her daughter in a variety of jobs—from bricklayer to licensed cosmetician—and sometimes having to depend on public assistance.

In 1983, Goldberg put together an hour-long, one-woman show. It was made up of four characters she had been developing for several years and was called *The Spook Show*. Its telling social satire was informed by a compassion that has since become characteristic of Goldberg. *The Spook Show* opened in Berkeley, went on the road in the United States and Europe, and ended up in New York as part of a workshop series at Dance Theatre Workshop. A popular and critical success, the show was seen by Mike Nichols, who asked to produce it on Broadway.

Goldberg did not immediately take Nichols up on his offer. First, she returned to Berkeley to appear as the great Moms Mabley in *Moms*, a show written by Goldberg and Ellen Sebastian. Then, for the 1984-85 Broadway season, she expanded *The Spook Show* and opened in it at the Lyceum Theatre as *Whoopi Goldberg*. Critical response was mixed. Some reviewers were enthralled by Goldberg's skills and her spirit. Others were frankly uncomplimentary about the quality of her material. Audiences loved it.

Her position was cemented when she was cast in the lead role in the film version of Alice Walker's *The Color Purple* (1985), directed by Steven Spielberg. She received an Academy Award nomination for her performance. Although her next few films were critical and/or box-office failures (*Jumpin' Jack Flash*, 1986; *Burglar* and *Fatal Beauty*, both 1987; *Clara's Heart* and *The Telephone*, 1988; *Homer & Eddie*, 1989), she scored a personal triumph in *Ghost* (1990), winning the Oscar for her supporting role and thereby becoming the first Black actress to win an Oscar since Hattie McDaniel in 1939 for *Gone with the Wind*. She has since appeared in *The Long Walk Home* (1990), *Soapdish* (1991), *Sister Act* (1992), and *Sarafina!* (1992).

Goldberg, who has always been politically aware and active, was a founding member of the Comic Relief benefit shows on cable's Home Box Office, which raise money to assist the homeless. In early 1992, she became the first African-American actor to star in a film shot on location in South Africa. Before she accepted the role—that of a Soweto high-school teacher in a movie version of the South African musical *Sarafina!*, which was a Broadway hit—she sought and received the permission of the African National

Whoopi Goldberg's first film performance, as Celie in Steven Spielberg's adaptation of Alice Walker's Pulitzer Prize novel The Color Purple, *earned her an Academy Award nomination as Best Actress of 1985. [Donald Bogle]*

Congress and, after some conflict, of the Azanian People's Organization.

Although she has done some television work—a short-lived series based on the film *Bagdad Cafe* and a recurring role on *Star Trek: The Next Generation*—Goldberg is best known for her work in motion pictures. There have been other great Black film actresses—Ethel Waters, Dorothy Dandridge, and Ruby Dee, to name only a few—but Goldberg's unique contribution and remarkable talent is her comic voice.

Black women found it once before in Moms Mabley, but it has been rare. The comic, as opposed to the clown, stands up and tells us what she thinks about life, death, politics, taxes, hairstyles, and the human condition. To be successful, the comic must be someone we are willing to hear. Until recently, the general public has not been willing to listen to Black women. Mabley was an exception, and her success was a tribute to her genius. With Goldberg's talents to lead the way, perhaps the rules are changing.

BIBLIOGRAPHY

Collier, Aldore. "Whoopi Goldberg," *Jet* (October 24, 1988); Contreras, Joseph. "Caught in the Crossfire," *Newsweek* (January 20, 1992); *Current Biography* (1985); *Jet*, "Whoopi Goldberg and Jean Stapleton" (April 23, 1990); *NA*; *NBAW*; *WWBA* (1992).

KATHLEEN THOMPSON

GORDON, NORA ANTONIA (1866-1901)

Nora Gordon was the first Spelman Seminary student to go to Africa. Her letters describing her experiences kept Africa alive in the minds of Spelman students who sang "Give a thought to Africa, 'Neath the burning Sun." The song typified a spirit prevalent throughout the institution, that of the duty of African-Americans to help Christianize and civilize their ancestral homeland.

Nora Antonia Gordon was born to former slaves in Columbus, Georgia, on August 25, 1866. In 1882, she entered Spelman Seminary (now Spelman College) in Atlanta, Georgia, and she graduated in 1888. She attended a missionary training institute in London before arriving at the Palabala mission in the Congo Free State (now Zaire) in 1889.

Nora Gordon was one of many brave and dedicated Black women who sacrificed their health and sometimes their lives to serve as missionaries in nineteenth-century Africa. [Sylvia Jacobs]

She was sent out by the Woman's Baptist Foreign Missionary Society of the West (today American Baptist Churches in the U.S.A.). At Palabala Gordon worked with Lulu Fleming. Gordon taught classes in the day and Sunday schools. In a report home Gordon echoed a recurring theme of women missionaries: "We very much need a girls' house. If we can save the women and the girls and have intelligent Christian wives and mothers, the atmosphere of the community will be greatly changed" (Read 1961).

Gordon was transferred to the Lukunga mission station in 1891. There she was in charge of the afternoon school and the printing office, where she set up type for printing the first arithmetic textbook in the local language. In 1893, Gordon took a furlough in the United States. Two years later she married S. C. Gordon of Jamaica and the couple returned to the

Congo under appointment by British Baptists. In 1900, she returned to the United States in poor health and died in Atlanta a year later, in January 1901, only thirty-four years old.

BIBLIOGRAPHY
Baptist Missionary Magazine (1890-1891); "Black Baptists in Mission." International Ministries, American Baptist Churches in the U.S.A. (pamphlet, 1971); Hartshorn, W. N., ed. *An Era of Progress and Promise, 1863-1910* (1910); Read, Florence Matilda. *The Story of Spelman College* (1961); *Woman's Baptist Foreign Missionary Society of the West* (1890-1891).

SYLVIA M. JACOBS

GORDON, ODETTA HOLMES FELIOUS *see* ODETTA

GORHAM, SARAH E. (1832-1894)

In Kissy Street Cemetery in Freetown, Sierra Leone, one tombstone has the following inscription: "She was early impressed that she should go to Africa as a missionary and that her life work should be there. She crossed the ocean five times, and ended her mission on the soil and among the people she so much desired to benefit." This was the message of Sarah Gorham's life.

Sarah E. Gorham was born on December 5, 1832, in Fredericktown, Maryland, or Fredericksburg, Virginia. Little is known of her life before 1880. In that year she visited relatives who had emigrated to Liberia and she spent a year traveling throughout the country preaching and comforting the needy. It was on this trip that she became interested in African mission work.

In 1888, Gorham applied to the African Methodist Episcopal (AME) Church for appointment as a missionary. Gorham, fifty-six years old, became the first woman missionary of the AME Church appointed to a foreign field. Soon after her arrival in Freetown in September of 1888, Gorham traveled to the Magbele mission where she was active in the Allen AME Church and worked among the Temne women and girls. It was at Magbele that she established the Sarah Gorham Mission School, which gave both religious and industrial training.

At the age of fifty-six, Sarah Gorham became the first woman appointed by the African Methodist Episcopal Church to serve as a missionary in Africa or any other foreign country. [Sylvia Jacobs]

In 1891, Gorham traveled to the United States to recuperate and regain her health. She later returned to Sierra Leone. In July 1894, Gorham was bedridden with malaria and died on August 10, 1894.

BIBLIOGRAPHY

Berry, Lewellyn L. *A Century of Missions of the African Methodist Episcopal Church, 1840-1940* (1942); Jacobs, Sylvia M. "Three Afro-American Women: Missionaries in Africa, 1882-1904." In *Women in New Worlds*, ed. Rosemary Skinner Keller, Louise L. Queen, and Hilah F. Thomas (1982); Kinch, Emily C. *West Africa, An Open Door* (1917); Parks, H. B. *Africa, The Problem of the New Century* (1899).

SYLVIA M. JACOBS

GOSPEL MUSIC

Black gospel music originated from slave songs, field hollers, and Black spirituals, which sustained and perpetuated the culture of rural Black Americans and provided a source of strength during the period of enslavement. By the twentieth century, it had evolved into a more emotional and jubilant Black religious music, an urban counterpart of the spiritual and the blues, representing the new freedom of religious, social, and political consciousness of Black Americans. Characterized by full-throated tones, blue notes, syncopation, and a performance style of call-and-response, gospel music elicits hand clapping, foot patting, and the "holy" dance, when the spirit is especially fervent.

One of the first gospel singers was Bessie Jones of the Georgia Sea Islands, who made a direct connection between the nineteenth-century spiritual and the twentieth-century gospel song. Her recording of "Beulah Land" illustrates the slides and turns that have become synonymous with gospel. Sallie Sanders and the blind Sister Arizona Dranes (c. 1905-c. 1960) of the Church of God in Christ were recording gospel as early as 1926. Dranes, singing in a high-pitched, pinched voice, would influence such later singers as Ernestine B. Washington and Alex Bradford. Her 1928 recording of "You Shall Wear a Golden Crown" not only illustrates the spirited singing of the saints, but introduces the piano into gospel. Dranes was followed by another blind singer, Mamie Forehand, who recorded gospel accompanied by her preacher husband on the guitar. Singing in a more bluesy style than Dranes, Forehand inspired Clara Hudmon (1897-c. 1960), known as the "Georgia Peach." Hudmon's dark contralto and refined sense of rhythm took her from her home in Atlanta to the stage of Radio City Music Hall in 1939.

Ernestine Beatrice Washington (1914-1983) of Arkansas was known as the "Song Bird of the East" during the 1940s and 1950s, after moving to New York City. Washington, heavily influenced by Dranes, sang in a voice similar to her mentor's but with bigger tones. Washington was responsible for introducing Gertrude Ward (1901-1981) and her daughters Willa (1922-) and Clara (1924-1973) to New York. Ward was contacted in 1935 by Thomas A. Dorsey (1899-), the "Father of Gospel," on one of his visits to Philadelphia, who suggested that she abandon the "light classics" that the family was singing and adopt the new gospel music he was composing. Clara emerged as the most talented member of the Ward family, playing the piano, teaching the other members their parts, and leading songs in a strong, metallic, alto voice. By 1943 Ward had added the young Marion Williams (1927-) of Miami and the alto Henrietta Waddy (c. 1907-1984) to create the Ward Singers. Through Clara's innovations, the Ward Singers became the leading gospel group of the 1940s and 1950s and was one of the first two gospel artists, with their recording of "Surely, God Is Able," to receive a gold record (for selling 500,000 recordings). Williams remained with the Ward Singers until 1958, when she left to organize her own group, the Stars of Faith, with Kitty Parham, Frances Steadman, and Henrietta Waddy. Still singing, Williams has retained her pure soprano voice and her ability to "growl."

Philadelphia is the home of two other important groups organized in the 1940s: the Angelic Gospel Singers and the Davis Sisters. Margaret Allison (1920-), a native of South Carolina, organized the Angelics in 1944 with her sister Josephine McDowell and two friends, Lucille Shird and Ella Mae Morris. Since their first recording in 1950, of "Touch Me, Lord Jesus," they have remained major proponents of the older style of gospel. The Davis Sisters, organized by the oldest sister, Thelma (1930 1963), in 1945, drew on their Fire Baptized Holiness church background for their music in addition to being one of the early progressive groups, employing harmonies and vocal devices that would not become popular until the 1960s. The soloist for the group was Ruth (1928-1970), called "Baby Sister," who introduced "hard" gospel (straining the voice for spiritual and dramatic effect) into female group singing. Pittsburgh was the home of another Pennsylvania group, the Mary Johnson Davis (1901-1982) Singers, known for their contemplative approach to gospel.

Gospel groups that were organizing in great numbers in the East were paying close attention to gospel activities in Chicago, which had emerged as the founding center of the movement. Before Dorsey decided to sever his relationship with blues luminaries Gertrude "Ma" Rainey and Tampa Red, Mollie Mae Gates and Magnolia Lewis Butts (c. 1885-c. 1949) were introducing gospel to choirs. Gates was the director of the Junior Choir at Metropolitan Community Church in Chicago, and among the singers from her choir who would influence gospel was Eugene Smith (1921-), one of the leaders of the Roberta Martin Singers. Hattie Parker, a member of Chicago's Pace Jubilee Singers, was drawn to the new gospel music and recorded Charles Albert Tindley's (1851-1933) "Stand by Me" in 1933.

There is little doubt that the most important woman in the Chicago gospel movement was the Arkansas native Roberta Evelyn Martin (1907-1969). Singer, pianist, composer, group leader, and music publisher, Martin participated in the transition from folk gospel to the refined, commercial style that is characteristic in the 1990s. She began as the pianist for Dorsey's Junior Gospel Chorus at Pilgrim Baptist Church in 1932 and organized the Martin and Frye Singers in 1933 (with Theodore R. Frye), changing the name to the Roberta Martin Singers in 1935. Possessing a mellow, dark contralto, Martin was equally at home moaning a Baptist hymn or sailing through a jubilee song. She was responsible for introducing Delois Barrett Campbell (1926-) into the gospel world when Barrett was only seventeen years old. Martin joined with Sallie Martin (no relation) in the early 1930s to present one of the first gospel concerts to charge an admission fee (at Chicago's DuSable High School) and thereby participated in the transition from "church" to "concert" gospel. Possessing a huge, rough-sounding alto, Sallie Martin (1895-1988) of Pittfield, Georgia, moved to Chicago in 1929 and joined with Dorsey to organize the National Convention of Gospel Choirs and Choruses in 1933. She traveled throughout the country teaching gospel to soloists and choirs, and earned the title "Mother of Gospel." The singer who was to elevate gospel from a folk music to a refined art was Mahalia Jackson (1911-1972), who came to Chicago from her native New Orleans at the age of sixteen. With her burnished alto, capable of executing both the softest whisper and the loudest wail, Jackson was the second gospel singer to earn a gold record for number of sales, with her recording "Move On Up a Little Higher" in 1950.

Gospel was still being created in the Deep South through such singers as "Mother" Willie Mae Ford Smith (1904-), who would later join with Dorsey and Martin in the gospel choir movement. (These three persons were celebrated in the film *Say Amen, Somebody* in 1982.) The first superstar in gospel, however, was Sister Rosetta Tharpe (c. 1915-1973) of Cotton Plant, Arkansas. With her mother, Katie Bell Nubin (1880-1969), Tharpe traveled the Church of God in Christ circuit, accompanying herself on guitar, before she was signed by Decca Records in 1938. Her light and lyric mezzo-soprano was particularly effective on such recordings as "Strange Things Happening Everyday." She later joined with Marie Knight (1916-) of Sanford, Florida, to record such hits as "Up above My Head" and "He'll Understand and Say, Well Done." Emily Bram, who was originally from Dallas, Texas and then lived in New Orleans, Louisiana, is known for her recording of "I've Been

Blessed and Brought Up." She possessed one of the most powerful voices in gospel.

Dorothy Love Coates (1928-) joined the popular Birmingham, Alabama, group the Original Gospel Harmonettes in the late 1940s, adding a preaching style and hard gospel element to the group. Her compositions "You Must Be Born Again" and "He's Right on Time" are considered gospel standards. The Caravans, a Chicago-based group, was organized in 1952 by Albertina Walker (1930-). During the group's fifteen-year existence, its members included, in addition to Walker, Inez Andrews, who popularized "Mary, Don't You Weep," Cassietta George, Bessie Griffin (1927-1990), remembered for her powerful recording of "Too Close to Heaven," and Shirley Caesar (1938-), who joined the group at age twenty. Caesar emerged in the 1990s as the principal singer of traditional gospel (a style incorporating elements of the Black spiritual and the Baptist lining hymn) and is famous for her rendition of such songs as "Sweeping through the City" and "Faded Roses."

Edna Gallmon Cooke (1918-1967), from Columbia, South Carolina, known as the "Sweetheart of the Potomac," specialized in the "song and sermonette," delivering the first half of a song as a sermon and singing the second half. Her best-known renditions are "Amen" and "Stop Gambler." Pearl Williams Jones (1931-1991) of Washington, D.C., possessed an alto not unlike that of the soul singer Nina Simone, while Sara Jordan Powell of Texas exploited the upper register of her lyric soprano voice. Delois Barrett Campbell joined with her sisters Billie Greenbey and Rhodessa Porter as the Barrett Sisters, bringing close group harmony back into the Chicago mainstream.

In the 1970s, Detroit became one of the principal gospel music centers, boasting such performers as Vanessa Bell Armstrong, Elbernita Clark, leader of the Clark Sisters, and CeCe Winans, of the duo CeCe and BeBe. San Francisco, California, gave the gospel world Tremaine Hawkins (1957-), known for her recording of "Changed," while Baltimore, Maryland, produced Myrna Summers, composer and singer of "God Gave Me a Song."

Although Black women have made the greatest impact on gospel as singers, they have also made contributions in other capacities. There are a number of outstanding women gospel pianists and organists. The gospel piano style was created by Arizona Dranes. Those who have built on her style include Clara Ward, who accompanied her group; Mildred Falls, the longtime accompanist for Mahalia Jackson; Evelyn Stark, pianist for the Original Gospel Harmonettes; Mildred Gay, accompanist for the Gay Sisters; Louise Overall Weaver, organist; and Elbernita Clark, pianist and organist. Roberta Martin was considered the premier gospel pianist and influenced a generation of pianists who were to follow her.

Among important women gospel music composers is Lucie Eddie Campbell (1885-1963), composer of over forty-five gospel songs, including "Touch Me, Lord Jesus" and "He'll Understand and Say, Well Done." Doris Akers (1923-) has a catalog of over 100 songs, including "Lead Me, Guide Me" and "Sweet, Sweet Spirit." Roberta Martin composed over forty songs, Dorothy Love Coates over fifty, and Margaret P. Douroux (1941-) over sixty, including the popular "Give Me a Clean Heart." Several of these composers owned publishing houses for the sale of their songs as well as those of other composers. Among these were Roberta Martin, Sallie Martin, Emma L. Jackson, and Louise Bowles (c. 1884-1949).

Women have also distinguished themselves as gospel choir directors. Mattie Moss Clark (1928-), the mother of the Clark Sisters, is responsible for the reputation of Detroit gospel choirs as the leaders in the field. LuDella Evans Reid has been the gospel choir director at Chicago's Fellowship Baptist Church since its founding, and Myrna Summers has directed choirs in both Baltimore and Memphis.

Important women disc jockeys in gospel have included Mary Mason of Philadelphia, Mary Dee of Baltimore, Mary Holt of Cleveland, June McCray of Miami, and the still popular Irene Joseph Ware, formerly of Mobile, Alabama, and now in Chicago. Managers and agents of gospel groups have included Lillian Cumber of Herald Attractions; Ruth Bowen, who also managed Dinah Washington; and Gertrude Ward, who managed her own group as well as other Philadelphia gospel singers. Vivian Bracken is the sole female owner of a record company and label, VeeJay Records of Chicago, which produced records by the most popular gospel singers of the 1950s and 1960s.

A small group of women scholars is dedicated to the study of gospel music. Among these are Pearl Williams Jones, Irene V. Jackson Brown, Joan Hillsman, author of *The Progress of Gospel Music* (1977), Bernice Johnson Reagon, Mellonnee Burnim, and Portia Maultsby.

BIBLIOGRAPHY

Baker, Barbara Wesley. "Black Gospel Music Styles," Ph.D. diss. (1978); Boyer, Horace Clarence. "Black Gospel Music." In *The New Grove Dictionary of American Music*, ed. H. Wiley Hitchcock and Stanley Sadie (1986); Burnim,

Mellonnee. "The Black Gospel Music Tradition: Symbols of Ethnicity," Ph.D. diss. (1977); Goreau, Laurraine. *Just Mahalia, Baby* (1975); Heilbut, Anthony. *The Gospel Sound—Good News and Bad Times* (1985); Jackson, Irene V. *Afro-American Religious Music—a Bibliography and Catalogue of Gospel Music* (1979); Oliver, Paul. *Songsters and Saints—Vocal Traditions on Race Records* (1984); Southern, Eileen. *The Music of Black Americans—a History* (1983); Walker, Wyatt Tee. *Somebody's Calling My Name: Black Sacred Music and Social Change* (1919).

DISCOGRAPHY

For discographies, see Anderson, Robert. *Gospel Music Encyclopedia* (1979); Scott, Frank. *The Down Home Guide to the Blues* (1991).

HORACE CLARENCE BOYER

GRAHAM, SHIRLEY *see* DU BOIS, SHIRLEY GRAHAM

GRANSON, MILLA (b. c. 1800)

Although Milla Granson was born a slave around 1800 in Kentucky, she became one of Black America's early pioneers of education. Teaching school at midnight, Granson risked her life to educate hundreds of Black children and adults in Kentucky and Mississippi.

Granson's interest in education began early. In Kentucky she learned firsthand the value of education. Impressed by the knowledge and power that white people possessed, Granson persuaded her master's children to teach her to read and write because she believed that education was the passage to freedom. Having acquired some rudimentary skills, Granson, with her master's permission, taught other slaves to read and write. With Granson's help many slaves wrote their own passes to freedom. Granson, however, remained a slave and on her master's death was sold to a plantation owner in Mississippi.

In Mississippi, Granson experienced hardships. Because she had been a house slave in Kentucky, she was unfamiliar with fieldwork and could rarely complete her assigned day's work in the Mississippi plantation fields. Consequently, she was beaten. Then, due to ailing health, Granson was made a house servant.

Granson's reassignment created the opportunity for the Black community on this Mississippi plantation to be educated. With more of her time available,

she initiated a teaching project in one of the small cabins in the back alley. Granson taught classes from midnight to two o'clock in the morning. When she had educated one group of students to the best of her ability, she graduated them and enrolled another group. Eventually, Granson's efforts led to the implementation of a Mississippi law which made it legal for slaves to teach slaves. To educate more slaves, Granson opened a Sabbath school for those who could not attend the midnight classes.

Although it is not clear when Granson died or whether she married, gave birth, or adopted a religious affiliation, it is apparent that she made a significant contribution to Black America. As one of the pioneers of Black education, Granson recognized the importance of self-help and through community effort and cooperation, she made a difference in the lives of Black people in Kentucky and Mississippi during slavery.

BIBLIOGRAPHY

Dannett, Sylvia G. L. *Profiles of Negro Womanhood, 1619-1900* (1964); Haviland, Laura S. *The Anti-Slavery Crusade in America: A Woman's Life-Work* ([1889] 1969); Spradling, Mary Mace, ed. *In Black and White* (1980).

VALERIE GRIM

GRANVILLE, EVELYN BOYD (1924-)

"I ... have had a very rich life. I have been blessed with a fine family, an excellent education, many friends ... and last, but by no means least, a happy (second) marriage." One of the first two Black women to earn a Ph.D. in mathematics (the other is Marjorie Lee Browne), Evelyn Boyd Granville's pioneering career and warm personality have inspired many.

She was born Evelyn Boyd on May 1, 1924, to William and Julia Walker Boyd in Washington, D.C. She and her older sister were raised primarily by their mother and their mother's twin sister, Louise Walker. After graduating from Dunbar High School in Washington, D.C., she won a partial scholarship to Smith College. She was able to afford her college education by living in a cooperative, by working summers at the National Bureau of Standards, and with financial help from her mother and aunt. In 1945, she graduated summa cum laude and was elected to Phi Beta Kappa.

She won awards for graduate study at Yale University, including a Smith College fellowship, a Julius

Rosenwald fellowship, and an Atomic Energy Commission fellowship. In 1949, she received her doctorate with a specialty in functional analysis, and she was elected to the scientific honorary society, Sigma Xi.

Although her advisor at Yale was a former president of the American Mathematical Society and her academic credentials were impeccable, she could not find a university with a Ph.D. program that would hire her. She taught for two years at Fisk University, inspiring at least two younger women (Etta Falconer and Vivienne Malone Mayes) to obtain Ph.D.s in mathematics. In 1952, she became an applied mathematician at the Diamond Ordnance Fuze Laboratories, and in 1956 she joined IBM to work on the formulation of orbit computations and computer procedures for the Project Vanguard and Project Mercury space probes.

She then participated in research studies on the methods of orbit computation with the Computation and Data Reduction Center of the U.S. Space Technology Laboratories. Later she became a research

Space beckoned mathematician Evelyn Boyd Granville as she worked on orbit computations and computer procedures for Project Vanguard and Project Mercury. [Patricia Kenschaft]

specialist in celestial mechanics, trajectory and orbit computation, numerical analysis, and digital computer techniques for Apollo engineers at the North American Aviation Space and Information Systems Division, followed by four more years with IBM as a senior mathematician.

In 1967, she joined the faculty of California State University in Los Angeles, from which she retired as a full professor in 1984. She and her husband bought a sixteen-acre farm in Texas, where they raised chickens. From 1985 to 1988, she taught mathematics and computer science full time at Texas College in Tyler. In 1990, she was appointed to the Sam A. Lindsey Chair at the University of Texas at Tyler and is currently a visiting professor at this institution.

Evelyn Boyd Granville was a member of the U.S. Civil Service Panel of Examiners of the Department of Commerce (1954-56); the psychology examining committee of the Board of Medical Examiners of the State of California (1963-70); an advisory committee of the National Defense Education Act Title IV Graduate Fellowship Program of the Office of Education (1966-69); and the board of trustees of the Center for the Improvement of Mathematics Education in San Diego (1975-79). She has been active in the National Council of Teachers of Mathematics and the California Mathematics Council. She was president of the Beverly Hills branch of the American Association of University Women from 1968 to 1970. In 1989, she became the first Black woman mathematician to receive an honorary doctorate when Smith College, her undergraduate alma mater, bestowed one on her.

BIBLIOGRAPHY

Dannett, Sylvia G. L. *Profiles of Negro Womanhood* (1966); Granville, Evelyn Boyd and Jason Frand. *Theory and Application of Mathematics for Teachers* (1975); Kenschaft, Patricia. "Evelyn Boyd Granville." In *Women of Mathematics: A Biobibliographic Sourcebook*, ed. Louise Grinstein and Paul Campbell (1987).

PATRICIA CLARK KENSCHAFT

GREENFIELD, ELIZABETH TAYLOR (c. 1819-1876)

They called her "The Black Swan" and an "African nightingale." She was courted by high society on both sides of the Atlantic. Born into slavery, she sang in a command performance before the Queen of England.

"The Black Swan," Elizabeth Taylor Greenfield, gave a command performance before Queen Victoria early in her career, astonishing Her Majesty with a range of more than three octaves. [Schomburg Center]

Elizabeth Taylor Greenfield, the first African-American musician to earn a reputation in both the United States and Britain, was born c. 1819 in Natchez, Mississippi, to a family named Taylor, who were slaves on the estate of Mrs. Holliday Greenfield. When Elizabeth was only a year old, Mrs. Greenfield, acting on her beliefs as a Quaker, manumitted the child's parents and sent them to Liberia; she took Elizabeth with her to Philadelphia. The child stayed with Mrs. Greenfield until she was eight, and then went to live with her own sister, Mary Parker. When she was in her late teens, she went back to Mrs. Greenfield as a companion.

The young woman's remarkable voice was noticed early by a neighbor—a Miss Price—who gave her musical instruction. The neighbor's father, Dr. Price, heard them practicing and decided that Mrs. Greenfield should know of her ward's gift. Elizabeth Greenfield was concerned that the older woman would disapprove of the secular music she was singing. How-

ever, Mrs. Greenfield encouraged the young singer's talent and, while a young woman, Elizabeth Greenfield began performing as a soloist at private parties. In 1844, Mrs. Greenfield died, leaving her companion an income of $100 a year for life. However, the will was contested, and Greenfield's inheritance was exhausted in lawyer's fees.

In about 1849, one of Philadelphia's leading musicians hired Greenfield to perform in Baltimore, where she advertised as a music teacher. The next stage of her life took place in Buffalo, New York, where she went either to hear Jenny Lind or to make contact with friends of Mrs. Greenfield's. She saved her money to make the journey and, on the boat, encountered Mrs. H. B. Potter. Potter, hearing her sing, invited Greenfield to her mansion. There she performed and was heard by a number of influential people. A group of them sponsored her in a series of concerts for the Buffalo Music Association. It was this series that brought Greenfield to the attention of the press. She was an immediate sensation, receiving the nickname that remained hers throughout her career—"The Black Swan." Soon she was giving concerts in New York City, Boston, and Toronto. Within a few years she had sung in all of the free states.

Though her voice was universally praised, her experiences were not always pleasant. She was criticized for her lack of training by reviewers whose racist bias was undisguised. She sang in halls to which other African-Americans were denied admittance. In New York, in 1853, she debuted at Metropolitan Hall, which held an audience of four thousand, white patrons only. Because of a threat that the building would be burned if she appeared, police were stationed in the hall during the concert. After the concert, Greenfield apologized to her own people for their exclusion from the performance and gave a concert to benefit the Home of Aged Colored Persons and the Colored Orphan Asylum.

Greenfield then went to England to perform, but her arrangements fell through. So she took matters into her own hands again and sought out Harriet Beecher Stowe, who was in London at the time. Stowe listened to her sing and was amazed by Greenfield's range, which spanned more than three octaves. Stowe was interested enough in Greenfield's artistry that she introduced the singer to the Duchess of Sutherland, who took her to Sir George Smart, the queen's musician. Smart was charmed and presented Greenfield in a concert at Stafford House.

This concert led to others, in London and in the provinces. Greenfield also studied extensively with Smart and attended concerts by other musicians. When the time came for her to return to the United States, Smart and the Duchess of Sutherland went to Queen Victoria, who arranged a command performance at Buckingham Palace on May 10, 1854. The queen gave Greenfield £20 for the performance, which helped to pay her way back to her own country.

Back in the United States, Greenfield went on tour again, including in her performance a well-known tenor, Thomas J. Bowers. The reception to her performances was again mixed. Certainly, Greenfield's remarkable range was something of a novelty. She amazed her audiences with vocal feats such as singing "Old Folks at Home" as a soprano and then as a baritone. Still, the reviews of her performances make it clear that she had much more than novelty appeal. Critics praised her emotional power and the weight and sweetness of her voice. Audiences seem to have responded also to her intelligence and personality. She was frequently compared to Jenny Lind. If she was not the best Black singer of the period—and many have said she was not—she was probably the most ambitious, and her accomplishments broke new ground for Black musicians. She also organized a troupe of Black musicians who performed in Washington, D.C., in 1862 and in Philadelphia in 1866.

In July of 1854, Greenfield returned to New York to perform and then to Philadelphia to live. She did not tour again until 1863. After that tour, she went back to teaching. She also sang for a variety of social causes, giving dozens of benefits for orphans, among others. She died in Philadelphia on March 31, 1876.

BIBLIOGRAPHY

CBWA; DANB; EBA; NAW; NBAW.

KATHLEEN THOMPSON

GREENFIELD, ELOISE (1929-)

Says Eloise Greenfield: "When I'm carrying a story around in my head, I feel as if I'm holding my head funny. Sometimes I want to explain to people on the street that I'm just trying to keep the words from spilling out until I get to a quiet place with pen and paper" (Holtze 1983). As a child Greenfield did not like to write, so she carried stories around in her head for many years before she actually began to write them down.

Eloise Greenfield was born on May 17, 1929, in Parmele, North Carolina, to Weston W. Little and Lessie Jones Little. They moved to Washington, D.C.,

when Little was only a few months old. She was educated at Miner Teachers College (1946-49). One of her first jobs was as a clerk-typist for the U.S. Patent Office (1949-56). It was partly because of her boredom with this job that she first began to write short stories. She continued at the Patent Office until 1960 as a supervisory patent assistant. From 1963 to 1964 she was a staff member of the Unemployment Compensation Board. She then went to work as a secretary, case-control technician, and administrative assistant for various employers from 1964 to 1968.

Then Greenfield began to work for the District of Columbia Black Writers' Workshop. She served as director of adult fiction (1971-73) and as director of children's literature (1973-74). In 1973, and again from 1985 to 1986, she was a writer-in-residence for the District of Columbia Commission on the Arts. It was during the 1970s that her love of reading and of words developed into a love of writing. *Bubbles*, her first book, was published in 1972. *Sister* appeared in 1974. Her first book of poems, *Honey, I Love and Other Love Poems* was published in 1978 and was recorded with music in 1982.

Greenfield's writing takes many forms: poetry, picture books, recordings, and biographies. She has collaborated with all of the most celebrated African-American illustrators, including Tom Feelings, Leo and Diane Dillon, Carole Byard, and John Steptoe. She writes about some of the most inspirational African-American historical figures: Paul Robeson, Rosa Parks, and Mary McLeod Bethune. Her commitment stems from her belief that "a true history must be the concern of every Black writer. It is necessary for Black children to have a true knowledge of their past and present, in order that they may develop an informed sense of direction for their future" (*Children's Literature Review* 1982).

Reviewers of children's literature have sometimes disagreed on the quality of Greenfield's writing. For example, *Childtimes: A Three-Generation Memoir* (the first of two books written with her mother) received almost universal acclaim. In contrast, some sharply criticized *She Come Bringing Me That Little Baby Girl* as propagating socially taught sexist behavior. More often than not, however, the world of children's literature has recognized the excellence of Eloise Greenfield's writing. She received the Carter G. Woodson Award for *Rosa Parks* in 1974. Despite the controversy it generated, *She Come Bringing Me That Little Baby Girl* won the Irma Simonton Black Award in 1974. *Me and Neesie* was named an American Library Association Notable Book of 1975. The same honor was given to *Honey, I Love* in 1978. In 1976,

Paul Robeson was recognized with the Jane Addams Children's Book Award. Greenfield's entire body of work has been celebrated formally, too, by the Council on Interracial Books for Children (1975), the District of Columbia Association of School Librarians (1977), and Celebrations in Learning (1977).

African-American children's literature is an important subcategory of children's literature in general. One of the most prestigious annual honors bestowed upon a Black writer and Black illustrator is the Coretta Scott King Award (awarded by the American Library Association). Greenfield has garnered this honor twice, for *Africa Dream* in 1978 and for *Nathaniel Talking* in 1990. *Nathaniel* is most notable because it is written largely in the form of "rap" lyrics, demonstrating Greenfield's concern with interpreting for children not only the past but also the present.

Eloise Greenfield married Robert Greenfield in 1950. They have one son, Steve, and one daughter, Monica. Greenfield has stated that her family and her efforts against racism are the two most important concerns in her life. Yet, in a very tangible way, she has adopted all Black children as her family by choosing to address racism through writing books especially for them. She is arguably the foremost African-American children's poet. She has secured her place in the history of African-American children's literature by writing consistently and truthfully about history, about social issues, and, perhaps most important, about family.

BIBLIOGRAPHY

CA; *Children's Literature Review* (1982); Holtze, Sally Holmes, ed. *Fifth Books of Junior Authors and Illustrators* (1983); Commire, Anne, ed. *Something about the Author* (1980); Kirkpatrick, D. L., ed. *Twentieth Century Children's Writers* (1983).

WORKS BY ELOISE GREENFIELD

Bubbles (1972); *Rosa Parks*. Illus. Eric Marlow (1973); *Sister*. Illus. Moneta Barnett (1974); *She Come Bringing Me That Little Baby Girl*. Illus. John Steptoe (1974); *Me and Neesie*. Illus. Moneta Barnett (1975); *Paul Robeson*. Illus. George Ford (1975); *Africa Dream*. Illus. Carole Byard (1977); *Mary McLeod Bethune*. Illus. Jerry Pinkney (1977); *Honey, I Love and Other Love Poems*. Illus. Leo and Diane Dillon (1978); *Childtimes: A Three-Generation Memoir* with Lessie Jones Little. Illus. Jerry Pinkney (1979); *Grandmama's Joy*. Illus. Carole Byard (1980); *Alesia* with Alesia Revis. Illus. George Ford, photographs by Sandra Turner Bond (1981); *Daydreamers*. Illus. Tom Feelings (1981); *Nathaniel Talking*. Illus. Jan Spivey Gilchrist (1988); *Night on Neighborhood Street* (1991).

DIANNE JOHNSON-FEELINGS

GRIER, ELIZA ANNA (1864-1902)

Eliza Anna Grier was born in North Carolina in July 1864. A former slave, she was the first Black woman physician licensed to practice medicine in the state of Georgia. In 1884, she enrolled in the Normal Course at Fisk University, in Nashville, Tennessee. Because of financial difficulties it took her seven years to complete her degree.

Following her graduation from Fisk University in 1891, Grier taught school for one year at the Paine Normal School and Industrial Institute (now Paine College) in Augusta, Georgia. In 1893, she matriculated at the Woman's Medical College of Pennsylvania. During the 1894-95 session she received a $100 stipend to cover some of her medical school costs. She graduated from the Woman's Medical College in 1897.

Grier set up practice in Greenville, South Carolina. Letters written by Grier in 1901 alluded to the fact that her practice was not very successful and that she was in need of financial assistance. She died of a stroke on April 14, 1902. She is buried in Charlotte, North Carolina.

Born into slavery, Eliza Anna Grier triumphed to become the first Black woman licensed to practice medicine in the state of Georgia. [Medical College of Pennsylvania]

BIBLIOGRAPHY

Eliza Grier file. Archives and Special Collections on Women in Medicine, Medical College of Pennsylvania, Philadelphia.

BRENDA GALLOWAY-WRIGHT

GRIFFIN, BESSIE (1922-1989)

"I'm a gospel singer in the old mold . . . traditional. I sing gospel songs that are taken from the hymnal, from the old *Gospel Pearl* book, gospel music that was started in the thirties." Regardless of where and for whom she sang, Bessie Griffin never strayed from her belief that "gospel was the good news that you did through your feelings" (Griffin 1987).

Born Arlette B. Broil on July 6, 1922, to Enoch Broil and Victoria Walker Broil in New Orleans, Louisiana, Bessie Griffin died April 10, 1989, in Los Angeles. She was educated in the Arlean Parish schools of Louisiana and was a graduate of McDonough Number 35 Senior High School. After her first marriage, to Willie Griffin, which ended after two years, she married Spencer James Jackson, Sr. They had one son, Spencer James Jackson, Jr., a railroad detective who died in New Orleans in 1981.

Because her mother died when she was five years old, Griffin was raised by her "grandmother" (actually her mother's cousin), Lucy Narcisse, from whom she learned to sing. Growing up in New Orleans, she sang in church choirs and various gospel singing groups (e.g., the Brent Quillon Four Gospel Singers and the Southern Harps). In 1951, Mahalia Jackson invited Griffin to Chicago to sing at Jackson's anniversary celebration. In 1953, she joined the Caravans, a female gospel group founded by Albertina Walker, and traveled with them for a year before settling in Chicago. Griffin left Chicago in 1955 and toured with W. Herbert Brewster, Jr., the son of gospel songwriter W. Herbert Brewster, Sr. Later she returned to New Orleans where she became the host of her own radio program and was crowned "Queen of the South."

Griffin first visited Los Angeles in June 1956 when she was invited to be one of the featured artists in a gospel festival ("Cavalcade of Gospel Singers") organized by the Simmons and Akers Singers who were associated with Eugene D. Smallwood's Opportunity Baptist Church. Griffin did not permanently move to Los Angeles until the late 1950s when she was invited by her agent, record producer Robert "Bumps" Blackwell, who made arrangements for her

Bessie Griffin, "Queen of the Los Angeles Gospel Singers," not only performed in churches and auditoriums, but also took gospel music into nightclubs with the Gospel Pearls, formed in 1950. [J. C. DjeDje]

to star in the musical *Portraits in Bronze*. Upon her arrival, she quickly became an important gospel figure in the Los Angeles area, performing in churches and auditoriums. When Griffin joined the Gospel Pearls, a Los Angeles-based gospel group formed in 1950, much attention was given to them because of their nightclub appearances. Taking gospel music into clubs offered Griffin the opportunity to make a unique contribution to her profession and it distinguished her from gospel singer Mahalia Jackson, to whom she was often compared. Both Griffin and Jackson were born in New Orleans, they had similar performance styles, and it was Jackson who introduced Griffin to the professional world of gospel music; but Jackson would never have performed in nightclubs.

Griffin recorded gospels, spirituals, and hymns. Some of her favorite songs included "The Days Are Passed and Gone," "It's Real," "Soon-ah Will Be Done with the Trouble of the World," "Sometimes I

Feel Like a Motherless Chile," and "Come Ye Disconsolate." In addition to worldwide concert tours and television and Broadway appearances, Griffin received many commendations and accolades for her achievements in gospel music, as well as a Grammy nomination. As a result, she has been honored with such titles as "Good Queen Bess," the "Thunderbolt of Gospel Singing," and the "Queen of the Los Angeles Gospel Singers."

BIBLIOGRAPHY

Broughton, Viv. *Black Gospel: An Illustrated History of the Gospel Sound* (1985); Brown, Clarence. "Bessie Griffin," *Lyric: A Magazine of the Fine Arts* (May 1976); DjeDje, Jacqueline Cogdell. "A Historical Overview of Black Gospel Music in Los Angeles," *Black Music Research Bulletin* (Spring 1988), and "Gospel Music in the Los Angeles Black Community: A Historical Overview," *Black Music Research Journal* (Spring 1989); Griffin, Bessie. Interview (October 1, 1987); Heilbut, Tony. *The Gospel Sound: Good News and Bad Times* (1975).

DISCOGRAPHY

Bessie Griffin and the Gospel Pearls, Portraits in Bronze: Excerpts from Robert "Bumps" Blackwell's Portraits in Bronze, Liberty Premiere LMM 13002 (1960); *The Fabulous Bessie Griffin and the Gospel Pearls*, Epic Records BN 26065 (1963); *Oh Glory Halleluia, the Sensational Gospel Singer, Bessie Griffin*, Epic Records BN 26101, LN 24101 (1964); *Bessie Griffin: It Takes a Lot of Love*, Decca Records DL 74947 (1967); *Bessie Griffin Live at the Montreux Blues Festival*, Nashboro Stereo 7115 (1972); *Bessie Griffin: Testimony*, Nashboro Stereo 7125 (1973); *Bessie Griffin Live*, AVI Gospel Records 50013 (1981); *Even Me: Four Decades of Recordings by Bessie Griffin*, Spirit Feel Records (1989); *All of My Life*, Bud Records BR 1004; *Bessie Griffin: Gospel Soul*, Sunset Records SUM-1195; *Bessie Griffin: Negro Spirituals, Gospel Songs, Live in Europe*, Carriere Record Company CA 641; *Bessie Griffin and the Consolaters: Heaven*, Specialty Records; *The Gospel Pearls Starring Bessie Griffin*, Epic Records.

JACQUELINE COGDELL DJEDJE

GRIMKÉ, ANGELINA WELD (1880-1958)

In Angelina Weld Grimké's poem "Under the Days," the persona asks who will ever find her because she is being crushed, covered, and smothered under ceaseless black, gray, and white days. Perhaps this poem best expresses Grimké's personal life, which was filled with feelings of rejection, alienation, and suppression. Although recent critics label Grimké as neurotic and paranoid, a close look at her life reveals a delicate and highly sensitive woman who felt pain more acutely than most. Her sensitivity found its way into her literary works. Grimké's play *Rachel* (1916), which was the first staged play by an African-American woman, illustrates the author's keen awareness that Black Americans are victimized.

Playwright, poet, and short-story writer Angelina Weld Grimké was born in Boston on February 27, 1880, to Archibald Henry and Sarah Stanley Grimké. Her father was from a prominent biracial family, and her mother was white. Three years after Grimké was born, her mother left her father and took Angelina with her. Four years later, she returned the seven year old to her father and never saw her again.

Grimké spent much of her childhood as the privileged child of Archibald Grimké, a nationally known lawyer and the executive director of the National Association for the Advancement of Colored People (NAACP). Under the tutelage of her white great-aunt, Angelina Grimké Weld, a noted abolitionist and suffragist, Grimké attended some of the finest schools in Massachusetts, including Carleton Academy in Ashburnham. A graduate of Boston Normal School of Gymnastics in 1902, Grimké moved to Washington, D.C., where she taught English at Armstrong Manual Training School.

In 1916, she transferred to Dunbar High School, where she developed close relationships with a host of Black women poets and playwrights who taught at the school. Grimké wrote and staged *Rachel* in her first year at Dunbar. Produced by the NAACP on March 3 and 4, 1916, at the Myrtill Miner Normal School, the play centers on the numerous humiliations that African-Americans suffer, ranging from lynchings to restricted job opportunities. Rachel, the play's heroine, vows never to bring Black children into the world because of the suffering they would have to endure. *Rachel* marked the beginning of staged or produced Black theater. Prior to *Rachel*, plays had been written without staging in mind, as was the case with William Wells Brown's costume dramas, which he read to white abolitionists. Grimké had responded to W.E.B. Du Bois's call for Black theater by, for, and near Black people.

Although Grimké's plays and fiction show evidence of race consciousness, the majority of her poems reflect a romantic influence, as does the poetry of many of her contemporaries, including Jessie Fauset, Georgia Douglas Johnson, Countee Cullen, and William Stanley Braithwaite. Her poems often contain images of isolation, no doubt the result of being abandoned by her mother.

Rachel, *by Angelina Grimké, was the first play by a Black writer to receive a fully staged professional production. Its heroine vows not to bring children into a world of racism and bigotry.* [Moorland-Spingarn]

Some of Grimké's unpublished poetry, mostly love poems, alludes to her lesbianism and resonates with signs of rejection, despair, and thoughts of death. She chose to suppress her emotions, with the possible exception of a love affair with poet, playwright, and co-worker at Dunbar High School, Mary Burrill, and her creativity was stifled long before she died.

BIBLIOGRAPHY

*AAW*1; Hatch, James V. and Ted Shine, eds. *Black Theater USA: Forty-Five Plays by Black Americans, 1847-1974* (1974); Hull, Gloria T. *Color, Sex, and Poetry: Three Women of the Harlem Renaissance* (1987), and " 'Under the Days': The Buried Life and Poetry of Angelina Weld Grimké," *Conditions: Five* (1979).

ELIZABETH BROWN-GUILLORY

GRIMKÉ, CHARLOTTE L. FORTEN (1837-1914)

Antislavery poet, educator, civil rights advocate, and minister's wife Charlotte L. Forten Grimké was a member of the prominent, activist Forten-Purvis family of nineteenth-century Philadelphia. Forten joined the antislavery crusade while attending school in Salem, Massachusetts. On June 4, 1854, she recorded a distressing event in her diary. The previous week, a Black newcomer to the city had been arrested and tried as a fugitive slave. The abolitionist community mounted a vigorous defense, but to no avail. The unfortunate man was returned to the South in chains. Deeply affected by this human tragedy, Forten renewed her dedication to the emancipation cause. Referencing these events, she wrote, "yet they shall be fresh incentive to more earnest study, to aid me in fitting myself for laboring in a holy cause, for enabling me to do much toward changing the condition of my oppressed and suffering people."

Charlotte Forten's grandfather was James Forten, Sr., a wealthy Philadelphia sailmaker and abolitionist, and Charlotte's parents, Robert Bridges Forten and Mary Woods Forten, were both activists. Besides his membership in several antislavery organizations, Robert Forten worked with his brother-in-law, Robert Purvis, on the Philadelphia Vigilant Committee, one link in the slave assistance network. When she died in 1840, Mary Woods Forten was a member of the Philadelphia Female Anti-Slavery Society.

Sent to Salem by her father to complete her education, Forten in New England led a life centered around school and antislavery activities. Higginson Grammar School on Beckford Street provided a fertile learning ground for the budding abolitionist. She was the only nonwhite student of 200 enrolled in 1854. Mary Shepard, the school's principal, and her three assistants stressed intellectual development through critical analysis. The Higginson curriculum consisted of history, geography, drawing, and cartography. When she completed her studies at Higginson, Charlotte enrolled in the Normal School at Salem. Beyond her classroom studies, she read many books, including some classics by Shakespeare and Milton and works by contemporary authors, Margaret Fuller and William Wordsworth.

Charlotte Forten's antislavery labors were extensive. As a member of the Salem Female Anti-Slavery Society, she attended sewing circles where the group prepared items for the annual fund-raising bazaars. She frequently attended antislavery lectures in Salem and sometimes traveled to nearby Haverhill or Boston to hear speakers such as Ralph Waldo Emerson, Henry Ward Beecher, Theodore Parker, and U.S. Senator Charles Sumner. Although she found Sumner to be a gifted speaker, she disagreed with his reverence for a constitution that condoned slavery.

Forten met many famous people as a boarder at the home of Black abolitionists John and Amy Remond. On May 31, 1854, she dined with *Liberator* editor William Lloyd Garrison, and his wife. The Garrisons extended an invitation for Charlotte Forten to visit them. On other occasions she met Wendell Phillips, the renowned antislavery orator, and antislavery activists Maria Weston Chapman and William Wells Brown.

During June 1856, dwindling finances threatened to curtail Forten's normal school studies. She accepted a teaching position at Epes Grammar School for a salary of $200 per year. Forten remained at Epes for two years before a reoccurring bout of tuberculosis forced her resignation and return to Philadelphia. Salem school officials promised to reassign her when her health permitted.

Charlotte Forten, like her aunt, Sarah Forten Purvis, was a gifted poet. When she was in Salem, her creative works began to appear in antislavery periodicals, including the *Liberator*, *National Anti-Slavery Standard*, and Bishop Daniel Payne's *Anglo African* magazine. Although the majority of her poems contained antislavery themes, she published works on a variety of subjects. Her poem "Wind among the Poplars" told the tragic story of young lovers. "Glimpses of New England" appeared in the *National Anti-Slavery Standard* in June 1858, and a choir sang her poem "Red, White, and Blue" at a Boston ceremony honoring Crispus Attucks and other heroes of the Boston Massacre.

With the outbreak of the Civil War, Charlotte Forten looked for a way to accelerate the end of slavery. The Port Royal Project in South Carolina gave her that opportunity. By spring 1862, Union forces had routed the Confederates from their stronghold on the South Carolina Sea Islands near Charleston. The planter class on those islands, most of whom were Confederate sympathizers, abandoned their homes and fled to the mainland. Thousands of slaves and a valuable cotton crop were left behind. Salmon Chase, Lincoln's secretary of the treasury, convinced the president that northern teachers and agriculture superintendents should be sent to prepare the Black population for citizenship. Forten applied for a teaching post. After some delay, on October 21, 1862, she received a note from James Miller McKim announcing her assignment with Philadelphia's Port

Royal Commission. She was the first Black teacher hired for the Sea Islands mission.

Charlotte Forten's two-year contribution to the project was substantial. She joined Laura M. Towne and Ellen Murray, two Philadelphia teachers, at a school held in the Central Baptist Church on St. Helena Island. The three women dedicated themselves to the enormous task at hand. From noon until three o'clock nearly one hundred students attended the school. Classes resumed in the evening when adults hurried from their daytime labors for tutoring in reading and spelling. Despite the hard work and long hours, Forten enjoyed her job. She hoped to inspire her students with lessons about Black liberators and heroes, like Haitian liberator Toussaint L'Ouverture. For their Christmas program in 1862, Forten taught the students a song written especially for them by New England poet John Greenleaf Whittier.

As an author, Charlotte Forten took the opportunity to record her Sea Islands experiences and observations for the northern reading public. Her essays entitled "Life on the Sea Islands," published in the May and June 1864 issues of *Atlantic Monthly*, provided a rare glimpse of the newly freed Black people's character and fitness for citizenship. Many northerners were skeptical that they could bridge the gap from slavery to freedom. Forten's work presented a firsthand account of a people who were eager to work, eager to learn, and eager to enjoy both the rights and the responsibilities of citizenship.

After the war, Forten held a variety of posts. During the late 1860s, as secretary of the Freedmen's Relief Association in Boston, she recruited teachers. From 1871 to 1872, she assisted Black educator Richard T. Greener, who was the principal of Sumner High School in Washington, D.C. Then, on July 3, 1873, the *New National Era and Citizen* reported Forten's new position as a clerk at the U.S. Treasury Department. She was one of fifteen selected out of a field of almost 500 candidates.

On December 19, 1878, at the age of forty-one, Charlotte Forten wed Francis J. Grimké, a promising Presbyterian minister and graduate of Pennsylvania's Lincoln University and the Princeton Theological Seminary. The major tragedy to mar their thirty-six years of married life was the death of their infant daughter, Theodora Cornelia, in June 1880. By all accounts Charlotte Grimké enjoyed her duties as a minister's wife. From 1885 until 1889, her husband served as pastor of the Laura Street Presbyterian Church in Jacksonville, Florida. Charlotte Grimké taught a Sunday school class for girls and organized a women's missionary group. In January 1889, the couple returned to Washington, D.C., where Francis Grimké assumed the pastorship of the Fifteenth Street Presbyterian Church.

True to her family's activist legacy, Charlotte Forten Grimké was a perennial advocate of Black civil rights. In October 1889, she responded to an *Evangelist* editorial entitled "Relations of Blacks and Whites: Is There a Color Line in New England?" Her response dismissed the editor's assertion that a color line had never existed. Charlotte recounted the harsh reality of segregated schools and separate public accommodations, in existence until the 1850s. Further, she rejected the editor's characterization of Black men and women as merely agricultural laborers, bootblacks, and chimney sweepers. As evidence of her statements, Grimké cited a dozen Black attorneys, including her brother-in-law, Archibald H. Grimké, who were practicing in the Boston area. She also listed other Black professionals residing in New England. She reminded the editor that Black Americans achieved in spite of overwhelming odds, and she rejected the notion that they wanted to force social integration. Above all else, she insisted, Black people desired their rights as American citizens and fair treatment from others in a Christian spirit.

[*See also* FORTEN SISTERS; FREEDMEN'S EDUCATION.]

BIBLIOGRAPHY
Annual Report for the School Committee of Salem, Massachusetts, Boston Public Library, Boston, Massachusetts (February 1854, 1858); Cooper, Anna J. *The Life and Writings of the Grimké Family* (1950); Forten, Charlotte. Letter to Ms. Chase, American Antiquarian Society, Boston, Massachusetts (June 8, 1867), and Letter to Edna Dow Cheney, Boston Public Library (December 15, n.y.), and the *Charlotte Forten Diary*, Moorland-Spingarn Research Center, Howard University, Washington, D.C.; *Liberator* (March 16, 1855; May 27, 1855; December 19, 1862); *New National Era and Citizen* (July 3, 1873); Stevenson, Brenda, ed. *The Journals of Charlotte Forten Grimké* (1988); Sumler-Lewis, Janice L. "The Forten-Purvis Women of Philadelphia and the American Anti-Slavery Crusade," *Journal of Negro History* (Winter 1981-82); Thomas, Benjamin P. *Theodore Weld, Crusader for Freedom* (1973).

JANICE SUMLER-EDMOND

GRIST, RERI (1932-)

Reri Grist was a successful product of the environment that nurtured her musical development from an early age. Beginning in musical theater, Grist went on to become a major figure on the 1960s opera stage.

Born in New York City in 1932, she danced in Broadway musicals, including *Carmen Jones, Shinbone Alley*, and *West Side Story*. She graduated from the High School for the Performing Arts and studied at Queens College; her voice teacher was Claire Gelda. Her successful transition to grand opera combined the power and stamina of a singer in musical theater with the facility and clarity of a coloratura. She made her operatic debut in 1959 as a soprano in the role of Blonde in Mozart's *The Abduction from the Seraglio* with the Santa Fe Opera Company, her San Francisco debut in 1963 as Susanna in Mozart's *The Marriage of Figaro*, and her Metropolitan Opera Company debut in 1966 as Rosina in Rossini's *The Barber of Seville*. She earned critical acclaim as Queen of the Night in Mozart's *The Magic Flute*, as Zerbinetta in Strauss's *Ariadne auf Naxos*, as Olympia in Offenbach's *The Tales of Hoffmann*, and as Norina in Donizetti's *Don Pasquale*. In New York she performed in oratorios and operas, including a City Center production of *Carmina Burana*. Favored by leading conductors, she was invited by Stravinsky to sing in his *Le Rossignol* and by Bernstein to sing in a New York Philharmonic

Beginning as a dancer on Broadway, Reri Grist rose to a career on the operatic stage. [Schomburg Center]

performance of Mahler's Fourth Symphony. She toured widely in Europe, singing regularly in Cologne and as a member of the Zurich Opera. She settled in Berlin in the 1960s after her marriage to musicologist Ulf Thompson. She gained the respect of critics and a reputation as a "demanding, nononsense artist for whom musical integrity was a high priority" (Story 1990).

BIBLIOGRAPHY

BDAAM; Slonimsky, Nicolas, ed. *Baker's Biographical Dictionary of Musicians* (1978); Story, Rosalyn M. *And So I Sing: African American Divas of Opera and Concert* (1990).

DISCOGRAPHY

For a discography, see Turner, Patricia. *Afro-American Singers: An Index and Preliminary Discography of Opera, Choral Music and Song* (1977).

REBECCA T. CUREAU

GUY, ROSA (c. 1925-)

Neighborhood children hurled insults and objects as Rosa Cuthbert Guy walked to school in New York City during the 1930s. Perhaps those children resented the Trinidadian accent or maybe they considered her an outsider even though they shared the same skin colors and many of the same experiences. Today, young adult readers shower her with praise and accolades for her novels. Some of the honors bestowed upon her novels include the American Library Association Notable Book Award for *The Friends* (1974) and the American Library Association's Best Books for Young Adults Award for *Ruby* (1976), *Edith Jackson* (1978), and *The Disappearance* (1979).

Rosa Cuthbert was born on September 1, 1925 or 1928 (the year is disputed and Guy has not resolved the discrepancy), in Trinidad, West Indies, to Henry and Audrey Gonzales Cuthbert. Her parents immigrated to the United States through Ellis Island in the early 1930s. Like many immigrants, Henry and Audrey Cuthbert came first and then sent for their children, Rosa and younger sister Ameze, in 1932. Audrey Cuthbert died when Rosa was nine years old. For a few years, she and Ameze lived with a cousin who was a follower of Marcus Garvey, an early advocate of Pan-African unity among the African diaspora. Her father remarried but then died in 1937. Thereafter, Rosa was shuttled back and forth among institutions and foster homes. She quit high school at age fourteen to help support her sister, taking a job in a brassiere factory. She married Warner Guy (now deceased) in 1941 and bore a son, Warner, in 1942. They moved to Connecticut in 1945 but Rosa Guy returned to New York City in 1950 after the dissolution of their marriage.

In the early 1940s, Guy began to study acting and eventually wrote a one-act play, *Venetian Blinds* (1954), that was staged off-Broadway.

She attended New York University to study writing and the theater and then became involved in the creation of the Harlem Writers' Guild. The guild has proven to be an important source of support for African-American writers, among them John O. Killens and Maya Angelou.

Guy speaks the Creole of her native Trinidad, as well as French and English. She travels extensively throughout the Caribbean and Africa. Currently, she resides off-and-on in New York City, gives readings of works, and occasionally teaches.

Few writers blend the literary, personal, and political in their novels as successfully as Guy. She avoids propaganda, overt didacticism, and strident tones, preferring instead to emphasize respect, pride, and knowledge about Africa, African-Americans, and Afro-Caribbeans. Guy maintains that the time she spent in her cousin's home profoundly affected her intellectual and political development. For Guy, that early exposure to the teachings of Marcus Garvey led her to seeing Malcolm X as a hero who symbolizes the "gold" (individuals) unsalvaged in America's ghettos.

Rosa Guy considers herself a storyteller. The stories she weaves are characterized by meticulous attention to the craft of writing. Guy explores a variety of themes, such as the conflicts that develop among people of color, the survival of children in hostile environments, love, coming of age, quests for identity and purpose in life, the relationships among family members and strangers, friendship, and many others. Her settings are vivid; the reader smells the stench of Harlem tenements or the fresh, fragrant air of middle-class enclaves. Her characters are complex and fully developed; she does not resort to stereotypes or one-dimensional figures to advance her plots. She captures the nuances of West Indian and African-American social dialects. Two novels, *The Friends* (1974), an exploration of the complicated and painful relationship between West Indian Phyllisia and African-American Edith, and *My Love, My Love* (1985), a retelling of *The Little Mermaid* set on a fictional Caribbean island, capture Guy's writing at its best.

Critics praise the naturalistic qualities of her work and the sensitivity with which she addresses complex issues such as defining the family and familial responsibilities, love and caring among family and friends, and the consequences of "coming of age" in an era when innocence is no longer a hallmark of childhood or adolescence.

Rosa Guy's legacy, in addition to the canon of quality literature she produced, is a body of work that takes artistic risks. Guy respects the ability of young adult readers to understand, analyze, and judge the themes, characters, and issues she incorporates into her novels. She trusts her readers and does not compel them to learn a lesson. Equally important, her personal political philosophy, commitment to justice, beliefs in freedom from oppression and in caring for those unlike oneself are not compromised. Her philosophy can be summed up in these words: "A novel to me is an emotional history of a people in time and place. If I have proven to be popular with young people, it is because when they have finished one of my books, they not only have a satisfying experience—they have also had an education" (Guy, "Young Adult Books," 1985).

BIBLIOGRAPHY

Commire, A., ed. "Rosa Guy." In *Something about the Author* (1978); Norris, Jerrie. *Presenting Rosa Guy* (1988); *WWBA* (1990).

SELECTED WORKS BY ROSA GUY

"All about Caring," *Top of the News* (Winter 1983); "Innocence, Betrayal, and History," *School Library Journal* (1985); "Young Adult Books: I Am a Storyteller," *Horn Book Magazine* (1985); *And I Heard a Bird Sing* (1989); *Bird at My Window* (1985); *Children of Longing* (1971); *The Disappearance* (1979); *Edith Jackson* (1978); *The Friends* (1974); *Measure of Time* (1983); *Mirror of Her Own* (1981); *Mother Crocodile: An Uncle Amadou Tale from Senegal* (1981); *My Love, My Love* (1985); *New Guys around the Block* (1983); *Paris, Pee Wee, and Big Dog* (1984); *Ruby* (1976).

VIOLET J. HARRIS

H

HACKLEY, EMMA AZALIA SMITH (1867-1922)

"The race needs daring, original people to think and speak"—these words were spoken by Azalia Hackley, concert soprano and pioneer music educator, during one of her inspirational lecture-recitals in the early decades of the twentieth century. Hackley believed that music could be a positive force in reclaiming Black ethnic and cultural pride.

Emma Azalia Smith was born June 29, 1867, in Murfreesboro, Tennessee. She and a younger sister, Marietta, were taken to Detroit, Michigan, about 1870 by their parents, Henry Smith and Corilla Beard Smith.

Azalia received her education in the Detroit public schools, where she graduated from Capital High School in 1886 and obtained a teaching certificate in 1887. She taught at the Clinton Elementary School from 1887 to 1894. Azalia was taught piano by her mother and took private lessons in voice and violin. She was a member of the Detroit Musical Society, she played in a Black orchestra, and she performed vocal recitals in Detroit and nearby cities.

After her marriage around 1894 to Edwin H. Hackley, a newspaper editor, the couple moved to Denver, Colorado, where Azalia Hackley received a bachelor of music degree from the Denver College of Music. The Hackleys moved to Philadelphia, Pennsylvania, in 1901 to further her singing career. She studied in Paris with Jean De Reszke in 1905 and 1907 and made a trip to London in 1909.

From 1910 to 1920, Hackley funded a "foreign scholarship for Black musicians," established the Normal Voice Culture Institute in Chicago, Illinois, and conducted mammoth folk festivals throughout the country to teach the Negro spiritual. Her name became synonymous with musical excellence and progress. She died in Detroit, Michigan, on December 13, 1922.

Her writings included *A Guide in Voice Culture* (1909); *Public School Lessons in Voice Culture* (n.d.); and *The Colored Girl Beautiful* (1916).

BIBLIOGRAPHY

Brown, Hallie Q. "Madam Emma Azalia Hackley." In her *Homespun Heroines* (1926); *DANB*; Dannett, Sylvia G. L. *Profiles of Negro Womanhood* (1964); Davenport, M. Marguerite. *Azalia: The Life of Madame E. Azalia Hackley* (1947); de Lerma, Dominique-René. "Hackley (née Smith), E(mma) Azalia." In *The New Grove Dictionary of American Music*, ed. H. Wiley Hitchcock and Stanley Sadie (1986); Hare, Maud Cuney. *Negro Musicians and Their Music* (1936); Lewis, Ellistine P. (Holly). "The E. Azalia Hackley Collection of Negro Music, Dance and Drama: A Catalogue of Selected Afro-American Materials," Ph.D. diss. (1978); *NAW*; Lovingood, Penman. *Famous Modern Negro Musicians* ([1921] 1978).

ELLISTINE P. LEWIS

Fervently believing that music could be a positive force in Black life, folk festival organizer Emma Hackley awakened awareness of the power of spirituals. [Schomburg Center]

HAINES NORMAL AND INDUSTRIAL INSTITUTE

The history of Haines Normal and Industrial Institute began in 1886 when Lucy Craft Laney opened a grammar school in a rented lecture hall in the basement of Christ Presbyterian Church in Augusta, Georgia. Laney's short-term goal was to establish a boarding school for girls, but her long-range vision was to create a training school for teachers. The evolution of Haines Institute, from a primary to secondary and finally a normal and industrial school, represented the fulfillment of Lucy C. Laney's dream.

Laney's goal and vision notwithstanding, when she welcomed her first pupils on January 6, 1886, the class comprised four girls and two poor ragged boys whom she did not have the heart to turn away. Although boys were admitted to the school from its inception, the institution remained predominantly female throughout its history.

After the first month of operation the school was overcrowded; consequently, in February 1886, Laney rented a house from the president of the Augusta Board of Education and moved the school. Overcrowding remained a problem as the number of students in attendance went from 75 at the end of the 1886 school year to 362 in 1887, but in that year Laney was able to rent a two-story frame house with a barn in the rear, and those two structures constituted the campus of Haines Institute until 1889.

Although the school was sanctioned by the Presbyterian board, Laney was left to her own devices and what she could collect for its support. She received no salary and was forced to live on the food provided by the parents of her students and to maintain the school on the contributions from the community. During the school's first year, Laney was the only teacher, and she worked around the clock, personally overseeing each student as well as managing the affairs of the institution.

Despite numerous problems, by 1887 Lucy C. Laney's vision began to take shape, and by the end of that year the primary, grammar, and elementary normal departments had been established. In addition, an industrial course had begun, an effort was under way to secure a foot-press, and plans for a class in printing had been finalized. Over the course of several years, Laney created a strong literary department and a well-planned scientifically based normal program. She organized a well-equipped kindergarten at Haines in 1890. In conjunction with the city hospital she had helped to create, she began a training program for nurses in 1892.

Between 1886 and 1889, Haines Institute operated out of various rented buildings, and as enrollment increased it became increasingly difficult to find adequate space. The institution's lack of property lent an air of uncertainty to the school's existence. In 1889, the Presbyterian board purchased a permanent site for Haines and erected the institution's first building, Marshall Hall. In 1906 McGregor Hall was constructed. The last major new building on the Haines campus was Cauley-Wheeler Hall, constructed in 1924.

Lucy C. Laney died in 1933 and was buried on the campus. Because of the Great Depression, the Presbyterian board withdrew support for the institution a few years thereafter. The school was able to continue through the support of alumni and friends, but they were unable to keep the school going after 1949.

[See also LANEY, LUCY CRAFT]

BIBLIOGRAPHY

Brawley, Benjamin. *Negro Builders and Heroes* ([1937] 1965); Cowan, E. P. "Haines Normal and Industrial School," *The Church Home and Abroad* (September 1887); *Crisis*, "Haines Institute" (August 1940); Gibson, J. W. and W. H. Crogman. *Progress of a Race* ([1902] 1965); Griggs, A. C. "Lucy Craft Laney," *Journal of Negro History* (January 1934); Haines Normal and Industrial School Commencement Program (1936); Haines Normal School and Industrial Institute Founder's Day Program (1934); Hartshorn, W. N. *An Era of Progress and Promise* (1910); *Home and Abroad*, "The Haines School" (August 1893); Murry, Andrew E. *Presbyterians and the Negro—A History* (1966); Ovington, Mary White. *Portraits in Color* (1927); Parker, Inez Moore. *The Rise and Decline of the Program of Education for the Black Presbyterian Church U.S.A., 1865-1970* (1977); *The Series*, "Haines Normal and Industrial Academy" (n.d.); Snively, Agnes Bell. "A Sketch of Lucy C. Laney," *Women and Missions* (April 1926); Thompson, Ernest Trice. *Presbyterians in the South* (1973).

JUNE O. PATTON

HALE, CLARA (MOTHER) McBRIDE (1904-)

Clara McBride Hale, known as Mother Hale and as the Mother Teresa of New York, is a Harlem housewife and licensed foster mother who for more than four decades has devoted her life to caring for many unwanted and drug-addicted Black babies. Born in Philadelphia, Clara McBride was orphaned at sixteen. She finished high school and then worked as a domestic because such work was the main work available for Black women. She married Thomas Hale and moved to Brooklyn, where he started a waxing business. After the birth of their third child in the 1940s, Thomas Hale died, leaving Clara Hale with three children (Lorraine, Nathan and Kenneth). In need of employment, she started taking care of foster children.

Mother Hale (who earned that affectionate nickname from her children) loves talking about her work with her babies and her foster children. She takes pride in having reared forty foster children and three natural children. Most of all, Mother Hale takes pride in the accomplishments of her work with unwanted, drug-addicted babies.

Mother Hale's career of caring for drug-addicted babies started in 1969, when one day a young woman appeared at her door with a drug-addicted baby. The woman had a note from Mother Hale's daughter, Lorraine, and left the baby on the floor. A few days later, the mother reappeared with two more children. Thereafter, other young mothers brought their babies, and word spread quickly about Mother Hale opening her home. At the time, Mother Hale was sixty-five years old and looking forward to retirement.

In 1970, Mother Hale founded Hale House, a home for drug-addicted babies. She and a small staff have cared for over 800 babies born addicted to drugs and children with AIDS, with funds from private and public sources. Hale House, formally the Hale House Center for the Promotion of Human Potential, is not an institution but a home where infants live in a loving environment. As a result of her dedication, former President Ronald Reagan in his 1985 State of the Union address hailed Mother Hale as an American hero. In addition, Mother Hale was awarded two of the Salvation Army's highest honors, the Booth Community Service Award and the Leonard H. Carter Humanitarian Award in 1987.

Mother Hale's daughter, Dr. Lorraine Hale, has a Ph.D. in child development and is director of Hale House.

BIBLIOGRAPHY

Beyette, Beverly. "Mother Hale's Solution," *Los Angeles Times* (March 8, 1990); Carcaterra, Lorenzo. "Mother Hale of Harlem Has Saved 487 Drug-addicted Babies with an Old Miracle Cure: Love," *People* (March 5, 1985); *Current Biography* (July 1985); Johnson, Herschel. "Clara (Mother) Hale: Healing Baby 'Junkies' with Love," *Ebony* (May 1986); Safran, Claire. "Mama Hale and Her Little Angels," *Reader's Digest* (September 1984); Spradling, Mary Mace, ed. *In Black and White* (1985); *WWBA* (1990).

LAVONNE ROBERTS-JACKSON

HALE, MAMIE ODESSA (1911-c. 1968)

Born in Pennsylvania in 1911, Mamie Odessa Hale attended teachers college to become a registered public health nurse. After working as a public health nurse in Pittsburgh, Hale attended the Tuskegee School of Nurse-Midwifery for Colored Nurses in Alabama. Graduating with a certificate in midwifery, she was recruited by the Arkansas State Board of Health to assist with maternal-child health programs.

From 1945 to 1950, Nurse Hale's primary task was to train Black granny midwives to safely deliver the babies of Arkansas Black women. Almost all the Black babies in Arkansas were delivered at home without medical supervision, resulting in very high death rates among Black women and their babies.

The task for Nurse Hale, as she was called by everyone, was particularly challenging. Granny midwives managed the deliveries and almost 75 percent of them were illiterate. Most were elderly, between sixty and eighty, and reluctant to change their ways. Undaunted by the mission ahead of her, and driven by the desire to prevent other deaths, Nurse Hale organized a series of classes for these granny midwives to improve their knowledge of and skill in midwifery.

Nurse Hale taught the midwives by songs, movies, and demonstration methods. She would simulate a birth to teach midwives how to care for the pregnant woman before, during, and after the delivery. She assembled a book full of illustrations to teach midwives about what they needed to take to deliveries. In the midwife bag were all the necessary items for a safe delivery. There were clean newspapers to protect the woman's bed, string to tie the baby's cord, dressings for the cord stub, and ampules of silver nitrate and cotton balls for the baby's eyes.

The State Board of Health required all midwives to take the program and be awarded a permit to deliver babies. By 1950 just over 1,000 midwives had such permits in Arkansas. The death rate for Arkansas's Black women and babies fell from 76 deaths in 1940 to 43 in 1950. Mamie Hale's efforts had resulted in dramatic improvements in the quality of obstetrical care in Arkansas.

BIBLIOGRAPHY

Arkansas State Board of Health. *Requirements for Midwife Permits* (September 19, 1940), and *Annual Report of the Arkansas State Board of Health* (1949, 1950, 1951), and "Negro Midwives Trained in State to Cut Death Rate," *Arkansas Health Bulletin* (February 1951); Burt, Marguerite. Interview by P. Bell, Wynne, Arkansas (September 1991); Hale, Mamie. "Arkansas Teaches Her Midwives," *Child* (October 1946), and "Arkansas Midwives Have All-Day Graduation Exercises," *Child* (October 1948); Hudson, Sarah. "Thoroughly Modern Midwives: Black Granny Midwives and Public Health in Arkansas 1920 to the Present," Special Collections, University of Arkansas for Medical Sciences Library, Little Rock, Arkansas (1984); Moòdy, Claire. "State's Midwife Schools Win U.N. Recognition," news clipping in the archives of the Arkansas Department of Health (c. 1951); Price, J., W. Martin, and T. Jones. "Report of Committee on Study of Midwifery," *Journal of the Arkansas Medical Society* (June 1946); Rothert, Frances. Interview by P. Bell, Hot Springs, Arkansas

(September 1991); Tuohey, Matilda. "Train Midwives to Aid Work of Health Division," *Arkansas Gazette* (November 1950).

PEGGE BELL

HALL, ADELAIDE (1901-)

"Flashing eyes, beautiful, witty, vivacious, and she can sing, too!" This description of Adelaide Hall was characteristic of the reviews and comments in the early 1920s when she appeared on and off Broadway as singer, chorine, and comedienne. It is appropriate today, although she is over ninety years old, because Hall is still active as a performer in London, where she has lived since the 1930s.

Born on October 20, 1901, to William and Elizabeth Hall in Brooklyn, New York, Hall has remained an active performer as an interpreter of popular ballads and stage songs for nearly sixty-five years. She began her career as a member of the chorus line in Sissle and Blake's *Shuffle Along*, the 1921 African-American musical that set the pattern for such shows for the next decade. She later had a featured role in *Runnin' Wild* (1923). *Chocolate Kiddies* (1925), which introduced her to European audiences, was the beginning of her successful captivation of the London theater cognoscenti. It was followed by *Brown Buddies* (1928) at the Liberty Theatre in London and the 1928 version of Lew Leslie's *Blackbirds*, in which Hall replaced the previous star, Florence Mills, who had died.

During the late 1920s and the 1930s, Hall performed in shows and as a single who sang, danced, and wisecracked to audiences in Paris, London, Chicago, and New York. Her appearances in musicals were interspersed with those at the Cotton Club as vocalist with the Duke Ellington Orchestra. Her most memorable performance with Ellington was her haunting vocals on the "Creole Love Call." She also performed with the Mills Blues Rhythm Band during that period. Paris and London were like magnets to the multitalented Hall, who also occasionally strummed the banjo in her act. She appeared at Paris's Alhambra Theatre along with the Willis Lewis 10 Entertainers, "le plus sensationnel orchestre de couleur." She claims to have introduced the dance rage from Harlem—Truckin'—to Parisians. In 1936, Hall and her husband, Wilbur Hicks, opened the Big Apple Club and the New Florida Club after they moved to London in 1938.

In the 1920s and 1930s, lively singer Adelaide Hall delighted American audiences in such Black musical theater productions as Sissle and Blake's Shuffle Along. *Since the late 1930s, she has lived and performed in London. [Schomburg Center]*

Hall has remained in London since the late 1930s, but she has returned to the United States to perform on Broadway on several occasions, including a dramatic role, Grandma Obeah, in *Jamaica*. She was active as an entertainer with the European version of the United Service Organizations (USO) during World War II. She has appeared in several British films and on British Broadcasting Company radio and television, and she has enjoyed an active participation in London night life as a vocalist renowned for her lush, sophisticated song styling. Her recordings are evidence of a vocalist of refined taste, romantic expressivity, and a sure sense of her musicianship. Her ability to keep abreast of contemporary trends in popular music is not unique but is certainly unusual for someone her age.

New York welcomed Hall home in spring 1992 for a solo performance.

BIBLIOGRAPHY

Chilton, John. *Who's Who of Jazz: Storyville to Swing Street* (1978); McKay, Claude. *A Long Way From Home* ([1937] 1970); Meeker, David. *Jazz in the Movies, 1917-1977* (1977); Woll, Allan. *Black Musical Theatre: From "Coontown" to "Dreamgirls"* (1989).

SELECTED DISCOGRAPHY

Creole Love Call, HMV [His Master's Voice] (1927); *Harlem Comes to London*, Sh 265, EMI (1977); *There Goes That Song Again*, Decca (1980).

DAPHNE DUVAL HARRISON

HALL, JUANITA (1901-1968)

Juanita Hall was born to Abram and Mary Richardson Hall on November 6, 1901, in Keyport, New Jersey. She was educated in the public schools of Keyport, but her formal musical training was to come later. Many persons recognized the unusual talent of

From her 1928 portrayal of the torch-carrying mulatto Julie in Show Boat *to her 1949 performance as the loud, bawdy, vital Bloody Mary in* South Pacific, *Juanita Hall showed herself to be a singer and actress of remarkable gifts. [Schomburg Center]*

the young mezzo-soprano as she sang in the local Catholic church choir. She also played the organ, although she could not yet read music. These early musical experiences led to her acceptance as a voice student at the Juilliard School of Music in New York City.

While still in her teens, she married Clement Hall, who died shortly thereafter, in 1920.

As a vocal performer, Hall's first successful role was Julie in *Show Boat* in 1928. She captured the attention of the eminent Hall Johnson, with whom she began a rewarding association. She appeared in *Green Pastures* in 1930 with the Hall Johnson Choir and became Johnson's assistant conductor until 1936. Her interest and success as a choral conductor resulted in her becoming the conductor of various choirs in the New York metropolitan area: the Works Progress Administration Chorus, 1935-44; the Westchester Chorale and Dramatics Association, 1941-42; and her own choir, the Juanita Hall Choir, in 1942.

Simultaneous with her radio performances with such personalities as Rudy Vallee and Kate Smith, Hall sang in a number of Broadway productions from 1943 to 1947: *The Pirate, Sing Out, Sweet Land, Saint Louis Woman, Deep Are the Roots,* and Kurt Weill's opera *Street Scene.*

Although classically trained, Hall turned her vocal talents to the nightclub scene, which for her became a fortunate venture. Not only was she a great success, but she was "discovered" by Richard Rodgers and Oscar Hammerstein II and cast in the role of Bloody Mary in their new musical, *South Pacific.* The first performance of the much-heralded new musical, which was an adaptation of the James Michener novel, was April 7, 1949, at the Majestic Theatre on Broadway. The stars of the production were the established Broadway star Mary Martin and the celebrated Metropolitan Opera bass Ezio Pinza, but Hall was a stunning success and was awarded the prestigious Donaldson Award for her supporting performance. She was later to play the same role in the film version of *South Pacific.*

Bloody Mary became Hall's signature role, although other successes were to follow: *Flower Drum Song* and her one-woman show, *A Woman and the Blues.* In addition, she continued her careers as a nightclub singer as well as a concert performer.

Juanita Hall's characters were always performed convincingly and with great authority. The eminent theater critic of the *New York Times* Brooks Atkinson wrote of her performance as Bloody Mary: "She plays a brassy, greedy, ugly, Tonkinese woman with harsh, vigorous authentic accuracy, and she sings one of Mr.

Rodgers's finest songs, 'Bali Hai,' with rousing artistry."

Cast as the flighty, mature Chinese lady Madam Liang in *Flower Drum Song*, Hall was so convincing that she was assumed by many Chinese to be of Chinese origin.

Complications from diabetes caused Hall's death on February 28, 1968, in Bay Shore, Long Island. Survived by a sister and a brother, Juanita Hall was buried in her home town of Keyport, New Jersey.

BIBLIOGRAPHY
DANB.

J. WELDON NORRIS

HALL, JULIA R. (JANE) (b. 1865)

Julia Hall's career spanned more than fifty years and involved a variety of medical practices. In 1889, she came with her husband, Reverend Jeremiah M. Hall, to the District of Columbia and entered the Howard University medical program the following year. She graduated in 1892 and entered the practice of medicine. She was appointed resident to the gynecology clinic at Howard—the first woman at that school to receive such an appointment—and for many years served as matron and medical advisor to the girls at Miner's Hall at Howard University. Hall was also distinguished by being the first woman to be appointed to the Board of Children's Guardians in the capital.

BIBLIOGRAPHY
Brown, Sara W. "Colored Women Physicians," *The Southern Workman* (December 1923); District of Columbia, Board of Education Personnel Records; *Journal of the College Alumnae Club of Washington, Twenty-Fifth Anniversary* (1935); Lamb, Daniel S., ed. *Howard University Medical Department: A Historical, Biographical, and Statistical Souvenir* (1900); Maher, Frank L. *Who's Who of the Colored Race* (1915); Majors, Monroe. *Noted Negro Women* (1893); *Polk's Directory of the District of Columbia* (1907-30); *Polk's Medical and Surgical Register of the United States and Canada* (1886-1920); Scruggs, Lawson A. *Women of Distinction* (1893).

GLORIA MOLDOW

HALL, KATIE BEATRICE GREEN (1938-)

"Men and women of good will on both sides of the aisle showed this was a human concern, not a political or racial issue," commented Katie Hall, representative from Indiana, when the U.S. House of Representatives passed the bill she had introduced designating the birthday of Martin Luther King, Jr., a federal holiday (*Congressional Quarterly* 1983). Signed into law by President Ronald Reagan on November 2, 1983, this legislation embodied the wishes of many Americans to honor the slain civil rights leader, following a legislative process mired in controversy since it was first introduced, shortly after King's assassination on April 4, 1968.

Katie Beatrice Green was born in Mound Bayou, Mississippi, on April 3, 1938, attended local schools, and graduated from Mississippi Valley State University in 1960. She married John W. Hall in August 1957. She received an M.S. from Indiana University in 1968. She spent her first years out of college as a teacher in the Gary, Indiana, public schools; later she taught social studies at the Edison School from 1964-75. A member of the Gary Council of Social Studies and vice chair of the Gary Housing Board of Commissioners, Hall became involved in politics while participating in the mayoral campaigns of Richard Hatcher. Eventually Hall entered electoral politics, serving as Indiana state representative (1974-76) from her northwestern Indiana district, state senator (1976-82), and chair of the Lake County Democratic Committee (1978-80).

Well connected in local Democratic politics, Hall was nominated to run for the U.S. House of Representatives seat left vacant by the death of Representative Adam Benjamin, Jr. In November 1982, she defeated the Republican candidate, Thomas Krieger, and immediately took the first district seat to complete the term in the Ninety-seventh Congress and serve in the succeeding term in the Ninety-eighth Congress.

While best remembered for her tireless efforts as floor manager in support of the King holiday, Hall also served on the House Committee on Post Office and Civil Service (as chair of the census and population subcommittee and as a member of the civil service subcommittee) and the Committee on Public Works and Transportation (aviation, economic development, and public buildings and grounds subcommittees). She focused her efforts on legislation that would remedy her district's significant unemployment rate and its associated social problems. Hall supported the Fair Trade in Steel Act, designed to infuse new energy into the lagging steel industry, and she supported the Humphrey-Hawkins bill for prevention of family violence and child abuse. She also supported the Equal Rights Amendment to the U.S. Constitution.

Running for reelection in 1984, Hall was defeated in the Democratic primary by Peter Visclosky. Again a resident of Gary, Indiana, Hall remains active in state and local politics, serving as state senator from Indiana's third district. She initiated two unsuccessful campaigns for a House seat, in 1986 and 1990.

BIBLIOGRAPHY

Congressional Quarterly Almanac, Ninety-eighth Congress (1983); *Congressional Staff Directory* (1984); *Women in Congress, 1917-1990* (1991).

LYNDA ALLANACH

HAMER, FANNIE LOU (1917-1977)

"I'm sick and tired of being sick and tired," the famous and radical words of Fannie Lou Hamer, summarized the essence of how many Black Americans had come to feel by the 1960s (Hamer 1964). Her speeches and singing influenced everyone who heard and saw her. For many Americans, Fannie Lou Hamer symbolized the best of what the civil rights movement became.

Most people familiar with the civil rights movement of the 1960s know of Fannie Lou Hamer: sharecropper, determined voter registrant, field worker for the Student Nonviolent Coordinating Committee (SNCC), a founder (along with Annie Devine, Victoria Gray, Aaron Henry, and others) of the Mississippi Freedom Democratic Party (MFDP), orator, and political activist. In addition to these contributions, Fannie Lou Hamer abided by strong religious teachings and often expressed that religious zeal through a sacred hymn before each of her speeches. She opened many gatherings with "This Little Light of Mine," one of her favorite songs.

Fannie Lou Townsend was born to Jim and Ella Townsend on October 6, 1917, in rural Montgomery County, Mississippi. Ella and Jim Townsend moved to Sunflower County, Mississippi, when Fannie Lou was two years old, and the child received her early education there. At the age of six, Fannie Lou began working in the cotton fields and worked many long years chopping and picking cotton until the plantation owner, W. D. Marlow, learned that she could read and write. In 1944, she became the time and record keeper for Marlow, and in 1945 she married Perry Hamer, a tractor driver on the Marlow plantation. For the next eighteen years, Hamer worked as sharecropper and time keeper on the plantation, four miles east of Ruleville, Mississippi, the place where she and Perry made their home. All this changed in 1962 when she suffered economic reprisals after an unsuccessful attempt to vote in the county seat of Indianola. Familiar with the physical violence that would often follow economic reprisals, and having received threats, Hamer left her family to stay with friends. The move did not stay the violence, however, and Hamer and her friends miraculously escaped rounds of gunshots fired into the friends' home when a person or persons yet unknown discovered her presence there.

Despite the denial of the right to vote and the subsequent violence and economic intimidation, Hamer became an active member of SNCC in Ruleville. She took the literacy test several times in order to repeatedly demonstrate her right to vote. In 1963, she became a field secretary for SNCC and a registered voter; both put her life in jeopardy. From this point onward Hamer worked with voter registration drives and with programs designed to assist economically deprived Black families in Mississippi.

The youngest of twenty siblings whose parents seldom were able to provide adequate food and clothing, Hamer saw a link between the lack of access to the political process and the poor economic status of Black Americans. She was instrumental in starting Delta Ministry, an extensive community development program, in 1963. The next year she took part in the founding of the MFDP, becoming vice chairperson and a member of its delegation to the Democratic National Convention in Atlantic City, New Jersey, in order to challenge the seating of the regular all-white Mississippi delegation. In this capacity she made a televised address to the convention. The 1964 challenge failed despite a compromise offered through Hubert Humphrey and Walter Mondale that would have seated two nonvoting MFDP members selected by Humphrey. Instead, the MFDP's actions resulted in an unprecedented pledge from the national Democratic party not to seat delegations that excluded Black delegates at the convention in 1968. Hamer also unsuccessfully ran for Congress in 1964. Because the regular Democratic party disallowed her name on the ballot, the MFDP distributed a "Freedom Ballot" that included all of the candidates' names, Black and white. Hamer defeated her white opponent, Congressman Jamie Whitten on the alternative ballot, but the state refused to acknowledge the MFDP vote as valid. In 1965, Hamer, Victoria Gray, and Annie Devine appealed to the U.S. Congress, arguing that it was wrong to seat Mississippi's representatives (who were all white) when the state's population was 50 percent Black. The three women watched as the House voted against the challenge, 228 to 143.

Hamer remained active in civic affairs in Mississippi for the remainder of her life and was a delegate to the Democratic National Convention in 1968 in Chicago. Her founding in 1969 of the Freedom Farms Corporation (FFC), a nonprofit venture designed to help needy families raise food and livestock, showed her concern for the economic plight of Black Americans in Mississippi. The FFC also provided social services, minority business opportunity, scholarships, and grants for education. When the National Council of Negro Women started the Fannie Lou Hamer Day Care Center in 1970, Hamer became its board's chairperson. As late as 1976, even as she struggled with cancer, Hamer served as a member of the state executive committee of the United Democratic party of Mississippi.

Fannie Lou Hamer in an interview in 1965 said: "I was determined to see that things were changed." Later in the same interview, and paraphrasing John F. Kennedy, she continued, "I am determined to give my part not for what the movement can do for me, but what I can do for the movement to bring about a change." On being tired, Hamer put it best when she said:

> I do remember, one time, a man came to me after the students began to work in Mississippi, and he said the white people were getting tired and they were getting tense and anything might happen. Well, I asked him, "how long he thinks we had been getting tired?" I have been tired for forty-six years, and my parents was tired before me, and their parents were tired; and I have always wanted to do something that would help some of the things I would see going on among Negroes that I didn't like and I don't like now.

Hamer consistently stated that she had always wanted to work to transform the South because she saw her parents work so hard to raise twenty children. Once her father bought two mules after much sacrifice, and simply because this meant he might experience semi-independence from the landowner, his mules were poisoned. Hamer said she never understood this kind of hatred, but fighting it gave her courage.

Fannie Lou Hamer's frankness, determination, courage, and leadership abilities made her a memorable figure in the 1960s civil rights struggle in general, particularly in the MFDP challenge to the Demo-

cratic party in August 1964, and especially in its challenge to white southern members of the party.

Fannie Lou Hamer received wide recognition for her part in bringing about a major political transformation in the Democratic party and raising significant questions that addressed basic human needs. In 1963, the Fifth Avenue Baptist Church in Nashville, Tennessee, presented her with one of the first awards that she received, for "voter registration and Hamer's fight for freedom for mankind." Other awards she received include the National Association of Business and Professional Women's Clubs National Sojourner Truth Meritorious Service Award as a tribute to Hamer's strong defense of human dignity and fearless promotion of civil rights. Delta Sigma Theta Sorority awarded her a life membership. Many colleges and universities honored her with honorary degrees, including Tougaloo College, in 1969.

Fannie Lou Hamer gave numerous speeches across the country into the 1970s. She suffered with cancer, but she continued to accept invitations to speak about the issue most dear to her, basic human rights for all Americans. Indeed, she remained tired of being sick and tired until her life ended. She died of cancer on March 14, 1977, at Mound Bayou Community Hospital.

[See also MISSISSIPPI FREEDOM DEMOCRATIC PARTY.]

For many Americans, sharecropper Fannie Lou Hamer, whose determination to vote led her to become a powerful political activist, symbolized the best of what the civil rights movement became. In 1967, she testified before the Senate's Subcommittee on Poverty. [Schomburg Center]

BIBLIOGRAPHY

"Autobiography of Fannie Lou Hamer." Fannie Lou Hamer papers, Amistad Research Center, New Orleans; Carson, Clayborne. *In Struggle: SNCC and the Black Awakening of the 1960s* (1981); DeMuth, Jerry. "Tired of Being Sick and Tired," *Nation* (June 1, 1964); De Veaux Garland, Phyl. "Builders of a New South," *Ebony* (August 1966); Golden, Marita. "The Sixties Live On: The Era of Black Consciousness Is Preserved as a State of Mind," *Essence* (May 1985); Hamer, Fannie Lou. Personal interviews (1964, 1965); Henry, Aaron. Interview by William M. Simpson (December 5, 1973). In Aaron Henry papers, Tougaloo College, Tougaloo, Mississippi; Ladner, Joyce A. "Fannie Lou Hamer: In Memoriam," *Black Enterprise* (May 1977); "Life in Mississippi: An Interview with Fannie Lou Hamer." In *Afro-American History: Primary Sources*, ed. Thomas R. Frazier ([1965] 1988); Locke, Mamie E. "Is This America? Fannie Lou Hamer and the Mississippi Freedom Democratic Party." In *Women in the Civil Rights Movement: Trailblazers and Torchbearers, 1941-1965*, ed. Vicki L. Crawford, Jacqueline Anne Rouse, and Barbara Woods (1990); McLemore, Leslie Burl. "The Mississippi Freedom Democratic Party: A Case Study of Grass-Roots Politics," Ph.D. diss. (1971); Norton, Eleanor Holmes. "Woman Who Changed the South: Memory of Fannie Lou Hamer," *Ms.* (July 1977); Reagon, Bernice Johnson. "Women as Culture Carriers in the Civil Rights Movement: Fannie Lou Hamer." In *Women in the Civil Rights Movement*, ed. Crawford, Rouse, and Woods (1990).

LINDA REED

HAMILTON, GRACE TOWNS (1907-1992)

There are many trailblazers and among them is Grace Towns Hamilton—Georgia's first Black female legislator. She brought power to minority voters and served as a catalyst for racial cooperation. She helped rewrite the Atlanta charter to give Black citizens self-government. "At a time when there was very little interracial cooperation and very little of any kind of discussion, she was a real pathfinder. . . . She set a standard for civic involvement that was difficult for any of her peers to meet and will be difficult for any who come after her to meet," said former Georgia state representative Julian Bond.

Grace Towns was born February 10, 1907, in Atlanta, the eldest of four children of George A. Towns and Nellis McNair Towns. Young Grace Towns graduated from American University in 1927, then enrolled in graduate school at Ohio State, paying her way by working as a Young Men's Christian

Association secretary. She earned a Master's degree in psychology in 1929.

In 1930, she married Henry Cooke Hamilton, dean and professor of education at LeMoyne College, now LeMoyne-Owen College, in Memphis.

Hamilton taught psychology at the Memphis college from 1930 to 1934, had a job making a Works Progress Administration survey of Black workers in Memphis in 1935-36, and was a YMCA employee helping to develop interracial programs on college campuses from 1936 to 1943. In 1943, her husband became a faculty member at Morehouse College in Atlanta, where they returned to live. Her husband of fifty-seven years died at the age of eighty-seven in 1987. They had a daughter, Eleanor Hamilton Payne, four grandchildren, and seven great-grandchildren.

Hamilton, the first Black woman to serve in the Georgia legislature, represented the Vine City area from 1966 to 1984. Hamilton was elected to the House after court-ordered reapportionment in 1965 that created eight new Fulton County seats and increased political opportunities for Black people. As executive director of the Atlanta Urban League and later as a legislator, she was a champion for fair housing, more job opportunities for Black workers, and the integration of Atlanta's Grady Memorial Hospital.

Hamilton was the major architect of the current Atlanta city charter, which became law in 1973. It reduced at-large representation and paved the way for Black self-government through district voting. She brought "one person, one vote" to local government. It was first actualized in a 1962 Georgia case before the Supreme Court and later swept Southern states and local governments.

Five years after she was elected to the Georgia House, Hamilton authored a bill creating an Atlanta Charter Commission. She served as vice-chairman of the twenty-seven-member commission during its deliberations in 1971-73. Hamilton and fellow Commissioner Everett Millican developed the current political map of Atlanta, with its twelve voting districts (the legislature later added six at-large seats). Before then, whites had used at-large voting to maintain control. Council members were not required to live in districts they represented. Consequently Atlanta had no Black council member until 1966. Seven years later in October 1973, Maynard H. Jackson was elected the first Black mayor of a major Southern city.

Hamilton was one of Atlanta's greatest activists as executive director of the Atlanta Urban League for eighteen years, from 1943 to 1961. As a fierce advocate of greater opportunities for Black school children, she waged a successful campaign in 1944-46 for the Black community to get a share of a $9.9 million school-bond issue. At the same time, she and others led a 1946 drive to register Black citizens to vote, as the federal courts were weighing a suit to outlaw the state's notorious white primary. Only whites could vote in the Democratic primary, which in a one-party state was tantamount to election.

During the pivotal 1954-55 period, when the Supreme Court was deliberating the *Brown* decision to eliminate segregated schools, Hamilton was on a leave of absence from the Urban League and was serving as associate director of the Atlanta-based Southern Regional Council, which worked to end discrimination.

She also was a seminar leader and member of the Executive Council of the Highlander Folk School in Monteagle, Tennessee. Liberals, Black and white, attended seminars at the school on voter registration and peaceful school integration. Hamilton's Highlander ties provoked racists. In 1957, segregationist Georgia governor Marvin Griffin sent a state employee to the school to photograph Black attendants. The governor then published a four-page hate sheet charging that Highlander was a hotbed of communism. Its principal news was that Dr. Martin Luther King, Jr., had visited the school, and Grace Hamilton was a member of the school's executive council.

Grace Towns Hamilton also was a champion of fair housing, more job opportunities for Black Americans, and the integration of Grady Memorial Hospital. She engaged in a struggle with the Fulton-Dekalb Hospital Authority over conditions at Grady Memorial Hospital many times. The Hughes Spalding Pavilion exists because Grace Hamilton convinced the authority that there had to be a place where Black patients who could afford to pay could receive medical treatment. At that time Grady Hospital was restricted to those too poor to pay. She was also primarily responsible for the hiring of Grady's first Black doctor in 1958.

Spurred by her triumph in recasting city government, she tried in 1975 to do the same with county government. She authored a bill to shorten the terms of county commissioners from four to two years. Not only did the commissioners get the bill defeated, they removed her from the Fulton-Dekalb Hospital Authority, a post she had held since 1971.

Political opposition began to mount in 1982 after she allied with Georgia House speaker Tom Murphy to oppose a congressional Reapportionment Committee. Hamilton's critical miscalculation, however, was her support of Walter Mondale, and not Jesse Jackson, for the Democratic nomination for president in 1984. That year, she sought a tenth term in the legislature from the 31st District. Mable Thomas, her opponent, charged that Hamilton was "out of touch with her district." Thomas led in a primary, 1,401 votes to 1,170, and won in a runoff, 2,483 to 983.

In 1989, Emory University in Atlanta, Georgia, honored Hamilton by inaugurating the Grace Towns Hamilton Lectureship, the first lecture series at a major university named for a Black woman. In 1990, she was honored again when Emory endowed a distinguished chair in her name. Both occurred through the initiative of the African-American and African Studies program at Emory.

Grace Towns Hamilton died at the age of eighty-five on July 17, 1992. Described as "the quiet warrior," she fought for better health facilities, improved education, help for the indigent, and rights for the disenfranchised.

BIBLIOGRAPHY

Bennett, Tom, and Charles Salter. "Former Legislator, Activist Grace Towns Hamilton Dies," *Atlanta Journal/Atlanta Constitution* (July 18, 1992); Hamilton, Grace Towns. Curriculum Vitae (1988), and Personal interview (Spring 1989); Hornsby, Alton. "Grace Towns Hamilton's Legacy in the Development of Atlanta," Grace Towns Hamilton Distinguished Lecture Series, Emory University (April 19, 1990); Jenkins, Harriet. Personal interview (Spring 1989); Payne, Eleanor Hamilton. Personal interview (Spring 1992); Treadway, Dan. "Burke Begins Hamilton Lecture Series," *Campus Report*, Emory University (November 6, 1989); *Who's Who of American Women* (1977-78).

DELORES P. ALDRIDGE

HAMILTON, VIRGINIA ESTHER (1936-)

Poised in gauzy pink, velvet, or taffeta dresses, five-year-old Virginia Esther Hamilton mesmerized family and friends with her singing voice. She loved performing at family gatherings and church socials. Now she astounds readers with the unique literary voices woven from what she remembers, knows, and imagines. Her literary career began at age nine or ten when she began to write stories for her pleasure. Her first published novel, *Zeely* (1967), helped alter the image of Africans in children's literature. Other novels followed: *The House of Dies Drear* (1968), a mystery that explored slavery, interrelationships, and the Underground Railroad through the experiences of a contemporary African-American family; *The Time-Ago Tales of Jadhu* (1969), an example of storytelling; *The Planet of Junior Brown* (1971), an exploration of genius, contemporary social problems, and survival; *W.E.B. Du Bois* (1972), a biography of a childhood hero; *Time-Ago Lost: More Tales of Jadhu* (1973); and the exceptional *M. C. Higgins, the Great* (1974).

Hamilton was born March 12, 1936, the fifth and youngest child of Kenneth James Hamilton and Etta Belle Perry Hamilton. Virginia adored her father and talks about him in many of her essays. Intelligent, well-read, and a musician, Kenneth Hamilton could not pursue the business career for which he trained (at Iowa State Business College) because of racism. He shared with his daughter a love of reading, music, travel, storytelling, and two personal heroes—Paul Robeson and W.E.B. Du Bois.

Her maternal relatives, the Perrys, settled in Yellow Springs, Ohio. Family lore related that an ancestress of the family, a leader in the Underground Railroad, guided her son out of slavery and into freedom in Ohio. This great grandfather married into one of the other families in the area and settled into farming. Future Perrys purchased land, became farmers, and raised children. Hamilton's early life in this circle of family love appears in vignettes in her work. She characterized her childhood as a "fine one" because of her experiences growing up in an extended family.

Few racial strictures penetrated this seemingly ideal existence. Hamilton's formal schooling included little of the contributions of African-Americans to culture and history, but she received what she labeled "the Knowledge" from home. The Knowledge supplanted what she received at school about African-Americans. Her father recounted the lives of famous African-Americans—especially Du Bois and Robeson, as well as entertainers Florence Mills and Blind Lemon Jefferson.

Hamilton attended a rural elementary school and high school. She performed well enough in school to receive a scholarship to attend Antioch College (1952-55), for her B.A. degree. She later enrolled at Ohio State University (1957-58) and the New School for Social Research.

Visiting and living in New York City were lifelong dreams for Hamilton and during her college years she worked summers in New York City as a bookkeeper. She moved there in the late 1950s and remained for fifteen years. Hamilton worked at a variety of occupations from bookkeeper to singer, all the while writing and enjoying community life in the East Village. During this time, Hamilton met and married Arnold Adoff, a Jewish teacher in Harlem, poet, graduate student, and manager of jazz musicians. Adoff won critical praise in children's literature for his stories about biracial families, the poetry anthologies he edited, and the volumes of poetry he created. He received the prestigious National Council of Teachers of English poetry award for his work. Adoff also serves as Hamilton's manager. They are the parents of a daughter, Leigh, and a son, Jamie. Hamilton and Adoff currently reside in Ohio.

M. C. Higgins, the Great (1974) secured Hamilton's literary reputation. This exceptional novel depicts a young male's concern for his family's safety (they live on a mountain ravaged by strip mining), his dreams of a singing career for his mother that will enable the family to leave the mountain, first love, relationships, and the quest to fulfill one's dreams. The book is filled with the sweet anguish of the family's love, music, and cultural traditions. It also contains a very gentle love relationship between parents. The novel garnered several major literary awards. Hamilton is the only author to receive the Newbery Medal (given by the American Library Association for the "most distinguished contribution to literature for children published in the United States during the preceding year"), the *Boston Globe-Horn Book Magazine* Award, the National Book Award, the Lewis Carroll Shelf Award, and the International Board on Books for Young People Award for the same book. Some of the original manuscripts of her books are housed in the Kerlan Collection at the University of Minnesota.

Hamilton considers herself a storyteller who carries on the tradition that enabled many African-Americans to survive slavery and postslavery experiences. The stories she weaves do not signify an ignoble people beaten down by poverty and racism. Instead, her stories reflect the myriad experiences of African-Americans, the bittersweet along with the triumphant. High John De Conqueror is a favorite image. This folklore character appears when needed most by his people. He is a trickster-hero who gives strength, courage, and laughter that sustains his people. She contends that he has emerged as a symbol of a new ethnic literature and that he represents the hunger for humor in African-American literature. Proponents of any single authentic literary depiction of African-Americans raise Hamilton's ire. She writes that she is "weary and wary" of cultural arbiters. Instead, she supports an artistic vision that enables her to write about the particulars of her "dreams, lies, myths, and disasters," in order to see and understand universal values and experiences.

Hamilton believes that the writer must grow and change, that it is the experience of living and partly living that illuminates the writer's art. This view prevents her from writing the same novel or repeating a set of characters in her novels. She has no desire to write about her family or her heritage indefinitely unless doing so enables her to explore new ideas, experiment with new forms or styles, or transform the source of an image. Hamilton chooses not to refer to African-Americans and other people of color as minorities. Rather, she uses the term "parallel culture" to connote the belief that people of color share in "American" culture as well as their own. The concept does not allow for presumed superiority or inferiority. The dreams, visions, myths, and ideas of a culture across the North American continent are referred to as being a component of the hopescape. Hopescape implies both the promise achieved and the promise unfulfilled.

Hamilton writes to entertain. The sharp humor and images in *Willie Bea and the Time the Martians Landed* (1983) provoke roll-in-the-aisles laughter. Though she always writes with humor, Hamilton has worked in a range of genres: contemporary realistic fiction, historical fiction, science fiction/fantasy, folk tales, and biographies. She has explored several themes in her books: the experiences and culture of African-Americans, surviving and survivors in a variety of milieus, quests of various types, coming of age, the struggles of famous African-Americans, first love, parent love, conflict between parent and child, attachment to one's homestead, environmental concerns, outsiders, and many others.

Folk tales have a significant presence in children's literature. Hamilton's contributions, *The People Could Fly* (1985), *In the Beginning* (1988), and *The Dark Way* (1990), found favor with readers and critics. The latter two were world tales about creation and the more malevolent elements of humans. *The People Could Fly*, a best-seller for Hamilton, recreates the language and beliefs of African-Americans in a manner that contrasts sharply with the traditional depictions of Joel Chandler Harris or the contemporary renditions of Julius Lester. The actor James Earl Jones joined with Hamilton to record some of the tales. Their voices, along with music, create haunting, vibrant, and memorable storytelling.

Biographies about great men have long been a staple of children's literature. Hamilton's offerings—*W.E.B. Du Bois: A Biography* (1972) and *Paul Robeson: The Life and Times of a Free Black Man* (1975)—are remarkable because of the extensive research Hamilton conducted, the choice of contro-versial subjects, and the candor apparent in the books' content. These biographies provide an excellent introduction to the lives of two phenomenal men.

Hamilton remains the only African-American who has written science fiction/fantasy for young readers. The Justice Trilogy books—*Justice and Her Brothers* (1978), *Dustland* (1980), and *The Gathering* (1981)—explore concepts such as good versus evil, psychic powers, the origin and development of various life forms, and the power unleashed when those of varying psychic abilities meld their talents.

Critics of Hamilton's work focus on content, style, and treatment. First, some argue that her subject matter is too complex for most children and that only the most gifted of readers enjoy her works. Second, some critics feel that some of the stylistic devices she uses—stream of consciousness, incomplete sentences, invented languages, and shifting settings and times—are distracting for many readers. Third, other critics suggest that her plots ramble occasionally, some plot twists seem contrived or forced, and some events are implausible or inappropriate for a particular setting. Few, however, criticize her characterizations or her vision.

Her critics aside, Hamilton has created an impressive and accomplished body of literature about African-American life and culture in all their complexities. She has helped to forge new standards of creative and literary excellence that inspire children and adults. Yet Hamilton has remained true to her initial reasons for writing: to entertain and to tell a good story while providing readers with new visions of the world.

BIBLIOGRAPHY

Apseloff, Marilyn. "A Conversation with Virginia Hamilton," *Children's Literature in Education* (1983); Commire, Ann, ed. "Virginia Hamilton," *Something about the Author* (1989); Heins, Paul. "Virginia Hamilton," *Horn Book Magazine* (August 1975); Sims, Rudine. *Shadow and Substance* (1982).

SELECTED WORKS BY VIRGINIA HAMILTON

Zeely (1967); *The House of Dies Drear* (1968); *The Time-Ago Tales of Jadhu* (1969); *The Planet of Junior Brown* (1971); *W.E.B. Du Bois: A Biography* (1972); *Time-Ago Lost: More Tales of Jadhu* (1973); *M. C. Higgins, the Great* (1974); *Paul Robeson: The Life and Times of a Free Black Man* (1975); "High John Is Risen Again," *Horn Book Magazine* (1975); "Newbery Award Acceptance," *Horn Book Magazine* (August 1975); *The Writings of W.E.B. Du Bois* (1976); *Arilla Sun Down* (1976); *Justice and Her Brothers* (1978); *Jadhu* (1980); *Dustland* (1980); *The Gathering* (1981); *Sweet Whispers, Brother Rush* (1982); *The Magical Adventures of Pretty Pearl* (1983); "The Mind of a Novel: The Heart of the Book,"

Children's Literature Association Quarterly (Winter 1983); *Willie Bea and the Time the Martians Landed* (1983); "Boston Globe-Horn Book Award Acceptance," *Horn Book Magazine* (February 1984); *A Little Love* (1984); *Junius Over Far* (1985); *The People Could Fly* (1985); "Coretta Scott King Award Acceptance," *Horn Book Magazine* (1986); "On Being a Black Writer in America," *The Lion and the Unicorn* (1986); "The Known, the Remembered, and the Imagined: Celebrating Afro-American Folk Tales," *Children's Literature in Education* (1987); *The Mystery of Drear House* (1987); *White Romance* (1987); *Anthony Burns* (1988); *In the Beginning* (1988); "Anthony Burns: Acceptance Speech for Boston Globe-Horn Book Award." *Horn Book Magazine* (March/April 1989); *The Bells of Christmas* (1989); *Cousins* (1990); *The Dark Way* (1990); *The All Jadhu Story Book* (1991).

VIOLET J. HARRIS

HANSBERRY, LORRAINE VIVIAN (1930-1965)

Lorraine Hansberry was a celebrated Black playwright who was born in Chicago, Illinois, on May 19, 1930, and died in New York City on January 12, 1965, at the age of thirty-four after a scant six years in the professional theater. Her first produced play, *A Raisin in the Sun*, has become an American classic, enjoying numerous productions since its original presentation in 1959 and many professional revivals during its twenty-fifth anniversary year in 1983-1984. The roots of Hansberry's artistry and activism lie in the city of Chicago, her early upbringing, and her family.

Lorraine Vivian Hansberry was the youngest of four children; seven or more years separated her from Mamie, her sister and closest sibling, and two older brothers, Carl Jr., and Perry. Her father, Carl Augustus Hansberry, was a successful real estate broker who had moved to Chicago from Mississippi after completing a technical course at Alcorn College. A prominent businessman, he made an unsuccessful bid for Congress in 1940 on the Republican ticket and contributed large sums to causes supported by the National Association for the Advancement of Colored People (NAACP) and the Urban League. Hansberry's mother, Nannie Perry, was a school teacher and later ward committeewoman who had come north from Tennessee after completing teacher training at Tennessee Agricultural and Industrial University. The Hansberrys were at the center of Chicago's Black social life and often entertained important political and cultural figures who were visiting the city. Through her uncle, Leo Hansberry, professor of African history at Howard University, Hansberry made early acquaintances with young people from the African continent.

The Hansberrys' middle-class status did not protect them from the racial segregation and discrimination characteristic of the period, and they were active in opposing it. Restrictive covenants, in which white homeowners agreed not to sell their property to Black buyers, created a ghetto known as the "Black metropolis" in the midst of Chicago's South Side. Although large numbers of Black Americans continued to migrate to the city, restrictive covenants kept the boundaries static, creating serious housing problems. Carl Hansberry knew well the severe overcrowding in the Black metropolis. He had, in fact, made much of his money by purchasing large, older houses vacated by the retreating white population and dividing them into small apartments, each one with its own kitchenette. Thus he earned the title "kitchenette king." In *A Raisin in the Sun*, Lorraine Hansberry used this type of apartment as the setting, with the struggle for better housing as the driving action of her plot.

Hansberry attended public schools, graduating from Betsy Ross Elementary School and then from Englewood High School in 1947. Breaking with the family tradition of attending southern Black colleges, Hansberry chose to attend the University of Wisconsin-Madison, moving from the ghetto schools of Chicago to a predominantly white university. She integrated her dormitory, becoming the first Black student to live at Langdon Manor. The years at Madison focused her political views as she worked in the Henry Wallace presidential campaign and in the activities of the Young Progressive League, becoming president of the organization in 1949 during her last semester there. Her artistic sensibilities were heightened by a university production of Sean O'Casey's *Juno and the Paycock*. She was deeply moved by O'Casey's ability to universalize the suffering of the Irish without sacrificing specificity and later wrote: "The melody was one that I had known for a very long while. I was seventeen and I did not think then of writing the melody as I knew it—in a different key; but I believe it entered my consciousness and stayed there" (*To Be Young, Gifted, and Black* 1969). She would capture that suffering in the idiom of the Negro people in her first produced play, *A Raisin in the Sun*. In 1950, she left the university and moved to New York City for an education of another kind.

In Harlem she began working on *Freedom*, a progressive newspaper founded by Paul Robeson, and turned the world into her personal university. In 1952, she became associate editor of the newspaper, writing and editing a variety of news stories that expanded her understanding of domestic and world problems. Living and working in the midst of the rich and progressive social, political, and cultural elements of Harlem stimulated Hansberry to begin writing short stories, poetry, and plays. On one occasion she wrote the pageant that was performed to commemorate the *Freedom* newspaper's first anniversary. In 1952, while covering a picket line protesting discrimination in sports at New York University, Hansberry met Robert Barro Nemiroff, a white student of Jewish heritage who was attending the university. They dated for several months, participating in political and cultural activities together. They married on June 20, 1953, at the Hansberry home in Chicago. The young couple took various jobs during these early years. Nemiroff was a part-time typist, waiter, Multilith operator, reader, and copywriter. Hansberry left the *Freedom* staff in 1953 in order to concentrate on her writing and for the next three years worked on three plays while holding a series of jobs: tagger in the garment industry, typist, program director at Camp Unity (a progressive, interracial summer program), teacher at the Marxist-oriented Jefferson School for Social Science, and recreation leader for the handicapped.

A sudden change of fortune freed Hansberry from these odd jobs. Nemiroff and his friend Burt d'Lugoff wrote a folk ballad, "Cindy Oh Cindy," that quickly became a hit. The money from that hit song allowed Hansberry to quit her jobs and devote full time to her writing. She began to write *The Crystal Stair*. This play about a struggling Black family in Chicago would eventually become *A Raisin in the Sun*.

Drawing on her knowledge of the working-class Black tenants who had rented from her father and with whom she had attended school on Chicago's South Side, Hansberry wrote a realistic play whose theme was inspired by Langston Hughes. In his poem "Harlem," he asks: "What happens to a dream deferred? . . . Does it dry up like a raisin in the sun? . . . Or does it explode?" Hansberry read a draft of the play to several colleagues. After one such occasion Phil Rose, a friend who had employed Nemiroff in his music publishing firm, optioned the play for Broadway production. Although he had never produced a Broadway play before, Rose and coproducer David S. Cogan set forth enthusiastically with their fellow novices on this new venture. They approached major Broadway producers, but the "smart money" considered a play about Black life too risky a venture for Broadway. The only interested producer insisted on

Young, gifted, and Black, Lorraine Hansberry changed the face of the American theater with her play A Raisin in the Sun. *[National Archives]*

directorial and cast choices that were unacceptable to Hansberry, so the group raised the cash through other means and took the show on tour without the guarantee of a Broadway house. Audiences in the tour cities—New Haven, Connecticut, Philadelphia, and Chicago—were ecstatic about the show. A last-minute rush for tickets in Philadelphia finally made the case for acquiring a Broadway theater.

A Raisin in the Sun opened at the Ethel Barrymore Theatre on March 11, 1959, and was an instant success with both critics and audiences. New York critic Walter Kerr praised Hansberry for reading "the precise temperature of a race at that time in its history when it cannot retreat and cannot quite find the way to move forward. The mood is forty-nine parts anger and forty-nine parts control, with a very narrow escape hatch for the steam these abrasive contraries build up. Three generations stand poised, and crowded, on a detonating-cap" (*New York Herald Tribune*, March 12, 1959). Hansberry became a celebrity overnight. The play was awarded the New York Drama Critics Circle Award in 1959, making Lorraine

Hansberry the first Black playwright, the youngest person, and the fifth woman to win that award.

In 1960, NBC producer Dore Schary commissioned Hansberry to write the opening segment for a television series commemorating the Civil War. Her subject was to be slavery. Hansberry thoroughly researched the topic. The result was *The Drinking Gourd*, a television play that focused on the effects that slavery had on the families of the slavemaster and the white poor as well as the slave. The play was deemed too controversial by NBC television executives and, despite Schary's objections, was shelved along with the entire project.

Hansberry was successful, however, in bringing her prize-winning play, *A Raisin in the Sun*, to the screen a short time later. In 1959, a few months after the play opened, she sold the movie rights to Columbia Pictures and began work on drafts of the screenplay, incorporating several new scenes. These additions, which were rejected for the final version, sharpened the play's attack on the effects of segregation and revealed with a surer hand the growing militant mood of Black America. After many revisions and rewrites, the film was produced with all but one of the original cast and released in 1961.

In the wake of the play's extended success, Hansberry became a public figure and popular speaker at a number of conferences and meetings. Among her most notable speeches is one delivered to a Black writers' conference sponsored by the American Society of African Culture in New York. Written during the production of *A Raisin in the Sun* and delivered on March 1, 1959—two weeks before the Broadway opening—"The Negro Writer and His Roots" is in effect Hansberry's credo. In this speech, since published in the *Black Scholar* (March/April 1981) as an essay, Hansberry declares that "all art is ultimately social" and calls upon Black writers to be involved in "the intellectual affairs of all men, everywhere." As the civil rights movement intensified, Hansberry helped to plan fund-raising events to support organizations such as the Student Nonviolent Coordinating Committee (SNCC). Disgusted with the red-baiting of the McCarthy era, she called for the abolition of the House Un-American Activities Committee and criticized President John F. Kennedy's handling of the Cuban missile crisis, arguing that his actions endangered world peace.

In 1961, amid many requests for public appearances, a number of which she accepted, Hansberry began work on several plays. Her next stage production, *The Sign in Sidney Brustein's Window*, appeared in 1964. Before that, however, she finished a favorite project, *Masters of the Dew*, adapted from the Haitian novel by Jacques Romain. A film company had asked her to do the screenplay; however, contractual problems prevented the production from proceeding. The next year, seeking rural solitude, she purchased a house in Croton-on-Hudson, forty-five minutes from Broadway, in order to complete work on *The Sign in Sidney Brustein's Window*.

Early in April 1963, Hansberry fainted. Hospitalized at University Hospital in New York City for nearly two weeks, she underwent extensive tests. The results suggested cancer of the pancreas. Despite the progressive failure of her health during the next two years, she continued her writing projects and political activities. In May 1963, she joined writer James Baldwin, singers Harry Belafonte and Lena Horne, and other Black and white individuals in a meeting in Croton to raise funds for SNCC and a rally to support the southern freedom movement. Although her health was in rapid decline, she greeted 1964 as a year of glorious work. On her writing schedule, in addition to *The Sign in Sidney Brustein's Window*, were *Les Blancs*, *Laughing Boy* (a musical adaptation of the novel), *The Marrow of Tradition*, *Mary Wollstonecraft*, and *Achnaton*, a play about the Egyptian pharaoh. Despite frequent hospitalization and bouts with pain and attendant medical conditions, she completed a photo-essay for a book on the civil rights struggle titled *The Movement: Documentary of a Struggle for Equality* (1964).

Then, in March 1964, she quietly divorced Robert Nemiroff, formalizing the separation that had occurred several years earlier. Only close friends and family had known; their continued collaboration as theater artists and activists had masked the reality of the personal relationship. Those outside their close circle only learned about the divorce when Hansberry's will was read in 1965.

Throughout 1964, hospitalizations became more frequent as the cancer spread. In May she left the hospital to deliver a speech to the winners of the United Negro College Fund's writing contest in which she coined the now-famous phrase, "young, gifted, and Black." A month later she left her sickbed to participate in the Town Hall debate "The Black Revolution and the White Backlash," at which she and her fellow Black artists challenged the criticism by white liberals of the growing militancy of the civil rights movement. She also managed to complete *The Sign in Sidney Brustein's Window*, which opened to mixed reviews on October 15, 1964, at the Longacre Theatre. Critics were somewhat surprised by this second play from a woman who had come to be identified with the

Black liberation movement. Writing about people she had known in Greenwich Village, Hansberry had created a play with a primarily white cast and a theme that called for intellectuals to get involved with social problems and world issues.

On January 12, 1965, Lorraine Hansberry's battle with cancer ended. She died at University Hospital in New York City at the age of thirty-four. Her passing was mourned throughout the nation and in many parts of the world. The list of senders of telegrams and cards sent to her family reads like a who's who of the civil rights movement and the American theater. *The Sign in Sidney Brustein's Window* closed on the night of her death.

Hansberry left a number of finished and unfinished projects, among them *Laughing Boy*, a musical adapted from Oliver LaFarge's novel; an adaptation of *The Marrow of Tradition* by Charles Chesnutt; a film version of *Masters of the Dew*; sections of a semiautobiographical novel, *The Dark and Beautiful Warriors*; and numerous essays, including a critical commentary written in 1957 on Simone de Beauvoir's *The Second Sex* (a book that Hansberry said had changed her life). In her will she designated her former husband, Robert Nemiroff, as executor of her literary estate.

Hansberry's reputation has continued to grow since her death in 1965 as the now late Nemiroff, who owned her papers, edited, published, and produced her work posthumously. In 1969, he adapted some of her unpublished writings for the stage under the title *To Be Young, Gifted, and Black*. The longest-running drama of the 1968-69 off-Broadway season, it toured colleges and communities in the United States during 1970-71; a ninety-minute film based on the stage play was first shown in January 1972.

In 1970, Nemiroff produced on Broadway a new work by Hansberry, *Les Blancs*, a full-length play set in the midst of a violent revolution in an African country. Nemiroff then edited *Les Blancs: The Collected Last Plays of Lorraine Hansberry*, published in 1972 and including *Les Blancs, The Drinking Gourd*, and *What Use Are Flowers?*, a short play on the consequences of nuclear holocaust. In 1974, *A Raisin in the Sun* returned to Broadway as *Raisin*, a musical, produced by Robert Nemiroff; it won an Antoinette Perry (Tony) Award.

In 1987, *A Raisin in the Sun*, with original material restored, was presented at the Roundabout Theatre in New York, the Kennedy Center in Washington, D.C., and other theaters nationwide. In 1989, this version was presented on national television. In March 1988, *Les Blancs*, also with much of the original

script restored, was presented at Arena Stage in Washington, D.C., the first professional production in eighteen years.

Hansberry made a very significant contribution to American theater, despite the brevity of her theatrical life and the fact that only two of her plays were produced during her lifetime. *A Raisin in the Sun* was more than simply a "first" to be commemorated in history books and then forgotten. The play was the turning point for Black artists in the professional theater. Authenticity and candor combined with timeliness to make it one of the most popular plays ever produced on the American stage. The original production ran for 538 performances on Broadway, attracting large audiences of white and Black fans alike. Also, in this play and in her second produced play, Hansberry offered a strong opposing voice to the drama of despair. She created characters who affirmed life in the face of brutality and defeat. Walter

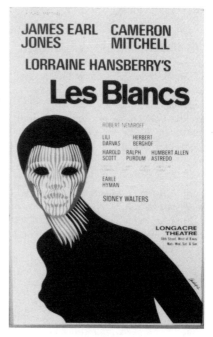

Les Blancs premiered on Broadway in 1970, five years after its author's death from cancer. The play is set in the midst of a violent revolution in an African country. In 1988, a revised version of the script was produced at Washington's Arena Stage. [Schomburg Center]

The Broadway production of A Raisin in the Sun *made Lorraine Hansberry a celebrity overnight. Drama critic Walter Kerr, in his opening night review, stated, "The mood is forty-nine parts anger and forty-nine parts control, with a very narrow escape hatch for the steam these abrasive contraries build up." [Schomburg Center]*

Younger in *A Raisin in the Sun*, supported by a culture of hope and aspiration, survives and grows; and even Sidney Brustein, lacking cultural support, resists the temptation to despair by a sheer act of will, by reaffirming his link to the human family.

With the growth of women's theater and feminist criticism, Hansberry has been rediscovered by a new generation of women in theater. Indeed, a revisionist reading of her major plays reveals that she was a feminist long before the women's movement surfaced. The female characters in her plays are pivotal to the major themes. They may share the protagonist role, as in *A Raisin in the Sun*, where Mama is coprotagonist with Walter; or a woman character may take the definitive action, as in *The Drinking Gourd*, in which Rissa, the house slave, defies the slave system (and Black stereotypes) by turning her back on her dying master and arming her son for his escape to the North. In *The Sign in Sidney Brustein's Window*,

Sidney is brought to a new level of self-awareness through the actions of a chorus of women—the Parodus sisters. Likewise, the African woman dancer is ever present in Tshemabe Matoeseh's mind in *Les Blancs*, silently and steadily moving him to a revolutionary commitment to his people. Hansberry's portrayal of Beneatha as a young Black woman with aspirations to be a doctor and her introduction of abortion as an issue for poor women in *A Raisin in the Sun* signaled early on Hansberry's feminist attitudes. These and other portrayals of women challenged prevailing stage stereotypes of both Black and white women and introduced feminist issues to the stage in compelling terms. Recently uncovered documents revealing Hansberry's sensitivity to homophobic attitudes have further stimulated feminist interest in her work. When more of her papers are released for publication, the full scope of Lorraine Hansberry's work will be appreciated and assessed.

A recent reprint of *A Raisin in the Sun* and *The Sign in Sidney Brustein's Window*, edited by Robert Nemiroff (1987), contains material restored to both scripts, a foreword by Nemiroff, an appreciation by Frank Rich, and critical essays by Amiri Baraka and John Braine. Hansberry's published works appear in various English language editions (as well as in French, German, Japanese, and other languages). The uncompleted *Toussaint* appears in *9 Plays by Black Women*, edited by Margaret B. Wilkerson (1968).

[This entry was originally published in *Notable Women in the American Theatre: A Biographical Dictionary*, ed. A. M. Robinson, V. Roberts, and M. S. Barranger (1989).]

BIBLIOGRAPHY

Anderson, Michael, et al. *Crowell's Handbook of Contemporary Drama* (1971); *AWW*; Bigsby, C.W.E. *Confrontation and Commitment: A Study of Contemporary American Drama 1959-1960* (1968); *Biographical Encyclopaedia and Who's Who of the American Theatre* (1966); Carter, Steven R. *Hansberry's Drama: Commitment Amid Complexity* (1991); *Current Biography* (1959); *DLB*; *Freedomways*, "Lorraine Hansberry: Art of Thunder, Vision of Light" (1979); Matlaw, Myron. *Modern World Drama: An Encyclopedia* (1972); May, Robin. *A Companion to the Theatre: The Anglo American Stage from 1920* (1973); *McGraw-Hill Encyclopedia of World Drama* (1972); Mitchel, Loften. *Black Drama: The Story of the American Negro in Theatre* (1967); *SBAA*; *Twentieth-Century American Literature* (1980); *Who's Who of American Women, 1964-1965* (1963); *Who Was Who in America, 1961-1968* (1968).

SELECTED WORKS BY LORRAINE HANSBERRY
"Willy Loman, Walter Lee Younger, and He Who Must Live," *Village Voice* (August 12, 1959); "On Summer,"

Playbill (June 27, 1960); "The Complex of Womanhood," *Ebony* (August 1960); "A Challenge to Artists," *Freedomways* (Winter 1961); "Images and Essences: 1961 Dialogue with an Uncolored Egghead Containing Wholesome Intentions and Some Sass," *Urbanite* (May 1961); "Genet, Mailer, and the New Paternalism," *Village Voice* (June 1, 1961); "The Black Revolution and the White Backlash," transcript of Town Hall Forum, *National Guardian* (July 1964); "The Nation Needs Your Gifts," *Negro Digest* (August 1964); "The Legacy of W.E.B. Du Bois," *Freedomways* (Winter 1965); "Original Prospectus for the John Brown Memorial Theatre of Harlem," *Black Scholar* (July/August 1979); "The Negro Writer and His Roots: Toward a New Romanticism," *Black Scholar* (March/April 1981); "All the Dark and Beautiful Warriors," *Village Voice* (August 16, 1983); "The Buck Williams Tennessee Memorial Association," *Southern Exposure* (September/October 1984).

AUDIOVISUAL MATERIALS
Lorraine Hansberry Speaks Out: Art and the Black Revolution, Caedmon Records TC1352 (1972); *Lorraine Hansberry: The Black Experience in the Creation of Drama*, Films for the Humanities, Princeton, New Jersey (1976); *A Raisin in the Sun*, distributed by Swann Films (1961); *To Be Young, Gifted, and Black*, production of NET, Educational Broadcasting Corp. (1972).

MARGARET B. WILKERSON

HARDIN, LILLIAN *see* ARMSTRONG, LILLIAN ("LIL") HARDIN

HARE, MAUD CUNEY (1874-1936)

Maud Cuney Hare dreamed of racial integration in the world of the performing arts—a seemingly impossible dream in the rigidly stratified and segregated Boston of the 1920s. Born in Galveston, Texas, in 1874, she was the daughter of Adelina Bowie and Norris Wright Cuney, a prominent businessman and leader in state and national politics. Maud Cuney Hare's goal was to propel young Black talent into the mainstream of art and music. "I abhor the segregated districts," she confided in a letter dated September 25, 1927, to the African educator and feminist Adelaide Casely. Surviving playbills suggest that Hare's dream was indeed realized in the form of the Allied Arts Center, which sponsored productions of Black playwrights' work.

In her own artistic right Maud Cuney Hare was a pianist trained at the New England Conservatory of Music in Boston and a musicologist who did research on Black musical expression in the Caribbean. Like contemporary Zora Neale Hurston, she traveled to Mexico, the Virgin Islands, Haiti, Puerto Rico, and Cuba in search of African survivals—instruments, rhythms, and popular dances—in the New World.

Hare was also a playwright, as revealed in the four-act romantic drama entitled *Antar of Araby* that appeared in 1930. This play tells of a legendary Arab, or perhaps Persian, desert poet who romances the daughter of an Arab chieftain. The issue is color, for Antar is a slave whose dark pigmentation and low social status are a barrier to winning her hand. It is more than likely that Antar is a metaphor for the tragedy of Black Americans, barred from the enjoyment of equality and privilege by a senseless color code.

In all of her writing, Hare expressed an unfailingly optimistic outlook. She believed that, as in the denouement of *Antar of Araby*, Black talent would succeed on its own merits and be accepted into the American mainstream. Records show that she died of cancer in Boston in 1936.

BIBLIOGRAPHY
Dannett, Sylvia G. *Profiles of Negro Womanhood* (1964); Ellis, Ethel M., comp. *Opportunity: A Journal of Negro Life* (1971); Hatch, James V. and Omanii Abdullah. *Black Playwrights, 1823-1977: An Annotated Bibliography of Plays* (1977); Herman, Kali, ed. *Women in Particular: An Index to American Women* (1984); Kellner, Bruce. *The Harlem Renaissance: A Historical Dictionary for the Era* (1984); Richardson, Marilyn. *Black Women and Religion* (1980); Roses, Lorraine Elena and Ruth Elizabeth Randolph. *Harlem Renaissance and Beyond* (1990); Spradling, Mary Mace, ed. *In Black and White* (1980).

LORRAINE ELENA ROSES

HARLEM RENAISSANCE

The decade of the "roaring twenties," a pivotal and turbulent one in American history, was also a period of unprecedented flowering of Black culture, encompassing literature, the visual and plastic arts, as well as the performing arts. Harlem, an area in upper Manhattan where the Black community had been residing since the beginning of the century, became the epicenter of Black cultural life. Like a magnet, Harlem's fame also drew aspiring Black writers from all over the United States and the West Indies into its precincts. For almost two decades (1917-1935), they supplied art to the world.

There was plentiful Black "renaissance" elsewhere in the country, but Harlem, with its nightlife, street corner speakers, and political ferment, was the showplace. Many Black women shared in the experiences of those heady years, although their presence has been inadequately recognized and historical research on them is just beginning.

Historians have focused on the confluence of disparate forces that produced this boom in Black creativity and an audience receptive to it. One factor was the arrival in Harlem of many southern rural Black Americans in search of economic opportunity and a haven from racial oppression. They brought with them a wealth of oral tradition, regional speech patterns, and rhythms, including the blues and jazz. Another factor was the stimulus provided by literary contests of Black magazines *Opportunity* and the *Crisis* and prizes (the Amy Spingarn and the Rosenwald, for example) for aspiring writers from all over the country. The smash hit success of the all-Black musical comedy *Shuffle Along* showed that there was a white audience for Black performers and Marcus Garvey's charismatic Pan-African movement instilled race pride and a sense of community in Black Americans of diverse social classes and ethnic origins. Catalytic, too, was the enthusiasm of such white literary critics and authorities on American literature as Carl Van Doren, whom Charles S. Johnson invited to the *Opportunity* prize dinners and Carl Van Vechten, whose best-selling novel on Harlem life, *Nigger Heaven* (1925), triggered the popularity of Harlem as a stomping ground for high livers. Yet the basis and quintessence of what Alain Locke baptized in 1925 as the "New Negro Renaissance" was the extraordinary wealth of talent compressed into a small section of the big city. Langston Hughes, Countee Cullen, Jean Toomer, Wallace Thurman, James Weldon Johnson, Rudolph Fisher, Willis Richardson, Walter White, and many others were beginning to publish and to have a following. The women cohorts of the movement—Jessie Fauset, Nella Larsen, Regina Andrews, May Miller, Georgia Douglas Johnson, Zora Neale Hurston and others—were eclipsed by these high-powered talents who by virtue of their gender had more social mobility and networks than women did.

Women shared only to a limited extent in the bounty of white mainstream publishing's discovery of Black writing—Alfred Knopf published Nella Larsen, Boni and Liveright published Jessie Fauset, and Christopher Publishing published Mercedes Gilbert. However, the vast majority of the Black women writers found outlets only in the pages of race magazines, and they often had to publish their work privately.

Likewise, the patronage of wealthy white women such as Charlotte Osgood Mason, who subsidized a number of young Black writers, including Zora Neale Hurston and Langston Hughes, was not available to most of the fledgling writers, who faced constraints different from those experienced by men. When Black women, like the men, flocked to New York from the rural South and from other parts of the country, they were often perceived by the white community solely as farm laborers, potential cooks, cleaning women, nannies who would work for $2 a week (at one point Zora Neale Hurston accepted work as a domestic). Within the Black community they were constrained in other ways, expected to lend moral support to the endeavors of Black men, to dedicate themselves to family and/or church activities, and to uphold an antiquated image of virtuous womanhood. White women were beginning to bob their hair, raise their hemlines, and dance the Charleston while the Black sisters were held to nineteenth-century codes of conduct.

It is thus not surprising that evidence of women's activity would be apparent primarily behind the scenes, instrumental in the making of the Harlem Renaissance, rather than in the limelight. For example, novelist Jessie Fauset (1882-1961), an editor of the *Crisis*, was credited by Langston Hughes for being one of the midwives of the Renaissance, encouraging new talents and bringing them to public attention. As literary editor of *The Brownies' Book*, she created a children's magazine that pioneered in addressing dark-skin children and portraying them in its pages. Poet Effie Lee Newsome (1885-1979) edited a children's column in *Opportunity* as well as in the *Crisis*. Dorothy West founded and edited *Challenge*, a magazine intended to revive the flagging forces of the Renaissance. In its first issue (March 1934), *Challenge* published some prestigious writers—Countee Cullen, Harry T. Burleigh, Arna Bontemps, Helene Johnson, and Langston Hughes. Its sequel, *New Challenge*, contained the much-discussed "Blueprint for Negro Writing" by Richard Wright, a link to the next Black literary renaissance that would follow decades later.

Black women were not usually included at gatherings such as Wallace Thurman's parties, attended by Black men and white women, but we can find them, again, behind-the-scenes, in the role of facilitators, hosting their own literary salons. Regina Anderson, who also worked with Charles S. Johnson on *Opportunity*, received writers in the apartment she shared with Ethel Ray Nance and Louella Tucker.

A'Lelia Walker, heiress daughter of the wealthiest Black woman of the period, Madam C. J. Walker, threw lavish parties and served bathtub gin in her townhouse, the Dark Tower, and Dorothy Peterson had her own gatherings in Brooklyn. At the same time, Georgia Douglas Johnson's salon, the Round Table, functioned similarly in Washington, D.C. These meeting places, offered by women for the benefit of their male fellow writers, were key in providing the Renaissance with energy and a shared repertory of themes. The female promoters, however, remained in the background, nearly invisible to present-day readers. Some came into their prime only much later, beyond the 1935 date often used to delimit the Harlem Renaissance period.

Exceptions to the rule of female invisibility were the Black women in the performing arts—dance orchestra conductors, pianists, composers, and singers. These performers, many of them young girls who, like Ida Cox, had run away from home in the South, were brilliantly visible in the New York scene. Much of the glamour of Harlem night life can be associated with women who danced and sang in clubs, some as small as the Glory Hole cabaret, with its ten-foot-square floor, or as capacious as the Cotton Club. Josephine Miles (1900-1965) played in *Shuffle Along*, Ethel Moses, the "Harlem Harlow," appeared in silent Black films directed by Oscar Micheax, and Ada Brown (1890-1950) from Kansas City became "the Queen of the Blues."

As writers, in contrast, women did not enjoy a prominence comparable to that of men. Recent research has identified many important women writers of this period, nonetheless. Major women writers of the era include Zora Neale Hurston, Nella Larsen, Jessie Fauset, and Dorothy West, and poets Georgia Douglas Johnson, Anne Spencer, Helene Johnson, and Gwendolyn Bennett.

The Renaissance-era woman who perhaps attained the most recognition for her achievements and who was probably the most prolific is Zora Neale Hurston. A consummate raconteur and spontaneous wit who arrived on the Harlem scene from Howard University, she published short pieces in *Opportunity* (1925) and *Fire!!* (1926) and went on to a scholarship at Barnard College, receiving her B.A. in 1928. Hurston turned her training in anthropology under Franz Boas to the study of her native Florida's Black rural traditions, eventually producing *Mules and Men* (1935), *Tell My Horse* (1938), and works of nonfiction filled with verve, irony, and folk wisdom. Her novels, *Jonah's Gourd Vine* (1934), *Their Eyes Were Watching God* (1937), and *Moses, Man of the Mountain* (1939)

came in quick succession, testimony to the originality, sense of humor, and poetic genius of this outstanding woman.

Perhaps her masterpiece is *Their Eyes Were Watching God*, a work that has become a classic in the feminist tradition, for it tells the tale of a woman, Janie Crawford, who matures as she learns about the transience of love and the magnitude of her own power to survive and create. The present-day success of this book contrasts with its cool reception by such Black critics as Alain Locke, Richard Wright, and Sterling Brown, who stipulated social content and critique as criteria for "how the Negro should be portrayed" in art and dismissed women's voices.

It is sad and puzzling that in Hurston's last manuscripts she strayed from her muse, those folk roots of the African-American heritage, and produced uninspired work that was rejected by publishers. She died penniless in a welfare home in Fort Pierce, Florida, and was buried in a nearly unmarked grave that many years later would be searched out and consecrated by Alice Walker, whose writing was influenced and inspired by Hurston. Because of Walker's efforts, Hurston has been rediscovered by a new generation of readers and her work has come back into print and popularity. She continues to set a shining example of devotion to intellectual inquiry and creative expression, with both fiercely individualistic and socially relevant dimensions.

Many women writers of the Harlem Renaissance continue to be overlooked. Carrie Williams Clifford (1862-1934) was a poet activist whose commentaries on the injustices and sufferings specific to women of color (such as sexual harassment and abuse) foreshadow late-twentieth-century protests. Mae Virginia Cowdery (1909-1953), from Philadelphia, was a promising writer who took her own life at the age of forty-four. Mercedes Gilbert Stevenson (1889-1952) made her mark as actress, songwriter, and novelist. Her only surviving novel, *Aunt Sara's Wooden God*, appeared in 1938 with a foreword by Langston Hughes. It is a portrait of a rural Georgia mother's anguished relationship with a son torn between noble impulses and a self-destructive streak. Marita Bonner, author of many short stories and plays, received little recognition during her lifetime (1898-1971)—her stories were not collected and published until 1987. Yet her portraits of women seeking self-realization and escape from entrapment describe qualities of women's experiences that continue to be relevant.

These are just a few of the Harlem Renaissance-era women. They belong to a larger field of writers that numbers well over one hundred in all genres—poets, novelists, essayists, short-story writers, biographers, and autobiographers. There were several other fine women writers in this period—Anne Spencer (1882-1975), Dorothy West (1907-) and her cousin Helene Johnson (1907-), May Miller Sullivan (1899-), Angelina Weld Grimké (1880-1958), and Octavia Wynbush (c. 1894-1972)—and still others wrote in so-called minor genres, including drama and children's literature.

Overall, the Harlem Renaissance women were very diverse. While some defined themselves as active protesters and were devoted to the struggle against the most virulent forms of discrimination and racism, others adopted a more contemplative stance. Ida B. Wells-Barnett epitomizes a lifetime of ceaseless struggle, whereas Aloise Barbour Epperson (?-1954), stung by the devastating experiences she knew as a Black American in the racist South, removed herself from the fray to write lyric poetry.

The Harlem Renaissance was a charmed moment in time, an oasis in a desert of widespread racist exclusion, one that vanished like a mirage in the late 1930s. The stock market crash of 1929 and the Great Depression that followed led indirectly to its demise. White patrons, customers, and business people had less money to spend or invest in publishing ventures. Riots in Harlem kept many others away. So the Black participants too drifted away, carrying not only bittersweet memories and disillusionment but also a rich and resplendent literary legacy that has yet to be fully appreciated. Some women drifted apart and many foresook literary endeavors for marriage, motherhood, or passing as white. Yet the experiences they had had both as cultural promoters and as authors in their own right modeled the roles women would occupy in the civil rights era of the 1950s and the Black Arts movement of the 1960s.

These women had quietly created their own renaissance. In their clubs, their literary enclaves, their private meetings and conversations, they cleared a space for female creativity to bud and flourish. The work they produced, often of a fragmentary character—some poems here and there rather than a complete volume—is suggestive of the conflicts inherent in the competing demands of family, work life, religious life, and social work. As Gertrude Elise Johnson McDougald wrote in a 1925 essay, "In Harlem, more than anywhere else, the Negro woman [was] free from the cruder handicaps of primitive household hardships and the grosser forms of sex and race subjugation" (McDougald 1925).

Black women lacked a network of mentors and a large, receptive audience that might have acknowledged them as professional writers; nor did they belong to a single coherent movement that could be called feminist. Without an established tradition for them to write freely of their experience as African-American women, they were less experimental and audacious in their writing than they might have wished to be. They could not easily assume a voice of their own. Evicted from Jim Crow trains, excluded from institutions of learning, taunted with racial epithets and libels, they wrote on pages tinged with tears. The opportunities to obtain interviews with them and to film or photograph them are forever lost, but not so the chance to search for lost manuscripts, extant photographs, and living descendants who can help piece together their story.

BIBLIOGRAPHY

Bontemps, Arna, ed. *The Harlem Renaissance Remembered* (1972); Kellner, Bruce. *The Harlem Renaissance: A Historical Dictionary for the Era* (1984); McDougald, Gertrude Elise Johnson. "The Double Task: The Struggles for Sex and Race Emancipation," *Survey* (March 1, 1925); Perry, Margaret. *The Harlem Renaissance: An Annotated Bibliography and Commentary* (1982); Roses, Lorraine. "An Interview with Dorothy West," *Sage* (Spring 1985); Roses, Lorraine Elena and Ruth Elizabeth Randolph. *Harlem Renaissance and Beyond: 100 Literary Biographies of Black Women Writers, 1900-1946* (1990); Watrous, Peter. "Harlem of the Twenties Echoes in America," *New York Times* (January 22, 1989).

LORRAINE ELENA ROSES

HARPER, FRANCES ELLEN WATKINS (1825-1911)

In "Sowing and Reaping" (1876-77), Frances Ellen Watkins Harper describes one of her characters as "a firm believer in the utility of beauty." Had she been talking about herself, she could not have chosen a more apt phrase. For sixty-eight years Frances Ellen Watkins Harper wrote, recited, and published poetry and fiction, essays, and letters, all designed to delight and to teach people how to live lives of high moral purpose and dedicated social service. She became an internationally recognized journalist, the nineteenth century's most prolific African-American novelist, and its best loved African-American poet. Frances Harper was known as the "bronze muse," but the publication of over a dozen books and innumerable poems, essays, and stories was but a part of her efforts to work for what she called "a brighter coming day." Harper was an active member of the Underground Railroad, one of the first African-American women to be hired as an abolitionist lecturer, a founder of the American Woman Suffrage Association, a member of the national board of the Women's Christian Temperance Union, and an executive officer of the Universal Peace Union. She was a founding member of the National Association of Colored Women, the director of the American Association of Educators of Colored Youth, and a tireless worker for the African Methodist Episcopal Church and the National Colored Women's Congress. By word and by deed, she became such a symbol of empowering and empowered womanhood that women across the nation organized F.E.W. Harper Leagues or, like the many Frances E. Harper Women's Christian Temperance Unions, named local chapters of national organizations after her. She was judged a "Woman of Our Race Most Worthy of Imitation," listed in *Daughters of America; or, Women of the Century*, and included in *Patriots of the American Revolution*. In his memorial tribute, the president of the Universal Peace Union, Alfred H. Love, reports that she had "acquired the title of 'Empress of Peace and Poet Laureate' " (Love 1911).

Frances Ellen Watkins was born to free parents in the slave city of Baltimore, Maryland, on September 24, 1825, but by the age of three, she was an orphan. It was a loss to which she was never reconciled. In a letter to a friend many years later, she wrote: "Have I yearned for a mother's love? The grave was my robber. Before three years had scattered their blight around my path, death had won my mother from me. Would the strong arm of a brother have been welcome? I was my mother's only child." In comparison with the majority of Black Americans of that time, however, Frances Ellen Watkins lived a privileged life. She was reared by relatives and attended the prestigious William Watkins Academy for Negro Youth, an institution founded by her uncle and noted for its emphasis upon biblical studies, the classics, and elocution as well as for the political leadership and social service of its graduates. As a young woman, Watkins was noted for her industry and intelligence. By the age of fourteen she had acquired an education superior to that of most nineteenth-century women of any color or class in the United States. She had gained a reputation locally as a writer and a scholar, but when she left the academy, the best employment she could obtain was as a seamstress and baby sitter for the owners of the local bookstore.

The slave city of Baltimore was never a comfortable place for free Black people to live, but by 1850, it had become perilous indeed. When her uncle closed his school and moved his family to Canada, Frances Watkins decided to leave also. She moved to Ohio and became the first female faculty person at the newly established Union Seminary, the precursor to what is now Wilberforce University. In his annual report, principal John M. Brown noted that "Miss Watkins . . . has been faithful to her trust, and has manifested in every effort a commendable zeal for the cause of education; and a sacrificing spirit, so that it may be promoted." After Union Seminary, she taught in Little York, Pennsylvania; then in 1853, she moved to Philadelphia in order to devote herself entirely to the abolitionist cause. The exact nature of her involvement there is not known, but we do know that she lived with the William Still family whose home was the main depot of the Philadelphia Underground Railroad. She frequented the local antislavery offices where she learned both the theory and practice of that organization, and she published several poems and essays in Frederick Douglass's paper the *Liberator*, the *Christian Recorder*, and other periodicals.

By 1854, Frances Ellen Watkins was in New Bedford, Massachusetts, lecturing on antislavery and equal rights topics, and shortly thereafter she was employed by the Maine Anti-Slavery Society as a traveling lecturer. Watkins's travels took her throughout the New England area and southern Canada, as far west as Detroit, Michigan, and Cincinnati, Ohio. She became a highly popular speaker and earned accolades from journalists who applauded her highly articulate and "fiery" speeches yet reported her delivery as "marked by dignity and composure" and "without the slightest violation of good taste." Frances Ellen Watkins often incorporated her own poetry into her lectures. This, combined with her regular publication in various newspapers and magazines, helped to create her national reputation as a poet. Thus, when *Poems on Miscellaneous Subjects* was published in 1854, it was printed in both Boston and Philadelphia, sold over 10,000 copies in three years, and was enlarged and reissued in 1857. Most likely it was her considerable contribution to the antislavery efforts that has made many scholars refer to her as an abolitionist poet, but this volume, and all of her subsequent collections, contained poems on a variety of subjects. In addition to well-known antislavery poems such as "The Slave Mother," "The Fugitive's Wife," and "The Slave Auction," the majority of the poems in *Poems on Miscellaneous Subjects* deal with issues such as religion, heroism, women's rights, Black achievement, and temperance. Some of the poems are responses to contemporary writers such as Harriet Beecher Stowe and Charles Dickens. Some are reinterpretations of Bible stories. Others comment on events such as the murder of Elijah Lovejoy in 1837, the Methodist church's expulsion of one of its ministers because of his antislavery stance, and the news report about a slave in Tennessee who was beaten to death because he would not testify about an escape attempt by other slaves.

The major themes of Harper's early writing and lectures are those that she expounded throughout her career: personal integrity, Christian service, and social equality. Far from repeating homilies and slogans, however, the full corpus of her work reveals a unique blend of idealism and pragmatism, faith and philosophy. Though she consistently wrote of being "Saved by Faith," of looking for "Light in Darkness," and of believing that "The Pure in Heart Shall See God," she also spoke crisply, even stridently, about the need for mass political action, the virtues of civil disobedience and economic boycotts, and the occasional necessity for physical confrontation. She argued that it was not enough to express sympathy without taking action. According to the Philadelphia press, she was one of the most liberal and able advocates of her day for the Underground Railroad and the slave. She was a longtime friend and colleague to activists such as Sojourner Truth, Susan B. Anthony, Frederick Douglass, and Henry Highland Garnet, and she remained a staunch and public supporter of John Brown after the failure of the Harpers Ferry raid. Her personal hero was Moses. "I like the character of Moses," she said, because "He is the first disunionist we read about in the Jewish scriptures" (*Moses* 1869).

Hers was not an assimilationist or a separationist creed; Frances Ellen Watkins Harper preferred education over violence. She believed, as one of her early essays declared, "We Are All Bound Up Together." The burdens of one group were "The Burdens of All" and as the poem of that name makes clear, without interracial cooperation, no group will be spared: "The burdens will always be heavy, / The sunshine fade into night, / Till mercy and justice shall cement / The black, the brown and the white."

Yet Frances Ellen Watkins Harper recognized the contradictions and complexities of issues and was not afraid to take controversial stands or to compromise when necessary. For example, she worked assiduously with the American Equal Rights Association but when the racism of Elizabeth Cady Stanton, Susan B. Anthony, and other white feminists became apparent in their disparaging remarks about Black men, she sided against them, urged the passage of the Fifteenth Amendment allowing Blacks to vote even though it excluded women, and ultimately contributed to the dissolution of that group and the formation of the American Woman Suffrage Association. Harper made her position widely known. She believed in equal rights for all, but if there had to be a choice between rights for Black Americans and rights for women, then she would not encourage any Black woman to put a single straw in the way to prevent the progress of Black men. She took this stance even though she also argued that her own close observation had shown that women are the movers in social reform, that while men talk about changes, the women are implementing them.

In 1860, Frances Ellen Watkins married Fenton Harper, a widower with three children. They moved to a farm outside Columbus, Ohio, and they had a daughter, Mary. Marriage and family responsibilities left her little time to lecture or to write, but during the Civil War years, Frances Harper did continue to speak out and to publish occasionally. Fenton Harper died in 1864 and that same year Harper returned to full-time lecturing. For the next several years, she traveled continuously throughout the North and in every southern state except Texas and Arkansas, lecturing and working for the Reconstruction effort. Papers throughout the nation advertised her appearances, reported on her travels, and published her letters about her experiences. Despite her hectic schedule, Frances Harper did some of her most experimental writing in the postbellum years. In 1869, she published a serialized novel, *Minnie's Sacrifice*, in the *Christian Recorder* and *Moses: A Story of the Nile*, a long dramatic poem that retells the Old Testament version of the Hebrews' Egyptian captivity and exodus. *Sketches of Southern Life* (1872), a pioneering effort in African-American dialect and folk characters that tells the story of slavery and reconstruction through a series of poems by "Aunt Chloe," is considered by many critics to be her most innovative and best literary contribution. In 1873, Harper began writing for the *Christian Recorder* a series of fictionalized essays called "Fancy Etchings." Using a cast of characters whose conversations upon current events and social mores served to expose the issues and propose solutions, Harper pioneered the journalistic genre that others such as Langston Hughes were to make popular a half century later.

Her experimentation with literary technique supplemented but did not replace her preference for lyrical ballads nor did her writing detract from her social involvement. In 1871, Harper arranged for the publication of the twentieth edition of *Poems on Mis-*

cellaneous Subjects and of the first collection of her published poetry since 1857, a volume simply titled *Poems*. About that time, she also bought a house, and 1006 Bainbridge, Philadelphia, Pennsylvania, became her address until she died. She had become a homeowner, but Frances Harper was rarely at home. She was in great demand as a speaker for lecture series and as a delegate to numerous conventions. She helped develop Sunday schools and Young Men's Christian Association groups in the Black community and she worked for the rehabilitation of juvenile delinquents and the security of the aged and infirm. In 1873, she became superintendent of the Colored Section of the Philadelphia and Pennsylvania Women's Christian Temperance Union and in 1883 she became national superintendent of work among the colored people. In this capacity she tried to help those who wished to join the white groups to do so and those who preferred to organize themselves separately to do that. For Frances Ellen Watkins Harper it was a matter of coalition building. She recognized and did not apologize for racism among some of the individuals with whom they might need to affiliate but declared this a "relic ... from the dead past." Her comments in

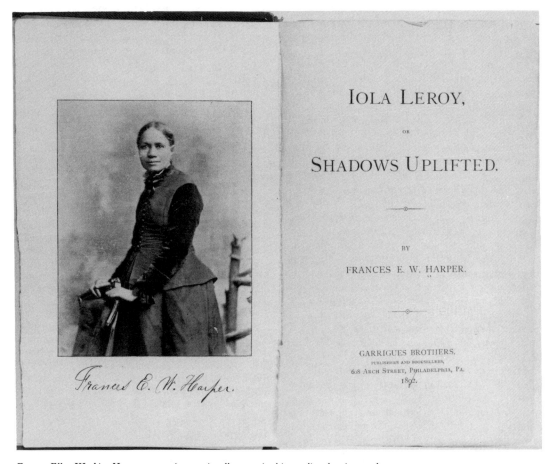

IOLA LEROY,

OR

SHADOWS UPLIFTED.

BY

FRANCES E. W. HARPER.

GARRIGUES BROTHERS,
PUBLISHERS AND BOOKSELLERS,
6.8 ARCH STREET, PHILADELPHIA, PA.
1892.

Frances E. W. Harper.

Frances Ellen Watkins Harper was an internationally recognized journalist, the nineteenth century's most prolific Black novelist, and its best-loved Black poet. Her novel Iola Leroy *was written to correct the record on slavery and Reconstruction, to inspire African-Americans to be proud of their past and diligent in their work toward a greater future, and to persuade all Americans that a stronger sense of justice was essential to the peace and prosperity of the country. [Moorland-Spingarn]*

"The Woman's Christian Temperance Union and the Colored Woman" (1888) are typical of her stance on this issue. In writing about the southern white women who would not work in harmony with Black women, Harper satirizes their pretentiousness and makes it clear that in failing to acknowledge their common interests these women are not only risking their political future but also their Christian rewards. "Let them remember," she writes, "that the most ignorant, vicious and degraded voter outranks, politically, the purest, best and most cultured woman in the South, and learn to look at the question of Christian affiliation on this subject, not in the shadow of the fashion of this world that fadeth away, but in the light of the face of Jesus Christ. And can any one despise the least of Christ's brethren without despising Him?" (*Sketches* 1872).

On issues of joint concern, Frances Harper believed in and worked with coalitions, but her priorities were always with the progress and elevation of African-Americans. Two of her serials, "Sowing and Reaping: A Temperance Story" (1876-77), whose title says it all, and "Trial and Triumph" (1888-89), a story about the Black middle class during the post-Reconstruction period, were written to that end. It was the 1892 novel, *Iola Leroy, Or, Shadows Uplifted*, a work that the *African Methodist Episcopal Church Review* called the crowning effort of her life, that became her best-known novel. Weaving her story from threads of fact and fiction, Harper wrote to correct the record on slavery and Reconstruction, to inspire African-Americans to be proud of their past and diligent in their work toward a greater future, and to persuade all Americans that a stronger sense of justice and a more Christlike humanity was essential to the peace and prosperity of the United States. Incorporating the patterns of antebellum slave narratives and of novels such as *Clotel, The Garies and Their Friends, The Royal Gentleman*, and *Bricks without Straw*—while refuting the themes of works such as *In Ole Virginia* and *Birth of a Nation*—Harper hoped to demonstrate yet again the utility of beauty.

Iola Leroy appears to have been Harper's last long literary project. After that work, she published at least five collections of poetry: *The Sparrow's Fall and Other Poems* (c.1894), *Atlanta Offering: Poems* (1895), *Martyr of Alabama and Other Poems* (c. 1895), *Poems* (1900) and *Light beyond the Darkness* (n.d.). However, these are generally rearrangements of previously published volumes supplemented by previously uncollected works.

At the beginning of the twentieth century, Frances Ellen Watkins Harper declared the beginning of a "woman's era" and clearly intended to be a part of that brighter coming day. She traveled less and published infrequently, but her counsel and her concern continued to be eagerly sought. During her last years, Harper was often sick. Believing that because of her failing health and her old age, she would not be able to support herself, many people offered her a place to live and continuing care. Always, Frances Ellen Watkins Harper gently but firmly declined, saying that she had always been independent, that she loved her liberty, and that she would support herself without charity, as she had always done.

Frances Ellen Watkins Harper died February 20, 1911. Her funeral was held at the First Unitarian Church in Philadelphia. She is buried in Eden Cemetery. She was a firm believer in the utility of beauty. She was independent, she loved liberty, she was self-supporting, and her record stands as a testimony to the strength, courage, and vision of African-American women who wrote and worked for a brighter coming day.

[*See also* ABOLITION MOVEMENT; SUFFRAGE MOVEMENT; TEMPERANCE WORK IN THE NINETEENTH CENTURY.]

BIBLIOGRAPHY

AAW1; Bacon, Margaret Hope. " 'One Great Bundle of Humanity': Frances Ellen Watkins Harper (1825-1911)," *Pennsylvania Magazine of History and Biography* (January 1989); Carby, Hazel V. *Reconstructing Womanhood: The Emergence of the Afro-American Woman Novelist* (1987); Christian, Barbara. *Black Woman Novelists: The Development of a Tradition, 1892-1976* (1980); *DANB*; Daniels, Theodora Williams. "The Poems of Frances E. W. Harper," Master's thesis (1937); Love, Alfred H. "Memorial Tribute to Mrs. Frances E. W. Harper," *The Peacemaker and Court of Arbitration* (June/July 1911); McDowell, Deborah E. " 'The Changing Same': Generational Connections and Black Women Novelists," *New Literary History* (Winter 1987); *NAW*; Redding, J. Saunders. *To Make a Poet Black* (1939); Still, William. *The Underground Rail Road* ([1871] 1970); Washington, Mary Helen, ed. *Invented Lives: Narratives of Black Women, 1860-1960* (1988); Williams, Kenny J. *They Also Spoke: An Essay on Negro Literature in America* (1970).

SELECTED WORKS BY FRANCES ELLEN WATKINS HARPER

Poems on Miscellaneous Subjects ([1854] 1871); *Moses: A Story of the Nile* (1869); "Minnie's Sacrifice," *Christian Recorder* (March 20, 1869-September 25, 1869); *Poems* ([1871] 1970); *Sketches of Southern Life* (1872); "Fancy Etchings," *Christian Recorder* (April 24, 1873-July 3, 1873); "Fancy Sketches," *Christian Recorder* (January 15, 1874); "Sowing and Reaping: A Temperance Story," *Christian Recorder* (August 10, 1876-February 8, 1877); "Trial and Triumph," *Christian Recorder* (October 4, 1888-February

14, 1889); "The Woman's Christian Temperance Union and the Colored Woman," *African Methodist Episcopal Church Review* (1888); *Iola Leroy, Or, Shadows Uplifted* ([1892] 1988); *The Sparrow's Fall and Other Poems* (c.1894); *Atlanta Offering: Poems* ([1895] 1969); *Martyr of Alabama and Other Poems* (c.1895); *Poems* (1900); *Light beyond the Darkness* (n.d.).

COLLECTIONS
Foster, Frances Smith, ed. *A Brighter Coming Day: A Frances E. W. Harper Reader* (1990); Graham, Maryemma, ed. *The Complete Poems of Frances E. W. Harper* (1988).

FRANCES SMITH FOSTER

HARRIS, BARBARA (1930-)

Barbara Harris was the first Black woman—indeed, the first woman—to become a bishop in the Episcopal church. She was born on June 12, 1930, in Philadelphia, Pennsylvania, to Walter Harris and Beatrice Price Harris. She attended the Philadelphia High School for Girls and, as a teenager, started a young adults group at her local church, Saint Barnabas Church. It quickly became the largest church youth group in Philadelphia. Her friends from school remember her as charming, spirited, and carefree. After graduating from high school, Harris took a job with Joe Baker Associates, a public relations firm. One of her responsibilities there was to edit a publication promoting historically Black colleges. At her church, she was active in the St. Dismas Society, a prison-visiting group, and belonged to the adult fellowship, which had grown out of her young adults group.

Harris went on to a position in public relations with Sun Oil Company and, back at her church, became a board member of the Pennsylvania Prison Society. She continued her volunteer work in prisons for fifteen years. In 1968, after Saint Barnabas merged with Saint Luke's, a primarily white parish, Harris decided that the resulting church was too sedate, and she became a member of the North Philadelphia Church of the Advocate. In that same year, a group of Black Episcopal ministers formed the Union of Black Clergy. Harris was one of several women who lobbied for membership in the organization and were admitted, adding "and Laity" to the name. Eventually, the group became the Union of Black Episcopalians, and Barbara Harris was an active member.

It seems likely that if women had been accepted as part of the Episcopal clergy earlier, Harris would never have worked in public relations. As soon as the ordination of women was approved, she began to

At the end of her ordination ceremony (February 12, 1989), Bishop Barbara Harris blessed the congregation. The first female Episcopalian bishop, she has been outspoken in her support of the rights of Black Americans, women, the poor, and other ethnic minorities. [AP/Wide World Photos]

study for the ministry. She attended Villanova University from 1977 to 1979 and the Urban Theology Unit in Sheffield, England. She was ordained a deacon in 1979, served as deacon-in-training at her own church until 1980, and was ordained a priest in that year. From 1980 to 1984, she was priest-in-charge at Saint Augustine-of-Hippo in Norristown, and attended Hobart and William Smith Colleges in 1981. For the five years after she left Norristown, she was executive director of the Episcopal Church Publishing Company. She was serving as interim rector at the Church of the Advocate when she was elected suffragan bishop of the diocese of Massachusetts.

Harris's election was surrounded by controversy. There were those who objected simply because she was a woman, but this objection was essentially futile because the General Convention of the Episcopal Church had opened all orders to women thirteen years earlier. Then there were those who complained that she was divorced. However, there had been divorced male bishops before. Those who opposed her election then criticized her educational background. However, Harris had followed an educational route that was approved by the church as an alternate to the more traditional one. If it made her fit for ordination, her supporters argued, it made her fit for the bishopric.

What may have been at the heart of some of the objections was her social activism rather than either her gender or her color. She has always been outspoken in her defense of the rights of Black Americans, women, the poor, and other ethnic minorities. She has fiercely attacked, in print, the firebombing of abortion clinics and those who excuse this sort of terrorism. She has spoken out on the issues surrounding acquired immune deficiency syndrome (AIDS) and people with AIDS. Many people are uncomfortable with her stands, and with good reason. She is an uncommonly challenging choice as the first Black woman bishop of the worldwide Anglican communion.

BIBLIOGRAPHY

NA; *NBAW*; *WWBA* (1992).

KATHLEEN THOMPSON

Tired of wages that averaged between five and six dollars a week, Export workers struck the company in August 1938. The eighteen-day strike galvanized Richmond's Congress of Industrial Organizations unions, which donated money for strike relief and bodies for the picket lines. The sight of picketing white women from the International Ladies' Garment Workers Union horrified the police and the Richmond elite, but it was the presence of hundreds of tobacco workers, all "black and evil" according to Harris, that won the strike.

Although little is known about her life, Louise "Mamma" Harris exemplified the numerous Black women workers who stepped forward in the South during the 1930s and 1940s to demand respect and an end to discrimination and exploitation. Black women dominated the tobacco factories, particularly those that processed the leaf for manufacture. For over a hundred years these plants had been their livelihood, and, despite the hardships, they developed a rich culture of mutuality and opposition. Commenting on the power of women during the 1938 strike, Harris observed, "They [the police and bosses] 'fraid of the women. You can out talk the men. But us women don't take no tea for the fever."

BIBLIOGRAPHY

Jackson, Augusta V. "A New Deal for Tobacco Workers," *Crisis* (October 1938); Poston, Ted. "The Making of Mamma Harris," *New Republic* (November 4, 1940).

ROBERT KORSTAD

HARRIS, LOUISE "MAMMA" (b.1891)

Louise "Mamma" Harris was a rank-and-file leader of the Tobacco Stemmers and Laborers Union at Export Leaf Tobacco Company in Richmond, Virginia. Workers organized this independent union in 1937 with the help of activists from the Southern Negro Youth Congress to help win higher wages and improved working conditions.

Born in 1891, Louise Harris left school at the age of eight to begin caring for younger children and cooking in the homes of white people in Richmond. She entered the tobacco factories in her early forties and quickly appreciated the conditions that would lead to her involvement in the union. "It took me just one day to find out," she told *New Republic* writer Ted Poston, "that preachers don't know nothing about hell. They ain't worked in a tobacco factory."

HARRIS, MARCELITE JORDON (1943-)

Marcelite Jordon Harris, a graduate of Spelman College in Atlanta, Georgia, served as a White House aide to President Jimmy Carter. She is also the first and only Black woman to earn the rank of general in the U.S. Air Force. While the native Texan may not yet be eligible for the title of Georgia's "favorite daughter," Atlanta Mayor Andrew Young was impressed enough to declare a Marcelite J. Harris Day on May 30, 1988; she was presented with the key to the city of Detroit in 1990; and Houston designated February 11, 1991, as Marcelite J. Harris Day. Marcelite J. Harris has made it to the top of her field, and in the process she has accumulated a succession of firsts.

Harris earned a B.A. in speech and drama from Spelman College in 1964 and a B.S. in business management from the University of Maryland, Asian Division in 1986. After teaching in the Head Start program in 1964-65, Harris joined the air force. Her initial assignments in administration were unchallenging, so she applied for the maintenance specialty hoping to repair airplanes. After two unsuccessful attempts, Harris was admitted into the military occupational specialty of maintenance. She was the first woman aircraft maintenance officer in the U.S. Air Force. Then, in December 1988, Harris became the first female wing commander of the Air Training Command at Keesler Air Force Base in Gulfport, Mississippi. The air force school at this command trains thousands from all branches of the military in highly technical fields such as computer science, communications, avionics, electronics, and air traffic control. To continually update her own training, she has attended Central Michigan University, the University of Maryland, Harvard University, and the National Defense Institute, among others.

General Harris is married to Air Force Lt. Colonel Maurice Harris and has a teenaged stepson, Steven, and a nine-year-old daughter, Tenecia.

BIBLIOGRAPHY

Alumnae Records, Spelman College, Atlanta, Georgia; Darby, Joe. "Woman Rises High in the Air Force," *New Orleans Times Picayune* (December 4, 1988).

LINDA ROCHELLE LANE

HARRIS, PATRICIA ROBERTS
(1924-1985)

An acute intelligence and tremendous confidence in herself led Patricia Roberts Harris to a brilliant political and academic career filled with "firsts"—the first Black woman to head a United States embassy, to serve in a president's cabinet, and to head a law school. She was born in 1924 in Mattoon, Illinois, to Bert and Chiquita Roberts. She and her brother were brought up by their mother after their father abandoned the family. The Roberts family was one of the few Black families in Mattoon, and Patricia was aware of racism by the age of six, though she was determined to do whatever she was able to do.

After graduating from a Chicago high school, Roberts went to Howard University. Four years later, she received her A.B. summa cum laude. While at Howard, Roberts participated in one of the first student sit-ins in an attempt to integrate the Little Palace cafeteria.

Back in Chicago, Roberts went to work for the Chicago Young Women's Christian Association and then became executive director of Delta Sigma Theta. She also met and married William Beasley Harris, a lawyer. Her husband encouraged her to go to law school and, in 1957, she enrolled in the George Washington University School of Law. Upon graduation, she went to work for the criminal division of the United States Department of Justice for about a year before joining the faculty of the Howard University Law School. In 1965, Harris was appointed ambassador to Luxembourg by President Lyndon Johnson. She served in that capacity until September 1967, when she returned to Howard. At this time she was also an alternate delegate to the United Nations.

For a brief time in 1969, Harris was dean of the School of Law at Howard, making her the first Black woman to head a law school. However, she resigned within a month after she was appointed, following student and faculty conflicts. She joined a prestigious Washington, D.C., law firm and practiced corporate law until she was appointed U.S. Secretary of Housing and Urban Development by President Jimmy Carter in 1977, a position she held until 1979, when

Patricia Roberts Harris was the first Black woman to head a law school, serve as a U.S. ambassador, and hold a cabinet position. [Moorland-Spingarn]

she became U.S. Secretary of Health, Education and Welfare until the Reagan administration in 1982.

In that year, Harris ran for mayor of the District of Columbia but was defeated by Marion S. Barry. The following year she joined the faculty of George Washington University. She taught there for less than two years before dying of cancer on March 23, 1985.

BIBLIOGRAPHY

CBWA; EBA; NA; NBAW.

KATHLEEN THOMPSON

HARRISON, HAZEL (1883-1969)

There are no recordings of the performances of Hazel Harrison, but historical evidence indicates that she was a remarkable pianist. She was certainly an inspiring and effective teacher.

Harrison was born on May 12, 1883, in La Porte, Indiana. Her parents, Hiram James and Olive J. Wood, recognized her musical talent early. She began to study the piano before she was five years old and was soon an accomplished pianist, performing for socials and in local musicales. Before long, she became a student of the well-known teacher Victor Heinze. While Harrison was in high school, Ferruccio Busoni, a great pianist of the time, made a tour of America. Through Heinze's efforts, Busoni agreed to listen to Harrison play. He was favorably impressed and urged her to complete high school and to concentrate on her musical technique, agreeing to see her again when she was older.

Three years after her high school graduation, Harrison was able to go to Europe, debuting at the Singakademie in Berlin to favorable reviews in October 1904 and returning to La Porte in January 1905. For six more years Harrison taught, practiced, and gave recitals. In 1911, she returned to Europe. She spent her first year in Berlin studying with a prominent German teacher, who arranged for her to play again for Busoni. She then worked with Busoni for two years until the outbreak of World War I, when she was forced to return home.

Beginning in 1914, Harrison toured the United States giving concerts. In addition to works from the standard classical repertoire, she included in her performances compositions by Black Americans such as William Dawson, Hall Johnson, and Elnora Manson. She also had the courage to perform the more radical contemporary composers of her day such as Stravinsky,

Extraordinary pianist Hazel Harrison salted the standard classical repertoire with the compositions of Black Americans and of then-radical composers such as Stravinsky and Ravel as she toured Europe and the United States in the 1910s and 1920s. [Schomburg Center]

Ravel, and Laszlo. In 1922, she joined the staff of Pauline James Lee's Chicago University of Music.

In 1926, Harrison made her final trip to Europe. This time she studied with a former student of Busoni's, Egon Petri. She stayed in Europe for ten months and returned to the United States to great acclaim. She was now recognized as a virtuoso and received many honors in the years that followed. During a Young Women's Christian Association leadership-of-women conference in 1929, she was chosen, from among women of all races, as a model for young people in the arts. In 1930, she made her Town Hall debut in New York City. She also performed that year at Boston's Jordan Hall, not a usual venue for Black Americans at that time.

Another career began for Harrison in 1931, when she was forty-eight years old. She began teaching at Tuskegee Institute in Alabama. After five years there, she went to Howard University. At both schools she overcame resistance to her lack of a degree through her expertise, artistry, and practical experience. She was at Howard until 1955 and became something of a legend to its students. During that time, she took a three-year sabbatical to go back on the concert circuit. After her retirement from Howard she lived briefly in New York but then, in 1958, went to teach at Alabama State College, where she remained until 1963. After her retirement at the age of eighty, she performed no more. She died on April 28, 1969, at the age of eighty-five.

BIBLIOGRAPHY

Abdul, Raoul. *Blacks in Classical Music* (1977); *BDAAM*; Bloom, Eric, ed. *Grove's Dictionary of Music and Musicians* (1954); Hare, Maud Cuney. *Negro Musicians and Their Music* ([1936] 1974); *International Cyclopedia of Music and Musicians* (1975); *NAW*; Sadie, Stanley, ed. *The New Grove Dictionary of Music and Musicians* (1980); Schonberg, Harold C. *The Great Pianists* (1963); Southall, Geneva. *Blind Tom: The Post Civil-War Enslavement of a Black Musical Genius* (1979); Southern, Eileen. *The Music of Black Americans: A History* (1983); Stewart, Ruth Ann. *Portia: The Life of Portia Washington Pittman, the Daughter of Booker T. Washington* (1976). Grainger Correspondence, 1930-1948, University of Melbourne, Grainger Museum, Parkeville, Australia.

DEBORRA A. RICHARDSON

HARRIS-STEWART, LUSIA (1955-)

High scorer Lusia Harris-Stewart led the American women's Olympic basketball team to a silver medal in the 1976 Montreal Olympics. This was the first time women's basketball appeared as an Olympic sport, and Harris-Stewart scored the first two points in Olympic women's basketball history. She also led her small, previously unknown, Delta State University (Cleveland, Mississippi) basketball team to three Association for Intercollegiate Athletics for Women (AIAW) National Collegiate Basketball Championships in 1975, 1976, and 1977. As a high scoring, six-foot three-inch-tall center she was the best of the new breed of star collegiate players. She broke hundreds of records and won numerous American and international honors. She was the dominant woman basketball player of her era.

Harris-Stewart was a pioneer woman player at Delta State University on an academic scholarship. Her ability was central to attracting large crowds to Delta State's basketball arena. As the only Black player on her school's team, and one of the few Black players on the collegiate basketball teams in the mid-1970s, she served as a lonely superstar role model for Black

girls and women. She was a member of the women's team that played at Madison Square Garden in New York in February 1976. Hers was the second women's team ever to do so (the first played in 1975). The fans came, in part, to watch Harris-Stewart, who at twenty-one years old was enjoying a three-year, fifty-game winning streak. She led Delta State to victory by scoring a dazzling forty-seven points, a high-score record that season for man or woman, college player or pro. Harris-Stewart, however, was not just a basketball player; she was an active leader at Delta State. She made a place for herself in the white community, not only as a top basketball recruit but also as an acknowledged leader on campus and as the first Black woman to be chosen homecoming queen.

Born in 1955, Lusia Harris grew up the seventh of nine children on a vegetable farm in Minter City, Mississippi, a town with a population of 200. Her love of sports and pursuit of excellence in school dominated her life. Her basketball career started in her backyard with her brothers and sisters. She played basketball at Tucker Young Junior High School and became a star player at Amanda Elzy High School. When she was about to enter Alcorn A & M, she was recruited away to Delta State and became a central player in building their basketball successes. Lusia graduated from Delta State with a B.S. and M.S. degree in physical education. While still a graduate student, she became an assistant basketball coach and admissions counselor at Delta State. For a brief time in 1980, Harris-Stewart played for the Houston Angels in a new Women's Pro League. Her husband, George E. Stewart, and their four sons live in Mississippi, where she teaches physical education and coaches women's basketball.

Lusia Harris-Stewart's achievements have merited many national honors and awards. As a college player, she was selected for the AIAW All-Tournament team; she was selected three times for the Kodak All-American team; and she was voted most valuable player at an AIAW National Championship. In 1976, she was Mississippi's first Amateur Athlete of the Year. The next year, she won the Broderick Award for the top basketball player in the AIAW, and she received the Broderick Cup for the outstanding female collegiate athlete. On the national and international level, Harris-Stewart was high scorer in the 1975 World University Games in Bogota, Colombia, in the Pan American games in Mexico City the same year, and in the 1976 Olympics. In May 1992, Harris-Stewart was one of the first two women basketball players inducted into the Springfield Basketball Hall of Fame. The other woman inducted was Nera White, an international player from the Amateur Athletic Union of the United States (AAU).

Lusia Harris-Stewart remains a basketball legend and is an active role model for young people. She speaks to the importance of accomplishing through sacrifice, working to overcome obstacles, and pursuing goals.

BIBLIOGRAPHY

CBWA; Damrosch, Barbara. "First Woman in History to Sink an Olympic Basket," *WomenSports* (November 1976); Salmon, Jacqui. "Wades Delta Team," *WomenSports* (December 1975); Tashima, Pat. "Delta State Rebounds for Glory," *Women's Sports* (December 1975); Trekell, Marianna and Rosalie M. Gershon. "Title IX, AIAW and Beyond—A Time for Celebration." In *A Century of Women's Basketball from Frailty to Final Four*, ed. Joan S. Hult and Marianna Trekell (1991).

JOAN HULT

HARSH, VIVIAN GORDON
(1890-1960)

She was called "the Lieutenant" by some of her colleagues and a taskmaster by many of the youths who did their research at the Chicago Public Library branch she headed. Yet Vivian G. Harsh was revered by a generation of prominent Black writers and scholars. She was eulogized as "the historian who never wrote" (Slaughter 1960), yet she succeeded in building one of the most important research collections on Black history and literature in the United States.

Born in Chicago on May 27, 1890, to Fenton W. Harsh and Maria L. (Drake) Harsh, Vivian Gordon Harsh grew up in the world of Chicago's Old Settlers, the tightly knit community of pioneer Black families in the city. Both of her parents were graduates of Fisk University; her mother was one of the first women to graduate from Fisk Normal School. The year after she graduated from Wendell Phillips High School on Chicago's South Side, Harsh began working for the only employer she would ever have, the Chicago Public Library. She started as a junior clerk in December 1909, rising slowly through the ranks during her first fifteen years of service. By 1921, she had graduated from Simmons College Library School in Boston, and on February 26, 1924, she became the first Black librarian for the Chicago Public Library.

In the late 1920s, George Cleveland Hall, then chief of staff at Provident Hospital and one of the founding members of the Association for the Study of

Negro Life and History headed by Carter G. Woodson, began pressing the Chicago Public Library to open a branch in the rapidly expanding South Side Black community. Hall convinced philanthropist Julius Rosenwald to donate land for the branch, but Hall died before construction was completed. On January 18, 1932, the building, now named the George Cleveland Hall branch, was opened to the public, with Vivian G. Harsh as its first head librarian.

Opening day created a sensation in the community, as thousands flocked to see the new library. Included among its holdings was a small but significant collection of books on Black history and literature, which Harsh called the Special Negro Collection. Even before the opening of the library, Harsh had received a fellowship from the Rosenwald Foundation to supplement her studies at the Graduate Library School of the University of Chicago with travels to other Black history collections. Harsh began to collect rare books, pamphlets, and documents on her journeys.

Aided by the Hall branch children's librarian, Charlemae Hill Rollins, Harsh tirelessly expanded the collection through subsequent Rosenwald Foundation grants, donations from supportive patrons, and her own purchases. The work continued throughout the 1930s, despite persistent antagonism from the Chicago Public Library's administration, which did not believe that public funds should be expended on such a project.

As the collection's reputation spread, the library became a meeting place for young Black writers and artists. The Works Progress Administration's (WPA) Federal Writers Project launched a study called "The Negro in Illinois," headed by Arna Bontemps; the library served as its unofficial headquarters. Many young scholars were attracted to the library's book review and lecture forum, begun by Harsh in 1934. Its bimonthly meetings featured an impressive array of Black speakers, including Richard Wright, Langston Hughes, Zora Neale Hurston, Arna Bontemps, Gwendolyn Brooks, Horace Cayton, William Attaway, Margaret Walker, Alain Locke, and St. Clair Drake.

Harsh encouraged these writers to help build the Special Negro Collection. Langston Hughes, a regular visitor to the collection in the 1940s, donated the typescripts and galley proofs of his autobiographical work *The Big Sea*. When Richard Wright's *Native Son* was published, he returned to the library to present Harsh with an inscribed copy, and he credited the collection with enriching his knowledge of the Black experience. Arna Bontemps, faced with the shutdown of the WPA Federal Writers Project in 1942, turned over nearly 100 boxes of research from the "Negro in Illinois" study to Harsh.

Throughout the 1930s and 1940s, Harsh was active in community and professional organizations. She served on the board of the Parkway Community Center and participated in the work of the National Association for the Advancement of Colored People, the Young Men's Christian Association, and the Young Women's Christian Association, and was a member of the influential Sixth Grace Presbyterian Church. After a serious illness, Harsh retired on November 10, 1958. She had never married and had no children, yet when she died two years later, on August 17, 1960, her funeral was crowded with friends and former library patrons.

In 1970, the Chicago Public Library renamed the Special Negro Collection as the Vivian G. Harsh

Eulogized as "the historian who never wrote," Vivian G. Harsh succeeded in building, within the Chicago Public Library system, one of the most important research collections on Black history and literature in the United States. [Vivian Harsh Collection, Chicago Public Library]

Collection of Afro-American History and Literature. By 1975, it was moved to the new Carter G. Woodson Regional Library, where a large photograph of Harsh hangs adjacent to one of Woodson. The collection has grown to some 70,000 volumes, with important holdings of rare Black journals and newspapers and an outstanding collection of archival materials on Illinois Black history.

As a Black bibliophile and collector, Harsh's achievements complement the work of Arthur Schomburg, Jesse Moorland, and other pioneers in the field. Even in the face of bureaucratic opposition and tight Depression-era finances, she was able to institutionalize her collection. Her greatest legacy is the extraordinary milieu she created, a meeting place that helped develop the work of so many Black writers and scholars.

BIBLIOGRAPHY

Chicago Public Library Staff News, "Notes from the Branches" (September 1931); *Dictionary Catalog of the Vivian G. Harsh Collection of Afro-American History and Literature, the Chicago Public Library* (1978); *EBA*; Joyce, Donald Franklin. "Vivian G. Harsh Collection of Afro-American History and Literature, Chicago Public Library," *Library Quarterly* (Winter 1988); Ottley, Roi. "Hall Library Becomes Negro Cultural Center," *Chicago Tribune* (February 21, 1954); *Proceedings of the Board of Directors of the Chicago Public Library*, "Resignation of Miss Vivian G. Marsh" (October 27, 1958); Slaughter, Adolph J. "Historian Who Never Wrote: The Vivian Harsh Story," *Chicago Defender* (August 29, 1960). See also the Vivian G. Harsh Research Collection of Afro-American History and Literature, Carter G. Woodson Regional Library, Chicago Public Library.

MICHAEL FLUG

HARTSHORN MEMORIAL COLLEGE

Hartshorn Memorial College for Women opened November 7, 1883, with fifty-eight students in the basement of Ebenezer Baptist Church, Richmond, Virginia. Soon thereafter eight acres of land were purchased on West Leigh Street and a building was erected for the 1884-85 school year. On March 13, 1888, Hartshorn was chartered by the Virginia State Legislature as "an institution of learning of collegiate grade for the education of young women, ... to confer such ... degrees as are wont to be conferred by colleges and universities in the United States," thus becoming the first Black women's college in the country.

The founding of Hartshorn Memorial College (HMC) answered the call in the Virginia African-American community for higher education for women. The Virginia Baptist State Convention (VBSC) and individual ministers such as Walter H. Brooks of Richmond had urged the American Baptist Home Mission Society (ABHMS) to provide for the advanced training of women, offering to raise the money for a women's dormitory to be constructed on the campus of Richmond Theological Institute (the forerunner of Virginia Union University) in order to open it to women. Brooks voiced the sentiments of the VBSC when he wrote, "We ask for no educational advantages for our sons which we do not ask for our daughters" (*Baptist Home Mission Monthly*, January 1881).

Joseph C. Hartshorn of Rhode Island founded the college in memory of his wife, Rachel, who had been a member of the board of directors of the Woman's American Baptist Home Mission Society (WABHMS) of New England. From the outset, Hartshorn and Lyman B. Tefft, president from 1883-1912, were clear that the school would be a *college* for Black women. Disavowing the focus on industrial education in many other Black seminaries and colleges, they set out to create a college curriculum equal to that at northern white women's schools, such as Wellesley College. While courses in sewing, cooking, and other domestic arts were required of all students, officials were quick to point out that "this does not mean a training school for servants in the kitchen, the chamber or the laundry" but rather the teaching of skills in cooking, sewing, and homemaking that they assumed every woman would need whether she became a homemaker, teacher, missionary, or laborer (*Catalogue*, 1884-85). Unlike female students in many other Black schools, Hartshorn students were not required to do their own laundry but could send it out if they could so afford and, though policy varied over time, were generally not required to do work around the school. In the 1920s, when school finances were especially low, the Domestic Science Department was the area of the curriculum that Hartshorn officials decided to eliminate.

This emphasis on liberal arts and collegiate-grade education, while responsive to an appeal from the Black community, also reflected the concern among northern white Baptists with producing a Black leadership class that could be the instrument of social reform and social control in southern Black communities, transforming illiterate, impoverished, and by many white northerners' perceptions, immoral, Black people into educated, industrious, pious, and refined

citizens. While northern white missionaries and teachers had initially assumed they themselves would fulfill this role, by the 1880s they increasingly acknowledged that this task would better be vested in carefully selected and trained African-Americans, because they would live in the communities, attend the churches, participate in the activities and create the community institutions that would establish rules, provide constant supervision, and maintain intimate enough contact to insure that the values taught in the schools would be reinforced throughout the community. The production of an industrious Black working class would be more effective if a Black middle class developed that would not only preach and teach but also model capitalist social values, thereby more rapidly transmitting them throughout the Black South. It was from this framework that northern white Baptists both coined the phrase "the talented tenth" and argued the importance of including women within that elite group. Black women became especially important in northern white Baptists' plans, for Black women, as teachers and community leaders, could be missionaries as well—going into the homes, training even those women who did not enter school and might not go to church—teaching the order and discipline of a home which northern white men and women believed would produce newly ordered, disciplined, and industrious family members and workers. In 1883, the ABHMS announced its commitment that "the education of women should advance alongside that of men. . . . Hence, if we had it in our power to educate one hundred, we would educate fifty men and fifty women rather than one hundred men" (Brooks 1984). That these ideas were central to Hartshorn's mission is reflected in Hartshorn teacher Mary A. Tefft's 1891 report to the WABHMS: "They [Black women] can help their own people in a way in which white women cannot, however consecrated they may be. The changes which are taking place in the South indicate that mission work must be done more and more by the colored women themselves. The color line is being drawn more stringently. In some parts of the South the colored people are becoming afraid to receive white missionaries, because they are made to suffer for receiving them. We hope some way may be found for educated colored women to do this work. . . . To provide for this need, the grade of the schools in which these workers are trained must be raised to keep pace with the . . . requirements of those who are to be leaders" (WABHMS annual report, 1891).

Despite its desire to be a college, Hartshorn, like most Black and women's schools of the time, had to provide precollege training to meet the educational level of its constituency. Thus the initial curriculum included a one-year Normal Preparatory Course, a three-year Normal Course, a College Preparatory Course, and a College Course. The college curriculum was to be offered directly on Hartshorn's campus. In 1884, its students were about evenly divided between Normal Prep (twenty-five) and Normal (twenty-three). Six were in College Prep, but none had yet enrolled in the College Course. In 1885, Hartshorn graduated its first four students, all of whom had completed the Normal Course. A Higher English and a Post-Normal Course were added in 1887, the latter designed to encourage women to continue their education even after teacher certification. At the same time Hartshorn officials renewed their commitment to the full intellectual development of Black women. They urged students to begin their education earlier, noting (without much compassion for the circumstances which made it necessary) that too many Black females started school at sixteen or eighteen and then "have not the time to complete advanced courses." Black women were warned not to "count their duty done" once they were able to teach in the lower grades of a county school. "The pressing needs of the people wait for women of broader education—and completer discipline. To meet this need, Hartshorn Memorial College was founded" (*Catalogue*, 1890-91). By 1891, Hartshorn had differentiated between the Bachelor of Science and Bachelor of Arts curriculums. The next year three women, Mary Moore Booze of Buchanan, Virginia; Harriet Amanda Miller of Charlottesville, Virginia; and Dixie Erma Williams of Milan, Tennessee, graduated with B.S. degrees, the first college degrees granted by a Black women's institution. Keeping up with the most current trends in women's education, the college's gymnasium was erected during the 1896-97 school year. Shortly thereafter Tefft laid out his visions for the future development of Hartshorn—included was the possibility of a medical school. This was not achieved but Hartshorn did continuously upgrade its curriculum; in the twentieth century it offered B.A., B.S., and B.A. in Education degrees; changed its Normal Course to a two-year post-high school program; and added a new course in African-American history to the core curriculum. Hartshorn's student body came from throughout the United States, the Caribbean, Africa, and South America. Hartshorn graduates became teachers, homemakers, nurses, real estate dealers, missionaries, and physicians.

That the founders of Hartshorn financed a separate school for women rather than funding the expansion of Richmond Theological to serve women equally, as many in the Black community had requested, is evidence of their concern that the Black women who were to become the leaders were also the products of these untransformed communities. Officials such as Lyman Tefft and Carrie Dyer, Lady Principal, or Dean, from 1883 to 1914, saw the entering students as embodying all the elements that had to be eliminated within the Black community—as Black women they were presumed to be immoral and to come from undisciplined homes and undeveloped communities. Thus in 1899, when ABHMS founded Virginia Union University and located it adjacent to Hartshorn's grounds, Hartshorn officials rejected the efforts to merge the two schools into one coeducational institution, contending that a separate school remained necessary to develop a curriculum tailored to the unique needs of Black women.

Hartshorn officials sought through the courses, extracurricular activities, discipline, and principles of the school to model an education that would "train the conscience, purge the mind from folly, make them strong to overcome evil" (*Catalogue*, 1891-92). Religious study, mission work, and activities viewed as improving the moral development of the pupils were highlighted. Bible study constituted a central part of the curriculum at all levels; attendance at the college's religious exercises was required, although students were also encouraged to attend services in the Richmond Black churches; and much emphasis was placed on achieving the conversion of all pupils. The first societies formed within the school were the Rachel Hartshorn Education and Missionary Society and the College Temperance Society. When the White Shield League (WSL) was founded in 1893, nearly all the pupils took its pledge "to uphold the law of purity as equally binding upon men and upon women; to be modest in language, behavior, and dress; to avoid all conversation, reading, art and amusements which may put impure thoughts into my mind; to guard the purity of others, especially of my companions and friends" (*Catalogue*, 1892-93). The WSL meetings served to indoctrinate students regarding appropriate dress and other matters; for example, in the twentieth century the meetings were used to combat the influence of ragtime music by introducing students to a "higher class" of music, including Negro folksongs.

Additionally, the students at Hartshorn were expected to involve themselves in social service work in the community. Through the Hartshorn Home Workers, students did house-to-house mission work and conducted sewing classes for boys, girls, and women in the neighborhood. The Hartshorn students were expected to teach more than needlework during these sessions; they used the time to teach class members hymns and Scripture; to lecture on temperance and morality; and to try to impart some of their lessons on dress, deportment, tasteful home furnishing, economical cooking, and wholesome recreation. In later years, they expanded their service work to include regular weekend trips to Peake's Turnout to work at Janie Porter Barrett's Virginia Industrial School for Colored Girls. Hartshorn officials considered this work an essential part of the students' training for leadership within their communities.

While these mission-focused societies continued throughout Hartshorn's existence, in the twentieth century a variety of other activities—debating teams, glee clubs, and an athletic association—were added. The latter developed both intramural and competitive teams. Negro Achievement Week and Negro History Week were celebrated in the 1920s.

The struggle of Hartshorn to fulfill its original mission as a college for Black women reflects many of the issues surrounding the development of Black higher education in the late nineteenth-early twentieth centuries. One of the most crucial issues was funding. Although Hartshorn received funds from WABHMS, ABHMS, the John Slater Fund, and the Virginia Black community through individual, church, and organizational donations, HMC was never a well-funded institution. HMC officials attributed this to their curriculum and its emphasis on liberal arts rather than vocational or industrial education. Comparatively speaking, HMC received about one-sixth the funding from WABHMS that Spelman Seminary in Atlanta received; the latter was an institution founded by WABHMS missionaries and was the pride of northern white Baptist women and also the symbol of their own power and influence. ABHMS funded more fully its own institution, Virginia Union University (VUU), and from the time of its founding urged merger. By the 1920s, when ABHMS support was crucial to Hartshorn's survival, ABHMS officials used their financial resources to push merger. Hartshorn never attracted the significant northern white philanthropic support that Spelman received from the Rockefellers and, though HMC received Slater Fund support for its domestic science courses, it did not receive the monetary support that institutions with fuller industrial education courses received.

While the Virginia African-American community offered its support to Hartshorn as an institution of higher education for Black women, there was little concern as to whether that higher education came through a separate or coeducational institution. Black Baptists, who had provided the initial impetus for the establishment of higher educational provisions for women, seem not to have been overly concerned on either side of the question of coeducation or separation as long as provisions were made for Black women. Thus when coordination or coeducation issues arose there was not a strong voice in the Richmond or Virginia African-American community arguing for the independence of Hartshorn Memorial College. This also reflects the position of HMC within the Black community. A few African-American women, including Mary Church Terrell and Maggie Lena Walker, served on the board; Rosa K. Jones had charge of the music department for forty years; and three Hartshorn graduates, Harriet Amanda Miller (Coleman), Ada Baytop, and Dixie Williams, joined the teaching staff for brief periods. Yet throughout Hartshorn's history it remained in the hands primarily of northern white Baptists, with white male presidents, white female deans, a principally white female teaching force, and a predominantly white board of trustees, while Virginia Union University developed with significant Black participation on its board and, by the 1920s, a significant group of Black faculty members. The latter became more fully an institution of the Black community and there was little opposition to ideas of Hartshorn's merger with VUU.

Additionally, the educational environment in which Hartshorn existed must be noted. Educational opportunities for Black youth in Virginia, while unequal to those for white youth, were generally better than in states further south. Richmond itself had a publicly funded high and normal school that dated from the Reconstruction era as well as the first fully state supported Black college, Virginia State, opened in Petersburg in 1882, the result of much pressure within the Black community for an institution to train Black teachers for the public schools.

Hartshorn officials' commitment to maintaining it as a college for Black women was not enough to sustain the institution. In 1918, students enrolled in the college department began doing their course work at Virginia Union University rather than on Hartshorn's campus and in 1922 Hartshorn entered into a temporary coordination with Virginia Union. In June 1928, in a last effort to avoid a merger, Hartshorn officials terminated the coordination agreement, closed its college department, and focused on high school while it struggled to get on more solid economic footing in order to resume its original mission as a college. They perhaps had reason to be hopeful because at the time of this decision the number of Black women enrolling in college was increasing and Hartshorn itself for the first time in its history had more college (187) than precollege (121 high school, 29 grammar school) students. However, Hartshorn was never to resume college courses on its own campus. In 1928, in response to the termination of the coordination agreement, Virginia Union University became coeducational and for the first time officially received women as part of its own student body. In that year VUU enrolled 521 college students, 215 of them female, and 19 law students, 8 of them female. In 1932, with all hope lost of reopening as an independent college, Hartshorn's trustees conveyed the college's property to VUU and merged with VUU, becoming Hartshorn Memorial College in the Virginia Union University.

BIBLIOGRAPHY

Annual Reports of Woman's American Baptist Home Mission Society; Archives, American Baptist Historical Society, Colgate Rochester Divinity School, Rochester, New York; Archives, Virginia Union University, Richmond, Virginia; *Baptist Home Mission Monthly; From Ocean to Ocean with the Representatives of the Woman's American Baptist Home Mission Society;* Brooks, Evelyn (Higginbotham). "The Women's Movement in the Black Baptist Church, 1880-1920," Ph.D. diss. (1984); Butcher, Beatrice. "The Evolution of Negro Women's Schools in the United States," M.A. thesis, Howard University (1936).

ELSA BARKLEY BROWN

HAWKINS, TRAMAINE (1951-)

Tramaine Aunzola Davis Hawkins, gospel singer and entertainer, was born October 11, 1951, in San Francisco, California. She is the daughter of Roland Duvall Davis and Lois Ruth Davis, who migrated to California from Houston, Texas, and Oklahoma City, Oklahoma, respectively. She is the mother of Jamie, a nineteen-year-old son who works with rap artist Hammer, and Trystan, a sixteen-year-old daughter who is in high school.

Throughout her life, Hawkins has remained close to family and the church, institutions from which she has received much of her training and professional development in gospel music. From birth to 1971, she was affiliated with the Ephesians Church of God in Christ (COGIC) in Berkeley where her grandfather, Bishop Elmer Elijah Cleveland, served as pastor.

During the 1970s and early 1980s, at the Love Center Church in Oakland, where her former husband, Walter Hawkins, is founder and pastor, she began to be recognized in the gospel music world. Since 1983, she has been a member of the Center of Hope Community Church, where her aunt Ernestine Cleveland Rheems is pastor. She has been singing contemporary gospel music since her early years as a vocalist with the Heavenly Tones.

Hawkins is fortunate to have worked with some of the most respected artists in contemporary gospel music: Andrae Crouch and the Disciples, the Edwin Hawkins Singers, and the Walter Hawkins Love Center Choir. While she sang on the first three *Love Alive* albums recorded by Walter Hawkins, it was her lead vocal performance on the songs "Changed" and "Going Up Yonder" on *Love Alive 1* (1975) that demonstrated her abilities as a soloist.

Over the past ten years, not only has she been involved with numerous concert tours in the United States and Europe as well as television appearances, but she has also recorded several albums: *Tramaine* (1980), *Determined* (1983), *The Search Is Over* (1986), *Freedom* (1987), *The Joy That Floods My Soul* (1988), and *Tramaine Hawkins, LIVE* (1990). Some of the major awards that Hawkins has received include two Grammys, two Dove Awards, two Communications Excellence to Black Audiences (CEBA) Awards, an NAACP Image Award, a Stellar Award, a British Gospel Music Award, and several awards from James Cleveland's Gospel Music Workshop of America.

Considered to be more daring than most gospel artists, Hawkins has experimented with songs such as "Fall Down (Spirit of Love)," which some critics consider to be overly secular. However, her recording of "What Shall I Do" by Quincy Fielding has become a best seller among churchgoers. For her 1990 album, she collaborated with musicians outside of the gospel music field—rock guitarist Carlos Santana, jazz organist Jimmy McGriff, and jazz tenor saxophonist Stanley Turrentine. Regardless of what and with whom she performs, her singing maintains a spiritual feeling with clarity and strength. She calls it music that ministers to the heart.

BIBLIOGRAPHY

Hawkins, Tramaine. Interview (November 27, 1991); Hildebrand, Lee. "In Concert—Going Up with the Spirit of Love," *East Bay Express* (May 18, 1990); "In Concert—Tramaine Hawkins—Singin' Her Heart Out!" *California Voice* (September 19, 1986); Magid, Lee. Interview (December 2, 1991); "Spreading the Word," *California*

Voice (April 4, 1986); "Tramaine Hawkins Produces Her First Album," *California Voice* (October 28, 1988).

DISCOGRAPHY

Tramaine. Light Records LC 5760 (1980); *Determined.* Light Records LS 5821 (1983); *The Search Is Over.* World Records 701-5009-293 (1986); *Freedom.* World Records 701-5019-299 (1987); *The Joy That Floods My Soul.* Sparrow Records SPR 1173 (1988); *Tramaine Hawkins, LIVE.* Sparrow Records SPR 1246 (1990).

JACQUELINE COGDELL DJEDJE

HAYNES, ELIZABETH ROSS (1883-1953)

Elizabeth Ross Haynes was a pioneering analyst of Black domestic and women workers, a writer, and a leader in the Young Women's Christian Association (YWCA) and the Democratic party. Born July 30, 1883, in Lowndes County, Alabama, to Henry and Mary Carnes Ross, prosperous farmers and freedpersons, Elizabeth Ross was valedictorian of the State Normal School in Montgomery, received an A.B. from Fisk University in 1903, and an M.A. in sociology from Columbia University in 1923. Ross married George E. Haynes, a sociologist and co-founder of the National Urban League, in 1910. Their interests in racial uplift, women's rights, and survey research were closely matched. Elizabeth Haynes worked in unsalaried positions after her marriage and the birth of her only child, George Jr., in 1912.

Elizabeth Ross Haynes was a persuasive advocate of job training and improved social services for Black urban women workers. Because of her skills as an organizer and her pragmatic approach to improving race relations, she accepted segregated social agencies if Black professionals were hired to staff them. This stance occasionally placed her at odds with more militant leaders, but it also made Haynes a vital link between white reform groups such as the YWCA and Black women's groups. From 1908 to 1910, Haynes was the YWCA's student secretary for work among colored women, and the number of Black YWCA branches increased because of her efforts. Appointed to the YWCA's new Council on Colored Work in 1922, Haynes served as the first Black person on its national board from 1924 to 1934. She also assisted her husband, who was head of the Federal Council of Churches' Department of Race Relations, from 1922 to 1946.

A dollar-a-year worker for the U.S. Department of Labor from 1918 to 1922, Haynes took part in

Elizabeth Ross Haynes was a pioneer advocate of Black urban women workers. [Schomburg Center]

some of the first systematic studies of Black women workers and served as domestic service secretary for the U.S. Employment Service. Her 1923 Master's thesis was the most comprehensive study of Black domestic workers until the 1970s. A New Deal Democrat, Haynes became coleader of Harlem's Twenty-first Assembly District in 1935, a member of the colored division of the national Democratic speakers' bureau by 1936, and in 1937 was the only woman appointed to the State Temporary Commission on the Condition of the Urban Colored Population. In 1952, she finished *The Black Boy of Atlanta*, a biography of Major Richard Robert Wright, college president and banker. Haynes died on October 26, 1953, in New York City.

BIBLIOGRAPHY

Haynes, Elizabeth Ross. *The Black Boy of Atlanta* (1952), and "Negroes in Domestic Service in the United States,"

Journal of Negro History (1923), and *Unsung Heroes* (1921); Katzman, David M. *Seven Days a Week: Women and Domestic Service in Industrializing America* (1978); *NAW*; Neverdon-Morton, Cynthia. *Afro-American Women of the South and the Advancement of the Race, 1895-1925* (1989); *New York Times*, "Mrs. G. E. Haynes, Active in YWCA. Obituary" (October 27, 1953); Salem, Dorothy. *Black Women in Organized Reform, 1890-1920* (1990).

FRANCILLE RUSAN WILSON

HEDGEMAN, ANNA ARNOLD
(1899-1990)

"I had been forced to spend my whole lifetime discussing the implications of color. . . . This was to me a waste of time and of whatever talent I had. . . . The opportunities I really wanted were closed to me" (Hedgeman 1964). Anna Arnold wanted to teach, but, because of her color, she could not find a teaching position in the North. She found a job with the Young Women's Christian Association (YWCA) in a branch located in a Black neighborhood, and from then on her varied career as educator, public servant, and civil rights advocate was determined by her race.

Anna Arnold was born in Marshalltown, Iowa, on July 5, 1899, the daughter of Marie Ellen Parker and William James Arnold II. Her father, born the son of slaves in South Carolina, had attended high school and then Clark College in Atlanta, Georgia, and was a strict disciplinarian. Anna grew up in an Irish neighborhood in Anoka, Minnesota, a small town without any signs of real poverty and without a Black community. Raised in a religious household, she was taught to read at home by her mother and did not attend school until the age of seven. Anna had reached high school when she first realized that hers was the only Black family in town. Because her father would not allow his daughters to date before college, the issue of a white boy dating a Black girl never emerged.

After she graduated from high school in June 1918, her father sent her to Hamline University, a Methodist college in St. Paul, Minnesota. Because she lived with white friends of her father's, Arnold never knew whether, as Hamline's first Black student, she would have been accepted in the dormitory. Her best friend at college was white, and her sense of her race was only incidental in her life. The fact that she was female, however, did limit her choice of a career, because teaching was the only occupation open to women at the time. Anna Arnold did her practice teaching at Hamline, learning only later that she would not have been allowed to do so at St. Paul High School because of her race.

Deciding she wanted to teach in the South, Arnold found a teaching job at Rust College, a Black school in Holly Springs, Mississippi. Her first experience with segregation came on the train trip south, in September 1922, when she was forced to change to the "colored" coach at Cairo, Illinois. Not only was racial segregation a constant affront in the South; Rust College was sex segregated as well. Anna Arnold lived with the women students, serving as their chaperone when they needed to go into town. Like many other southern towns, Holly Springs's Black grade school was inferior and, because town leaders assumed that Black children neither needed nor were capable of high school training, there was no Black high school. Consequently, in addition to its college offerings, Rust maintained a grade school and high school for Black students. Many came from sharecropping families, so they could not begin classes until after harvest, and they left early in the school year for spring planting. Parents paid tuition out of their often meager earnings.

Disillusioned by southern segregation, Arnold decided to return to the Midwest to teach in 1924. After learning that racism prohibited her from getting a teaching job in the North, Arnold accepted a position with a YWCA in Springfield, Ohio, beginning in the fall of 1924. The Springfield YWCA was segregated by neighborhood and lacked a gym, swimming pool, cafeteria, and adequate staff. Anna Arnold found it difficult to give Black children confidence in the face of such discrimination and even more difficult to give lectures on race relations because there were no relations. Yet, the national YWCA was ahead of its time for even hiring Black executives, and her relationship with the YWCA, where she helped develop a variety of international programs in education, lasted on and off for twelve years.

Having spent time in the summer of 1926 in the freer atmosphere of New York, Arnold was eager to return. Requesting a transfer from the national YWCA, she became the executive director of a Black branch in Jersey City. There Black Americans were represented on all committees, and there were even a few Black teachers in the public schools. Her days off were spent in Harlem where she became acquainted with the culture of the Harlem Renaissance at A'Lelia Walker's soirées. In 1927, Anna Arnold became membership secretary of the Harlem YWCA. Endowed by the Rockefellers, the Harlem YWCA had a well-equipped physical plant, a business school, a beautician training program, an employment agency, and meeting rooms. Because African-Americans were barred from white branches of the YWCA just as they were from other public accommodations, this branch was particularly important to the community. For two years Arnold had a good job and was surrounded by Black colleagues and friends. The Great Depression, however, brought more difficult times. The branch's membership shrank dramatically as people could no longer afford to pay for its services. Yet the community was now faced with the reality of starvation and a burgeoning Harlem population that had increased more than 600 percent in twenty-five years.

In fall 1933, Arnold became the executive director of the Black branch of the Philadelphia YWCA. She made the Black branch a vital part of the life of the community but only stayed one year. She returned to New York City in November 1933 to marry Merritt A. Hedgeman, a concert artist, an interpreter of Black folk music and opera, and a former member of the Fisk Jubilee Singers. By this time, her parents and siblings had also settled in New York. By fall 1934, the city's Emergency Relief Bureau had begun to hire a few Black supervisors, and Anna Hedgeman began working for the agency as the city's first consultant on racial problems. Hedgeman served Jews and Italians as well as Black Americans. In fall 1937, the Emergency Relief Bureau became the Department of Welfare, whereupon Hedgeman resigned and accepted the directorship of the Black branch of the Brooklyn YWCA. She used this position to organize a citizens' coordinating committee to seek provisional appointments for Black Americans to the Department of Welfare. They secured the first 150 provisional appointments the city had ever given to the Black community. With the aid of white women on the race relations committee of the Federation of Protestant Churches, she also succeeded in expanding employment opportunities for Black clerks in Brooklyn department stores. Hedgeman resigned from the Brooklyn YWCA, however, after her activities became a point of contention with the central board. Her organizing tactics—including picket lines and challenges to the old guard leadership—proved too militant.

Anna Hedgeman continued to lobby for change. She defended the picketing of a local defense plant that refused to hire Black workers on the grounds that government contracts should be denied to contractors who discriminate against Black workers. She joined the civilian defense program as a race relations assistant. Then she joined A. Philip Randolph's March on Washington Committee, designed to fight segregation and discrimination against African-Americans

in defense industries and the military. In 1944, Randolph offered Hedgeman the job of executive director of the National Council for a Permanent Fair Employment Practices Committee (FEPC). Because she had come to believe that permanent legislation was needed to outlaw discrimination in employment, Hedgeman took the job and moved to Washington, D.C., and began lobbying on behalf of FEPC. The National Council was unable to obtain a permanent FEPC, and after a major legislative drive in 1946 failed, she resigned and then became dean of women at Howard University.

In summer 1948, Congressman William L. Dawson, vice chair of the Democratic National Committee, asked Hedgeman to join the presidential campaign of Harry Truman by becoming executive director of the national citizens' committee to raise funds among African-Americans. Pollsters predicted that Truman would lose, and Hedgeman was reluctant to align with racist southern Democrats, but Dawson had supported FEPC, and she accepted the offer. After the election, Hedgeman received a patronage appointment as assistant to Oscar R. Ewing, administrator of the Federal Security Agency (later the Department of Health, Education and Welfare). She was sworn in on February 12, 1949, the first Black American to hold a position in the Federal Security Agency administration. At the request of Ambassador Chester Bowles, Hedgeman spent three months in India in 1952 as an exchange leader for the State Department. She resigned upon her return to the United States, following the Republican victory in the presidential election.

Hedgeman returned to New York City after a ten-year absence and was met by a Harlem delegation that urged her to delve into city politics. So, on January 1, 1954, when Robert F. Wagner invited her to be a mayoral assistant, she accepted. She was responsible for eight city departments, acting as their liaison with the mayor, and she remained in the post until 1958. As the first Black woman at the cabinet level, Hedgeman gave speeches, represented the mayor at conferences and conventions, hosted United Nations' visitors to the city, and participated in weekly cabinet meetings. In 1955, when Mayor Wagner was on a European tour, Hedgeman was designated as his representative at the tenth-anniversary meeting of the United Nations in San Francisco. In 1956, she was invited on a study tour of Israel and the Middle East through the American Christian Committee on Palestine. Because she was a board member of the United Seamen's Service, she continued on to Munich, Germany, where she chaired a panel at the International

Conference of Social Work as a representative of the Seamen's Service. In the same capacity, she attended the International Conference of Social Work in Japan in 1958. Hedgeman served as secretary to the board of the United Seamen's Service from 1955 to 1960.

By fall 1958, frustrated by City Hall's lack of response to Black concerns and the Black community, Hedgeman accepted the offer of S. B. Fuller to join his cosmetics firm as a public relations consultant and an associate editor and columnist for the *New York Age*, one of the oldest Black papers in the United States.

In 1960, a group of Black and Puerto Rican reformers asked Hedgeman to run for Congress as an insurgent from the East Bronx. She ran, but she lost.

That same year, Hedgeman was invited to be the keynote speaker at the First Conference of African Women and Women of African Descent held in Accra, Ghana, in July. She also became a consultant for the division of higher education of the American Missionary Association to help six Black colleges prepare for their centennial anniversaries in 1966, and she had her own radio program, "One Woman's Opinion," on a local New York City station.

In February 1963, Hedgeman played a key role in conceptualizing the 1963 march on Washington as a joint effort. A. Philip Randolph had called for a march on Washington for job opportunities to be held in October 1963. When Hedgeman learned that Martin Luther King, Jr., was planning a march for that July to pressure public opinion on behalf of a strong civil rights bill, she suggested that they combine efforts into a March on Washington for Jobs and Freedom to be held in August. Hedgeman was the only woman on the organizing committee of the march; indeed the heads of all the sponsoring organizations and all of the proposed speakers were male, even though women had played major roles in fund-raising. While plans for the march were taking shape, Hedgeman was appointed to the newly formed commission on religion and race of the National Council of Churches as coordinator of special events. The intent of the commission was to mobilize the resources of Protestant and Orthodox churches to work against racial injustice in American life. Her first assignment was to relate the march on Washington to this renewed commitment of Protestant churches to justice for all. In this capacity she was asked to help mobilize 30,000 white Protestant church leaders to march. About a third of the 250,000 marchers were white; some credit for that figure certainly belongs to Hedgeman.

In 1965, granted a leave from the commission on religion and race, Hedgeman campaigned unsuccess-

fully for president of the City Council of New York on the Reform Democratic ticket. She was the first woman and the first Black woman to run for the office. In 1968, she unsuccessfully ran in the Democratic party primary for an assembly seat.

On December 31, 1967, Hedgeman retired from her work with the National Council of Churches. She and her husband established Hedgeman Consultant Services in 1968. Their clients included educational institutions and civic, business, and community organizations.

The recipient of many honors and awards for her work in race relations, Hedgeman garnered, among others, the Frederick Douglass Award from the New York Urban League, the National Human Relations Award from the State Fair Board of Texas, and awards from the Schomburg Collection of Negro Literature and the American Federation of Labor-Congress of Industrial Organizations (AFL-CIO). She received citations from the National Association for the Advancement of Colored People (NAACP), the Southern

The only woman on the organizing committee of the 1963 march on Washington, Anna Hedgeman had a long career in community service which began with Black chapters of the YWCA and progressed through government service in New York City and on a national level. Though she protested the sexual discrimination to the committee, no woman made a major address at the march. [Moorland-Spingarn]

Christian Leadership Conference (SCLC), the National Council of Negro Women, and United Church Women. In 1948, she was awarded an honorary doctorate of humane letters by Hamline University, the first woman graduate of Hamline to be so honored. In 1983, she received a "pioneer woman" award from the New York State Conference on Midlife and Older Women. Hedgeman was also a board member of the National Council of Christians and Jews. In 1964, she published her autobiography and study of Black leadership, *The Trumpet Sounds*, following it with an assessment of the civil rights movement from 1953 to 1974, *The Gift of Chaos* (1977).

In later years, Hedgeman used a restaurant at 22 West 135th Street as her unofficial office and meeting place for friends during the breakfast and dinner hours. From there she continued her efforts to improve conditions for the people of Harlem. After fifty-four years of marriage, Merritt Hedgeman died in 1988; Anna Hedgeman died on January 17, 1990, at the age of ninety.

Despite her indisputable accomplishments, Hedgeman never received the recognition due her. Partly from her own desire to better her situation and partly forced by circumstances, she constantly changed jobs, never remaining in one long enough to achieve prominence as a leader. Still, her long career as a civil rights advocate deserves further attention.

BIBLIOGRAPHY

CA; Hedgeman, Anna Arnold. *The Trumpet Sounds: A Memoir of Negro Leadership* (1964), and *The Gift of Chaos: Decades of American Discontent* (1977); NA; *New York Amsterdam News* (February 10, 1990); *New York Times* (January 26, 1990); Pfeffer, Paula F. *A. Philip Randolph: Pioneer of the Civil Rights Movement* (1990); Anna Arnold Hedgeman papers, Schomburg Center for Research in Black Culture, New York Public Library, New York.

PAULA F. PFEFFER

HEIGHT, DOROTHY IRENE (1912-)

For nearly half a century, Dorothy Irene Height has given leadership to the struggle for equality and human rights for all people. Her life exemplifies her passionate commitment to a just society and her vision of a better world.

Born in Richmond, Virginia, March 24, 1912, and educated in the public schools in Rankin, Pennsylvania, a small town near Pittsburgh, where her family moved when she was four, Dorothy Irene Height established herself early as a dedicated student with exceptional oratorical skills. With a $1,000 scholarship for winning a national oratorical contest sponsored by the Elks and a record of scholastic excellence, she enrolled in New York University and earned Bachelor's and Master's degrees in four years. She did further postgraduate work at Columbia University and the New York School of Social Work.

Employed in many capacities by both government and social service associations, she is known primarily for her leadership role with the Young Women's Christian Association (YWCA) and the National Council of Negro Women (NCNW). While working as a caseworker for the New York welfare department, she was the first Black American named to deal with the Harlem riots of 1935 and became one of the young leaders of the National Youth Movement of the New Deal era. It was during this period that Height's career as a civil rights advocate began to unfold, as she worked to prevent lynching, desegregate the armed forces, reform the criminal justice system, and guarantee free access to public accommodations. The turning point in the life of Dorothy Height came on November 7, 1937. That day, Mary McLeod Bethune, founder and president of the NCNW, noticed the assistant director of the Harlem YWCA, who was escorting Eleanor Roosevelt into an NCNW meeting. Height answered Bethune's call for help and joined Bethune in her quest for women's right to full and equal employment, pay, and education.

This was the beginning of her dual role as YWCA staff and NCNW volunteer, integrating her training as a social worker and her commitment to rise above the limitations of race and sex.

Height quickly rose through the ranks of the YWCA, from the Emma Ransom House in Harlem to the Phyllis Wheatley Branch in Washington, D.C. By 1944 and until 1977, Height was a staff member of the National Board of the YWCA of the USA, where she held several leadership positions and assumed responsibility for developing leadership training activities for volunteers and staff as well as programs to promote interracial and ecumenical education. In 1965, she inaugurated and became director of the Center for Racial Justice, a position she held until 1977 when she retired from the national YWCA.

Height was elected national president of Delta Sigma Theta sorority in 1947 and carried the sorority to a new level of organizational development throughout her term, which ended in 1956. Her leadership training skills, social work background, and knowledge of volunteerism benefited the sorority as it moved into a new era of activism on the national and international scenes. From the presidency of Delta Sigma Theta, Height assumed the presidency of the NCNW in 1957, a position she holds today.

As the fourth president of the NCNW, Height has led a crusade for justice for Black women and since 1986 has worked to strengthen the Black family. Under the leadership of Height, NCNW achieved tax-exempt status; raised funds from thousands of women in support of erecting a statue of Bethune in a federal park; developed several model national and community-based programs (ranging from teenage parenting to swine "banks" that address hunger in rural areas) that were replicated by other groups; established the Bethune Museum and Archives for Black Women, the first institution devoted to Black women's history; and established the Bethune Council House as a national historic site. In the 1960s, Height placed the organization on an action course of issue-oriented politics, sponsoring "Wednesdays in Mississippi" when interracial groups of women would help out at Freedom Schools; promoting voter education drives in the North and voter registration drives in the South; and establishing communication between Black and white women.

Her international travels and studies throughout Africa, Asia, Europe, and Latin America began as early as 1937. As vice-chair of the United Christian Youth Movement of North America, she was chosen as one of ten American youth delegates to the World Conference on Life and Work of the Churches in Oxford, England. Two years later Height was a YWCA representative to the World Conference of Christian Youth in Amsterdam, Holland. These early international experiences and activities as a leader of the youth movement left her with heightened confidence and the conviction that her goals and vision should be broadened to encompass international perspectives.

By the early 1950s, her leadership and understanding of the need to move the woman's agenda beyond the boundaries of the United States were evident. While she served as a YWCA staff member, she represented the NCNW at a meeting of the Congress of Women in Port-au-Prince, Haiti, in connection with Haiti's bicentennial exposition; while there, she arranged for the initiation of the first international chapter of Delta Sigma Theta. In 1952, Height arranged a four-month visiting professorship at the University of Delhi, India, in the Delhi School of Social Work, which was founded by the YWCA of India, Burma, and Ceylon to learn firsthand the needs of Indian women. Height became known for her internationalism and humanitarianism, and became the YWCA representative to conduct international

A leader in the struggle for equality and human rights, Dorothy Irene Height is best known for her work with the Young Women's Christian Association, especially as a staff member of the National Board of the YWCA of the USA, and for her work with the National Council of Negro Women. As president of the latter organization since 1957, she has worked for justice for Black women and has sought to strengthen the Black family. [National Council of Negro Women, Inc.]

studies and travel to expand the work of the YWCA. In 1958, she was one of a thirty-five-member Town Meeting of the World on a special people-to-people mission to five Latin American countries. Because of her expertise in training, she was sent to study the training needs of women's organizations in five West African countries.

These early international and human relations experiences helped prepare her for moving the NCNW agenda into one of cooperation and collaboration in response to the needs of the people, both domestically and internationally. But her experiences also caught the attention of the human rights community as well as the federal government. In 1966, Height served on the Council to the White House Conference "To Fulfill These Rights"; went to Israel to participate in a twelve-day study mission sponsored by the Institute on Human Relations of the American Jewish Committee; and attended an Anglo-American Conference on Problems of Minority Integration held by the Ditchley Foundation. In 1974, she was a delegate to the United Nations Educational, Scientific, and Cultural Organization (UNESCO) Conference on Woman and Her Rights held in Kingston, Jamaica; in 1975, she participated in the Tribunal at the International Women's Year Conference of the United Nations at Mexico City. As a result of this experience, under Height's leadership the NCNW was awarded a grant from the United States Agency for International Development to hold a conference for women from the United States, Africa, South America, and the Caribbean in Mexico City and to arrange a site visit with rural women in Mississippi. Under the auspices of the United States Information Agency, Height lectured in South Africa after addressing the National Convention of the Black Women's Federation of South Africa near Johannesburg in 1977.

Her distinguished service and contributions to making the world more just and humane have earned her over fifty awards and honors from local, state, and national organizations and the federal government. With Vice President Hubert H. Humphrey she received the John F. Kennedy Memorial Award of the National Council of Jewish Women in 1965; and in 1964, she was awarded the Myrtle Wreath of Achievement by Hadassah. For her contributions to the interfaith, interracial, and ecumenical movements for over thirty years, she was awarded the Ministerial Interfaith Association Award in 1969; she received the Lovejoy Award, the highest recognition by the Grand Lodge, I.B.P.O. Elks of the World for outstanding contribution to human relations in 1968. In 1974, *Ladies' Home Journal* named her "Woman of the Year" in human rights; and the Congressional Black Caucus presented Height the William L. Dawson Award for "Decades of public service to people of color and particularly women."

Working closely with Dr. Martin Luther King, Jr., Roy Wilkins, Whitney Young, A. Philip Randolph, and others, Height participated in virtually all the major civil and human rights events of the 1960s. For her tireless efforts on behalf of the less fortunate, President Ronald Reagan presented her with the Citizens Medal Award for distinguished service in 1989, the year she also received the Franklin Delano Roosevelt Freedom Medal from the Franklin and Eleanor Roosevelt Institute. Her awards also include the Essence Award, 1987; the Stellar Award, 1990; the

Camille Cosby World of Children Award, 1990; the Caring Award by the Caring Institute, 1989; and the Olender Foundation's Generous Heart Award, 1990.

Dr. Height has received over twenty honorary degrees, from such institutions as Spelman College, Lincoln University (Pennsylvania), Central State University, and Princeton University.

As a result of her extraordinary leadership in advancing women's rights, her dedication to the liberation of Black America, and her selfless determination, Height has carried out the dream of her friend and mentor, Mary McLeod Bethune, to leave no one behind. As a self-help advocate, she has been instrumental in the initiation of NCNW-sponsored food drives, child care and housing projects, and career and educational programs that embody the principles of self-reliance. She is proud that the NCNW established and maintains the Fannie Lou Hamer Day Care Center in Ruleville, Mississippi. As a promoter of positive Black family life, Height conceived and organized the Black Family Reunion Celebration in 1986 to reinforce the historic strengths and traditional values of the African-American family. Now in its sixth year in seven cities, the Black Family Reunion Celebration has made a difference in the lives of four million participants. Dorothy Height, too, has made a difference during her six decades of public life as dream giver, earth shaker, and crusader for human rights.

[*See also* NATIONAL COUNCIL OF NEGRO WOMEN.]

BIBLIOGRAPHY
CBWA; *NBAW*; *WWBA*.

ELEANOR HINTON HOYTT

HEMINGS, SALLY (1773-c. 1835)

It is believed by some that Sally Hemings, a Black American woman who lived and died as a slave, was the mistress of Thomas Jefferson and the mother of several children by him. Although not nearly enough is known about the specific facts of her life, what is known suggests a woman of considerable interest and character whether or not the legends that surround her are true.

Born in 1773, she was the daughter of Betty Hemings and John Wayles. Her mother was the daughter of "a full-blooded African" woman and an English ship captain; her father was both her mother's master and the father-in-law of Thomas Jefferson. When Wayles died in the year of Sally's birth, Hemings and her family became the property of Jefferson, and she thus grew up in the household of her half-sister, Martha Wayles Jefferson. When Jefferson's daughter, Maria, joined him in 1787 on his diplomatic mission in France, Hemings attended her. Abigail Adams, who helped them travel from London to Paris, described the fourteen-year-old Sally as "quite a child" but who "seems fond of [Maria] and appears good natured." Upon returning to America, Hemings became a house servant at Monticello, where she bore five children, Harriet (1795-97), Beverley (b.1798), Harriet (b.1801), Madison (1805-77), and Eston (b.1805). These are the children supposedly fathered by Jefferson, but strong evidence points to their paternity by Samuel Carr, Jefferson's nephew who lived nearby. Sally Hemings seems to have figured at Monticello, however, more because of her abilities and character than because of the identity of her lover. Jefferson's *Farm Book* indicates that, at Monticello in 1796, Hemings had with her Edy, the daughter of Isabel, who was then employed elsewhere on the farm, and she seems to have cared briefly in 1799 for Thenia, the daughter of Abram and Doll, who similarly were working elsewhere. Sally's caring nature seems to have made her a significant presence in the life of the Black people at Monticello even as it made an impression on her white cousins.

Various descendants of Betty Hemings became free over the years, but as Jefferson's finances grew more troubled the contradictions of chattel slavery asserted themselves. When Jefferson died on July 4, 1826, his will freed her sons Madison and Eston; Harriet and Beverley apparently had been permitted to run away four years earlier. Sally Hemings was not freed at this time, partly because she was no longer Jefferson's property but that of his granddaughter, Ellen Randolph Coolidge, and partly because under Virginia law at the time she would have had to leave the state if freed. Surviving family correspondence from the decade after 1826 reveals genuine concern for her and for accommodating her wishes about where and how she would live; however, trapped in the economic wreckage of the Jefferson family, her life ended in 1835 or 1836 as it began, in slavery.

The accusations that Sally Hemings was Jefferson's concubine were first made in 1802 by James T. Callender, a sensational journalist and disappointed office-seeker. They found wide circulation in the mudslinging political campaign of 1804 and subsequently entered the fabric of American folklore. William Wells Brown's novel *Clotel, or the President's*

Daughter (1853) fictionalized the tale in the interest of the abolition movement, and Barbara Chase-Riboud's prize-winning novel *Sally Hemings* (1979) reinvented Hemings against the background of a new Black consciousness and an emerging feminism. Fawn Brodie's 1974 biography of Jefferson attempted to assert the relationship as historical fact, but most professional historians fault her analysis of the evidence and find little convincing proof of the relationship. If stories like these about Sally Hemings have made her place in American history, they should not be allowed to obscure either the intelligent, caring woman behind them or the situation in which she lived.

BIBLIOGRAPHY

Bear, James A., Jr. "The Hemings Family of Monticello," *Virginia Cavalcade* (1979), and *Jefferson at Monticello* (1967); Betts, Edwin Morris, ed. *Thomas Jefferson's Farm Book* (1953); Brodie, Fawn M. *Thomas Jefferson: An Intimate History* (1974); Dabney, Virginius. *The Jefferson Scandals: A Rebuttal* (1981); Langhorne, Elizabeth C. *Monticello: A Family Story* (1987); Miller, John Chester. *The Wolf by the Ears: Thomas Jefferson and Slavery* (1977).

FRANK SHUFFELTON

HEMPHILL, JESSIE MAE (1933-)

Jessie Mae Hemphill has preserved a family tradition of music stretching over four generations and has helped to bring the sound of traditional Mississippi blues to modern listeners throughout the United States and abroad. Within this folk tradition she has created a unique style and has composed many original songs based on her life experiences. Her sound features melismatic, mostly pentatonic melody lines sung in a sweet voice, usually followed by repeated short figures on the electric guitar. Her powerful guitar rhythms, sometimes augmented by a tambourine attached to her foot, are influenced by the rhythms of fife and drum music, which she also plays.

She was born October 18, 1933, near Como, Mississippi, where she still lives. Her grandfather, Sid Hemphill (c. 1876-1963), was a prominent blind musician in the area and the son of a fiddler. Sid Hemphill played fiddle, banjo, guitar, fife, panpipes, drums, and several other instruments, and for over fifty years led a string band that also played fife and drum music. His three daughters, Sidney Lee, Rosa Lee, and Virgie Lee (Jessie Mae's mother) all learned to play guitar, drums, and various stringed instruments from him. Jessie Mae learned to play guitar and drums from her grandfather, mother, and aunts, especially her aunt Rosa Lee. Her father, James Graham, was a blues pianist around Como and later in Memphis. Most of her music was confined to local house parties and picnics near Como and in Memphis, where she sometimes lived. At an early age she was briefly married to L. D. Brooks and was known as Jessie Mae Brooks. She changed her name back to Hemphill in order to emphasize the family's musical heritage when she decided to pursue a career in music in 1979. Since then she has performed in concerts and festivals in over twenty states, Canada, and nine European countries. In 1987 and 1988, she was voted winner of the Handy Award for Best Female Traditional Blues Artist. She has recorded two 45 rpm records and an album (*Feelin' Good*) for the High Water label of the United States, an album (*She-Wolf*) for the Vogue label of France, and various album tracks for the Black & Blue label of France and the Au-Go-Go label of Australia. Her album *Feelin' Good* won a Handy Award in 1991 in the Best Country Blues Album category.

BIBLIOGRAPHY

Evans, David. "Jessie Mae Hemphill," *Living Blues* (March-April 1985), and Notes to Jessie Mae Hemphill, *She-Wolf*, Vogue 513501 (France, 1981), and Notes to Jessie Mae Hemphill, *Feelin' Good*, High Water LP 1012 (USA, 1990); Mitchell, George. *Blow My Blues Away* (1971).

DAVID EVANS

Jessie Mae Hemphill has preserved a family tradition of music stretching over four generations and has helped to bring the sound of traditional Mississippi blues to modern listeners around the world.

HENDRICKS, BARBARA (1948-)

Growing up Black means being compassionate, Barbara Hendricks has stated. It is not a handicap but it does include an obligation to give something back to the people.

The soprano was born on November 20, 1948, in Stephens, Arkansas, where her father served as Methodist minister. She enrolled at the University of Nebraska, carrying a double major in mathematics and chemistry, not taking her singing seriously until she was nineteen, when friends urged her to study with Jennie Tourel.

Following their advice and with the resulting encouragement, she resolved to dedicate her attention to music. Although not wealthy during these student days, she invested in attending every concert and opera performance she could manage, and began serious study of foreign languages, acting, music theory, and piano.

In 1973, when only twenty-five years old, she made her debut with the Metropolitan Opera for twelve performances as St. Settlement in *Four Saints in Three Acts* by Virgil Thomson, an opera calling for an all-Black cast. Following this, she performed in San Francisco's production of Cavalli's *Ormindo* (1974) and in various productions in England, the Netherlands, Germany, Austria, and the United States, with particular success in Paris as Juliette in Gounod's *Roméo et Juliette* (1982). In 1986, she returned to the Metropolitan Opera as Sophie in *Der Rosenkavalier* (Richard Strauss), moving to the Teatro alla Scala in Milan the next year to appear as Susanna in Mozart's *Le nozze di Figaro*. A highlight of 1988 was the release on film of Puccini's *La bohème*, directed by Luca Canonici, in which she was cast with José Carreras (because of health problems, the tenor was represented only on the sound track). She was offered the leading role in the film *Diva* (which was accepted by Wilhelmenia Fernandez); she declined so that she would not be thought a film actress who sings. She is attracted to films, however, because of the greater potential to pursue her interest in acting. For the same reason, she prefers the smaller opera houses and rarely schedules more than five operas per season.

Her recorded repertoire gives emphasis to French composers, as well as Mozart, Gershwin, Handel, Schubert, and Puccini. The first recordings to attract a large following were of Mahler's Fourth Symphony (London LDR-10004) in 1979, and Daniel del Tredici's *Final Alice* (London LDR-71018) in 1981.

She was appointed Goodwill Ambassador by the United Nations, working for human rights. The French government named her Commandeur des Arts et des Lettres in 1986 and she was awarded honorary doctorates by the Nebraska Wesleyan University (1988) and Belgium's Louvain University (1990).

She currently lives in Switzerland with her husband and children.

BIBLIOGRAPHY

Forbes, Elizabeth. "Hendricks, Barbara." *The New Grove Dictionary of American Music*, ed. H. Wiley Hitchcock and Stanley Sadie (1986); Turner, Patricia. *Afro-American Singers: An Index and Preliminary Discography of Opera, Choral Music and Song* (1977).

DOMINIQUE-RENÉ de LERMA

HEWITT, GLORIA CONYERS
(1935-)

"They were so busy loving me that they didn't notice that they didn't respect me—so, of course, neither did I," said mathematician Gloria Conyers Hewitt of her all-male, all-white colleagues at the University of Montana at Missoula in the mid-1970s (Hewitt 1991). One of them had recommended her for a merit award, her department had supported her, but the dean had denied the award.

In preparation for an appeal, she was asked if she could prove that the widespread recognition she had received was not *just* because of her sex/race. "Nobody around here knew more math than me," she remembered in a 1991 interview. "They weren't doing that much research either. One day I got mad. 'I don't care what you think,' I said, and I meant it. 'I'm tired of trying to please you. What you think of me doesn't matter to me any more.' Then they *had* to begin *respecting* me. I believe now that my colleagues both respect and like me." Eleven years after she was denied the aforementioned merit award, she received one initiated by the dean. Now she chairs the graduate committee and was asked to consider becoming the department chair. She declined.

Gloria Conyers was born to Crenella and Emmett Conyers, Sr., in Sumter, South Carolina, on October

One of the first Black women to receive the Ph.D. in mathematics, Gloria Conyers Hewitt has served for many years on the Educational Testing Service's Graduate Record Examination Committee. [Patricia Kenschaft]

26, 1935. She attended Fisk University from 1952 to 1956. There she took mathematics courses from Lee Lorch, who, though he was dismissed at the end of her second year, had recommended her for graduate study without consulting her. She was amazed in her senior year when she was offered a fellowship at the University of Washington in Seattle without applying for it, but she accepted it.

In 1962, she became the third Black woman in the United States to receive a Ph.D. in mathematics. In fall 1961, she joined the faculty of the University of Montana in Missoula. She became a full professor in 1972.

She was a visiting lecturer for the Mathematical Association of America from 1964 to 1972, giving lectures and colloquia at many institutions. She was on the executive council of Pi Mu Epsilon, the mathematical honor society from 1972 to 1975. From 1976 to 1986, she was a member of Educational

Testing Service's Graduate Record Examination Committee, which planned and made up questions for the subject test in mathematics. From 1984 to 1986, she chaired this committee. She served on the College Board's Advanced Placement Calculus Development Committee from 1987 to 1991, planning questions for the AP calculus examination.

In 1980-81, she spent a sabbatical year at Case Institute, studying algebraic topology and homological algebra. She has taught a course and supervised a doctoral dissertation in homological algebra at the University of Montana. She coauthored a publication with a student, a copy of which she saw at the mathematical institute in Beijing when she visited there with the Women in Mathematics tour of China in 1990.

BIBLIOGRAPHY

Hewitt, Gloria Conyers. Personal interview (October 1991); Hewitt, Gloria Conyers, and Frank Hannick. "Characteristics of Generalized Noetherian Rings," *Acta Mathematica Hungarica* (1989); Kenschaft, Patricia C. "Black Women in Mathematics in the United States," *American Mathematical Monthly* (October 1981).

PATRICIA CLARK KENSCHAFT

HIGGINS, BERTHA G. (1872-1944)

Suffragist and political activist Bertha G. Higgins worked tirelessly in Providence, Rhode Island, politics to benefit African-Americans and women. Her activities spanned four decades, from the turn of the century until 1940. As a political activist, her goals included votes for women, political patronage for Black men and women, antilynching legislation, and increased social services and jobs for the people of her community.

Bertha G. Dillard was born in Danville, Virginia, on November 18, 1872. A seamstress and clothing designer, she studied in London and Paris and for a time operated a clothing shop of her own after her marriage to physician William Harvey Higgins. The couple was married in Charlotte, North Carolina, in 1896, lived in Harlem for a time around 1899, and settled in Providence in 1906. They had one daughter, Prudence, who became a musician and a social worker.

Bertha Higgins began her political and community work shortly after moving to Providence by joining other Black women, in 1907, to petition the mayor and the school committee to hire a Black teacher. She became involved in the Rhode Island Black women's club movement, leading both cultural and political activities within a few years of her arrival in the city.

By 1914, Higgins was a suffragist, and with the support of her husband she led efforts to foster the work of the Woman Suffrage Party of Rhode Island. She wrote letters to federal and state elected officials and helped raise funds in support of the votes for women campaign. Several other Black women worked in the Rhode Island woman suffrage movement during this period, including Mary E. Jackson, Susan E. Williams, and Maria Lawton. Of these women, however, Higgins was a prime mover. In 1916, for example, Higgins persuaded the Twentieth-Century Art and Literary Club, a group of Black Providence women, to sponsor a minstrel show. Funds raised from this event benefited the Woman Suffrage Party, a racially integrated association.

Bertha Higgins was a founder and leader of several women's political organizations, including the Political League and, after the ratification of the Nineteenth Amendment, the Julia Ward Howe Republican Women's Club. Higgins cooperated with nationally known Republican women such as Mary Church Terrell, who had significant roles not only in working for the passage of the amendment but also in helping elect Warren G. Harding to the presidency in 1920. In appreciation of her work during the campaign, Harding invited the Higginses to his inauguration.

Through her various associations, Higgins fought for Black women's political patronage in the Republican party. However, in 1932 she became disillusioned with the failure of the party to recognize Black political patronage and, as a result, led the women in her organization to the Democratic party. Eventually, they changed the name of their organization to the Julia Ward Howe Democratic Women's Club.

Political activism was also a means for Higgins to push for legislation to improve Black human rights. As president of her association, she pressured Congressman Clark Burdick and Senator Le Baron Colt to support the Dyer antilynching bill that went before Congress several times between 1918 and 1925. Burdick supported the bill, which managed to get through the House of Representatives a few times. Colt did not support the bill, which never passed the Senate.

During the 1930s and 1940s, Higgins worked diligently to gain meaningful employment for Black people in her community. Numerous individuals sought her assistance in their efforts to gain state employment because they knew she would lobby on their behalf. As a result of her efforts, for example, in 1937 Higgins's daughter, Prudence, became the first Black social worker at the Rhode Island Department of Public Welfare. Furthermore, in Bertha's efforts to end poverty among Black people in Providence, she was instrumental in bringing the Urban League to the city during the 1930s.

By the end of the 1930s, Bertha Higgins had begun to slow down. In 1938, her husband passed away, and she withdrew to mourn for eighteen months. In 1942, at the age of seventy, she withdrew permanently from public life. She died December 30, 1944, at her home in Providence. This formidable woman never allowed barriers to hinder her battles to strengthen the rights of women and the people of her race.

BIBLIOGRAPHY

Terborg-Penn, Rosalyn. "African American Women's Networks in the Anti-Lynching Crusade." In *Gender, Class, Race, and Reform in the Progressive Era*, ed. Noralee Frankel and Nancy S. Dye (1991), and "African Feminism: A Theoretical Approach to the History of Women in the African Diaspora." In *Women in Africa and the African Diaspora*, ed. Rosalyn Terborg-Penn, et al. (1987). The Bertha G. Higgins papers are in the Rhode Island Black Heritage Society, Providence, Rhode Island.

ROSALYN TERBORG-PENN

HIGHLANDER FOLK SCHOOL

After attending a summer workshop on school desegregation at Highlander Folk School (HFS) in 1954, a Black school teacher from Columbia, South Carolina, reported to her community: "I always knew what I wanted to get done, but now I feel like I know how I'm going to get it done" (Glen 1988). Highlander provided both a gathering place and a philosophy of social change that engaged and supported the Black freedom movement as it expanded in the aftermath of the 1954 *Brown* v. *Board of Education* decision. During the 1950s, interactions between Highlander and southern Black communities helped foster the development of indigenous local leaders. Women such as Rosa Parks, Septima Clark, and Bernice Robinson played a pivotal role in fusing Highlander's resources with the needs and aspirations of their communities in ways that helped to fundamentally shape the tactics and goals of the civil rights movement.

Cofounder Myles Horton described Highlander as a place "where people can share their experiences and learn from each other and learn to trust their own judgement" as they worked toward a more democratic and economically just society (Horton 1989). HFS was established in Grundy County, Tennessee, in 1932 to serve industrial and rural workers in southern Appalachia. Through its dynamic and flexible program of workshops and extension programs, Highlander quickly developed into a regional center for workers' education. Highlander became the primary training school for labor organizers who led the Congress of Industrial Organizations (CIO) drives to organize southern industry. Although HFS was always open to all races, most unions were reluctant to sponsor interracial schools; Black people did not begin to attend Highlander as students until 1944. The efforts of the 1930s and 1940s had demonstrated with increasing frequency, however, that racism was the main obstacle to achieving a democratic and economically just society in the South. By the late 1940s, Highlander's firm commitment to interracial unionism and its refusal to accommodate postwar anticommunism left it estranged from an increasingly conservative CIO, leading to a complete reassessment of HFS's program and goals.

Highlander was prepared to respond to the important developments in race relations that the 1950s would bring. In anticipation of the U.S. Supreme Court's ruling on *Brown* v. *Board of Education*, the HFS executive council resolved to focus its efforts on promoting the desegregation of public schools. Highlander initiated its new program in 1953 with a series of summer workshops to help prepare Black and white representatives of civic, labor, church, and interracial groups to lead in the transition to an integrated school system. In contrast to earlier days, at least half of the workshop participants were Black. The workshops provided a valuable forum for individuals from throughout the South to share their experiences and frustrations, address common problems, and develop strategies and tools for achieving public school desegregation in their communities. For many, HFS workshops also created a unique experience of interracial community. Reflecting on her participation in a Highlander workshop during the summer of 1955, Rosa Parks recalled: "That was the first time I had lived in an atmosphere of complete equality with the members of the other race" (Glen 1988). Within months of her stay at Highlander, Rosa Parks's defiance of segregation would spark the legendary Montgomery bus boycott.

HFS's flexible program and workshop networks offered fertile ground for new ideas and new leadership to grow even as southern states organized their

Rosa Parks (right) participated in a school desegregation workshop at Highlander Folk School in the summer of 1955. Several months later, back home in Montgomery, Alabama, Parks's refusal to give up her seat on a bus triggered the Montgomery bus boycott. Seated at the table (left to right) are Septima Clark; Dr. Parrish, University of Louisville; and Dr. Fred Patterson, president of Tuskegee Institute. Legend has it at Highlander that Parks remarked during the workshop "Nothing ever happens in Montgomery." [Emil Willimetz]

resistance to the implementation of the *Brown* decision, along with a concerted assault on the National Association for the Advancement of Colored People (NAACP). When NAACP member and HFS workshop participant Septima Clark was fired from her job with the Charleston public schools in 1956, Myles Horton immediately hired Clark as full-time director of Highlander's workshop program. Septima Clark, along with Esau Jenkins and Bernice Robinson, two other workshop participants, gave substance to HFS's extension program to develop community leadership

when they joined it to the concrete needs and aspirations of the people of the Sea Islands. Esau Jenkins, self-educated farmer and long-time community activist and leader on St. Johns Island, was convinced that the right to vote was the key to addressing other problems confronting the island's Black community, and adult illiteracy was the primary barrier to meeting voting requirements. Jenkins's appeal to Highlander, first made during a 1954 summer workshop, resulted in the establishment of the first citizenship school on St. Johns Island in January 1957 as part of Highlander's extension program. Bernice Robinson, who served as the first teacher, and Septima Clark developed an adult literacy curriculum and program that provided the basis for citizenship schools throughout the South.

Bernice Robinson, a beautician and dressmaker, developed a curriculum around the life experiences and needs of her students. She and Septima Clark produced workbooks that included sample money order and mail order forms and voter registration applications, along with pertinent sections of the state's voting requirements, and short chapters on political parties, social security, taxes, the function of the county school board, and other topics. Robinson also rehearsed registration and voting procedures with the students. Jenkins, Robinson, and Clark organized mass meetings throughout the Sea Islands and in Charleston to build enthusiasm for the program and recruit

teachers. Highlander ran workshops for more than 220 potential teachers, who represented a variety of occupational backgrounds and ages. By 1961, there had been thirty-seven citizenship schools in South Carolina alone, with 1,300 participants, which translated into a dramatic increase in the number of registered Black voters. On St. Johns Island alone, Black voter registration more than tripled between 1956 and 1960. Starting in 1959, Clark and Robinson produced materials for use in citizenship schools in Tennessee and Georgia, and they worked directly in helping to establish programs in Huntsville, Alabama, and Savannah, Georgia.

On April 1, 1960, Highlander's seventh annual student workshop hosted participants in the wave of sit-ins that swept the South earlier in the year. During the next year, Highlander sponsored several workshops for the new generation of activists and provided

Septima Clark (shown here on the left with a "civil rights group") became the director of the Highlander Folk School's workshop program in 1956. The Highlander workshops provided a valuable forum for individuals to share their experiences, address common problems, and develop strategies and tools for achieving change in their communities. [State Historical Society of Wisconsin]

an important forum for addressing the role of white students in the movement. Ella Baker, Dorothy Cotton, Ruby Doris Smith, and Diane Nash were among the participants. In January 1961, fifty-two Black beauticians from Tennessee and Alabama met at Highlander for a "new leadership responsibilities" workshop and explored how they and other women whose incomes were not dependent on white people could participate more effectively in the movement.

Highlander held its last workshop in May 1961. Years of harassment by state officials culminated in a Tennessee Supreme Court ruling revoking the school's charter and confiscating its property. Yet Highlander's contribution to the civil rights movement could not be so easily contained. The citizenship school program was transferred to the Southern Christian Leadership Conference (SCLC), where it continued to flourish under the leadership of Septima Clark. Bernice Robinson continued to work with the program from her position on the HFS staff, later joining the staff of the SCLC. Highlander reincorporated as the Highlander Research and Education Center and is currently located in New Market, Tennessee. Since the 1970s, it has worked primarily with the people of Appalachia, seeking to address labor, environmental, and health problems and concerns in the continuing struggle for social and economic justice.

BIBLIOGRAPHY

Crawford, Vicki L., Jacqueline Anne Rouse, and Barbara Woods, ed. *Women in the Civil Rights Movement: Trailblazers and Torchbearers, 1941-65* (1990); Glen, John M. *Highlander: No Ordinary School, 1932-1962* (1988); Horton, Myles. "Thou Shalt Not Teach." In *It Did Happen Here: Recollections of Political Repression in America*, ed. Bud Schultz and Ruth Schultz (1989).

PATRICIA SULLIVAN

HINARD, EUFROSINA (b. 1777)

While no one knows for sure what Eufrosina Hinard thought of slavery, her actions as a slaveholder challenge any easy assumptions about her views. Born in New Orleans in 1777, she was the offspring of both slavery and freedom, the descendant of a Black slave woman and a free white man. Because her mother had been freed, Hinard was free, never personally witnessing the exploitation of slavery. Instead, Hinard understood slavery from what she learned from her mother and from her experiences as a slaveholder. What brings her assumptions about the institution of slavery into question is the extraordinary way in which she balanced slavery and its antithesis, emancipation.

In 1791, when Hinard was fourteen years old, she, like so many other free women of color in the frontier Spanish port of New Orleans, was placéed (committed) to the Spaniard Don Nicolás Vidal, *auditor de guerra*, the military legal counselor to the governor. Hinard's arrangement was not unusual for women of her caste, especially in the Spanish colonies. There, as in the French colonies, interracial marriage was against the law; thus the institutions of *plaçage* and *concubinato*, both forms of de facto marriage, were regularly practiced. Both offered some political, legal, economic, and social protection to the women who participated in the practice, and to their offspring.

Eufrosina bore two quadroon daughters, Carolina (1793) and Merced (1795). When Vidal died in 1806 in Spanish Pensacola, where he had taken his family after Louisiana was ceded to the United States with the Louisiana Purchase in 1803, he left his estate to Hinard and their daughters. It was after Vidal's death that Hinard's abilities as an astute businesswoman and a slaveholder became evident, and she combined her business sense and her view of slavery in seemingly antagonistic ways.

Like other urban slaveholders, Hinard rented out the slaves she owned or allowed them to live out, bringing a portion of their profits to her. While the Spanish governed Louisiana and the Floridas, they offered slaves the right to purchase their own freedom, and several thousand urban slaves were able to accumulate enough money to buy themselves out of slavery. After Spanish Louisiana and Florida were ceded to the United States and joined the southern states, slaves no longer had that right. In fact, as the antebellum period progressed, freedom became more and more difficult to acquire. State after state clamped down on manumission, leaving few avenues to freedom.

Eufrosina Hinard, however, had lived much of her life as a Spanish subject and by Spanish tradition freedom was a natural right. Slavery, in that view, was an unfortunate condition. All slaves had the right to purchase themselves, if they could pay their estimated value. Yet by the time Hinard became a slaveowner, a slave's right to purchase his or her own freedom had been annulled. That, however, did not prevent Hinard from continuing the practice. Throughout the antebellum period, Hinard regularly bought slaves, allowing them to pay her their purchase price, plus interest. Then she freed them. Thus while Hinard could understandably be viewed as a slaveholder, her method of slaveholding actively challenged the assumptions behind the southern institution that defined slavery as a natural condition and the slave as having no rights.

BIBLIOGRAPHY

Deeds. Pensacola City Court, Pensacola, Florida (1820-60); Gould, Lois Virginia Meacham. "In Full Enjoyment of Their Liberty: The Free Women of Color of the Gulf Ports of New Orleans, Mobile, and Pensacola, 1769-1860," Ph.D. diss. (1991); Macdonald, Robert, John Edward Kemp, and Edward Haas. *Louisiana's Black Heritage* (1979); Macdonald, Robert, and Edward Haas. *Louisiana's Legal Heritage* (1983); Mills, Gary B. *The Forgotten People: Cane River's Creoles of Color* (1977); Rankin, David C. "The Forgotten People: Free People of Color in New Orleans, 1850-1870," Ph.D. diss. (1976); Will books, Escambia County Court. Escambia County, Pensacola, Florida (1820-60); Sterkx, H. E. *The Free Negro in Antebellum Louisiana* (1972); Sutton, Leora. "Eufrosina Hinard." Unpublished paper, Escambia County Court House (n.d.); Vidal, Don Nicolás. Will. New Orleans Notarial Archives, Notary Pedro Pedesclaux (April 25, 1798).

VIRGINIA GOULD

Natalie Hinderas began as a child prodigy, giving her first full-length public recital at the age of eight. This highly respected pianist went on to become a strong advocate of the work of Black composers. [Schomburg Center]

HINDERAS, NATALIE LEOTA HENDERSON (1927-1987)

Born June 15, 1927, in Oberlin, Ohio, Natalie Henderson was born into the musical household of Abram and Leota (Palmer) Henderson. Her parents were both students at Oberlin—her father was a jazz pianist and her mother was a classical pianist who taught at the Cleveland Institute of Music.

As a child, Natalie was surrounded by music and musicians. She began playing the piano at the age of three. Her formal piano studies began at six and she also studied violin and voice at an early age. Natalie was a child prodigy at the piano and played a full-length public recital at the age of eight. She played a concerto with the Cleveland Women's Symphony at the age of twelve. She was musically educated in the public schools of Oberlin, Ohio. She later received the B.Mus. in 1945 from Oberlin Conservatory as their youngest graduate. (She had been admitted as a special student at the age of eight.) Assuming the name Natalie Hinderas, she did postgraduate work in piano at the Juilliard School of Music with Olga Samaroff and at the Philadelphia Conservatory with Edward Steuermann. She also studied composition with Vincent Persichetti.

In 1954, she made her Town Hall debut and received critical acclaim. Thereafter she toured extensively as a concert pianist in the United States, Europe, and the West Indies. The U.S. Department of State sponsored two tours abroad that included Africa and Asia as well as Europe. In the mid-1950s, Hinderas signed a contract with NBC to travel to their owned and operated stations in the various major cities to play solo recitals, concertos, and variety shows.

Hinderas made a debut with the Philadelphia Orchestra in four concerts in 1971. She was the first Black female instrumental soloist to appear with the orchestra in subscription concerts. Her debut piece was the contemporary Ginastera Concerto. Many concerts followed with the Los Angeles Philharmonic Orchestra, the Cleveland, Atlanta, New York, San Francisco, and Chicago symphony orchestras, and others. Her orchestral performances featured

Rachmaninoff's Concerto no. 2 in C Minor, the Schumann Piano Concerto, Gershwin's *Rhapsody in Blue,* and George Walker's Piano Concerto no. 1, which she commissioned in 1975. Her recording debut came in 1971 with the album *Natalie Hinderas Plays Music by Black Composers* (DESTO); other recordings followed on the Orion and Columbia labels. She was hailed as an extremely intelligent and thorough pianist with comprehensive technical ability and honest musical instincts (*Musical Courier* 1954). Throughout her career she promoted and recorded works by Black performers and composers, among them R. Nathaniel Dett, William Grant Still, John W. Work, and George Walker, whose works she recorded.

She received numerous awards and fellowships, including the Leventritt, John Hay Whitney, Julius Rosenwald, Martha Baird Rockefeller, and Fulbright fellowships. She also received an honorary doctorate of music degree from Swarthmore College (1976). In 1968, Hinderas joined the faculty of Temple University, where she was a full professor at the time of her death on July 22, 1987.

BIBLIOGRAPHY

BDAAM; Black Perspective in Music (Fall 1987); Felton, J. "Philadelphia Orchestra (Ormandy) Natalie Hinderas," *High Fidelity/Musical America* (February 1972); Fleming, Shirley. "Natalie Hinderas: Musician of the Month," *High Fidelity/Musical America* (October 1973); *Musical Courier* (December 1, 1954); *New York Times* (obituary) (July 23, 1987); *Saturday Review* (December 26, 1970); *Variety* (obituary) (July 29, 1987); *WWBA* (1978).

DISCOGRAPHY

For a discography, see de Lerma, Dominique-René. "The Hinderas Discography," *Sonorities in Black Music* (1980).

MARVA GRIFFIN CARTER

HINKSON, MARY (1930-)

Mary Hinkson, dancer, teacher, and choreographer, was born in Philadelphia, Pennsylvania, in 1930. She attended the University of Wisconsin, which had a budding dance program. After graduation, Hinkson moved to New York to study with Martha Graham, the modern dance pioneer and visionary. Hinkson danced with the Martha Graham Dance Company in many roles that Graham created specifically for her, such as *Ardent Song* (1955), *Acrobats of God* (1960), *Samson Agonistes* (1962), and *Phaedra* (1969). Hinkson

is best remembered for her role as Circe in the dance of the same name in 1963.

Hinkson has worked as a guest artist with many dance companies in the United States and in Europe. Some of the other choreographers she worked with were Pearl Lang (*Chosen People,* 1952), Donald McKayle (*Rainbow 'Round My Shoulder,* 1959, in which she created the female lead), John Butler (*Carmina Burana,* 1966), George Balanchine (*Figure in the Carpet,* 1960), and Anna Sokolow (*Seven Deadly Sins,* 1975) in which Hinkson danced in *The Dance of Anna.*

Hinkson remains known for her long and outstanding work with Graham, which began in 1951. She has taught the Graham technique at the Martha Graham School in New York. Although Hinkson is known primarily as a dancer and a teacher, she has choreographed several dances. She performed her most notable dance, *Make the Heart Show,* in 1951. Hinkson also has taught at the Dance Theatre of Harlem's school, the Juilliard School, and at the High School of Performing Arts, all in New York City.

BIBLIOGRAPHY

Clarke, Mary and David Vaughan, eds. *The Encyclopedia of Dance and Ballet* (1977); Cohen-Stratyner, Barbara Naomi. *Biographical Dictionary of Dance* (1982); *EBA*; Emery, Lynne Fauley. *Black Dance in the United States from 1619 to Today* (1988); Goodman, Saul. "Dancers You Should Know," *Dance Magazine* (1964); Long, Richard. *The Black Tradition in American Concert Dance* (1990); McDonagh, Don. *The Complete Guide to Modern Dance* (1976); Thorpe, Edward. *Black Dance* (1990); Toppin, Edgar A. *A Biographical History of Blacks in America since 1528* (1971); Willis, John, ed. *Dance World* (1976).

KARIAMU WELSH ASANTE

HOBSON, ANN (1943-)

During the 1960s, Ann Hobson broke ground as one of four African-American musicians in the nation's leading symphony orchestras. Born in Philadelphia on November 6, 1943, Hobson began to study the harp at age fourteen. During her senior year at Philadelphia's Girls High, she was noted as being of concert caliber. After high school, she enrolled at the Philadelphia Musical Academy and continued her harp study through the summer at the Maine Harp Colony (which had rejected her years earlier because of her race). In Maine she met a teacher, Alice Chalifoux, whose protégé she later became. She transferred to the Cleveland Institute of Music in order to study with the noted harpist and teacher, who later recommended her for principal harpist of the National Symphony.

In 1966, Hobson was selected to fill a one-year assignment as a master harpist with the National Symphony, but, because of her fine musicianship, that initial year was extended for several seasons. In 1969, she competed against thirty harpists for the position of second harpist with the Boston Symphony Orchestra. Her competition performance was so outstanding, however, that she was offered a higher position as associate principal harpist and then eventually became principal harpist with the Boston Pops Orchestra.

In addition to her professional affiliation with the National Symphony and the Boston Symphony/Boston Pops Orchestras, Hobson has been a member of the Boston Symphony Chamber Players, and she founded the New England Harp Trio (cello, flute, harp) based in Boston. She has performed throughout the United States and, in 1979, traveled to Shanghai and Peking, China, where she also taught master classes. Throughout her career she has taught privately and been affiliated with several outstanding musical institutions, including the Philadelphia Musical Academy and the New England Conservatory of Music.

Ann Hobson has recorded with the Boston Symphony Chamber Players on the Deutsche Grammophon label, performing Debussy, and has received numerous favorable reviews of her concert performances. After a 1977 appearance, the *Wichita Eagle* (Wichita, Kansas) wrote, "Miss Hobson is an incredible technician, but more, she is able to tear the harp out of its traditional raiment and give it new and vital voices."

She currently resides outside Boston.

BIBLIOGRAPHY

BDAAM; Handy, D. Antoinette. *Black Women in American Bands and Orchestras* (1981).

IRENE JACKSON-BROWN

HOLIDAY, BILLIE (1915-1959)

Billie Holiday never won a jazz popularity poll. Readers of *Metronome*, *Melody Maker*, and *Downbeat* magazines consistently chose Holiday second, third, even tenth after Ella Fitzgerald, Mildred Bailey, Helen O'Connell, and Jo Stafford, singers who typically performed with the commercially popular big bands. With jazz critics, however, there is little question that

Billie Holiday was the greatest jazz singer ever recorded. Coming into her own a generation after the classic blues singers, like Bessie Smith, Holiday created a place for herself outside the confines of the big band "girl singer" role, setting standards by which other jazz singers continue to be judged and influencing singers as far-ranging in style as Sarah Vaughan, Frank Sinatra, Carmen McRae, and Lena Horne.

Holiday began recording during the big band era, and although her work with Count Basie attests to her ability to perform with such ensembles, her style was better suited to small combos in which she found the freedom to be a true jazz soloist. Recordings made during her twenty-six-year career reveal her skill as a re-composer of melody and a rhythmic innovator, the hallmarks of any great jazz improviser.

Born Eleanora Fagan in Philadelphia, Pennsylvania, on April 7, 1915, to teenagers Sadie Fagan and Clarence Holiday, Billie grew up in Baltimore, Maryland, where she took the name of her screen idol, Billie Dove. Her father, later a guitarist with Fletcher Henderson's orchestra, never lived with the family, and Holiday was raised by her mother and other relatives. Her childhood was one of deprivation and even cruelty during a year spent at the Catholic-run House of the Good Shepherd for Colored Girls, ostensibly for truancy. As a teenager she joined her mother, who had moved to New York City, and she may have worked for a time as a prostitute while learning to be a performer.

Her autobiography, *Lady Sings the Blues*, written with the help of journalist William Dufty and published in 1956, is often factually inaccurate, and the 1972 movie based on it likewise served to sensationalize aspects of Holiday's tragic private life at the expense of her musical talent. Nonetheless, the autobiography provides a pointed critique of American society, with its portrayal of Holiday as a Black performer facing racism and as a female performer facing sexism in the male-dominated world of jazz.

The beginnings of her career are unclear. Holiday claimed not to read music, but family friends remember her singing as a child, and by her early teens she was performing for tips and jamming with other musicians in Baltimore's waterfront entertainment district. In her autobiography, Holiday stresses the early influences of recordings by Louis Armstrong and Bessie Smith. Although not a true blues singer, Holiday certainly shares with blues singers like Smith an identification with the text, a gift for emphasizing particular words and syllables in performance, and a fondness for slow tempos. Similarly, although she did not imitate Louis Armstrong's vir-

Though she never won a jazz popularity poll in Downbeat *or* Melody Maker, *jazz critics consider Billie Holiday the greatest jazz singer ever recorded. [Schomburg Center]*

tuoso scatting technique, Holiday's singing is marked by rhythmic flexibility and the swing characteristic of Armstrong's trumpet performances. Holiday was not a big-voiced belter like Armstrong or Smith, but she used the distinctive timbre and limited range of her voice to their best advantage, producing solos marked by subtlety and nuance.

By 1931, Holiday was singing in New York City accompanied solely by piano. For a time she was part of a floor show featuring bassist George "Pops" Foster and tap dancer Charles Honi Coles. In 1933, John Hammond, jazz record producer and critic, heard the then eighteen-year-old Holiday singing in Monette Moore's club accompanied by the house pianist, Dot Hill. Hammond immediately wrote about her in the British journal *Melody Maker*, describing the individual vocal style and delivery that set Holiday apart from other mainstream pop singers of the time.

Hammond, who as a record producer was always looking for new talent, arranged for Holiday to record, and she cut two sides in 1933. Ironically, Hammond recorded Holiday within twenty-four hours of producing Bessie Smith's final recordings. Although Holiday's sidemen included Jack Teagarden, Benny Goodman, and Gene Krupa, the songs she was given to record, "Your Mother's Son-in-Law" and "Riffin'

the Scotch," were second-rate Tin Pan Alley tunes. However, for her first time in front of a recording microphone, accompanied by musicians she did not know and in a manner to which she was unaccustomed, Holiday sounds assured and confident, if lacking in the rhythmic freedom that marks her later work.

Before Holiday returned to a recording studio in 1935, she took part in Duke Ellington's short film *Symphony in Black*, depicting African-American life. (The film received little distribution at the time but is now available on video.) Holiday performed "Big City Blues," a twelve-bar blues chorus sung during the second scene, entitled "A Triangle," and her brief appearance demonstrates her growing talent as a singer with a captivating stage presence. Holiday made one other screen appearance eleven years later, in the movie *New Orleans* (1946). Playing opposite her musical mentor Louis Armstrong, Holiday performed three numbers in an otherwise demeaning role as a singing maid with few substantive lines.

In July 1935, Hammond arranged for Holiday to return to the recording studio with pianist Teddy Wilson and his pick-up ensemble. Holiday found these musicians and their spontaneous approach suited to her style. She particularly enjoyed working with

Count Basie's sideman, saxophonist Lester Young, whose vocal-like approach was ideal for providing instrumental responses and counter melodies during her solos, as in "When a Woman Loves a Man" or "I'll Never Be the Same." Young, who began recording with Holiday in 1937, gave her the nickname "Lady Day," by which she was known from then on. Between 1935 and 1938, she released some eighty titles on the Brunswick label for marketing to the Black jukebox audience, earning a reputation as a one-take artist who learned material quickly and had a fantastic ear. Although still rarely given well-known songs to record, her performances demonstrated her improvisatory skill and contributed to her growing popularity with nightclub audiences. Also in 1935, she made the first of many successful appearances at Harlem's Apollo Theatre. By 1936, she was recording under her own name, as well as with Teddy Wilson.

John Hammond also championed the work of Count Basie, and in 1937 he took Basie to hear Holiday and encouraged him to take her on as a singer with his band. Basie enthusiastically agreed, and Holiday performed with the band for a year. Due to contractual problems the two were not able to record together, but three air checks from Savoy and Meadowbrook Ballroom performances show that Holiday was capable of meeting the rhythmic challenges of one of the hottest bands of the era. The reasons given for her departure vary, depending on the source, but Holiday and Basie remained friends, and she made occasional appearances with the band in the 1940s.

Holiday went on to perform with Artie Shaw's band in 1939, becoming one of the first Black performers to integrate an all-white ensemble. Contractual problems again kept Holiday from recording with the band, however, and her time with Shaw's band was fraught with tensions over her style, which remained less popular with his big band audiences (who were used to a mainstream pop style), and over her race. Shaw hired white performer Helen Forrest as a back-up singer when establishments refused to allow Holiday to perform with the all-white ensemble or when conflicts over Holiday's approach to her material arose, and that did little to alleviate tensions. Holiday's descriptions of her time with Shaw, particularly on tour, are some of the most poignant parts of her autobiography.

By 1939, when she was just twenty-four, Holiday had gained significant recognition through her appearances at Café Society, a club opened by Barney Josephson in December 1938 for the express purpose of providing entertainment to integrated audiences. It was within this context that Holiday came to be identified with the song "Strange Fruit." Written by Lewis Allan, "Strange Fruit" is about lynching; in it, lynched bodies are described as "strange fruit," the "bitter crop" of southern racial politics. The song was unusual for the directness of its message, and many critics, including Hammond, were uncomfortable with Holiday's adoption of it as a kind of theme song, which she performed in a dramatic manner. Columbia Records held her contract at the time and was unwilling to record "Strange Fruit," but Holiday

Billie Holiday enjoyed working with saxophonist Lester Young, whose vocal-like approach was ideal for providing instrumental responses and counter melodies to her solos. It was Young who gave her the nickname "Lady Day." [National Archives]

managed to record the song on Milt Gabler's independent Commodore label. The recording sold well, with one of Holiday's blues numbers, "Fine and Mellow," on the flip side. Following her time at Café Society, Holiday became a much sought after performer in New York City and elsewhere.

She signed with Decca in 1944, a label with a reputation for mainstream popular music rather than jazz but where Gabler now worked. Holiday decided she wanted strings as part of her back-up, and Gabler complied. "Lover Man," her first recording in this new style, became her best-selling record to date. During her six years with Decca, Holiday recorded her own compositions, "God Bless the Child" and "Don't Explain," and had success with the material of others, such as "Good Morning, Heartache," by Irene Higginbotham (whom she had met when Higginbotham was married to Teddy Wilson) as well as some standards.

In 1947, Holiday entered a private clinic to try and kick her drug habit, but some three weeks following her discharge she was arrested for possession. Circumstances surrounding her arrest are unclear, but rather than receive treatment, she was sentenced to a year and a day at the Federal Reformatory for Women at Alderson, West Virginia. She served nine and one-half months, and upon her release for good behavior New York City authorities revoked her cabaret card, thus making it impossible for her to perform in local clubs. The loss of the nightclub venue was a blow to the singer, who had been one of the performing lights of the New York entertainment scene, but Holiday found work outside New York City and in special concerts in the city, such as appearances at Carnegie Hall, as well as on national and European tours.

Decca records let Holiday's contract lapse in 1950, and she was without a recording label until 1952, when she signed with Norman Granz's Verve label. Granz wanted Holiday's recordings to recapture the spontaneity of the earlier sessions with Teddy Wilson, and so he shed the rehearsed orchestral arrangements of the Decca releases. With the formidable back-up talent of Oscar Peterson, Bobby Tucker, Ben Webster, Paul Quinichette, Harry "Sweets" Edison, and others, Holiday recorded some 100 songs for Granz. Although these recordings share the jam-like informality of the Brunswick releases, her material consisted of standards, like "Blue Moon" and "Stormy Weather," as well as remakes of some of her earlier numbers, such as "What a Little Moonlight Can Do," which provide an opportunity to hear how she continued to recompose her material.

In 1958, Holiday recorded her last and most popular album, *Lady in Satin*, featuring lush string arrangements by Ray Ellis. Holiday's voice is noticeably different from her Verve releases, and its cracked, almost harsh timbre, so apparent when accompanied by the strings, has led several critics to call it her worst album. Holiday's talent shines through the harsh timbre, however, and her rhythmic flexibility and careful shaping of the text remain as true as ever.

Prior to her *Lady in Satin* release, Holiday made one other recording that stands as a testament to her career as a jazz soloist. In December 1957, she took part in a special CBS program, *The Sound of Jazz*. Produced by Robert Herridge with the advice of Whitney Balliett and Nat Hentoff, the show presented nine performances by the leading jazz musicians of the time. Holiday performed her famous "Fine and Mellow" blues with assisting solos by Ben Webster, her old friend Lester Young, Vic Dickerson, Gerry Mulligan, Doc Cheatham, Coleman Hawkins, and Roy Eldridge. On the program, which is available on videocassette, Holiday performs in a circle with the other musicians. Her singing is true and rhythmically flexible, and she takes obvious delight in the work of the others. On her remaining choruses, she enters, not as a singer carrying the blues text, but as a distinctive soloist in the jazz ensemble.

Holiday died in New York City on July 17, 1959, from the long-term effects of drug addiction; she was only forty-four years old. A lifelong Roman Catholic, she is buried in Saint Raymond's Catholic Cemetery in the Bronx. Her funeral, a formal requiem high mass held at Saint Paul the Apostle Cathedral, was attended by thousands of friends and fans.

BIBLIOGRAPHY

Chilton, John. *Billie's Blues* (1975); Holiday, Billie and William Dufty. *Lady Sings the Blues* (1956); Jepsen, Jorgen Drunnet. *Discography of Billie Holiday* (1960); O'Meally, Robert. *Lady Day: The Many Faces of Billie Holiday* (1991); Schuller, Gunther. *The Swing Era: The Development of Jazz, 1930-1945* (1989); White, John. *Billie Holiday: Her Life and Times* (1987); Williams, Martin. *The Jazz Tradition* (1983).

SELECTED DISCOGRAPHY

The Billie Holiday Songbook, Verve/Polygram Records 823246-2 (1986); *Billie Holiday—The Complete Decca Recordings*, 2 cd, (1991); *Billie Holiday—The Legacy*, Columbia 3 cd, 47724, (1991).

VIDEOS

The Long Night of Lady Day (British documentary featuring reminiscences by many who knew and worked with Holiday, BBC television, 1985); *Duke Ellington and His Orchestra* (Jazz Classics JCVC 101, 1987; contains

Symphony in Black); *Lester Young and Billie Holiday* (Jazz and Jazz Video, Vidjazz 12, 1990; contains the three performances from the movie *New Orleans* as well as performances from the 1950s with Count Basie, Mal Waldron and His All Stars, and The Seven Lively Arts program, "The Sound of Jazz," featuring Holiday's performance of "Fine and Mellow" with Lester Young, broadcast from CBS Studio 58 on December 8, 1957); *The Sound of Jazz* (Vintage Jazz Classics, 1990; also contains the 1957 performance of "Fine and Mellow"); *Lady Day: The Many Faces of Billie Holiday* (Masters of American Music Series, distributed by Kultur International Films, 1991; documentary film based on the book by Robert O'Meally and directed by Matthew Selig, featuring reminiscences by Buck Clayton, Harry Edison, Milt Gabler, Carmen McRae, Albert Murray, Annie Ross, and Mal Waldron).

SUSAN C. COOK

HOLLAND, ANNIE WELTHY DAUGHTRY (c. 1871-1934)

"Please do not mention to any one that I may get any publicity from friend or foe," wrote Annie Holland to Charlotte Hawkins Brown, December 31, 1920, in support of Brown's fund-raising campaign to build the Alice Freeman Palmer building. Annie Welthy Daughtry Holland, Jeanes Fund teacher and supervisor, first Black female supervisor of Negro elementary education in North Carolina, and the founder of North Carolina's Colored Parent Teachers' Association, was driven by a commitment to improve public education for Black Americans rather than a desire for recognition for herself. This commitment and philosophy enabled her to influence Black and white southerners during the Jim Crow era.

Although other sources list Holland as the oldest of seven children of John and Margaret Daughtry, a death certificate completed by her son-in-law, Dr. F. N. Harris, lists her mother's name as Sarah Daughtry and her father as J. W. Barnes. She was born around 1871 in Isle of Wight County, Virginia. After her mother and father separated, she lived with her grandparents, Friday and Lucinda Daughtry, until she completed her education at the county school. In 1883, at the age of eleven, she entered Hampton Institute in Hampton, Virginia, where she stayed for a year and a half. Due to financial difficulties and a bout with malaria, she never graduated from Hampton.

Around 1886, she took the teacher's examination in Isle of Wight County and received a second grade certificate. In 1888, she married Willis Bird Holland,

For more than two decades, Annie Holland was in charge of Black elementary education for North Carolina. Her influence reached a white administration, teachers, future teachers, students, and parents. [Valinda Littlefield]

an 1884 Hampton graduate. Their marriage was nontraditional. From 1897 to his death in 1925, they kept dual residences, allowing each other to pursue individual careers—even in separate states. Between 1886 and 1900, she organized a temperance association and a Christian Endeavor Society, and she helped to organize a Kings' Daughters Society. From 1892 to 1897, she worked as an assistant to her husband at Franklin Public School. After her fifth year, the school board honored her request to teach at a school in the country because she felt that it would be better for her health. In 1905 she succeeded her husband as principal when he went into the insurance and real estate business—a position she held for at least five years.

She became the Jeanes Fund state supervisor in Gates County, North Carolina, in 1911 and by 1915 was the North Carolina State Home Demonstration Agent, responsible for supervising forty-four county supervisors. In 1921, she was appointed North Carolina State Supervisor for Negro Elementary Education, a position she held until her death. In 1927, she founded North Carolina's Colored Parent Teachers' Association. In its first year, 784 local associations were established and 15,770 people became members. In two years, the association raised $116,115. Monies were used to purchase such items as pianos, sewing machines, stoves, tables, chairs, shoes and clothing for children, as well as to support health clinics and school lunch rooms.

Holland died suddenly on January 6, 1934, while addressing a countywide meeting of Black teachers in Louisburg, North Carolina. Over 800 people attended a memorial for her in Raleigh, North Carolina. She was buried in Franklin, Virginia.

Her influence on education for Black North Carolinians reached a white administration, teachers, future teachers, students, and parents. As State Supervisor of Negro Elementary Education, she was responsible for visiting and assisting nineteen county training schools, ten city schools, and three state normal schools. As founder of the Colored Parent Teachers' Association, she was responsible for creating a climate in which parents and teachers worked to raise money, improve child health care, and improve the quality of life for Black children in rural homes. Her ability as a peacemaker and her organizational skills allowed her to forge a cooperative arrangement between the Colored Parent Teachers' Association and the white Parent Teachers Association decades before the 1969 unification of these groups. She used her resources to improve education for Black North Carolinians when funding for and attention to the problems of educating Black Americans in the South were overlooked or blatantly ignored by many educational boards. Remembered by her colleagues as a vibrant, practical, cultured, and capable organizer and peacemaker, Holland was able to achieve many of her accomplishments because she desired publicity from neither friend nor foe.

BIBLIOGRAPHY

Brown, Charlotte Hawkins. C. H. Brown Papers. North Carolina Department of Cultural Resources, Raleigh; Brown, Hugh Victor. *A History of the Education of Negroes in North Carolina* (1961); Crowell, Dorothy M. and Nora E. Lockhart. *This Too Is Our Heritage* (1973); Gavins, Raymond. "A 'Sin of Omission': Black Historiography in North Carolina." In *Black Americans in North Carolina and the South*, ed. Jeffrey J. Crow and Flora J. Hatley (1984); Hampton University Archives. Correspondence of Hollis Burke Frissell, in Annie W. Daughtry Holland and Willis Bird Holland files, Hampton, Virginia; *Journal and Guide*, "N.C. Educator Dies" (January 13, 1934); Murray, Percy. *History of the North Carolina Teachers' Association*. Washington, D.C. (1984); *NBAW*; Newbold, N. C., ed. *Five North Carolina Negro Educators* (1939); North Carolina Department of Archives. Records of the Division of Negro Education, Raleigh (1911-1934); North Carolina Parent and Teachers' Library. Records of Parent and Teachers' Association, Raleigh (1919-1969); Powell, William S., ed. *Dictionary of North Carolina Biography* (1988); *Wilmington Star*, "Colored Parents and Teachers to Attend Sessions" (February 27, 1927).

VALINDA ROGERS LITTLEFIELD

HOLT, NORA DOUGLAS (1885-1974)

Music critic, composer, and performer, Nora Douglas Holt lived by a creed that said, "Music is one of the greatest refiners of the Race" (*Chicago Defender*, November 9, 1918). During a long and successful career as a classical music critic for the *Chicago Defender* (1917-23) and the *New York Amsterdam News* (1944-52), Holt challenged and inspired numerous young Black musicians and urged her readers to culture themselves in the arts.

Born Nora Douglas in Kansas City, Kansas, in 1885, she was influenced to study piano at an early age by her mother, Grace (Brown), and her father, C. N. Douglas, presiding officer with the Puget Sound, African Methodist Episcopal (AME) Church. Further encouragement came from her secondary school music teacher, N. Clark Smith, who took her to hear symphony concerts.

In 1916, she graduated from Western University in Quindaro, Kansas (B.A.), and, in 1918, from the Chicago Musical College (M.Mus.). Holt is credited as being the first Black musician to earn the M.Mus. degree.

For her Master's thesis Holt composed a symphonic rhapsody for string orchestra based on the Negro spiritual "You May Bury Me in the East." Unfortunately, her music library and original manuscripts were stolen while she was traveling in Europe and the Far East in the early 1930s. However, one of her four "Negro Dances" for piano survives in her publication *Music and Poetry*, copies of which are housed in the James W. Johnson Memorial Collection of Yale University's Beinecke Library. Her musical settings for four Paul Laurence Dunbar poems, "My Love Is Like a Cry in the Night," "A Florida Night," "Who Knows," and "The Sandman," were very successful. "A Florida Night" became a favorite of the renowned Black tenor Roland Hayes.

During her graduate studies (1917-18) under Felix Borowsky, musicologist, president of Chicago Musical College, and, later, music critic for the *Chicago Sun-Times*, she began to demonstrate a growing curiosity for music criticism while her interest in composing and performing gradually diminished.

Holt joined the *Chicago Defender* in November 1917. Her first feature article, "Cultivating Symphony Concerts," appeared on November 10, 1917, on the "Woman's Page" under the byline Lena James Douglas. She had married George W. Holt (her third husband) a few months prior, however, and she later changed her name to Nora Douglas Holt.

As the only woman writing for a leading Black newspaper in a male-dominated profession, she immediately recognized the enormity of the responsibilities she would encounter. Asked to summarize her philosophy on the role of the music critic, she said her goal was always to offer expert musical judgments; to teach and awaken musical interest in her public; to advance young artists and the music of African-Americans; and, finally, to provide both Black and white communities with quality appraisals in order to prove her competency as a critic.

Between 1917 and 1923, young and seasoned artists performed in the Windy City (many of whom she would review again during her tenure with the *New York Amsterdam News*), and Holt evaluated their performances by comparing them to what she believed were the necessary standards for measuring artistic growth.

Holt did not accept the insurgence of jazz and blues during the early 1920s, and because of this was often perceived as snobbish. Unashamed, she considered herself an initiate and remained faithful to her creed to advance young Black musicians into what she described as wholesome artistic realms.

On March 9, 1919, she invited several Black Chicago musicians to her home to consider forming a national association to exchange views and ideas, evaluate standards in performance and teaching, and encourage Black youth. This meeting resulted in the founding of the Chicago Musical Association, and Holt was voted its first president. In May of that year, other renowned musicians met in Washington, D.C., to consider forming a second temporary association, and Holt strongly objected because she thought it might lead to divisions within the associations. In July, at her invitation, musicians met at her home to establish what is now the National Association of Negro Musicians (NANM). Among the charter members were Henry L. Grant, Nora Douglas Holt, Carl Diton, Alice Carter Simmons, Clarence C. White, Deacon Johnson, and R. Nathaniel Dett.

Music and Poetry was first published and edited by Holt in January 1921. Although the publication was short lived, it encouraged research, and it contained an array of articles by brilliant Black artists with expertise in various genres, such as violin, voice, poetry, harmony, dance, and composition.

In 1923, Holt, now widowed, married Joseph Luther Ray, secretary to Bethlehem Steel magnate Charles Schwab, and retired as a music critic in order to honeymoon abroad. This marriage, however, lasted only one year, ending in divorce. Holt later returned to Europe, performing in the posh nightclubs of Paris, Monte Carlo, London, and Italy. She also went to the Far East, playing for Chinese audiences in Shanghai. She returned to Chicago and Los Angeles intermittently over the next twelve years and finally settled in Los Angeles, where she taught in the California school system for several years.

As classical music critic for the Chicago Defender *(1917-23) and the* New York Amsterdam News *(1944-52), Nora Holt was dedicated to awakening musical tastes and encouraging Black musicians. [Moorland-Spingarn]*

She left California for New York City in 1944 in order to join the *New York Amsterdam News* as senior music critic. Her first article, "Carmen Jones, Magnificent with Quips, says Nora Holt," appeared on January 9, 1944.

Holt was the first Black person to work as a music editor and critic under union contract with the American Newspaper Guild, CIO. In 1945, sponsored by composer Virgil Thomson, she became the first Black member to join the Music Critics Circle of New York, and from 1953 to 1964 she was producer-musical director of radio station WLIB's "Concert Showcase."

Through her reviews, Holt welcomed hundreds of young musicians into New York City, some of whom were seasoned artists. Many were students of artists she had reviewed twenty-one years earlier in the *Chicago Defender* and who now taught in Black colleges and universities in the South, Howard, Fisk, Hampton, and Florida A & M universities as well as Spelman, Morehouse, and many white conservatories in the United States and Europe. Nora Douglas Holt was indeed a pioneer who provided a rich legacy of music criticism.

BIBLIOGRAPHY

Abdoul, Raoul. *Blacks in Classical Music* (1977); *BDAAM*; Dannett, Sylvia G. *Profiles of Negro Womanhood* (1964-66); McGuire, Phillip. "Black Music Critics and Classic Blues of the 20s." Transcript, NEH Summer Seminar, Howard University (1984); Spearman, Rawn, ed. "Music Criticism by Nora Douglas Holt in the *New York Amsterdam News*: Saturday Edition, 1944-1952." Transcript, NEH Summer Seminar for College Teachers, Howard University (1984), and "Music Criticism by Nora Douglas Holt in the *Chicago Defender*: Saturday Edition, 1917-1923," unpublished paper (1991).

RAWN SPEARMAN

HOOKS, JULIA BRITTON
(1852-1942)

Julia Hooks was one of the pioneer Black clubwomen in Memphis, Tennessee. Through various organizations and institutions, she worked to help alleviate the social ills that befell the increasingly segregated and destitute Black Americans who migrated from rural Tennessee, Mississippi, Arkansas, and Alabama during the post-Reconstruction era. Because of her tireless efforts, she is fondly remembered as "The Angel of Beale Street."

Julia Amanda Morehead Britton was born free in Frankfort, Kentucky, in 1852. Julia's mother, Laura Marshall, had been freed by her mistress, Elizabeth Marshall, in 1848, and she married a free carpenter named Henry Britton in the same year. Julia inherited musical talent from her mother and received professional training in classical music. Julia's parents enrolled her in the interracial program in Berea College in 1869, and from 1870 to 1872, Julia Britton was listed as the faculty instructor of instrumental music, making her one of the first Black professors to teach white students in Kentucky. In 1872, Julia moved to Greenville, Mississippi, to marry Sam Werles, a public school teacher. Both Julia and Sam taught school, but Sam died suddenly in the yellow fever epidemic of 1873. Eventually, Julia accepted a position with the Memphis Public School system in 1876. Four years later she married Charles Hooks, who had been born a slave in the city circa 1849.

One of the first associations Julia Hooks was involved with was cultural. In 1883, she and her close friend Anna Church (the wife of Robert Church, one of the country's first Black millionaires) started the Liszt-Mullard Club. This was probably the first Black organization in the city entirely devoted to music. The club promoted classical music and raised money to provide scholarships for aspiring musicians. Several years later Julia established the Hooks School of Music, an integrated institution that fostered some well-known pupils: W. C. Handy (the father of the blues); Sidney Woodward (one of the first Black concert artists to tour Europe); and Nell Hunter (known for her work on Broadway in the Pulitzer Prize-winning play, *The Green Pastures*).

Julia Hooks was also committed to the education of Black children. She taught at several public schools and served as principal, but she was always dissatisfied with the poor quality of education parceled out to the underprivileged. Julia's position was that separate would never be equal because the idea was based on the superiority of one race over another. Children in Black Memphis were short-changed due to poorly prepared teachers, lack of books and supplies, overcrowded classrooms, low standards and attendance, and inferior shelter, food, and clothing. Sometimes there were over sixty children in a classroom; many were recent migrants who had never before been inside a school. In 1892, Julia Hooks opened her own private kindergarten and elementary facility, the Hooks Cottage School.

A few years before, in 1887, Julia Hooks wrote an article on character building, the responsibility of government toward its neglected citizens, and the necessity of instilling morality in children. Entitled "The Duty of the Hour," Hooks's essay was so popular that she was asked to give public readings at numerous churches, functions, and organizations throughout the Black community. "Duty of the Hour" was later published in the 1895 edition of the *African-American Encyclopedia*.

Social services were another of Julia Hooks's concerns. She was especially interested in the plight of orphans and the elderly, since there were no orphanages or homes for the elderly for Black Memphis. Hooks decided that combining the two would be a good idea, and she established and became one of the charter members of the Colored Old Folks and Orphans Home Club in 1891. The members purchased twenty-five acres and erected buildings to provide shelters for orphans and elderly women. Julia Hooks gave concerts to raise the money that helped pay off the debt in three years.

Because of her compassionate social service work, Hooks was selected to serve as an officer of the court when the city established a Black juvenile court in 1902. She and husband Charles, who became a truant officer, supervised the court's detention home, which was built next to their residence. One of the inmates shot and killed Charles a year later. Julia Hooks remained committed to the institution, sometimes being called to advise in cases involving Black youth. She gained the trust and cooperation of young and adult inmates due to her compassion, gentleness, and calm manner.

Julia Hooks remained active for over fifty years in club work and social services until her death at the age of ninety in 1942. She and Charles Hooks had two sons, Henry and Robert. They became photographers and founded the Hooks Brothers' Photographers Studio on Beale Street, the first of its kind in Black Memphis, and they photographed decades of Black Memphis history. Julia and Charles Hooks's most famous descendent is the Reverend Benjamin L. Hooks, who served as the city's first Black judge since Reconstruction. In 1977, he became the executive director of the National Association for the Advancement of Colored People—a fitting tribute to grandmother Julia who sixty years earlier had been one of the charter members of the NAACP's Memphis branch.

BIBLIOGRAPHY

Church, Robert, and Ronald Waters. *Nineteenth-Century Memphis Families of Color, 1850-1900* (1987); Giddings, Paula. *When and Where I Enter: The Impact of Race and Sex on Black Women in America* (1984); Hamilton, Greene. *The Bright Side of Memphis* (1908); Hine, Darlene Clark, ed. *The State of Afro-American History* (1986); Lee, George W. *Beale Street: Where the Blues Began* (1969); Lewis, Selma and Morgan G. Kremer. *The Angel of Beale Street: A Biography of Julia Ann Hooks* (1986); Nelson, Paul D. "Experiment in Interracial Education at Berea College, 1858-1908," *Journal of Negro History* (January 1974).

EARNESTINE JENKINS

HOPE, LUGENIA BURNS (1871-1947)

"It is difficult for me to understand why my white sisters so strenuously object to this honest expression of colored women as put forth in the discarded preamble," Lugenia Burns Hope lamented in the 1920s, referring to the hesitation of white women to support antilynching legislation. "After all, when we yield to public opinion and make ourselves say only what we think the public can stand, is there not a danger that we may find ourselves with our larger view conceding what those with the narrow view demand?" (Rouse 1989)

Lugenia Burns Hope was still a young woman when she became a community activist, work that would later distinguish her as one of the most effective African-American social reformers in the South. Born in 1871 to Louisa and Ferdinand Burns, Lugenia Burns spent her formative years in St. Louis, Missouri, and later Chicago, Illinois. The last of seven children, she was able to attend school, where she focused on photography, printing/drawing, sculpting, and business management. When her family's economic situation changed, however, she was forced to quit school and work full time. She worked with several charitable settlement groups for more than twelve years, including the Kings Daughters and Hull House in Chicago, which helped develop her interest in community building and public service.

In 1893, she met John Hope, a native Georgian and a theological student at Brown University. They married during the Christmas holidays of 1897 and then moved to Nashville, Tennessee, where John Hope had accepted a professorship at Roger Williams University. During their one-year stay in Nashville, Lugenia Hope became involved in community activities through her relationship with families such as the Crosthwaits and the Napiers, and she taught physical education and arts and crafts classes to the female students at Roger Williams University. However, because of John Hope's desire to return to his native Georgia, the Hopes moved in 1898 to

Atlanta, where he had accepted a position as an instructor in classics at Atlanta Baptist College (later to become Morehouse College). For the next thirty-five years the Hopes lived on campus, beginning in Graves Hall, a dormitory, and ending in the president's house as John Hope's career took him from the classroom to the office of the presidency.

Lugenia Hope immediately became involved in the West Fair community as a result of the Conferences on African-American life that were hosted by Atlanta University and that featured W.E.B. Du Bois and Gertrude Ware. Spurred on by conference sessions on child welfare, Hope and a core group of women began to organize kindergartens and day care centers for working mothers of the West Fair community. The group persuaded Atlanta Baptist College to donate land for playgrounds for neighborhood children. Later, as their community work grew, the core group organized themselves into the Neighborhood Union, Hope's most important legacy.

For twenty-five years Hope led the Neighborhood Union—*her* organization—as it became an international model for community building and race/gender activism. Adopting the motto "Thy Neighbor as Thyself," the union offered services to Atlanta's African-American communities that were not provided by the state, county, or city. The union divided into zones, districts, and neighborhoods in order to ascertain the cultural, medical, educational, recreational, social, religious, and economic needs of the city. Students from the local Black colleges, Morehouse, Spelman, and Atlanta University, were instrumental in organizing classes for young and elderly citizens. The union participated in the drive for equal education, instruction, and facilities, supporting Black students as they produced community- and citywide rallies and confrontations. The Union joined with many prominent male leaders, churches, and local organizations to fight the discrimination of separate-but-equal education. Their efforts to educate Black Atlantans about the double and triple sessions of Black schools, the shortage and low pay of Black teachers, the poor physical condition of the school buildings, and the limited funds appropriated to Black schools led to successful campaigns to block bond issues in municipal elections. Limited successes enabled the African-American community to appreciate the importance of being organized and united in order to overcome the odds.

As the Neighborhood Union grew, Hope acquired a national reputation as a social reformer and community leader. She took her place alongside Mary Church Terrell, Mary McLeod Bethune, Charlotte Hawkins Brown, Margaret Murray Washington, Nannie Helen Burroughs, and other African-American women who were fighting for equal rights and freedom. In the southern network of African-American female activists, Hope was a major force in challenging racism and initiating interracial cooperation.

Hope's interracial work is best illustrated by two separate campaigns: the creation of African-American Young Women's Christian Association (YWCA) branches in the South, and the antilynching movement, especially her alliance with Southern Methodist women and the Association of Southern Women for the Prevention of Lynching (ASWPL). In both campaigns Hope believed that she and her counterparts, representing more than 300,000 Black southern women, could speak without reservation in order to bring about immediate change. They first challenged the racist policies of the YWCA, which did not allow African-American autonomy, and threatened to withdraw from the movement and to return to their churches as bases of support. Hope worked for years to eliminate discriminatory practices and to demand Black women's participation in administrative functions. Her steadfastness often led to charges of inflexibility and hampering the progress of racial harmony and compromise, but Hope did not relent. She continued the struggle until the direction of Black YWCAs in the South was controlled from the national office in New York and not the regional and state offices. Southern Black women were soon able to determine the types of young women they would help and the areas where their services were most needed, a right that was not automatic prior to 1924.

While working on the second campaign, to outlaw lynching, Hope came to believe that southern white women did not accept enough responsibility for the continued use of lynching in the region. Given the widespread assertion that lynching "protected white womanhood," Hope and her network expected enlightened southern white women to do more than speak out against this so-called act of chivalry and merely hint at feminist jargon. They expected them to control their husbands, sons, brothers, uncles, and grandfathers, who were maliciously murdering Black men. They also expected white women to include the rape of Black women in their view of female liberation. The manner in which Black domestics were treated in some white women's homes, and their low wages, were important issues for Black southern women who were determined to awaken southern

The alliance with Atlanta University's sociology department helped Atlanta's Neighborhood Union to develop scientific methods to determine community needs. Here, Neighborhood Union founder Lugenia Burns Hope (center) and her husband, John Hope, pose with graduates of the Atlanta School of Social Work. [Atlanta University Archives]

progressive white women to the fact of their own racism. Joining with such figures as Jessie D. Ames and the ASWPL, Hope tried to convince this group that the most expedient measure was a national bill to prohibit lynching, one that called for the prosecution of local law officials in towns where such acts occurred. Championing states rights, however, Ames and the ASWPL opposed federal intervention, believing that state laws prohibiting lynching would be more likely to pass local legislatures and to be enforced by local law enforcement officials. As a result, Hope came away with deep misgivings about southern white women's commitment to equality and the elimination of racism, but she forced them to face their own role as participants and as beneficiaries of racism.

Lugenia Hope was a member/official in several of the traditional race protest organizations. For example, she was First Vice President of the Atlanta chapter of the National Association for the Advancement of Colored People (NAACP) in 1932. In this capacity she created citizenship schools, establishing six-week classes on voting, democracy, and the Constitution that were taught by professors of Atlanta University. The success of the Atlanta program triggered citizenship classes in other branches. That same year Hope was nominated to receive the Spingarn Award, the NAACP's highest honor, but the award was not given. However, the strategies developed by Hope were reused in the civil rights movement of the 1950s and 1960s. Representatives of the Student Nonviolent Coordinating Committee (SNCC) and the Congress of Racial Equality (CORE) canvassed the South, educating rural and urban African-Americans about their rights and voting procedures and enabling them to become politically active. The Highlander School/Center in Monteagle, Tennessee, used citizenship training to prepare many of the activists who led heroic efforts to repeal Jim Crow laws in the South. Although the connection is seldom made, the civil rights movement had its origin in the political activism of early-twentieth-century women such as Hope and those in the Neighborhood Union.

Hope the mother, wife, and "first lady" of Morehouse College had to balance Hope the social activist and reformer. She supported her husband's work as professor, college president, spokesman for the YWCA, race leader, and educator. She traveled with her husband nationally and abroad, especially on fund-raising trips, and when the opportunity arose she persuaded him to accept the position of president of Atlanta University. Having helped to establish Morehouse College, he could now help create new opportunities for more Black students and at the same time build a major Black higher educational center, the Atlanta University Center. Creating the country's first African-American graduate school, Atlanta University, was an opportunity of a lifetime, one that Hope believed her husband could not overlook or decline.

As a mother, Hope was not one to spare the rod, but she believed in negotiating and building expectations more than instilling fear as a means of establishing discipline. Although her community work often took her away from home, she sewed most of her children's clothing and ran her home herself. She instilled in her two sons respect and courage. She trained them to think independently, and not in terms of gender roles, when viewing themselves, women, and society.

In relation to the young men of Morehouse, Hope followed the African-American female tradition of the othermother, nurturing these young men as she took time to acquaint them with their different world. By forcing them to take lessons in etiquette and to work with young children through the Neighborhood Union programs, Hope was instrumental in creating the mystique of the Morehouse man.

After John Hope's death in 1936, Lugenia moved to New York City, Chicago, and then to Nashville to be near relatives. She died in August 1947. In compliance with her wishes, her cremated ashes were thrown from the tower of Graves Hall over the campus of Morehouse College.

Lugenia Hope exemplified the strong-spirited race woman who worked for racial justice in the early years of the twentieth century. She was a determined woman who recognized and utilized her abilities and who expected the same from others. She succeeded as a leader because of her ability to work with diverse groups of people and because of her great executive skills. She was successful in African-American communities because of her access to the white power structure and her ability to use that access. Poor and voiceless Black Atlantans expected her to be their voice at board and city council meetings. Thus, part of her appeal was her radical, undaunting activism; the other was her genuine love and concern for all children and her willingness to struggle to improve their lives. However, her radical style of activism made her far more outspoken than her peers, more demanding, and less willing to compromise on the issues of racial justice and gender equality. She was more accusatory, and more direct, in interracial meetings than were most of her colleagues. In fact, her voice spoke what other Black women felt but could not risk saying. Her peers praised her courage, her frankness, and the forthright manner in which she exposed deceit, prejudice, and injustice. Her refusal to allow misunderstandings and injustice to pass unchallenged sometimes cost her support and allies, but because of Hope the African-American women's agenda was always clear, its priorities always visible.

Lugenia Hope's dominating nature also cost her allies within the Neighborhood Union, but no one could produce the results she could. Oral and written accounts of the union's successes and failures reflect a respect and fear of Hope, for the group always deferred to her. Under her leadership, however, the community witnessed major reforms, including the establishment of the first African-American high school in 1924 and the first public housing for African-Americans in the country.

Whether her steadfast and forthright leadership was politically correct is debatable. It did, however, take its toll on Hope's health, and it did put a strain on her family. Lugenia Hope was a product of Victorian America, and she worked to improve the image of her class versus those whose actions she viewed as immoral and a detriment to the race. She imparted and enforced her values on others so that they could use them to clean up their lives and uplift the race. At the same time, she presented an alternative to the southern white view of conciliatory, conservative Black southerners. She openly opposed segregation and discrimination, and her efforts helped the growth of racial cooperation and intraracial solidarity in the New South of the late twentieth century. Without question Hope's work was instrumental in improving the lives of African-American Atlantans during the early years of this century.

BIBLIOGRAPHY
Lerner, Gerda. "Early Community Work of Black Clubwomen," *Journal of Negro History* (April 1974); Lerner, Gerda, ed. *Black Women in White America* (1972); Neverdon-Morton, Cynthia. *Afro-American Women of the South and the Advancement of the Race, 1895-1925* (1989); Rouse,

Jacqueline A. "The Legacy of Community Organizing: Lugenia Burns Hope and the Neighborhood Union," *Journal of Negro History* (Summer, Fall 1984), and *Lugenia Burns Hope: Black Southern Reformer* (1989); Torrence, Ridgley. *The Story of John Hope* (1948).

COLLECTIONS

John and Lugenia Burns Hope papers, Woodruff Library, Atlanta University Center, Atlanta, Georgia; Neighborhood Union Collection, Woodruff Library, Atlanta University Center, Atlanta, Georgia.

JACQUELINE A. ROUSE

HOPKINS, PAULINE ELIZABETH (1859-1930)

"The true romance of American life and customs is to be found in the history of the Negro upon this continent," Pauline Elizabeth Hopkins asserted in 1901 ("Famous Men" 1901). This sentiment reverberates throughout Hopkins's novels, short stories, plays, and nonfiction, all of which capture the heroism, the drama, and the struggles against evil and racial oppression implicit in her term "romance." A remarkably prolific, talented, and pioneering writer, Hopkins sharpened awareness both of Blacks' accomplishments and of racial issues with her lively, compelling fiction, drama, and essays aimed at a wide audience.

Born in Portland, Maine, in 1859 to William A. and Sarah Allen Hopkins, Hopkins was the great-grandniece of poet James Whitfield. Her mother was a descendant of Nathaniel and Thomas Paul, who founded Baptist churches in Boston. When Pauline was a child, the Hopkins family moved to Boston, where Pauline attended elementary and secondary school, graduating from Girls High School.

Pauline's writing talents emerged when she was only fifteen and entered a writing contest sponsored by Boston's Congregational Publishing Society. The contest was supported by William Wells Brown, an escaped slave who wrote one of the first Black novels, *Clotel* (1853). Brown wished to promote temperance, believing it to be a virtue that would enhance the Black community. Pauline's essay, an eloquent, if moralistic, response to the contest theme, "The Evils of Intemperance and Their Remedy," won the first prize of ten dollars.

Hopkins was only twenty years old when she completed her first play, *Slaves' Escape: or The Underground Railroad*. Just one year later, on July 5, 1880, *Slaves' Escape* was produced at Boston's Oakland Garden by the Hopkins Colored Troubadours. The play is a musical comedy celebrating the bravery and ingenuity of those slaves, such as Harriet Tubman and Frederick Douglass, who escaped bondage. The cast included Hopkins's mother, stepfather, and Pauline herself, who later achieved fame being billed as "Boston's Favorite Colored Soprano."

For twelve years Hopkins performed with the Colored Troubadours. During this time she wrote another play entitled *One Scene from the Drama of Early Days*, dramatizing the Biblical story of Daniel in the lion's den. At this point, she decided to leave the stage and train herself as a stenographer to better support her writing. In the 1890s, she worked at the Bureau of Statistics and developed a career as a public lecturer.

At the turn of the century, Hopkins became instrumental in the development of a new publication, *The Colored American Magazine*. Aimed at predominantly Black audiences, *The Colored American* contained short stories, articles, and serialized novels, all designed to simultaneously entertain and educate. The magazine was a medium for Black writers to demonstrate their talents. Hopkins was not only a founding member and editor of *The Colored American*, she also published three novels, seven short stories, and numerous biographical and political sketches there. The sketches, which reflect her skill as a dramatist, flesh out the positive fictional images that appear in her fiction by applauding the achievements of luminaries such as William Wells Brown, Sojourner Truth, Harriet Tubman, and Frederick Douglass. The sketches also combine her scholarly and literary talents.

In May 1900, the first issue of *The Colored American* carried her short story "The Mystery within Us." At the same time, the Colored Co-operative Publishing Company, a Boston firm which produced the magazine, brought out Hopkins's *Contending Forces: A Romance Illustrative of Negro Life North and South*.

Contending Forces showcases the themes and techniques that inform all of Pauline Hopkins's fiction. In her effort to present "the true romance of American life . . . the history of the Negro," Hopkins employs strategies used in popular historical romances of her day. Suspenseful, complicated plots involving superhuman heroes, imperiled heroines, and incomparable villains inform the audience about Black history and about social issues and concerns. *Contending Forces* is an ambitious story about several generations of a Black family from their pre-Civil War Caribbean and North Carolina origins to their later life in the North. The main plot involves Will and Dora Smith, brother and sister, and their friend Sappho Clark, with whom

Will falls in love. In addition to the formula plot of boy meets girl, boy loses girl, boy marries girl, the narrative dramatizes essential American historical realities: slavery, lynching, hidden interracial blood lines, post-Reconstruction voting disenfranchisement, and job discrimination against Blacks.

Underlying these themes and techniques is Hopkins's announced purpose in the preface to *Contending Forces* "to raise the stigma of degradation from my race." To that end, her Black characters are admirable and intelligent, and many are educated. Writing at a time when Black writers struggled with the nearly inescapable color prejudice that exalted an ideal of beauty based on Anglo-Saxon features, skin, and hair, Hopkins invariably described her heroines as light-skinned, sometimes so much so that they themselves were unaware of their racial origins. Sappho Clark, and the characters in much of Hopkins's fiction, exemplified the cultural contradictions in which Black writers were often caught in their efforts to recast Black cultural identity.

Hopkins's three other novels, all of which were serialized in *The Colored American*, employ additional romance techniques. Cliff-hangers, episodes concluding with an unresolved question, such as who the murderer really was, enticed the reader to anticipate the next issue of the magazine. Mistaken identities and disguise typify these novels, as do outrageous coincidences, supernatural occurrences, and evil schemes.

Hagar's Daughter: A Story of Southern Caste Prejudice (serialized in 1901-2) is a generational novel like *Contending Forces*. The characters in *Hagar's Daughter* are, however, mostly white. Anticipating today's romance novels and soap operas, *Hagar's Daughter* concerns a glamorous leisure class preoccupied with clothes, gambling, and intrigue. In each generation, an adored, beautiful woman, fully entrenched in a white, wealthy culture, discovers herself to be Black, forcing her to cope with racism and rejection. *Hagar's Daughter* strongly implies that wealth and status do not equate with ethics. Moreover, the novel concludes with a bitter indictment of American racism, even among white Americans supposedly sensitive to racial issues.

Winona: A Tale of Negro Life in the South and Southwest (serialized during 1902) is a historical romance set during slavery. Hopkins surrounds the love story about a Black woman and an antiracist white Englishman with dramatic incidents involving slave traders, the Underground Railroad, and John Brown's Free Soilers. Judah, a militant Black man described as "a living statue of a mighty Vulcan" stands proudly at the center of the novel, telegraphing Blacks' positive historical roles during slavery. Judah not only embodies resistance against slavery, he transmits Hopkins's notion that Blacks should always resist oppression.

Of One Blood: or The Hidden Self (serialized in 1902-3) explores Hopkins's belief that Blacks should revere their African origins. Reuel, who has never identified himself as Black, visits Africa. There he becomes aware of the superiority of African civilization and culture and begins to embrace his heritage. Reuel's emergence as a descendent of African kings underscores Hopkins's belief that Black Americans should ignore racist messages of inferiority. *Of One Blood* not only encourages racial pride for Black Americans, it also voices a Pan-African vision, unifying and celebrating Black people all over the world.

During the time that Hopkins serialized her novels in *The Colored American*, she published seven short stories in the magazine. The stories echo many themes and techniques found in her novels. The unmasking of Black characters passing for white, such as those in "As the Lord Lives, He Is One of Our Mother's Children" and "A Test of Manhood," reiterates Hopkins's insistence that racial barriers are irrational. Black characters are extraordinary and ethical, contributing to Hopkins's urge to create positive images of African-Americans. The stories contain the devices of romance and popular fiction, such as coincidence and the supernatural. Hopkins's stories, like her sketches, complement the aims and tactics of her novels to form a coherent body of work.

Hopkins's contributions to *The Colored American* thus included her voluminous fiction and nonfiction, her editorial talents, and her business skills. Hopkins promoted the magazine through Boston's Colored American League, which she founded. She also went on tour in 1904 to promote the magazine. In fact, the extent to which she wielded power over *The Colored American* was significantly underestimated until the 1980s. As a woman, Hopkins struggled against many odds, including the discrediting and suppression of her work by scholars.

When Booker T. Washington bought *The Colored American* in 1903, Hopkins's influence began to fade. By September of 1904, her dissatisfaction with this situation, combined with her poor health, led her to resign. During the next fifteen years, Hopkins published several other pieces, including "The Dark Races of the Twentieth Century" (1905) and the novella "Topsy Templeton" (1916). At the time of her death, she was a stenographer for the Massachusetts Institute of Technology.

Hopkins died on August 3, 1930, "when the liniment-saturated red flannel bandages she was wearing to relieve the neuritis she suffered were ignited by an oil stove in her room," writes Ann Allen Shockley. Equally tragic as Hopkins's death is the critical neglect she suffered afterwards. Despite her impressive career as a poet, playwright, novelist, essayist, lecturer, editor, and actor, Hopkins was virtually forgotten until Shockley rediscovered her work in 1972. Since then, Hopkins's reputation has gradually reemerged. A feminist and Pan-Africanist dedicated to celebrating and preserving her racial history, Hopkins prefigured such writers as Jessie Fauset, Zora Neale Hurston, and Alice Walker. Moreover, her work is as serious, timely, and accessible today as it was nearly a century ago.

BIBLIOGRAPHY

Campbell, Jane. *Mythic Black Fiction: The Transformation* (1986), and "Pauline Elizabeth Hopkins, 1859-1930," *Heath Anthology of American Literature*, ed. Paul Lauter (1990); Carby, Hazel V. *Reconstructing Womanhood: The Emergence of the Afro-American Woman Novelist* (1987); *DANB*; *DLB*; Shockley, Ann Allen. "Pauline Elizabeth Hopkins: A Biographical Excursion into Obscurity," *Phylon* (1972); Tate, Claudia. "Pauline Hopkins: Our Literary Foremother." In *Conjuring: Black Women, Fiction, and Literary Tradition*, ed. Marjorie Pryse and Hortense J. Spillers (1985).

SELECTED WORKS BY PAULINE ELIZABETH HOPKINS

Contending Forces: A Romance Illustrative of Negro Life North and South ([1900] 1988); Pauline Hopkins, *The Magazine Novels of Pauline Hopkins* (1988); "Bro'r Abr'm Jimson's Wedding, A Christmas Story." In *Invented Lives: Narratives of Black Women 1860-1960*, ed. Mary Helen Washington (1987); "The Mystery within Us," *The Colored American Magazine* (May 1900); "Talma Gordon," *The Colored American Magazine* (October 1900); "George Washington, A Christmas Story," *The Colored American Magazine* (December 1900); "A Dash for Liberty," *The Colored American Magazine* (August 1901); [Sarah A. Allen], "The Test of Manhood, A Christmas Story," *The Colored American Magazine* (December 1902); "As the Lord Lives, He Is One of Our Mother's Children," *The Colored American Magazine* (November 1903); "Topsy Templeton," *New Era* (1916); "Famous Men of the Negro Race," series in *The Colored American Magazine* (February 1901-September 1902); "Famous Women of the Negro Race," series in *The Colored American Magazine* (November 1901-October 1902); "William Wells Brown," *The Colored American Magazine* (January 1901).

JANE CAMPBELL

HORN, SHIRLEY (1934-)

Many long years of styling harmonious songs at the piano began to pay off handsomely in the late 1980s, as Shirley Horn became a virtual overnight sensation with her much-acclaimed recordings for the Verve label. Beginning with the 1986 live album *I Thought about You: Live at Vine St.*, Horn began to craft an incandescent series of recordings, which included a rare guest appearance by her friend and supporter, the late trumpet master Miles Davis, along with the brothers Marsalis, Wynton and Branford, and harmonica man Toots Thielemans.

Author Kitty Grime summed it up succinctly when she wrote, "Shirley Horn must be *the* cult performer. A near-legendary figure, seldom seen outside Washington, she's just about everybody's favorite singer-player" (Grime 1983). Horn certainly was a favorite of Davis. When he made a guest appearance on her 1991 recording, *You Won't Forget Me*, it was the culmination of an artistic love affair that began decades earlier when, after hearing her 1960 debut album, *Embers and Ashes*, Davis insisted that she open engagements for his quintet at the Village Vanguard.

After that stint, Horn was in demand at jazz clubs across the country. She also found herself in the recording studio working with Quincy Jones, then vice president of Mercury Records, which opened up the world of movie soundtracks, and she sang on *For Love of Ivy* and *A Dandy in Aspic*. Never one for the road, Horn took great comfort in her Washington, D.C., home life and was determined to raise her daughter, Rainy. This effectively kept her out of the music scene during the late 1960s and the entire decade of the 1970s.

Born, raised, and still living comfortably in Washington, D.C., Horn showed her talent at the piano at a very early age, even before kindergarten. As a teenager she studied composition at Howard University, eventually garnering a scholarship to Juilliard in New York City. A tight family budget forced her to return to Howard, however, and she later left school to pursue a professional career in local clubs.

Long one of the treasures of Washington night life, Horn's tender, swinging vocal style is second only to her enormous talent at the piano. So singular is her approach to the piano that she once became very uncomfortable in the studio when an insistent record producer wanted her to be accompanied by another pianist; she simply could not fathom another pianist backing her vocals.

Much more than a vocalist, Horn has made her mark as a pianist who sings, rather in the mold of Nat

"King" Cole, though unlike Cole, she never considered abandoning the piano in order to increase her visibility as a singer. Her piano talent received even greater recognition during the early 1990s, when she was called upon to back jazz vocal master Carmen McRae and harmonica player Toots Thielemans on their respective recordings.

Shirley Horn possesses an intuitive sense of swing that blends harmoniously with her honeyed voice. Her phrasing is impeccable, and her ease with a lyric, always tender and touching, is the mark of a true song stylist. Equally at home with Tin Pan Alley and jazz, Shirley Horn is one of the singular talents of jazz voice and piano.

BIBLIOGRAPHY

Grime, Kitty. *Jazz Voices* (1983); Kernfield, Barry, ed. *The New Grove Dictionary of Jazz* (1988).

SELECTED DISCOGRAPHY

Close Enough for Love. Verve 837 933-1 (1989).

WILLARD JENKINS

HORNE, LENA (1917-)

"There were always people around reminding me that I was a symbol of certain Negro aspirations," Lena Horne said in a 1965 *Ebony* interview. "When those reminders were made too often I would try to assert myself and say, in effect: 'All right, I'm a symbol. But I'm a person, too. You can't push me so hard. I've got a right to my own happiness, too'." Lena Horne's position as a symbol of and for her race has worked hand in hand with racism to limit her possibilities as a performer and a person. However, she has managed to go beyond those limitations to carve out an impressive stage, film, and recording career and a life of personal fulfillment.

Lena Calhoun Horne was born on June 17, 1917, in Brooklyn, New York. Her father was, in her words, a gambler and a racketeer. Her mother was a struggling actress. Both of them, however, came from respectable middle-class families, and, as a very little girl, Horne was surrounded by that respectability. She and her parents lived with her paternal grandparents until her mother and father divorced when she was three. Then Lena remained while her mother tried to make a career as an actress.

Cora Calhoun Horne was a suffragist and a bold defender of Black rights. "My grandmother took me to her meetings," said Horne in an interview for *I Dream a World,* "from the time I was little until I was

fifteen. She was in the Urban League, the NAACP, and the Ethical Culture Society. I was surrounded by adult activities. . . . if I hadn't had that from her, then the other side of my life, which was more bleak, might have finished me" (Lanker 1989). There are probably few other Hollywood legends who were members of the National Association for the Advancement of Colored People at two years old.

Unfortunately, Horne was not able to stay permanently with her grandmother, or anyone else for that matter. When she was about seven, she rejoined her mother and spent the next few years traveling with her as she pursued her career as an actress. They had no home and, because of Jim Crow laws, could seldom find a hotel to stay in as they traveled. So they slept in the homes of relatives, friends, and even strangers, a common practice in the southern Black community, where hospitality stretched to try to fill the void created by prejudice. Horne then spent several years in Brooklyn, living with relatives, attending the Brooklyn public schools and the Girls High School. When she was fourteen, her mother remarried, returning from a tour in Cuba with her new husband, Miguel Rodriguez. The new family moved to a poor section of the Bronx, having been rebuffed by Brooklyn's Black middle class.

At sixteen, Horne had to quit school. Her mother had become very ill, and the household needed money. A friend of her mother's, Elida Webb, was choreographer at the Cotton Club and got young Horne a job, solely on the basis of her spectacular looks. While Horne was working there, she began to take music lessons. She said later that she was never a natural singer and that it took a lot of hard work and a number of years for her to hone her skills. In the meantime, she danced in the chorus on bills with Count Basie, Cab Calloway, Billie Holiday, and Ethel Waters. However, when she was only seventeen she was cast in *Dance with Your Gods* (1934) on Broadway. At eighteen, she left the Cotton Club for good, to be a singer with Noble Sissle's Society Orchestra in Philadelphia. Her father was not far away, operating a hotel in Pittsburgh. The two became reacquainted, and he remained an important part of her life until he died.

On the road with the orchestra, Horne was constantly confronted with the harsh realities of racism. Possibly to escape, she married a friend of her father's, Louis Jones. They remained married for four years, long enough for Horne to bear two children. In 1939, she took a starring role in the revue *Blackbirds of 1939,* and in 1940 she left her husband. When she first went to New York, she left her children with their father so that she could make a start and find a place for the three of them to live. Late in the year, she became chief vocalist for the Charlie Barnett band and began recording. Able to provide a home for her children, she went back to Pittsburgh to get them, but Jones would give up only her daughter. Horne agreed to settle for visiting rights with her son.

While with Barnett's band, she started recording. One of her most popular early records, "Haunted Town," was made with Barnett. Next, she went to the Café Society Downtown, an engagement that might be said to have made her name. There she met Paul Robeson and Walter White, both on the same night. Both of them, as her friends, helped increase her awareness of the political struggles of Black people. She also met and started dating boxer Joe Louis. Within the year, she got an offer of a booking at the Trocadero Club in California.

The decision to take the offer and go to Hollywood was a difficult one. She knew it might lead to work in films, but she had serious doubts about battling what she expected would be the rampant racism of the film community. Walter White persuaded her that she would be doing a service to her people if she

Lena Horne began her career as a dancer at the Cotton Club, hired for her spectacular looks. She then studied music and honed her skills as a singer, becoming a successful recording artist and club and concert performer. [Schomburg Center]

could break into films. He made her think of the possibility as a challenge. Sure enough, two months after arriving in Los Angeles she was auditioning for Metro-Goldwyn-Mayer (MGM). Soon she was signing a seven-year contract with a starting salary of $200 per week and a clause saying she did not have to perform in stereotypical roles. "My father had them scared to death. I think that was the first time a black man had ever come into Louis B. Mayer's office and said, 'I don't want my daughter in this mess.' . . . He was so articulate and so beautiful, they just said, 'Well, don't worry.' "

Then the problem was how to use her. She lost her first chance for a speaking role in a mixed-cast movie because she was too light. She did not get another shot until 1956. All her performances in between were guest spots in which she sang only. These scenes never included the principals of the film in any important way and were easily edited out so that the films could be shown in southern theaters. Horne did do one speaking part at MGM, an all-Black film entitled *Cabin in the Sky* (1943), and she was loaned out for another, *Stormy Weather* (1943).

The guest spots had a tremendous impact. Her job, as Walter White had seen it, was to change the American image of Black women, and she did. She fit white society's standards of beauty as well as the most beautiful white women, but she was clearly a woman of color. She was also a woman of great charm and dignity who was conscious of her position as a representative of Black America. Her choices about the way she presented herself were influenced by that role. It seemed important at the time to show that a Black woman did not have to sing spirituals or earthy, overtly sexual laments; Horne sang Cole Porter and Gershwin. It seemed important that a Black woman could be cool, glamorous, and sophisticated; Horne always looked as though she had stepped out of the pages of *Vogue*. "The image that I chose to give them was of a woman who they could not reach" (*BAFT*).

When not singing on screen, she was singing in clubs. "Each year in New York's after-dark world of supper clubs," *Life* magazine reported in 1943, "there appears a girl singer who becomes a sensation overnight. She stands in the middle of a dance floor in a white dress and a soft light, and begins to sing. The room is hushed and her voice is warm and haunting. Her white teeth gleam, her eyes move back and forth, and her softly sung words seem to linger like cigaret smoke. This year that girl is Lena Horne."

Horne turned out to have staying power. During the 1940s, she could command $10,000 a week at the clubs. Her recordings, including "Birth of the Blues,"

"Moanin' Low," "Little Girl Blue," and "Classics in Blue," were highly successful, and she was in demand on the radio. During World War II, she traveled extensively to entertain the troops, an experience that was not always salubrious. "When at a performance in Fort Riley, Kansas," Donald Bogle wrote in *Brown Sugar*, "she spotted German prisoners of war sitting in the best seats in the front of the house, she stepped from the stage, whisked past them, then sang to the black soldiers in the back" (1980).

In 1947, Horne secretly married Lennie Hayton, whom she had been seeing for years. Hayton was white, and Horne's position as symbol rose up to haunt her again. She did not reveal her marriage until 1950, and when she did her mail filled with hate letters from white racists and bitter reproaches from Black Americans. It was a reaction she had anticipated. "Isn't it ironic?" she said in a 1965 *Ebony* article. "For three years I preferred to let the world think I was a woman living in sin than admit that I had married a white man." While her comments in later years show that she clearly understood the source of the anger felt by other Black people at her marriage, she had found that there were limits to her ability to tailor her life to fit what she and others thought of as her responsibilities as a public figure.

As the 1950s arrived, Horne was at the top of her form. By 1948, she received $60,000 a week for appearing at the Cibacabano in New York. In 1950, she made her first television appearance, on Ed Sullivan's *Toast of the Town*. In 1956, she had her first speaking role in a mixed-cast film, *Meet Me in Las Vegas*. In 1957, she starred on Broadway for the first time in *Jamaica*. However, she lost the film role she had most hoped for, the mulatto Julie in *Show Boat*, probably because of her marriage. Also, because she remained loyal to friends who were being blacklisted for supposed Communist sympathies, she was eventually blacklisted herself from television work. Her second appearance in that medium was nine years after her first, on *The Perry Como Show* in 1959.

As she went into the 1960s, Horne, like many others, became more and more involved in civil rights. She was at the march on Washington in 1963. In the atmosphere of change, she also separated from her husband. "I took a chance," she told *Ebony* in 1968. "I said, 'Lennie, I'm going through some changes as a black woman. I can't explain them. I don't know what they're going to mean, what they're going to do to me, but I've got to be by myself to work it out'." They remained apart for three years and then came back together to go on with their twenty-four-year marriage. In the meantime, she toured for the National

Legendary performer Lena Horne broke through countless racial barriers but had to live with the pressures of being a symbol to both Black and white Americans. [Schomburg Center]

Council of Negro Women, speaking to Black women all over the South. Her autobiography, *Lena*, which she wrote with Richard Schickel, appeared in 1965. In these years, her music began to develop in different directions. The constraints of her position loosened, and she was able to explore areas she had once kept rigidly under control.

In 1970, Horne's father died, followed, in just a few months, by her son. Less than a year later, her husband died. The next few years were filled with grief and sorrow. She had lost the two people she most depended on and three of the people she most loved.

In 1974, Horne was back on Broadway, performing with Tony Bennett. Four years later, she played Glinda, the Good Witch, in the film *The Wiz*. On April 30, 1981, at the age of sixty-four, she opened on Broadway with *Lena Horne: The Lady and Her Music*, which became the longest-running one-woman show in Broadway history and won her a special Tony Award, the New York City Handel Medallion, the Drama Desk Award, and a Drama Critics' Circle citation. She has continued to appear on television regularly. She has received both an Image Award and the Spingarn Medal from the NAACP, and in 1979 she accepted an honorary doctorate from Howard University.

It is difficult to assess the historical importance of Lena Horne's life and work. In part, this is because she is, even today, so remarkably contemporary. Thinking of her as a historical figure strains the imagination. Her image as a beautiful, proud, self-assured Black woman suggests that nothing (not even history) could or would dare impinge on her. She responded to this idea when she talked about the time she struck a white man in a Hollywood nightclub for a racist insult. The incident was widely reported by journalists. "I got telegrams from Black people saying, 'How wonderful, we didn't know.' I just automatically thought that Black people knew that if you were Black, you were going to catch hell. They thought because I was me I wasn't catching hell. It was a damn fight everywhere I was, every place I worked, in New York, in Hollywood, all over the world" (Pierce 1968).

The mission Lena Horne accepted more than half a century ago was to show that Black people could be on top, could be winners. Her job was to make people look at the triumph and not just the struggle. She succeeded.

BIBLIOGRAPHY

BAFT; Bogle, Donald. *Brown Sugar* (1980); Buckley, Gail Lumet. *The Hornes: An American Family* (1986); *EBA*; Feinstein, Herbert. "Lena Horne Speaks Freely," *Ebony* (May 1963); Horne, Lena. "My Life with Lennie," *Ebony* (November 1965); Lanker, Brian. *I Dream a World: Portraits of Black Women Who Changed America* (1989); *Life*, "Young Negro with Haunting Voice Charms New York with Old Songs" (January 4, 1943); Mapp, Edward. *Directory of Blacks in the Performing Arts* (1990); *NA*; *NBAW*; Pierce, Ponchitta. "Lena Horne at 51," *Ebony* (July 1968); *WWBA* (1992).

SELECTED DISCOGRAPHY

Jamaica. RCA (1958). *Stormy Weather: The Legendary Lena, 1941-1958.* Bluebird BMG (1990).

KATHLEEN THOMPSON

HOUSEWIVES' LEAGUE OF DETROIT

The Great Depression of the 1930s was one of the most catastrophic periods in American history. All Americans suffered economic hardships, but especially African-Americans. The thousands of Black men and women who had left the South for northern cities and midwestern communities in search of a better future for themselves and their families as early as the mid-1920s found themselves embroiled in a fierce struggle for jobs, housing, education, and first-class citizenship. As their economic status worsened, African-Americans in cities across the country encountered an increase in incidences of brutal violence, race riots, and blatant racial discrimination and segregation. It was during these dire times that Black women in Detroit created an ingenious organization based upon the principles of mutual aid, economic nationalism, and self-determination: the Housewives' League of Detroit.

The greatest weapon Detroit Black women had at their disposal during the height of the Depression was the leadership and organizing skill they had cultivated during the previous four decades of involvement in club work. Black women's culture taught them how to identify issues needing to be addressed, how to mobilize their sisters, how to develop persuasive arguments, and how to fight for the survival and well-being of their families and communities. Grounded in a social welfare-oriented cultural tradition, they appreciated the necessity for collective action. As Black women in Detroit experimented with new strategies to serve their people and to enhance their status as women, they seized upon the idea of harnessing their economic power.

On June 10, 1930, a group of fifty Black women responded to a call issued by Fannie B. Peck, wife of Reverend William H. Peck, pastor of the 2,000-member Bethel African Methodist Episcopal Church and president of the Booker T. Washington Trade Association. Out of this initial meeting emerged the Detroit Housewives' League. Peck had conceived the idea of creating an organization of housewives after hearing a lecture by M.A.L. Holsey, secretary of the National Negro Business League. Holsey had described the successful efforts of Black housewives of Harlem to consolidate and exert their considerable economic power. Peck became convinced that if such an organization worked in Harlem, it should work in Detroit. As an admirer later recalled, Peck "focused the attention of women on the most essential, yet most unfamiliar factor in the building of homes, communities, and nations, namely—'The Spending Power of Women.'"

The organization grew with phenomenal speed. From the original fifty members, its membership increased to 10,000 by 1934. Peck maintained that the growth was "due to the realization on the part of Negro women of the fact that she has been travelling through a blind alley, making sacrifices to educate her children with no thought as to their obtaining employment after leaving school."

Essentially the Housewives' League combined economic nationalism and Black women's self-determination to help Black families and businesses survive the Depression. The only requirement for membership was a pledge to support Black businesses, buy Black products, and patronize Black professionals, thereby keeping the money in the community. The leadership acknowledged that Black women were the most strategically positioned group to preserve and expand the Black internal economy. Members held the conviction that "it is our duty as women controlling 85 percent of the family budget to unlock through concentrated spending closed doors that Negro youth may have the opportunity to develop and establish businesses in the fields closest to them."

Each Black neighborhood in Detroit had its own chapter of the Housewives' League. The community leaders attended monthly meetings of the executive board. Any woman who pledged to "help build bigger and better Negro businesses and to create and increase opportunities for employment" was welcomed to membership. "A belief in the future of Negro business and a desire to assist in every way by patronizing and encouraging the same is all that is necessary to become a member." The organization took pains to make sure that all interested women had the opportunity to join and participate in the league's work. This tactic lessened the development of class-based hierarchies within the organization.

The requirement for membership in the Housewives' League of Detroit was a commitment to support Black businesses, buy Black products, patronize Black professionals, and keep Black money in the Black community. Founded in 1930, the league grew to a membership of 10,000 by 1934. Housewives' Leagues exerted major influences in other large cities as well. [Detroit Public Library]

Fulfilling the duties of membership in the league required considerable effort and commitment. Members of each chapter canvassed their neighborhood merchants, demanding that they sell Black products and employ Black children as clerks or stockpersons. In addition, chapter leaders organized campaigns to persuade their neighbors to patronize specific businesses owned by African-Americans or white businesses with Black employees. Across the city, league officers organized lectures, planned exhibits at state fairs, discussed picketing and boycotting strategies, and disseminated information concerning the economic self-help struggles of African-Americans in other sections of the country. The Research Committee gathered data and made recommendations as to the types of businesses needed in various communities and neighborhoods and reported the results of "directed spending" tactics.

Black women's activism through the Housewives' League remained securely attached to concern for home, family, and community uplift. By the time of the modern civil rights movement, therefore, Black women in Detroit perceived their advancement as being grounded upon the tripartite base of home, family, and community.

The League had an even more material impact however. During the Great Depression, historian Jacqueline Jones explains, the Housewives' Leagues "in Chicago, Baltimore, Washington, Detroit, Harlem, and Cleveland relied on boycotts" to secure "an estimated 75,000 new jobs for Blacks." Jones also notes that during the Depression these leagues "had an economic impact comparable to that of the CIO in its organizing efforts, and second only to government jobs as a new source of openings."

The league continued its work throughout the 1950s and into the 1960s. Ironically, however, just as the Black Power movement gathered momentum in the late 1960s, the Housewives' League of Detroit faded from view.

BIBLIOGRAPHY

Hine, Darlene Clark. *Black Women in the Middle West: The Michigan Experience* (1990); Jones, Jacqueline. *Labor of Love, Labor of Sorrow: Black Women, Work, and the Family from Slavery to the Present* (1985); Thomas, Richard M. *Life for Us Is What We Make It: Building Black Community in Detroit, 1914-1945* (1992). Information on the league can be found in the Housewives' League of Detroit Manuscript Collection, Burton Historical Collection, Detroit Public Library, Detroit, Michigan.

DARLENE CLARK HINE

HOUSTON, DRUSILLA DUNJEE (1876-1941)

Drusilla Dunjee Houston is the earliest known Black woman to author a multivolume study of the history of ancient Africa and its people. A teacher, journalist, and self-trained historian, she was the daughter of John William Dunjee and Lydia Taylor Dunjee. In her father's expansive library, she first read and began to master what she would later call "the dry bones of history." At twenty-two, she married Price Houston, a storekeeper, and they had a daughter. With her brother Roscoe Dunjee, she helped establish the *Black Dispatch*, a weekly Oklahoma City newspaper. As a columnist, she frequently researched and wrote articles of historical interest.

She is best known as the author of *Wonderful Ethiopians of the Ancient Cushite Empire* (1926). Beginning with the origin of civilization, *Wonderful Ethiopians* examines the links among Egypt, Ethiopia, and the ancient Black populations in Arabia, Persia, Babylonia, and India. Two other volumes written on similar themes were completed but never published. Both are now lost.

Drusilla Houston approached world history by first recognizing the blood and cultural ties that connect African people the world over. In this sense, she anticipates and shares views articulated by today's Pan-Africanist scholars.

Drusilla Houston was a significant and unique writer of ancient history. Her contribution to Black historiography and women's history has yet to be adequately appraised, in part because information on Drusilla Houston and her work is difficult to locate. An introduction to her life and work, along with a commentary and an afterword, can be found in the republished edition of *Wonderful Ethiopians* (Black Classic Press, 1985).

W. PAUL COATES

HOWARD, CLARA A. (1866-1935)

"My girls and women, you should live that the world may be better by your having lived in it," were words that Clara A. Howard heard in 1887 as valedictorian of the first graduating class of the Spelman Seminary in Atlanta, Georgia. As a member of a new generation of educated women in the postslavery era, this moment marked a turning point in Howard's life. From that day forward she was inspired to dedicate her life to humanity, and she spent the next forty-eight years establishing a remarkable record as an educator, a missionary in foreign fields, and an inspirational advisor to countless numbers of young people whose lives she touched.

Born in Greenville, Georgia, on January 23, 1866, Howard was raised along with nine siblings in Atlanta by parents who held a deep commitment to Christian values and family. Howard also embraced these values and spent her life nurturing young people as a teacher, surrogate mother, advisor, and friend. Significant among Howard's contributions, however, was her pioneering work as a missionary in the French Congo from 1890 to 1895 and in Panama from 1896 to 1897. Totally committed to serving communities in dire need, Howard hazarded dangerous conditions as a woman traveling alone during this era. Howard was one of the very few women of her generation who held a missionary appointment in a foreign field in her own right rather than by means of a husband's appointment.

By 1897, Howard was forced to end her missionary career because of continuing bouts with malaria. Nevertheless, she left behind a legacy of international service, service as a long-term staff member of Spelman College and as a member of the Atlanta community, in which she continued to be active until her death on May 3, 1935. On November 23, 1969, Spelman College dedicated a dormitory, Howard-Harreld, in honor of Clara A. Howard, its first seminary graduate, and Claudia White Harreld, its first college graduate, both of whom had distinguished themselves in their professions as well as in their daily lives.

BIBLIOGRAPHY

Guy-Sheftall, Beverly, and Jo Moore Stewart. *Spelman: A Centennial Celebration, 1881-1981* (1981); Read, Florence Matilda. *The Story of Spelman College* (1961); Spelman College Archives, Atlanta, Georgia.

JACQUELINE JONES ROYSTER

HOWARD UNIVERSITY

Established by an act of the U.S. Congress in 1867, Howard University, located in Washington, D.C., was designated as "a university for the educa-

Howard University has, since its founding in 1867, been open to women, both as students and as faculty members. This 1893 portrait shows students posing on the steps of Miner Hall. [Moorland-Spingarn]

The only constraint on female participation in Howard's administrative and educational systems, from the beginning until the present, was the availability of qualified women candidates. This photograph of a women's tennis team dates from the early 1930s. [Scurlock Studio]

tion of youth in the liberal arts and sciences." Consisting of four principal campuses totaling 241 acres, Howard is a comprehensive, research-oriented institution. Women comprise approximately thirty-seven percent of the more than two thousand faculty members, and represent fifty-seven percent of employed staff members.

Founded primarily to provide postsecondary educational opportunities to the newly emancipated slaves and free persons of color, Howard University serves the educational needs of students without regard to race, sex, creed, or nationality. From an initial enroll-

ment of four white female students in 1867, the university today enrolls a multiracial female population exceeding seven thousand, more than fifty-seven percent of the total student body. Women students enroll in the university's seventeen schools and colleges, selecting courses from a diverse curriculum offering degree programs in more than two hundred specialized subjects.

Howard University's women students, coming from various states and foreign nations, participate in undergraduate, graduate, and professional programs. Preparing female educators, lawyers, doctors, dentists, and other educated women, especially to work within the Black community, has been a Howard tradition since the late nineteenth century. In contrast to many other postsecondary institutions during that period, Howard not only included women as students but also included them as faculty members. Beginning in the late 1860s and early 1870s, female faculty members taught in the fine arts and medical fields. During the 1880s a woman served as the administrator of the university's normal department. Howard's first graduates from its normal and collegiate departments in the early 1870s were women. The university graduated a female doctor in 1872 and 1874, a female lawyer in 1872, a female pharmacist in 1887, and a female dentist in 1896 and 1900. The only constraint on female participation in the university's administrative and educational systems, from this early period until the present, was the availability of qualified women candidates.

Howard University's historic mission symbolizes its ongoing adherence to the belief in female inclusion in the postsecondary educational process. Howard alumnae serving worldwide are living testimonies to the university's incalculable contribution to both the American and world communities. Individuals such as Debbie Allen, Mary Frances Berry, Sharon Pratt Dixon, Frankie M. Freeman, Lois Mailou Jones, Toni Morrison, Jessye Norman, Eleanor Holmes Norton, Dorothy Porter Wesley, and Jeanne C. Sinkford reflect the high caliber of women graduates from Howard, a university forever mindful of its female tradition and its commitment to educating this important component of its student constituency.

BIBLIOGRAPHY

Dyson, Walter. *Howard University, The Capstone of Negro Education: A History, 1867-1940* (1941); *Howard University Blue Book* (1990); *Howard University Bulletin: Graduate School of Arts and Sciences, 1989-91* (1989); *Howard University Centennial Commission, Howard in the Second Century: Answer to a National Need* (1966); Logan, Rayford W. *Howard University: The First Hundred Years, 1867-1967* (1969); Patton, William W. *The History of Howard University, Washington, D.C., 1867 to 1888* (1896); Williams, Charles E. *The Howard University Charter Annotated: Upon the Centenary of Howard University* (1967); *WWBA* (1990).

CLIFFORD MUSE

HUGGINS, ERICKA (1948-)

"I would like to see education given top priority for Black and poor children, for all children." These were the words of Ericka Huggins, grass-roots activist, educator, and poet, after she won a seat in 1976 on the Alameda County Board of Education in Oakland, California. However, Huggins began her crusade to educate children long before 1976.

Ericka Huggins, born January 5, 1948, in Washington, D.C., was the oldest of three children. She began her undergraduate education at Cheyney State College in West Chester, Pennsylvania, with the intention of becoming a teacher of learning-impaired children and director of a school for them. In 1966 Huggins transferred to Lincoln University, in Oxford, Pennsylvania, where she worked toward a degree in special education. She completed her degree in 1979.

In the midst of her academic studies she became aware of the Oakland-based Black Panther Party (BPP) and, during her junior year in November 1967, left Lincoln University to actively involve herself in the struggle to improve conditions in Black communities in America. Nevertheless, she did not lose sight of her dream to educate children, but rather began realizing her dream within the context of the BPP.

She married Jon Huggins in 1968, and they joined the Los Angeles chapter of the BPP in February 1968; in December 1968 she gave birth to a daughter, Mai. After her husband was murdered in January 1969, Huggins moved to his home in New Haven, Connecticut. She opened a BPP Liberation School for children where the children received meals in addition to an education. Huggins's BPP work was interrupted on May 22, 1969, however, when the New Haven police illegally arrested and incarcerated her. Huggins's case was dismissed May 25, 1971.

Ericka Huggins moved to Oakland, California, and resumed her grass-roots activism. Before her June 1972 election to the Berkeley Community Development Council Board of Directors, Huggins taught English and creative writing at the BPP-sponsored Oakland Community School, then called the Intercommunal Youth Institute. In 1973, she became editor of the *Black Panther Intercommunal News Service*.

From 1973 until 1981, she was director of the accredited Oakland Community School, the alternative school for Oakland youth established January 1971 by the BPP. As a consequence of the success of the model school, Huggins became a consultant for other alternative educational programs. In June 1976, Huggins became the first Black person to serve on the Alameda County School Board. She was also a member of alternative school associations such as the Pacific Regional Association of Alternative Schools.

Ericka Huggins lives in Oakland, California. She has been teaching part-time since fall 1990 in the Women's Studies Department at San Francisco State University. She also directs a program in underprivileged areas of San Francisco for individuals and families with Human Immunodeficiency Virus (HIV).

[*See also* BLACK PANTHER PARTY.]

BIBLIOGRAPHY

Anthony, Earl. *Picking up the Gun: A Report on the Black Panthers* (1970); *Black Panther Intercommunal News Service* (1969-79); *Essence* (May 1990); Freed, Donald. *Agony in New Haven: The Trial of Bobby Seale, Ericka Huggins, and the Black Panther Party* (1973); Huggins, Ericka. Interview (December 2, 1991); Newton, Huey. *Insights and Poems with Ericka Huggins* (1974); Sheehy, Gail. *Panthermania: The Clash of Black against Black in One American City* (1971).

ANGELA D. BROWN

HUNTER, ALBERTA (1895-1984)

Born in Memphis, Tennessee, on April 1, 1895, Alberta Hunter enjoyed a long and successful career, primarily as a blues singer, until her death on October 17, 1984, in New York City.

Hunter's career began around 1914 in Chicago and continued in New York in 1921. In both cities she sang in clubs and cabarets, but after moving to New York she began to record. Hunter recorded for Gennett, as well as other labels, and was accompanied by musicians such as Louis Armstrong, Sidney Bechet, and Fletcher Henderson. In order to record on labels other than Gennett (Hunter was under contract to Gennett), she used two different aliases, May Alix and Josephine Beatty.

From 1927 to 1953, Hunter sang both in Europe and the United States, including several United Service Organizations (USO) tours, and she appeared in the 1936 film *Radio Parade*. Hunter was semiretired from 1954 to 1977, having become a nurse; during

The great blues singer Alberta Hunter, whose career spanned seven decades, was also the composer of "Downhearted Blues" (1922), made famous by Bessie Smith in 1923. She is shown here performing in Carnegie Hall on June 27, 1978, as part of the Newport Jazz Festival's Salute to the American Song. [AP/Wide World Photos]

this time she recorded only with Lovie Austin in 1961 and Jimmy Archey in 1962. She resumed her musical career in 1977 and continued to sing in clubs, make television appearances, and record until her death in 1984.

In addition to her vocal talent, Hunter also was a composer. She wrote at least one classic composition, "Downhearted Blues," in 1922, a composition that became famous after Bessie Smith recorded it in 1923.

BIBLIOGRAPHY

Albertson, C. "Roots of Jazz," *Stereo Review* (1977); Darden, N. J. "No Tea for the Fever: Alberta Hunter Is Back and Happy to Sing the Blues," *Essence* (1978); Driggs, F. "Alberta Hunter," *SV* (1975); Jeske, C. "Alberta Hunter: Singer of Songs," *Downbeat* (1980); Placksin, S. "Alberta Hunter." In *American Women in Jazz, 1960 to the Present: Their Words, Lives, and Music*, ed. Sally Placksin (1982); Radano, Ronald M. "Alberta Hunter." In *The New Grove Dictionary of Jazz*, ed. Barry Kernfeld (1988); Reynolds, J. "Alberta Hunter with Jimmy Daniels," *Interview* (1978); Taylor, F. C., and G. Cook. *Alberta Hunter: A Celebration of Blues* (1987); Wilson, J. S. "Alberta Hunter" (obituary), *New York Times* (October 19, 1984).

SELECTED DISCOGRAPHY

Downhearted Blues, Paramount-12005 (1922); *Jazzin' Baby Blues*, Paramount-12006 (1922); *Stingaree Blues*, Paramount-12049 (1923); *Texas Moaner Blues*, Gennett-5594 (1924); *Your Jelly Roll Is Good*, Okeh-8268 (1925); *Sugar Blues*, Victor-20771 (1927); *Alberta Hunter with Lovie Austin and Her Blues Serenaders*, Riverside-9418 (1961).

EDDIE S. MEADOWS

HUNTER, CLEMENTINE
(1886-1988)

"If Jimmy Carter wants to see me, he knows where I am. He can come here." This reply, to President Carter's invitation that she come to Washington for the opening of an exhibition of her work, is vintage Clementine Hunter. Her disregard for fame and the famous was part of her special charm and did not change, even after she became known worldwide for her colorful folk paintings of Black life in the Cane River region of north Louisiana.

Clementine Hunter was born on Hidden Hill Plantation, near Cloutierville, Louisiana, in December 1886. Her mother, Mary Antoinette Adams, was the daughter of a slave, brought to Louisiana from Virginia; her father, John Reuben, had an Irish father and a Native American mother. Hunter considered herself a Creole. When she was a teenager, she moved with her family from Hidden Hill to Yucca Plantation, renamed Melrose, seventeen miles south of Natchitoches, Louisiana. Hunter lived and worked at Melrose until 1970, when the plantation was sold; then she moved to a small trailer a few miles away, where she lived until her death on January 1, 1988.

Charles Dupree, the father of Hunter's first two children—Joseph (Frenchie) and Cora—died about 1914. In January 1924, Clementine married Emmanual Hunter, by whom she had five children: Agnes, King, Mary, and two who died at birth. Emmanual Hunter died in 1944. Clementine Hunter outlived all her children except Mary (called Jackie).

Hunter's mentor was François Mignon, a French writer who lived on Melrose Plantation from 1938 to 1970. According to Mignon, Hunter did her first painting in 1939. From then until a few months before her death, Hunter painted continually, on any surface she could find. Her output was prodigious; estimates are that she completed more than 5,000 paintings. Like many folk artists, however, Hunter painted the same scenes over and over. Her works fall into roughly five thematic categories: work scenes from plantation life; recreation scenes; religious scenes; flowers and birds; and abstracts. The quality of her work varies greatly, but her paintings are prized for their vibrant colors and whimsical humor.

The first exhibit of Hunter's work was at the New Orleans Arts and Crafts show in 1949. After three exhibits in the 1950s, her work received little attention until the early 1970s, when it was shown at the Museum of American Folk Art in New York City (1973) and in the Los Angeles County Museum of Art's exhibit "Two Centuries of Black American Art" (1976). In the last fifteen years of her life, Hunter had many one-woman shows at colleges and galleries throughout Louisiana; was featured on local and national television shows; was included in two oral Black-history projects (Fisk University, 1971; Schlesinger Library, Radcliffe College, 1976); and was part of the photographic portrait exhibition "Women of Courage by Judith Sedwick," shown in 1985 in New York and Boston. Also in 1985, Hunter was awarded an honorary doctor of fine arts from Northwestern State University of Louisiana, in Natchitoches.

Although the quality of Hunter's paintings is uneven, the historical value of her work is beyond question.

BIBLIOGRAPHY

Archives and Special Collections, Cammie G. Henry Research Center, Eugene P. Watson Memorial Library,

Northwestern State University of Louisiana, Natchitoches (François Mignon Collection, James Register Collection, Melrose Collection, Thomas N. Whitehead Collection); Bailey, Mildred Hart. "Clementine Hunter." In *Four Women of Cane River: Their Contributions to the Cultural Life of the Area* (1980); "Clementine Hunter and the Cane River Country," WDSU-TV, New Orleans (February 10, 1974); Jones, Anne Hudson. "The Centennial of Clementine Hunter," *Woman's Art Journal* (Spring/Summer 1987), and personal interview with Clementine Hunter (June 21, 1986), and personal interviews with Mildred Hart Bailey and Thomas N. Whitehead (June 17, 21, 1986); Mignon, François. *Plantation Memo: Plantation Life in Louisiana, 1950-70, and Other Matters* (1972); Mills, Gary B. *The Forgotten People: Cane River's Creoles of Color* (1977); "Miss Clemmie," KSLA-TV, Shreveport, Louisiana (March 9, 1984); Rankin, Allen. "The Hidden Genius of Melrose Plantation," *Reader's Digest* (December 1975); Read, Mimi. "Clementine Hunter: Visions from the Heart," *Dixie Magazine*, New Orleans *Times-Picayune* Sunday Supplement (April 14, 1985); Ryan, Bob and Yvonne Ryan. "Clementine Hunter: A Personal Story," *Louisiana Life* (September/October 1981); Wilson, James L. *Clementine Hunter: American Folk Artist* (1988).

ANNE HUDSON JONES

Trained as a nurse, Jane Edna Hunter distinguished herself as the founder and executive director of the Phillis Wheatley Association in Cleveland, Ohio. The association opened its first home for Black women in 1913, and became the model for a network of clubs, residences, and employment services throughout the United States. [Phillis Wheatley Association]

HUNTER, JANE EDNA (1882-1971)

I believe firmly in the philosophy of Booker T. Washington, namely, "to teach a man to do something and to do it well. To make him efficient in whatever he undertakes to do so no man coming after him can do the job any better" (Jane Hunter 1945).

Jane Edna Harris Hunter devoted her entire adult life to improving conditions for Black women. Although the above quotation, from a letter she wrote to a white benefactor, refers to men, she applied the philosophy in every respect to her work as founder and executive director of the Phillis Wheatley Association in Cleveland, Ohio. The independent association, which opened its first home for Black women in 1913, became the model for a network of clubs, residences, and employment services throughout the country, sponsored by the National Association of Colored Women (NACW). Between 1913 and 1950, Hunter was a major figure in the Black women's club movement as well as in local politics and race relations. Her Phillis Wheatley Association was home to hundreds of women moving into the city for work opportunities, especially during World Wars I and II.

Jane Harris was born on December 13, 1882, on the Woodburn Plantation near Pendleton, South Carolina, the second of four siblings born to Edward and Harriet Milner Harris. Edward Harris, Jane's father, the son of a slave woman and the plantation overseer, named his first daughter after his English grandmother, Jane McCrary. According to her own account, young Jane, with her light complexion and keen features, resembled her father and felt a strong kinship with him and the grandmother she barely knew. Unfortunately, the same features alienated her from her dark-skinned mother. In her autobiography, she confessed that because she despised the "poverty, contempt, and subjugation of the race," she rejected her "racial heritage as a Negro." Later, after years of personal struggle, she dedicated her life to "give the world what [she] had failed to give her [mother]" (Hunter 1941).

Jane was only able to attend school for a short time before her father's death when she was ten years old. However, when she was fourteen, she was invited by missionaries to attend a small Presbyterian school, Ferguson-Williams College, in Abbeville, South Carolina, where she could work in exchange for her education. In 1902, after a failed marriage, she enrolled at the Canon Street Hospital and Training School for Nurses in Charleston, South Carolina, and two years later she moved to the Dixie Hospital and Training School at Hampton Institute.

When Hunter arrived in Cleveland in 1905, she found that Black nurses were not accepted in the hospitals and were barely tolerated for private duty. Even more devastating was the lack of available decent housing, especially for Black women. She turned to the Young Women's Christian Association (YWCA) for help but was refused because of her race. As a result, she vowed to find a way to help other young Black women avoid similar problems. After several years, she approached the YWCA again for help. This time, rather than ask them to allow Black Americans into their facilities, she convinced the leadership to help her open a separate home. The white women eagerly embraced the idea.

The Phillis Wheatley Home, named in honor of the Black slave poet, opened its doors in 1913. Jane Hunter was appointed secretary and manager by an interracial board of trustees, headed by the president of the YWCA. As director of the Phillis Wheatley Association, Hunter gained local and national attention as a master negotiator between the races. Although some Black Americans denounced her servile manner with whites and her accommodationist ideology, none could deny her ability to maintain cordial relations with wealthy donors or her strength as head of the city's largest Black institution. Under her leadership the association grew from a twenty-three-room rented house to a new eleven-story, half-million-dollar residence and training facility, built in 1927—the largest independent facility for Black women in the country.

Hunter remained executive director of the Phillis Wheatley Association until 1946, when she was forced to retire. During her tenure the institution expanded its services to include a beauty school, a fine dining room, and gymnasium, a music school, a nursery school, a large summer camp, three branch facilities, two training cottages, and the Booker T. Washington playground. The association was also well known for its controversial employment bureau, which emphasized placement for domestic workers. Hunter also established the Phillis Wheatley Department in the National Association of Colored Women (NACW). She served as state president and national vice president of the NACW during the 1930s and 1940s and edited its state organ, the *Queen's Garden*.

In addition to her activities as executive director of the Phillis Wheatley Association, Hunter also maintained active leadership in business and social service organizations. She was a founding member of the Board of the Colored Welfare Association of Cleveland, which later affiliated with the National Urban League; a founder of Saint Mark's Presbyterian Church; a trustee of Central State University; an active partner in the Empire Savings and Loan Association (a Black banking organization); a member of the Progressive Business Alliance; a member of the International Council of Women of the Darker Races; and an officer and national figure with the Republican party's Colored Women's Committee. In addition, she was active in real estate as a director of the Black-owned Union Realty Company and as a landlord with several properties in the city's central area.

Hunter also continued her education. She often participated in training events for Black branch directors sponsored by the YWCA National Board, and she took courses in social work at the School of Social Work at Western Reserve University. She graduated from the Cleveland School of Law at Baldwin-Wal-

Under Jane Edna Hunter's inspired leadership, the Phillis Wheatley Association in Cleveland grew from a twenty-three-room rented house to an eleven-story, half-million-dollar residence and training facility, the largest independent residence facility for Black women in the country. [The Western Reserve Historical Society, Cleveland, Ohio]

lace College and passed the Bar in 1926. Honorary degrees in recognition of her outstanding work were presented by Wilberforce, Fisk, and Allen universities and Tuskegee Institute. She was also nominated for the prestigious Spingarn Award of the National Association for the Advancement of Colored People in 1937.

After retirement, Hunter established the Phillis Wheatley Foundation, a scholarship fund for women. Although her yearly salary never exceeded $3,000, she left an estate at her death of nearly half a million dollars, most of which went to the foundation. According to her attorney, the money accumulated from real estate and stock investments. Tragically, after over fifty years of activism and service, she began to experience increasing periods of confusion and was judged to be mentally incompetent in 1960. She died of natural causes on January 19, 1971.

BIBLIOGRAPHY

Davis, Russell. *Black Americans in Cleveland* (1972); Hunter, Jane Edna. *A Nickel and a Prayer* (1941); Jones, Adrienne Lash. *Jane Edna Hunter: A Case Study of Black Leadership, 1905-1950* (1989); Kusmer, Kenneth. *A Ghetto Takes Shape: Black Cleveland, 1870-1930* (1978); Western Reserve Historical Society Manuscript Collections: Phillis Wheatley, Jane Edna Hunter, and Young Women's Christian Association.

ADRIENNE LASH JONES

HUNTER, KRISTIN (1931-)

Kristin Hunter began her professional writing career at the age of fourteen as a columnist and feature writer for the Philadelphia edition of the *Pittsburgh Courier*. She had been writing poetry and articles for school publications, having learned how to read by the age of four. She has won critical acclaim for her short stories, novels for adults and young adults, and documentaries.

Kristin Eggleston was born in Philadelphia on September 12, 1931, to George Lorenzo and Mabel Eggleston. She was the only child of parents who were both school teachers, and her father insisted that she also become a teacher. She acquiesced and received her B.S. in education from the University of Pennsylvania in 1951. She accepted a position as a third-grade teacher but resigned before the school year had ended to pursue her dream of writing. She accepted a position at the Lavenson Bureau of Advertising, where she worked as a copywriter. She later worked as an information officer for the City of Philadelphia and as director of comprehensive health services at Temple University.

In 1955, Hunter entered her television documentary, *Minority of One*, in a competition sponsored by CBS and won first place. This award attracted a great deal of attention, and Hunter continued to combine copywriting and freelance writing until 1964, when she published her first novel, *God Bless the Child*. Perhaps her most critically acclaimed work, *God Bless the Child* is the tragic story of the rise and fall of Rosalie Fleming as she works untiringly to escape the slum into which she is born.

In her second novel, *The Landlord*, Hunter portrays Elgar Enders, a wealthy white misfit who purchases a dilapidated tenement in the ghetto. Gradually his interactions with the Black tenants transform Enders into a humanitarian who finds acceptance and a niche in the most unlikely of worlds. In 1970, United Artists released the movie adaptation of the novel, for which Hunter wrote the screenplay.

Hunter has also written at least four works for young adults. One million copies were sold of her first young adult book, *The Soul Brothers and Sister Lou*, written in 1968. The novel, which also won the Council on Interracial Books Children's Award in 1968, has been translated into several languages. The work chronicles the emergence of a group of young, aspiring Black musicians who sing their way out of the ghetto. In a 1981 sequel, *Lou in the Limelight*, Hunter examines the entanglements that often beset pop artists in their struggle to maintain success.

A member of the Philadelphia Art Alliance, Hunter has been the recipient of numerous awards. In 1955 she received the Fund for the Republic Prize for her television documentary, *Minority of One*. She also won the Philadelphia Athenaeum Award in 1964. The 1968 publication of *The Soul Brothers and Sister Lou* brought several important awards in addition to those mentioned above: the Mass Media Brotherhood Award from the National Conference of Christians and Jews in 1969 and the Lewis Carroll Shelf Award in 1971. Hunter's young adult novel *Guests in the Promised Land* was a National Book Award finalist in 1974 and winner of the Christopher Award in 1975. The novel also received the Chicago Tribune Book World Prize in 1973.

Hunter also has written several critically acclaimed short stories and articles. Her article "Pray for Barbara's Baby," first printed in *Philadelphia Magazine*, received the Sigma Delta Chi Best Magazine Reporting Award in 1969.

As a journalist and creative writer, Kristin Hunter has produced works in many genres. In addition, she continues to teach creative writing at the University of Pennsylvania, where she has taught since 1968. Married to a photojournalist, John Lattany, Sr., she is the mother of one stepson, John, Jr.

BIBLIOGRAPHY

DLB; Harris, Trudier. *From Mammies to Militants: Domestics in Black American Literature* (1982); "Kristin (Eggleston) Hunter." In *Contemporary Literary Criticism*, ed. Daniel G. Marowski (1985); Polak, Maralyn Lois. "Kristin Hunter: A Writer and a Fighter," *Philadelphia Inquirer* (November 24, 1974).

SHIRLEY JORDAN

HUNTER-GAULT, CHARLAYNE (1942-)

"Whatever I have faced as a woman," Charlayne Hunter-Gault said, "is probably a lot more subtle than what I have faced as a Black person" (Lanker 1989). By the time she and Hamilton Holmes became

Kristin Hunter's children's book The Soul Brothers and Sister Lou *sold over a million copies and won the Council on Interracial Books Children's Award in 1968. [Schomburg Center]*

the first Black students to enter the University of Georgia, Athens, in January 1961, Charlayne Hunter had endured two years of legal maneuvering and bureaucratic delays. After the riots and unrest that followed, many journalists interviewed the two Black students, and Hunter's interest in becoming a journalist grew. She joined the staff of the *New Yorker* in 1963 as a secretary. Her writing talent enabled her to advance rapidly at the *New Yorker*, at the *New York Times*, and in other news positions, to become a leading journalist.

The oldest of three children, Charlayne Hunter was born on February 27, 1942, in Due West, South Carolina, to Charles S. H. Hunter, Jr., a Methodist chaplain in the U.S. Army, and Althea Hunter. In 1954, the Hunters moved to Atlanta, Georgia, where the mother was secretary in a real estate firm. The father's long tours of duty abroad left the rearing of Charlayne and her two younger brothers to the mother and grandmother.

From 1954 to 1959, Hunter attended Henry McNeal Turner High School, where she was an honor student and editor of the student newspaper. She became a Roman Catholic at age sixteen. Her ambition to be a reporter led Hunter to seek admission to the University of Georgia. A group of prominent civil rights activists supported Hunter and Holmes in the fight to integrate the university. While waiting for the court order, she studied at Wayne State University in Detroit, Michigan. At the University of Georgia she worked on weekends for the Atlanta *Inquirer*, founded by Georgia college students, including Julian Bond.

She received a B.A. in journalism from the University of Georgia in 1963, became secretary at the *New Yorker*, and the next year was promoted to staff writer. After receiving a Russell Sage Fellowship in 1967 to study social science at Washington University, St. Louis, she left the *New Yorker*. In St. Louis she edited articles for *Trans-Action* magazine, which sent her to cover the Poor People's Campaign in Washington, D.C. Later that year she became investigative reporter and anchorwoman of the local evening news broadcast of WRC-TV, and in 1968 she joined the metropolitan staff of the *New York Times*. In the early 1970s, she took a leave of absence to become codirector of the Michele Clark Fellowship program for minority students in journalism at Columbia University, returning later to spend a total of nine years with the *Times*. Hunter-Gault joined *The MacNeil/Lehrer Report* on PBS in 1978 and was named national correspondent in 1983, when the show was expanded to *The MacNeil/Lehrer NewsHour*.

Hunter-Gault has received numerous major journalism awards: the *New York Times* Publisher's Award, the National Urban Coalition Award for Distinguished Urban Reporting, two national news and documentary Emmy Awards, and the George Foster Peabody Award for Excellence in Broadcast Journalism.

In addition to her print and broadcast work as a journalist, she has written articles for *Change, Essence, Life, Ms., Saturday Review,* the *New Leader,* and other magazines. She married Walter Stovall, a white student, while in college. They had one daughter, Susan, born a few years later. In 1971, she married Ronald Gault, a Black Chicagoan, and they have one son, Chuma.

Charlayne Hunter-Gault set a goal early in life, which, coupled with her talent and tenacity, led her to become a leading journalist. The University of Georgia, though it once denied her admission and was the site of violent protests against her presence on campus, now accepts and honors Hunter-Gault.

BIBLIOGRAPHY

Current Biography Yearbook (1987); Dreifus, Claudia. "A Talk with Charlayne Hunter-Gault," *Dial* (February 1987); Dupree, Adolph. "Language of an Evening Star: Charlayne Hunter-Gault," *About Time* (July 1986); Fraser, C. Gerald. "Charlayne Hunter-Gault: From the Front Line to the Firing Line," *Essence* (March 1987); Hunter-Gault, Charlayne. *In My Place* (1992); Lanker, Brian. *I Dream a World: Portraits of Black Women Who Changed America* (1989); *NBAW; WWBA* (1990-91).

JESSIE CARNEY SMITH

HUNTON, ADDIE WAITS
(1866-1943)

Addie Waits Hunton described another woman as "gifted and favored by the gods" yet having "resolved to make her life full through work in this movement." Hunton's words could have described herself. The movement she referred to was the National Association of Colored Women (NACW). Through the NACW and the Young Women's Christian Association (YWCA) Addie Hunton challenged those who denigrated Black women, worked for the uplift of all Black people, primarily by uplifting Black women, and fought for Black women's suffrage, among other activities. Educated and cultured, she was also a teacher and a writer who used her pen to publicize, to educate, and to proselytize for Black women.

Born in Norfolk, Virginia, on June 11, 1866, Addie D. Waits was the eldest of three children of Adeline Lawton and Jesse Waits. She graduated from Boston Girls Latin School and from the Spencerian College of Commerce in Philadelphia, where she was the only Black student in the 1889 class. She held several educational posts: teacher in the public schools of Portsmouth, Virginia; principal at the State Normal and Agricultural College in Normal, Alabama; and registrar and accountant at Clark University in Atlanta, Georgia (1905-6).

On July 19, 1893, in Norfolk she married William Alphaeus Hunton, the first Black international secretary for the Young Men's Christian Association (YMCA). The couple moved to Atlanta in 1899 with high hopes for the future of Black people, but their hopes were soon dashed with the brutal lynching near Atlanta of Sam Hose. While her husband traveled, organizing college men for the YMCA, Addie Hunton combined motherhood, club work, and education. She bore four children. Only two lived, Eunice Roberta and William Alphaeus, Jr., both born in Atlanta.

During the 1900s and 1910s her articles about the women's club movement and topics germane to Black women appeared in the *Atlanta Independent,* the *Voice of the Negro,* the *Colored American Magazine,* and the *Crisis.* In one of her most important pieces, "Negro Womanhood Defended," she took to task those who accused Black women of immorality:

> For centuries the Negro woman was forced by cruelty too diverse and appalling to mention to submit her body to those who bartered for it. She was voiceless, and there was no arm lifted in her defense. ... In the face of all this ignominy—she has staggered up through the ages ladened with the double burden of excessive maternal care and physical toil, and she has, while climbing, thrown off much of the dross. ... Work, pray and hope—this seems to be woman's part in the uplift of the race (Hunton 1904).

Hunton attended the NACW's 1895 founding convention in Boston and carried its mission to the Deep South, serving as president of the Atlanta and Georgia bodies and as board member of the Southern Federation. She organized in southern states and later, during 1906-10, throughout the United States.

Referring to the work of southern women she wrote, "About them the air is surcharged with the smoke of the battle. Around them they hear the heart-throbs and sighs of a people crying for right." Yet, unprepared for turn-of-the-century violence, the Huntons left the South after the 1906 Atlanta riot, never to live again "in the midst of the great racial conflict" (Hunton 1905).

From 1907 to 1915, she was a national official for the YWCA, serving as city secretary and student secretary to Black youth. During 1908-9, she studied at Kaiser Wilhelm University in Germany. The Huntons established their permanent home, which was to remain Addie Hunton's until her death, in Brooklyn, New York. However, William Hunton contracted tuberculosis and after two years of treatment died in 1916. She stayed with him during most of his illness and later memorialized him in a loving biography, *William Alphaeus Hunton: A Pioneer Prophet of Young Men* (1938).

She once again returned to the civic and club life that motivated her. Under the auspices of the YWCA, she and two other women went to France to head up the work with American Black troops during the World War I years, 1917-18. She and Kathryn Johnson chronicled their experiences in *Two Colored Women with the American Expeditionary Forces* (1920).

Home from the war, in the early 1920s she worked as field secretary for the National Association for the Advancement of Colored People (NAACP) on behalf of Black women who were being denied their suffrage rights. In particular, she confronted the National Woman's party and its leader, Alice Paul, to support voting rights for Black women. In correspondence she wrote, "Five million [Black] women in the United States can not be denied their rights without all the women of the United States feeling the effect of that denial. No women are free until all women are free."

In the 1920s, Hunton was also active on behalf of African peoples, observing the occupation of Haiti by the United States, writing of race relations in occupied Haiti (1926), and working as a principal organizer for the 1927 Pan-African Congress in New York City and as a member of the Women's International League for Peace and Freedom. In the 1920s and 1930s, she also kept up her club work, serving for a time as president of the Empire State Federation of Women's Clubs and the International Council of Women of the Darker Races. At age seventy-seven she died of diabetes in Brooklyn on June 21, 1943, and was buried in Cypress Hills Cemetery.

Her daughter, Eunice Hunton Carter (1899-1970), was a lawyer and an active Republican and clubwoman, and was married to Lyle S. Carter. Addie Hunton's son, William Alphaeus Hunton, Jr. (1903-1970), taught at Howard University, was jailed for five years for refusing to cooperate with the McCarthy committee, and wrote *Decision in Africa* (1960).

BIBLIOGRAPHY
CBWA; Clark University and Biographical Files, Special Collections, Woodruff Library, Atlanta University Center; *DANB*; Giddings, Paula. *When and Where I Enter: The Impact of Black Women on Race and Sex in America* (1984); Hunton, Addie. "Negro Womanhood Defended," *Voice of the Negro* (July 1904), and "The Southern Federation of Colored Women," *Voice of the Negro* (December 1905), and "Woman's Part in the Uplift of the Negro Race," *Colored American Magazine* (January 1907); Maher, Frank L. *Who's Who of the Colored Race* ([1915] 1976); *NAW*; U.S. Census, Manuscripts, Tenth Census, Norfolk County, Virginia (1880), and Twelfth Census, Fulton County, Georgia (1900).

GRETCHEN E. MACLACHLAN

HURLEY, RUBY (c. 1913-)

In 1955, alone in Klan country, National Association for the Advancement of Colored People field representative Ruby Hurley went from plantation to plantation, asking questions about the death of Emmett Till. Her life was at risk, and she knew it; but she was just doing her job. That job began in 1939 when the Washington, D.C., native began organizing an NAACP youth council in her hometown. She was then about twenty-six years old. A few years later, in 1943, she became the national youth secretary of that organization. During the time she held that position, the number of youth councils and college chapters grew from 86 to 280.

It was in 1951 that Hurley went into the deep South. Racial tension and violence were intense as the white population struggled to maintain the most extreme state of oppression. When, in 1955, the Reverend George W. Lee encouraged thirty-one of his parishioners to register to vote and then to hold their ground against opposition, he was murdered. Hurley went to investigate. She saw Lee's body in the casket—reportedly the victim of a traffic accident—and wrote, "I saw his body in the casket—I will not be able to forget how the whole lower half of his face had been shot away. A man killed because he, as a minister, said that God's children had rights as God's children and as American citizens."

In the same year, young Emmett Till was lynched for supposedly whistling at a white woman. Hurley, along with Medgar Evers and Amzie Moore, found witnesses to the alleged crime in spite of the threat to themselves. Evers himself was murdered eight years later.

A few months after the Emmett Till investigation, Hurley stood next to Autherine Lucy as thousands of white racists tried to prevent that young woman from entering the University of Alabama. When Hurley went back to her home office in Birmingham, she was subjected to continual threats and harassment, from which she could expect no protection from the police department under the notorious commissioner "Bull" Conner. Eventually, she developed situational stress disorder, losing weight and suffering almost constant illness. She had to close the Birmingham office because of legal maneuvers against the organization.

In Atlanta, to which she moved, Hurley became involved in the struggles between the NAACP and the younger Student Nonviolent Coordinating Committee and Southern Christian Leadership Conference. For the rest of her thirty-nine years in service to the NAACP, she found herself defending the older generation and trying to make the younger generation aware of civil rights activity before 1960.

BIBLIOGRAPHY

CBWA; *NBAW*; Raines, Howell. *My Soul Is Rested* (1977); *WWBA* (1991).

KATHLEEN THOMPSON

HURSTON, ZORA NEALE (1891-1960)

Zora Neale Hurston was a colorful and flamboyant figure in the 1920s and 1930s who created controversy whenever and wherever she appeared. She also created a remarkable body of writings—folklore, anthropological studies, plays, short stories, essays, novels, and an autobiography.

Born on January 7, 1891, in the all-Black town of Eatonville, Florida, she was the fifth of eight children of John Hurston and Lucy Potts Hurston. In her autobiography, Hurston described her childhood as a safe and secure world where her imagination was unencumbered by the restrictions of race or gender and where she had the opportunity to develop her own individuality. This idyllic childhood was shattered by the death of her mother around 1904 and the disintegration of her family. Her father, Reverend John Hurston, sent her off to boarding school, and her sisters and brothers scattered into marriages, schools, and journeys of their own. Her father's remarriage several months after her mother's death destroyed her family life and some educational op-

portunities, and catapulted her out of the safe world of Eatonville. This was a major experience in Hurston's life, marking the beginning of her wanderings in search of freedom from the constraints of race and gender that the larger world imposed upon African-Americans.

For several years, Hurston wandered from job to job and lived in the homes of family members and strangers. She worked as a maid in a traveling Gilbert and Sullivan theater company. While working as a maid and a manicurist, she finished her high school education at Morgan Academy in Baltimore, Maryland, and her college education at Howard University in Washington, D.C., and she earned a graduate degree from Barnard College in New York City. With the assistance of such luminaries as Charles S. Johnson and Alain Locke, she began her career by publishing several short stories in *Opportunity* magazine, including "Drenched in Light" in December 1924, "Spunk" in June 1925, and "Muttsy" in August 1926. In collaboration with other writers, including Langston Hughes and Wallace Thurman, Hurston edited the short-lived magazine *Fire!* in which her short story "Sweat" appeared in November 1926. In 1930, in collaboration with Langston Hughes, she wrote a play entitled *Mule Bone*, a comedy about African-American life. It was never performed during her lifetime. After developing her skills as an anthropologist, she wrote a volume of folklore, *Mules and Men*, which was not published until 1935, and a second volume of Caribbean folklore, *Tell My Horse*, published in 1938. Hurston then turned her attention to the novel.

In 1934, she published her first novel, *Jonah's Gourd Vine*, loosely based on the life of her parents, particularly her father. Her masterpiece, *Their Eyes Were Watching God*, was published in 1937; *Moses, Man of the Mountain* in 1939; and *Seraph on the Suwanee*, the least successful of her writings, in 1948. Equally important in Hurston's canon is her autobiography, *Dust Tracks on a Road*, published in 1942.

In these novels, set within an all-Black or mostly Black background, Hurston rejects color and race identity as important to her situation, although the implications of these factors are woven skillfully into her work. It is in the response to the reality of race and racism that this all-Black community comes into existence. Yet within this world, Hurston brings forward gender as critical in influencing African-American women's and men's ability to come to self-realization. She creates characters who deal with gender in an African-American, rural, middle-class world. Poverty is not at the core of their problem, as it is for the majority of African-Americans. Rather their struggle is for an internal sense of freedom—of spirit and body. In her novels, this struggle of African-Americans for both spiritual and physical freedom is carried out behind the walls of segregation.

Although Hurston presents gender as central to identity, her works also reveal the construction of race and its relationship to class behind the walls of segregation. The tension among color, class, and gender is revealed further in her autobiography, *Dust Tracks on a Road*. Shaping and molding these meditations on gender, race, color, and class is Hurston's search and struggle for freedom—freedom as an artist, as a woman, as an African-American, freedom as a space to be enlarged upon. How to be Black without being limited by that reality; how to be woman without the constraints of womanhood; and how to remain true to both of these identities and still be an educated artist plagued Hurston all her life.

Hurston's work, coupled with the details of her life, suggests that she accepted the legitimacy of African-American culture and by doing so established the authenticity of this cultural formation. For Hurston, this culture had its own internal logic and moral code. She did not challenge the ideology of racism by attempting to prove the humanity of African-Americans, but rather she challenged the hegemonic power of the dominant culture to represent African-American people negatively. Her literary works particularly establish Hurston as a keen observer of African-Americans and the world in which they lived.

Hurston challenged and contested the notion that the integrity of the African-American race needed defending and that the responsibility for this defense must be borne by each individual Black person. She believed that such a burden originated from essentially the same racist ideology: that is, that Black people were deficient and had to be uplifted for approval by the dominant society and that each representative Negro must assume the burden of both uplifting and defending the race even at the cost of personal wishes and needs. These views were developed and shaped to a considerable extent by her anthropological training at Barnard College under the direction of the renowned anthropologist Franz Boas. Boas believed in the value and legitimacy of all cultures and trained his students to discover the internal logic of the cultures they studied. Hurston, one of his most devoted students, was strongly influenced by this perspective, which led her to reject the prevailing notion of Black culture as inferior and immoral. For Hurston, the race needed no improvement or justification.

Hurston also contested the gender conventions that required a ladylike image for women, confining them to both the private sphere of marriage and motherhood and the public sphere of nurturing roles as teachers, nurses, and other homespun heroines uplifting the African-American race. She refused, in other words, to be a female "race man," at least in her public persona. This defiance is embedded in both her artistic and autobiographical writings. Unlike characters in the novels of two of her contemporaries, Richard Wright and Jessie Fauset, Hurston's characters are not engaged in race relations. They seek to build, quite deliberately, worlds where African-American people concern themselves with life issues outside the control and purview of white hegemonic structures. Race moves from an all-controlling factor to one that influences but does not wholly determine day-to-day existence. Instead, Hurston's characters struggle through life in spite of race, drawing on their own communities and culture for strength and direction. They focus on gender, family, and community relationships in an effort to find space for the individual. This view of race is in sharp contrast to the reality of her life, where white patrons required demeaning behavior of her before granting the financial support she needed to complete her work. Yet, she looked to her own strengths in her private struggle in gender, family, and community relationships where she sacrificed marriage, family connections, motherhood, and community acceptance in order to be a scholar and artist.

Hurston was a rural, southern, Black woman attempting to be an artist in a world controlled by white people and men. Her struggle, as evidenced by her artistic, ethnographic, and autobiographical writings, dealt with how love is possible, how color can liberate and imprison at the same time, how ambiguous an identity it is to be an American, how genius can or cannot be borne, and how womanhood can both adorn and strangle a life. Hurston refused to be confined by gender and racial roles. Her critics misunderstood her public behavior and also missed the meaning of her scholarly and artistic production. It is in her novels that one finds the key to her understanding and confusion surrounding the realities of gender, race, and class.

In the introduction to her folklore collection, *Mules and Men*, Hurston provides insight into the mind of Black rural people. Black people "are most reluctant at times to reveal that which the soul lives by and the Negro, in spite of his open-faced laughter, his seeming acquiescence, is particularly evasive.... The Negro offers a feather-bed resistance. That is, we let the probe enter, but it never comes out. It gets smothered under a lot of laughter and pleasantries." Hurston suggests that this "onstage" consciousness of African-Americans was distinctly different from their "offstage" consciousness. She argues for a deliberate deception constructed by African-Americans that establishes mental protection from the intrusion of the outside world. If African-Americans could not protect themselves totally from physical and economic exploitation, they could resist intrusion into their inner lives, into their soul: "I'll set something outside the door of my mind for him to play with and handle. He can read my writing but he sho' can't read my mind."

Mules and Men and Hurston's other folklore writings are humorous and informative collections of the conversations, sermons, and joke-telling as well as the cultural behavior, religious customs, and local characters in Florida and Louisiana. The humor and seeming triviality of the stories conceal important discussions on gender and race in community life. The discourse on race is far different from the one found in the dominant culture. In this discourse, race is not a badge of inferiority; instead it is a trick to be played on the arrogant, a way of referencing race and class, and a way of protecting the inner lives of Black people. Gender tensions rest uneasily beneath an apparent male dominance in these tales, and a sensitivity to color is also evident. These folktales establish Hurston's understanding and respect for African-American culture and her acute awareness of racial and gender constructions in rural culture.

Hurston's most famous and popular novel is *Their Eyes Were Watching God*, published in 1937 and set in the all-Black world of Eatonville, Florida. The central character is a woman, Janie, who struggles to realize her true self in a world where self-definition is filtered through race and gender. It is an African-American world to be sure, but within that world there are those who seek their identity, and therefore their freedom, in models drawn from the white, male-dominated world outside of Eatonville. The idioms and foundation for their freedom are sought in that external world and are then interpreted within a Black context. Janie's grandmother, her first two husbands, and some members of the community seek to impose lifestyles and definitions of self on Janie that restrict and confine her. Hurston explores and unpacks the basis of spiritual and physical freedom in this story.

Freedom in this work is intimately tied to the question of land and how land is a symbol for freedom, yet land must be shared in common. Janie (and through her Zora) saw the world through community eyes, and that structured how she conceived love, ownership of property, justice, and labor. For Janie, freedom remains an elusive quest as long as she is outside or above the Black community. Only when she is part of a whole community, one in which men and women work in concert with the human needs of each other, can she be free to be herself.

Throughout the narrative, freedom for Nanny Crawford, Logan Killicks, and Jody Starks, people central to Janie's life, is defined in material terms. For Janie, freedom means love and fulfillment, and she first witnesses both in the pollination of the pear tree. For Nanny, who has only known the horrors of slavery and the meaning of women's oppression, the major concern and fear is that Janie will live a similar life of despair and deprivation. She knows that women have often been a "spit cup" for men and white folks. Marriage and security represent freedom for Nanny and escape for Janie. Deprived of material security, Nanny knows that property and class offer protection in the white world and position in the Black world. It is not that she wants to make Janie literally "like white folks"; she wants what white represents. She forces Janie, therefore, to marry the aged but wealthy (as defined by the Black community) Logan Killicks.

Killicks takes Janie to a lonely and isolated existence, away from people, unconnected to anyone; she is simply another piece of property. She is not free to be a person, and neither is he. Killicks stifles Janie, and the environment robs her of any lifegiving force. She runs away with the handsome Jody Starks, hoping to find her freedom in his promise of love. Jody plans to be a big man with a big voice. He buys land, builds a town, installs himself as the head official, and puts Janie on a pedestal. She sits on the pedestal that Nanny envisioned for her; but she is just as alone and unsatisfied as she was on Killicks's farm. Janie is not permitted to take part in the stories that the local folk participate in because she serves as a showpiece for Jody.

Slowly the marriage dies from a lack of connectedness. Jody's deathbed scene after twenty years reveals the price he paid to be a "big man with a big voice." Janie insists that he know the mistake he made before he dies. With skillful use of Black dialect, Hurston captures the rhythm and texture of the African-American cultural spirit as Janie forces Jody to witness their life together: "You wouldn't listen. You done lived wid me for twenty years and you don't half know me atall. And you could have but you was so busy worshippin' de works of yo' own hands, and cuffin folks around in their minds till you didn't see uh whole heap uh things you could have had." In spite of

Jody's anguish and wish for silence, Janie insists on having her say: "you wasn't satisfied wid me the way Ah was. Naw! Mah own mind had tuh be squeezed and crowded out tuh make room for yours in me."

Jody dies as "the icy sword of the square-toed one had cut off his breath and left his hands in a pose of agonizing protest." Janie ponders their life together and the price Jody paid for his power and success: " 'Dis sittin in the rulin chair is been hard on Jody,' she muttered out loud. She was full of pity for the first time in years. Jody had been hard on her and others, but life had mishandled him too." Starks had bought land and set himself above the people; he was not a part of them. He had not labored with or loved with them. His model of freedom and leadership had been drawn from outside the community.

After Jody dies, leaving Janie materially secure, she enters into a relationship with Teacake, a penniless younger "ne'er-do-well," and with him she finds her freedom. Her freedom comes not as a possessor of land but as part of a community connected to the land and laboring on the land. It is a self-actualized community. The home that Teacake and Janie share on the "muck" is always alive with people. They come to gamble, tell stories, and listen to music. Janie is a part of the life there, and she wonders what Eatonville would think of her in "her blue denim overalls and heavy shoes? The crowd of people around her and a dice game on her floor!" Here she can listen and laugh and tell her own stories. Life on the "muck" shows people in motion—singing, talking, playing—with peripheral vision. It is a community where negative conflict occurs only when idioms based on color and class enter and are filtered through gender.

A careful reading of her texts reveals that, for Hurston, real freedom can only occur in a whole, self-actualized community. She explores this discussion of the meaning of freedom in texts constructed within the Black world. The white world encases this world to be sure, intruding at times with its values and definitions, but Hurston locates her focus squarely in the Black world, and this shapes her understanding of freedom, gender, and race. It is an idealized world, one where Hurston works out her views of race, class, and gender. By using this approach, Hurston addresses how gender relations are constructed in this world, the role that class plays in gender identity, and how the ways of talking about these issues are embedded in folk material. What she discovers is that while many sought their identity in the values of white society, others struggled for self-realization in the "muck" of the African-American world.

Further, Hurston's discussion of these issues connects with the larger discussion going on in the world inhabited by African-Americans: How should women manage their encounters with men and other women? How should men and women deal with Jim Crow in the North and South? How can one move up in social class and deal with the jagged edges of social mobility? How should one think about humble origins? Writers and activists such as Anna Julia Cooper, W.E.B. Du Bois, Ida B. Wells-Barnett, James Weldon Johnson, Langston Hughes, and others pondered these concerns in their writings. Massive numbers of southern peasants and northern workers were also pondering these concerns as they moved to urban communities in the North and South and struggled to define freedom in spiritual and material terms. These questions, too, are taken up in Hurston's autobiography, *Dust Tracks on a Road*.

When J. B. Lippincott approached Hurston in 1941 with the idea of writing her autobiography, her response was less than enthusiastic. She was uncomfortable exposing her inner self to the world and initially resisted the idea. The request came in the middle of her career, she protested, and her career was hardly over. Two books of folklore, two novels, and a series of articles and short stories had established her as a major literary figure. Despite her success, however, Hurston was still very dependent on patronage for her writing and artistic endeavors. Financial stability continued to be elusive. Her only means of earning additional money was to comply with Lippincott's request for the autobiography.

Katherine Mershon, a wealthy friend in California, offered her a place to live and work on the autobiography, so Hurston moved there from New York in the spring of 1941. She completed a draft of the manuscript by mid-July. However, rewriting took over half a year, which was unusual for Hurston. Her biographer, Robert Hemenway, has suggested that much rewriting became necessary after the bombing of Pearl Harbor because Hurston disliked the colonial and imperialist implications of World War II. Her dislike of war is evident in her satirical comments about American marines who "consider machine gun bullets good laxatives for heathens who get constipated with toxic ideas about a country of their own" and Americans who sang "Praise the Lord and Pass the Ammunition" (*Dust Tracks on a Road*, 1942). Lippincott deleted such passages from the final version of her autobiography. What remained and was finally published in November 1942 was a document that some have argued is the most problematic piece in Hurston's canon.

Dust Tracks on a Road is a simulated story of Hurston's life. Facts are often missing or distorted in this text. For example, she portrays herself as younger than she actually was when her mother died. She states that she was nine years old, but census records establish her age as probably thirteen. *Dust Tracks on a Road* is her life played out in full view of the white world, the world that defined images and determined which works received acceptance. It was a world in which only primitive Black people were authentic. It is the life of a woman resisting the confinement of rigid gender conventions that required the appearance of submission by women to male and white authority. In this work she attempted to discuss an idyllic childhood where neither race nor poverty was central; a disrupted family caused by the death of her mother that sent her wandering in search of education and self; the creation of a woman scholar and artist aided by patrons; and a southern individual who would not be contained or transformed. She attempts to do this in a manner acceptable to a white audience that was a necessary part of the story. What emerges from this autobiography is what her former employer, writer Fannie Hurst, called a "woman half in shadow."

Navigating between the Black and white worlds was not an easy task. If she exposed the pain and anger that Black women invariably felt when trying to enter doors blocked by racism and sexism, no admittance would ever have been possible. Her entrance into the privileged world of academic degrees would have been forever denied. Her dilemma was to unblock that passageway and at the same time retain the essence of herself that included her southern identity and her intellectual independence. In commenting on her years at Barnard, she referred to herself as Barnard's sacred Black cow. She once stated, "I feel most colored when I am thrown against a sharp white background." Her essays, "How It Feels to Be Colored Me" (1928), "The Pet Negro System" (1943), and "My Most Humiliating Jim Crow Experience" (1944), are testimony to her understanding that racism confined and restricted and that the struggle for a healthy existence is a lifelong engagement for African-Americans.

The decades of the 1940s and 1950s were not easy for Hurston. After the publication of *Seraph on the Suwanee* in 1948, she struggled to write a novel about Herod the Great, which she never completed. She left the literary world of New York and returned to Florida, where she continued to write articles for various newspapers and magazines. Her finances were low, and by the mid-1950s her health began to deteriorate.

Hurston spent some of the last years of her life responding to the U.S. Supreme Court's 1954 decision to desegregate public schools. On August 11, 1955, the *Orlando Sentinel* in Orlando, Florida, published a letter Hurston had written to express her disapproval of the court decision. For most African-Americans and Euro-Americans alike, the decision represented the culmination of over fifty years of struggle to end segregation by law. For Hurston, the decision was deplorable and an insult to her people. Hurston defended the job done by African-American teachers, arguing that unless there was some quality or facility in white schools that could not be duplicated in Black schools, there was simply no reason to desegregate. She contested, "I can see no tragedy in being too dark to be invited to a white school social affair. The Supreme Court would have pleased me more if they had concerned themselves about enforcing the compulsory education provisions for Negroes in the South as is done for white children." Embedded in these comments was the fierce racial pride that others had thought was missing from her consciousness. Recognizing that her comments would not be well received by the civil rights leadership, Hurston defended her views and made clear the basis for her opposition. She stated, "Them's my sentiments and I am sticking by them. Ethical and cultural desegregation. It is a contradiction in terms to scream race pride and equality while at the same time spurning Negro teachers and self-association."

During the last decade of her life, Hurston fell into obscurity—she was poor, ill, alone, but still proud. She remained virtually unknown for two decades after her death in 1960. Her burial in an unmarked commoner's grave belied the genius of a gifted and rich life that had once captured the hearts and minds of thousands. Her life and work yield a mosaic of gender, racial, and class images that reveals much about the mental state, social realities, and political tensions of African-American life.

[*See also* HARLEM RENAISSANCE.]

BIBLIOGRAPHY

Awkward, Michael, ed. *Their Eyes Were Watching God* (1990); Bloom, Harold. *Zora Neale Hurston's* Their Eyes Were Watching God (1987); Glassman, Steve and Kathryn Lee Seidel, eds. *Zora in Florida* (1991); Hemenway, Robert. *Zora Neale Hurston: A Literary Biography* (1977); Howard, Lillie P. *Zora Neale Hurston* (1980); Nathiri, N. Y. *Zora! A Woman and Her Community* (1991); Turner, Darwin T. *In a Minor Chord* (1971).

SELECTED WORKS BY ZORA NEALE HURSTON

Jonah's Gourd Vine (1934); *Mules and Men* (1935); *Their Eyes Were Watching God* (1937); *Tell My Horse* (1938);

Moses, Man of the Mountain (1939); *Mule Bone: A Comedy of Negro Life*, with Langston Hughes (1990); *Dust Tracks on a Road* (1942); *Seraph on the Suwanee* (1948); *I Love Myself: When I Am Laughing . . . and Then Again When I Am Looking Mean and Impressive: A Zora Neale Hurston Reader* (1979); *The Sanctified Church: The Folklore Writings of Zora Neale Hurston* (1981); *Spunk: The Selected Stories of Zora Neale Hurston* (1985).

TIFFANY R. L. PATTERSON

HUTSON, JEAN BLACKWELL (1914-)

One of the foremost librarians in the country and a noted authority on Black life and culture, Jean Hutson was born in Summerfield, Florida, on September 4, 1914, to Paul O. Blackwell and Sarah Myers Blackwell, but spent much of her early life in Baltimore. An exceptional student, she was always ahead of her classmates because of her love of reading. She graduated from high school at the age of fifteen and enrolled in the University of Michigan with the intention of studying psychiatry. However, because of the Great Depression and the high cost of medical school, Hutson, on the advice of her mother who was a great influence, transferred to Barnard College, where she received a B.A. in 1935. A year later she received a B.S. from the Columbia University School of Library Service.

Her first professional assignment following graduation was as a high school librarian in Baltimore. Later she worked for the New York Public Library system in Manhattan and in the Bronx. While in the Bronx, she observed that the Spanish-speaking people in the neighborhood had difficulty making use of library services. She subsequently began ordering materials in Spanish, which resulted in greater use of the library by residents of the neighborhood. These efforts did not go unnoticed by the administrators of the library system and led them to consider her when efforts were made to increase services to other underserved populations in the city.

In 1955, Hutson became curator of the Schomburg Collection of Negro Literature and History at the New York Public Library (now called the Schomburg Center for Research in Black Culture), where she remains. The author of many short stories and introductions to books, Hutson's proudest accomplishment was overseeing the development of the Schomburg's *Dictionary Catalog*, which has made it possible for scholars and researchers around the world

to review the collection's holdings and more easily pursue their own research interests.

During 1964-65, Hutson was assistant librarian at the University of Ghana. After her return to New York, she served as chair of the Harlem Cultural Council and lectured at City College of the City University of New York. She belonged to numerous organizations that promoted the study of the heritage of Africa. Hutson retired from the Schomburg in 1984.

BIBLIOGRAPHY

Hutson, Jean. Manuscript collection, Schomburg Center for Research in Black Culture, The New York Public Library, New York City, and manuscript collection, Clark Atlanta University, Atlanta, Georgia; Schomburg Center for Research in Black Culture. *Jean Blackwell Hutson: An Appreciation* (1984).

ARTHUR C. GUNN

HYERS, ADAH M. *see* CONCERT MUSIC

HYERS, EMMA *see* THEATER

HYMAN, FLORA (1955-1986)

"The floor wasn't a good friend of mine," said Flora Hyman when describing the demanding sport of volleyball. She was born in Inglewood, California, in 1955 and began to play volleyball as a teenager.

Hyman studied math and physical education at the University of Houston for three years. She then decided to pursue volleyball instead, thinking that she could resume her academic career later in life. Hyman was a "three-time all-American at the University of Houston and was named the outstanding collegiate player of 1976, but it was only after years of work on the United States team that she came to her full potential" (Thomas 1986). She was a member of the U.S. team in the 1978 and 1982 world championships and the world cup tournaments in 1977 and 1981. In 1983, she and the coach of the women's volleyball team, Dr. Arie Selinger, accepted the Team of the Year Award from the Women's Sports Foundation.

One of the foremost librarians in the country and a noted authority on scholarship about Blacks, Jean Blackwell Hutson was curator of the Schomburg Center for Research in Black Culture for nearly thirty years. She is shown here with Langston Hughes. [Schomburg Center]

Hyman was a dedicated athlete who insisted on learning as much as possible about the game and practicing at every opportunity. She was described as "one of the world's strongest hitters at the net, who spikes the ball the way Julius Erving dunks a basketball" (Vecsey 1983). She was faced with limited prospects as a female athlete after the U.S. team won the silver medal in the 1984 Olympics, so she and several of her teammates traveled to Japan to join a semiprofessional team, "Daiei," sponsored by a Japanese supermarket chain.

It was in Japan at a game on January 24, 1986, that Hyman died of Marfan Syndrome. She was survived by her father and seven brothers and sisters.

Hyman brought a vigor, vitality, and aggressiveness to women's athletics that helped pave the way for women in sports.

BIBLIOGRAPHY

Demark, Richard. "Marfan Syndrome: A Silent Killer," *Sports Illustrated* (February 17, 1986); *Newsweek*, Obituary (February 3, 1986); *Time*, Obituary (February 3, 1986); Thomas, Robert, Jr. "Flo Hyman Volleyball Star for the 1984 U.S. Olympic Team," *New York Times* (January 25, 1986); Vecsey, George. "America's Power in Volleyball," *New York Times Biographical Service* (October 1983).

FLORA R. BRYANT

I

INFANTICIDE AND SLAVE WOMEN

Infanticide is seemingly anomalous in the history of slavery in the United States, and yet it is highly topical in inquiries about the nature of captive women's experiences in the antebellum South. Testimonies by Black women about their attempts to determine their role as mothers and their relationship to their sexuality within the planter economy echo insistently from the past. Deeply painful and contradictory choices, such as infanticide, often were thrust upon women in their need to negotiate the brutality of forced breeding, the separation of families, sexual coercion, and material conditions adverse to the health and sustenance of human life.

Many voices attest to this reality. One Gullah woman, whose full identity is lost to us, recounted having suffered frequent beatings on the orders of her mistress, against which she claimed to have retaliated by bringing "not one nigger to Maussa" (Creel 1988). Susannah, another woman from the South Carolina Sea Islands, spoke about the pain of having her only three surviving sons sold away. In expressing her grief, she said she had been pregnant twenty-two times. What truth is encoded in the relaying of these particular experiences?

While neither woman explicitly reveals the choices made to control her fate as a mother or the fate of her children, certainly their methods included forms of contraception and abortion as a means to create sites of resistance and self/family protection within a system that routinely exploited their womanhood. Could infanticide have been one means of resistance? Certainly infanticide must be examined within the range of reproductive control that was available to, and sometimes exercised by, captive women.

One of the most explicit and widely recognized incidents of infanticide is that committed by Margaret Garner. It is Garner's story that Toni Morrison takes up in her novel *Beloved* (1987), a largely fictional, mythic revisioning of this woman's psychical experience of bondage and her desperate act. In the winter of 1856, a pregnant Margaret Garner, her husband, Simeon Garner, their four children, and her husband's parents fled from bondage in Kentucky to Cincinnati, Ohio, taking advantage of the frozen Ohio River in crossing into free territory. At the crossing they were joined by nine other fugitives from Kentucky. Soon after arriving in Cincinnati, the Garners were tracked down by a large posse, including their slaveholders and U.S. marshals who sought to restore them to bondage. Under the Fugitive Slave Law passed by Congress in 1850, slaveowners had the right to track fugitives in free states, claim and capture them, and return them to their ownership.

A fierce struggle ensued at the house of a relative, an ex-slave, where they were being temporarily sheltered, but the Garners were overcome. As a desperate defense, Margaret Garner slit the throat of her infant daughter and then took a shovel and struck two of the boys, all in an attempt to keep them from having to return to their brutal life. Garner, who was immediately brought to court, was described as appearing "very calm . . . very serene" in the wake of the tragedy (Rothstein 1987). It is recorded that she testified, "if they had given me time, I would have killed them all," bearing witness to her struggle to claim her children, even if her claim was a final and violent act. Despite attempts by abolitionists and other benevolent community members to protect the family from repatriation to Kentucky, the court ruled that Garner be restored to her former master. In a final attempt to free herself and her children, Garner threw herself and at least one child into the Ohio River as they recrossed it on their return to Kentucky. Ironically, that same river had once mercifully carried them to free territory. Their captors recovered them, and Garner eventually was sold to a planter in the Deep South and separated from her family.

Margaret Garner's story is perhaps the most thoroughly documented case of infanticide. Tracing it in the historical accounts, one finds an unusual breadth of accounts by the many people who interviewed her and reported on the trial. From these accounts emerge a historiographical pattern: the use of her case as a shocking example to support various political and social platforms on the issue of slavery. Despite this broad knowledge of Garner, there are many holes in our record of her struggles, and discrepancies, particularly in the secondary materials that are available, in the details of the case and the facts of her life. What is most painfully absent is Garner's voice—her own telling of what this act meant to her on an intimate level.

However, what we know from other cases of infanticide adds to our understanding of what the act meant to captive women both as ontological fact and response. Fannie, a slave woman characterized as being particularly defiant, was to be sold as a result of attacking her mistress and thereby be separated from her infant. One of Fannie's daughters recalled the events of the struggle that occurred when Fannie learned she was about to be sold:

> Ma took the baby by its feet, a foot in each hand, and with the baby's head swinging downward, she vowed to smash its brains out before she'd leave it. Tears were streaming down her face. It was seldom that Ma cried, and everyone knew that she meant every word. Ma took the baby with her. (Hine and Wittenstein 1981)

Although born out of a sense of pain and desperation, and a will much like that of Garner's, which was decidedly resistant to violation, Fannie's actions, however unwittingly, proved effective in gaining some measure of power over her owner and subverting his attempts to determine her fate and that of her baby. In another instance, a woman named Lucy gave birth but, supported by the attending midwife, denied ever being pregnant. Her suspicious master had her examined by a physician to see if there was any evidence of her having given birth, and when his charges were verified, a desperate search for the infant was begun. Twelve days later, the decomposing body of a newborn was uncovered. Lucy, her mother, and the midwife all were brought to court. They were never convicted of the murder, however, because the court was unable to shatter their collective defense that the child had been stillborn. Similarly, Lou Smith, a freedman from South Carolina, recounted his knowledge of a woman who had had one child after another had been sold away from her. Resolute to end this pain, she poisoned the next child she bore and determined to have no more. Smith recalled that others in the captive community knew what she had done and protected her.

Although many important details of these two incidents are lost to us, and thus prevent our being able to fully reconstruct what occurred, they do express a communal recognition that infanticide was bred by a system that unjustly exploited Black women by trying to control their sexuality and their capacity and will to be mothers. And yet, it is difficult to fully uncover how these communities contained or reconciled the moral and social contradictions that were seemingly inherent in these collaborative acts.

In combing the historiography of slavery, and searching through primary documents such as planters' journals, court depositions, narratives, and other sources, one can uncover significant evidence of infanticide. Scholars have approached this material from a range of disciplines and thus have broadened the critical framework from which to approach our many queries about the subject. Among the theoretical discourses are compelling studies that explore infanticide in relation to planter neglect and its correlation to infant mortality, specifically Sudden Infant Death Syndrome (SIDS). In addition, there has been important speculation about the relationship between material deprivation and the mental health of captive women as it affects a woman's ability to mother.

What is clear from what these incidents do reveal is the very complex and, on some level, impervious nature of captive women's experiences as chattel, as

One of the most widely recognized instances of infanticide among slave women is the case of Margaret Garner, "the modern Medea." Garner's story inspired Toni Morrison's novel Beloved. *[Library of Congress]*

mothers, as women, and as individuals within a system that exacted an inordinate price for their existence. The choice of infanticide signals a convergence of the many aspects of a particular woman's predicament as the weight of all her roles collided with a will and a need for self-determined choice.

Examining this collision in the contexts of motherhood, bondage, violence, and sexuality allows us to approach another aspect of the multifaceted experience of African-American women, because it allows us to approach the captive subject from outside the mythic, monolithic, and idealized notions of who Black women are. For does not the woman who with one hand holds her child at her breast but with the other kills her child defy simple notions of Black womanhood? We cannot read these acts simply, for they are not wholly acts of resistance, or proof of capitulation, or evidence of waywardness. An examination of infanticide insists that we redefine paradigms in approaching the broad questions of who captive women were and, thus, revise the theoretical discourse on slavery itself.

BIBLIOGRAPHY

Coleman, J. Winston, Jr. *Slavery Times in Kentucky* (1940); Creel, Margaret Washington. *"A Peculiar People": Slave Religion and Community-Culture among the Gullahs* (1988); Dannett, Sylvia G. L. *Profiles of Negro Womanhood, Volume I, 1619-1900* (1964); Genovese, Eugene. *Roll, Jordan, Roll* (1972); Harris, Middleton, et al., eds. *The Black Book* (1974); Hine, Darlene and Kate Wittenstein. "Female Slave Resistance: The Economics of Sex." In *The Black Woman Cross-Culturally*, ed. Philomena Chioma Steady (1981); *Liberator* (January-April 1856); McDougall, Marion Gleason. *Fugitive Slaves, 1619-1865* (1891); McKinley, Catherine. *Sethe and Margaret: Infanticide and the Economy of Mothering in the Narratives of Captive Women*, Master's thesis (1992); *New York Daily Tribune* (January-April 1856); Rothstein, Mervyn. "Toni Morrison, in Her New Novel, Defends Women," *New York Times* (August 26, 1987); Yanuck, Julius. "The Garner Fugitive Case," *Mississippi Valley Historical Review* (1953).

CATHERINE McKINLEY

INSTITUTE FOR COLORED YOUTH, PHILADELPHIA

The Institute for Colored Youth, the oldest private high school established for African-Americans, was founded in 1832 by a $10,000 bequest of Richard Humphreys, a Philadelphia goldsmith. A thirteen-member Quaker board was established to carry out the terms of Humphreys's will, and in early 1840 a 136-acre farm was purchased seven miles from Philadelphia by the trustees of the school. Five boys from the Shelter for Colored Orphans in Philadelphia were enrolled in this farm school. The stringent rules and regulations resulted in a series of runaways, and by 1846 the unsuccessful farm school had closed.

In 1848, a group of African-American mechanics in Philadelphia approached the Quaker board with a proposal to establish an educational institution in Philadelphia where Black students could be apprenticed with them to learn various trades and also have an opportunity to study the literary and "higher branches." The board agreed to the proposal, and by 1849 a Black man, Ishmael Locke, was hired as a teacher for the evening school that opened in South Philadelphia. Within a month, thirty pupils were enrolled, and by the end of the 1850 term forty-three boys had attended. With the success of this venture, the Black tradesmen were able to convince the Quaker managers to establish a day school that would be available to both boys and girls. In 1852, a building was erected at Sixth and Lombard streets in the heart of the Philadelphia Black community and named the Institute for Colored Youth (ICY). Charles A. Reason, a distinguished African-American educator from New York, was named principal, and Grace A. Mapps, also of New York, was named head of the female department.

Under Reason's principalship the institute developed into a strong academic institution. Reason was succeeded as principal in 1856 by Ebenezer Bassett, a graduate of Connecticut State Normal School and a former student at Yale College. Bassett continued the high academic standards of the school. Because the school offered a classical, college preparatory curriculum, the institution drew attention from persons throughout the nation, and visitors to Philadelphia frequently stopped by the school to observe the students. In 1869, Bassett was appointed U.S. minister to Haiti, and he was replaced by Fanny Jackson, an 1865 Oberlin College graduate. Fanny Jackson (later Coppin) joined the faculty of the institute in 1865 as principal of the female department. Her skills as a teacher were quickly recognized, and her appointment as principal of the entire school resulted in her

heading the school for thirty-two years, until she retired in 1901.

During Coppin's principalship the institute grew to attract a national and international student body and always maintained a long waiting list of applicants. The all-Black faculty represented some of the best-educated Black Americans of the time, including Mary Jane Patterson, the first Black woman college graduate (Oberlin 1862); Richard T. Greener, the first Black graduate of Harvard University (1870); and Edward Bouchet, the first Black person to earn a Ph.D. (Yale 1876, physics). As a result of the institute's strong science faculty, numerous male and female students became physicians. In addition, the strong teacher-training program of the institute contributed to producing most of the Black teachers in the Philadelphia and New Jersey areas.

When Coppin retired as principal in 1901, the Quaker managers were persuaded by Booker T. Washington to abolish the classical thrust of the institution and replace it with a more industrial curriculum. Consequently, ICY closed its doors in Philadelphia in 1902 and moved to Cheyney, Pennsylvania, where it subsequently became Cheyney State College.

[See also COPPIN, FANNY JACKSON.]

BIBLIOGRAPHY

Conyers, Charlene. "A History of the Cheyney State Teachers College, 1837-1951," Ed.D. diss (1960); Coppin, Fanny Jackson. *Reminiscences of School Life and Hints on Teaching* (1913); Perkins, Linda M. *Fanny Jackson Coppin: The Institute for Colored Youth, 1865-1902* (1987).

LINDA M. PERKINS

INSTRUMENTALISTS

The following table lists pioneer Black female instrumentalists, with their pre-1940 band/orchestral affiliation.

STRING PLAYERS	
Violin	
Pamora Banks (12)	Penelope Johnson (10)
Grazia Bell (11)	Lelia Julius (12)
*Mae Brady (11)	Florence Lewis (14)
Marjorie Ferrell (11)	*Gertrude E. Martin (10) (11)
Elizabeth Foster (plus mandolin and bass) (1)	Pamela Moore (12)
	Mazie Mullen (7)
Mildren Franklin (2)	Julia Lewis Nickerson (plus cello) (14)
Marie Guilbeau (14)	
Emma Harris (14)	Gertrude Palmer (18)
Ruth Jackson (10)	Alberta Riggs (15)

Angelina Riviera (10)
(Mrs.) Jesse Scott (1)
Dorothy Smith (9)

Jean Taylor (12)
Marie Wayne (2) (10)

Viola

Maude Shelton (2)

Cello

Minnie Brown (2) (10)

String Bass

Marge Backstrom (12)
Jamesetta Humphrey (11)
Lillian Humphrey (11)
Gertrude H. Martin (7) (11)

*Olivia Porter Shipp (plus cello)
(2) (7) (10) (11)
Gwen Twiggs (13)

Harp

Myrtle Hart (1)

Olivette Miller (11)

Guitar/Banjo/Ukulele

*Minnie ("Memphis Minnie")
Douglas (11)
Laura Dukes (11)
Vanzula ("Van") Carter
Hunt (11)

Betty Lomax (7)
Fanny Wiley (1)

WIND PLAYERS

Cornet/Trumpet

*Viola Allen (19)
*Estella Harris (18)
*Leora Meoux Henderson
(2) (5) (7) (11) (16)
*Gertrude Irene Howard (3)
(15)
Gertrude Hughes (11)
Laurie Johnson (11)
(Mrs.) Roper Johnson (20)

*Dolly Jones (Armendar) (11)
(16)
Dyer Jones (11)
Nettie Lewis (20)
Carrie Melvin (plus violin) (11)
Alice Proctor (13)
Mary Shannon (12)
Mattie Simpson (11)
*Valaida Snow (11)

Saxophone

Margaret Backstrom (12)
Mildred Creed (11)
Lula Edge (12)
Gertrude Grigsby (11)
Ophelia Grigsby (11)
Hattie Hargrow (20)
Elizabeth King (12)

Helen Murphy (11)
*Alma Long Scott (8) (16)
Gladys Seals (7)
*Isabele Taliaferro Spiller (plus
trumpet) (4) (11)
May Yorke (11)
Irma Young (11)

Clarinet

Bea Acheson (11)

Geneva Moret (11)

Trombone

Nettie Goff (11)
*Marie Lucas (2) (11)
Susie Stokes (20)

Della Sutton (6) (7)
Anna Wells (20)

Baritone

Ada Low (20)

Tuba

Ella Clifford (20)

PERCUSSIONISTS

Lottie Brown (2)
Jennie Byrd (13)
Alice Calloway (2)
Mary Alice Clarke (11)
Clothilde Hart (1)
Hazel Hart (1)

Bettie May (11)
*Marian Pankey (17)
Beverly Sexton (11)
Florence Sturgess (2)
Maggie Thompson (19)

KEY

* indicates group leader
(1) Family Orchestra
(2) Lafayette Theatre Ladies Orchestra
(3) Chicago Colored Women's Band
(4) Excelsior Temple Band
(5) The Vampires
(6) Della Sutton's All-Girls Band
(7) Negro Women's Orchestral and Civic Association
(8) American Creolians
(9) Cleveland Women's Orchestra
(10) Martin-Smith Music Schools Orchestra/Ladies Staff Orchestra
(11) Mainstream (Male-Dominated Orchestra)
(12) Harlem Playgirls
(13) Dixie Sweethearts
(14) Nickerson Ladies Orchestra
(15) N. Clark Smith's Ladies Mandolin & String Club Ladies Orchestra
(16) Lil Hardin Armstrong's All-Girl Orchestra
(17) Marian Pankey's Female Orchestra
(18) Estella Harris's Jass Band
(19) Colored Female Brass Band (East Saginaw, Michigan)
(20) Bailey's Female Brass Band

D. ANTOINETTE HANDY

INTERNATIONAL COUNCIL OF WOMEN OF THE DARKER RACES

Our object is the dissemination of knowledge of peoples of color the world over, in order that there may be a larger appreciation of their history and accomplishments and so that they themselves may have a greater degree of race pride for their own achievements and touch a greater pride in themselves. The constitution declares that the membership shall be one hundred fifty American women of color and fifty foreign women of color. . . .

A most interesting Committee of Seven . . . for the past year have been studying conditions on the West Coast of Africa paying special attention to Sierra Leone. Liberia and Ethiopia and also questions of India have come in for study as well as several books of great importance on conditions of American Colored people. (Margaret Murray Washington, 1924)

The historical notes written in 1924 by Margaret Murray Washington (wife of Booker T. Washington) captured the essence of Black women's commitment to the "racial uplift" movement of the late nineteenth and early twentieth century. Through their organizational life, the leaders of the Black women's club movement created a powerful network of women of color. This historic movement began in Boston in 1895 when a convention of Black women—organized at the urging of Josephine St. Pierre Ruffin, president of the New Era Club—resulted in the formation of a National Federation of Afro-American Women. In 1896, the National Association of Colored Women (NACW) was formed as a result of the merging of the Federation and Mary Church Terrell's National League of Colored Women of Washington, D.C. Terrell was elected the first president of NACW and later held the position of second vice-president of the International Council of Women of the Darker Races. The council, an outgrowth of the Black women's club movement, was created in the early 1920s to advance racial pride through the study and dissemination of information about people of color. Black clubwomen believed that their efforts to inform and be informed would lead to a greater appreciation and understanding of the races. The desire for connections to other women of color was articulated through this small, short-lived organization, the International Council of Women of the Darker Races. Members of the council were among the former leaders of the NACW who understood the role education could play in liberation struggles throughout the world. The leadership of the council was in the hands of Margaret Murray Washington, its first president and the former president of NACW (1914-18).

Margaret Washington (1865-1925) was born in Macon, Georgia, to a poverty-stricken family that included ten children. She began teaching at age fourteen, graduated from Fisk University in 1889, and during the same year became the Director of Girls' Industries and later Dean of Women at Tuskegee

Institute. She became Booker T. Washington's third wife in 1893, and was to become an important force, along with her husband, in the building of Tuskegee Women's Club. In addition to organizing the council, she was responsible for the development of a course at Tuskegee on the conditions of women in foreign lands.

Correspondence from some of the women on the council reveals Washington to have been the catalyst and sustaining force in the development of the council and its activities. A letter written by Addie Hunton of Brooklyn, New York, prominent clubwoman and later active in the Young Women's Christian Association and the National Association for the Advancement of Colored People, praised Washington's persistent "efforts to stimulate interest in the Council for the study of race literature and the many books now being published on the subject of race" (Hunton 1925). In the same letter Hunton admitted how difficult it was to be active in yet another organization. Study groups and other community and club work made major time demands on this select group of women, who had been very active during the previous two to three decades. However, most members shared the sentiments Hunton expressed in a letter to Washington in 1924: "I want you to know my heart is with you and that I will stand close beside you in whatever you undertake. As I study present day problems and touch them, I am more and more convinced that we need just such an organization as you are fostering." She also expressed her desire for the council to send goods to Germany at Christmas. "If we are to be a part of the world's program and find favor for our needs we must also learn to share our little."

Lugenia Burns Hope, founder of the Neighborhood Union in 1908 and active clubwoman, also encouraged Washington's leadership while acknowledging the importance of the council. In an emotional appeal, Hope begged Washington not to permit the organization to function another year without her undivided attention. Having gained experience both locally and nationally, Hope realized that the council could be the vehicle through which to promote race literature in the public schools. The formation of study groups, which were called Committees of Seven, became the organizational strategy for curriculum integration projects in what we would now call Black Studies. Teachers were organized; recommended reading lists were distributed; discussions were held; and school boards were lobbied.

Understanding the conditions and status of women and children in West Africa, Haiti, Cuba, and India was also a concern addressed by the council's study groups through field trips to selected countries and fund-raising campaigns for international educational projects. One such project cooperated with the Chicago Women's Club in 1924 by supporting the efforts of Adelaide Casely-Hayford, wife of African nationalist Joseph Casely-Hayford, to build a school in Sierra Leone, West Africa.

The importance of this historic organization as part of the general history of the Black women's club movement has not been determined. This is due in part to the paucity of information on the council. However, the historical evidence suggests a profound understanding on the part of these clubwomen of the importance of analyzing the intersection of race and gender on a global basis. According to Beverly Guy-Sheftall, "this forward looking organization is reminiscent of recent attempts by contemporary Black feminists to establish linkages with other women of color throughout the world and to struggle for the elimination of sexism on a global level" (Guy-Sheftall 1986). The desire to understand and bond with other women of color across geographical boundaries is yet another manifestation of both feminist and Pan-African impulses on the part of earlier Black women activists.

BIBLIOGRAPHY

Guy-Sheftall, Beverly. "Remembering Sojourner Truth: On Black Feminism," *Catalyst* (Fall 1986); Mary Church Terrell papers, Moorland-Spingarn Research Center, Howard University, Washington, D.C.: Letter from Lugenia Burns Hope to Mrs. Margaret M. Washington (January 5, 1925); Letter from Addie W. Hunton to New York members of the National Association of Colored Women (March 24, 1925); Letter from Addie W. Hunton to Mrs. Margaret M. Washington (August 5, 1924).

ELEANOR HINTON HOYTT

INTERNATIONAL LADIES' AUXILIARY, BROTHERHOOD OF SLEEPING CAR PORTERS

These Black women trade unionists believed the American labor movement was not only for men but also for their wives and families. "Marching Together" (the title of the auxiliary's official anthem), the wives and female relatives of sleeping car porters, attendants, and maids helped the Brotherhood of Sleeping Car Porters (BSCP) American Federation of Labor become the first successful national Black trade union. Membership figures varied, but in 1945 the auxiliary had more than 1,500 dues-paying members in the United States and Canada. Chicago, the largest local, claimed nearly 175 members, while smaller districts such as Portland, Norfolk, and St. Paul had core memberships of more than forty. Active between 1925 and 1957, the auxiliary also affiliated with the National Women's Trade Union League and American Federation of Women's Auxiliaries to Labor.

The Hesperus Club of Harlem became the first auxiliary in October 1925, with the encouragement of A. Philip Randolph, publisher of the *Messenger* and general organizer of the six-week-old BSCP. Other women's groups soon followed, along with Brotherhood locals in Philadelphia, Washington, D.C., Chicago, St. Louis, Omaha, Kansas City, Los Angeles, and elsewhere. For twelve years these auxiliaries, known formally as the Colored Women's Economic Councils, kept the faith during the "dark days" of the union's struggle for recognition.

Council activities varied with the Brotherhood's needs and differing locales. The new union always needed money. Often evicted, frequently without funds for heat and light, the struggle to keep the union going often fell to the councils. Using fund-raising methods learned in church and other women's groups, they sponsored dances, bazaars, silver teas, chitterlings and chicken dinners, and apron and pajama sales to send Brotherhood officials on cross-country organizing tours. When Randolph and other organizers arrived in Washington, D.C., for example, Brotherhood women such as Rosina Corrothers Tucker (1881–1987) housed and fed them. Lucy Bledsoe Gilmore, a porter's widow who sold insurance at the St. Louis Pullman yards and who was a popular speaker, had a knack for collecting large sums—even from Pullman Company spies—by passing the hat at mass meetings. In Los Angeles, Mrs. Tinie Upton, a Pullman maid fired for her labor activities, collected union dues and with her husband, a Pullman porter, preached the Brotherhood to the unconverted.

The Women's Economic Councils operated as local units until 1938, when President Randolph called women together in Chicago to found the International Ladies' Auxiliary Order to the Brotherhood of Sleeping Car Porters, "the first international labor organization of Black women in the world" as Tucker wrote in her unpublished autobiography. Delegates from twenty-seven cities elected Halena Wilson as president, Rosina Corrothers Tucker as secretary-treasurer, and recognized twelve other faithful wives with international offices. Brotherhood President Randolph became the international counselor to the auxiliary, maintaining his central advisory role in the women's organization.

Under the international structure, President Wilson, with Counselor Randolph's approval, developed a three-part program of organization, legislation, and cooperation designed to educate Black women about the labor movement. The Ladies' Auxiliary believed labor solidarity meant family unity. The Brotherhood brought domestic security to porters' families through increased wages and better working conditions for husbands. The assumption was that women should take responsibility for the labor movement because women spent 85 percent of the family income; wives should spend their husbands' wages on union-label goods and services to guarantee organized labor's success. Members studied the consumers' cooperative movement; the Chicago and Denver auxiliaries founded cooperative buying clubs. One meeting each month focused on workers' education; each summer as many as a dozen members or their daughters received labor school scholarships to learn labor history, economics, union leadership, public speaking, and union homemaking.

Securing passage of federal and state legislation to advance labor and civil rights causes constituted the second part of the auxiliary's program. At each biennial convention, the Ladies' Auxiliary passed resolutions on poll taxes, lynching, lily-white primaries, the Fair Employment Practice Committee, desegregation of the armed forces, the Taft-Hartley Act, extending the Social Security Act to domestic and agricultural workers, and other current issues. As trade unionists, they voted against the Equal Rights Amendment and in favor of eight-hour-day labor laws for women. Through the auxiliary's page of the *Black Worker* the legislative committee kept members informed of recent congressional actions. President Wilson, a member of the executive board of the Chicago Women's Trade Union League, lobbied for legislation regularly in the state capital. Addie Booth of Seattle worked tirelessly for passage of a Washington State Fair Employment Practice Committee bill.

Armed with new consciousness, many porters' wives joined in labor and civil rights struggles. In Washington, D.C., they helped organize commercial laundry workers; in St. Louis and Oakland, they picketed discriminatory public utilities and defense plants; and in Little Rock, Arkansas, they often drove the Black students who desegregated Central High School.

Auxiliary membership was open to wives and women relatives of any Brotherhood member, without regard to race, creed, or color. In Los Angeles, Mrs. T. B. Soares, wife of the local BSCP secretary-treasurer, and other Mexican-American and Filipino women joined; in Canada, several white women participated in the auxiliary. Pullman maids and other female members of the Brotherhood received complimentary auxiliary membership; Ada V. Dillon, a former Pullman maid on the Twentieth Century Limited, became president of the New York Ladies' Auxiliary in 1946. Husband-wife teams formed the leadership in several local auxiliaries and brotherhoods, but most union officials' spouses were rank-and-file members.

Before the Brotherhood gained recognition in 1937, porters earned less than $75 per month. Their wives often worked as domestics, laundresses, and seamstresses; Nora Fant, Auxiliary Executive Board member from Jersey City, New Jersey, also belonged to Local No. 25 of the International Ladies' Garment Workers Union. During World War II, many did defense work—jobs opened up as a result of Randolph's successful pressure on President Franklin D. Roosevelt to issue Executive Order 8802 banning race (but not sex) discrimination in defense industries. By 1949, porters' annual wages were in the top quarter of median Black family incomes. The majority of auxiliary members were housewives, some held secretarial and factory operative jobs, and a very few held professional jobs or owned small businesses.

The Ladies' Auxiliary Constitution declared subordination to the Brotherhood, but men and women contested women's proper role in the union. Many men objected when Randolph announced he would encourage women to join the union's fight, believing that women's participation would complicate matters. In some locals, Brotherhood men appear to have deliberately sabotaged the women's efforts; in other locals, a few in the Ladies' Auxiliary insisted they had a right to attend the men's union meetings and to vote. Yet when the Chicago auxiliary debated the Brotherhood in 1951 on "Who Makes a Better Union Member, Man or Woman?" the women won by a majority vote.

BIBLIOGRAPHY

Anderson, Jervis B. *A. Philip Randolph: A Biographical Portrait* ([1973] 1986); Bracey, John, and August Meier, eds. *The Brotherhood of Sleeping Car Porters Series A: Holdings of the Chicago Historical Society and the Newberry Library, 1925-1969* (1990); Brazeal, Brailsford. *The Brotherhood of Sleeping Car Porters: Its Origin and Development* (1946); Harris, William Hamilton. *Keeping the Faith: A. Philip Randolph, Milton P. Webster, and the Brotherhood of Sleeping Car Porters, 1925-1937* (1977); McKissack, Frederick. *A Long Hard Journey: The Story of the Pullman Porter* (1989); Pfeffer, Paula F. *A. Philip Randolph: Pioneer of the Civil*

These two line drawings come from the sheet music of Rosina Corrothers-Tucker's "Marching Together."
The chorus says it all: "We're the Auxiliary, the ladies' Auxiliary of the B.S.C.P. Together we are
marching proudly; Proudly marching as one pow'rful band; Singing our Union songs so loudly that they
vibrate throughout the land. We are determined and won't turn away, But will steadfastly face the new
day; And courage and unity shall lead us to victory." [M. Chateauvert]

Rights Movement (1990); Santino, Jack. *Miles of Smiles, Years of Struggle: A Folklore Study of Pullman Porters* (1989); Santino, Jack with Paul Wagner. Rosina Tucker, narrator. *Miles of Smiles, Years of Struggle: The Untold Story of the Black Pullman Porter.* Benchmark Films (1982); Tucker, Edgar Edgerton. "Brotherhood of Sleeping Car Porters, 1945-1961." M.A. thesis (1963); Wilson, Joseph F., ed. *Tearing Down the Color Bar: An Analysis and Documentary History of the Brotherhood of Sleeping Car Porters* (1989).

MANUSCRIPT COLLECTIONS

Bancroft Library. C. L. Dellums Papers. Brotherhood of Sleeping Car Porters Papers. U. of California, Berkeley, California; Chicago Historical Society. International Ladies' Auxiliary Papers. Brotherhood of Sleeping Car Porters Papers. Chicago, Illinois; Leadership Conference on Civil Rights. Rosina Corrothers Tucker Papers. Rosina C. Tucker, "My Life As I Have Lived It." Private collection, Washington, D.C.; Library of Congress, Manuscript Division. A. Philip Randolph Papers. Brotherhood of Sleeping Car Porters Papers. Washington, D.C.; Newberry Library. Pullman Company Records. Chicago, Illinois; New York Public Library. Schomburg Center for Research in Black Culture. Benjamin McLaurin Papers. New York City.

M. MELINDA CHATEAUVERT

INTERNATIONAL SWEETHEARTS OF RHYTHM

The International Sweethearts of Rhythm was a late 1930s-40s Black female swing band that was conceived, created, and managed (initially) by Laurence C. Jones. The band was originally based at Piney Woods Country Life School (founded in 1909 by Jones) in Piney Woods, Mississippi. A work-your-way-through coeducational institution (elementary, secondary, and, for a brief period, junior college), the

Even while they still represented Piney Woods Country Life School, the International Sweethearts of Rhythm broke attendance records at such places as Washington, D.C.'s Howard, Chicago's Regal, and Detroit's Paradise theaters, as well as Los Angeles's Plantation Club. When the group went on to the "big time," seasoned performer Annie Mae Winburn was brought from Omaha, Nebraska, to front the band. [Schomburg Center]

doors of Jones's school were open to the materially impoverished, social misfits, physically disabled, and the blind as well as the more affluent. Jones began sending out Piney Woods singing groups in the early 1920s on fund-raising missions of the school. Noting the tremendous public response to the all-girl, all-white orchestras, including the Hormel Girls Caravan (Darlings of the Airwaves), Phil Spitalny, and Ina Ray Hutton orchestras, Jones decided to celebrate girls of tan and brown orchestrally. A fourteen- to sixteen-piece girls' swing band was culled from the school's forty-five-piece marching and concert bands, led by Piney Woods graduate Consuella Carter, who offered musical instruction on all instruments. The swingsters, whose ages ranged from fourteen to nineteen, became the school's primary musical messengers and fund-raisers during the 1938-39 school year. Thus began the extraordinary saga of the International Sweethearts of Rhythm. Originally appearing at dances, conventions, winter resorts, and all-day frolics throughout the South, by the winter of 1940 the band was completing a nationwide tour and competing successfully in various band polls (otherwise exclusively male).

The roster included saxophonists Willie Mae Wong, Alma Cortez, twins Irene and Ione Grisham, and sisters Lucy and Ernestine Snyder; trumpeters Sadie Pankey and Nova Lee McGee; trombonists Helen Jones, Ina Belle Byrd, and sisters Lena and Corine Posey; pianist Johnnie Mae Rice; bassist Bernice Rothchild; drummer Pauline Braddy; vocalist Virginia Audley; and entertainer Nina de la Cruz. Multitalented Edna Armstead Williams was designated leader/vocalist. Brought from Omaha, Nebraska, to chaperon was Rae Lee Jones and from Ohio, as instructor in academic subjects, Vivian Crawford. Joining the band (and the school) later were saxophonists Helen Saine, and sisters Judy and Grace Bayron. The first non-Piney Woods student to join the band was saxophonist Jennie Lee Morse; the second, vocalist Evelyn McGee.

Traveling in a unique palatial semitrailer, the band was soon declared one of the nation's best draws—a sweetheart for the box offices. They were breaking attendance records at such places as the District's Howard, Chicago's Regal, and Detroit's Paradise Theatres, as well as Los Angeles's Plantation Club. Replacements on all instruments remained on call back at Piney Woods Country Life School. By early 1941, school officials and supporters were raising questions about the girls' academic development. The girls were questioning graduation possibilities, as well as their wages. In April 1941, the following headline appeared in the Black press: "Seventeen-Girl Band Which Quit School at Piney Woods, Rehearses for Big Time." Homebase was now Arlington, Virginia. Seasoned performer Annie Mae Winburn was brought in from Omaha, Nebraska, to front the band. Veteran arranger Eddie Durham was brought in as music director, to be followed by Jesse Stone and Maurice King. Appearances now included New York City's Apollo Theatre and the Savoy Ballroom; cross-country tours continued. Most memorable was a 1945 six-month United Service Organizations (USO) tour of France and Germany.

The first member who was not Black was trumpeter Toby Butler, who joined in 1943. Following one year later was saxophonist Rosalind Cron. Other non-Black members included trumpeters Mim Polak, Nancy Brown, Norman Carson, and Flo Dreyer; saxophonist Pat Stulken; and drummer Fagel Lieberman. Other Black performers who appeared on the band's roster before its demise in 1949 included saxophonists Vi Burnside, Marge Pettiford, Amy Garrison, Myrtle Young, and Geneva Perry; trumpeters Ernestine "Tiny" Davis, Marian Carter, Johnnie Mae Stansbury, Ray Carter, Jean Starr, and Augusta Perry; trombonists Jean Travis and Esther Cooke; bassists Lucille Dixon, Helen Coles, Margo Gipson, and Edna Smith; guitarists Roxanna Lucas and Carline Ray; pianist Jackie King; and vocalists Betty Sheppard and Betty Givens. Following three decades of undeserved obscurity, the International Sweethearts of Rhythm were saluted at the Third Women's Jazz Festival (March 1980) in Kansas City, Missouri, where pianist Marian McPartland released her booklet "The Untold Story of the International Sweethearts of Rhythm." Its activities were chronicled in D. Antoinette Handy's 1981 publication *Black Women in American Bands and Orchestras* and its history documented in her 1983 publication *The International Sweethearts of Rhythm*. In 1984, Rosetta Records released a two-record album of sixteen cuts. The thirty-minute film *International Sweethearts of Rhythm*, produced and directed by Geta Schiller and Andrea Weiss, was released in 1986.

BIBLIOGRAPHY

Handy, D. Antoinette. *Black Women in American Bands and Orchestras* (1981), and *International Sweethearts of Rhythm* (1984).

D. ANTOINETTE HANDY

INVENTORS

Women inventors have often been overlooked in the history of invention. The word *inventor* itself carries definite masculine overtones, and reference works use exclusively the inventions of men as examples of the act or process of inventing. Yet there have been women inventors throughout American history. As early as 1715, patents were granted by the British government to Thomas Masters for "a new invention found out by Sybilla, his wife, for cleaning and curing the Indian Corn growing in the several colonies in America," and in 1809 Mary Kies, another white woman, received a U.S. patent for a process of weaving silk.

African-American women have been successful in this field, demonstrating creativity and problem-solving skills that have been recognized by U.S. patents over the years. There have been obstacles, however. Just as African-American men often faced discrimination in getting their new ideas tried and accepted, so did these women face the obstacle of race. In addition, they confronted discrimination against women in a domain that, because it required mechanical and technical skills, was thought to be for men only. Because they were not expected or encouraged to be interested in technology, women were generally excluded from studies and opportunities in this field. African-American women, then, had three hurdles to overcome—resistance to new ideas (one that all inventors face), discrimination because of race, and discrimination because of gender. Added to all this is the cost of patenting, which could involve making a model or having drawings made by a draftsperson. Many talented Black women may not have had the financial resources to complete applications for patents.

Without the mechanical or technical apprenticeships, training, and experience that men had, women have had to rely on creative spirits and the determination to turn ideas for solving problems into the solutions themselves. Not infrequently, they have been unable to exploit their inventions to the fullest.

Ellen Elgin is an example. In the 1880s, Elgin, who lived in Washington, D.C., and was a member of the Women's National Industrial League, invented a clothes-wringer. She sold her invention to an agent for $18, and he manufactured it. The clothes-wringer was a success, and Elgin was asked why she sold it so cheaply. She had, after all, devoted years of time to its development. Elgin replied that she was afraid that if it was known to be the invention of a Black woman, the wringer would not be bought by white women.

While the number of recorded inventions by African-American women is small, the variety is impressive, ranging from domestic items to complex mechanical devices to health aids.

Between 1885 and 1898, five African-American women received U.S. patents. The first was Sara E. Goode, owner of a Chicago furniture store. Goode designed a "Folding Cabinet Bed," similar to today's sofabed. The second patent awarded to an African-American woman went to Miriam E. Benjamin in 1888 for a "Gong and Signal Chair" for hotels. This chair was adopted by the U.S. House of Representatives for signaling pages.

Four years after Benjamin received her patent, Anna Mangin of Woodside, New York, patented an improved pastry fork. In that same year, a patent was awarded to Sarah Boone of New Haven, Connecticut, for an improved ironing board.

Among the inventions that were patented by African-American women in the next half century were an "Apparatus for Holding Yarn Skeins" (Julia F. Hammonds), a hair brush that permitted easy cleaning (Lydia D. Newman), a fruit press for extracting juice (Madeline Turner), a form of central heating (Alice H. Parker), and a permanent wave machine (Marjorie S. Joyner).

In 1945, Henrietta Bradbury broke new ground, going well beyond the areas of "women's work." She developed a "Torpedo Discharge Means" using compressed air.

The most prolific African-American woman inventor to date is Mary B. D. Kenner, who patented five inventions between 1956 and 1987, devices ranging from health aids to household conveniences. "It [invention] runs in my family," Kenner has said. "Both my father and grandfather were inventors, so I inherited it." Kenner's sister Mildred A. Smith is also an inventor. She received a patent grant in 1980 for a game teaching family relationships and history.

In the 1960s and 1970s, African-American women invented, among other things, a home security system (Marie Van Brittan Brown), an attachment for rotary floor washers that cleans corners and baseboards (Gertrude Downing), and a pain reliever (Mary A. Moore).

In 1980, Valerie Thomas received a patent for her "Illusion Transmitter." Her invention is a "three-dimensional illusional television-like system for transmitting an illusion of an object" before your eyes (Hayden 1992). Thomas has a degree in physics from Morgan State University and is a data analyst for the National Aeronautics and Space Administration. On the job, she has worked on the development of the Landsat image processing systems for more than ten years. The sophistication of her invention reflects the training she has received and is clear evidence of a changing situation. Even though African-American women have been inventing social and political tools for hundreds of years, their efforts to create new material realities are only just beginning to be recognized.

BIBLIOGRAPHY

Hayden, Robert C. "Valerie Thomas and Other Women Inventors." In his *9 African American Inventors* (1992); Sluby, Patricia C. "Black Women and Invention," *Sage: A Scholarly Journal on Black Women* (Fall 1989).

ROBERT C. HAYDEN

J

JACK AND JILL OF AMERICA, INC.

For the young—a chance to see where life can go. (*Up the Hill* 1988)

Jack and Jill of America, Inc., began as an African-American children's play group in Philadelphia. The club organizers were professional African-American mothers and the wives of professional African-American men. The goal was to provide their children with social, cultural, and educational programs in a time of de facto segregation in northern cities. As the club grew into a national organization, the goals expanded to include service and charitable projects of an educational, literary, and scientific nature, financed through a nationally supported foundation.

Miriam Stubbs Thomas called the first meeting of sixteen women to her Philadelphia home in January 1938. A concert pianist during the 1930s, Thomas taught piano in her own studio while her children were young. Along with several women of the Philadelphia Black elite, she agreed that most of the women who associated socially and professionally had children who did not know one another. Developing a mothers' club for children ages two to twenty-two, the women sponsored cultural events and opportunities for their children to meet and mingle. The club provided a network for parents and children. The Black elite in Philadelphia extended to networks of Black professionals in other cities, where plans to organize similar clubs were in the making. As a result, the New York chapter was founded in 1939. Like their Philadelphia friends, a group of New York City African-American mothers had been meeting and bringing their children together for activities. When Philadelphia named its group Jack and Jill, the New Yorkers decided to adopt this name also. By the time of the fiftieth anniversary in 1988, Jack and Jill of America had expanded to 187 chapters nationwide.

In less than a decade from the founding, the Jack and Jill concept had spread so quickly that a national organization became needed. The first national officers were selected in 1946, with Dorothy B. Wright of Philadelphia, president; Emilie B. Pickens of Brooklyn, vice president; Edna Seay of Buffalo, secretary-treasurer; Constance Bruce of Columbus, corresponding secretary; and Ida M. Smith Peters of Baltimore, editor of *Up the Hill*, the national journal. The chapters were organized into eight regions with emphasis on building leadership opportunities for the children. Mothers remained in the club until their children had graduated from high school and then became Jack and Jill alumni. Teen groups were organized with a leadership structure similar to that of the parent organization. Teens met with mothers at the yearly regional meetings and at the biannual national conventions.

After thirty years, Jack and Jill became one of the first national organizations of African-American women to establish a foundation. In 1968, Jacqueline J.

Robinson of the District of Columbia chaired the foundation steering committee and became the first foundation president. Articles of incorporation were drafted and the foundation announced its purpose as a self-help organization designed to help eliminate some of the contemporary obstacles that confront Black youth. Many of the projects sponsored by the foundation are centered at historically Black colleges around the nation. From 1968 to 1988, the foundation awarded $600,000 in grants to communities, serving thousands of youth, preschool to college in age. Among the projects funded in the late 1980s were the Saturday Academy at Central State University, Project "Get Smart" at Florida A & M University, the Saturday Academy at Kansas City Community College, and the Los Angeles Young Black Scholars program, cosponsored by Los Angeles chapters of Jack and Jill and 100 Black Men.

In reflecting upon the legacy of Jack and Jill over fifty years from the founding, Miriam Stubbs Thomas believes the organization has become an important link for Black leaders today. Many Jack and Jill alumni became professionals who then joined Jack and Jill chapters to promote the social and cultural development of their children. This process has continued for three generations. The organization also provides a haven for African-American parents and youth who are confronted with the loneliness of working in integrated corporate America and living in upper-middle-class communities. For African-American professionals who are still connected to Black institutions and communities, providing leadership in educational development for those in the community who are disadvantaged is a significant goal. Like the Greek organizations founded by African-American college women in the early 1900s for social reasons, Jack and Jill goals by the 1990s expanded to provide service to the larger Black community.

BIBLIOGRAPHY

Philadelphia Inquirer (April 29, 1979); Thomas, Miriam Stubbs. Personal Interview (August 1, 1991); *Up the Hill: Journal of Jack and Jill of America* (1988).

ROSALYN TERBORG-PENN

JACKET, BARBARA J. (1935-)

When Barbara J. Jacket became head coach for the U.S. women's track and field team at the 1992 Olympic games in Barcelona, Spain, she became the second African-American woman to hold that honor.

The first was Jacket's coach and mentor, Nell Jackson. No stranger to pioneering roles in athletics, Jacket holds many honors and awards as athlete, coach, and manager. In 1990, she became the first and only female athletic director in the Southwestern Athletic Conference (SWAC) when Prairie View A & M University in Prairie View, Texas, named her to that position.

Barbara Jacket, daughter of Eva Getwood, was born in Port Arthur, Texas, on December 26, 1935. She was educated at Port Arthur's Lincoln High School and then went to Tuskegee University, where her track and field abilities led to her induction into the Tuskegee Athletic Hall of Fame (1987). However, Jacket is even better known for her work as a coach. She has been named National Association of Intercollegiate Athletics (NAIA) Coach of the Year in various categories on twenty-seven different occasions. She had Olympic assistant coaching responsibilities for U.S. teams in 1973 meets in Germany, Poland, and Russia; in 1975 in Russia; and in 1977 in Bulgaria. She was assistant coach in the Pan-American games in 1979; and head coach in the World University games (Japan 1975); the World Championships (Italy 1987); and the World University games (England 1991). Her Prairie View women's track teams have won the following national championships: NAIA, 1974 and 1976; U.S. Track and Field Federation, 1975 and 1976; Track and Field Association-USA, 1979 and 1980; NAIA Indoor, 1984, 1987, and 1991; and NAIA Outdoor, 1982-90.

BIBLIOGRAPHY

Houston Defender, "PV Sports Hall of Fame Inducts 15 New Members" (May 13, 1992); *Houston Informer*, "Discipline Is the Answer for U.S. Olympic Track Coach from PV" (June 6, 1992); *Waller County Newscitizen*, "Jacket Heads to Olympics" (June 10, 1992).

JEWEL LIMAR PRESTAGE

JACKSON, MAHALIA (1911-1972)

Mahalia Jackson, destined to become one of the greatest gospel singers of all time, was born in poverty in a three-room "shotgun" shack on Water Street between the railroad tracks and the Mississippi River levee in New Orleans. She was the third of six children. Her father, John A. Jackson, was a stevedore, barber, and preacher. Her mother, Charity Clark, died at twenty-five when Mahalia was only four.

The church was always the central focus in Jackson's life, and she began singing at the age of four in the children's choir at Plymouth Rock Baptist. After her mother's death, Mahalia was raised by her mother's sisters, Mahalia "Aunt Duke" Paul, for whom Mahalia was named, and Bessie Kimble, both of New Orleans. They lived in the section of the city upriver from Audubon Park that is known today as Black Pearl.

She attended McDonough School No. 24 until the eighth grade; then she worked as a laundress and cook. She began attending Mt. Moriah Baptist Church, where she was very active, singing and "shouting its members" even before she was baptized in the Mississippi River at the age of twelve. She was also actively singing at other churches in the community. Even when she was young, her voice was recognized as something special.

As a young girl growing up in New Orleans, Jackson absorbed the musical sounds of her family's Baptist church, the Sanctified church next door, and the local legends-to-be King Oliver, Kid Ory, and Bunk Johnson. Louis Armstrong was not even in his teen years and was already playing trumpet in the New Orleans Waifs' Home Band. Famous brass bands such as the Tuxedos, Eagle, and Eureka rode around town in advertising wagons and played at funerals, picnics, fish fries, lodge parties, and parades of all types. The Mardi Indians also marched with their unique sounds on Fat Tuesday. Musicians like Jelly Roll Morton and King Oliver were playing in cabarets and cafes, and there was ragtime music on the showboats on the Mississippi.

Many people were buying gramophones at this time, and everybody had records of blues singers like Bessie Smith and Ma Rainey. Although Jackson grew up among people who were serious about religion, she was an admirer of Bessie Smith, and it was difficult not to hear the amalgam of sounds in her community. She was definitely influenced by this powerful music of the Delta.

Jackson experienced and was influenced by many styles of music at an early age; however, the most significant was that of the Sanctified church. A Sanctified church was near her home, and she could hear spirited singing and the drum, the cymbal, the tambourine, and the steel triangle. They did not have a choir or organ, however; the whole congregation participated by singing, clapping, and stamping their feet—in essence, utilizing the whole body. She has commented on several occasions that the church literally interprets the psalmist in the Bible, just as she does: "Make a joyful noise unto the Lord" and "Praise

"When you sing gospel you have a feeling there is a cure for what's wrong," said the great Mahalia Jackson, explaining her refusal to sing secular music. "But when you are through with the blues, you've got nothing to rest on." [Moorland-Spingarn]

the Lord with the instruments." Jackson also said that the powerful beat and rhythms of the Sanctified church are retentions from the antebellum era of slavery and that the music is so expressive it brought tears to her eyes. The sacred and secular sounds in her community blended together, and when she left New Orleans, she carried this African-American musical matrix with her to Chicago.

In 1927, following the traditional pattern of African-American migration, Jackson moved to Chicago, where she lived with another aunt, Hannah Robinson. She worked as a laundress, a maid in a hotel, and a date packer, and she studied beauty culture. Soon after she arrived in Chicago, she joined the choir of the Greater Salem Baptist Church. After the director heard her sing "Hand Me Down My Silver Trumpet, Gabriel," she immediately became the choir's first soloist.

During the 1930s, she toured the "storefront church circuit," singing to congregations that could not afford conventional places of worship. She married her first husband in 1935 and in later years she married and divorced again. She also became a member of a gospel quintet, the Johnson Singers, at Greater Salem Baptist Church. In addition, she caught the attention of Professor Thomas A. Dorsey, later known as the "Father of Gospel Music." Dorsey was a gospel composer and publisher, who from then on served as her mentor and publisher. He wrote over 400 songs and needed singers to sing and popularize them. Jackson, with other singers like Roberta Martin and Sallie Martin, began performing and demonstrating Dorsey's songs for the Baptist conventions and various churches around the country. Dorsey was previously the accompanist for Ma Rainey, the classic blues singer, which accounts for his musical orientation and why he and his music were shunned by some middle-class congregations.

Jackson, Dorsey, and the other talented gospel singers and composers of this period revitalized African-American religious music by extending the developments that transpired within the sanctified churches to the more established denominations. They helped bring back into African-American church music the sounds and the structure of antebellum street cries and field hollers, folk spirituals and work songs; they borrowed freely from ragtime, blues, and jazz of the secular world; they helped keep alive the stylistic and aesthetic continuum that has characterized African-American music in the United States.

Jackson was criticized for hand clapping and stomping and for bringing "jazz into the church" because it was not dignified. Of course, being the feisty person that she was, she always retaliated, usually with scripture. Her favorite psalm to justify her performance practices was "Oh clap your hands, all ye people! Shout unto the Lord with the voice of triumph!" She said she had to praise God with her whole body, and she did.

Jackson bridged the gap between the sacred and the secular in her performance without compromising her deep-rooted fundamentalist faith. Numerous persons encouraged her to abandon her commitment to gospel music and switch from the church to the nightclub circuit. After hearing her sing in church, some of her relatives offered to teach her minstrel jazz tunes, and a jazz band leader offered her $100 per week. Decca Records wanted her to sing the blues and offered her $5,000 to play at the Village Vanguard. In addition, she was offered as much as $25,000 per performance in Las Vegas clubs. She turned down all offers. Mahalia knew that basically sacred gospels

and secular blues flow from the same bedrock of experience. However, she explained the difference: "When you sing gospel you have a feeling there is a cure for what's wrong. But when you are through with the blues, you've got nothing to rest on."

Her first recording was for Decca, in 1934. The song was "God Shall Wipe Away All Tears." In 1946, she brought gospel singing out of the storefront and basement congregations by recording on the Apollo label "Move On Up a Little Higher," which sold over 8 million copies. This song made her commercially successful, and her career was launched. Jackson, who had sung gospel songs in neighborhood churches since her childhood, turned her attention from her Chicago beauty parlor to push her professional career. African-American disc jockeys played her music, African-American ministers praised it from their pulpits. When sales passed one million, the African-American press hailed Jackson as "the only Negro whom Negroes have made famous." Few Euro-Americans had ever heard her; she had come to fame by singing only in African-American communities. From the start, audiences ackowledged her, as did London's *New Statesman*, as "the most majestic voice of faith" of her generation.

The obvious sincerity of Jackson's faith and belief moves audiences even when they cannot understand the lyrics. Her warm, uninhibited contralto voice carries a strong emotional message. Jackson's sound depends on the employment of the full range of expression of the human voice—from the rough growls employed by blues singers to the shouts and hollers of folk cries to the most lyrical, floating tones of which the voice is capable. She utilized to the fullest extent half-tones, glissandi, blue notes, humming, and moaning. Her performance also embodied pronunciation that was almost of the academy one instant and of the broadest southern cottonfield dialect the next. Her style of singing has a broad rhythmic freedom and accents the lyric line to reinforce her emotional genuineness.

Many of these vocal characteristics were exemplified in Jackson's other multimillion sellers such as "Upper Room," "Didn't It Rain," "Even Me," and "Silent Night." Some of her earliest and best work, recorded originally at 78 rpm, has been reissued on LP and CD. On *Mahalia Jackson* (Grand Award 326), she sings "It's No Secret" and other songs that first gained her popularity in her own community. On *In the Upper Room* (Apollo 474), she performs "His Eye Is on the Sparrow" and, accompanied by a male quartet with a basso profundo, offers an unequaled version of the title song. She recorded about thirty albums (mostly for Columbia Records) during her career, and she acquired a dozen gold records (million sellers) from the 45 rpm records she recorded.

By the time of World War II, she was nationally known and was also recognized in many countries in Europe. After the war, with breakthroughs in communications, she became better known as a recording and performing artist. Jackson was also an entrepreneur/producer. She had her own CBS radio program and television show, which aired from 1954 to 1955. Thus she helped to prime the mass public for later gospel and soul singers. After attending beauty culture school she managed her own beauty shop, florist shop, and also owned a substantial amount of real estate. She has appeared in movies such as *Imitation of Life*, *St. Louis Blues*, *The Best Man*, and *I Remember Chicago*. Two books have been published on her life, *Movin' On Up* (1966) and *Just Mahalia, Baby* (1975).

By 1953, Jackson received international acclaim on a European concert tour. When one of her recordings won the French Academy Award, Jackson consented to the European tour, though she was not convinced that foreign audiences would understand the sacred music of her people. In Paris, she had twenty-one curtain calls. She doubled the number of her originally scheduled performances when thousands were turned away from her concerts. Greetings came from Queen Elizabeth I and Winston Churchill before an Albert Hall concert. She also gave a command performance before the king and queen of Denmark.

For years, a Mahalia Jackson concert assured promoters of sell-out crowds at Carnegie Hall in New York, where she was a favorite. In Madison Square Garden, she moved a packed house from tears to thunderous applause. At the 1958 Newport Jazz Festival, the jazz world came to Mahalia on her own terms. Thousands of jazz buffs gave her standing ovations, and when she closed with "The Lord's Prayer," the crowd stood breathless. During two days in 1960, Mahalia taped a show for the Voice of America and gave two sell-out concerts at the hall of the Daughters of the American Revolution and one in Constitution Hall. She also appeared on many television shows.

With the advent of the civil rights era, she yielded to the requests of Martin Luther King, Jr. She supported the liberation fight by traveling and singing at fund-raising rallies all over the nation with King. Mahalia Jackson would encourage the people with songs like "We Shall Overcome" and "If I Can Help Somebody." She would also quietly slip money to leaders who she believed were "for real." She emerged as one of the symbols for the movement when in 1963 millions of television viewers watched as she accompanied King at the famous March on Washington. Immediately before King began his "I Have a Dream" speech at the Lincoln Memorial, Mahalia sang "I Been 'Buked and I Been Scorned." With the lyrics of this traditional spiritual, she summed up the frustrations and aspirations of the entire movement.

As an eighth-grade drop-out, one of her major concerns was educating poor youth. She established the Mahalia Jackson Scholarship Fund and reportedly helped about fifty young adults to obtain college educations.

Jackson died of heart failure at the age of sixty in 1972. She was honored with funerals in Chicago and New Orleans and was finally entombed in Providence Memorial Park in Metairie, Louisiana. Jackson believed that she was "ordained to sing the gospel," but she did much more than just sing the gospel. She was an ambassador of goodwill wherever she traveled. People all over the world were attracted to her. Perhaps it was the simplicity of her ways; she said she was "just a good strong Louisiana woman who can cook rice so every grain stands by itself." Perhaps it was the explicit faith and conviction with which she delivered her messages in song. Jackson brought a wider acceptance and popularity to gospel music in the United States, which gave it more international prominence. She also helped make the gospel music industry a multimillion-dollar one while leaving her imprint on the African-American sacred music culture. She achieved a universality by living faithfully within the confines of a particular tradition in singing the songs of her people in her own unique style. Aretha Franklin ended the funeral service by singing for Jackson one of the songs she loved so well, "Precious Lord, Take My Hand."

BIBLIOGRAPHY

Ellison, Ralph. "As the Spirit Moves Mahalia," *Saturday Review* (September 27, 1958); Haley, Alex. "She Makes a Joyful Music," *Reader's Digest* (November 1961); Jackson, Mahalia. "I Can't Stop Singing," *Saturday Evening Post* (December 5, 1959); "Moving On Up," *Time* (February 7, 1972); "Moving On Up," *Newsweek* (February 7, 1972); "To Europe and the Holy Land with Mahalia Jackson," *Ebony* (October 1961); "Two Cities Pay Tribute to Mahalia Jackson," *Ebony* (April 1972).

DISCOGRAPHY

For a discography, see Cooper, David Edwin. *International Bibliography of Discographies* (1975).

JOYCE MARIE JACKSON

JACKSON, MARY E. *see* WORLD WAR I

JACKSON, MAY HOWARD (1877-1931)

"There is among us one woman who is far less known than is her rightful due . . . temperamental, withdrawn, and shunning publicity . . . yet endowed with unusual ability." This observation was made in *Crisis* magazine in September 1927. As is the case with great talent and vision, May Howard Jackson was a woman far ahead of her time.

She was born in Philadelphia, Pennsylvania, in 1877, the daughter of Floarda Howard and Sallie Durham. She attended public schools in Philadelphia and then entered Todd's Art School. In 1895, Jackson became the first Black woman to receive a scholarship to attend the Pennsylvania Academy of Fine Arts, where she studied for four years with William Merritt Chase, Charles Grafly, and John Joseph Boyle. After

An artist far ahead of her time, sculptor May Howard Jackson expressed in her work her fascination with the complex and varied physiognomy of Black people as a result of the mixing of the races in the aftermath of slavery. [Moorland-Spingarn]

graduating in 1899, she married William Sherman Jackson, head of the mathematics department at the M Street High School in Washington, D.C., and set up a studio in their home.

Counter to the tradition of that era, Jackson did not travel to Europe for further training as a sculptor. Some critics, such as Alain Locke, speculated that this decision might have deterred the development of her technical skills, if not her recognition and credibility as an artist. Ironically, Jackson's isolation, and the absence of direct European influences, actually freed her, both intellectually and artistically, and thus enabled her to develop a distinctly personal style. The corpus of her work centered on Jackson's own ancestry, her fascination with the complex and varied physiognomy of Black people as a result of the mixing of the races in the aftermath of slavery. Her factual execution of Black subjects was not favorably received, however, especially at a time when stereotypical images of Black people were rampant in the public arena. The generally negative attitude toward her work elicited in her immense frustration and anger.

In her portrait busts, Jackson tried to evoke more than the neoclassical training she had received at the Pennsylvania Academy of Fine Arts; she went far beyond the realist traditions of the day, imbuing her subjects with the psychological dimensions of the individual's personality, identity, and humanity. At a time when African-Americans were considered to have nothing substantive to contribute to society, portraiture of this nature was hardly appreciated.

May Howard Jackson executed numerous portrait busts in her lifetime, among them, representations of Paul Laurence Dunbar (1919), W.E.B. Du Bois, Rev. Francis J. Grimké, Kelly Miller (1929), Rev. H. M. Joseph, Sherman Jackson (1929), and W. H. Lewis. She also rendered abstract portraits, such as *Head of a Negro Child* (1929), *Mulatto Mother and Her Child* (1929), and *Shell-Baby in Bronze* (1929). Jackson was a pioneer in establishing the first stylistic movement identified by Alain Locke as a departure from "academic cosmopolitanism" in favor of a "frank and deliberate racialism." Her efforts to address, without compromise and without sentimentality, the issues of race and class, especially as they affected mulattos, make her the founder of the first movement toward an Afrocentric aesthetic.

In her active years, Jackson's successful exhibitions included the Corcoran Gallery in Washington, D.C. (1915), the Veerhoff Gallery in New York City (1919), and the National Academy of Design (1916, 1928). In 1928, Jackson won the Bronze award from the Harmon Foundation's Achievements for Negroes

In her portrait busts, May Howard Jackson went beyond the realist traditions of her day, imbuing her subjects with the psychological dimensions of individual personality, identity, and humanity. Pictured here is her bust of the Rev. Francis J. Grimké. [Moorland-Spingarn]

in the Fine Arts. The current locations of many of her sculptures are unknown, but she is represented in the Barnett-Aden Collection at Dunbar High School in Washington, D.C., and at Howard University, where she taught.

W.E.B. Du Bois, an ardent supporter of Black visual artists, eloquently eulogized Jackson in a 1931 issue of *Crisis*: "In the case of May Howard Jackson the constrictions and idiotic ramifications of the Color Line tore her soul asunder. It made her at once bitter and fierce with energy, cynical of praise, and, above all, at odds with life and people. She met rebuffs in her attempts to study and in her attempts at exhibition, in her chosen ideal of portraying the American mulatto type; with her own friends and people she faced continual doubt as to whether it was worthwhile. ... She accomplished enough to make her fame firm in our annals." Little did May Howard Jackson realize that the tenacity of her spirit, the brilliance of her vision, and the genius of her techni-

cal skills would one day make her the heir apparent to a truly original African-American imagery.

BIBLIOGRAPHY

Bardolph, Richard. *Negro Vanguard* (1961); Butcher, Margaret Just. *The Negro in American Culture* (1972); Cederholm, Theresa Dickason. *Afro-American Artists: Bio-Bibliographical Directory* (1973); *Crisis*, "Men of the Month" (June 1912), and "Poetry and Painting" (September 1927); Du Bois, W.E.B. "Postscript: May Howard Jackson," *Crisis* (October 1931); Igoe, James, and Lynn Moody. *250 Years of Afro-American Art—An Annotated Bibliography* (1981); Lewis, Samella. *Art: African American* (1978); Locke, Alain. *The Negro and His Music/Negro Art Past and Present* ([1936] 1969); Porter, James. *Modern Negro Art* ([1943] 1969).

LESLIE KING-HAMMOND

JACKSON, NELL CECILIA
(1929-1988)

Nell Cecilia Jackson, one of the pioneers in women's track and field, was born July 1, 1929, in Athens, Georgia, to Dr. Burnette and Wilhemina Jackson. The second of three children, she spent most of her early life and college days in Tuskegee, Alabama, where her father was a dentist and her mother worked at the Veterans Administration Hospital. Nell loved sports, and by the time she was fourteen she was a member of the Tuskegee Institute Track and Field Club. The club was for talented girls at both the high school and college levels and was the avenue for their entry into national meets. From then on, Nell Jackson's life revolved around track as she became a competitor, educator, coach, and official.

As a competitor, she was an All-American sprinter who was a member of the 1948 U.S. Olympic team. She competed in the first Pan-American games in 1951, placing second in the 200-meter relay and winning a gold medal as a member of the 400-meter relay team. In 1949, Jackson set an American record time of 24.2 for the 200-meter relay that lasted for six years.

Jackson received a Bachelor's degree from Tuskegee Institute in 1951, a Master's degree from Springfield College in 1953, and a Ph.D. from the University of Iowa in 1962. She taught physical education and coached track at the Tuskegee Institute, Illinois State University, the University of Illinois, and Michigan State University. She also was women's athletic director at Michigan State University and, at the time of her death in 1988, professor and director of athletics and physical education at the State University of New York at Binghamton. A renowned scholar, she wrote many track articles for periodicals and books, and she authored a definitive text, *Track and Field for Girls and Women* (1968).

In addition to her collegiate experience, she was coach of the U.S. women's track team at the 1956 Olympic games in Melbourne, Australia, the first Black head track coach of an Olympic team and, at twenty-seven, one of the youngest head coaches of any sport. Nell Jackson was also head women's track coach at the 1972 Olympic games in Munich, Germany. In 1980, she was one of five Americans selected to attend the International Olympic Academy in Olympia, Greece. In 1987, she was manager of the U.S. women's track team that competed in the Pan-American games. She also conducted innumerable track workshops and clinics all over the country.

As an official, Jackson served in many capacities. She was the first of two women to serve on the board of directors of the U.S. Olympic Committee, was a vice president of The Athletic Congress (TAC), and, at the time of her death, was secretary of TAC. She also served in varying committee assignments for the American Alliance for Health, Physical Education, Recreation, and Dance, the National Association for Girls and Women in Sports (NAGWS), and the National Collegiate Athletic Association.

Through the years Nell Jackson received many honors. She was inducted into the Black Athletes Hall of Fame, and she won the NAGWS Honor Award twice for her track contributions. Tuskegee Institute (now Tuskegee University) honored her three times, the last time with its Outstanding Alumni Award. The University of Iowa also recognized her with its Alumni Merit Award.

Nell Jackson epitomized loyalty, honesty, dedication, and excellence. Her untimely death from the flu occurred on April 1, 1988, in Binghamton, New York. She was survived by two brothers, Dr. Burnette L. Jackson, Jr., and Thomas P. Jackson, both of Philadelphia. Posthumously, on December 1, 1989, Nell Jackson was inducted into TAC's National Track and Field Hall of Fame and was awarded its highest honor, the Robert Giegengack Award, given for outstanding leadership and contributions in track and field.

BIBLIOGRAPHY

Ashe, Arthur R., Jr. *A Hard Road to Glory: A History of the African-American Athlete since 1946* (1988); Bortstein, Larry. *After Olympic Glory* (1978); Davenport, Joanna. "The Lady Was a Sprinter." Conference paper, American Alliance for Health, Physical Education, Recreation, and Dance, Atlanta, Georgia (April 19, 1985), and personal interview with Nell C. Jackson (April 1985); Green, Tina Sloan et al. *Black Women in Sports* (1981); Jackson, Nell C. *Track and Field for Girls and Women* (1968); funeral program, Tuskegee, Alabama (April 9, 1988).

JOANNA DAVENPORT

JACKSON, REBECCA COX (1795-1871)

Rebecca Cox Jackson was a charismatic itinerant preacher, the founder of a religious communal family in Philadelphia, and a religious visionary writer. Though an important example of Black female religious leadership and spirituality in the nineteenth century, she was virtually unknown after her death until the rediscovery and publication of her manuscript writings in 1981.

Jackson was born into a free Black family in Horntown, Pennsylvania, near Philadelphia. She lived at different times in her childhood with her maternal grandmother, and with her mother, Jane Cox (who died when Rebecca was thirteen). In 1830, she was married (to Samuel S. Jackson), but apparently childless, and living with her husband in the household of her older brother, Joseph Cox, a tanner and local preacher of the Bethel African Methodist Episcopal (AME) Church in Philadelphia. Jackson cared for her brother's four children while earning her own living as a seamstress.

As the result of the powerful religious awakening experience in a thunderstorm in 1830 with which her autobiography begins, Jackson became active in the early Holiness movement. She moved from leadership of praying bands to public preaching, stirring up controversy within AME church circles not only as a woman preacher, but also because she had received the revelation that celibacy was necessary for a holy life. She criticized the churches, including the AME church and its leaders, for "carnality."

Jackson insisted on being guided entirely by the dictates of her inner voice, and this ultimately led to her separation from husband, brother, and church.

After a period of itinerant preaching in the later 1830s and early 1840s, Jackson joined the United Society of Believers in Christ's Second Appearing (the Shakers), at Watervliet, New York. She was attracted by the Shakers' religious celibacy, their emphasis on spiritualistic experience, and their dual-gender concept of deity. With her younger disciple and lifelong companion, Rebecca Perot, Rebecca Jackson lived at Watervliet from June 1847 until July 1851. However, she was increasingly disappointed in the predominantly white Shaker community's failure to take the gospel of their founder, Ann Lee, to the African-American community. Jackson left Watervliet in 1851, on an unauthorized mission to Philadelphia, where she and Perot experimented with seance-style spiritualism. In 1857, she and Perot returned to Watervliet for a brief second residence, and at this time Jackson won the right to found and head a new Shaker "outfamily" in Philadelphia. This predominantly Black and female Shaker family survived her death in 1871 by at least a quarter of a century.

Rebecca Jackson's major legacy is her remarkable spiritual autobiography, *Gifts of Power*, describing her spiritual journey as a woman with a divine calling. Jackson records in vivid detail a wide variety of visionary experiences, including mysterious prophetic dreams and supernatural gifts. Her visionary writing has received recognition as spiritual literature of great power. Alice Walker has described Jackson's autobiography as "an extraordinary document" which "tells us much about the spirituality of human beings, especially of the interior spiritual resources of our mothers" (Walker 1983). In her review of Jackson's writings, however, Walker questioned the editor's speculation that Jackson's relationship with Perot, in the modern age, might have been understood as lesbian. In this context, Walker first coined the term "womanism" to distinguish a specifically Black feminist cultural tradition that includes women's love for other women but is not separatist.

BIBLIOGRAPHY

Braxton, Joanne. *Black Women Writing Autobiography* (1989); Duclow, Geraldine. "The Philadelphia Shaker Family," *Shaker Messenger* (forthcoming); Hull, Gloria T. "Rebecca Cox Jackson and the Uses of Power," *Tulsa Studies in Women's Literature* (Fall 1982); Humez, Jean McMahon. *Gifts of Power: The Writings of Rebecca Cox Jackson, Black Visionary, Shaker Eldress* (1981), and "Visionary Experience and Power: The Career of Rebecca Cox Jackson." In *Black Apostles at Home and Abroad*, ed. David M. Wills and Richard Newman (1982); McKay, Nellie Y. "Nineteenth-Century Black Women's Spiritual Autobiographies: Religious Faith and Self-Empowerment." In *Interpreting Women's Lives: Feminist Theory and Personal Narratives*, ed. Personal Narratives Group (1989); Sanders, Cheryl J., Katie G. Cannon, Emilie M. Townes, M. Shawn Copeland, bell hooks, and Cheryl Townsend Gilkes. "Roundtable Discussion: Christian Ethics and Theology in Womanist Perspective," *Journal of Feminist Studies in Religion* (1984); Sasson, Diane. "Life as Vision: The Autobiography of Mother Rebecca Jackson." In *The Shaker Spiritual Narrative*, ed. Sarah D. Sasson (1983); Walker, Alice. "Gifts of Power: The Writings of Rebecca Cox Jackson." In her *In Search of Our Mothers' Gardens* (1983); Williams, Richard E. *Called and Chosen: The Story of Mother Rebecca Jackson and the Philadelphia Shakers* (1981). Jackson's manuscripts are in the Shaker collections of the Western Reserve Historical Society, Cleveland, Ohio; the Library of Congress; and the Berkshire Athenaeum, Pittsfield, Massachusetts.

JEAN McMAHON HUMEZ

JACOBS, HARRIET ANN (1813-1897)

Harriet Ann Jacobs is now known as the author of *Incidents in the Life of a Slave Girl: Written by Herself* (1861), the most important slave narrative by an African-American woman. Jacobs is also important because of the role she played as a relief worker among Black Civil War refugees in Alexandria, Virginia, and Savannah, Georgia. Throughout most of the twentieth century, Jacobs's autobiography was thought to be a novel by a white writer, and her relief work was unknown. With the 1987 publication of an annotated edition of her book, however, Jacobs became established as the author of the most comprehensive antebellum autobiography by an African-American woman.

Harriet Ann Jacobs was born into slavery in Edenton, North Carolina, in 1813. Her mother was Delilah, daughter of Molly Horniblow (slave) and slave of Margaret Horniblow (mistress); her father was Daniel, a carpenter, probably a son of the white Henry Jacobs and slave of Andrew Knox, a doctor. *Incidents* is a first-person pseudonymous account of a slave woman's sexual oppression and of her struggle for freedom. Written in the first person by Jacobs's pseudonymous narrator "Linda Brent," the book is a remarkably accurate (although incomplete) rendering of Jacobs's life up to her 1853 emancipation. It shows her as a slave and fugitive in the South, and as a fugitive in the North. In her narrative, Jacobs's Linda Brent credits her family, and especially her grandmother (who had gained her freedom and established a bakery in the town), with sustaining her and her younger brother, John S. Jacobs, in their youthful efforts to achieve a sense of selfhood despite their slave status.

When Jacobs was six years old, her mother died, and she was taken into the home of her mistress, who taught her to sew and to read, skills she later used to support herself and to protest against slavery. But when in 1825 Jacobs's mistress died, the slave girl was not freed, as she had expected. Instead, her mistress's will bequeathed her, along with a "bureau & work table & their contents," to a three-year-old niece, and Jacobs was sent to live in the Edenton home of the little girl's father, Dr. James Norcom ("Dr. Flint" in *Incidents*). As the slave girl approached adolescence, the middle-aged Norcom subjected her to unrelenting sexual harassment and, when she was sixteen, threatened her with concubinage. To stop him, Jacobs became sexually involved with a neighboring white attorney, young Samuel Tredwell Sawyer ("Mr. Sands"). Their alliance produced two children: Joseph (c. 1829-?), called "Benny," and Louisa Matilda (1833-1917), called "Little Ellen" in the narrative. When Jacobs was twenty-one, Norcom said if she did not agree to become his concubine, he would send her away to one of his plantations. Jacobs again rejected his sexual demands and was taken to a plantation. After she learned that Norcom also planned to send her children out to the country, fearing that once they became plantation slaves they would never be free, she decided to act.

In June 1835, Jacobs escaped. She reasoned that if she was missing, Norcom would be willing to sell her and the children and that their father would buy and free them all. Joseph and Louisa were indeed bought by Sawyer, who permitted them to continue living in town with Jacobs's grandmother. Jacobs was hidden by neighbors, both Black and white, but with Norcom searching for her, she was unable to escape from Edenton. As the summer wore on, her grandmother and uncle built her a hiding place in a tiny crawlspace above a porch in their home. For almost seven years, Jacobs hid in this space, which, she wrote, measured seven feet wide, nine feet long, and—at its tallest—three feet high.

Finally, in 1842, she escaped and was reunited with her children, who had been sent north. In New York City, Jacobs found work as a domestic in the family of litterateur Nathaniel Parker Willis. In 1849, she moved to Rochester to join her brother, who had also become a fugitive from slavery. John S. Jacobs was now an antislavery lecturer and activist, and through him, Harriet Jacobs became part of the Rochester abolitionist circle surrounding Frederick Douglass's newspaper, the *North Star*. After passage of the 1850 Fugitive Slave Law, she left Rochester for New York, where her North Carolina masters tried to seize her and her children on the streets of Manhattan and Brooklyn. Determined not to be sent back into slavery or to bow to the slave system by permitting herself to be bought, Jacobs fled to Massachusetts. In 1852, however, without her knowledge, Cornelia Grinnell Willis arranged for her and her children to

be bought from Norcom's family. Jacobs and her children were free.

Amid conflicting emotions—determination to aid the antislavery cause, humiliation at being purchased, and a deep impulse perhaps prompted by the death of her beloved grandmother in Edenton—Jacobs decided to make public the story of her sexual abuse in slavery. A few years earlier, she had whispered her history to Amy Post, her Rochester Quaker abolitionist-feminist friend, and Post had urged her to write a book informing northern women about the sexual abuse of women slaves. Now Jacobs was ready. Harriet Beecher Stowe's newly published *Uncle Tom's Cabin* (1852) had become a runaway best-seller, and Jacobs's first thought was to try to enlist Stowe to write her story. When she learned that Stowe planned to incorporate her life story into *The Key to Uncle Tom's Cabin* (1853), however, Jacobs decided instead to write her story herself. After practicing her writing skills in letters she sent to the *New York Tribune*, she began her book. Five years later, it was finished. Soliciting letters of introduction to British abolitionists from Boston antislavery leaders, Jacobs sailed to England to sell her manuscript to a publisher. She returned home unsuccessful. Finally, with the help of African-American abolitionist William C. Nell and white abolitionist Lydia Maria Child, early in 1861 Jacobs brought the book out herself. *Incidents in the Life of a Slave Girl: Written by Herself* was published for the author, with an Introduction by L. Maria Child, who was identified as editor on the title page. Although Jacobs's authorship was later forgotten, she was from the first identified as "Linda Brent." Reviewed in the abolitionist and African-American press, *Incidents* made Jacobs a minor celebrity among its audience of antislavery women.

Within months, however, the nation was at war, and in the crisis, Jacobs launched a second public career. Using her new celebrity, she approached northern antislavery women for money and supplies for the "contrabands"—Black refugees crowding behind the Union lines in Washington, D.C., and Alexandria, Virginia (which had been occupied by the army). With the support of Quaker groups and of the newly formed New England Freedmen's Aid Society, in 1863 Harriet Jacobs and her daughter Louisa went to Alexandria. There they provided emergency health care and established the Jacobs Free School, a Black-owned and Black-taught institution for the children of the refugees.

Throughout the war years, Jacobs and her daughter reported on their southern relief efforts in the northern press and in England, where in 1862 her book had been published as *The Deeper Wrong: Incidents in the Life of a Slave Girl, Written by Herself*. In May 1864, Jacobs was named a member of the Executive Committee of the Women's National Loyal League, an antislavery feminist group mounting a mass petition campaign to urge Congress to pass a constitutional amendment ending chattel slavery. In July 1865, the mother-daughter team left Alexandria, and in 1866 they moved to Savannah, where they again worked to provide educational and medical facilities for the freedpeople. The following year, Jacobs's daughter Louisa joined Susan B. Anthony and Charles Lenox Remond to campaign for the Equal Rights Association—a group of radical feminists and abolitionists who worked for the inclusion of the enfranchisement of African-Americans and women in the New York State Constitution.

In 1868, Harriet and Louisa Jacobs went to London to raise money for an orphanage and home for the aged in the Black Savannah community. Aided by British supporters of Garrisonian abolitionism, they raised £100 sterling for the Savannah project. Despite their success, however, they recommended to their New York Quaker sponsors that the building not be built. The Ku Klux Klan was riding and burning; it would not tolerate the establishment of new Black institutions.

In the face of the increasing violence in the South, Jacobs and her daughter retreated to Massachusetts. In Boston, Jacobs was briefly employed as clerk of the fledgling New England Women's Club, perhaps with the patronage of her old employer and friend Cornelia Grinnell Willis and her New England Freedmen's Aid Society colleague Ednah Dow Cheney, both club members. As the new decade began, Jacobs settled in Cambridge, where for several years she ran a boardinghouse for Harvard students and faculty.

When Harriet and Louisa Jacobs later moved to Washington, D.C., Harriet continued to work among the destitute freedpeople, and Louisa was employed in the newly established "colored schools," then at Howard University. They did not return south, and in 1892, Jacobs sold her grandmother's house and lot in Edenton, property that her family had managed to arrange for her to inherit, despite her earlier status as a fugitive. When in 1896 the National Association of Colored Women held organizing meetings in Washington, D.C., Louisa Jacobs apparently attended. The following spring, Harriet Jacobs died at her Washington home. She is buried in the Mount Auburn Cemetery, Cambridge.

Harriet Jacobs's life spanned her experiences before the Civil War as a slave in the South, as a fugitive in the South and in the North, and as an abolitionist activist and slave narrator in the North. She served as a relief worker among Black refugees in the South during the Civil War and Reconstruction and as a public commentator on their condition. Later she was involved as an adjunct to the post-Civil War club movement among white women and witnessed the birth of the Black women's club movement. No other woman is known to have possessed this range of experience

[*See also* AUTOBIOGRAPHY; FREEDMEN'S EDUCATION; SLAVE NARRATIVES.]

BIBLIOGRAPHY
Andrews, William L. *To Tell a Free Story: The First Century of Afro-American Autobiography* (1986); Braxton, Joanne. "Harriet Jacobs's *Incidents in the Life of a Slave Girl*: The Re-Definition of the Slave Narrative Genre," *Massachusetts Review* (1986); Carby, Hazel. *Reconstructing Womanhood: The Emergence of the Afro-American Woman Novelist* (1987); Christian, Barbara. *Black Feminist Criticism* (1980); Foster, Frances Smith. " 'In Respect to Females': Differences in the Portrayals of Women by Male and Female Narrators," *Black American Literature Forum* (1981); Fox-Genovese, Elizabeth. *Within the Plantation Household: Black and White Women of the Old South* (1988); hooks, bell. *Feminist Theory: From Margin to Center* (1984); Jacobs, Harriet A. *Incidents in the Life of a Slave Girl: Written by Herself*, ed. Jean Fagan Yellin ([1861] 1987); Sekora, John and Darwin T. Turner, eds. *The Art of Slave Narrative* (1982); Smith, Valerie. *Narrative Authority in Modern Afro-American Fiction* (1987); Washington, Mary Helen. "Meditation on History: The Slave Narrative of Linda Brent." In her *Invented Lives: Narratives of Black Women, 1860-1960* (1987); White, Deborah Gray. *Ar'n't I a Woman? Female Slaves in the Plantation South* (1985); Yellin, Jean Fagan. "*Legacy* Profile: Harriet Ann Jacobs," *Legacy* (1988), and "Text and Context of Harriet Jacobs's *Incidents in the Life of a Slave Girl: Written by Herself*." In *The Slave's Narrative*, ed. Charles T. Davis and Henry Louis Gates, Jr. (1985), and "*Written by Herself*: Harriet Jacobs's Slave Narrative," *American Literature* (1981).

MANUSCRIPT COLLECTIONS
Manuscript sources on Harriet Jacobs can be found at the Boston Public Library; the Sydney Howard Gay papers, Rare Book and Manuscript Library, Columbia University Libraries, New York; the Massachusetts Historical Society, Boston; the Norcom Family papers, North Carolina State Archives, Raleigh; the Isaac and Amy Post Family papers, Department of Rare Books and Special Collections, Rush Rhees Library, University of Rochester, Rochester, New York; Schlesinger Library, Radcliffe College, Cambridge, Massachusetts; and the Sophia Smith Collection, Smith College, Northampton, Massachusetts.

JEAN FAGAN YELLIN

JAMES, ETTA (1938-)

From her musical roots in the Black gospel tradition Etta James has forged a musical career that has spanned almost forty years. She is as comfortable with the gospel music she used to sing in church choir as she is with rhythm and blues, jazz, rock 'n' roll, ballads, and contemporary sounds. Critics have had a hard time defining her style, but there can be no doubt that the power, honesty, and sexual double entendres of her music evoke reminiscences of Trixie Smith and Victoria Spivey, the great classic blues singers of the 1920s.

Etta James was born in Los Angeles in 1938. Like many young African-American singers, she received her musical training in the church choir, at Saint Paul's Baptist Church. In fact, her musical style was developing in an era when gospel reformed the country's listening habits and when the term "race music" was replaced by rhythm and blues. When Etta was performing with her girlfriends on San Francisco's street corners, the stage was being set for her professional debut. Disk jockeys were becoming important players in the entertainment field, with recordings reaching larger and larger audiences avid for tunes to fuel the post-Depression dance crazes that swept the country.

James's career was launched at age fourteen when she became a member of Johnny Otis's rhythm and blues band, Etta and the Peaches, based in Los Angeles. Her first recording, "Roll with Me Henry," with the legendary band leader made her an instant success. Originally banned by radio stations coast to coast for its suggestive content, it was later released by Modern Records in 1954 as "The Wallflower," an answer to Hank Ballard's "Work with Me Annie," a 1954 hit. James's popularity was at its height in the 1950s. In fact, from then until the 1970s no other female rhythm and blues artist, except Dinah Washington and Ruth Brown, had more top ten hits. In the 1960s, she toured with Little Richard, James Brown, Little Willie John, and Johnny Guitar Watson. By 1969, James was one of *Billboard*'s top seven female artists.

As the 1960s wore on, however, it became apparent to the public that James was struggling with heroin addiction. As a result, she stopped recording and made very few public appearances from 1964 to 1968. She was eventually able to free herself from the habit through years in a drug rehabilitation program. In 1973, she picked up the pieces of her career and recorded her first album in two years, entitled *Etta James* and produced by Gabriel Mekler.

Once her rehabilitation was complete, there was no turning back. For the last twenty years, James has been active performing, touring widely in the United States and Europe and recording and appearing in concert halls, festivals, and clubs. In 1988, she cut her first solo album in more than ten years, *Seven Year Itch*. She has more than thirty albums and twenty charted hits to her credit. In 1990, the National Association for the Advancement of Colored People named her "Best Blues Artist" for her new album *Stickin' to My Guns*.

BIBLIOGRAPHY

BWW; Hoare, Ian, ed. *The Soul Book* (1975); Liventen, Sharon. "Inside Rock and Roll: R & B's Etta James Is Back; You Just Have to Look for Her," *Los Angeles Times* (November 30, 1988); Shaw, Arnold. *The World of Soul* (1971).

DISCOGRAPHY

1954-60 singles: "Roll with Me Henry"/"Hold Me Squeeze Me," Modern Records (1954) (later titled "The Wallflower"); "Hey Henry," "Good Rockin' Daddy," "Do Something Crazy," "Tough Lover." *At Last*, Cadet LP 4003 (1961); *Etta James*, Argo 4013 (1962); *Etta James Sings for Lovers*, Argo LP 4018 (1962); *Rocks the House*, Chess

Among female singers, from the 1950s to the 1970s only Dinah Washington and Ruth Brown had more top ten rhythm and blues hits than Etta James. [Schomburg Center]

CRL 4502 (1963); *Top Ten*, Cadet LP 4025 (1963); *Queen of Soul*, Argo LP 4040 (1964); *Etta James Sings Funk*, Chess LP (1965); *Call My Name*, Cadet LP 4055 (1966); *Tell Mama*, Cadet LP 802 (1967); *Losers Weepers*, Cadet LPS 847 (1970); *Etta James*, Chess CH 50042 (1973); *Come a Little Closer*, Chess CH 60029 (1974); *Peaches*, Chess CH 6004 (1975) (reissued by MCA); *Etta Is Better Than Evvah!*, Chess ACH 19003 (1976); *Deep in the Night*, Warner Bros. BSK 3156 (1978); with Tony Orlando on "Let the Good Times Roll" and "Bring It on Home to Me," Electra 6E-149 (1978); appeared on Allen Toussaint's *Motion* with Rosemary Butler and Bonnie Raitt singing backup (1978); *Changes*, MCA LP 3244 (1981); with Eddie "Cleanhead" Vinson on *Blues in the Night*, Fantasy LP (1986); with Eddie "Cleanhead" Vinson on *The Late Show*, Fantasy LP (1987); *Seven Year Itch*, Island 91018 (1988).

ROBERT STEPHENS

JAMISON, JUDITH (1944-)

Judith Jamison was appointed as artistic director of the Alvin Ailey American Dance Theater in 1990 and has been a vital force in the dance community for

An international symbol of American modern dance, Judith Jamison has been an inspiration for generations of aspiring young African-American women dancers. Here she performs in Nubian Lady. *[Schomburg Center]*

over twenty years. Although her early training was in ballet, she went on to become an international symbol of American modern dance and provided inspiration for generations of aspiring young African-American female dancers.

Jamison, a striking six-foot-tall, cocoa-colored woman with a short-cropped natural hair style, was an appropriate image to emerge from the 1960s and 1970s cultural revolution. She helped to redefine the image of a dancer with her African appearance and carriage. In the tradition of Katherine Dunham and Pearl Primus, she proudly acknowledged her heritage through her own choreography with works like *Divination* and *Ancestral Rites*. *Cry*, the magnum opus created by the late choreographer Alvin Ailey for Jamison, epitomized the struggle of Black women in America and symbolized for the world the dignity and strength of Black women through four hundred years of oppression and victory. In the 1980s she starred in the Broadway hit *Sophisticated Ladies* (with music by Duke Ellington) with Gregory Hines.

After a distinguished career as a dancer, Jamison went on to establish her own company, the Jamison Project, in 1987, before becoming the artistic director of the Alvin Ailey American Dance Theater. Jamison is the first African-American woman to direct a major modern dance company. She and her contemporaries, choreographers Dianne McIntyre (Sounds in Motion), Kariamu Welsh Asante (National Dance Company of Zimbabwe), and JaWolle Willa Jo Zollar (Urban Bush Women), have extended the lineage of Katherine Dunham and Pearl Primus to ensure the artistic legacy of African-Americans.

[*See also* DANCE COMPANIES, ARTISTIC DIRECTORS.]

BIBLIOGRAPHY

Clarke, Mary and David Vaughan, eds. *The Encyclopedia of Dance and Ballet* (1977); Cohen-Stratyner, Barbara Naomi. *Biographical Dictionary of Dance* (1982); *EBA*; Emery, Lynne Fauley. *Black Dance in the United States: From 1619 to Today* (1988); Long, Richard. *The Black Tradition in American Concert Dance* (1990); McDonagh, Don. *The Complete Guide to Modern Dance* (1976); Thorpe, Edward. *Black Dance* (1990); *WWBA*; Willis, John, ed. *Dance World* (1967, 1976).

KARIAMU WELSH ASANTE

JAZZ *see*
BLUES AND JAZZ

JEANES FUND AND JEANES TEACHERS

The Negro Rural School Fund was established in 1907 by Quaker heiress Anna Jeanes to improve small rural schools for southern African-Americans. Commonly known as the Jeanes Fund, its trustees included Booker T. Washington, Andrew Carnegie, Robert Moton, and James Dillard. With the financial support of the fund, hundreds of Blacks became Jeanes teachers in the first decades of the twentieth century and significantly improved the quality of education available to Black children throughout the rural South.

Jackson Davis, school superintendent of Henrico County, Virginia, requested and received a Jeanes Fund grant after being denied county funds to implement new teaching methods in Black schools. The methods were those of Virginia Randolph, the daughter of ex-slaves, who had graduated from high school and was teaching by age sixteen. In addition to academic subjects, she taught gardening, cooking, laundering, and sewing to encourage students to value labor and maximize their meager resources. She urged community members of both races to support the students' activities, and she visited community members' homes, teaching health care, nutrition, homemaking, and needlework. In 1908, Randolph became the first Jeanes Supervising Industrial Teacher, with the responsibility of assisting and directing county teachers in efforts to improve Black communities.

Other Jeanes teachers were employed, and their success led to increased financial support from local governments, resulting in the hiring of more women throughout the South. By 1936, 426 Jeanes teachers in fourteen southern states earned an average annual salary of $850. Although normal school degrees were not required, 45 percent had Bachelor's degrees, earned primarily through summer courses at Hampton Institute, paid for by the fund. Teachers were required to file annual reports of school activities and to present public exhibits of students' projects.

In 1937, the Jeanes Fund merged with others and is currently known as the Southern Educational Foundation, Incorporated, headquartered in Atlanta, Georgia.

BIBLIOGRAPHY

Aptheker, Herbert, ed. *Documentary History of the Negro People in the United States, 1910-1932* (1973); Bergman, Peter M. *The Chronological History of the Negro in America* (1969); Neverdon-Morton, Cynthia. *Afro-American Women of the South and the Advancement of the Race, 1895-1925* (1989); Quarles, Benjamin. *The Negro in the Making of*

Quaker heiress Anna Jeanes established the Negro Rural School Fund to improve small rural schools for southern Blacks. With financial support from the fund, hundreds of Blacks in the early twentieth century became Jeanes teachers. Of these teachers, 45 percent had Bachelor's degrees, earned primarily through summer courses at Hampton Institute, where this group photograph was taken. [Donna Hollie]

America (1987); Woodson, Carter Godwin and Charles H. Wesley. *The Negro in Our History* (1972); Wright, Arthur D. *The Jeanes Fund and the Jeanes Teachers* (1936).

DONNA HOLLIE

JEMISON, MAE C. (1956-)

Because of her background, education, talent, and interests, Mae C. Jemison would be a valuable asset to any private corporation. That she has chosen instead to build a career in public service, as the first Black female astronaut at the National Aeronautics and Space Administration (NASA), is America's good fortune.

Born on October 17, 1956, in Decatur, Alabama, to Charlie and Dorothy Jemison, Mae moved to Chicago with her parents at an early age. A graduate of Morgan Park High School in Chicago, she earned a National Achievements Scholarship to Stanford Uni-

versity. She graduated from Stanford in 1977 with a B.S. in chemical engineering while at the same time fulfilling all requirements for a B.A. in African and Afro-American Studies. From Stanford, she went on to Cornell University Medical School, earning her M.D. in 1981. Along the way, Jemison received a host of awards for involvement in activities as far-flung as working in a refugee camp in Thailand. She completed her internship at the University of Southern California Medical Center in Los Angeles.

In January 1985, after a brief period spent in private practice, Jemison joined the Peace Corps. Until 1985, she served as the area Peace Corps medical officer in Sierra Leone and Liberia in West Africa. Then she took a position managing the health care delivery system for both Peace Corps and U.S. Embassy personnel as well as developing self-help information for local constituents.

In 1987, NASA selected Jemison as an astronaut candidate. She completed her one-year training and evaluation program in August 1988, qualifying as a mission specialist on space shuttle crews. Jemison was then a mission specialist on STS-47, Spacelab-J, a cooperative mission between the United States and Japan. As part of her training for work in space, Jemison helped prepare space shuttles for launch. Her responsibilities included preparing launch payloads and thermal protection systems as well as verifying the integrity and performance of shuttle computer software.

On September 12, 1992, she was aboard the space shuttle *Endeavor* when it was launched on a one-week mission to study the effects of zero gravity on people and animals. The first Black woman in space took with her an Alvin Ailey American Dance Theater poster depicting the dance *Cry*, explaining to Judith Jamison, the director of the company, that the dance was created for Jemison and "all Black women everywhere."

The first Black woman in space, Mae C. Jemison qualified as a mission specialist on space shuttle crews in August 1988. As part of her training for work in space, Jemison helped prepare space shuttles for launch. [UPI/Bettmann]

BIBLIOGRAPHY

Biographical data supplied by the National Aeronautics and Space Administration (NASA), Lyndon B. Johnson Space Center, Houston, Texas; *New York Times* (September 16, 1992).

CHRISTINE A. LUNARDINI

JESSYE, EVA (1895-1992)

"Oh, I Can't Sit Down," the picnic song from *Porgy and Bess*, aptly characterizes the life of this Black American musical phenomenon. For almost a century, Eva Jessye made a peerless contribution to the world of music, pushing herself, and anyone associated with her, at a relentlessly swift pace in order to achieve the perfection she demanded. A forceful woman, she was known to exclaim, "Time is fleeting! I have no time to waste or to spare!" and her achievements attest to that fact.

She was born Eva Alberta Jessye on January 20, 1895, in Coffeyville, Kansas, a small town bordering Oklahoma. Her father supported the family as a chicken picker. As a small child Eva sang and was an avid reader. She wrote her first poem at the age of seven and won a poetry contest when she was thirteen. By this time her musical talents also had begun to surface, for she organized a girls' quartet when she was twelve years old.

She studied choral music and music theory at the now defunct Western University in Quindaro, Kansas, graduating in 1914, and she received a degree from Langston University in Langston, Oklahoma.

Earning what was then a generous salary of $52.50 a month, she taught elementary school in Taft, Oklahoma, and later was employed at schools in Haskell and Muskogee, Oklahoma. Jessye also taught at Claflin College in Orangeburg, South Carolina, and at Morgan State College in Baltimore, Maryland, where she served as director of the music department. During that time she also was on the staff of Baltimore's *Afro-American* newspaper.

In 1926, the young teacher decided to move to New York in search of musical and theatrical opportunities. She got her first big break at the Capitol Theatre playing with Major Bowles. It was here that she met and became the protégé of Will Marion Cook, an early Black classical jazz composer.

Eva Jessye immediately began to attract attention as a trail blazer. Her personality, her demeanor, and her talent declared to all: "I am a woman. I am a woman of African descent. I am a Black woman. And

I am happy to be exactly as God made me" (Burroughs 1985). The music world was never the same.

An expert in harmonics, Jessye's literary and musical accomplishments spanned well over three quarters of a century. She was internationally renowned in the areas of poetry, musical composition, drama and choral directing and was an acclaimed authority on American music and folklore. She also was an actress and an inspirational lecturer. In addition, she was known as the unofficial guardian of the *Porgy and Bess* score, having been appointed choral conductor by the composer, George Gershwin, and having officiated in that capacity since the premiere of the Gershwin-Heyward operetta in 1935 and continuing through numerous productions around the world. Jessye contributed many authentic touches to the score, thereby deepening the cultural flavor of the African-American

A monumental figure in Black music, Eva Jessye was the first musical director of a motion picture starring Black actors, Metro-Goldwyn-Mayer's Hallelujah, *written and directed by King Vidor. The Eva Jessye choir was the first to interpret the Virgil Thomson-Gertrude Stein opera,* Four Saints in Three Acts *(1934), and was the official choir for the historic 1963 March on Washington. [Schomburg Center]*

experience so miraculously discovered and translated by Gershwin. The choral pattern set in the original production by the Eva Jessye choir is still closely followed. At the thirtieth anniversary celebration by the cast at the Royal Alexandria Theatre in Toronto, Canada, then Vice President Hubert Humphrey wired Jessye to express his appreciation for her role in spreading Gershwin's great music around the country.

The artists Eva Jessye discovered, coached, and guided to success are legion. She was a pioneer in radio, writing and directing her own shows on major networks. She also was the first musical director of a motion picture starring Black actors, Metro-Goldwyn-Mayer's *Hallelujah*, written and directed by King Vidor, and she and her choir were the first to interpret the 1934 Virgil Thomson-Gertrude Stein opera, *Four Saints in Three Acts*.

She was featured in 1944 in the first annual I Am an American Day initiated by Fiorello LaGuardia, the mayor of New York City. Jessye also wrote and directed the New York City theme song for Order of the Day, a postwar celebration sponsored by the Organization for American-Soviet Friendship held in 1944 at New York's Madison Square Garden and at the Watergate Hotel in Washington, D.C., with American and Soviet dignitaries participating. In 1963, she directed the official choir for the historic March on Washington, recordings of which were used by Tom Muboya in the struggle for independence in Kenya. She also was cited by the cities of Detroit and Windsor, Canada, for her participation in their first annual freedom festival.

The Eva Jessye choir has performed in concert at major universities and colleges for more than forty years. In 1952, as the ensemble of the State Department-sponsored tour of *Porgy and Bess*, the choir was hailed by the Berlin press as ambassadors of good will.

In 1972, Jessye directed her original folk oratorio, "Paradise Lost and Regained," based on the epic poem by John Milton, at the Washington Cathedral, and it was hailed by the *Washington Post*. That same year, the Eva Jessye collection of Afro-American music was established at the University of Michigan. In May 1976, Jessye was awarded a Degree in Determination by the Department of Afro-American Studies at the University of Michigan, and she was cited by the International Women's Year for her contributions to the arts, women's progress, and peace. She was the recipient of numerous other awards from organizations and government agencies. In 1987, after receiving an honorary Doctor of Arts from Eastern Michigan University at the age of ninety-two, she

wrote in a letter, "You see I am still cuttin' cane and choppin' cotton—with might and main—with wide acclaim!" (Personal collection).

Jessye was a constant, honored guest at conventions of the National Association of Negro Musicians in recent years at the special invitation of her good friend William Warfield, who is national president.

In 1990, she was selected as one of seventy-six Black American women to be photographed in *I Dream a World: Portraits of Black Women Who Changed America*. Her portrait also is featured for the month of January in the 1991 "I Dream a World" calendar.

Throughout her life Eva Jessye shared her wisdom and her talents. Often to the amazement of many half her age, her resonant voice, the twinkle in her eye, the alertness of her mind, and the accuracy of her ear articulated the depth and breadth of her greatness. Professionally a very public person, Jessye never publicly dwelled on her personal life, although she outlived two husbands and had no children. She died on February 21, 1992.

BIBLIOGRAPHY

Burroughs, Margaret. "And Ring the Whole Wide World Around" (August 9, 1985); Campbell, Cynthia. "Livin' Not Easy, but Exciting for Famed Choral Director," *Baton Rouge Morning Advocate* (June 27, 1976); Marsh-Ellis, Frances. Personal collection of letters from Eva Jessye, Baton Rouge, Louisiana; Nolan, Robert L. "Music and Musicians," *Detroit Chronicle* (April 1972); Price, Anne. "Porgy and Bess Has Ups and Downs," *Baton Rouge Morning Advocate* (June 30, 1976); Treml, William B. "As I See It," *Ann Arbor News* (July 27, 1975); "Whatever Happened to . . . Eva Jessye?" *Ebony* (May 1974). See also the Eva Jessye Afro-American Music collection, University of Michigan, Ann Arbor; Eva Jessye collection, Clark College, Atlanta, Georgia; Eva Jessye collection, Oklahoma Public Schools, Taft, Oklahoma; Eva Jessye collection, Pittsburg State College, Pittsburg, Kansas.

FRANCES MARSH-ELLIS

JIM CROW LAWS

Jim Crow laws mandated separate public and private facilities that led to racial ostracism from the mainstream of public affairs for Black women and men in the United States between the 1896 *Plessy v. Ferguson* and the 1954 *Brown v. Board of Education* U.S. Supreme Court decisions. Although there were local laws, customs, and practices supporting segregation before *Plessy v. Ferguson*, this decision made separate but equal facilities in interstate railroad transportation legal, and it justified past segregation activities, as in the 1884 Ida B. Wells-Barnett case. Wells-Barnett charged that the Chesapeake and Ohio Railroad had discriminated against her when she had been asked to move to the smoking car. At the next stop Wells-Barnett got off the train, returned to Memphis, and filed suit. She should have won the case because the Civil Rights Act of 1875 forbade discrimination in public places and conveyances against persons within the jurisdiction of the United States. After *Plessy* v. *Ferguson*, many court challenges filed under the 1875 law were lost. In 1913, the thirty-eight-year-old civil rights law was ruled unconstitutional by the Supreme Court when it ruled against Emma Butts, a Black woman who sued the steamship company Merchants' and Miners' Transportation Company for denying her accommodations equal to those provided for white passengers.

Plessy v. *Ferguson* paved the way for a broader interpretation of the separate but equal doctrine and the passage of Jim Crow laws that facilitated the creation of two separate and unequal societies in which babies were born in segregated hospitals, grew up in a segregated world, and were buried by segregated mortuaries in segregated cemeteries. Black women and men were denied the right to shape public policy as voters or consumers. The goal of such laws was the separation of the races in every aspect of life, including religion, economics, education, entertainment, recreation, transportation, lodging, housing, and dining. These practices were accompanied by public signs and constant reminders, including the use of a different Bible for swearing in white and Black witnesses during court trials. There were also public signs that read "whites only," "colored only," "colored, back door," "colored water," and "white water." Parks had signs that read "no Negroes allowed on these grounds except as servants." Southern Black women, especially domestic workers who took white children to the parks and zoos during the week, were denied the privilege of taking their own children to the parks on Sunday afternoons. One Black woman wrote that it was "pitiful, pitiful customs and laws that made war on women and babes. There is no wonder that we die; the wonder is that we persist in living" (Romero 1978).

Jim Crow laws and the climate they created permitted white people to express their anger violently against Black men, Black women, and their families. Jim Crow laws not only denied Black Americans access to public facilities, they permitted the lynching of Black men and women. Fourteen Black women were lynched in Mississippi between 1880 and 1945,

and more than 550 Black males, including many adolescents, were lynched during the same period.

Many crimes against Black Americans went unpunished because intimidation prevented victims from filing charges. When a charge was filed by a Black person against a white person, witnesses would not testify, and the authorities, including the courts, were often hostile toward Black citizens. Because they were without legal protection, Black Americans of this era sought ways to avoid confrontations with white people. For example, in order to avoid the sexual abuse of Black women by white men, many Black families attempted to protect young women by educating them for jobs that kept them away from frequent contact with white men. When given a choice, Black women preferred not to work as domestics or field hands, even though most jobs available to Black workers in Jim Crow society were in this category.

Black women were subjected to the worst situations in employment under Jim Crow laws. Between 70 and 90 percent of all Black women workers were agricultural and domestic employees without minimum wages or Social Security. Black women generally received one-third to one-half of white women's pay, which was one-third to two-thirds of white men's pay. Even the National Recovery Codes at the end of the Great Depression permitted segregation because some employers did not want to pay Black women the minimum wages that the codes required.

Jim Crow laws were aimed at the race rather than the gender of Black women, and they infected so-called egalitarian perspectives, too. The goal of the white feminist movement between 1896 and 1920 was the right to vote for white women. During this twenty-four-year period, white suffragists cultivated the support needed to get the Nineteenth Amendment added to the U.S. Constitution. Suffragists often exploited racial prejudices and frequently excluded Black women from their organizations and activities. White racist suffragists assured the nation that they would maintain the status quo relative to the enforcement of Jim Crow laws in the South. However, the Nineteenth Amendment as passed in 1920 did not explicitly exclude Black women. So in many of the border states Black women began to vote in large numbers after 1920, and they played a significant part in electoral activities. After the death of West Virginia legislator E. Howard Harper in 1927, his wife, Minnie Buckingham-Harper, was appointed to serve his unexpired term. She became the first Black female legislator in a U.S. legislative body.

While suffragists and the courts left Black women to make their own way with Jim Crow laws, Black women worked collectively to challenge Jim Crow laws through social agitation and self-help organizations. For example, the Mississippi Federation of Colored Women's Clubs, under the leadership of Grace Jones, wife of Piney Woods Country Life School founder Laurence C. Jones, initiated an effort that created a state commission for blind Black residents. The commission later appropriated $3,000 to start a school for blind Black students at Piney Woods in 1929. Further, under Grace Jones's leadership, the Federation of Colored Women's Clubs initiated a project to change Jim Crow laws that placed Black male youth offenders in the same facility with adults. Governor Paul B. Johnson gave his approval, and the state legislature appropriated money to build Oakley Training School as a separate facility for incorrigible Black boys and girls in 1940. The facility was opened in 1943.

The personal and interracial achievements of Mary McLeod Bethune (1875-1955), a founder of Bethune-Cookman College in Daytona Beach, Florida, exemplify the courage of those Black women who rose above Jim Crow laws. Bethune's commanding presence once caused an Atlanta ticket agent to sell her a train ticket in a white waiting room. The same commanding presence caused Bethune to express her displeasure when she was called "Mary" at the first meeting of the Southern Conference for Human Welfare. She responded, "I do not care what anyone calls me as an individual, but as a delegate from Florida I must insist on respect of that sovereign state, and since there are probably dozens of Marys at this Conference, I ask that it be entered on the record that the resolutions were presented by Mrs. Mary Bethune" (Dannett 1964).

Among the national positions held by Bethune was her appointment by President Franklin Roosevelt as administrator for the Office of Minority Affairs in the National Youth Administration. A popular speaker, she often spoke of uniting people across color barriers, and in 1935 she created the National Council of Negro Women to work actively toward this ideal. Bethune's racial and personal dignity, her faith and hope in God and her people, her respect for power, her desire to live harmoniously with all humanity, and her sense of responsibility for educating young people were characteristics that epitomized some Black women's accommodation to Jim Crow laws. Bethune's commitments symbolize the spirit of Black women who worked to lift the race through service within the prescribed legal system. Gladys Noel Bates, Linda Brown, Daisy Bates, Elizabeth Eckford, and Rosa Parks are among the Black women who confronted Jim Crow laws and practices and thus opened the way to overturning them.

Gladys Noel Bates filed a lawsuit against the Jackson, Mississippi, School Board of Trustees on behalf of Black teachers in March 1948 to eradicate inequity in teachers' salaries because of race. Bates started teaching in the Jackson school system in 1943-44 and earned a salary of $350. By 1946-47, she was earning an annual salary of $900, and by 1947-48 she was earning an annual salary of $1,260. White teachers of equal experience and education earned almost $2,000. Because Bates had sued her employer, her contract was not renewed for fall 1948, and she left the state.

Richard Jess Brown, the continuing plaintiff, received a salary of $2,205 for 1949-50 while one white teacher with similar experience and educational background received a salary of $2,450 and two others received salaries of $3,600 each. Lawyers for Bates and Brown argued that there were differences in salaries ranging from approximately 45 percent to as much as 1,000 percent. They won their case and, though Bates did not benefit directly, Black teachers in Mississippi thereafter were given larger percentages of annual salary increases until their pay was equal to that of their white counterparts.

Perhaps the single most important act that led to the overturn of Jim Crow laws was Linda Brown's question to her father asking why she could not attend the school closest to her. Her question prompted her father to file the suit against the Topeka, Kansas, school system in 1953 that resulted in the U.S. Supreme Court's declaring separate but equal schools to be inherently unequal. The 1954 *Brown* v. *Board of Education* landmark decision was the beginning of the end of Jim Crow laws.

Although segregation and Jim Crow laws had become illegal, a series of acts followed that challenged the emotions, creativity, and willingness of women and men to move to a new era. On December 1, 1955, Rosa Parks, mother of the modern civil rights movement, sat in the Black section of a Montgomery, Alabama, bus, as was the custom. However, when the bus driver asked her to give her seat to a white man, she refused. This quiet act of defiance, following on the heels of Black Americans' successes in court, began the modern civil rights movement that has led to the death of many practices and customs associated with Jim Crow laws.

Between 1896 and 1954, the period of legal segregation under Jim Crow laws, many Black women struggled with the negative situations created by these laws while accommodating these same laws. Some Black women turned these impediments into challenges and became involved in improving the situation for Black Americans, often with the hope of helping the race become more acceptable to white Americans. Other Black women pursued activities to encourage interracial harmony. After 1954, most Black women increasingly worked to eradicate Jim Crow laws altogether.

Although the 1954 *Brown* v. *Board of Education* decision was the beginning of the end of Jim Crow laws, courageous individuals and groups continued to help develop a more just society. Yet it was not until the 1964 Civil Rights Act that the last vestiges of Jim Crow laws became illegal. However, the social and economic heritage of Jim Crow—Black women and men still receive the lowest pay for comparable skills, experience, and work—lives on.

BIBLIOGRAPHY

Bates, Daisy. *The Long Shadow of Little Rock* (1962); *Bates, Gladys Noel and Richard Jess Brown, individually, etc. Appellants,* v. *John C. Batee et al.* U.S. Court of Appeals for the Fifth Circuit, N 13,215 (February 15, 1951); Dannett, Sylvia G. L., ed. *Profiles of Negro Womanhood, 1619-1990* (1964); Harrison, Alferdteen. *Piney Woods School: An Oral History* (1982); McMillen, Neil R. "The Migration and Black Protest in Jim Crow Mississippi." In *Black Exodus: The Migration from the American South,* ed. Alferdteen Harrison (1991), and *Dark Journey: Black Mississippians in the Age of Jim Crow* (1989); Rhode, Deborah. *Justice and Gender: Sex Discrimination and the Law* (1989); Romero, Patricia W., ed. *I, Too, Am American: Documents from 1619 to the Present* (1978); Trotter, Joe W. "On the Road North: Black Migration to Southern West Virginia, 1915-1932." Jackson State University symposium paper, Jackson, Mississippi (September 1989); Wesley, Charles Harris. *The Quest for Equality: From Civil War to Civil Rights* (1968); White, Geneva Brown Blalock and Eva Hunter Bishop, eds. *Mississippi's Black Women: A Pictorial Story of Their Contributions to the State and Nation* (1976).

ALFERDTEEN B. HARRISON

JOHNSON, ANN BATTLES (b. 1815) AND KATHERINE JOHNSON

Ann Battles was born into slavery in Concordia Parish, Louisiana, in 1815. Her mother, Harriet Battles, struggled for years to secure her own freedom and that of her daughter, achieving it only in Cincinnati in 1829, when Ann was fourteen. Even though their freedom redefined their lives, offering them opportunities that they could only have imagined as slaves, it did not distinguish them from the hundreds of thousands of other free women of color who lived in the hostile environment of the South.

What distinguishes Ann Battles Johnson and her daughter, Katherine Johnson, from their neighbors is the collection of letters and the diary that they left to their descendants. Perhaps the Johnsons knew that their experiences as free women of color in a society that defined slavery by race were significant. Perhaps they did not. Either way, they accumulated and jealously protected the letters that their family members regularly sent. Most of the letters were from Ann Johnson's nieces in New Orleans—Emma, Octavia, and Lavinia Miller. Katherine Johnson left her own contribution by writing and preserving a diary.

The letters and the diary are significant because none of the authors stepped outside the bounds that circumscribed the lives of southern women, slave or free. The documents are invaluable because few free women of color were allowed the education necessary to correspond with their families and friends. Only those free women of color who lived in the predominantly Catholic-Creole lower South were regularly educated in the skills of reading and writing, and only the Johnson collection offers an extensive set of writings.

The letters of the Miller women describe the experiences of free women of color of urban New Orleans. They also include glimpses into the lives of their aunt, Ann Battles Johnson, who devoted her life to her husband and children, and of family members and friends scattered up and down the Mississippi River. The community was united by color and condition, by its freedoms despite the conventions of the dominant culture. The letters also tell the story of women, in Natchez and New Orleans, who were freed slaves who owned slaves, who were accomplished musicians or accomplished seamstresses, but who struggled to make ends meet. Most poignantly, these women turned to each other for comfort and support because, as the letters suggest, the women lived in an uneasy truce with their white neighbors.

Katherine Johnson's diary was written later than the letters and offers a glimpse into the life of a young woman who devoted herself to her community by becoming a schoolteacher. Her diary begins during the Civil War and continues, sporadically, for ten years. It offers the reader an invaluable glimpse of the dilemmas that faced the small community of elite free people of color who lost their elite status with the war.

BIBLIOGRAPHY

Alexander, Adele Logan. *Ambiguous Lives: Free Women of Color in Rural Georgia, 1789-1879* (1991); Gatewood, Willard B. *Aristocrats of Color: The Black Elite, 1880-1920* (1990); Gould, Lois Virginia Meacham. "In Full Enjoyment of Their Liberty: The Free Women of Color of the Gulf Ports of New Orleans, Mobile, and Pensacola, 1769-1860," Ph.D. diss. (1991), and *Chained to the Rock of Adversity: The Letters that Family and Friends Wrote to Anne and Anna Johnson and the Diary of Katherine Johnson, 1844-1900* (forthcoming), and "Urban Slavery-Urban Freedom: The Manumission of Jacqueline Lemelle." In *Black Women in Slavery and Freedom in the Americas* (forthcoming); Leslie, Kent Anderson. "Woman of Color, Daughter of Privilege: Amanda America Dickson," Ph.D. diss. (1990). All papers of Ann Battles Johnson and Katherine Johnson are preserved in the William T. Johnson collection, Hill Memorial Library, Louisiana State University, Baton Rouge, Louisiana.

VIRGINIA GOULD

JOHNSON, GEORGIA DOUGLAS (1877-1966)

In 1927, Alice Dunbar-Nelson described her friend Georgia Douglas Johnson as having "as many talents as she has aliases. . . . One is always stumbling upon another nom de plume of hers." Johnson did sometimes publish under various pseudonyms, but the merit of Dunbar-Nelson's comment lies in her recognition of Johnson's many gifts as musician, poet, playwright, columnist, short-story writer, wife, mother, and friend.

This multitalented woman began her life as Georgia Blanche Douglas Camp on September 10, 1877, in Atlanta, Georgia. She grew up in Rome, Georgia. Her mother was Laura Jackson, of Indian and Black ancestry, and her father was George Camp, whose wealthy and musical father had moved to Marietta, Georgia, from England. Her mixed ancestry prompted Georgia's lifelong preoccupation with miscegenation.

Georgia Camp attended elementary schools in Atlanta, and then entered Atlanta University's Normal School, from which she graduated in 1893. During these years, she was particular about her friends and chose to remain primarily alone, teaching herself to play the violin. Her interest in music took her to Oberlin, Ohio, to train at the Oberlin Conservatory (1902-3).

On September 28, 1903, Georgia Camp married Henry Lincoln Johnson. "Link" was born to ex-slaves in 1870, and became a prominent attorney and member of the Republican party. The couple had two children, Henry Lincoln, Jr., and Peter Douglas. In 1910, the family moved from Atlanta to Washington, D.C., where Link not only established a law practice but also, in 1912, accepted President William Howard Taft's appointment to serve as recorder of deeds for the District of Columbia.

Moving to Washington was the stimulus Georgia Johnson needed to begin her literary career. In 1916, three of her poems appeared in *Crisis*, and in 1918, her first book of poetry, *The Heart of a Woman*, was published. In the introduction, William Stanley Braithwaite praised the work for "lifting the veil" from women. Johnson's musical gifts are evident in the lyrical quality of poems that reveal the difficulties and frustrations faced by women and that echo Johnson's youthful isolation.

Johnson's first book did not explore racial themes, a choice for which she was criticized. During this time of the "New Negro," Black writers were expected to address racial issues to expose and overturn prejudice. In 1922, Johnson responded to her critics with a book of poetry titled *Bronze: A Book of Verse*, which addresses miscegenation as well as mothering in a racist world. She was praised by W.E.B. Du Bois and Jessie Redmon Fauset for this work, but Johnson herself admitted in a letter to Arna Bontemps that she preferred not to write on racial themes, saying that "if one can soar, he should soar, leaving his chains behind" (Cullen-Jackman collection 1941).

During this productive period, Georgia Douglas Johnson struggled to balance her roles as housewife and writer. She was an unconventional wife and mother, preferring reading to cooking, and her husband was not always sympathetic to her creative efforts, though he did financially support her in them. After the death of Henry Lincoln Johnson, Sr., on September 10, 1925, her difficulties intensified as she divided her day between earning a living and writing, a struggle that would follow her to her death. She put Peter through Williston Seminary, Dartmouth College, and Howard University's medical school, while Henry Lincoln, Jr., went to Asburnham Academy, Bowdoin College, and Howard University's law school.

During this difficult period, Johnson accepted an appointment by President Calvin Coolidge in 1925 to work for the U.S. Department of Labor as Commissioner of Conciliation, requiring her to investigate the living conditions of laborers. Working full-time caused her to feel that she never had enough time to write. However, she did produce a third book of poetry in 1928, *An Autumn Love Cycle*, considered to be her finest. She again avoided racial themes, returning instead to the theme of a woman in love. The best-known poem in this volume is "I Want to Die While You Love Me."

While Johnson refused to limit her poetry to racial themes, she greatly contributed to the New Negro Renaissance by opening her home at 1461 S Street Northwest, Washington, D.C., as a salon. Every week, writers such as Jean Toomer, Langston Hughes, Angelina Grimké, and Alice Dunbar-Nelson gathered for a meeting of the Saturday Nighters' Club. She also invited prisoners with whom she had corresponded to the weekly gatherings, once they were released. In fact, Johnson named her home "Half-Way Home," in part because she saw herself as half-way between everybody and everything and trying to bring them together, and also because she wanted to make her home a place where anyone who would fight half-way to survive could do so.

Zona Gale—a white writer to whom *An Autumn Love Cycle* was dedicated—encouraged Johnson to try writing plays, which she did with success. In 1926, Johnson received an honorable mention in the *Opportunity* play contest for *Blue Blood*, a drama about miscegenation through rape in the South. Her most famous play, *Plumes*, was awarded *Opportunity*'s first prize in 1927. This drama is a folk tragedy that pits modern medicine against folk customs. Other published plays include *A Sunday Morning in the South* (1974), which was a "lynching play," and the historical dramas *Frederick Douglass* (1935) and *William and Ellen Craft* (1935). While these are the only plays published, Johnson did produce many more dramas about "average Negro life," "brotherhood" between the races, and the intermixture of races. One of her great contributions to drama is the representation of authentic folk speech rather than stereotypical mutilated English.

Life, of course, grew harder for Johnson after the Harlem Renaissance with the onset of the Great Depression. She tried ceaselessly to obtain fellowship money, but with the exception of an honorable mention from the Harmon Foundation in 1928, she never succeeded. Nevertheless, she continued to be productive. She wrote a weekly newspaper column from 1926 to 1932 titled "Homely Philosophy" that was syndicated to twenty newspapers. Though it was somewhat clichéd, Johnson tried to bring cheer into the homes of Americans during economic devastation, with such columns as "A Smile on the Lips" or "Find Pleasure in Common Things." She was listed in the 1932 edition of *Who's Who of Colored America*. She was also asked to join the D.C. Women's Party, Poets League of Washington, and Poet Laureate League.

The home of poet, playwright, and novelist Georgia Douglas Johnson served as a salon to Harlem Renaissance writers such as Jean Toomer, Langston Hughes, Angelina Grimké, and Alice Dunbar-Nelson. [Schomburg Center]

Losing her position with the U.S. Department of Labor in 1934, Johnson was forced to turn to temporary work, but she continued to write. She won third prize in 1934 in a poetry contest sponsored by the D.C. Federation of Women's Clubs. Georgia Douglas Johnson was also a member of several literary social clubs and organizations, such as the American Society of African Culture and the League of American Writers.

During World War II, she continued to publish poetry as well as to read her poems over the radio. She also returned to music during this period and tried her hand at short story writing. Her three extant stories are "Free," "Gesture," and "Tramp"; the last two were published under the pseudonym "Paul Tremaine," and are derived in large part from the life of Gypsy Drago, a man who did not discover that he was Black until the age of thirty. These stories predominantly focus on relationships and not on racial themes, however. Johnson tried in vain to locate a publisher for the biography of her late husband, *The Black Cabinet*, and for her novel, *White Men's Children*. Her last book of poetry, *Share My World*, was published in 1962. One year before her death, in 1965, she was awarded an honorary doctorate from Atlanta University. During these later years, she developed into a local institution, widely known as "the old woman with the headband and the tablet around her neck." The tablet was for her to write down any idea that came to her.

When Georgia Douglas Johnson died of a stroke on May 14, 1966, she left a multitude of papers that were literally thrown out. Much of what she wrote is lost, but she lived a remarkable and unselfish life.

BIBLIOGRAPHY

AAW2; Adoff, Arnold, ed. *The Poetry of Black America: An Anthology of the Twentieth Century* (1973); Brown, Sterling A., Arthur P. Davis, and Ulysses Lee, eds. *The Negro Caravan: Writings by American Negroes* (1941); *Catalog of Writings by Georgia Douglas Johnson* (n.d.); Cullen, Countee, ed. *Caroling Dusk: An Anthology of Verse by Negro Poets* (1927); Cullen-Jackman collection. Robert W. Woodruff Library, Atlanta University, Atlanta, Georgia; Davis, Theresa Scott and Charles Y. Freeman. "A Biographical Sketch of Georgia Douglas Johnson and Some of Her Works" (1931); Dover, Cedric. "The Importance of Georgia Douglas Johnson." *Crisis* (December 1952); Ellington, Mary Davis. "Plays by Negro Authors with Special Emphasis upon the Period 1916 to 1934," Master's thesis (1934); Fletcher, Winona. "From Genteel Poet to Revolutionary Playwright: Georgia Douglas Johnson as a Symbol of Black Success, Failure, and Fortitude," *Theatre Annual* (February 1985); Hughes, Langston, and Arna Bontemps, eds. *The Poetry of the Negro, 1746-1970* (1970); Hull, Gloria T. *Color, Sex, and Poetry: Three Women Writers of the Harlem Renaissance* (1987); Johnson, James Weldon, ed. *The Book of American Negro Poetry* (1931); Kerlin, Robert T. *Negro Poets and Their Poems* (1923); Lewis, David Levering. *When Harlem Was in Vogue* (1981); Shockley, Ann Allen, ed. *Afro-American Women Writers: 1746-1933* (1988); White, Newman Ivey and Walter Clinton Jackson, eds. *An Anthology of Verse by American Negroes* (1924).

SELECTED WORKS BY GEORGIA DOUGLAS JOHNSON

Verse: *The Heart of a Woman and Other Poems* (1918); *Bronze: A Book of Verse* (1922); *An Autumn Love Cycle* (1928); *Share My World* (1962). Plays: *Blue Blood* (1927); *Plumes* (1928); *Frederick Douglass Leaves for Freedom* (1940); "Frederick Douglass" and "William and Ellen Craft." In *Negro History in Thirteen Plays*, ed. Willis Richardson and May Miller (1935); "Plumes." In *Plays of Negro Life: A Source-Book of Native American Drama*, ed. Alain Locke and Montgomery Gregory (1927); "A Sunday Morning in the South." In *Black Theatre, U.S.A.: Forty-five Plays by Black American Playwrights, 1947-1974*, ed. James V. Hatch and Ted Shine (1974).

JOCELYN HAZELWOOD DONLON

JOHNSON, HALLE TANNER DILLON (1864-1901)

"[I] try to keep before [myself] the possibility of failing but unless some harder and more complex than anything they have given me yet I feel that I can not, but, if they mark me fairly, get thro" (Harlan 1972). With this determination and self-confidence, Halle Tanner Dillon passed the state medical examinations in Alabama in 1891 and became the first woman licensed to practice medicine in the state. Her concern for social justice led her to establish a training school and dispensary at Tuskegee Institute in Alabama, where she became resident physician.

Halle (Hallie) Tanner was born in Pittsburgh, Pennsylvania, on October 17, 1864, to Benjamin Tucker Tanner and Sarah Elizabeth (Miller) Tanner. She was the eldest daughter of nine children, two of whom died in infancy. The Tanners were a prominent family whose home in Philadelphia was a rest haven for travelers and a meeting place for Black intellectuals, including leading Black and white clergy. The parents created a culturally developed and intellectually stimulating atmosphere by introducing their children to the works of prominent African-American artists such as Edward Bannister and Edmonia Lewis. The Tanners' son, Henry Ossawa (1859-1937), was guided by the experience; the gifted artist became a celebrated painter of landscape, religious, and genre paintings.

Benjamin Tucker Tanner, a successful minister in the African Methodist Episcopal (AME) Church, edited the *Christian Recorder* beginning in 1868; he was first editor of the *AME Church Review* in 1884 and two years later was elected a bishop in the church. He had worked incessantly on the *Review* with daughter Halle as an office staff member. She soon met Charles E. Dillon, of Trenton, New Jersey, and after a brief courtship they married in the Tanner home in June 1886. Halle gave birth to the Dillons' only child, Sadie, in 1887. The marriage ended with Charles Dillon's death, although the details and date of death are unknown. Halle Dillon and her daughter returned to the Tanner home on Diamond Street, where they remained for several months.

Determined to put her life back in order, Dillon, then twenty-four years old, enrolled in the Woman's Medical College of Pennsylvania. The only Black student in her class of thirty-six women, she completed the three-year course and graduated with high honors on May 7, 1891. Booker T. Washington, president of Tuskegee Institute, had searched for four years for a Black resident physician to provide health care for the local community. He had written to the dean of the Woman's Medical College for a nomination, who apparently mentioned it to Dillon. Dillon was interested in the position and wrote to Washington.

Washington's letters to Halle Dillon introduced her to the social and economic climate in Tuskegee and the responsibilities of the position. Washington preferred a Black woman, and he offered a salary of $600 a year with board included. The resident physician would teach two classes each day, administer the health department, and compound the medicines needed to serve the sick. Additional compensation was to be derived from the physician's private practice. Much of the work would be missionary in spirit; thus, the physician would need to come for the good of the cause. The physician would need to pass the local or state medical examination and begin work on September 1, 1891.

Halle Dillon found the offer appealing, accepted the challenge, and arrived in Tuskegee in August 1891. Washington had arranged for her to prepare for the strenuous medical board examination through study with Cornelius Nathaniel Dorsett, a practicing physician in Montgomery where the examinations were to be held. Dorsett was the first Black physician to pass the Alabama medical board. Both Bishop Tanner and Halle Dillon were confident of Dillon's ability to pass any reasonable and just examination; however, they were more concerned about the examining board. Halle Dillon's impending appearance before the examiners caused a public stir. Some questioned her daring to sit for the examination. The curious wanted to know how she looked.

The ten-day examinations tested her on a separate subject each day. At the end the board supervisor was impressed with Halle Dillon's neatness and cleanliness in work. Three weeks after her return to Tuskegee, she learned that she had passed with an average of 78.81. Confident of her accuracy and completeness in response to the examination questions, Dillon felt that the examiner might have been too critical and too rigid in evaluating her papers. The press took notice of Dillon's success and recognized her as the first woman of any race to become licensed as a medical doctor in Alabama and the first Black woman to practice medicine in the state. Dillon's achievement called attention to a double standard regarding the races, for Anna M. Longshore, a white woman who failed the medical examination earlier, had practiced medicine in Alabama without a license before Dillon took the test.

From 1891 to 1894, Halle Dillon was resident physician at Tuskegee. During this time she established a nurses' training school and the Lafayette Dispensary to provide for the health care needs of the local residents and the campus. She also compounded many of her own medicines. In 1894, she married Reverend John Quincy Johnson, who in 1893-94 was a mathematics teacher at Tuskegee. The next year, John Quincy Johnson became president of Allen University, a private school for Black students in Columbia, South Carolina. He received a B.D. from Hartford Divinity School, Hartford, Connecticut, and the D.D. from Morris Brown College, Atlanta, Georgia. Halle Johnson joined her husband when he did postgraduate work at Princeton Theological Seminary.

Halle Tanner Johnson was an Alabama pioneer: the first Black woman to sit for—and pass—a medical board examination, and the first woman of any race to be licensed to practice medicine in the state. As resident physician at Tuskegee Institute, she established a nurses' training school and a dispensary to care for the needs of the community as well as the campus population. [Medical College of Pennsylvania]

The Johnsons moved to Nashville, Tennessee, where John Quincy Johnson was pastor of Saint Paul AME Church from 1900 to 1903. They had three sons, who were named after their noted father, grandfather, and uncle—John Quincy, Jr., Benjamin T., and Henry Tanner. Complications of childbirth and dysentery led to Halle Johnson's death in her Nashville home on April 26, 1901, when she was thirty-seven years old. She is buried in Nashville's Greenwood Cemetery. Three grandchildren and two grandnieces survive her today.

Halle Tanner Dillon Johnson, a member of a noted and highly respected Black family of the nineteenth century, is a notable figure in Black and American history and in the racial history of the South. She became an Alabama pioneer when she became the first woman in the state to pass the medical board examination. She withstood the curiosity of a questioning society that had not seen a Black woman sit for a medical examination; she opened public discussion of racial discrimination in the medical profession; and she improved significantly the health care of a racially segregated community by providing training for nurses, building a dispensary, and ministering to the needs of the residents.

BIBLIOGRAPHY

Alexander-Minter, Ray. "The Tanner Family," *Henry Ossawa Tanner Exhibition Catalog* (1991); Atlanta University. *Bulletin* (November 1891); Brown, Hallie Quinn, comp. *Homespun Heroines and Other Women of Distinction* (1926); Harlan, Louis, ed. *The Booker T. Washington Papers* (1972); *NBAW*; Wright, R. R., Jr., ed. *Encyclopedia of African Methodism* (1916).

JESSIE CARNEY SMITH

JOHNSON, HAZEL WINIFRED
(1927-)

Interested in travel and changing her outlook, Hazel Johnson entered the Army in 1955, five years after completing basic nurses' training at New York's Harlem Hospital. She received a direct commission as a first lieutenant in the U.S. Army Nursing Corps in May 1960. Nineteen years later the one-star insignia representing brigadier general was pinned on her uniform. Thus, at age fifty-two, Hazel Winifred Johnson became the first Black woman general in the history of the U.S. military.

Taking advantage of the educational opportunities provided by the military, she earned a Bachelor's degree in nursing from Villanova University, a Master's degree in nursing education from Columbia University, and a Ph.D. in education administration through Catholic University. She was chief of the Army Nurse Corps from 1979 to 1983, the first Black American to hold the corps' most powerful position. The promotion to brigadier general was recommended by a military board and approved by Congress.

In 1983, the general retired and rejoined civilian life as director of the government affairs division of the American Nursing Association. Three years later she left to assume a professorship of nursing at George Mason University in Virginia. Her retirement from the army created a void in top female leadership, leaving only two women generals, neither of whom was Black. After Hazel Johnson's retirement, two years elapsed before another Black woman, in any branch of the military, pinned on the coveted star—Sherian G. Cadoria.

Although retired from army service, military mementos adorn the Clifton, Virginia, home of Johnson and her husband, David Brown. The Distinguished Service Medal, the Legion of Merit, the Meritorious Service Medal, and an Army Commendation Medal with an oak leaf cluster are among the general's decorations, awards, and badges.

BIBLIOGRAPHY

Army Records. General Officer Management Office, Headquarters, Department of the Army, Washington, D.C.; Reynolds, Barbara A., ed. *Delta Journal* (Winter 1986-87).

LINDA ROCHELL LANE

JOHNSON, KATHERINE *see*
JOHNSON, ANN BATTLES

JOHNSON, KATHRYN MAGNOLIA
(1878-1955)

Lecturer, author, fieldworker for the National Association for the Advancement of Colored People (NAACP), and public school teacher, Kathryn Magnolia Johnson was born December 15, 1878, in the Drake County Colored Settlement near Greenville, Ohio. She attended public schools in New Paris, Ohio, and went on to study at Wilberforce University during 1897-98 and 1901-2. She studied at the University of North Dakota during the summer of 1908.

Johnson began teaching in 1898, and worked in the Ohio and Indiana public school systems until 1901. She taught at the State Normal School in Elizabeth City, North Carolina, 1904-5, and then accepted a position as Dean of Women at Shorter College in Little Rock, Arkansas, 1906-7. From 1907 until 1910, Johnson instructed high school students who were attending summer school.

In 1910, Johnson, having moved to Kansas City, Kansas, shifted her career to "race work." Mary White Ovington, one of the white founders of the NAACP, credits Johnson as the first fieldworker of the NAACP. Johnson earned her living by making small commissions on branch memberships and *Crisis* (the official publication of the NAACP) subscriptions. Beginning in 1913, Johnson traveled extensively throughout the South and West, establishing branches, instigating educational campaigns to raise the consciousness of southern Blacks, and drumming up support for the national headquarters of the NAACP in New York City. In February of 1915 Johnson became a "reimbursed" field agent—she earned a small salary in addition to her commissions.

In January 1916 the NAACP publicly commended Johnson for her fruitful organization of all-Black branches. Six months later, however, the NAACP dismissed her. Although no definitive explanation of this decision exists, some historians believe that Johnson's forceful personality, blunt conversational style, and emphatic beliefs that the NAACP leadership should be all-Black hastened, if not caused, her dismissal.

Johnson and Addie Hunton were two of three Black women who worked for the YMCA in France during World War I to guard the rights of the Black American soldiers abroad. Hunton and Johnson co-authored *Two Colored Women with the American Expeditionary Forces* (1922) that detailed their observations and experiences.

After World War I, Johnson undertook a nationwide campaign to disseminate Black literature. She traveled as a sales representative for Associated Publishers and the Association for the Study of Negro Life and History in Washington, D.C. She championed what she called her "two foot shelf of Negro literature," which consisted of fifteen books published by the association.

Johnson continued to teach, lecture, and agitate for social justice throughout her life. She was a member of the Independent Order of St. Luke, the African Methodist Episcopal church, and the Republican party.

Possibly the first fieldworker for the NAACP, Kathryn Magnolia Johnson firmly believed that the leadership of the organization should be all-Black. Her outspokenness on this matter may have caused her dismissal from the organization in 1916. [Schomburg Center]

BIBLIOGRAPHY

Aptheker, Herbert, ed. *The Correspondence of W.E.B. Du Bois* (1973); Du Bois, W.E.B. "A *Crisis* Agent and Organizer," *Crisis* (July 1914); Johnson, Kathryn and Addie Hunton. *Two Colored Women with the American Expeditionary Forces* (1922); Kellogg, Charles Flint. *NAACP: A History of the National Association for the Advancement of Colored People* (1967); *New York Times*. Obituary (May 12, 1955); Ovington, Mary White. "The National Association for the Advancement of Colored People," *Journal of Negro History* (April 1924), and *The Walls Came Tumbling Down* (1947); Robb, Frederic. *The Negro in Chicago, 1779-1927*. In *Black Biographical Dictionaries, 1790-1950* (microfiche 1987); Salem, Dorothy. *To Better Our World: Black Women in Organized Reform, 1890-1920* (1990); *WWCA*.

THEA ARNOLD

JOHNSON, NORMA HOLLOWAY

President Jimmy Carter appointed Louisiana native Norma Holloway Johnson to the U.S. District Court for the District of Columbia in March 1980. When the Senate confirmed her appointment that July, she became the first Black woman to be appointed to the federal bench in the District of Columbia. Since her appointment, Holloway, in addition to presiding over trials, has served on two judicial conferences and assisted committees concerned with judicial management.

After graduating from Miner Teachers College in 1955, and inspired by the 1954 U.S. Supreme Court decision in *Brown* v. *Board of Education*, Johnson decided against a career in dentistry and chose instead to enter the Georgetown University Law Center. Motivated by a passion to pursue legal equality for African-Americans, her initial goal was to become an attorney for the legal defense fund of the National Association for the Advancement of Colored People (NAACP).

After becoming the first Black woman to graduate from Georgetown's law school in 1962, Johnson became a trial attorney in the civil division of the U.S. Department of Justice, where she served until 1967. She then went to the Office of the Corporation Counsel for the District of Columbia, where she eventually became chief of the juvenile division. In 1970, President Richard Nixon asked her to accept a judgeship on what would become the Superior Court for the District of Columbia. She served in that court until her appointment to the federal bench.

Norma Johnson has played numerous roles other than that of federal judge. She is a founding member of the National Association of Black Women Attorneys and the National Association of Women Judges, and she is active in many professional and public interest organizations. Juvenile justice continues to be a major concern, and she spends much of her spare time attempting to reform the juvenile justice system.

BIBLIOGRAPHY

The American Bench (1987-88); *NBAW*; *Who's Who in American Law* (1990-91); *WWBA* (1990).

PHILIP A. PRESBY

JOHNSON, VIRGINIA (1950-)

Virginia Johnson was born January 25, 1950, in Washington, D.C. She attended New York University and the Washington School of Ballet. Johnson made her debut with the Washington Ballet in 1965 and the Capitol Ballet in 1968. She is known best for her work with the Dance Theatre of Harlem, for which she has danced since 1971. Johnson, a lyrical dancer, is a premier Black ballerina. Her versatility as a dancer has allowed her to move successfully from classical ballet roles like the *Don Quixote* pas de deux to contemporary dramatic ballets like Valerie Bettis's *A Streetcar Named Desire*. Johnson also created the role of Giselle in Arthur Mitchell's reinterpretation of the romantic ballet *Giselle*. As Giselle, she plays the sheltered, half-caste daughter of a recently freed African slave. The ballet is set in the bayous of Louisiana. Deborah Jowitt, dance critic for the *Village Voice*, applauded Johnson's representation of Giselle as a "triumph of intelligence, sensitivity, and good taste."

Johnson found her niche in dramatic ballets, and she mastered many of the classics, including Agnes De Mille's *The Accused* in *Fall River Legend*. *The Accused* is a dramatic rendition of the celebrated case of Lizzie Borden. Anna Kisselgoff of the *New York Times* lauded Johnson's performance and pronounced the production "a sheer triumph." Johnson continues to dance the technical, emotional, and dramatic spectrum of ballets and continuously extends her artistic range from historic classical to contemporary experimental ballets.

Johnson received the Young Achiever Award of 1985 from the National Council of Women of the United States for her work with young dancers, in master classes, and in lecture demonstrations.

BIBLIOGRAPHY

Clarke, Mary and David Vaughan, eds. *The Encyclopedia of Dance and Ballet* (1977); Cohen-Stratyner, Barbara Naomi. *Biographical Dictionary of Dance* (1982); *EBA*; Emery, Lynne Fauley. *Black Dance in the United States: From 1619 to Today* (1988); Long, Richard. *The Black Tradition in American Concert Dance* (1990); McDonagh, Don. *The Complete Guide to Modern Dance* (1976); Toppin, Edgar A. *A Biographical History of Blacks in America since 1528* (1971); Willis, John, ed. *Dance World* (1976).

KARIAMU WELSH ASANTE

JONES, CLARA STANTON (1913-)

The year 1976 was an eventful one for Black librarians. As the American Library Association celebrated its centennial and the country celebrated its bicentennial, a Black woman, Clara Stanton Jones, became the first Black president of the American Library Association (ALA).

She was born in St. Louis, Missouri, May 1913, to Ralph and Etta Clara Stanton. She received a B.A. from Spelman College and an A.B.L.S. in Library Science from the University of Michigan. She married Alfred Jones in 1938 and they had three children. Her library career began at a historically Black college, Dillard University in New Orleans. Her next position was at Southern University in Baton Rouge, Louisiana, where she served as associate librarian and instructor in library science.

She took a position in 1944 at the Detroit Public Library, where she was first a children's librarian and then rose through the ranks to become a library neighborhood consultant in late 1968. In 1970, she was elected director of the Detroit Public Library, the fifth largest public library in the United States, by the Detroit Library Commission. After her appointment Jones later commented: "You might say that in a sense I was the dark horse candidate, both figuratively and literally. My appointment was unconventional because I am Black, I am a woman, and I come from middle management in our own system" (*Current Biography* 1976). As director of the library, she was instrumental in creating the Information Place, commonly known by public librarians as TIP, a pioneering information and referral service that was established as an integral part of every branch. As director, she continued to use creative leadership to maintain viable library service for the people of Detroit in a period of fiscal problems. She became a well-known speaker in Detroit and a champion of that city's revitalization and cultural development.

She has received numerous awards including the Distinguished Alumnus Award of the University of Michigan School of Library Science. She has also been associated with the National Association for the Advancement of Colored People, Women's International League for Peace and Freedom, and the American Civil Liberties Union.

She served as acting president of the American Library Association in 1975 and served as president from 1976 to 1977. As the first African-American president of the ALA, Clara Stanton Jones provided sterling leadership in the development and promotion of appropriate activities for the centennial celebration of the association.

BIBLIOGRAPHY

ALA Yearbook of Library and Information Services. A Review of Library Events (1977, 1980, 1984); "Campaigning for ALA Presidency: Clara Jones Speaks Out," *Library Journal* (1975); Croneberger, Robert J. and Carolyn Luck. "Defining Information and Referral Service," *Library Journal* (1975); *Current Biography* (1976); "Detroit's Top Librarian," *Ebony* (November 27, 1971); "The Emancipated Librarian," *McCall's* (April 1971); Gell, Marilyn. "Five Women," *Library Journal* (1975); Jones, Clara S. "Reflections on Library Service to the Disadvantaged." Manuscript (1974), and "Ruminations and Relevancies: Public Libraries and Cities," *Illinois Libraries* (1971); *Who's Who of American Women* (1975-76).

JOYCE C. WRIGHT

JONES, CLAUDIA (1915-1965)

Claudia Jones was among a tiny cadre of Black women to rise within the ranks of the Communist party of the United States. Born in Port of Spain, British West Indies (Trinidad), Jones was only nine years old when her family migrated to Harlem in 1924. As a teenager she earned a reputation as a promising journalist, but her education was cut short by the Depression—she was forced to drop out of school in order to work. Like many working-class Harlem residents, she was attracted to the Communist party (C.P.) through the International Labor Defense's campaign to free the Scottsboro Nine, and at eighteen she joined the Young Communist League (YCL). Jones rose quickly within the ranks of the Harlem C.P., becoming editor of the YCL *Weekly Review* and the *Spotlight* and assuming the posts of chairperson of the national council of the YCL, YCL education officer for New York State, and eventually national director of the YCL.

As one of the preeminent young Black Communists in Harlem during the popular front, Jones actively supported the National Negro Congress (NNC) from its inception, serving as a leader of the NNC youth council in Harlem. Although she had been associated with issues pertaining to African-American rights and was among the first to criticize Earl Browder's decision to abandon self-determination in the Black belt, during World War II Jones developed a reputation as a relentless critic of male chauvinism and a leading party spokesperson for women's rights. After the war she was appointed to the women's commission, briefly serving as its secretary.

Following a series of arrests and attempted deportations beginning in 1948, she was eventually indicted in 1951 for violating the Smith Act and imprisoned in Alderson Federal Reformatory for Women. Although her case did not attract as much attention as Angela Davis's did two decades later, Jones became a symbol for a generation of radical Black women who came of age on the eve of the civil rights upsurges of the 1960s, many of whom marched and petitioned on her behalf. Her incarceration is one of the clearest examples in history of an African-American woman serving time as a political prisoner in the United States.

Despite her deteriorating health, Jones was not released from prison until she had served her complete one-year sentence. In December 1955, she was deported to London, where she continued to work for radical Black causes, including the Caribbean Labour Congress, the West-Indian Workers and Students Association, and the Communist party. She served as editor of the left-wing *West Indian Gazette* during the late 1950s and in 1962 was guest editor of *Soviet Women*. Jones's life came to an end on Christmas day, 1965; her death was caused in part by tuberculosis contracted as a teenager but aggravated by prison conditions in the United States.

BIBLIOGRAPHY

Davis, Angela. *Women, Race, and Class* (1981); Elean, Thomas. "Remembering Claudia Jones," *World Marxist Review* (March 1987); Haywood, Harry. *Black Bolshevik: Autobiography of an Afro-American Communist* (1978); Johnson, Buzz. *"I Think of My Mother": Notes on the Life and Times of Claudia Jones* (1985); Naison, Mark. *Communists in Harlem During the Depression* (1983); North, Joe. "Communist Women," *Political Affairs* (March 1971).

ROBIN D. G. KELLEY

JONES, GAYL (1949-)

For Gayl Jones, fiction and storytelling are different. "I say I'm a fiction writer if I'm asked, but I really think of myself as a storyteller. When I say fiction, it evokes a lot of different kinds of abstractions, but when I say storyteller, it always has its human connections" (Harper 1977). Those human connections were made for Jones when, as a child, her mother, grandmother and other adults introduced her to the art of telling stories.

Gayl Jones was born in Lexington, Kentucky, on November 23, 1949, to Lucille and Franklin Jones. In her childhood, Jones "first knew stories as things that were heard." Her mother wrote stories to be read aloud to Gayl and her brother, Franklin. Gayl's favorite was called "Esapher and the Wizard," but all of them contrasted greatly with some of the "really un-

Calling herself a storyteller, poet and novelist Gayl Jones used the blues as a thematic undercurrent in her novels Eva's Man *and* Corregidora. *[Schomburg Center]*

fortunate kinds of books . . . children learned to read out of" when she was growing up (Harper 1977).

Jones's mother and grandmother were important early influences, but teachers and educational institutions also provided encouragement. Jones began writing her own stories in the second or third grade, but she gives credit to her fifth-grade teacher, Mrs. Hodges, for encouraging her efforts to write. As a student at Connecticut College she won an award for writing the best original poem and became one of four undergraduate poets who toured the Connecticut poetry circuit. After earning a B.A. at Connecticut College, she continued her education at Brown University in Providence, Rhode Island, where she earned an M.A. (1973) and a D.A. (1975).

Although Jones is best known for her two novels, *Corregidora* (1975) and *Eva's Man* (1976), she also has written short stories, poetry, and plays. While still a student at Brown, she began to explore the themes and experiment with the techniques that later bore fruit in her novels. In short stories such as "The Welfare Check" (1970), "The Roundhouse" (1971), and "The Return: A Fantasy" (1971), Jones assumes the storyteller's voice and writes in the first person. The technique of writing in the first person allows Jones to minimize authorial intrusion while achieving the directness of the storyteller's relationship to her audience. *Chile Woman*, Jones's first play, was produced at Brown in 1973 by Rites and Reason, a university/community arts project. In *Chile Woman*, Jones explores the legacy of slavery and examines the devastation it wreaked on human relationships. Her use of blues music as a means of voicing and structuring the themes of the play is a device to which she returned in her first novel, *Corregidora*.

Corregidora is a challenging book to read. Its central character, blues singer Ursa Corregidora, is the last in a line of women fathered, and debauched, by the Portuguese slavemaster Simon Corregidora. Stories about the incest and prostitution that are her heritage have been handed down from mother to daughter for four generations. An accidental fall makes it impossible for Ursa to bear children and triggers her search for a means of coming to terms with her past. Jones uses blues as the means by which Ursa gives voice to her pain, and it becomes the means of her transcendence as well.

Reviewers of *Eva's Man*, Jones's second novel, tended to see it as too similar in tone and subject matter to *Corregidora*. In *Eva's Man*, however, Jones merely shows herself to be the kind of musician who can play endless variations on a central group of themes. As a blues singer, Ursa Corregidora is able to use language as an instrument of regeneration, whereas Eva, the central character of *Eva's Man*, is imprisoned within her own silence. Eva listens to blues music but does not speak of her own pain. As a result, the sexual violence that is transcended in *Corregidora* results in murder and madness in *Eva's Man*.

Gayl Jones returns to Brazil as a setting for other stories in her two book-length poems, *Song for Anninho* (1981) and *Xarque* (1985). The background of *Song* is the story of a Portuguese attack on Palmares, a settlement founded by African slaves who had escaped from their masters, but at the forefront is the story of two lovers who affirm their love in spite of the brutality that they cannot escape. In *Xarque*, the remarkable spiritual energy that is present in *Song* is now dissipated by intergroup disharmony. Thus, in this pair of story-poems, as in her pair of novels, Jones concentrates on theme and variation.

In addition to her prolific career as novelist, playwright, and poet, Jones is also an academic. She was a professor of English at the University of Michigan, Ann Arbor, 1975-81. *Liberating Voices* (1991) is a scholarly work about the use of the oral tradition in the work of African-American writers.

BIBLIOGRAPHY
Bell, Roseann P. "Gayl Jones Takes a Look at *Corregidora*: An Interview." In *Sturdy Black Bridges: Visions of Black Women in Literature*, ed. Roseann P. Bell, Bettye J. Parker, and Beverly Guy-Sheftall (1979); Harper, Michael. "Gayl Jones: An Interview," *Massachusetts Review* (1977); Rowell, Charles H. "An Interview with Gayl Jones," *Callaloo* (October 1982); Smith, Cynthia J. "Gayl Jones." In *African American Writers*, ed. Valerie Smith, Lea Baechler, and A. Walton Litz (1991); Tate, Claudia C. "An Interview with Gayl Jones," *Black American Literature Forum* (1979).

SELECTED WRITINGS BY GAYL JONES
Fiction: *Corregidora* (1975); *Eva's Man* (1976); *White Rat: Short Stories* (1977). Drama: *Chile Woman*. Shubert Playbook Series (1974); "The Ancestor: A Street Play." *B(lacks) O(n) P(aper)*, No. 1 (1974); "Beyond Yourself (The Midnight Confession)—for Brother Ahh." *B(lacks) O(n) P(aper)*, No. 3 (1975). Poetry: *Song for Anninho* (1981); *The Hermit Woman* (1983); *Xarque and Other Poems* (1985).

CYNTHIA J. SMITH

JONES, LOIS MAILOU (1905-)

An active and acclaimed painter for more than six decades, Lois Mailou Jones enjoyed two impressive careers, one as a professor of art and the other as an artist. Her teaching gave her financial security and served as an inspiration and a challenge.

Lois Jones was born on November 3, 1905, in Boston to Caroline Dorinda Adams and Thomas Vreeland Jones. Her father was superintendent of a large office building and attended night classes at Suffolk Law School, where he received his law degree in 1915 at age forty. "I think that much of my drive surely comes from my father," says Jones, "wanting to be someone, having an ambition" (Benjamin 1986). Her mother was a beautician and Jones's first mentor. She filled the Jones home with color and freshly cut flowers, instilling in her daughter a love of beauty.

With the assistance of four annual tuition scholarships, Jones earned a diploma from the High School of Practical Arts (HSPA). During her high school years, she also attended the Boston Museum Vocational Drawing Class, on a scholarship. While at HSPA, she was apprenticed to Grace Ripley, a well-known costume designer and professor at the Rhode Island School of Design. She assisted Ripley in creating costumes for the Ted Shawn School of Dance and a branch of the Bragiotti School in Boston. Working on Saturdays and after school, she designed dance costumes, especially masks. She recalls that "very early I was introduced to Africa through creating the masks with the Ripley studio" (Benjamin 1986).

In 1923, Jones was admitted to the Boston Museum of Fine Arts, where each year from 1923 to 1927 she won the coveted Susan Minot Lane Scholarship in Design. Here she studied design concepts, life drawing, and portraiture under such artists as Anson Cross, Phillip Hale, Alice Morse, and Henry Hunt Clark. She graduated from the museum school with honors in 1927. During her last year at the museum school, Jones enrolled in evening classes at the Boston Normal Art School (now the Massachusetts College of Art), receiving a teaching certificate in 1927. That same year she won a scholarship to the

Designers Art School of Boston, where she continued graduate study with Ludwig Frank, internationally known designer of textiles. Her studies were extended at Harvard University during the summer of 1928. Jones created a series of designs for cretonne—a strong, unglazed cotton or linen cloth that is used especially for curtains and upholstery—and other fabric and textile patterns.

That year, two eminent educators, Henry Hunt Clark and Charlotte Hawkins Brown, told Jones to "go south" and help her people. She had been disappointed by Clark when she applied for a position at the museum school; none was available, and Clark pointed the young designer toward the South and its

Noted artist-educator Lois Mailou Jones is seen here in her studio, surrounded by works exemplifying her expressive, colorful, hard-edged style, which fuses abstraction with decorative patterns and naturalism. [Scurlock Studio]

needs. She balked. Next, she applied to Howard University. She was informed that they had recently hired James A. Porter and had no other positions available. Then she heard Brown speak in Boston, urging college students to take their talents to the youth of the South. This time she accepted the challenge. Although thought by some to be too young and inexperienced, she was hired by Brown to develop the art department at the Palmer Memorial Institute, one of the nation's first preparatory schools for African-Americans, in Sedalia, North Carolina. Jones established the curriculum, served as chairperson of the department, and provided instruction to a small, eager class. In addition to her other duties, Jones also taught dancing, coached a basketball team, and played the piano for Sunday morning worship services.

During the spring of 1930, James Vernon Herring, founder and head of the Department of Art at Howard University, was invited by Jones to lecture at Palmer. He was impressed by the work of her students and recruited her to serve as an instructor of design at Howard. Jones joined the Howard faculty in 1930 and remained there until her retirement in 1977. She, James A. Porter, and James Lesesne Wells constituted the art department and forged a curriculum unique among historically Black colleges and universities.

For her first sabbatical Jones chose the Académie Julian in Paris. During a summer on Martha's Vineyard, she had met sculptor Meta Warrick Fuller and composer Harry T. Burleigh. They advised her that, if she wanted to find a niche in the art world, she should travel to Paris for recognition. Also, of course, study in Paris was a tradition for American artists who could manage the expense. With the aid of a General Education Board fellowship, Jones sailed for France on the S.S. *Normandie* on September 1, 1937. Her sojourn there marked a shift in her career from that of designer, illustrator, and teacher to that of painter. The experience allowed her, as Jones said, "to be shackle free, to create and to be myself" (Benjamin 1986).

Many of her works from that year were painted on location. It was during one of her painting exercises on the Seine that Jones met Emile Bernard, the father of French Symbolist painting. He encouraged her and criticized her work. Albert Smith, an African-American artist in Paris, also became a friend during Jones's stay and after her return to the United States.

Jones made such progress that, toward the end of the academic year, her friends and instructors urged her to submit paintings to the annual Salon de Printemps of the Société des Artistes Français, one of the most important exhibits of the year. Although her work of this era reveals a commitment to the organizing principles and preferred palette of the Impressionists and Post-Impressionists, her paintings were clearly personal interpretations. As James Porter, author of *Modern Negro Art*, observed: "Thus far her painting has been in the tradition, but not in the imitation of Cezanne. . . . Miss Jones wishes to confirm Cezanne but at the same time to add an original note of her own. . . . Sensuous color delicately adjusted to the mood indicates the artistic perceptiveness of this young woman" (Porter 1952).

Soon after her return to the United States in September 1938, Jones exhibited at the Robert Vose Galleries in Boston. Her work received high praise, and her reputation grew as she exhibited throughout the United States. After her return to Washington, she met Alain Locke, poet laureate of the Harlem Renaissance, or New Negro Movement, and head of the philosophy department at Howard. Telling her of his plans to include one of her Parisian street scenes in his forthcoming book, *The Negro in Art* (1940), Locke strongly encouraged her to reevaluate her subjects and take her own heritage more seriously. An early advocate of Black consciousness, Locke was perhaps the most influential voice on art in the African-American community at that time. Jones's response to Locke's challenge produced works focused on the Black American. The artist refers to the 1940s as her Locke period. Also during this decade, Jones took classes at Howard, receiving an A.B. in art education, graduating magna cum laude in 1945.

When Lois Jones married the noted Haitian graphic artist and designer Louis Vergniaud Pierre-Noel in 1953, both her life and her art were transformed. They took advantage of an invitation from the Haitian government to teach at the Centre d'Art and the Foyer des Arts Plastiques so that they could honeymoon in Haiti. The experience was the beginning of a new way of seeing for Jones, and, from her first visit, she "fell increasingly in love with Haiti and its people" (Benjamin 1986). Her early Haitian paintings explored the picturesque elements of the marketplace and its people. Although the essence of Europe was still, at the beginning, very much apparent, the palette and the formal organization of her paintings gradually evolved into a brilliantly spirited style, fresh, energetically fluid, and highly individual. This new style signaled clearly that Europe did not yield the exuberance so vital to expressing the vigor found in this African-oriented culture.

Jones's work in the 1960s drew more upon her knowledge of design techniques and her passion for

When Lois Mailou Jones married the noted Haitian graphic artist and designer Louis Vergniaud Pierre-Noel in 1953, her life and her art were transformed. From her first visit, she fell in love with Haiti and its people. Peasants on Parade *(1962) reflects her fascination with the marketplace and its people. The painting is in the collection of the artist. [Tritobia Benjamin]*

In the summer of 1989, Jones returned to France. The works that resulted recall an earlier era. Reminiscent of the Impressionist/Post-Impressionist style abandoned by Jones more than thirty years earlier, the paintings created during that visit illustrate her continued fascination with nature and her desire to capture the fleeting beauty of place. In 1990, a major retrospective, "The World of Lois Mailou Jones," was sponsored by Meridian House International in Washington, D.C. It opened in January and traveled for two years across the United States.

Lois Mailou Jones has received innumerable awards for her work in competitions, including the National Thayer Prize for excellence in design. She has also received honorary degrees from a number of universities, including Howard. In 1954, the government of Haiti awarded her the Diplome and Decoration de l'Ordre Nationale "Honneur et Mérite au Grade de Chevalier." Her work is represented in museums and private collections across the country and the world, including the Metropolitan Museum of Art in New York; the Museum of Fine Arts and the Museum of the National Center of Afro-American Artists in Boston; the National Museum of American Art, the National Museum of Women in the Arts, the National Portrait Gallery, and the Hirshhorn Museum and Sculpture Garden in Washington, D.C.; and the Palais Nationale in Port-au-Prince, Haiti.

It is difficult to estimate the impact of any given artist during his or her lifetime. About Lois Jones, however, certain things are clear. While teaching and communicating a love of art to generations of students, she has created a body of work characterized by technical virtuosity, consummate skill, versatility, elegance, vitality, structure, design, and clarion color.

color while synthesizing the diverse religious and ritualistic elements of Haitian life and culture. It showed a more expressive, colorful, hard-edged style that fused abstraction with decorative patterns and naturalism. These characteristics asserted themselves even more powerfully in the 1970s.

In 1969, Jones received a grant from Howard University to conduct research on contemporary artists in Africa. Between April and July, she compiled biographical material on African artists, photographing their work, conducting interviews, and visiting museums in eleven African countries. More than 1,000 slides were given to the Howard University archives upon completion. Jones said her trip "proved to be a revelation and a rich experience" (Benjamin 1986). During the 1970s and into the 1980s, she maintained an intense interest in Africa. Undoubtedly this was in part due to the African-American's quest for cultural identity. The Black cultural movement of these years was even more profound and widespread than that which occurred during the Harlem Renaissance.

BIBLIOGRAPHY

"Artists of Sunlit Canvases," *Ebony* (November 1968); Benjamin, Tritobia. Personal interviews with Lois Mailou Jones (September 28, 1986; October 29, 1986; November 2, 1986); Davis, John P. *American Negro Reference Book* (1966); Dover, Cedric. *American Negro Art* (1960); Driskell, David C. *Two Centuries of Black American Art* (1976), and *Hidden Heritage: Afro-American Art, 1800-1950* (1985); Fine, Elsa Honig. *The Afro-American Artist* (1973), and *Women and Art: History of Women Painters and Sculptors from the Renaissance to the 20th Century* (1978); Heller, Nancy G. "Lois Mailou Jones, American Painter," *Museum and Arts Washington Magazine* (July/August 1988), and *Women Artists: An Illustrated History* (1987); LaDuke, Betty. "Lois Mailou Jones: The Grand Dame of African-American Art,"*Women's Art Journal* (Fall 1986/1987); Lewis, Samella. *Art: African-American* (1978); Locke, Alain. *The Negro in Art: A Pictorial Record of the Negro Artist and of the Negro Theme in Art* (1969); "One Hundred and Fifty Years of Afro-American

Art." UCLA Art Galleries, Dickson Art Center, Los Angeles (1966); Porter, James A. Prefatory comments in *Lois Mailou Jones Peintures 1937-1951* (1952), and *Modern Negro Art* (1969); Robinson, Wilhemina, ed. *International Library of Negro Life and History: Historical Negro Biographies* (1969); Rubinstein, Charlotte S. *American Women Artists form Early Indian Times to the Present* (1982); "The World of Lois Mailou Jones." Meridian House International, Washington, D.C. (1990); Wardlaw, Alvia, Barry Gaither, Regina Perry, and Robert Farris Thompson. *Black Arts, Ancestral Legacy: The African Impulse in African-American Art* (1990).

TRITOBIA HAYES BENJAMIN

JONES, NANCY (b. 1860)

As she states in a letter to E. M. Cravath, president of the American Board of Commissioners for Foreign Missions (ABCFM, now United Church of Christ), Nancy Jones contemplated mission work before applying to the ABCFM: "I have prayed to the Lord and asked Him what He would have me to do ever since I became a Christian and I believe He has given me the work of a missionary and He directs my mind and heart to Africa the land of my Forefathers" (ABCFM papers, March 20, 1887). Jones had decided at the age of twelve that she wanted to become a missionary.

Nancy Jones was born in Christian County, Kentucky, on January 8, 1860, but her family moved to Memphis, Tennessee, during her childhood. Jones graduated from the normal department course at Fisk University (Nashville, Tennessee) in 1886. Although a Baptist, she applied to the Congregational American Board for a missionary appointment. Jones served the board in Mozambique from 1888 to 1893 and in Southern Rhodesia from 1893 to 1897.

In 1888, as the first unmarried Black woman commissioned by the Congregational American Board, Jones joined Benjamin and Henrietta Ousley, an African-American couple, at the Kambini station in southeastern Mozambique. Jones and the Ousleys worked at the segregated station for five years. At Kambini, Jones began teaching and soon took charge of the school's primary department. She also visited nearby areas to work with the women and children. However, Jones never realized her dream of setting up a boarding school for girls and boys.

When the Ousleys retired in 1893, Jones was transferred to the new Gazaland mission in Southern Rhodesia (now Zimbabwe). At the Mt. Silinda station, Jones was the only Black person. Initially, she worked as a teacher in the day school but she eventually was relieved of that duty. Finally, in 1897, Jones resigned from the East Central African Mission stating that she was unable to work in harmony with the mission because of the prejudice against her by some of her white missionary coworkers. Jones returned to Memphis. Her death date is unknown.

BIBLIOGRAPHY

Goodsell, Fred Field. *You Shall Be My Witness: An Interpretation of the History of the American Board, 1810-1960* (1959); Harvard University, Houghton Library, American Board of Commissioners for Foreign Missions Papers, Nancy Jones Papers, Cambridge, Massachusetts (1887); Jacobs, Sylvia M. "Give a Thought to Africa: Black Women Missionaries in Southern Africa." In *Complicity and Resistance: Western Women and Imperialism*, ed, Nuper Chaudhuri and Margaret Strobel (1992); Strong, William E. *The Story of the American Board: An Account of the First Hundred Years of the American Board of Commissioners for Foreign Missions* (1910); Williams, Walter L. *Black Americans and the Evangelization of Africa, 1877-1900* (1982).

SYLVIA M. JACOBS

JONES, ROSABELLE DOUGLASS SPRAGUE *see* SPRAGUE, FREDERICKA DOUGLASS (PERRY) AND ROSABELLE DOUGLASS (JONES)

JONES, SARAH GARLAND (d. 1905)

Sarah Garland Jones, the first woman to be licensed to practice medicine in the state of Virginia, was born in Albemarle County, Virginia, soon after the end of the Civil War. Her parents were Ellen and George W. Boyd. George Boyd was a distinguished Black contractor and builder in Richmond.

Sarah Jones attended public school in Richmond and graduated from the Richmond Normal School in 1883, after which she taught locally for nearly five years. In 1888, she married Miles Berkley Jones, then secretary of the True Reformers. Her desire to pursue a medical career prompted her to resign her teaching position and enter Howard Medical School in 1890. Following her graduation in 1893, she passed the Virginia State Board examinations, which granted her the right to practice medicine in the state. She and her husband, also a physician, operated a lucrative practice in Richmond for many years and were well respected within the Black community.

In 1898, the Joneses founded a patient-care facility called the Women's Central Hospital and Richmond Hospital. The hospital had twenty-five beds and catered primarily to the needs of female patients. A training school for nurses was affiliated with the hospital in 1901, graduating its first class that same year. Incorporated in 1912, the hospital changed its name to the Sarah Jones Memorial Hospital. The school stayed open until 1920.

At the time of her death in 1905, Jones was still the only Black woman practicing medicine in the state of Virginia.

BIBLIOGRAPHY

Jones, Sarah Garland. Archives and Special Collections on Women in Medicine. Medical College of Pennsylvania, Philadelphia, Pennsylvania.

BRENDA GALLOWAY-WRIGHT

JONES, SISSIERETTA JOYNER (1868-1933)

Sissieretta Jones once summarized her love of singing by comparing her life to the life of flowers. "The flowers absorb the sunshine because it is their nature. I give out melody because God filled my soul with it." Distinguished by over ten years of solo performances at locations ranging from the White House (President Harrison) to Covent Garden, England; by her travels to the West Indies and South America; by enthusiastic reviews from the Black and white press alike; by over eighteen years of travel in America as a prima donna with the Black Patti Troubadours (later the Black Patti Musical Comedy Company) with one of the most difficult schedules on the road, Sissieretta Jones became a major Black concert and theatrical pioneer on the American stage. She was hailed as America's leading prima donna. She was nicknamed the Black Patti by the *New York Clipper*, a theatrical journal, after a writer heard Sissieretta in a private concert-audition at Wallack's Theater, July 15, 1888, and compared her to Italian singer Adelina Patti.

Born in Portsmouth, Virginia, in 1868 to Henrietta Beale and Malachi Joyner, Sissieretta Jones's unique talent was identified by northern visitors who persuaded her father to move to Providence, Rhode Island.

In this new environment, Sissieretta, fondly called "Sissy" and "Tilly" by her classmates, became well known as a singer at school events when her sweet and bell-like voice could be heard above all the rest.

After voice study with Ada Baroness Lacombe at the Academy of Music, she married David Richard Jones, who suggested that she continue her voice study at Boston Conservatory. Here, for approximately two years, 1886-88, she studied and broadened her contacts with other artists, such as Flora Batson, the leading star of the Bergen Star Company. It was this concert series that first featured Jones, billed as "the rising soprano from New England," in a New York City concert that brought her to the attention of concert managers Abbey, Schoffel, and Grau, who then scheduled her for a Wallack Theater debut on July 15, 1888. Henry Abbey, manager for Adelina Patti, attended this performance and recommended a tour to the West Indies with the Tennessee Jubilee Singers. This tour gave birth to Sissieretta Jones's professional concert career.

Engagements in the famous African Jubilee in Madison Square Garden, a career managed by Major Pond for the 1892-94 seasons, and performances across America (including appearances at the Pittsburgh, Buffalo, and Toronto Expositions) followed. Reviews of her performances, although sometimes tinged with the racial myths of the day, were positive. For instance, John van Cleve, a respected Boston-trained musician and critic, defined her style of singing and her particular attributes as being of "high and genuine ability both as concerns the gift of nature and the supplementary additions of art." She was possibly the first Black performer to appear at Carnegie Concert Hall. She performed with Antonín Dvořák and the National Conservatory of Music in the United States and she performed abroad at the Wintergarten in Berlin and at Covent Garden, England.

Frustrated by the conditions of performance on the serious concert stage, and disturbed by the mistreatment of Black people by the Metropolitan Opera, Jones surrounded herself with approximately forty Black performers and formed the Black Patti Troubadours. Managed by Rudolph Voelckel and John J. Nolan, this company opened its first season on July 25, 1896. First adopting the format of a loose skit (as in *A Rag-time Frolic at Ras-bury Park* [1898-99]), with comedy, dancing, and acrobatic fun, the company featured an operatic kaleidoscope and highlighted Sissieretta and a chorus in excerpts from such works as *Cavalleria Rusticana*, *Chimes of Normandy*, and *Faust*. As the shows became more organized, a definite plot

Known as the Black Patti, Sissieretta Jones formed her own company when she found herself limited by racism. The Black Patti Troubadours, who performed an eclectic mix that ranged from grand opera to ragtime, toured the country successfully for almost twenty years. [Moorland-Spingarn]

and musical comedy appeared. Jones began to appear in the storyline rather than exclusively in the kaleidoscope.

With shows such as *A Trip to Africa* (1909-10), *In the Jungles* (1911-12), *Captain Jasper* (1912-13), and *Lucky Sam from Alabam'* (1914-15), the Black Patti company appeared in the new Black-owned theaters (such as the Howard in Washington, D.C.) and its future course and popularity seemed assured. However, an illness prevented Jones's full participation in the 1913-14 season, and her return in the 1914-15

season was cut short after a production in Church's Auditorium in Memphis, Tennessee, when the company was disbanded.

With the close of the Black Patti company, Jones gave a performance at the end of 1915 at the Grand Theater in Chicago, followed by her last performance, at the Lafayette Theater in New York City in October 1915. Jones promised her audiences that she would return, but she went into total retirement, quietly living with her ill mother until her mother died. Sissieretta Jones died on June 24, 1933. To those who worked with her, she struggled to establish racial pride and self-esteem in young performers during a most depressing and difficult period in American history.

BIBLIOGRAPHY

Daughtry, Willia E. *Sissieretta Jones: Profile of a Black Artist* (1972), and "Sissieretta Jones: A Study of the Negro's Contribution to Nineteenth-Century American Concert and Theatrical Life," Ph.D. diss. (1968); Hughes, Glenn. *A History of the American Theatre: 1700-1950* (1951); Jones, Sissieretta. Press scrapbook. Moorland-Spingarn Collection, Howard University, Washington, D.C.; Nathan, Hans. *Dan Emmett and the Rise of Negro Minstrelsy* (1952); Sampson, Henry. *Blacks in Blackface* (1980).

WILLIA E. DAUGHTRY

JONES, SOPHIA BETHENE
(1857-1932)

Born in Ontario, Canada, in 1857, Sophia Bethene Jones entered the University of Toronto in 1879. Around 1881, she came to the United States and studied medicine at the University of Michigan. After she graduated in 1885, Jones went to Spelman College in Atlanta, Georgia. She became the first Black woman to teach at Spelman and was in charge of the college infirmary and setting up a nurses' training course. She taught there from 1885 to 1888.

Sophia Jones also practiced in St. Louis, Philadelphia, and Kansas. While in Kansas, her health began to fail, and she moved to California with her brothers and sisters. She lived for fifteen more years and died in 1932.

BIBLIOGRAPHY

Jones, Sophia Bethene. Archives and Special Collection on Women in Medicine. Medical College of Pennsylvania, Philadelphia, Pennsylvania.

MARGARET JERRIDO

JONES, VERINA MORTON HARRIS (1865-1943)

Physician, clubwoman, civil rights activist, and suffragist, Verina Morton-Jones was born in Cleveland, Ohio, January 28, 1865, and attended State Normal School in Columbia, South Carolina, followed by the Woman's Medical College of Pennsylvania in Philadelphia—then widely acknowledged to be one of the best medical colleges for women in the country—from 1884 to 1888. She received her M.D. in 1888 and began practice in the Black community at Rust College in Holly Springs, Mississippi. Morton-Jones was the first woman, Black or white, to practice medicine in the state of Mississippi. She married twice; the first time in 1890 to W. A. Morton, M.D.,

The distinguished Verina Morton was the first woman, Black or white, to practice medicine in the state of Mississippi, but her greatest achievement was her leadership of the Lincoln Settlement House in Brooklyn, which offered, among other services, a clinic and a day nursery and free kindergarten. [Moorland-Spingarn]

who died in 1895, and the second time in 1901 to Emory Jones, who died in 1927. She had one child from her first marriage, Franklin W., who was born in 1892.

Among the first Black women in the U.S. to receive her degree in medicine, Morton-Jones moved to New York to practice in Brooklyn and on Long Island during the Progressive era. She was the first Black woman to practice medicine in Nassau County on Long Island, and she played an active role in the largely white, male-dominated Kings County Medical Society. In the 1941-44 edition of *Who's Who in Colored America*, Morton-Jones is described as "the oldest colored physician in Brooklyn in point of practice as well as age." In spite of her long and active career in medicine and healing, Morton-Jones also devoted her time to club work, education, suffrage, community "uplift," and civil rights.

Morton-Jones headed the Lincoln Settlement House in Brooklyn from its founding in May 1908. Lincoln House began as an extension of white social reformer and nurse Lillian Wald's Henry Street Settlement House on the Lower East Side of New York City. The primary sponsor of this self-help, community-based program, Morton-Jones contributed the down payment on the property for the settlement house and pioneered the first social service organization in Brooklyn that sought to address the needs of the growing Black population. Under her directorship, Lincoln House offered a clinic, a day nursery and free kindergarten, a lecture series on health and hygiene, and classes in carpentry, cooking, embroidery, folk dancing, and sewing; it also sponsored choral and debating clubs. It appealed not only to Black youth but also to the adults of the community. The settlement house incorporated in 1914 and moved from its original quarters at 129 Willoughby Street to 105 Fleet Place, where there was a more spacious building and a nearby lot for a playground.

Morton-Jones nurtured diverse social and political commitments. As a Black clubwoman, she played an active part in the National Association of Colored Women (NACW, founded in 1896). She was the director of the NACW's Mothers' Club in Brooklyn and was part of the female auxiliary of the radical Niagara Movement in 1905 and 1906. She also participated in the work of the Committee for Improving Industrial Conditions of Negroes in New York City (founded in 1906), which in 1911 merged with two other social reform groups to become the National Urban League. Morton-Jones fought to win the vote for all women and fought to protect the right to vote of all Black Americans. She rejected the notion that

Black women had no interest in voting. She assisted in conducting voter education programs, noted instances of race discrimination at the polls, and testified before congressional investigatory committees. Like many other Black clubwomen of the Progressive era, Morton-Jones drew on the tradition of self-help in the Black community in her tenure as president of the Brooklyn Equal Suffrage League.

Morton-Jones was elected to the National Association for the Advancement of Colored People (NAACP) Board of Directors in 1913 and worked on the executive committee until 1925. Mary White Ovington, a white social reformer and one of the founders of the NAACP, in her 1947 autobiography *The Walls Came Tumbling Down*, reminisced about a typical 1917 board meeting in which Morton-Jones was the only "colored woman." Morton-Jones was not the only woman of color to have membership in the interracial Cosmopolitan Club, however. This social and political group of New York City and Brooklyn reformers met regularly to discuss racism, civil rights, and reform stratagems. Morton-Jones, Ovington, *Independent* editor Hamilton Holt, prominent socialist John Spargo, and the *Evening Post*'s Oswald Garrison Villard were among the members of this club. Both Black and white reformers active in groups such as the NAACP and the Urban League attended meetings of this club. Morton-Jones also held membership in the Association for the Protection of Colored Women, and volunteered for the "Phillis Wheatley" chapters of the Young Women's Christian Association (YWCA).

Morton-Jones is at once an outstanding and a typical example of the Black professional and clubwomen who sought to "uplift" their communities by working within both Black and interracial protest groups to combat racism and protect civil rights. An Episcopalian and a Republican, Morton-Jones died in 1943.

BIBLIOGRAPHY

Aptheker, Herbert, ed. *The Correspondence of W.E.B. Du Bois* (1975); Cash, Floris. "Womanhood and Protest: The Club Movement among Black Women, 1892-1922," Ph.D. diss. (1986); Connolly, Harry X. *A Ghetto Grows in Brooklyn* (1977); Giddings, Paula. *When and Where I Enter: The Impact of Black Women on Race and Sex in America* (1984); *New York Times*, "Brooklyn's Black Women" (October 22, 1985); *New York Times*, "The Role of Black Women in Brooklyn's History" (October 19, 1985); Ovington, Mary White. *The Walls Came Tumbling Down* (1947); Salem, Dorothy. *To Better Our World: Black Women in Organized Reform, 1890-1920* (1990); Scuggs, Lawson A. *Women of Distinction, 1892.* In *Black Biographical Dictionaries, 1790-1950* (1987); Sterling, Dorothy, ed. *We Are Your Sisters: Black Women in the Nineteenth Century* (1984); Weiss, Nancy. *The National Urban League, 1910-1940* (1974); *WWCA*. Morton-Jones's archives are at the Moorland-Spingarn Research Center, Howard University, Washington, D.C.

THEA ARNOLD

JONES, VIRGINIA LACY (1912-1984)

Among library educators, Virginia Lacy Jones was known as "the Dean of Deans." Diminutive in stature, Dean Jones was a giant in library education. A wise counselor, inspired teacher, patient mentor, and demanding scholar, she was a courageous leader who pointed the way to achievement and success against barriers that most would have considered insurmountable.

Born in Cincinnati, Ohio, on June 25, 1912, the daughter of Edward Lacy and Ellen Louise Parker Lacy, Virginia grew up in Clarksburg, West Virginia, where she had an early exposure to books at home and at the library. Her school years were spent first in Clarksburg and then in St. Louis, Missouri, when her family relocated.

While a student at Summer High School, in doing research for an essay contest, she came into contact with a reference librarian at the St. Louis Public Library whose knowledge, resourcefulness, and dedication made a lasting impression. Although she had earlier intended to enroll in Stowe Teachers College after graduation in 1929, fired with the desire to become a librarian, she entered Hampton Institute in Virginia. During her fourth year at Hampton, she met Florence Rising Curtis, director of the library school. Curtis's personal interest in her professional advancement had a lifelong impact on Jones.

After graduation from Hampton in 1933, she began her professional career at Louisville Municipal College in Kentucky as assistant librarian. In 1935, she returned to study at Hampton. During 1935-36, she worked part time in the Hampton Institute Library and accompanied Curtis to the American Library Association (ALA) Conference in Richmond, Virginia. At the meeting, she and other African-American librarians experienced the degradation of institutional racism in the South during that era. As a result of protests about the humiliating treatment of Black librarians at the Richmond conference, ALA made it a policy not to convene in cities where all librarians could not participate fully in all facets of the meeting.

Returning to Louisville Municipal College in the fall of 1936, after receiving a Bachelor's degree in education at Hampton, Virginia became head librarian. Later, with a fellowship from the General Education Board and with a leave of absence from the College, she studied for and received an M.L.S. from the University of Illinois in 1938. After a year at Louisville again, she became catalog librarian at Atlanta University's Trevor Arnett Library in 1939, where she remained for two years. When the Atlanta University School of Library Service opened in 1941, Jones was one of the original faculty members, teaching cataloging and classification, school library service, and children's literature. In the same year, she married Edward Allen Jones, professor of French and chairman of the Department of Modern Language at Morehouse College.

In 1943, Jones was awarded a fellowship from the General Education Board to study at the graduate library school of the University of Illinois, and in 1945 she became the second African-American to receive a doctorate in library service. She was named dean of the School of Library Service at Atlanta University, a position she held until December 1981, when she became the first director of the Atlanta University Center Robert W. Woodruff Library.

Jones was a prolific contributor to library literature. Believing that ethnic and racial barriers should be broken down from within professional organizations, she worked untiringly in the ALA to make it an organization responsive to all its members. She held various offices within the ALA, including posts on the ALA Council in 1946-69 and on the executive board in 1970-76. Her 1976 honorary membership award citation from the ALA stated: "In your pursuit of excellence for librarianship, you have conducted institutes, persuaded foundation officials, pressured state library associations to drop discriminatory practices, and insisted that your students demonstrate both commitment and scholarship." She also won the Melvil Dewey, Joseph E. Lippincott, and Beta Phi Mu awards, among others. President Lyndon B. Johnson appointed Jones a member of the President's Advisory Committee on Library Research and Training Projects during 1967-70.

For her contributions to American librarianship, Jones received an honorary doctorate of humane letters from Bishop College and an honorary doctorate of letters from the University of Michigan, both in 1979. She retired from active service to the profession in 1984. She died December 3, 1984.

BIBLIOGRAPHY

Jones, Virginia Lacy. "A Dean's Career." In *The Black Librarian in America*, ed. E. J. Josey (1970), and Manuscript Collection, Clark Atlanta University, Atlanta, Georgia.

ARTHUR C. GUNN

JORDAN, BARBARA CHARLINE (1936-)

Barbara Jordan was born in the Fifth Ward of Houston, Texas, to a Black Baptist minister, Benjamin Jordan, and a domestic worker, Arlyne Jordan. Barbara attended Roberson Elementary and Phyllis Wheatley High School. While at Wheatley, she was a member of the Honor Society and excelled in debating, and she graduated in 1952 in the upper five percent of her class. In 1956, she graduated magna cum laude from Texas Southern University with a double major in political science and history. She earned her J.D. from Boston University in 1959.

Jordan taught political science at Tuskegee Institute in Alabama for one year before returning to Houston in 1960 to take the bar examination and set up a private law practice.

Barbara Jordan's interest in politics was solidified in 1965 when she received her first public appointment as administrative assistant to the county judge of Harris County. Following this appointment she was elected to the Texas state senate in 1966, the first Black Texan to serve in that august body since 1883. Then, in 1972, she was elected to the U.S. House of Representatives.

Her brief record in the Texas state senate is viewed as somewhat of a phenomenon. On March 21, 1967, she became the first Black elected official to preside over that body; she also was the first Black state senator to chair a major committee, Labor and Management Relations, and the first freshman senator ever named to the Texas Legislative Council. When the Texas legislature convened in special session in March 1972, Senator Jordan was unanimously elected president pro tempore. In June of that year, she was honored by being named Governor for a Day. Shortly thereafter, she decided to run for Congress and was elected, in November 1972, from Houston's Eighteenth Congressional District.

Both as a state senator and as a U.S. congresswoman, Jordan sponsored bills that championed the cause of poor, Black, and disadvantaged people. One of her most important bills as a senator was the Workman's Compensation Act, which increased the

"What did the president know and when did he know it?" This was the question raised again during the House of Representatives hearings into the impeachment of President Richard M. Nixon. Representative Barbara Jordan spoke eloquently and passionately of her belief in the Constitution during these hearings. [Schomburg Center]

maximum benefits paid to injured workers. As a congresswoman she sponsored legislation to broaden the Voting Rights Act of 1965 to cover Mexican-Americans in Texas and other southwestern states and to extend its authority to those states where minorities had been denied the right to vote or had had their rights restricted by unfair registration practices, such as literacy tests.

Jordan gained national notoriety for the position she took, and the statement she made, at the 1974 impeachment hearing of President Richard Nixon. In casting a "yes" vote, Jordan stated, "My faith in the Constitution is whole, it is complete, it is total." Having become a national celebrity, Jordan was chosen as keynote speaker for the Democratic National Convention in 1976 and again in 1992.

Along with, and because of, her political accomplishment, Jordan has received fifteen honorary doctorate degrees. She was named the Democratic Woman of the Year by the Women's National Democratic Club. *Ladies' Home Journal* picked her as 1975

Woman of the Year in Politics. *Time* magazine recognized her that same year as one of its ten women of the year, and a poll conducted by *Redbook* (1979) magazine selected Jordan as one of the top women who could be president.

Barbara Jordan retired from public office in 1978 and gave her congressional papers and memorabilia to her alma mater, Texas Southern University. She then went on to become a visiting professor at the Lyndon B. Johnson School of Public Affairs at the University of Texas at Austin, a post she still holds.

BIBLIOGRAPHY

Bryant, Ira B. *Barbara Charline Jordan: From the Ghetto to the Capital* (1977); Jordan, Barbara and Shely Hearn. *Barbara Jordan: Self Portrait* (1979); *Journal of House of Representatives Sixty-first Legislature*; *Journal of the United States House of Representatives of the Ninety-fourth Congress*; Smith, Garland. *Black Texans of Distinction* (n.d.); *WWBA*.

MERLINE PITRE

JORDAN, JUNE (1936-)

In addition to her successful career as a college professor, June Jordan is famous for her writing, particularly her poetry, her children's and young people's fiction, and her essays. Her social and political awareness, combined with her prodigious literary skill, have earned Jordan both critical praise and popular acceptance.

Born in Harlem, New York, on July 9, 1936, June Jordan is the only child of Granville Ivanhoe Jordan and Mildred Maud (Fisher) Jordan, who came to America from Jamaica. Jordan grew up in the Bedford-Stuyvesant section of Brooklyn, but as a teenager she traveled to Midwood High School in southeast Brooklyn, where she was the only Black student. After one year at Midwood, her parents enrolled her in the Northfield School for Girls, a preparatory school now part of Mount Hermon, in Massachusetts.

After graduating from high school in 1953, Jordan entered Barnard College in New York City. While

Versatile writer June Jordan began to attract wide attention with her first book of poetry, Who Look at Me, *which explores Black-white relations and a Black person's process of self-definition in a white-dominated society. [Schomburg Center]*

there, she met Michael Meyer, a white Columbia University student, whom she married in 1955. Later that year, when Meyer left New York to attend the University of Chicago, Jordan went too and also enrolled in the university. In 1956, Jordan returned to Barnard for one more semester before finally leaving in February 1957. In 1958, the couple's only child was born, Christopher David Meyer. Jordan and Michael Meyer divorced in 1963. Also in 1963, Jordan became employed as production assistant on the crew of Shirley Clarke's film about Harlem, *The Cool World.*

In 1966, Jordan began her academic career teaching English at the City University of New York. Two years later she moved to New London, Connecticut, to teach English at Connecticut College as well as direct the Search for Education, Elevation, and Knowledge (SEEK) program. Later that year she joined the writing faculty of Sarah Lawrence College in Bronxville, New York, where she remained until 1974. She was a visiting professor at Yale University in 1974-75 and later became assistant professor of English at City College of New York. In 1976, she took a faculty position at the State University of New York and was promoted to a full professorship in 1982. In 1989, Jordan became professor of Afro-American Studies and Women's Studies at the University of California, Berkeley.

Jordan established her writing career with the publication of her stories and poems (under the name June Meyer) in magazines such as *Esquire,* the *Nation,* and the *New York Times Magazine.* Her writing began to attract national attention in 1969, when Crowell published her first book of poetry, *Who Look at Me,* a collection of works that portrays Black-white relations and a Black person's process of self-definition in a white-dominated society. In 1970, she edited *Soulscript: Afro-American Poetry,* a collection of poems by young people aged twelve to eighteen. Jordan has published nineteen works to date, including poetry, books for children and young people, and collected essays, articles, and lectures. Among these are the award-winning *His Own Where,* a novel for young adults (1971); *Some Changes,* poems (1971); *Fannie Lou Hamer,* a biography (1972); *New Room: New Life,* a book for children (1975); *Living Room: New Poems, 1980-1984* (1985); and *On Call: New Political Essays, 1981-1985* (1985). Jordan also is the author of several plays, including *The Spirit of Sojourner Truth,* staged at the Public Theater in New York City in 1979, and *For the Arrow That Flies by Day,* performed during 1981 by the New York Shakespeare Festival.

Taking her place among the radical poets who emerged during the 1960s, Jordan is esteemed for her political and aesthetically Black stance as well as for her technical verve and control. Much of her poetry grapples with the issue of Black self-identity as well as the powerful, and often problematic, influence that parents have on their children. In her works for children, Jordan displays a commitment to the use of Black English and the promotion of what she describes as "Black-survivor consciousness" (*DLB*). In her work Jordan also has examined such biographical topics as her mother's suicide in 1966 and her father's death in 1974.

June Jordan has received many prizes, grants, and fellowships for her writing, including a Rockefeller grant for creative writing in 1969. She also received a fellowship in poetry from the National Endowment for the Arts in 1982 and a fellowship award in poetry from the New York Foundation for the Arts in 1985. *His Own Where* was selected by the *New York Times* as one of 1971's most outstanding works for young adults and was nominated for the National Book Award. Jordan is an executive board member of the American Writers Congress, a board member of both the Center for Constitutional Rights and the Nicaraguan Culture Alliance, and a member of the International Association of Poets, Playwrights, Editors, Essayists, and Novelists (PEN). She also is a regular political columnist for the *Progressive* magazine.

BIBLIOGRAPHY

CA; Deveaux, Alexis. "Creating Soul Food: June Jordan," *Essence* (April 1981); *DLB*; Jordan, June. "Notes of a Barnard Dropout," Reid Lecture, Barnard College (1975), and *Things That I Do in the Dark* (1977), and *Soulscript: Afro-American Poetry* (1970).

FENELLA MACFARLANE

JOSEPH-GAUDET, FRANCES
(1861-1934)

Frances Joseph-Gaudet was born in a log cabin in Holmesville, Pike County, Mississippi. A seamstress by profession, she became known throughout the country at the turn of the century for her work in reforming prisons and the juvenile court system and for founding the Gaudet Normal and Industrial School for Black youth in New Orleans, Louisiana, in 1902.

The young Frances moved to New Orleans from Mississippi when she was eight years old. She attended public schools in uptown New Orleans and then enrolled at Straight University, but she was unable to finish because she and her brother were needed to help her mother support the younger children. Married at twenty-three, she lived happily with her husband for ten years until alcohol, "the curse of America" (Gaudet 1913), caused the Josephs to seek a legal separation.

Following her separation in 1894, she began work for prison reform. She visited the prisons for weekly prayer meetings for the next eight years and was dismayed by the plight of young Black boys who were housed with inveterate criminals. The Prison Reform Association supported her efforts to improve the prisons and the conditions of the indigent insane, and she founded the city's first juvenile court.

As president of the Louisiana Negro chapter of the Women's Christian Temperance Union (WCTU), Joseph was a delegate to the International WCTU Convention in Edinburgh in 1900. For five months she toured England and Europe; spoke in Ireland, Paris, and London about the welfare of poor children; and visited prisons and juvenile detention homes abroad. Shortly after her return to New Orleans, she bought 105 acres of farmland on Gentilly Avenue to build a school devoted to saving homeless Negro children and teaching them a craft by which they could make a living.

In founding the Colored Industrial and Normal School (later called Gaudet School) in 1902, Joseph had the support of the *Times-Democrat* and of Ida A. Richardson, wife of Tobias G. Richardson, dean of the Louisiana State University School of Medicine. The first secretary of the board was Adolphe P. Gaudet, whom Frances Joseph later married.

Because much of her support for founding the school had come from members of the Episcopal Church, Joseph-Gaudet decided to offer the school to the Episcopal Diocese in 1919 for a long-lasting sponsorship. She continued as principal for a short while, but, becoming increasingly blind, she felt compelled to resign. She moved to Chicago to live with relatives but returned to New Orleans several times to see the progress of the school before her death on December 24, 1934. At the 1935 Episcopal convention, a Memorial Minute was adopted in tribute to Joseph-Gaudet "in which her unselfish service in behalf of her own people was gratefully acknowledged" (*Churchwork*, September 1963).

BIBLIOGRAPHY

Bryan, Violet Harrington. "Frances Joseph-Gaudet: Black Philanthropist," *Sage* (Spring 1986); Carter, Hodding and Betty Werlein Carter. *So Great a Good: A History of the Episcopal Church in Louisiana and of the Christ Church Cathedral, 1805-1955* (1955); *Churchwork*, "The History of Gaudet School and Home" (September 1963), and "Mrs. Frances Joseph Gaudet: Courageous Crusader" (August 1963); Episcopal Diocese of Louisiana Manuscript Volumes. Special Collections, Howard-Tilton Library, Tulane University, New Orleans; Gaudet, Frances Joseph. *He Leadeth Me* (1913); Labouisse, S. S. "Gaudet Can Be the First Approved Negro High School in New Orleans," *Louisiana Forth* (April 1949); *Louisiana Weekly*, "Expansion Program for Gaudet High School" (February 5, 1949); *New Orleans Item*, "Frances Joseph Gaudet" (December 27, 1934).

VIOLET HARRINGTON BRYAN

JOURNALISM

Black women's ascent into journalism is a story of privation, persistence, and opportunity, starting with Mary Ann Shadd Cary, who published a Black abolitionist newspaper in Canada in the 1850s. Although the 1850s marked the official entry of African-American women into journalism, it is likely they turned to journalistic writing as early as 1827 when Samuel Cornish and John Russwurm founded the first Black newspaper, *Freedom's Journal.*

During the antebellum period, Black women contributed their efforts to Frederick Douglass's *North Star* and white-owned abolitionist newspapers, including William Lloyd Garrison's *Liberator.* Maria Stewart, the first American-born woman to lecture in defense of women's rights, published her essays in the *Liberator.* Other, anonymous, contributors in the antebellum period, conscious of sexual oppression, expressed considerable unhappiness with women's status. Although some identified themselves simply as "a young woman of color," "Zillah, a Young Lady of Color" and "Matilda," their letters to editors provided cultural and psychological insights into the thoughts of literate, free, northern Black women.

Like their brothers in the struggle, Black women also recognized the power of newspapers to move the word beyond specific places and time, beyond the pulpit and the platform, which relied heavily on audiences being present to witness what was said and when. With a different medium, the newspaper, Black women increased their audience. They denounced slavery, and they addressed political and economic discrimination in the North.

Unlike Black men, however, African-American women's protest extended beyond the horrors of sla-very and discussions of race and education to the issues of sex, gender, and class. As the debate over slavery intensified, Black women also began to struggle for changes in their own status. In this sense, Black women used newspapers in a radically different form than their Black brothers. By introducing the issue of sex into the public domain, Black women shifted their symbolic environment significantly by calling attention to the double-bind of being both Black and female.

After the Civil War, Black women became more immersed in printed matter, more diverse in their creativity. Frances Ellen Watkins Harper not only published her poetry and short stories in the 1850s, but she also published her novel, *Iola Leroy*, in 1892. Harper, Stewart, Douglass, and other Black American women writers showcased their intellectual and creative talents in journals and magazines, including the *Repository of Religion and Literature and of Science and the Arts*, a journal of the African Methodist Episcopal Church begun in 1858, and the *Anglo-African* magazine founded in 1859. Scores of other women followed the print tradition, among them, professor Mary V. Cook, editor of the education section of *Our Women and Children*, Meta E. Pelham, reporter for the *Detroit Plain Dealer*, Gertrude Mossell, correspondent for the *Indianapolis Freeman*, and Lillian A. Lewis, who wrote a fascinating column, "They Say," for the *Boston Advocate* under the pen name Bert Islew.

As the problems of the freedpersons intensified during post-Reconstruction, Black women focused even more vigorously on themes and ideas essential to their uplift—self-reliance, temperance, education, home building, and the creation of organizations such as the National Association of Colored Women—as vehicles for mobilizing women. Josephine St. Pierre Ruffin, editor of *Woman's Era*, the official paper of the National Federation of Afro-American Women, played a pivotal role in the development of the Black women's club movement of the 1890s by providing women such as Mary Church Terrell, Gertrude Mossell, Fannie Barrier Williams, and others with outlets for their talents. In addition to Ruffin's *Woman's Era*, the *National Notes*, founded in 1897 in Tuskegee, Alabama, served as the organ for the National Association of Colored Women. Indeed, in her *A Voice from the South* (1892), Anna Julia Cooper insisted that Black women should "have the sole management of the primal lights and shadows!"

Unlike the white press, which often relegated white women to marginalized positions—sob sisters, stunt women, or editing the women's pages—the Black press offered more varied opportunities. One woman, however, dominated journalism at the end of the nineteenth century, Ida B. Wells-Barnett, the fiery, intrusive editor of *Free Speech and Headlight*, a small weekly in her hometown of Memphis, Tennessee. Wells-Barnett used scathing language in her crusading efforts against lynching. In fact, Wells-Barnett, by introducing the idea that white women were culpable in these crimes, redefined lynching, its causes and consequences. At considerable cost, with the burning of the *Free Speech* office and her subsequent exile from Tennessee (induced by letters to editors all over the South that warned she would be torched next if she returned), Wells-Barnett became only the second Black female journalist (Cary preceded her) to step outside the content boundaries reserved for women, and to successfully mobilize both Black and white readers through print.

In addition to Wells-Barnett's contributions, the post-Reconstruction period also introduced the first periodicals targeting a female audience and featuring the work of Black women. In 1887, A. E. Johnson, a woman poet from Baltimore, Maryland, founded a monthly literary journal, *The Joy*, perhaps the earliest of these efforts. The magazine was published until 1889-90, and received complimentary reviews from both Black and white contemporaries, a striking testament to the journalistic skills of Black women.

By the close of the nineteenth century, an increasing number of Black women were firmly entrenched in the Black press. Yet, writer and activist Gertrude Mossell admonished her female colleagues for remaining "willing captives, chained to the chariot wheels of the sterner element," and she criticized Black men for not fully including their female colleagues.

Greater opportunities were available to Black women in the next century as the Black press evolved into a thriving institution. In the early 1900s there were close to fifty newspapers and forty magazines and periodicals published by African-Americans, and women played a central role in their publication. These women journalists represented the cultural, political, and economic diversity of the larger Black community.

In 1900, for example, the *Colored American Magazine* hired the young novelist and writer Pauline Hopkins to edit the women's section of the Boston-based magazine. Three years later Hopkins was literary editor of the magazine, and today she is best known for her four novels serialized in its pages. Despite her efforts to spark a Black literary movement, Hopkins was unable to sustain her journalistic career, supported herself as a stenographer, and died in obscurity.

In contrast, Margaret Murray Washington began as editor of *National Notes*. She was the wife of Booker T. Washington as well as the dean of women at Tuskegee Institute. Washington figured prominently in the women's club movement and Black self-help activities, and she continued as editor until 1922.

The first decade of the twentieth century witnessed the publication of two Black women's periodicals in states west of the Mississippi. *Women's World* was founded in Fort Worth, Texas. *Colored Women's Magazine* began in Topeka, Kansas, in 1907 and was edited by two women, C. M. Hughes and Minnie Thomas, as a monthly family magazine. It was published until at least 1920, and women maintained editorial control throughout its history.

Black women also figured prominently in periodicals targeted for a more general audience. Josephine Silone Yates, a teacher at Lincoln Institute in Missouri and a two-term president of the National Association of Colored Women, served as associate editor of the *Negro Educational Review*, founded in Vincennes, Indiana, in 1904. Agnes Carroll, a music teacher in Washington, D.C., helped edit the *Negro Music Journal*, published in that city during the same period. Amanda Berry Smith, an evangelist, itinerant preacher, and perhaps the most colorful woman journalist of the period, published the *Helper* (1900-1907), a magazine that focused on the issues of child care, temperance, and religion.

The turn of the century brought an era of development and growth for influential African-American newspapers, such as the Baltimore *Afro-American*, the *Chicago Defender*, and the *New York Age*. The polemical, romantic writing of nineteenth-century American journalism gradually was replaced with a quest for objective reporting of the news, and powerful Black newspapers were part of this developing professionalism. Black women were reporters, columnists, and editors for these papers but little is known about their efforts beyond the heroic story of Ida Wells-Barnett.

Some Black women writers of the early 1900s included journalism among the other literary forms they employed. Alice Dunbar-Nelson, wife of poet Paul Laurence Dunbar, is not often identified as a journalist, but she wrote for both Black and white newspapers at the beginning of the century, including the *Pittsburgh Courier*, the *Washington Eagle*, the *Chicago Daily News*, the *Chicago Record-Herald*, and the *New York Sun*. She published poetry and short stories in numerous periodicals, and she wrote reviews of other Black writers' works as well as news stories. She also edited the Wilmington *Advocate*, served as an associate editor for the *AME Church Review*, and later tried unsuccessfully to launch her own syndicated newspaper column.

Other of Dunbar-Nelson's contemporaries devoted their energies more exclusively to journalism, including Delilah Beasley, who began her career writing for a Black newspaper, the Cleveland *Gazette*, and went on to contribute to white-owned papers such as the Cincinnati *Enquirer*. After moving to California, Beasley wrote a regular column for the Oakland *Tribune*—the state's largest circulation daily at the time—from 1915 to 1925.

California was home base for another journalist, Charlotta Bass, who is thought to be the first Black woman to own and publish a newspaper in the United States. Bass started her career in 1910 as a writer for the *California Eagle*, a Black-owned weekly in Los Angeles, and she purchased the paper two years later. She supported Marcus Garvey's Universal Negro Improvement Association and numerous civil rights organizations on the West Coast. Bass published the *Eagle* for nearly forty years, but she is perhaps best known as the first Black woman to run for vice-president when she joined the Progressive party ticket in 1952.

Political activism frequently became a partner to Black women's journalistic work. Marvel Jackson Cooke began her career as an editorial assistant to W.E.B. Du Bois at the *Crisis* in 1926. Two years later Du Bois helped Cooke obtain a position at the *New York Amsterdam News* where she struggled to improve the newspaper's quality and expand coverage of the Black community. Her efforts to organize a union local and lead a strike against the paper in 1935 prompted a move to the *People's Voice*, founded by Adam Clayton Powell, where she served as assistant managing editor. In 1950, Cooke became the first African-American full-time woman reporter for a mainstream newspaper when she joined the staff of the *Daily Compass*, where she worked with the renowned journalist I. F. Stone.

By the 1940s Black women had seized new challenges within the Black press. Hazel Garland broke into the newspaper business as a stringer for the *Pittsburgh Courier*. In 1946, she was hired as a full-time reporter, and she traveled the country to cover crucial issues such as lynching and African-Americans' responses to World War II. In one interview she recalled writing an award-winning series titled "The Three I's: Ignorance, Illiteracy, Illegitimacy," based on her travels through poor Black communities in the South. During her years at the *Courier*, Garland served as entertainment editor, radio-television edi-

tor, women's editor, and finally editor-in-chief. Garland's daughter, Phyllis, also became a journalist, beginning her career at *Ebony* magazine in 1966, and then teaching in Columbia University's Graduate School of Journalism.

Elizabeth Murphy Moss was connected with one of the Black newspaper giants at mid-century, her family's paper, the Baltimore *Afro-American*. She began her career at the paper at age eleven and was a correspondent from England during World War II. She eventually rose to the position of vice-president and treasurer for the *Afro-American* newspaper chain.

Alice Allison Dunnigan became the first African-American woman to cover the White House when she was the Washington correspondent for the *Chicago Defender*. In the mid-1960s, Ethel L. Payne spent ten weeks in Vietnam covering the war. She traveled extensively throughout Asia and Africa during her career and became one of the first Black women in broadcasting when she provided commentary to CBS News.

The death of Philippa Duke Schuyler in Vietnam in May 1967 at the age of thirty-four, as she tried to evacuate Vietnamese children trapped in an orphanage, is a tragic episode among the stories of Black women journalists. Schuyler was best known as a child prodigy who performed as a classical pianist when barely in her teens. She began her second career as a journalist in the 1960s, first covering the war in the Congo, and later Vietnam, for the *Manchester Union Leader*.

These diverse and courageous women served as role models for a new generation of journalists who emerged in the 1960s and 1970s. Individuals like Dorothy Gilliam, the first Black woman columnist for the *Washington Post*, and Pamela M. Johnson, the first Black woman publisher of a white-owned daily newspaper, the *Ithaca Journal*, have continued this pioneering legacy. Black women have also become increasingly visible in broadcast news, following the lead of Charlayne Hunter-Gault in public broadcasting, and Carol Jenkins, Renee Poussaint, and others associated with the networks. Today's Black women journalists face the challenge of increasing their numbers and visibility in every facet of the news business. Their predecessors demonstrated that Black women are a vital link in the nation's quest for free expression and social justice.

BIBLIOGRAPHY

Belford, Barbara. *Brilliant Bylines: A Biographical Anthology of Notable Newspaperwomen in America* (1986); Bullock, Penelope L. *The Afro-American Periodical Press:*

1838-1909 (1981); Cooper, Anna Julia. *A Voice from the South* (1892); Diggs-Brown, Barbara. *Philippa Duke Schuyler, African-American Woman Martyr,* Unpublished manuscript (n.d.); Dunnigan, Alice E. "Early History of Negro Women in Journalism," *Negro History Bulletin* (May 1965); Duster, Alfreda M., ed. *Crusade for Justice: The Autobiography of Ida B. Wells* (1970); Giddings, Paula. *When and Where I Enter: The Impact of Black Women on Race and Sex in America* (1984); Harding, Vincent. *There Is a River: The Black Struggle for Freedom in America* (1983); Hull, Gloria T. *Color, Sex, and Poetry: Three Women Writers of the Harlem Renaissance* (1987); "Lady of Color," *Liberator* (May 11, 1833); Lerner, Gerda, ed. *Black Women in White America: A Documentary History* (1973); "Matilda," *Freedom's Journal* (August 1827); Marzolf, Marion. *Up From the Footnote: A History of Women Journalists* (1977); Penn, I. Garland. *The Afro-American*

Using scathing language in her crusading efforts against lynching, Ida B. Wells-Barnett dominated journalism at the end of the nineteenth century. She was the editor of the Memphis, Tennessee, paper Free Speech and Headlight. *This reproduction was published in I. Garland Penn's book* The Afro-American Press and Its Editors *(1891). [Schomburg Center]*

Press and Its Editors ([1891] 1968); Rhodes, Jane. "Mary Ann Shadd Cary and the Legacy of African-American Women Journalists." In *Women Make Meaning: The New Feminist Scholarship in Communication*, ed. Lana Rakow (forthcoming); Still, William Grant. *The Underground Railroad* (1872); Streitmatter, Rodger. "Alice Allison Dunnigan: Pioneer Black Woman Journalist," Paper presented to the Association for Education in Journalism and Mass Communication, Minneapolis, Minnesota (August 1990); Streitmatter, Rodger, and Barbara Diggs-Brown. "Marvel Cooke: An African-American Woman Journalist Who Agitated for Racial Reform," Paper presented to the Association for Education in Journalism and Mass Communication, Boston, Massachusetts (August 1991); Wilson, Clint C. *Black Journalists in Paradox: Historical Perspectives and Current Dilemmas* (1991); *Woman's Era* (May-June 1895).

JANE RHODES
CAROLYN CALLOWAY-THOMAS

JOYNER, FLORENCE GRIFFITH
(1959-)

Born in Los Angeles in 1959, Olympic medalist Florence Griffith Joyner, the seventh of eleven children, began running track at age seven, through a program at the Sugar Ray Robinson Youth Foundation. At fourteen and fifteen she won the Jesse Owens National Youth Games Awards and while at Los Angeles's Jordon High School set records in sprinting and long jumping.

In 1979, Joyner attended California State University in Northridge, but was forced to drop out because of lack of funds in 1981. Fortunately, University of California at Los Angeles Assistant Track Coach Bob Kersee recognized her athletic talents and engineered an athletic scholarship to UCLA for her in 1981. While attending classes on the Westwood campus, Joyner won the National Collegiate Athletic Association 200-meter championship in 1982 and the 400-meter championship in 1983.

After graduating as a psychology major in 1983, she was not very successful when she competed in the U.S. nationals and the world championship games. Later to become well known for her flamboyant clothes, nails, and hair, Joyner first caused a stir when she ran the first two rounds of the 1984 World Championship games in Rome wearing a skin-tight leotard-like suit.

At the XXIII Olympiad in Los Angeles in 1984, Joyner garnered a silver medal in the 200-meter race.

After the 1984 Olympic games, Joyner worked at a bank during the day and styled hair and nails for clients in the evenings. From September 1986 to April 1987 she was retired from athletic competition.

Joyner resumed training by spending endless hours watching a tape of Ben Johnson's 100-meter world-record run in order to improve her start. Success came at the 1987 World Championship games, when she was a member of the winning relay team and won a second-place award for the 200-meter event.

A gold medalist in the 1988 Olympic games in Seoul, Korea, Florence Griffith Joyner is noted not only for her prowess on the track but for her sometimes flamboyant fashion sense. [UPI/ Bettmann]

It was at the Olympic trials in Indianapolis, however, that Joyner's flamboyant beauty and exciting taste in track attire combined with her athletic performance to capture the attention of the world press. Her outfits included a sparkling apple green "one-legger" bodysuit, a plum purple "one-legger" bodysuit, a fluorescent gold bodysuit, and a white lace bodysuit with see-through tights and midriff. She came in first in the 100- and 200-meter events and shattered the world record for the 100-meter race in the quarter finals.

Wearing the conventional American uniform at the XXIV Olympiad in Seoul (1988), Joyner won the 200-meter event, setting new world records in both the semifinals and the final race. In addition, she established a new world record in the 100-meter heat and won the gold in the final event. The gold was again cinched in the 400-meter relay (4 x 100) and silver was garnered in the 1,600-meter relay (4 x 400). Following her multiple victories in Seoul, Joyner received the Sullivan Award and the *Track and Field News* Athlete of the Year award.

Joyner is currently coaching her husband, Al Joyner (brother of Olympic medalist Jackie Joyner-Kersee), designing clothing, and writing children's books; in August 1992 she began an acting stint on the television soap opera *Santa Barbara*. Although she did not participate in the 1992 Olympics, she is reported to be considering training for the marathon event in the 1996 Olympic games to be held in Atlanta, Georgia.

BIBLIOGRAPHY

"Florence Griffith Joyner." *Women's Track and Field Biographies*, NBC Sports (1990); Lindstrom, Sieg. "Woman Athlete of the Year: Nobody But Flo Jo," *Track and Field News* (February 1989); Mallon, Bill. "Florence Griffith Joyner," *TAC/TAFWA Bio Data Sheet* (1990).

D. MARGARET COSTA
JANE D. ADAIR

JOYNER-KERSEE, JACKIE (1962-)

As she ran a victory lap at the 1992 Summer Olympics, the tall Illinois native was approached by Olympic decathlon champion Bruce Jenner. "You're the greatest athlete in the world," he told her. "Man or woman, the greatest athlete in the world" (Janofsky 1992). Seven times in the history of the Olympic games a woman has scored more than 7,000 points in the challenging and grueling heptathlon. Six of those times, the woman was Jackie Joyner-Kersee. More

than a superb athlete, more than a repeated winner of Olympic gold medals, she is a legend.

Jacqueline Joyner was born on March 3, 1962, in East St. Louis, Illinois. Joyner's grandmother insisted that the child be named after First Lady Jacqueline Kennedy because "some day this girl will be the first lady of something" (*Current Biography* 1987). Her parents, Alfred and Mary Joyner, were seventeen and nineteen years old and had been married for three years. Life was difficult for the teenaged parents. Mary Joyner worked as a nurse's assistant, and Alfred Joyner traveled to other cities to work in construction before he got a job as a railroad switch operator.

At the age of nine, she ran in her first track competition. Soon she was bringing home first prizes every time, sometimes four or five of them. When she was fourteen, she won her first National Junior Pentathlon Championship. Then she won it three more times. At Lincoln High school, she set a state record for the long jump and played on a basketball team that defeated its opponents by an average of 52.8 points a game. All this time, she excelled in her academic work as well, graduating in the top ten percent of her class.

The University of California at Los Angeles recruited the remarkable young athlete, offering her scholarships in either basketball or track. She chose basketball and went off to UCLA as star forward. She qualified for the 1982 Olympics and was disappointed when the U.S. boycotted the games. However, a much greater sorrow overshadowed that loss. During Joyner's freshman year, her mother died of meningitis at the age of thirty-eight.

Joyner was concentrating on basketball and the long jump when she was spotted by assistant track coach Bob Kersee. He was stunned by her abilities but dismayed that they were not being encouraged to their fullest. After receiving special permission to coach her, he persuaded Joyner to begin heptaphlon training; she set collegiate records in 1982 and 1983. In 1983, she and her older brother, Al, were both chosen to compete in the world track and field championships in Helsinki. There, Joyner discovered that she was not invulnerable. She experienced her first serious injury, a pulled hamstring, and was unable to compete. However, a year later, she qualified for the 1984 Olympics.

Joyner arrived at the Los Angeles stadium with another hamstring injury. In spite of that, and two fouls in her best event—the long jump—she went into the final event of the second day neck-to-neck with Glynnis Nunn of Australia. With her brother running beside her on the final leg of the 800-meter

In 1992, at the age of thirty, Jackie Joyner-Kersee became the first woman in Olympic history to win back-to-back gold medals in the heptathlon. [AP/Wide World Photos]

run, urging her on, she came within .06 seconds of winning the gold medal. Al, however, did win a gold, in the triple jump. It was the first time in Olympic history that a sister and brother and won medals on the same day and the first time an American woman had won any multievent medal. Joyner went home with the silver medal and the recognition by many of her peers that she was someone very special.

In 1986, Joyner and her coach, Bob Kersee, got married. That same year, she gave up basketball to concentrate on the heptathlon and changed her training to avoid hamstring pulls. Her performance

immediately improved, peaking at the Goodwill Games in Moscow, where she shattered the 7,000-point mark—the heptaphlon equivalent of running the four-minute mile. From that time on, she did it regularly. That same year she won the Sullivan Award for top amateur athlete. She also received the 1986 Jesse Owens Award.

For the next two years, Joyner-Kersee racked up wins and records. At the 1988 Summer Olympics in Seoul, she won a gold medal in the heptathlon. Then, in 1992, she did the unprecedented. At the age of thirty, after eleven years of competition, she won the gold for the second time. This time, she was ahead after every single event. Her closest competitor, Irinia Belova, finished 199 points behind her. No woman had ever before won back-to-back medals in the heptaphlon.

Jackie Joyner-Kersee is not finished, however. "Wouldn't it be great," she said moments after her win, "to complete my career back on American soil, in Atlanta in 1996?"

BIBLIOGRAPHY

Current Biography (1987); Freeman, Patricia. "Is She the Greatest of Them All?" *Women's Sports and Fitness* (January 1987); Janofsky, Michael. "American's Seventh Wonder of Games," *New York Times* (August 3, 1992); Moore, Kenny. "Dash to Glory," *Sports Illustrated* (August 10, 1992), and "The Ties That Bind," *Sports Illustrated* (April 27, 1987); Steffens, Don. "Joyous Junction for Joyners," *Track and Field News* (August 1984); *Time.* "League of Her Own" (July 27, 1992); Willman, Howard. "Track and Field News Interview," *Track and Field News* (September 1986).

D. MARGARET COSTA
JANE D. ADAIR

K

KANSAS FEDERATION OF COLORED WOMEN'S CLUBS

African-American women began organizing in Kansas cities in the 1880s and 1890s. Literary and art clubs offering self-expression and education were initially popular with elite Black women eager to meet the ideal of Victorian womanhood. Kansans were also active in the first national meetings of African-American women.

In 1900, under the leadership of Elizabeth Washington and the Oak Leaf Club of Topeka, the Black women of Kansas formed their first statewide organization. Twenty-eight official delegates attended, representing ten clubs from Topeka, Leavenworth, Paoli, and Kansas City, Kansas. Initially called the State Federation of Women's Art Clubs, the group's first meeting featured elaborate displays of the women's paintings and needlework and a banquet for several hundred guests.

The federation quickly spread beyond northeastern Kansas, and by 1904, fifty-one clubs were represented at the annual meeting. Although the state organization continued to emphasize art and needlework, its concerns also expanded to include programs on such topics as domestic science. Members also assisted Black Americans who lost their homes in floods in 1903 and began annual donations to homes for the elderly, orphanages, and scholarship funds. By 1913, local clubs were competing over which had

done the most for charity as well as over the value of their art work.

The 1920s marked a high point in the development of the Kansas federation. As state president, Beatrice Childs expanded membership opportunities for Black women in rural areas. Under her leadership, the Kansas federation also joined the National Association of Colored Women (NACW). Art Chairman Susie Bouldin enlarged the annual art displays and added fashion shows, and Marie Fines, the music chairman, organized large music contests for local and state meetings. Scholarship donations remained a significant priority. Local clubs also continued their service activities, and the state organization supported projects such as the first Florence Crittenton Home for Colored Girls in Topeka. Among the activities of the federation's twenty-fifth anniversary celebration were a recognition ceremony by the governor and the organization of an interracial committee, but the state organization seldom engaged in formal political activities or challenged segregation.

Because of its commitment to provide role models and opportunities to train young Black women as future leaders of their race, the Kansas federation was one of the first state organizations to create junior clubs. Often the daughters of members became junior club members, and they engaged in music and art projects and held their own statewide conventions

Elizabeth Washington came to be known as "Mother Washington" in recognition of her leadership in the movement to form a statewide women's organization in Kansas in 1900.

where they discussed issues such as child labor, interracial relationships, and involvement in churches.

During the 1930s, activities at the state level declined as Childs, Bouldin, and Fines devoted most of their energy to the NACW. Local and junior clubs, however, remained active, especially in service projects. The clubwomen of Topeka and elsewhere purchased clubhouses that served as community centers in their segregated cities. In 1931, the state organization changed its name to the Kansas Federation of Colored Women's Clubs.

The Kansas federation and its local clubs continue their activities, exhibiting the practice of "rowing, not drifting," which they proclaim in their state motto.

BIBLIOGRAPHY

"Afro-American Clubwomen in Kansas: Achievements against the Odds." Pamphlet, Women's Studies Program, University of Kansas (1985); Brady, Marilyn Dell. "Kansas Federation of Colored Women's Clubs," *Kansas History* (Spring 1986), and "Organizing Afro-American Girls Clubs in Kansas in the 1920s," *Frontiers* (1987), and "The Topeka Federation of Colored Women's Clubs," *Shawnee County Historical Society Bulletin* (November 1984).

MARILYN DELL BRADY

KECKLEY, ELIZABETH (1818-1907)

Few events are more likely to stir up controversy in the nation's capital than the publication of the personal memoirs of a first lady's confidante. This was as true in 1868 as it is today. One of the first, and still one of the most controversial, of all the "serve-and-tell" books was *Behind the Scenes: or Thirty Years a Slave and Four Years in the White House*. This book revealed the often prickly opinions of Mary Todd Lincoln and information about the Lincolns' family life that many who idolized the president did not want to know.

There is a continuing argument about who actually formed the words and sentences of this startling publication, but there is no disagreement about whose story it tells. Elizabeth Keckley was Mary Todd Lincoln's dressmaker and close friend for a span of seven years that included the Civil War and the death of President Abraham Lincoln. That friendship ended with the publication of *Behind the Scenes*.

Elizabeth Keckley was born Elizabeth Hobbs in 1818 at Dinwiddie Court House in Virginia. She was a slave and the daughter of slaves. Her owners, the Burwell family, sold her while she was in her teens to a North Carolina slaveowner by whom she had a son. She was repurchased by one of the Burwell daughters, Anne Burwell Garland, shortly thereafter and taken to St. Louis. There she began her career as a dressmaker, helping to support her owners and their five daughters. Against her better judgment, she married James Keckley, who claimed to be a free man, but who turned out to be a slave and a bad husband. The two soon separated.

Keckley was so popular with her dressmaking customers that several of them offered to lend her the money to buy her freedom and that of her son, George. On November 15, 1855, at the age of thirty-seven, Keckley paid Mrs. Garland $1,200 for her freedom. Her dressmaking business thrived, and she soon paid off her loan. She also learned to read and write and, in 1860, left St. Louis for Baltimore. Six months later, she went to Washington, D.C., where she rented an apartment and began to attract an elite group of customers, including the wife of Jefferson Davis.

The Lincolns had been in Washington, D.C., a mere two weeks before Mary Todd Lincoln heard of and sent for Keckley. The first gown she designed for the first lady met with approval, as did Keckley's quiet, good-natured temperament. Keckley began to make all of Mary Todd Lincoln's clothes and also to be her traveling companion and friend. During this time, George Keckley was killed in action while fighting for the Union.

In 1862, Keckley helped to found the Contraband Relief Association, an organization of African-American women formed to provide assistance to former slaves who had come to the District of Columbia. Mary Todd Lincoln donated $200 to the effort. Keckley also garnered financial support from Wendell Phillips and other prominent white abolitionists and philanthropists as well as the great Frederick Douglass and other prominent African-Americans. She even received donations of goods from England.

On April 5, 1865, Mary Todd Lincoln and Keckley left Washington on the steamer *Monohasset* for City Point. They met President Lincoln the next day, on board the steamer *River Queen*, and continued by special train to Petersburg. On the morning of

Few events are more likely to stir up controversy in the nation's capital than the publication of the personal memoirs of a confidante of a First Lady. One of the first, and still one of the most controversial, of all the "serve-and-tell" books was Behind the Scenes *by Elizabeth Keckley, which revealed the often prickly opinions of Mary Todd Lincoln. [Moorland-Spingarn]*

April 14, Mary Todd Lincoln told Keckley that she was going to the theater in the evening with the president. At 11:00 that night, Keckley was awakened and given the news of the president's assassination. She spent the night torn by grief and concern. In the morning, she was called to her friend's side and remained with her in the days that followed.

After Lincoln's assassination, his wife turned to Keckley for comfort, and though she could no longer afford to keep the dressmaker with her, the two remained friends. When Mary Todd Lincoln, believing herself to be in serious financial trouble, decided to sell part of her White House wardrobe, Keckley met her in New York to help her organize the auction. Keckley turned to her own friends to find help for Lincoln, and, at her urging, Frederick Douglass agreed to lecture to raise money for the president's widow.

Then *Behind the Scenes* was published. Keckley insisted that her purpose was to present a sympathetic picture of the former first lady, but the book caused a permanent rift between the two women. Keckley's business also suffered. Many other African-Americans believed she had betrayed their honored and beloved hero, President Lincoln. The book, however, is considered by scholars to be a valuable source of information about the Lincolns.

The controversy about whether Keckley wrote *Behind the Scenes* herself has never centered on the accuracy of the observations in the book. Indeed, it contains forty letters from Mary Todd Lincoln to Elizabeth Keckley. However, there are those who have argued that a greater degree of education and skill than Keckley possessed might have been necessary to produce the book. At any rate, Keckley's importance in history does not depend on whether hers was the hand that held the pen that wrote the words. It derives from her position in the Lincoln household and her participation in the events surrounding the Civil War.

During the last years of Keckley's life, she lived on a small pension which she received as the mother of a fallen Union soldier. She died in 1907 of a paralytic stroke at the Home for Destitute Women and Children, an institution which she had helped found.

BIBLIOGRAPHY

Brown, Hallie Q. *Homespun Heroines and Other Women of Distinction* ([1926] 1988); *CBWA*; *DANB*; Keckley, Elizabeth. *Behind the Scenes: or Thirty Years a Slave and Four Years in the White House* (1868); *NAW*; *NBAW*.

KATHLEEN THOMPSON

KEIN, SYBIL (1939-)

"I wonder if they know something we don't know" is a line spoken by several characters from the older generation in Sybil Kein's play *Get Together* (1970). The implication is that the young are better equipped to deal with interracial or interethnic relationships than their parents. Kein maintains that once the mask is removed, people of all races and ethnic groups discover that while each ethnic group has certain culture-specific attributes, human beings are more alike than different. Her literary works celebrate diversity while underscoring the common ground or shared experiences among humanity.

Named Consuela Moore at birth, Sybil Kein was born on September 29, 1939, in New Orleans to Frank and Augustine Boudreaux Moore. One of thirteen children, Kein grew up in the seventh ward of New Orleans, an area historically inhabited by *gens du couleur* (free people of color, Creoles, or Black Creoles). Kein, a Creole of Native American, French, and African ancestry, grew up speaking a French patois primarily and English secondarily.

Educated at Corpus Christi Elementary School and Xavier Preparatory High School, Kein went on to Xavier University in New Orleans to earn a Bachelor's degree in instrumental music in 1958 and to the University of New Orleans to earn a Master's degree in theater arts and communication in 1972. Between 1958 and 1972, Kein had three children, Elizabeth, David, and Susan, and struggled through a divorce. At the age of thirty-three, Kein left New Orleans and three years later received a doctorate in American ethnic literature from the University of Michigan at Ann Arbor. She has taught English and theater at the University of Michigan-Flint since 1972.

A performing artist, poet, playwright, scholar, and recording artist, Sybil Kein has dedicated her life to researching the history and culture of Louisiana Creoles of color as well as writing poems and plays about them. Kein has published several volumes of poetry written in Creole and English, including *Visions from the Rainbow* (1979), *Gumbo People: Poésie Creole de la Nouvelle-Orleans* (1981), and *Delta Dancer* (1984). Many of her poems can be heard on two recordings: *Poetry and Music by Sybil Kein* (1979), by the National Federation of Community Broadcasters Program Service, and *Serenade Creole* (1987) by Mastertracks.

Kein's educational grounding is apparent in her twenty-eight plays, which incorporate poetry, music, and dance. Her most frequently produced plays include *Saints and Flowers* (1965), *Projection One* (1966), *The Black Box* (1967), *The Christmas Holly* (1967), *Deep River Rises* (1970), *The Reverend* (1970), *Get Together* (1970), *When I Grow Up!* (1974), *Rogues along the River Flint* (1977), and *River Rogues* (1979). Kein's plays explore such subjects as the ramifications of slavery, miscegenation, teenage pregnancy, and, especially, class and color biases.

Garnering for her a Best Playwright Award from the University of New Orleans in 1970, Kein's play *Get Together* is representative of her wit. Her central message in this play is that members of different races are not very different from each other in that they all want good health, decent jobs, and security for their children. Kein pokes fun at African-Americans and white Americans who have preconceived, racist notions about each other, which she further satirizes by bringing up the possibility that they may be related to each other because of mixed ancestry.

Kein has also won the Avery Hopwood Award for poetry (1975), the Creative Achievement Award (1978), the Amoco Foundation Grant (1979), the Michigan Council of the Arts Artist Award (1981), and the Michigan Association of Governing Boards Award (1982).

Sybil Kein is an important figure in the development of African-American theater and poetry, particularly because of the local color in her work. She travels throughout the country performing and singing, often in English, French, Spanish, Kreyol, and Creole, her poetry about the family-oriented, education-minded, fun-loving, religious, and proud Creoles of color whose history, culture, and traditions are deeply entrenched in New Orleans and in Creole settlements across the country. A regionalist of the first rank, Sybil Kein's works are as important to understanding Louisiana culture as are the works of Flannery O'Connor and Ernest Gaines.

BIBLIOGRAPHY

Brown-Guillory, Elizabeth, ed. *Wines in the Wilderness: Plays by African-American Women from the Harlem Renaissance to the Present* (1990); Bryan, Violet Harrington. "Evocations of Place and Culture in the Works of Four Contemporary Black Louisiana Writers: Brenda Osbey, Sybil Kein, Elizabeth Brown-Guillory, and Pinkie Gordon Lane," *Louisiana Literature* (Fall 1987).

ELIZABETH BROWN-GUILLORY

KELLOR, FRANCES A. *see* ASSOCIATIONS FOR THE PROTECTION OF NEGRO WOMEN

KELLY, LEONTINE T. C. (1920-)

The family of Leontine T. C. Kelly, the first Black woman to be bishop of a major religious denomination in the United States, tells a story about her baptism. "The second black bishop elected in the Methodist church baptized me when I was three years old. The story goes that when he handed me back to my mother, he said, 'How I wish you were a boy, so that my mantle could fall on you' " (Lanker 1989). Kelly herself speculates that the bishop would turn over in his grave if he knew what happened to that little girl baby.

Leontine Turpeau was born on March 5, 1920, in the parsonage of Mount Zion Methodist Episcopal Church in Washington, D.C. Her father, David D. Turpeau, was minister of the church. Her mother, Ila Turpeau, was one of the cofounders of the Urban League in Cincinnati, Ohio, where the family moved in the late 1920s.

As a child, Kelly was constantly reminded of the richness of her heritage. At one point, while living in Cincinnati, she and her sister discovered a station of the Underground Railroad in the basement of their parsonage. Their father said that the real witness of that church was in the cellar. Kelly also remembered sitting on the floor playing, at the age of eight, while her mother talked with a visitor, Mary McLeod Bethune.

Kelly attended the Harriet Beecher Stowe School and Woodward High School in Cincinnati, then went to West Virginia State College. She did not receive a college degree until she graduated from Virginia Union University in 1960, when she was forty years old. She was early married and divorced from Gloster Current and then remarried, to James David Kelly. Her second husband was pastor of the Galilee United Methodist Church in Edwardsville, Virginia, until his death in 1969. One year later, the people of the church asked Kelly to be their minister.

Kelly, who had been a certified lay speaker in the church for twelve years, attended Union Theological Seminary in New York City and was ordained in the Methodist Church. When the district superintendent asked Kelly's youngest son what he thought of his mother's going into the ministry, he said, "She's been preaching all my life."

Kelly served the Galilee church and later became a member of the staff of the Virginia Conference Council on Ministries. From 1976 to 1983, she was pastor of the Asbury United Methodist Church in Richmond, Virginia. She then became a member of the national staff of the United Methodist Church. In 1984, Kelly was elected bishop of the United Methodist Church in the San Francisco area. Her bishopric comprised nearly 400 churches and 100,000 members. She served as bishop until she retired in 1988 and then became a visiting professor at Pacific School of Religion in Berkeley, California.

"For me," Kelly has said, "the crux of the gospel message is the way we share power. One of the things women bring to the situation in terms of sharing power is new styles of leadership. I am no less the bishop. I know where the buck stops and who is responsible. But that doesn't mean that I have to exert power in such a way that other people feel they are less than who they are because of who I am."

BIBLIOGRAPHY

Lanker, Brian. *I Dream a World: Portraits of Black Women Who Changed America* (1989); Marshall, M. "First Black Woman Bishop," *Ebony* (November 1984); *NBAW*; *Who's Who of American Women* (1971).

KATHLEEN THOMPSON

KELLY, SHARON PRATT (1944-)

The first Black woman mayor of Washington, D.C., Sharon Pratt Kelly admires Franklin Delano Roosevelt and Martin Luther King, Jr., for their power to shape public policy. A resolute and optimistic newcomer to political office, Kelly is charged by her firm belief in the possibility of creating a more caring and responsible society.

She was born in Washington, D.C., on January 30, 1944, the oldest child of Carlisle and Mildred Pratt. Following her mother's death when Sharon was four, she and her younger sister, Benaree, moved in with their paternal grandmother and aunt. Her father, a former Washington, D.C., superior court judge, proved to be an important influence in her childhood—when she was still a girl he gave her a copy of *Black's Law Dictionary* as a birthday present. Sharon Pratt attended Gage and Rudolph elementary schools, MacFarland Junior High School, and Roosevelt High School. In 1965, she graduated from Howard University with a B.A. in political science and went on to the Howard University School of Law, receiving a J.D. in 1968. While in law school, she married Arrington Dixon, with whom she had two daughters, Aimee Arrington Dixon, who was born in 1968, and Drew Arrington Dixon, who was born in 1970. The couple divorced in 1982. Sharon Pratt Kelly married James Kelly III in late 1991.

The first Washington, D.C., native as well as the first woman to be elected mayor of the nation's capital, Sharon Pratt Kelly promised voters that, if elected, she would "clean house with a shovel, not a broom." [Reuters/Bettmann]

Kelly began her legal career in 1970 as house counsel for the Joint Center for Political Studies in Washington, D.C. In 1971, she became an associate with the Pratt and Queen legal firm and a year later joined the faculty of Antioch School of Law. She held both positions until 1976, when she became employed by the general counsel's office at Potomac Electric Power Company (PEPCO). In 1979, PEPCO appointed Kelly director of consumer affairs and then, in 1983, vice president of consumer affairs. She was both the first Black person and the first woman to be named to that position. In 1986, Kelly became vice president of public policy for the company, and in that capacity she worked to develop programs to assist low-income and senior citizens.

Sharon Pratt Kelly has a long record of involvement in many different organizations. Between 1985 and 1989, she was the first woman to serve as national treasurer of the Democratic party. She served as Democratic national committeewoman from the District of

Columbia from 1977 to 1980 and was vice chairperson of the District of Columbia Law Revision Committee from 1970 to 1971. She has been a member of the National Women's Political Caucus and the American Bar Association. Her other affiliations include the Legal Aid Society, the American Civil Liberties Union (ACLU), and the United Negro College Fund. Kelly also is a member of Holy Comforter Church. She is a recipient of the Falk Fellowship, Howard University, 1962-65; the Federation of Women's Club's Distinguished Service Award, 1986; and the Presidential Award from the National Association for the Advancement of Colored People, 1983.

In 1990, she stepped down from her vice presidency with PEPCO in order to make a long-shot bid for the office of mayor of Washington, D.C. An outsider in the field of politics, Dixon ran for office promising "I'll clean house with a shovel, not a broom" (*Time* 1990), a statement that reflected both her concern about the city's cumbersome and ineffectual administration and the enormous social and economic problems affecting its citizens. Kelly's election on November 6, 1990, was not only a triumphant win for a contender with less money and a smaller staff than any of her four rivals; it also resulted in two historic firsts: she became the first Washington, D.C., native as well as the first woman to be elected mayor of the nation's capital.

BIBLIOGRAPHY
Essence. "Who Is Sharon Pratt Dixon?" (April 1991); *Georgetowner.* "Sharon Pratt-Dixon: Fresh Alternative," (June 29-July 12, 1990); *Jet.* "D.C. Mayor Sharon Pratt Marries Businessman James Kelly, III in Massachusetts" (December 23, 1991), and "Election Results: Blacks Make New Gains across U.S." (November 26, 1990); McCraw, Vincent. "Anxious Dixon on Mission to Cure D.C.'s Ills," *Washington Times* (April 17, 1990); *Time.* "A Pick with a Shovel" (September 29, 1990); *Washington Post.* "Why Not a Ms. Mayor?" (July 10, 1990); *WWBA* (1990).

FENELLA MACFARLANE

KENNEDY, FLO (1916-)

Florynce Rae Kennedy was born on February 11, 1916, in Kansas City, Missouri, the daughter of Wiley and Zella Kennedy. Her father was a Pullman porter who later owned a taxi business. Her mother worked outside the home only during the Great Depression. Her parents were fiercely proud and protective of their children. No one ever hit the Kennedy children, not their parents and not their teachers. They grew up feeling that they were precious and important and that authority and respect were earned, not granted. These teachings have stood her in good stead as she has demanded respect and gained authority through her civil rights, feminist, and gay rights activism.

Kennedy attended public schools in Missouri and in California during the two or three years her family lived there. After graduating at the top of her class from Lincoln High School in Kansas City, she worked at a variety of jobs, owned a little hat shop, sang on the radio, and generally had a good time. In 1942, after her mother's death, she moved to New York City. Two years later she began taking prelaw courses at Columbia University. From there she went to Columbia Law School, after turning a rejection into an acceptance by implying to the dean that a lawsuit based on racism was a possibility.

When she graduated in 1951, Kennedy worked first as a clerk in a law firm and then opened her own office. It was not easy—one Christmas she worked at Bloomingdale's to pay the rent on the office—and by the end of the decade the end of her time as a practicing lawyer was fast approaching. "Not only was I not earning a decent living," she wrote in her autobiography, "there began to be a serious question in my mind whether practicing law could ever be an effective means of changing society or even of simple resistance to oppression" (1976).

In the early 1960s, Kennedy began to get politically involved. In 1966, she created the Media Workshop, the purpose of which was to fight discrimination in and through the media. From the very beginning, Kennedy had the knack of knowing what would get people's attention, and she was not afraid to do it, whatever it was. "When you want to get to the suites," she said repeatedly, "start in the streets."

In the suites, on the streets, in the courts, and wherever else she went, Kennedy soon learned that it does not pay to be polite. She developed a reputation for being rude, outrageous, foul-mouthed, and effective. "In 1967 I was up in Montreal at an anti-war convention," she explained in her autobiography, "and I got very mad because they wouldn't let Bobby Seale speak. He was more radical than the rest of the people there, and wanted to talk about racism, instead of limiting the discussion to the war. When they tried to stop him, I went berserk. I took the platform and started yelling and hollering. As a result, I was invited out to Washington to speak, for a fee of $250 plus expenses, and that was the beginning of my speaking career" (1976).

That career has continued to parallel Kennedy's political involvement. She has spoken, and acted, for

After becoming politically active in the 1960s, Flo Kennedy discovered that it doesn't pay to be polite. She has spoken out, sometimes rudely, sometimes outrageously, but often effectively, on behalf of prostitutes, ethnic minorities, and the poor. [AP/ Wide World Photos]

Black civil rights, feminism, and gay rights. She has been an advocate for prostitutes, ethnic minorities, and the poor. During the 1970s, she was a frequent speaking partner with Gloria Steinem. She formed the Feminist party to support Shirley Chisholm as a presidential candidate. She also coauthored one of the first books on abortion, *Abortion Rap* (1976).

BIBLIOGRAPHY

CBWA; Kennedy, Flo. *Color Me Flo: My Hard Life and Good Times* (1976); *NBAW*; *WWBA* (1992).

KATHLEEN THOMPSON

KIDD, MAE STREET

Even though Mae Street Kidd was very active in Louisville and civic affairs, she had no real interest in elective politics until she was drafted by the Democratic party to run for the Kentucky legislature in 1967. Once seated in the Kentucky House of Representatives, she candidly affirmed that she was there to get all she could for her constituents. Serving on the banking and insurance and the cities and rules committees, and as vice chair of the elections and constitutional amendments committee, Kidd sponsored or co-sponsored bills on women's rights, collective bargaining for public employees, education, welfare, age discrimination, civil rights, law and order, and housing. Two housing bills bear her name. One provided for open housing, the other for low-cost housing.

Born in Bourbon County, Kentucky, and educated at Lincoln Institute of Kentucky at Lincoln Ridge, Kidd served as assistant club director for the American Red Cross in Europe during World War II. After the war she became a public relations consultant and businesswoman. She is married to J. Meredith Kidd III. She is a vibrant activist in the Plymouth Congregational Church; a member of Iota Phi Lambda sorority, the Urban League, and the Young Women's Christian Association (YWCA); and a recipient of the Louisville Kennedy-King Award (1968). She retired in 1984 and devotes her time to local civic matters.

BIBLIOGRAPHY

Powell, Bill. "Bill Powell's Notebook: Mrs. Kidd Is Again Seeking Cure for Housing Ills" (May 11, 1970); Prestage, Jewel L. Personal interview with Mae Street Kidd, Louisville Kentucky, and telephone interviews with Dr. Cassie Osborne, Kentucky State University (October/November 1991, February 1992).

JEWEL LIMAR PRESTAGE

KINCAID, JAMAICA (1949-)

Bring together the West Indies and the *New Yorker*, and you have Jamaica Kincaid, one of the Caribbean-American writers who have emerged in the last few decades.

Born Elaine Potter Richardson on May 25, 1949, in St. Johns, Antigua, Kincaid was the daughter of Annie Richards. She did not know of or meet her biological father until later in her life and was brought up thinking that her mother's husband, a carpenter, was her father. When she was nine years old, her mother gave birth to the first of three sons, whom Kincaid seems to have experienced as intruders. When she was sixteen, Kincaid left Antigua. She went to New York and began trying to establish herself as a writer. Her entrée into the New York literary scene was the *New Yorker*, to which she sent clever descrip-

tions of African-American and Caribbean life, which were published regularly between 1974 and 1976.

In 1976, Kincaid became a *New Yorker* staff writer. In 1983, a collection of her short stories and other short pieces, most of which had been published in the *New Yorker*, was published under the name *At the Bottom of the River*. It received generally positive reviews. In 1985, Kincaid's first novel, the autobiographical *Annie John*, was published. It was a lyrical re-creation of her childhood with her mother. Five years later, *Lucy* was published. It is in many ways a sequel to the earlier book, though the protagonist has a different name. In the meantime, Kincaid also wrote and published *A Small Place*, a political analysis of Antigua that is highly critical of European and American exploitation of the island. The emotional content of her books deals almost entirely and intensely with relationships between women. Kincaid is married to Allen Shawn, son of William Shawn, who was editor when she began working for the *New Yorker*. They have two children.

BIBLIOGRAPHY

NBAW; Tyler, Anne. "Mothers and Mysteries," *New Republic* (December 31, 1983); *WWBA* (1992).

KATHLEEN THOMPSON

KING, CORETTA SCOTT (1927-)

The founding president of the Martin Luther King, Jr., Center for Nonviolent Social Change in Atlanta, Georgia, Coretta Scott King emerged as an African-American leader of national stature after the death in 1968 of her husband, Martin Luther King, Jr.

Born on April 27, 1927, in Marion, Alabama, Coretta Scott spent her childhood on a farm owned by her parents, Obie Leonard Scott and Bernice McMurry Scott. By the early 1940s, her father's truck-farming business had become increasingly successful, prompting harassment from white neighbors. The family suspected that resentful whites may have been responsible for a 1942 fire that destroyed the Scott family's home. Hoping for better opportunities for their offspring, Obie and Bernice Scott encouraged their three children to excel in school. Coretta Scott graduated from Lincoln High School, a private Black institution with an integrated faculty, and then followed her older sister Edyth to Antioch College in Ohio, where she received a B.A. in music and elementary education. An accomplished musician and singer, Scott held her concert debut in 1948 in Springfield,

Ohio, performing as a soloist with the Second Baptist Church.

Enrolling in 1951 at Boston's New England Conservatory of Music with a grant from the Jessie Smith Noyes Foundation, Scott developed her singing talent and eventually earned a Mus.B. in voice. While there, she also began dating Martin Luther King, Jr., a doctoral candidate at Boston University's School of Theology. Despite the initial objections of King's parents, who wanted him to marry a woman from his hometown of Atlanta, the two were married at the Scott family home near Marion on June 18, 1953.

During the period of her husband's public career, Coretta King usually remained out of the public spotlight, raising the couple's four children: Yolanda Denise (born November 17, 1955), Martin Luther III (October 23, 1957), Dexter Scott (January 30, 1961), and Bernice Albertine (March 28, 1963). While her primary focus was on raising children, in 1962 she served as a voice instructor in the music department of Morris Brown College in Atlanta, Georgia.

Coretta King also worked closely with her husband and was present at many of the major civil rights events of the 1950s and 1960s. In 1957, she accompanied her husband on a trip to Europe and to Ghana to mark that country's independence. In 1959, the Kings traveled to India, where Coretta King sang spirituals at events where her husband spoke. In 1960, after the family moved from Montgomery to Atlanta, she helped gain her husband's release from a Georgia prison by appealing to presidential candidate John F. Kennedy for his assistance. Kennedy's willingness to intervene to help the jailed civil rights leader contributed to the crucial support he received from African-American voters in the 1960 election. In 1962, Coretta King expressed her long-standing interest in disarmament efforts by serving as a Women's Strike for Peace delegate to the seventeen-nation Disarmament Conference held in Geneva, Switzerland. She also attended the 1964 ceremony in Oslo, Norway, awarding Dr. King the Nobel Peace Prize. In the mid-1960s, Coretta King's involvement in the civil rights movement increased as she participated in "freedom concerts," which consisted of poetry recitation, singing, and lectures demonstrating the history of the civil rights movement. The proceeds from the concerts were donated to the Southern Christian Leadership Conference. In February 1965, while Martin Luther King was jailed during voting rights protests in Alabama, she met with Black nationalist leader Malcolm X shortly before his assassination. Prior to 1968, Coretta King also maintained speaking commitments that her husband could not fill.

After the assassination of Martin Luther King, Jr., in Memphis on April 4, 1968, Coretta King devoted her life to actively propagating her husband's philosophy of nonviolence. Just a few days after the assassination she led a march on behalf of sanitation workers in Memphis, substituting for her husband, and, later in the month, she kept his speaking engagement at an anti-Vietnam war rally in New York. In May she also helped launch the March on Washington of the Poor People's Campaign, and thereafter participated in numerous antipoverty efforts. In addition, during 1969, she published her autobiography, *My Life with Martin Luther King, Jr.*

In 1969, Coretta King began mobilizing support for the Martin Luther King, Jr., Center for Nonviolent Social Change. Her plans included an exhibition hall, a restoration of the King childhood home, an Institute for Afro-American Studies, a library containing King's papers, and a museum. As founding president of the center, she guided the construction of its permanent home, located on Auburn Avenue next to Ebenezer Baptist Church where Dr. King had served as copastor with his father.

Always a strong force in the civil rights movement, after her husband's death Coretta Scott King moved into the spotlight to help fulfill his dreams. [Schomburg Center]

By the 1980s, Coretta King had become one of the most visible and influential African-American leaders, often delivering speeches and writing nationally syndicated newspaper columns. In 1983, she led an effort that brought more than a half-million demonstrators to Washington, D.C., to commemorate the twentieth anniversary of the 1963 march on Washington for jobs and freedom, where Martin Luther King had delivered his famous "I Have a Dream" speech.

Also during the 1980s, Coretta King reaffirmed her long-standing opposition to the apartheid system in South Africa. She participated in a series of sit-in protests in Washington that prompted nationwide demonstrations against South African racial policies. In 1986, she traveled to South Africa to investigate apartheid. Several Black opposition leaders criticized her plans to meet with President P. W. Botha and with Chief Buthelezi, who was viewed by many as an accommodationist. Consequently, King canceled her meetings and, instead, met with African National Congress leader Winnie Mandela. After her return to the United States, she met with President Ronald Reagan to urge him to approve sanctions against South Africa.

Perhaps the most notable achievement of Coretta King's public life was her participation in the successful effort to establish a national holiday in honor of Martin Luther King, Jr. In 1984, she was elected chairperson of the Martin Luther King, Jr., Federal Holiday Commission, which was established by an act of Congress to formalize plans for the annual celebrations that began in 1986. Also notable are Coretta King's speeches at London's St. Paul's Cathedral in 1969 and at Harvard University's Class Day exercises. She was the first woman to speak at each of the events. King has also been involved in various women's organizations such as the National Organization for Women, the Women's International League for Peace and Freedom, and United Church Women.

BIBLIOGRAPHY

Branch, Taylor. *Parting the Waters: America in the King Years: 1954-63* (1988); Hampton, Henry and Steve Fayer. *Voices of Freedom: An Oral History of the Civil Rights Movement from the 1950s Through the 1980s* (1990); King, Coretta Scott. *My Life with Martin Luther King., Jr.* (1969); Reddick, L. D. *Crusader Without Violence: A Biography of Martin Luther King, Jr.* (1959); Vittoriano, Larry M. "Coretta Scott King: Keeping the Road to Freedom Clear," *Class* (February 1992).

CLAYBORNE CARSON
ANGELA D. BROWN

KING, SUSIE *see*
TAYLOR, SUSIE KING

KITT, EARTHA (1928-)

From her initial stage appearances in the early 1950s to the recent and often ironic reflections on her life as America's Black "sex kitt(en)" (Kitt 1991), Eartha Kitt has maintained an awkward public stature, coupling ideals of Black female liberation with lurid stereotypes of the mainstream sexual imagination. By simultaneously fulfilling and challenging the expectations of a male-centered popular culture, Kitt has negotiated a fine line between supplication and defiance, poignancy of insight and simple desires for public approval.

Born on January 26, 1928, in North, South Carolina, Kitt was raised in a foster family until 1936, when she moved to New York to live with her aunt. After attending Metropolitan High School (later the High School for the Performing Arts), she toured South America and Europe as a dancer and singer of "ethnic songs" with Katherine Dunham (1946-50). In Paris, she left the troupe in order to work in clubs and theater, notably on stage and on tour with Orson Welles. Returning to New York, Kitt appeared at the Village Vanguard—at the time, a popular folk venue—and with John Carradine in Leonard Sillman's Broadway show *New Faces of 1952* (film version, 1954). These appearances vitalized her career as she quickly grew into a celebrated public figure. Articles, interviews, and reviews focused on her urbane sophistication, linguistic fluency, and haughty, aloof manner, all of which helped to shape a racially ambiguous image that stood at odds with the sambo stereotypes more commonly informing mainstream white perspectives. At the same time, gossipy references to her "feline seductiveness," alleged preference for white men, and contempt for her rural and racial past reinforced social hierarchies that placed male over female, urban over rural, white over Black.

From the mid-1950s to the mid-1960s, Kitt worked regularly in nightclubs, cabarets, and hotels, both in the United States and abroad. Her appearances in film, on television (notably in the feline role of Catwoman on episodes of *Batman*, a television program from 1967), and on record—*The Bad Eartha* (1955), *Bad But Beautiful* (1961), *At the Plaza* (1965)—helped to reinforce her image as the sophisticated Black seductress. Undermining both the sex kitten and uppity, color-struck themes, however, was her scandalous public appearance at a White House func-

By simultaneously fulfilling and challenging the expectations of a male-centered popular culture, Eartha Kitt has negotiated a fine line between supplication and defiance. She made her television acting debut in 1955 as Salome on CBS-TV's Omnibus. *[AP/Wide World Photos]*

tion hosted by Lady Bird Johnson in 1968. Castigating a group of prominent women for their myopic views of American racial and social problems and an unjust Vietnam war, Kitt became virtually overnight the pariah of conservative politics as well as a hero of the antiwar and civil rights movements. For such acclaim she would pay dearly, subjected to press ridicule, an alleged blacklisting, and investigations by both the CIA and FBI. Reviews of her activities after 1968 reveal, in fact, that Kitt worked principally overseas, although appearances in domestic clubs, film, and on television continued to a greater extent than has been commonly reported. Furthermore, while

her 1972 performance in South Africa helped somewhat to restore her reputation in the American press—named in a *Life* essay, South Africa's "Honorary White"—her seemingly naive acceptance of white South African hospitality refueled skepticism about her sense of obligation to Black Americans.

Aside from a brief return to Broadway in 1978, Kitt has worked intermittently and mainly as a cabaret singer. Her Carnegie Hall appearance in 1985 represented a public revival of sorts, while her album *I Love Men* (1984) was popular in the gay disco community of the late 1980s.

BIBLIOGRAPHY

Ebony. "Why Negroes Don't Like Eartha Kitt," (December 1954); Kitt, Eartha. *Confessions of a Sex Kitten* (1991), and *Alone with Me* (1976); Kitt, Eartha and Louie Robinson. "Fame Can Be Lonely," *Ebony* (December 1957); *Life.* "Eartha Kitt as an 'Honorary White'" (June 2, 1972); *Time.* "The First Lady: Down to Eartha" (January 26, 1968).

DISCOGRAPHY

For discographies, see Pitts, Michael. *Hollywood on Record: The Film Stars Discography* (1978); Skowronski, J. *Black Music in America: A Bibliography* (1981).

RONALD M. RADANO

KNEELAND, FRANCIS M.
(b. c. 1873)

Francis M. Kneeland was one of the pioneer Black women physicians to graduate from Meharry Medical College in Nashville, Tennessee. Kneeland was part of the first generation of Black women doctors who practiced in the United States in the late nineteenth and early twentieth centuries. However, only sketchy information exists about their experiences. The first Black women physicians not only were the first women of their race to practice medicine, but also were among the first female physicians in the country.

Born in Tennessee c. 1873, Francis Kneeland lost her parents at an early age. Where or exactly when she was born, when she was orphaned, or the names of her parents are unknown. She raised her younger siblings and educated them and herself. She graduated from Meharry, one of the foremost training institutions of Black physicians in the country, with honors in 1898. A few years earlier, in 1893, Dr. Georgiana Patton and Dr. Annie D. Gregg had become the first women to receive medical degrees from Meharry. Dr. Patton went on to become the first Black woman licensed to practice surgery and medicine in Tennessee. She located in Memphis, becoming the city's first Black woman physician. Dr. Patton established a large and successful practice, and she remained in the city until her death in 1900 at the age of thirty-six.

Dr. Francis Kneeland followed closely on the trail blazed by Patton and by 1907-8 her name appears in the Memphis directory as Dr. Francis M. Kneeland, physician and surgeon, with an office at 168 Beale Avenue. In addition to her private practice,

Dr. Kneeland was closely associated with the University of West Tennessee in Memphis. The university was a medical school (founded by Miles V. Lynk in 1901) that provided training for minorities for sixteen years. Although the school was established as an institution of higher learning for Black Americans, other minorities received training, and so, for instance, six Japanese students graduated with the class of 1923. The university had conferred 216 medical degrees by 1924. Dr. Kneeland served as the head instructor of the nursing program.

She was an excellent lecturer and was known for her involvement in associations that worked for the uplift and improvement of Black women. Because she was the only Black woman physician in the city, she was seen as an important role model who demonstrated what women with character could achieve professionally. She was the favored physician of hundreds of women in the city and apparently successfully combined a private practice with teaching, nurses' training, and public service work.

In addition, Dr. Kneeland made a good business decision to locate her office on Beale Street, important not only as the birthplace of the blues, but also as a uniquely diverse and multiethnic area of the city where Black and white, European and Asian, urban and rural, and wealthy and poor people all lived and worked. By 1908, there were over forty Black doctors in Memphis with offices located on or near Beale Street. Most were, like Dr. Kneeland, graduates of Meharry who located in Memphis because its Black population (about 52,500 in 1910) needed access to, and could pay for, medical care. Black physicians formed the upper crust of the Black community. Evidently Dr. Kneeland was able to benefit from these opportunities, for she purchased her own home in one of the more prosperous sections of the city. However, for reasons unknown, Dr. Kneeland left Memphis (it is not known exactly when) to reside in Chicago with relatives.

BIBLIOGRAPHY

Church, Roberta and Ronald Waters. *Nineteenth Century Memphis Families of Color, 1850-1900* (1987); Hamilton, Greene. *The Bright Side of Memphis* (1908); Hine, Darlene Clark. "Co-Laborers in the Work of the Lord: Nineteenth Century Black Women Physicians." In *"Send Us a Lady Physician": Women Doctors in America, 1835-1930,* ed. Ruth Adams (1985); LaPointe, Patricia M. *From Saddlebags to Science: A Century of Health Care in Memphis, 1803-1930* (1984).

EARNESTINE JENKINS

KOONTZ, ELIZABETH DUNCAN
(1919-1989)

Elizabeth Duncan Koontz served as president of the National Education Association (NEA) in 1968-69 and set as her theme, "A time for Educational Statesmanship." She called on teachers "to make use of their united power to bring about change." In her acceptance speech in Dallas, Texas, she further emphasized "that educators . . . men and women . . . young and old . . . black and white . . . stand together."

Born in Salisbury, North Carolina, on June 3, 1919, to Samuel and Lean Duncan, Elizabeth Duncan attended the Salisbury public schools and Livingstone College. She received a Bachelor's degree in English and elementary education in 1938, a Master's degree in elementary education from Atlanta University in 1941, and did further study at both Columbia University and Indiana University. She pursued additional training in education for the mentally retarded at North Carolina College in Durham, now North Carolina Central University (NCCU). On November 26, 1947, she married Harry Lee Koontz.

Devoting her entire life to the field of education, Koontz taught in the following North Carolina schools: Harnett County Training School, 1938-40; Aggrey Memorial School, Landis, 1940-41; Fourteenth Street School, Winston-Salem, 1941-1945; Price High School, Salisbury, 1945-49; Monroe School, Salisbury, 1949-65; and Price Junior-Senior High School, Salisbury, 1965-68.

Her involvement in teaching led her to become active in the local and state teachers' organizations for African-Americans and the North Carolina Teachers Association. Koontz served as president of the North Carolina Association of Classroom Teachers (NCACT) from 1959 to 1963. Under her leadership NCACT published its first edition of *Guidelines for Local Associations of Classroom Teachers* in 1961. Other accomplishments during her tenure included passage of a resolution against segregated accommodations at NEA-DCT (Department of Classroom Teachers) regional meetings of the Southeastern Region; the resolution was cosponsored by the Florida Teachers Association. Other firsts for this African-American woman included being the first North Carolina Teachers Association member appointed to the NEA Commission. Her participation at NEA-DCT meetings led to her appointment to the advisory committee by Margaret Stevenson, executive secretary of NEA-DCT.

In 1960, she was elected secretary of the NEA-DCT, a position she held for two years. Then, after serving one year as vice-president and one year as president-elect, Koontz served as president of NEA-DCT from 1965 to 1966. She represented 825,000 teachers nationwide. She was the first African-American to serve in each of these national offices.

In 1968, she was elected president of the NEA, another first for her and for African-Americans. As NEA president, she outlined a nine-point program for her tenure in which she called for a unified, secure, respected, informed, and socially aware profession; a profession that also ensured adequate income after retirement, protected against unjust attacks, had teacher-leaders, and was undivided by artificial differences.

A statesperson for education, Koontz was one of sixteen Americans who visited the Soviet Union at the request of *Saturday Review* in 1964. She held membership in the North Carolina Council of Human Relations and the North Carolina Governor's Com-

A lifelong educator, during the Nixon administration Elizabeth Koontz headed the Women's Bureau of the Department of Labor and in 1970 served as a delegate to the United Nations Commission on the Status of Women. [Schomburg Center]

mission on the Status of Women, and in 1965 was a member of the President's Advisory Council on Education of Disadvantaged Children.

During the presidential administration of Richard M. Nixon, Koontz headed the Women's Bureau of the Department of Labor and served as a delegate to the United Nations Commission on the Status of Women in 1970. Her last career appointment was as assistant superintendent for the Department of Public Instruction. She retired from this position in 1982. Koontz not only served the educational system in North Carolina, but she also served the nation and the world. She received many awards, citations, honors, and honorary degrees that give testimony to the esteem and appreciation felt by those she served. Elizabeth Duncan Koontz died in 1989 of a heart attack.

BIBLIOGRAPHY

Brown, Hugh Victor. *A History of the Education of Negroes In North Carolina* (1961); *CB* (1989); Duncan, Bernadine Moses. "Libby Koontz Retires: An Era Comes to an End," *North Carolina Education* (May/June 1982); Gilbert, Lynn and Gaylen Moore. "Particular Passions," *Crown* (1981); Interviews with Elliot B. Palmer, Bernard Allen, Edna Richards, and Ruth Jones (1981-82); Koontz, Elizabeth. "Women of a Minority." In *Voices of the New Feminism,* ed. Mary Lou Thompson (1971); Koontz, Elizabeth Duncan. Personal interview (March 1982), and *The Best Kept Secret of the Past 5,000 Years: Women Are Ready for Leadership in Education* (1972); McNeil, Barbara. *Biography and Genealogy Master Index, 1986-1990* (1990); Murray, Percy. *History of the North Carolina Teachers Association* (1984); *WWBA.*

PERCY E. MURRAY

L

LaBELLE, PATTI (1944-)

Patti LaBelle is a Grammy-winning, bona fide diva. Her voice is wide ranging, passionate, and, after more than thirty years in the business, showing no signs of becoming tame.

Patti LaBelle was born Patricia Louise Holte on May 24, 1944 (some sources list October 4), in Philadelphia, Pennsylvania. As a shy young girl, she first began singing in front of the mirror and later in a choir at Beaulah Baptist Church in Philadelphia. In 1960, Patti and Cindy Birdsong (who joined the Supremes in 1967) were members of the Ordettes. A year later, the two were teamed with their friends Nona Hendryx and Sarah Dash as the BlueBelles. In 1962 the group became known as Patti LaBelle and the BlueBelles.

The decade of the 1970s brought dramatic changes for the group. Under new management in 1970, the group changed its name to LaBelle and burst on the scene provocatively dressed in leather, feathers, and glitter, singing disco anthems of progressive funk and rock. "Lady Marmalade," a widely played song, was a number-one hit for LaBelle in 1974. The group disbanded in 1977, however, as a result of artistic and personal differences.

Patti LaBelle, as a solo artist, continues to successfully record—winning her first Grammy in 1992—and perform before enthusiastic full houses. She also is an accomplished actress, having appeared in film (*A Soldier's Story*, *Beverly Hills Cop*), on Broadway (*Your Arms Too Short to Box with God*), and on television (most recently as Dwayne Wayne's mother on *A Different World*). She also has had her own television special and stars in the television series *Out All Night* (NBC).

In 1969, she married Armstead Edwards, who manages her career. They have three sons, Zuri, their natural child, and Stanley and Dodd, who are adopted.

BIBLIOGRAPHY

Clark, Donald, ed. *The Penguin Encyclopedia of Popular Music* (1989); Clifford, Mike. *The Illustrated Encyclopedia of Black Music* (1982); Ebert, Alan. "Girlfriend: A Down-Home Diva!" *Essence* (March 1991); Moritz, Charles, ed. *Current Biography Yearbook 1986* (1986); Smart-Grosvenor, Vertamae. "Patti!" *Essence* (October 1985).

LAWRENCE J. SIMPSON

LABOR MOVEMENT

Throughout American history, Black wives, mothers, sisters, and daughters have had to labor outside their own homes in order to ensure the survival of their families. Racial and sexual discrimination have marginalized this work force, relegating Black women to the bottom of the occupational hierarchy, to agricultural work and domestic service and, more recently, to the unskilled service sector. For these reasons, laboring Black women have been systematically excluded from industrial jobs targeted by the labor movement and forced to work in the least desirable jobs in factories, such as janitors or tobacco stemmers, unprotected by unions dominated by white laborers.

Nevertheless, Black women have organized collective actions—beyond the parameters of the national labor movement—wherever they have found employment, drawing on a legacy of slave women's resistance to do so. Black women fieldworker strikes date back to 1862; Black washerwomen in Jackson, Mississippi, organized in 1866. The Washerwomen's Association of Atlanta strike in 1881 involved 3,000 Black women. More covert methods of resistance among domestic workers included careless work and a blacklist against notoriously abusive white women. Even during the Great Depression, when Black women subjected themselves to "slave markets"—streetcorners where white women chose one woman among many to work at radically depressed wages—efforts at collective self-protection persisted in several cities. The standard contract that the New York Domestic Workers' Association recommended, although it was impossible to enforce, included a minimum wage, a sixty-hour work week, and "last, but not least, no window-washing" (Lerner 1972). Dorothy Bolden continued in this tradition more successfully when she organized Atlanta domestic workers in 1968.

Black women have also played important supportive roles in labor agitation. During United Mine Workers strikes in the early twentieth century and steelworkers' strikes in the 1930s and 1940s, Black women cooked, juggled family budgets, assumed additional jobs, and picketed, thus enabling their menfolk to strike. During the Depression, boycotts by the housewives' leagues were integral to the success of don't-buy-where-you-can't-work campaigns—protests against white-owned ghetto businesses that resulted in some 75,000 new jobs for Black workers.

Because of racial, gender, and professional biases, Black women workers were not organized into the American Federation of Labor (AFL) when it was founded in 1881. Although labor shortages during World War I enabled some Black women (6.7 percent of all women working in manufacturing) to acquire industrial jobs, the AFL ignored marked differentials in wages between men and women and between races, as well as the poorer working conditions of Black female laborers. Unprotected by unions, Black women's brief occupational progress was wiped out in the 1920s.

When the Congress of Industrial Organizations (CIO) broke away from the AFL in 1935, it focused its gaze on unskilled workers, the South, and Black workers. Consequently, during the Depression and through World War II, interracial labor efforts became a reality in the steel, auto, garment, laundry, and tobacco industries, among others. Black women employed in industries—although a mere 5 percent of the Black female work force in 1930—were crucial to this interracial organizing.

CIO affiliates influenced by the Communist party and its inclusion of women were particularly likely to draw on Black women's organizing skills. For example, Connie Smith and 3,000 nut pickers, 85 percent of whom were Black women, organized the Food Workers' Industrial Union, a CIO affiliate in St. Louis. Manager "Boss Funsten" failed to break the interracial strike by offering white women more money if they returned to work, marking a departure in management's traditionally successful manipulation of the racial caste system. Scores of rural Black women were active in the interracial Southern Tenant Farmers Union (STFU), which protested the disastrous effects that federal agricultural policies had on poor people in the rural South. Carrie Dilworth and Henrietta McGee spoke for the STFU and made the plight of the displaced sharecropper a national issue.

Black women were most visible as labor activists during the 1930s and 1940s in the tobacco industry, which had been characterized by a rigid sex- and race-determined occupational hierarchy since the nineteenth century. Louise "Mamma" Harris, a Black tobacco stemmer, initiated spontaneous walkouts at the I. N. Vaughn Company in Richmond, Virginia, in 1938. Richmond police were appalled to see white International Ladies Garment Workers Union (ILGWU) women "parading for niggers." Harris's walkouts-turned-strikes led to the establishment of the Tobacco Workers Organizing Committee, a CIO affiliate through which workers won major concessions.

In 1943, Black women Theodosia Simpson, Velma Hopkins, Viola Brown, Ruby Jones, and Miranda Smith were among the union activists who were central to the strike that brought Winston-Salem, North Carolina, tobacco giant R. J. Reynolds to the negotiating table with Local no. 22 of the Food, Tobacco, Agricultural, and Allied Workers of America (FTA). Smith later became the FTA's southern regional director, the highest position a Black woman had held in the labor movement.

During the labor shortages of World War II, the percentage of Black females in the industrial labor

*A strike was usually the only way manual workers could hope to improve their working
conditions. These women (and men) represent the range of people employed as laundry workers.
[Archives of Labor and Urban Affairs, Wayne State University]*

force tripled, and interracial efforts begun in the 1930s
escalated. During these years, therefore, Black women
began to struggle against racial and sexual discrimination within the context of organized labor. In 1943,
the CIO established the Committee to Abolish Racial
Discrimination; that same year Detroit's United Auto
Workers co-sponsored with the National Association
for the Advancement of Colored People a rally at
which 10,000 workers demanded that war industry
jobs be opened to Black women. Between 1940 and
1945, Black union membership rose from 200,000 to
1.25 million. Miranda Smith explicitly linked civil
rights and labor activism in her address to the CIO in
1947: "We want to stop lynching in the South. We
want people to walk the picket lines unafraid" (Lerner
1972).

Even during the 1940s, however, the national
labor movement was unwilling to endorse the link
between civil rights and labor activism or make the
fate of Black workers a priority. Wartime labor shortages notwithstanding, Black women were the "last
hired, first fired," and they were underpaid. The racism of white women periodically erupted into so-called
hate strikes against Black women workers, which

unions did little to counter. Efforts to segregate workers in organized labor endured, particularly in the
AFL. "They're trying to have Jim Crow unions," said
tobacco stemmer Luanna Cooper in 1943. "They
wanted me to join. I told them: 'I get Jim Crow free. I
won't pay for that' " (Lerner 1972).

During demobilization and into the 1950s, Black
women workers faced severe setbacks. Unions worked
with management to eliminate women from the work
force; the CIO capitulated to anti-Communist hyste-
ria and expelled eleven so-called suspect unions—all
with strong records for interracial organizing; and the
passage of the Taft-Hartley Act in 1947 further limited organized labor. Even organized labor's postwar
southern organizing drives—"Operation Dixie"—primarily targeted the all-white textile industry
or expected Black workers to accept their second-
class status. By 1947, accusations of Communist-
domination, a House Un-American Activities
Committee investigation, and competition with the
AFL had severely eroded the power of the FTA's
egalitarian Local 22 in Winston-Salem; three years
later, nonunion forces were victorious at R. J. Reynolds. By 1948, most of the economic advances made

by Black women during the war had eroded, and by 1950, 41 percent of laboring Black women worked as domestics.

Black women were among the labor leaders who tried to resist red-baiting in the National Negro Labor Council (NNLC), formed in 1951. The short-lived NNLC sought to put pressure on industries to comply with the Fair Employment Practices Committee nondiscrimination policies in peacetime and stressed the ongoing need for Black workers to organize. One third of its initial delegates were Black women; Octavia Hawkins, a garment worker active in the Amalgamated Clothing Workers, was the organization's first treasurer. A series of successful NNLC strikes in the early 1950s opened jobs as stewardesses and cashiers to Black women. In these and other organizations, Black women and men united to advance their collective interests and to challenge economic racism comprehensively, something organized labor had failed to do. These efforts would culminate in the national civil rights movement.

Since the 1960s, Black women have brought a heritage of activism from the civil rights movement, as well as their own rich tradition of collective resistance, to organizing efforts in occupations opened to them by civil rights legislation. The southern textile industry continues to be difficult to organize, but unions are more viable in interracial mills, where Black women often initiate organizing drives. When thousands of mostly Black hospital employees in Charleston, South Carolina, initiated a strike in 1969, Coretta Scott King, the Southern Christian Leadership Conference (SCLC), the AFL-CIO, and Charleston's Black community came together in support of the women. The dramatic 113-day action echoed the country's most bitter civil rights and organized labor struggles, including mass arrests and a "jail, no bail" pledge. "We were forgotten women," strike leader Ann Moultrie said, but using the union as their vehicle, the strikers demonstrated that "we can and will overcome" (Foner 1982).

In the 1970s and 1980s, Black women's collective efforts to transform the workplace continued: in the Coalition of Black Trade Unionists, formed in 1972 to address racism on the job and in unions; in the Coalition of Labor Union Women, formed in 1974 to resist sexism in unions; in evolving Black feminist theory; and in the homes and offices of Black women. These diverse organizations and methods demonstrate the multiple struggle of Black women—as workers, as Black people, and as women.

Organized labor has never comprehensively addressed the economic problems of Black workers, and it has never been able to help the many needy Black women who remain outside the industrial economy—the domestic worker of the 1920s and 1950s, the displaced sharecropper of the 1930s, or the unemployed young mother mired in poverty in the 1990s. Indeed, while the gap in wages and job occupations between Black and white women has narrowed considerably, Black women continue to rank lowest in earnings in the occupational hierarchy of white men, Black men, and white women. Throughout the century, however, organized labor has been one of many collective strategies that Black women have used to survive, to protect their families, and to challenge inequities of class, race, and sex. For the 22.9 percent of the Black female work force represented by labor unions in 1989 (relative to 13.7 percent of white women), union membership echoes an age-old legacy of collective resistance.

BIBLIOGRAPHY

AFL-CIO. "Women in the Workforce." Publication No. 98-P0890-30 (1990), and "Blacks in the Workforce." Publication No. 28-R0290-5 (1990); Anderson, Karen. "Last Hired, First Fired: Black Women Workers During World War II," *Journal of American History* (June 1982); Black Women Oral History Project. Schlesinger Library, Radcliffe College, Cambridge, Massachusetts; Clark-Lewis, Elizabeth. " 'This Work Had a End': African-American Domestic Workers in Washington, D.C., 1910-1940." In *"To Toil the Livelong Day": America's Women at Work, 1780-1980*, ed. Carol Groneman and Mary Beth Norton (1987); Davis, Angela Y. *Women, Race and Class* (1983); Foner, Philip S. *American Socialism and Black Americans: From the Age of Jackson to World War II* (1977), and *Organized Labor and the Black Worker, 1619-1973* (1974), and *Women and the American Labor Movement, Volume 1: From Colonial Times to the Eve of World War I* (1979), and *Women and the American Labor Movement, Volume 2: From World War I to the Present* (1982); Foner, Philip S. and Ronald L. Lewis, eds. *American Communism and Black Americans: A Documentary History, 1930-1934* (1991), and *Black Workers: A Documentary History from Colonial Times to the Present* (1989); Frederickson, Mary. " 'I Know Which Side I'm On': Southern Women in the Labor Movement in the Twentieth Century." In *Women, Work and Protest: A Century of U.S. Women's Labor History*, ed. Ruth Milkman (1985); Frederickson, Mary and Joyce Kornbluh, eds. *Sisterhood and Solidarity: Workers' Education for Women, 1914-1984* (1984); Gabin, Nancy F. *Feminism in the Labor Movement: Women and the United Auto Workers, 1935-1975* (1990); Giddings, Paula. *When and Where I Enter: The Impact of Black Women on Race and Sex in America* (1984); Groneman, Carol and Mary Beth Norton, eds. *"To Toil the Livelong Day": America's Women at Work, 1780-1980* (1987); Hartmann, Susan M. "Women's Organizations During World War II: The Interaction of Class, Race and Feminism." In *Woman's Being, Woman's*

Place: Female Identity and Vocation in American History, ed. Mary Kelley (1979); Hawks, Joanne V. and Sheila L. Skemp, eds. *Sex, Race, and the Role of Women in the South* (1983); Haynes, Elizabeth Ross. "Negroes in Domestic Service in the United States," *Journal of Negro History* (October 1923); Henry, Alice. *The Trade Union Woman* (1915); Hine, Darlene Clark, ed. *Black Women in American History: From Colonial Times through the Nineteenth Century, Volumes 1-4* (1990), and *Black Women in American History: The Twentieth Century* (1990); hooks, bell. *Ain't I a Woman: Black Women and Feminism* (1981); Janiewski, Dolores E. " 'Seeking a New Day and a New Way': Black Women and Unions in the Southern Tobacco Industry." In *"To Toil the Livelong Day": America's Women at Work, 1780-1980*, ed. Carol Groneman and Mary Beth Norton (1987), and "Sisters Under Their Skins: Southern Working Women, 1880-1950." In *Sex, Race, and the Role of Women in the South*, ed. Joanne V. Hawks and Sheila L. Skemp (1983), and *Sisterhood Denied: Race, Gender, and Class in a New South Community* (1985); Jones, Jacqueline. *Labor of Love, Labor of Sorrow: Black Women, Work and the Family from Slavery to the Present* ([1985] 1986); Katzman, David M. *Seven Days a Week: Women and Domestic Service in Industrializing America* (1978); Kessler-Harris, Alice. *Out to Work: A History of Wage-Earning Women in the United States* (1982); Kessler-Harris, Alice and J. Carroll Moody, eds. *Perspectives on American Labor History: The Problems of Synthesis* (1989); Korstad, Robert and Nelson Lichtenstein. "Opportunities Found and Lost: Labor, Radicals and the Early Civil Rights Movement," *Journal of American History* (December 1988); Lerner, Gerda, ed. *Black Women in White America: A Documentary History* (1972); Lewis, Ronald. *Black Coal Miners in America: Race, Class and Community Conflict* (1987); Lynd, Alice and Staughton Lynd, eds. *Rank and File: Personal Histories by Working-Class Organizers* (1973); Milkman, Ruth. *Gender at Work: The Dynamics of Job Segregation by Sex During World War II* (1987); Milkman, Ruth, ed. *Women, Work and Protest: A Century of U.S. Women's Labor History* (1985); Miller, Marc S., ed. *Working Lives: The "Southern Exposure" History of Labor in the South* (1980); Naison, Mark. *Communists in Harlem During the Depression* (1983); Sitkoff, Harvard. *A New Deal for Blacks: The Emergence of Civil Rights as a National Issue* (1978); Terborg-Penn, Rosalyn. "Survival Strategies among African-American Women Workers: A Continuing Process." In *Women, Work and Protest: A Century of U.S. Women's Labor History*, ed. Ruth Milkman (1985); Terborg-Penn, Rosalyn and Sharon Harley, eds. *The Afro-American Woman: Struggles and Images* (1978); Wallace, Phyllis A. *Black Women in the Labor Force* (1980); White, Deborah Gray. *Ar'n't I a Woman?: Female Slaves in the Plantation South* (1985).

RUTH FELDSTEIN

LAFONTANT-MANKARIOUS, JEWEL STRADFORD (1922-)

"Well, I don't know about this tokenism. People say to your face, 'They selected you because you are a twofer.' It means two for one—a black and a woman—and I laugh about it. But they are serious. I can't look into the person's mind, why they selected me. All I can say is, 'thank you.' It is up to me to turn tokenism into something real" (Travis 1981). Jewel Lafontant-Mankarious has not only turned her opportunities into something real, she has opened the doors for others to follow behind. Lafontant-Mankarious's career in law, business, and government has been marked by firsts. She has not only broken through barriers of race and sex, she has worked within the system to attempt positive change for minorities and women.

Jewel Stradford Lafontant-Mankarious was born on April 28, 1922 in Chicago, Illinois, to Cornelius Francis and Aida Carter Stradford. Jewel was born into a family of successful lawyers and businessmen. Her grandfather and father were both Oberlin College graduates, attorneys, and active in Republican politics. She continued the family tradition when she received a B.A. from Oberlin College in 1943 and a J.D. from the University of Chicago in 1946. While in law school, Jewel Stradford was one of the founding members of the Congress of Racial Equality (CORE). She also participated in sit-ins during the early 1940s.

Jewel Stradford began her career after admission to the Illinois state bar in 1947, as the first Black trial attorney for the Legal Aid Bureau of the United Charities of Chicago (1947-53) where she worked on a volunteer basis. She also worked in the law firm of Rogers, Rogers, and Strayhorn, the firm of her husband John Rogers, from 1952 to 1954, and served as precinct captain for the sixth ward of Chicago. President Dwight D. Eisenhower appointed her Assistant U.S. Attorney for the North District of Illinois, where she served from 1955 to 1958. She left her appointment after the birth of her son, John Rogers, Jr., and practiced with her father's firm. Married to Ernest Lafontant in 1961, they opened a law office and she practiced there until 1983. Ernest Lafontant died in 1976. Jewel Lafontant was a senior partner in the law firm of Vedder, Price, Kaufman, Kammholz, and Day from 1983 to 1989 where she practiced corporate and labor law.

In addition to her legal career, Lafontant-Mankarious, a lifelong Republican, seconded the nomination of Richard M. Nixon for president in

1960, as an alternate delegate to the Republican National Convention. She served as U.S. representative to the United Nations from September 1972 to December 1972. President Nixon also appointed her to the position of Deputy Solicitor General of the United States in 1973, where she became the first woman to argue a case before the U.S. Supreme Court. As Deputy Solicitor General, she was chairperson of federal women's programs for the Department of Justice. She served as Deputy Solicitor General from February 1973 to June 1975.

In 1968, Lafontant-Mankarious was elected to the board of directors of Jewel Foods. Prior to her appointment as an ambassador, she served as a corporate director of seventeen major corporations. She used her influence on these boards not only to provide leadership to the corporations but also to increase minority hiring, among other concerns.

Lafontant-Mankarious served as commissioner of the Martin Luther King, Jr., Federal Holiday Commission and chair of the Illinois Advisory Committee to the U.S. Civil Rights Commission. In recognition of her professional achievements and civic service, she has received numerous awards including awards from OICs of America (Opportunities Industrialization Centers), the National Coalition of Black Women, and PUSH (People United to Save Humanity). She is also the recipient of honorary degrees from fourteen universities including Howard University, Providence College, Loyola University, and the University of Chicago.

Lafontant-Mankarious is currently Ambassador at Large and United States Coordinator for Refugee Affairs. Her appointment was confirmed by the U.S. Senate on June 15, 1989. She is responsible to the president for the development of overall U.S. refugee assistance, admission, and resettlement policy. She also negotiates on behalf of the United States with foreign governments and international organizations concerning refugee affairs.

Ambassador Lafontant-Mankarious is married to Naguib S. Mankarious, an international business consultant. Her son, John W. Rogers, Jr., is president and chief executive officer of Ariel Capital Management.

BIBLIOGRAPHY
Lafontant, Jewel. Interview by Dempsey J. Travis. In *An Autobiography of Black Chicago* (1981); Lafontant-Mankarious, Jewel. Biographical data, Department of State, Washington, D.C.; Mankarious, Jewel Lafontant. "Chicago Sets the Stage for a Career of Helping the Helpless," *Chicago Tribune* (July 21, 1991); *NA*; *Who's Who in America* (1990-91).

SONYA RAMSEY

LAMPKIN, DAISY ELIZABETH ADAMS (c. 1884-1965)

When Daisy Elizabeth Adams Lampkin died at her Pittsburgh home on March 10, 1965, the whole nation took note. The Pittsburgh *Post-Gazette* carried an editorial stating: "Americans owe a debt to Mrs. Daisy Lampkin." The editors credited her with being "instrumental in advancing the cause of the National Association for the Advancement of Colored People, and indirectly, the case which led to legally enforced desegregation of public schools." The *New York Times* characterized her as a "Negro leader," calling attention to her contributions to civil rights, to her thirty-six years as vice-president of the once-powerful *Pittsburgh Courier*, and to her work with the National Council of Negro Women (NCNW) and the National Association of Colored Women (NACW).

On August 9, 1983, the Pennsylvania Historical and Museum Commission dedicated a ten-foot-high, shining blue-and-gold official historical marker bearing the state insignia in front of her home at 2519 Webster Avenue, which was a mecca for national African-American activists for half a century. Lampkin was the first Black woman to be so honored by the Commonwealth of Pennsylvania, which has erected more than 1,500 markers. Then Governor Dick Thornburgh (later U.S. attorney general) wrote in a statement issued for the ceremony, "Daisy Lampkin courageously sought full equality for Blacks and women throughout the country. Today her work stands as an inspiration for countless citizens." Former Pennsylvania House Speaker K. Leroy Irvis recalled how Lampkin had guided young men like himself and Supreme Court Justice Thurgood Marshall in their public careers. Officials of city and county government, the Urban League, NCNW, Delta Sigma Theta sorority, The Links, and the Lucy Stone Civic League, as well as church and neighborhood groups, gave testimony of her numerous humanitarian achievements.

Daisy Elizabeth Adams was born in the District of Columbia in March 1884, according to the 1900 census for Reading, Berks County, Pennsylvania, which lists her as the stepdaughter of John Temple and his wife, Rosa. The record indicates that the couple had been married one year and that the sixteen-year-old girl was housekeeper for the adults who were employed as cooks. However, there have been several conflicting published reports, especially the data in *WWCA* 1950 stating that she was born in Reading, August 9, 1888, daughter of George and Rosa Anne (Proctor) Adams. She completed high school in Reading and is remembered as an active member of the Presbyterian Church. In 1909, Adams moved to Pittsburgh where she married William Lampkin, a native of Rome, Georgia, in 1912. That same year, the *Pittsburgh Courier* (December 20) ran

an article commending her for promoting a successful woman's suffrage event. In 1913, Lampkin began her life-long association with the noted publisher and politician, attorney Robert L. Vann. She won a cash award for selling the most new subscriptions to the *Courier* and traded it in for stock in the publishing company, continually augmenting her investment until she was named vice president of the corporation in 1929, a post she held for the rest of her life.

Lampkin was best known for her work as national field secretary for the National Association for the Advancement of Colored People (NAACP), but

Best known for her work as national field secretary for the NAACP in the 1930s and 1940s, Daisy Lampkin was a tireless fund-raiser and fighter for American civil rights organizations, as well as a longtime vice-president of the Pittsburgh Courier. *She is shown here addressing the 1947 National Council of Negro Women convention. [Bethune Museum and Archives]*

she had established herself as a prominent national figure long before Walter White recruited her for the civil rights association. She had gained recognition for her leadership ability in Liberty bond drives during World War I, when the Black community of Allegheny County raised more than 2 million dollars. She started her political career as president of the Negro Women's Franchise League in 1915, affiliated early with the National Suffrage League, and held top positions in the women's division of the Republican party. She was elected president of the National Negro Republican Convention in Atlantic City, New Jersey, in July 1924, when, according to the *New York Times*, the assembly passed a strong antilynching resolution. She was elected delegate-at-large to the Republican National Convention in Cleveland, Ohio, in 1926.

Before she joined the NAACP staff, Lampkin served as national organizer and chair of the executive board of the NACW. When James Weldon Johnson organized a group of African-American leaders to meet with President Calvin Coolidge at the White House in 1924 in an attempt to secure justice for the Black soldiers accused in the 1917 Houston riot, he summoned Lampkin, the only woman among the twelve or more national leaders. Lampkin also was a delegate along with Mary McLeod Bethune, Nannie Burroughs, Alice Dunbar-Nelson, and Addie Dickerson, all noted clubwomen, when Sallie Stewart, NACW president, was elected a vice president of the National Council of Women of the United States, whose membership extended to the International Council of Women. This November 1929 meeting marked the first formal recognition of African-American women as official participants in world affairs.

When the January 1930 edition of the *Crisis* announced the appointment of Lampkin as NAACP regional field secretary, the periodical noted, "The name of Daisy Lampkin will be known wherever colored women meet together. Her achievements have been so unusual that they have long been the subject of public knowledge and comment."

Significantly, Lampkin had been named vice president of the Pittsburgh Courier Publishing Company just a few months earlier and had been working closely with Walter White, then acting NAACP executive secretary, before she was hired by the board of directors.

She was able to use the connecting forces of the NAACP and the *Courier*—the two most effective civil rights institutions of the era—to assure success in numerous important campaigns. In fact, records show that Lampkin mediated numerous bitter fights among the men, which threatened the viability of a united African-American front in the battle against Jim Crow. Her devotion to the overarching cause of Black progress earned Lampkin the respect of rivals and opponents throughout the community. Lampkin plunged into massive membership and fund-raising drives, using the NAACP's role in the defeat of U.S. Supreme Court nominee Judge John J. Parker of North Carolina as a rallying cry.

The NAACP announced that its staff and members would do everything possible to defeat senators who had voted for Judge Parker, whom they considered to be an archenemy of the race, and in 1930 Lampkin played a major role in the defeat of Senator Roscoe McCullough of Ohio. Even before she was hired, she had begun to reorganize the Ohio State NAACP Conference by working in twenty-three towns and cities, speaking two and three times a day, maximizing her superb oratorical skills. At the same time, Roy Wilkins, editor of the Kansas City *Call*, was out in front in the battle to bring down Senator Henry J. Allen of Kansas. His resounding victory in helping the NAACP make good its threat brought Wilkins into the NAACP fold as assistant secretary to White. Lampkin, Wilkins, and White formed a dynamic triumvirate whose relentless efforts laid the foundation for civil rights triumphs on battlefronts all over the nation.

Named national field secretary in 1935, Lampkin embarked on an astonishing fund-raising membership campaign schedule, often reporting more than forty meetings in one month. Almost as remarkable was her ability to garner nearly all of her expense money from the branches, thus keeping costs at the national office extremely low. Throughout her tenure as field secretary, Lampkin remained active with the NACW and NCNW, serving as a vice president of the former and on the board of directors and education foundation chair of the latter. She headed the drive to establish an NCNW headquarters in 1945 and turned over a check for $49,000 at the Washington, D.C., annual workshop. She also chaired the 1952 campaign to raise funds for Delta Sigma Theta's national home, sharing her triumph in a letter to her life-long friend, Nannie Burroughs.

Lampkin entered the Democratic party camp along with Robert L. Vann and the *Courier* during the New Deal era of President Franklin Delano Roosevelt, skillfully skirting around NAACP nonpartisan directives to staff members. She asserted her right to speak for the women, telling White, "the public knows that I have many other interests in addition to the NAACP." However, in 1947 she used the NAACP nonpartisan stance to decline repeated efforts by Congressman William Dawson to recruit her for the committee to elect Harry Truman.

It is true that Lampkin's fund-raising ability was unmatched, but observers have grossly underestimated her worth to the civil rights movement by focusing only on this facet of her work. Due to extreme fatigue she finally resigned her field position in 1947, despite fervent pleas from White, Wilkins, and Marshall that she hold on. To their great satisfaction she immediately accepted an assignment with the board of directors and continued to conduct membership drives in branches where leaders made it clear that they wanted no other person.

Lampkin began her job at $50 a week in 1930, and her salary never was higher than a meager $5,200 annually. During all those years she gave herself totally to what she always referred to as "the cause," the elevation of Black people all over the world. C.L.R. James, the noted author, recognized her great influence when, in 1956, he wrote to her requesting that she make sure the Negrophobic pamphlet "Ordeal of the South" by England's Alistair Cooke was refuted. James described the articles as sneers and slanders, extremely harmful to international race relations. The NAACP's Henry Moon was joined by Black journalists everywhere in voicing scathing rebuttals of Cooke's stories published by the *Manchester Guardian*.

Keeping her finger on the political pulse of the nation, Lampkin switched back to the Republican party in 1952 when the Democrats ran a segregationist, John J. Sparkman of Alabama, for vice president. Her switch was reported in the *New York Times* with a headline announcing, "Woman Newspaper Executive and Democrat Opposes Sparkman" (October 16).

Still campaigning for the NAACP in October 1964, Lampkin collapsed on the stage of a Camden, New Jersey, auditorium moments after delivering a stirring appeal. Lampkin was too feeble to attend the elaborate ceremony in New York's Waldorf-Astoria Hotel when the NCNW presented her its first Eleanor Roosevelt-Mary McLeod Bethune Award the following December 22. Lena Horne, who had formed a close friendship with Lampkin when the young singer lived in the same Pittsburgh neighborhood, accepted the tribute for her.

During the remaining few months of her life, Lampkin was cared for by her adopted family, Dr. and Mrs. Earl Childs, and their son, Earl Douglas Childs, who lived with her in the Daisy Lampkin apartment building, now a historic site.

BIBLIOGRAPHY

McKenzie, Edna B. "Daisy Lampkin: A Life of Love and Service," *Pennsylvania Heritage* (Summer 1983), and "Servant Well Done," Unpublished manuscript (1992); NAACP papers, Library of Congress, Washington, D.C.; *Twelfth Census of the United States*. Schedule No. I, *Population*, Berks County, Pennsylvania.

EDNA CHAPPELL McKENZIE

LANEY, LUCY CRAFT (1854-1933)

"To woman has been committed the responsibility of making the laws of society, making environments for children. She has the privilege and authority, God-given, to help develop into a noble man or woman the young life committed to her care. There is no nobler work entrusted to the hands of mortals" (Laney 1897). This conviction, expressed by Lucy Craft Laney in 1897, reflected the beliefs and principles of one of the most important African-American female educators in the late-nineteenth-century South.

Early in her development Laney concluded that women's most profound power derived from their roles as mothers and wives. She saw a relationship between the progress of the race and the need to defend, preserve, and strengthen the moral integrity of Black women. Laney was convinced that women molded the character of the nation, that highly moral, educated Black women were a prerequisite for uplift of the race, and that the first line of defense was the home. In Lucy's view, "The home [was] the nearest approach on earth to heaven. The chief joy of home [was the] mother" (Laney 1897). These convictions not only shaped Lucy Craft Laney's character and inspired her choice of a career but also provided the basic ideas to which she devoted her life's work. Laney's respect for the home, the major role of women in sustaining it, and the significance of the home and family in the struggle to uplift the Black race were instilled in her during her youth.

Born in Macon, Georgia, on Thursday, April 13, 1854, Lucy was the seventh of ten children of David and Louisa Laney. Her father, who had succeeded in purchasing his freedom and that of his wife during slavery, was a carpenter by trade. A deeply religious man, David Laney served as a preacher among his people before the Civil War and on May 13, 1866, was ordained as a Presbyterian minister. During the following year, he cofounded the John Knox Presbytery, the first all-Black Presbyterian Synod in the United States, which was received into the Northern Assembly in 1868. David Laney was a renowned religious and community leader in Georgia who retired in the early 1890s and died in 1902.

Louisa, Lucy's mother, was purchased by the Campbell family of Macon from a group of nomad Indians when she was a small child. Mr. Campbell bought the little girl at the urging of his daughter, to whom Louisa became a personal maid. A cute and likeable child, Louisa and the Campbells' daughter developed an amicable relationship. Louisa not only mastered the skills necessary to perform her duties, but also, with the assistance of her mistress, she learned to read and write. When Louisa was about fifteen years old, she married David Laney and, in spite of her small frame and frail body, gave birth to ten healthy children, four boys and six girls, one of whom was Lucy Craft.

Lucy C. Laney spent her childhood in Macon, Georgia, where she was reared in a large, warm, loving, nourishing, closeknit, Christian family that stressed sharing, responsibility, sacrifice, and education. She received her first formal education at the Lewis School, an institution opened by missionary teachers in 1865, and from which she was graduated in 1869. When the American Missionary Association opened a Black college in Atlanta, Georgia, Lewis was one of the schools asked to send its best and brightest students for advanced education. Lucy C. Laney was one of the twenty-seven women among the first eighty-nine students admitted to Atlanta University in fall 1869.

Lucy and a fellow Lewis graduate, William S. Scarborough, quickly earned the reputation of being the most intelligent students at the university. In 1873, Laney and three other women in the "Higher Normal Course" became the first students to receive degrees from Atlanta University.

Lucy C. Laney began her teaching career in Milledgeville, Georgia, but between 1873 and 1877 she also taught at schools in Macon and Savannah. When illness necessitated a more healthful climate, she moved to Augusta where she secured a position as a grammar school teacher in the public school system. During her initial tenure in Augusta (1877-80), Laney played a major role in the successful fight for Georgia's first Black public high school. She was also instrumental in the selection of Richard R. Wright as the institution's first principal.

Laney returned to Savannah in 1880, but a few years later moved back to Augusta and opened a private school for Black children. Haines Normal and Industrial Institute, as the school was later named,

was opened in a rented hall at Christ Presbyterian Church on January 6, 1886. The idea for the school was rooted in Lucy C. Laney's convictions about the need for educated women in the struggle to uplift the race, and was prompted by her concern over the increasing number of young Black "children out of school without the care of parents, [who were] left to grow up idle and ignorant." The school was chartered by the state of Georgia in 1886 and during the same year Laney succeeded in having the distinction of being the only Black woman at the head of a major school affiliated with the Presbyterian Church.

Although Lucy C. Laney never married or had a family of her own, she loved children, and devoted her career to improving their chance in life. Through self-sacrifice, devotion, faith, and hard work Lucy Craft Laney developed Haines Institute into one of the best secondary schools in the South. In the course of accomplishing this feat she earned the title "mother of the children of the people." Fired with boundless zeal for the elevation of her race and a keen sense of the welfare of women and of the larger society, Laney's activities were not confined to her school. She was a member of the National Association of Colored Women, the Southeastern Federation of Women's Clubs, the Georgia State Teachers Association, and the National YWCA, and she chaired the Colored Section of the Interracial Commission of Augusta. Lucy Craft Laney was the first woman to be awarded honorary degrees from Atlanta University (1898) and Lincoln University (1904). She was similarly honored by South Carolina State College (1925) and Howard University (1930). Although she was never a recipient, Laney was nominated for the prestigious William E. Harmon Award for Distinguished Achievement among Negroes in 1928, 1929, and 1930.

After a lingering illness, on Tuesday, October 24, 1933, Lucy C. Laney died of nephritis and hypertension. Two days later, funeral services were held in the Chapel of Haines Institute and she was buried on the campus of the school.

[See also HAINES NORMAL AND INDUSTRIAL INSTITUTE.]

BIBLIOGRAPHY

Cowan, E. P. "Haines Normal and Industrial School," *The Church Home and Abroad* (September 1987); Daniel, Sadie Iola. *Women Builders* (1931); Griggs, A. C. "Lucy Craft Laney," *Journal of Negro History* (January 1934); Haynes, Elabeth Ross. *The Black Boy of Atlanta* (1952); *Home and Abroad.* "The Haines School" (August 1893); Johnson, William Hallock. "A Friend of Boys and Girls," *Women and Missions* (April 1926); Laney, Lucy C. "Address before the Women's Meeting," *Proceedings of the Second*

Atlanta Conference on the Negro Way, May 25-26 (1887), and "The Burden of the Educated Colored Women." In *Black Women in Nineteenth-Century American Life*, ed. Bert James Loewenberg and Ruth Bogin (1976), and "Miss Laney's Address," *Haines Journal* (1903); McCrorey, Mary Jackson. "Lucy Laney," *Crisis* (June 1934); Notestein, Lucy Lilian. *Nobody Knows the Trouble I See* (n.d.); Ovington, Mary White. *Portraits in Color* (1927); Parker, Inez Moore. *The Rise and Decline of the Program of Education for Black Presbyterian Church, U.S.A., 1865-1970* (1977); Patton, June O. "Augusta's Black Community and the Struggle for Ware High School." In *New Perspectives on Black Educational History*, ed. Vincent P. Franklin and James D. Anderson (1978); Rouse, Jacqueline Ann. *Lugenia Burns Hope: Black Southern Reformer* (1989); Thompson, Ernest Trice. *Presbyterians in the South* (1973). See also the Lucy C. Laney file, William E. Harmon Foundation Papers, Manuscript Division, Library of Congress, Washington, D.C.

JUNE O. PATTON

LANGE, ELIZABETH CLOVIS (1784-1882)

Elizabeth Clovis Lange was the founder and the initial "Superior-general" of the Oblate Sisters of Providence, the first Black Roman Catholic order to operate in the United States. Mother Mary Elizabeth, as she was known, was a towering figure in nineteenth-century educational circles around Baltimore, Maryland, for over fifty years. Elizabeth was born in the French colony Saint Domingue, to Clovis and Annette Lange in 1784. She migrated to eastern Cuba and lived near the city of Santiago, Cuba. Because of the Haitian revolution, she had to flee eastern Cuba, coming to the United States in 1817 and settling in Baltimore in 1827.

Soon after arriving in Baltimore, she opened the first school for the city's French-speaking immigrants using her inheritance in spite of strong attempts to discourage Black education in antebellum Maryland. Elizabeth's persistent service to her church and help to the educationally deprived won approbation from Rome under Pope Gregory XVI to organize the Oblate Sisters of Providence Order.

Although she ran primarily an educational order she became involved in many needy community outreach programs. During the Civil War years, she also became local superior of Saint Benedict's School in Baltimore and later spearheaded the establishment of other schools in Baltimore, Philadelphia, and New Orleans. During 1880, she began the order's first mission school in St. Louis, Missouri. By the time she

died, the influence of the Oblate order had extended across the United States, the Caribbean, and Central America. More than one hundred years after her death there are attempts to make her the first African-American female to be canonized by the Roman Catholic Church.

[*See also* CATHOLIC CHURCH; OBLATE SISTERS OF PROVIDENCE.]

BIBLIOGRAPHY

Dedeaux, Mary Liberta. "The Influence of St. Francis Academy on Negro Catholic Education in the Nineteenth Century," M.A. thesis (1944); Gillard, John T. *Colored Catholics in the U.S.* (1941); Hadrick, Mary Emma. "Contributions of the Oblate Sisters of Providence to Catholic Education in the U.S. and Cuba, 1829-1962," M.A. thesis (1964); Helmes, Winifred G., ed. *Notable Maryland Women* (1977); Marrow, Gloria R. "A Narrative of the Founding and Work of the Oblate Sisters of Providence," M.A. thesis (1976); Oblate Archival Materials and Josephite Archival Materials, *Annals of Oblate Sisters* (1836-77), Baltimore, Maryland; O'Neil, Michael. *Some Outstanding Colored People* (1943); Porterfield, Anne M. "The Oblate Sisters of Providence." Unpublished paper (1975); Sherwood, Grace. *The Oblates' Hundred and One Years* (1931); Warnagiris, M. Clare. "Marie Becraft and Black Catholic Education, 1820-1833," M.A. thesis (1977).

GLENN O. PHILLIPS

LARSEN, NELLA (1891-1964)

Novelist and shorty-story writer Nella Larsen created images of Black women that dispelled the myth of the typical and simplistically caricatured tragic mulatto of American literature. Like her heroines, Larsen felt out of place and was in search of a firm foothold in a world that seemed not to understand the inner conflicts associated with mixed ancestry. Literary critics and authors who were acquaintances of Larsen praised her for adeptly portraying the life of bourgeois African-Americans of mixed ancestry, a class for which a paucity of literature is extant.

Nella Larsen was born in Chicago on April 13, 1891, to a West Indian father and a Danish mother. Larsen's father died when she was two years old, and her mother later married a white man with whom she had a second daughter. Growing up among a family of European descent was uncomfortable for Larsen, who rarely spoke of her family except to recall that she attended a private school in Chicago with her white half-sister.

Nella Larsen was the first Black woman to win a creative writing award from the Guggenheim Foundation. Herself the product of a mixed marriage, she wrote two novels that broke ground in exploring the alienation of people of mixed ancestry. [Schomburg Center]

After attending high school in Chicago, Larsen studied science from 1909 to 1910 at Fisk University in Nashville, Tennessee. From the all-Black world of Fisk, Larsen moved to Copenhagen, where her relatives lived and where she studied at the University of Copenhagen between 1910 and 1912. Larsen's odyssey next found her in New York City, where she studied nursing at Lincoln Hospital from 1912 to 1915 before serving as assistant superintendent of nurses at Tuskegee Institute in Alabama from 1915 to 1916. Returning to New York City, Larsen worked at

Lincoln Hospital from 1916 to 1918 and for the New York City Department of Health from 1918 to 1921.

Never feeling connected to her mother and half-sister and a stepfather who viewed her as an embarrassment, Larsen found solace in her relationship with physicist Elmer S. Imes, whom she married on May 3, 1919. She worked as a library assistant and children's librarian from 1921 to 1926, a career that inspired her to read voluminously and write. Her favorite authors included James Joyce, John Galsworthy, eighteenth-century playwright Carlo Goldoni, Marmaduke Pickthall, Taylor Gordon, Rudolph Fisher, Walter White, and Carl Van Vechten, who was instrumental in securing a contract for Larsen's novels from Alfred A. Knopf.

As a socialite wife, Larsen became acquainted with a cadre of Black authors in New York City who encouraged her to write, including James Weldon Johnson, Jessie Fauset, Jean Toomer, and Langston Hughes. With strong support from Black author Walter White and the leading white patron of New Negro authors, Carl Van Vechten, Larsen published her first novel, *Quicksand*, in 1928.

Substantially autobiographical, *Quicksand* focuses on a mulatto of Danish and West African parentage, named Helga Crane, whose quest in search of self takes her from Naxos, a southern Black college, to Chicago to seek white relatives, to Harlem to mingle with African-Americans, to Copenhagen to live with white relatives, to Harlem again, and finally to rural Alabama, where she marries the arrogant, despicable, and unkempt Reverend Pleasant Green. Her husband minimally fulfills her spiritual as well as sexual needs, which she has repressed because of Victorian notions of womanhood. The novel concludes with Helga, still weak and bedridden from the birth of her fourth child, preparing to give birth to a fifth.

Larsen's novel skillfully captures the lives of many northern middle-class African-Americans at the turn of the century who, because they were formally educated, cultured, and of mixed parentage, found themselves alienated from white Americans and from the masses of Black Americans, many of whom had rural southern roots. In addition to exploring race and class-related conflicts, Larsen also treats gender issues in *Quicksand*. The delicate, fickle, and passionate Helga seems not only to be running from her divided racial self but from her own sexuality. When Helga has an opportunity to take a lover on several occasions, she bolts. Larsen's novel shows the limitations of Black bourgeois women in the 1920s who were forced to choose marriage at any cost as the only way to express their sexuality. The ending of *Quick-*

sand is less than satisfying because Helga, who has progressively become stronger and more self-assured, reverts to self-doubt. She becomes a pathetically helpless woman whose destiny will be determined by a man she does not love and with whom she has very little in common.

With the publication of Larsen's second novel, *Passing*, in 1929, just thirteen months after the national acclaim of *Quicksand*, the thirty-eight-year-old novelist was hailed as a major New Negro author. *Passing* centers on women's friendship, women's sexuality, mixed ancestry, and preoccupation with respectability and materiality. *Passing* illustrates that African-Americans who pass for white often yearn to be part of the Black community. Born in poverty and raised by her white aunts, Clare Kendry risks losing her wealthy white husband, daughter, and social standing for the chance to socialize with her Harlem friends. Irene Redfield, Clare's friend who passes for white when it is expedient, ruins her marriage because she fears change and because of her obsession with maintaining middle-class standing. Like *Quicksand*, *Passing* has a weak ending. Larsen leaves unresolved whether Clare has fallen, jumped, or been pushed out of the window by Irene, who suspects her friend of having had an affair with her husband. In spite of the less-than-satisfying ending, *Passing* depicts the dilemmas and complexities of a growing Black middle class.

Following the success of her two novels, Nella Larsen, in 1930, became the first Black woman to win a creative writing award from the prestigious Guggenheim Foundation. Shortly before Larsen was to leave for Europe to do research in Spain and France for her third novel, she was accused of plagiarism in one of her short stories published in *Forum*. Though she responded to the attack with an essay in *Forum* and was supported by her editor, Larsen's public humiliation stifled her writing and she never completed another novel. A marriage that had begun to show signs of deterioration in 1930 ended in divorce in 1933 when rumors spread that Larsen's husband was having an affair with a white woman and that Larsen had tried to kill herself by jumping out of a window. This second public humiliation apparently weakened Larsen's self-confidence and diminished her productivity as a writer.

From 1941, Larsen worked as a nurse at several hospitals on the East Side of Manhattan. She died in New York City on March 30, 1964.

Larsen made a significant contribution to Black history and culture by capturing in impressive detail the mannerisms, values, concerns, and emotional conflicts of the Black bourgeoisie, underscoring that even members of this class were victimized by racism. Especially important is Larsen's exploration of Black women's lives of her time. Her legacy is a map of the complex lives of America's Black nouveau riche during the New Negro movement.

BIBLIOGRAPHY

*AAW*2; McDowell, Deborah E. "Introduction," *Quicksand and Passing* (1986); Perry, Margaret. *Silence to the Drums: A Survey of the Literature of the Harlem Renaissance* (1976); Soto, Hiroko. "Under the Harlem Shadow: A Study of Jessie Fauset and Nella Larsen." In *Harlem Renaissance Remembered*, ed. Arna Bontemps (1972); Tate, Claudia. "Nella Larsen's *Passing*: A Problem of Interpretation," *Black American Literature Forum* (Winter 1980); Washington, Mary Helen, ed. *Invented Lives: Narratives of Black Women 1860-1960* (1987).

ELIZABETH BROWN-GUILLORY

LATIMER, CATHERINE ALLEN
(c. 1895-1948)

In 1920, Catherine Allen Latimer became the first Black professional librarian at the New York Public Library. She was assigned to the 135th Street branch, which is now the Schomburg Center for Research in Black Culture. In her twenty-six years there she created a clipping file that continues to be an important source of information on Black Americans; she incorporated Arthur Schomburg's personal library into the branch's Negro Collection; and she inspired many with her knowledge, competence, and professional methods.

Born in Nashville, Tennessee, about 1895 to H.W. Allen and Minta Bosley Trotman, Latimer grew up in Brooklyn. She attended Howard and Columbia universities, and worked as an assistant librarian at Tuskegee Institute in Alabama before returning to New York. At the 135th Street branch of the New York Public Library during the Harlem Renaissance, when interest in and material about the New Negro was burgeoning, Latimer created and developed what is known as the Clipping File. It was maintained during the 1930s by Works Progress Administration (WPA) workers who mounted the clippings in scrapbooks that are still in use. She also actively sought periodicals that featured articles on aspects of the Black experience. This file was never weeded, and so it grew into a most unusual resource. Latimer was an experienced reference librarian who was sought after by writers and researchers, and she

The first Black professional librarian at the New York Public Library, Catherine Latimer created and developed the famous Clipping File at the Schomburg Center for Research in Black Culture. She is seated fourth from the right (with crossed ankles) at the unveiling at the Center in 1936 of Pietro Calvi's bust of actor Ira Aldridge as Othello. Arthur A. Schomburg is standing, second from right. [Schomburg Center]

was mentioned in the writings of Langston Hughes and Elise J. McDougald. She wrote for *Crisis, Looking Forward,* and the *Negro History Bulletin.*

Latimer was married to Benton R. Latimer and had one son, Bosley. She retired in 1946 because of poor eyesight and illness and died in 1948.

BIBLIOGRAPHY

Kaiser, Ernest D. "The Genesis of the Kaiser Index." In *The Kaiser Index to Black Resources, 1948-1986* (1992); *NBAW*; Sinnette, Elinor Des Verney. *Arthur Alfonso Schomburg: Black Bibliophile and Collector* (1989).

SELECTED WORKS BY CATHERINE ALLEN LATIMER

Crisis. "Where Can I Get Material on the Negro?" (June 1934); *Looking Forward.* "Negro Life through Books

and Art" (March 1935); *Looking Forward.* "Some Recent Books on the Negro" (September 1935); *Negro History Bulletin.* "Catherine Ferguson" (November 1941); *The Negro: A Selected Bibliography* (1943).

BETTY K. GUBERT

LATTIMER, AGNES D. (1928-)

"Many things we need can wait," Agnes Lattimer once observed, but "the children cannot" (*Chicago Defender* 1984). An abiding concern for the welfare of children motivated Lattimer to become a pediatrician, to work tirelessly for systems of preventative medicine for children, and, ultimately, because of her talents and efforts, to become the medical director of Cook County Hospital, one of the nation's largest public hospitals.

Agnes Lattimer was born on May 13, 1928, in Memphis, Tennessee. Her father, who worked in the insurance industry, and her mother, Hortense, had four other children as well. Agnes's mother recalled that as early as age ten her daughter had expressed a firm desire to become a doctor, a pilot, and a pianist—all of which she became. Lattimer graduated magna cum laude from Fisk University in 1949 with a B.S. in biology. Heading north to Chicago, she entered the Chicago Medical School, where she earned her M.D. in 1954. Over the next four years, Lattimer did her internship and residency in pediatric medicine at Cook County Hospital. In 1960, she became a fellow of the American Board of Pediatrics.

With her appointment as medical director of Cook County Hospital in Chicago, Illinois, one of the nation's largest public hospitals, Agnes D. Lattimer became the only Black woman in the United States to hold the top medical post in a major hospital in a major city. [Cook County Hospital]

In addition to a demanding practice in pediatric medicine, Lattimer also embarked on a teaching career at both the University of Illinois School of Public Health and the University of Chicago School of Medicine. She still holds a full professorship in the University of Chicago's Department of Pediatrics.

Over the course of her career, Lattimer also has become more and more committed to health care for poor people. Throughout her years as a practicing physician and as an administrator, Lattimer has insisted that medical personnel treat all patients with respect and dignity, regardless of their ability to pay. "People often refer to care for the poor as free care, but too often we exact the most significant coin ... from these patients ... their self-respect" (*Chicago Defender* 1984).

After serving as associate director of ambulatory care and as director of the Fantus Health Center, both at Cook County Hospital, Lattimer was appointed temporary medical director of the hospital in February 1986; in March 1986, when that appointment became permanent, Lattimer became the only Black woman in the country to hold the top medical post in a major hospital in a major city. As medical director she oversees the activities of 350 doctors and 475 interns and residents in the 1,200-bed facility. Her role, she has said, is that of problem-solver. "There is a constant barrage of problems that occur at a hospital, and the medical director is the one who develops options and plots a course of action."

Agnes Lattimer's work schedule leaves little time for her family, which includes a grown son, Bernard Goss, or for her two favorite hobbies, flying and bridge, but she says she would have it no other way. "It's a very demanding job. ... It's what I wanted ... and I like it" (*Chicago Defender* 1984).

BIBLIOGRAPHY

Chicago Defender (February 16, 1984); *Michigan Chronicle* (September 4, 1967); Whitaker, Charles. "Cook County's Top Doctor," *Ebony* (September 1986).

CHRISTINE A. LUNARDINI

LAURIE, EUNICE RIVERS
(1899-1986)

In 1958, public health nurse Eunice Rivers Laurie received the U.S. Department of Health, Education and Welfare's (HEW) highest honor, the Oveta Culp Hobby Award, for her "notable service covering twenty-five years during which through selfless devotion and skillful human relations she has sustained the interest and cooperation of the subjects of a venereal disease control program in Macon County, Alabama." Fourteen years later, media coverage revealed what is often considered this country's most heinous medical experiment: Nurse Rivers, as she was known, had been crucial in sustaining a forty-year study by the U.S. Public Health Service of late stage syphilis in nearly 400 Black men that kept the men ignorant of their disease while denying them treatment. Her role in the "Tuskegee Experiment" is still debated by the public, media, and scholars alike, even becoming the subject of an often produced play and of television documentaries.

Eunice Verdell Rivers was born on November 12, 1899, in Early County, Georgia, the oldest child of three in the family of Albert and Henrietta Rivers. Rivers's mother died when she was fifteen and her father gained a modicum of independence by working a small farm while he held onto his job in a sawmill. Eunice Rivers remembers that after her father was wrongly accused of aiding the escape of a Black man wanted for the murder of a white policeman, a Ku Klux Klan member shot a bullet into their home. To save the family, Albert Rivers moved them into a rented house while he protected their home.

Eunice Rivers first went to a school under the tutelage of a cousin in Fort Gaines, Georgia, and then to a mission boarding school in Thomasville. When Albert Rivers discovered that the mission school had only white teachers in the upper grades, he pulled his daughter out (one year shy of high school graduation) and sent her on to the Tuskegee Institute in Alabama in 1918.

Eunice Rivers spent her first year at Tuskegee learning handicrafts in keeping with the school's philosophy of vocational education. In response to her father's urging she switched to nursing. Graduating from Tuskegee Institute in 1922, she did some private nursing and then was hired to travel with Tuskegee's Moveable School, a truck that carried an agricultural extension agent, a home demonstration agent, a public health nurse, and their equipment into Alabama's countryside. Rivers focused primarily on the health needs of Black women and children, teaching basic health education, simple sanitation methods, and well child care. She also demonstrated cleanliness techniques to Alabama's extensive network of granny midwives. At the time she was one of only four Black public health nurses in the entire state. She also worked for the state's Bureau of Vital Statistics, devising techniques to have the midwives report births accurately. For many, Rivers's great skill was her

nonjudgmental understanding of the medical beliefs of rural Black people and her support for their dignity and individual needs in medical encounters. By 1931, the state had cut its work force and Rivers had lost her position. She was then hired as a night supervisor at Tuskegee Institute's Andrews Hospital.

Eight months and many sleepless nights later, she was offered a half-time day position: scientific assistant for the Public Health Service's study formally called "Untreated Syphilis in the Male Negro." Rivers's job for the next forty years was to help in finding men for the study, following up their conditions, assisting in their examinations, gaining agreement from their families for autopsies, and modifying the primarily white physicians' behaviors toward their "subjects." Nurse Rivers was central to securing the compliance of the men to painful spinal taps and diagnostic procedures, providing rubs and aspirin, and ensuring that they did not receive treatment for their disease.

When the story of the experiment broke on the Associated Press wire on July 26, 1972, it caused an uproar across the country. Charges of racism, genocidal medicine, paternalism gone awry, and the health care system's notorious willingness to use poor and illiterate people for experimentation without informed consent were debated. Senator Edward Kennedy convened hearings in the U.S. Senate, an HEW investigation condemned the study, the institutions and medical groups involved offered varying justifications, and a class-action civil suit filed by prominent civil rights attorney Fred Gray ended in a $10 million out of court settlement for survivors and their families. Nurse Rivers never testified before the Senate hearings nor was she named in the suit.

Eunice Rivers spent almost all of her adult life in Tuskegee, Alabama, turning down an opportunity to work in a New York City hospital in 1932. She spent half of her time in maternal and child health clinics at the Andrews Hospital. In 1952, she married Julius Laurie, an orderly at the hospital. She was also active in the Red Cross and the Greater St. Mark Missionary Baptist Church in Tuskegee. Numerous awards testified to her nursing skills. Eunice Rivers died in Tuskegee on August 28, 1986.

Differing interpretations exist of the reasons why Eunice Rivers participated in the syphilis research for so long. For some, she is the naive nurse deferring to male physicians' authority, rationalizing the racism because of her status in the Black community. Others suggest she was less deferential and was moved by her ability to provide some medical attention to a community that usually received none at all. For still others, her story symbolizes the constraints on moral decision-making. More complex interpretations will have to give greater weight to her dignity, her power over the white physicians who needed her, the context of the Black health movement of the early twentieth century, and her own understanding of her efforts.

BIBLIOGRAPHY

Feldshuh, David. "Miss Evers' Boys," *American Theatre* (November 1, 1990); "Interview with Eunice Rivers Laurie, October 10, 1977." Black Women Oral History Project, Schlesinger Library, Radcliffe College, Cambridge, Massachusetts (1991); Jones, James. *Bad Blood: The Tuskegee Syphilis Experiment* (1981); Rivers, Eunice, et al. "Twenty Years of Follow-up Experience in a Long-Range Medical Study," *Public Health Reports* (April 1953); Smith, Susan Lynn. " 'Sick and Tired of Being Sick and Tired': Black Women and the National Negro Health Movement, 1915-1950," Ph.D. diss. (1991).

SUSAN M. REVERBY

LAVEAU, MARIE (c. 1790-1881)

Marie Laveau, the Voodoo Queen of New Orleans, was perhaps the most powerful Black woman in nineteenth-century America. Even as thousands of her contemporaries, Black and white, slave and free, feared her and the Voodoo that she practiced, they regularly turned to her for her mystical powers. Her followers believed that she could cure their ills with her *gris-gris*, that she could bring them luck with her charms, amulets, or *mascots*, and that she could see into the future. It has been said that slaves who hoped to escape bondage sought her blessings and charms for safe passage, that ladies sought her advice on love, and that local politicians wore her amulets of bone and wood for luck. Certainly, there can be little doubt that Laveau had considerable power and influence over the population of New Orleans. Her power was not so much mystical as it was a product of her common sense, her ability to organize, and her considerable sphere of influence.

Born in New Orleans in the last decade of the eighteenth century, Marie Laveau was a free woman of color, a quadroon. She married Jacques Paris, a carpenter and a free man of color, in 1819. Laveau did not stay with Paris; instead, she left him and began calling herself the widow Paris long before Paris died. During this interval, Laveau lived with Christophe Glapion, a free man of color from Saint Domingue, with whom she reputedly had fifteen children. Be-

sides her duties as a wife and a mother, Laveau was a hairdresser and a cook for the city jail. Both trades placed her in the private and public lives of the Black and white population where she collected the bits of news and gossip that served as the foundation of her powers of influence and manipulation.

Most certainly, Laveau's power was derived from her intimate knowledge of life in the city. It was the particular expression that her knowledge and influence took, the Voodoo, that instilled the respect and fear that she received from her followers. Like most other free women of color of French descent in New Orleans, Laveau was Catholic. She also shared a common African heritage with much of the community where she, perhaps more than any other single person in the city, represented the retention of African culture and religious beliefs. African religious beliefs, influenced by Catholicism and expressed as the practice of Voodoo, inspired her neighbors, friends and foes alike, to at once fear and revere her.

Marie Laveau lived until she reached her nineties, dying in 1881, having passed her influence and her knowledge to her daughter. The second Marie Laveau, who was born in 1827, became the more notable of the two women, serving as the high priestess of the voodoo cult that is most often portrayed in the popular literature of the city.

BIBLIOGRAPHY

Castellanos, Henry. *New Orleans As It Was: Episodes of Louisiana Life* ([1979] 1990); Gehman, Mary. *Women and New Orleans: A History* (1988); Johnson, Jerah. "New Orleans's Congo Square: An Urban Setting for Early Afro-American Culture Formation," *Louisiana History* (Spring 1991); Logsden, Joseph. New Orleans *States-Item* (February 12, 1980); Saxon, Lyle. *Fabulous New Orleans* (1988).

VIRGINIA GOULD

LAW: OPPRESSION AND RESISTANCE

"The law" is, of course, more than the words in the Constitution or the words in the statutes that are enacted by legislatures. It is also how the courts interpret those words, and how the enforcement authorities decide to enforce them. In addition, it is how the Constitution and the statutes and the governmental regulations as written, interpreted, and enforced operate together. Thus, determining what "the law" is with respect to any particular group is a complicated matter. Nonetheless, it is possible to discern two clear strains in the way Black women have been treated by American law.

First, the law has not been on the side of Black Americans in this country. It has upheld slavery, created gerrymandered voting districts, and forced Black Americans into segregated schools and neighborhoods. Second, the law has not been on the side of those Americans who are women. It has denied them the right to vote, the right to own property, the right to control their own reproductive systems. Clearly, then, Black women will suffer in the American legal system by virtue of their membership in two groups that are disfavored in this society and under its laws, for Black women are both Black and women. In addition, the law disfavors Black women through statutes and regulations that have explicitly singled them out, as a group, for oppression.

These are the ways in which the legal system explicitly oppresses Black women; but the legal system also oppresses Black women in less explicit, more subtle ways. One way in which this takes place is through the interaction of laws that, on their face, do not directly address the lives of Black women. Another way is through manipulation by legal actors: how a judge construes a law, or how the enforcement authority decides to enforce it.

Because the pattern of oppression against Black women has been a complicated one, the pattern of resistance to this oppression also has been complicated. Black women have struggled along with white women for their rights as women, have struggled along with Black men for their rights as African-Americans, and have struggled on their own to protect the group "Black women." They have worked in various roles—as attorneys, organizers, lobbyists and activists—to force the law to address their lives in a less harmful, and more protective way.

Today, the law no longer explicitly grants or withholds benefits based on the race and gender of the person affected by the statute, but it once did. As early as 1644, both Maryland and Virginia passed laws stating that they would tax those persons who farmed, whether they were slave or free—and that those persons included all adult men and Black women. Thus, whatever protection this statute offered for white women—either not farming or not having to pay taxes—the legislature was clear that it was a benefit Black women would not get. Later on, after the Civil War, the federal government created the Freedman's Bureau, in order to help former slaves make the transition to a productive life as free people. The administrative regulations of the Freedman's Bureau, however, distinguished between Black men

and Black women who had been slaves. In the wage labor agreements for employers who wanted to hire former slaves, the government recommended that Black adult men receive $10-12 per month, but that Black women be paid only $8 per month.

Thus, the basic patterns were set early. Black women would suffer whatever Black men or white women suffered. They would be slaves because they were Black; they would be worth less money than men in a free economy because they were women; but there was more. In the unlikely event that Black men were to get any benefit under the law, Black women would not get it, for they were women. In the unlikely event that white women were to receive a legal benefit, Black women would again be ignored, for they were also Black.

There are many examples of these basic patterns in the early years. Many of them revolve around issues of reproduction, voluntary sex, and rape. Three statutes that were in force in Virginia before the Civil War show the effect those laws might have had on the lives of a Black woman. The first law provided that it was not unlawful for a white man to have sex with a Black female slave; the second stated that it *was* unlawful for whites to marry Blacks, whether those Blacks were slave or free; and the third law stated that the decision as to whether a newborn infant would be slave or free would depend on the legal status of the mother. If the mother of the baby was a slave, then the child would be a slave; if the mother was free, the child would be free.

Considering the historical context and the fact that laws do not exist independently but interact with each other to achieve certain results, it is clear that these three laws made it possible to do incalculable harm to Black women. The first law made it clear to the white slaveowner that he had total license with respect to the sexual exploitation of his Black female slaves. The second emphasized that his sexual relations with Black women could *only* be exploitative because it was illegal for a white man to marry a Black woman. Thus, the law provided a disincentive for any white man who wanted to legalize a sexual relationship with a Black woman through marriage, for that was the one sexual relationship that was forbidden: she could not be his wife. The third law provided a financial incentive for white slaveowners to exploit Black slave women sexually, for any child born to these women would be another slave, that is, another source of work and income for the master. Thus, these three laws operated together to encourage the rape, concubinage, and breeding of Black women by white men, and to discourage marriage—the one act that would dignify these sexual liaisons and offer some legal protection to Black women.

Even when a statute is written in a way that appears to protect Black women, it is possible for a judge to interpret the law in a way that denies protection. One example of this took place in Missouri and involved a young Black slave named Celia.

Celia was fourteen years old in 1850 when she was bought by Robert Newsom, a seventy-year-old farmer. On the way home from the slave auction, he raped her. He raped her repeatedly after that, until the night of June 23, 1855, when she resisted him with force. At that time, Celia, nineteen years old, was pregnant for the third time, and had been ill for at least four months. According to court testimony, Celia had told Newsom that she would hurt him if he raped her while she was still sick. Despite her warning, he came to her cabin that night to force sexual intercourse upon her. Celia, who had armed herself with a stick, struck him twice. He died immediately thereafter, and Celia was charged with first-degree murder.

In Missouri, at this time, the law stated that it was unlawful for a man to force sex upon "any woman." The law also provided that if a woman killed a man who was trying to rape her, that would be considered a legitimate act of a self-defense, not a crime. Celia's lawyer used the law as it was written on the books. He argued that because the law protected "any woman" in this situation, the legislators must have meant to protect slave women too. The judge disagreed. Because Celia was a slave, that statute could not apply to her: she was not included in the phrase "any woman." A slave woman had no rights over her body and could not legally resist her master's sexual assaults. Celia was sentenced to death and hanged.

This case shows how the law has operated to the detriment of Black women. It shows that even where the law as written offered protection to all women, a court might interpret it in a way to deny that protection. A benefit granted to white women was not extended to Black women. The term "any woman" did not include Celia.

Another way in which the law operated to encourage sexual attacks upon Black women was to provide, as many states did, that Blacks were not allowed to testify in court against whites. Thus, even in a state where "any woman" might be interpreted to include Celia, she could not testify against the white rapist, and so, in effect, the law did not protect her.

The ways in which the law encouraged sexual attacks on Black women were cruelly completed by laws that refused to punish the rape of a slave woman by another slave. A statute that was in force in Mis-

souri while Celia was alive stated that any "negro or mulatto" who even tried to rape a white women would be castrated. Black women, slave or free, had no legal protection from rape, even from rape by other slaves. In 1859, the Mississippi Supreme Court held that a slave woman held no rights to her body and so could not be violated by rape. If another slave raped her, that was simply not a crime. Thus with regard to issues of sex and reproduction, the law worked in varied ways to oppress Black women.

There are many other areas of the law where this pattern of oppression can be seen if one looks behind the words of the legal document to find the impact on Black women. One very important example is the struggle for the right to vote.

In 1870, soon after the end of the Civil War, the Fifteenth Amendment was added to the Constitution. That amendment states that "the right of citizens to vote shall not be denied based on race." It was added to provide important citizenship rights for Black people who had formerly been slaves. Once again, the law meant something different for Black men and Black women, for in 1870, "citizen" did not mean woman: only men could be citizens. Therefore only Black men won the right to vote in 1870. Black women still did not have this most basic right of citizenship.

In the early twentieth century, during the debate over the amendment giving women the right to vote, it was still not clear that the term "women" would include Black women. Many white legislators were outspoken in their belief that the right to vote should go to white women only. As one senator from Idaho stated, "Nobody intends that the two and a half million Negro women of the South shall vote." He was wrong. The constitutional amendment stating that "the right to vote shall not be denied because of sex" has been interpreted to include Black women too. Thus, in 1920, when the Nineteenth Amendment to the Constitution came into force, Black women finally obtained this most basic citizenship right, which Black men—their sons and husbands and brothers—had held for fifty years. A law that had granted a benefit to Black people did not include those Black people who were women, and a law that protected women almost did not protect those women who were Black.

This pattern continues into the present. There is currently a heated debate in our society about the right of women to control their own reproductive systems. Should laws be passed to limit the right to abortion, or to expand it? How should the courts interpret the abortion laws which already exist? The laws that surround abortion rights affect all women, including black women. Similarly, there is passionate debate about the problem of drug abuse. How should it be treated? Is drug abuse a crime? Should drug abusers be sent to prison or should they be sent to medical facilities? How much is society willing to pay to rehabilitate them? Because laws in this country are enforced in ways that oppress Black people, decisions in this area tend to have a disproportionate impact on Black Americans, again including Black women. If we put together restrictive reproductive laws designed to control women, and drug laws that are enforced in ways to oppress African-Americans, one might expect to find a negative impact on the lives of Black women.

Indeed, this has been the result. For example, in Florida, state laws make it very difficult for women to get abortions. In related legislation, Florida law states that pregnant drug abusers will be jailed for harming the fetus through their drug use. This law has been applied almost entirely to Black women, despite the fact that almost half of the women drug users in that state are white. Thus, laws written and enforced in ways that oppress Black Americans and women separately, work together to oppress Black women in even more harmful ways.

Because the law is such an important tool for organizing social structure, for solidifying the definitions of who will be powerful and who will not, the law has been an important locus of resistance for Black women. Because the patterns of oppression through which the law affects the lives of Black women are complicated, so too the pattern of resistance has been a complicated one.

The struggle for the right to vote is a good example of the dual nature of the struggle that Black women must wage to resist the oppression of the law. Many Black women supported the constitutional amendment that gave the right to vote to Black men, for they knew that if Black men never got the vote because they were Black, Black women would never get it either. Similarly, some fifty years later, Black women fought along with white women for the constitutional amendment that would give all women the right to vote, even though the Black women were forced to work in segregated chapters of the women's organizations, forced to walk at the back of parades organized by white women. This could not have been easy. Still, Black women were there in the struggle, because they also knew that if white women did not get the vote, neither would they.

Black women, along with Black men, have engaged in the struggle for civil rights. A good example is the participation of Black women in the long legal struggle to desegregate the public schools. Constance Baker Motley, for example, was the attorney for the National Association for the Advancement of Colored People Legal Defense Fund who represented James Meredith in his fight for admission to the University of Mississippi. Daisy Bates organized the nine high school students who integrated Central High School in Little Rock in 1957.

Black women, along with white women, have been active in the struggle for reproductive freedom. Faye Wattleton, former national president of Planned Parenthood, and Byllye Avery, the founder and director of the National Black Women's Health Project, have spoken out and organized for reproductive choice for women. The National Council of Negro Women and other groups of Black women have filed briefs with the Supreme Court on this issue. They have lobbied against the efforts of legislators and judges to enact and enforce laws in ways that limit their reproductive choices.

Black women work with Black men and with white women in an effort to protect their interests as black women. Black women also have been active in efforts to get the legal system to provide the group "Black women" with greater protection. The legal system that participated in creating the social disability which limits them must also participate in undoing that harm.

One area where this kind of resistance has taken place is around the law that prohibits employment discrimination. The federal statute that was enacted to end employment discrimination forbids discrimination based on race or on sex. This is helpful to Black women, for they are often treated badly by employers because they are Black or because they are women.

But studies of the workplace show that there are many employers who give Black women different jobs than they do white men and women or Black men—jobs that pay less and with worse working conditions. Indeed, some employers refuse to hire Black women at all. For these reasons, many black women have gone into court to complain about employment discrimination against them. However the law against employment discrimination does not speak about discrimination based on race *and* sex, which is what Black women often face. Initially, when dealing with this issue, the courts were confused. How should they interpret a statute that protected Black women against sex discrimination, or against race discrimination, but did not speak to the issue of discrimination based on both? Group after group of Black women went to court arguing that the courts could not refuse to protect Black women under that statute simply because the legislators who drafted it had not thought about the likelihood that some employers would discriminate against Black women as a group; and they won. The courts determined that the federal statute prohibiting employment discrimination based on race *or* sex must also be interpreted to prohibit discrimination based on race *and* sex. This was a major legal breakthrough fought for, and won by, Black women.

There are other ways in which Black women have struggled to resist the harm that the legal system has done, or might do, to black women. One technique is lobbying. Black women who lobbied for the passage of the 1990 Civil Rights Act fought for changes that would increase the likelihood that Black women would find protection under that statute. Another technique is legal scholarship. Within the past ten years, the number of Black women law professors in law schools in this country has increased dramatically. Now that these women have a voice in academia, many of them are writing articles and books criticizing court opinions and legal doctrines that have operated to limit the life chances of Black women. Among other things, they have written about how the right to privacy should be re-thought to protect Black women who are prosecuted for fetal drug abuse; about the weaknesses in a court decision that said it was lawful to fire a pregnant single Black woman who was considered a poor role model for the young Black women in her charge; and about how the courts should reinterpret the Constitution to provide more protection for Black women. The arguments in these publications provide more weapons to those who are willing to fight against the legalized oppression of Black women.

The law no longer explicitly sanctions the oppression of Black people as a group, although Black women are still restricted by laws that affect women's conduct with respect to sex and reproduction. It continues, however, to operate in more hidden, subtle ways to oppress black women—through discriminatory enforcement of supposedly neutral laws and through the intersection of laws that affect groups based on race as well as gender. Yet, history shows that Black women have always opposed this oppression whenever and however they could—whether by organizing bus-loads of women to travel to Washington, D.C., to protest laws restricting the right to abortion or by filing suit to protect themselves against sexual harassment or by insisting on an interpretation of employment discrimination law that recognizes their existence and the harm that they suffer as a group.

BIBLIOGRAPHY

Austin, Regina. "Sapphire Bound!" *University of Wisconsin Law Review* (May-June 1989); Crenshaw, Kimberle Williams. "Demarginalizing the Intersection of Race and Sex: A Black Feminist Critique of Antidiscrimination Doctrine, Feminist Theory and Antiracist Politics," *University of Chicago Legal Forum* (1989); Giddings, Paula. *When and Where I Enter: The Impact of Black Women on Race and Sex in America* (1984); Harris, Angela P. "Race and Essentialism in Feminist Legal Theory," *Stanford Law Review* (February 1990); Higginbotham, A. Leon, Jr. *In the Matter of Color: Race and the American Legal Process, The Colonial Period* (1978), and "Race, Sex, Education and Missouri Jurisprudence: *Shelley v. Kraemer* in a Historical Perspective," *Washington University Law Quarterly* (Fall 1989); Higginbotham, A. Leon, Jr. and Barbara A. Kopytoff. "Racial Purity and Interracial Sex in the Law of Colonial and Antebellum Virginia," *Georgetown Law Review* (August 1989); Jones, Jacqueline. *Labor of Love, Labor of Sorrow: Black Women, Work, and the Family from Slavery to the Present* (1985); Roberts, Dorothy E. "Punishing Drug Addicts Who Have Babies: Women of Color, Equality, and the Right of Privacy," *Harvard Law Review* (May 1991); Scales-Trent, Judy. "Black Women and the Constitution: Finding Our Place, Asserting Our Rights," *Harvard Civil Rights—Civil Liberties Law Review* (Winter 1989); White, Evelyn C., ed. *The Black Women's Health Book: Speaking for Ourselves* (1990); Winston, Judith A. "Mirror, Mirror on the Wall: Title VII, Section 1981 and the Intersection of Race and Gender in the Civil Rights Act of 1990," *California Law Review* (May 1991).

JUDY SCALES-TRENT

LEAGUE OF WOMEN FOR COMMUNITY SERVICE, BOSTON

The League of Women for Community Service has had a long and creditable record of community service in Boston dating back to 1918 when it functioned as the Soldier's Comfort Unit. The central focus of the league was on local problems, but their activities also addressed the national arena. For example, the league consistently opposed lynching, sometimes collaborating with the National Association of Colored Women (of which their body was a member); sometimes working with the National Association for the Advancement of Colored People; and at other times acting alone. At the funeral services for Geraldine Trotter (wife of Monroe Trotter), the congregation, which included clubwomen, passed a resolution in her name appealing to President Woodrow Wilson to ask Congress to pass an antilynching law and to implement measures to end discrimination against Black Americans in the Navy, Army, and civilian life.

The league was comprised of women whose families represented the stable element in Black America. Their husbands tended to be professionals and they valued property, education, and gracious living. They had access, through their spouses, to economic, political, and legal resources and they used these to help those less fortunate than themselves. Prominent women among them included Josephine St. Pierre Ruffin, who had a national reputation, and Maria Louise Baldwin, who had statewide prominence. Ida Parker and Elizabeth Harley Forbes became well known locally because of the long years that they had contributed to the league as recording secretaries. Dorothy Clarke earned the respect of the Boston community by guiding the latter-day league into education-related activities.

Historically, the members of the league had a sense of civic responsibility and usually belonged to other social clubs as well. Several of them held positions of authority in other bodies and came to the league with expertise in club management. Although the by-laws did not set any limits on the size of the body, the league unofficially restricted itself to fifty to sixty working members. Membership was by invitation only and invitations went to women of a certain stable family, professional, and class background. Clubwomen helped where the needs were greatest and they were willing to shift their agenda to reflect the changing needs of Boston's Black community.

At its inception in spring 1918, when it was called the Soldier's Comfort Unit, the most pressing need was to assist the Black soldiers stationed in and near Boston. These Boston women wanted to render patriotic service and race help at the same time. They established several committees, each headed by a chairwoman in charge of such functions as publicity, hospitality, entertainment, music, supplies, soldiers' and sailors' visiting, junior comfort unit, printing, knitting, and Red Cross. There was a loving service committee that was always notified by the military authorities whenever Black soldiers were brought to area hospitals. League women protested, on the soldiers' behalf, any racial slights.

After the war, when the unit purchased its own building and changed its name to the League of Women for Community Service, it opened its physical facilities to many different community action groups in Boston. It refrained from partisan politics, but since the building was the meeting place of many other groups that were active politically, they all strengthened one another.

The women operated a day nursery, sought the protection and welfare of young Black girls along the lines of the Young Women's Christian Association, started a Girl's Business Club, sponsored lectures on "How to Cast an Intelligent Ballot" (since women had received the right to vote under the Nineteenth Amendment to the Constitution in 1920), established a committee that would give clothing and food to needy families, added a soup kitchen during the Great Depression, and provided dorm facilities for young Black college women (to whom many college residence halls were closed in the 1940s and 1950s). Coretta Scott King once boarded in the league's dormitories in Boston. In more recent years, members have assisted in tutoring schoolchildren and have held leadership seminars to encourage young women to do volunteer work.

The cardinal commitment of these clubwomen was to continue the club's work and they did not tolerate members who were not active. Their rationale for continuing as a group is the same now as it was in the second decade of this century—that much work remains to be done along social and civil lines.

BIBLIOGRAPHY

Babchuck, Nicholas and Ralph Thompson. "The Voluntary Associations of Negroes," *American Sociological Review* (October 1962); Blalock, H. M. and Ann B. Blalock. "Situational Factors and Negro Leadership Activity in a Medium Sized Community," *Journal of Negro Education* (Winter 1960); Brown, Hallie Q., ed. *Homespun Heroines and Other Women of Distinction* ([1926] 1971); Daniel, Sadie Iola. *Women Builders* (1970); Farley, Ena L. "Caring and Sharing since World War I: The League of Women for Community Service—A Black Volunteer Organization in Boston," *Umoja* (Summer 1977); Fields, Emma L. "The Women's Club Movement in the United States, 1877-1900," Master's thesis (1948); Gulley, William H. "Relative Effectiveness in Negro and White Volunteer Associations," *Phylon* (Summer 1963); Hill, Adelaide Cromwell. "The Negro Upper Class in Boston: Its Development and Present Social Structure," Ph.D. diss. (1952); Lerner, Gerda, ed. *Black Women in White America: A Documentary History* (1972), and "Early Community Work of Black Clubwomen," *Journal of Negro History* (April 1974); McAlpine, Margaret Alice. "Negro Citizenship in Massachusetts," Master's thesis (1941); Minutes of the League of Women for Community Service. Schlesinger Research Library, Radcliffe College, Cambridge, Massachusetts (the larger collection is housed in the League's own vaults on its premises in Boston); Rice, Hattie M. "The Negro as Portrayed in the *Boston Evening Transcript*, 1901-1919," Master's thesis (1951); Solomons, Olivia S. "Maria Louise Baldwin," *Negro History Bulletin* (October 1941).

ENA L. FARLEY

LEE, JARENA (b. 1783)

Jarena Lee, the first female known to petition the African Methodist Episcopal (AME) Church for authority to preach, was seminal in her gospel labors. She was born February 11, 1783, at Cape May, New Jersey, and is recorded to have made a first request to preach in 1809 at Bethel African Methodist Church of Philadelphia. The denial of this request did not stop Lee from preaching, and neither did her family life.

She married Reverend Joseph Lee, an AME pastor, in 1811 and moved to Snow Hill, New Jersey. In the sixth year of marriage, Joseph Lee died, and Jarena was left with two children and a commitment "to preach his gospel to the fallen sons and daughters of Adam's race" (Lee 1849).

Jarena Lee returned to Philadelphia and renewed her request to preach. Reverend Richard Allen, who at Lee's first request could find no precedent in Methodist discipline for women preaching, was now bishop of the newly organized African Methodist Episcopal Church. Lee asked "to be permitted the liberty of holding prayer meetings in my own hired house, and of exhorting as I found liberty" (Lee 1849). Bishop Allen granted the request and was affirmed in the decision when Lee was moved to speak when Reverend Richard Williams, the assigned preacher for Bethel Church, appeared to lose the spirit. She spoke so well and so linked the text to her life that Bishop Allen publicly proclaimed her gifts.

Lee went on to preach throughout the northeastern region. Although she often traveled alone, her autobiography reports constant companionship among African-American evangelical women. Because Lee was an itinerant preacher and because she carried out her ministry with and among other "sisters in Christ," she was a pathfinder for future preaching women, particularly women of the AME Church. The constant and successful preaching efforts of AME women eventually forced the denomination to create gender-specific positions where no organizational authority for women had previously existed.

[See also AFRICAN METHODIST EPISCOPAL PREACHING WOMEN OF THE NINETEENTH CENTURY.]

BIBLIOGRAPHY

Lee, Jarena. *Life and Religious Experience of Jarena Lee, A Coloured Lady, Giving an Account of Her Call to Preach* (1836), and *Religious Experience and Journal of Mrs. Jarena Lee, Giving an Account of Her Call to Preach the Gospel* (1849).

JUALYNNE E. DODSON

Initially denied permission to preach because she was a woman, Jarena Lee persisted. Bishop Richard Allen of the African Methodist Episcopal Church granted her request and publicly praised her preaching. [Moorland-Spingarn]

LEE, JULIA (1902-1958)

Julia Lee, jazz pianist, vocalist, and composer for nearly three decades, was one of the most popular musicians in Kansas City. Born on October 31, 1902, in Kansas City, Missouri, she began playing the piano at the age of ten and as a teenager joined the George E. Lee Orchestra, the popular band of her older brother. Lee worked with her brother from 1920 to 1934 when she struck out on her own as a result of her aversion to airplane travel.

Julia Lee recorded "Waco Blues" and "Just Wait til I'm Gone" in Chicago for the Okeh label in June 1923, becoming the first Kansas City jazz musician to record; however, because the records were not released, she is often not credited with that distinction. Lee reached the peak of her popularity between 1946 and 1949, selling nearly one million records, including her first major recording, "Snatch and Grab It"

(Capitol Records), which sold more than 500,000 copies. During this period she toured the country and, in 1949, played at the White House during the term of fellow Missourian, President Harry S. Truman. In 1957, she appeared in the Robert Altman film *The Delinquents*, performing "A Porter's Love Song."

Julia Lee had a distinctive and powerful singing style. She is best known for performing songs with suggestive lyrics, often using double entendre, for example, "King Size Papa" and "My Man Stands Out." Nonetheless, she was a fine and accomplished musician.

In 1919, Lee married Frank Duncan, catcher and manager of the Kansas City Monarchs of the Negro Baseball League. Their nine-year union resulted in the birth of one son, Frank Duncan, Jr.

Julia Lee, known as the Empress of Kansas City, of whom it was said that she liked her whiskey—and her men—straight, died of a heart attack in her Kansas City apartment on December 8, 1958 (Haddix 1990).

BIBLIOGRAPHY

Carr, Ian, Digby Fairweather, and Brian Priestly. *Jazz: The Essential Companion* (1987); Chilton, John. *Who's Who of Jazz* (1978); Feather, Leonard. *The Encyclopedia of Jazz* (1960); *Goin' to Kansas City: A Catalogue for the Goin' to Kansas City Exhibit*, Mid-America Arts Alliance, Kansas City, Missouri (1980); Haddix, Charles J. "Julia Lee: The Empress of Kansas City," *Association for Recorded Sound Collectors Journal* (Spring 1990); Kinkle, Roger D. *The Complete Encyclopedia of Popular Music and Jazz, 1900-1950* (1974); Murray, Albert. *Stomping the Blues* (1976).

LAWRENCE J. SIMPSON

LEE, REBECCA *see* CRUMPLER, REBECCA LEE

THE LEFT

In much of the history and historiography of the U.S. Left, African-American women have remained invisible, lost in the cracks somewhere between the "Negro question" and the "woman question." Most white and Black male Communists, Socialists, and even New Leftists of the 1960s have tended to view African-American struggles through the lens of race, saving the category of gender (when it was applied at all) for white women. Thus, in most left-wing movements, where African-Americans as a whole and women of various ethnic groups have struggled to remain visible and find an authoritative voice, Black women radicals were probably the most invisible of all.

From the rise of the U.S. branch of the First International Workingmen's Association in 1864 to the collapse of its successor—the Second International Workingmen's Association—in the aftermath of World War I, the U.S. Left did not take an interest in the specific struggles of African-American women, nor did Black women figure prominently in left-wing movements. In retrospect, the best-known Black woman radical of the late nineteenth and early twentieth centuries was Lucy Parsons, although it was only later in her life that the fair-skinned Parsons even claimed her African heritage. Indeed, although she would eventually become an avid fighter for the rights of all women and actively protest racist attacks, at the height of her popularity she regarded issues of race and sex as secondary to the class struggle.

By the first two decades of the twentieth century, there was some limited Socialist activity among African-American women in Harlem and, to a lesser degree, in parts of the Midwest, especially in Oklahoma, where a large number of independent Black towns were located. A handful of Harlem women, including housewives, schoolteachers, and full-time domestics, listened to street-corner lectures by Black Socialists Hubert Harrison, A. Philip Randolph, Chandler Owen, and Frank Crosswaith. However, with the possible exception of Helen Holman (of whom virtually nothing is known), Black women played no substantive leadership roles in the Socialist party.

There are several reasons why the Socialists failed to attract many Black working-class women or men to their ranks. First, the Socialists' official position subordinated both race and gender issues to the needs of the class struggle. Second, leading Black male Socialists, despite their support for woman suffrage, directed their attention to the condition of male industrial workers, the relationship between African-Americans and the labor movement, and southern lynchings. Third, white Socialist women showed little if any interest in the specific problems of Black working women. Although the publication of August Bebel's *Women under Socialism* (1883) provided a theoretical framework with which white women within the Socialist party could discuss the woman question in a Marxist context, there was no effort to examine the disproportionate numbers of African-American women engaged in wage work, the racist character of early birth control and suffrage movements, the ways in which race hinders the possibility of a radical sisterhood, or the dominant racist views of Black women's sexuality and the unequal treatment Black women received in courts of law in incidents of rape and other cases. Moreover, there was no serious attempt to challenge the tendency among many white Socialist women to employ Black female domestic workers.

African-American women became slightly more visible with the founding of the African Blood Brotherhood (ABB) in 1918 by West Indian immigrant Cyril Briggs. Under Briggs's editorship, ABB published a radical newspaper called the *Crusader*, in which Bertha DeBasco edited a short-lived women's column. Leading Black female activists in ABB included Gertrude Hall and Harlem schoolteacher Grace Campbell, both of whom joined the Communist party in 1924 after ABB leaders decided to liquidate ABB. Although we know very little about the role Black women played within ABB, the organization's public rhetoric couched the entire struggle in terms of Black male redemption. A secret underground organization of radical Black nationalists, ABB advocated armed defense against lynchings, the right to vote in the South, the right to organize, equal rights for Black Americans, and the abolition of Jim Crow laws. Though it is plausible that Black women in the ABB might have carved out autonomous spaces for themselves within the organization, much as Garveyite women had done within the Universal Negro Improvement Association (UNIA), ABB left very little documentation. Besides, by 1924 most of its leadership had joined forces with the newly created Communist Party of the United States of America (CPUSA).

Initially, CPUSA's official position on the Negro question hardly differed from that of the Socialists, and throughout most of the 1920s the woman question was almost nonexistent. Before 1928, the party's discussion of women's problems centered primarily on their role as wage laborers, although the CPUSA platform included a list of demands unique to working mothers (e.g., maternity leave, nurseries, and feeding times at factories). By the onset of the Great Depression, the Communists, with some nudging from Comintern (the international organization of Communist parties), began to pay more attention to both the woman question and the Negro question. However, the party's position on Black liberation after 1928—namely, their insistence on self-determination for African-Americans in the southern Black belt—essentially precluded a serious theoretical framework combining both the Negro and woman

questions. The party's advocacy of Black self-determination conjured up masculine historical figures such as Toussaint L'Ouverture, Denmark Vesey, and Nat Turner; and writers such as Eugene Gordon and V. J. Jerome portrayed the movement as a struggle for manhood.

Though it never occurred to most leading Communists that there could be a "Negro woman question" distinct from other categories, the party's shift in the way it conceived of class struggle opened up at least a few free spaces in which African-American working-class women could pursue their own agenda and find their own autonomous voice. Although CPUSA's early forays into labor organizing via the Trade Union Unity League ignored the majority of African-American women, who were concentrated in domestic work and agriculture, Black women joined the Communist-led unemployed councils, neighborhood relief committees, and a variety of housewife organizations and auxiliaries. In cities such as Chicago, Birmingham, Los Angeles, Detroit, and especially Harlem, Black working women participated in relief demonstrations, resisted eviction efforts, confronted condescending social workers, and fought utilities shut-offs. Working through a variety of Communist-led mass organizations—from the Housewives League and the International Labor Defense to the Hands Off Ethiopia Campaign—the Harlem Communist party produced a significant group of Black women leaders, including Louise Thompson Patterson, Claudia Jones, Audley Moore, and Bonita Williams. African-American women also participated in Communist-led strikes, the most famous of the period being the St. Louis nut-pickers' strike of 1933, which involved at least 1,200 Black women.

For committed Black women in CPUSA, the Marxist education they received nurtured an incipient, though somewhat muted, feminist consciousness. The Communists not only encouraged working-class women's participation as activists, they also offered Black women an empowering language with which to define and critique gender oppression. On both a personal and collective level, Black women activists appropriated from the party's tabloid, *Working Woman*, such terms as the "woman question" and "male chauvinism" as weapons with which to negotiate relationships, the sexual division of labor, and their participation in the movement. It was out of such discussions and actions that Black working-class women developed an incipient class-conscious Black feminist—or, more appropriately, womanist—perspective.

This unique perspective that emerged within CPUSA found its strongest voice in the South. The party gained its largest Black female following in rural Alabama, where more than 5,000 women joined the Communist-led Share Croppers Union (SCU), Young Communist League (YCL), and/or the Communist party during the first half of the Depression decade. Founded in 1931 by African-American tenant farmers and sharecroppers in Tallapoosa County, Alabama, SCU attracted a substantial number of rural women from the outset, many of whom had been radicalized by the deterioration of the rural economy and its effects on their proscribed roles in the division of labor. Women were burdened not only with field work and housework but also with the responsibility for providing meals for their families with whatever food was available. Although planters usually provided food and cash advances, malnutrition and outright starvation were common in the rural South during the 1930s. To make matters worse, New Deal agricultural policies intended to keep cotton prices at market level resulted in the evictions of thousands of tenant and sharecropper families. The crisis prompted a group of Black women SCU activists to form a "Committee of Action," which marched down to the Tallapoosa County Civil Works Administration office in Camp Hill and won demands for relief.

The success and direction of SCU depended to a large degree on women's participation. Women's social and cultural networks served as conduits for radical organization; women activists possessed indispensable organizing skills (as they tended to have higher rates of literacy); and women's concerns constituted the very fabric of SCU's program in the cotton belt. Black women's religious and social organizations were prototypes for the women's auxiliaries. Frequently called "sewing clubs," the women's auxiliaries exercised considerable power within the union. Although they met separately to divert the suspicions of local authorities and to divide child-care responsibilities, the sewing clubs provided forums for women to discuss conditions and formulate strategy.

African-American women played more than an auxiliary role in SCU; they proved to be indispensable local and national leaders. The best known was undoubtedly the niece of martyred SCU founder Ralph Gray, Eula Gray, who at nineteen assumed leadership of the union for nearly a year after it had been driven underground in 1931. Although she was replaced by a Black male comrade in 1932, she continued her union work and led YCL in Alabama, serving as a delegate to the party's eighth national convention in April 1934. Moreover, Black women in SCU were sometimes the target of antiradical violence. Tallapoosa County police brutally beat Estelle Milner, a young schoolteacher and Communist organizer, after discovering in her possession a newspaper clipping about the Scottsboro case. Likewise, Annie Mae Merriweather, whose husband was killed during SCU's cotton-pickers' strike in 1934, was attacked, stripped naked, beaten with a knotted rope while hanging from a wooden beam, and probably raped.

Ironically, the party's shift to popular front politics after 1935—a period known for emphasizing the woman question—spelled disaster for rural Alabama women. The party's central committee disbanded SCU in 1937 and divided its 12,000 members between the all-white Alabama Farmers' Union and an American Federation of Labor-led farm laborers' union—the latter becoming a section of the United Cannery, Agricultural, Packing, and Allied Workers of America (UCAPAWA), an affiliate of the Congress of Industrial Organizations (CIO). Although the old SCU kept most of its locals intact, it now had to conform to the standards of the farmers' union or the CIO. The social movement reflecting women's concerns gave way to simple trade unionism, and the critical role women once played as decision-makers was taken over by unfamiliar white male bureaucracies.

Just as SCU collapsed, the Southern Negro Youth Congress (SNYC) emerged as an important platform for the elaboration of a class-conscious Black womanist perspective. Founded in 1937, the Communist-led SNYC attracted a number of Black women activists, many of whom were young middle-class intellectuals who came of age in the South during the New Deal era. Although SNYC chapters were located throughout the South, its organizational centers were in Richmond, Atlanta, New Orleans, and Birmingham—the latter serving as national headquarters from 1939 until SNYC's demise in 1948.

From the time of its founding, SNYC's Communist and non-Communist leadership adopted a program that proved more radical than most other civil rights organizations of the period. Despite its rather traditional slogan of "Freedom, Equality, and Opportunity," SNYC's program emphasized the right to vote, job security, the right of Black workers to organize, and general improvement in the health, education, and welfare of Black citizens. SNYC also opposed regional wage differentials, police brutality, and segregation in public places. Although socialism was rarely mentioned in SNYC literature, it remained a point of discussion within congress circles throughout its eleven-year history.

Women also held more substantial leadership positions in SNYC than in any other non-gender-specific civil rights organization of the day. The most important national leaders in SNYC were Communist women such as Esther Cooper, who rose to the position of executive secretary during the war; Augusta Jackson, editor of the SNYC newspaper *Cavalcade*; and executive board members Grace Tillman, Dorothy Burnham, and Thelma Dale. Ethel Lee Goodman, Communist party member and former organizer of relief workers in Birmingham, assumed leadership of SNYC's rural committees, whose members consisted of many former SCU members. Leaders of the local rural councils consisted largely of young women who devoted most of their time to quilting and soliciting used books and magazines to stock local rural schools. Non-Communist women also held critical leadership roles. Bertha Boozer, the primary strength in the Atlanta chapter, attempted to organize Black domestic workers, assisted a strike of garbage collectors, and led a boycott of department stores that refused to hire African-Americans. Mildred McAdory led a group of five SNYC activists to protest segregation on public transportation in Fairfield (a suburb of Birmingham), for which she was beaten and arrested. Sallye Davis, a young schoolteacher in Birmingham whose daughter Angela would become the most celebrated Black Communist in history, was also a vital force in the Birmingham SNYC local.

The Southern Negro Youth Congress was founded at an auspicious time with respect to the Communist position on the woman question. During the popular front (1935–39), party leadership encouraged more debate on women's oppression, and its publications placed greater emphasis on women's rights and the sexual division of labor in working-class households. These issues were brought to the forefront within the party by Communists such as Margaret Cowl, director of CPUSA's women's commission during the period, and Mary Inman, whose influential book, *In Woman's Defense* (1940), still stands out as a pioneering effort to wed Marxism and feminism. The newfound importance of the woman question during the popular front prompted challenges to traditional gender relations within the party as well as in other Communist-led organizations. Men were criticized more frequently for male chauvinism, and efforts to recruit and involve women were more pronounced. Within SNYC in particular, some Black women and men strove to eradicate sexist relations in their personal lives; Black Communist couples who led SNYC during the 1940s recalled sharing household duties and child care.

It is possible that the prominent roles Black women played in leadership positions partly account for SNYC's tendency to focus its legal defense activities on cases involving Black women. This marked a substantial shift in left-wing legal defense work on behalf of African-Americans, which had grown out of the Communists' defense of Black men falsely accused of rape (e.g., the Scottsboro and Willie Peterson cases). During and after the war, SNYC's most important cases were its defense of Nora Wilson, a Black Alabama domestic worker convicted of assaulting her boss with intent to kill, and of Recy Taylor, a young Black woman who had been kidnapped and raped by six white men in Abbeville, Alabama.

SNYC's emphasis on legal justice for Black women also had an impact on the actions of the Civil Rights Congress (CRC), a left-wing legal defense organization founded in 1946, just two years before SNYC's demise. One of CRC's better known campaigns centered on Rosie Lee Ingram, a Black Georgia tenant farmer and widowed mother of twelve who, along with two of her sons, was convicted and sentenced to death for the murder of a neighboring white tenant farmer, John Stratford. Stratford had initiated the altercation on Ingram's property in November 1947, assaulting her with the butt of a rifle and, by some accounts, sexually harassing her. One of Ingram's sons intervened, wrested the gun from Stratford, and struck a blow to his head that proved fatal. Throughout the country, African-Americans, white liberals, and radicals rallied in defense of Ingram and her sons, angered especially by the speedy and unconstitutional trial that resulted in their convictions, the racist application of the death penalty in a clear-cut case of self-defense, and the conviction of all three defendants when the responsibility for Stratford's death lay with only one of the sons. Black women in particular viewed the case as proof that the courts did not recognize their right to defend themselves against physical assault or sexual violence. The case spurred the creation of a number of radical women's organizations linked to the CRC campaign, founded primarily by Black women who had some association with the Communist party. Perhaps the most important of these organizations was Sojourners for Truth and Justice, initiated by Charlotta Bass, Shirley Graham Du Bois, Louise Thompson Patterson, Alice Childress, and Rosalie McGee.

Despite these breakthroughs in Communist-led movements during and after World War II, African-American women and issues affecting them still remained the most invisible component of party work. In 1949, for example, Black CPUSA leader Claudia

Jones published a scathing critique, "An End to the Neglect of the Problems of Negro Women!," in the party's theoretical journal, *Political Affairs*. Indeed, the article stands out as one of the clearest articulations of a class-conscious womanist perspective to emerge from the Communist party. Jones insisted that Black women's struggles should be foremost on the CPUSA agenda because they were the most exploited segment of the American working class. Black women not only earned less than all men and white women, she argued, but also postwar economic restructuring had had the effect of forcing large numbers of Black women into domestic work for white families. She railed against left-wing labor organizers for refusing to organize domestic workers and noted with disgust that "many progressives, and even some Communists, are still guilty of exploiting Negro domestic workers" (Jones 1949). Jones was especially critical of the casual, allegedly unconscious racist and sexist remarks directed at Black women within the party and demanded that African-American women hold more substantial leadership positions. The latter demand was crucial to Jones's argument, for she suggested that Black women's position in the hierarchies of race, gender, and class uniquely situated them to push the party in the most progressive direction.

Nevertheless, just as in the early 1930s, radical Black working-class women found free spaces within certain left-wing trade unions in which to resist multiple forms of oppression. Two of the most important unions in the postwar period were the Food, Tobacco, Agricultural, and Allied Workers (FTA), especially Local no. 22 at R. J. Reynolds Tobacco Company in Winston-Salem, and the Drug, Hospital, and Health Care Employees Union's Local no. 1199 in New York City. Led by a number of militant Black women closely associated with CPUSA, including Miranda Smith, Velma Hopkins, Theodosia Simpkins, and Viola Brown, Local no. 22 waged strikes, resisted sexual harassment in the workplace, taught worker education classes, set up a library stocked with volumes on African-American history and Marxist literature, registered Black voters, refused to sign anti-Communist affidavits required by the Taft-Hartley Act after the war, and supported the Progressive party's 1948 presidential candidate, Henry Wallace. As a radical union in the age of the Cold War, FTA was eventually expelled from the CIO in 1950.

While Local no. 22 grew out of a predominantly Black female work environment, Local no. 1199 was initially made up of white male pharmacists, clerks,

soda men, Black porters, and retail hospital workers in New York's Harlem. Founded in the 1930s by Jewish Communists active in the CPUSA Trade Union Unity League, its composition changed dramatically by the late 1950s, when a left-wing breakaway group within the union began organizing Black and Latino hospital service workers and waged a partially successful strike in 1959. Although it eventually abandoned its ties to the Communist party, Local no. 1199 retained a left-wing political culture, struggled against racial and gender inequality in the workplace and beyond, opposed the Vietnam War, actively supported the civil rights movement, and pledged solidarity with democratic movements in Central American and South African solidarity committees. Local no. 1199 was also among the first to support Jesse Jackson's presidential candidacy in 1988.

In the aftermath of the Communist party's decline in the 1950s—a decline due largely to postwar repression and general disillusionment with the Soviet Union after Stalin's crimes were revealed in 1956—there were very few Marxist organizations in which African-American women figured prominently. Nevertheless, a handful of radical Black female intellectuals, artists, and organizers continued to work relatively autonomously. Among this group were Esther Cooper Jackson, former SNYC activist and cofounder of *Freedomways* magazine; Elizabeth Catlett, one of the most important visual artists of the postwar period; and the extraordinary poet and playwright Lorraine Hansberry. Hansberry had been a supporter of left-wing causes ever since she was a teenager. She protested the House Un-American Activities Committee hearings, studied at the Communist party's Jefferson School of Social Science, joined the editorial staff of Paul Robeson's *Freedom*, and eventually married Robert Nemiroff, then director of the left-wing Camp Unity in upstate New York. In addition to writing, she participated in a number of progressive political campaigns until her untimely death in 1965.

Finally, left-leaning African-American women also participated in, and at times influenced, mainstream civil rights organizations. Former Communist Mae Mallory, for instance, provided critical support for Robert Williams during his armed self-defense campaign in Monroe, North Carolina, in 1957. Marvel Cooke, a former CRC activist, continued to offer her talents to various civil rights movements during the 1960s. Perhaps the most powerful radical female voice within both the Student Nonviolent Coordinating Committee (SNCC) and the Southern Christian Leadership Conference (SCLC) was Ella Baker, whose experience with left-wing politics began in Harlem during the 1930s. By example, she prompted a number of young militants in SNCC to pay closer attention to the struggles of the poor and working class and to challenge male chauvinism within the movement.

Although the activities of radical Black women in particular and Communist-led movements in general had the potential of inspiring the new generation of militants in the 1960s and 1970s, the lessons of the past were largely (though not entirely) lost to Black New Leftists. In an age when the metaphors for Black liberation were increasingly masculinized and Black movement leaders insisted on privileging race over class and gender oppression, even the most Marxist of the Black nationalist movements of the time—the Black Panther party—initially ignored or belittled the woman question. Yet, in spite of these adverse circumstances, when it was possible radical Black women sustained the tradition of carving out free spaces within existing male-dominated organizations in order to articulate a class-conscious womanist perspective and to challenge the multiple forms of exploitation Black working-class women and men faced daily. Whether it was the Panthers' free breakfast and educational programs or antiwar movements like the Harlem-based Black Women Enraged, African-American women radicals devised strategies that, in varying degrees, challenged capitalism, racism, and patriarchy. In some instances, African-American women radicals rose to positions of prominence and, sometimes by sheer example, contributed toward developing a militant, class-conscious Black feminist perspective. The most important figures in this respect include Kathleen Cleaver, Ericka Huggins, and Assata Shakur (formerly JoAnne Chesimard) of the Black Panther Party, and Communist leader Angela Davis.

When it was not possible to build progressive, class-conscious womanist movements within radical nationalist organizations, a number of leading Black woman activists collectively organized autonomous Black feminist organizations, the most notable being the National Black Feminist Organization (NBFO) founded in 1973. Yet, though NBFO provided a forum to challenge racism and gender oppression, its leaders tended to ignore the specific struggles of poor and working-class women and limited their discussions to the problems of heterosexual women. Thus, in 1977 the Combahee River Collective, a radical group of Black lesbian feminists, split from NBFO and issued a challenge to the Black feminist movement to consider the inherently exploitative character of capitalism and to take issues of sexual politics and identity more seriously. The Collective's statement of purpose marked the most sophisticated Black socialist-feminist articulation of the multiple dimensions of Black women's oppression to date. "The inclusiveness of our politics," the Collective asserted, "makes us concerned with any situation that impinges upon the lives of women, Third World, and working people. We are of course particularly committed to working on those struggles in which race, sex, and class are simultaneous factors in oppression. We might, for example, become involved in workplace organizing at a factory that employs Third World women, or picket a hospital that is cutting back on already inadequate health care to a Third World community, or set up a rape crisis center in a Black neighborhood. Organizing around welfare and day-care concerns might also be a focus. The work to be done and the countless issues that this work represents merely reflect the pervasiveness of our oppression."

Thus, by the early 1970s and 1980s, there really was no single, identifiable Black socialist-feminist movement. On the contrary, African-American women on the left worked within an endless number of left-wing groups, welfare rights campaigns, regional organizations such as the Southern Organizing Committee for Economic Justice, predominantly white feminist movements, militant trade unions, and a variety of Marxist and left-leaning Black nationalist organizations, including the Republic of New Africa, African People's party, Patrice Lumumba Coalition, All-African People's Revolutionary party, National Black Independent Political party (whose steering committee included none other than former Harlem Communist Audley "Queen Mother" Moore), and more recently the Rainbow Coalition, to name a few. Although they continue to participate in a variety of different movements and to articulate a wide range of radical positions, both within and without the U.S. Left, today's Black women radicals share with their predecessors a commitment to simultaneously challenging racism, capitalism, and patriarchy and highlighting the unique struggles of African-American working-class women.

BIBLIOGRAPHY

Boyd, Herb. "The Black Left in Struggle: 1980-1985." In *The Year Left 2: Toward a Rainbow Socialism*, ed. Mike Davis, Manning Marable, Fred Pfeil, and Michael Sprinker (1987); Dixler, Elsa. "The Woman Question: Women and the Communist Party, 1929-1941," Ph.D. diss. (1974); Echols, Alice. *Daring to Be Bad: Radical Feminism in America, 1967-1975* (1989); Evans, Sara. *Personal Politics: The Roots of Women's Liberation in the Civil Rights Movement and the New Left* (1979); Foner, Philip. *American Socialism and Black Americans: From the Age of Jackson to World War II* (1977);

Giddings, Paula. *When and Where I Enter: The Impact of Black Women on Race and Sex in America* (1984); Horne, Gerald. *Communist Front? The Civil Rights Congress, 1946-1956* (1988); Inman, Mary. *In Woman's Defense* (1940); Jones, Claudia. "An End to the Neglect of the Problems of Negro Women!" *Political Affairs* ([1949] March 1974); Kelley, Robin D. G. *Hammer and Hoe: Alabama Communists during the Great Depression* (1990); King, Deborah. "Multiple Jeopardy, Multiple Consciousness: The Context of a Black Feminist Ideology," *Signs* (Autumn 1988); Nekola, Charlotte and Paula Rabinowitz, eds. *Writing Red: An Anthology of American Women Writers, 1930-1940* (1987); North, Joe. "Communist Women," *Political Affairs* (March 1971); Richards, Johnetta. "The Southern Negro Youth Congress: A History," Ph.D. diss. (1987); Schaffer, Robert. "Women and the Communist Party, USA, 1930-1940," *Socialist Review* (May-June 1979).

ROBIN D. G. KELLEY

LeNOIRE, ROSETTA OLIVE BURTON (1911-)

"Bubbling Brown Sugar in a Crystal Ball" is the nickname that Rosetta LeNoire's godfather, Bill "Bojangles" Robinson, gave her when she was growing up in Harlem. Decades later she reclaimed her nickname for *Bubbling Brown Sugar* (1975), the award-winning musical revue that celebrates the African-American music and performers of her youth with "Uncle Bo." Rosetta LeNoire became well known in the 1980s and early 1990s through television sitcoms, appearing as Nell's mother on *Gimme a Break*, as Rolly's wife on *Amen*, and as the grandmother on *Family Matters*. At the age of eighty, she had become a nationally recognized television star after fifty years of theater successes, bouts with discrimination, numerous awards, and humanitarian work in the arts. She has made significant contributions to every major phase of the Black experience in American theater history, serving as her own manager.

Rosetta Olive Burton LeNoire was born in "Hell's Kitchen," Fifty-ninth Street in New York City, on August 8, 1911, to Marie Jacque and Harold Charles Burton shortly after they migrated from Dominica, British West Indies, to the United States. Her early years dancing with Uncle Bo and singing lead in her church choir gave her the confidence to audition for the Federal Theatre Project in 1935, her entry into professional theater in New York City.

She became a member of the acclaimed Harlem unit of the Federal Theatre Project in 1936, performing the role of the First Witch in Orson Welles and John Houseman's production of *Haitian Macbeth*. Other Federal Theatre Project (1935-39) productions in which LeNoire performed were *Bassa Moona*, *Bluebirds*, *Haiti*, *Sing for Your Supper*, and *Underground Railroad*.

After Congress closed the Federal Theatre Project in 1939, LeNoire made her Broadway debut in a principal role with Uncle Bo. The production was *The Hot Mikado* and was produced by Michael Todd. She completed the tour of *The Hot Mikado* after the bombing of Pearl Harbor and went on to perform in several productions of the United Service Organizations (USO) during World War II.

With her role as Rheba in *You Can't Take It with You*, she began performing female servant roles in some of the most prominent productions in New York. She became highly respected as an actress who contributed to changing the stage image of the Black female servant by performing with dignity and self-pride. This reputation has continued to the present. Included among the plays in which she performed are *Decision* and *Three's a Family* with the New York Subway Circuit; *Four Twelves Are 48* (1948); *The Easiest Way* (1949); *Kiss Me, Kate* (1950); *Show Boat*, *Anything Goes*, and *Happy Birthday* (1951) stock; *The Ceremony of Innocence* (1954) and *The Name of the Game* (1967) off Broadway; and the following Broadway productions: *Finian's Rainbow* (1955), *The White Devil* (1955), *Destry Rides Again* (1959), *Sophie* (1963), *I Had a Ball* (1964), *The Great Indoors* (1966), *Show Boat* (1966), *The Sunshine Boys* (1972), *God's Favorite* (1974), *The Royal Family* (1976), and *The Little Foxes* (1983).

She performed in numerous off-Broadway shows by Black writers and in plays written specifically for a Black cast. After *Hot Mikado*, she was featured in a principal role in Abram Hill's adaptation of Philip Yordan's *Anna Lucasta*, which was transferred from the American Negro Theatre to Broadway. It opened August 30, 1944, and became the most successful production in the 1940s using a Black cast. Intertwined with her servant roles, she obtained principal roles in the following plays for mixed or an all-Black cast off-Broadway: *O Distant Land* (1952), *Supper for the Dead* (1954), *Mister Johnson* (1955), *Take a Giant Step* (1956), *The Bible Salesman* (1960, 1961), *The Oldest Trick in the World* (1961), *Clandestine on the Morning Line* (1961), *Cabin in the Sky* (1964), and *Lady Day* (1972). On Broadway she had roles in *Lost in the Stars* (1958), *South Pacific* (1961), *Tambourines to Glory* (1963), *Blues for Mr. Charlie* (1964), *A Cry of Players* (1968), *Hallelujah Baby* (1968), and *Lost in the Stars* (1972).

Early in Rosetta LeNoire's career, Bill "Bojangles" Robinson called her "Bubbling Brown Sugar in a Crystal Ball." Fifty years later, this star of stage, screen, and television conceived the idea for the award-winning musical revue Bubbling Brown Sugar. *Here she appears in the Broadway musical* Double Entry. *[Schomburg Center]*

LeNoire was instrumental in establishing two of the most prominent organizations that contributed to the development of and more opportunities for Black performers, the Negro Actor's Guild (NAG) and the Coordinating Council for Negro Performers (CCNP). She was one of the charter members of NAG, a welfare organization for performers in need, and she was one of the founders of CCNP, a political action organization that in 1955 led a boycott against television to sensitize the sponsors to provide a fair share of jobs for Black performers. In more recent years, she has been an active member of the Actor's Fund, the interracial welfare organization for performers.

Her proudest contribution to her profession was the establishment of Amas Repertory Theatre in 1969 to encourage cultural pluralism and love in the world. The name of the theater, Amas, means "you love" in Latin and its musical theater productions reiterate that theme. LeNoire's primary reason for continuing to work as an actress, with all of the physical complications of her age, is to help subsidize the theater company, which is her greatest love. As she continues to work at Amas, refusing to accept a salary, her most immediate concern is finding a permanent building to house her institution.

LeNoire's contributions have not gone unrecognized. She has received almost as many major awards as the number of years she has been in theater. Since 1981, she has received thirty distinguished career awards including the Johnny Walker Award (1981); the Harold Jackman Award (1981); the St. Genesius Award from the Catholic Actor's Guild (1981); the Outstanding Pioneer Award (1982), Board of Directors' Award (1982), and Outstanding Musical Production of the Year (1979-84, 1991) from AUDELCO (Audience Development Committee); the Hoey Award from the Catholic Interracial Council (1985); Sojourner Truth Award from the Council of Negro Professional Women (1986); Mayor's Award for Arts and Culture (1986); Woman of the Year from the Caribbean Cultural Association (1986); Actor's Equity Award created especially for her called the Rosetta LeNoire Award (1989); the Living Legend Award from the National Black Theatre Festival (1991); and the Lucille Lortel Career Achievement Award (1991). The variety of presenters of these prestigious awards demonstrates that LeNoire has made an indelible mark on her profession and on her home, New York City.

BIBLIOGRAPHY

LeNoire, Rosetta Olive Burton. Personal interviews (1981, 1992); Norflett, Linda. "The Theatre Career of Rosetta LeNoire: Fifty Years of the Black Experience in the American Theatre," Ph.D. diss. (1982).

LINDA NORFLETT

LEWIS, MARY EDMONIA "WILDFIRE" (b. c. 1843)

Her dual heritage and accomplished marble sculpture distinguish Edmonia Lewis as the first major sculptress of African-American and Native American heritage. Her early biographical circumstances are sketchily known at best. Although Lewis claimed 1854 as her birthdate, it is more likely that she was born in 1843 or 1845. Various sources, including the artist herself, have noted Greenhigh, Ohio, and Greenbush, New York, as well as the vicinity of Albany, New York, as her birthplace, but none can be verified.

Lewis's father was a full-blooded African-American employed as a gentleman's servant, and her mother was a Chippewa Indian who may have been born near Albany. It was she who presumably named her daughter "Wildfire." Lewis appears to have spent little if any time with her father, and instead lived with her mother's tribe. Orphaned before she was five, Lewis remained with the Chippewas until she was about twelve years old. As "Wildfire," she learned to fish, swim, make baskets, and embroider moccasins. Typically, she sold her crafts as the tribe followed its nomadic lifestyle throughout New York State.

During the 1850s Lewis left the Chippewas because her brother "Sunrise," a California gold miner, had arranged for her schooling near Albany. Adapting to her new circumstances proved difficult, but her brother persisted in efforts to educate her. Thus in 1859 Lewis entered Oberlin College in Oberlin, Ohio, with his financial assistance. This event triggered her name change, and the school's records indicate that she assumed the name Mary Edmonia Lewis. Throughout her career, however, she seldom used her new first name, as reflected in her correspondence as well as the signatures on her sculptures.

Lewis was a moderately successful student, completing the preparatory department's high-school courses and pursuing the college department's liberal arts program. Her only extant drawing, *The Muse Urania*, still in the Oberlin College Archive, was done in 1862 as a wedding present for her classmate, Clara Steele Norton. She may have been inspired by optional drawing courses offered by the Young Ladies' Course. Later in life Lewis recalled that "I had always wanted to make the form of things; and while I was at school I tried to make drawings of people and things" (Child 1865).

Although Oberlin College and its namesake village actively promoted racial harmony, Lewis became the focus of a racially motivated controversy in 1862, when two white female students accused her of poisoning them. Lewis subsequently was beaten by vigilantes. John Mercer Langston—a prominent lawyer also of African-American and Native American

Raised as "Wildfire" by Chippewa Indians, Edmonia Lewis was the first major sculptress of African-American and Native American heritage. She spent most of her adult life working in Europe. [Schomburg Center]

heritage—came to her defense and she was exonerated because of insufficient evidence. A year later she was accused of stealing art supplies. Despite her second acquittal, the college refused to allow her to graduate.

Shortly thereafter, Lewis moved to Boston, in part because her brother believed that the city's resources could support her interest in becoming a sculptor. Upon her arrival, she was greatly inspired by seeing Richard Greenough's life-size statue of Benjamin Franklin at City Hall. Using letters of introduction from Oberlin College, Lewis met William Lloyd Garrison, the abolitionist writer, who introduced her to Edward Brackett, a well-known portrait sculptor at that time. Brackett lent Lewis fragments of sculptures to copy in clay and critiqued her early efforts, then a customary alternative to academic training. Equipped only with this limited preparation, Lewis began to establish herself in Boston as a sculptor, and was listed as such in the city's directories in 1864 and 1865. According to these same directories, she worked in the Studio Building, where African-American painter Edward Mitchell Bannister and other artists maintained studios during the 1860s. To date, however, the extent of her interaction with this artistic community and specifically with Bannister has not been established.

Exposure to Edward Brackett's sculpture and the impact of the Civil War combined to determine Lewis's first sculptures—medallion portraits of white anti-slavery leaders and Civil War heroes, which she modeled in plaster and clay. She also attempted her first portrait bust during this period. Its subject was Colonel Robert Gould Shaw, the young Boston Brahmin who was killed as he led his all-Black battalion in battle against Confederate forces. The city's liberal white community subsequently lionized Shaw. Lewis's bust of Shaw, and most of her early efforts, are still unlocated, despite the fact that she made numerous plaster copies to help finance her move to Europe in 1865.

Lewis initially considered living in England because of its active abolitionist community. Following visits to London, Paris, and Florence, however, she established her studio in Rome during the winter of 1865-66. She was barely twenty years old at the time. Her interest in Italy and the decision to settle in Rome were not unique. Since the 1820s, American sculptors led by the example of Hiram Powers had been attracted by Italy's venerable artistic traditions, classical sculpture, abundant marble, and inexpensive artisan labor. Moreover, American women artists and writers considered Rome particularly congenial because it disregarded the sexist restrictions of their Anglo-American world.

Settled into a large studio near the Piazza Barberini, Lewis quickly began learning to carve in marble, experimenting with the challenge of creating full-length figures. To increase her skills, she followed the common practice of copying classical sculptures in public collections. Proving adept in this direction, Lewis made copies of classical statuary, which she regularly sold to Americans who visited artists' studios in Italy as part of their European tours.

Lewis, however, shunned other customs of the art community. She avoided instruction or criticism from her peers and refused to hire native artisans to enlarge her small clay and plaster models and to carve the final marbles. Fierce pride in her heritage and the desire to achieve legitimacy as a sculptor persuaded her that her sculptures would not be considered original if she did not execute them. This attitude limited her production, but to date research documents forty-six different compositions (she may have done more; in any case most of the actual works are still unlocated).

Commissions for small portrait busts in terra cotta and marble became Lewis's most reliable means of support. Patrons in Boston, especially prominent white male abolitionists and social reformers, were her most regular clients and she shipped work to them. She also recognized the American market for "conceits" or "fancy pieces"—sculptures that used mythological children to convey human, often sentimental themes. *Poor Cupid* (or *Love Ensnared*) of 1876 (National Museum of American Art, Washington, D.C.) is probably her best-known effort in this vein.

Financial security, however, was not Lewis's principal concern. Slavery and racial oppression were the central issues of her sculptures, a focus greatly facilitated by her distance from America. It also distinguished Lewis from her fellow sculptors in Italy, who derived their ideas and images from classical literature, history, and art. Between 1866 and 1883, Lewis created at least six major figurative groups featuring either African-Americans or Native Americans. *The Freed Woman and Her Child* of 1866 (location unknown) and *Forever Free* of 1867 (Howard University, Washington, D.C.), for example, both capture the powerful emotion of emancipation; the latter's title actually adapts phrasing from Abraham Lincoln's Emancipation Proclamation.

Lewis's exploration of the Black figure reached as far as the African continent, when in 1868 she sculpted *Hagar*, a marble also known as *Hagar in the Wilderness* (National Museum of American Art collection). Egyp-

Edmonia Lewis's Forever Free *(1867) captures the powerful emotion of emancipation. The title adapts phrasing from Abraham Lincoln's Emancipation Proclamation. [Schomburg Center]*

social commentary and ethnographic accuracy of her Black figures, however, Lewis took a more literary, sentimental approach when carving her small-scale Indian groups such as *Old Arrow Maker* of 1872, also known as *The Old Arrow Maker and His Daughter* (National Museum of American Art). Lewis was greatly influenced by the narrative poem, "The Song of Hiawatha" (1855) by Henry Wadsworth Longfellow. He posed for his portrait bust, which she began carving in Rome in 1869 and finished in 1871 (Harvard University portrait collection, Cambridge, Massachusetts).

Lewis's career in Rome coincided with those of other American women artists and writers who gathered around the neoclassical sculptor Harriet Hosmer and actress Charlotte Cushman. Both women welcomed Lewis to Rome, and it is widely believed that their influential circle greatly benefitted her. Social reformer Lydia Maria Child, one of Lewis's longtime patrons in Boston, nonetheless wondered if American artists abroad would free themselves of "American prejudice" to help Lewis when she was deeply in debt. By 1865 it had became evident that Cushman and others would not come to her aid.

During the height of her popularity in the late 1860s and 1870s, Lewis's studio was a frequent stop for those who visited American artists abroad. She was also well-received during her several return visits to the United States between 1870 and 1876 when she exhibited works in Chicago, California, Boston, and Philadelphia. Perhaps the American high point of her career came in 1876 when her ambitious sculpture, *The Death of Cleopatra* (Forest Park Historical Society, Forest Park, Illinois) was exhibited and awarded a medal at the Centennial Exposition in Philadelphia.

From the outset, however, Lewis was considered "an interesting novelty . . . in a city [Rome] where all our surroundings are of the olden time" (Wreford, "A Negro Sculptress," 1866). Dressed in her rakish red cap and mannish costumes, Lewis captivated both Europeans and Americans, who regularly described her as childlike, charming, and picturesque. In 1863, she had already recognized the pitfalls of her triple heritage as a Black Indian woman when she asked that her sculpture not be praised solely because of her background. Unfortunately, Lewis represented a tempting opportunity to those in Boston and Rome eager to demonstrate their support of human rights, and the encouragement she subsequently received ranged from sincere belief in her talents to well-meant but misguided indulgence.

Equally diverse, if not confused, were the interpretations of Lewis's appearance. Some described her

tians such as Hagar, the biblical maidservant to Abraham, were considered Black by the nineteenth-century Western world, and in this sculpture, Lewis included the issues of gender and women's rights in her interpretation of oppression.

She also reacted against the period's negative stereotypes of Native Americans as murderous savages or a dying primitive race. Eschewing the direct hair as being black and straight like an Indian's and associated her complexion and willfully proud character with her mother's ancestry, while others believed that her facial features and hair reflected her father's background. Lewis herself was amused by a Bostonian's observation that "as her father had been a 'man of color' it would have seemed as though she ought to have been a painter, had it not been that her mother was a 'Chippe-e-way' Indian, and that made it natural for her to be a sculptor" (Wyman 1914).

In 1883, Lewis received her last major commission, *Adoration of the Magi* (location unknown), for a church in Baltimore, no doubt a reflection of her conversion to Catholicism in Rome in 1868. After 1883, demand for her work declined, as it did for neoclassical sculpture in general. Her presence in Rome was reported in 1911, but the activities of her final decades are barely documented and the date and place of her death are unknown even today.

Following a visit to Lewis's studio, an anonymous American writer wondered in 1867 if "the youthful Indian girl" would create a "distinctive if not original style in sculpture" (Tuckerman 1867). Lewis indeed represented a fresh approach to the neoclassical sculpture tradition, injecting as she did timely yet universal human rights issues and developing a more emotional, naturalistic style than her contemporaries.

BIBLIOGRAPHY

Blodgett, Geoffrey. "John Mercer Langston and the Case of Edmonia Lewis: Oberlin, 1862," *Journal of Negro History* (July 1968); Child, Lydia Maria. "Letter from L. Maria Child," *National Anti-Slavery Standard* (February 27, 1864), and "Edmonia Lewis," *Broken Fetter* (March 13, 1865); Gerdts, William H. *American Neo-Classic Sculpture: The Marble Resurrection* (1973); Goldberg, Marcia. "A Drawing by Edmonia Lewis," *American Art Journal* (November 1977); Hartigan, Lynda Roscoe. *Sharing Traditions: Five Black Artists in Nineteenth-Century America* (1985); James, Henry. *William Wetmore Story and His Friends* (1903); Leach, Joseph. *Bright Particular Star: The Life and Times of Charlotte Cushman* (1970); Locke, Alain. *The New Negro in Art* (1940); *NAW; Revolution,* "Edmonia Lewis" (April 20, 1871); Sterling, Dorothy, ed. *We Are Your Sisters: Black Women in the Nineteenth Century* (1984); Tuckerman, Henry T. *Book of the Artists: American Artist Life, Comprising the Biographical and Critical Sketches of American Artists* (1867); Waterston, Anna Quincy. "Edmonia Lewis (the young colored woman who has successfully modeled the bust of Col. Shaw)," *National Anti-Slavery Standard* (December 24, 1864); Wreford, Henry. "Lady Artists in Rome," *Art-Journal* (March 1866), and "A Negro Sculptress," *Athenaeum* (March 3, 1866); Wyman, Lillie Buffum Chase and Arthur Crawford Wyman. *Elizabeth Buffum, 1806-1899* (1914).

Archival resources include the James Thomas Fields collection, F1650, Huntington Library, San Marino, California; Oberlin College archives, Oberlin, Ohio; Robie-Sewall papers, Massachusetts Historical Society, Boston, Massachusetts; and Anne Whitney papers, Wellesley College archives, Wellesley, Massachusetts.

LYNDA ROSCOE HARTIGAN

LIBRARIANSHIP

Librarians, especially in the modern age, are far more than keepers of books. They are responsible for an ever-changing instrument of communication that has tremendous potential to help, or harm, the community at large. With regard to women and minorities, this responsibility is particularly grave.

A librarian's most basic task is providing books that inspire and inform and that provide a sense of heritage and models for achievement. Simply stocking the shelves is not enough, however. "Librarians cannot afford to be passive," Ann Steward Watt said about the school librarian in *What Black Librarians Are Saying*. "Involvement in world, community and school affairs is mandatory. . . . Instead of waiting for clients to come to the library or to ask for material, it is incumbent upon the librarian to reach out to clients with an informed anticipation of their needs and adequate means for meeting them." Libraries have the potential for undermining bigotry by empowering people—bigots have always known this. In many southern states, for example, it was once unlawful for Black citizens to use public libraries. Indeed, as children many of today's Black librarians could only stand outside the library and watch while white children climbed up the stairs toward the door. Thus the modern librarian has the duty of making sure that the bigot's fears are realized.

In addition, the librarian also has a responsibility of seeing that oppressed groups are represented fairly, completely, and in a nonprejudicial way. "For centuries," wrote Dharthula H. Millender in *Library Journal* in 1967, "literature has been valued for introducing readers to each other. . . . Tragically, however, books have often planted false images in the minds of readers." It is the librarian's obligation to make sure that books with accurate images of women, Black people, and other minority groups find their way into the hands of readers.

Black women have a special stake in this area, and since the days of Susan Dart Butler (1888-1959) and Sadie Peterson Delaney (1889-1958), they have taken on a special responsibility to their community, even though this sometimes has entailed personal as well as professional sacrifices. As Ella Gaines Yates pointed out in the early 1970s, "A very large percentage of the librarians working in community and outreach services to the 'disadvantaged' are black. . . . The 'minority' librarian seems to be the one who can best function and offer the most relevance to our 'disadvantaged' population. Yet the librarians delegated to this type of service are far too often among the lower echelon of staff in terms of status, rank, and title, and too often rank among the lower paid." In addition, according to Yates, the community experience these librarians receive is not considered appropriate grounding for higher level positions. It is wiser to avoid community involvement if a librarian is interested in advancement, but hundreds of Black women have refused to avoid such involvement and, in fact, have committed themselves to making public libraries active participants in the lives of the people in their communities. School librarians, too, face this challenge. Watt has argued that the Black librarian can be a particularly strong force in successfully integrating a school and/or ensuring a quality education for Black students.

Nonetheless, there have not been and still are not enough Black women receiving training in the field. The 1991 edition of the *Statistical Handbook on Women in America* reported statistics for the year 1986–87, breaking women down into several ethnic groups. In the group called "black non-Hispanic," only 121 women received Master's degrees in library and archival science, and only one woman received a doctorate. The paucity of Black women in the profession is particularly disturbing when one considers the need for more trained staff in Black colleges and universities as well as in public libraries in Black communities.

Many Black women who have overcome the obstacles and become librarians have made their mark on the profession and advanced in their professional organizations. Alma Jacobs was elected president of the Pacific Northwest Library Association in 1957, president of the Montana Library Association in 1960, and became the first Black member of the executive board of the American Library Association (ALA) in 1964. Also in 1957, Charlemae Rollins was elected the first Black president of the Children's Services Division of the ALA. Hannah D. Atkins was elected first Black president of the Oklahoma Chapter of the Special Libraries Association in 1967 and president of the Southwestern Chapter of the Association of Law Librarians in 1969. Virginia Lacey Jones was

chosen president of the Association of American Library Schools in 1967. All of these women achieved leadership roles before the formation of the Black Caucus of the ALA in 1970.

In 1971, Effie Lee Morris was elected president of the Public Library Association Division of the ALA, and Rebecca T. Bingham was named president of the Kentucky Library Association. In 1974, Georgia McClaron was elected president of the Tennessee Library Association, and, in 1975, Clara S. Jones was elected vice president/president-elect of the ALA. In 1976, Lucille C. Thomas became president of the New York Library Club and, the following year, president of the New York Library Association. Also that year, Jessie Carney Smith, who would later edit *Notable Black American Women*, was elected president of Beta Phi Mu, a professional sorority for Black librarians.

BIBLIOGRAPHY

Bauer, Henry C. "Seasoned to Taste," *Wilson Library Bulletin* (February 1955); Gunn, Arthur C. "A Black Woman Wants to Be a Professional . . .," *American Libraries* (February 1989); Josey, E. J., ed. *The Black Librarian in America* (1970), and *What Black Librarians Are Saying* (1972); Josey, E. J. and Ann Allen Shockley, eds. *Handbook of Black Librarianship* (1977); Taeuber, Cynthia, ed. *Statistical Handbook on Women in America* (1991).

LEE SELLERS

LIGHTNER, GWENDOLYN

Born in Brookport, Illinois, Gwendolyn Rosetta Capps Lightner (gospel pianist, arranger, and choir director) displayed talents in playing the piano at an early age. "When I was small, we didn't have a piano. So I would make music on everything I saw—my father's razor stand, behind the stove, my mother's sewing machine, whatever. I would get there and imagine it was a piano and I would play and make music with my mouth" (Lightner 1988). Little did she know that these early childhood experiences would serve as the foundation for a career that would include world concert tours and television appearances as pianist for the legendary gospel singer Mahalia Jackson.

Lightner is the daughter of Mase and Florence Capps. In personal interviews, she has declined to give her birthdate. She is married to Peter Lightner and the mother of six children (Deborah, Ricke, Donna, Copelia, Raphael, and Barron). While two children (Ricke and Copelia) have begun to establish professional careers in music, the others are pursuing careers in the medical field, business, politics, and civil service.

As a youngster, Lightner studied Western art music, church hymnody, and spirituals. After completing high school, she attended Southern Illinois University in Carbondale, Illinois, and Lyon and Healy Music School in Chicago. The move to Chicago during the early 1940s introduced her to gospel music through contacts with gospel giants in the city (e.g., Kenneth Morris, Sallie Martin, Mahalia Jackson, and Roberta Martin), and Lightner's membership with the Chicago gospel group the Emma L. Jackson Singers gave her the opportunity to travel to Los Angeles where she has remained since 1946.

Lightner's gospel music career blossomed after her move to the West Coast. Initially, she managed and taught music at a studio (Los Angeles Gospel Music Mart) in the city. During the late 1940s, she was credited with introducing a new style of playing gospel music on the piano when she became the first pianist for the highly acclaimed Echoes of Eden Choir at Saint Paul Baptist Church (1947-49), a group that revolutionized the Los Angeles gospel music community. After leaving Saint Paul, she worked as choir director and pianist at Grace Memorial Church of God in Christ as well as Mount Moriah Baptist Church. Since 1956, she has been the minister of music at Bethany Baptist Church.

Among the Los Angeles-based groups with whom Lightner has been affiliated are the Rose of Sharon (1946-47), a female gospel trio; the J. Earle Hines Goodwill Singers (1947-49); the J. Earle Hines Goodwill Community Choir (1950s); and the Sallie Martin Singers (1952-53). Between 1957 and 1974, she and Thurston G. Frazier organized and served as codirectors of the Voices of Hope, a community choir initially established to raise funds for the March of Dimes; it later became well known on the West Coast as a result of numerous concert appearances and recordings on Capitol Records. During the 1950s, she played piano on several gospel recordings by the Pilgrim Travelers, the Soul Stirrers, and Brother Joe May for Specialty Records. In the 1960s, she recorded with Doris Akers on RCA Records. Nationally, she is probably known best for her work as pianist for the legendary gospel singer Mahalia Jackson (1968-72), including several world concert tours and many television appearances.

At present she is an instructor at Victory Baptist Day School and holds several offices within the Baptist church, including director of music for the

Gwendolyn Lightner is probably best known for her work from 1968 to 1972 as pianist for Mahalia Jackson, but her career has also included work with the Echoes of Eden Choir, the Rose of Sharon, and the Sallie Martin Singers, and recordings with Doris Akers, the Pilgrim Travelers, and Brother Joe May. [J. C. DjeDje]

Western Baptist State Convention and Congress of Christian Education and pianist for the National Baptist Convention, USA, and National Congress of Christian Education.

BIBLIOGRAPHY

DjeDje, Jacqueline Cogdell. "A Historical Overview of Black Gospel Music in Los Angeles," *Black Music Research Bulletin* (Spring 1988), and "Gospel Music in the Los Angeles Black Community: A Historical Overview," *Black Music Research Journal* (Spring 1989); Lightner, Gwendolyn. Interviews (January 25, 1988, and November 27, 1991).

JACQUELINE COGDELL DJEDJE

LINCOLN, ABBEY (1930-)

Abbey Lincoln/Aminata Moseka is a uniquely talented vocalist, actress, and songwriter, as well as a student of African music. Scholar and night-life sophisticate, Aminata Moseka creates thoughtful cultural mirrors and shapes that are very reminiscent of the creative and explorative work of two other multi-

Vocalist, actor, and songwriter Abbey Lincoln has been compared to Billie Holiday and Betty Carter for her dramatic and innovative jazz song stylings. [Schomburg Center]

disciplined innovators, Zora Neale Hurston and Katherine Dunham.

Born Gaby Lee in Chicago in 1930, Lincoln, who began her career during the 1950s, is often likened to Billie Holiday and Betty Carter, since her engaging dramatic interpretations goad, seduce, and inform. However, her voice is distinctively her own. Skilled and practiced control affords her a wide range of expression: playful, sultry, angry, and despairing

qualities all live in Lincoln's deep voice and share access to that instrument's clarity.

The 1965 film *Nothing But a Man* starred Lincoln, Ivan Dixon, and Gloria Foster. Aminata co-starred with Sidney Poitier in the 1968 film *For Love of Ivy*.

Teamed for thirty years with a formidable array of forceful jazz instrumentalists, Abbey Lincoln works to create a space beyond the role of "singer with the band" to become a true collaborator. In the 1960 landmark recording *We Insist! Freedom Now*, with master drummer/composer Max Roach, she was at once a strong member of the ensemble sound, an innovative soloist, and the narrative center of the presentation.

People in Me, Talking to the Sun, The World Is Falling Down, and *You Gotta Pay the Band* are recent examples of Lincoln's strengths as a leader and songwriter.

BIBLIOGRAPHY

Giddings, Paula. "Continues an Exciting Career," *Encore* (January 1982); *New Grove Dictionary of Jazz* (1988); *New York Amsterdam News*. "Abbey Lincoln: 'What Happens to My People Happens to Me' " (January 9, 1982); Seymour, Gene. "Now's the Time for Abbey Lincoln," *Fan Fare* (November 17, 1991).

WILLIAM LOWE

THE LINKS, INC.

At the end of World War II, considerable racial tension and discrimination existed in the United States. Although large numbers of African-Americans had fought and died to "make the world safe for democracy," they returned home to find that little had changed in the area of race relations. Nevertheless, many Americans began to view in a new light the age-old questions of civil rights, human rights, and social and racial injustice, which had been ignored for decades. It was in this atmosphere that The Links, Inc., a public service, nonpartisan, volunteer organization, was founded.

On November 9, 1946, Margaret Roselle Hawkins and Sarah Strickland Scott founded the organization in Philadelphia. The original members were Frances Atkinson, Katie Green, Margaret Hawkins, Marion Minton, Myrtle Manigault, Sarah Scott, Lillian Stanford, Lillian Wall, and Dorothy Wright. These women chose to "link" their friendship and resources in an attempt to improve the quality of life and provide hope for disadvantaged African-Americans.

By 1949, fourteen groups of women had developed chapters and gathered in Philadelphia for their first national meeting. Delegates attended from various chapters in Delaware, Maryland, Missouri, New Jersey, North Carolina, Ohio, Pennsylvania, Virginia, and Washington, D.C. In 1951, the organization was incorporated, and in 1954 it was decentralized into four geographic areas: Central, Eastern, Southern, and Western. At present, The Links is an organization of approximately 8,000 women with over 240 chapters in 40 states, the District of Columbia, the Bahamas, and Frankfurt, Germany. The following have served as president: Sarah Strickland Scott, Margaret Roselle Hawkins, Pauline Weeden Maloney, Vivian J. Beamon, Helen Gray Edmonds, Pauline Allen Ellison, Julia Brogdon Purnell, Dolly Desselle Adams, and Regina Jolivette Frazier. Marion Schultz Sutherland was elected as the tenth president in 1990. The theme for the organization under her leadership is "Cherishing the Past, Cultivating the Present, Creating the Future."

The Links is committed to promoting educational, cultural, and civic activities. Over the years the organization has adopted specific programs such as Service to Youth, the Arts, National Trends and Services, and International Trends and Services. All chapters initiate, support, and participate in programs designed to address the needs of their communities in these areas.

The Service to Youth program, adopted by the national group in 1958, was an outgrowth of a White House conference on the wasted potential of minority youth. The Links launched the program under the theme "Educating for Democracy," with the purpose of supporting over 2,000 gifted minority youth. Over the years, programs in this area have been broadened and expanded to address issues in the following areas: teenage pregnancy, juvenile crime and delinquency, alcohol and drug abuse, mental and emotional disorders, breakdown of the family, unemployment, and education. Since 1982, a primary focus has been the development of programs in drug and alcohol abuse prevention. In an effort to empower youth to reject a variety of negative influences, the organization is spearheading Operation SEED (Self-Esteem Enrichment Day). It also is in partnership with the Library of Congress in its national literacy campaign.

National Trends and Services became a program facet in 1962 as a result of the organization's interest in public affairs, especially in promoting human rights, quality of life, and first-class citizenship for all. Links chapters across the country have developed programs concerning education, poverty, unemployment, spouse abuse, voter registration, crime, leadership, citizenship, civic concerns, consumer education, women, housing, nutrition, economics, the survival of Black colleges, health education, and the Black family. Local chapters and the national organization cooperate with other community groups to provide conferences, seminars, workshops, and funding in order to address these concerns. Recent programs include cancer prevention awareness for African-Americans in partnership with the National Cancer Institute, wellness in the African-American family, a letter-writing campaign in support of the passage of the Civil Rights Act of 1991, and glaucoma screening in partnership with the Eye Institute.

In 1964, a program to encourage interest in the arts was added. Cultural enrichment programs have been developed throughout the United States. The Links provides scholarships for talented individuals, sponsors opportunities for the display of talent by new artists, supports the inclusion of African-American artists in public and private art institutions, and sponsors programs and projects for young people.

Originally a part of National Trends and Services, International Trends and Services became a separate facet in 1978. Its main goal is to involve Links in international events, affairs, and issues. The organization has provided more than $30,000 to support the African Water Wells Project through the International Drinking Water Supply and Sanitation Decade (1981-90). It also collaborates with other organizations in sponsoring international projects such as the Southern Africa Initiative in cooperation with AFRICARE. In recent years it has been actively involved in initiating community support programs for the adjustment and rehabilitation of Haitian nationals. The organization also supports foreign students studying in the United States. The Links participated in the planning of the 1985 International Women's Decade Conference held in Nairobi, Kenya, supported the United States Commission on Women's Programs and Activities, and endorsed the goals of the International Women's Decade. The Links accepted status as a Non-Governmental Organization of the United Nations in May 1985.

In 1985, the organization developed the program entitled Project LEAD (Links Erase Alcohol and Drug Abuse): High Expectations!, funded in 1987 by the Office of Substance Abuse Prevention, the Alcohol, Drug Abuse, and Mental Health Administration, and the Department of Health and Human Services. Targeted for high-risk African-American youth, Project

LEAD seeks to provide field-tested, community-based educational outreach to prevent drug and alcohol abuse, premature sexual activity, unintended pregnancies, and sexually transmitted diseases. A sixty-hour, five-module curriculum was developed by Links chapters and other Black fraternal, professional, and service organizations and was implemented in 107 cities and 139 sites.

A grant from the Lilly Foundation made it possible for The Links to join forces with fifteen of the nation's largest African-American women's organizations to form Black Women's Consultation. The purpose of this group was to address issues considered vital to the survival of African-Americans. Conferences were convened in 1980, 1982, 1983, and 1985, addressing topics such as "Black Women's Response to Global Concerns"; "Programming for Surviving in the New Federalism"; "Making History through Coalescence: Black Women's Organizations in Parallel Programming"; and "Black Women: Leadership, Responsibility, and Response."

The Links provides financial support for many organizations, educational institutions and programs throughout the United States through its Links' National Grants-in-Aid program. Since its creation, the organization and its chapters have made contributions of over $10 million, of which over $1 million has been donated to the United Negro College Fund. A similar amount has been pledged to the NAACP Legal Defense and Education Fund.

The national headquarters are located in Washington, D.C., and the chief administrative officer in 1992 was Mary Polly Douglass.

BIBLIOGRAPHY

Parker, Marjorie. *A History of The Links, Incorporated* (1982); Thompson, Nancy Bowen, ed. *Southern Area History: The Links, Incorporated, 1949-1989* (1989).

DOROTHY COWSER YANCY

LISETTE *see*
FORTH, ELIZABETH DENISON

LISTON, MELBA (1926-)

"It's like Jackie Robinson," Melba Liston once said in an interview comparing the impossible standards set for female jazz instrumentalists to those set for African-American athletes. "You've got so much to prove before you get a chance. It shouldn't be like that. You go in there just like anybody else, and if you can't make it, then you get put out. But don't keep you out until you become a Charlie Parker or something. That's not fair!"

In spite of the unfair conditions and pressures she has faced in the male-dominated field of jazz, Melba Liston has become a pioneer female jazz trombonist of distinction and one of the greatest inspirations to female jazz writer/arrangers and brass players. Noted for eliciting a warm, robust tone from her instrument and putting together sensitive, personal, and often difficult arrangements, Liston has performed, composed, or arranged for Gerald Wilson, Dizzy Gillespie, Duke Ellington, Count Basie, Quincy Jones, Johnny Griffin, Clark Terry, Freddie Hubbard, Randy Weston, Dinah Washington, Gloria Lynne, Charlie Mingus, Sarah Vaughan, Aretha Franklin, Art Blakey, J. J. Johnson, Budd Johnson, Tony Bennett, and Jon Lucien, among others. She also has arranged symphonic music for Clark Terry and the Buffalo Symphony Orchestra, Randy Weston and the Boston Pops, and the Brooklyn Philharmonic.

Melba Doretta Liston was born in Kansas City, Missouri, on January 13, 1926, to Lucile and Frank Liston. Her father was a lawyer and a musician who played string instruments, and she grew up hearing Duke Ellington, Count Basie, Cab Calloway, and the swing music of the day. One of Liston's chief early influences was Ellington trombonist Lawrence Brown, and her mother bought her her first trombone when she was seven. Liston went on to excel at the trombone, an instrument that traditionally was considered unacceptable for women because it came out of the male brass band/marching band tradition. Self-taught at first, Liston began to pick out church songs, such as "Deep River" and "Rocked in the Cradle of the Deep," as well as folk tunes. In 1937, her family moved to Los Angeles, where she joined a youth band sponsored by the parks and recreation department and began to study with Alma Hightower, who had been a friend of Bert Williams. Hightower taught the band comedy and straightman routines, to dance and sing, and to recite poetry by Paul Laurence Dunbar. The group played on street corners, at YMCA dances, and at supermarket openings. Even then, however, the taboo on women's involvement with the business side of music was evident. "The boys would steal all the money," Melba said in an interview,"'cause the girls weren't allowed to pass the hats."

A trombonist whose talent allowed her to crack that male-dominated musical province, Melba Liston has performed, composed, or arranged for a veritable Who's Who of American music, ranging from Duke Ellington and Count Basie to Aretha Franklin and the Boston Pops. [Schomburg Center]

The late 1930s and early 1940s were a time, she recalled, when "blacks didn't look forward to a musical career—especially a female! A female white didn't even look forward to it too tough. And I wasn't like Paul Robeson. . . . I wasn't one of those fighters. . . . The music that I gravitated to was what was available to me, what I was listening to at the little parties and dances and records, that seemed to be a possibility." At sixteen Melba joined the musicians union and got a job in the pit band in the Lincoln Theatre, playing for such acts as Dusty Fletcher and Pigmeat Markham. The theater closed, and in 1943 the members of the band joined the band of arranger/

composer Gerald Wilson. Liston stayed with Wilson from 1943 to 1948, when the unit disbanded. She wrote and copied music for him while he taught her, he once said in an interview, "things that weren't in books."

Although highly respected by many musicians, Liston has said that she was a reluctant soloist, preferring pencil and paper and the chance to concentrate on her writing, making "the lines individually beautiful . . . all the parts sort of free and special—melodic," sometimes breaking up sections in order to blend one saxophone with the trumpets and one with the trombones. Undoubtedly, however, the conditions under which women jazz musicians had to labor also played some part in shaping this preference. "I was scared of the guys, too," Liston admitted in an interview. "They get so jealous of a girl. Once or twice, I had been threatened on the band from some of the older musicians, I mean, because I was a little old girl, I suppose. I would play my solo, and I would get an encore, and people would applaud, and then the older dude would go up there, and maybe he didn't get as much response, and once or twice I was threatened and had to run off the bandstand. So I really wasn't very aggressive about this solo business." It is widely agreed among musicians that Liston has never received the credit she deserves, and composer Hale Smith speculated in an interview that one reason for this was that "she could write most of the guys under the table without trying, and I'm talking about some of the best out there."

In 1947, while still with the Wilson band, Liston was persuaded to take some solos when she recorded with saxophonist Dexter Gordon in his Dial session. Later, in 1948 and 1949, she accompanied Billie Holiday on a southern tour, as assistant director and arranger for Wilson's big band. In an interview she recalled that, as the band traveled deeper and deeper south, the audiences got smaller and smaller. "We sat in the bus for days in Charleston, South Carolina," she said, "and then came home." By the early 1950s, tired of the sexism of the music business, and with her family encouraging her to leave the world of jazz, Liston got a job with the board of education in Los Angeles and stayed there for four years. She also married during this time, but in a business where steady work usually means long stretches of time on the road touring, riding buses, and doing one-nighters, she experienced the difficult struggle of work versus family life. It is not surprising, then, that Liston has been married three times; "trying to do those kinds of ordinary things," she admitted in an interview, "didn't work too well."

Also during the 1950s, Liston appeared in the movies *The Prodigal* (1955) with Lana Turner and *The Ten Commandments* (1956), and then Dizzy Gillespie asked her to join his band for two U.S. State Department Tours, one to the Middle East in 1956, the other to South America in 1957. On tour she arranged standards, ballads, and vocal backgrounds, work that fell to her, according to Liston, because she was a woman; she was not offered more dramatic kinds of pieces, she recalled, just the "mushy business." Nonetheless, her outstanding arrangements from this period include Claude Debussy's "My Reverie," "Stella by Starlight," and "Annie's Dance."

After the tours, Liston led her own all-woman unit for several months, and then in 1959 she joined a European tour of the Harold Arlen folk opera *Free and Easy* with Quincy Jones as music director. The group barnstormed through Europe for eleven months after the tour unexpectedly closed early. After returning to the United States in the early 1960s, she did arrangements for Johnny Griffin's album *White Gardenia*, a tribute to Billie Holiday, as well as for Riverside, Motown, and Bluenote records, for such artists as Ray Charles, Dakota Staton, Milt Jackson, Kim Weston, and Billy Eckstine. She also began a long and continuing association with pianist/composer Randy Weston. Liston has done arrangements for his albums *Little Niles, Blues to Africa, High Life, Uhuru Africa, Tanja, Open House at the Fivespot with Coleman Hawkins and Kenny Durham*, and most recently, *The Spirits of Our Ancestors* (1992), which features guest appearances by Dizzy Gillespie and Pharoah Sanders. Liston also did the charts for his work, "Three African Queens," performed by Weston and the Boston Pops.

In the early 1970s, Liston visited Jamaica and was invited back in 1973 to start the African American Division of the Jamaica School of Music. In 1978, she returned to the United States to play at the Kansas City's Women's Jazz Festival, and in 1979 she moved back to New York City, where she led her own group, Melba Liston and Company. In the mid-1980s, Liston suffered a stroke, which necessitated a lengthy convalescence. Later, in 1989, she moved back to Los Angeles, where, in 1990, she resumed writing. Liston wrote some arrangements for a 1991 New York City tribute to Dexter Gordon, and her first major undertaking was arranging the charts for the Randy Weston African Rhythms Orchestra concert "Blues to Africa," which, on September 13, 1991, inaugurated the first season of Jazz at Lincoln Center.

Like many women in jazz, Liston's multiple talents have enabled her to survive. When there was no work playing, her writing saved her, and when there was no work writing, out came her horn again. "The horn has always saved me from any sadness," she has said. "Anytime I need a lift, the trombone takes care of me. I'm not so good to it as it is to me. The trombone set me up for an arranger, and then when I'm writing I forget the trombone. But when things get dull, I go back to the trombone and it saves me again."

Passing the music and its history and traditions along to future generations has always been important to Liston, who has taught at Jazzmobile in New York City and the Pratt Institute Youth-In-Action

Orchestra in Brooklyn. She also has been honored by several musical organizations. She received the Universal Jazz Coalition, Inc. Award for Outstanding Contributions to Jazz at the fifth Annual Women's Jazz Festival on June 20, 1982; the Annual Black Musicians Conference Distinguished Achievement Award on April 23, 1984; a Triple Talent award, as arranger/composer/musician, at Freddie Jetts Pied Piper in 1971; and, in 1977, the Conductor/Christian Achievement Award for Outstanding Service. She also was a recipient of a certificate of award as an honored participant in the Philadelphia High School Gospel Choir Festival of 1976, and she was honored as a participant at the Jamaica Jazz Festival in 1975. In 1988, she was honored in the exhibition "Black Visions '88—Lady Legends in Jazz" in New York City.

BIBLIOGRAPHY

Feather, Leonard. "This Melba Is a Peach," *Downbeat* (September 19, 1956); Feather, Leonard and Ira Gitler, eds. *Encyclopedia of Jazz in the Seventies* (1976); "Melba Liston." In *The New Grove Dictionary of Jazz*, ed. Barry Kernfeld (1988); Paige, Benjamin S. "A Toast to Melba," *Downbeat* (January 5, 1961); Placksin, Sally. *American Women in Jazz, 1900 to the Present* (1982), and Personal interviews with Melba Liston (1984), Gerald Wilson (1984), and Hale Smith (1984); Williams, Martin. "Recording with Bags," *Downbeat* (August 29, 1963).

SALLY PLACKSIN

LITTLE ROCK NINE

Few people know their names, but the nine Black students who became known as the Little Rock Nine helped to bring widespread integration to public schools in the United States. In the fall of 1957, Americans who were impressed with their courage and curious about the confrontations they caused watched as these nine students braved repeated threats and other indignities from segregationists as they tried to attend classes at the all-white Little Rock Central High School. The determination of the Little Rock Nine in challenging Arkansas Governor Orval Faubus, who used armed troops to bar the nine students from entering the school, is legendary. Despite the obstacles they faced, the Little Rock Nine eventually entered the school and were able to attend classes, and as they did, their experiences continued to be documented and preserved as a testament to their characters.

In 1954, the U.S. Supreme Court ruled in *Brown v. Board of Education* that segregation in public schools was unconstitutional and that school systems should begin plans to desegregate. However, during the early years of his administration, President Dwight D. Eisenhower did not focus on education and, therefore, many states were slow to implement plans for or actively to pursue desegregation. Civil rights organizations like the National Association for the Advancement of Colored People (NAACP) continued to pressure state and federal officials about integration while implementing their own plans to facilitate the process. The Arkansas state president of the NAACP, Daisy Bates (who was elected in 1952), organized a youth council that included the first nine students to desegregate Little Rock Central High. Bates visited seventeen homes of Black students selected by public school officials for their scholastic achievement and emotional stability to ask their parents whether they would allow their children to be assigned to Central High. The parents of nine of these students—Ernest Green, Elizabeth Eckford, Gloria Ray, Melba Patillo, Carlotta Walls, Terrance Roberts, Thelma Mothershed, Minnijean Brown, and Jefferson Thomas—agreed to enroll their children in Central High. The Little Rock Nine, as they became known, were to start school at Central High in September 1957.

Along with the worries of attending a new school, the Little Rock Nine also faced threats from Governor Faubus that he would take action to block integration of Arkansas schools and that he would use National Guard troops if necessary. On September 2, 1957, Faubus kept his promise and ordered units of the National Guard to bar the nine Black students from entering Central High. Later that evening the school board issued a statement asking Black students not to attempt to enroll at any of the white public schools. Faubus's action and others made by Arkansas officials (including an August 29 injunction against integration granted by Judge Murray Reed) were flagrant violations of the Supreme Court's decision, prompting a response from President Eisenhower. The Nine were now in the midst of a state/federal confrontation, with Faubus on one side claiming states rights and Eisenhower on the other side issuing a petition for "preliminary injunction against further interference with integration" and ordering Faubus to remove his troops (*New York Times* 1957).

Members of the Black community in Little Rock also took action to counteract Faubus's actions. In response to Faubus's order to block the entrance with troops on September 2, Bates organized a group of ministers to escort the students from her house to Central the next day. She called the parents of all the students except Elizabeth Eckford to alert them of the change in plans. Too tired to drive to the Eckfords' (who had no phone), Bates retired for the evening. The next morning, Elizabeth went to Central High alone, and was taunted and berated by hundreds of white students and citizens in front of cameras, reporters, and photographers from around the world.

National Guard troops were not the only hindrances to the Nine's entrance to Central High. On September 24, 1957, the day after Faubus withdrew the Guard in order to allow the students to enter Central, the Nine and their police escorts attempted unsuccessfully to enter the school. This time, they were forced to retreat by an angry mob consisting primarily of white students, their parents, and members of the local community. As the Nine approached the school's entrance, the mob became more violent and the situation more chaotic; both Black and white newsmen were injured by mobsters trying to lessen the publicity the incident was receiving. Several white students protested by boycotting their classes. Virgil Blossom, the district's superintendent and the spearhead for the "Blossom Plan," which called for phased integration, expressed doubts that the Nine would attempt or even be able to attend classes the next day. Blossom underestimated the Nine's determination and persistence, and the next day (September 25), the Nine once again tried to enter the school. They succeeded with the assistance of National Guard troops who had been federalized by President Eisenhower.

Three of the Little Rock Nine talk with National Guardsmen during the Little Rock Central High School crisis in 1957. From left to right they are Carlotta Walls, unidentified student, Gloria Ray, and Ernest Green. [Benita Ramsey]

All but one of the Little Rock Nine stayed in school for the rest of the year, but they were continually harassed by groups of white students inside the school. Nevertheless, they had attempted to provide "a model of orderly transition for the thousands of other school districts across the South" who were "just beginning to face up to the reality of the mandate the United States Supreme Court had handed down" (Huckaby 1980). These "likeable, admirable young people," as they were called by Elizabeth Huckaby, a former teacher at Central High who taught the Nine, had changed the policy of a nation and triumphed over bigotry.

BIBLIOGRAPHY

Bates, Daisy. *The Long Shadow of Little Rock* (1964); Huckaby, Elizabeth. *Crisis at Central High, Little Rock, 1957-1958* (1980); *New York Times* (September 21, 1957); Spring, Joel. *American Education: An Introduction to Social and Political Aspects* (1985).

BENITA RAMSEY

LIVINGSTON, MYRTLE ATHLEEN SMITH (1902-1973)

Myrtle Athleen Smith Livingston was one of the first Black American playwrights to place the controversial question of interracial marriage squarely on the stage. "For Unborn Children," published in the *Crisis* in July 1926, provocatively explores the situation of a Black lawyer who has fallen in love with a white woman and who plans to marry her over the opposition of his sister and grandmother. When he learns that his own mother was white and may have abandoned him because of his color, he begins to realize the cost of crossing the color line. As the play concludes, a lynch mob clamors outside his door and the audience realizes that it may be too late for him to escape being lynched.

Born in Holly Grove, Arkansas, on May 8, 1902, to Samuel Isaac and Lula C. Hall Smith, Myrtle Athleen Smith lived in Denver as a child, studied pharmacy at Howard University from 1920-22, and transferred to Colorado Teachers College in Greeley. There she organized a dance group and began her lifelong involvement with theater arts. In 1925, she married William McKinley Livingston. In 1928, she joined the faculty of Lincoln University, Jefferson City, Missouri, as the sole member of the physical education and dance department and the director of women's athletics. During her forty-four years of teaching, she also wrote plays, directed performances, and spent several sabbaticals studying in New York, at Columbia University and New York University.

Livingston died in July 1973 in Honolulu. In accordance with Hawaiian custom, her ashes were scattered in the Pacific Ocean.

BIBLIOGRAPHY

Harambee, "Three Professors to Retire" (April 1972), and "Mrs. Livingston Dies in Hawaii" (March 1974); *WWCA*. See also the Inman E. Page Library Archives, Lincoln University, Jefferson, Missouri.

LORRAINE ELENA ROSES

LOGAN, ADELLA HUNT (1863-1915)

"My busy life has been without romantic event," Adella Hunt Logan said of herself in 1902, but others might disagree (Logan 1902). She was born in Sparta, Georgia, in 1863, the daughter of a free mulatto woman and a white planter—the fourth of their eight children. During her childhood, she lived on Hunt's Hill, an enclave where the town's more comfortably situated African-American population resided.

Adella attended Bass Academy in her hometown and became a certified teacher at sixteen. She acquired a scholarship to Atlanta University, and in 1881 she completed the normal course there—four-year programs were closed to women. The school later awarded her an honorary M.A. degree for her continuing work in education.

She taught for several years in an American Missionary School and in 1883 declined a teaching opportunity at her alma mater, choosing instead to go to Alabama's new Tuskegee Institute. During the early years at Tuskegee, Hunt filled a number of positions. She taught English and social sciences, became the institute's first librarian, and was "Lady Principal" for a short time. She also met Warren Logan, a schoolmate and old friend of Booker T. Washington. Warren Logan became the treasurer of Tuskegee Institute and served on its board of trustees.

These two educators married in 1888. The impoverished new school could not support two-salary families; since Adella's work was considered less critical, she subordinated her career to her husband's. In 1890 she gave birth to the first of nine children; the last was born in 1909 when she was forty-six.

Adella Hunt Logan taught only intermittently between difficult pregnancies and was limited as well

In the early years of Tuskegee Institute, Adella Hunt Logan filled a number of positions, including serving for a time as Lady Principal. This family photograph, which includes her husband, Warren, and six of their nine children, was taken in Tuskegee, Alabama, in 1913; she is third from the left. [Photo by Arthur Bedou; Collection of Adele Logan Alexander]

by domestic demands and official responsibilities as the wife of Tuskegee's second-ranking official. Teaching remained her greatest passion, however, and she was the creative force behind Tuskegee's model school and teachers' training facility.

She immersed herself in activities of the Tuskegee Women's Club, a chapter of the National Association of Colored Women (NACW), as well.

Logan's most important work centered around the club's efforts on behalf of local farm women and their children. She advocated health care for all and education for every child.

Logan's other major interest was woman's suffrage. At the turn of the century, most white Alabamans vehemently opposed votes for women, but Logan led regular forums about suffrage at Tuskegee and encouraged students to debate and participate in demonstrations of participatory democracy. She lectured at NACW conferences as well and served briefly as that group's national director of both suffrage and rural affairs. She also wrote about suffrage in the *Colored American* and the *Crisis*.

Because of her predominantly white ancestry, Adella Hunt Logan looked white. When the National American Woman Suffrage Association (NAWSA) held conventions in the segregated South, she attended without identifying herself as "colored." Subsequently, she brought back information from those meetings to share with colleagues in the African-American community. For a decade she was the only Life Member of the NAWSA from the state of Alabama. She also contributed articles about NACW activities to that organization's newspaper.

Logan became swept up in the ideological feud between Booker T. Washington and W. E. B. Du Bois over the direction of the Black community, but she managed to maintain her philosophical alliance with Du Bois even while remaining a personal friend, professional associate, and next-door neighbor to Washington.

A combination of events, including defeats for the suffrage movement and tensions in her marriage, led to an emotional collapse in September 1915, when Adella Hunt Logan was sent to a Michigan sanitarium. A few weeks later, however, news of Booker T. Washington's precipitously declining health summoned her home. After her friend's death, Logan never recovered. On December 12, as visiting dignitaries assembled at Tuskegee to attend a memorial service for Washington, Logan jumped to her death from the top floor of one of the school's buildings.

[*See also* LOGAN, MYRA ADELE; ROBERTS, RUTH LOGAN.]

BIBLIOGRAPHY

Alexander, Adele Logan. *Ambiguous Lives: Free Women of Color in Rural Georgia, 1789-1879* (1991). Articles by Adella Hunt Logan appeared in *Atlanta University Publications, No. 2, Social and Physical Condition of Negroes in Cities* (1987); *The Colored American* (September 1905); *The Crisis* (September 1912); *The Negro Farmer* (April 14, 1914); *Twentieth Century Negro Literature*, ed. D. W. Culp (1902); *The Woman's Journal* (January 26, 1901, and January 17, 1903); and *Work for the Colored Woman of the South*, comp. Mrs. Booker T. Washington (1984). Booker T. Washington papers, Manuscript Division, Library of Congress; Emily Howland Collection, Cornell University.

ADELE LOGAN ALEXANDER

LOGAN, MYRA ADELE (1908-1977)

"If you're interested in any field of humanity," physician Myra Logan said of her chosen profession, "you can't miss if you go into medicine" (*Compass* 1952). She followed in the family tradition: her mother, an aunt, and a sister were deeply involved with health issues, and a brother and a brother-in-law were physicians.

Myra Adele Logan was born in 1908 in Tuskegee, Alabama, the eighth child of Warren and Adella Hunt Logan. She completed her early education at Tuskegee and then obtained a Bachelor's degree at Atlanta University in 1929.

She moved to New York City and earned a Master's degree from Columbia University, working as well with the Young Men's Christian Association (YMCA). Logan then attended and graduated from the school of medicine of New York's Flower Fifth Avenue Hospital. She spent most of her professional career at Harlem Hospital. Her work in developing antibiotics and her achievements in open heart surgery brought her great respect in the medical community. She had a private practice and belonged to a joint medical insurance group as well. She worked with both Planned Parenthood and the National Association for the Advancement of Colored People (NAACP), was published in numerous medical journals, and was one of the first Black females elected to the American College of Physicians and Surgeons.

Logan had little time to play, but she was, nonetheless, a skilled classical pianist. In 1943, she married painter Charles Alston; the couple had no children. She died of lung cancer in 1977.

[*See also* LOGAN, ADELLA HUNT; ROBERTS, RUTH LOGAN.]

BIBLIOGRAPHY

Compass (New York) (September 17, 1952). Private papers are in the possession of Adele Logan Alexander.

ADELE LOGAN ALEXANDER

LORDE, AUDRE (1934-)

Among contemporary writers, there are few who so completely challenge the categorization and consequent repudiation of individuals as does Audre Lorde. Her challenge takes the interesting and powerful form of embracing all the categories into which she herself fits or can be squeezed. "I am a Black lesbian feminist poet," she says and demands recognition of the fact that she has not uttered a paradox. "I am a Black Lesbian," she says, and then goes on, "and I *am* your sister." To those who would deny familial connection with her, metaphorical though it might be, she presents an infuriating and, usually, sensitizing determination to define herself and, by so doing, to define the world around her.

Audre Lorde was born in Harlem on February 18, 1934. From the beginning, her sense of her identity was unusually complex. Her parents had come to New York from their home country of Grenada and for many years firmly believed that they would one day go home. When, during the Great Depression, they realized that they would probably never go back, a permanent sorrow entered their household. Their nostalgia for the country of their birth provided the background of Lorde's childhood. For this young New York girl, there was an island in the West Indies—an island she had never seen—that she was expected to think of as home.

One of Lorde's books, *Zami: A New Spelling of My Name*, presents a clear picture of her early life. A fictionalized biography—or biomythography, as she calls it—the work graphically retells racist incidents the author suffered as a child. It also describes with wonder her discovery of language and its power. At an early age, she began to use the latter as a tool to exclude, resist, and even manipulate racist attitudes.

The strictness of her parents' home, along with her own sense of herself as an outsider, led Lorde into rebellion as a teenager. She began to seek out others who felt as she did and she found them at Hunter College High School. One companion misfit was poet Diane Di Prima.

After graduation from high school, Lorde moved to her own apartment and began to support herself. The jobs she was able to find were low-paying and unsatisfying. She endured great loneliness because of her inability to find a world in which she felt at home. It was during this time that she had her first lesbian affair, in Connecticut, while she was working in a factory.

Another affair with a woman, one that occurred while she was in Mexico in 1954, led Lorde wholeheartedly into the Greenwich Village "gay-girl" scene. It was the closest she had yet come to a sense of belonging, and she found it in a sea of almost entirely white faces. This irony, and the conflict it aroused in her, provoked years of thinking, writing, and feeling. At this time, she also went to college and began to work as a librarian, and she wrote her poetry.

The poetry led her, for a time, to involvement with the Harlem Writers Guild. Its members, includ-

ing Langston Hughes, were the vanguard of a growing movement in African-American literature. Here was another possible home for the aspiring young writer. Hughes himself showed an interest in her work. Yet, according to Lorde, the homophobia of the Guild members alienated her once again.

In 1959, Lorde received her B.A. from Hunter College. In 1960, she was awarded an M.L.S. from Columbia University's School of Library Service. For a number of years, Lorde wrote poetry and worked as a librarian, ending up as head librarian at the Town School in New York. She also got married and had two children. The marriage and its circumstances are not recorded in Lorde's writing and therefore little is known of it. Then, in 1968, *The First Cities*, her first book of poetry, was scheduled for publication by the Poet's Press. Her old high school friend, Diane Di Prima, was instrumental in its being published. At about the same time, Lorde was invited to Tougaloo College, in Mississippi, to be poet-in-residence.

Lorde was at Tougaloo for only six weeks, but during that time her life changed suddenly and radically. Public recognition of her poetry, in the form of her book's publication, was one of the foremost reasons. Another was her experience teaching the students of Tougaloo—a historically Black institution—about poetry, an experience that she wrote of movingly in the poem "Blackstudies." The third significant factor was meeting Frances Clayton; the two women would become life partners.

Upon her return to New York City, Lorde continued teaching. She gave courses in writing at City College and on racism at Lehman College and John Jay College. Her second book of poetry, *Cables to Rage*, came out in 1970.

In 1971, Lorde read publicly a lesbian love poem. The subject had never before appeared in her public work. The same poem was published later in *Ms.* It was not, however, included in her next volume of poetry, *From a Land Where Other People Live*, having been rejected by the editor of that volume. In 1974, the book was nominated for a National Book Award, bringing Lorde greater recognition for her work and, after two more publications with small presses, a contract with W. W. Norton.

Norton brought out *Coal*, a collection of new poems and poems from her first two, hard-to-find books, with a jacket blurb written by Adrienne Rich. Rich was at that time one of Norton's most prominent poets, and the association between Lorde and Rich continued over the years. The same blurb appeared on Lorde's second book with Norton, *The Black Unicorn*, published in 1978. In the summer of

1981, Rich published an interview with Lorde in *Signs: Journal of Women in Culture and Society*, thereby introducing her to a large white readership.

The Black Unicorn is probably Lorde's most successful poetic attempt to merge her different worlds. She uses the image of the unicorn (which she believes Europeans took from the African agricultural goddess Chi-Wara, a one-horned antelope) to explore the influences of European and African cultures upon each other. She delves into the sexual significances of the symbol, pointing out how the European myth divides meaning into the masculine, the phallic horn, and the feminine, the pale virgin who alone can tame the animal. In contrast, African culture combines those meanings to emphasize the power of growth.

With the appearance of *The Black Unicorn*, Lorde became an acknowledged, widely reviewed poet. Critical articles began to be written about her work, often alongside that of other poets belonging to one of her "categories" and sometimes alone. Her prose, too, though published by small presses, began to command attention and respect. *Zami* was published in 1982 and reviewed in the *New York Times*. A different audience grew out of the publication of a collection of essays titled *Sister Outsider* (1984). It was widely adopted in women's studies courses and quickly achieved the status of a feminist classic.

During the 1970s, Lorde traveled in Africa, the Caribbean, Europe, and Russia. In 1980, her autobiographical work *The Cancer Journals* was published. In it, she describes her feelings during and after her affliction with breast cancer. The experience had added yet one more identity to her long list. In another prose work, *A Burst of Light* (1988), she recounts her decision not to undergo further surgery after a return of the disease and her experience with alternative methods of treatment. Again, during this time, Lorde traveled extensively, teaching and giving readings.

The stubborn reality of her own experiences and her own feelings serves as the basis of Lorde's worldview. Where political oversimplifications collide with her personal affections and loyalties, she sees a reason to challenge the politics, as in her essay "Man Child: A Black Lesbian Feminist's Response." In that work, she explores, among other issues, the ramifications of her motherhood of a son in a cultural milieu in which her primary identification is lesbian.

Lorde's focus as a writer and a person has been to strive for unity by embracing diversity. She challenges all political and social actions that arbitrarily separate one individual from another, that exclude and ostracize. She has done this by fervently defending the individual's right to define herself and her

"I am a Black lesbian feminist poet," declares Audre Lorde with deliberation. She creates a world of eroticism, sensuality, and symbolism in her work, which defies categorization. [Schomburg Center]

possibilities. In her prose, this position has often been set forth explicitly. In her poetry, she has created a world of eroticism, sensuality, and symbolism that, ultimately, aspires to the same goal.

[Editor's note: Audre Lorde died on November 17, 1992.]

BIBLIOGRAPHY

Abod, Jennifer and Angela Brown. "A Radio Profile of Audre Lorde." Profile Productions (1988); Annas, Pamela. "A Poetry of Survival: Unnaming and Renaming in the Poetry of Audre Lorde, Pat Parker, Sylvia Plath, and Adrienne Rich," *Colby Library Quarterly* (1982); Avi-ram, Amitai F. "*Apo Koinou* in Audre Lorde and the Moderns: Defining the Differences," *Callaloo* (Winter 1986); Bowles, Juliette, ed. *In the Memory and Spirit of Frances, Zora, and Lorraine: Essays and Interviews on Black Women and Writing* (1979); Brooks, Jerome. "In the Name of the Father: The Poetry of Audre Lorde." In *Black Women Writers (1950-1980): A Critical Evaluation*, ed. Mari Evans (1984); Carruthers, Mary J. "The Re-Vision of the Muse: Adrienne Rich, Audre Lorde, Judy Grahn, Olga Broumas," *Hudson Review* (1983); Chinosole. "Audre Lorde and Matrilineal

Diaspora: 'moving history beyond nightmare into structures for the future. . . .' " In *Wild Women in the Whirlwind: Afro-American Culture and the Contemporary Literary Renaissance*, ed. Joanne M. Braxton and Andrée Nicola McLaughlin (1990); Christian, Barbara. "The Dynamics of Difference: Review of Audre Lorde's *Sister Outsider*." In her *Black Feminist Criticism: Perspectives on Black Women Writers* (1985); Hammond, Karla. "Audre Lorde: Interview," *Denver Quarterly* (Spring 1981); Hull, Gloria T. "Living on the Line: Audre Lorde and *Our Dead Behind Us*." In *Changing Our Own Words: Essays on Criticism, Theory, and Writings by Black Women*, ed. Cheryl A. Wall (1989); McDowell, Margaret. "The Black Woman as Artist and Critic: Four Versions," *Kentucky Review* (1987); Martin, Joan. "The Unicorn Is Black: Audre Lorde in Retrospect." In *Black Women Writers (1950-1980): A Critical Evaluation*, ed. Mari Evans (1984); Perreault, Jeanne. " 'that the pain not be wasted': Audre Lorde and the Written Self," *A/B: Auto/Biography Studies* (Fall 1988); Stepto, Robert. "The Phenomenal Woman and the Severed Daughter," *Parnassus* (1979); Tate, Claudia, ed. *Black Women Writers at Work* (1983); Winter, Nina. "On Audre Lorde" and "Audre Lorde." In *Interview with the Muse: Remarkable Women Speak on Creativity and Power* (1978).

SELECTED WORKS BY AUDRE LORDE

Poetry: *The First Cities* (1968); *Cables to Rage* (1970); *From a Land Where Other People Live* (1973); *New York Head Shop and Museum* (1975); *Between Ourselves* (1976); *Coal* (1976); *The Black Unicorn* (1978); *Chosen Poems, Old and New* (1982); *Our Dead Behind Us* (1986). Prose, Essays, Journals: *The Cancer Journals* (1980); *Zami: A New Spelling of My Name* (1982); *Sister Outsider* (1984); "My Words Will Be There." In *Black Women Writers (1950-1980): A Critical Evaluation*, ed. Mari Evans (1984); *A Burst of Light* (1988). Speeches: "Sisterhood and Survival." Conference keynote address, The Black Woman Writer and the Diaspora. *The Black Scholar* (1988); "A Question of Survival." Commencement speech, Oberlin College, May 1989. *Gay Community News* (August 1989).

MARGARET HOMANS

LOVING, MILDRED (1942-)

Mildred Loving gained notoriety when the U.S. Supreme Court decided *Loving* v. *Virginia*, a case that declared antimiscegenation laws unconstitutional.

In October 1958, a Virginia grand jury indicted Mildred Loving and her white husband for violating the state's antimiscegenation laws. The Lovings pleaded guilty, and each received a one-year sentence. The trial judge suspended their sentences on the condition that the Lovings leave Virginia and not return to the state together for twenty-five years. The Lovings initially agreed to the conditions set by the trial judge and moved to the District of Columbia. However, they later became unhappy in Washington and moved back to Virginia, where they decided to fight to have the antimiscegenation statutes declared unconstitutional and have their convictions reversed. They were unsuccessful in the Virginia state court system, which upheld the constitutionality of the statutes. The Lovings appealed the Virginia court's decision to the U.S. Supreme Court, which, in a unanimous 1967 opinion, struck down the Virginia antimiscegenation laws and, by extension, similar laws that fifteen other states had in force at the time. Chief Justice Earl Warren wrote that the laws at issue were nothing more than "measures designed to maintain White Supremacy" and that restricting the freedom to marry along racial lines violated the equal protection clause of the Fourteenth Amendment. At the time of this decision, miscegenation was the last social institution still governed by *de jure* segregation laws. Loving's lawsuit put an end to such regulations.

Mildred Loving has led a quiet life since 1967. She and her husband had three children before he died in a car accident in 1975. In early 1992, her Central Point, Virginia, church awarded her a plaque to commemorate her struggle, and her minister compared her to Rosa Parks. Loving tends to downplay the role she played, suggesting that she really had no choice but to proceed as she did. Nonetheless, her efforts helped forge a world in which interracial relationships face one less barrier. Indeed, her daughter, Peggy Loving Fortune, married a man of mixed parentage.

BIBLIOGRAPHY

Duke, Lynn. "Mixed Marriage Broken Up by Death," *Washington Post* (June 12, 1992), and "25 Years after Landmark Decision, Still the Rarest of Wedding Bonds," *Washington Post* (June 12, 1992); Margolick, David. "A Mixed Marriage's 25th Anniversary of Legality," *New York Times* (June 12, 1992).

PHILIP A. PRESBY

LUCY, AUTHERINE *see* FOSTER, AUTHERINE JUANITA LUCY

In Loving v. Virginia, *the U.S. Supreme Court in 1967 ruled unanimously that a Virginia law prohibiting marriages between Blacks and whites was unconstitutional, thereby nullifying similar laws in fifteen other states. The case was brought by Mildred Loving, of Black and Native American ancestry, and her husband, Richard, who was white. [UPI/Bettmann]*

LUPER, CLARA (1923-)

In Oklahoma, the name Clara Luper is synonymous with civil rights sit-ins. As is true of many civil rights leaders of her generation, Luper is also closely associated with education and the Black church. Perceived to be an agitator and vilified for leading the demonstrations on August 19, 1958, in Oklahoma City, which would continue off and on for more than ten years, Luper is now accorded the status of respected elder and is seen as a moderating voice in racial issues.

The daughter of Ezell and Isabell (Wilkerson) Shepard, she was born May 3, 1923, in rural Okfuskee County, Oklahoma. Clara Shepard grew up in the small community of Hoffman in Okmulgee County, Oklahoma. Her father was a laborer who did farmwork, drove buses, moved houses, chopped cotton on contract, and picked pecans, to name but a few of the jobs he would do. Her mother took in laundry.

She went to a segregated school and wrote in her autobiography, *Behold the Walls* (1979), this account of those days: "The books . . . had been mainly discarded from the white elementary school. We were separate and we possessed through Education Calculated Manipulation an overabundance of *promises* for better books, equipment, and supplies that never came. We were Separate and Unequal."

She attended a segregated high school five miles away at Grayson. The microscope had no lenses, pages were missing from the handed-down history books, and the outdated encyclopedias and dictionaries were without some letters of the alphabet. After graduating with five other Black seniors, she went on to Langston University, then a segregated institution in central Oklahoma. It also had inferior equipment, books, and supplies as compared to the white universities in the state. She earned her B.A. in mathematics with a minor in history in 1944. When she went to the University of Oklahoma, where she completed her Master's degree in secondary education and history in 1951, Luper encountered separate restrooms and separate sections in the cafeteria. Classrooms had bars to segregate Black and white students.

Luper's first marriage, to Bert Luper, an electrician, ended in divorce after thirteen years. In 1977, she married Charles P. (C. P.) Wilson, a truck driver. She has three children.

When she reviews her experiences, Luper tells about the twenty-six times she was jailed for her part in nonviolent demonstrations to end segregation. Her civil rights work began in earnest on August 19, 1958, when she and the local National Association for the Advancement of Colored People (NAACP) Youth Council carried out their first sit-in at the Katz Drug

Store in Oklahoma City. When the group was refused service at the lunch counter and, in turn, refused to leave, police were called and the media came. Two days later, Katz announced that its thirty-eight outlets in Oklahoma, Missouri, Kansas, and Iowa would serve all people, regardless of race.

The sit-ins grew to involve hundreds of young Black Americans and some white supporters. Participants would set out on foot from Calvary Baptist Church for various downtown establishments. Frequently, they would be jailed for trespassing, but they always kept coming back. Starting in August 1960, general boycotts were used as another tactic to force the end of segregation. Luper helped spread the word and build support with her regular radio broadcast. Sit-in demonstrations continued off and on for almost six years until the Oklahoma City Council enacted a public accommodations ordinance on June 2, 1964, to resolve problems with hold-out establishments resisting integration.

Luper continued her efforts in other areas, working for a fair housing ordinance and establishing a Freedom Center for Youth Council activities—and rebuilding it after it was fire-bombed on September 10, 1968. At the insistence of the predominantly Black

sanitation workers, she led them in their strike in 1969 for better pay and working conditions. Though she had no lack of causes in Oklahoma, she joined the danger-filled civil rights march from Selma to Montgomery, Alabama, in 1965, among many other national activities. In 1972, she ran for the U.S. Senate from Oklahoma, but was not elected.

Throughout her many years of civil rights involvement, Luper taught in public schools and often drew criticism for her outside activities. For seventeen years she taught at Dunjee High School, a Black school in Oklahoma City. She spent two years at Northwest Classen High School and then taught at John Marshall High School, both in Oklahoma City. In spring 1989, she was honored with a retirement dinner after forty-one years in education.

Clara Luper has received the NAACP Youth Council Advisor of the Year national award several times. Other honors include the Langston University Alumni Award, 1969; Zeta Phi Beta, Chi Zeta Chapter Woman of the Year, 1970; and Sigma Gamma Rho Service to Mankind Award, 1980.

In June 1961, Luper wrote down the following thoughts in the thick of her sit-ins: "As I see it, Blacks must become the active conscience of America, but

In Oklahoma, Clara Luper's name is synonymous with civil rights sit-ins; she was jailed twenty-six times for her participation in nonviolent demonstrations to end segregation. Luper, left, received hugs and words of appreciation from her acquaintances and admirers after she spoke in April 1992 at a Watonga High School Heritage Club program commemorating the civil rights struggle in Oklahoma. [Watonga Republican]

conscience is a drowsy thing. It stirs, turns over, takes another nap and falls into a deep, dead sleep. 'Leave me alone,' conscience cries. 'Let me sleep, let me sleep,' conscience cries. 'Let time take care of it—time, time is the answer. Maybe ten years or maybe another hundred years.' Oh, no, America, your conscience, like old Pharaoh's of old, will not rest or sleep until we can eat here at John A. Brown's. We will arouse your conscience and will not let you rest until we can eat" (*Behold the Walls* 1979).

Clara Luper did not rest, and Oklahoma has been different for it ever since.

BIBLIOGRAPHY

Daily Oklahoman (November 27, 1989); *Ebony Tribune* (May 12, 1989); Graves, Carl R. "The Right to Be Served: Oklahoma City's Lunch Counter Sit-ins, 1958-1964." In *We Shall Overcome: The Civil Rights Movement in the United States in the 1950s and 1960s*, ed. David J. Garrow (1989); Luper, Clara. *Behold the Walls* (1979); Rice, Darrell. Telephone interview with Clara Luper (July 18, 1992); *Watonga Republican* (April 23, 1992).

DARRELL RICE

LYLE, ETHEL HEDGEMAN
(1887-1950)

"As long as life lasts and beyond, I shall see the beautiful deeds done to help others less fortunate and the lovely hands of all the women of Alpha Kappa Alpha outstretched to the aid of others who, mentally, morally, and physically, are still poor and needy; and I will always thank God that I had some small part in it," Ethel Hedgeman Lyle once said. Although she would never say so herself, playing a role was something Ethel Hedgeman Lyle did well and often. Far from making a cameo appearance, however, Lyle was the leading lady, and her most memorable performance was as the founder of Alpha Kappa Alpha

(AKA) sorority, the first Greek-letter organization for Black women. Lyle believed that women united by a common bond could organize their talents and strengths for the betterment of themselves and humankind. It was this philosophy that led the honor student to establish AKA at Howard University in 1908, and the debut brought rave reviews.

Her performance in the educational arena also brought critical acclaim. After receiving her A.B. in English from Howard in 1909, she became the first college-trained Black woman to teach in a normal school in Oklahoma and to receive Oklahoma's Teacher's Life Certificate. Yet Lyle's longest running appearances came in Philadelphia. She taught in the public schools from 1921 to 1948, and seeing her students achieve and garner honors gave Lyle "the greatest happiness and thrill of my life!" (Boyer 1941). Her civic performances brought additional plaudits, including a mayoral appointment as chair of the committee of 100 women charged with planning the 150th anniversary of the Constitution. At home, she played the traditional roles of wife and mother to her husband, George Lyle, a Philadelphia school principal, and son, George Hedgeman Lyle.

The daughter of Albert Hedgeman and Marie Hubbard Hedgeman of St. Louis, Missouri, Lyle grew up in a family that actively worked through their church and community to improve conditions for their children and those who were less fortunate. She spent her life continuing that commitment. She died on November 28, 1950.

BIBLIOGRAPHY

Boyer, Sallie C. Personal interview with Ethel Hedgeman Lyle, (Spring 1941); *Ivy Leaf.* "Life of Alpha Kappa Alpha's Founder Given against Colorful, Historical Background" (December 1948), and "A Living Memorial" (March 1951); Parker, Marjorie. *Alpha Kappa Alpha through the Years, 1908-1988* (1990).

EARNESTINE GREEN McNEALEY